# GMAT®

## PREMIUM PREP

**2022 Edition**

The Staff of The Princeton Review

PrincetonReview.com

Penguin Random House

The Princeton Review
110 East 42nd St, 7th Floor
New York, NY 10017



Published in the United States by Penguin Random House, LLC, New York, and in Canada by Random House of Canada, division of Penguin Random House Ltd., Toronto.



ISBN: 978-0-525-57046-2
eBook: 978-0-525-57086-8
ISSN: 2687-9646



The material in this book is up-to-date at the time of publication. However, changes may have been instituted by the testing body in the test after this book was published.

If there are any important late-breaking developments, changes, or corrections to the materials in this book, we will post that information online in the Student Tools. Register your book and check your Student Tools to see if there are any updates posted there.

Editor: Eleanor Green
Production Artist: Jason Ullmeyer
Production Editors: Kathy Carter and Sarah Litt

Printed in the United States of America.

10 9 8 7 6 5 4 3 2 1

2022 Edition

**Editorial**
Rob Franek, Editor-in-Chief
David Soto, Director of Content Development
Stephen Koch, Student Survey Manager
Deborah Weber, Director of Production
Gabriel Berlin, Production Design Manager
Selena Coppock, Director of Editorial
Aaron Riccio, Senior Editor
Meave Shelton, Senior Editor
Chris Chimera, Editor
Anna Goodlett, Editor
Eleanor Green, Editor
Orion McBean, Editor
Patricia Murphy, Editorial Assistant

**Penguin Random House Publishing Team**
Tom Russell, VP, Publisher
Alison Stoltzfus, Publishing Director
Amanda Yee, Associate Managing Editor
Ellen Reed, Production Manager
Suzanne Lee, Designer

For customer service, please contact **editorialsupport@review.com**, and be sure to include:

- full title of the book
- ISBN
- page number

# Acknowledgments

Our GMAT course is much more than clever techniques and powerful computer score reports; the reason our results are great is that our teachers care so much about their students. Thanks to all the teachers who have made the GMAT course so successful, but in particular the core group of teachers and development people who helped get it off the ground: Alicia Ernst, Tom Meltzer, Paul Foglino, John Sheehan, Mark Sawula, Nell Goddin, Teresa Connelly, Phillip Yee, Kimberly Beth Hollingsworth, Bobby Hood, Chris Chimera, Chris Hinkle, Peter Hanink, Cathy Evins, and Doug Scripture.

Special thanks to John Fulmer and Kyle Fox for their valuable contributions to the 2022 edition of this book.

Special thanks to Adam Robinson, who conceived of and perfected the Joe Bloggs approach to standardized tests and many of the other successful techniques used by The Princeton Review.

We are also, as always, very appreciative of the time and attention given to each page by Jason Ullmeyer, Kathy Carter, and Sarah Litt.

# Contents

# Get More (Free) Content

## at **PrincetonReview.com/prep**

## As easy as 1·2·3

**1** Go to PrincetonReview.com/prep or scan the **QR code** and enter the following ISBN for your book: **9780525570462**

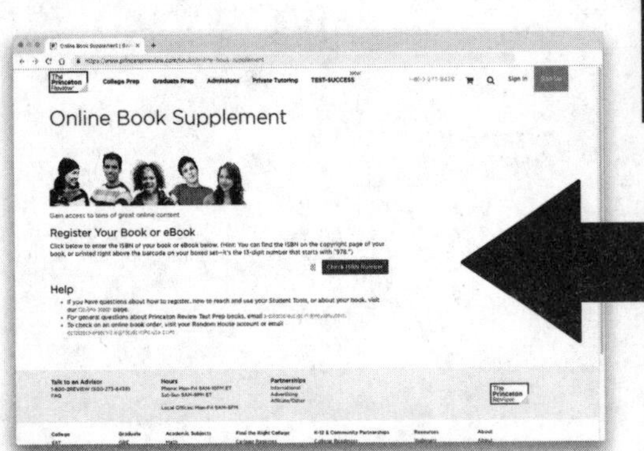


**2** Answer a few simple questions to set up an exclusive Princeton Review account. *(If you already have one, you can just log in.)*

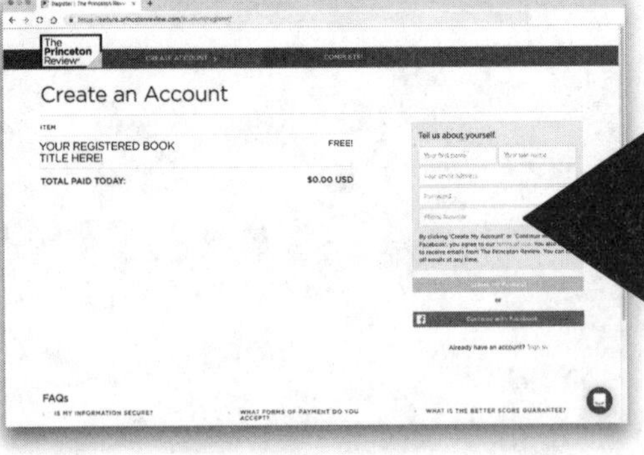


**3** Enjoy access to your **FREE** content!

# Once you've registered, you can...

- Take 6 full-length practice GMAT exams
- Download additional practice material excerpted from 3 other Princeton Review GMAT titles
- Plan your review sessions with study guides based on your schedule—4 weeks, 8 weeks, 12 weeks
- Watch short video tutorials in which top-notch Princeton Review teachers discuss GMAT question types and strategies, working through problems step by step
- Research admissions rates and average test scores for dozens of popular business schools
- Access the Business School Insider, our guide to financial aid, admissions, writing winning application essays, MBA job prospects, and more
- Check to see if there have been any corrections or updates to this edition
- Get our take on any recent or pending updates to the GMAT

## Need to report a potential **content** issue?

Contact **EditorialSupport@review.com** and include:

- full title of the book
- ISBN
- page number

## Need to report a **technical** issue?

Contact **TPRStudentTech@review.com** and provide:

- your full name
- email address used to register the book
- full book title and ISBN
- Operating system (Mac/PC) and browser (Firefox, Safari, etc.)

## Look For These Icons Throughout The Book

 PREMIUM PORTAL

 ONLINE VIDEO TUTORIALS

 ONLINE ARTICLES

 ONLINE PRACTICE DRILLS

 ONLINE PRACTICE TESTS

 PROVEN TECHNIQUES

 APPLIED STRATEGIES

 TIME-SAVING TIP

 OTHER REFERENCES

 WATCH OUT

Dear Test-Taker,

There is a lot of content that could be tested on the GMAT.

Virtually all that content is covered in this book.

Therefore, this book is very long.

We set out to create a book with a simple goal in mind: we want you to achieve the GMAT score of your dreams. After diligently reading this book from cover to cover, we want you to have seen enough practice questions and heard enough discussion about the GMAT that nothing you see on test day is a surprise to you. We also want you to be confident that the GMAT is the right test for you to take to help achieve your career goals.

But how do you know you've improved if you don't know where you started? Moreover, how do you navigate a nearly 1,000-page book designed to help you shore up weaknesses and challenge strengths if you don't know what your strengths and weaknesses are?

And let's just be honest with each other. Some of you are going to attack your GMAT studies with machine-like tirelessness. You are going to thoroughly comb through every page, take every practice test, send questions to our editorial team, and think about nearly nothing else until test day. If this sounds like you, then you're going to love this book. You might even give it a permanent spot on your mantle.

But others of you want a book that helps you triage how to spend your time. You have only so many hours a day or week to devote to your studies. You're going to see a book this big, that feels this heavy, and know you are unlikely to see every page and work through every question. If this sounds like you, then we have good news. You are also going to love this book. The opening diagnostic test is going to give you a good sense of where you are with each question type and help you determine where to focus your efforts. The closing diagnostic test is going to let you know just how far you've come and what you still may need to brush up on to maximize your score.

In short, we created a book that you can use to maximize your time in order to maximize your score. We think you'll love it. But don't take our word for it. See for yourself.

Happy studying,

The Princeton Review

# Part I
# Diagnostic Test 1

# Chapter 1
# Diagnostic Test 1

## TAKING THE DIAGNOSTIC

No matter your circumstances, you should begin this book by taking the first diagnostic test found in this chapter. The goal of the diagnostic is to give you a sense of the types of questions you might see on the GMAT and to give you a baseline to evaluate your performance. While working through this test, take stock of what types of questions you find the most challenging. Understanding what you find difficult will help ensure that you can give appropriate attention to any areas with which you are currently struggling.

Before you dive into the diagnostic, there are a couple things you should keep in mind. This test does not include an essay or integrated reasoning section. The diagnostic is separated into different content sections. Each section has a mix of question types ranging in difficulty from easy to hard.

There are two primary ways you can use the diagnostic test to focus your studies. The first is by knowing the sheer volume of questions you get correct and incorrect for each content segment. If you get a large volume of questions incorrect on a certain content segment, it is a good idea to think about giving those sections of this book a thorough review. The second way to use this test is for timing. On test day, you will need to average about 2 minutes per question to finish each section in the allotted amount of time. While taking the diagnostic, keep track of how long a question has taken you. Getting a correct answer is great! But getting a correct answer in under 2 minutes is fantastic. If you find a problem that is taking you longer than 2 minutes to answer, don't just give up! Continue to solve the problem but make a note for yourself about this content. You may want to give that content area a little bit more attention while you work your way through this book.

## HOW TO SCORE THE DIAGNOSTIC

At the end of the diagnostic, we provide both an answer key and explanations for each question. Keep track of the number of questions you get correct and the content areas of the questions that you missed. Review the length of time it took you to answer questions, taking note of those content areas for which many questions took you longer than two minutes to answer. The total number of questions you get correct is considered your "score." While this is not an accurate representation of an actual GMAT score, it is a way for you to monitor progress and compare your performance on Diagnostic Test 1 with that on Diagnostic Test 2 found near the end of the book. Once you've made your way through the content of the book, take the second diagnostic and compare the results to the first!

Keeping tabs on the content areas of the questions that you missed provides you the opportunity to seek out those trouble areas in this book and give them the extra attention they need to become areas of strength. This is an incredibly important step to take, so don't skip it.

Grab some paper and a pencil, set your egg timer, and get ready to begin your journey to GMAT success!

## Diagnostic Test 1

**59 Questions**

---

### Arithmetic

1. If $p$ is an integer such that $-8 < p < 8$, what is the product of all the possible even values of $p$ ?

- ⬭ −14,746
- ⬭ −2,304
- ⬭ −384
- ⬭ −64
- ⬭ 0

2. If $x$, $y$ are distinct positive integers, then which of the following must be true about $x^2 + y + 1$ ?

- ⬭ It is odd when $x$ is a factor of $y$
- ⬭ It is even when $x$ is odd and $y$ is odd
- ⬭ It is odd when $y$ is a factor of $x$
- ⬭ It is even when $x$ is even and $y$ is odd
- ⬭ It is odd when $x$ is odd and $y$ is even

3. If the three children in the Yao family are all at least one year apart in age, are they all less than 11 years old?

(1) The sum of the children's ages is less than 22

(2) The age of the oldest child is twice that of the youngest child.

- ⬭ Statement (1) ALONE is sufficient, but statement (2) alone is not sufficient.
- ⬭ Statement (2) ALONE is sufficient, but statement (1) alone is not sufficient.
- ⬭ BOTH statements TOGETHER are sufficient, but NEITHER statement ALONE is sufficient.
- ⬭ EACH statement ALONE is sufficient.
- ⬭ Statements (1) and (2) TOGETHER are not sufficient.

4. If $x$ is a positive integer such that $x = \sqrt[3]{k}$, then what is the value of $x$ ?

(1) $200 < k < 1{,}100$

(2) $x$ is prime

- ⬭ Statement (1) ALONE is sufficient, but statement (2) alone is not sufficient.
- ⬭ Statement (2) ALONE is sufficient, but statement (1) alone is not sufficient.
- ⬭ BOTH statements TOGETHER are sufficient, but NEITHER statement ALONE is sufficient.
- ⬭ EACH statement ALONE is sufficient.
- ⬭ Statements (1) and (2) TOGETHER are not sufficient.

5. For the first month of a three-month period, Judy used 19 gallons of gas and her car averaged (arithmetic mean) 24 miles per gallon. For the second month of the three-month period, she used 31 gallons of gas and her car averaged 26 miles per gallon. At the end of the three-month period, Judy used a total of 72 gallons of gas and her car averaged 27 miles per gallon. How many miles per gallon did Judy average in the third month?

- ⬭ 28
- ⬭ 29
- ⬭ 30
- ⬭ 31
- ⬭ 32

GO ON TO THE NEXT PAGE.

6. Claudio wants to arrange his book collection on a bookshelf such that all books of the same genre are grouped together. He has 3 fantasy novels, 2 biographies, and 4 science fiction novels. How many ways can the books on his bookshelf be arranged?

- 32
- 48
- 124
- 288
- 396

7. If $xy = -1$, then what is $|x - y|$ ?

(1) $x$ is an integer

(2) $y$ is an integer

- Statement (1) ALONE is sufficient, but statement (2) alone is not sufficient.
- Statement (2) ALONE is sufficient, but statement (1) alone is not sufficient.
- BOTH statements TOGETHER are sufficient, but NEITHER statement ALONE is sufficient.
- EACH statement ALONE is sufficient.
- Statements (1) and (2) TOGETHER are not sufficient.

8. If $m = \dfrac{\left(\frac{1}{6} + \frac{3}{8} - \frac{1}{4}\right)}{\left(\frac{7}{3}\right)}$, then $\sqrt[3]{\frac{1}{m}} =$

- $2$
- $\frac{1}{2}$
- $2\sqrt[3]{2}$
- $\frac{\sqrt[3]{4}}{2}$
- $\frac{\sqrt[3]{2}}{7}$

9. 450 is what percent greater than 15 ?

- 30
- 290
- 300
- 2,900
- 3,000

10. Amy, Barb, and Claire are going on an 800-mile trip in Amy's car. They agree to split the cost for gas such that Barb and Claire each pay twice the amount that Amy pays. Amy's car averages 25 miles to the gallon, and gas costs $1.25 per gallon. If Barb and Claire each pay twice the amount for gas that Amy pays, how much does Barb pay for gas?

- $8
- $16
- $24
- $32
- $40

11. Is $P$ divisible by 15 ?

(1) The greatest common prime factor of $P$ and 65 is 13

(2) The greatest common prime factor of $P$ and 95 is 19

- Statement (1) ALONE is sufficient, but statement (2) alone is not sufficient.
- Statement (2) ALONE is sufficient, but statement (1) alone is not sufficient.
- BOTH statements TOGETHER are sufficient, but NEITHER statement ALONE is sufficient.
- EACH statement ALONE is sufficient.
- Statements (1) and (2) TOGETHER are not sufficient.

GO ON TO THE NEXT PAGE.

**Geometry**

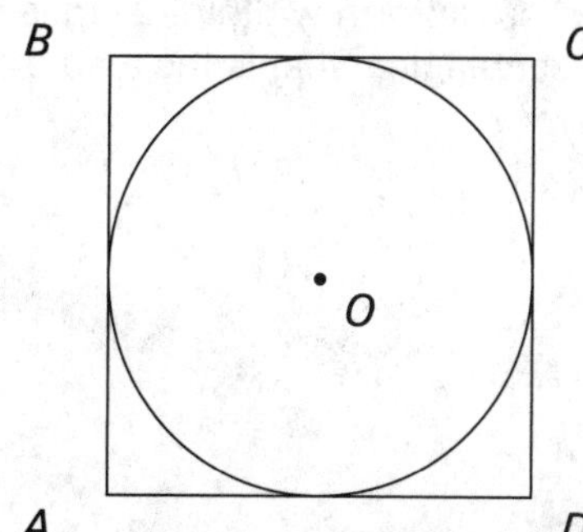


1. In the figure above, the circle with center $O$ is inscribed in square $ABCD$. If square $ABCD$ has an area of 64, what is the area of the circle?

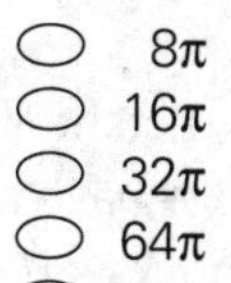

- $8\pi$
- $16\pi$
- $32\pi$
- $64\pi$
- $96\pi$

2. If the surface area of a cube is 384 square centimeters, what is the volume of the cube?

- 64 $cm^3$
- 216 $cm^3$
- 288 $cm^3$
- 384 $cm^3$
- 512 $cm^3$

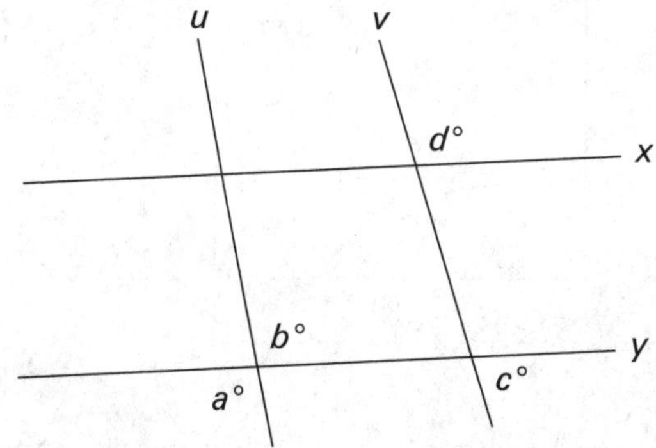


3. In the figure above, $u \parallel v$ and $x \parallel y$. What is the value of $d$ ?

(1) $a + d = 180$

(2) $a + c = 180$

- Statement (1) ALONE is sufficient, but statement (2) alone is not sufficient.
- Statement (2) ALONE is sufficient, but statement (1) alone is not sufficient.
- BOTH statements TOGETHER are sufficient, but NEITHER statement ALONE is sufficient.
- EACH statement ALONE is sufficient.
- Statements (1) and (2) TOGETHER are not sufficient.

GO ON TO THE NEXT PAGE.

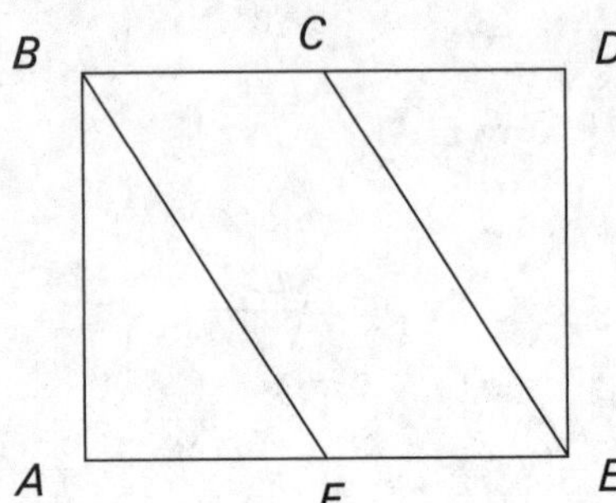


4. In the figure above, if $ABDE$ is a rectangle, and $BF$ is parallel to $CE$, what is the area of region $BCEF$ ?

(1) $AB = 8$ and $AF = 6$

(2) $F$ is the midpoint of $AE$

- Statement (1) ALONE is sufficient, but statement (2) alone is not sufficient.
- Statement (2) ALONE is sufficient, but statement (1) alone is not sufficient.
- BOTH statements TOGETHER are sufficient, but NEITHER statement ALONE is sufficient.
- EACH statement ALONE is sufficient.
- Statements (1) and (2) TOGETHER are not sufficient.

5. A rectangular box has side lengths $l$, $w$, and $h$, and a cube has side lengths $s$. If $l$, $w$, $h$, and $s$ are integers, how many of these cubes are needed to completely fill this rectangular box?

(1) $4s^2 = lw$ and $6s^2 = wh$

(2) $w = 3s$

- Statement (1) ALONE is sufficient, but statement (2) alone is not sufficient.
- Statement (2) ALONE is sufficient, but statement (1) alone is not sufficient.
- BOTH statements TOGETHER are sufficient, but NEITHER statement ALONE is sufficient.
- EACH statement ALONE is sufficient.
- Statements (1) and (2) TOGETHER are not sufficient.

6. The ratio of the length and width of a rectangle is 4:3 and the length of its diagonal is 25 cm. If a border with a uniform width of 2 cm is placed around the rectangle, what is the area of the border, in cm$^2$ ?

- 74
- 156
- 300
- 374
- 456

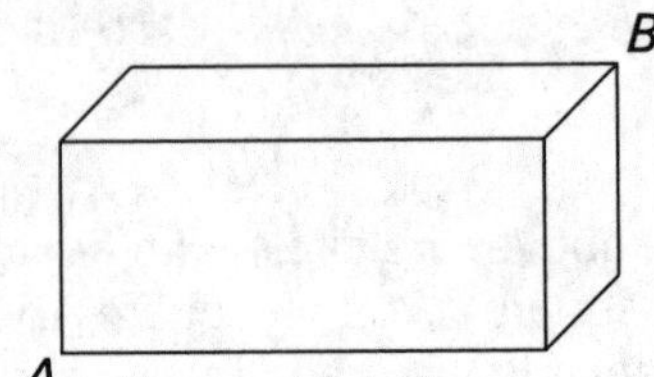


7. The length, width, and height of the rectangular solid with vertex $A$ and $B$ shown above have a ratio of 4:3:2 respectively. If the length of $AB$ is $\sqrt{58}$, what is the surface area of the solid?

- 52
- 104
- 116
- 332
- 348

GO ON TO THE NEXT PAGE.

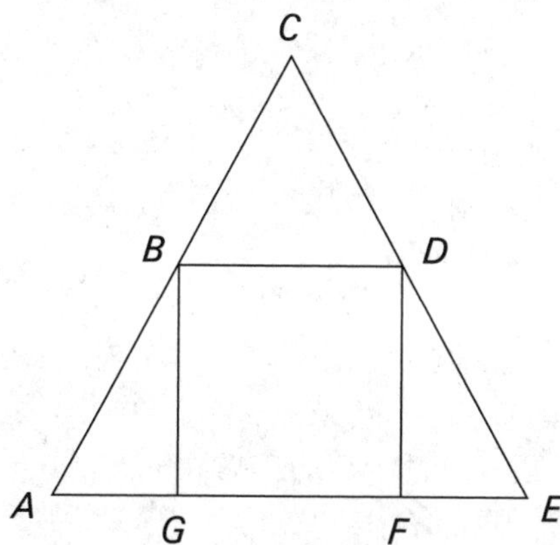


8. Square *BDFG* is inscribed in equilateral triangle *ACE.* What is the area of triangle *ACE* ?

(1) The area of triangle *BCD* is $9\sqrt{3}$

(2) $DE = 4\sqrt{3}$

- Statement (1) ALONE is sufficient, but statement (2) alone is not sufficient.
- Statement (2) ALONE is sufficient, but statement (1) alone is not sufficient.
- BOTH statements TOGETHER are sufficient, but NEITHER statement ALONE is sufficient.
- EACH statement ALONE is sufficient.
- Statements (1) and (2) TOGETHER are not sufficient.

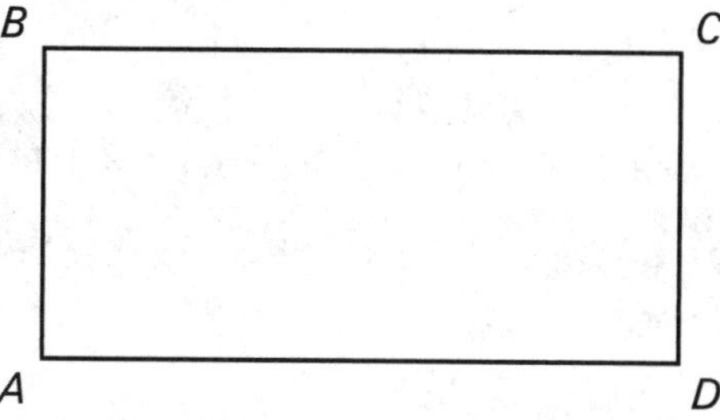


9. What is the area of rectangle *ABCD* ?

(1) $\frac{AD}{CD} = \frac{4}{3}$

(2) $AC = 10$

- Statement (1) ALONE is sufficient, but statement (2) alone is not sufficient.
- Statement (2) ALONE is sufficient, but statement (1) alone is not sufficient.
- BOTH statements TOGETHER are sufficient, but NEITHER statement ALONE is sufficient.
- EACH statement ALONE is sufficient.
- Statements (1) and (2) TOGETHER are not sufficient.

GO ON TO THE NEXT PAGE.

## Algebra

1. If $7y = 4x + 1$ and $z + 3 = 3y + 2$, then what is the value of $x$ when $z = 8$ ?

   - 1
   - 2
   - 3
   - 4
   - 5

2. What is the value of $w$ ?

   (1) $w$ is a factor of 51

   (2) $w > 17$

   - Statement (1) ALONE is sufficient, but statement (2) alone is not sufficient.
   - Statement (2) ALONE is sufficient, but statement (1) alone is not sufficient.
   - BOTH statements TOGETHER are sufficient, but NEITHER statement ALONE is sufficient.
   - EACH statement ALONE is sufficient.
   - Statements (1) and (2) TOGETHER are not sufficient.

3. Is $k \leq p$ ?

   (1) $k > 0$

   (2) $k^3 = p$

   - Statement (1) ALONE is sufficient, but statement (2) is not sufficient.
   - Statement (2) ALONE is sufficient, but statement (1) alone is not sufficient.
   - BOTH statements TOGETHER are sufficient, but NEITHER statement ALONE is sufficient.
   - EACH statement ALONE is sufficient.
   - Statements (1) and (2) TOGETHER are not sufficient.

4. What is the value of $k$ ?

   (1) $2k^2 + 7k + 6 = 0$

   (2) $4k^2 + 12k + 9 = 0$

   - Statement (1) ALONE is sufficient, but statement (2) alone is not sufficient.
   - Statement (2) ALONE is sufficient, but statement (1) alone is not sufficient.
   - BOTH statements TOGETHER are sufficient, but NEITHER statement ALONE is sufficient.
   - EACH statement ALONE is sufficient.
   - Statements (1) and (2) TOGETHER are not sufficient.

5. If $x$, $y$, and $z$ are consecutive negative odd integers such that $x > y > z$, is $xy > |z|$ ?

   (1) $z < -5$

   (2) $|x| > 1$

   - Statement (1) ALONE is sufficient, but statement (2) alone is not sufficient.
   - Statement (2) ALONE is sufficient, but statement (1) alone is not sufficient.
   - BOTH statements TOGETHER are sufficient, but NEITHER statement ALONE is sufficient.
   - EACH statement ALONE is sufficient.
   - Statements (1) and (2) TOGETHER are not sufficient.

GO ON TO THE NEXT PAGE.

6. If $x$ and $y$ are distinct non-zero integers, is $x < \left(x^2 - y^2\right)^{\frac{1}{3}}$ ?

(1) $x^2 > y^2$

(2) $x^3 < y^3$

- Statement (1) ALONE is sufficient, but statement (2) alone is not sufficient.
- Statement (2) ALONE is sufficient, but statement (1) alone is not sufficient.
- BOTH statements TOGETHER are sufficient, but NEITHER statement ALONE is sufficient.
- EACH statement ALONE is sufficient.
- Statements (1) and (2) TOGETHER are not sufficient.

7. In the equation $ax^2 + bx + c = (3x - d)^2$, $x$ is a non-zero variable and $a$, $b$, $c$, and $d$ are constants. What is the value of $d$ ?

(1) $c = 9$

(2) $a - x = 10$

- Statement (1) ALONE is sufficient, but statement (2) alone is not sufficient.
- Statement (2) ALONE is sufficient, but statement (1) alone is not sufficient.
- BOTH statements TOGETHER are sufficient, but NEITHER statement ALONE is sufficient.
- EACH statement ALONE is sufficient.
- Statements (1) and (2) TOGETHER are not sufficient.

8. What is the cube root of the square root of 128 ?

- $\sqrt[6]{2}$
- $2\sqrt[6]{2}$
- $2\sqrt[3]{2}$
- $2\sqrt{2}$
- $2$

GO ON TO THE NEXT PAGE.

**Sentence Correction**

1. Rap artists had trouble breaking into the daily rotation of videos on television channels such as MTV in the 1980s, despite the fact that they had been gaining exposure on radio charts and in record stores for several years.

   - despite the fact that they had been gaining exposure on radio charts and in record stores for several years.
   - even though for several years they had gained exposure on radio charts and in record stores.
   - despite the fact that they had gained exposure for several years with radio charts and record stores.
   - despite the fact that for several years these artists gained exposure on radio charts and in record stores.
   - even though these artists had been gaining exposure on radio charts and in record stores for several years.

2. Writing in a style blending historical fiction and scientific dystopia, the novels of Octavia Butler, who has been called "the godmother of Afrofuturism," have won Hugo and Nebula awards as well as critical acclaim from sociologists for their exploration of racial and environmental issues.

   - the novels of Octavia Butler, who has been called "the godmother of Afrofuturism," have won Hugo and Nebula awards as well as critical acclaim from sociologists for their exploration of racial and environmental issues.
   - the novels of "the godmother of Afrofuturism," Octavia Butler, have won Hugo and Nebula awards as well as critical acclaim from sociologists for exploring racial and environmental issues.
   - Octavia Butler, who has been called "the godmother of Afrofuturism," has won Hugo and Nebula awards, as well as critical acclaim from sociologists for her novels' exploration of racial and environmental issues.
   - Octavia Butler, whose novels have won Hugo and Nebula awards as well as critical acclaim from sociologists for their exploration of racial and environmental issues, has been called "the godmother of Afrofuturism."
   - Octavia Butler's novels, called "the godmother of Afrofuturism," have won Hugo and Nebula awards as well as critical acclaim from sociologists for exploring racial and environmental issues.

GO ON TO THE NEXT PAGE.

3. Keeping a daily journal improves the organization of one's thoughts and yields quite a few spontaneous ideas about self-reflection that, in turn, becomes the basis of new ambitions and initiatives.

- that, in turn, becomes the basis of new ambitions and initiatives.
- that, in turn, become the basis of new ambitions and initiatives.
- becoming, in turn, the basis of new ambitions and initiatives.
- so as to become, in turn, the basis of new ambitions and initiatives.
- that becomes the basis of new ambitions and initiatives in turn.

4. Research into information pollution—a term popularized by web usability experts—have determined that the impact of disrupting information pollutants such as unsolicited electronic messages (spam) is less than that caused by information overload due to the proliferation of social media platforms.

- have determined that the damage caused by disrupting information pollutants such as unsolicited electronic messages (spam) is less than that caused by
- have determined that the damage caused by disrupting information pollutants such as unsolicited electronic messages (spam) is less than that of
- has determined that the damage caused by disrupting information pollutants such as unsolicited electronic messages (spam) is less than
- has determined that the damage caused by disrupting information pollutants such as unsolicited electronic messages (spam) is less than that of
- has determined that the damage caused by disrupting information pollutants like unsolicited electronic messages (spam) is less than that of

5. The leopard geckos that are native to dry and semi-desert areas in Afghanistan, unlike the Gold Dust Day Geckos found in Hawaii, is crepuscular, as evidenced by its habit of "cruising" in search for food at dawn and dusk, even though those held in captivity long term may adapt to their owners' schedules.

- is crepuscular, as evidenced by its habit of "cruising" in search for food at dawn and dusk,
- is crepuscular, in its habit of "cruising" in search of food at dawn and dusk,
- are crepuscular, as evidenced by their habit of "cruising" in searching for food at dawn and dusk,
- are crepuscular, in its habit of "cruising" in search of food at dawn and dusk,
- is crepuscular, as evidenced by the habit of "cruising" in searching for food at dawn and dusk,

6. When held up to the backdrop of the night sky, the circumference of an ordinary quarter held at arm's length appears greater than other much more distant objects, such as the full moon.

- the circumference of an ordinary quarter held at arm's length appears greater than other much more distant objects, such as the full moon.
- the circumference of an ordinary quarter held at arm's length appears greater than other much more distant objects, like the full moon.
- the circumference of an ordinary quarter held at arm's length appears greater than that of other much more distant objects, such as the full moon.
- the full moon seems smaller than the circumference of an ordinary quarter held at arm's length, as it is more distant.
- the full moon seems smaller than the circumference of an ordinary quarter held at arm's length, even though it is more distant.

GO ON TO THE NEXT PAGE.

7. The comedian's sharp movements and clipped delivery showed that he was equally prone to show disrespect with his manager than an audience member.

- equally prone to show disrespect with his manager than
- equally prone to show disrespect toward his manager just as he is with
- equally prone to show disrespect with his manager as
- as prone to show disrespect to his manager as
- as prone to show disrespect to his manager as to

8. Known primarily to locals before being discovered by MTV in the late 1980s, in Manhattan Blue Man Group, who started with a troupe of three performers, expanded to a rotating company of eight to nine professionals, who appeared in trios at performances nationwide.

- Known primarily to locals before being discovered by MTV in the late 1980s, in Manhattan Blue Man Group, who started with a troupe of three performers, expanded to a rotating company of eight to nine professionals, who appeared
- Known primarily to locals in Manhattan before being discovered by MTV in the late 1980s, Blue Man Group started with a troupe of three performers and has since expanded to a rotating company of eight to nine professionals who appear
- In Manhattan, Blue Man Group was known primarily to locals before being discovered by MTV in the 1980s, starting with a troupe of three performers, expanded to a rotating company of eight to nine professionals, who appeared
- Originally a troupe of three performers who has since expanded to a rotating company of eight to nine professionals, Blue Man Group was known primarily to locals before being discovered by MTV in the 1980s in Manhattan, who appear
- Blue Man Group was known primarily to locals in Manhattan before being discovered by MTV in the 1980s, and starting with a troupe of three performers, they expanded to a rotating company of eight to nine professionals, who appeared

GO ON TO THE NEXT PAGE.

9. A sea urchin can crawl slowly on its tube feet, sometimes propelling itself with its spine, and feeds primarily on algae, occasionally eating slow moving animals such as periwinkles or mussels.

- algae, occasionally eating slow moving animals such as
- algae, and will on occasion eat slow moving animals like
- algae, and occasionally they will eat slow moving animals such as
- algae, so that it occasionally eats slow moving animals like
- algae, on occasion it does eat slow moving animals such as

10. Standardized tests in elementary school were once administered every other year, but it was found by an educational commission to be both economical plus reliable to reduce the testing schedule to only two of the six elementary school years.

- Standardized tests in elementary school were once administered every other year, but it was found by an independent educational commission to be both economical plus reliable to reduce the testing schedule to only two of the six elementary school years.
- Although standardized tests in elementary school were once administered every other year, an independent educational commission found that reducing the testing schedule to only two of the six elementary school years was both economical and reliable.
- Since standardized tests in elementary school were once administered every other year, reducing the testing schedule to only two of the six elementary years was found by an educational commission both economical and reliable to reduce the testing schedule to only two of the six elementary school years.
- Once administered every other year in elementary school, an independent educational commission found that reducing the standardized testing schedule to only two of the six elementary school years was both economical and reliable.
- An independent educational commission, having found it to be both economical plus reliable to reduce the standardized testing schedule only two of the six elementary school years, which were once administered every other year in elementary school.

GO ON TO THE NEXT PAGE.

11. Use of renewable energy has gained popularity in the past decade, but in the United States <u>alternative energy sources, primarily hydroelectric, account for only ten percent of energy use</u>.

- alternative energy sources, primarily hydroelectric, account for only ten percent of energy use.
- alternative energy sources account for only ten percent of energy use, primarily being from hydroelectric sources.
- ten percent of energy use is only from alternative energy sources, primarily hydroelectric.
- primarily hydroelectric alternative energy sources only accounts for ten percent of energy use.
- only ten per cent of alternative energy sources, primarily hydroelectric, account for energy use.

GO ON TO THE NEXT PAGE.

**Reading Comprehension**

Questions 1–3 are based on the following passage:

A mysterious new material is surprising scientists with its ability to conduct electricity without resistance (a measure of an object's opposition to the flow of electric current) at close to room temperature, about 60 degrees Fahrenheit. While known superconductors typically function only in extremely frigid temperatures, though at atmospheric pressures, the new material only survives under very high pressures, such as those near the center of the Earth. Still, while the compound composed of carbon, sulfur, and hydrogen isn't immediately feasible for use, it demonstrates the possibility of zero-resistance materials that are functional at normal temperatures. Known technological uses for superconductors abound and include generators for wind turbines as well as magnetic resonance imaging machines. But the need for temperatures below –140 degrees Celsius for these common superconductors currently poses a significant limitation to their usage. Previously tested materials that demonstrated superconductivity comprised only two elements, and the copious research on such compounds means that they are well-understood. This three-component compound has expanded the possibilities for future superconductor research. Since such a combination is unique in its superconductivity, scientists cannot yet explain this material's properties or how it can function at such unusually high temperatures.

1. The primary purpose of the passage is to

- ⬭ compare technologies in one field to those in another field
- ⬭ determine the ideal temperature for a material
- ⬭ evaluate the implications of a scientific discovery
- ⬭ enumerate potential applications of a new technology
- ⬭ speculate about potential future scientific developments

2. The author mentions the highlighted phrase most likely in order to

- ⬭ explain how pressures vary in different regions of the Earth
- ⬭ highlight a drawback of common superconductors
- ⬭ compare the requirements of different superconductors
- ⬭ describe the primary location in which superconductors function
- ⬭ emphasize the difficulty of achieving extremely low temperatures

3. Each of the following is mentioned in the passage as a characteristic of the new material EXCEPT

- ⬭ It is composed of three elements.
- ⬭ It can function at temperatures above freezing.
- ⬭ It requires high amounts of pressure.
- ⬭ It could lead to new and useful technologies.
- ⬭ It is well-understood.

GO ON TO THE NEXT PAGE.

Questions 4–6 are based on the following passage:

Mitochondrial DNA from both ancient and modern chicken specimens may provide evidence about the origin of these birds in South America. Cooper's contradiction of Storey's hypothesis that the chicken was introduced to the region by traveling Polynesians hundreds of years ago is bolstered by evidence that chickens found in the two regions are genetically distinct. Cooper also challenges Burley's contention that Polynesians must have reached the New World because they found Easter Island and share common flora, such as the bottle gourd and sweet potato, with South America. Cooper's claim that a connection between the South Pacific islands and the South American continent does not exist is based upon his team's comparison of the DNA from chicken bones collected at Polynesian archaeological sites and feathers from modern Polynesian chickens with the DNA of both ancient and modern South American chickens.

However, modern DNA has limited applicability in determining the origin of a species in one part of the world. For instance, chickens, among other animals and objects, moved around the world as people traveled; the chickens on the Pacific Islands today do not necessarily represent those that existed in the region several centuries ago. Furthermore, Cooper's belief severs the historical connection between the regions and displaces the South American plants that are generally accepted as products of Polynesian trade. Therefore, Cooper's dispute may require a broader view of the strong research supporting both sides of the chicken origin debate.

4. The author of the passage mentions plants that are common to both South America and Polynesia most likely in order to

- suggest that DNA evidence is mainly useful for comparing modern species
- point out a potential challenge to the idea that South American chickens did not originate in Polynesia
- suggest that animals were involved in local, as opposed to international, trade
- suggest that the chicken probably arrived in South America not from Polynesia but from another region
- provide evidence that disproves Cooper's claim about the South American chicken's origin

5. The passage suggests which of the following about Cooper's DNA evidence?

- It did not provide a definitive indication of whether Polynesians traded with South Americans.
- It demonstrated that modern chickens in Polynesia were not related to ancient South American chickens.
- It used primarily modern, rather than ancient, genetic material.
- It is consistent with the prevailing theory regarding plants that occur in Polynesia and South America.
- It bolstered the theory that Polynesians introduced chickens to South America.

6. According to the passage, Cooper and Burley disagree on which of the following points?

- Whether voyaging Polynesians traveled to South America
- The idea that the South American sweet potato exists in Polynesia
- The time period in which chickens appeared in South America
- How Polynesians located Easter Island
- The extent to which modern DNA is useful in ascertaining the regional origin of a species

GO ON TO THE NEXT PAGE.

Questions 7–10 are based on the following passage:

Over the past century, the United States population has continued to grow and so has the amount of hurricane activity along the Gulf and Atlantic coastlines. For meteorologists, a better understanding of storm frequency and characteristics can assist in hurricane forecasts, which in turn guides infrastructure planning and even insurance rates. Unfortunately, fewer than 200 years of historical weather records exist in the U.S., and in that time only a handful of category 5 hurricanes—the most destructive tropical cyclones—have made landfall. This paucity of data presents a challenge in accurately predicting the likelihood of future devastating storms. Consequently, some researchers have turned to a relatively new field, paleotempestology, which examines geologic evidence of prehistoric hurricane landfalls to better understand the frequency with which they occur.

In one early study, Liu and Fearn extracted sediment samples from a lake in Louisiana that was isolated from the Gulf of Mexico by a narrow barrier beach: only a storm could cause water and materials to flow from the ocean to the lake. By analyzing the overwash layers, the layers of coarse beach sediment observable on the bottom of the lake, the scientists were able to produce a rough storm history for the region, dating back several thousand years. Some have questioned this method, however, as it does not conclusively verify the sediments' provenance.

Another paleotempestological strategy relies on offshore-indicative foraminifera, single-celled organisms that are similarly thought to have arrived in a body of water via storm surges. Unlike sediments, which may be of unknown origin, if a species of foraminifera is native to the sea, its presence in a body of water adjacent to a barrier beach provides more compelling evidence as to the necessity of a historic storm. Nonetheless, Hippensteel's and Martin's method, too, must be qualified: scientists disagree about precisely which taxa are considered "offshore-indicative," and dating methods used on foraminifera fossils merely demonstrate the age of the fossils, not necessarily when a hurricane might have occurred.

Although scientists have produced estimates of hurricane recurrence rates, the limitations of paleotempestological research temper the reliability of such predictions. Moreover, long-term changes in weather and climate affect the frequency of tropical storms, which further casts doubt on the field's ability to relate past storm data to the potential for future hurricanes.

7. Which of the following best describes the organization of the passage?

- ⬭ After introducing an area of research, the author outlines its history and then casts doubt on its credibility.
- ⬭ The author describes a problem, evaluates two approaches to the problem, and then questions the usefulness of a field of study.
- ⬭ The author explains the origins of a scientific field and refutes potential criticisms to the field.
- ⬭ After comparing two methodologies, the author demonstrates why one is superior to the other.
- ⬭ After illustrating a scientific dilemma, the author explores differing perspectives on the dilemma and then reconciles the viewpoints.

8. According to the passage, which of the following is a potential drawback to the sediment analysis method mentioned in the second paragraph?

- ⬭ Scientists' inability to easily access overwash layers deep below a lake
- ⬭ The difficulty in proving precisely where the sediments came from
- ⬭ Incomplete knowledge regarding what types of sediments might have oceanic origins
- ⬭ Disagreement among researchers as to the validity of fossil evidence
- ⬭ The lack of reliability in current methods for dating sediments

GO ON TO THE NEXT PAGE.

9. It can be inferred from the passage that the two research methods described in the passage have which of the following in common?

- They involved bodies of water that were not connected to oceans.
- They were conducted in Louisiana.
- They did not provide useful paleotempestological data.
- They used historical records in conjunction with ecological data to construct storm timelines.
- Their validity has been rejected by most meteorologists.

10. Each of the following is mentioned as a potential benefit of paleotempestological research EXCEPT

- the ability to predict hurricanes
- accurate regional insurance rates
- planning of structural facilities
- a greater understanding of hurricane patterns
- preventing destructive hurricanes

GO ON TO THE NEXT PAGE.

## Critical Reasoning

1. **Grocer:** Organic produce requires less pesticide use than conventionally grown produce. Pesticides impact the health of the ecosystem, which affects the health of consumers. Shoppers can realize health benefits by buying produce that is organically grown and can become more health-wise and prone to choose organic produce through strategic marketing. Therefore, a nationwide mailing campaign of a brochure extolling the benefits of organic produce will help the ecosystem of our entire country.

   Which of the following, if true, poses the most serious challenge to the argument?

   - ⬭ The negative impact on the ecosystem from the pollution and waste generated by the national mailing campaign will meet or exceed the positive environmental impacts from more people eating organic produce.
   - ⬭ Eating a healthy diet is only one part of what it takes to lead an environmentally-friendly lifestyle.
   - ⬭ Organic produce is already available in nationwide grocery chains in every major city.
   - ⬭ The exact health benefits realized by consuming organic produce cannot be estimated for the nation as a whole.
   - ⬭ Conventional produce will make up a smaller proportion of the produce departments in grocery stores in the future.

2. The Mohs scale of mineral hardness categorizes the ability of one natural sample of mineral to make a visible scratch on another mineral. To measure the hardness of a certain mineral *X* on the scale, one finds the hardest mineral that mineral *X* can scratch, or the softest mineral that can scratch mineral *X*. However, at times, minerals that are classed as lower hardness on the Mohs scale can create microscopic disruptions on minerals that have a higher Mohs hardness. These microscopic disruptions can sometimes damage the structural integrity of the harder mineral.

   Which of the following, if true, most helps to explain how minerals lower on the Mohs scale can still affect minerals that are higher on the Mohs scale?

   - ⬭ Microscopic disruptions are not considered "scratches" for the determination of a Mohs scale number.
   - ⬭ The Mohs scale was created in 1812 without the more complete knowledge of mineral hardness that exists today.
   - ⬭ The softer minerals' impact on the harder minerals is imperceptible to the naked eye.
   - ⬭ Such anomalies do not exist when using the Vickers scale, which is a more precise measure of mineral hardness than the Mohs scale.
   - ⬭ Minerals that are scratched often bear some residue of the mineral that inflicted the scratch.

GO ON TO THE NEXT PAGE.

3. A student response survey found that students who paid for 10 or more in-person tutoring sessions on an hour-by-hour basis missed or rescheduled a session on average once every five sessions. By contrast, those students who purchased tutoring sessions in ten-hour packages missed or rescheduled a session on average only once every ten sessions. This indicates that students are at least partly motivated by the amount of money they have invested for in-person tutoring.

   Which of the following, if true, calls into question the explanation above?

   - The price per hour was slightly more expensive for those who bought individual hours.
   - Many students who missed or rescheduled sessions did so although they made a strong verbal commitment beforehand to be present.
   - All students must pay a 10% fee for rescheduling any tutoring session, but if a student cancels a session entirely, the entire cost is forfeited.
   - Upon purchase of any tutoring hours, students are required to immediately schedule all the purchased hours.
   - Students who try to reschedule tutoring sessions without enough notice may not be able to make up the session in a timely fashion, so that it counts as a missed session.

4. **Graduate Student:** While there is no doubt that the themes in my new thesis *An Examination of Warp Protocols* echo the themes in the latest quantum physics textbook of my respected mentor, titled *Hypotheses in Hyperspace*, the accusations of plagiarism I face from the committee are invalid. Although both works take similar positions on a relatively new field, I had never read my mentor's textbook, which was published three months ago, before completing my thesis.

   Which of the following, if true, provides the most support for the graduate student's position?

   - An abstract of *Hypotheses in Hyperspace* had appeared in a widely circulated physics journal a year and a half prior to the book's publication.
   - The themes explored in the thesis and the textbook are both founded on, and extensions of, prior research by a renowned physicist.
   - The textbook was published by a company that devotes most of its catalogue to chemistry texts.
   - Since the book's publication, other students who have been mentored by the author of *Hypotheses in Hyperspace* wrote papers exploring themes in that book.
   - The author began writing *Hypotheses in Hyperspace* before the graduate student began writing *An Examination of Warp Protocols.*

GO ON TO THE NEXT PAGE.

5. **Psychologist:** Negotiators who lie regularly to cover up mistakes or to form new business alliances know that "truth adherence"—the closeness with which a story aligns to the known facts—is more likely to win a listener's trust than a completely unfamiliar story with corroboration from others. Clearly, people are more willing to trust a story that feels familiar but has a few inconsistencies, than a story that is entirely new but completely verifiable.

   Which of the following most seriously calls into question the psychologist's conclusion?

   - Negotiators who are regular liars are only slightly more likely than others to use stories that have "truth adherence" to form new business alliances.
   - Although an entirely false story would immediately put the listener on guard, negotiators who are regular liars would never use such a tactic.
   - Most people who negotiate do lie once in a while, but only a very few do so regularly.
   - People tend not to become negotiators unless they already have a tendency to lie on a regular basis.
   - People are more likely to trust a negotiator if they have been referred by friends in common or trusted business acquaintances.

6. The aeronautics commission recently released a report detailing a problem with the thrusters on the newly developed XR rocket. The rocket was designed to explore the near planets in the solar system but not within the orbit of the Moon. Federal regulations require the public to be alerted about any flaw in the design of spacecraft intended primarily to traverse space within the Moon's orbit, but not further out in space. However, the aeronautics commission decided to release its report as soon as the flaw was discovered.

   Which of the following, if true, most helps to explain the decision by the aeronautics commission?

   - Until the government decided on the current regulations, the regulatory committee considered implementing stricter regulations that would require public disclosure of problems with any sort of spacecraft.
   - Spacecraft designed for traversing space solely within the orbit of the Moon have a greater likelihood of impacting the earth in the event of a problem.
   - The admission of a design flaw is not enough to deter the public from supporting future developments in space exploration technology.
   - Funding for future spacecraft might be affected if the flaws in the current rockets are made public.
   - The aeronautics commission has recently received negative publicity for a lack of transparency regarding craft design.

GO ON TO THE NEXT PAGE.

7. Prima ballerinas typically begin training between the ages of five and eight. Many ballet enthusiasts believe there is a distinct advantage not only in sheer years of training but also because the early exposure to dance shapes help young muscles develop. However, even though many prima ballerinas begin their overall training at a younger age, **they do not go on pointe any earlier than other ballerinas, typically between the ages of 10 and 12.** Since the bones of the foot require time to mature, many ballet instructors delay pointe work until this age. Therefore, it's more likely that instead of early work shaping the ballerina's muscles towards expertise, **the gifted young performer naturally gravitates toward ballet classes.**

   The portions in bold play which of the following roles in the argument?

   - ◯ The first is a claim that the argument sets out to dispute, the second is the conclusion formed on the resolution of that dispute.
   - ◯ The first is evidence against a common belief, the second is that common belief.
   - ◯ The first is evidence in support of a position with which the argument disagrees, the second is that position.
   - ◯ The first is evidence that supports an alternative explanation for a phenomenon, the second is the refutation of that explanation.
   - ◯ The first offers support for a position the argument advocates, the second is that position.

8. There are many websites that offer metrics for evaluating college-level writing. Nevertheless, professors should never allow students to use these websites to evaluate the merits of their own essays assigned in the course. While the metrics are written to allow easy comprehension, the proper application of the metrics to the specifics of the essay requires a disinterested, objective perspective.

   Which of the following, if true, most strengthens the argument?

   - ◯ The student who spent time researching and crafting an essay is usually in a better position to evaluate the merits of the essay than a professor who typically only reads the essay once.
   - ◯ In order to evaluate an essay, one must have some knowledge of the background topic of the essay.
   - ◯ Few students evaluate the essays that other students have written for the same assignment and so lack a broad perspective on what makes an essay worth merit.
   - ◯ Any essay written by a college student, when evaluated using these metrics, will demonstrate less merit than would an essay written by a professional writer.
   - ◯ For the purposes of a college course, anonymous peer review is the best method of assessing the merits of an assigned essay.

GO ON TO THE NEXT PAGE.

9. Running shoes have to be replaced periodically since the repeated force of impact wears down the sole and collapses the insole. High-tech running shoes that incorporate memory foam and gel inserts adapt to the individual stride, last much longer, and contribute to improved running performance. However, ordinary running shoes cost much less and casual runners do not get enough use out of high-tech shoes to justify the expense of the materials. Therefore, for most runners, high-tech running shoes do not save money.

Which of the following would be most useful to know in evaluating the argument?

- ⬭ If there are shoe materials that increase running performance but do not cost as much as memory foam and gel inserts
- ⬭ Whether casual runners are interested in improved running performance
- ⬭ How the price of the materials typically used in high-tech running shoes compares to that of materials used in high tech shoes tailored to other sports
- ⬭ The length of time an ordinary running shoe and a high-tech running shoe can be used before needing to be replaced
- ⬭ Whether the shoes would be used for any other sport or recreational activity aside from running

10. The election committee in the country of Jana analyzed the records of the Ostrich political party in light of new information about the opposing political party, the Prawn party. The analysis revealed that every year for the last 40 years, the Ostrich party's projections of what Prawn party political donations would be 3 years later was wrong by an average of 22%. The review also revealed that in every year for the last 40 years, the Ostrich party estimate of the Prawn party political donations for the previous year—which the Prawn party never released for public information—was only off by an average of 0.2%.

Which of the following claims is most strongly supported by the information given?

- ⬭ Prawn party political donations fluctuated widely in the last 40 years.
- ⬭ Prior to the new information, the Prawn party had not intentionally released data intended to mislead the Ostrich party's projections.
- ⬭ The average percent by which the Ostrich party's projections of the Prawn party political donations were wrong increased over time.
- ⬭ Even before the new information was released, the Ostrich party had reason to believe their projections were incorrect.
- ⬭ The Ostrich party's projections had no impact on the country of Jana.

**END OF DIAGNOSTIC TEST**

# Chapter 2
# Diagnostic Test 1: Answers and Explanations

# DIAGNOSTIC TEST 1 ANSWER KEY

| Arithmetic | Geometry | Algebra |
|---|---|---|
| 1. E | 1. B | 1. E |
| 2. D | 2. E | 2. C |
| 3. C | 3. A | 3. E |
| 4. C | 4. C | 4. B |
| 5. D | 5. C | 5. D |
| 6. D | 6. B | 6. C |
| 7. C | 7. B | 7. E |
| 8. A | 8. D | 8. B |
| 9. D | 9. C | |
| 10. B | | |
| 11. E | | |

| Sentence Correction | Reading Comprehension | Critical Reasoning |
|---|---|---|
| 1. E | 1. C | 1. A |
| 2. C | 2. C | 2. A |
| 3. B | 3. E | 3. A |
| 4. D | 4. B | 4. B |
| 5. C | 5. A | 5. E |
| 6. C | 6. A | 6. E |
| 7. E | 7. B | 7. E |
| 8. B | 8. B | 8. E |
| 9. A | 9. A | 9. D |
| 10. B | 10. E | 10. D |
| 11. A | | |

## ARITHMETIC

1. **E** Since $p$ is an integer between –8 and 8, the possible even values of $p$ are –6, –4, –2, 0, 2, 4, and 6. Since one of those integers is 0, the product of these integers is 0. The correct answer is (E).

2. **D** Plug In values for $x$ and $y$ according to the information in the answer choices, looking for ways to eliminate each. For (A), if $x = 2$ and $y = 4$, then the result of the expression in the question stem is 9 which makes (A) true. However, if $x = 3$ and $y = 6$, then the result of the expression in the question stem is 16. Now (A) is false. Eliminate it. For (B), if $x = 3$ and $y = 5$ then the result is 15. (B) is false, so eliminate it. For (C), if $y = 3$ and $x = 6$, then the result is 40. (C) is false, so eliminate it. For (D), if $x = 2$ and $y = 3$, then the result is 8. No matter what values for $x$ and $y$ are used, (D) is true. Keep it. (E) is false when $x = 3$ and $y = 2$, so eliminate (E). The correct answer is (D).

3. **C** This is a Yes/No data sufficiency question, so be prepared to Plug In more than once. The known information is that the three children in the Yao family are all at least one year apart in age. The statements need to provide a way to determine the ages. Consider Statement (1). Given that the sum of the children's ages is less than 22, Plug In three values for the children that add to less than 22. If the children are 5, 6, and 7, then the sum of the ages is 18. In this case all 3 children are less than 11, so the answer to the question is Yes. Now Plug In different values trying to get an answer of No. If the children are 3, 4, and 12 years old, then the sum of the ages is 19. In this case not all of the children are less than 11 years old, so the answer is No. The statement produces both a Yes and a No answer to the question, so the statement is insufficient. Write down BCE. Now consider Statement (2). Given that the oldest child is twice as old as the youngest child, Plug In three values for the children. If the children are 5, 7, and 10, then all 3 children are less than 11, so the answer to the question is Yes. Now Plug In different values in an attempt to get an answer of No. If the children are 6, 8, and 12 years old, then not all of the children are less than 11 years old, so the answer is No. The statement produces both a Yes and a No answer to the question, so the statement is insufficient. Eliminate (B). Now consider both statements together. The statements combine to dictate that the sum of the children's ages is less than 22 and the oldest child is twice as old as the youngest child. Plug In values that satisfy both statements. If the youngest child is 4, the oldest 8, and the middle child 6, the sum of the ages is 18. In this case, all 3 children are less than 11, so the answer to the question is Yes. Now Plug In again in attempt to get an answer of No. If the oldest child is 11, that makes the youngest child 5.5 and the middle child at least 6.5 years old. This totals 23, which violates Statement (1). All the numbers that satisfy both statements produce an answer of Yes to the question. The statements combined are sufficient. The correct answer is (C).

4. **C** This is a value data sufficiency question, so begin by determining what is known and what is needed to answer the question. The question states that $x = \sqrt[3]{k}$ and asks for the value of $x$. To answer the question, the statements need to provide a value of $x$ or $k$. Consider Statement (1). If $k = 1{,}000$, then $x = \sqrt[3]{1{,}000} = 10$. However, if $k = 216$, then $x = \sqrt[3]{216} = 6$. Statement (1) produces two different answers to the question. Statement (1) is insufficient. Write down BCE. Consider Statement (2). If $x = 5$, then the answer to the question is 5. If $x = 13$, then the answer to the question is 13. So, Statement (2) is insufficient. Eliminate (B). Now consider Statements (1) and (2) together. If $x = 7$, then both Statements (1) and (2) are satisfied, and the answer to the question is 7. If $x = 5$ or if $x = 11$, then Statement (2) is satisfied, but Statement (1) is not. The only value for $x$ that satisfies both Statements (1) and (2) is 7, which means that Statements (1) and (2) together are sufficient. The correct answer is (C).

5. **D** Begin the question by determining how many total miles Judy drove in the first two months of the three-month period and the total for the three-month period. In the first month, Judy averaged 24 miles per gallon and used 19 gallons, so she drove $24 \times 19 = 456$ miles. In the second month, she averaged 26 miles per gallon and used 31 gallons, so she drove $26 \times 31 = 806$ miles. For all three months, Judy averaged 27 miles per gallon and used 72 gallons, so she drove $27 \times 72 = 1{,}944$ miles. This means she drove $1{,}944 - 456 - 806 = 682$ miles in the third month. Judy used a total of 72 gallons of gas for the three-month period, which means she used $72 - 19 - 31 = 22$ gallons of gas in in the third month. So, Judy's average miles per gallon for the third month is $\frac{682}{22} = 31$. The correct answer is (D).

6. **D** This is a permutation problem, so evaluate it one step at a time. The problem states that the novels must be grouped by genre. There are 3 fantasy novels. Determine how many different ways the fantasy novels can be arranged. There are 3 options for the first fantasy novel, 2 options for the second, and 1 option for the third, so there are $3 \times 2 \times 1 = 6$ ways to arrange the fantasy novels. Repeat this for each of the different genres. There are $2 \times 1 = 2$ ways to arrange the biographies and $4 \times 3 \times 2 \times 1 = 24$ ways to arrange the science fiction novels. The total number of ways the books can be arranged is the product of all the arrangements by genre. The total number of ways to arrange the books is $6 \times 2 \times 24 = 288$. The correct answer is (D).

7. **C** This is a value data sufficiency question, so begin by determining what is known and what is needed to answer the question. The question provides that $xy = -1$ and asks for the value of $|x - y|$. The statements need to give specific values of $x$ and $y$. Because there are variables, Plug In. Consider Statement (1). If $x = 2$, then $y = -\frac{1}{2}$ and the value of $|x - y|$ is $\frac{5}{2}$. However, if $x = 3$, then $y = -\frac{1}{3}$ and the value of $|x - y|$ is $\frac{10}{3}$. The statement produces more than one value for the question, so it is insufficient. Write down choices BCE. Consider Statement (2). If $y = 2$, then $x = -\frac{1}{2}$ and the value of $|x - y|$ is $\frac{5}{2}$. However, if $y = 3$, then $x = -\frac{1}{3}$ and the value of $|x - y|$ is $\frac{10}{3}$. The statement produces more than one value for the question, so it is insufficient. Eliminate (B). Now work with both statements together. The only number that allows for both $x$ and $y$ to be integers and $xy = -1$ is if one of the values is 1 and the other is $-1$. No matter which variable is equal to 1 and which to $-1$, the result of $|x - y|$ is always 2. Because the two statements combined produce one value for the answer, the statements combined are sufficient. The correct answer is (C).

8. **A** The question states that $m = \frac{\left(\frac{1}{6} + \frac{3}{8} - \frac{1}{4}\right)}{\left(\frac{7}{3}\right)}$. Multiply the fraction by the reciprocal of the fraction in the denominator, which yields $m = \frac{3}{7}\left(\frac{1}{6} + \frac{3}{8} - \frac{1}{4}\right)$. Before applying the

distributive property, find common denominators for all the fractions inside the parentheses,

which makes $m=\frac{3}{7}\left(\frac{1}{6}+\frac{3}{8}-\frac{1}{4}\right)=\frac{3}{7}\left(\frac{4}{24}+\frac{9}{24}-\frac{6}{24}\right)$. Now add and multiply to find that

$m=\frac{3}{7}\left(\frac{4}{24}+\frac{9}{24}-\frac{6}{24}\right)=\frac{3}{7}\left(\frac{7}{24}\right)=\frac{1}{8}$. Use this value in the expression and solve to find that

$\sqrt[3]{\frac{1}{m}}=\sqrt[3]{\frac{1}{\left(\frac{1}{8}\right)}}=\sqrt[3]{8}=2$. The correct answer is (A).

9. **D** This question asks for the percent greater than of two numbers, so use the percent change formula. The percent change formula is $\frac{\textit{difference}}{\textit{original}}\times 100$. In this question, 15 is the original number, so the percent change is $\frac{450-15}{15}\times 100=\frac{435}{15}\times 100=2{,}900$ percent. The correct answer is (D).

10. **B** Divide 800 miles by 25 miles/gallon to determine that 32 gallons of gas are needed for the trip. Multiply 32 gallons by $1.25/gallon to find that it costs $40 total for the gas for the trip. If Barb and Claire each pay twice what Amy pays, then Barb and Claire each pay 40% of the cost of the gas, and Amy pays 20%. Barb's cost equals $40 × 40% = $16. The correct answer is (B).

11. **E** This is a Yes/No data sufficiency question, so be prepared to Plug In more than once. The question asks if $P$ is divisible by 15. The prime factorization of 15 is $3 \times 5$, so for $P$ to be divisible by 15, $P$ must have at least one 3 and one 5 as part of its prime factorization. Consider Statement (1). The prime factorization of 65 is $5 \times 13$. Plug In numbers for $P$ that satisfy the statement. If $P = 39$, then the greatest common prime factor of $P$ and 65 is 13. The statement is satisfied. The prime factorization of 39 is $3 \times 13$. In this case, the answer to the question is No because $P$ does not have a prime factor of 5. Plug In again in an attempt to get a Yes answer to the question. If $P =$ 195, then the prime factorization of $P$ is $3 \times 5 \times 13$. In this case, the answer to the question is Yes because $P$ has both 3 and 5 as prime factors. This statement provides two different answers to the question, so it is not sufficient. Write down BCE. Consider Statement (2). The prime factorization of 95 is $5 \times 19$. Plug In numbers for $P$ that satisfy the statement. If $P = 57$, then the greatest common prime factor of $P$ and 95 is 19. The statement is satisfied. The prime factorization of 57 is $3 \times 19$. In this case, the answer to the question is No because $P$ does not have a prime factor of 5. Plug In again in an attempt to get a Yes answer to the question. If $P = 285$, then the prime factorization of $P$ is $3 \times 5 \times 19$. In this case, the answer to the question is Yes because $P$ has both 3 and 5 as prime factors. This statement provides two different answers to the question, so it is not sufficient. Eliminate (B). Consider the two statements combined. If $P = 3 \times 5 \times 13 \times 19 = 3{,}705$, then both statements are satisfied and the answer to the question is Yes because $P$ has both 3 and 5 as prime factors. However, if $P = 3 \times 13 \times 19 = 741$, then both statements are satisfied but the answer to the question is No because $P$ does not have 5 as a prime factor. The two statements combined do not produce a consistent Yes or No answer to the question, so the statements combined are insufficient. The correct answer is (E).

## GEOMETRY

1. **B** The area of a square is found using the formula $A = s^2$, where $s$ is the length of one of the sides of the square. Use this information to determine the length of the sides of the square. Because $64 = 8^2$, one side of the square has a length of 8. The problem states the circle is inscribed in the square, which means that the midpoint of each side of the square is tangent to the circumference of the circle. Therefore, the diameter of the circle has the same length as the side of the square. The diameter is 8. The area of a circle is determined by the formula $A = \pi r^2$, where $r$ is the radius of the circle. The radius is half the length of the diameter, so the radius is 4. Therefore, the area of the square is $A = 4^2\pi = 16\pi$. The answer is (B).

2. **E** A cube has six square faces. Divide the surface area by 6 to find that the area of one face of the cube is $\frac{384}{6} = 64$. The formula for the area of a square is $A = s^2$, where $s$ is the length of one of the sides of the square. The sides of the squares, which are the edges of the cube, equal 8 cm. The volume of a cube is found by the formula $V = s^3$, so the volume is 8 cm × 8 cm × 8 cm = 512 cm$^3$. The answer is (E).

3. **A** This is a value data sufficiency problem. Determine what is known from the information in the problem and what is needed to solve the problem. The problem provides a figure with parallel lines that intersect each other. When lines intersect each other in this manner, all the big angles are equal and all the small angles are equal. Additionally, the sum of any big and any small angle is 180 degrees. Because of this, it is known that angle *a*, *b*, and *d* are all equal and that angle *c* is the difference between angle *a*, *b*, or *d* and 180. The problem asks about the value of *d*. In order to determine this value, the statements must provide a way to solve for *d*. Statement (1) is $a + d = 180$. Because *a* and *d* are congruent angles and are equal, both *a* and *d* are 90° angles. This provides a single answer to the question, so Statement (1) is sufficient. Write down AD. Statement (2) is $a + c = 180$. Angles *a* and *c* are supplementary angles, so the sum is always going to be 180. However, this statement does not provide any way to determine specific values of *a* or *c*. Without specific values of either, there is no way to solve for the value of *d*. Statement (2) is not sufficient. Eliminate (D). The answer is (A).

4. **C** This is a value data sufficiency question, so determine what is known and what is needed in order to answer the question. The question provides that *ABDE* is a rectangle which means all the angles are 90°, and *BAF* and *CDE* are both right triangles. Since *BF* is parallel to *CE*, the two lines maintain a constant distance from each other at all points. Therefore, segment *BC* is equal to segment *EF*. The area of region *BCEF* can be found by subtracting the areas of triangles *ABF* and *CDE* from the total area of *ABDE*. Thus, the statements need to provide the base and height of each triangle as well as the length and width of the rectangle. Consider Statement (1). This statement provides the base and height of triangle *ABF*, which is enough information to determine the area of triangle *ABF*. However, this statement provides no information about the area of the rectangle, so this statement is insufficient. Write down BCE. Now consider Statement (2). Statement (2) provides the information that *F* is the midpoint of *AE*, which means that *AF* = *AE*. But this statement doesn't provide the length of *AB*, which is needed to find the area of the rectangle. This statement by itself is insufficient. Eliminate (B). Now consider both statements combined. Statement (1) provides enough information to determine the area of triangle *ABF*, and Statement 2 indicates that *F* is the midpoint of *AE*. This means that $AE = 12$ and $EF = 6$. Thus, the area of the entire rectangle can be determined because the base *AE* and the height *AB* have known values. Furthermore, since $EF = 6$, $BC = 6$, and both *AE* and *BD* equal 12, segment *CD* is 6. Additionally, because $AB = 8$, the opposite side, *DE*, is also 8. The area of triangle *CDE* can

be found with the base of 6 and the height of 8. Therefore, with the combined information from Statement (1) and Statement (2), the areas of triangle *ABF*, triangle *CDE*, and rectangle *ABDE* can all be determined. The correct answer is (C).

5. **C** This is a value data sufficiency question, so determine what is known from the question and what is needed to answer the question. The question presents a rectangular box with side lengths *l*, *w*, and *h* and a cube with side lengths *s*. The question asks about the number of cubes needed to fill the rectangular box. In order to answer the question, values for *l*, *w*, *h*, and *s* need to be determined. Once these values are determined the volume of the rectangle can be calculated as $l \times w \times h$ and the volume of the cube can be calculated as $s^3$. Therefore, the number of cubes needed to completely fill the box is equal to $\frac{lwh}{s^3}$. Consider Statement (1). If $4s^2 = lw$ and $6s^2 = wh$, then $l = \frac{4s^2}{w}$ and $l = \frac{6s^2}{w}$. The number of cubes needed to completely fill the rectangular box is equal to $\frac{\left(\frac{(4s^2)(6s^2)(w)}{(w)(w)}\right)}{s^3} = \frac{24s^4}{s^3 w} = \frac{24s}{w}$. There is no information on how many factors of *s* are in *w*, which means that Statement (1) is insufficient. Write down BCE. Consider Statement (2). If $w = 3s$, then the number of cubes needed to completely fill the box is equal to $\frac{lh(3s)}{s^3} = \frac{3lh}{s^2}$. There is no information about *l* or *h*, so Statement (2) is insufficient. Eliminate (B). Consider both statements combined. From Statement (1), the number of cubes equals $\frac{24s}{w}$, and from Statement (2), $w = 3s$. Plug In $3s$ for *w*. So, $\frac{24s}{w} = \frac{24s}{3s} = 8$, which means that Statements (1) and (2) together are sufficient. The correct answer is (C).

6. **B** The problem asks for the area of the border, so it is necessary to find specific values of the length and width of the rectangle and the rectangle with the border. Begin by drawing the figure. Label the length and width of the rectangle as $4x$ and $3x$, respectively. The diagonal splits the rectangle in half to create a triangle with legs of length $3x$ and $4x$ and a hypotenuse of 25 cm. Use the Pythagorean Theorem to solve for the value of *x*. In this case, $(3x)^2 + (4x)^2 = 25^2$. Solving this equation yields $x = 5$. If *x* is 5 then the rectangle has dimensions 20 cm by 15 cm and an

area of 300 cm$^2$. The border adds 2 cm to the length and width on both sides of the rectangle, so the rectangle with the border has dimensions of 24 cm by 19 cm and an area of 456 cm$^2$. The area of the border is 456 cm$^2$ – 300 cm$^2$ = 156 cm$^2$. The answer is (B).

7. **B** The surface area of a rectangular solid is calculated using the formula *Surface Area* = $2(lw + wh + lh)$. To solve this problem, determine the length, width, and height of the rectangular solid. If the length of the solid is $4x$, then the width is $3x$ and the height is $2x$. This information can be used in the equation for surface area to produce $2[(4x)(3x) + (3x)(2x) + (4x)(2x)] = 2[12x^2 + 6x^2 + 8x^2]= 2[26x^2] = 52x^2$. The problem gives the length of the line that connects the two vertices, so use the Super Pythagorean Theorem to determine the value of $x^2$. The Super Pythagorean Theorem is $a^2 + b^2 + c^2 = d^2$. For this rectangular solid, the equation is $(4x)^2 + (3x)^2 + (2x)^2 = (\sqrt{58})^2$. This simplifies to $16x^2 + 9x^2 + 4x^2 = 58$, which equals $29x^2= 58$. Therefore, $x^2 = 2$. Since $x^2 = 2$, the surface area is 52(2) or 104. The answer is (B).

8. **D** This is a value data sufficiency question, so determine what is known and what is needed to answer the question. The question provides that *BDFG* is a square and *ACE* is an equilateral triangle. The area of a triangle is calculated by the formula $A = \frac{1}{2}$ (*base*) (*height*). For an equilateral triangle, the height is equal to $\frac{1}{2}$ (*base*) $\sqrt{3}$ and the formula for the area of an equilateral triangle can be written as $A = \frac{1}{2}(base)\left(\frac{1}{2}base\sqrt{3}\right) = \frac{\sqrt{3}}{4}base^2$. To find the area of triangle *ACE*, the statements need to provide a way to find the length of the side of triangle *ACE*. It also helpful to note that triangles *ABG* and *FDE* are 30:60:90 triangles so their sides are in the ratio of $x : x\sqrt{3} : 2x$. Now, evaluate the statements. Statement (1) provides the area of triangle *BCD*, which is an equilateral triangle. Using the formula above, $9\sqrt{3} = \frac{\sqrt{3}}{4}b^2$. Solving yields that $b = 6$. Because triangle *BCD* is equilateral, *BD*, the side of the square, is equal to 6. If *DF* = 6, then using the 30:60:90 relationships, *FE* = $2\sqrt{3}$ and *DE* = $4\sqrt{3}$. Hence, each side of the equilateral triangle is $6 + 4\sqrt{3}$. Statement (1) is sufficient. Write down AD. For statement (2), if *DE* = $4\sqrt{3}$, then *FD* = 6 and the side of the triangle is $6 + 4\sqrt{3}$. Statement (2) is also sufficient.

The correct answer is (D).

9. **C** This is a value data sufficiency question, so determine what is known from the problem and what is needed from the statements to solve the problem. The problem provides rectangle *ABCD* and nothing else. The problem asks for the area of rectangle *ABCD*. The area of a rectangle is calculated by the equation *area* = *length* × *width*. To solve the area, the statements need to provide a value for the length and width of the rectangle, or a way to solve for the

length and width. Statement (1) provides a relationship between the length and the width of the rectangle. If the dimensions of the rectangle are 3 by 4, then the area is 12. But, because this is a relationship and not static values, the dimensions could also be 6 by 8 which makes the area 48. Because the statement produces more than one possible value for the answer, the statement is not sufficient. Write down BCE. Statement (2) provides the length of the diagonal of the rectangle. Because this is a rectangle, the diagonal line creates a right triangle. Therefore, the side lengths of the triangles created by the diagonal can be solved with the Pythagorean Theorem. Using the information in Statement (2), the equation is $AB^2 + BC^2 = 10^2$. If the length of $AB$ and $BC$ are 6 and 8, the statement is satisfied because 36 + 64 = 100. This makes the area of the rectangle 48. But the dimensions could also be 1 and $\sqrt{99}$. This also satisfies the statement because 1 + 99 = 100. However, the area of the rectangle is now $\sqrt{99}$. Because this statement provides more than one possible value for the answer to the question, the statement is not sufficient. Eliminate (B). Now consider the two statements combined. The only dimensions that can satisfy both Statement (1) and Statement (2) are 6 and 8. The area of the rectangle is 48. Both statements combined produce a single answer to the question. The answer is (C).

## ALGEBRA

1. **E** If $z = 8$, then $z + 3 = 3y + 2$ becomes $8 + 3 = 3y + 2$ and $y = 3$. Use the value of $y$ in the first equation to find that $7(3) = 4x + 1$ and $x = 5$. The correct answer is (E).

2. **C** This is a value data sufficiency question so determine what is known and what is needed to answer the question. The question asks about the value of $w$. The statements need to provide a way to solve for a single value of $w$. Evaluate each statement individually. Statement (1) is that $w$ is a factor of 51. The factors of 51 are 1, 3, 17, and 51. There are no further restrictions on this, so $w$ can be equal to 1, 3, 17 or 51. Statement (1) is insufficient. Write down BCE. Statement (2) provides that $w$ is greater than 17. This can be any value, which means that Statement (2) is insufficient. Eliminate (B). Consider Statements (1) and (2) together. From Statement (1), $w$ is 1, 3, 17, or 51, and from Statement (2), $w$ is greater than 17. When combined, these statements provide enough information to determine that $w = 51$. Statements (1) and (2) together are sufficient. The correct answer is (C).

3. **E** This is a Yes/No data sufficiency question, so be prepared to Plug In more than once. The question asks if $k \leq p$. Evaluate the statements individually. Consider Statement (1). The inequality $k > 0$ doesn't give any information about $p$, which means that Statement (1) is insufficient. Write down BCE. Consider Statement (2). Plug In. If $k = 2$ and $p = 8$, then this statement is $2^3 = 8$. In this case, Statement (2) is satisfied and the answer to the question is Yes. Plug In again in an attempt to get an answer of No to the question. If $k = \frac{1}{2}$ and $p = \frac{1}{8}$, then the statement is $\left(\frac{1}{2}\right)^3 = \frac{1}{8}$. This is true so Statement (2) is satisfied. However, the answer to the question is now No. The statement produces both a Yes and a No answer to the question, so the statement is insufficient. Eliminate (B). Consider Statements (1) and (2). The values used to Plug In for Statement (2) also satisfy Statement (1). This means that both statements combined can create both a Yes and No answer

to the question. Both statements combined are insufficient to answer the questions. The correct answer is (E).

4. **B** This is a value data sufficiency question, so determine what is known and what is needed in order to answer the question. The question asks for the value of *k*. There is no other information known from the question. To be sufficient, the statements need to provide a way to solve for a single value of *k*. Consider Statement (1). This is a quadratic. Factor $2k^2 + 7k + 6 = 0$ to get $(2k + 3)(k + 2) = 0$, which means that $k = -\frac{3}{2}$ or $k = -2$. Because there is more than one possible value of *k*, Statement (1) is insufficient. Write down BCE. Consider Statement (2). Factor $4k^2 + 12k + 9 = 0$ to get $(2k + 3)(2k + 3)$ and $k = \frac{3}{2}$. There is a single value of *k*, which means that Statement (2) is sufficient. The correct answer is (B).

5. **D** This is a Yes/No data sufficiency question, so be prepared to Plug In more than once. The question states that *x*, *y*, and *z* are consecutive negative odd integers such that $x > y > z$. The question asks if $xy > |z|$. Because *xy* are both negative and the question asks for $|z|$, both values are positive numbers. Consider Statement (1). Plug In values that satisfy the statement. If $z = -7$, then $y = -5$ and $x = -3$. In this case, the answer to the question is Yes because $15 > 7$. In fact, no matter what number is Plugged In for *z*, the answer to the question is always Yes because the product of *xy* is greater than *z*. Statement (1) produces a consistent Yes answer to the question, so the statement is sufficient. Write down AD. Consider Statement (2). Plug In a value for *x* that satisfies the statement. If $x = -3$, then $y = -5$ and $z = -7$. Like Statement (1), this produces a Yes answer to the question. Any value of *x* that satisfies the statement results in an answer of Yes to the question. Statement (2) produces a consistent Yes answer to the question, so the statement is sufficient. The correct answer is (D).

6. **C** This is a Yes/No data sufficiency question, so be prepared to Plug In more than once. If $x < (x^2 - y^2)^{\frac{1}{3}}$, then the question can be rewritten as asking if $x^3 < x^3 - y^2$. Consider Statement (1). If $x^2 < y^2$ and *x* and *y* are positive, then $x > y$. However, if *x* and *y* are negative, then $x < y$. Plug In $x = 3$ and $y = 2$. This satisfies Statement (1). The answer to the question is No because $27 < 9 - 4$ is false. Plug In again. If $x = -3$ and $y = 2$, then the statement is satisfied. Now the answer to the question is Yes because $-27 < 9 - 4$ is true. Because the statement produces two different answers to the question, the statement is insufficient. Write down BCE. Consider Statement (2). Plug In $x = 2$ and $y = 3$. This satisfies Statement (2). The answer to the question is No because $8 < 4 - 9$ is false. Plug In again. If $x = -3$ and $y = 2$, then the statement is satisfied. The answer to the question is Yes because $-27 < 9 - 4$ is true. Because the statement produces two different answers to the question, the statement is insufficient. Eliminate (B). Consider Statements (1) and (2) together. Plug In $x = -3$ and $y = 2$, which satisfies Statement (1) and Statement (2). The answer to the question is Yes because $-27 < 9 - 4$ is true. Plug In again in an attempt to get a No answer to the question. If *x* and *y* are both positive, then Statement (1) is

satisfied only when $x > y$. In that case, Statement (2) is not satisfied. If $x$ and $y$ are both negative, then Statements (1) and (2) are satisfied only when $x < y$. If $x$ is positive and $y$ is negative, then Statement (2) is not satisfied. When $x$ is negative and $y$ is positive, Statements (1) and (2) are satisfied if $|x| > |y|$. In order to satisfy both statements, $x$ must be negative, and $y$ can be positive or negative. If Statement (1) is satisfied, then $x^2 - y^2$ is positive, which means that $x$ is always less than $x^2 - y^2$, and the answer to the question is Yes. Statements (1) and (2) together are sufficient. The correct answer is (C).

7. **E** This is a value data sufficiency question, so determine what is known and what is needed in order to answer the question. If $ax^2 + bx + c = (3x - d)^2$, then $ax^2 + bc + bx + c = 9x^2 - 6dx + d^2$, which means that $a = 9$, $b = -6d$ and $c = d^2$. Subtract $9x^2 - 6dx$ from both sides which results in $c = d^2$. The statements need to provide a way to solve for the value of $d$ given this information. Consider Statement (1). If $c = 9$, then $9 = d^2$, and $d = 3$ or $d = -3$. Statement (1) produces two different answers to the question, so it is insufficient. Write down BCE. Consider Statement (2). If $a - x = 10$ , then $9 - (-1) = 10$ and $x = -1$. This does not provide any information regarding how to solve for $d$, which means that Statement (2) is insufficient. Eliminate (B). Now consider Statements (1) and (2). From Statement (1), $9 = d^2$ and Statement (2) provides no information about how to solve for $d$. Statements (1) and (2) together are insufficient. Eliminate (C). The correct answer is (E).

8. **B** Translate the question into an expression and solve. The expression in the question can be translated to . $\sqrt[3]{\sqrt{128}}$ A root is the same thing as a fractional exponent. Therefore, the square root of 128 can be written as $128^{\frac{1}{2}}$. The cube root of this number can be written as $\left(128^{\frac{1}{2}}\right)^{\frac{1}{3}}$. Use the Power-Multiply rule of exponents to find that $\left(128^{\frac{1}{2}}\right)^{\frac{1}{3}} = 128^{\frac{1}{6}}$. All of the answer choices have a base of 2, so rewrite 128 as its prime factorization, which is $2^7$. Now the expression can be written as $\left(2^7\right)^{\frac{1}{6}} = 2^{\frac{7}{6}}$. Factor out $2^{\frac{6}{6}}$ from the expression and manipulate to find that $2^{\frac{7}{6}} = \left(2^{\frac{6}{6}}\right)\left(2^{\frac{1}{6}}\right) = 2\sqrt[6]{2}$ . The correct answer is (B).

## SENTENCE CORRECTION

1. **E** The underlined portion of the sentence contains the pronoun *they,* so look for agreement or ambiguity errors. The pronoun *they* could refer to *artists* or *videos,* so eliminate (A) and look for any obvious repeaters. Choices (B) and (C) repeat the error, so eliminate these as well. Evaluate the remaining answer choices individually, looking for reasons to eliminate each. Choice (D) has the simple past tense verb *gained* which is incorrect since this action happened further in the past than the other action *had trouble.* Eliminate (D). Choice (E) has the correct past perfect verb *had been gaining* and makes no new errors. The correct answer is (E).

2. **C** The underlined portion of the sentence begins with *the novels* following the modifying phrase *Writing in a style*, which indicates that the *novels* are *writing*. This is a misplaced modifier error. Eliminate (A) and look for any obvious repeaters. Choices (B) and (E) repeat the error, so eliminate these choices. Evaluate the remaining answer choices individually, looking for reasons to eliminate each. Choice (C) correctly places *Octavia Butler* as the noun modified by the opening participial phrase, and it makes no other errors. Keep this choice. Choice (D) contains the plural pronoun *their*, which is ambiguous, as it could refer to *novels* or *sociologists*. Eliminate (D). The correct answer is (C).

3. **B** The underlined portion contains the verb *becomes* which does not agree with the subject *ideas*. This is a subject-verb agreement error. There is an error in the sentence, so eliminate (A) and look for any obvious repeaters. Choice (E) obviously repeats the error, so eliminate it. Evaluate the remaining answer choices, looking for reasons to eliminate each. Choice (B) fixes the original error and makes no new errors, so retain this choice. Choice (C) contains the participle *becoming*. This is a misplaced modifier as it is unclear whether *becoming* modifies *self-reflection* or *ideas*. Eliminate (C). Choice (D) contains the construction *so as to become*. The idiom *so as...to* indicates degree, which is not appropriate in this sentence. This is an idiom error, so eliminate this choice. The correct answer is (B).

4. **D** This underlined portion contains the plural verb *have determined* which does not agree with the singular subject *research*. This is a subject-verb agreement error, so eliminate (A) and look for any obvious repeaters. Choice (B) repeats the error so eliminate it as well. Evaluate the remaining answer choices, looking for reasons to eliminate each. Choice (C) results in the construction *the impact of disrupting information pollutants such as unsolicited electronic messages (spam) is less than information overload*. This incorrectly compares *impact of disrupting information pollutants* to *information overload*, so eliminate this answer. Choice (D) has the correct singular verb *has determined* and makes no new errors, so keep this answer choice. Choice (E) contains the idiom *like*. The idiom *like* is used to compare nouns. The correct idiom to introduce examples is *such as*. Eliminate this answer. The correct answer is (D).

5. **C** The underlined portion contains the singular verb *is* which does not agree with the plural subject *leopard geckos*, so eliminate (A) and look for any obvious repeaters. Choices (B) and (E) repeat the error, so eliminate these choices as well. Evaluate the remaining answer choices, looking for reasons to eliminate each. Choice (C) repairs the error with the plural verb *are* and creates no new errors, so keep this answer. Choice (D) contains the singular pronoun *its* which does not agree with the plural *leopard geckos*, so eliminate this answer. The correct answer is (C).

6. **C** The underlined portion compares *the circumference of an ordinary quarter* to *other much more distant objects*. This is a comparison error, so eliminate (A) and look for any obvious repeaters. Choice (B) repeats the error, so eliminate it as well. Evaluate the remaining answer choices individually, looking for reasons to eliminate each. Choice (C) corrects the comparison by including *that of* and creates no new errors, so keep this answer choice. Choice (D) yields the construction *When held up to the backdrop of the night sky, the full moon* which is a modifier error. The noun *the full moon* is now modified by *held up to the backdrop of the night sky*. Eliminate (D). Choice (E) contains a modifier error as *the full moon* is now modified by *held up to the backdrop of the night sky*. Eliminate (E), and the correct answer is (C).

7. **E** The underlined portion contains the construction *equally...than* which is not idiomatically correct and also not a parallel comparison. Eliminate (A) and look for obvious repeaters. There are no obvious repeaters, so evaluate the remaining answer choices individually, looking for reasons to eliminate each. Choice (B) is not parallel, as the first item is *show disrespect toward* and the

second item is *just as he is with.* Eliminate (B). Choice (C) is not parallel as it is constructed to compare *to show disrespect with his manager* with *an audience member.* This makes it unclear whether the *audience member* is also one to *show disrespect.* Eliminate (C). Choice (D) is also not parallel as it suggests the comedian would *show disrespect...as an audience member.* Eliminate this choice. Choice (E) corrects the original error and makes no new errors. The correct answer is (E).

8. **B** This sentence contains the modifier *Known primarily to locals before being discovered by MTV in the late 1980s,* followed by the phrase *in Manhattan.* This is a misplaced modifier, so eliminate (A) and look for any obvious repeaters. No other answers contain this construction, so examine the remaining answers for new errors. Choice (B) repairs the original modifier error by positioning the noun *Blue Man Group* after the modifying phrase *Known primarily to locals before being discovered by MTV in the late 1980s* and creates no additional errors. Keep (B). Choice (C) contains the construction *was known primarily...starting with a troupe...expanded to a rotating company...who appeared.* This is a list that does not keep the intended meaning of the sentence nor is it parallel in construction. Eliminate (C). In (D), the pronoun *who* is ambiguous. It is not clear whether *who* refers to the *locals* or the *professionals.* Eliminate (D). Choice (E) contains the pronoun *they* which is ambiguous. The pronoun could refer to the *troupe*, the *locals*, or the *performers.* Eliminate (E). The correct answer is (B).

9. **A** This sentence contains the proper idiomatic construction *such as* to mean "for example" and makes no verb or construction errors, so retain (A) and look for differences in the answers or a 2/3 split that indicates a common error. In this case two answers contain *like* instead of *such as.* The idiom *like* is used to compare nouns whereas the idiom *such as* is to introduce examples. *Such as* is the correct idiom in this sentence, so eliminate (B) and (D). Choice (C) uses the pronoun *they*, which does not agree with the singular noun *sea urchin*, so eliminate this choice. Choice (E) uses the verb form *does eat* which is not parallel with either *feeds* or *propelling*, so eliminate this choice. The correct answer is (A).

10. **B** This underlined portion of the sentence contains the idiom construction *both...plus.* The proper construction is *both...and.* Therefore, eliminate (A) and look for any obvious repeaters. Choice (E) repeats this error, so eliminate (E). Evaluate the remaining answer choices, looking for reasons to eliminate each. Choice (B) repairs the idiom with the construction *both...and* and creates no new errors, so keep it. Choice (C) has the construction *both economical and reliable* modifying *an educational commission.* This is a misplaced modifier error, so eliminate (C). Choice (D) has the phrase *Once administered every other year in elementary school,* modifying the noun *an independent educational commission.* This is a misplaced modifier error, so eliminate this choice. The correct answer is (B).

11. **A** The underlined portion correctly contains the plural verb *account* to agree with *sources* and contains no obvious errors, so keep (A) for now and examine the remaining answers for errors. Choice (B) places *primarily being from hydroelectric sources* so that it modifies *energy use.* This is a misplaced modifier error. Eliminate (B). Choice (C) moves *only* so that it modifies *alternative energy sources* instead of *ten percent.* This is a modifier error. Eliminate (C). Choice (D) uses the singular verb *accounts* for the plural subject *sources*, so eliminate this choice. Choice (E) now has the phrase *ten percent* modifying *alternative energy sources* instead of *energy use*, so eliminate (E). The correct answer is (A).

## READING COMPREHENSION

1. **C** The subject of the question is the passage as a whole and the task of the question is indicated by the phrase *primary purpose*, so this is a primary purpose question. The passage introduces a *mysterious new material* that is *surprising scientists with its ability to conduct electricity without resistance…at close to room temperature*. The passage then compares this substance with other *superconductors* and then states that the material *demonstrates the possibility of zero-resistance materials that are functional at normal temperatures*. The remainder of the passage discusses the different aspects of the new material and how they may impact the use of superconductors. Evaluate the answer choices individually, looking for one that reflects the primary purpose of the passage. Choice (A) is a no-such comparison answer as the passage does not *compare technologies in one field to those in another field*. Eliminate (A). Choice (B) is a memory trap as the passage does mention *temperature* in multiple places. But temperature is not the primary purpose of the passage. Eliminate (B). Choice (C) is a good paraphrase of the primary purpose of the passage, so keep it. Choice (D) is a reversal of the information in the passage. The passage states that *scientists cannot yet explain this material's properties or how it can function at such unusually high temperatures*. If scientists cannot yet explain how the material functions at the temperatures it is found at, then they cannot yet discuss applications of the material. Eliminate (D). Choice (E) is a memory trap. The passage does speculate about potential impacts of the material's discovery, but this is not the primary purpose of the passage. Eliminate (E). The correct answer is (C).

2. **C** The subject of the question is the phrase *"atmospheric pressures"* and the task of the question is referenced by the phrase *most likely in order to*, so this is a purpose question. Determine why the author uses the phrase *atmospheric pressures*. The sentence in question is *While known superconductors typically function only in extremely frigid temperatures, though at atmospheric pressures, the new material only survives under very high pressures, such as those near the center of the Earth*. In this sentence, the conditions in which *known superconductors typically function* are compared to the conditions in which *the new material only survives*. One of the conditions in which known superconductors function is *at atmospheric pressures*, while the new material only survives *under very high pressures, such as those near the center of the Earth*. Therefore, the passage mentions *atmospheric pressures* to compare the conditions for the function of known superconductors and the conditions for the survival of the new material. Evaluate the answer choices individually, looking for one that reflects this idea. Choice (A) is a memory trap as the passage does mention different regions of the Earth but this is not the purpose of discussing atmospheric pressures. Eliminate (A). Choice (B) is a reversal of the information in the passage as functioning at atmospheric pressures is one the reasons common superconductors are used. Eliminate (B). Keep (C) because it is a good paraphrase of the purpose of mentioning *atmospheric pressures*. Choice (D) is a memory trap. Atmospheric pressures is listed as one of the conditions in which common superconductors function, but the purpose of mentioning atmospheric pressures is not to *describe the primary location*. Eliminate (D). Choice (E) is another memory trap. The passage does mention *extremely frigid temperatures* and atmospheric pressures as conditions for common superconductors. The passage also mentions *the need for temperatures below –140 degrees Celsius* for common superconductors to function as an issue. But *atmospheric pressures* is not mentioned to *emphasize the difficulty of achieving extremely low temperatures*. Eliminate (E). The correct answer is (C).

3. **E** The subject of the question is *characteristic(s) of the new material* and the task is referenced by the phrase *mentioned in the passage*, so this is a retrieval question. Determine what the passage says about the characteristics of the new material. The passage says the new material has the *ability*

*to conduct electricity without resistance...at close to room temperature* and *survives under very high pressures.* The material is *composed of carbon, sulfur, and hydrogen* and has *expanded the possibilities for future superconductor research* despite that scientists *cannot yet explain this material's properties or how it can function at such unusually high temperatures.* This is an except question, so evaluate the answer choices individually, looking for that one not mentioned in the passage. Eliminate (A) because the passage says the material is *composed of carbon, sulfur, and hydrogen.* Eliminate (B) because the passages says the material can function *at close to room temperature.* Eliminate (C) because the material *survives under very high pressures.* Choice (D) can also be eliminated as the material has *expanded the possibilities for future superconductor research.* Choice (E) is a reversal of the information in the passage that scientists *cannot yet explain this material's properties or how it can function at such unusually high temperatures.* The correct answer is (E).

4. **B** The subject of the question is *plants that are common to both South America and Polynesia* and the task of the question is referenced by the phrase *most likely in order to*, so this is a purpose question. Determine what the passage says about these plants. The first paragraph says that Cooper *challenges Burley's contention that Polynesians must have reached the New World because they found Easter Island and share common flora, such as the bottle gourd and sweet potato, with South America.* The second paragraph states that *Cooper's belief severs the historical connection between the regions and displaces the South American plants that are generally accepted as products of Polynesian trade.* Therefore, plants are mentioned as another piece of evidence regarding the contested connection between South America and Polynesia. Evaluate the answer choices individually, looking for one that reflects this idea. Choice (A) is a memory trap from the passage, which states *modern DNA has limited applicability in determining the origin of a species in one part of the world.* This is not a reason why the passage mentions plants, so eliminate (A). Choice (B) is a good paraphrase of the information in the passage, so keep (B). Choice (C) is a reversal of the information in the passage, which states *chickens, among other animals and objects, moved around the world as people traveled.* Eliminate (C). Choice (D) is a memory trap. While the passage does mention plants to *suggest that the chicken probably arrived in South America not from Polynesia but from another region*, the passage also mentions the plants as a reason why there is a connection between South America and Polynesia. This answer choice does not address both claims about the plants in the passage. Eliminate (D). Choice (E) is also a memory trap as the plants are considered *evidence that disproves Cooper's claim about the South American chicken's origin.* But the plants are also mentioned as an argument in support of Cooper's claim. Eliminate (E). The correct answer is (B).

5. **A** The subject of the question is *Cooper's DNA evidence* and the task of the question is referenced by the word *suggests*, so this is an inference question. Determine what the passage says about Cooper's DNA evidence. Cooper's team conducted a *comparison of the DNA from chicken bones collected at Polynesian archaeological sites and feathers from modern Polynesian chickens with the DNA of both ancient and modern South American chickens* as evidence of *Cooper's contradiction of Storey's hypothesis that the chicken was introduced to the region by traveling Polynesians hundreds of years ago.* The passage then states *modern DNA has limited applicability in determining the origin of a species in one part of the world* and that *Cooper's dispute may require a broader view of the strong research supporting both sides of the chicken origin debate.* Evaluate the answer choices, looking for one that reflects this idea. Choice (A) is a good paraphrase of the information in the passage. Keep (A). Choice (B) is a reversal of the information in the passage that says *modern DNA has limited applicability in determining the origin of a species in one part of the world.* Eliminate (B). Choice (C) is a reversal of the information in the passage that Cooper's team used *DNA of both ancient and modern South American chickens.* Eliminate (C). Choice (D) is a reversal of the information in the passage as the *prevailing theory regarding plants that occur*

*in Polynesia and South America* is also part of the debate on the origin of chickens in South America. Eliminate (D). Choice (E) uses the recycled language *bolstered,* but this is used to state that *chickens found in the two regions are genetically distinct* and not as a boon to Cooper's DNA evidence. Eliminate (E). The correct answer is (A).

6. **A** The subject of the question is what *Cooper and Burley disagree on* and the task of the question is referenced by the phrase *According to the passage.* This is a retrieval question, so determine what the passage says about Cooper and Burley's disagreement. According to the passage, Cooper *challenges Burley's contention that Polynesians must have reached the New World because they found Easter Island and share common flora, such as the bottle gourd and sweet potato, with South America.* Look for an answer that reflects this idea. Choice (A) is a good paraphrase of the information in the passage. Keep (A). Choice (B) is a reversal of the information in the passage as it is not explicitly stated that Cooper believes the South American sweet potato does not exist in Polynesia. Eliminate (B). Choice (C) is a reversal of the information in the passage. Cooper and Burley disagree on *if* chickens appeared in South America from Polynesia, not the *time period.* Eliminate (C). Choice (D) uses the recycled language *Easter Island,* but the passage does not give any indication that either disagree the Polynesians located the island. Eliminate (D). Choice (E) is a memory trap. One of the contentions in the passage is regarding *the extent to which modern DNA is useful in ascertaining the regional origin of a species.* However, this is not a disagreement between Cooper and Burley. Eliminate (E). The correct answer is (A).

7. **B** The subject of the question is the passage as a whole and the task of the question is referenced by the phrase *describes the organization,* so this is a structure question. Identify the key sentences in each paragraph. The first paragraph's last two sentences are the key sentences. They state *This paucity of data presents a challenge in accurately predicting the likelihood of future devastating storms. Consequently, some researchers have turned to a relatively new field, paleotempestology, which examines geologic evidence of prehistoric hurricane landfalls to better understand the frequency with which they occur.* The second paragraph introduces *one early study* of paleotempestology that involved extracting sediment samples *from a lake in Louisiana that was isolated from the Gulf of Mexico by a narrow barrier beach.* The second paragraph's key sentence is the last, which states *Some have questioned this method, however, as it does not conclusively verify the sediments' provenance.* The third paragraph introduces a*nother paleotempestological strategy.* The passage mentions in the last sentence that this method is also *called into question* by scientists. The final paragraph concludes the *limitations of paleotempestological research temper the reliability of such predictions.* Evaluate the answer choices individually, looking for one that reflects the structure of the passage. Choice (A) can be eliminated because the passage does not begin by *introducing an area of research.* Choice (B) is a good outline of the organization of the passage. Keep (B). Eliminate (C) because it is a reversal of the information in the passage. The passage does not *refute potential criticisms.* Choice (D) is a no-such comparison answer. The passage does not compare two methodologies and *demonstrate why one is superior to the other.* Eliminate (D). Choice (E) is incorrect because the passage does not reconcile different viewpoints. Eliminate (E). The correct answer is (B).

8. **B** The subject of the question is *the sediment analysis method,* and the task is referenced by the phrase *according to the passage.* This is a retrieval question. The question asks about *a potential drawback* of the analysis, so look for the information in the second paragraph that mentions a drawback. The second paragraph states s*ome have questioned this method, however, as it does not conclusively verify the sediments' provenance.* The word *provenance* means place of origin, so the potential drawback is that the analysis does not indicate where the sediment came from. Evaluate the answer choices individually, looking for one that reflects this idea. Choice (A)

contains the recycled language *overwash layers,* but the claim that scientists were unable to *easily access* these layers is a reversal of the information in the passage. The passage does not give any indication of any issue accessing the overwash layers. Eliminate (A). Choice (B) is a good paraphrase of the information in the passage, so keep (B). Choice (C) contains a memory trap regarding oceans. While the paragraph does mention ocean sediment, it is not concerned with *knowledge regarding* the types of sediment. Eliminate (C). Choice (D) is a memory trap of the third paragraph. The third paragraph discusses *fossils* and the potential drawback cited in the third paragraph is the *validity of fossil evidence.* Eliminate (D). Choice (E) is a reversal of the information in the passage, which states that from sediment *scientists were able to produce a rough storm history for the region, dating back several thousand years.* Eliminate (E). The correct answer is (B).

9. **A** The subject of the question is *the two research methods described in the passage* and the task of the question is referenced by the word *inferred,* so this is an inference question. The question asks what the two research methods have in common, so determine what the passage says about each method. The first method involved *sediment samples from a lake in Louisiana that was isolated from the Gulf of Mexico by a narrow barrier beach* that resulted in the ability to *produce a rough storm history for the region, dating back several thousand years.* The first method also has a drawback noted in the passage. The second method involved *offshore-indicative foraminifera, single-celled organisms that are similarly thought to have arrived in a body of water via storm surges* and also contains a drawback outlined in the passage. Evaluate the answer choices individually, looking for one that describes something in common between the two methods. Choice (A) is true as both methods *involved bodies of water that were not connected to oceans.* Keep (A). Choice (B) uses the recycled language *Louisiana.* While the first method was conducted with samples from a lake in Louisiana, the second method does not mention a specific location. Eliminate (B). Choice (C) is a reversal of the information as the methods did produce useful data but there were questions about the methodology. Eliminate (C). Choice (D) is a memory trap. The first method was able to *construct storm timelines* but the second method was only able to *demonstrate the age of the fossils, not necessarily when a hurricane might have occurred.* Eliminate (D). Eliminate (E) as well as it contains the extreme language *rejected.* The validity was not rejected by any scientists. The scientists only raised questions about the data. Eliminate (E). The correct answer is (A).

10. **E** The subject of the question is *a potential benefit of paleotempestological research,* and the task of the question is referenced by the word *mentioned.* This is a retrieval question. Determine what the passage says about this research. The research was turned to in response to the *challenge in accurately predicting the likelihood of future devastating storms.* The passage describes the research as a *relatively new field* which *examines geologic evidence of prehistoric hurricane landfalls to better understand the frequency with which they occur.* It states that *the limitations of paleotempestological research temper the reliability of such predictions* and *long-term changes in weather and climate affect the frequency of tropical storms, which further casts doubt on the field's ability to relate past storm data to the potential for future hurricanes.* This is an except question, so the correct answer will not be mentioned in the passage. Choice (A) is a reversal of the information in the passage regarding the research. Eliminate (A). Choices (B) and (C) are both reversals of the same sentence in the passage, which states that *a better understanding of storm frequency and characteristics can assist in hurricane forecasts, which in turn guides infrastructure planning and even insurance rates.* Eliminate (B) and (C). Choice (D) is a reversal of the information in the passage that states the field *examines geologic evidence of prehistoric hurricane landfalls to better understand the frequency with which they occur.* Choice (E) is not mentioned as one of the potential benefits of the research, so keep it. The correct answer is (E).

## CRITICAL REASONING

1. **A** The question task is indicated by the phrase *poses the most serious challenge*, so this is a weaken question. Find the conclusion, premise, and pattern or assumption. The conclusion of the argument is *doing a nationwide mailing campaign of a brochure extolling the benefits of organic produce will help the ecosystem of our entire country.* The premise is *pesticides impact the health of the ecosystem, which affects the health of consumers.* This argument follows a Planning pattern, since the conclusion is about what course of action to take. The assumption is that there is no problem with the plan to *help the ecosystem of our entire country* with *a nationwide mailing campaign of a brochure.* The correct answer will expose a problem with the plan.

   (A) Correct. This answer reveals a problem with the plan. If the negative impact of the mailing campaign meets or exceeds the positive impact of more people eating organic produce, then the plan is not effective.

   (B) No. The impact of eating a healthy diet on how close an individual is to leading an environmentally-friendly lifestyle is out of scope.

   (C) No. This answer strengthens the argument. If *Organic produce is already available in nationwide grocery chains*, then the plan is more likely to work.

   (D) No. This answer is out of scope. This answer choice weakens the connection between organic produce and health benefits.

   (E) No. This answer strengthens the argument. If there is less conventional produce in the store, then there may be more organic produce. If there is more organic produce, then the plan is more likely to work.

   The correct answer is (A).

2. **A** The question task is referenced by the phrase *most helps to explain,* so this is a resolve/explain question. Specifically, the task is to find the answer that explains *how minerals lower on the Mohs scale can still affect minerals that are higher on the Mohs scale.* Find the conflict in the argument. The argument states *However, at times minerals that are classed as lower hardness on the Mohs scale can create microscopic disruptions on minerals that have a higher Mohs hardness.* The correct answer will explain how minerals can have a lower classification yet still damage harder minerals.

   (A) Correct. This answer explains that the damaging *microscopic disruptions* don't count as *scratches* for purposes of Mohs classification.

   (B) No. This answer would make the conflict worse because it questions the validity of the Mohs scale.

   (C) No. This answer choice addresses only one side of the argument. The answer confirms that the disruptions can't be seen by the *naked eye*; however, it doesn't explain whether *naked eye* is the standard for a *visible scratch* that determines the Mohs classification.

   (D) No. This answer is giving an alternative to the Mohs scale, but this choice is out of scope of the task as it does not explain *how minerals lower on the Mohs scale can still affect minerals that are higher on the Mohs scale.*

   (E) No. This answer explains only one side—that softer minerals can damage the integrity of harder minerals—but this choice doesn't explain why the minerals are classed as harder and softer on the Mohs scale.

   The correct answer is (A).

3. **A** The question task is referenced by the phrase *calls into question,* so this is a weaken question. Find the conclusion, premise, and assumption or pattern. The conclusion is *that students are at least partly motivated by the amount of money they have invested for in-person tutoring* and the premise is the findings of the *student response survey.* This argument follows a sampling pattern. The standard assumption of a sampling pattern is that the sample is representative. The correct answer will give new evidence that shows the sample is not representative or cannot be trusted.

(A) Correct. If those who bought individual hours paid more per hour, then they have a greater financial incentive, and yet the group with individual hours has more sessions that are missed or rescheduled.

(B) No. The *strong verbal commitment* a student made to be present is out of the scope of the argument.

(C) No. The rescheduling fee or cancellation fee for a session is out of the scope of the argument.

(D) No. This answer suggests that scheduling purchased hours one hour at a time might lead to a lower missed or rescheduled rate when compared to purchasing 10 hours all at once.

(E) No. How sessions are classified as rescheduled or missed is out of the scope of the argument.

The correct answer is (A).

4. **B** The question task is referenced by the phrase *provides the most support,* so this is a strengthen question. Find the conclusion, premise, and pattern or assumption in the argument. The conclusion is *the accusations of plagiarism I face from the committee are invalid.* The premise is *I had never read my mentor's textbook, which was published three months ago, before completing my thesis.* The graduate student is arguing against the committee's claim of plagiarism. The committee's argument follows a causality pattern. The committee assumes the cause of the *similar positions* in the two works is *plagiarism.* The standard assumption of a causality pattern is that there is no other cause and it's not a coincidence. To support the student's defense against this assumption, the correct answer needs to weaken the committee's assumption of causality. Therefore, the correct answer will provide an alternate cause for the *similar positions* in the mentor's text and the student's thesis.

(A) No. This weakens the student's position, as it suggests there was ample time to become exposed to the ideas in the mentor's work.

(B) Correct. This indicates that both the student's and the mentor's works were influenced by a third scientist, which would support that the student has not plagiarized the mentor.

(C) No. This answer indicates that the mentor's physics book was published by a company that doesn't usually publish physics. This information is out of scope of the question.

(D) No. This weakens the student's position. If other students had time to write papers on the mentor's book, then it is possible for this student to write a thesis based on the same work.

(E) No. This weakens the student's position. This indicates the mentor's work was started before the student's thesis, so the student might have had some exposure to the ideas before publication.

The correct answer is (B).

5. **E** The question task is referenced by the phrase *calls into question,* so this is a weaken question. Find the conclusion, premise, and patterns or assumption. The conclusion is *people are more willing to trust a story that feels familiar but has a few inconsistencies, than a story that is entirely new but completely verifiable.* The premise is *"truth adherence"—the closeness with which a story aligns to the known facts—is more likely to win a listener's trust than a completely unfamiliar story with corroboration from others.* In this argument, the language shifts from people's *trust* being connected to the *closeness with which a story aligns to the known facts* to people's *trust* being connected to *trust a story that feels familiar but has a few inconsistencies.* The argument fits the causality pattern, as it assumes the root cause of *trust* in a story is whether it *aligns to the known facts* and therefore *feels familiar* even though it may have *a few inconsistencies.* The standard assumption of a causality pattern is that there is no other cause and it's not a coincidence. The correct answer will provide evidence to weaken this assumption by bringing up another cause of *trust* in a story.

(A) No. This answer is out of scope. This answer targets the incidence of *"truth adherence,"* which is just a part of the premise, rather than the assumption that *trust* in a story is caused by whether it *aligns to the known facts* and therefore *feels familiar.*

(B) No. This answer strengthens the premise that *negotiators who lie regularly* know that *"truth adherence"...is more likely to win a listener's trust.*

(C) No. This answer is out of scope. This answer targets the premise that there are *negotiators who lie regularly.*

(D) No. This answer introduces a new causal relationship, that people who *become negotiators* are those who already *have a tendency to lie,* which may strengthen the premise that there are *negotiators who lie regularly.*

(E) Correct. This answer provides another reason for *trust* in a story from a negotiator: the source or person who tells the story, rather than whether the story has *"truth adherence"* or *aligns to the known facts.*

The correct answer is (E).

6. **E** The question task is referenced by the phrase *most helps to explain,* so this is a resolve/explain question. The argument presents a contradiction. The contradiction is that *the aeronautics commission decided to release its report as soon as the flaw was discovered* despite the rocket being *designed to explore the near planets in the solar system but not within the orbit of the Moon* even though *Federal regulations require the public to be alerted about any flaw in the design of spacecraft intended primarily to traverse space within the Moon's orbit, but not further out in space.* The correct answer will provide new information that bridges both sides and gives a reason for the commission to release the report.

(A) No. This answer gives more information about the regulations, but not why the commission decided to release a report about the flaw. This answer only explains one side of the conflict.

(B) No. This answer explains why the regulations only apply to spacecraft within the Moon's orbit, but not why the commission decided to release a report about the flaw. This answer only explains one side of the conflict.

(C) No. This answer choice is out of scope. It rules out a possible consequence of the commission's decision but doesn't explain why the commission decided to release the report about the flaw when it wasn't required.

(D) No. This answer makes the conflict worse, as it is a reason for the commission not to release the report.

(E) Correct. If the *commission has recently received negative publicity for a lack of transparency,* then the commission has another reason to release the report about the flaw.

The correct answer is (E).

7. **E** The task of this question is referenced by the phrase *roles in the argument,* so this is an identify the reasoning question. Identify the conclusion and premise. The conclusion is *it's more likely that instead of early work shaping the ballerina's muscles towards expertise, the gifted young performer naturally gravitates toward ballet classes.* The second bolded phrase is a part of the conclusion. The premises are *they do not go on pointe any earlier than other ballerinas, typically between the ages of 10 and 12* and *Since the bones of the foot require time to mature, many ballet instructors delay pointe work until this age.* The first bolded phrase is a premise that supports the conclusion.

(A) No. While the second bolded phrase is a conclusion, the first bolded phrase is a premise that supports the conclusion, not a claim that the argument sets out to dispute. This answer is only a partial match.

(B) No. While the first bolded phrase is evidence against the common belief *many think* in the second sentence, the conclusion containing the second bolded phrase disagrees with that common belief. This answer is only a partial match.

(C) No. This answer does not match the structure of the passage. The first phrase is a premise that supports the argument itself, not the position it disagrees with.

(D) No. While the first bolded phrase is evidence that supports the alternative explanation of *the gifted young performer naturally gravitates toward ballet classes* found in the conclusion, the second phrase is not a refutation of that explanation. This answer is only a partial match.

(E) Correct. The first phrase is a premise in support of the conclusion, and the second phrase is the explanation or position the author advocates.

The correct answer is (E).

8. **E** The question task is referenced by the phrase *strengthens the argument,* so this is a strengthen question. The conclusion is *professors should never allow students to use these websites to evaluate the merits of their own essays assigned in the course,* and the premise is *the proper application of the metrics to the specifics of the essay requires a disinterested, objective perspective.* Thus, the argument fits the causality pattern. The standard assumption of a causality pattern is that there is no other cause and it's not a coincidence. The argument assumes that the cause of being able to *evaluate the merits of their own essays* is a *disinterested, objective perspective,* which the students do not have. The correct answer will uphold this assumption by ruling out another cause or confirming the link between a *disinterested, objective perspective* and a student *evaluating the merits* of his or her own essay.

(A) No. This answer weakens the conclusion, as it states that students are better at evaluating their own essays.

(B) No. This answer weakens the conclusion, as it suggests that it is *knowledge of the background topic,* not *a disinterested, objective perspective,* that is needed to evaluate an essay.

(C) No. This answer is out of scope. The answer choice suggests that students are unskilled at evaluating essays of *other students.* However, this argument is about the assumption that they lack the requirements to *evaluate the merits of their own essays.*

(D) No. This answer is out of scope. It suggests that the student *essay will demonstrate less merit* than *an essay written by a professional.* However, this argument is about how skilled students are at evaluating their own essays, not how skilled they are at writing those essays.

(E) Correct. If *anonymous peer review is the best method of assessing the merits of an assigned essay,* then the this supports the assumption that the cause of being able to *evaluate the merits* of a student essay is *a disinterested, objective perspective.*

The correct answer is (E).

9. **D** The task of the question is referenced by the phrase *useful to know in evaluating the argument,* so this is an evaluate question. Find the conclusion, premise, and assumption or pattern. The conclusion is *for most runners, high-tech running shoes do not save money,* and the premise is *ordinary running shoes cost much less and casual runners do not get enough use out of high-tech shoes to justify the expense of the materials.* The correct answer will bring up a consideration that connects the conclusion and the premise.

(A) No. Other *shoe materials that increase running performance but do not cost as much* is out of the scope of the argument.

(B) No. The interests of casual runners are out of the scope of the passage.

(C) No. This answer is out of scope as it contrasts the materials used in shoes of *other sports.*

(D) Correct. This answer ties the conclusion and the premise together. If most runners do not save money by purchasing the high-tech running shoes, then knowing the length of time a shoe lasts is integral to understanding how often a new shoe must be purchased.

(E) No. This answer is out of scope as it targets whether these shoes *would be used for any other sport.*

The correct answer is (D).

10. **D** The task of the question is referenced by the phrase *strongly supported,* so this is a strengthen question. The passage discusses the Ostrich party's projections of Prawn party political donations *for the last 40 years.* The passage states that the projections were for *3 years later* and were *wrong by an average of 22%.* The passage also states that the Ostrich party estimated *Prawn party political donations for the previous year* and these estimates were *only off by an average of 0.2%.* The correct answer will be something that is true based on the information in the passage.

(A) No. How much the *Prawn party political donations fluctuated* is out of the scope of the passage and not supported by the information given.

(B) No. This statement is weakened by the information in the passage. If the Prawn party had not intentionally released data intended to mislead the projections of the Ostrich party, then there must be another reason for the projections to be off by 22%.

(C) No. The *average percent* of how *wrong* the Ostrich party's projections are is out of the scope of the passage.

(D) Correct. If the Ostrich party had accurate estimates for the previous year, then they would know that their 3-year projections were wrong.

(E) No. The *impact on the country of Jana* is out of scope.

The correct answer is (D).

# Part II Orientation

# Chapter 3 Introduction

Congratulations on your decision to attend business school, and welcome to *GMAT Premium Prep, 2022 Edition*! Preparing for the GMAT is an important part of the process, so let's get started. This chapter will provide you with a strategic plan for acing the GMAT, as well as an overview of the test itself, including question formats and information on how the test is scored.

# HOW TO USE THIS BOOK: A STRATEGIC PLAN FOR ACING THE GMAT

**Need a Study Plan?**
Go to your Student Tools to download our study plans—tailored for 4, 8, and 12 weeks of available prep time! See pages viii-ix for instructions.

## 1. Learn the Famed Princeton Review Test-Taking Strategies

In the next few chapters, you'll find the strategies that have given our GMAT students the edge for over 20 years.

## 2. Learn the Specific Math and Verbal Skills You'll Need

Our courses include an extremely thorough review of the math and verbal skills our students need to ace the GMAT, and this book will give you that same review.

## 3. Practice Each Type of Question—at the Difficulty Level You Need to Master

Two of the GMAT's sections, the Quantitative and Verbal sections, are computer adaptive. These sections quickly hone in on your ability level and then mostly give you questions at or just above that level. It makes sense for you to practice on the level of problem you will actually see during the test. *GMAT Premium Prep* is the only book out there with practice questions grouped by difficulty. Page after page of practice questions are arranged at the back of this book in difficulty "bins"—just like the questions on the real GMAT—so that you can concentrate on the question level you will have to answer on the actual test in order to get the score you need.

The Integrated Reasoning section of the GMAT is *not* computer adaptive. We've provided two complete Integrated Reasoning sections at the back of this book to help you prepare for this section of the test.

**Important Phone Numbers:**
To register for the GMAT:
800-717-GMAT

To reach GMAC Customer Service:
866-505-6559 or
703-668-9605

## 4. Periodically Take Simulated GMATs to Measure Your Progress

As you work through the book, you'll want to take our online practice tests to see how you're doing. These tests closely mimic the GMAT so you can become familiar with the test's content and structure. Our tests include adaptive sections for the Quantitative and Verbal sections and a non-adaptive section for the Integrated Reasoning section. Our practice tests can be found at PrincetonReview.com. In addition, we actively encourage students to use *The Official Guide for GMAT Review,* which is published by the Graduate Management Admission Council (GMAC). It contains actual test questions from previous administrations of the GMAT. You should also take at least one of the real practice tests available through the GMAT website, www.mba.com.

Make sure that you register your book to access your tests. Please refer to the "Get More (Free) Content" on pages viii-ix to learn how to do just that.

## 5. Hone Your Skills

Using the detailed score reports from your practice exams, you'll be able to zero in on problem areas and quickly achieve mastery through additional practice. And as your score rises on the adaptive sections, this book is ready with more difficult question bins to keep you on track for the score you need. You can use the two practice Integrated Reasoning sections in this book to help you prepare for your practice tests and your real GMAT.

**Important Websites**
To register for the GMAT:
www.mba.com

## 6. Keep Track of the Application Process

Throughout the book, you will find informative sidebars explaining how and when to register for the test, how and when to apply to business school, the advantages and disadvantages of applying early, and much more. Plus, at PrincetonReview.com, you'll be able to take advantage of our powerful web-based tools to match yourself with schools that meet your needs and preferences.

# WHAT IS THE GRADUATE MANAGEMENT ADMISSION TEST?

The Graduate Management Admission Test (GMAT) is a standardized test that business schools use as a tool to decide whom they are going to accept into their MBA programs.

**More Great Resources!**
Check out our online guide, The Best Business Schools, for profiles of the nation's top b-schools: www.princetonreview.com/business-school-rankings/best-business-schools

## Where Does the GMAT Come From?

The GMAT is published and administered by the Graduate Management Admission Council (GMAC), a private company. We'll tell you more about them later on in this book.

## What Does the Test Look Like?

The GMAT is offered only on computer. The 3.5-hour test is administered at a secure computer terminal at an approved testing center. You enter your multiple-choice answers on the screen with a mouse; you must compose your essay for the Writing Assessment section on the computer as well.

1. One 30-minute essay to be written on the computer with a generic word-processing program
2. One 30-minute, 12-question, multiple-choice Integrated Reasoning section. Some Integrated Reasoning questions can have multiple parts.
   (optional break)
3. A 62-minute, 31-question multiple-choice Quantitative section
   (optional break)
4. A 65-minute, 36-question multiple-choice Verbal section

On average, this would give you two minutes for each quantitative question and a little less than two minutes for each verbal question—but you will find that our Princeton Review strategies will slightly revise these times. You must answer a question in order to get to the next question—which means that you can't skip a question and come back to it. And while you are not required to finish any of the sections, your score will be adjusted downward to reflect questions you do not complete.

On each of the Quantitative and Verbal sections, approximately one-quarter of the questions you encounter will be experimental and will not count toward your score. These questions, which will be mixed in among the regular questions, are there so the test company can try out new questions for future tests. We'll have much more to say about the experimental questions later.

## But Wait, There's More

One of the first options you'll encounter when taking the GMAT is the option to choose from one of three possible orders for the exam sections. You pick your preferred section order on the day of the test.

Here are the possible section orders:

<table>
<tr><th>Order #1 (Classic Order)</th><th>Order #2 (Verbal First)</th><th>Order #3 (Quantitative First)</th></tr>
<tr><td>Analytic Writing Assessment</td><td rowspan="2">Verbal</td><td rowspan="2">Quantitative</td></tr>
<tr><td>Integrated Reasoning</td></tr>
<tr><td colspan="3">Optional 8 minute break</td></tr>
<tr><td>Quantitative</td><td>Quantitative</td><td>Verbal</td></tr>
<tr><td colspan="3">Optional 8 minute break</td></tr>
<tr><td rowspan="2">Verbal</td><td>Integrated Reasoning</td><td>Integrated Reasoning</td></tr>
<tr><td>Analytical Writing Assessment</td><td>Analytical Writing Assessment</td></tr>
</table>

## How Do You Know What Order to Pick?

The answer to that depends on your goals for the test and your level of comfort with the different sections. Are you looking to get a high Quantitative score, but you don't care so much about the Verbal? Has your school told you they never consider the essay and Integrated Reasoning section? Are you good at Verbal but not so good at Quantitative?

The answer to these questions and other questions like them help to inform your section order choice.

## How Does This Impact Your Studying?

We recommend that you take your first two tests using the classic order. A major goal of your first practice test is to simply get acquainted with the sections, question types, content, and timing of the GMAT. A major goal of your second practice test is to start putting into use some of the basic approaches for important question types.

Taking your first two tests using the classic section order provides a baseline score. Having established a baseline score, you can then try out different section orders for the remaining tests. Compare the results of the tests with different section orders to the results of the tests with the classic section order and see if there are any improvements.

In addition to looking for score improvements, you should also pay attention to a handful of other factors about your preferences in test taking.

For instance, do you like to ease into a test or hit the ground running? If you like to ease into a test, you may want to stick with the classic section order. While all parts of your GMAT score are important, most schools do attach less importance to your AWA (Analytical Writing Assessment) and Integrated Reasoning scores than your Quantitative and Verbal scores. Remember, as well, that only the Quantitative and Verbal scores are used in calculating the overall score. So, if you like to ease into a test, the AWA and Integrated Reasoning can provide that way to ease in.

Do you like to do the section you're most worried about first? Some test-takers like to get the section that they are most worried about out of the way. If that's you, you'll probably want to pick either the Verbal First or Quantitative First orders, depending on which section you are most worried about!

Are you worried about fatigue? Most test-takers find the GMAT both fast-paced and tiring. Fatigue can be a very real issue. If you are worried about fatigue, you probably want to do either the Verbal First or Quantitative First orders as they place the two least consequential sections at the end of the test.

## What Information Is Tested on the GMAT?

You will find several different types of multiple-choice questions on the GMAT.

**Quantitative (31 questions total)**

- Problem Solving—approximately 16 questions
- Data Sufficiency (a strange type of problem that exists on no other test in the world)—approximately 15 questions

**Verbal (36 questions total)**

- Reading Comprehension (tests your ability to answer questions about a passage)—approximately 12 questions
- Sentence Correction (a grammar-related question type)—approximately 14 questions
- Critical Reasoning (a logic-based question type recycled from the LSAT)—approximately 10 questions

**Integrated Reasoning (12 questions total)**

- Table Analysis—data is presented in a sortable table (like an Excel spreadsheet); each question usually has three parts.
- Graphics Interpretation—a chart or graph is used to display data; each question usually has two parts; answers are selected from drop-down boxes.
- Multi-Source Reasoning—information (a combination of charts, text, and tables) is presented on two or three tabs; each set of tabbed information is usually accompanied by three questions.
- Two-Part Analysis—each question usually has five or six options of which you need to pick two.

## How Is the GMAT Scored?

As soon as you've finished taking the GMAT, your computer will calculate and display your unofficial results, not including your Writing Assessment score. You can print a copy of your unofficial results to take with you. Within 20 days, you will receive your score report online; a written report will be available only by request.

Most people think of the GMAT score as a single number, but in fact there are five separate numbers:

1. Quantitative score (reported on a scale that runs from 6 to 51 in one-point increments)
2. Verbal score (reported on a scale that runs from 6 to 51 in one-point increments)
3. Total score (reported on a scale that runs from 200 to 800 and is based only on the results of Quantitative and Verbal sections)
4. Analytic Writing Assessment score (reported on a scale of 0 to 6, in half-point increments; 6 is the highest score)
5. Integrated Reasoning score (reported on a scale from 1 to 8 in one-point increments)

The report will look something like this:

| Quantitative | % | Verbal | % | Total | % | AWA | % | Integrated Reasoning | % |
|---|---|---|---|---|---|---|---|---|---|
| 36 | 42 | 30 | 56 | 550 | 48 | 4.5 | 38 | 6 | 75 |

**Where Will Your Scores Take You?**
Get The Princeton Review's definitive list of admissions rates and average test scores for dozens of top business schools. Visit your Student Tools for more info.

Scores in the Quantitative and Verbal sections of the test are based on three factors: the number of questions you answer, whether you answered the question correctly, and the parameters of the question (such as difficulty). Your score improves if you answer more questions, answer them correctly, and answer them at a higher level of difficulty. Recently, the GMAT updated their scoring system making it possible to score between a 6 and a 51 only.

Many business schools tend to focus on the total score, which means that you may make up for weakness in one area by being strong in another. For example, if your quantitative skills are better than your verbal skills, they'll help pull up your total score—although some of the more selective schools say they prefer to see math and verbal sub-scores that are balanced. According to GMAC, two-thirds of test-takers receive a total score between 400 and 600. Total scores go up or down in ten-point increments. In other words, you might receive 490 or 500 on the GMAT, but never 494 or 495.

The Integrated Reasoning section is scored from 1 to 8 in one-point increments. Questions have multiple parts, and you must answer each part correctly to get credit for the question. The Integrated Reasoning score is not included in the Overall score.

The score on the Analytical Writing Assessment section is based on the submission of one Analysis of an Argument essay. The essay is scored independently twice, and the average of the scores is taken. One of the scorers for the essay may be an automated essay-scoring engine.

You will also see a percentile ranking next to each score. For example, if you see a percentile of 72 next to your Verbal score, it means that 72 percent of the people who took this test scored lower than you did on the Verbal section.

## WHAT IS THE PRINCETON REVIEW?

The Princeton Review is a test-preparation company founded in New York City. It has branches in more than 50 cities across the country, as well as abroad. The Princeton Review's techniques are unique and powerful, and they were developed after a study of thousands of real GMAT questions. They work because they are based on the same principles that are used in writing the actual test. The Princeton Review's techniques for beating the GMAT will help you improve your scores by teaching you to:

- think like the test-writers
- take full advantage of the computer-adaptive algorithms upon which the GMAT is based
- find the answers to questions you don't understand by using Process of Elimination
- avoid the traps that test-writers have set for you (and use those traps to your advantage)

## A Warning

Many of our techniques for beating the GMAT may be very different from the way that you would naturally approach problems. Some methods may even seem counterintuitive. Rest assured, however, that many test-takers have used our methods to get great GMAT scores. To get the full benefit of our techniques, you must trust them. The only way to develop this trust is to practice the techniques and persuade yourself that they work.

## Practice with Real Questions

One reason coaching books do not use real GMAT questions is that GMAC won't let them. So far, the council has refused to let anyone (including us) license actual questions from old tests. As we mentioned above, the council has its own review book, *The Official Guide for GMAT Review*, which we heartily recommend that you purchase. GMAC also puts out preparation software called *GMATPrep*, which can be downloaded for free from www.mba.com. This software includes two computer-adaptive tests plus additional practice sets, all of which feature real GMAT questions. By practicing our techniques on real GMAT items, you will be able to prove to yourself that the techniques work and increase your confidence when you actually take the test.

And, remember, by using The Princeton Review's practice questions grouped by level of difficulty at the back of this book, you'll be able to concentrate on the types of questions you are actually likely to see.

## Additional Resources

In addition to the material in this book, we offer a number of other resources to aid you during your GMAT preparation.

**Premium Student Tools**
To gain access, follow the instructions on page viii.

Register your book at PrincetonReview.com to gain access to your Student Tools, the companion website to this book. There you will find 6 full-length GMAT exams, assorted videos that demonstrate step-by-step approaches to GMAT question types and strategy, extra drills and practice, and tons of useful articles, essays, and information.

# Summary

- By using a combination of The Princeton Review's Integrated Reasoning introduction, math and verbal reviews, the practice questions contained in this book, and periodic simulated tests, you will be able to improve your score on the GMAT.
- The test itself is taken on computer. It consists of the following:

| **Analytical Writing Assessment** | | | |
|---|---|---|---|
| • Analysis of an Argument | 1 essay on business or a topic of general interest | 30 minutes | Scoring: 0–6 in half-point increments |
| **Quantitative Section** | | | |
| • Problem Solving<br>• Data Sufficiency | 31 questions total; roughly 50% Problem Solving | 62 minutes | Scoring: 6–51 |

<table>
<tr><th colspan="4">Verbal Section</th></tr>
<tr><td>• Sentence Correction<br>• Critical Reasoning<br>• Reading Comprehension</td><td>36 questions total; roughly 40% Sentence Correction and 30% each for Reading and Critical Reasoning</td><td>65 minutes</td><td>Scoring: 6–51</td></tr>
<tr><td colspan="4">Overall score: 200–800 (based only on the Quantitative and Verbal sections)</td></tr>
<tr><th colspan="4">Integrated Reasoning Section</th></tr>
<tr><td>• Table Analysis<br>• Graphics Interpretation<br>• Multi-Source Reasoning<br>• Two-Part Analysis</td><td>12 questions total, but most questions require multiple responses</td><td>30 minutes</td><td>Scored on a scale from 1 to 8 in one-point increments</td></tr>
</table>

# Chapter 4
# How to Think About the GMAT

If you think the GMAT tests your business knowledge or shows how smart you are, you're in for a surprise. This chapter will give you a new way to look at the GMAT to guide your studies in the right direction.

## How Do You Think About Standardized Tests?

If you're like most people, you think standardized tests measure how smart you are. If you score 800 on the GMAT, you may think of yourself as a genius (and the future manager of a corporate empire). If you score 200, you may think of yourself as an idiot (and the future manager of...well...nothing). You may think that the GMAT measures your verbal and math abilities. At the very least, you probably believe the GMAT is an accurate predictor of how you'll do in business school.

## What Does the GMAT Measure?

The GMAT is not a test of how smart you are. Nor is it a test of your business acumen or even a predictor of your grades in business school. It's simply a test of how good you are at taking the GMAT. In fact, you will learn that by studying the very specific knowledge outlined in this book, you can substantially improve your score.

## The GMAT as a Job Interview

The first axiom of any how-to book on job interviewing is that you must always tell your interviewer what he or she wants to hear. No matter whether this is good job-hunting advice, it happens to be a very useful strategy on the GMAT. The test-writers think in predictable ways. You can improve your score by learning to think the way they do and anticipating the kinds of answers that they think are correct.

## How Closely Does The Princeton Review Monitor the GMAT?

Very closely. Each year, we publish a new edition of this book to reflect the subtle shifts that happen over time, or, in the case of the introduction of the Integrated Reasoning section, the major changes to the GMAT. For the latest information on the GMAT, please visit our website PrincetonReview.com.

## Is This Book Just Like The Princeton Review Course?

No. You won't have the benefit of taking 10 computer-adaptive GMATs that are scored and analyzed by our computers. You won't get to sit in small classes with only three other highly motivated students who will spur you on. You won't get to work with our expert instructors who can assess your strengths and pinpoint your weaknesses. There is no way to put these things into a book.

What you *will* find in this book are some of the techniques and methods that have enabled our students to crack the system—plus a review of the essentials that you cannot afford not to know.

If at all possible, you should take our course. If that is not possible, there is this book.

## How to Crack the System

In the following chapters, we're going to teach you our method for cracking the GMAT. Read each chapter carefully. Some of our ideas may seem strange at first. For example, when we tell you that it is sometimes easier to answer GMAT questions without actually working out the entire problem, you may think, "This isn't the way I conduct business."

## Remember: The GMAT Isn't About Business

We're not going to teach you business skills. We're not going to teach you math and English. We're going to teach you the GMAT.

# Chapter 5
# Cracking the Adaptive Sections: Basic Principles

This chapter will show you how the computer-adaptive sections of the GMAT really work. You will learn to pace yourself and to take advantage of the test's limitations.

## HOW THE COMPUTER-ADAPTIVE GMAT SECTIONS WORK

To understand how to beat the computer-adaptive sections (Math and Verbal) of the GMAT, you have to understand how they work.

Unlike paper-and-pencil standardized tests that begin with an easy question and then become progressively tougher, the computer-adaptive sections always begin by giving you a medium question. If you get it correct, the computer gives you a slightly harder question. If you get it wrong, the computer gives you a slightly easier question, and so on. The idea is that the computer will zero in on your exact level of ability very quickly, which allows you to answer fewer questions overall and allows the computer to make a more finely honed assessment of your abilities.

To check out which b-schools are the "Toughest to Get Into," take a look at the Business School Ranking lists at PrincetonReview.com.

### What You Will See on Your Screen

During the test itself, your screen will display the question you're currently working on, with little circles next to the five answer choices. To answer the question, you use your mouse to click on the circle next to the answer choice you think is correct. Then you press a button at the bottom of the screen to verify that this is the answer you want to pick.

### What You Will Never See on Your Screen

What you will *never* see is the process by which the computer keeps track of your progress. When you start each adaptive section, the computer assumes that your score is average. So, your starting score for each section is around a 30. As you go through the test, the computer will keep revising its assessment of your score based on your responses.

Let's watch the process in action. In the left-hand column on the next page, you'll see what a hypothetical test-taker—let's call her Jane—sees on her screen as she takes the test. In the right-hand column, we'll show you how GMAC keeps track of how she's doing. (We've simplified this example a bit in the interest of clarity.)

Note: The answer choices on the actual GMAT don't have letters assigned to them. Instead, you select your response by clicking on an adjacent oval. For the sake of clarity and brevity, we'll refer to the five answer choices as (A), (B), (C), (D), and (E).

### What Jane Sees:

To regard the overwhelming beauty of the Mojave Desert is <u>understanding the great forces of</u> nature that shape our planet.

- ⬭ understanding the great forces of
- ⬭ to understand the great forces to
- ⬭ to understand the great forces of
- ⬭ understanding the greatest forces in
- ⬭ understanding the greater forces on

## What Jane *Doesn't* See:

When you start each adaptive section, the computer assumes that your score is average. So, your starting score for each section is around a 30. Jane gets the first question correct, (C), so her score goes up to a 35, and the computer selects a harder problem for her second question.

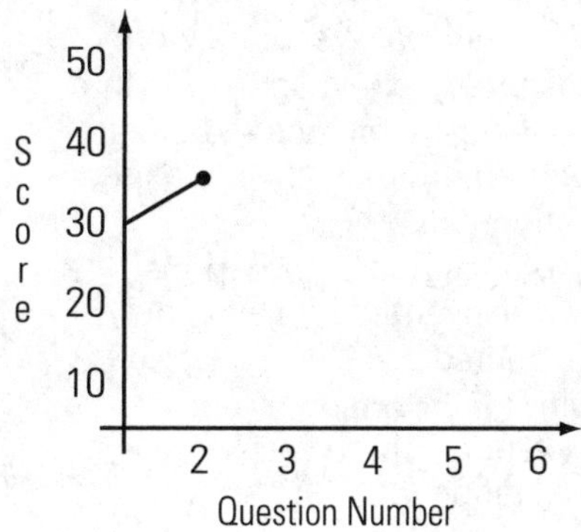


### What Jane Sees:

Hawks in a certain region depend heavily for their diet on a particular variety of field mouse. The killing of field mice by farmers will seriously endanger the survival of hawks in this region.

Which of the following, if true, casts the most doubt on the conclusion drawn above?

- ⬭ The number of mice killed by farmers has increased in recent years.
- ⬭ Farmers kill many other types of pests besides field mice without any adverse effect on hawks.
- ⬭ Hawks have been found in other areas besides this region.
- ⬭ Killing field mice leaves more food for the remaining mice, who have larger broods the following season.
- ⬭ Hawks are also endangered because of pollution and deforestation.

### What Jane *Doesn't* See:

The computer happens to select a Critical Reasoning problem.

Oops. Jane gets the second question wrong (the correct answer is (D)), so her score goes down to a 32, and the computer gives her a slightly easier problem.

*current score: 32*

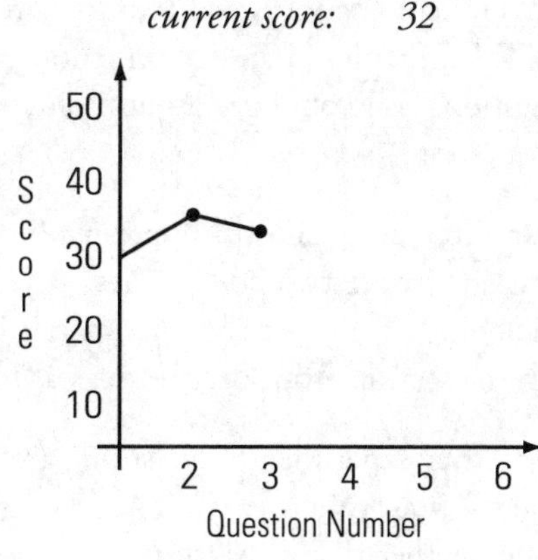

**WHAT JANE SEES:**

<u>Nuclear weapons being invented, there was wide expectation in the scientific community that</u> all war would end.

- ◯ Nuclear weapons being invented, there was wide expectation in the scientific community that
- ◯ When nuclear weapons were invented, expectation was that
- ◯ As nuclear weapons were invented, there was wide expectation that
- ◯ Insofar as nuclear weapons were invented, it was widely expected
- ◯ With the invention of nuclear weapons, there was wide expectation that

**WHAT JANE *DOESN'T* SEE:**

Jane has no idea what the correct answer is on this third question, but she guesses (E) and gets it correct. Her score goes up to a 33.

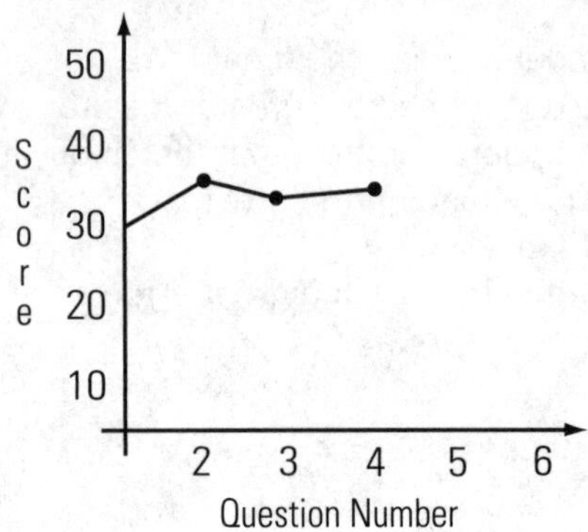


You get the idea. At the very beginning of the section, your score moves up or down in larger increments than it does at the end, when GMAC believes it is merely refining whether you deserve, say, a 42 or a 43. The questions you will see on your test come from a huge pool of questions held in the computer in what the test-writers call "difficulty bins"—each bin with a different level of difficulty.

## The Experimental Questions

Unfortunately, approximately one-fourth of the questions in each adaptive section (Math and Verbal) won't actually count toward your score; they are experimental questions being tested out on you. The difficulty of an experimental question does not depend on your answer to the previous question. You could get a question correct and then immediately see a fairly easy experimental question.

So, if you are answering mostly upper-medium questions and suddenly see a question that seems too easy, there are two possibilities: a) you are about to fall for a trap, or b) it's an experimental question and really is easy. That means it can be very difficult for you to judge how you are doing on the section. Your best strategy is to simply try your best on every question.

Remembering that experimental questions are included throughout the adaptive sections can also help you use your time wisely. When you get stuck on a question—even one of the first 10 questions—remember that it might be experimental. Spending an inordinate amount of time on one question could cause you to rush and make silly mistakes later. Would you really want to do that if the question turned out to be experimental?

In those situations, eliminate as many answer choices as you can, guess, and move on to the next question.

## What the Computer-Adaptive GMAT Uses to Calculate Your Score

How much can leaving questions at the end unanswered damage your score? GMAC says that somebody who was on track to score in the 91st percentile will drop to the 77th percentile by leaving just five questions unanswered. Answer every question!

The GMAT keeps a running tally of your score as it goes, based on the number of questions you get correct and their levels of difficulty—but there are two other important factors that can affect your score:

- Early questions count more than later questions.
- Questions you leave unanswered will lower your score.

## Why Early Questions Count More Than Later Questions

At the beginning of the test, your score moves up or down in larger increments as the computer hones in on what will turn out to be your ultimate score. If you make a mistake early on, the computer will choose a much easier question, and it will take you awhile to work back to where you started. Similarly, if you get an early problem correct, the computer will then give you a much harder question.

However, later in the test, a mistake is less costly—because the computer has decided your general place in the scoring ranks and is merely refining your exact score.

While it is not impossible to come back from behind, you can see that it is particularly important that you do well at the beginning of the test. Answering just a few questions correctly at the beginning will propel your interim score quite high.

## Pace Yourself

Make sure that you get these early questions correct by starting slowly, checking your work on early problems, and then gradually picking up the pace so that you finish all the problems in the section.

Still, if you are running out of time at the end, it makes sense to spend a few moments guessing intelligently on the remaining questions using Process of Elimination (POE) rather than random guesses or (let's hope it never comes to this) not answering at all. You will be pleased to know that it is possible to guess on several questions at the end and still end up with a 700.

On the next page, you'll find our pacing advice for Math and Verbal. The charts will tell you how much time you should spend for each block of 10 questions based on a practice test score.

| QUANTITATIVE PACING | | | |
|---|---|---|---|
| Latest Score | Questions 1–10 | Questions 11–20 | Questions 21–31 |
| Under 35 | 30 min. | 22 min. | 10 min. |
| 35–42 | 28 min. | 20 min. | 14 min. |
| Above 42 | 25 min. | 20 min. | 17 min. |

| VERBAL PACING | | | | |
|---|---|---|---|---|
| Latest Score | Questions 1–10 | Questions 11–20 | Questions 21–30 | Questions 31–36 |
| Under 28 | 30 min. | 22 min. | 10 min. | 3 min. |
| 28–34 | 26 min. | 20 min. | 15 min. | 4 min. |
| Above 34 | 25 min. | 20 min. | 15 min. | 5 min. |

## The Princeton Review Approach to the GMAT

**General Test Strategies**
Go to your Student Tools to watch a video on effective ways to approach and tackle the GMAT exam, no matter which section you're in.

To help you ace the computer-adaptive sections of the GMAT, this book is going to provide you with:

- test-taking techniques that have made The Princeton Review famous and that will enable you to turn the inherent weaknesses of the computer-adaptive sections of the GMAT to your advantage
- a thorough review of all the major topics covered on the GMAT
- a short practice test to help you predict your current scoring level
- practice questions to help you raise your scoring level

## Know Your Bin

According to classic theory, average test-takers spend most of their time answering questions at their level of competency (which they get correct) and questions that are just above their level of competency (which they get wrong). In other words, most test-takers will see questions from only a few difficulty "bins."

This means that to raise your score, you must learn to answer questions from the bins immediately *above* your current scoring level. At the back of this book, you will find a short diagnostic test to determine your current scoring level, as well as bins filled with questions at various scoring levels. When combined with a thorough review of the topics covered on the GMAT, this should put you well on your way to the score you're looking for.

But first, let's learn some test-taking strategies.

# Summary

- The computer-adaptive sections of the GMAT always start you off with a medium question. If you get it correct, you get a harder question; if you get it wrong, you get an easier question. The test assigns you a score after each answer and quickly (in theory) hones in on your level of ability.
- Mixed in with the questions that count toward your score will be experimental questions that do not count toward your score. The testing company is using you as an unpaid guinea pig to try out new questions. Approximately one-fourth of the questions in each of the adaptive sections are experimental.
- Because the test is taken on a computer, you must answer each question to get to the next question—you can't skip a question or come back to it later.
- Because of the scoring algorithms, early questions count more than later questions—so check your work carefully at the beginning of the test.
- The GMAT computer-adaptive sections select questions for you from "bins" of questions at different levels of ability. The Princeton Review method consists of finding your current bin level through diagnostic tests and then practicing questions from that bin, gradually moving to higher bins as you become more proficient.

# Chapter 6 Cracking the Adaptive Sections: Intermediate Principles

This chapter provides an introduction to one of the key Princeton Review techniques: Process of Elimination.

Imagine for a moment that you are a contestant on *Jeopardy*. You are hoping to stumble upon a coveted Daily Double, but first you've got to answer every question that gets thrown your way.

As you answer assorted questions about myriad topics (including "Potent Potables," no doubt), you wish that there were some way that you could know where the Daily Doubles are placed on the board and jump to those. But you can't—you can't opt to skip any of the questions and continue to dominate that game.

## Let's Make a GMAT

Normally when you don't know the correct answer on a test, you skip the question and come back to it later. But on the computer-adaptive sections of the GMAT, as in *Jeopardy*, you can never skip the question.

## To Get to the Next Question, You Have to Answer This One

Because of the way the computer-adaptive sections of the GMAT's scoring algorithm works, the question you see on your computer screen at any particular moment depends on your response to the previous question. This creates an odd situation for the test designers: if they allowed you to skip a question, they wouldn't know which question to give you next.

It's clear from articles published by GMAT test designers that they know test-takers are at a real disadvantage when they can't skip a problem and come back to it later. Still, the idea of using a computer to administer tests was too tempting to give up. In the end, GMAC decided that you should generously be willing to make the sacrifice in the name of progress.

So whether you know the answer to a problem or not, you have to answer it in order to move on.

This means that, like it or not, you may have to do some guessing on the GMAT. Ah, but there's guessing, and then there's *guessing*.

## If You Don't Know the Correct Answer, Don't You Dare Just Pick an Answer at Random

This may sound a little loony, but it turns out that you don't always have to know the correct answer to get a question correct.

Try answering the following question:

> What is the unit of currency in Sweden?

What? You don't know?

Unless you work for an international bank or have traveled in Scandinavia, there is no reason why you would know the unit of currency in Sweden. (By the way, the GMAT doesn't ask such factual questions. We're using this one to make a point.) As it stands now, because you don't know the answer, you would have to answer this question at random, right?

Not necessarily. GMAT questions are written in multiple-choice format. One of the five choices has to be the answer. You just have to find it.

**Inappropriate Use of GMAT Scores**

The following is a list of what GMAC considers "inappropriate uses" of GMAT scores:

1. As a requisite for awarding a degree
2. As a requirement for employment, for licensing or certification to perform a job, or for job-related rewards (raises, promotions, etc.)
3. As an achievement test

Source: *Graduate Management Admission Council*

## Look for Wrong Answers Instead of Correct Ones

Let's put this question into multiple-choice format—the only format you'll find on the GMAT—and see if you still want to answer at random.

What is the unit of currency in Sweden?

- the dollar
- the franc
- the pound sterling
- the yen
- the krona

## PROCESS OF ELIMINATION

Suddenly this question isn't difficult anymore. You may not have known the correct answer, but you certainly knew enough to eliminate the wrong answers. Wrong answers are often easier to spot than correct answers. Sometimes they just sound weird. Other times they're logically impossible. While it is rare to be able to eliminate all four of the incorrect answer choices on the GMAT, you will almost always be able to eliminate at least one of them—and frequently two or more—by using Process of Elimination. Process of Elimination (POE for short) will enable you to answer questions that you don't have the time to figure out exactly. We will refer to POE frequently throughout this book. It is one of the most important and fundamental tools you will use to increase your score.

Process of Elimination is a key strategy that can play a huge role in helping you to find the correct answer choice!

Try another example:

Which of the following countries uses the peso as its unit of currency?

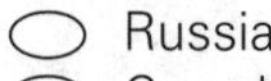

- Russia
- Canada
- Venezuela
- England
- Chile

This time you can probably get rid of only three of the five answer choices using POE. The answer is clearly *not* Russia, Canada, or England, but most people probably don't know for sure whether the answer is Venezuela or Chile.

You've got the question down to two possibilities. What should you do?

## Heads or Tails

A Chilean might flip a peso. You have a 50/50 chance of getting this question correct, which is much better than if you had guessed at random. And because the GMAT forces you to guess anyway, it makes sense to guess intelligently.

In the chapters that follow, we'll show you specific ways to make use of POE to increase your score. You may feel uncomfortable about using these techniques at first, but the sooner you make them your own, the sooner you'll start to improve your score.

## Is It Fair to Get a Question Correct When You Don't Know the Answer?

If you took any math courses in college, you probably remember that the correct answer to a problem, while important, wasn't the only thing you were graded on. Your professor was probably more interested in *how* you got the answer, whether you wrote an elegant equation, or if you used the right formula.

If your equation was correct but you messed up your addition at the end, did you get the entire question wrong? Most college professors give partial credit for an answer like that. After all, what's most important is the mental process that goes into getting the answer, not the answer alone.

On the GMAT, if you don't click the correct circle with your mouse, you're wrong. It doesn't matter that you knew how to do the problem or that you clicked the wrong answer by mistake. GMAC doesn't care: you're just wrong. And a wrong answer means that the running score GMAC is keeping on you will go down by 10 or 20 points, and you'll be forced to answer several easier questions correctly before you get back to the level at which you were.

This really isn't fair. It seems only fitting that you should also be able to benefit from the flip side of this situation: if you click on the correct circle, GMAC doesn't care how you got that answer either.

## Scratch Work

Process of Elimination is a powerful tool, but it's powerful only if you keep track of the answer choices you've eliminated. On a computer-adaptive test, you obviously can't cross off choices on the screen—but you can cross them off on your scratch paper. Don't be afraid to use it!

You only have so many tools at your disposal, and the scratch paper the testing center provides is one of them. Many test-takers often ignore the scratch paper—especially on the Verbal side of the test. Don't be one of them! Use the scratch paper to keep track of eliminated answer choices, jot down notes about questions and passages, and keep yourself organized.

The bottom line about scratch paper:

Make the test easier on your brain by writing things down instead of keeping them in your head.

**So, What Are the Appropriate Uses of Your GMAT Score?**

1. Selection of applicants for graduate study in management
2. Selection of applicants for financial aid on the basis of academic potential
3. Counseling and guidance

Source: *Graduate Management Admission Council*

# Summary

- Because of the way the GMAT is designed, you will be forced to answer questions whether or not you know the correct answer.
- However, not knowing the exact answer to a question does not mean that you have to get it wrong.
- When you don't know the correct answer to a question, look for wrong answers instead. This is called POE, or Process of Elimination.

# Chapter 7
# Cracking the Adaptive Sections: Advanced Principles

In this chapter, you will learn how the GMAT is constructed with obvious answers. You will also learn how to use this information to radically increase your score.

The people who write the computer-adaptive section of the GMAT think that this part of the test is wonderful—and not just because they wrote it, or because it makes them a lot of money. They like it because it ensures that the only problems test-takers get to see are problems at, and slightly above and below, their level of ability. One of the things test-writers always hated about the paper-and-pencil test was that a student scoring 300 could guess the correct answer to a 700-level question.

## But They Have This Little Problem

The questions on the GMAT are still multiple-choice.

That may not seem like a problem to you, but consider the following situation. Suppose a student takes the GMAT. She's answered 30 of the 31 problems on the Quantitative section. There's one left, and as she looks at this last question, she realizes she has absolutely no idea how to answer it. However, one of the answer choices just "seems" correct. So she picks it.

And she gets it correct.

The test-writers get nightmares just thinking about this situation. Say that student was supposed to get 500. She "deserved" 500. But by guessing the correct answer to one last problem, she may have gotten 510.

Ten points more than she "deserved."

## GMAC's Solution

GMAC's tests wouldn't be worth much if students could routinely guess the correct answer to difficult questions by picking answers that seemed correct.

So the test-writers came up with a wonderful solution:

On some difficult questions, answer choices that seem correct are wrong.

## Choosing Answers That Seem Correct

Almost everybody gets stuck on at least a few questions when they take the computer-adaptive sections of the GMAT. After all, the questions keep getting harder as you get questions right. Sooner or later, you may run into a question that you just don't know how to do. If you're like most people, you'll get as far as you can, and then choose the answer that seems correct. In other words, you play a hunch. For some questions, you may pick an answer because it "just looks right" or something about it seems to go naturally with the question.

## What Happens When a Person Takes the GMAT?

Many people pick the answer that seems correct on every problem. Sometimes these hunches are correct; sometimes they are not.

- On easy questions, the obvious answer tends to be the correct answer.
- On medium questions, the obvious answer is correct only some of the time.
- On difficult questions, the obvious answer is almost always wrong.

**Question Difficulty**
GMAT questions are rated according to the number of people who get them wrong, not the question content.

Hard = 70 percent or more of people get it wrong

Medium = about 50 percent of people get it wrong

Easy = fewer than 30 percent of people get it wrong

## What Do Most People Think About the GMAT?

Most people have a few preconceived notions about the GMAT.

- The GMAT is constructed to be fair.
- Knowing the content is enough to get most questions right.
- GMAC wants you to get the questions right if you have the knowledge needed.

Unfortunately, none of these is true.

## The Truth about the GMAT

- The GMAT is constructed to make you miss questions you *should* get right.
- You can completely understand the content behind the question and still get it wrong. In fact, almost all GMAT test-takers miss some questions this way.
- GMAC wants to trick you into getting the question wrong, even if you understand the concepts.

## Don't Be Predictable

Because most people trust the test, they feel confident reading a problem, solving it in a way that seems correct, and picking the answer that appears in the answer choices.

To ace the GMAT, it is not enough to know how to read and to understand math and grammar topics. You have to be able to dodge GMAC's traps. In this section, we'll discuss how to use the traps to your advantage and make yourself more likely to pick the right answer, since understanding the content is not a guarantee that you will get the question right. First, let's understand how GMAC constructs these traps.

## Put Yourself in GMAC's Shoes

Imagine you are writing a multiple-choice test. Here is a problem you've written:

> During a sale, a store sells $\frac{1}{5}$ of its books. The following day, the sale continues and the store sells $\frac{1}{5}$ of the remaining books. What fraction of the original books remains in the store?

Because you enjoy making people miserable, you decided to write a question that was very tricky. To solve this problem correctly, a student needs to understand that the second $\frac{1}{5}$ is coming out of the books that are remaining after the first day. That is, there are $\frac{4}{5}$ of the books left after the first day, and the store sells $\frac{1}{5}$ of those books, not another $\frac{1}{5}$ of the total.

$\frac{1}{5}$ of $\frac{4}{5}$ is $\frac{4}{25}$ (solve by replacing "of" with multiplication). So the store sold $\frac{1}{5}$ of the total and then another $\frac{4}{25}$ of the total, for a final total of $\frac{9}{25}$ of the original books sold. Then the student has to subtract that from 1 because the question asks what fraction *remains* in the store: the answer is $\frac{16}{25}$.

So that is already a pretty tough question. By itself, it would be rated a high medium. You have to make one of the answer choices $\frac{16}{25}$, since that's the answer, but how should you come up with the other answer choices? You could make up random fractions, but if a student did the problem wrong, his or her answer probably wouldn't be one of the choices, and the student would realize that he or she did it wrong. Then the student might figure out the correct way to solve the problem or even decide to take a random guess and get the answer right. You can't allow that.

## Making the Problem Extra Tricky Just Because You Can

You want to make sure that this student doesn't get the answer right. You only want a student who understood the question the first time to get it right and to weed out students who could get it right if they realized they'd made a mistake.

To do that, you create answer choices based on what a student might do wrong. So let's figure out what that is.

A student might think the second $\frac{1}{5}$ was coming from the total and add $\frac{1}{5}+\frac{1}{5}$, and get $\frac{2}{5}$. That would be a good answer choice to use.

Another student might get that same part wrong but understand that the question was asking about how many are left: $\frac{3}{5}$ would be another good answer to use.

A student who really doesn't understand the problem might just multiply the two fractions. $\frac{1}{5}\times\frac{1}{5}=\frac{1}{25}$. Make another answer choice $\frac{1}{25}$.

How about a student who did everything correct but misread the question? The student gets that the store sold $\frac{9}{25}$ of the books over the two days and is so excited that he or she didn't fall into a trap in the first couple steps that the student sees $\frac{9}{25}$ in the answer choices and goes ahead and picks it without rereading the question.

So now you've made sure that most students who don't know how to solve the problem don't get it right. Either they do it wrong but don't realize it because their answer is there, or they look at the answer choices and find one that seems like it could be correct based on the numbers in the problem. But your correct answer is disguised—it isn't obvious how to get to it because it's the result of several steps. This bumps up the difficulty level to medium-hard because you've ensured that it would be almost impossible for a student to get the problem right without knowing exactly how to do it and carefully avoiding your traps.

Here's your finished question:

> During a sale, a store sells $\frac{1}{5}$ of its books. The following day, the sale continues and the store sells $\frac{1}{5}$ of the remaining books. What fraction of the original books remains in the store?
>
> - $\frac{1}{25}$
> - $\frac{9}{25}$
> - $\frac{2}{5}$
> - $\frac{3}{5}$
> - $\frac{16}{25}$

## Use GMAC's Tricks Against Them

Knowing how these questions are constructed makes you GMAC's worst nightmare. Now, rather than a great trap question, this just became much easier than it was without the trap choices. Why? Because you might not be able to solve the problem yourself, but you know how **not** to solve it!

You see the phrase *of the remaining books* and you realize that something tricky is happening. You add the fractions, get (C), subtract them from 1, get (D), and eliminate both of them, because you *know* there's a trick that you're not seeing, so *those answers can't be right.* A little quick estimating can eliminate (A) too—there' s no way those numbers are going to get **that** low.

Now this medium-hard question just became a 50/50 shot, and you had no idea how to solve it.

Nice job.

## No Relief on the Verbal Portion

Let's pretend again: you still work for GMAC, and you write a reading passage. Let's use a short one, to keep it simple.

> For most of this century, big companies dominated an American business scene that seemed to thrive on its own grandness of scale. The expansion westward, the growth of the railroad and steel industries, an almost limitless supply of cheap raw materials, plus a population boom that provided an ever-increasing demand for new products (although not a cheap source of labor) all coincided to encourage the growth of large companies.

Then you write a question:

> To what does the passage credit as bolstering the growth of large companies?

And you write the correct answer:

> The combination of a variety of conditions favorable to big businesses

Why did you write an answer choice like that instead of something that is explicitly stated in the passage? Well, because you're thinking like GMAC. You only want students who have a good understanding of the passage as a whole and read the answer choices carefully to get the question correct.

**B-School Lingo**

*back of the envelope:* a quick analysis of numbers, as if scribbled on the back of an envelope

*benchmarking:* comparing a company to others in the industry

*burn rate:* the amount of cash a money-losing company consumes during a period of time

Source: *The Best 294 Business Schools*

## Read Carefully...Or Else

Next you make some trap answers to direct students away from the correct answer. Would you write a trap answer like, *The lack of government intervention prior to the Sherman Antitrust Act?* No, because nothing in there was mentioned in the passage and a student isn't likely to pick it.

You want to write trap answers that a student will find tempting. How about:

> The high cost of labor for expanding businesses

The passage says this more or less, but it doesn't answer this particular question because high labor costs don't help businesses grow. It's a trap because students might pick it if they forget what the question is actually asking, or if they misunderstand the meaning of the word *bolster.*

You might also write:

> Large companies' ability to transport steel via railroads
>
> Greater demand for new products in the West than in the East
>
> Cheap labor as a result of a population boom

Notice that all of these are not supported by the passage but have some elements that are found within the passage. In fact, they are, respectively, examples of the common GMAT trap answer types: Recycled Language, No Such Comparison, and Reversal. We'll go into much greater detail on these later on. Your correct answer, however, is 100% supported by what is in the passage but doesn't have a lot of memory traps that make you want to pick it immediately after reading the passage.

## How to Use This to Your Advantage

Now that you know how GMAC constructs wrong answers, you can use that to your advantage to avoid picking them.

Here are two examples of how you might do that.

1. You read a problem and immediately know what to do. You do one step on paper or solve quickly in your head and see that answer in the answer choices. You're super excited to click on the answer and you're sure you got such an obvious problem correct.

   Stop! Don't pick that answer. You aren't likely to see many, if any, questions that are so easy you barely have to do any work. If you think you know the answer right away, go back and reread the problem carefully. Reread the question and the answer choices as well. You have probably made a mistake.

   If you have been doing well on the last few questions, the questions are going to get harder, and that means less obvious answers!

2. You can't figure out why your "obvious" answer is wrong OR you have no idea how to actually solve the problem.

   Look at the answer choices and eliminate anything that is obvious. Ask yourself what answer choice you could get by doing one or two simple steps. Or maybe you know the first step of the problem and see that answer on there but you know there's more to do. Eliminate any answer choices that you can tell are not correct and take a guess among whatever is left.

   This approach applies to the Verbal as well. You should never just pick out an answer choice that immediately seems correct. It is probably a trap. Use POE and think carefully about what the passage actually means.

## What This Means for Your Bin

Higher-level questions tend to have more trap answers. In fact, that's often what makes a higher-level question rated as so difficult. It's not that the math is hard or the passage is complex, but that many students are fooled and miss the question.

If you know most of your questions are coming from the medium-hard and hard bins, look out for those trap answers. If you've noticed a trap and avoided it, you can feel more confident that your answer is correct.

**Harvard and the GMAT**

For 12 years, Harvard University's Business School would not even look at the GMAT scores of its applicants. The class of 1997 was the first in more than a decade that was required to submit GMAT scores.

If your questions are drawing mostly from the easy and medium bins, there will still be trap answers. The most important thing to keep in mind is that while GMAC considers those questions easier, they're not easy for you since the test is designed to give you questions at or above your appropriate level. Even if the questions are more straightforward, answer choices are always constructed based on common errors and misreadings.

Be honest with yourself! Practice, evaluate your performance, and develop a solid understanding of what bins you can reasonably handle. The techniques you will learn and practice will increase what you can handle, but don't try to jump ahead of yourself. What kind of practice is more likely to improve your score? What kind of practice is more likely to just be frustrating?

- Correctly answering 90% of the problems in a challenging bin
- Incorrectly answering 90% of the problems in a *really* challenging bin

Even if you want your score to go up significantly, take it one step at a time.

# Summary

- Almost everyone approaches the GMAT by choosing the answer that seems correct, all things considered.
- The GMAT is constructed with incorrect answer choices that the test-writers think you might like. If it's a mistake a person might easily make on a problem, it's probably an answer choice.
- If a question seems easy to you, STOP, and reread the question. Make sure you haven't fallen into a trap. If you caught a twist or trick along the way, you can feel more confident.
- Knowing why an answer choice is a trap can help you eliminate and improve your chances—even on problems you don't know how to solve.

# Chapter 8
# Taking the GMAT

How do you register and practice for the GMAT? What is taking the actual test really like? What do you do if something goes wrong? This chapter will answer these and other practical questions.

To register for the GMAT, call 1-800-717-GMAT or visit the website at www.mba.com.

The registration fee increased in February 2020! Stay updated of the latest test changes through your Student Tools or by checking the GMAT website.

## REGISTERING TO TAKE THE GMAT

The easiest way to register for the exam is by telephone or online. You will be given a list of dates, times, and testing centers that are located near you. One of the actual advantages of the GMAT is that you get to schedule the time of the exam. If you are not a morning person, ask for an afternoon time slot. If you can't think after midday, ask for a morning time slot.

Keep in mind that certain slots get filled quickly, so be sure to call ahead of time. The registration fee is $275 (worldwide). Those who schedule an exam in certain countries will incur taxes. Tax rate information is available at www.mba.com in the GMAT registration section. Note that checks or money orders payable in U.S. dollars must be drawn from banks located in the United States or Canada.

## PRACTICING TO TAKE THE GMAT

As you prepare for the GMAT, it's important to know—in advance—what the experience of taking the test is like so that you can mimic those conditions during practice tests. When you are taking a practice test, turn off your telephone, and try to strictly observe the time limits of the test sections, and even the time limits of the breaks in between sections. To mimic the experience of working with a scratch booklet, buy a spiral notebook filled with grid paper. If you know what time you will be taking the real GMAT, try to schedule your practice tests around the same time of day.

If you are the sort of person who likes to have a mental picture of what a new experience will be like, you might even consider visiting the test center ahead of time. This serves two purposes: first, you'll know how to get there on the day of the test, and second, you'll be familiar with the ambiance in advance.

### The Days Before the Test

Try to keep to your regular routine. Staying up late to study the last few nights before the test is counterproductive. It's important to get regular amounts of exercise and sleep. Continue the study plan you've been on from the beginning, but taper off toward the end. You'll want to take your last practice exam no later than several days before the real test, so you'll have time to go over the results carefully. The last day or so should be devoted to any topics that still give you trouble.

## The Night Before the Test

Get together the things you will need to take with you for the test: a government-issued ID card, directions to the test center (if you haven't already been there), a mental list of the five schools you wish to receive your test scores (if you can't identify these when you take the test, you will have to pay $28 extra per school to get scores sent out later), and a snack and some water. Snacks and water are not allowed in the testing room, but they can be placed in your locker and consumed during a break. Don't bother to take a calculator—no calculators are permitted for the adaptive sections (Quantitative and Verbal) of the GMAT. An on-screen calculator is provided for the Integrated Reasoning section.

**What to Take to the Test Center**

1. A government-issued ID
2. A snack
3. A bottle of water

Once you have gathered everything you need, take the night off. Go to a movie. Relax. There is no point in last-minute cramming. You are as ready as you are going to be.

## The Day of the Test

If you are taking the test in the morning, get up early enough so you have time to eat breakfast, if that is your usual routine, and do a couple of GMAT questions you've already seen in order to get your mind working. If you are taking the test in the afternoon, make sure you get some lunch, and, again, do a few GMAT problems. You don't want to have to warm up on the test itself.

Take a snack to the test center. Use your breaks to eat the food you've brought or to run to the bathroom.

## At the Testing Center

Unlike testing sessions you may have attended in the past, where hundreds of people were lined up to take the same test, you may well be the only person at your testing center taking the GMAT. You'll be asked to present your government-issued ID, and an employee will take your photograph and scan your palm using a palm vein scanner. Finally, you'll be led to the computer station where you will take the test. The station consists of a desk with a computer monitor, a keyboard, a mouse, the equivalent of five erasable noteboards, and a noteboard pen. The marker they will give you to write in your scratch booklet has tendency to dry up when left uncapped—so during breaks, remember to cap it. If you need another marker or another scratch booklet during the test, simply raise your hand, and a proctor will bring it. However, the timer won't stop while the proctor brings you another scratch booklet or marker. Therefore, use your practice tests to learn to fit your scratch work into one scratch booklet. Before the test starts, make sure you're comfortable. Is there enough light? Is your desk sturdy? Don't be afraid to speak up; you're going to be spending four hours at that desk.

There will almost certainly be other people in the same room at other computer stations taking other computer-adaptive tests. You might be seated next to someone taking the licensing exam for architects, or a test for school nurses, or even a test for golf pros.

None of the people in the room will have necessarily started at the same time. The testing center employee will show you how to begin the test, but the computer itself will be your proctor from then on. It will tell you how much time you have left in a section, when your time is up, and when to go on to the next section.

The test center employees will be available if you have a question. They will also monitor the room for security purposes. Just in case their eagle eyes aren't enough, video and audio systems will record everything that happens in the room.

The process sounds less human than it really is. Our students have generally found the test center employees to be quite nice.

## What Your Screen Will Look Like

During most of the test, your screen will look a lot like this:

**Admissions Insight No. 1: Timeline**

**January–May:** Research schools; study for the GMAT

**June–July:** Take the GMAT; request official undergraduate transcripts; ask mentors for recommendations

**July–August:** Start essays; follow up with recommenders; update résumé

**September:** Fine-tune essay; make sure recommenders meet deadlines

**October:** Begin to submit applications; send thank-you notes to recommenders

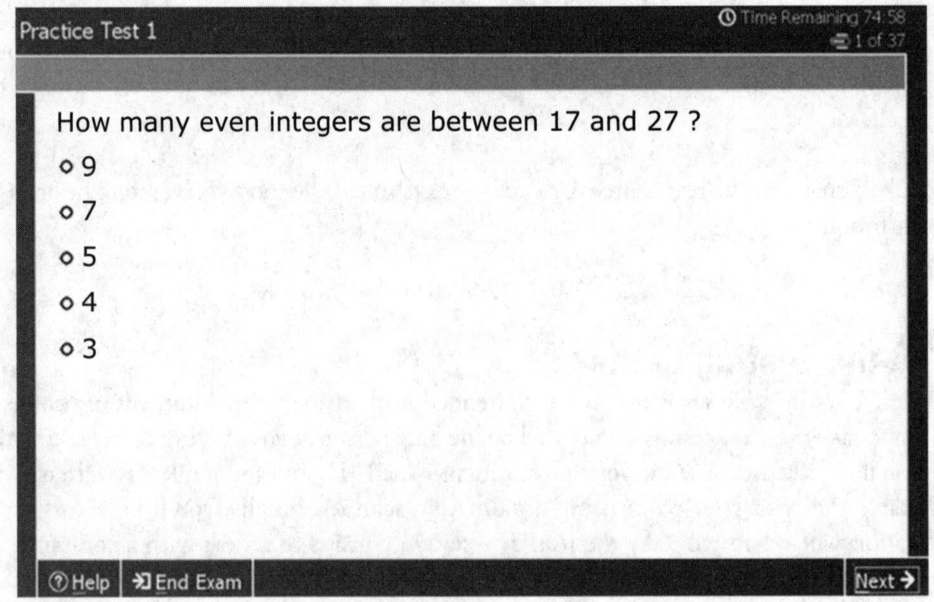


The problem you're working on at any particular moment will be near the top of the screen (by the way, the answer to this one is the third choice). At the top right will be a readout of the time remaining in the section, the number of the question you're working on, and how many total questions there are in the section. Here are the main interface items you will see on the screen:

End Exam—By clicking on this button, you can end the test at any moment. We don't recommend that you do this unless you actually become ill. Even if you decide not to have your test scored (an option they will give you at the end of the exam), you might as well finish—it's great practice, and besides, GMAC has no intention of giving you a refund.

Time—The time you have left to complete the section is displayed in the upper right of the screen. You can hide the time by clicking on it, and you can make it reappear by clicking on the icon that appears in its place. During the last few minutes of the test, the time is automatically displayed and you cannot hide it.

Question Number—The number of the question that you are working on is also displayed in the upper right, and it works just like the time display: you can hide it by clicking on it or make it reappear by clicking on the icon. During the last few minutes of the test, the question number is automatically displayed and cannot be hidden.

Help—During the test, this button provides test and section directions and information about using the software.

Next—When you've answered a question by clicking on the small bubble in front of the answer you think is correct, press this button.

Confirm—After you press "Next," a pop-up window will open and ask you to confirm your answer. Select "yes" to continue to the next question.

## What Happens If You Get Stuck on a Question?

Everyone knows that sinking feeling of not knowing how to do a test problem, but before you start panicking, there are a few things to bear in mind about the GMAT.

First of all, as any Princeton Review graduate will tell you, seeing hard questions on the adaptive (Math and Verbal) sections of the GMAT is a good sign. Because these sections are adaptive, you don't get a hard question until you've answered a bunch of increasingly difficult medium questions correctly—which means you are probably already on track for a good score.

Second, if you have gone through this book and taken the practice tests, then chances are good that if you reread the question and think about it for a few seconds, you may get an idea of how to start it (and starting is half the battle).

Third, you should remember that approximately one-fourth of the questions on the adaptive sections of this test don't even count. They are "experimental questions" being tried out for future versions of the GMAT, so there's no point in getting too upset over a question that might not even get scored.

And fourth, if you are really stuck, then you can pull out The Princeton Review's arsenal of POE (Process of Elimination) techniques to do some very shrewd guessing.

**Admissions Insight No. 2: Research**
All business schools are NOT alike. To begin your admissions research, go to PrincetonReview.com, and take advantage of our Advanced Business School Search tool. Our school profiles present detailed facts and figures on admissions, academics, student body, and career outlook.

## What Happens If You Don't Get to Every Question in a Section?

If you run out of time without having answered all the questions in one of the adaptive sections, the computer just moves you on to the next section. As we said earlier, for adaptive sections, the computer keeps an updated estimate of your score as you move through the section. If you don't get to answer some questions, the computer deducts points (based on an algorithm) and gives you a score based on the questions you *have* answered. So, you could get a score on the adaptive sections by answering only one math and one verbal question. Of course, that score would be pretty low!

The same is true for the Integrated Reasoning section: you cannot skip a question and move on to the next question. For questions that have multiple parts, you also need to answer every part of the question before you move onto the next question. Like the adaptive sections, you can run out of time, and end up leaving questions unanswered. Doing so, however, can have a drastic impact on your Integrated Reasoning score. With scores that range from only 1 to 8, and only 12 questions that are scored all or nothing, answering every question is important on this section.

## It Is Actually in Your Interest to Answer *All* the Questions—Even If You Have to Guess

You might think it would be better to skip any questions you don't have time to answer at the end of an adaptive section—but in fact, the reverse is true: if time is running out, you will almost certainly get a higher score by clicking through and answering any remaining questions at random. This is because the penalty for getting a question wrong diminishes sharply toward the end of each adaptive section (when the computer has already largely decided your score). The penalty for each question skipped at the end of an adaptive section is actually greater than the penalty for getting one of those last questions wrong.

## But You Can Do Much Better Than Guessing at Random

In the following chapters, we will give you all the specific math and verbal skills you need to ace the Math, Verbal, and Integrated Reasoning sections. We will also raise the Process of Elimination to a fine art—in case you have to guess.

## Zen and the Art of Test Taking

As you begin each new question, put the previous question behind you. Don't get rattled if you think you got the previous question wrong. Even if your current question seems easier, it could be experimental. Just do your best to answer the current question correctly.

## At the End of the Test

When you finish your exam, you will be provided a Score Preview that contains four of the five scores: Integrated Reasoning, Quantitative, Verbal, and Total scores. Your essay score is not included. The test will prompt you to decide if you'd like to accept your scores. You have two minutes to decide. If you say no, or you allow the two minutes to expire, the scores will be canceled, and you will not be able to send those scores to your prospective schools. If you were to take the exam again, your future official score reports would not show this test. You can reinstate previously canceled scores up to four years and 11 months after your exam date for a $50 fee.

Before beginning your exam, you may have selected up to five schools to receive your official score report. Deciding you want the test to count will prompt the computer to provide your unofficial score report on the screen and send your official scores to the selected schools. Within 20 days, you will receive your official results online and can send them to other schools for free. If you decide to accept the scores but later decide you want to cancel them, you can do so within 72 hours for a $75 fee.

## If Something Weird Happens at the Test Center...

We have found that almost nothing ever goes wrong at the test centers. They are professionally run. But in the unlikely event that there is a technical glitch with your assigned computer, or if you want to complain about test center conditions or some other anomaly, it is best to start the process before you leave the test center by filing a complaint immediately after the test is over. If possible, get the test center staff to corroborate your complaint. Then, as soon as possible after the test is over, contact either Pearson VUE or GMAT Customer Service by one of the following methods:

**Email:** pvtestsecurity@pearson.com
**Web:** www.pearsonvue.com/contact/gmat/security
**Phone:** 800-717-GMAT or 952-681-3680

**Admissions Insight No. 3: When to Apply**
Although many schools have a filing range that stretches from six to eight months, early applications often have a better chance. This is because there are more spots available in the beginning of the process.

## One Final Thought Before You Begin

No matter how high or low you score on the test and no matter how much you improve your performance with this book, you should *never* accept the score GMAC assigns you as an accurate assessment of your abilities. The temptation to see a high score as evidence that you're a genius, or a low score as evidence that you're an idiot, can be very powerful.

When you've read this book and practiced our techniques on real GMAT questions, you'll be able to judge for yourself whether the GMAT actually measures much besides how well you do on the GMAT.

Think of this as a kind of game—a game you can win.

# Summary

- Register for the GMAT either online or by telephone. Schedule the test for a time that is convenient for you, but that meets your schools' deadlines.
- In the days leading up to the test, follow the study plan you set up in the beginning. Be sure to get plenty of rest, particularly the night before the test.
- Get together all the things you'll need on the day of the test: directions to the test center, a list of five schools to which you want to submit scores, a snack, water, and photo ID.
- At the testing center, make sure you are comfortable at the computer they assign to you. Tune out everyone else. Start working through the test. It should look exactly like the practice tests you have taken online. If you get stuck on a question, use POE to make an educated guess and move on. Remember, some of the questions are experimental and may not count toward your score.
- Because there is a penalty for unanswered questions at the end of the test, it makes sense to use POE to guess on any remaining questions rather than to leave them blank.

# Part III How to Crack the Quantitative GMAT

# Chapter 9
# GMAT Math: Basic Principles

If *absolute value* sounds familiar, but you can't quite remember it, this chapter can help. It provides a comprehensive review of the math terms and rules you haven't had to think about since high school.

## Math and the Integrated Reasoning Section

Before we start talking about the Quantitative section of the GMAT, let's take a moment to talk about the Integrated Reasoning section. The Integrated Reasoning section tests a blend of math and critical reasoning (verbal) skills. However, some questions test just math skills. The good news is that those math skills are the same math skills that the GMAT has been testing for years. So, while we'll be mostly discussing the Quantitative section in this and the following chapters, remember that you'll also use the math reviewed in these chapters to answer some of the Integrated Reasoning questions.

**B-School Lingo**
*cold call*: an unexpected, often dreaded request by the professor to open a case discussion

*cycle time*: how fast you can turn something around

Source: *The Best 294 Business Schools*

## What's Covered in the Quantitative Section

The 31 math questions on the GMAT come in two different formats. About half of the questions are regular Problem Solving questions of the type you're familiar with from countless other standardized tests, such as the SAT. The questions in the other half, mixed in among the regular Problem Solving questions, are of a type unique to the GMAT: they're called Data Sufficiency questions, and they ask you to determine whether you can answer a math question based on two pieces of information. We've devoted two entire chapters to Data Sufficiency.

But whether the question falls into the category of Problem Solving or Data Sufficiency, GMAT questions test your general knowledge of three subjects:

1. Arithmetic
2. Basic algebra
3. Basic geometry

## What Isn't Covered in the Quantitative Section

The good news is that you won't need to know calculus, trigonometry, or any complicated geometry. The bad news is that the specialized, business-type math you're probably good at isn't tested, either. There will be no questions on computing the profit on three ticks of a particular bond sale, no questions about amortizing a loan, no need to calculate the bottom line of a small business.

**A Note on Noteboards:**
Please check out our introduction to the use of GMAT's version of scratch paper (called noteboards) in your Student Tools.

## Ancient History

For the most part, what you'll find on the GMAT is a kind of math that you haven't had to think about in years: junior high school and high school math. Because most people who apply to business school have been out of college for several years, high school math may seem a bit like ancient history. In the next few chapters, we'll give you a fast review of the important concepts, and we'll show you some powerful techniques for cracking the system.

## The Princeton Review Approach

Because it's probably been a long time since you've needed to reduce fractions or remember how many degrees there are in a quadrilateral, the first thing to do is review the information tested on the GMAT by going through our math review. Along the way, you'll learn some valuable test-taking skills that will allow you to take advantage of some of the inherent weaknesses of standardized testing.

When you've finished the math review, you should read our chapter on Data Sufficiency and then take our Warm-Up Questions. Based on your approximate score on our diagnostic, you can then practice working through problems at, or just above, your scoring range. By becoming familiar with the general level of difficulty of these problems and the number of steps required to solve them, you can increase your score on the real GMAT.

**Stay Focused!**
Always keep in mind that if your purpose is to raise your GMAT score, it's a waste of time to learn math that won't be tested. Don't get us wrong, we think the derivation of π is fascinating, but....

## Extra Help

Although we can show you which mathematical principles are most important for the GMAT, this book cannot take the place of a basic foundation in math. We find that most people, even if they don't remember much of high school math, pick it up again quickly. Our drills and examples will refresh your memory if you've gotten rusty, but if you have serious difficulties with the following chapters, you should consider a more thorough review, like *Math Workout for the GMAT*, from The Princeton Review. This book will enable you to see where you need the most work. Always keep in mind, though, that if your purpose is to raise your GMAT score, it's a waste of time to learn math that won't be tested.

**No Calculators on Quant!**
One form of extra help you won't be allowed during the Quantitative section of the GMAT is a calculator. (For the Integrated Reasoning section, there's an onscreen calculator.) All calculations for the Quant section must be done the old-fashioned way—by hand. To get used to this, you should retire your calculator (especially during practice tests) until after you have finished with your real GMAT.

## BASIC INFORMATION

Try the following problem:

How many even integers are between 17 and 27 ?

- 9
- 7
- 5
- 4
- 3

**Extra Practice**
Visit your Student Tools to download a free excerpt from *Math Workout for the GMAT.*

This is an easy GMAT question. Even so, if you don't know what an integer is, the question is impossible to answer. Before moving on to arithmetic, you should make sure you're familiar with some basic terms and concepts. This material isn't difficult, but you must know it cold. (The answer, by the way, is (C).)

### Integers

Integers are the numbers we think of when we think of numbers. Integers are sometimes called whole or natural numbers. They can be negative or positive. They do not include fractions. The positive integers are:

1, 2, 3, 4, 5, etc.

The negative integers are:

−1, −2, −3, −4, −5, etc.

Zero (0) is also an integer. It is the only number that is neither positive nor negative. Sometimes the GMAT will reference a number that is not positive, or non-negative. That is another way to refer to zero as a potential part of a question.

**Ancient History 101**
The GMAT will test your (probably rusty) knowledge of high school math.

Positive integers become greater as they move away from 0; negative integers become lesser. Look at this number line:

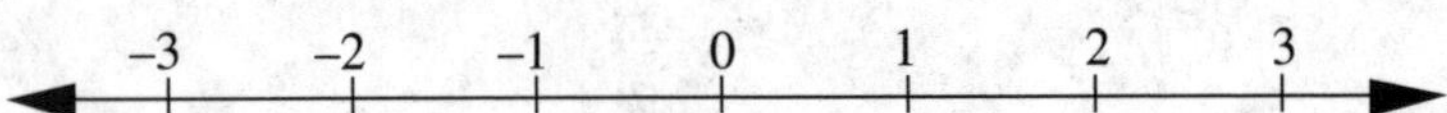


2 is greater than 1, but −2 is less than −1.

## Positive and Negative

Positive numbers lie to the right of zero on the number line. Negative numbers lie to the left of zero on the number line.

There are three rules regarding the multiplication of positive and negative numbers:

positive × positive = positive

positive × negative = negative

negative × negative = positive

**Having Trouble Memorizing?**
If you're having trouble memorizing GMAT math terminology, consider making flashcards to help you review.

If you add a positive number and a negative number, subtract the number with the negative sign in front of it from the positive number.

$$4 + (-3) = 1$$

If you add two negative numbers, you add them as if they were positive, and then put a negative sign in front of the sum.

$$-3 + -5 = -8$$

## Digits

There are ten digits:

0, 1, 2, 3, 4, 5, 6, 7, 8, 9

All integers are made up of digits. In the integer 246, there are three digits: 2, 4, and 6. Each of the digits has a different name:

6 is called the units (or ones) digit.
4 is called the tens digit.
2 is called the hundreds digit.

A number with decimal places is also composed of digits, although it is not an integer. In the decimal 27.63, there are four digits:

2 is the tens digit.
7 is the units digit.
6 is the tenths digit.
3 is the hundredths digit.

## Remainders

If an integer cannot be divided evenly by another integer, the integer that is left over at the end of division is called the **remainder**. Thus, remainders *must* be integers.

$$\begin{array}{r} 3 \\ 2\overline{)\ 7} \\ \underline{-6} \\ 1 \end{array} \quad \leftarrow \text{remainder}$$

## Odd or Even

**Even numbers** are integers that can be divided evenly by 2, leaving no remainder. Here are some examples:

−6, −4, −2, 0, 2, 4, 6, etc.

Q: 20,179.01792
In the number above, which of the following two digits are identical?

(A) The tens digit and the hundredths digit
(B) The ones digit and the thousandths digit
(C) The hundreds digit and the tenths digit
(D) The thousands digit and the tenths digit
(E) The thousands digit and the hundredths digit

*Turn to page 108 for the answer.*

Any integer, no matter how large, is even if its last digit is divisible by 2. Thus 777,772 is even.

**Odd numbers** are integers that cannot be divided evenly by 2. Put another way, odd integers have a remainder of 1 when they are divided by 2. Here are some examples:

−5, −3, −1, 1, 3, 5, etc.

Any integer, no matter how large, is odd if its last digit is not divisible by 2. Thus 222,227 is odd.

There are several rules that always hold true for even and odd numbers:

even × even = even

odd × odd = odd

even × odd = even

even + even = even

odd + odd = even

even + odd = odd

It isn't necessary to memorize these, but you must know that the relationships always hold true. The individual rules can be derived in a second. If you need to know *even* × *even*, just try 2 × 2. The answer in this case is even, as *even* × *even* always will be.

## Consecutive Integers

**Consecutive integers** are integers listed in order of increasing value without any integers missing in between. For example, –3, –2, –1, 0, 1, 2, 3 are consecutive integers. Only integers can be consecutive.

Some consecutive even integers: –2, 0, 2, 4, 6, 8, etc.

Some consecutive odd integers: –3, –1, 1, 3, 5, etc.

## Distinct Numbers

If two numbers are **distinct**, they cannot be equal. For example, if $x$ and $y$ are distinct, then they must have different values.

## Prime Numbers

A **prime number** is a positive integer that is divisible only by two numbers: itself and 1. Thus 2, 3, 5, 7, 11, and 13 are all prime numbers. The number 2 is both the least and the only even prime number. Neither 0 nor 1 is a prime number. All prime numbers are positive.

## Divisibility Rules

If there is no remainder when integer $x$ is divided by integer $y$, then $x$ is said to be **divisible** by $y$. Put another way, divisible means you can evenly divide the greater number by the lesser number with no remainder. For example, 10 is divisible by 5.

A: D. Both the thousands digit and tenths digit are 0.

**Some Useful Divisibility Shortcuts:**

- An integer is divisible by 2 if its units digit is divisible by 2. Thus, 772 is divisible by 2.
- An integer is divisible by 3 if the sum of its digits is divisible by 3. We can instantly tell that 216 is divisible by 3, because the sum of the digits $(2 + 1 + 6)$ is divisible by 3.
- An integer is divisible by 4 if the number formed by its last two digits is divisible by 4. The number 3,028 is divisible by 4, because 28 is divisible by 4.
- An integer is divisible by 5 if its final digit is either 0 or 5. Thus, 60, 85, and 15 are all divisible by 5.
- An integer is divisible by 6 if it is divisible by both 2 and 3, the factors of 6. Thus, 318 is divisible by 6 because it is even, and the sum of $3 + 1 + 8$ is divisible by 3.
- Division by zero is undefined. The test-writers won't ever put a zero in the denominator. If you're working out a problem and you find yourself with a zero in the denominator of a fraction, you've done something wrong. By the way, a 0 in the numerator is fine. Any fraction with a 0 on the top is 0.

$$\frac{0}{1} = 0$$

$$\frac{0}{4} = 0$$

$$\frac{4}{0} = \text{undefined}$$

## Factors and Multiples

An integer, $x$, is a factor of another integer, $y$, if $y$ is divisible by $x$. So, in other words, $y = nx$, where $y$, $n$, and $x$ are all integers. For example, 3 is a factor of 15 because $15 = (3)(5)$. All the factors of 15 are 1, 3, 5, and 15.

Q: Which of the following numbers is prime?
0, 1, 15, 23, 33

*Turn to page 110 for the answer.*

The **multiples** of an integer, $y$, are all numbers 0, $\pm 1y$, $\pm 2y$, $\pm 3y$…, etc. For example, 15 is a multiple of 3 $(3 \times 5)$; 12 is also a multiple of 3 $(3 \times 4)$. When you think about it, most numbers have only a few factors, but an infinite number of multiples. The memory device you may have learned in school is "factors are few; multiples are many."

Every integer greater than 1 is both its own greatest factor and least positive multiple.

## Least Common Multiples

If an integer, $x$, is divisible by two integers, $n$ and $m$, then $x$ is a common multiple of $n$ and $m$. For example, 30 is a common multiple of 5 and 6. The lowest multiple that two numbers have in common is called the **least common multiple**. For our example, 30 is also the least common multiple of 5 and 6.

The most straightforward way to find a least common multiple is to simply start listing the positive multiples of both integers. When you find a number that is on both lists, that number is the least common multiple.

For example, here's how you find the least common multiple of 4 and 6.

**Multiples of 4:** 4, 8, 12, 16, 20,...

**Multiples of 6:** 6, 12,...

Since 12 is on both lists, 12 is the least common multiple of 4 and 6.

## Greatest Common Factor

If two integers, $n$ and $m$, are both divisible by an integer, $x$, then $x$ is a common factor of $n$ and $m$. For example, 6 is a common factor of both 12 and 18. The highest factor that two numbers have in common is referred to as the **greatest common factor**. For our example, 6 is also the greatest common factor of 12 and 18.

The most straightforward way to find a greatest common factor is to simply list the factors of both numbers. Then you just need to find the greatest number that is on both lists.

For example, here's how you find the greatest common factor of 12 and 18.

**Factors of 12:** 1, 2, 3, 4, 6, 12

**Factors of 18:** 1, 2, 3, 6, 9, 18

Since 6 is the greatest number on both lists, 6 is the greatest common factor of 12 and 18.

## Prime Factors

If an integer, $x$, that is a factor of an integer, $y$, is also prime, then $x$ is called a **prime factor** of $y$. For example, 3 and 5 are prime factors of 15.

To find the prime factors of an integer, use a factor tree:

A: 23. Remember, neither 0 nor 1 is prime.

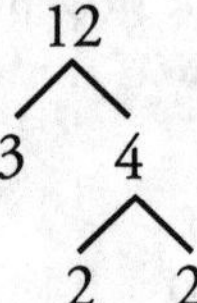


All positive integers greater than 1 have unique prime factorizations, a fact that the GMAT frequently tests. So, it doesn't matter which pair of factors you start with when you use the factor tree.

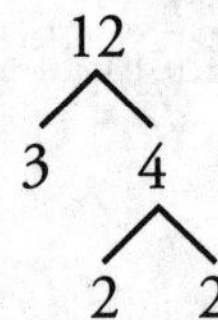


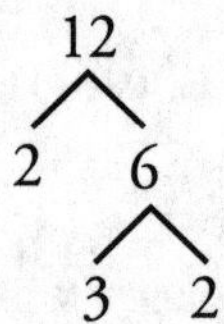


Here are some symbols you should know for the GMAT:

| Symbol | Meaning |
| --- | --- |
| = | is equal to |
| ≠ | is not equal to |
| < | is less than |
| > | is greater than |
| ≤ | is less than or equal to |
| ≥ | is greater than or equal to |

The prime factorization of 12 is $2 \times 2 \times 3$.

## Absolute Value

The **absolute value** of a number is the distance between that number and 0 on the number line. The absolute value of 6 is expressed as $|6|$.

$$|6| = 6$$

$$|-5| = 5$$

## Challenge Question #1

Find the answers to all Challenge Questions in Part VII!

*x* and *y* are integers less than 60 such that *x* is equal to the sum of the squares of two distinct prime numbers, and *y* is a multiple of 17. Which of the following could be the value of $x - y$ ?

- ⬭ −19
- ⬭ −7
- ⬭ 0
- ⬭ 4
- ⬭ 9

## NOW LET'S LOOK AT THE INSTRUCTIONS

During the test, you'll be able to see test instructions by clicking on the "Help" button at the bottom of the screen. However, to avoid wasting time reading these during the test, read our version of the instructions for Problem Solving questions now:

> Problem Solving Directions: Solve each problem and choose the best of the answer choices provided.
>
> Numbers: This test uses only real numbers; no imaginary numbers are used or implied.
>
> Diagrams: All problem solving diagrams are drawn as accurately as possible UNLESS it is specifically noted that a diagram is "not drawn to scale." All diagrams are in a plane unless stated otherwise.

# Summary

- Without a review of the basic terms and rules of math tested on the GMAT, you won't be able to begin to do the problems.
- Study the vocabulary and rules in the preceding chapter to get this stuff back into your head. If you find that you need an even more comprehensive review, consider getting *Math Workout for the GMAT* or *Math Smart*, both published by The Princeton Review.

# Chapter 10 POE and GMAT Math

This chapter delves deeper into Process of Elimination for GMAT Math problems, focusing on what to look for when eliminating incorrect answer choices.

In Chapter 5, we introduced you to Process of Elimination—a way to increase your chances of picking a correct answer by eliminating incorrect answers. We delved into POE a little more deeply by exploring the mind of the test-writer and showing you ways to use GMAC's tricks against them by not being predictable.

In this chapter, we are going to focus on what to look for when using POE on GMAT math problems.

But, first things first.

## Break Glass in Case of Emergency

The strategies we're going to outline for you in this chapter are often misunderstood by students. It's not that the concepts are overly difficult or foreign. In fact, they rely mostly on straightforward logical reasoning and simply paying close attention to the problem.

However, many students believe that these strategies are a one-stop shop for GMAT success. This is emphatically not the case.

When you are confronted with a GMAT math problem, your goal should be to solve the problem using the math concepts and strategies covered in this book. Solving the question should be your goal every time a new math question appears on your screen. You should take an internal inventory of the question—determine the kind of math being tested, the possible steps for completing the problem, the information provided by the problem—and then you should reach into your math toolkit to pull out the appropriate tools to solve the problem.

So, these POE strategies are not a silver bullet to solving math problems. They should not be your first resort.

These strategies should be considered an emergency valve. They are a rip cord for you to pull when you need it the most. That usually means that you are either stuck—the solution isn't working out—or that you are running out of time.

## Hard Questions

Unless you are a truly masterful mathematician, or for some reason the adaptive portion of the GMAT testing algorithm is broken that day (hint: it won't be), you will eventually run into a math problem that you don't know how to solve. What do you do? Spending a lot of time hammering away at a problem is not necessarily the best idea, as you have other problems that you need to work on that may be easier to solve. So, you decide to guess and move on. That's a good idea!

But wait! Before you make a blind guess, take a second and apply the POE strategies outlined in this chapter to see whether you can eliminate any answer choices. You may still need to guess but your odds of guessing correctly will be greater if you've already eliminated some answer choices. This way, you have the best possible chance at answering an additional hard question correctly, which will improve your score.

## Running Out Of Time

Let's say you're nearing the end of the allotted time for the Quantitative section and you look up only to realize that you have more questions left than you have time to work on. You know it's in your best interest to click on an answer for all the questions on the test, so you decide to guess on the remaining questions.

But wait! Don't guess blindly. Try some of these POE strategies for these remaining questions. If you can eliminate some answers before you guess, great!

## Let's Get to Work

Now that we've established when you should use these POE strategies, it's time to discuss the actual strategies. For the remainder of this chapter, we are going to assume that you have already tried to answer the question using math concepts and that you were unsuccessful. Or, that you are running out of time and need to make quick, educated guesses about the answers. You are ready to break the glass and use your emergency tools. But what are those tools and how do you wield them?

Take a look at the following question. Using the knowledge you gained from Chapter 5, are there any answer choices that you can eliminate using POE?

> Twenty-two percent of the cars produced in the United States are manufactured in Michigan. If the United States produces a total of 40 million cars, how many of these cars are produced outside of Michigan?
>
> ◯ 8.8 million
> ◯ 18 million
> ◯ 31.2 million
> ◯ 48.8 million
> ◯ 62 million

## Ballparking

Let's see if we can eliminate any answer choices from this problem quickly and without doing any heavy lifting. The problem is asking for the number of the 40 million cars produced in the United States that are produced outside of Michigan. The problem also states that 22 percent of the cars produced in the United States are produced in Michigan, so you know that 78 percent of the cars produced in the United States are produced outside of Michigan. Even if you're unfamiliar with percentages, are there any answer choices that could be easily eliminated using this information? Well, if there are only 40 million cars produced in the entire United States, is it possible for any combination of states outside Michigan to produce more than 40 million cars? No, it's not, so (D) and (E) can be eliminated because they are greater than the total number of cars.

This tactic is called Ballparking. Ballparking usually involves either making rough comparisons of numbers or rough estimates of the size of an answer. In this case, comparing the answer choices to the total number of cars produced, which is stated in the problem, eliminates two answer choices.

Are there any other answer choices that can be eliminated using Ballparking? Let's try a rough estimate of the size of the answer. If 78 percent of the cars produced in the United States are produced outside of Michigan, then you know that more than three-fourths of the 40 million cars produced in the United States are produced outside of Michigan. Three-fourths of 40 million is 30 million. Two of the answer choices, (A) and (B), are less than half of the total number of cars produced in the United States. Therefore, it is impossible that (A) and (B) represent the number of cars produced outside of Michigan. Choices (A) and (B) can be eliminated. The only answer that remains is (C), which is the correct answer. Note that (C) is also close to our estimate of the answer.

While Ballparking won't usually get you to a single answer, it can often help you to eliminate some answers.

## Partial Answers

Let's look at that same problem again, but for a different reason:

> Twenty-two percent of the cars produced in the United States are manufactured in Michigan. If the United States produces a total of 40 million cars, how many of these cars are produced outside of Michigan?
>
> ◯ 8.8 million
> ◯ 18 million
> ◯ 31.2 million
> ◯ 48.8 million
> ◯ 62 million

So, let's now assume that you are running low on time for the Quantitative section of the test and you come across this question. You're comfortable with percentages, so you decide that you can rush your way through this question. You quickly realize the first step in this problem is to find out how many actual cars are produced in Michigan; in other words, you need to know what 22 percent of 40 million equals. You do the calculation to determine that 8.8 million is 22% of 40 million. Your eye catches (A), which is an exact match for the number you just got, so you select (A) and move on to the next question.

The only problem is that you got the question wrong because you fell for a partial answer.

Partial answers are answer choices that match a correct calculation for part of a question. The GMAT test-writers love to include partial answers. Partial answers are particularly tricky when you're in a rush as they are designed to be appealing to test-takers who don't read the full question, or who are in a hurry.

How can you use this information to your advantage? When you are looking to guess on a question, it helps to think critically about the answer choices. Does a certain answer choice look too obvious or easy? If so, there's a good chance it's a partial answer and, absent doing the actual problem, would be a good candidate to be eliminated before you guess.

Many times partial answers also come in the form of answers that can be derived from one step, or answers that contain numbers or variables that are similar to those found in the problem. If you're pressed for time and looking to guess, look for these types of answer choices to eliminate.

Finally, the best way to avoid partial answers is to get into the habit of reading the question stem one more time before selecting your answer. That way, you can be sure that you are answering the question that was asked!

## Putting It All Together

Try the following problem and look for ways to eliminate answer choices using Ballparking and partial answers.

---

The output of a factory is increased by 10% to keep up with rising demand. To handle the holiday rush, this new output is increased by 20%. By approximately what percent would the output of the factory now have to be decreased in order to restore the original output?

- ○ 20%
- ○ 24%
- ○ 30%
- ○ 32%
- ○ 70%

### Here's How to Crack It

The factory raises its output by 10% and then raises it again by 20%. The problem is asking for the amount the factory will need to lower its output to return to the original level. For this example, don't worry about solving the problem. Just practice eliminating incorrect answer choices using Ballparking or partial answers.

Choice (A) is just a repeat of the numbers in the question, which is a warning sign of a partial answer, so eliminate (A). Choice (C) is the result of adding the two percentages in the question together. This is too easy and a warning sign of a partial answer, so eliminate (C). Choice (E) is significantly greater than the information in the problem would suggest. Even if it's unclear by how much the factory needs to lower its output, the amount by which the factory raised its output is not even close to 70%. Eliminate (E).

The remaining answer choices, (B) and (D), are not as easily eliminated as (A), (C), and (E). Figuring out which answer to eliminate next would require solving the problem. However, if you are in a rush or do not know how to answer this question, you could have eliminated three of the five answer choices and given yourself a 50/50 shot at correctly guessing the answer to the question. Those are better odds than guessing blindly! The correct answer, by the way, is (B).

---

Look at another example:

---

A student took 6 courses last year and received an average (arithmetic mean) grade of 100 points. The year before, the student took 5 courses and received an average grade of 90 points. To the nearest tenth of a point, what was the student's average grade for the entire two-year period?

- ◯ 79
- ◯ 89
- ◯ 95
- ◯ 95.5
- ◯ 97.2

### Here's How to Crack It

Again, assume you're running out of time or are unsure how to solve this problem. Can you eliminate any answer choices to improve your odds of correctly guessing the answer? The problem states that the student received average grades of 100 and 90 in a two-year period. The question wants to know the average grade of the student for the entire two-year period. If the least grade the student averaged is 90, it is not possible for the student's average to be less than 90, so (A) and (B) can be eliminated. Choice (C) has all the warning signs of a partial answer, as 95 is just the average of 100 and 90, the two numbers found in the problem, so (C) is also a good candidate to be eliminated.

The remaining answer choices are not as easy to eliminate. But again, by applying these POE strategies, you were able to give yourself a 50/50 shot at correctly guessing the answer! The correct answer here is (D).

---

# Summary

- Process of Elimination allows you to eliminate answer choices even when you don't know how to do a problem or you are running out of time. There are two types of answer choices to look for in these situations: Ballparking and partial answers.
  - **Ballparking:** Some GMAT answer choices can easily be found to be false by using rough estimates of numbers in the problem that make the numbers easier to work with.
  - **Partial answers:** GMAC likes to include, among the answer choices, answers that are partial completions of the problem. Recognize these answer choices by looking for choices that require little or no work, or are similar to the numbers in the problem.

# Chapter 11
# Data Sufficiency: Basic Principles

Data Sufficiency is a question type you've never seen before. This chapter will show you how to use basic POE techniques to make this format your new favorite kind of math.

Almost half of the 31 math questions on the GMAT will be Data Sufficiency questions. We're about to show you how to use POE to make this strange question type easy.

## WHAT IS DATA SUFFICIENCY?

If you've never heard of Data Sufficiency, that's because this question type is unique to the GMAT, and these questions definitely require some getting used to. If you have already taken a GMAT practice exam, or the actual GMAT, you may have spent several minutes just trying to understand the directions for Data Sufficiency questions.

However, Data Sufficiency questions really just test the same math concepts as Problem Solving questions, but with a twist—a strange question format.

Here's what a Data Sufficiency question looks like on the GMAT:

---

What is the value of $y$ ?

(1) $y$ is an even integer such that $-1.5 < y < 1.5$

(2) Integer $y$ is not prime

- ⬭ Statement (1) ALONE is sufficient, but statement (2) alone is not sufficient.
- ⬭ Statement (2) ALONE is sufficient, but statement (1) alone is not sufficient.
- ⬭ BOTH statements TOGETHER are sufficient, but NEITHER statement ALONE is sufficient.
- ⬭ EACH statement ALONE is sufficient.
- ⬭ Statements (1) and (2) TOGETHER are not sufficient.

Each Data Sufficiency question consists of a question followed by two statements. There are also five possible answer choices, as shown. The answers are the same for every Data Sufficiency question, so once you learn what each means, you won't need to spend time rereading them. You'll just be able to think about them as answers (A), (B), (C), (D), and (E), which is how we'll refer to them.

Notice that there are two words that the answer choices keep repeating—*alone* and *sufficient.* So, it looks like we're supposed to evaluate the statements on their own—at least at first. Moreover, our task is evidently to determine whether we have sufficient information to answer the question.

That's how Data Sufficiency differs from Problem Solving. In Problem Solving questions, you are asked to give a numerical answer to the question. In fact, the inclusion of five numerical answer choices tells you that you can assume that the question can be solved. For Data

Sufficiency questions, however, you're not being asked to solve the question but to decide WHETHER the question can be solved. It may, in fact, turn out that the statements do not provide sufficient information to answer the question.

**Data Sufficiency: How To**
To watch tips and strategies on how to more easily solve complex Data Sufficiency problems, visit your Student Tools.

### Here's How to Crack It

The first answer choice—(A)—indicates that we should first look at Statement (1) by itself to see if it is sufficient to answer the question.

In fact, the best way to work Data Sufficiency problems is to look at *one statement at a time.* So, ignore Statement (2). Here, we've replaced Statement (2) with question marks to indicate that we are looking only at the first statement—almost as though we had covered up the second statement.

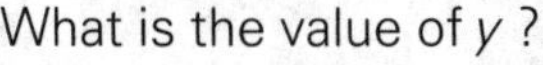

What is the value of $y$ ?

(1) $y$ is an even integer such that $-1.5 < y < 1.5$.

(2) ????

Now, we're ready to evaluate Statement (1) alone. There are three integers between $-1.5$ and $1.5$: $-1$, $0$, and $1$. Of those, as you may recall from Chapter 9, only 0 is even. So, Statement (1) does provide sufficient information to answer the question.

We're not ready to choose the first answer—(A)—yet, however, because the second part of the answer choice states that Statement (2) alone is not sufficient. Now, forget that you have ever seen Statement (1).

What is the value of $y$ ?

(1) ????

(2) Integer $y$ is not prime.

The second statement tells us only that $y$ is not prime. So, possible values for $y$ include 1, 4, 6, 8, etc. Do we know the value of $y$? No way. So, Statement (2) is not sufficient. Because (1) is sufficient and (2) is not, the answer to this question is

○ Statement (1) ALONE is sufficient, but statement (2) alone is not sufficient.

Or, in other words, the correct answer is (A).

## DATA SUFFICIENCY: GETTING STARTED

Now that you've seen and worked a Data Sufficiency question, it's time to learn how to make this weird question type your own. The first step is to understand what each of the answer choices means.

By making small changes to the example you've just seen, we can provide examples of each of the answer choices. Next to each example, you'll find a graphic that provides a quick and dirty way to understand and remember each answer choice. Here's the example for (A) again:

◯ Statement (1) ALONE is sufficient, but statement (2) alone is not sufficient.

What is the value of $y$ ?

(1) $y$ is an even integer such that $-1.5 < y < 1.5$.

(A) ① ~~2~~

(2) Integer $y$ is not prime.

Now, let's make some changes to the statements, to get an example of (B).

◯ Statement (2) ALONE is sufficient, but statement (1) alone is not sufficient.

What is the value of $y$ ?

(1) Integer $y$ is not prime.

(B) ~~1~~ ②

(2) $y$ is an even integer such that $-1.5 < y < 1.5$.

As you can see from this example, (B) is pretty much the flip side of (A). In this case, the first statement provides no help in determining the value of $y$, but the second statement tells us that $y = 0$.

A few more changes produce an example of (C).

◯ BOTH statements TOGETHER are sufficient, but NEITHER statement ALONE is sufficient.

What is the value of $y$ ?

(1) $y$ is an even integer.

(C) (~~1~~ ~~2~~)

(2) $-1.5 < y < 1.5$

The first statement tells us that $y$ is even, but there are a lot of even integers. The second statement gives us a range of values for $y$, but, by itself, we don't even know that $y$ is an integer from the second statement. So, neither statement is sufficient on its own. But, when we put them together, we know that $y = 0$.

Now, let's get an example of (D).

◯ EACH statement ALONE is sufficient.

What is the value of $y$ ?

(1) $y$ is an even integer such that
$-1.5 < y < 1.5$.

(2) For any integer $a \neq 0$, $ay = 0$.

As pointed out in previous examples, the information in Statement (1) allows us to conclude that $y = 0$. The information in the second statement also tells us that $y$ is 0, because the only way for the product of $ay$ to equal 0 is if either $a$ or $y$ is 0. Since $a$ can't be 0, $y$ must be 0. Note how the statements independently allow us to arrive at the conclusion that $y = 0$ for (D).

Finally, let's look at an example of (E).

◯ Statements (1) and (2) TOGETHER are not sufficient.

What is the value of $y$ ?

(1) $y$ is an even integer.

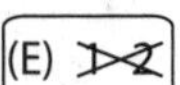

(2) Integer $y$ is not prime.

For this example, there's no way to determine the value of $y$. The first statement doesn't work because $y$ could be any even integer. The second statement also doesn't help because $y$ can be any integer that isn't prime. Even when we combine the statements, we don't know the value of $y$ because any even integer except 2 fits the conditions. So, (E) is the no way, no how answer.

Below, you'll find the full graphic for all of the answers. You may find it helpful to keep the graphic handy until you are completely comfortable with what each answer choice means.

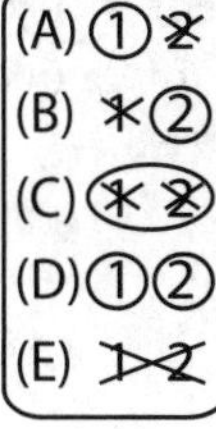

## DATA SUFFICIENCY: BASIC POE STRATEGY

One of the reasons the test-writers decided to include Data Sufficiency questions on the GMAT is that when this format was first dreamed up they thought these questions would be immune to Process of Elimination (POE). Were they ever wrong! If anything, it's even easier to apply POE to Data Sufficiency questions. Let's see why.

First, however, let's restate one of the most important strategies for working any Data Sufficiency question: *Evaluate the statements one at a time before you think about combining them.* Many people mistakenly pick (C)—you need both statements together—when it would have been possible to answer the question with only the information in the first statement or the second statement. Generally, people make this mistake when they read both statements right after reading the question stem. In fact, this mistake is the most common mistake that test-takers make when working Data Sufficiency questions.

To avoid this common mistake, *read the question stem and only the first statement.* Ignore the second statement. Pretend it isn't there. You may even go as far as covering Statement (2) with your finger if you find the temptation to read both statements too overpowering. Once you have evaluated Statement (1), forget it. Ignore it. It doesn't exist anymore. Cover it up if you need to and read and evaluate Statement (2).

Apply POE to Data Sufficiency questions like this one.

What happens when you evaluate the statements one at a time? Something magical, that's what! POE comes roaring back. Consider the following partial example:

What is the value of $x$ ?

(1) $x + 7 = 12$

We don't even have Statement (2), but we can still do a lot with this partial question. (Don't worry. There won't be any partial questions on the real test!) First, you want to see if the statement is sufficient to answer the question. In this case, you could subtract 7 from both sides of the equation to discover that $x = 5$. We'll take this as an opportunity to remind you, however, that you don't really need to solve the equation—you just need to know that you *can* solve the equation. After all, to pick an answer to the problem, you just need to know if you have sufficient information.

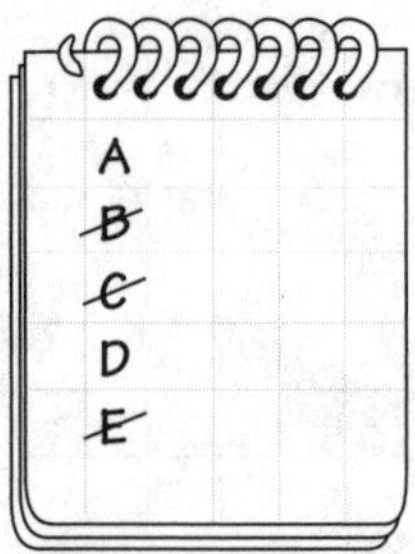


Since Statement (1) is sufficient in this case, which answer choices can be eliminated? From the chart on the previous page, you can see that there are only two answer choices—(A) and (D)—that have Statement (1) circled to indicate that, for that answer choice, Statement (1) is sufficient. So, you no longer need to worry about (B), (C), or (E). They've been eliminated! If the first statement is sufficient, the answer to the problem must be (A) or (D)! You're down to 50/50 just based on looking at the first statement!

Now, check out this example:

What is the value of $x$ ?

(1) $x$ is an integer.

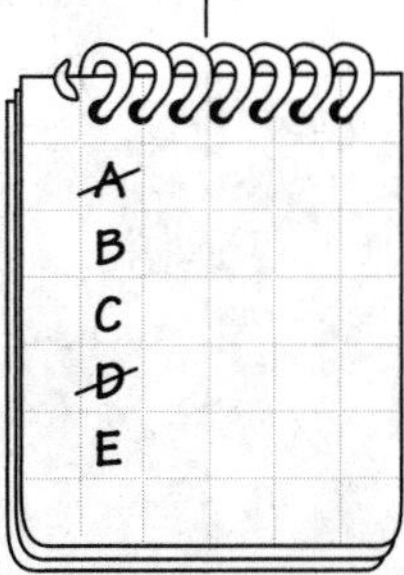


Now, what are the possible answers? If you said (B), (C), or (E), you are well on your way to getting this Data Sufficiency stuff under control. If you said something else, take a look at the steps outlined previously. In this case, the first statement is insufficient to determine the value of $x$. So, you want the answer choices that have 1 crossed off, and that is (B), (C), or (E).

## DRILL 1: (AD/BCE)

In the following drill, each question is followed by only one statement. Based on the first statement, decide if you are down to AD or BCE. The answers can be found in Part VII.

1. What is the value of $x$ ?

   (1) $y = 4$

   (2) ????

2. Is $y$ an integer?

   (1) $2y$ is an integer.

   (2) ????

3. A certain room contains 12 children. How many more boys than girls are there?

   (1) There are three girls in the room.

   (2) ????

4. What number is $x$ percent of 20 ?

   (1) 10 percent of $x$ is 5.

   (2) ????

## From AD or BCE to the Answer

Every time you start a Data Sufficiency question, you should read the question and only the first statement. If the first statement is sufficient, your possible answers are (A) or (D). If the first statement is insufficient, your possible answers are (B), (C), or (E). So, you can always get rid of either two or three answer choices just by evaluating the first statement. The AD/BCE split is so important that you'll want to write down AD or BCE on your noteboard as you work every Data Sufficiency question.

But what happens next? How do you get to the answer? Let's take a look.

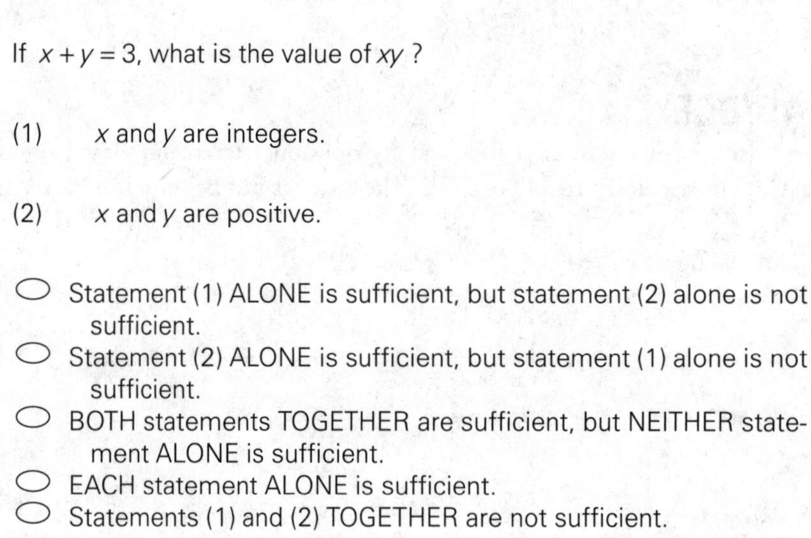

If $x + y = 3$, what is the value of $xy$ ?

(1) $x$ and $y$ are integers.

(2) $x$ and $y$ are positive.

- Statement (1) ALONE is sufficient, but statement (2) alone is not sufficient.
- Statement (2) ALONE is sufficient, but statement (1) alone is not sufficient.
- BOTH statements TOGETHER are sufficient, but NEITHER statement ALONE is sufficient.
- EACH statement ALONE is sufficient.
- Statements (1) and (2) TOGETHER are not sufficient.

### Here's How to Crack It

As always, ignore Statement (2) and look only at Statement (1). If $x$ and $y$ are integers and $x + y = 3$, do we know what they are? Not really—$x$ could be 1 and $y$ could be 2 (in which case, $xy$ would be 2). But $x$ could also be 0 (yes, 0 is an integer) and $y$ could be 3 (in which case, $xy$ would be 0). Because Statement (1) alone is not sufficient, we are down to BCE, a one in three shot.

Now, ignore Statement (1) and look at Statement (2). By itself, this statement doesn't begin to give us values for $x$ and $y$—$x$ could be 1 and $y$ could be 2, but $x$ could just as easily be 1.4 and $y$ could be 1.6. Because there is still more than one possible value for $xy$, cross off (B).

We're down to (C) or (E). Now it's finally time to look at both statements at the same time. See how late in the process we combine the statements? Get into the habit of physically crossing off (B) before you think about combining the statements. That's how you can avoid making the most common GMAT Data Sufficiency mistake of putting the statements together too early.

Because we know from the first statement that $x$ and $y$ are integers, and from the second statement that they must be positive, do we now know specific values for $x$ and $y$?

Well, we do know that there are only two positive integers that add up to 3: 2 and 1. (Remember, zero is an integer but it is neither positive nor negative.)

Do we know if $x = 1$ and $y = 2$, or vice versa? Not really, but frankly, it doesn't matter in this case. The question is asking us the value of $xy$.

Because neither statement by itself is sufficient, but both statements together are sufficient, the answer is (C).

---

Here's a handy flowchart that shows you what to do for any Data Sufficiency problem. You should keep the flowchart next to you and consult it as you first start practicing Data Sufficiency questions. After you have done 10 or 20 questions, you'll probably find that you have learned the basic POE process well enough that you don't need the chart anymore. However, if you ever find yourself having trouble with Data Sufficiency, pull out the chart again and do some more problems, using it as a guide.

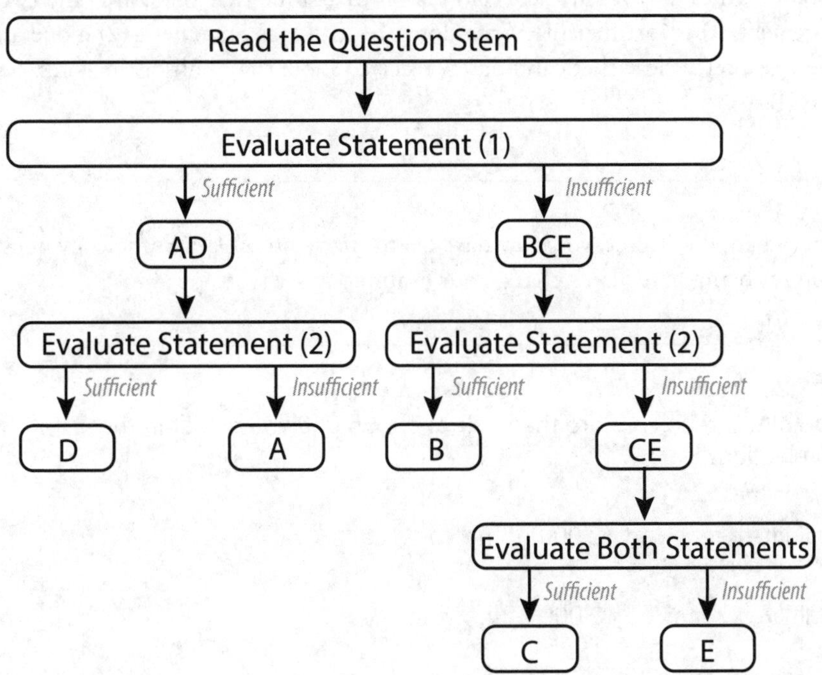

**Combining the Statements**
Notice how late in the process you combine the statements. Remember that one of the most common mistakes on Data Sufficiency is combining the statements before you have properly evaluated each statement on its own.

## YES/NO DATA SUFFICIENCY: THE BASICS

If you were going to provide the answer to most Data Sufficiency questions, your response would be a number. However, as many as half of all the Data Sufficiency questions that you will see on your test will ask a yes-or-no question instead.

Leave it to GMAC to come up with a way to give you five different answer choices on a yes-or-no question. Let's look at an example.

Did candidate *x* receive more than half of the 30,000 votes cast in the general election?

(1) Candidate *y* received 12,000 of the votes cast.

(2) Candidate *x* received 18,000 of the votes cast.

### Here's How to Crack It

When all is said and done, the answer to this question is either yes or no. Start by ignoring Statement (2) and evaluating Statement (1). Does Statement (1) alone answer the question? If you were in a hurry, you might think so. Many people assume that there are only two candidates in the election. They reason that if candidate *y* got 12,000 votes, then candidate *x* must have received 18,000 votes. However, there's no reason to assume that there are only two candidates. So, Statement (1) is insufficient. Write down BCE. Does Statement (2) alone answer the question? Yes, it's pretty clear that candidate *x* received more than half of the votes. So, the correct answer is (B).

That didn't seem so bad, did it? Yet, you may have heard that yes/no Data Sufficiency questions have a reputation for being hard. Let's change our example to see why.

Did candidate *x* receive more than half of the 30,000 votes cast in the general election?

(1) Candidate *y* received 12,000 of the votes cast.

(2) Candidate *x* received 13,000 of the votes cast.

### Here's How to Crack It

As always, start by ignoring Statement (2) so that you can properly evaluate Statement (1) alone. As in our previous example, Statement (1) is insufficient, so be sure to write down BCE. Statement (2) seems pretty straightforward. Candidate *x* received fewer than half of the votes cast. At this point many people say, "Since the guy clearly got fewer than half the votes, this statement doesn't answer the question, either." But those people are wrong!

## Just Say No

Broken down to its basics, the question we were asked was, "Did he get more than half of the vote—yes or no?"

Statement (2) *does* answer the question. The answer is, "No, he didn't." So, the answer is the same as that of the first example. The answer is (B).

---

On a yes/no Data Sufficiency problem, if the statement answers the question in either the affirmative or the negative, it is sufficient.

## Yes/No/Maybe

Yes/no questions really should be called yes/no/maybe questions. Even if that's not their "official" name, it's still worthwhile to think about them in that fashion.

Let's look at one last example to see why.

---

Did candidate $x$ receive more than half of the 30,000 votes cast in the general election?

(1) Candidate $y$ received 12,000 of the votes cast.

(2) Candidate $x$ received at least 13,000 of the votes cast.

### Here's How to Crack It

Since the first statement of this question is the same as that of the previous two examples, we know that it is insufficient. So, write down BCE. Now, let's tackle Statement (2). Based on Statement (2), candidate $x$ could have received exactly 13,000 votes, which would make the answer to the question "No, he did not receive more than half the votes cast." However, he could have also received 16,000 votes, and that would make the answer to the question, "Yes, he did receive more than half the votes cast." So, based on Statement (2), the best we can really say is that candidate $x$ may have received more than half the votes. "Maybe" isn't good enough—we need a definitive yes or no answer. So, Statement (2) is insufficient. Cross off (B). What if we combine the statements? We still have the same problem. We've accounted for at least 25,000 of the votes between the two candidates, but we don't know about the other 5,000. All of those votes could have gone to candidate $x$, making the answer to the question "yes." However, there could have been a third candidate who received those 5,000 votes. In that case, $x$ would have received only 13,000 votes and the answer to the question is "no." Combining the statements didn't get us to a definitive answer. If the answer is sometimes "yes" and sometimes "no," the statement is not sufficient. Cross off (C). The correct answer is (E).

---

## MORE ON DATA SUFFICIENCY

Although Data Sufficiency problems test the same material covered by regular Problem Solving questions, some readers find it distracting to learn the more complicated subtleties of this new question type at the same time that they are learning (or relearning) math concepts. That's why we've put our main chapter on Data Sufficiency at the end of our math review.

However, you will find Data Sufficiency problems sprinkled throughout the math drills—and you should feel free at any time to dip into Chapter 18, where you'll find everything in one place, including more advanced strategy, several more drills, and some great techniques to handle the most complicated yes/no questions.

# Summary

- “Data Sufficiency” means just that, sufficiency. These questions are asking you if the data presented is enough to solve the problem.
- Every Data Sufficiency problem consists of a question followed by two statements. You must decide whether the question can be answered based on the information in the two statements.
- The best strategy for Data Sufficiency problems is to look at one statement at a time. Cover up the other statement with your hand, so that you can completely focus on one statement at a time.
- AD or BCE: These are always your options when you first start eliminating. Memorize them.

# Chapter 12
# Arithmetic

Do you remember all the rules for exponents? This chapter will review rules for those and other important mathematical concepts and teach you how to solve problems involving fractions, proportions, decimals, ratios, percentages, averages, medians, modes, standard deviation, exponents, and radicals.

Although arithmetic is only one of the three types of math tested on the GMAT, arithmetic problems comprise about half of the total number of math questions.

Here are the specific arithmetic topics tested on the GMAT:

1. Axioms and Fundamentals (properties of integers, positive and negative numbers, even and odd). These were covered in Chapter 9.
2. Arithmetic Operations
3. Fractions
4. Decimals
5. Ratios
6. Percentages
7. Averages
8. Exponents and Radicals

In this chapter, we will first discuss the fundamentals of each topic and then show how the test-writers construct questions based on that topic.

## ARITHMETIC OPERATIONS

There are six arithmetic operations you will need for the GMAT:

| | | |
|---|---|---|
| **1.** | **Addition (2 + 2)** | The result of addition is a sum or total. |
| **2.** | **Subtraction (6 – 2)** | The result of subtraction is a difference. |
| **3.** | **Multiplication (2 × 2)** | The result of multiplication is a product. |
| **4.** | **Division (8 ÷ 2)** | The result of division is a quotient. |
| **5.** | **Raising to a power ($x^2$)** | In the expression $x^2$, the little 2 is called an exponent. |
| **6.** | **Finding a square root $\left(\sqrt{4}\right)$** | $\sqrt{4} = \sqrt{2 \times 2} = 2$ |

### Which One Do I Do First?

In a problem that involves several different operations, the operations must be performed in a particular order, and occasionally GMAC likes to see whether you know what that order is. Here's an easy way to remember the order of operations:

**P**lease **E**xcuse **M**y **D**ear **A**unt **S**ally
or
PEMDAS

The first letters stand for Parentheses, Exponents, Multiplication, Division, Addition, and Subtraction. Do operations that are enclosed in parentheses first; then take care of exponents; then multiply and divide; finally add and subtract, going from left to right.

## DRILL 2

Just to get you started, solve each of the following problems by performing the indicated operations in the proper order. The answers can be found in Part VII.

1. $74 + (27 - 24) =$

2. $(8 \times 9) + 7 =$

3. $2(9 - (8 \div 2)) =$

4. $2(7 - 3) + (-4)(5 - 7) =$

### The Drill on Drills

- You can't use a calculator on the Quantitative section of the GMAT, so please don't use one as you work through the math drills in this book.
- To mimic the actual conditions of the test, get used to using scratch paper rather than writing in the book directly.

Here's an easy question that shows how GMAC might test PEMDAS.

5. $4(-3(3 - 5) + 10 - 17) =$

    ◯ −27
    ◯ −4
    ◯ −1
    ◯ 32
    ◯ 84

It is not uncommon to see a Data Sufficiency problem like this on the GMAT:

6. What is the value of $x$?

    (1) $x^3 = 8$

    (2) $x^2 = 4$

    ◯ Statement (1) ALONE is sufficient, but statement (2) alone is not sufficient.
    ◯ Statement (2) ALONE is sufficient, but statement (1) alone is not sufficient.
    ◯ BOTH statements TOGETHER are sufficient, but NEITHER statement ALONE is sufficient.
    ◯ EACH statement ALONE is sufficient.
    ◯ Statements (1) and (2) TOGETHER are not sufficient.

There are two operations that can be done in any order, provided they are the only operations involved: *when you are adding or multiplying a series of numbers, you can group or regroup the numbers any way you like.*

$2 + 3 + 4$ is the same as $4 + 2 + 3$
and
$4 \times 5 \times 6$ is the same as $6 \times 5 \times 4$

This is called the **Associative Law,** but the name will not be tested on the GMAT.

Another law that GMAC likes to test states that

$a(b + c) = ab + ac$ and $a(b - c) = ab - ac$.

This is called the **Distributive Law** but, again, you don't need to know that for the test. Sometimes the Distributive Law can provide you with a shortcut to the solution of a problem. If a problem gives you information in "factored form"—$a(b + c)$—you should distribute it immediately. If the information is given in distributed form—$ab + ac$—you should factor it.

## DRILL 3

If the following problems are in distributed form, factor them; if they are in factored form, distribute them. Then do the indicated operations. Answers are in Part VII.

1. $x^2 + x$

2. $(55 \times 12) + (55 \times 88)$

3. $a(b + c - d)$

4. $abc + xyc$

A GMAT problem might look like this:

5. If $x = 6$, what is the value of $\frac{2xy - xy}{y}$ ?

    - ⬭ −30
    - ⬭ 6
    - ⬭ 8
    - ⬭ 30
    - ⬭ It cannot be determined from the information given.

It is not uncommon to see a Data Sufficiency problem like this on the GMAT:

6. If $ax + ay + az = 15$, what is $x + y + z$ ?

(1) $x = 2$

(2) $a = 5$

- Statement (1) ALONE is sufficient, but statement (2) alone is not sufficient.
- Statement (2) ALONE is sufficient, but statement (1) alone is not sufficient.
- BOTH statements TOGETHER are sufficient, but NEITHER statement ALONE is sufficient.
- EACH statement ALONE is sufficient.
- Statements (1) and (2) TOGETHER are not sufficient.

## Challenge Question #2

A device calculates the worth of gemstones based on quality such that a gem with a quality rating of $q - 1$ is worth 5 times more than a gem with a quality rating of $q$, and a gem with a quality rating of $q - 4$ is worth 625 times more than a gem with a quality rating of $q$. According to this device, the worth of a gem with a quality rating of $p - r$ is how many times greater than that of a gem with a rating of $p$ ?

- $p^5 - r^5$
- $r^5$
- $(p - r)^5$
- $5^r$
- $5r$

# FRACTIONS

Fractions can be thought of in two ways:

- A **fraction** is just another way of expressing division. The expression $\frac{1}{2}$ is exactly the same thing as 1 divided by 2. $\frac{x}{y}$ is nothing more than $x$ divided by $y$. In the fraction $\frac{x}{y}$, $x$ is known as the **numerator** and $y$ is known as the **denominator**.
- The other important way to think of a fraction is as $\frac{\text{part}}{\text{whole}}$. The fraction $\frac{7}{10}$ can be thought of as 7 parts out of a total of 10 parts.

## Adding and Subtracting Fractions with the Same Denominator

To add two or more fractions that have the same denominator, simply add the numerators and put the sum over the common denominator. For example:

$$\frac{1}{7}+\frac{5}{7}=\frac{(1+5)}{7}=\frac{6}{7}$$

Subtraction works exactly the same way:

$$\frac{6}{7}-\frac{2}{7}=\frac{6-2}{7}=\frac{4}{7}$$

## Adding and Subtracting Fractions with Different Denominators

Before you can add or subtract two or more fractions with different denominators, you must give all of them the same denominator. To do this, multiply the numerator and denominator of each fraction by a number that will give it a denominator in common with the others. If you multiplied each fraction by any old number, the fractions wouldn't have their original values, so the number you multiply by has to be equal to 1. For example, if you wanted to change $\frac{1}{2}$ into sixths, you could do the following:

$$\frac{1}{2}\times\frac{3}{3}=\frac{3}{6}$$

We haven't actually changed the value of the fraction, because $\frac{3}{3}$ equals 1.

If we wanted to add:

$$\frac{1}{2}+\frac{2}{3}$$

$$\frac{1}{2}\times\frac{3}{3}+\frac{2}{3}\times\frac{2}{2}$$

$$\frac{3}{6}+\frac{4}{6}=\frac{7}{6}$$

## The Bowtie

The Bowtie method has been a staple of The Princeton Review's materials since the company began in a living room in New York City in 1981. It's been around so long because it works so simply.

To add $\frac{3}{5}$ and $\frac{4}{7}$, for example, follow these three steps:

**Step One:** Multiply the denominators together to form the new denominator.

$$\frac{3}{5}+\frac{4}{7}=\frac{\quad}{5\times7}=\frac{\quad}{35}$$

**Step Two:** Multiply the first denominator by the second numerator (5 × 4 = 20) and the second denominator by the first numerator (7 × 3 = 21) and place these numbers above the fractions, as shown below.

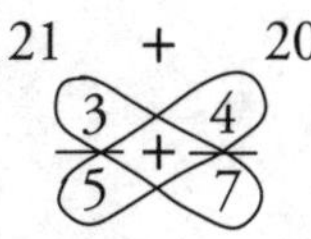

See? A bowtie!

**Step Three:** Add the products to form the new numerator.

$$\frac{3}{5}+\frac{4}{7}=\frac{21+20}{5\times7}=\frac{41}{35}$$

Subtraction works the same way.

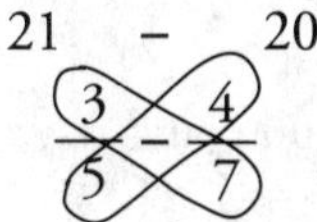


Note that with subtraction, the order of the numerators is important. The new numerator is 21 – 20, or 1. If you somehow get your numbers reversed and use 20 – 21, your answer will be $-\frac{1}{35}$, which is incorrect. One way to keep your subtraction straight is to always multiply **up** from denominator to numerator when you use the Bowtie.

## Multiplying Fractions

To multiply fractions, just multiply the numerators and put the product over the product of the denominators. For example:

$$\frac{2}{3} \times \frac{6}{5} = \frac{12}{15}$$

## Reducing Fractions

When you add or multiply fractions, you often end up with a big fraction that is hard to work with. You can usually reduce such a fraction. To reduce a fraction, find a factor of the numerator that is also a factor of the denominator. It saves time to find the biggest factor they have in common, but this isn't critical. You may just have to repeat the process a few times. When you find a common factor, cancel it. For example, let's take the product we just found when we multiplied the fractions above:

$$\frac{12}{15} = \frac{4 \times \cancel{3}}{5 \times \cancel{3}} = \frac{4}{5}$$

Get used to reducing all fractions (if they can be reduced) *before* you do any work with them. It saves a lot of time and prevents errors in computation.

For example, in that last problem, we had to multiply two fractions together:

$$\frac{2}{3} \times \frac{6}{5}$$

Before you multiplied 2 × 6 and 3 × 5, you could have reduced $\frac{2}{3} \times \frac{6}{5} = \frac{2 \times \cancel{6}}{\cancel{3} \times 5} = \frac{2 \times 2}{5} = \frac{4}{5}$.

## Dividing Fractions

To divide one fraction by another, just invert the second fraction and multiply:

$$\frac{2}{3} \div \frac{3}{4}$$

which is the same thing as...

$$\frac{2}{3} \times \frac{4}{3} = \frac{8}{9}$$

You may see this same operation written like this:

$$\frac{\frac{2}{3}}{\frac{3}{4}}$$

Again, just invert and multiply. This next example is handled the same way:

$$\frac{6}{\frac{2}{3}} = \frac{6}{1} \times \frac{3}{2} = \frac{18}{2} = 9$$

When you invert a fraction, the new fraction is called a **reciprocal.** $\frac{2}{3}$ is the reciprocal of $\frac{3}{2}$. The product of two reciprocals is always 1.

## Converting to Fractions

An integer can be expressed as a fraction by making the integer the numerator and 1 the denominator: $16 = \frac{16}{1}$.

The GMAT sometimes gives you numbers that are mixtures of integers and fractions, for example, $3\frac{1}{2}$. It's easier to work with these numbers if you convert them into fractions. Simply multiply the denominator by the integer, then add the numerator, and place the resulting number over the original denominator.

$$3\frac{1}{2} = \frac{(3 \times 2) + 1}{2} = \frac{7}{2}$$

## Comparing Fractions

In the course of a problem, you may have to compare two or more fractions and determine which is greater. This is easy to do as long as you remember that you can compare fractions directly only if they have the same denominator. Suppose you had to decide which of these three fractions is greatest:

$$\frac{1}{2}, \frac{5}{9}, \text{ or } \frac{7}{15}$$

To compare these fractions directly, you need a common denominator, but finding a common denominator that works for all three fractions would be complicated and time consuming. It makes more sense to compare these fractions two at a time. We showed you the classical way to find common denominators when we talked about adding fractions earlier.

Let's start with $\frac{1}{2}$ and $\frac{5}{9}$. An easy common denominator for these two fractions is 18 (9 × 2).

$$\frac{1}{2} \qquad \frac{5}{9}$$

$$\frac{1}{2}\times\frac{9}{9} \qquad \frac{5}{9}\times\frac{2}{2}$$

$$=\frac{9}{18} \qquad =\frac{10}{18}$$

Because $\frac{5}{9}$ is greater, let's compare it with $\frac{7}{15}$. Here the easiest common denominator is 45. But before we do that...

## Two Shortcuts

Comparing fractions is another situation in which we can use the Bowtie. The idea is that if all you need to know is which fraction is greater, you just have to compare the new numerators. Again, simply multiply the denominator of the first fraction by the numerator of the second and the denominator of the second by the numerator of the first, as shown here.

$$9 \times 1 = 9 \quad \frac{1}{2} \times \frac{5}{9} \quad 2 \times 5 = 10$$

$$10 > 9\text{, therefore } \frac{5}{9} > \frac{1}{2}$$

You could also have saved yourself some time on the last problem by a little fast estimation. Again, which is greater? $\frac{1}{2}$, $\frac{5}{9}$, or $\frac{7}{15}$?

Let's think about $\frac{5}{9}$ in terms of $\frac{1}{2}$. How many ninths equal a half? To put it another way, what is half of 9? 4.5. So $\frac{4.5}{9} = \frac{1}{2}$. That means $\frac{5}{9}$ is *greater* than $\frac{1}{2}$.

Now let's think about $\frac{7}{15}$. Half of 15 is 7.5. $\frac{7.5}{15} = \frac{1}{2}$, which means that $\frac{7}{15}$ is *less* than $\frac{1}{2}$.

## PROPORTIONS

A fraction can be expressed in many ways. $\frac{1}{2}$ also equals $\frac{2}{4}$ or $\frac{4}{8}$, etc. A **proportion** is just a different way of expressing a fraction. Here's an example:

**Proportions and Ratios**
Proportions are really ratios. Where a proportion question asks about the number of shirts *per* box, a ratio question might ask about the number of red shirts to blue shirts in a box.

---

If 2 boxes hold a total of 14 shirts, how many shirts are contained in 3 boxes?

### Here's How to Crack It

The number of shirts per box can be expressed as a fraction. What you're asked to do is express the fraction $\frac{2}{14}$ in a different way.

$$\frac{2\text{ (boxes)}}{14\text{ (shirts)}} = \frac{3\text{ (boxes)}}{x\text{ (shirts)}}$$

To find the answer, all you need to do is find a value for $x$ such that $\frac{2}{14} = \frac{3}{x}$. The easiest way to do this is to cross-multiply.

$2x = 42$, which means that $x = 21$. There are 21 shirts in 3 boxes.

---

## DRILL 4

The answers to these questions can be found in Part VII.

1. $5\frac{3}{4} + \frac{3}{8} =$

2. Reduce $\frac{12}{60}$

3. Convert $9\frac{2}{3}$ to a fraction

4. Solve for $x$ in $\frac{9}{2} = \frac{x}{4}$

A relatively easy GMAT fraction problem might look like this:

5. $\dfrac{\left(\dfrac{\frac{4}{5}}{\frac{3}{5}}\right)\left(\dfrac{\frac{1}{8}}{\frac{2}{3}}\right)}{\frac{3}{4}} =$

- $\frac{3}{100}$
- $\frac{3}{16}$
- $\frac{1}{3}$
- 1
- $\frac{7}{16}$

## Fractions: Advanced Principles

Now that you've been reacquainted with the basics of fractions, let's go a little further. More complicated fraction problems usually involve all of the rules we've just mentioned, with the addition of two concepts: $\frac{\text{part}}{\text{whole}}$, and the rest. Here's a typical medium fraction problem:

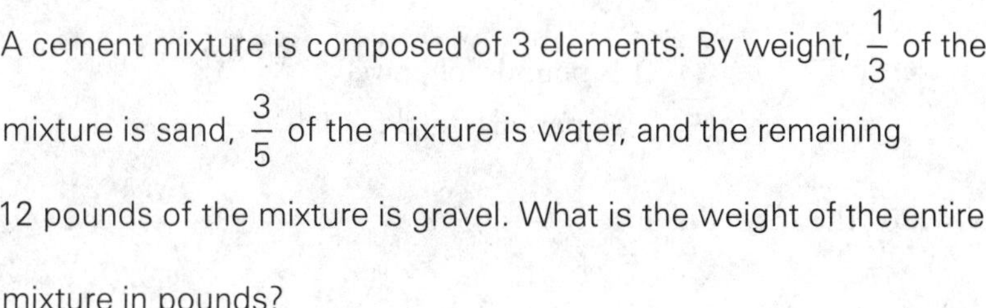
A cement mixture is composed of 3 elements. By weight, $\frac{1}{3}$ of the mixture is sand, $\frac{3}{5}$ of the mixture is water, and the remaining 12 pounds of the mixture is gravel. What is the weight of the entire mixture in pounds?

- 4
- 8
- 36
- 60
- 180

Q: There are only roses, tulips, and peonies in a certain garden. There are three roses to every four tulips and every five peonies in the garden. Expressed as a fraction, what part of the flowers in the garden are tulips?

*Turn to page 149 for the answer.*

### Easy Eliminations

Before we even start doing serious math, let's use some common sense. The weight of the gravel alone is 12 pounds. Because we know that sand and water make up the bulk of the mixture—sand $\frac{1}{3}$, water $\frac{3}{5}$ (which is a bit more than half)—the entire mixture must weigh a great deal more than 12 pounds. Choices (A) and (B) are out of the question. Eliminate them.

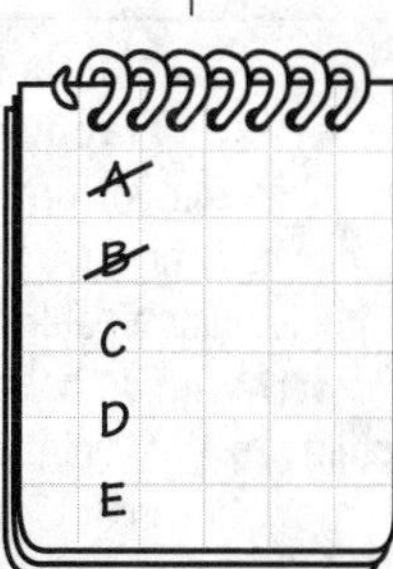


### Here's How to Crack It

The difficulty in solving this problem is that sand and water are expressed as fractions, while gravel is expressed in pounds. At first there seems to be no way of knowing what fractional part of the mixture the 12 pounds of gravel represent; nor do we know how many pounds of sand and water there are.

The first step is to add up the fractional parts that we do have:

$$\frac{1}{3}+\frac{3}{5}=\frac{1}{3}\left(\frac{5}{5}\right)+\frac{3}{5}\left(\frac{3}{3}\right)=\frac{14}{15}$$

Sand and water make up 14 parts out of the whole of 15. This means that gravel makes up what is left over—the rest: 1 part out of the whole of 15. Now the problem is simple. Set up a proportion between parts and weights.

$$\frac{1}{15}=\frac{12}{x}\ \begin{matrix}\text{pounds (of gravel)}\\ \text{pounds (total pounds)}\end{matrix}$$

Cross-multiply: $x = 180$. The answer is (E).

---

## DECIMALS ARE REALLY FRACTIONS

A decimal can be expressed as a fraction, and a fraction can be expressed as a decimal.

> **Decimals or Fractions**
> Whether you prefer decimals or fractions, you must be able to work with both. The ability to work comfortably and confidently with decimals and fractions is vital to GMAT success.

$$0.6=\frac{6}{10},\text{ which can be reduced to }\frac{3}{5}$$

$$\frac{3}{5}\text{ is the same thing as }3 \div 5$$

Which would you rather figure out—the square of $\frac{1}{4}$ or the square of 0.25? There may be a few of you out there who've had so much practice with decimals in your work that you prefer decimals to fractions, but for the rest of us, fractions are infinitely easier to deal with.

Occasionally, you will have to work with decimals. Whenever possible, however, convert decimals to fractions. It will save time and eliminate careless mistakes. In fact, it makes sense to memorize the fractional equivalent of some commonly used decimals:

$$0.2 = \frac{1}{5} \qquad 0.6 = \frac{3}{5}$$
$$0.25 = \frac{1}{4} \qquad 0.\overline{66} = \frac{2}{3}$$
$$0.\overline{33} = \frac{1}{3} \qquad 0.75 = \frac{3}{4}$$
$$0.4 = \frac{2}{5} \qquad 0.8 = \frac{4}{5}$$
$$0.5 = \frac{1}{2}$$

A: The relationship between roses, tulips, and peonies was expressed as a ratio. To find the fractional part, first find the *whole*. We know the parts are 3 roses, 4 tulips, and 5 peonies. $3 + 4 + 5 = 12$ = the whole. What fractional part of the flowers are tulips? 4 out of a total of 12, otherwise known as $\frac{4}{12}$ or $\frac{1}{3}$.

## Adding and Subtracting Decimals

To add or subtract decimals, just line up the decimal points and proceed as usual. Adding 6, 2.5, and 0.3 looks like this:

$$\begin{array}{r} 6.0 \\ 2.5 \\ +\ 0.3 \\ \hline 8.8 \end{array}$$

## Multiplying Decimals

To multiply decimals, simply ignore the decimal points and multiply the two numbers. When you've finished, count all the digits that were to the right of the decimal points in the original numbers you multiplied. Now place the decimal point in your answer so that there are the same number of digits to the right of it. Here are two examples:

$$\begin{array}{r} 0.3 \\ \times\ 0.7 \\ \hline 0.21 \end{array}$$

There were a total of two digits to the right of the decimal point in the original numbers, so we place the decimal so that there are two digits to the right in the answer.

$$\begin{array}{r} 14.3 \\ \times\ 0.232 \\ \hline 3.3176 \end{array}$$

There were a total of four digits to the right of the decimal point in the original numbers, so we place the decimal such that there are four digits to the right in the answer.

## Dividing Decimals

The best way to divide one decimal by another is to convert the number you are dividing by (in mathematical terminology, the **divisor**) into a whole number. You do this simply by moving the decimal point as many places as necessary. This works as long as you remember to move the decimal point in the number that you are *dividing* (in mathematical terminology, the **dividend**) the same number of spaces.

For example, to divide 12 by 0.6, set it up the way you would an ordinary division problem: $0.6\overline{)12.}$

To make 0.6 (the divisor) a whole number, you simply move the decimal point over one place to the right. You must also move the decimal one place to the right in the dividend. Now the operation looks like this:

$$0.6\overline{)12.}$$

$$6\overline{)120}$$

$$\begin{array}{r} 20 \\ 6\overline{)120} \end{array}$$

## Rounding Decimals

9.4 rounded to the nearest whole number is 9.
9.5 rounded to the nearest whole number is 10.

**Rounding**
To round a decimal, look at the digit to the right of the digits place you are rounding to. If that number is 0–4, there is no change. If that number is 5–9, round up.

When GMAC asks you to give an approximate answer on an easy question, it is safe to round numbers. But you should be leery about rounding numbers on a difficult question. If you're scoring in a high percentile, rounding off numbers will be useful to eliminate answer choices that are out of the ballpark, but not to decide between two close answer choices.

## DRILL 5

The answers to these questions can be found in Part VII.

1. $\begin{array}{r} 34.26 \\ -\ 0.96 \\ \hline \end{array}$

2. $\begin{array}{r} 27.3 \\ \times 9.75 \\ \hline \end{array}$

3. $\frac{19.6}{3.2} =$

4. $\frac{\frac{4}{0.25}}{\frac{1}{50}} =$

On the GMAT, there might be questions that mix decimals and fractions:

5. $\frac{\frac{3}{10} \times 4 \times 0.8}{0.32}$

- 0.96
- 0.333
- 3.0
- 30.0
- 96.0

6. If $x$ and $y$ are reciprocals, what is the value of $x + y$ rounded to the nearest hundredth?

(1) $x = 0.2$

(2) $y = 5$

- Statement (1) ALONE is sufficient, but statement (2) alone is not sufficient.
- Statement (2) ALONE is sufficient, but statement (1) alone is not sufficient.
- BOTH statements TOGETHER are sufficient, but NEITHER statement ALONE is sufficient.
- EACH statement ALONE is sufficient.
- Statements (1) and (2) TOGETHER are not sufficient.

**First Things First**

On *all* questions, before you do any serious calculations, take a moment to see whether the answer choices make sense. Eliminate trap answer choices. Do this first because those "trap" choices usually reflect the result of a common (but incorrect) approach to the problem. Eliminate first and you won't think (falsely), "Aha, I've got it." Instead, you'll know you took a misstep somewhere.

## RATIOS

**Ratios** are close relatives of fractions. A ratio can be expressed as a fraction and vice versa. The ratio 3 to 4 can be written as $\frac{3}{4}$ as well as in standard ratio format: 3:4.

### There Is Only One Difference Between a Ratio and a Fraction

A fraction compares a part to whole relationship. A ratio compares a part to part relationship. It's that simple. Check out the box below for a handy visual representation.

| **Fraction:** | **Ratio:** | |
|---|---|---|
| part: 3 women | part: 3 women | |
| whole: 7 people | part: 4 men | (The whole is 7.) |

### Aside from That, All the Rules of Fractions Apply to Ratios

A ratio can be converted to a percentage or a decimal. It can be cross-multiplied, reduced, or expanded—just like a fraction. The ratio of 1 to 3 can be expressed as:

$$\frac{1}{3}$$

1:3

$$\frac{2}{6}$$

$$\frac{3}{9}$$

## An Easy Ratio Problem

The ratio of men to women in a room is 3 to 4. If there are 20 women, what is the number of men in the room?

### Here's How to Crack It

No matter how many people are actually in the room, the ratio of men to women will always stay the same: 3 to 4. What you're asked to do is find the numerator of a fraction whose denominator is 20, and which can be reduced to $\frac{3}{4}$. Just set one fraction equal to another and cross-multiply:

$$\frac{3}{4} = \frac{x}{20} \qquad 60 = 4x \qquad x = 15$$

The answer to the question is 15 men. Note that $\frac{15}{20}$ reduces to $\frac{3}{4}$.

## A More Difficult Ratio Problem

The ratio of women to men in a room is 3 to 4. If there are a total of 28 people in the room, how many are women?

This problem is more difficult because, while we are given the ratio of women to men, we are not given a specific value for either the women or the men. If we tried to set up this problem as we did the previous one, it would look like this:

$$\frac{3}{4} = \frac{x}{y}$$

Of course, you can't solve an equation that has two variables.

### Here's How to Crack It

You need a way to see how the total number of people in the room, which you know is 28, can be broken down into groups of 3 women and 4 men.

A good way to solve the problem is to use a Ratio Box. Here's what that looks like for the information provided by the problem:

| | **Women** | **Men** | **Total** |
|---|---|---|---|
| Ratio | 3 | 4 | |
| Multiplier | | | |
| Actual Number | | | 28 |

To use a Ratio Box, you need a ratio and an actual number. Now, remember that ratios compare parts to parts. So, if you add up the parts, you get a group (or total) of 7 people.

Next, the key idea of a ratio is the multiplier, which allows you to make the group greater or lesser while keeping everything in the same ratio. For this problem, you don't want a group of 7 people. You want a group of 28. So, you multiply $7 \times 4 = 28$.

To keep everything in the same ratio, you just need to remember that whatever you do to one part, you need to do to every part. So, multiply the ratio numbers for both the women and men by 4.

Here's what the box looks like when it is completed:

| | **Women** | **Men** | **Total** |
|---|---|---|---|
| Ratio | 3 | 4 | 7 |
| Multiplier | 4 | 4 | 4 |
| Actual Number | $12 = (3 \times 4)$ | $16 = (4 \times 4)$ | $28 = (7 \times 4)$ |

There are 12 women in the room.

## PERCENTAGES

A **percentage** is just a fraction in which the denominator is always equal to 100. Fifty percent means 50 parts out of a whole of 100. Like any fraction, a percentage can be reduced, expanded, cross-multiplied, converted to a decimal, or converted to another fraction: $50\% = \frac{1}{2} = 0.5$.

### An Easy Percent Problem

Q: What is $\frac{1}{4}$% of 40?

*Turn to page 157 for the answer.*

5 is what percent of 20 ?

#### Here's How to Crack It

Whenever you see a percent problem, you should be thinking $\frac{\text{part}}{\text{whole}}$. In this case, the question asks you to expand $\frac{5}{20}$ into another fraction in which the denominator is 100.

$$\frac{\text{part}}{\text{whole}} = \frac{5}{20} = \frac{x}{100}$$

$$500 = 20x$$

$$x = 25$$

$$\frac{25}{100} = 25\%$$

## Percent Shortcuts

In the last problem, reducing $\frac{5}{20}$ to $\frac{1}{4}$ would have saved you time if you knew that $\frac{1}{4} = 25\%$. Here are some fractions and decimals whose percent equivalents you should know:

$$\frac{1}{4} = 0.25 = 25\%$$

$$\frac{1}{2} = 0.50 = 50\%$$

$$\frac{1}{3} = 0.333\ldots \text{ (a repeating decimal)} = 33\frac{1}{3}\%$$

$$\frac{1}{5} = 0.20 = 20\%$$

Some percentages simply involve moving a decimal point. To get 10 percent of any number, simply move the decimal point of that number over one place to the left:

10% of 6 = 0.6
10% of 60 = 6
10% of 600 = 60

- To get 1 percent of any number, just move the decimal point of that number over two places to the left:
  1% of 600 = 6
  1% of 60 = 0.6
  1% of 6 = 0.06

- To find a more complicated percentage, break the percentage down into easy-to-find chunks:
  20% of 60: 10% of 60 = 6; 20% of 60 is double 10%, so the answer is 2 × 6, or 12.
  30% of 60: 10% of 60 = 6; 30% of 60 is three times 10%, so the answer is 3 × 6, or 18.
  3% of 200: 1% of 200 = 2; 3% of 200 is just three times 1%, so the answer is 3 × 2, or 6.
  23% of 400: 10% of 400 = 40. Therefore, 20% equals 2 × 40, or 80. 1% of 400 = 4. Therefore, 3% equals 3 × 4, or 12. Putting it all together, 23% of 400 equals 80 + 12, or 92.

## A Medium Percent Problem

Like medium and difficult fraction problems, medium and difficult percent problems often involve remembering the principles of $\frac{\text{part}}{\text{whole}}$ and the rest.

A: There are a number of ways to calculate the answer, but the simplest is to first calculate 1% of 40 by moving the decimal point two places to the left. This gives 0.4 as a result. Dividing this result by 4 gives us 0.1—the answer.

A motor pool has 300 vehicles of which 30 percent are trucks. 20 percent of all the vehicles in the motor pool are diesel, including 15 trucks. What percent of the motor pool is composed of vehicles that are neither trucks nor diesel?

- 165%
- 90%
- 65%
- 55%
- 10%

### Here's How to Crack It

Do this problem one sentence at a time.

1. A motor pool has 300 vehicles, of which 30% are trucks. Thirty percent of 300 = 90 trucks, which means that 210 (the rest) are *not* trucks.
2. Twenty percent of all the vehicles are diesel, including 15 trucks. Twenty percent of 300 = 60 diesel vehicles, 15 of which are trucks, which means there are 45 diesel vehicles that are *not* trucks.
3. What percent of the motor pool is composed of vehicles that are neither truck nor diesel? We know from sentence number 1 that there are 210 nontrucks. We know from sentence number 2 that of these 210 nontrucks, 45 are diesel. Therefore, 210 – 45, or 165, are neither diesel nor truck.

There's a handy formula for calculating mixed groups. It isn't a priority for you to memorize (you just saw the problem calculated without it), but the formula can be helpful on some questions. Here it is: **Group 1 + Group 2 – both + neither = total.** Here's what that looks like using the numbers from the vehicle problem. 90 trucks + 60 diesel – 15 diesel trucks + $x$ = 300. 135 + $x$ = 300. $x$ = 165, or 55% of 300.

The question asks what percent of the entire motor pool these 165 nondiesel nontrucks are.

$$\frac{165}{300} = \frac{x}{100} \qquad 300x = 16{,}500$$

$x = 55$, so the answer is (D).

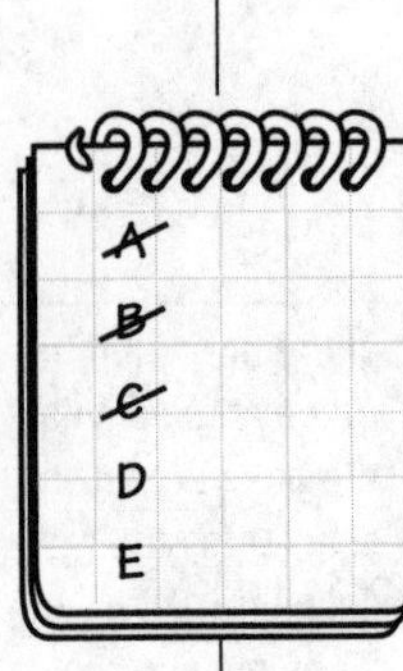


**Easy Process of Elimination**

1. Because the problem asks us to find a portion of the entire motor pool, it's impossible for that portion to be greater than the motor pool itself. Therefore, (A), 165%, can be eliminated via Ballparking.
2. If the problem simply asked what percent of the motor pool was not made up of trucks, the answer would be 70%. But because there is a further condition (the vehicles must be both nontruck and nondiesel), the answer must be even less than 70%. So, (B) can be eliminated via Ballparking as well.
3. Choice (C) is a partial answer that you can get by simply adding 30 + 20 + 15, all numbers found within the problem. Choice (C) can be reasonably eliminated.

## Percent Increase or Decrease

Another type of percent problem you may see on the GMAT has to do with *percent increase* or *percent decrease.* In these problems, the trick is always to put the increase or decrease in terms of the *original* amount. See the following example:

The cost of a one-family home was $120,000 in 1980. In 1988, the price had increased to $180,000. What was the percent increase in the cost of the home?

- 60%
- 50%
- 55%
- 40%
- 33.3%

### Here's How to Crack It

The actual increase was \$60,000. To find the percent increase, set up the following equation:

$$\frac{\text{amount of increase}}{\text{original amount}} = \frac{x}{100}$$

In this case, $\frac{\$60{,}000}{\$120{,}000} = \frac{x}{100}$. So, $x = 50$ and the answer is (B).

**What's the Original Amount?**
GMAT test-writers like to see if they can trick you into mistaking which number was the original amount. On percent decrease problems (sometimes called "percent less" problems), the original is the larger number; on percent increase problems (sometimes called "percent greater" problems), the original is the smaller number.

To solve a percent *decrease* problem, simply put the amount of the decrease over the original amount.

## Compound Interest

Another type of percent problem involves **compound interest**. If you kept \$1,000 in the bank for a year at 6% simple interest, you would get \$60 in interest at the end of the year. Compound interest would pay you slightly more. Let's look at a compound-interest problem:

Ms. Lopez deposits \$100 in an account that pays 20% interest, compounded semiannually. How much money will there be in the account at the end of one year?

- \$118.00
- \$120.00
- \$121.00
- \$122.00
- \$140.00

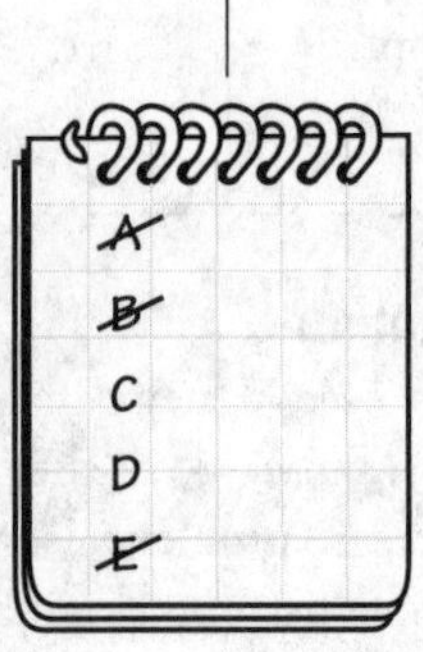


**Easy Process of Elimination**
How would you work this problem if you were running out of time, or not sure how to find compound interest? Look for answer choices that can be eliminated via POE. The question asks for compound interest but (B) is the calculation of simple interest. Because finding simple interest is how to start a compound interest problem, (B) is a partial answer and can be eliminated. If you know that compound interest is always a *little bit* more than simple interest, you can eliminate (A) and (E) via Ballparking. Solving this problem from here requires knowledge of calculating compound interest. But, if you were having difficulty with this problem or were running out of time, POE can make this a 50/50 guess!

### Here's How to Crack It

To find compound interest, divide the interest into as many parts as are being compounded. For example, if you're compounding interest semiannually, you divide the interest into two equal parts. If you're compounding quarterly, you divide the interest into four equal parts.

When Ms. Lopez deposited \$100 into her account at a rate of 20% compounded semiannually, the bank divided the interest into two equal parts. Halfway through the year, the bank put the first half of the interest into her account. In this case, because the full rate was 20% compounded semiannually, the bank deposited 10% of \$100 (10% of \$100 = \$10). Halfway through the year, Ms. Lopez had \$110.

For the second half of the year, the bank paid 10% interest on the \$110 (10% of \$110 = \$11). At the end of the year, Ms. Lopez had \$121.00 in her account. She earned \$1 more than she would have earned if the account had paid only simple interest. The answer is (C).

## AVERAGES

To find the **average** of a list of *n* numbers, simply add the numbers and divide by *n*. For example:

$$\text{The average of 10, 3, and 5 is } \frac{10+3+5}{3}=6.$$

**Reminder!**
Averaging problems often have easy eliminations, so be sure to look for them—*before* you solve.

A good way to handle average problems is to set them up in the same way every time. Whenever you see the word *average*, you should think:

$$\frac{\text{total sum of the items}}{\text{total number of the items}} = \text{average}$$

## A One-Step Average Problem

In a simple problem, GMAC will give you two parts of this equation, and it will be up to you to figure out the third. Let's warm up those old average skills.

What is the average (arithmetic mean) of the numbers 3, 4, 5, and 8 ?

### Here's How to Crack It

In this case they've given us the actual numbers, which means we know the total sum (3 + 4 + 5 + 8 = 20) and the total number of items (there are four numbers). What we're missing is the average.

$$\frac{\text{total sum of the items}}{\text{total number of the items}} = \text{average} \qquad \frac{20}{4} = x \quad x = 5$$

Here's another one:

If the average (arithmetic mean) of 7 numbers is 5, what is the sum of the numbers?

### Here's How to Crack It

In this case we know the total number of items and the average, but not the total sum of the numbers.

$$\frac{\text{total sum of the items}}{\text{total number of the items}} = \text{average} \qquad \frac{x}{7} = 5 \quad x = 35$$

**The Average Test-Taker**

A common mistake by the average test-taker is thinking he or she can take the average of two averages. Take a look at the following question:

If Fred's average score on his first two tests was 70, and his average score on his next three tests was 80, what was his average score on all the tests?

The average test-taker wants to say the answer is 75, which is just the average of 70 and 80. This test-taker either forgets, ignores, or misses the information that the first average was based on two tests, while the second average was based on three tests. Therefore, the average score is not 75, and the average test-taker would get this question wrong.

Avoid this mistake by slowing down and reading the full question!

## A Two-Step Average Problem

This is the same problem you just did, made a little more difficult:

---

The average (arithmetic mean) of 7 numbers is 5. If two of the numbers are 11 and 14, what is the average of the remaining numbers?

### Here's How to Crack It

Always set up an average problem the way we showed you above. With more complicated average problems, take things one sentence at a time. The first sentence yields:

$$\frac{\text{total sum of the items}}{\text{total number of the items}} = \text{average} \qquad \frac{x}{7} = 5 \quad x = 35$$

The sum of *all* the numbers is 35. If two of those numbers are 11 and 14, then the sum of the remaining numbers is 35 – (11 + 14), or 10. The question asks, "What is the average of the remaining numbers?" Again, let's set this up properly:

$$\frac{\text{total sum of the remaining numbers}}{\text{total number of the remaining numbers}} = \text{average} \qquad \frac{10}{5} = y \quad y = 2$$

Why did we divide the total sum of the remaining numbers by 5? There were only 5 remaining numbers!

---

## Medians and Modes

Calculating the average of a list of numbers is one way to find the "middle" of these numbers, but there are two other ways that yield slightly different results. To find the **median** of a list of *n* numbers, just reorder the numbers from least to greatest, and pick the middle number.

If *n* is odd, this is a piece of cake:

The median of 4, 7, 12, 14, 20 = 12.

If $n$ is even, it's still easy—just add the two middle numbers together and divide by 2:

$$\text{The median of 4, 12, 14, 20} = \frac{12+14}{2} = 13.$$

To find the **mode** of a list of $n$ numbers, just pick the number that occurs most frequently...

The mode of 5, 6, 3, 9, 3, 28, 3, 5 = 3.

...but remember that a list of numbers *can* have more than one mode:

The modes of 3, 3, 3, 4, 5, 5, 5 = both 3 and 5.

Here's a relatively easy problem:

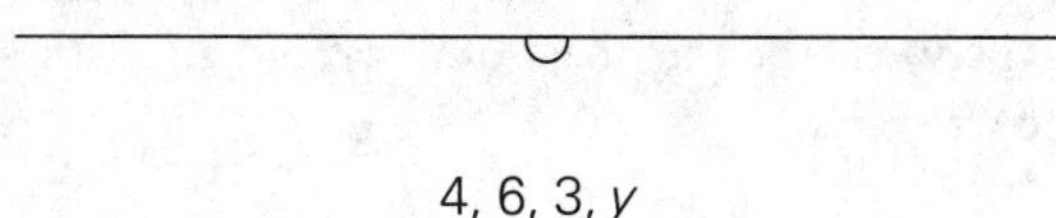

4, 6, 3, $y$

If the mode of the list of numbers above is 3, then what is the average (arithmetic mean) of the list?

- ○ 7
- ○ 3
- ○ 4
- ○ 9
- ○ 12

### Here's How to Crack It

The mode of the list of numbers is 3, which means that $y$ must also equal 3 (because the mode is the number that occurs most frequently in the list). So now all we have to do is find the average of 4, 6, 3, and 3. The correct answer is (C).

**Mean**
When a question refers to an average, the words "arithmetic mean" will often follow in parentheses. This is not just to make the problem sound scarier. **Arithmetic mean** is the precise term for the process of finding an average that we've illustrated in the problems above.

## RANGE

To find the range of a list of $n$ numbers, take the least number and subtract it from the greatest number. This measures how widely the numbers are dispersed.

The range of 4, 3, 8, 12, 23, 37 = 37 − 3 = 34.

## STANDARD DEVIATION

Standard deviation is another way that the dispersion of a group of numbers is calculated. The prevalence of standard deviation questions on the GMAT is small, and though the GMAT might ask you questions about standard deviation, you'll never have to actually calculate it. Instead, you'll just need a basic understanding of what standard deviation is and how it's tested on the GMAT. Generally, the GMAT treats standard deviation as a measure of spread.

### A Question of Spread

The first thing to know is what is meant by standard deviation on the GMAT. Standard deviation is a measure of the amount of spread, or variation, of a set of data values. A low standard deviation indicates that the data values tend to be close to the mean (thus, to have little spread), while a high standard deviation indicates that the values are spread out over a wider range. So, the further the distance between the members of a set and the set's average, the greater the standard deviation of the set.

**Means, Medians, and Modes, Oh My!**

Q: For the list of numbers {3, 2, 5, 8, 2, 16}, find the mean, the mode, the median, and the range.

*Turn to page 166 for the answer.*

Consider two sets of numbers, {4,4,4} and {3,4,5}. The first set, {4,4,4}, has a mean value of 4, as $\left(\frac{4+4+4}{3}\right)$ is equal to 4. However, since each member of the set is equal to the mean (and thus to each other member of the set), there is no distance between the members of the set and the mean of the set, so there is no spread among the numbers. Now look at the second set, {3,4,5}. This set also has a mean of 4, as $\left(\frac{3+4+5}{3}\right)$ is equal to 4. However, in this group, instead of all numbers being equal to the mean, two members of the set have some distance from the mean (3 and 5 are not equal to the mean of 4). Therefore, since the second set has more spread (the members of the set have more distance from the mean), the second set has a greater standard deviation.

Here's an example of how GMAC might test standard deviation:

---

What is the standard deviation of set *R* ?

- ◯ The value of all elements of set *R* is between 5 and 20.
- ◯ The mean of set *R* is 12.

#### Here's How to Crack It

This is a Value Data Sufficiency question, so begin by determining what is known from the question stem and what is needed from the statements in order to answer the question. Begin by determining what is known. The question stem only provides that there is a set *R*. Next, determine what is needed. In order to be sufficient, the statements need to provide information necessary to determine the standard deviation. In order to determine the standard deviation, the statements need to provide a way to determine the values in set $R$. Evaluate the statements individually.

Statement (1) provides a range of the value of all elements of set $R$, but does not state how many elements there are, or what the average is, so there is no way to determine the standard deviation of set $R$ from this information. Write down BCE.

Statement (2) provides the mean of set $R$. However, this does not provide information that indicates the actual values of $R$ or how many elements are in set $R$, so eliminate (B).

The statements combined provide a range of values and a mean for set $R$. However, this information is still not sufficient. For example, the values of set $R$ could be 11 and 13, which are between 5 and 20 and have an average of 12. Alternatively, set $R$ could contain 6 instances of the number 12. Both options satisfy the statements, but there is not a consistent answer for the question. Therefore, the statements combined are not sufficient. Eliminate (C).

The correct answer is (E).

---

Now, let's try a question that deals with standard deviation differently.

---

For a certain distribution, the value 12.0 is one standard deviation above the mean and the value 15.0 is three standard deviations above the mean. What is the mean of the data set?

- 9.0
- 9.5
- 10.0
- 10.5
- 11.0

### Here's How to Crack It

This one's a little tougher than the previous question. The question provides neither the individual data points nor the mean, and GMAC is hoping that this will throw you off. But remember that standard deviation deals with the distance from the mean. Start by determining the size of one standard deviation. Since 12.0 is one standard deviation above the mean and 15.0 is three standard deviations above the mean, then the difference between the data values represents the difference in the number of standard deviations. Therefore:

$$15.0 - 12.0 = 3.0 \text{ st dev} - 1.0 \text{ st dev, so } 3.0 = 2.0 \text{ st dev}$$

Now set up a proportion to find the size of one standard deviation:

$$\frac{3.0}{2.0 \text{ st dev}} = \frac{x}{1 \text{ st dev}}$$

Solve to find that $x = 1.5$, which means that one standard deviation for this data set is equal to 1.5. Since 12.0 is one standard deviation above the mean, the mean of the data set is $12.0 - 1.5 = 10.5$, so the answer is (D).

## EXPONENTS

An **exponent** is a short way of writing the value of a number multiplied several times by itself. $4 \times 4 \times 4 \times 4 \times 4$ can also be written as $4^5$. This is expressed as "four to the fifth power." The large number (4) is called the base, and the little number (5) is called the exponent.

There are several rules to remember about exponents:

- **Multiplying numbers with the same base:** When you multiply numbers that have the same base, simply add their exponents.

$$6^2 \times 6^3 = 6^{(2+3)} = 6^5 \qquad (y^4)(y^6) = y^{(4+6)} = y^{10}$$

- **Dividing numbers with the same base:** When you divide numbers that have the same base, simply subtract the bottom exponents from the top exponents.

$$\frac{3^6}{3^2} = 3^{(6-2)} = 3^4 \qquad \frac{x^7}{x^4} = x^{(7-4)} = x^3$$

**Means, Medians, and Modes, Oh My!**
A: Always remember to reorder the numbers.
In the list of numbers {2, 2, 3, 5, 8, 16}:
The mean is 6.
The mode is 2.
The median is 4.
The range is 14.

- **Raising a power to a power:** When you raise a number with an exponent to another power, simply multiply the exponents.

$$(4^3)^2 = 4^{(3\times 2)} = 4^6 \qquad (z^2)^4 = z^{(2\times 4)} = z^8$$

There are several operations that ***seem*** like they ought to work with exponents, but don't.

- Does $x^2 + x^3 = x^5$? NO!
- Does $x^6 - x^2 = x^4$? NO!
- Does $\dfrac{(x^2 + y^2 + z^2)}{(x^2 + y^2)} = z^2$? NO!

But note that in the first example, $x^2 + x^3$ can be written in another form, using the distributive property: $x^2 + x^3 = x^2(1 + x)$.

### The Strange Powers of Powers

If you raise a positive integer to a power, the result is *greater* than the original integer. For example, $6^2 = 36$. However, raising a number to a power can sometimes have unexpected results:

- If you raise a positive fraction that is less than 1 to a power, the result is *less* than the original fraction.

$$\left(\frac{1}{3}\right)^2 = \frac{1}{3} \times \frac{1}{3} = \frac{1}{9}$$

- If you raise a negative number to an odd power, the result is *less* than the original number.

  $$(-3)^3 = (-3)(-3)(-3) = -27$$

  (Remember, −27 is smaller than −3.)

- If you raise a negative number to an even power, the result is positive.

  $$(-3)^2 = (-3)(-3) = 9$$

  (Remember, negative times negative = positive.)

- Any number to the first power = itself.

- Any nonzero number raised to the 0 power = 1.

**Strange Powers Revealed!**

Why is any number to the 0 power equal to 1 when any other time we multiply by 0 the result is 0? The answer is that we aren't multiplying by 0 at all. Watch closely now: $3^0$ should equal $3^{-1} \times 3^1$, because when you add the exponents you get $3^0$. Now, $3^{-1} \times 3^1$ can be rewritten $\frac{1}{3} \times 3 = \frac{3}{3} = 1$.

## RADICALS

The **square root** of a positive number $x$ is the number that, when squared, equals $x$. By definition, you can take the square root of only a nonnegative number and the square root function returns only nonnegative values. The symbol for a square root is $\sqrt{\ }$. A number inside the $\sqrt{\ }$ is called a **radical**. Thus, in $\sqrt{4} = 2$, 4 is the radical and 2 is its square root.

The **cube root** of a positive number $x$ is the number that, when cubed, equals $x$. For example, the cube root of 8 is 2, because $2 \times 2 \times 2 = 8$. The symbol for a cube root is $\sqrt[3]{\ }$. Thus, the cube root of 27 would be represented as $\sqrt[3]{27} = 3$, because $3 \times 3 \times 3 = 27$. The cube root of −27 would be represented as $\sqrt[3]{-27} = -3$ because $-3 \times -3 \times -3 = -27$.

There are several rules to remember about radicals:

1. $\sqrt{x}\sqrt{y} = \sqrt{xy}$. For example, $\sqrt{12}\sqrt{3} = \sqrt{36} = 6$.

2. $\sqrt{\frac{x}{y}} = \frac{\sqrt{x}}{\sqrt{y}}$. For example, $\sqrt{\frac{3}{16}} = \frac{\sqrt{3}}{\sqrt{16}} = \frac{\sqrt{3}}{4}$.

3. To simplify a radical, try factoring. For example, $\sqrt{32} = \sqrt{16}\sqrt{2} = 4\sqrt{2}$.

4. The square root of a positive fraction less than 1 is actually larger than the original fraction. For example, $\sqrt{\frac{1}{4}} = \frac{1}{2}$.

**Even More Strange Powers**

A radical can be rewritten as a fractional exponent, and vice versa. That is: $\sqrt[3]{5} = 5^{\frac{1}{3}}$.

## DRILL 6

The answers to these questions can be found in Part VII.

1. If 2 men and 1 woman drop out of a certain class, the ratio of men to women in the class would be 8 to 7. If the current ratio of men to women in the class is 6 to 5, then how many men are currently in the class?

   - 14
   - 16
   - 18
   - 20
   - 22

2. The average (arithmetic mean) of five numbers is 7. If the average of three of the numbers is 5, then what is the average of the other two numbers?

   - 5
   - 10
   - 12
   - 15
   - 20

3. $\dfrac{\left(\frac{1}{3}\right)^6 - \left(\frac{1}{3}\right)^4}{\left(\frac{1}{3}\right)^5} =$

   - $\left(\frac{1}{3}\right)^{-3}$
   - $-\frac{8}{27}$
   - $-\frac{8}{9}$
   - $-\frac{8}{3}$
   - $-\left(\frac{1}{3}\right)^{-3}$

4. The ratio $\frac{\sqrt{147}+\sqrt{75}}{14}$ to $\frac{28}{7\sqrt{3}}$ is equal to

- $\sqrt{74}$ to 2
- 24 to 7
- 14 to 9
- 9 to 14
- 7 to 24

5. If $5,000 is invested in an account that earns 8% interest compounded semiannually, then the interest earned after one year would be how much greater than if the $5,000 had been invested at 8% simple yearly interest?

- $4
- $8
- $12
- $16
- $432

6. If the average of ten numbers is 10, then which of the following could be the standard deviation of the ten numbers?

I. 0
II. 10
III. 20

- I only
- I and II
- I and III
- II and III
- I, II, and III

7. List I: {$y$, 2, 4, 7, 10, 11}
List II: {3, 3, 4, 6, 7, 10}

If the median of List I is equal to the sum of the median of List II and the mode of List II, then $y$ equals

- 5
- 7
- 8
- 9
- 10

## Challenge Question #3

A bar over a digit in a decimal indicates an infinitely repeating decimal.

$333{,}333.\overline{3} \times (10^{-3} - 10^{-5}) =$

- ◯ $3{,}333.\overline{3}$
- ◯ 3,330
- ◯ $333.\overline{3}$
- ◯ 330
- ◯ 0

# Summary

- The six arithmetic operations are addition, subtraction, multiplication, division, raising to a power, and finding a square root.
- These operations must be performed in the proper order (**P**lease **E**xcuse **M**y **D**ear **A**unt **S**ally).
- If you are adding or multiplying a group of numbers, you can regroup them in any order. This is called the **Associative Law**.
- If you are adding or subtracting numbers with common factors, you can regroup them in the following way:

  $$ab + ac = a(b + c)$$
  $$ab - ac = a(b - c)$$

  This is called the **Distributive Law**.
- A fraction can be thought of in two ways:
  - another way of expressing division
  - as a $\frac{\text{part}}{\text{whole}}$
- You must know how to add, subtract, multiply, and divide fractions. You must also know how to raise them to a power and find their roots.
- Always reduce fractions (when you can) before doing a complicated operation. This will reduce your chances of making a careless error.
- In tough fraction problems, always think $\frac{\text{part}}{\text{whole}}$ and *the rest.*
- A decimal is just another way of expressing a fraction.
- You must know how to add, subtract, multiply, and divide decimals.
- In general, it is easier to work with fractions than with decimals, so convert decimals to fractions.

- A ratio is a fraction in all ways but one:
  - A fraction is a $\frac{\text{part}}{\text{whole}}$.
  - A ratio is a $\frac{\text{part}}{\text{part}}$.
  - In a ratio, the whole is the sum of all its parts.
- A percentage is just a fraction whose denominator is always 100.
- You must know the percentage shortcuts outlined in this chapter.
- In tough percent problems, like tough fraction problems, think $\frac{\text{part}}{\text{whole}}$ and *the rest.*
- In a percentage increase or decrease problem, you must put the amount of the increase or decrease over the *original* amount.
- In compound interest problems, the answer will always be *a little bit more* than it would be in a similar simple interest problem.
- To find the average of several values, add the values and divide the total by the number of values.
- Always set up average problems in the same way:

$$\frac{\text{total sum of the items}}{\text{total number of the items}} = \text{average}$$

- To find the median of a list of $n$ numbers, reorder the numbers from least to greatest, and pick the middle number if $n$ is odd. Take the average of the two middle numbers if $n$ is even.
- To find the mode of a list of $n$ numbers, pick the number that occurs most frequently.
- To find the range of a list of $n$ numbers, subtract the smallest number from the greatest number.
- Standard deviation is a measure of spread of a set of numbers.

- An exponent is a shorter way of expressing the result of multiplying a number several times by itself.
- When you multiply numbers with the same base, simply add the exponents.
- When you divide numbers with the same base, simply subtract the exponents.
- When you raise a power to a power, multiply the exponents.
- You *cannot* add or subtract numbers with the same or different bases by adding their exponents.
- The three radical rules you need to know:
    - $\sqrt{x}\sqrt{y} = \sqrt{xy}$
    - $\sqrt{\frac{x}{y}} = \frac{\sqrt{x}}{\sqrt{y}}$
    - $\sqrt{x^2 y} = x\sqrt{y}$
- There are some unusual features of exponents and radicals:
    - The square root of a positive fraction that's less than 1 is larger than the original fraction.
    - When you raise a positive fraction that's less than 1 to an exponent, the resulting fraction is smaller.
    - When you raise a negative number to an even exponent, the resulting number is positive.
    - When you raise a negative number to an odd exponent, the resulting number is still a negative number.

# Chapter 13
# Algebra

Algebra is usually all about writing equations. In this chapter, we'll show you a foolproof way to write the equations you *need* to write, give you a review of the quadratic formula, and teach you how to do simultaneous equations.

Approximately one-fourth of the problems on the computer-adaptive GMAT Quantitative section involve traditional algebra. Your algebra skills may also be tested by some questions in the Integrated Reasoning section. This chapter introduces the algebraic concepts that you will need to know in order to answer questions on the GMAT. This chapter focuses on ways to find algebraic solutions to common problems on the GMAT. Familiarizing yourself with these concepts is an important step to cracking the Quantitative section of the test.

Chapter 14 discusses a strategy that you can employ to make algebra problems easier to work with. However, you need a firm foundation to most effectively deploy that strategy. When you are finished working through this chapter, you will have been exposed to all the tools you need to excel on algebra questions on the GMAT.

## BASIC ALGEBRA

You can solve most GMAT algebra problems using some form of Plugging In, which we'll cover in Chapter 14. However, there are some questions that you may need to solve using some relatively basic algebra.

**Avoiding Common Errors**

We'll add a third rule that you won't find written in any math book.

3. Equations cannot become expressions.

If you've ever started working with one side of an equation without writing down both sides of the equation, you've broken this rule. By always writing down both sides of the equation, you can avoid wasting time and making silly mistakes.

### Two Simple Rules

Before we review some very specific types of algebra that GMAC likes to test, let's review the two basic rules that are true for any algebraic situation. These two rules are used pretty much any time that you solve a problem algebraically.

1. Collect like terms. Get all the $x$'s on one side of the equals sign and all the numbers on the other.
2. Whatever you do to one side of an equation, you need to do to the other side of the equation. Did you multiply one side by 5? Then you need to multiply the other side of the equation by 5, as well.

### Solving Equalities

Even the simplest equalities can be solved by Plugging In the Answers, which is also covered in Chapter 14, but it's probably easier to solve a simple equation algebraically. If there is one variable in an equation, isolate the variable on one side of the equation and solve it. Let's try an example of this type, although a question this easy wouldn't actually be seen on the GMAT. This one is just for practice.

If $x - 5 = 3x + 2$, then $x =$

- $-8$
- $-7$
- $-\frac{7}{2}$
- $\frac{7}{5}$
- $\frac{10}{3}$

### Here's How to Crack It

Get all of the *x*'s on one side of the equation. If we subtract *x* from both sides we have:

$$\begin{aligned} x - 5 &= 3x + 2 \\ -x \quad &\quad -x \\ -5 &= 2x + 2 \end{aligned}$$

Now subtract 2 from both sides:

$$\begin{aligned} -5 &= 2x + 2 \\ -2 \quad &\quad -2 \\ -7 &= 2x \end{aligned}$$

Finally, divide both sides by 2:

$$\frac{-7}{2} = \frac{2x}{2}$$

$$x = -\frac{7}{2}$$

The answer is (C).

## Solving Inequalities

To solve inequalities, you must be able to recognize the following symbols:

| | |
|---|---|
| $>$ | is greater than |
| $<$ | is less than |
| $\geq$ | is greater than or equal to |
| $\leq$ | is less than or equal to |

As with an equation, you can add a number to or subtract a number from both sides of an inequality without changing it; you can collect similar terms and simplify them. In fact, an inequality behaves just like a regular equation except in one way:

If you multiply or divide both sides of an inequality by a negative number, the direction of the inequality symbol changes.

For example,

$$-2x > 5$$

To solve for $x$, you would divide both sides by $-2$, just as you would in an equality. But when you do, the sign flips:

$$\frac{-2x}{-2} < \frac{5}{-2}$$

$$x < -\frac{5}{2}$$

## Solving Simultaneous Equations

Simultaneous equations are almost always tested in Data Sufficiency format on the GMAT. It is generally impossible to solve one equation with two variables, and later we will discuss the rare opportunity to do so. But if there are two equations, both of which have the same two variables, then it is possible to solve for both variables. An easy problem might look like this:

If $3x + 2y = 6$ and $5x - 2y = 10$, then $x = ?$

To solve simultaneous equations, add or subtract the equations so that one of the variables disappears.

$$\begin{array}{r} 3x + 2y = 6 \\ \underline{+\ 5x - 2y = 10} \\ 8x \qquad = 16 \end{array}$$

$$x = 2$$

Q: Are the following equations distinct?
(1) $3x + 21y = 12$
(2) $x + 7y = 4$

*Go to page 181 for the answer.*

In more difficult simultaneous equations, you'll find that neither of the variables will disappear when you try to add or subtract the two equations. In such cases, you must multiply both sides of one of the equations by some number in order to get the coefficient in front of the variable that you want to disappear to be the same in both equations. This sounds more complicated than it is. A difficult problem might look like this:

If $3x + 2y = 6$ and $5x - y = 10$, then $x = ?$

Let's set it up the same way:

### Equation Tricks and Traps

$x + 3y - 7 = x^2(x^{-1}) + y$

This looks like two variables in one equation, which would mean we need at least one more equation to solve, but look again. Because $x^2(x^{-1}) = x^{(2-1)} = x$, each side of the equation has only one $x$. The $x$s can be subtracted, leaving you with just one variable, $y$. The equation can be solved.

$$3x + 2y = 6$$

$$5x - y = 10$$

Unfortunately, in this example, neither adding nor subtracting the two equations gets rid of either variable. But look what happens when we multiply the bottom equation by 2:

$$\begin{array}{c} 3x + 2y = 6 \\ (2)5x - (2)y = (2)10 \end{array} \quad \text{or} \quad \begin{array}{r} 3x + 2y = 6 \\ \underline{+\ 10x - 2y = 20} \\ 13x \qquad = 26 \end{array} \quad x = 2$$

## Building Algebraic Expressions

One of the prerequisites for Plugging In (covered in the next chapter) or using algebra to solve algebraic expressions or equations is, of course, having an algebraic expression or equation for which to solve. Sometimes, the GMAT provides an equation for you that contains all the information you need to solve the problem. In this case, you can go straight to working the equation by simplifying, substituting, factoring, or whatever method is necessary to solve the equation. For instance, the following equations provide everything you need to know in order to solve for $x$:

$$7 = x - 2$$
$$2x = 8$$
$$\frac{x+2}{4} = 12$$

When presented with an equation that looks like one of the above, there is no preparation work to be executed in order to solve for $x$. However, the GMAT does not always provide fully written out equations like those above. Consider the following statements that describe equations:

7 is 2 less than $x$

Twice the value of $x$ is 8

The sum of 2 and $x$, divided by 4, is 12

Statements like these do not lend themselves to immediately having mathematical operations done to them. Before completing any algebraic work, the sentences need to be built into algebraic expressions. Similar work needs to be done for problems that give information such as the following:

*If $y = 2x$ and $7 = y + 5$, then what value is 4 less than $x$?*

The problem above combines two algebraic equations and a statement that describes an expression. Before working this question or the three prior statements, you need to build algebraic expressions and equations from the information provided.

## Translating from English to Math

One of the skills required to build algebraic expressions correctly is to translate phrases or sentences into expressions or equations. This is a skill most commonly used on word problems, but it also shows up when you are working with data sufficiency questions. Use the following table to help translate some of the more common words into a familiar math operation.

| Word | Equivalent Symbol |
|---|---|
| percent | $\frac{}{100}$ |
| is | = |
| of, times, product | × |
| what (or any unknown value) | any variable ($x$, $k$, $b$) |
| sum | + |
| difference | – |
| fraction | $\frac{x}{y}$ |

A: No. Look at what equation #2 looks like multiplied by 3: $3(x + 7y) = 3(4)$ or $3x + 21y = 12$. Multiply both sides by 3 and equations #1 and #2 are identical. When one equation can be multiplied to produce the other, the equations are identical, not distinct.

## Less Than, Greater Than

Depending on the context, the phrases *less than* and *greater than* yield different math symbols. For example, in the phrase *7 is less than 9*, the phrase *is less than* indicates an inequality. This is translated as $7 < 9$ and the phrase *is less than* is represented by the symbol <. However, in the phrase *7 less than x is 9*, the phrase *less than* indicates subtraction. This phrase can be rewritten as $x - 7 = 9$, and the phrase *less than* is represented by the subtraction symbol –.

The same is true of the phrases *is greater than* and *greater than*. The phrase *is greater than* is represented by the symbol >. However, the phrase *greater than* indicates addition and is translated to the addition symbol, +.

## Order of Operations

The order of operations is the standard rule that dictates which operations are performed in what order. Applying the correct order of operations can dramatically impact the outcome of a set of operations in an equation or expression. As explained earlier, the correct order of operations is most commonly remembered by the acronym PEMDAS, which stands for Parentheses, Exponents, Multiplication, Division, Addition, Subtraction. Begin solving all equations with anything in parentheses, then work with any exponents, then multiply and divide together, working from left to right, and finally add and subtract together, also working from left to right.

When providing information that needs to be used to build algebraic expressions, the GMAT is not going to be as explicit as stating what operation goes where. For instance, the GMAT is not going to provide information that says "3 minus the parenthetical value of 2 plus *x*." Instead, the GMAT is more likely to write "3 minus the sum of 2 and *x*." The placement of the word *sum* in the expression implies the parentheses to bracket off the 2 and *x*. Written out, this expression looks like this:

$$3 - (2 + x)$$

Writing an expression such as the previous one incorrectly can have disastrous consequences. For instance, if $x = 1$, then the previous expression evaluates to $3 - (2 + 1) = 3 - 3 = 0$. However, if you had not set off $2 + x$ in parentheses, then the previous expression is $3 - 2 + 1 = 1 + 1 = 2$. The answer changes because the order of operations changes.

Instead of explicitly telling you to set off items in parentheses, the GMAT uses terms of aggregation, such as *sum*, *difference*, and *product* to indicate that the value of two items should be calculated first. For instance, the expression "2 times the sum of 4 and 5" is written as $2 \times (4 + 5)$ and is calculated as $2 \times (9) = 18$. This is very different than the expression "2 times 4 plus 5," which is written and calculated as $2 \times 4 + 5 = 8 + 5 = 13$.

## Putting It All Together

Let's take another look at the question presented earlier:

*If $y = 2x$ and $7 = y + 5$, then what value is 4 less than $x$?*

This question wants to know what value is 4 less than $x$. Writing this phrase as an expression yields $x - 4$. The word *is* indicates an equal sign, so this can be written as $x - 4 =$. The phrase *what value* indicates a variable, which is what you are solving for. You need to solve for the value of $x$ in order to answer the question. There is only one equation that involves the variable $x$ and that requires a value of $y$. Solve for $y$ using the equation that has one value of $y$. If $7 = y + 5$, then $y = 2$. If $y = 2$, then the first equation is $2 = 2x$ and $x = 1$. Therefore, the answer to the question *what value* is *4 less than x* is $1 - 4 = -3$.

Now that you've gotten an introduction to building algebraic expressions, take a look at the following quiz and build the appropriate equations.

## Algebraic Expressions Quiz

The answers can be found in Part VII.

1. The sum of $x$ and 4 is 3 less than the sum of $y$ and 8
2. 35 is what percent of $z$ ?
3. 8 plus the product of 3 and 4 is what percent of $y$ ?
4. 5 less than the difference between $x$ and 8 is 14
5. What number is $x$ percent of $y$ ?

## Using Substitution to Solve

As discussed in the section on solving simultaneous equations, it is almost always impossible to solve a single equation that has two variables. For instance, the equation $x + y = 9$ cannot be solved for either $x$ or $y$ because both variables could be any value so long as the sum is 9. In algebra, if a problem asks to solve for the value of either $x$ or $y$, there are several ways in which to complete the task. The most commonly known, and widely used, path is to identify a value for one of the variables and use that information to solve for the other variable.

Replacing a variable with a known value is the essence of substitution. In the example above, if you were told that $x = 3$, then it is just a matter of substitution to solve for the value of $y$. Use the known value of $x$ to replace the variable and solve: $3 + y = 9$, so $y = 6$.

### It's All About Relationships

Using substitution to solve for a variable when the known value is an integer or other real number is accomplished by replacing the variable with the known value. But what if the known value of a variable is not an integer or a real number? What if, instead, it is a relationship? For instance, in the equation above, would you be able to solve for $y$ if you knew the value of $x$ is one-half the value of $y$ ?

You can! The information provided is enough to solve for the value of $y$. Write out the equation for the value of $x$: $x = \frac{1}{2}y$ . Apply the rules of substitution for the value of $x$ in the equation to find that $\frac{1}{2}y + y = 9$. Multiply both sides by 2 to produce $y + 2y = 18$ and then combine to find that $3y = 18$ and $y = 6$.

### Integers Not Required

When using substitution to solve an algebraic equation or manipulate an expression, you replace a variable with a known quantity for that variable. However, as demonstrated above, the known value does not always need to be an integer or any real number. Knowing the relationship of the variables is enough to use substitution to solve. When the known value is a relationship, the process to apply substitution is no different than when the known value is an integer. Simply replace the variable with the known value and solve!

### Solving with Algebra

A key difference between when the known value is a relationship and when it is an integer is how the equation is solved once substitution is complete. It is often easier to solve the equation when the known value is an integer than when it is a relationship to the other variable. When the known value is a relationship, solving can require a more adept use of algebra. However, the use of algebra can be mitigated in certain scenarios by applying the principles of Plugging In. If you are unfamiliar with the Plugging In skill set, check out Chapter 14. It takes a deep dive into how to use this powerful technique to make algebra more like arithmetic, thus making the process of finding solutions to the nastiest of algebra problems far more accessible.

Test out your new skills below.

## Substitution Quiz

Solve each of the following equations using substitution. The answers can be found in Part VII.

1. What is the value of $x$ in the equation $x + 3y = 6$ if $y$ is one-third the value of $x$ ?

2. If $y = 2x$ and $x + y = 24$, then what is the value of $3x$ ?

3. If $4x - 2y = 16$ and $12x + 6y = 48$, then what is the value of $(x, y)$ ?

4. What is the value of $x$ if $-6x - 2y = 2$ and $10 = 10x + 10y$ ?

5. If the area of a rectangle is 18 and the length is twice the width, what is the width of the rectangle?

6. The rate of car $A$ is 3 times that of car $B$ and the combined rate is 88 miles per hour. If car $A$ traveled for 2 hours and car $B$ traveled for 1 hour, then what is the total combined distance the cars traveled?

### Hey! What's Up with Those Last Two Questions?

The first four questions in the drill above, as well as all the examples before the drill, all presented two obvious equations that are solvable using substitution. The final two questions of the drill deviated from that pattern. Instead of providing equations, the questions required that you construct common equations and use the information provided to substitute to find the answer.

Presenting a substitution problem in this format is well within the confines of the content that can be tested on the GMAT. Not all substitution problems are going to contain obvious equations. You may be asked to use substitution in all types of questions, such as geometry and rates.

## Three's a Crowd

In addition to asking about substitution in different contexts, the GMAT can also ask about more than two equations and variables. Consider how to solve for $x$ given the following information:

$$x + 2z = 24$$
$$y + x = 12$$
$$4z + 2y = 8$$

There are two equations that contain the variable $x$. One of the equations also contains the variable $z$ and the other also contains the variable $y$. In order to solve for $x$, one of these equations must be set equal to $x$. The second equation is the simplest, so rewrite that equation as $x = 12 - y$.

Now you need a value for $y$ that is expressed in terms of $x$. The only other equation that contains the variable $y$ is the third equation. Setting this equation equal to $y$ yields results in terms of $z$. Divide both sides of the equation by 2 and isolate the $y$ to rewrite this equation as $y = 4 - 2z$. Use this value of $y$ in the rewritten second equation, so $x = 12 - 4 - 2z = 8 - 2z$. The first equation contains values of $z$ and of $x$, so work there next. The rewritten second equation expresses $x$ in terms of $2z$. The first equation contains $2z$, so rewrite the first equation to provide a value of $2z$. This rewritten first equation is $2z = 24 - x$. Use this value for $2z$ in the rewritten second equation. This yields $x = 8 - 24 - x$. Now solve for $x$: $2x = 8 - 24 = -16$ and $x = -8$.

When working on substituting with more than two equations, work with the equations one at a time. Begin by isolating the information you want to solve for first and then through each equation systematically, looking for ways to solve for values present in other equations.

## Solving by Factoring

The building blocks for solving algebraic equations are addition, subtraction, multiplication, and division. These tools work great when solving for the variable in equations such as $x + 10 = 4$ or $3x = 6$. However, there are occasions when an equation is constructed in such a way that these basic operations alone are not enough to solve the problem. For example, how could you solve for $x$ in the following:

$$2x^2 + 3x = 0$$

Simply subtracting and dividing is not enough to find the value of $x$. Not even more advanced operations, such as taking the square root, produce a way to solve for the value of $x$. In this case, solving for $x$ requires factoring out an $x$ from the left-hand side of the equation to produce the following:

$$x(2x + 3) = 0$$

Solving for $x$ in the above equation produces two results. One result is $x = 0$. The other result is $2x + 3 = 0$ and $x = -\frac{3}{2}$.

In the above equation, there were two solutions for $x$. When a variable is factored out of an equation, that variable must be considered as equal to the answer independently from the rest of the equation. In the above example, the $x$ was factored out of the left-hand side of the equation, so the $x$ is considered independently.

When factoring out a variable or value, the variable or value must be present in each of the elements of the expression. For example, in the equation $2x^2 + 4x = 0$, a value of $2x$ can be factored out of the left-hand side of the equation to create $2x(x + 2) = 0$. There are now two separate expressions that need to be considered equal to 0: $2x$ and $x + 2$. Two separate values for $x$ can now be calculated with the basic operations.

The ability to factor out a value is due to the Distributive Law. This law and a different law, the Associative Law, are discussed in the Arithmetic chapter. We are not going to discuss either of these laws in detail here. If you'd like to know more about either law, and test your skills with a drill, check out the Arithmetic Operations section of the Arithmetic chapter.

Consider the following, more complicated, equation and use factoring to solve for $x$.

$$x^3 + 6x^2 + 8x = 0$$

The variable $x$ is present in each element of the expression $x^3 + 6x^2 + 8x$, so $x$ can be factored out of the expression on the left-hand side of the equation above to produce $x(x^2 + 6x + 8) = 0$. As before, there are now two expressions that need to be considered equal to 0: $x$ and $x^2 + 6x + 8$. Setting $x$ equal to 0 reveals one of the possible solutions for $x$, which is $x = 0$. The other expression is a quadratic.

In the section on solving quadratics (later in this chapter), we discuss the techniques and methodology for solving quadratics. If you are unfamiliar with those techniques, we recommend checking out that section. The quadratic $x^2 + 6x + 8 = 0$ factors to $(x + 4)(x + 2) = 0$. There are now two more expressions that need to be evaluated as equal to 0: $x + 4$ and $x + 2$. When $x + 4 = 0$, then $x = -4$. When $x + 2 = 0$, then $x = -2$. Therefore, there are three possible solutions for $x$ in the equation above. Those solutions are 0, –4, and –2. Below are all the steps taken to solve this problem written out in order, so you can better visualize them:

$$x^3 + 6x^2 + 8x = 0$$
$$x(x^2 + 6x + 8) = 0$$
$$x((x + 4)(x + 2)) = 0$$
$$x = 0$$
$$x + 4 = 0; x = -4$$
$$x + 2 = 0; x = -2$$
$$x = \{0, -4, -2\}$$

## Factoring Equations Not Equal to 0

Thus far, all the examples have been equal to 0. The following equation is not equal to 0. How would your approach to solving this problem differ from your approach for the problem above?

$$2x^3 + 16x^2 - 3x = -24$$

The first step to take is to set the equation equal to 0 by adding 24 to both sides to produce:

$$2x^3 + 16x^2 - 3x + 24 = 0$$

At first glance, there is nothing that can be factored out of this equation. However, you can group items together that do have common factors. Group $2x^3$ and $16x^2$ together and group $3x$ and 24 together. By doing this, you can see that $2x^3 + 16x$ has a $2x^2$ in common and $3x + 24$ has a –3 in common. So, this equation can be rewritten as:

$$2x^2(x + 8) - 3(x + 8) = 0$$

Because the two terms contain the same factors, you can then combine the factors together. This produces:

$$(2x^2 - 3)(x + 8) = 0$$

Now solve for each of these individually:

$$2x^2 - 3 = 0$$

$$2x^2 = 3$$

$$x^2 = \frac{3}{2}\ x = \pm\sqrt{\frac{3}{2}}$$

AND

$$x + 8 = 0$$

$$x = -8$$

The solutions for this equation are $x = \pm\sqrt{\frac{3}{2}}$ or −8.

## Solving Absolute Value Equations and Inequalities

Knowing how to solve absolute value equations and inequalities is a good skill to have for test day. Before considering how to solve these types of questions, let's revisit absolute values and establish a working definition.

In Chapter 9, GMAT Math: Basic Principles, a number line is used to illustrate positive and negative integers. In that same chapter, absolute value is defined as *the distance between a number and 0 on the number line.* Represented visually by the bolded line below, the absolute value of 3 (|3|) is 3 because that is how far that number is from 0 on the number line:

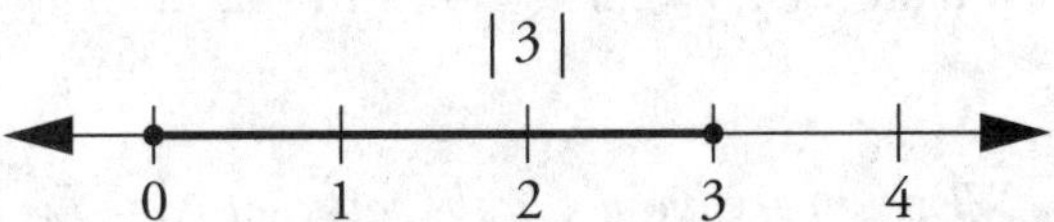


However, the definition of absolute value is not limited to positive numbers only! In fact, the definition states that the absolute value is the distance between *a number and 0.* Therefore, the absolute value of −3 is also 3 because that is how far that number is from 0 on the number line. This is represented again by the bolded bar in the visual below.

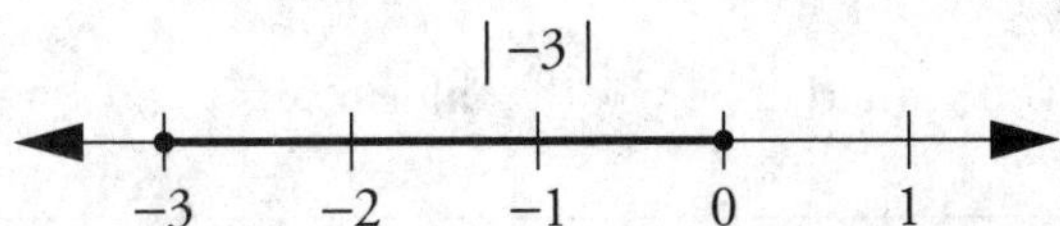

Considering the information above, finding the absolute value of real numbers is an uncomplicated process: simply take the positive value of the number. So, $|6| = 6$, $|-6| = 6$, $\left|-\frac{3}{2}\right| = \frac{3}{2}$, and so on. It stands to reason then that the absolute value of a variable follows the same pattern, right?

Let's look at the number line again, but this time map the distance between a positive variable $x$ and 0.

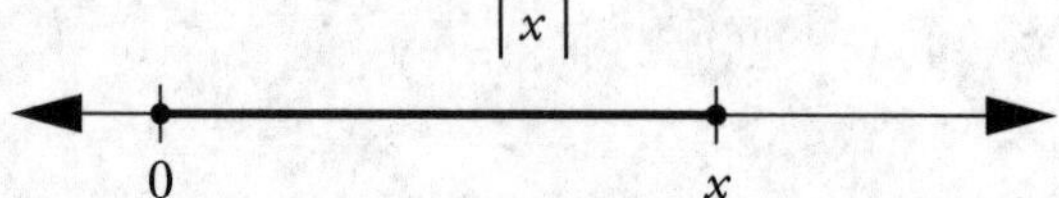


In the example above, the value inside the absolute value brackets is $x$. The absolute value distance between $x$ and 0 is the positive value of $x$, so it is true that $|x| = x$. But what happens if the value inside the absolute value brackets is $-x$?

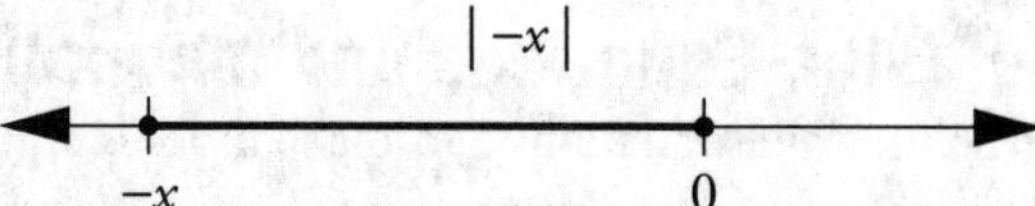


In this case, the absolute distance between $-x$ and 0 is still $x$. So, it is true that both $|x|$ and $|-x|$ equal $x$, just like both $|4|$ and $|-4|$ equal 4.

## Variable Absolute Values with Real Number Solutions

Now that the basics of absolute values have been covered, let's talk about the first of two specific rules for working with absolute values we'll establish in this chapter. Consider the following question:

*What is the value of x in the equation $|x| = 4$?*

While the gut reaction to this question is often that $x = 4$, that is not the case. As we established above, there are two values of $x$ that make the equation $|x| = 4$ true. If $x = 4$, then $|4| = 4$ is true. But, if $x = -4$, then $|-4| = 4$ is also true. Therefore, there are two possible values of $x$: 4 and $-4$. This is the first specific rule of working with absolute values.

> For the equation $|x| = y$, the value of $x = y$ and $x = -y$

## Solving Absolute Value Inequalities

The visual representation of absolute value inequalities is slightly more complicated than the visual representations of absolute values. Consider the inequality $|x| < 4$. The visual representation of all values of $x$ is:

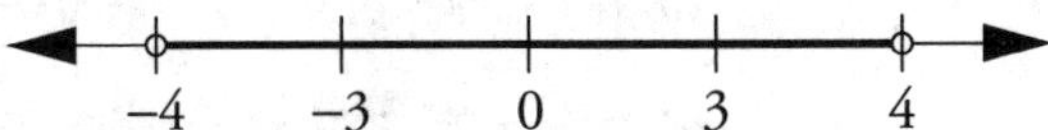


This is true because of the first of the two specific rules stated above. If $|x| < 4$, then $x < 4$, but $x > -4$. When working with absolute value inequalities, the direction of the inequality is always flipped when the value of the number that the variable is being compared to is switched from positive to negative.

The same is true for more complicated absolute value inequalities. What is the range of possible values of $x$ given the following inequality?

$$|x + 4| > 10$$

Because this is an absolute value that involves a variable, there are two solutions for the variable. In this case, both solutions are inequalities. The possible values of $x$ are represented by the inequalities:

$$x + 4 > 10$$
$$x + 4 < -10$$

Solving these inequalities yields both $x > 6$ and $x < -14$. The range of possible values of $x$ is represented by the following number line:

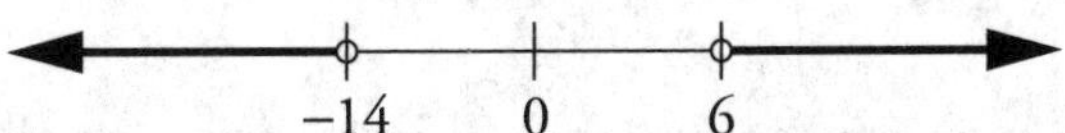


This is the second specific rule for working with absolute values.

> For the equation $|x| > y$, the range of possible values of $x$ is $x > y$ and $x < -y$

The GMAT may ask for values of $x$ in an absolute value inequality multiple-choice question. In this case, if there is only one possible correct answer, look for a value that falls into either range. In this case, the above rule can be read as follows: for the equation $|x| > y$, the possible value of $x$ is $x > y$ OR $x < -y$.

## Quadratic Equations

On the GMAT, quadratic equations always come in one of two forms: factored or expanded. Here's an example:

$$\underset{\textit{factored}}{(x+2)(x+5)} = \underset{\textit{expanded}}{x^2+7x+10}$$

The first thing to do when solving a problem that involves a quadratic equation is to see which form the equation is in. If the quadratic equation is in an unfactored form, factor it immediately. If the quadratic equation is in a factored form, unfactor it. The test-writers like to see whether you know how to do these things.

To unfactor a factored expression, just multiply it using FOIL (First, Outer, Inner, Last):

$$\begin{aligned}(x+2)(x+5) &= (x+2)(x+5) \quad \text{F, O, I, L}\\ &= (x \text{ times } x) + (x \text{ times } 5) + (2 \text{ times } x) + (2 \text{ times } 5)\\ &= x^2 + 5x + 2x + 10\\ &= x^2 + 7x + 10\end{aligned}$$

To factor an unfactored expression, put it into the following format and start by looking for the factors of the first and last terms.

$$\begin{aligned}&x^2+2x-15\\ &=(\quad)(\quad)\end{aligned}$$

For the first term of the unfactored expression to be $x^2$, the first term of each parentheses of the factored expression has to be $x$.

$$\begin{aligned}&x^2+2x-15\\ &=(x\quad)(x\quad)\end{aligned}$$

For the last term of the unfactored expression to be 15, the last term in each parentheses of the factored expression must be either 5 and 3 or 15 and 1. Since there is no way to get a middle term for the unfactored expression with a coefficient of 2 if the terms were 15 and 1, we are left with

$$\begin{aligned}&x^2+2x-15\\ &=(x\quad 5)(x\quad 3)\end{aligned}$$

To decide where to put the pluses and minuses in the factored expression, look to see how the inner and outer terms of the factored equation would combine to form the middle term. If we put a minus in front of the 5 and a plus in front of the 3, then the middle term would be $-2x$ (not what we wanted). Therefore, the final factored expression looks like this:

$$\begin{aligned}&x^2+2x-15\\ &=(x+5)(x-3)\end{aligned}$$

Quadratic equations are usually set equal to 0. Here's an example:

What are all the values of $x$ that satisfy the equation $x^2 + 4x + 3 = 0$ ?

- −3
- −1
- −3 and −1
- 3 and 4
- 4

### Here's How to Crack It

This problem contains an unfactored equation, so let's factor it.

$$x^2 + 4x + 3 = 0$$
$$(x \quad)(x \quad) = 0$$
$$(x \quad 3)(x \quad 1) = 0$$
$$(x + 3)(x + 1) = 0$$

In order for this equation to be correct, $x$ must be either −3 or −1. The correct answer is (C).

**Note:** This problem would also have been easy to solve by Plugging In the Answers (covered in Chapter 14). It asked a specific question, and there were five specific answer choices. One of them was correct. All you had to do was try the choices until you found the right one. Bear in mind, however, that in a quadratic equation there are usually two values that will make the equation work.

**The Equation Rule**
For most easy to medium level questions, you must have as many equations as you have variables for the data to be sufficient. For example, $x = y + 1$ cannot be solved without another *distinct* equation.

## Favorites of GMAT Test-Writers

There are three types of quadratic equations the GMAT test-writers find endlessly fascinating. These equations appear on the GMAT with great regularity in both the Problem Solving format and the Data Sufficiency format:

$$(x + y)^2 = x^2 + 2xy + y^2$$

$$(x + y)(x - y) = x^2 - y^2$$

$$(x - y)^2 = x^2 - 2xy + y^2$$

Memorize all three of these. As with all quadratic equations, if you see the equation in factored form, you should immediately unfactor it; if it's unfactored, factor it immediately.

Here's an example:

If $\frac{x^2 - 4}{x + 2} = 5$, then $x =$

- 3
- 5
- 6
- 7
- 9

**Here's How to Crack It**
It is unfactored, so let's factor it:

$$\frac{(x+2)(x-2)}{(x+2)} = 5$$

The $(x + 2)$s cancel out, leaving us with $(x - 2) = 5$. So $x = 7$, and the answer is (D).

## Algebraic Functions

The most common notation for function questions on the GMAT is $f(x)$—read as $f$ of $x$. There are other notations, such as $g(x)$ and $h(x)$, but $f(x)$ is the most common. Additionally, there are other ways that functions are tested. Those are covered in the functions section of the Applied Arithmetic chapter. For more information on those, check out that chapter section.

Many test-takers are tripped up by function questions because their unfamiliar structure can be intimidating. Before diving into the specifics about solving algebraic functions, let's discuss the components of the function. While knowing the different components of the function is not strictly necessary to solve function questions, knowing this information can be a powerful tool for building familiarity with the topic.

Functions on the GMAT are comprised of two components: domain and range. In the function $f(x) = x + 4$, the domain of the function is all the allowable values of $x$. The range of the function is all the corresponding values of $x + 4$. The true definitions of domain and range are more complicated than the above information suggests. However, for the purposes of the GMAT, these definitions are sufficient.

A GMAT problem that provides the function $f(x) = x + 4$ and asks to solve for the value of $x$ when $f(x) = 6$ is really asking to solve for the domain in the function $f(x)$ when the range of the function is equal to 6. The range of the function is $x + 4$, so this can be set equal to 6 to yield $x + 4 = 6$. This means that $x = 2$ and the domain of the function $f(x) = 6$ is 2.

The implications of the relationship between the domain and range mean that if a function is defined and then a value for the domain or range is given, the missing piece of information can be solved for. For instance, if a function is defined as $f(x)=\frac{x}{2}$ and you are asked to solve the function for $f(2)$, it could be stated that the domain is 2 and the range is $f(2)=\frac{2}{2}=1$.

Solving GMAT function questions is rarely more complicated than following directions. If a function is defined, and the domain or range of that function is provided, then solve for whatever piece of information is missing. If the question contains only variables in the definition of the function, then Plug In.

| The information given is... | So, solve by... |
|---|---|
| the domain | Plugging In the value of the variable in the function (the domain) for all instances of that variable in the range (what the function is equal to) |
| the range | Setting the known value of the range equal to the range defined in the function and solving for the variables (the domain) |
| only variables | Plugging In |

If you're not already familiar with Plugging In and Plugging In the Answers (PITA), check out Chapter 14 to learn all about these helpful strategies!

Let's try a couple of examples:

For which of the following functions does $f(x) = f(-x)$ for all values of $x$?

- ○ $f(x) = x^3 + 3$
- ○ $f(x) = -x$
- ○ $f(x) = 2x + 3$
- ○ $f(x) = (-x)^2 + 2$
- ○ $f(x) = 5x - 4$

### Here's How to Crack It

This question only provides variables in the definition of the function, so solve by Plugging In for the variables. Begin with (A). If $x = 2$, then $f(2) = 2^3 + 3 = 11$ and $f(-2) = -2^3 + 3 = 5$. In this case, $f(2) \neq f(-2)$. Eliminate (A). For (B), if $x = 2$, then $f(2) = -2$ and $f(-2) = -(-2) = 2$. The functions are not equal, so eliminate (B). For (C), $f(2) = 2(2) + 3 = 7$ and $f(-2) = 2(-2) + 3 = -1$. Eliminate (C). For (D), $f(2) = (-2)^2 + 2 = 4 + 2 = 6$ and $f(-2) = (-(-2))^2 + 2 = 2^2 + 2 = 4 + 2 = 6$. The functions are equal, so keep (D). For (E), $f(2) = 5(2) - 4 = 10 - 4 = 6$ and $f(-2) = 5(-2) - 4 = -10 - 4 = -14$. The functions are not equal, so eliminate (E). The correct answer is (D).

Let's try another.

---

If the function $h(x)$ is defined as $h(x) = 3 - \frac{1}{x}$, then what is the value of $g(h(x))$ ?

(1) $x = 1$

(2) $g(2) = 2$

### Here's How to Crack It

This is a data sufficiency question, so begin by determining what is known and what is needed to solve the problem. Start by determining what is known. The problem defines $h(x)$ as $h(x) = 3 - \frac{1}{x}$ but does not provide any further information. Now consider what is needed from the statements to solve the problem. The problem asks for the value of $g(h(x))$, so the problem needs to define a value for the function $g$ and a way to solve for the value of $h(x)$. Now consider each statement independently.

Don't forget! We discuss the strategies of Plugging In and Plugging In the Answers (PITA) in depth in the next chapter!

Statement (1) provides a value of $x$. This value can be used to Plug In to the function $h(x)$ to solve for $h(x)$ such that $h(1) = 3 - \frac{1}{1} = 3 - 1 = 2$, so $h(1) = 2$. Now the function $g(h(x))$ can be rewritten as $g(2)$. However, this statement does not provide any further information about the definition of the function $g$. Because there is no way to determine the value of the function, this statement is insufficient. Eliminate (A) and (D), and write down BCE.

Now consider Statement (2). This statement states that $g(2) = 2$. While this may seem sufficient to solve the problem, there is no way to verify that $h(x) = 2$ using the information in Statement (2). Because there is no way to determine a value for $h(x)$, there is no way to solve for the value of $g(h(x))$. Eliminate (B).

Now consider both statements together. Statement (1) establishes that $x = 1$. The equation in the question stem can be rewritten as $g(h(1))$. Because $x = 1$, it is true that $h(1) = 2$. The equation in the question stem can be rewritten again as $g(2)$. Statement (2) establishes that $g(2) = 2$. While neither statement provides a definition for the function $g$, the statements combined are enough to determine that $g(h(x)) = g(2) = 2$. The two statements combined are sufficient. The correct answer is (C).

---

## DRILL 7 (Algebra)

The answers to these questions can be found in Part VII.

1. 5 years ago, Joe was twice as old as Jessica. If in 4 years Joe will be one and a half times as old as Jessica, then how old is Joe now?

 - 23
 - 25
 - 27
 - 29
 - 31

2. If $\frac{x^2 + 2x - 9}{3} \leq x + 1$, then $x$ could be represented by which of the following?

 - $-4 \leq x \leq -3$
 - $-4 \leq x \leq 3$
 - $-3 \leq x \leq 3$
 - $-3 \leq x \leq 4$
 - $3 \leq x \leq 4$

3. If $x > 0$ and $x$ percent of $a$ is $b$, then, in terms of $x$, $a$ is how many times $b$ ?

 - $100x$
 - $10x$
 - $x$
 - $\frac{10}{x}$
 - $\frac{100}{x}$

4. John has $s$ pairs of shoes, which is $\frac{1}{3}$ as many as Sheila and twice as many as James. In terms of $s$, how many pairs of shoes do the three of them have combined?

 - $\frac{7}{3}s$
 - $\frac{10}{3}s$
 - $\frac{7}{2}s$
 - $4s$
 - $\frac{9}{2}s$

## Challenge Question #4

A dealer once sold identical cars at a price of $x$ dollars each (including sales tax). However, the pretax price was recently increased by \$2,500 such that 18 cars purchased at the old price would cost the same as purchasing three fewer cars at the new price. If the sales tax rate is 8%, what is the new price of the dealer's cars, including sales tax, in dollars?

- \$10,800
- \$12,500
- \$13,500
- \$16,200
- \$16,750

# Summary

- The difficulty of many GMAT questions is reliant on some of the basics of algebra, such as like terms, ensuring you perform operations on both sides of an equation, building algebraic equations, order of operations, and substitution.
- If you see a problem with a quadratic equation in factored form, the easiest way to get the answer is to expand the equation immediately. If the equation is expanded, factor it immediately.
- Memorize the factored and expanded forms of the three most common quadratics on the GMAT:

$$(x + y)^2 = x^2 + 2xy + y^2$$
$$(x + y)(x - y) = x^2 - y^2$$
$$(x - y)^2 = x^2 - 2xy + y^2$$

- On problems containing inequalities, remember that when you multiply or divide both sides of an inequality by a negative number, the sign flips.
- In solving simultaneous equations, add or subtract one equation to or from another so that one of the two variables disappears.
- Problems that involve functions such as $f(x)$ typically require you to follow the directions in the problem or Plug In values for the variable in the function.

# Chapter 14
# Plugging In

In this chapter, you'll learn two fantastic techniques that will allow you to avoid writing equations on most GMAT questions: Plugging In and Plugging In the Answers (PITA).

In this chapter, we'll show you some powerful techniques that will enable you to solve certain types of algebra problems without using traditional algebra. If you are uncomfortable with algebra, you'll find a lot of these techniques valuable as they can make some of the toughest algebra questions far easier to solve. Even if you are an algebra whiz, mastery of these techniques can be a big timesaver for certain questions and can be a failsafe if you run into a question you're not quite sure how to solve.

## NOT EXACTLY ALGEBRA: BASIC PRINCIPLES

Algebra is used to come up with general solutions to problems. For example, you might know (for whatever reason) that the price of a new pair of shoes in relation to the cost of a pair of jeans is $3j + 20$, where $j$ is the cost of the jeans. Based on this formula, if you know that the jeans cost \$50, then you know that the shoes cost \$170. But, you also know the cost of the shoes if the jeans cost \$75.

In most algebra problems, you need to find an algebraic expression that matches the description of the relationship given in the problem. For the situation above, the problem might read as follows:

> At a certain store, the price of a pair of shoes is twenty dollars more than three times the price of a pair of jeans. If the price of a pair of jeans is $j$ dollars at this store, then what is the price, in dollars, of a pair of shoes, in terms of $j$ ?
>
> ⬭ $20 - 3j$
> ⬭ $3j + 20$
> ⬭ $3j - 20$
> ⬭ $3j + 60$
> ⬭ $20j + 3$

You might consider this question a fairly easy algebra question. To solve it, you might just start translating the phrase "the cost of a pair of shoes is twenty dollars more than three times the cost of a pair of jeans." But, you need to be careful while doing that. If you get confused about whether you should add 20 or subtract 20, you'll pick the wrong answer. The test-writers have put a lot of thought into the ways that the key statement in the question can be misinterpreted.

Plugging In is a great way to avoid making mistakes when you are manipulating variables.

If it's so easy to make a mistake while doing the algebra, is there a more foolproof way to do this question? Of course! Instead of trying to come up with a general solution—the algebraic approach—let's pick a number and come up with a specific solution. Then, we'll just choose the answer that matches.

We call this approach **Plugging In**. It is perhaps our most powerful math technique and will allow you to solve complicated problems more quickly than you might have ever thought possible. Plugging In is easy. There are three steps involved.

**Plugging In**

1. Pick numbers for the variables in the problem.
2. Using your numbers, find an answer to the problem. At The Princeton Review, we call this the target answer.
3. Plug your numbers into the answer choices to see which choice equals the answer you found in step 2.

Let's look at the same problem again:

At a certain store, the price of a pair of shoes is twenty dollars more than three times the price of a pair of jeans. If the price of a pair of jeans is $j$ dollars at this store, then what is the price, in dollars, of a pair of shoes, in terms of $j$?

- ○ $20 - 3j$
- ○ $3j + 20$
- ○ $3j - 20$
- ○ $3j + 60$
- ○ $20j + 3$

### Here's How to Crack It

Let's pick a number for *j*. Let's say that the jeans cost $10. (We don't need to worry about being realistic!) Write down "$j = 10$." We've now transformed the problem from an algebra problem into an arithmetic problem.

Here's what the problem now asks:

At a certain store, the price of a pair of shoes is twenty dollars more than three times the price of a pair of jeans. If the price of a pair of jeans is **10** dollars at this store, then what is the price, in dollars, of a pair of shoes, ~~in terms of *j*~~?

You'll notice that we've substituted 10 for the variable *j* in the original problem. You'll also notice that we've crossed out the phrase "in terms of *j*." Once we put a number into the problem, the phrase "in terms of" has no meaning so we can ignore it.

Using $10 for the price of the jeans, the price of the pair of shoes is $50. All we did was translate the phrase "the price of a pair of shoes is twenty dollars more than three times the price of a pair of jeans." Three times the price of the pair of jeans is 3 × $10 = $30. Twenty dollars more is just $30 + $20 = $50. The numerical answer to our problem is $50. Write that number down on your noteboard and circle it to indicate that it is your target answer.

Now you just need to find the answer that matches \$50 when you substitute 10 for $j$. You should write down A, B, C, D, E on your noteboard and work out each answer choice. Here's what that looks like:

A) $20 - 3j = 20 - 3(10) = -10$
B) $3j + 20 = 3(10) + 20 = 50$
C) $3j - 20 = 3(10) - 20 = 10$
D) $3j + 60 = 3(10) + 60 = 90$
E) $20j + 3 = 20(10) + 3 = 203$

Choice (B) is the only answer that matches the target answer, so it is the answer to this problem. You'll note that we checked all five answer choices. We did that to be sure we were picking the correct answer.

---

## Scratch Work

The students in our GMAT course learn to automatically do scratch work. When Plugging In, always write down the numbers you are plugging in for each variable. Be sure to clearly label the number for each variable by writing down something like $j = 10$. Next, do the work for each step in the problem. When you find the numerical answer to the problem, write that down and circle it. Then, try each of the answer choices, crossing them off as you eliminate them. Here's what your scratch work should have looked like for the last problem:

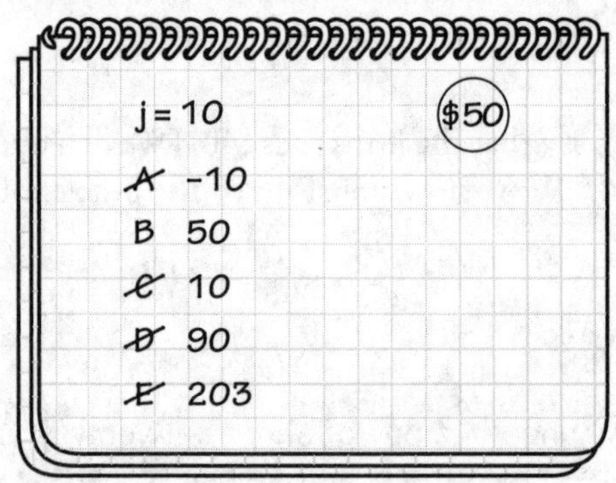

## Why Plug In? Because It Makes Difficult Problems Easy!

You might be thinking, "Wait a minute! It was just as easy to solve this problem algebraically. Why should I Plug In?" To see why, let's take a look at another version of the problem.

**Another Reason to Plug In**

Plugging numbers into a problem is a much more natural way to think for most folks than algebra. Has any high school coach ever told their team, "Run 6*x* sprints, where *x* equals two full lengths of the field?" The players might comply, but you can be sure they'd have to think about the instructions first. Complicate the request with *y*, the number of players on the team, and *z*, the number of meters of the field, and you've got a real headache. Essentially, Plugging In is a matter of putting numbers back into a form that you are used to working with.

---

At a certain store, the price of a pair of shoes is twenty dollars more than three times the price of a pair of jeans and the price of a sweater is fifty percent more than the price of a pair of shoes. If the price of a pair of jeans is $j$ dollars at this store, then what is the price, in dollars, of a pair of shoes, a sweater, and a pair of jeans, in terms of $j$ ?

- ⬭ $1.5j + 10$
- ⬭ $3j + 20$
- ⬭ $4.5j + 30$
- ⬭ $5.5j + 30$
- ⬭ $8.5j + 50$

### Here's How to Crack It

This version of the problem is wordier and that helps to make it more confusing. Let's try Plugging In. As before, we'll start by making $j = 10$. So, the jeans cost \$10. Next, we know the relationship between the price of the jeans and the cost of the shoes. The price of the shoes is "twenty dollars more than three times the price of the jeans." So, the price of the shoes is \$50. Finally, the sweater costs "fifty percent more than the price of the shoes." So, the sweater is \$50 + \$25, or \$75. So, the cost of all three items is \$10 + \$50 + \$75 = \$135. Be sure to circle \$135.

Now, it's time to find the answer that equals 135 when $j = 10$. Choice (A) is 25, so cross it off. Choice (B) is 50, so it's wrong. Choice (C) is 75, so it's also wrong. Choice (D) is 85, so it can be eliminated. Finally, (E) is 135. Choice (E) matches the target and is the correct answer.

By the way, (D) is what you get if you misread how to calculate the cost of the sweater. If you were doing the algebra, the cost of the shoes is $3j + 20$. It would be pretty easy to think that the price of the sweater is then $1.5j + 10$, which is fifty percent of the cost of the shoes rather than fifty percent *more*. Of course, you could make this mistake while working with the numbers too. But, what's easier—to see that \$25 is not more than \$50 or to see that $1.5j + 10$ is not more than $3j + 20$?

---

To recap, there are two reasons why you'd want to Plug In even if you are pretty good at algebra.

1. Plugging In can make even the hardest algebra problems much easier to solve.
2. The test-writers have thought about all the possible ways you might mess up the algebra while working the problem. If you make one of those mistakes, your answer will be among the answer choices and you'll most likely wind up picking the wrong answer.

**What to Plug In**

- Numbers that make the math easy!
- Small simple numbers such as 2, 5, or 10
- Percents? Try 100
- Hours or Minutes? 30 or 120

**What NOT to Plug In**

- Avoid using 0 or 1
- Numbers in the problem or in the answer choices

## What Number Should I Plug In?

While you can plug in any number, you'll find that certain numbers work better than others. Ideally, you want a number that makes it easy to perform the calculations for the problem. For most problems, you can just use small, simple numbers such as 2, 5, or 10. However, you also want numbers that make sense within the context of the problem. For example, for a problem that uses percents, plugging in 100 would be a good idea. Different numbers work for different types of problems. As you practice, you'll get better at picking good numbers—especially if you keep asking yourself "What number will make this problem easy?" You also shouldn't be afraid to change your number if the calculations start to get messy.

Q: If 80% of a certain number $x$ is 50% of $y$ and $y$ is 20% of $z$, then what is $x$, in terms of $z$?

A. $5z$
B. $3z$
C. $z/4$
D. $z/5$
E. $z/8$

*Turn to page 206 for the answer.*

Sometimes the best way to select a number is to use a little common sense. Here's an example:

If Jim drives $k$ miles in 50 minutes, how many minutes will it take him to drive 10 miles, at the same rate?

- $\frac{500}{k}$
- $\frac{k}{500}$
- $60k$
- $10k$
- $\frac{50}{k}$

### Here's How to Crack It

GMAC would like you to use the formula *distance* = *rate* × *time*. There are variables in the answer choices, so we can Plug In. Since it's a good bet that at least a few of the wrong answers are based on using the formula, let's Plug In.

Any number you choose to plug in for *k* will eventually give you the answer to this problem, but there are some numbers that will make your task even easier.

We need to find a good number for *k*. Notice that we know that Jim is going to drive 10 miles. Suppose we just made *k* equal to half of 10? The question now reads as follows:

If Jim drives 5 miles in 50 minutes, how many minutes will it take him to drive 10 miles, at the same rate?

Now the problem is pretty easy. Since Jim is going to drive twice the distance, it's going to take him twice the time. So, the target is 100 minutes. Now, all we need to do is find the answer that matches the target when $k = 5$. Start with (A). Divide 500 by 5 to get 100. Bingo! To double check, plug 5 into the other answer choices as well. None of them match the target.

The answer to this question is (A).

## More Times to Plug In

So far, we've been looking at questions that have explicit variables in both the problem and the answer choices. When you see variables in the problem or answer choices, that's one of the signs to Plug In.

However, sometimes GMAC expects you to use algebra to answer a question that doesn't have explicit variables. You can still Plug In on these problems. In fact, *you should consider Plugging In whenever you feel the urge to do algebra.* The urge to do algebra is the ultimate sign that the problem can be cracked using some form of Plugging In.

Let's take a look at some other ways to Plug In.

## Plugging In with Hidden Variables

Some problems have a hidden variable. For these problems, all the calculations are usually based off one item but you don't know the value of that item. There's a simple solution—just plug in a value for the item!

Let's look at an example:

A: The answer is (E). If you plugged in 100 for $x$, then you found $y$ must equal 160. The question tells us 160 (our $y$) equals 20% of $z$. That means $z$ equals 800. Now it should be simple to see that $x$ equals $z$ divided by 8.

A merchant reduces the original price of a coat by 20 percent for a spring sale. Finding that the coat did not sell, the merchant reduces the spring price by a further 15 percent at the start of the summer. The coat's summer price is what percent of its original price?

- 35%
- 64%
- 65%
- 68%
- 80%

### Here's How to Crack It

You may have noticed that this problem never gave us the coat's original price. You may have felt the urge to do algebra starting to kick in as you read the problem. For example, you might have started to say to yourself "Well, if the price of the coat is $x$, then the spring price is...." That's your sign that you can do this problem as a Plug In! All you need to do is pick a price for the coat.

Let's make the original price of the coat $100. *When you are solving a percent problem, 100 is a great number to plug in.* The merchant discounts the price of the coat by 20% for the spring sale. Twenty percent of $100 is $20, so the spring price is $80. For the summer, the spring price of the coat is discounted by another 15%. Fifteen percent of $80 is $12, making the summer price $68.

The question asks for the summer price as a percent of the original price. In other words, $68 is what percent of $100? 68%. The answer is (D).

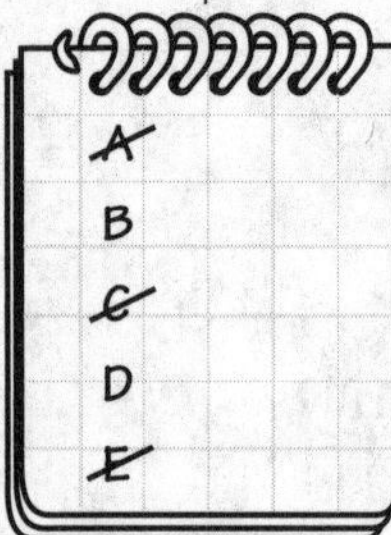


**Easy Eliminations**

If you were running out of time, you'd need to make a guess. But you could eliminate some obviously wrong answers first. When you read the problem fast, you might be tempted to think that the overall reduction is 20% + 15% = 35%, but that's too easy. So, cross off (A). Choice (C) is just 100 – 35 = 65. Also, too easy. Finally, (E) is what you get after the first reduction. The answer is probably (B) or (D).

Another way to tell that you can probably solve a question as a Hidden Plug In is to look at the answer choices. The answer choices for Hidden Plug In questions are typically percents, fractions, or sometimes ratios. How can you tell that this problem is a Hidden Plug In?

At College P, one–fourth of the students are seniors and one–fifth of the seniors major in business. If two–fifths of all students at the college major in business, the business majors who are not seniors are what fraction of all business majors?

- $\frac{1}{20}$
- $\frac{1}{8}$
- $\frac{7}{20}$
- $\frac{7}{15}$
- $\frac{7}{8}$

### Here's How to Crack It

You may have noticed that while this problem provides lots of fractions to work with, it never reveals how many students attend College P. Of course, knowing the total enrollment at the college would make solving the problem fairly straightforward. So, before you start setting up equations based on *x* students at College P, let's plug in a number for the total students.

An easy way to come up with a good number when the problem has fractions is to simply multiply the denominators of the fractions together. In this case, that's $4 \times 5 \times 5 = 100$. Don't worry, by the way, that some of the denominators are not distinct. Multiplying by the extra 5 may help us to avoid getting a result that leads to some fractional part of a student!

So, if there are 100 students at the college, there are 25 seniors and 75 students who are not seniors. Next, you know that one-fifth of the seniors major in business, so that's 5 seniors who are business majors. Since two-fifths of all students are business majors, the college has 40 business majors. Of those 40 business majors, $40 - 5 = 35$ of the business majors are not seniors. So, the fraction of business majors who are not seniors is $\frac{35}{40} = \frac{7}{8}$. The correct answer is (E).

#### It Works for Ratios, Too!

You can also Plug In when the answer choices are expressed as ratios. Here's how a similar question would be written as a ratio problem.

At College P, one-fourth of the students are seniors and one-fifth of the seniors major in business. If two-fifths of all students at the college major in business, then what is the ratio of senior business majors to non-senior business majors?

- 1 : 3
- 1 : 5
- 1 : 7
- 1 : 8
- 7 : 8

As before, just plug in 100 for the number of students. There are 5 seniors who are business majors and 35 business majors who are not seniors. The ratio is 5:35, which reduces to 1:7. The answer is (C).

## Plugging In the Answers (PITA)

Some algebra questions ask for a numerical answer. GMAC expects you to write an equation, solve it, and then pick the answer. However, the person who wrote the problem had to do all of that hard work. So, rather than duplicate all of the work the question writer did, why not just test out the answers to see which one works?

Proven Technique: PITA

We call this method of solving the problem **Plugging In the Answers** (or PITA for short). You'll find that solving problems this way can save you a lot of time and help you to avoid common algebra mistakes. There are three steps involved when you Plug In the Answers.

**Plugging In the Answers**

1. Write down the answers, determine what they represent, and label them.
2. Start with (C) and work the steps of the problem.
3. Look for some sort of condition that must be met to make the answer correct.

Let's take a look at an example.

At a certain restaurant, the price of a sandwich is $4.00 more than the price of a cup of coffee. If the price of a sandwich and a cup of coffee is $7.35, including a sales tax of 5%, what is the price of a cup of coffee, EXCLUDING the sales tax?

- $1.50
- $3.00
- $4.00
- $5.50
- $7.00

**Scratch Work**

When you Plug In the Answers, make your scratch work looks like an Excel spreadsheet. Label your columns and put your results for each column next to the answer choice you are checking. Doing so will help you to cut down on mistakes and check subsequent answer choices more quickly.

### Here's How to Crack It

If there were no answer choices, you'd be forced to write an equation and solve it. However, because you know the answer must be one of the five provided choices, it will be easier and faster to simply try the answers.

Start by writing down the answers and labeling them as "coffee." Now, start with (C). If the cup of coffee costs $4.00, what can you figure out? The problem states that the sandwich costs $4.00 more than the cup of coffee, so the sandwich is $8.00. Make a column for "sandwich" and write down $8.00 next to (C). You now know that the cost for the sandwich and the cup of coffee is $12.00. Choice (C) is too big because the cost for the sandwich and the cup of coffee is supposed to be only $7.35 including the sales tax. Go ahead and cross off (C).

So far, your work should look like this:

| Coffee | Sandwich | Total |
|---|---|---|
| A) $1.50 | | |
| B) $3.00 | | |
| ~~C) $4.00~~ | $8.00 | $12.00 |
| D) $5.50 | | |
| E) $7.00 | | |

Now it's time to decide if you need a bigger number or a smaller number. It's a pretty easy choice for this problem. Since $4.00 turned out to be too big, it makes sense to try a smaller number. Choices (D) and (E) are out of the question, so cross them off. There's no need to debate over (A) or (B). One of them must be correct, so just try (B). If it works, you're done. If it doesn't, choose (A) and you're still done.

If the cup of coffee costs $3.00, as in (B), then the sandwich is $7.00. That would make the total cost for both items $10.00. That's still too big! The answer must be (A).

Here's what the work should look like at this point:

| Coffee | Sandwich | Total |
|---|---|---|
| A) $1.50 | | |
| ~~B) $3.00~~ | $7.00 | $10.00 |
| ~~C) $4.00~~ | $8.00 | $12.00 |
| ~~D) $5.50~~ | | |
| ~~E) $7.00~~ | | |

There's really no need to test (A). However, if the coffee costs $1.50, then the sandwich costs $5.50. Together the two items cost $7.00. The tax on the two items is 5% of $7.00 or $0.35. So, the total with tax is $7.35, which meets the condition stated in the problem. The answer is (A).

## Plugging In the Answers: Advanced Principles

When you solve a problem using Plugging In the Answers (PITA), you'll usually know if you need a bigger or smaller number if (C) doesn't work. However, there are times when you won't be sure. Rather than wasting time trying to decide if you need a bigger or smaller number, just pick an answer choice and try it. You'll actually waste less time testing an extra answer choice or two than you will trying to decide which type of number to try next.

Jim is now twice as old as Fred, who is two years older than Sam. Four years ago, Jim was four times as old as Sam. How old is Jim now?

- 8
- 12
- 16
- 20
- 24

### Here's How to Crack It

This question has numbers in the answers and you probably started to think "Well, if Jim is *x* years old, then Fred is...." The urge to do algebra means that it's time to Plug In the Answers. Start with (C).

**When to Plug In the Answers**

- There are numbers in the answer choices.
- The question asks for a specific amount.
- You have the urge to set up and solve an equation.

The answers represent possible ages for Jim. If Jim is 16 years old, then Fred is 8 because Jim is twice as old as Fred. Next, you know that Fred is two years older than Sam, so Sam is 6. Now, you need to compare Jim's age and Sam's age four years ago. Four years ago, Jim was 12 and Sam was 2. Remember that there's always a condition in the problem that must be met by the correct answer.

In this case, Jim's age four years ago must be four times that of Sam. Is 12 four times 2? No. So, (C) can be eliminated.

Here's what your work should look like up to this point.

| | **Now** | | **4 years ago** | |
|---|---|---|---|---|
| **Jim** | **Fred** | **Sam** | **Jim** | **Sam** |
| A) 8 | | | | |
| B) 12 | | | | |
| ~~C) 16~~ | 8 | 6 | 12 | 2 |
| D) 20 | | | | |
| E) 24 | | | | |

Now, it's time to choose a bigger or smaller number. But, it isn't really clear which direction to go, is it? So, rather than waste a lot of time trying to figure that out, just pick an answer and try it. If Jim is 20 years old now, as in (D), then Fred is 10 and Sam is 8. Four years ago, Jim was 16 and Sam was 4.

Here's what your work should look like.

| | Now | | | 4 years ago | |
|---|---|---|---|---|---|
| Jim | Fred | Sam | | Jim | Sam |
| A) 8 | | | | | |
| B) 12 | | | | | |
| ~~C) 16~~ | 8 | 6 | | 12 | 2 |
| D) 20 | 10 | 8 | | 16 | 4 |
| E) 24 | | | | | |

Since 4 × 4 = 16, the condition in the problem is met. Choice (D) is the correct answer.

---

Most of the time, starting at (C) when doing PITA makes the most sense. By starting at (C), you can usually cut down on the number of answer choices that you need to test. However, there can be times when it makes sense to start with a different answer choice.

---

If $x$ is a positive integer such that $x^2 + 5x - 14 = 0$, what is the value of $x$ ?

- ○ –7
- ○ –5
- ○ 0
- ○ 2
- ○ 5

### Here's How to Crack It

Notice that the question states that $x$ is a positive integer. Don't waste time with (A), (B), or (C)—cross them off immediately. For this problem, it makes sense to start with (D). Plug 2 into the equation for $x$ to get $(2)^2 + 5(2) - 14 = 0$. Since the equation is true when $x = 2$, (D) is the correct answer.

---

## Challenge Question #5

A certain game requires players to collect both blue tokens, which are worth $b$ points each, and red tokens, which are worth $r$ points each. If $p$ percent of Player A's points are from blue tokens and $q$ percent of Player A's tokens are red, which of the following is an expression for the value of $p$, in terms of $b$, $r$, and $q$ ?

- $\dfrac{100bq}{bq + 100r - qr}$
- $\dfrac{10{,}000b - 100bq}{100b - bq + qr}$
- $\dfrac{bq + 100r - qr}{100bq}$
- $\dfrac{100b - bq}{100r - 100bq - qr}$
- $\dfrac{100b - bq + qr}{10{,}000b - 100bq}$

### Plugging In the Answers Advanced Tips

1. If you're not sure whether you need a bigger or smaller number, don't waste time. Just pick another answer choice and try it.
2. You may be able to eliminate some numbers that are too big or too small before you start Plugging In. If you can, just start with the middle number that you have left.
3. If you have both easy to work with numbers and messy numbers in the answer choices, try the easy to work with numbers first.

## Must Be

Some questions will use the words "must be." For example, the question may ask which of the expressions in the answers *must be* even or *must be* divisible by 3. These questions can be solved easily by Plugging In. However, you'll probably need to Plug In at least twice to find the answer.

Here's all you need to do.

**Must Be Plugging In**

1. Pick numbers for the variables in the problem. Be sure to satisfy any restrictions for the variables.
2. Eliminate any answer choices that don't match what you are looking for.
3. Plug in the most different kind of number you are allowed to try. For example, if you tried an even number, try an odd number.
4. Repeat until only one answer remains.

---

If $n$ is a positive integer, which of the following must be even?

- $(n - 1)(n + 1)$
- $(n - 2)(n + 1)$
- $(n - 2)(n + 4)$
- $(n - 3)(n + 1)$
- $(n - 3)(n + 5)$

### Here's How to Crack It

Start by picking a value for $n$. How about $n = 2$? Now, evaluate each answer choice. For (A), the expression equals 3, so cross it off. For (B), the expression equals 0. Remember that 0 is an even number, so keep this answer choice. But you aren't done yet. Just because you've found one case where this answer choice is even doesn't mean it will always be even. Keep checking the answers. Choice (C) is also equal to 0, so keep it as well. Choice (D) equals –3. Don't be fooled by the negative sign. Negative integers can also be even or odd. Since –3 is odd, cross this answer off. Choice (E) equals –7 and can also be eliminated.

**Try the ZONEF Numbers**

For some "must be" questions, the different number you need is one of the ZONEF numbers. These are the numbers that most people forget to think about.

Zero
One
Negatives
Extremes (like 100)
Fractions

Next, try a new number. Since this problem is about even and odd numbers, it makes sense to try an odd number next. How about $n = 3$? You need to check only the two answers that remain. Choice (B) equals 4, which is still even. However, (C) now equals 7, so it can be eliminated. The correct answer is (B).

Here's what your work should look like once you have worked through the entire problem.

| | $n = 2$ | $n = 3$ |
|---|---|---|
| ~~A) $(n - 1)(n + 1)$~~ | 3 | |
| B) $(n - 2)(n + 1)$ | 0 | 4 |
| ~~C) $(n - 2)(n + 4)$~~ | 0 | 7 |
| ~~D) $(n - 3)(n + 1)$~~ | –3 | |
| ~~E) $(n - 3)(n + 5)$~~ | –7 | |

---

## Which Plugging In Method Should I Use?

The problems that can be solved with the different Plugging In methods have a cadence that is unique to them. Being able to quickly identify the presence of this cadence will enable you to more easily determine which Plugging In method can be employed to solve the problem.

Below is a table that lays out these cues and the Plugging In method that is associated with them. While familiarity with this table can help you learn to identify what Plugging In method may be useful for a given problem, the only way to become more efficient at utilizing these methods is to do practice problems. Immediately following this table is a short quiz on identifying Plugging In problems and which Plugging In method to choose. At the end of the Plugging In section is a 10-question drill on Plugging In problems. Both the short quiz and the drill are excellent primers for using Plugging In, but they may not be enough. Make sure to work through the practice tests and employ the Plugging In strategies where possible.

| When the problem contains... | Then, you should consider... |
| --- | --- |
| variables in the question stem and answer choices | Plugging In |
| a missing value that the entire problem is based on or answer choices that are percents, fractions, or ratios | Plugging In for the hidden value |
| numbers in the answer choices, a question that asks for a specific amount, answer choices that represent that amount, and information that makes you want to write an equation | Plugging In the Answers |
| the phrase *must be* | Plugging In more than once using ZONEF numbers |

Using the table above and the knowledge provided in the section thus far, identify which of the following questions can be solved with Plugging In methods and which Plugging In method could be used. Finding the correct solution is not the point of this drill, so no answer choices are provided. There is a 10-question Plugging In drill with full questions and answer choices later in this section.

## Which Plugging In Method Should I Use? Quiz

| Question | Should You Plug In? | Plugging In Method |
|---|---|---|
| 1. If Mark's current age is three times greater than Jenny's age was 5 years ago, then, in terms of Jenny's current age, what is Mark's current age? | | |
| 2. What number is 625% of 3,420? | | |
| 3. If $x^2 > 17$ and $x^3 > -512$, then which of the following must be true of $x$ ? | | |
| 4. The original price of a shirt was increased by 25% and then decreased by 15% to a final price of $105. What was the original price of the shirt? | | |
| 5. A certain square has an area of 24 and a height that is 1.5 times its width. What is the perimeter of the square? | | |

## DRILL 8 (Plugging In)

Work your way through the following 10-question drill and use a Plugging In method for each of the questions. Remember, for many Plugging In questions, there are multiple ways to solve the problem and the problem can always be solved without Plugging In. The point of this drill is not to get as many questions correct as you can. The point of this drill is to practice the Plugging In techniques. So, even if you think you know a faster way to solve the problem, try to solve it using Plugging In. The answers can be found in Part VII.

1. List $L$ : 1, $\sqrt{2}$, $x$, $x^2$

   In list $L$, if $x > 0$ and the range of numbers is 4 then what is the value of $x$ ?

   - 5
   - 4
   - 2
   - $\sqrt{5}$
   - $\sqrt{4}$

2. If $r \neq s$ and $t > 0$, which of the following must be true?

- $(r - s)t > 0$
- $(r - s)t \neq 0$
- $rt + st > 0$
- $(r^2 - s^2)t > 0$
- $(r - s)t > \dfrac{r - s}{t}$

3. Is $xy > 0$ ?

(1) $|x| + 8|y| = 0$

(2) $8|x| + |y| = 0$

- Statement (1) ALONE is sufficient, but statement (2) alone is not sufficient.
- Statement (2) ALONE is sufficient, but statement (1) alone is not sufficient.
- BOTH statements TOGETHER are sufficient, but NEITHER statement ALONE is sufficient.
- EACH statement ALONE is sufficient.
- Statements (1) and (2) TOGETHER are not sufficient.

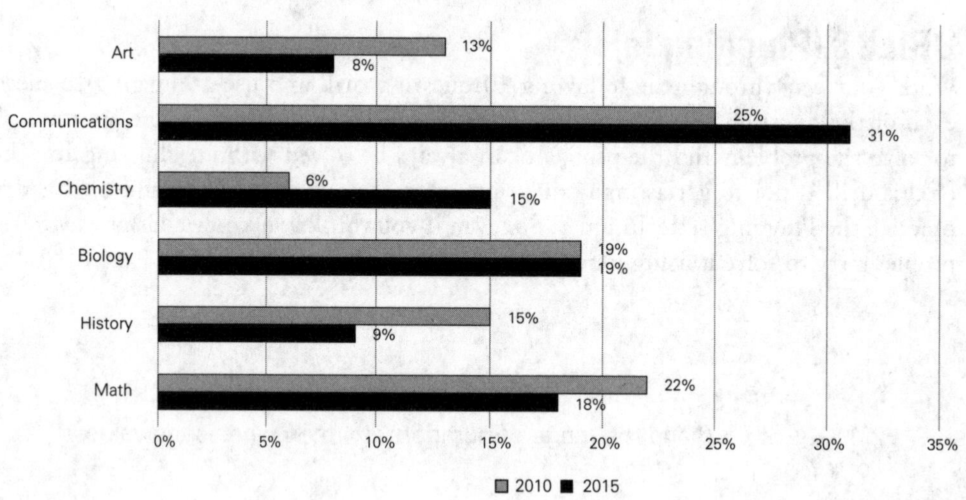


4. In 2015, if $\frac{2}{6}$ of the majors in math focused on statistics, approximately what percent of all majors focused on statistics?

- 3%
- 6%
- 9%
- 12%
- 15%

5. If $x$ and $y$ are integers such that $x^2 + y^2 < 46$ and $0 < x \leq 5$, then which of the following represents all possible values of $y$ ?

- $-6 \leq y \leq 6$
- $-6 \leq y \leq 5$
- $-5 \leq y \leq 5$
- $5 \leq y \leq 4$
- $-4 < y \leq 4$

6. Are the integers $x$, $y$, and $z$ consecutive?

(1) The average (arithmetic mean) of $x$, $y$, and $z$ is $y$.

(2) $y - x = z - y$

- Statement (1) ALONE is sufficient, but statement (2) alone is not sufficient.
- Statement (2) ALONE is sufficient, but statement (1) alone is not sufficient.
- BOTH statements TOGETHER are sufficient, but NEITHER statement ALONE is sufficient.
- EACH statement ALONE is sufficient.
- Statements (1) and (2) TOGETHER are not sufficient.

7. If the probability of selecting, without replacement, 2 red marbles from a bag containing only red and blue marbles is $\frac{3}{55}$ and there are 3 red marbles in the bag, what is the total number of marbles in the bag?

- 10
- 11
- 55
- 110
- 165

8. When integer $y$ is divided by 2, is the remainder 1 ?

(1) $y > 5$

(2) $y$ is prime

- Statement (1) ALONE is sufficient, but statement (2) alone is not sufficient.
- Statement (2) ALONE is sufficient, but statement (1) alone is not sufficient.
- BOTH statements TOGETHER are sufficient, but NEITHER statement ALONE is sufficient.
- EACH statement ALONE is sufficient.
- Statements (1) and (2) TOGETHER are not sufficient.

9. One-fourth of the cars that an automobile manufacturer produces are sports cars, and the rest are sedans. If one-fifth of the cars that the manufacturer produces are red and one-third of the sports cars are red, then what fraction of the sedans are red?

- $\frac{7}{45}$
- $\frac{5}{36}$
- $\frac{1}{4}$
- $\frac{7}{20}$
- $\frac{1}{2}$

10. Line $l$ is a line on the $xy$-plane. Does line $l$ pass through the second quadrant?

(1) Line $l$ has a negative slope

(2) The absolute value of the $x$-intercept is greater than 3

- Statement (1) ALONE is sufficient, but statement (2) alone is not sufficient.
- Statement (2) ALONE is sufficient, but statement (1) alone is not sufficient.
- BOTH statements TOGETHER are sufficient, but NEITHER statement ALONE is sufficient.
- EACH statement ALONE is sufficient.
- Statements (1) and (2) TOGETHER are not sufficient.

# Summary

- Most of the algebra problems on the GMAT are simpler to solve *without* algebra, using two Princeton Review techniques: **Plugging In** and **Plugging In the Answers**.
- Plugging In is easy. There are three steps:
    - Pick numbers for the variables in the problem.
    - Using your numbers, find an answer to the problem. (Write that answer down and circle it.)
    - Plug your numbers into the answer choices to see which choice equals the answer you found in the previous step.
- When you Plug In, try to choose convenient numbers—those that are simple to work with and make the problem easier to manipulate.
- When you Plug In, avoid choosing 0, 1, or a number that already appears in the problem or in the answer choices.
- On problems with variables in the answers that contain the words "must be" or "could be," you may have to Plug In more than once to find the correct answer.
- Plugging In the Answers is easy. There are three steps:
    - Always start with (C). Plug that number into the problem and see whether it makes the problem work.
    - If (C) is too small, try the next larger number.
    - If (C) is too big, try the next smaller number.
    - If you're not sure which way to go, don't sweat it. Just pick a direction and try it out!
    - If the question asks for the least or greatest number, start with the least or greatest answer choice.

# Chapter 15
# Applied Arithmetic

Applied arithmetic involves knowing how to solve word problems involving rate and work, functions, probability, permutations, and combinations. In this chapter, we cover the important facets of each type of problem and show you how they appear on the GMAT.

It's time to look at some applied arithmetic subjects that the GMAT test-writers love to use. In this chapter, we'll cover these topics:

1. Rate problems
2. Work problems
3. Function problems
4. Probability problems
5. Permutation and Combination problems

## RATE PROBLEMS

Any problem that mentions planes, trains, cars, bicycles, distance, miles per hour, or any other travel-related terminology is asking you to solve a rate problem. You may remember that you can use the formula *distance* = *rate* × *time* to solve these types of problems.

We're going to use a **Rate Pie** to keep track of the information in a rate problem. Here's what it looks like:

**Two Out of Three Ain't Bad**
For Data Sufficiency problems, as soon as you have two of the pieces of the Rate Pie, you have sufficient information to find the other piece.

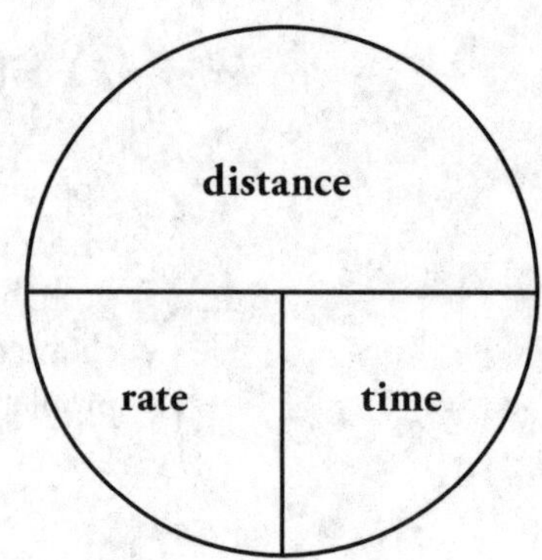


If a problem gives you the rate and time, the pieces on the bottom, you multiply to get the distance. If you have the distance, the piece on the top, and one of the pieces on the bottom, you divide to get the other bottom piece. As soon as you know that you are dealing with a rate problem, draw a Rate Pie and start filling in what you know.

The Rate Pie is really just a different way of writing the *distance* = *rate* × *time* formula. It works well for GMAT problems, however, because GMAT problems often involve multiple steps. So, the pie helps you to see what information you have and what you need to find.

Let's try a problem:

Pam and Sue drove in the same car to a business meeting that was 120 miles away. Pam drove to the meeting at 60 miles per hour and Sue drove back, along the same route, at 50 miles per hour. How many more minutes did it take Sue to drive the distance than it took Pam?

- 4
- 10
- 20
- 24
- 30

### Here's How to Crack It

Since the problem deals with rates, you need a Rate Pie. In fact, since there is rate information for both Pam and Sue, you need two Rate Pies—one for Pam and one for Sue.

Pam

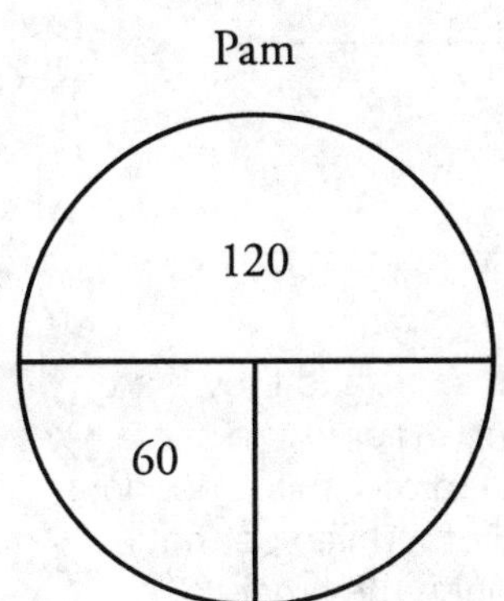


Sue

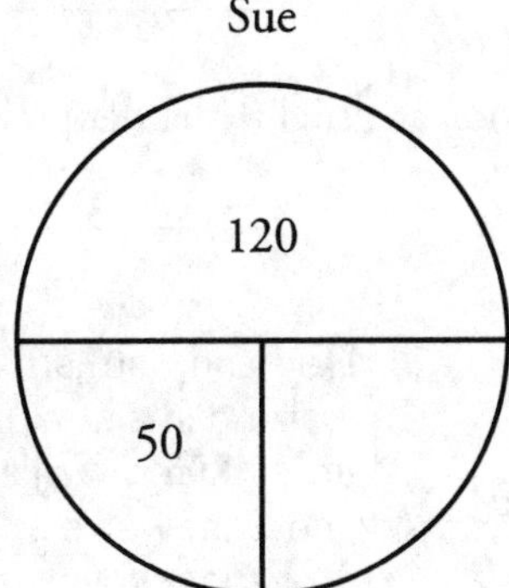


Once you draw the pies, you can transfer the information that you know to each pie. Since Pam and Sue drove along the same route, the distance is 120 miles for each pie. Pam's rate is 60 miles per hour and Sue's rate is 50 miles per hour. Transfer that information to the pies too.

To use the pie, remember that if you have the piece at the top and one of the pieces on the bottom, you divide to find the other piece. So, Pam's time is $120 \div 60 = 2$ and Sue's time is $120 \div 50 = 2\frac{2}{5}$. The pies made it easy to see how to find the time for each driver.

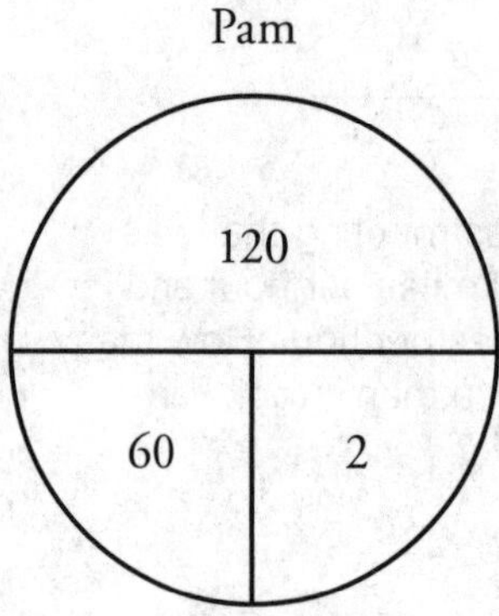


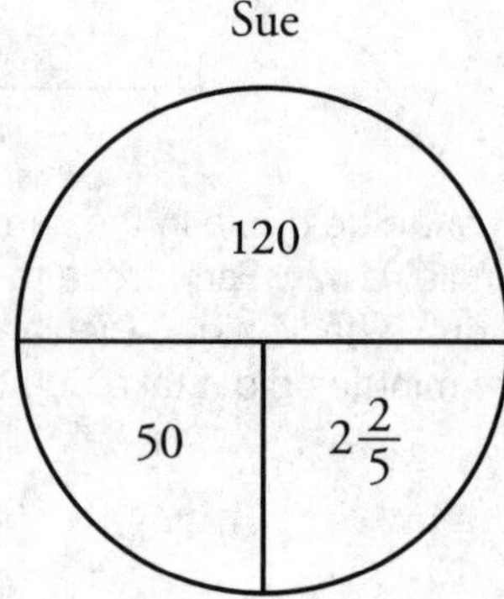


The problem asks how many more minutes it took Sue to drive the distance than it took Pam. Start by subtracting $2\frac{2}{5} - 2 = \frac{2}{5}$ to find that it took Sue $\frac{2}{5}$ of an hour longer. Now, just convert to minutes: $60 \times \frac{2}{5} = 24$. The answer is (D).

---

Now, let's look at a slightly harder problem:

---

**Easy Eliminations**
Choices (A) and (E) are unlikely because they are numbers in the problem. Choice (B) is just 45 ÷ 5, which is Fred's time to walk the whole distance.

Fred and Sam are standing 45 miles apart and they start walking in a straight line toward each other at the same time. If Fred walks at a constant speed of 4 miles per hour and Sam walks at a constant speed of 5 miles per hour, how many miles has Sam walked when they meet?

- 5
- 9
- 25
- 30
- 45

### Here's How to Crack It

Since the problem is about rates, draw a Rate Pie. In this case, you may be wondering if you need one pie or two. You actually need one. Here's why: when dealing with rates, it is often helpful to think about what happens in a certain amount of time such as an hour. In one hour, Fred walks 4 miles and Sam walks 5 miles. Since they are walking toward each other in a straight line, they have covered 9 miles of the distance between them at the end of an hour. Wait! Nine miles in an hour? That means that their combined rate is 9 miles per hour. That's what goes on the pie for the rate.

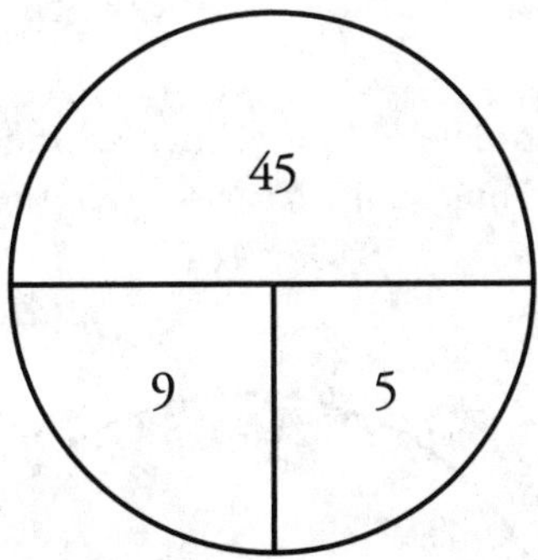

**Here's A Tip!**
When two items travel in a straight line toward each other, you can add their rates.

The other piece that you could fill in on the pie from the problem was the distance, 45 miles. Then, use the pie to find that Fred and Sam walk for 5 hours before they meet. (Remember that you divide the top piece of the pie by one of the pieces on the bottom to find the other bottom piece.)

The problem wants to know how many miles Sam had walked when he met Fred. So, set up one more pie. This time you know Sam's rate, 5 miles per hour, and you know that he walked for 5 hours.

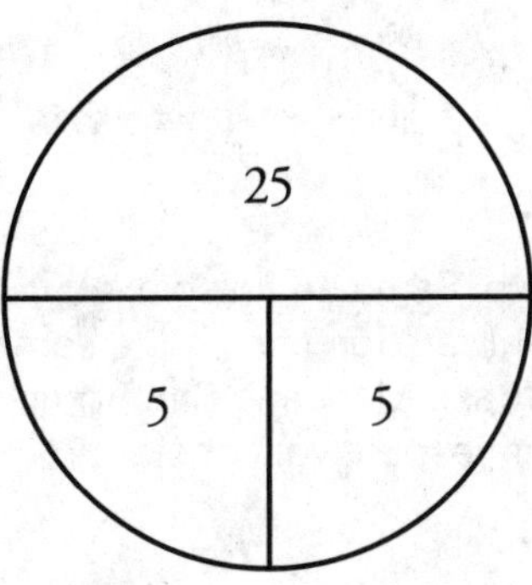


So, Sam walks 25 miles when he meets Fred. The answer is (C).

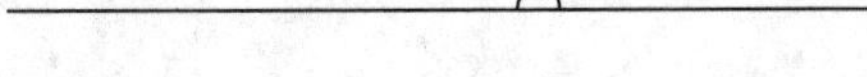

## WORK PROBLEMS

Work problems are a type of rate problem. Rather than asking about a distance, these problems ask about a job or a part of a job. You can use a variation of the Rate Pie to solve these problems. Here's what it looks like:

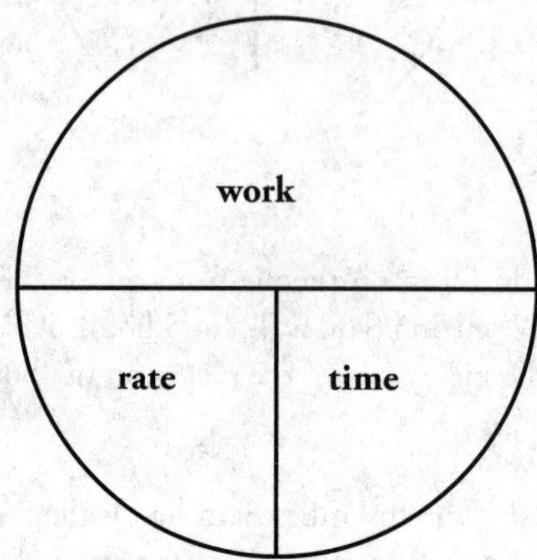


All that changes is that *work* replaces *distance* at the top of the pie. You use the **Work Pie** in the same way as the Rate Pie.

---

Working at a constant rate, Sam can finish a job in 3 hours. Mark, also working at a constant rate, can finish the same job in 12 hours. How many hours does it take Mark and Sam to finish the job if they work together each at his respective, constant rate?

- ◯ 1
- ◯ $2\frac{2}{5}$
- ◯ $2\frac{5}{8}$
- ◯ $3\frac{1}{4}$
- ◯ 4

Since the problem mentions a job being completed, you can use a Work Pie. You'll actually need two pies for the first step of the problem since you must find each worker's individual rate. Once you draw your pies, you can put each worker's time on the pie. You can also put 1 for the work since they each complete 1 job.

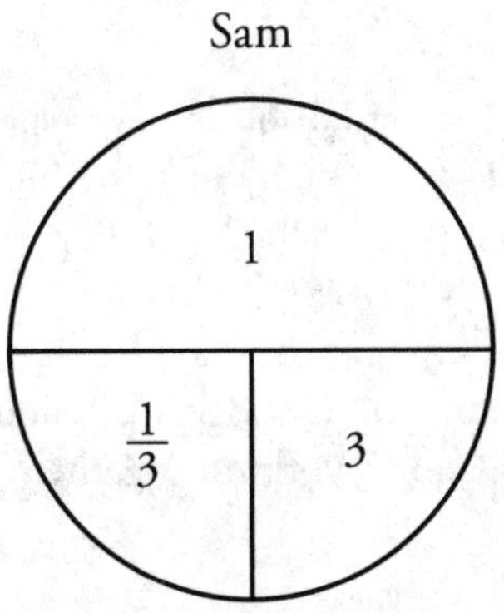


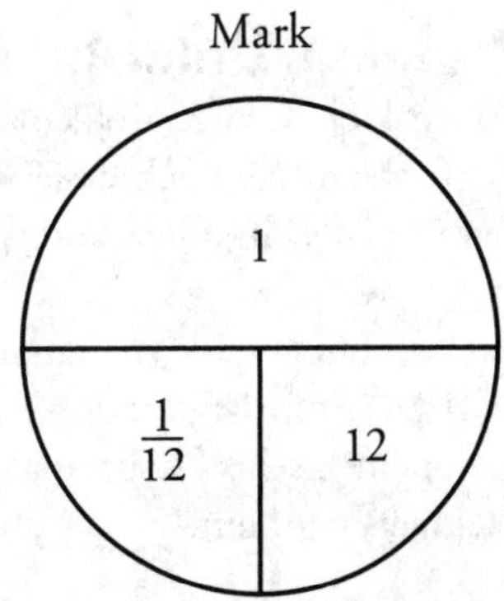


So, Sam's rate is $\frac{1}{3}$ and Mark's rate is $\frac{1}{12}$. What does that mean? Well, it means that Sam completes $\frac{1}{3}$ of the job every hour, while Mark completes $\frac{1}{12}$ of the job every hour.

To finish the problem, note that Mark and Sam work together. Since they are working together, you can combine their rates to find that they complete $\frac{1}{3}+\frac{1}{12}=\frac{5}{12}$ of the job every hour. When people work together, you can combine their rates. Now, set up one more Work Pie. Use 1 for the amount of work and $\frac{5}{12}$ for the rate.

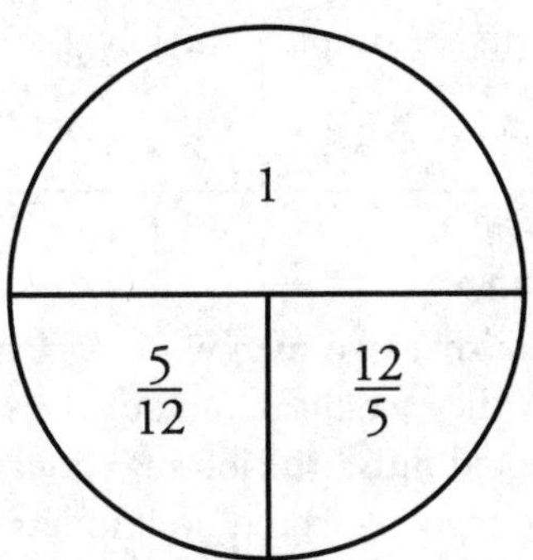


Divide the amount of work by the combined rate to find that the time to complete the job is $1 \div \frac{5}{12}=\frac{12}{5}=2\frac{2}{5}$ hours. The correct answer is (B).

## Same Problem, Different Approach

Another way to look at this problem is to realize that the actual job is never specified. But, wouldn't the problem be much easier to solve if you knew how many of something Sam and Mark needed to make? In other words, this problem can be approached as a Plug In.

Suppose that Sam and Mark were making widgets. Let's say that the complete job is to make 24 widgets. If Sam finishes the job in 3 hours, then he makes 8 widgets per hour. If Mark finishes the job in 12 hours, he makes 2 widgets per hour. Working together, they make $8 + 2 = 10$ widgets per hour.

Now, let's set the last step up using a Work Pie.

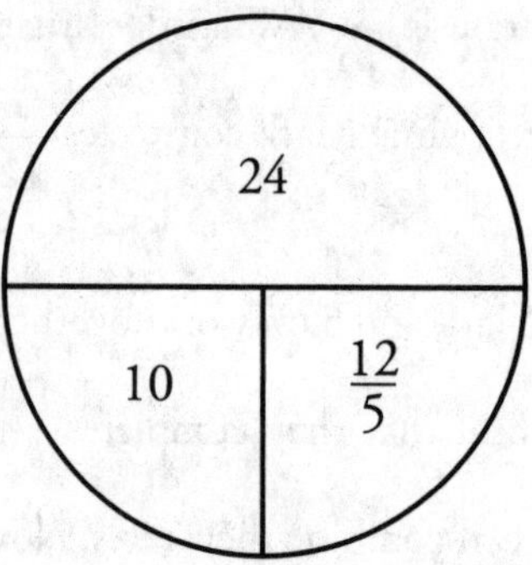


Again, it takes them $\frac{12}{5} = 2\frac{2}{5}$ hours to complete the job. The answer is (B).

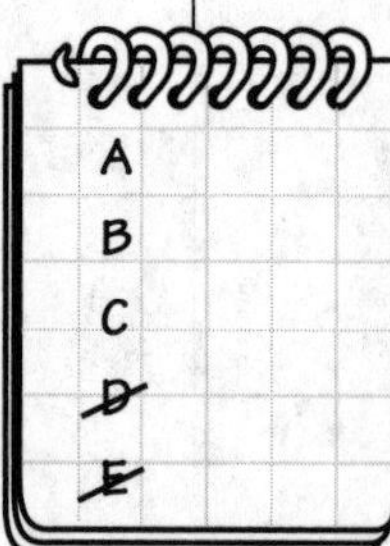


**Easy Eliminations**

It stands to reason that two men working together would take less time to finish a job than they would if each of them worked alone. Because Sam, working alone, could finish the job in 3 hours, it must be true that the two of them, working together, could do it in less time. The answer to this question has to be less than 3. Therefore, we can eliminate (D) and (E).

Here's a slightly harder version of the previous problem:

Working at a constant rate, Sam can finish a job in 3 hours. Mark, also working at a constant rate, can finish the same job in 12 hours. If they work together for 2 hours, how many minutes will it take Sam to finish the job, working alone at his constant rate?

- 5
- 20
- 30
- 60
- 120

### Here's How to Crack It

This problem starts in the same way so you can use the same Work Pies to find each worker's rate.

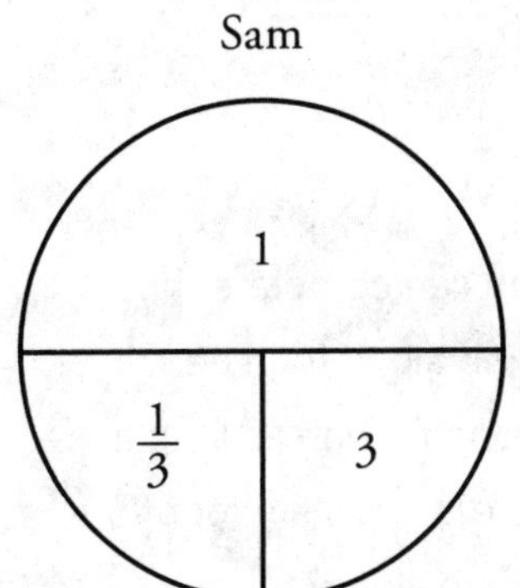


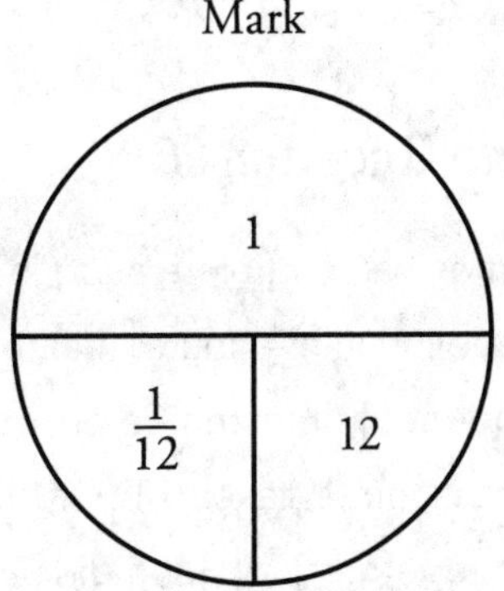


Now you need a new pie. For this pie, you know the combined rate, $\frac{1}{3} + \frac{1}{12} = \frac{5}{12}$, and that they work together for two hours.

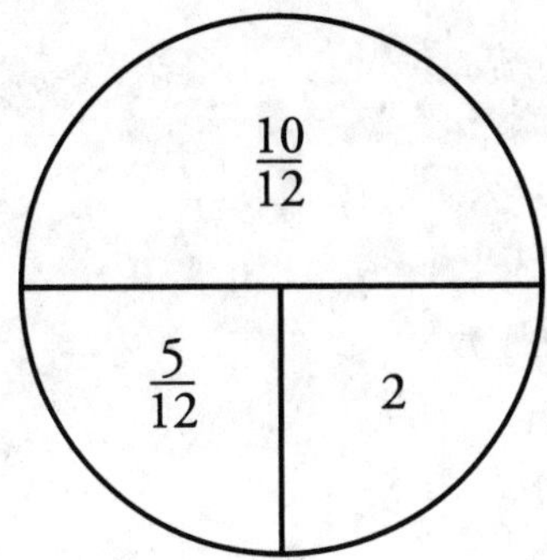

So, you now know that $\frac{5}{12} \times 2 = \frac{10}{12} = \frac{5}{6}$ of the job has been completed when Mark goes home. Sam must finish $\frac{1}{6}$ of the job on his own. Of course, you know Sam's rate, so just set up one last Work Pie.

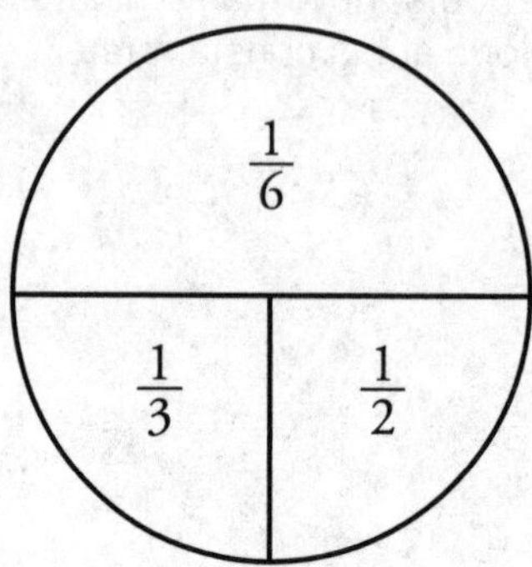


To find the time for Sam to finish the job, use the pie to find that $\frac{1}{6} \div \frac{1}{3} = \frac{1}{2}$, or 30 minutes. The correct answer is (C).

---

## Challenge Question #6

James can complete a job in 6 hours and Sarah can complete the same job in $4\frac{1}{2}$ hours. If James works on the job alone for a certain amount of time and Sarah works on the job alone for half as long as James, and it takes 1 hour for them to complete the remainder of the job together, how long did James work on the job alone?

- 1 hour, 6 minutes
- 1 hour, 10 minutes
- 2 hours, 12 minutes
- 2 hours, 20 minutes
- 3 hours, 18 minutes

## FUNCTIONS

You know you've hit a function problem by the sensation of panic and fear you get when you see some strange symbol (# or * or Δ) and say, "I studied for two months for this test and somehow managed to miss the part where they told me about # or * or Δ." Relax. Any strange-looking symbol on the GMAT is just a function question. For more information on how to solve function questions, check out that section in the Algebra chapter.

**Functions? No Problem**

If you can follow a recipe, you can do a GMAT function problem. Many students are uncomfortable with function questions. But, if you can master these questions, you can pick up a couple points on a question that may trip up some other people.

A function is basically a set of directions. Let's look at an example:

---

If $\Delta x = x$ for $x \geq 0$ and $2x$ for $x < 0$, $\dfrac{\Delta 30}{\Delta(-5)} =$

- −12
- −6
- −3
- 6
- 30

### Here's How to Crack It

A function is basically a set of directions. In this case, the directions tell you what to do with the number that comes after the symbol Δ. If the number that follows the symbol is greater than or equal to 0, then the output of the function is just the number $x$. However, if the number that follows the symbol is negative, the output of the Δ function is $2x$. So, we can evaluate the given expression thus:

$$\frac{\Delta 30}{\Delta(-5)} = \frac{30}{2(-5)} = \frac{30}{-10} \text{ or } -3. \text{ The answer is (C).}$$

**Mistakes of the Average Test-Taker**

The average test-taker has no idea what to do with Δ, so she just ignores it. Because $\frac{30}{-5} = -6$, the average test-taker picks (B). On the other hand, the average test-taker might also think she can reduce functions. In other words, she might think she can do this:

$$\frac{\Delta 30}{\Delta(-5)} = \Delta(-6)$$

The function of −6 = −12, so she might also select (A).

---

## Challenge Question #7

For positive integers $x$, $y$, and $z$, the function $x * y * z$ means that $\frac{z}{x^y}$ is an integer, but $\frac{z}{x^{y+1}}$ is not. If $x * 2 * 144$, then which of the following is NOT a possible value of $x$ ?

- 2
- 3
- 4
- 6
- 12

# PROBABILITY

## Probability, Part 1

Just the word is enough to cause math-phobes to run for the exits—but, at least as it appears on the GMAT, probability really isn't all that bad. Check out the easy example below:

> A fair, six-sided die with faces numbered one through six is rolled once. What is the probability that this roll results in a 2 ?

Well, of course, there's only one possibility of this happening, and there are six possible outcomes, so there's a one-in-six chance. In essence, this is all that probability is about. On the GMAT, probability is usually expressed as a fraction: the total number of possibilities is always the denominator. The number of possibilities that match what you want is the numerator. In the example above, that translates to $\frac{1}{6}$.

$$\text{Basic probability formula} = \frac{\text{number of outcomes you want}}{\text{total number of possible outcomes}}$$

Let's make this example a little harder:

> A fair, six-sided die with faces numbered one through six is rolled once. What is the probability that this roll results in either a 2 or a 3 ?

The total number of possible outcomes (the denominator) is still the same: 6. But the numerator is different now. There are two possibilities that would match what we want, so the numerator becomes 2. The probability is $\frac{2}{6}$, or $\frac{1}{3}$.

Let's make the example a little harder still.

> A fair, six-sided die with faces numbered one through six is rolled twice. What is the probability that both rolls result in a 2 ?

Obviously, the odds of this happening are much smaller. How do you figure out the probability of something happening over a series of events? To find the probability of a series of events, you multiply the probabilities of each of the individual events. Let's start with the first roll of the die. We already figured out that the probability of the die landing with its "2" side facing up on a single toss is $\frac{1}{6}$. Now, let's think about the second toss. Well, actually, the probability of this happening on the second toss is exactly the same: $\frac{1}{6}$.

However, to figure out the probability of the "2" side facing upward on *both* tosses, you multiply the first probability by the second probability: $\frac{1}{6} \times \frac{1}{6} = \frac{1}{36}$.

The probability that A **and** B will both happen:
p(A and B) = p(A) × p(B)

Here's an example of a moderately difficult GMAT problem.

**Admissions Insight No. 4: Letters of Recommendation, Part 1**

Most MBA programs require two to three letters of recommendation. The best recommendations are from people who know you well in a professional capacity and can discuss the same points you have already made in your essays.

Unlike admissions committees for other graduate programs, MBA admissions committees generally prefer professional recommendations to academic ones.

There are 8 job applicants sitting in a waiting room—4 women and 4 men. If 2 of the applicants are selected at random, what is the probability that both will be women?

- $\frac{1}{2}$
- $\frac{3}{7}$
- $\frac{1}{4}$
- $\frac{3}{14}$
- $\frac{1}{10}$

### Here's How to Crack It

Let's take the first event in the series. The total number of possibilities for the first selection is 8, because there are 8 applicants in the room. Of those 8 people, 4 are women, so the probability that the first person chosen will be a woman is $\frac{4}{8}$, or $\frac{1}{2}$. You might think that the probability would be exactly the same for the second choice (in which case you would multiply $\frac{1}{2} \times \frac{1}{2}$ and choose (C)), but in fact, that's not true. Let's consider: the first woman has just left the room, and they are about to choose another applicant at random. How many total people are now in the room? Aha! Only 7. And how many of those 7 are women? Only 3. So the probability that the second choice will be a woman is actually only $\frac{3}{7}$, which is (B). But we aren't done yet. We have to figure out the probability that BOTH choices in this series of two choices will be women. The probability that the first will be a woman is $\frac{1}{2}$. The probability that the second will be a woman is $\frac{3}{7}$. The probability that they both will be women is $\frac{1}{2} \times \frac{3}{7}$, or $\frac{3}{14}$. The answer is (D).

**Easy Eliminations**

The GMAT test-writers like to see if they can trick you into picking partial answers—i.e., numbers that you get in the course of solving a problem that are not quite the final answer. The probability that the first choice will be a woman is $\frac{1}{2}$, (A)—but does it feel like you've done enough work to "deserve" to get this problem right yet? Nope—this is only an intermediate step. The probability that the second choice will be a woman is $\frac{3}{7}$, (B). But again, this is just another intermediate step. Don't fall for these trick choices—cross off (A) and (B).

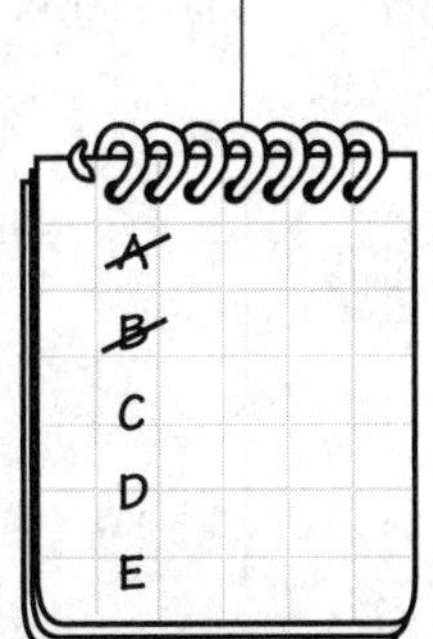


## Probability, Part 2: One Thing or Another

So far, we've been dealing with the probability of one event happening and then another event happening (for example, in that last problem, the first event was choosing a female job applicant; the second event was choosing ANOTHER female job applicant). But what if you are asked to find the probability of either one thing OR another thing happening? To solve this type of problem, you simply add the probabilities. Note that pure versions of these "or" problems are incredibly rare on the GMAT. Understanding the idea can be helpful on other problems, however.

The probability that A or B will happen: p(A or B) = p(A) + p(B).
This is the formula used if the probabilities are mutually exclusive, that is, if they cannot happen together. Use this formula because **on the GMAT, probabilities are almost always mutually exclusive.** In case you're curious, the formula used to show the probability that A or B will happen, if the events are NOT mutually exclusive, is
p(A or B) = p(A) + p(B) – p(A and B).

Here's an example:

Sally and Sam are watching a magician perform with 16 of their friends. If the magician chooses one audience member at random to assist with a trick, what is the probability that either Sally or Sam is chosen?

### Here's How to Crack It

By this point, you should have no problem figuring out that the probability of Sally being chosen is $\frac{1}{18}$. And the probability of Sam being chosen? That's right: $\frac{1}{18}$. So what is the probability of Sally or Sam being chosen?

$$\frac{1}{18}+\frac{1}{18}=\frac{2}{18}\ or\ \frac{1}{9}$$

## Probability, Part 3: The Odds That Something Doesn't Happen

But what if you are asked to find the probability that something will NOT happen? Well, think of it this way: if the probability of snow is 70%, or $\frac{7}{10}$, what's the probability that it won't snow? That's right: 30%, or $\frac{3}{10}$. To figure out the probability that something won't happen, simply figure out the probability that it WILL happen and then subtract that fraction from 1.

p(event happens) + p(event does NOT happen) = 1

Here's an example:

Sally and Sam are watching a magician perform with 16 of their friends. If one audience member is chosen at random to assist with a trick, what is the probability that neither Sally nor Sam is chosen?

### Here's How to Crack It

As we already know, the probability that Sally will be chosen is $\frac{1}{18}$. The probability that Sam will be chosen is also $\frac{1}{18}$. So what is the probability that neither Sally nor Sam will be chosen?

$$1-\frac{2}{18}=\frac{16}{18}=\frac{8}{9}$$

## Probability, Part 4: The Odds That at Least One Thing Will Happen

What if the problem asks the probability of something happening at least once? To calculate the probability of at least one thing happening, just use this equation: the probability of what you WANT to happen plus the probability of what you DON'T want to happen equals one. Or, to put it another way:

p(event happens) = 1 − p(event does NOT happen)

Here's an example:

Nine boys and nine girls are watching a magician perform. Four times during the performance a child is chosen at random to assist with a trick. If any of the children can be chosen to assist with each of the four tricks, what is the probability that at least one girl is chosen?

### Here's How to Crack It

To find the odds of at least one girl being chosen, let's begin by figuring out the odds that a girl isn't chosen. The magician will make a total of four choices. What are the odds that the magician will not pick a girl in the first round? If you said $\frac{9}{18}$ *or* $\frac{1}{2}$, you are doing just fine. And what are the odds that the magician will not pick a girl the second, third, and fourth round? Each time, the odds of not picking a girl stay the same, because the children are returned to the pool of possible candidates, so each time the odds will be $\frac{9}{18}$ *or* $\frac{1}{2}$. The probability of not picking a girl all four times is:

$$\frac{1}{2}\times\frac{1}{2}\times\frac{1}{2}\times\frac{1}{2}=\frac{1}{16}$$

But we aren't done. The probability of a girl being picked at least once is 1 minus the probability that she will not be picked. So the correct answer is:

$$1-\frac{1}{16}=\frac{15}{16}$$

## Challenge Question #8

If there are $g$ girls and $b$ boys on a team, and two members of the team are randomly selected, then what is the probability, in terms of $g$ and $b$, that at least one selected player is a girl?

- $\frac{g(g-1)}{(b+g)(b+g-1)}$
- $\frac{b(b-1)}{(b+g)(b+g-1)}$
- $\frac{2bg}{(b+g)(b+g-1)}$
- $\frac{g(2b+g-1)}{(b+g)(b+g-1)}$
- $\frac{b(2g+b-1)}{(b+g)(b+g-1)}$

# PERMUTATIONS AND COMBINATIONS

In general, permutation and combination problems tend to show up as medium-hard to hard problems on the GMAT.

Here's a very simple example of a combination problem:

At a certain restaurant, a meal consists of one appetizer, one main course, and one dessert. If the restaurant has 2 appetizers, 3 main courses, and 5 desserts, then how many different meals could the restaurant serve?

- 60
- 30
- 10
- 6
- 3

### Here's How to Crack It

You could just carefully write down all the different combinations:

Shrimp cocktail with meatloaf with cherry pie
Shrimp cocktail with meatloaf with ice cream
Shrimp cocktail with meatloaf with…

You get the idea. But first of all, this is too time consuming, and second of all, there's a much easier way.

> For a problem that asks you to choose a number of items to fill specific spots, when each spot is filled from a different source, all you have to do is multiply the number of choices for each of the spots.

So, because there were 2 appetizers, 3 main courses, and 5 possible desserts, the total number of combinations of a full meal at this restaurant would be $2 \times 3 \times 5$, or 30. The answer is (B).

## Permutations: Single Source, Order Matters

The same principle applies when you're choosing from a group of similar items—with one slight wrinkle. Take a look at this easy permutation problem:

Three basketball teams play in a league against each other. At the end of the season, how many different ways could the 3 teams end up ranked against each other?

- ○ 1
- ○ 3
- ○ 6
- ○ 36
- ○ 72

### Here's How to Crack It

You could just carefully write down all the different combinations. If we call the three teams A, B, and C, then here are the different ways they could end up in the standings:

ABC  ACB  BAC  BCA  CAB  CBA

**Admissions Insight No. 5: Letters of Recommendation, Part 2**

What to give to your recommenders:

1) Background information about yourself, such as a résumé or statement of purpose, plus talking points (if appropriate) to get them started
2) A list of schools to which you're applying
3) Stamped envelopes already addressed to the schools
4) The recommendation deadlines for each of the schools
5) A thank-you note, mailed after the letters are submitted

In general, it is best to waive your right to see the recommendations, because this will give the schools more confidence in their veracity.

But again, this approach is time consuming (even more so for more difficult problems). As you probably suspected, there's a simpler and faster way to solve this problem.

> For a problem that asks you to choose from the same source to fill specific spots, all you have to do is multiply the number of choices for each of the spots—but the number of choices keeps getting smaller.

Let's think for a moment about how many teams could possibly end up in first place. If you said 3, you're doing just fine.

Now, let's think about how many teams could finish second. Are there still 3 possibilities? Not really, because one team has already finished first. There are, in fact, only 2 possible teams that could finish second.

And finally, let's think about how many teams could finish third. In fact, there is only 1 team that could finish third.

To find the number of different ways these teams could end up in the rankings, just multiply the number of choices for first place (in this case, 3) by the number of choices for second place (in this case, 2) by the number of choices for third place (in this case, 1).

$$3 \times 2 \times 1 = 6$$

The correct answer is (C).

---

In general, no matter how many items there are to arrange, you can figure out the number of permutations of a group of $n$ similar objects with the formula:

$$n(n - 1)(n - 2)\ldots \times 3 \times 2 \times 1, \text{ or } n!$$

So if there were 9 baseball teams, the total number of permutations of their standings would be $9 \times 8 \times 7 \times 6 \times 5 \times 4 \times 3 \times 2 \times 1$, also sometimes written as 9!. If 4 sailboats sailed a race, the total number of permutations of the orders in which they could cross the finish line would be $4 \times 3 \times 2 \times 1$, also sometimes written as 4!.

## Single Source, Order Matters but Only for a Selection

The problems we've shown you so far were necessary to show you the concepts behind permutation problems—but were much too easy to be on the GMAT. Here's a problem that would be more likely to appear on the test:

---

Seven basketball teams play in a league against each other. At the end of the season, how many different arrangements are there for the top 3 teams in the rankings?

- 6
- 42
- 210
- 5,040
- 50,450

### Easy Eliminations

If you were to see this problem on the computer-adaptive section of the actual GMAT, you should first stop and give yourself a pat on the back, because it means you're doing pretty well—permutation and combination problems usually show up only among the more difficult problems. But after you've congratulated yourself, stop and think for a moment. Could the answer to this difficult problem simply be a matter of finding $7 \times 6 \times 5 \times 4 \times 3 \times 2 \times 1$, (D)? Too easy. Because the question is asking for the permutations for only 3 of the 7 slots, the number must be less than that. So get rid of (D) and (E).

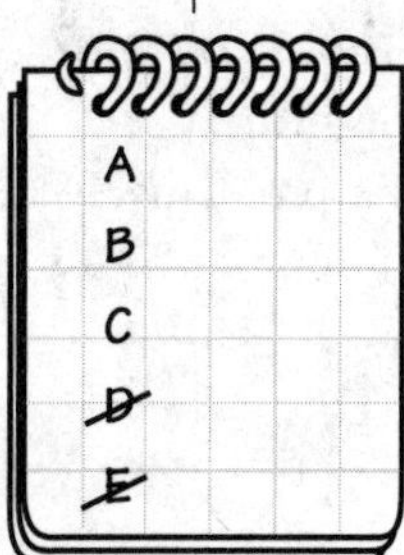


### Here's How to Crack It

To find all the possible permutations of the top 3 out of 7 baseball teams, simply multiply the number of combinations for each spot in the standings. How many teams are possibilities for the first place slot? If you said 7, you're right. How about for the second slot? Well, one team is already occupying the first place slot, so there are only 6 contenders left. And for the third place slot? That's right: 5.

So, the correct answer is $7 \times 6 \times 5 = 210$, or (C).

---

In general, no matter how many items there are to arrange, you can figure out the number of permutations of $r$ objects chosen from a set of $n$ objects with the formula:

$$n(n-1)(n-2)\ldots \times (n-r+1)$$

So if there were 9 baseball teams (*n*), the total number of permutations of the top 4 teams (*r*) would be $9 \times 8 \times 7 \times 6$. If 4 sailboats sailed a race (*n*), the total number of permutations of the first 3 boats to cross the finish line (*r*) would be $4 \times 3 \times 2$. Here is another way to write this same formula:

$$\frac{n!}{(n-r)!}$$

(where $n$ = total items and $r$ = the number selected)

Because $9 \times 8 \times 7 \times 6$ is the same as $\frac{9 \times 8 \times 7 \times 6 \times \not{5}!}{\not{5}!}$

## Combinations: Single Source, Order Doesn't Matter

In the previous problems, the order in which the items are arranged actually matters to the problem. For example, if the order in which the three teams finish a season is Yankees, Red Sox, Orioles—that's entirely different than if the order were Red Sox, Yankees, Orioles, especially if you're from Boston.

But combination problems don't care about the order of the items.

**Not Sure If It's a Permutation or a Combination Problem?**
Here's a good clue:
Permutation problems usually ask for "arrangements."
Combination problems usually ask for "groups."

Six horses are running in a race. How many different groups of horses could make up the first 3 finishers?

- 6
- 18
- 20
- 120
- 720

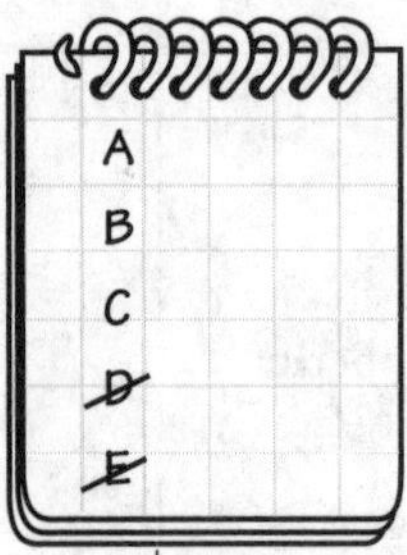


**Easy Eliminations**
If we cared about the order in which the top 3 horses finished the race, then the answer would be the number of permutations: $6 \times 5 \times 4$, or 120. But in this case, we care only about the number of *unique* permutations, and that means the number will be smaller because we don't have to count the set of, for example, (Secretariat, Seattle Slew, and Affirmed) and the set of (Seattle Slew, Secretariat, and Affirmed) as two different permutations. If the correct answer must be smaller than 120, then we can eliminate (D) and (E)—they're too big.

### Here's How to Crack It

To find the number of combinations, first find the number of permutations. If 6 horses run in the race, and we are interested in the top 3 finishers, then the number of permutations would be $6 \times 5 \times 4$, or 120. But if we don't care about the order in which they finished, then a bunch of these 120 permutations turn out to be duplicates.

How many? Let's think of one of those permutations. Let's say the first 3 finishers were Secretariat, Seattle Slew, and Affirmed. How many different ways could we arrange these 3 horses? If you said 6, you're thinking like a permutation master. There are 3!, or $3 \times 2 \times 1$ permutations of any 3 objects. So, of those 120 permutations of the top 3 horses, each combination is being counted 3!, or 6 times. To find the number of combinations, we need to divide 120 by 6. The correct answer is (C).

In general, no matter how many items there are to arrange, you can figure out the number of combinations of $r$ objects chosen from a set of $n$ objects with the formula:

$$\frac{n(n-1)(n-2)\ldots\times(n-r+1)}{r!}$$

So if there were 9 baseball teams, the total number of combinations of the top 4 teams would be:

$$\frac{9\times8\times7\times6}{4\times3\times2\times1}$$

Another way to write this same formula is:

$$\frac{n!}{r!(n-r)!}$$

because $\frac{9\times8\times7\times6}{4\times3\times2\times1}$ is the same as $\frac{9\times8\times7\times6\times\cancel{5}!}{(4\times3\times2\times1)\times\cancel{5}!}$

## Challenge Question #9

On a certain two-part test, a student must choose one of 4 short essays and one of 2 long essays in Part One, and then choose one of $x$ short essays and one of $y$ long essays in Part Two. If there is a total of 144 different lineups of essays that the student could choose, and the ratio of available long essays to short essays remains constant in both parts of the test, then what is the value of $x$ ?

- 3
- 6
- 8
- 9
- 12

## DRILL 9 (Applied Arithmetic)

The answers to these questions can be found in Part VII.

1. If Teena is driving at 55 miles per hour and is currently 7.5 miles behind Joe, who is driving at 40 miles per hour in the same direction, then in how many minutes will Teena be 15 miles ahead of Joe ?

- 15
- 60
- 75
- 90
- 105

2. If the operation $\Delta$ is defined by $a \Delta b = \frac{(b-a)^2}{a^2}$ for all numbers $a$ and $b$, and $a \neq 0$, then $-1 \Delta (1 \Delta -1) =$

- −1
- 0
- 1
- 9
- 25

3. At a local office, each trainee can stuff $\frac{2}{3}$ as many envelopes per day as a full-time worker. If there are $\frac{2}{5}$ as many trainees as there are full-time workers, then what fraction of all the envelopes stuffed in a day did the trainees stuff?

- $\frac{2}{19}$
- $\frac{2}{17}$
- $\frac{4}{19}$
- $\frac{4}{17}$
- $\frac{4}{15}$

4. A focus group is currently made up of $x$ men and $y$ women. If 2 men and 4 women are added to the group, and if one person is selected at random from the larger focus group, then what is the probability that a man is selected?

- $\frac{x}{x+2}$
- $\frac{x}{x+y}$
- $\frac{x+2}{x+y+2}$
- $\frac{y+4}{x+y+6}$
- $\frac{x+2}{x+y+6}$

# Summary

- Rate problems and work problems can be solved using your handy Rate or Work Pies.
- The key to work problems is to think about how much of the job can be done in one hour. But remember, it is often easier to simply Plug In.
- A function problem may have strange symbols like Δ or *, but it is really just a set of directions.
- Probability problems can be solved by putting the total number of possibilities in the denominator and the number of possibilities that match what you are looking for in the numerator.
- Permutation and combination problems ask you to choose or arrange a group of objects.
  - To choose a number of items to fill specific spots, when each spot is filled from a different source, multiply the number of choices for each of the spots.
  - To choose from a set of *n* objects from the same source to fill specific spots, when order matters, multiply the number of choices for each of the spots—but the number of choices keeps getting smaller, according to the formula:

    $n(n-1)(n-2)\ldots\times 3\times 2\times 1$, or $n!$
  - To find the number of permutations of *r* objects chosen from a set of *n* objects, when order matters, use the formula $n(n-1)(n-2)\ldots\times(n-r+1)$, also expressed as $\frac{n!}{(n-r)!}$.
  - To find the number of combinations of *r* objects chosen from a set of *n* objects, use the formula $\frac{n(n-1)(n-2)\ldots\times(n-r+1)}{r!}$

# Chapter 16
# Geometry

The geometry tested on the GMAT is but a small fraction of the geometry you probably studied during high school. In this chapter, we cover the geometry the test-writers actually test: angles, triangles, circles, quadrilaterals, volume, surface area, and coordinate geometry.

Fewer than one-quarter of the problems on the computer-adaptive Quantitative section of the GMAT will involve geometry. And while this tends to be the math subject most people remember least from high school, the good news is that the GMAT tests only a small portion of the geometry you used to know. It will be relatively easy to refresh your memory.

The bad news is that unlike some standardized tests, such as the SAT, the GMAT does not provide you with the formulas and terms you'll need to solve the problems. You'll have to memorize them.

The first half of this chapter will show you how to eliminate answer choices on certain geometry problems without using traditional geometry. The second half will review all the geometry you need to know in order to answer the problems that must be solved using more traditional methods.

## TRAP ANSWERS

Eliminating choices that don't make sense has already proven to be a valuable technique on arithmetic and algebra questions. On geometry questions, you can develop this technique into an art form. The reason for this is that many geometry problems come complete with a diagram *drawn to scale.*

Most people get so caught up in solving a geometry problem geometrically that they forget to look at the diagram to see whether their answer is reasonable.

## Trap Answers on Easy Questions

How big is angle *x*?

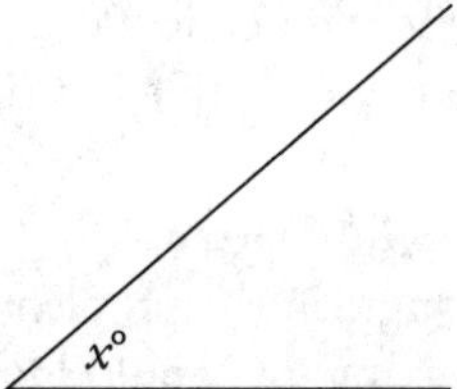


Obviously, you don't know exactly how big this angle is, but it would be easy to compare it with an angle whose measure you *do* know exactly. Let's compare it with a 90-degree angle:

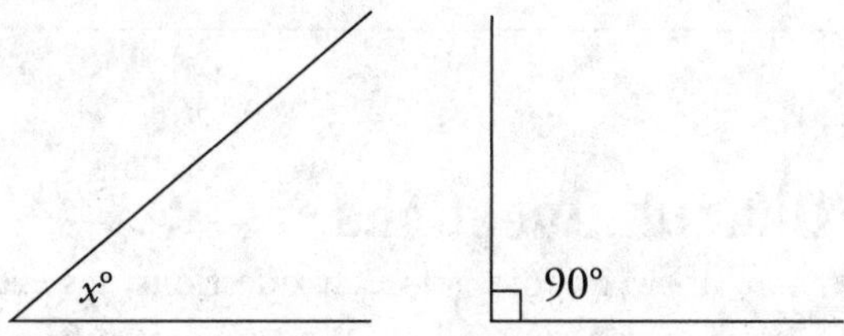


Angle *x* is less than 90 degrees. How much less? It looks as though it's about half of a 90-degree angle, or 45 degrees. Now look at the following problem that asks about the same angle, *x*.

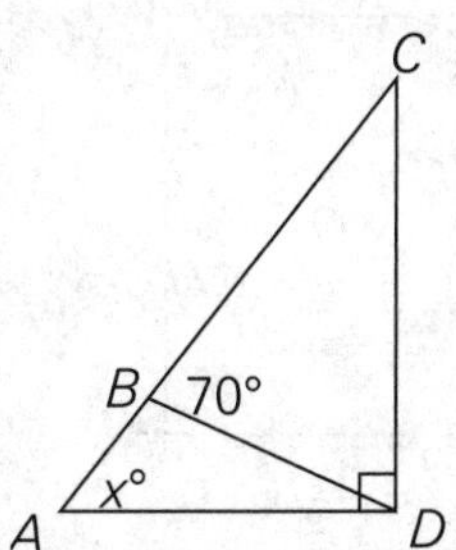


In the figure above, if $BC = CD$ and angle $ADC = 90$ degrees, then what is the value of $x$ ?

- 45
- 50
- 70
- 75
- 100

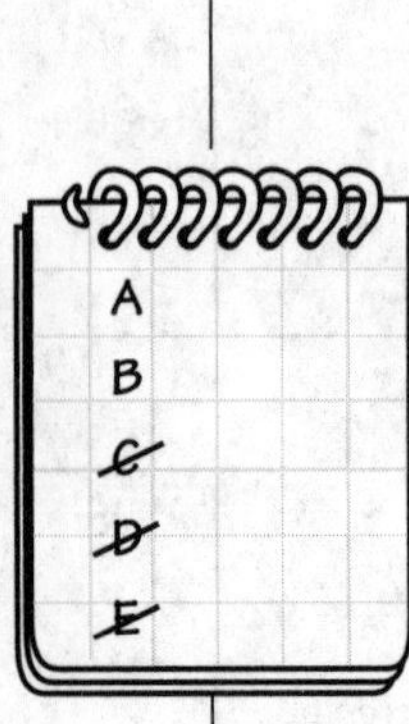


**Easy Eliminations**

We've already decided that angle $x$ is less than 90 degrees, which means that (E) can be eliminated. How much less is it? Well, we estimated before that it was about half, which rules out (C) and (D) as well.

There is another way to eliminate (C) and (D). We can compare angle $x$ with the other marked angle in the problem—angle $DBC$. If the answer to this problem is (C), then angle $x$ should look like angle $DBC$. Does it? No. Angle $x$ looks a little bit smaller than angle $DBC$, which means that both (C) and (D) can be eliminated.

Eliminating trap answers will prevent you from making careless mistakes on easy problems.

## Trap Answers on Difficult Questions

If it's important to cross off trap answer choices on easy questions, it's even more important to eliminate trap answer choices when you're tackling an average or difficult geometry problem. On these problems, you may not know how to find the answer geometrically, and even if you do, you could still fall victim to one of the traps the test-writers have placed in your path. Take a look at the following difficult geometry problem:

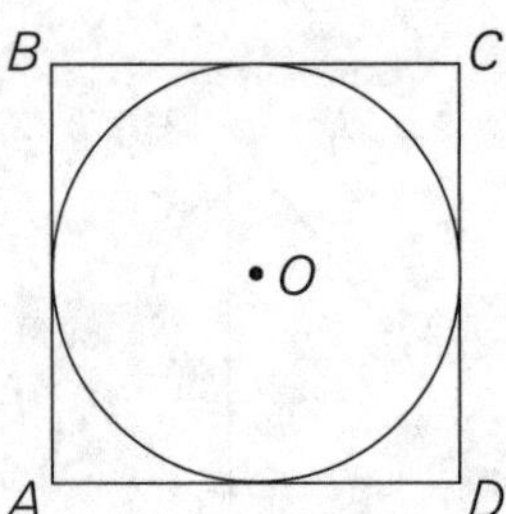


In the figure above, the circle with center $O$ is inscribed inside square $ABCD$ as shown. What is the ratio of the area of circle $O$ to the area of square $ABCD$ ?

- $\frac{\pi}{2}$
- $\frac{4}{\pi}$
- $\frac{\pi}{3}$
- $\frac{\pi}{4}$
- $\frac{\pi}{5}$

**Easy Eliminations**

Let's say that you knew how to do this problem, but it's near the end of the section and you don't have enough time to do it. Let's see whether you can eliminate any of the answer choices just by looking at the diagram and using some common sense.

The problem asks you for the ratio of the area of the circle to the area of the square. Just by looking at the diagram, you can tell that the circle is smaller than the square. The correct answer to this question has to be the ratio of a smaller number to a bigger number. Let's look at the answer choices.

In (A), the ratio is $\pi$ over 2. An approximate value of $\pi$ is 3, so this really reads $\frac{3}{2}$.

Is this the ratio of a smaller number to a bigger number? Just the opposite. Therefore, (A) is a trap answer. Eliminate it.

In (B), the ratio is 4 over $\pi$. This really reads $\frac{4}{3}$.

Is this the ratio of a smaller number to a bigger number? No. Choice (B) is a trap answer. Eliminate it.

In (C), the ratio is $\pi$ over 3. This really reads $\frac{3}{3}$.

Is this the ratio of a smaller number to a bigger number? No. Choice (C) is a trap answer. Eliminate it.

Choices (D) and (E) both contain ratios of smaller numbers to bigger numbers, so they're both still possibilities. However, we've eliminated three of the answer choices without doing any math. If you know how to solve the problem geometrically, then proceed. If not, guess and move on. (By the way, we will show you how to solve this problem using geometry later in the chapter.)

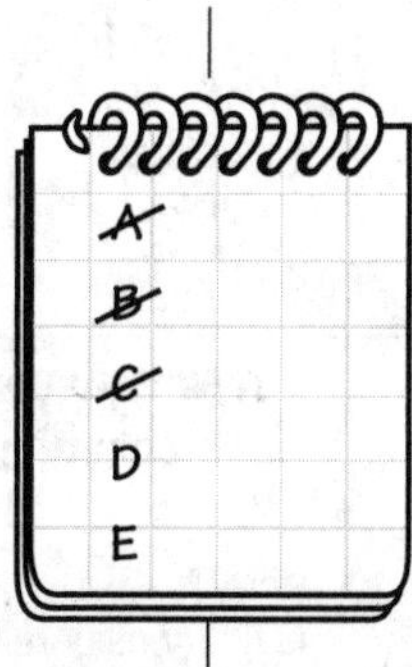


**How to Drive Math Teachers Insane**

Teachers will never know if you use our approximations. We promise. Use them. Many students freeze up when they see $\pi$: it's just a number. Think of it as 3 (and a little extra).

## The Basic Tools

In eliminating trap answers, it helps to have the following approximations memorized.

$$\pi \approx 3$$
$$\sqrt{1} = 1$$
$$\sqrt{2} \approx 1.4$$
$$\sqrt{3} \approx 1.7$$
$$\sqrt{4} = 2$$

It's also useful to have a feel for the way certain common angles look:

**A Note About Measuring:**
Remember that measuring a diagram is not considered cheating. If a diagram in the Problem Solving format does not have the words "not drawn to scale," then it's fair game to use a pen or pencil and measure it!

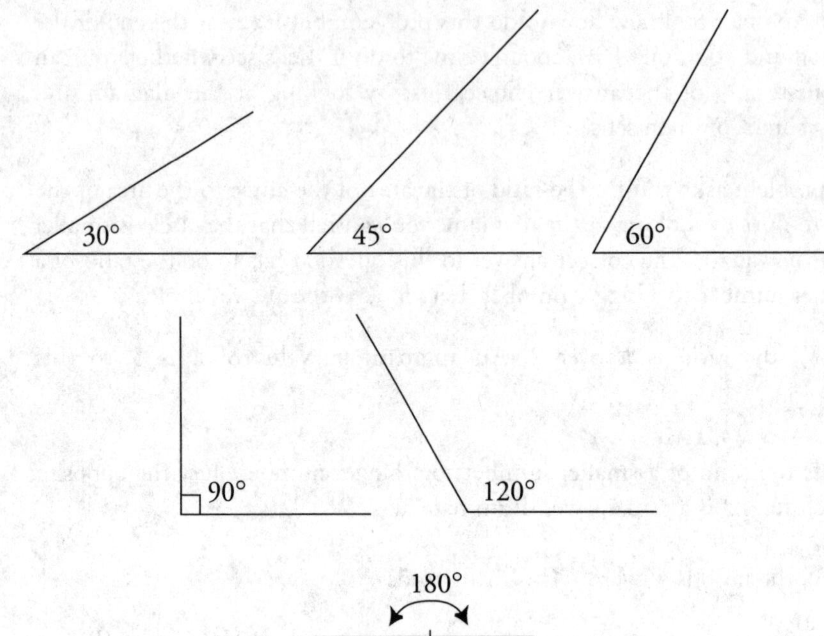


## Getting More Precise

When a geometry problem contains a diagram that's drawn to scale, you can get even more precise in eliminating wrong answer choices.

How? By measuring the diagram.

Look at the problem below:

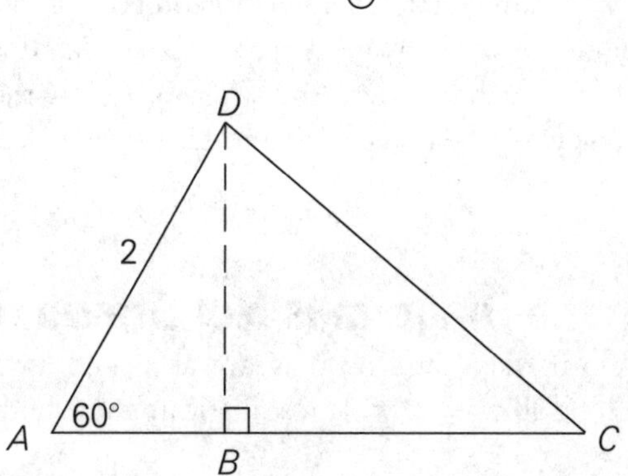


In the figure above, if a line segment connecting points $B$ and $D$ is perpendicular to $AC$ and the area of triangle $ADC$ is $\frac{3\sqrt{3}}{2}$, then $BC =$

- $\sqrt{2}$
- $\sqrt{3}$
- 2
- $3\sqrt{3}$
- 6

### Here's How to Crack It

Practice measuring the diagram with your pen or pencil. If you measure carefully, you'll notice that the distance between *A* and *D* is the same as the distance between *B* and *C*—exactly 2. Let's look at the answer choices. Because you memorized the values we told you to memorize earlier, you know that (A) is equal to 1.4. Eliminate it. Choice (B) is equal to 1.7. This is close enough for us to hold on to it while we look at the other choices. Choice (C) is exactly what we're looking for—2. Choice (D) is 3 times 1.7, which equals 5.1. This is much too large. Choice (E) is even larger. Eliminate (D) and (E). We're down to (B) and (C). The correct answer is (C). By the way, we'll show you how to do this problem geometrically later on the chapter.

## Three Important Notes

1. Diagrams in questions using the Problem Solving format are drawn to scale (unless otherwise indicated).
2. Diagrams marked "not drawn to scale" cannot be measured. In fact, the drawings in these problems are often purposely misleading to the eye.
3. Data Sufficiency geometry diagrams have their own rules, which we will discuss in Chapter 18.

## What Should I Do If There Is No Diagram?

**Geometry Hint**
If there's no diagram, draw one yourself.

Draw one. It's always difficult to imagine a geometry problem in your head. The first thing you should do with any geometry problem that doesn't have a diagram is sketch it out in your scratch booklet. And when you draw the diagram, try to draw it to scale. That way, you'll be in a position to estimate.

## What Should I Do If the Diagram Is Not Drawn to Scale?

The same thing you would do if there were no diagram at all—draw it yourself. Draw it as accurately as possible so you'll be able to see what a realistic answer should be.

## Basic Principles: Fundamentals of GMAT Geometry

The techniques outlined above will enable you to eliminate many incorrect choices on geometry problems. In some cases, you'll be able to eliminate every choice but one. However, there will be some geometry problems in which you will need geometry. Fortunately, GMAC chooses to test only a small number of concepts.

For the sake of simplicity, we've divided GMAT geometry into six basic topics:

1. degrees and angles
2. triangles
3. circles
4. rectangles, squares, and other four-sided objects
5. solids and volume
6. coordinate geometry

**The 180° Rule, Part I**
When you see a geometry problem that asks about angles, always look to see if two angles form a line, which tells you that the total of the two angles is 180 degrees. This is often the crucial starting point on the road to the solution. The test-writers like to construct problems in such a way that it is very easy to miss this.

## DEGREES AND ANGLES

There are 360 degrees in a circle. No matter how large or small a circle is, it still has precisely 360 degrees. If you drew a circle on the ground and then walked a quarter of the distance around it, you would have traveled 90 degrees of that circle. If you walked halfway around the circle, you would have traveled 180 degrees of it.

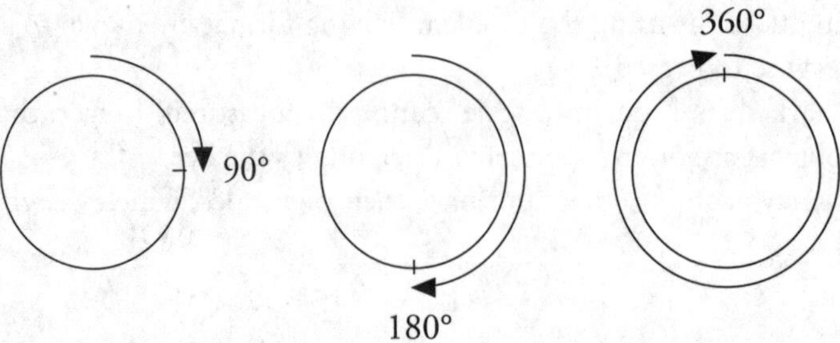

An angle is formed when two line segments extend from a common point. If you think of that point as the center of a circle, the measure of the angle is the number of degrees enclosed by the lines when they pass through the edge of the circle.

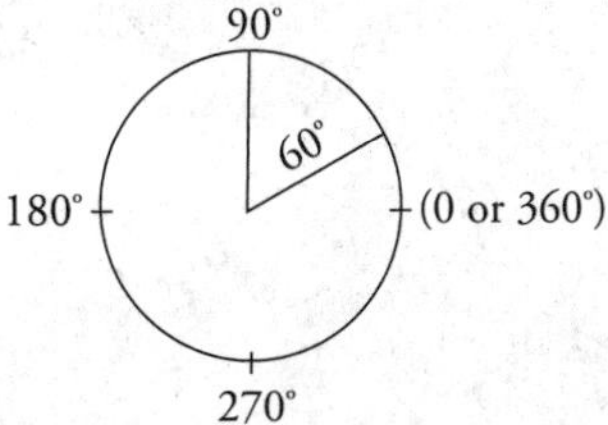


A line is just a 180-degree angle.

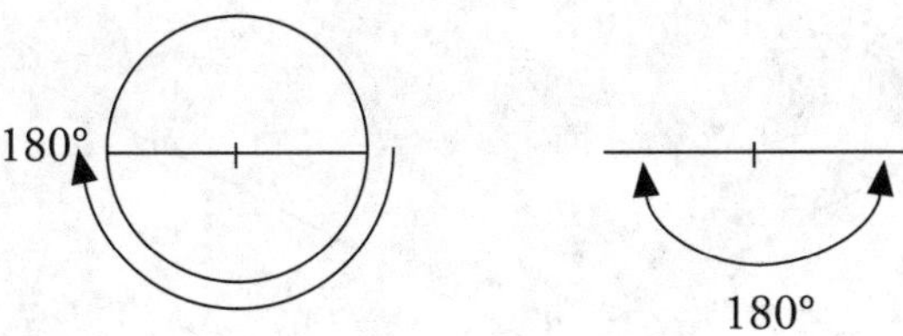


$\ell$ is the symbol for a line. A line can be referred to as $\ell$ or by naming two points on that line. For example, in the diagram below, both points $A$ and $B$ are on the line $\ell$. This line could also be called line $AB$. Also, the part of the line that is between points $A$ and $B$ is called a line segment. $A$ and $B$ are the end points of the line segment.

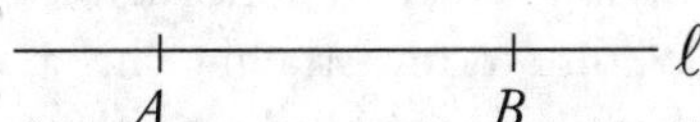


If a line is intersected by another line, as in the diagram below, angle $x$ and angle $y$ add up to one straight line, or 180 degrees. So, for example, if you know that angle $x$ equals 120 degrees, you can find the measure of angle $y$ by subtracting 120 degrees from 180 degrees. Thus, angle $y$ would equal 60 degrees.

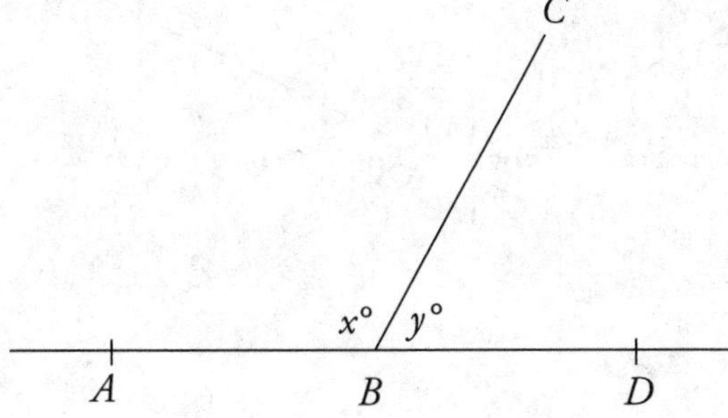


Note that in the diagram above, angle $x$ could also be called angle $ABC$, with $B$ being the point in the middle.

When two lines intersect—as in the diagram below—four angles are formed. The four angles are indicated by letters.

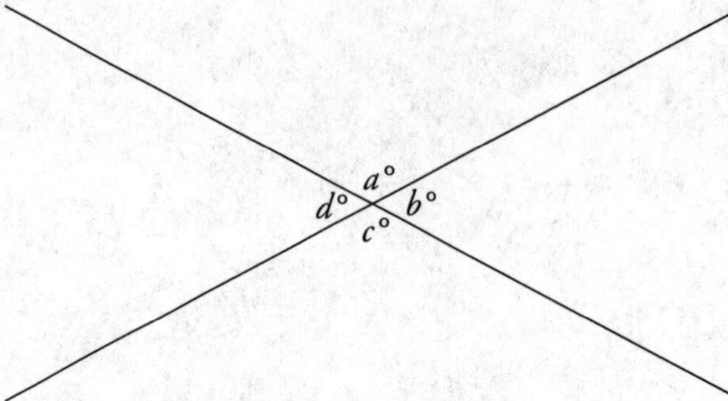


The four angles add up to 360 degrees (remember the circle).

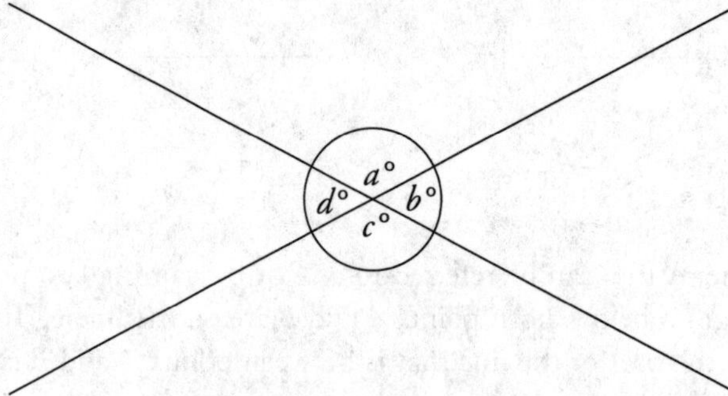


$a° + b° + c° + d° = 360$ degrees. Angle *a* and angle *b*, because they form a straight line, are equal to 180 degrees. Angle *b* and angle *c* also form a straight line, as do $c + d$ and $d + a$. Angles that are opposite each other are called *vertical angles* and have the same number of degrees. For example, in the diagram above, angle *a* is equal to angle *c*. Angle *d* is equal to angle *b*.

Therefore, when two lines intersect, there appear to be four different angles, but there are really only two:

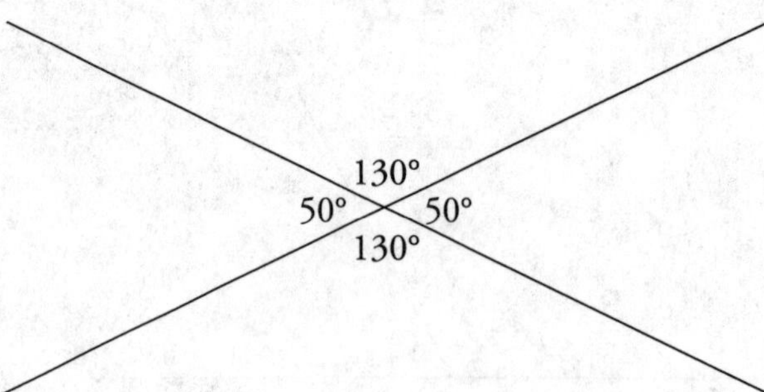

Two lines in the same plane are said to be parallel if they extend infinitely in both directions without intersecting. The symbol for parallel is ||.

Look at the diagram below:

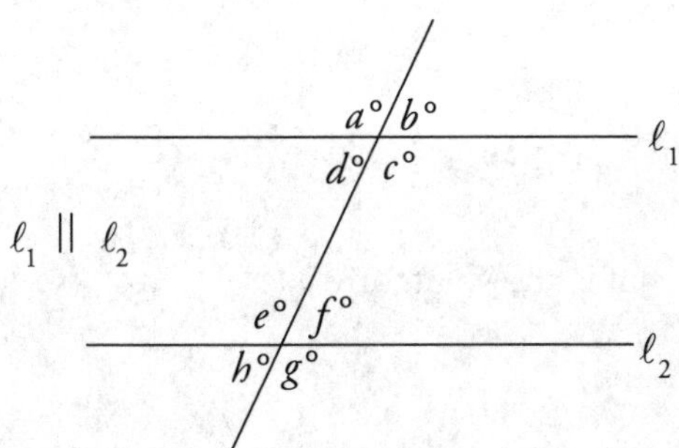


> When two parallel lines are intersected by a third line, there appear to be eight different angle measurements, but there are really only two.

There is a big one (greater than 90°) and a little one (less than 90°). Angle *a* (a big one) is equal to angles *c, e,* and *g.* Angle *b* (a little one) is equal to angles *d, f,* and *h.*

If two lines intersect in such a way that one line is perpendicular to the other, all the angles formed will be 90-degree angles. These are also known as right angles:

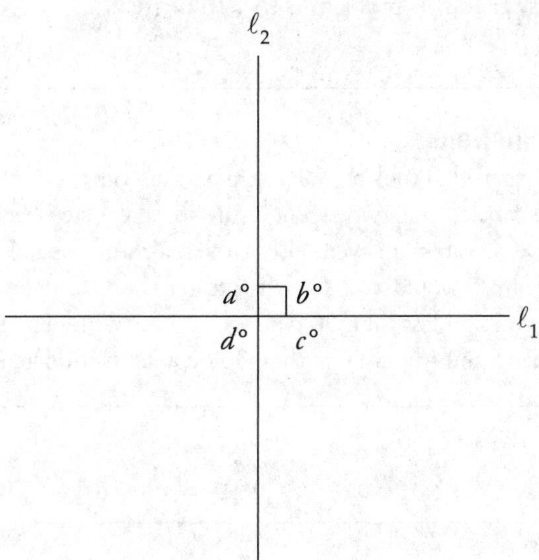


Angles *a, b, c,* and *d* each equal 90 degrees. The little box at the intersection of the two lines is the symbol for a right angle.

Let's practice on a problem:

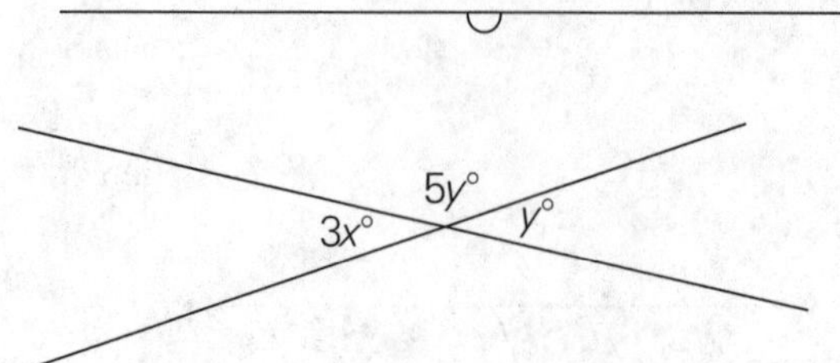


In the figure above, what is the value of $x$ ?

- 10
- 15
- 20
- 30
- 40

### Here's How to Crack It

On a GMAT geometry problem, you may not know exactly how to solve at first glance, but there is almost always something you can do to get started. Did you notice that $5y$ and $y$ together make up a straight line? In other words, $6y = 180$ degrees. Noticing this is the key to solving the problem. If $6y = 180$ degrees, then $y$ equals 30 degrees. You might be tempted to pick (D), but remember—that we're looking for the value of $x$, not the value for $y$. Opposite angles formed by two straight lines are always equal, so $y$ is equal to $3x$. Therefore, $3x$ also equals 30 degrees, and the correct answer to this problem is (A), 10 degrees.

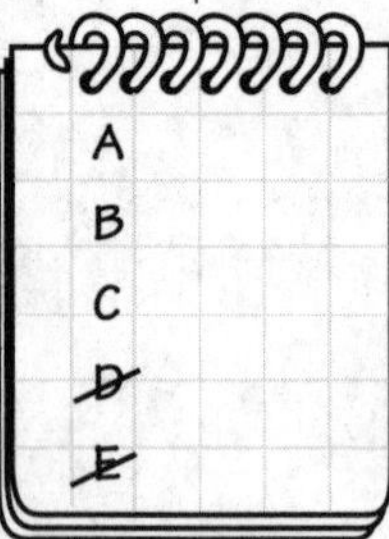


**Easy Eliminations**

Remember that all Problem Solving diagrams on the GMAT are drawn to scale unless labeled otherwise. So be sure to take a step back and think about which answer choices are even within the realm of possibility. Looking at the angle labeled $3x$, would you say it is greater than 90 degrees or less than 90 degrees? If you said less than 90 degrees, you are doing just fine. So if $3x$ is less than 90, then $x$ must be smaller than 30 degrees. Eliminate (D) and (E).

## DRILL 10 (Angles and Lengths)

In the following figures, find numbers for all the variables. The answers to these problems can be found in Part VII.

1. 2.

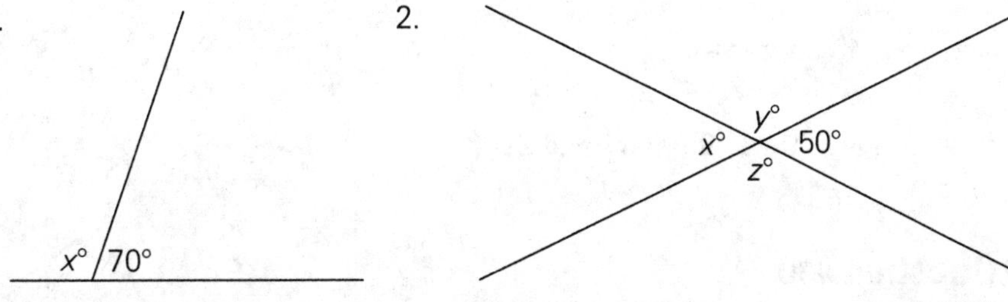


3.

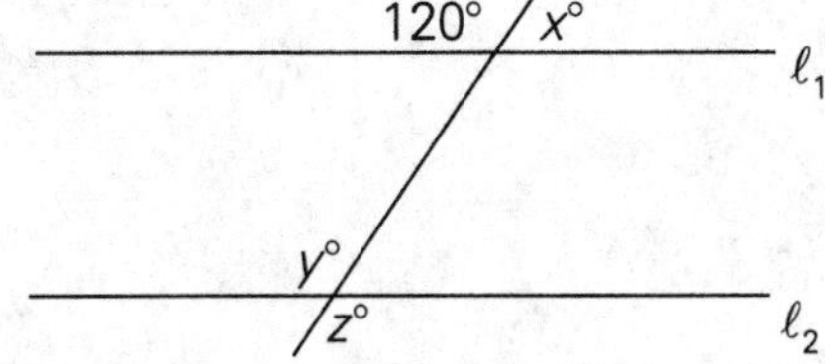


4. If a driver has traveled 270 degrees around a circular race track, what fractional part of the track has he driven?

A real GMAT angle problem might look like this:

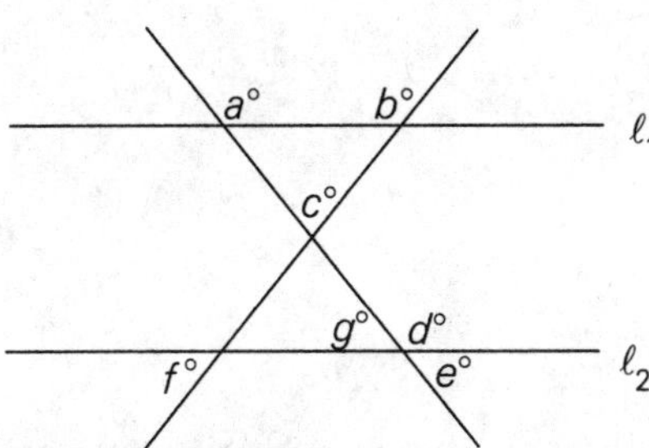


Note: Figure not drawn to scale.

5. In the figure above, if $\ell_1 \parallel \ell_2$, then which of the following angles must be equivalent?

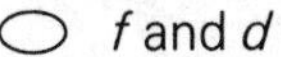

- *a* and *b*
- *g* and *f*
- *d* and *e*
- *a* and *d*
- *f* and *d*

**Drawn to Scale?**
In a Problem Solving question, if it doesn't say *not drawn to scale,* then it *is* drawn to scale. When they give you a scaled drawing, use it to eliminate answers that are out of proportion.

You might see a very straightforward Data Sufficiency problem like this on the GMAT:

6. What is the degree measure of angle $x$ ?

   (1) Angle $y = 40$ degrees.

   (2) Angle $x$ and angle $y$ form a straight line.

## Challenge Question #10

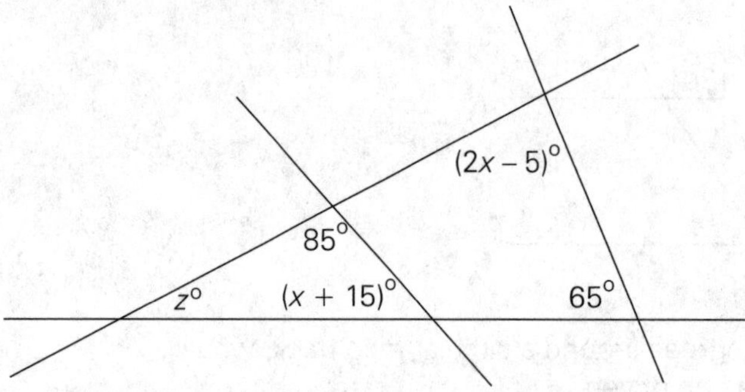


In the figure above, what is the value of $z$ ?

- 40
- 45
- 50
- 55
- 65

## TRIANGLES

A triangle is a three-sided figure that contains three interior angles. The sum of the degree measures of the three angles in a triangle is 180 degrees. Several kinds of triangles appear on the GMAT:

An **equilateral triangle** has three sides that are equal in length. Because the angles opposite equal sides are also equal, all three angles in an equilateral triangle are equal.

**The 180° Rule, Part II**
When a question involving angles has a triangle or several triangles in it, remember that the interior angles of a triangle add up to 180 degrees. Apply that rule in every possible way you can. It is one of the things that the GMAT writers love to test most.

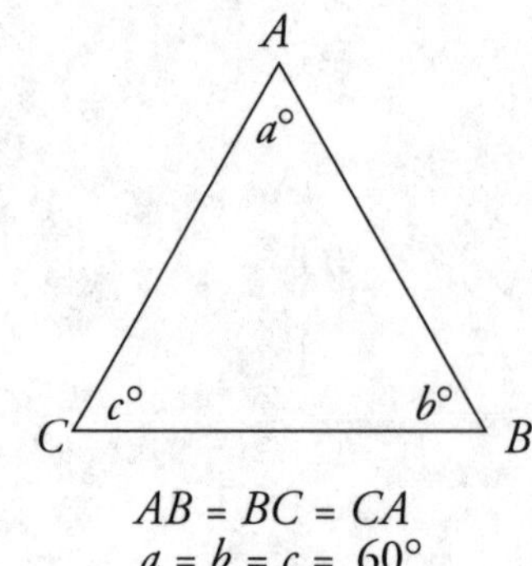


$AB = BC = CA$
$a = b = c = 60°$

An **isosceles triangle** has two sides that are equal in length. The angles opposite the two equal sides are also equal.

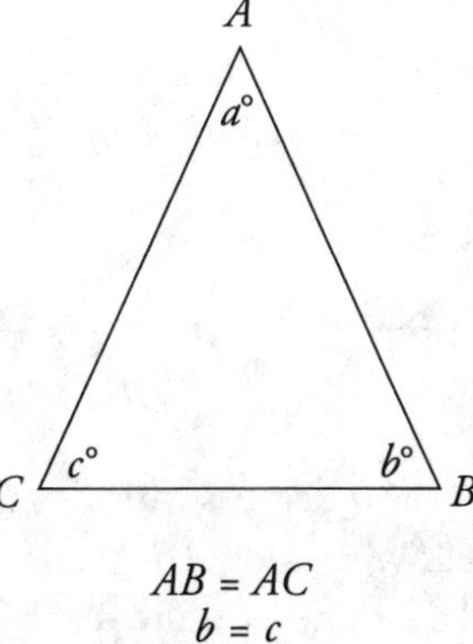


$AB = AC$
$b = c$

A **right triangle** has one interior angle that is equal to 90 degrees. The longest side of a right triangle (the one opposite the 90-degree angle) is called the *hypotenuse*.

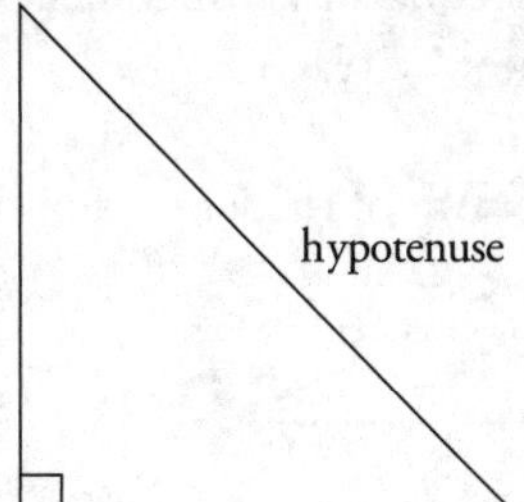

**Triangles**
Triangles are by far the test-writers' favorite geometric shape. If you get stuck on a geometry problem that doesn't have triangles in it, ask yourself: can the figure in this problem be divided into triangles (especially right triangles) that I can work with? This will sometimes be the key to the solution.

## Everything Else You Need to Know About Triangles

1. The sides of a triangle are in the same proportion as its angles. For example, in the triangle below, which is the longest side?

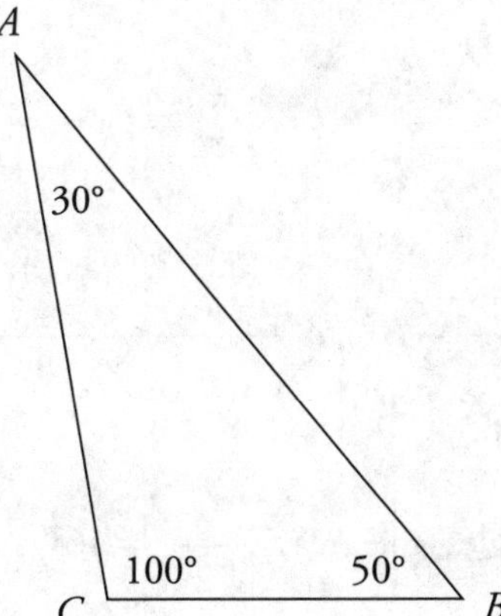


The longest side is opposite the largest angle. The longest side in the triangle above is *AB*, which is opposite the largest angle of 100 degrees. The next longest side is *AC*.

2. One side of a triangle can never be longer than the sum of the lengths of the other two sides of the triangle, or less than their difference. Why? Look at the diagrams below:

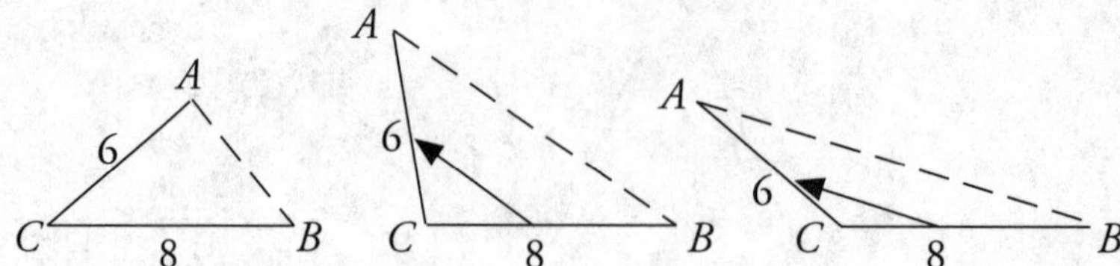


At the point where angle $ACB = 180$ degrees, this figure ceases to be a triangle. Angle $ACB$ becomes 180 degrees when side $AB$ equals the sum of the other two sides, in this case $6 + 8$. Side $AB$ can never quite reach 14.

By the same token, if we make angle $ACB$ smaller and smaller, at some point, when angle $ACB = 0$ degrees, the figure also ceases to be a triangle. Angle $ACB$ becomes 0 degrees when side $AB$ equals the difference of the other two sides, in this case $8 - 6$. So $AB$ can never quite reach 2.

3. The *perimeter* of a triangle is the sum of the lengths of the three sides.

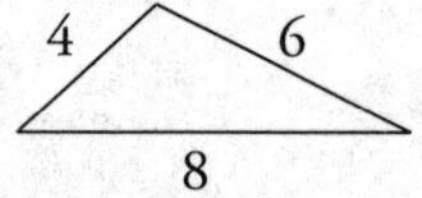


perimeter = 18

4. The *area* of a triangle is equal to $\frac{height \times base}{2}$. By definition, the base and height must be perpendicular to each other.

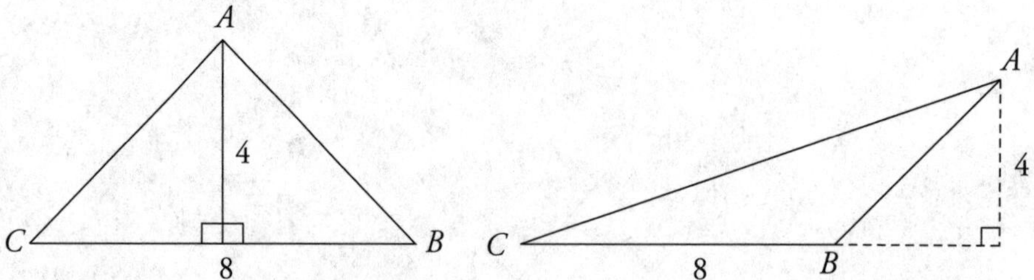


In both of the above triangles, the area $= \frac{4 \times 8}{2} = 16$.

In a right triangle, the height also happens to be one of the sides of the triangle:

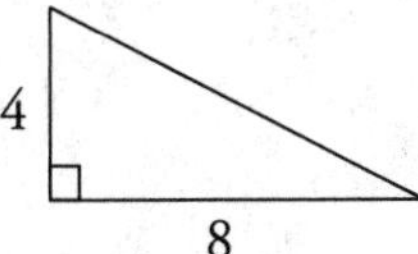


5. Don't expect triangles to be right side up:

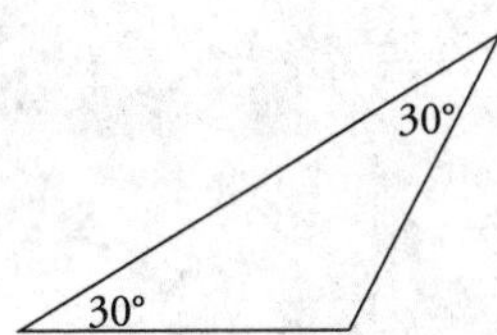


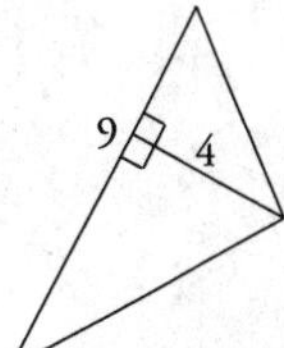


This is an isosceles triangle.

The area of this triangle is $A = \frac{9 \times 4}{2}$, or 18.

6. The degree measurement of an exterior angle that is adjacent to an angle of a triangle is equal to the sum of the degree measures of the other two angles of the triangle. This is called the **exterior angle rule**. Let's take a look at the rule using a diagram.

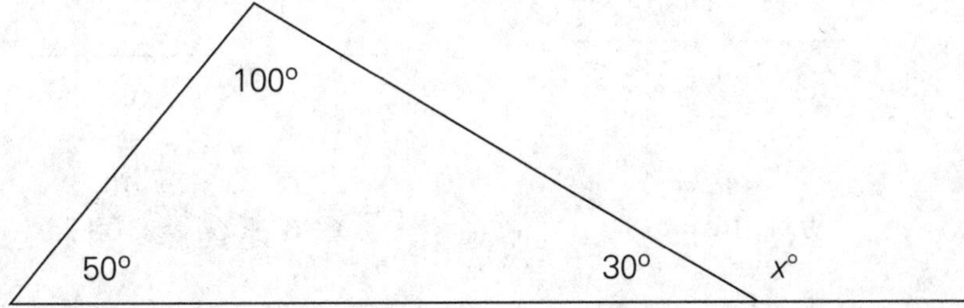


In the figure above, the angle $x$ is an exterior angle that is adjacent to an angle of a triangle. According to the exterior angle rule of triangles, the degree measure of $x$ is equal to the sum of the two angles of the triangle that angle $x$ is not adjacent to. Therefore, the measure of angle $x$ is $100 + 50 = 150$ degrees.

Another way to think about this is to consider that the degree measure of a line is 180 degrees. Angle $x$ creates a straight line with the 30-degree angle of the triangle. This means the measure of angle $x$ is $180 - 30 = 150$ degrees.

7. In a right triangle, the square of the hypotenuse equals the sum of the squares of the other two sides. In the triangle below:

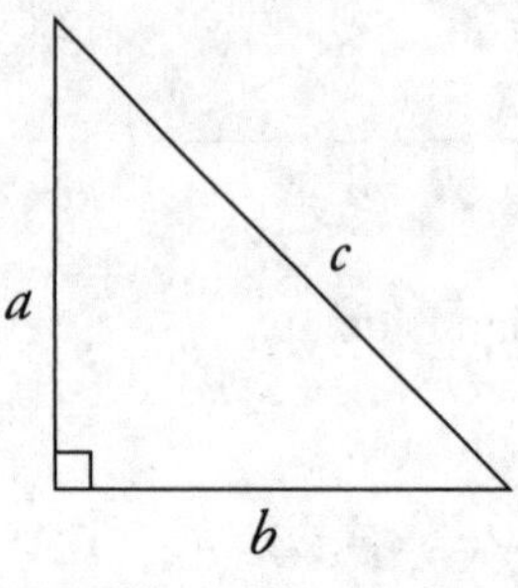


$$a^2 + b^2 = c^2$$

**Pythagoras's Other Theorem**
Pythagoras also developed a theory about the transmigration of souls. So far, this theory has not been proven.

This is called the **Pythagorean Theorem**. The test-writers love to test this theorem, but usually you won't actually have to make use of it if you've memorized a few of the most common right-triangle proportions.

The Pythagorean triangle that comes up most frequently on the GMAT is one that has sides of lengths 3, 4, and 5, or multiples of those numbers. Look at the following examples:

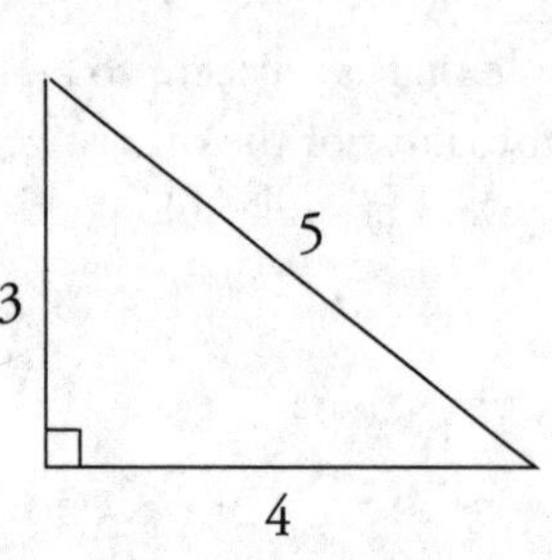


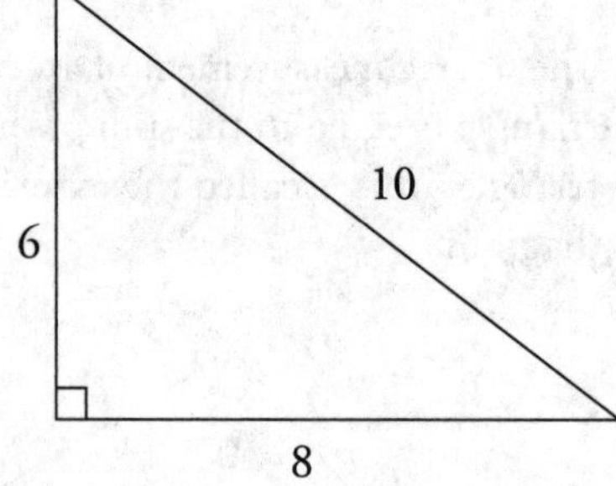


$$3^2 + 4^2 = 5^2$$
$$9 + 16 = 25$$

$$6^2 + 8^2 = 10^2$$
$$36 + 64 = 100$$

**Pythagorean Triples**

The right triangle in the ratio 3:4:5 is the most common Pythagorean triple, but it's not the only one that shows up on the GMAT. Here are the three triples you need to know:

3:4:5
5:12:13
7:24:25

There are two other kinds of right triangles that GMAC loves to test. These are a little complicated to remember, but they come up so often that they're worth memorizing.

8. A right isosceles triangle always has proportions in the ratio $x{:}x{:}x\sqrt{2}$. This kind of triangle may also be referred to as a 45-45-90 right triangle.

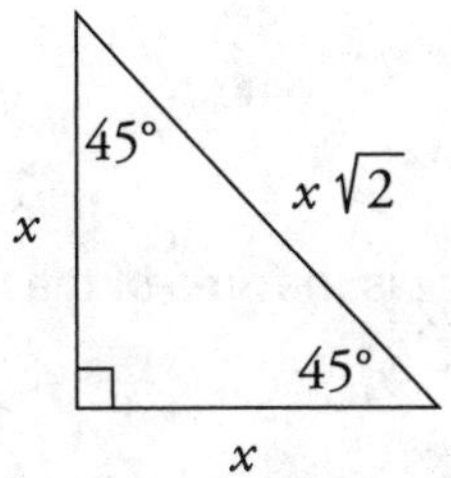


For example:

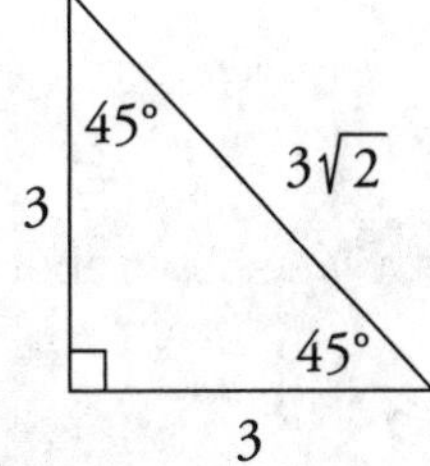


9. The second special right triangle is called the **30-60-90** right triangle. The ratio between the lengths of the sides in a 30-60-90 triangle is constant. If you know the length of any of the sides, you can find the lengths of the others. The ratio of the sides is always $x{:}x\sqrt{3}{:}2x$.

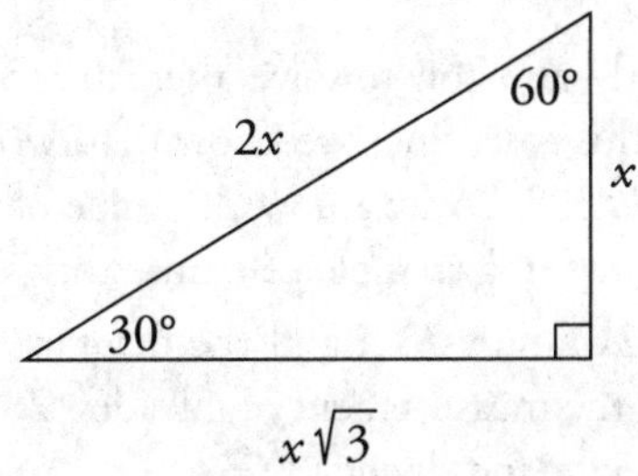


**How to Label a 30-60-90 Triangle**

Remembering how to label the 1, 2, $\sqrt{3}$ sides of a 30-60-90 triangle is easy if you remind yourself that the largest side goes opposite the largest angle and the smallest side opposite the smallest angle, *and* if you remind yourself that $\sqrt{3}$ is roughly 1.7, okay?

That is, if the shortest side is length $x$, then the hypotenuse is $2x$, and the remaining side is $x\sqrt{3}$.

Try this problem:

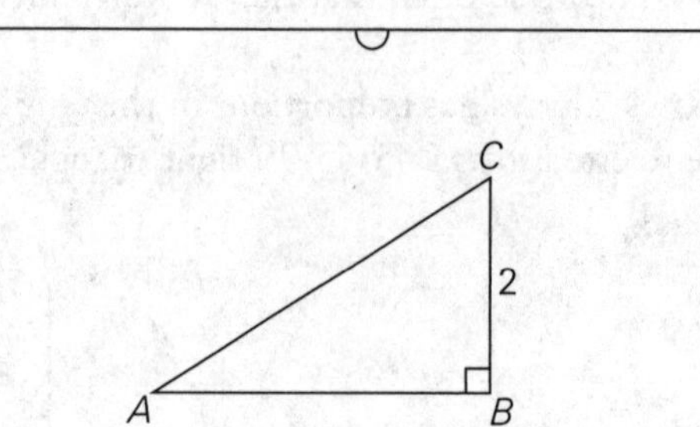


In $\Delta ABC$ shown above, if $\angle CAB$ equals 30°, then what is the area of the triangle?

- 2
- $2\sqrt{2}$
- $2\sqrt{3}$
- $3\sqrt{2}$
- 4

### Here's How to Crack It

As with all geometry problems, even if you aren't exactly sure how to solve, there may be something you can do to get started—always half the battle. In this case, since we know that $\Delta ABC$ is a right triangle, and the problem tells you that $\angle CAB$ equals 30°, do we know the value of $\angle ACB$? We do—it must be 60° (since there are a total of 180 degrees in a triangle). Because this is a 30-60-90 triangle (which always has sides in proportion of $x$, $2x$, and $x\sqrt{3}$), and the diagram gives us the measurement of one of those sides, we actually know the measurement of all sides: $2, 2\sqrt{3}$, and 4. To find the area, we simply multiply the base by the height and divide by 2:

$A = \dfrac{2 \times 2\sqrt{3}}{2} = 2\sqrt{3}$, and the answer is (C).

## DRILL 11 (Triangles)

Find the value of the variables in the following problems. The answers can be found in Part VII.

1. 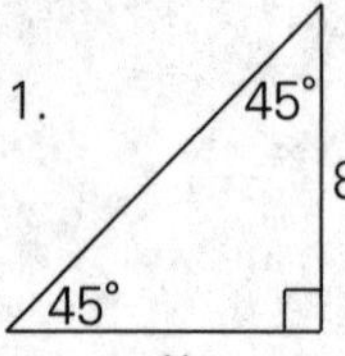


2. 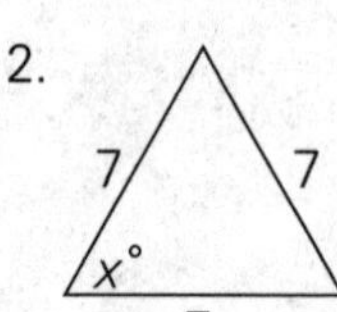


3. 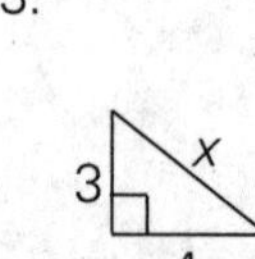

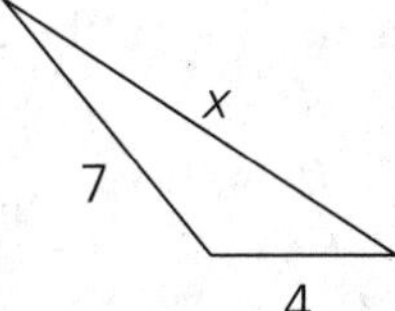


4. What value must $x$ be less than in the triangle above? What value must $x$ be greater than?

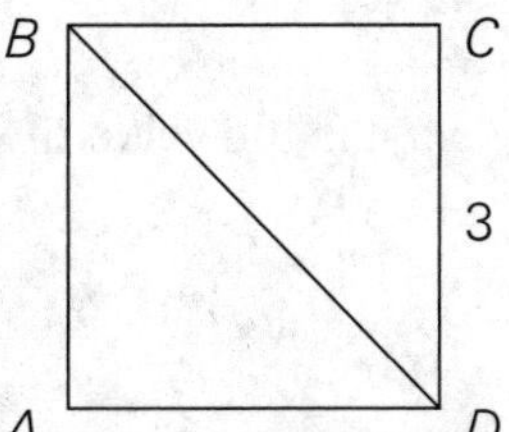


5. In square *ABCD* above, what is the length of line segment *BD* ?

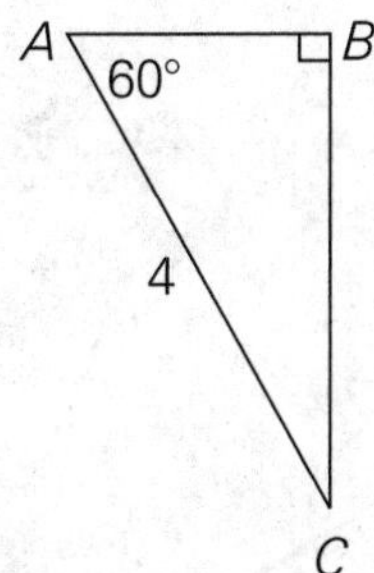


6. In the triangle above, what is the length of the line segment *BC* ?

A real GMAT triangle problem might look like this:

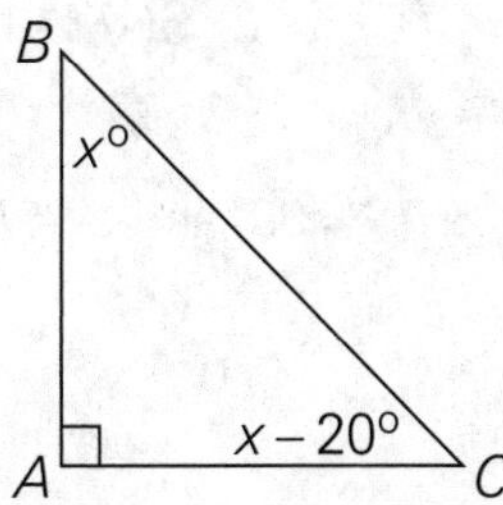


7. In the figure above, what is the ratio of the measure of angle *A* to the measure of angle *C* ?

- 1 to 3
- 2 to 1
- 3 to 1
- 9 to 3.5
- 9 to 5.5

You might see a Data Sufficiency problem like this on the GMAT:

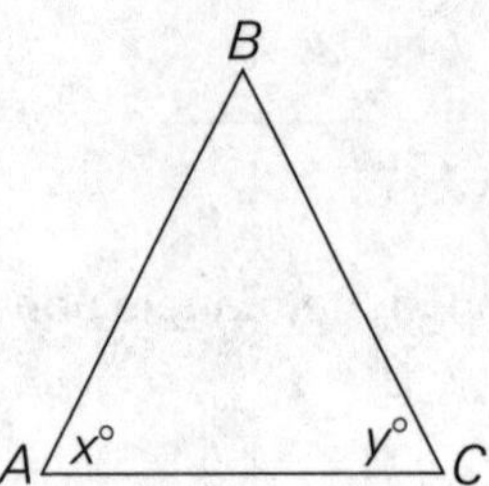


8. In triangle *ABC* shown above, what is the value of $x$ ?

(1) $y = 80$

(2) $AB = BC$

## Challenge Question #11

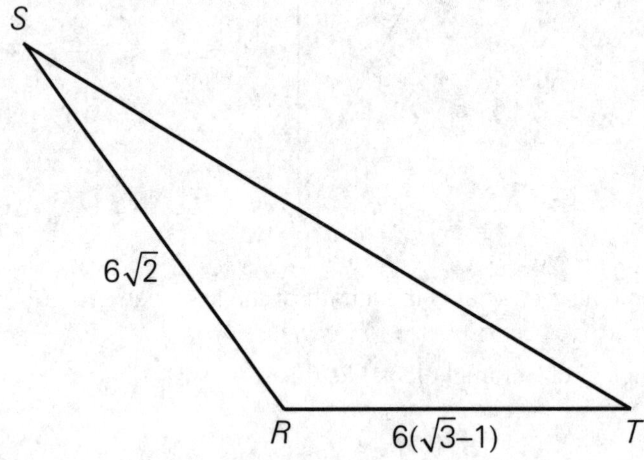


In triangle *RST*, shown above, $\angle RTS = 30°$ and $\angle RST = 15°$. What is the length of *ST* ?

- 6
- 12
- 24
- 36
- 72

## CIRCLES

A line segment whose endpoints lie on a circle is called a **chord**. The distance from the center of the circle to any point on the circle is called the **radius**. The distance from one point on the circle through the center of the circle to another point on the circle is called the **diameter**. The diameter is equal to twice the radius.

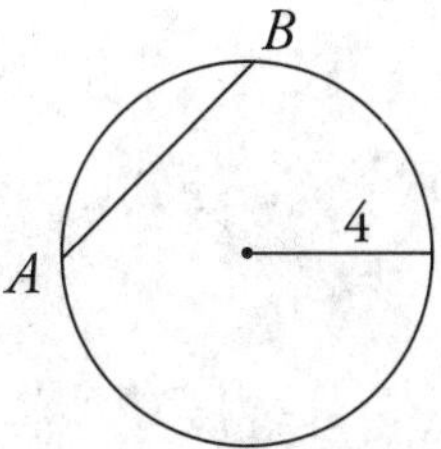


radius = 4

diameter = 8

*AB* is a chord.

**A Perfect Circle**
During the 14th century, Pope Boniface VIII commissioned artists to send samples of their work to demonstrate their abilities. One of the artists, Giotto, responded by dipping his paintbrush in red ink and in one continuous stroke created "a perfect circle." When the pope saw it, he instantly perceived that Giotto surpassed all other painters of his time.

The **circumference** (the length of the entire outer edge of the circle) = $2\pi r$ or $\pi d$.

The rounded portion of the circle between points *A* and *B* is called an **arc**.

The **area** of a circle = $\pi r^2$.

A circle cut in half by a diameter is called a **semicircle**.

A triangle is said to be **inscribed** inside a semicircle when one of its sides is the diameter of the circle itself, with the two other sides meeting at any point on the circle. A triangle inscribed inside a semicircle is always a **right triangle**.

Let's try a circle problem:

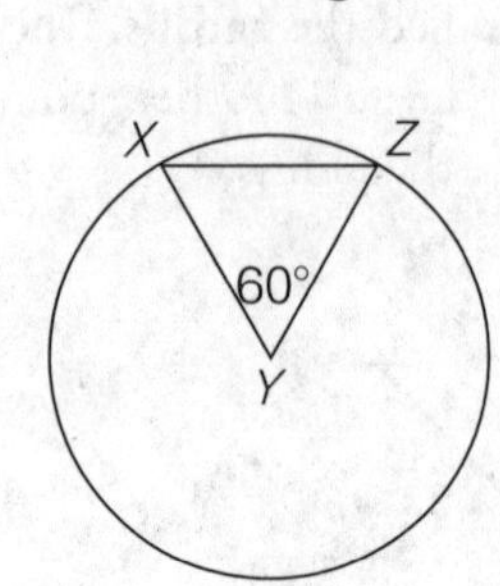


If the circle above has center $Y$ and area $4\pi$, then what is the perimeter of triangle $XYZ$ ?

- 2
- $2\pi$
- 4
- 6
- $6\pi$

### Here's How to Crack It

As always, the solution to this problem will probably only become apparent once you've started doing the problem. The only information you've been given is the area of the circle, $4\pi$. Since the formula for the area of a circle is $\pi r^2$, set that equal to $4\pi$. Can you figure out what $r$ equals? That's right, 2. And since both sides $XY$ and $YZ$ are radii of the circle, they must both equal 2. To find the perimeter of the triangle, the last thing we need to do is find the length of $XZ$. You might not think that you know what $XZ$ equals, but the diagram tells us that angle $XYZ$ equals 60 degrees. Since we know sides $XY$ and $YZ$ are equal, that means that this triangle must be equilateral: all three sides have the same length, 2. Therefore, the perimeter of triangle $XYZ$ is 6, and the answer is (D).

## Central and Inscribed Angles

The central angle of a circle is the angle that is formed by two radii and the vertex at the center of the circle. In the circle below, angle $AOB$ with degree measure $x$ is a central angle of the circle with center $O$.

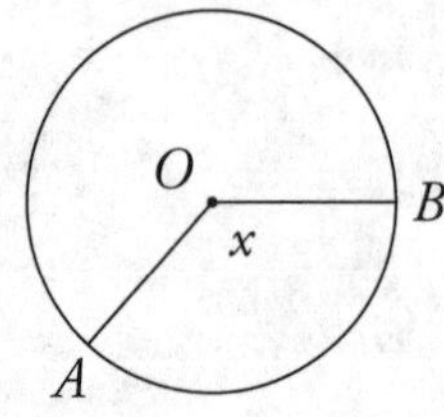

The proportion of the central angle and the total degrees in the circle is the same as the proportion of the arc and the circumference of the circle. In the circle above, if the degree measure of angle $x$ is one-sixth the total degree measure of the circle, then arc $AB$ is one-sixth the length of the circumference. Similarly, the area contained within the segment sectioned off by angle $AOB$ has the same proportion to the entire area of the circle as the degree measure of the central angle does to the total degrees in the circle.

The inscribed angle of a circle is an angle that has a vertex "on" the circle, typically formed by two intersecting chords. In the figure below, angle $ABC$ with degree measure $x$ is an inscribed angle on the circle with center $O$.

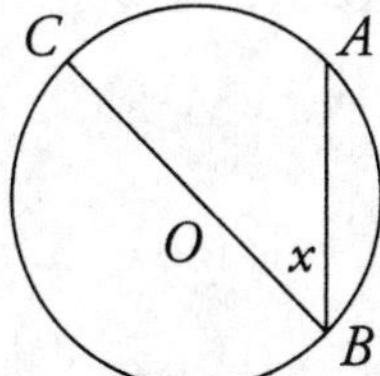


There are a handful of quirks about inscribed angles. First, an inscribed angle of a semicircle is a right angle, as shown in the figure below.

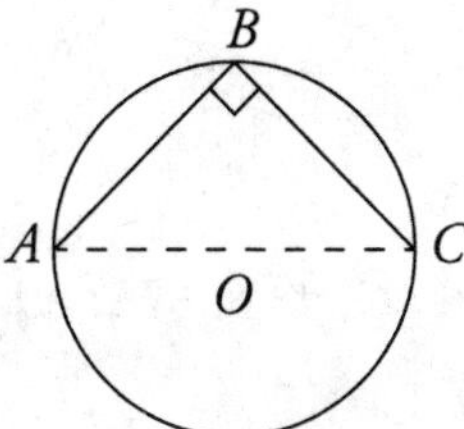


Secondly, inscribed angles that intercept the same arc are congruent. In the figure below, angle $ACB$ is equal to angle $ADB$.

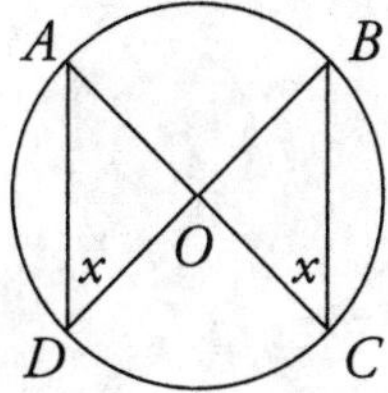

## DRILL 12 (Circles)

Answer the following questions. The answers can be found in Part VII.

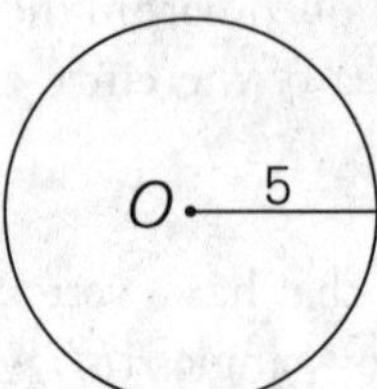


1. In the circle above with center $O$, what is the area of the circle? What is the circumference?

2. If the area of a circle is $36\pi$, what is the circumference?

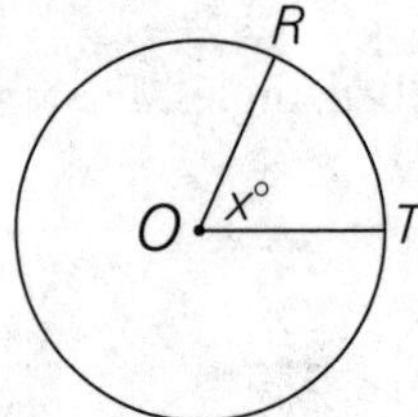


3. In the circle above with center $O$, if arc $RT$ is equal to $\frac{1}{6}$ of the circumference, what is the value of $x$ ?

A real GMAT circle problem might look like this:

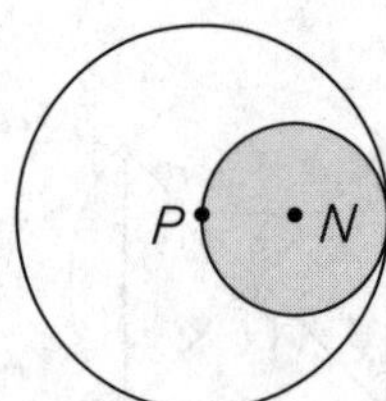


4. In the figure above, $P$ is the center of the larger circle, and $N$ is the center of the smaller, shaded circle. If the radius of the smaller circle is 5, what is the area of the unshaded region?

   - $100\pi$
   - $75\pi$
   - $25\pi$
   - $20\pi$
   - $10\pi$

You might see a Data Sufficiency problem like this on the GMAT:

5. What is the area of circle *P* ?

   (1) The diameter of circle *Q* is 6.

   (2) The radius of circle *Q* is twice the radius of circle *P*.

## RECTANGLES, SQUARES, AND OTHER FOUR-SIDED OBJECTS

A four-sided figure is called a **quadrilateral**. The perimeter of any four-sided object is the sum of the lengths of its sides. A **rectangle** is a quadrilateral whose four interior angles are each equal to 90 degrees. Opposite sides of a rectangle are always equal.

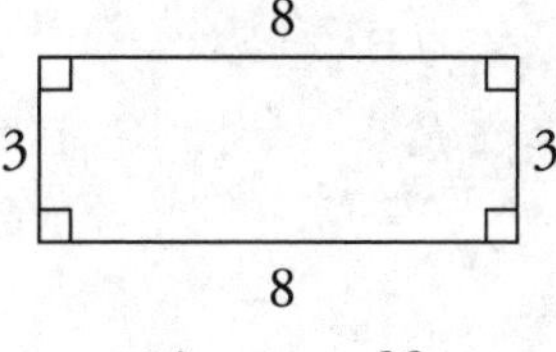

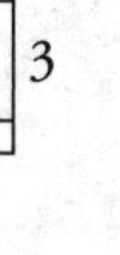


perimeter = 22

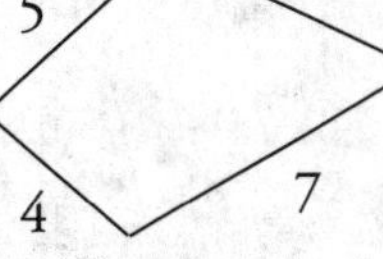


perimeter = 22

The area of a rectangle is *length* × *width*. The area of the rectangle above is therefore 3 × 8, or 24.

A **square** is a rectangle whose four sides are all equal in length. The *perimeter* of a square is therefore just four times the length of one side. The *area* of a square is the *length* of one of its sides squared. For example:

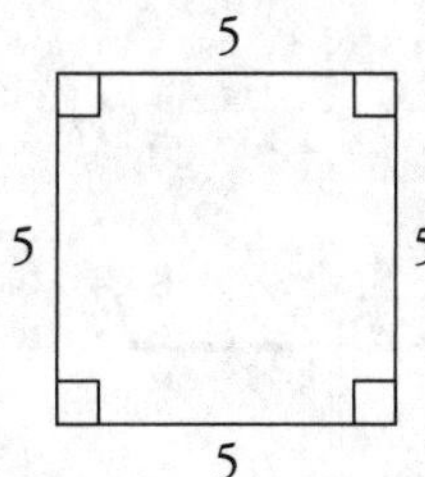


perimeter = 4 × 5 = 20

area = 5 × 5 = 25

## Parallelograms

Parallelograms on the GMAT often look like this:

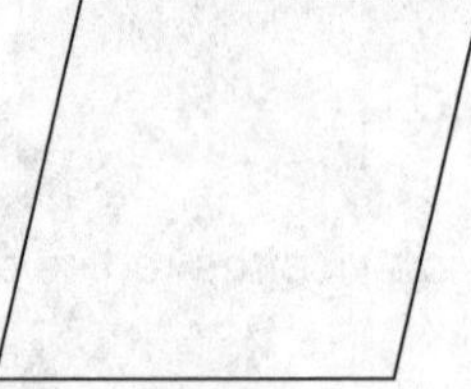

The sides of a parallelogram that are opposite each other are parallel. Finding the perimeter and area of a parallelogram requires the height of the figure. The height of the figure is used to determine the area of the figure or the length of the slanted side of the figure.

To find the area of a parallelogram, it is necessary to determine the height by dropping a line from one of the corners straight down, as shown by the dotted line below:

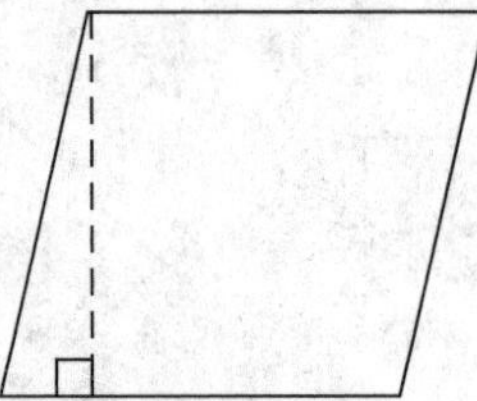

The dotted line in the figure above is the height of the figure. Where the dotted line intersects with the base is a right angle. To find the area of the parallelogram, multiply the height by the length of one of the bases. The equation for the area of a parallelogram is:

$$Area = base \times height$$

The base is the top or the bottom of the figure, as indicated by the bolded lines below:

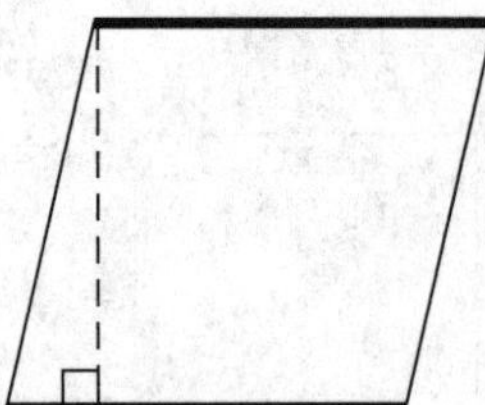

The height of a parallelogram creates a right triangle with one of the sides of the parallelogram. If the parallelogram provides the length of the slanted side of the figure and the length of the base of the right triangle, you can solve for the height of the parallelogram by using the Pythagorean Theorem. The figure below has sides labeled $a$, $b$, and $c$ to represent the different variables of the Pythagorean Theorem.

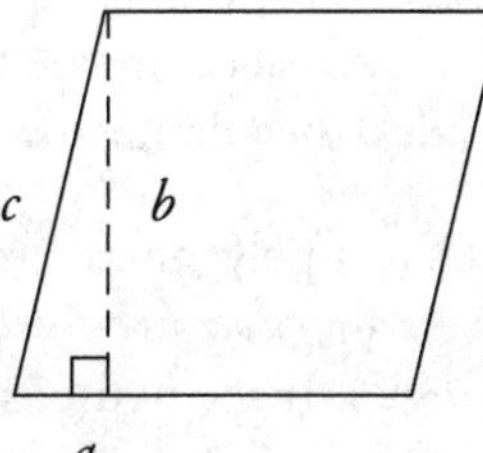


Solving for the perimeter of a parallelogram follows a similar pattern. You can use the height of the figure and the base of the triangle created by the height to solve for the length of the slanted edge.

## Trapezoids

A trapezoid is a quadrilateral with only one set of parallel sides. A trapezoid could look like this:

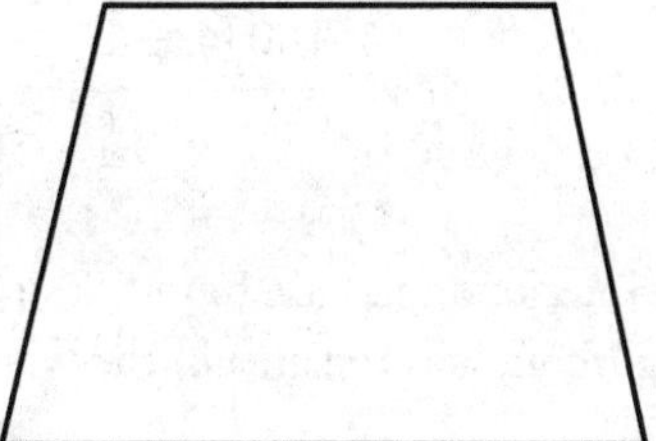

In the case of the figure above, the parallel sides are the top and the bottom of the figure. The GMAT tests the area and perimeter of trapezoids. The most effective way to solve for the area of the figure is to split the trapezoid into more familiar shapes and solve for the area of each of those shapes individually. For instance, the trapezoid above can be split into two right triangles and a rectangle:

Anytime there is an unfamiliar figure, look for ways to split that figure up into more familiar shapes.

You can then solve for the area of each of these familiar shapes individually and add them together to get the area of the trapezoid.

Finding the perimeter of a trapezoid follows a similar pattern to finding that of a parallelogram. Finding the lengths of the sides typically involves using the Pythagorean Theorem.

## Polygons

Polygons are figures like pentagons, hexagons, and octagons. A polygon is a figure with at least three straight sides and angles, and typically five or more. For the purposes of this discussion, we are going to focus on polygons with more than four sides. The GMAT sometimes refers to these figures by name, such as labeling a figure a hexagon. Other times, the GMAT mentions the number of sides of the figure, instead of the name of the figure. Typically, if the GMAT references the name of the figure, the name is accompanied by a figure. However, if the GMAT refers to the figure by the number of sides, they do not always show a figure.

Sometimes the GMAT refers to a polygon as a *regular* figure. For instance, they may reference a *regular pentagon* or a *regular five-sided figure.* The word *regular* means the figure has equal sides and angles. If the figure is not regular, then the lengths of the sides and the angles are not necessarily equal.

This equation actually works for any polygon, including triangles, rectangles, and squares. However, it is best to commit to memory the total angle measure for triangles, rectangles, and squares.

One kind of problem asked about polygons involves determining the degree measure of the angles inside the figure. The equation for determining the measure of the total angles in a polygon is:

$$180(n-2)$$

where $n$ is the number of sides in the figure. By extension, if you want to find out the measure of a single interior angle in a regular polygon, the equation is:

Polygons that are not regular polygons cannot use this equation. A regular polygon has an even distribution of the total angle of the figure between all of its sides because all side lengths are equal.

$$\frac{180\left(n-2\right)}{n}$$

Once the measures of interior angles are found, it's possible to determine several different measures of the figure such as the area of the whole figure or the area of a section.

## Area of Figures with More Than Four Sides

Solving for the area of a figure with more than four sides can be tricky. Take a look at the following regular six-sided figure:

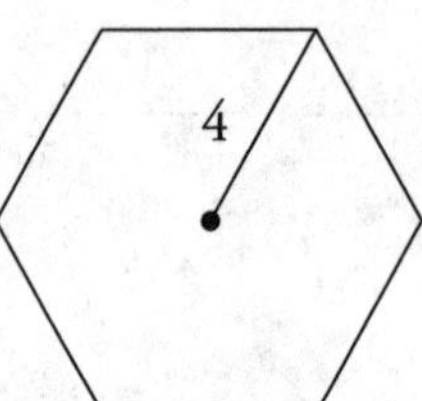


How would you go about solving for the area of the entire figure?

This process begins by realizing that the straight-line distance between the center of the figure and each of the corners of the figure is the same. This is true of all regular polygons. A triangle with two equal sides can be created using this piece of knowledge.

Because the two lengths inside the figure are equal, the angles opposite both lengths are equal.

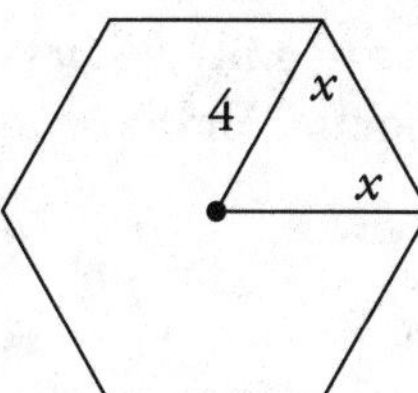


The central angle created by the intersection of the two lengths inside the figure is a portion of the entire area of the figure. There are 6 sides to the figure, so the entire area is 180(6 – 2) = 180(4) = 720. The degree measure of each interior angle is $\frac{720}{6} = 120$. If the figure is split up into 6 equal triangles, a total of 12 angles is created. Each 120-degree angle is split in half. Therefore, each interior angle is 60 degrees, which means the third angle is also 60 degrees since a triangle has a total of 180 degrees. If the triangle has three equal angles, it is equilateral and also has three equal sides, so all sides are 4.

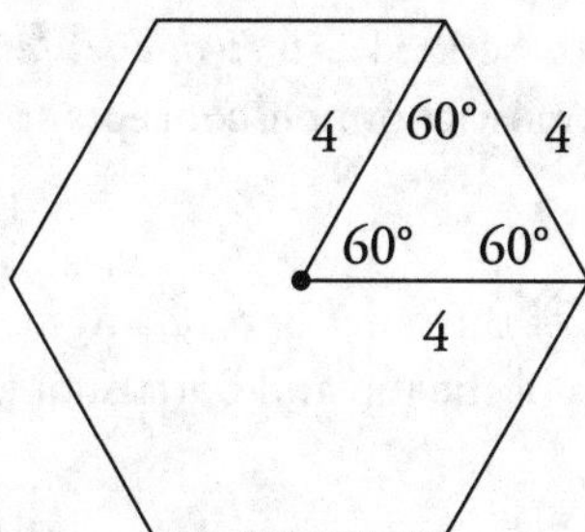


Draw in the height of the triangle that splits the base in half and this creates a 30-60-90 degree right triangle with side lengths $2 : 2\sqrt{3} : 4$. The area of this triangle is $\frac{1}{2}(4)(2\sqrt{3}) = 4\sqrt{3}$. Since there are six equal triangles in all, multiply the area of this triangle by 6. So, the area of the whole figure is $24\sqrt{3}$.

# 3D FIGURES

3D figures on the GMAT typically come in one of two forms: cylinders or rectangular solids. In order to answer most questions regarding 3D figures, you'll need to know how to calculate the surface area and volume of each figure, and how to find the length of the diagonal of a rectangular solid or cube.

## Cylinder

When represented visually, cylinders look like some variation of the following:

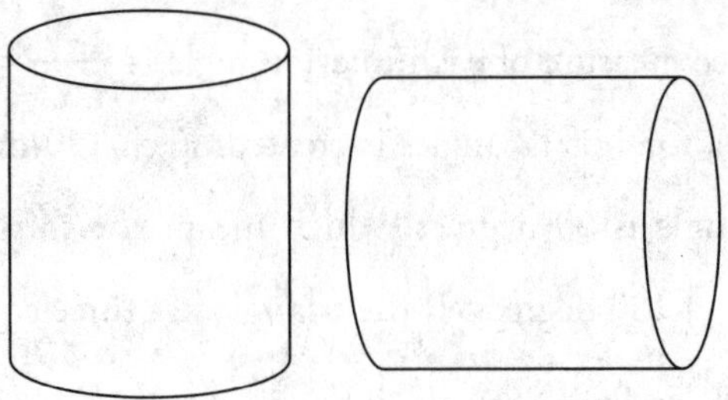

A cylinder may also be described as a *right circular cylinder.* No matter how a cylinder is represented, the most common concepts to test about this figure are surface area and volume.

> The GMAT also uses the concept of circular cylinders in word problems and refers to them as a word that describes a cylinder, such as "tanks," "circular cylindrical tank," "tubes," and "pipes."

Surface area is the area of the outer part of a figure. For example, the surface area of a can of soup is the area of the top and bottom of the can plus the area of the curved sides of the can.

Volume is the amount of space that a substance could occupy. The volume of a can of soup is the amount of soup that can fit inside the can.

### Surface Area

The surface area of a cylinder is calculated by the equation:

$$\textit{Surface Area} = 2\pi r(\textit{height}) + 2(\pi r^2)$$

This equation looks like a lot. But, let's break it down into its individual components.

The surface area of a cylinder is the sum of the area of the top of the cylinder, the area of the bottom of the cylinder, and the area of the curved side of the cylinder. The curved side of the cylinder is actually a rectangle that has been curved. Imagine taking a rectangular piece of paper and rolling it so two opposing edges now touch. Alternatively, imagine what would result if you removed the top and bottom from a can of soup, cut the resulting piece straight down just one side, and flattened it out. The height of the resulting rectangle is the same as the height of the can. However, the length of the rectangle is equal to the circumference of the top or bottom of the can. The circumference of a circle is found by the expression $2\pi r$.

Visually, the length and height of a cylinder can be represented by something like this:

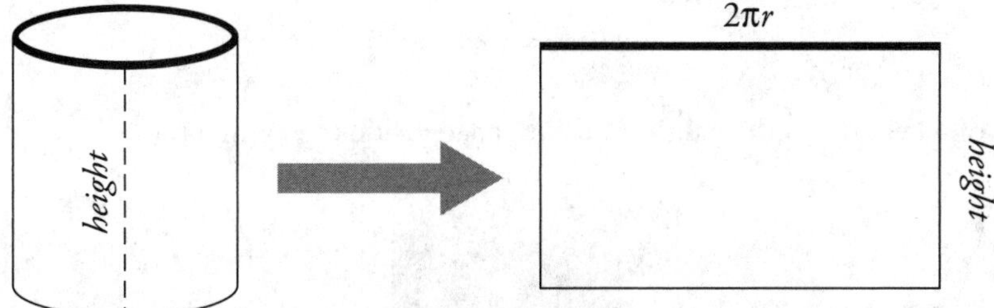


On the GMAT, the area of the top of the cylinder and the area of the bottom of the cylinder are equivalent circles.

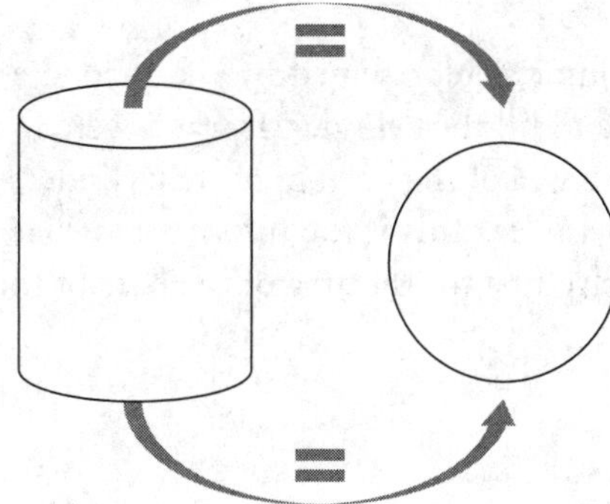


The equation for surface area given above is just the sum of the areas of all these individual components. This can be represented graphically as:

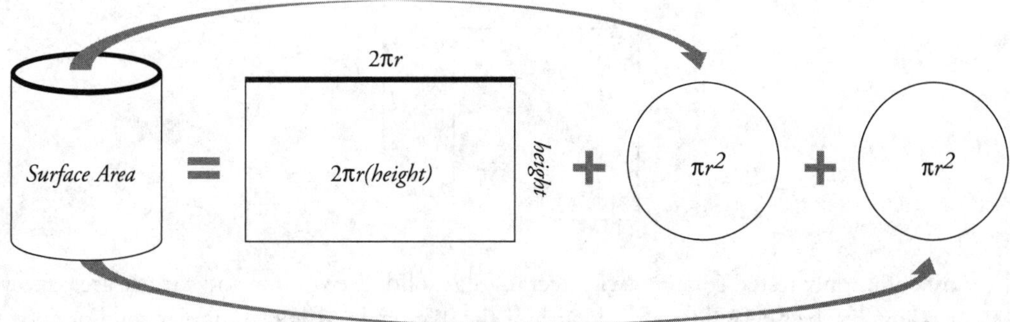


In order to solve for the surface area of a circular cylinder, it is necessary to have, or be able to derive, a value for the radius of the top or bottom of the cylinder as well as the height of the cylinder.

## Volume

The volume of a cylinder is calculated by the equation:

$$Volume = \pi r^2(height)$$

The volume of a cylinder is the value of all the space inside the cylinder.

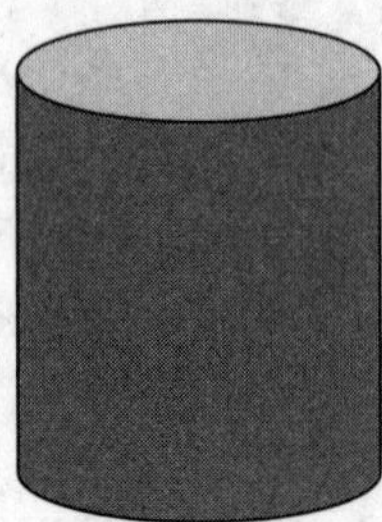

In the cylinder above, the volume is represented by the shaded area. Consider volume as the amount of water it would take to fill the cylinder. If water were to be poured into the cylinder, the water would first fill up the area of the bottom of the cylinder and then fill that area for the entirety of the height of the cylinder. This is the information that the equation for the volume of a cylinder is asking for—solve first for the area of the base of the cylinder and then multiply it by the height.

## Rectangular Solids

When represented visually, rectangular solids or cubes look like this:

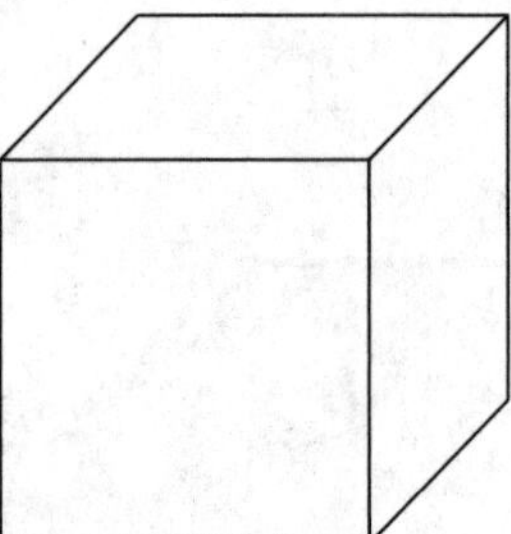

The most commonly tested concepts with rectangular solids are volume and surface area. However, occasionally the GMAT tests the length of the diagonal of the rectangular solid or cube.

Surface area is the area of the outer part of the rectangular solid. This is represented by the area of the top and bottom, front and back, and both sides of the figure.

Volume is the amount of space inside the figure. This is the amount of space that could be occupied by a substance placed inside the rectangular solid.

It is easier to visualize the items required to calculate the surface area and volume by placing dotted lines in the figure to represent the missing edges. This makes it clear that there are 6 faces (flat sides) that create the outside of the figure. The sum of the areas of each of these six sides is the surface area.

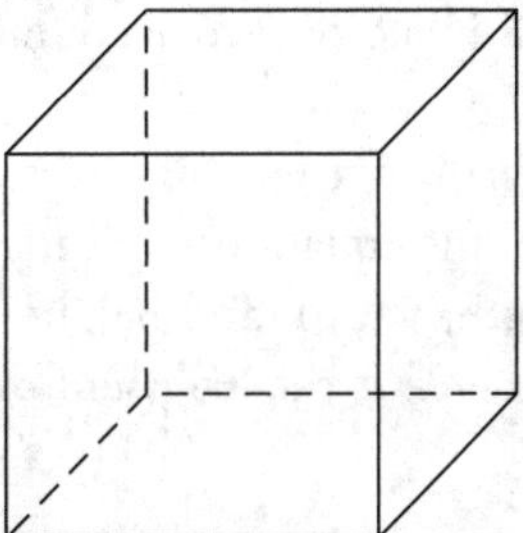

Don't be afraid to draw in these dotted lines on your own figure during the test if it makes it easier to look at.

The diagonal of the rectangular solid or cube is the longest distance between two corners. This is represented by the bold dotted line below.

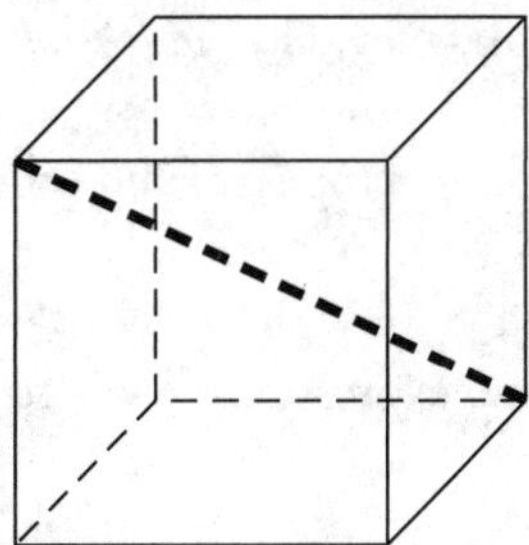

## Surface Area

The surface area of a rectangular solid is calculated via the equation:

$$\textit{Surface Area} = 2(\textit{length} \times \textit{width}) + 2(\textit{length} \times \textit{height}) + 2(\textit{width} \times \textit{height})$$

For a regular rectangular solid, the side lengths are labeled as follows:

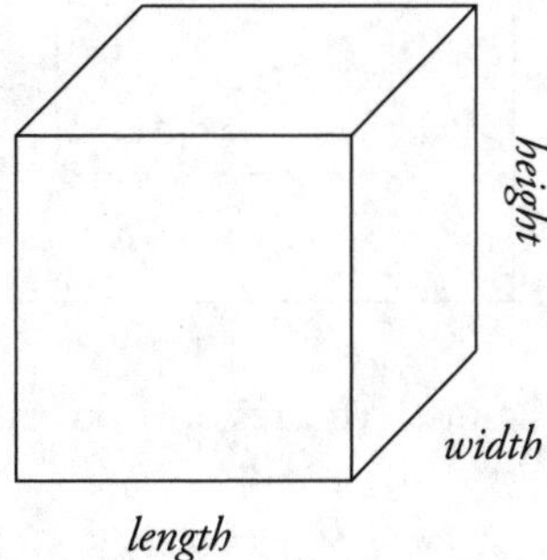


Let's look at each of the components of the equation for surface area independently.

The expression *length* × *width* produces the area for the top or the bottom of the figure. The equation for surface area multiplies this by 2 to represent the area of both the top and bottom of the figure. The expression *length* × *height* represents the area of the front or back of the rectangular solid and this is also multiplied by 2 to represent the front and the back. Finally, the expression *width* × *height* represents the area of one of the sides of the rectangular solid. The product is multiplied by 2 to account for both faces on the sides.

The formula for the surface area of a cube is just the formula for the area of a square multiplied by 6.

Ultimately, the surface area of a rectangular solid or cube is the sum of the areas of the faces. For a cube, this equation is greatly simplified. A cube is a rectangular solid that has equal length, width, and height. To find the surface area of a cube, the expression is $6(s^2)$, where $s$ is the length of one of the edges of the cube.

## Volume

The equation for the volume of a rectangular solid is simpler than that of the surface area of the rectangular solid. The equation for the volume of a rectangular solid is:

$$Volume = length \times width \times height$$

Therefore, calculating the volume of a rectangular solid only involves figuring out the values of the length, width, and height.

The volume of a cube is found by the expression $s^3$, where $s$ is the value for either the length, width, or height of the cube.

## Diagonal

In the figure below, the diagonal of a rectangular solid is depicted by the bold dotted line. The diagonal of a rectangular solid is the straight-line distance between points *A* and *B*. This is the longest length inside a rectangular solid.

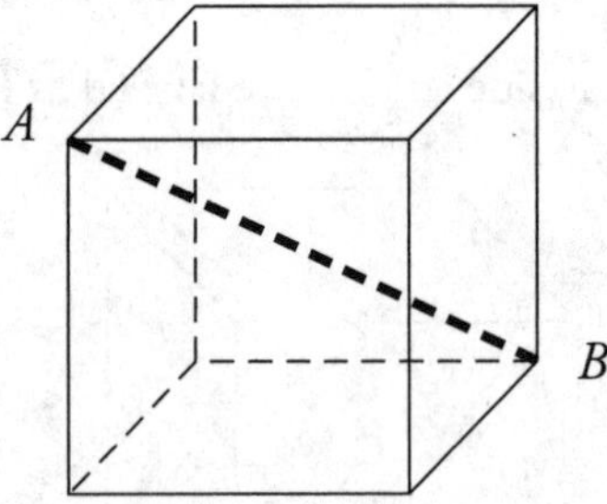


Solving for the distance between *A* and *B* requires only one equation. The equation is:

$$a^2 + b^2 + c^2 = d^2$$

In the equation, $d$ is the value of the diagonal distance while $a$, $b$, and $c$ are the dimensions of the rectangular solid. If you're familiar with right triangles, this equation will remind you a lot of the Pythagorean Theorem. In fact, this equation is called the Super Pythagorean Theorem.

## COORDINATE PLANE

In a coordinate system, the horizontal line is called the ***x*-axis** and the vertical line is called the ***y*-axis**. The four sections of the coordinate plane formed by the intersection of these axes are called **quadrants**. While it is not strictly necessary to know the ordering of the quadrants for most coordinate plane problems, occasionally the quadrant numbers are asked about directly or mentioned as a compass on a question. So being familiar with them is a good idea. The point where the axes intersect is called the **origin** and its coordinates are (0, 0). This is what it looks like:

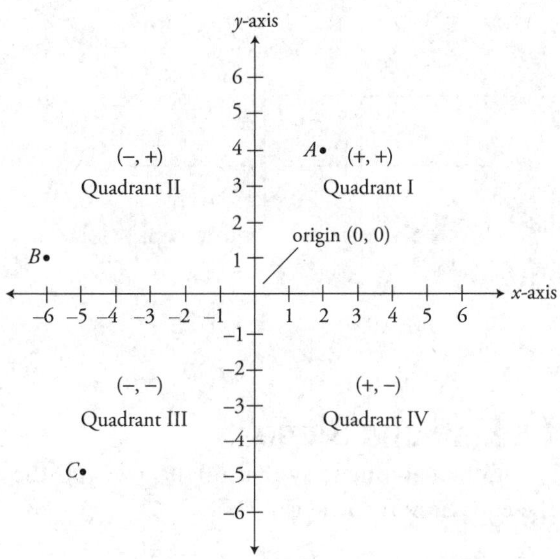


To express any point in the coordinate system, you first give the horizontal value, which is the value of the point associated with the *x*-axis. Next, you provide the vertical value, which is the value of the point associated with the *y*-axis. This creates the coordinates of the point, or (*x*, *y*). In the diagram above, point *A* can be described by the coordinates (2, 4). That is, the point is two spaces to the right of the origin and four spaces above the origin. Point *B* is described by the coordinates (–6, 1). That is, it is six spaces to the left and one space above the origin. What are the coordinates of point *C*?

The coordinate plane is often used to test shapes drawn onto the plane, such as circles, triangles, or rectangles. However, information about lines found on the plane, such as intercepts, the equation of a line, slope, points on a line, and perpendicular and parallel lines is also fair game for the GMAT.

In case you're curious, the coordinates of point *C* are (–5, –5)

## Intercepts

The ***x*-intercept** and ***y*-intercept** are the points at which a line on the coordinate plane crosses the *x*-axis or *y*-axis, respectively. The point at which a line crosses the *x*-axis happens when the coordinate of the point has a *y*-value of 0. The point at which a line crosses the *y*-axis happens when the coordinate of the point has an *x*-value of 0. Therefore, in order to determine the *x*-intercept or *y*-intercept, find the value of the *x*- or *y*-coordinate when the *y*- or *x*-coordinate is equal to 0.

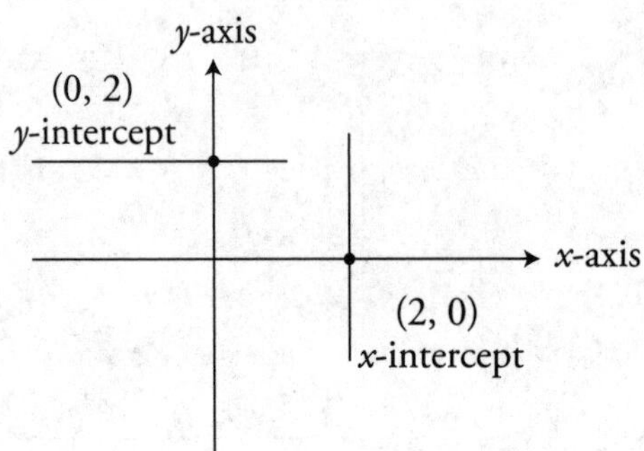


## The Equation of a Line and Slope

Trickier questions involving the coordinate system might give you the equation for a line on the coordinate plane. The **equation of a line** is:

$$y = mx + b$$

Sometimes on the GMAT, *m* is written instead as *a*, as in $y = ax + nm$. If you see this, don't worry. Nothing has changed about the equation for the line or the slope if *m* is written as *a*.

In this equation *x* and *y* are both points on the line, *b* stands for the *y*-intercept, and *m* is the slope of the line. **Slope** is defined as the vertical change divided by the horizontal change, often called "rise over the run" or "the change in *y* over the change in *x*."

$$Slope = \frac{rise}{run} = \frac{y_2 - y_1}{x_2 - x_1}$$

Slope can be any number, positive or negative, and this designation dictates how a line appears on the coordinate plane. A line with a positive slope trends upwards from Quadrant III to Quadrant I and a line with a negative slope trends downwards from Quadrant II to Quadrant IV.

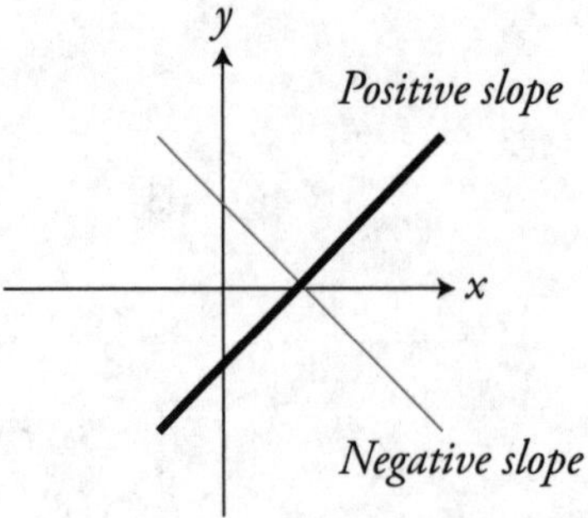

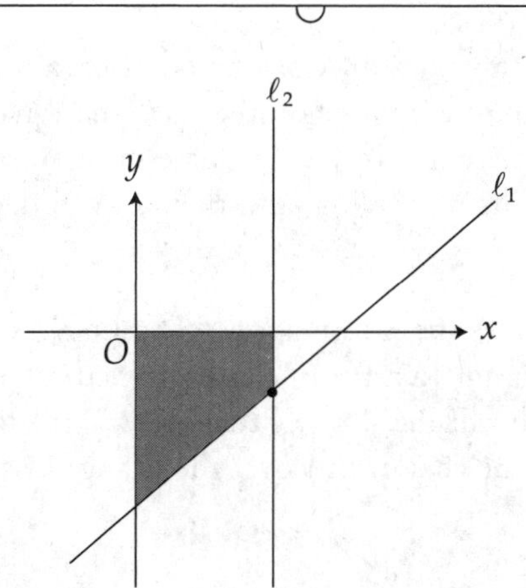


In the coordinate plane above, if the equation of $\ell_1$ is $y = x - 3$ and the equation of $\ell_2$ is $x = 2$, then what is the area of the shaded region?

- 3
- 4
- $3\sqrt{2}$
- 4.5
- 5

### Here's How to Crack It

First, draw your own coordinate axes. The equation for $\ell_1$ is $y = x - 3$, which means that the $y$-intercept is $-3$ and the slope is 1. That means the bottommost point of the large triangle is point (0, −3), and the rightmost point of the large triangle is (3, 0). What we have here is an upside-down right triangle with base 3 and height 3. The area of this entire triangle is $\frac{b \times h}{2}$ or $\frac{9}{2}$, which is (D), but we aren't done yet. Now we have to find the area of the small triangle and subtract it from the area of the large triangle. What remains will be the shaded region.

The equation for $\ell_2$ is $x = 2$, which means that $\ell_2$ is a vertical line running parallel to the $y$-axis. The small triangle therefore must also be an upside-down right triangle. Its base is 1 (from point (2, 0) to point (3, 0)). Eyeballing it, you might decide that its height is 1 too. The way to know for sure is to realize that these two right triangles (the small one and the large one) share an angle formed by the $x$-axis and $\ell_1$. The large triangle is isosceles, so its angles must measure 90-45-45. And since the small triangle shares one of the large triangle's 45-degree angles, we know that the small triangle's third angle must be 45 degrees as well. That means that the small triangle is an isosceles triangle, too, and that its height equals 1, the length of its base. Equipped with this information, we can calculate that the small triangle's area is $\frac{1}{2}$. Thus, the area of the shaded region is $\frac{9}{2} - \frac{1}{2}$, or 4. The correct answer is (B).

## Points on a Line

If the problem provides two points on a line, or one point on a line and the slope, it is possible to determine the location of other points on the line. The equation of a line can be used, in combination with the information provided, to determine missing points. Typically, the GMAT provides one of the points on the line and then asks to determine either the *x*- or *y*-coordinate of a missing point.

For instance, if a question provides the information that a line passes through the origin and has a slope of 3, you could determine that the line also passes through the point (1, 3). You can do this by setting up a proportion. If the slope of the line is 3, the line passes through the origin, and the slope of the line is the change in *y* over the change in *x*, then the following equation can be written:

$$\frac{y_2 - 0}{x_2 - 0} = 3$$

The slope can be rewritten as $\frac{3}{1}$. If you solve for the slope, you determine that $y_2 = 3$ and $x_2 = 1$. The value of the missing point can be any $(x, y)$ combination that results in a value of 3 for the expression $\frac{y}{x}$. Alternatively, if a problem provides to you two points on a line, it is possible to find a third point. Use the two points to determine the slope and then use one of the points and the slope in the same manner shown above.

## Perpendicular and Parallel Lines

**Perpendicular lines** are lines with slopes that are negative reciprocals of each other. These lines intersect at a right angle. **Parallel lines** are lines with the same slope. Parallel lines will never intersect.

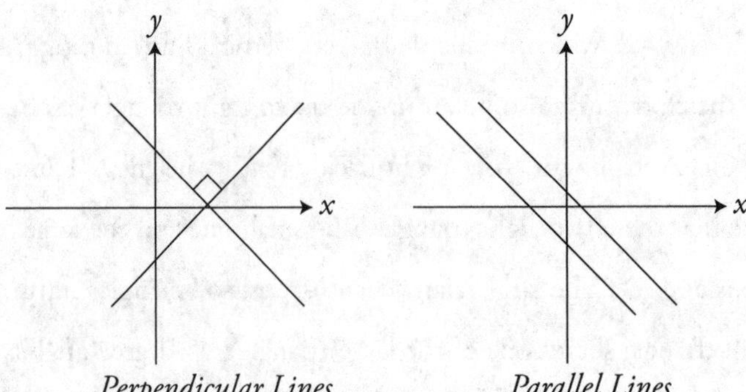


*Perpendicular Lines* *Parallel Lines*

## Graphs of Quadratics

Quadratic equations are covered in more detail in the Algebra chapter, so we are not going to spend much time exploring these here. However, as a reminder, a quadratic equation is an equation in the form:

$$ax^2 + bx + c = 0$$

Like linear equations, quadratic equations can be represented on the coordinate plane. When expressed on the coordinate plane, a quadratic equation has its own distinct shape—a parabola:

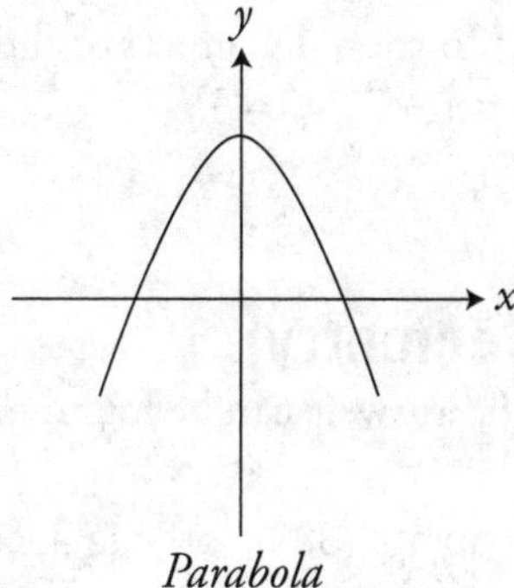


*Parabola*

Most problems that contain quadratic equations on the GMAT do not need to be plotted in order to solve. Mostly, the ability to draw the parabola is useful in order to test individual points on a graph by using different $x$ or $y$ values. For instance, consider the following quadratic equation:

$$y = x^2 + 2x - 8$$

Based on this equation, you can begin plotting points on the coordinate plane to create a parabola. A quadratic equation passes through the $y$-axis only once and that point is when $x = 0$, so the graph of the equation above passes through the point (0, –8). Determining other points on the graph is achieved by either solving for the roots of the equation or plugging in. For instance, if $x = 2$, then the equation is $y = 2^2 + 2(2) - 8 = 2 + 2 - 8 = 0$. So, when $x = 2$, $y = 0$ and the point (2, 0) is also on the graph. Similarly, if $x = -4$ then $y = -4^2 + 2(-4) - 8 = 16 - 8 - 8 = 0$ and the point (–4, 0) is on the graph. These three points can be plotted in order to produce the outline of the parabola:

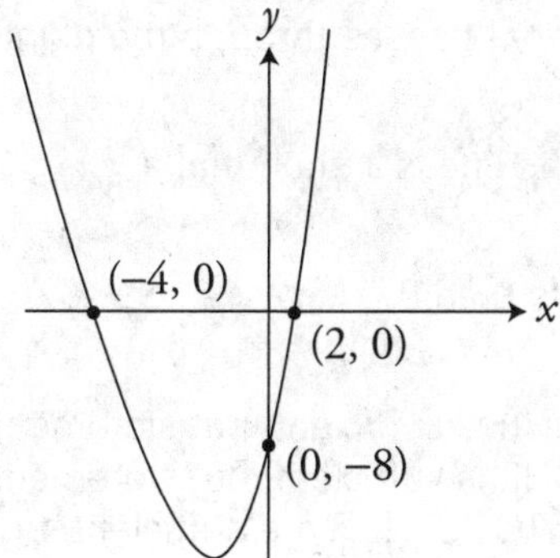

There is one additional point on the graph of a parabola that is important to be aware of and that point is the vertex of the parabola. The vertex is the bottom- or topmost point of a parabola. The vertex is the maximum absolute value of the $y$-coordinate. The vertex is related to the $x$-intercepts of the parabola. This relationship is defined by the *line of symmetry*. The line of symmetry is the vertical line that passes through the vertex of the parabola. The $x$-coordinates of the $x$-intercepts are equal distance from the line of symmetry. In the parabola on the previous page, the distance between the $x$-intercepts is $2 - (-4) = 6$. Half the distance between the $x$-intercepts is the distance between one of the $x$-intercepts and the line of symmetry. In the example above, the $x$-coordinate of the vertex is $-1$ because that point is equal distance away from both $x$-intercepts. Once you've determined the $x$-coordinate of the vertex, you can determine the $y$-coordinate by Plugging In the value of $x$. For the parabola above, the $y$-coordinate of the vertex is $y = -1^2 + 2(-1) - 8 = 1 - 2 - 8 = -9$.

## DRILL 13 (Coordinate Geometry)

Answer the following questions. The answers can be found in Part VII.

1. Line $l$ passes through the point $(-3, 8)$ and has a slope of $-2$. Which of the following could be another point on line $l$?

   - $(-2, 6)$
   - $(-1, 7)$
   - $(1, 4)$
   - $(2, 4)$
   - $(4, -22)$

2. A parabola has one $x$-intercept at $(3, 0)$. If the vertex is at point $(-1, 6)$, then what is the $x$-coordinate of the other $x$-intercept?

   - $-4$
   - $-5$
   - $-6$
   - $-7$
   - $-8$

3. Is the slope of the line that passes through the point $(x, y)$ negative?

   (1) The $x$-intercept of the line is $a$ such that $a < x$

   (2) Both $x$ and $y$ are less than 0

   - Statement (1) ALONE is sufficient, but statement (2) alone is not sufficient.
   - Statement (2) ALONE is sufficient, but statement (1) alone is not sufficient.
   - BOTH statements TOGETHER are sufficient, but NEITHER statement ALONE is sufficient.
   - EACH statement ALONE is sufficient.
   - Statements (1) and (2) TOGETHER are not sufficient.

4. What is the equation of the line that passes through the points (18, 5) and (10, 10) ?

A. $y=\frac{5}{8}x+\frac{25}{4}$

B. $y=-\frac{5}{8}x-\frac{65}{4}$

C. $y=-\frac{8}{5}x-10$

D. $y=\frac{8}{5}x+10$

E. $y=-\frac{25}{8}x-\frac{5}{4}$

5.

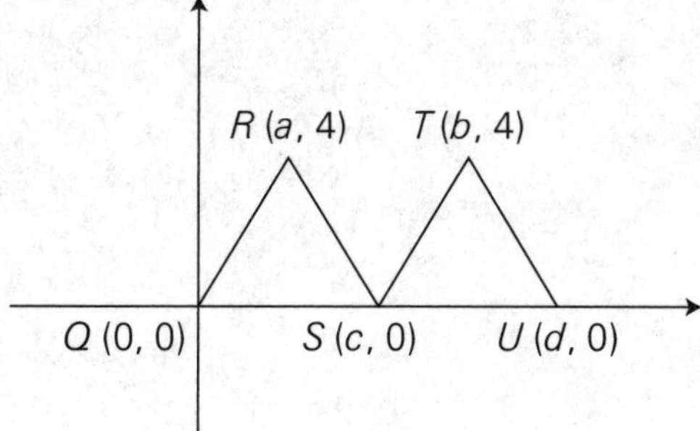


In the figure above, do triangles *QRS* and *STU* have the same area?

(1) $b = 2a$

(2) $d = 2c$

- ○ Statement (1) ALONE is sufficient, but statement (2) alone is not sufficient.
- ○ Statement (2) ALONE is sufficient, but statement (1) alone is not sufficient.
- ○ BOTH statements TOGETHER are sufficient, but NEITHER statement ALONE is sufficient.
- ○ EACH statement ALONE is sufficient.
- ○ Statements (1) and (2) TOGETHER are not sufficient.

## Challenge Question #12

A circle with center ($h$, $k$), in which $k = 2h$, lies tangent to the $y$-axis in the ($x$, $y$) coordinate system. What is the distance from the origin to the center of the circle, in terms of $k$ ?

- $\frac{k\sqrt{3}}{2}$
- $\frac{k\sqrt{5}}{2}$
- $k$
- $k\sqrt{3}$
- $k\sqrt{5}$

## GMAT GEOMETRY: ADVANCED PRINCIPLES

All geometry problems (even easy ones) involve more than one step. Remember the first problem we looked at in this chapter?

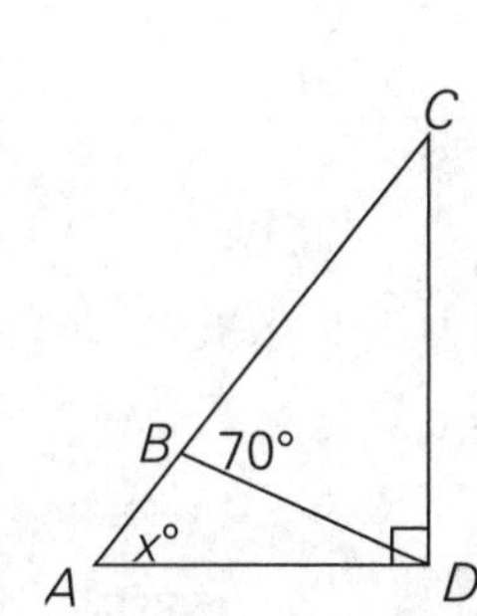


In the figure above, if $BC = CD$ and angle $ADC = 90$ degrees, then what is the value of $x$ ?

- ○ 45
- ○ 50
- ○ 70
- ○ 75
- ○ 100

### Here's How to Crack It

Just by looking at the figure, we were able to eliminate (C), (D), and (E). Now let's solve the problem using geometry. The figure includes two—actually three—different triangles: *ABD, BCD*, and *ACD*. The test-writers want even this easy problem to be a little challenging; there must be more than one step involved. To find angle *x*, which is part of triangles *ABD* and *ACD*, we must first work on triangle *BCD*.

What do we know about triangle *BCD*? The problem itself tells us that $BC = CD$. This is an isosceles triangle. Because angle *DBC* equals 70, so does angle *BDC*. Angle *BCD* must therefore equal 180 minus the other two angles. Angle $BCD = 40$.

Now look at the larger triangle, *ACD*. We know that angle $ACD = 40$ and that angle $ADC = 90$. What does angle *x* equal? Angle *x* equals 180 minus the other two angles, or 50 degrees. The answer is (B).

## Walking and Chewing Gum at the Same Time

Most GMAT geometry problems involve more than one geometric concept. A problem might require you to use both the properties of a triangle and the properties of a rectangle, or you might need to know the formula for the volume of a cube in order to find the dimensions of a cube's surface area. The difficult geometry problems do not test more complicated concepts—they just pile up easier concepts.

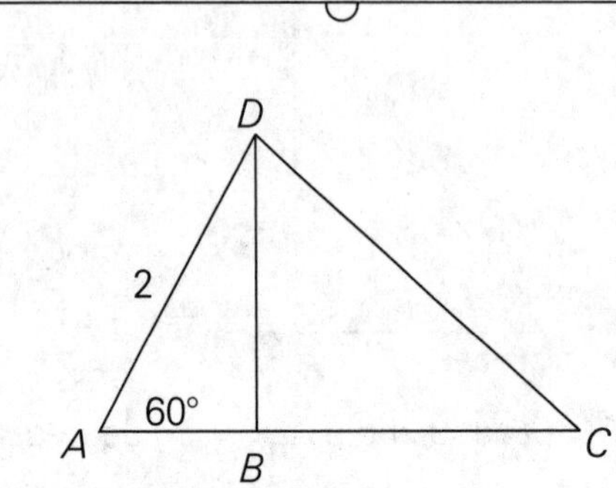


In the figure above, if a line segment connecting points *B* and *D* is perpendicular to *AC* and the area of triangle *ADC* is $\frac{3\sqrt{3}}{2}$, then *BC* =

- ◯ $\sqrt{2}$
- ◯ $\sqrt{3}$
- ◯ 2
- ◯ $3\sqrt{3}$
- ◯ 6

### Here's How to Crack It

You may remember that earlier in this chapter, we got an approximate answer to this question by measuring; now let's solve it using geometry. Because line *BD* is perpendicular to line *AC*, the angle *DBA* is 90 degrees, which means triangle *ADB* a 30-60-90 triangle. The hypotenuse of this triangle is 2. Using the rules we've learned about 30-60-90 triangles, we can conclude that the measurements of triangle *ADB* are as follows:

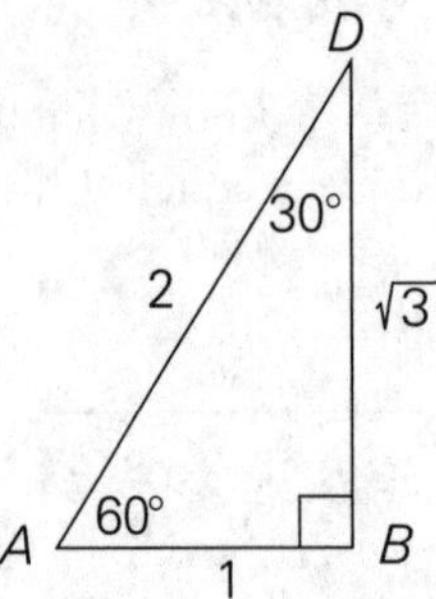


Thus, $BD = \sqrt{3}$. At first you might think we're no closer to the solution, but don't despair. Just look for somewhere else to start. The problem tells us that the area of triangle *ADC* is $\frac{3\sqrt{3}}{2}$.

The area of a triangle is $\frac{\text{base} \times \text{height}}{2}$. *BD* is the height. Let's find out what the base is. In other words, $\frac{\text{base} \times \sqrt{3}}{2} = \frac{3\sqrt{3}}{2}$, so the base equals 3. We know from the 30-60-90 triangle that $AB = 1$. What is *BC*? 2. The answer is (C).

## Plugging In on Geometry?

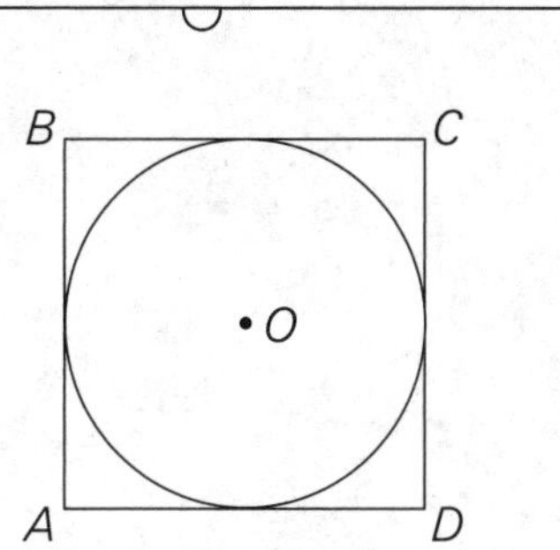


In the figure above, circle *O* is inscribed inside square *ABCD* as shown. What is the ratio of the area of circle *O* to the area of square *ABCD* ?

- $\frac{\pi}{2}$
- $\frac{4}{\pi}$
- $\frac{\pi}{3}$
- $\frac{\pi}{4}$
- $\frac{\pi}{5}$

### Here's How to Crack It

We already saw this problem in the first half of the chapter when we discussed eliminating trap answers. As you may recall, we were able to eliminate (A), (B), and (C) because we determined that the correct answer had to be the ratio of a smaller number to a bigger number.

Now let's solve this problem completely. You may have noticed that the answer choices do not contain *specific numbers* for the areas of the two figures—all we have here are *ratios* in the answer choices. Sound familiar? That's right! This is just another Plugging In problem.

**Bite-Sized Pieces**

With GMAT geometry, you shouldn't expect to see what every step a problem involves before you start solving it. Often, arriving at the right answer involves saying, "I have no idea how to get the answer, but because the problem says that $BC = CD$, let me start by figuring out the other angle of that triangle. Now what can I do?" At some point, the answer usually becomes obvious. The main point is not to stare at a geometry problem looking for a complete solution. Just wade in there and start, one bite-sized piece at a time.

To find the area of the circle, we need a radius. Let's just pick one—3. If the radius is 3, the area of the circle is $9\pi$. Now let's tackle the square. The circle is inscribed inside the square, which means that the diameter of the circle is also the length of a side of the square. Because the radius of the circle is 3, the diameter is 6. Therefore, the side of the square is 6, and the area is 36.

The problem asks for the ratio of the area of the circle to the area of the square:

$$\frac{9\pi}{36} = \frac{\pi}{4}$$

The answer is (D).

# Summary

- While the geometry found on the GMAT is rudimentary, you will have to memorize all of the formulas that you'll need because they are not provided on the test.
- Always study any problem drawn to scale very closely in order to eliminate trap answer choices.
- You must know the following approximate values: $\pi \approx 3$, $\sqrt{2} \approx 1.4$, and $\sqrt{3} \approx 1.7$.
- You must be familiar with the size of certain common angles:

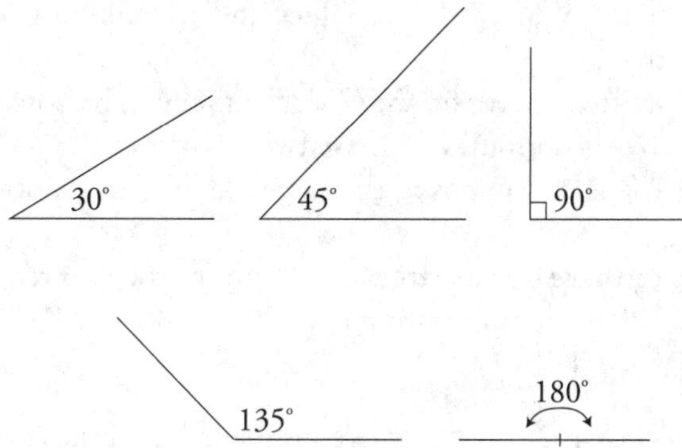


- You can estimate Problem Solving diagrams drawn to scale very precisely by using the marker that comes with your scratch booklet.
- When no diagram is provided, draw your own, and make it to scale.
- When the diagram is not drawn to scale, redraw it.
- Degrees and angles:
  - A circle contains 360 degrees.
  - A line is a 180-degree angle.
  - When two lines intersect, four angles are formed, but in reality there are only two pairs of identical angles.
  - When two parallel lines are cut by a third line, eight angles are formed, but in reality there are only two sets of identical angles: a set of big ones and a set of little ones.

- Triangles:
  - Every triangle contains 180 degrees.
  - An equilateral triangle has three equal sides and three equal angles, each of which measures 60 degrees.
  - An isosceles triangle has two equal sides, and the angles opposite those sides are also equal.
  - A right triangle contains one 90-degree angle.
  - The perimeter of a triangle is the sum of the lengths of its sides.
  - The area of a triangle is $\frac{height \times base}{2}$.
  - In a right triangle, the Pythagorean Theorem states that the square of the hypotenuse equals the sum of the squares of the other two sides, or $a^2 + b^2 = c^2$.
  - Some common right triangles are 3-4-5 triangles and multiples of 3-4-5 triangles, 5-12-13 triangles, and 7-24-25 triangles.
  - Two other triangles that often appear on the GMAT are the right isosceles triangle and the 30-60-90 triangle. Memorize the formulas for these two triangles.
  - The longest side of a triangle is opposite the largest angle; the shortest side is opposite the smallest angle.
  - One side of a triangle can never be as large as the sum of the two remaining sides, nor can it ever be as small as the difference of the two remaining sides.

- Circles:
  - The circumference of a circle is $2\pi r$ or $\pi d$, where $r$ is the radius of the circle and $d$ is the diameter.
  - The area of a circle is $\pi r^2$, where $r$ is the radius of the circle.

- Rectangles, squares, and other four-sided objects:
  - Any four-sided object is called a quadrilateral.
  - The perimeter of a quadrilateral is the sum of the lengths of the four sides.
  - The area of a rectangle, or of a square, is equal to *length* × *width*.
  - The area of a parallelogram is equal to *height* × *base*.
- Solids and volume:
  - The volume of most objects is equal to their two-dimensional *area* × their *depth*.
  - The volume of a rectangular solid is equal to *length* × *width* × *depth*.
  - The volume of a cylinder is equal to the *area* of the circular base × *height*.
- GMAT geometry problems always involve more than one step, and difficult GMAT geometry problems may layer several concepts. Don't be intimidated if you don't see the entire process that's necessary to solve the problem. Start somewhere. You'll be amazed at how often you arrive at the answer.

# Chapter 17
# Number Theory

Number Theory topics don't apply to one specific type of GMAT question. They are general principles about numbers and how they interact that are necessary to unlock the answers to a wide variety of Quantitative questions across all question types. These principles are the Fundamental Theorem of Arithmetic, Least Common Multiples, Greatest Common Factors, Tests for Multiples and Factors, and the Role of Shared Prime Factors.

## WHAT IS NUMBER THEORY?

For the purpose of the GMAT, number theory is information about various types of numbers and the interactions between those numbers. An understanding of number theory allows you to work through various problems on the GMAT that may otherwise be inaccessible.

### Why Does This Matter?

Many GMAT questions involve number theory topics. Consider the following examples:

What is the remainder when integer $n$ is divided by 13 ?

(1) When $n$ is divided by 91, the remainder is 83.

(2) When $n$ is divided by 52, the remainder is 18.

If $x$ is an integer, is $n$ prime?

(1) $x! = n$

(2) $0 \leq x \leq 2$

If $\frac{17!}{7^m}$ is an integer, what is the greatest possible value of $m$ ?

- ◯ 2
- ◯ 3
- ◯ 4
- ◯ 5
- ◯ 6

If $a$ is a multiple of 7, is $ab$ a multiple of 21 ?

(1) Every factor of 65 is also a factor of $b$.

(2) $b$ is divisible by 51.

Don't worry about answering these questions now. We'll return to them later in this chapter. What is important to know is that each of the questions above can be answered through the application of number theory. This chapter covers the Fundamental Theorem of Arithmetic, Least Common Multiple (LCM), Greatest Common Factor (GCF), Tests for Multiples and

Factors, and the Role of Shared Prime Factors. By the end of this chapter, you will understand how to work through problems like the four shown above.

## Fundamental Theorem of Arithmetic

The Fundamental Theorem of Arithmetic (also known as the Unique Prime Factorization Theorem) is the cornerstone of factorization. It states that every integer greater than 1 is either prime or can be written as the unique product of primes. A prime number has only itself and 1 as factors. Because of this, the number 1 is not prime and the number 2 is the only even prime number. The list of prime numbers is a familiar cast of characters: 2, 3, 5, 7, 11, …, 73, 79, 83, 89, 97, ….

Numbers that are not prime are called composite numbers. Each composite number can be factored into a unique set of prime factors that, when multiplied together, equal the number. For example, the prime factors of 42 are 2, 3, and 7. Note that order does not matter. $3 \times 7 \times 2 = 7 \times 3 \times 2 = 42$. The prime factors of 144 are 2, 2, 2, 2, 3, and 3. That is, $2 \times 2 \times 2 \times 2 \times 3 \times 3 = 144$. Every factorization of a composite number is unique to that number, that is, no two distinct composite numbers have the same prime factors.

In order to factor an integer, start with the least prime number and continue until all factors are prime. For example, to factor 308, first divide by 2 to get 154, then divide by 2 again to get 77, then divide by 7 to get 11, which means that the prime factors of 308 are 2, 2, 7, and 11.

## How to Determine If an Integer Is Prime

In order to determine if an integer is prime, start with the least prime number 2 and test whether the number is divisible by 2. Continue testing prime numbers up to the square root of the number. If none of the prime numbers less than or equal to the square root divide into the number, the number is prime.

Let's try 383. Start with the least prime number 2. The number 383 is not divisible by 2. The square root of 383 is less than 20, which means that it is not necessary to test any prime greater than 20. Try 3, 5, 7, 11, 13, 17, and 19. None of the primes from 2 to 19 are factors of 383, which means that 383 is prime.

Suppose we want to determine if 3,119 is prime. The square root of 3,119 is less than 56. This means that if we test the prime numbers from 2 to 56 and find that none of those are factors of 3,119, then 3,119 is prime. As is turns out, 3,119 is prime.

How about 3,127? The square root of 3,127 is less than 56. Test to determine if any of the prime numbers from 2 to 56 is a factor of 3,127. When we test 53, we find out that 3,127 divided by 53 equals 59, which means that 3,127 is not prime.

At this point, you may be wondering how you are going to test all the prime factors between 2 and 53 in a reasonable time frame on test day. The good news is the GMAT rarely tests prime factors on numbers greater than 400. So, you'll likely only have to work with the prime numbers up to 20. In addition, knowing a few simple rules about how to determine if certain numbers are factors of another number is useful. These rules are covered in the section on Test for Multiples and Factors in this chapter.

### Factorization

The factors of an integer *x* are comprised of all integers less than *x* that divide evenly into *x*. This includes the integer itself and 1. For example, the factors of 12 are 1, 2, 3, 4, 6, and 12. The prime factors of 12 are 2, 2, and 3. The GMAT may ask about distinct prime factors. The distinct prime factors of 12 are 2 and 3.

Every factor pairs with another factor. In the above example, 1 pairs with 12 ($1 \times 12 = 12$), 2 pairs with 6, and 3 pairs with 4.

Let's try another example. What are all the factors of 72? Start with 1 and 72, then 2 and 36, 3 and 24, 4 and 18, 6 and 12, and finally, 8 and 9. The factors of 72 are 1, 2, 3, 4, 6, 8, 9, 12, 18, 24, 36, and 72. The prime factors are 2, 2, 2, 3, and 3. The distinct prime factors are 2 and 3.

## Least Common Multiple (LCM)

The least common multiple (LCM), also known as the lowest common multiple, or smallest common multiple of two or more integers, is the least positive integer that is divisible by at least two integers. For example, the LCM of 4 and 6 is 12, because 12 is the least number that is divisible by both 4 and 6.

In order to find the LCM of two numbers, determine the prime factorization of each number. The LCM is the product of each prime factor in either number raised to the higher power in either number. For example, what is the LCM of 36 and 45? The prime factors of 36 are 2, 2, 3, and 3, or $2^2 \times 3^2$. The prime factors of 45 are 3, 3, and 5, or $3^2 \times 5$ . This means that the LCM has the factors of $2^2$, $3^2$ , and 5. The LCM of 36 and 45 is $2^2 \times 3^2 \times 5 = 180$.

In order to find the LCM of three or more numbers, follow the same method as above. For example, what is the LCM of 12, 15, and 20? The prime factors of 12 are 2, 2, and 3, or $2^2 \times 3$. The prime factors of 15 are $3 \times 5$. The prime factors of 20 are 2, 2, and 5, or $2^2 \times 5$ . This means that the LCM of 12, 15, and 20 has the factors $2^2$, 3, and 5. So the LCM of 12, 15, and 20 is $2^2 \times 3 \times 5 = 60$.

Here's an example of a GMAT question that requires use of LCM:

A certain light has three bulbs that light up at different intervals. The first lights up every 6 minutes, the second lights up every 8 minutes, and the third lights up every 14 minutes. If all three bulbs lit up simultaneously at 11:04 A.M., at what time will all three bulbs light up simultaneously next?

- 12:48 P.M.
- 1:48 P.M.
- 1:52 P.M.
- 2:48 P.M.
- 2:52 P.M.

### Here's How to Crack It

In order to answer this question, determine the LCM of 6, 8, and 14. The prime factors of 6 are 2 and 3; the prime factors of 8 are 2, 2, and 2, or $2^3$; the prime factors of 14 are 2 and 7. The LCM of 6, 8, and 14 is $2^3 \times 3 \times 7 = 168$, which means the three bulbs light up together every 168 minutes, or every 2 hours and 48 minutes. They all lit up together at 11:04 A.M.. Adding 2 hours and 48 minutes means that they will light up together again at 1:52 P.M.. The correct answer is (C).

Here's another one:

Boris has the same number of orange, purple, and green marbles that he wants to arrange in groups. He wants to arrange the orange marbles in groups of 15, the purple marbles in groups of 13, and the green marbles in groups of 14. What is the least number of marbles of each color Boris must have in order to make these groups and have no marbles leftover?

- 546
- 910
- 1,365
- 2,730
- 5,460

### Here's How to Crack It

Begin by determining the LCM of 13, 14, and 15. The only prime factor of 13 is 13. The prime factors of 14 are 2 and 7, and the prime factors of 15 are 3 and 5. All three numbers have no prime factors in common. The LCM of 13, 14, 15 equals $2 \times 3 \times 5 \times 7 \times 13 = 13 \times 14 \times 15 =$ 2,730. The correct answer is (D).

## Greatest Common Factor (GCF)

The greatest common factor (also known as highest common factor and greatest common divisor) of two or more positive integers is the greatest positive factor they have in common. One way to determine the GCF is to find the product of all the prime numbers that appear in the prime factorization of at least two numbers. For example, to find the GCF of 78 and 130, first determine the prime factors of each number. The prime factors of 78 are 2, 3 and 13, and the prime factors of 130 are 2, 5, and 13. Both numbers have the prime factors 2 and 13 in common, which means the GCF of 78 and 130 is $2 \times 13 = 26$.

Here's an example question that requires use of GCF:

---

The greatest common factor of 8 and positive integer *k* is 2, and the greatest common factor of *k* and 105 is 7. Which of the following could be the greatest common factor of *k* and 120 ?

- ◯ 2
- ◯ 3
- ◯ 4
- ◯ 5
- ◯ 6

### Here's How to Crack It

The prime factors of 8 are 2, 2, and 2, or $2^3$. The GCF of 8 and *k* is 2. Because the GCF of 8 and *k* is 2, *k* only has one factor of 2. If *k* had more than one factor of 2, then the GCF of 8 and *k* would be a multiple of 2. The prime factors of 105 are 3, 5, and 7. The GCF of 105 and *k* is 7. Because the GCF of 105 and *k* is 7, *k* does not have factors of 3 and 5. If *k* had factors of 3 or 5, then the GCF of 105 and *k* would be a multiple of 7. The prime factors of 120 are 2, 2, 2, 3, and 5. The question asks which of the following could be the GCF of *k* and 120. Now look at the answer choices. We know that 2 is a factor of *k*, so keep (A). Because the GCF of 105 and *k* is 7, it has already been established that 3 is not a factor of *k*. Therefore, it is not possible for the GCF of *k* and 120 to be 3. Eliminate (B). Similarly, because the GCF of *k* and 8 is 2, 4 is not a factor of *k*. Eliminate (C). Eliminate (D) because 5 is not a factor of *k*. Finally, eliminate (E) because 6 is a multiple of 3 and 3 is not a factor of *k*. The correct answer is (A).

---

Here's one more:

Is $m$ divisible by 14 ?

(1) The greatest common factor of $m$ and 42 is 6.

(2) The greatest common factor of $m$ and 72 is 24.

### Here's How to Crack It

This is a Yes/No Data Sufficiency question, so be prepared to Plug In more than once. The question asks if the variable $m$ is divisible by 14. Begin by finding the prime factors of 14, which are 2 and 7. For $m$ to be divisible by 14, both 2 and 7 must be factors of $m$.

Statement (1) states that the GCF of $m$ and 42 is 6. The prime factors of 42 are 2, 3, and 7. Because the GCF of $m$ and 42 is 6 and $2 \times 3 = 6$, two of the factors of $m$ are 2 and 3. Alternatively, $m$ does not have 7 as a factor. Because 7 is not a factor of $m$, it is impossible for $m$ to be divisible by 14. Therefore, the answer to the question is "No." There is no way to produce an answer of "Yes" to the question. When a statement consistently produces the same answer to a question, that statement is sufficient. Write down AD.

Statement (2) states that the GCF of $m$ and 72 is 24. The prime factors of 72 are 2, 2, 2, 3, and 3, or $2^3 \times 3^2$, and the prime factors of 24 are 2, 2, 2, and 3, or $2^3 \times 3$, which means that the prime factors of $m$ include $2^3$ and one factor of 3. This information does not provide enough data to determine if $m$ is divisible by 14 because it does not give any indication if 7 is a factor of $m$. If $m$ has a factor of 7, then the answer to the question is "Yes." However, if $m$ does not have a factor of 7, then the answer to the question is "No." The statement produces two different answers to the question, so the statement is insufficient. Eliminate (D). The correct answer is (A).

## Relation Between LCM and GCF

One interesting property of the LCM and GCF of any two positive integers is that the product of the LCM and GCF of positive integers $x$ and $y$ is equal to the product of $x$ and $y$. For example, the LCM of 21 and 35 is $3 \times 5 \times 7 = 105$. The GCF of 21 and 35 is 7. The product of 7 and 105 is equal to 735, which is equal to the product of 21 and 35. This property does not hold true for more than two integers.

In other words, for any two positive integers $m$ and $n$, $mn = \text{LCM}(m, n) \times \text{GCF}(m, n)$. This means that if you know either the LCM or the GCF of any two positive integers, you can determine the other by dividing it into the product of the integers. For example, the GCF of 72 and 48 is 24. What is the LCM? The product of 72 and 48 is 3,456. Divide 3,456 by 24 to get 144, which is the LCM of 72 and 48.

## Prime and Coprime Numbers

A number is prime if its factors are only 1 and itself. Two integers are coprime (also known as relatively prime or mutually prime) if the only positive integer that is a factor of both numbers is 1. In other words, two integers are coprime if the GCF of both numbers is 1. For example, 51 and 286 are coprime because they have no common factors other than 1. The numbers 51 and 374 are not coprime, because they both have a factor of 17.

## Patterns and Cycles

The GMAT frequently asks questions that require you to recognize various patterns and cycles. For example, consider powers of 7. $7^0 = 1$; $7^1 = 7$; $7^2 = 49$; $7^3 = 343$; $7^4 = 2{,}401$; $7^5 = 16{,}807$, etc. Notice the pattern of the units digit of each power of 7: 1, 7, 9, 3, and then the same cycle repeats. Here are some of the frequent examples of patterns that may appear on the GMAT.

### Remainder Cycles When Dividing by Integers

When dividing by an integer $s$, there are $s$ possible remainders, 0 through $s - 1$. These remainders cycle in an infinite loop. For example, 17 divided by 5 has a remainder 2, 18 divided by 5 has a remainder 3, 19 divided by 5 has a remainder 4, 20 divided by 5 has a remainder 0, 21 divided by 5 has a remainder 1, and then the cycle repeats.

### Units Digit Cycles

The GMAT sometimes asks questions that require you to determine the units digit of a number raised to a very high power. For example, if integer $g > 0$, what is the remainder when $49^{16g+3}$ is divided by 5? In order to answer the question, we need to know the units digit of $49^{16g+3}$. Plug in $g = 1$. $16 \times 1 + 3 = 19$, which means that we need to know the units digit of $49^{19}$. Consider the patterns of the unit digit of powers of 9. They are as follows: $9^1 = 9$; $9^2 = 81$; $9^3 = 729$, and so on. The pattern is 9, 1, 9, 1, etc. When 9 is raised to any even power, the units digit is 1, and when 9 is raised to any odd power, the units digit is 9. 19 is odd, so the units digit of $49^{19}$ is 9. The remainder when 5 is divided into any integer ending in 9 is 4. Plug In $g = 2$. $16 \times 2 + 3 = 35$, which is odd. This means that the units digit of $49^{19}$ is 9, and the remainder when $49^{19}$ is divided by 5 is 4.

## Tests for Multiples and Factors

The GMAT frequently asks questions that require knowing whether a number is divisible by commonly used integers. The chart below shows divisibility shortcuts for the integers 2 through 13.

| Number | Test for divisibility | Examples |
|---|---|---|
| 2 | All even numbers (numbers ending in 0, 2, 4, 6, and 8) are divisible by 2. | 4,832 (even) is divisible by 2. 4,831 (odd) is not divisible by 2. |
| 3 | If the sum of the digits of a number is divisible by 3, then the number is divisible by 3. | The sum of the digits of 6,711 is 15, which is divisible by 3. So 6,711 is divisible by 3. |
| 4 | If the last two digits of a number are divisible by 4, then the number is divisible by 4. | The last two digits of 4,776 are 76, which is divisible by 4. So 4,776 is divisible by 4. |
| 5 | Any number ending in 0 or 5 is divisible by 5. | 3,745 and 2,670 are divisible by 5. |
| 6 | Any even number divisible by 3 is divisible by 6. | The sum of the digits of 2,778 is 24, which is divisible by 3. So 2,778 is an even number divisible by 3, which means it is divisible by 6. |
| 7 | Remove the last digit, double it, and then subtract it from the truncated original number. Repeat until what remains is either divisible by 7 or not. | Consider 3,248. 324 – 16 = 308; 30 – 16 = 14, which is divisible by 7. So 3,248 is divisible by 7. |
| 8 | If the last three digits of a number are divisible by 8, then the number is divisible by 8. | The last three digits of 103,488 are 488, which is divisible by 8. So 103,488 is divisible by 8. |
| 9 | If the sum of the digits of a number is divisible by 9, then the number is divisible by 9. | The sum of the digits of 8,343 is 18, which is divisible by 9. So 8,343 is divisible by 9. |
| 10 | Any number ending in 0 is divisible by 10. | 450, 9,230, and 107,770 are divisible by 10. |
| 11 | Remove the last digit and subtract it from the remaining truncated number. Repeat until what remains is either divisible by 11 or not. | Consider 8,173. 817 – 3 = 814; 81 – 4 = 77, which is divisible by 11. So 8,173 is divisible by 11. |
| 12 | Any number divisible by 3 and 4 is also divisible by 12. | Consider 38,424. The sum of the digits is 21, which is divisible by 3. The last two digits are 24, which is divisible by 4. So 38,424 is divisible by 3 and 4, which means it is divisible by 12. |
| 13 | Remove the last number, multiply it by 4, and then add it to the remaining truncated number. Repeat until what remains is divisible by 13 or not. | Consider 18,902. 1,890 + 8 = 1,898; 189 + 32 = 221; 22 + 4 = 26, which is divisible by 13. So 18,902 is divisible by 13. |

Here's an example for which divisibility tests may prove useful:

---

*b* is a multiple of 7. Is *ab* a multiple of 1,638 ?

(1) *a* is divisible by 39

(2) Every factor of 42 is a factor of *a*

### Here's How to Crack It

This is a Yes/No Data Sufficiency question, so be prepared to Plug In more than once. Begin by working with the question. In order to solve this problem, we need to find the prime factors of 1,638. It is even, so it is divisible by 2. Divide 1,638 by 2 to get 819. The sum of the digits of 819 is 18, which means that 819 is divisible by 9. Divide 819 by 9 to get 91, which is equal to $7 \times 13$. The prime factors of 1,638 are 2, 3, 3, 7, and 13. In order for *ab* to be a multiple of 1,638, which is another way of asking if 1,638 is a factor of *ab*, *ab* must share factors with 1,638. In other words, *ab* must have factors of 2, 3, 3, 7, and 13. We know that *b* is a multiple of 7, which means that 7 is a factor of *ab*. If *a* or *b* has the factors 2, 3, 3, and 13, then *ab* has all the factors of 1,638. Evaluate each statement individually.

Statement (1) states that *a* is divisible by 39, which is equal to $3 \times 13$. This means that *ab* is a multiple of 3, 7, and 13. However, this provides no information about if *ab* is a multiple of 2 or the second factor of 3. If *ab* is a multiple of 2 and the second factor of 3, then the answer to the question is "Yes." If *ab* is not a multiple of 2 or the second factor of 3, then the answer to the question is "No." Because this statement produces two different answers to the question, the statement is insufficient. Write down BCE.

Statement (2) states that every factor of 42 is a factor of *a*, which is another way of stating that *a* is divisible by 42. The prime factors of 42 are 2, 3, and 7. This statement does not provide any information about if *ab* is a multiple of 13 or the second factor of 3. If *a* is a multiple of 13 and the second factor of 3, then the answer to the question is "Yes." If *a* is not a multiple of 13 or the second factor of 3, then the answer to the question is "No." Because the statement produces two different answers to the question, the statement is insufficient. Eliminate (B).

Now evaluate the statements together. From Statement (1), we know that 3, 7, and 13 are factors of *ab*, and from Statement (2), we know that 2, 3, and 7 are factors of *ab*. Taken together, 2, 3, 7, and 13 are factors of *ab*. However, this does not provide any information about if *ab* is a multiple of the second factor of 3. This means that statements (1) and (2) together are insufficient. Eliminate (C).

The correct answer is (E).

---

## Back to the Beginning

Now that you've worked with number theory topics, let's take another look at the questions from the beginning of this chapter.

What is the remainder when integer $n$ is divided by 13 ?

(1) When $n$ is divided by 91 the remainder is 83.

(2) When $n$ is divided by 52 the remainder is 18.

### Here's How to Crack It

This is a Value Data Sufficiency question, so begin by determining what is known and what is needed to answer the question. The question asks for the remainder when integer $n$ is divided by 13. So, determining possible values of $n$ is necessary to solve the question. Evaluate the statements individually.

Statement (1) states that when $n$ is divided by 91, the remainder is 83, which means that $\frac{n}{91} = k + \frac{83}{91}$, and that $n = 91k + 83$ for some integer $k$. Plug In. If $k = 1$, then $n = 91(1) + 83 = 174$. When 174 is divided by 13, the remainder is 5 because $13 \times 13 = 169$ and $174 - 169 = 5$. Plug In again. If $k = 0$, then $n = 83$. The remainder when 83 is divided by 13 is 5 because $13 \times 6 = 78$ and $83 - 78 = 5$. In fact, no matter what number is used for $k$, the remainder when $n$ is divided by 13 is always 5. This statement produces the same result no matter what the numbers are, so the statement is sufficient. Write down AD.

Statement (2) states that when $n$ is divided by 52 the remainder is 18, which means that $\frac{n}{52} = j + \frac{18}{52}$, and that $n = 52j + 18$ for some integer $j$. Plug In. If $j = 1$, then $n = 52(1) + 18 = 70$. When 70 is divided by 13, the remainder is 5 because $13 \times 5 = 65$ and $70 - 65 = 5$. Plug In again. If $k = 0$, then $n = 18$. The remainder when 18 is divided by 13 is 5 because $13 \times 1 = 13$ and $18 - 13 = 5$. Plug In one more time. If $j = 2$, then $n = 122$. The remainder when 122 is divided by 13 is 5 because $13 \times 9 = 117$ and $122 - 117 = 5$. No matter what number is used for the value of $j$, this statement produces the same answer to the question. When a statement produces the same answer to the question, that statement is sufficient. Eliminate (A). The correct answer is (D).

If $x$ is an integer, is $n$ prime?

(1) $x! = n$

(2) $0 \le x \le 2$

### Here's How to Crack It

This is a Yes/No Data Sufficiency question, so be prepared to Plug In more than once. The question asks if $n$ is prime and provides that $x$ is an integer. Evaluate the statements individually.

Consider Statement (1), which states that $x! = n$. This means that $x$ could be equal to 2 or any other number. Statement (1) is not sufficient. Write down BCE.

Statement (2) states that $0 \le x \le 2$, which means that $x$ could be equal to 2, 1, or 0. This does not provide any information about $n$, so eliminate (B).

Now consider both statements together. According to Statement (2), $x$ could be equal to 0, 1, or 2. Any of these values for $x$ satisfies Statement (1). Plug In. If $x = 1$, the answer to the question is "No." If $x = 2$, the answer to the question is "Yes." The statements combined result in two different answers to the question, so the statements combined are insufficient. Eliminate (C). The correct answer is (E).

If $\frac{17!}{7^m}$ is an integer, what is the greatest possible value of $m$ ?

- 2
- 3
- 4
- 5
- 6

**Here's How to Crack It**

The questions states that $\frac{17!}{7^m}$ is an integer, so expand this factorial to find that $\frac{17!}{7^m} = \frac{17 \times 16 \times 15 \times 14 \times 13 \times 12 \times 11 \times 10 \times 9 \times 8 \times 7 \times 6 \times 5 \times 4 \times 3 \times 2 \times 1}{7^m}$. In order for $\frac{17!}{7^m}$ to be an integer, 17! must be divisible by $7^m$. Because 7 is prime, there must be at least as many factors of 7 in the numerator as in the denominator. The numerator has two factors of 7, one at 7 and one at 14. For $\frac{17!}{7^m}$ to be an integer, the denominator can have at most two factors of 7. The correct answer is (A).

If *a* is a multiple of 7, is *ab* a multiple of 21 ?

(1) Every factor of 65 is also a factor of *b.*

(2) *b* is divisible by 51.

### Here's How to Crack It

This is a Yes/No Data Sufficiency question, so be prepared to Plug In more than once. The prime factors of 21 are 3 and 7, which means that for *ab* to be a multiple of 21, it must have factors of 3 and 7. The question states that *a* is a multiple of 7, which means that *ab* has at least one factor of 7. So, it is necessary to find out if either *a* or *b* has a factor of 3.

Statement (1) states that every factor of 65 is also a factor of *b.* The prime factors of 65 are 5 and 13. If these are the only factors of *b,* then the answer to the question is "No." However, if *b* has a factor of 3 as well, the answer to the question is "Yes." The statement produces two different answers to the question, so it is insufficient. Write down BCE.

Statement (2) states that *b* is divisible by 51. The prime factors of 51 are 3 and 17, which means that *b* has at least one factor of 3. Statement (2) is sufficient. Eliminate (C) and (E). The correct answer is (B).

# Summary

- Number theory is information about various types of numbers and the interactions between those numbers.
- The Fundamental Theorem of Arithmetic states that every integer greater than 1 is either prime or can be written as the unique product of primes.
- The Least Common Multiple is the least positive integer that is divisible by at least two integers.
- The Greatest Common Factor of two or more positive integers is the greatest positive factor they have in common.
- Prime numbers only have factors of 1 and itself. Coprime numbers are two integers for which 1 is the only positive, common factor.
- Be on the lookout for remainder patterns, units digit patterns, and opportunities to apply divisibility rules to make challenging questions.

# Chapter 18 Advanced Data Sufficiency

In this chapter, we'll show you how to master Data Sufficiency problems, how to decipher the intermediate and advanced math hidden beneath the unfamiliar format, and how to use POE to eliminate tempting traps.

Now that you've reviewed all the important math concepts covered on the GMAT, it's time to take a second look at how these concepts are used in Data Sufficiency questions.

First, a quick review:

Every Data Sufficiency problem consists of a question followed by two statements:

What is the value of $x$ ?

(1) $x^2 = 4$
(2) $x$ is negative.

You have to decide NOT what the answer is, but WHETHER the question can be answered based on the information in the two statements. There are five possible answer choices:

- ○ Statement (1) ALONE is sufficient, but statement (2) alone is not sufficient.
- ○ Statement (2) ALONE is sufficient, but statement (1) alone is not sufficient.
- ○ BOTH statements TOGETHER are sufficient, but NEITHER statement ALONE is sufficient.
- ○ EACH statement ALONE is sufficient.
- ○ Statements (1) and (2) TOGETHER are not sufficient.

The best way to answer Data Sufficiency problems is to look at one statement at a time—so ignore Statement (2), and look only at Statement (1). Based on Statement (1), $x^2 = 4$, can we answer the question, "What is $x$?"

At first glance, you might think so. If $x^2 = 4$, then $x = 2$, right?

Well, not necessarily; $x$ could also equal −2. And when different numbers that satisfy a statement yield different answers to the question, the statement is insufficient. Choices (A) and (D) can be eliminated; the only remaining possible correct choices are (B), (C), and (E).

**AD or BCE**

Just by evaluating Statement (1) we have already eliminated several answer choices:

If Statement (1) is sufficient, we are down to (A) or (D).

If Statement (1) is NOT sufficient, we are down to (B), (C), or (E).

AD or BCE. Memorize it; these are always your options. And it makes sense to write it down this way in your scratch book.

Now, ignore Statement (1) and look ONLY at Statement (2). Based on Statement (2), "$x$ is negative," can we answer the question, "What is $x$?"

Nope, $x$ could be any negative number. For instance, $x$ could be −2 or −3. When different numbers that satisfy a statement yield different answers to the question, the statement is insufficient. We are now down to (C) or (E).

Look at both statements together. If $x^2 = 4$ and $x$ is negative, can we answer the question, "What is $x$?"

Yup! Now there is only one unique number in the world that $x$ could be: −2. The correct answer is (C).

Here's a flowchart that walks you through each step of solving a Data Sufficiency question. If you need more information about how to use the chart or the basic strategy for solving a Data Sufficiency question, check out Chapter 11.

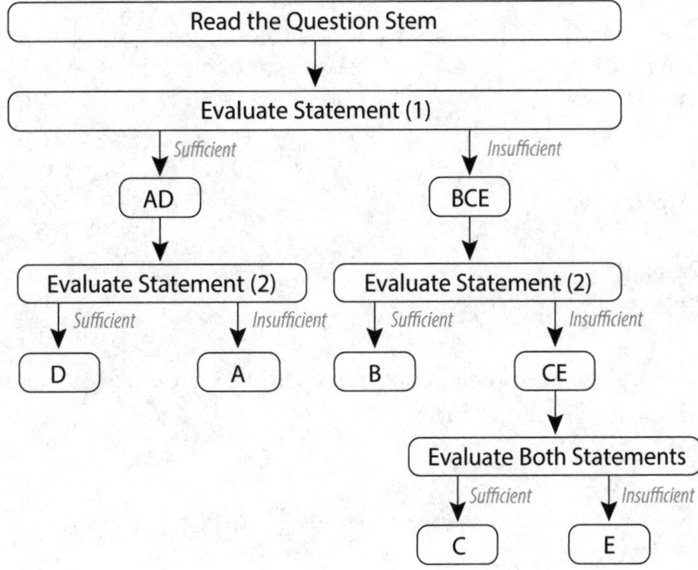


## DATA SUFFICIENCY: PIECES OF THE PUZZLE

In terms of mathematical content, Data Sufficiency questions test the same kinds of topics tested by Problem Solving questions (as we told you in Chapter 9). You'll find problems involving integers, percents, averages, ratios, algebra, and geometry. Only the format is different.

Proven Technique: Pieces of the Puzzle

Your familiarity with the math content, however, can give you an advantage when working a Data Sufficiency question. Most people read the question and then immediately read the statements. But that's not how you would normally work a math problem. Normally, you would read the problem and then ask yourself, "What do I already know?" and "What do I need?"

You should always attempt to do the same thing when working a Data Sufficiency question. Before proceeding to the statements, take stock of the information that you already know. Then, see if you can determine what sort of information the statements need to provide so that you could solve the problem.

We call this approach Pieces of the Puzzle. In a sense, Data Sufficiency questions are just like jigsaw puzzles. When you work a jigsaw puzzle, you know what piece you are looking for based on the shapes of the pieces that fit around it. In a Data Sufficiency question, you'll often know what sort of information you need from the statements based on what you already know from the question stem.

Here's an example:

If a store sold 30 more televisions this month than last month, by what percent has the number of televisions sold increased from last month to this month?

(1) This month the store sold 150 televisions.
(2) Last month the store sold 80% as many televisions as this month.

### Here's How to Crack It

Start by asking, "What do I know?"

You know two things. First, the problem asks for a percent increase. That should get you thinking about the formula for percent change:

$$\% \text{ change} = \frac{\text{difference}}{\text{original}} \times 100$$

Next, notice that you already know the change, since the question states that the store sold 30 more televisions this month than last month. So, you can plug the difference into the formula to get:

$$\% \text{ change} = \frac{30}{\text{original}} \times 100$$

**Pieces of the Puzzle**

*What do you know?*

The difference is 30.

*What do you need?*

The sales for last month, the original.

Now it's time to ask yourself, "What do I need?" By looking at the formula, you can see that you'll be able to answer the question if the statements give you a way to determine the original. So, as soon as you know how many televisions the store sold last month, you have sufficient information.

Remember to read only Statement (1). If the store sold 150 televisions this month and that represents an increase of 30 televisions, you know that the store sold 120 televisions last month. So, write down AD.

Now forget about Statement (1) and read Statement (2). This statement is a little trickier than the first. If last month's sales were 80% of this month's sales, you know that the additional 30 televisions that were sold this month represent 20% of the total. Now, you set up a part-to-whole relationship:

$$\frac{\text{part}}{\text{whole}} = \frac{20}{100} = \frac{30}{x}$$

Can you find the value of *x* from this equation? Of course. Therefore, Statement (2) is also sufficient and the answer to this question is (D).

Let's try the approach again on a difficult question.

What is the average (arithmetic mean) of a list of 6 consecutive two-digit integers?

(1) The remainder when the fourth integer is divided by 5 is 3.
(2) The ratio of the largest integer to the smallest integer is 5:4.

### Here's How to Crack It

As before, apply the Pieces of the Puzzle approach by asking, "What do I know?"

Since the question asks you to find the average, you should remember that you can find an average if you have the sum of the items being averaged and the number of those items. In this case, you know that there are six integers. You also know that the integers are consecutive. Finally, since the question states that the integers are two-digit, you know that each integer is between 9 and 100.

Now, it's time to ask, "What do I need?" There are lots of possibilities. The statements could give you the sum of the six numbers. Or, the statements could give you the value of one of the integers and its position in the list. For example, if you know that the second integer is 12, you could certainly find the average.

Now, read and evaluate only Statement (1). It's best to think about the information in this statement by plugging in some possible numbers. For example, the fourth integer could be 18 because the remainder when 18 is divided by 5 is 3. If the fourth integer is 18, the first integer is 15. The complete list would be 15, 16, 17, 18, 19, 20 with an average of 17.5. However, the fourth integer could also be 33, making the first integer 30 and the average of the six integers 32.5.

So, Statement (1) does not provide sufficient information to find the average of the six integers. Write down BCE.

Now, forget what you know from the first statement and evaluate only Statement (2). At first, Statement (2) may not seem like much help either. After all, if you are going too quickly, you may be tempted to think that the largest integer could be 15 and the smallest 12 or the largest could be 20 and the smallest 16.

However, here's where you need to remember the puzzle piece that you already have—there are *six* consecutive integers on the list. So, while 12 and 15 may seem to fit the ratio provided in the second statement, those numbers really don't satisfy the statement and the problem because there wouldn't be six numbers for the list.

The only way to satisfy the information in the second statement and in the problem is to make the smallest number 20 and the largest number 25.

Therefore, the answer to this difficult question is (B).

---

## DRILL 14 (Data Sufficiency Parts and Wholes)

The answers can be found in Part VII.

1. If only people who paid deposits attended the Rose Seminar, how many people attended this year?

    (1) 70 people sent in deposits to attend the Rose Seminar this year.
    (2) 60% of the people who sent deposits to attend the Rose Seminar this year actually went.

    - Statement (1) ALONE is sufficient, but statement (2) alone is not sufficient.
    - Statement (2) ALONE is sufficient, but statement (1) alone is not sufficient.
    - BOTH statements TOGETHER are sufficient, but NEITHER statement ALONE is sufficient.
    - EACH statement ALONE is sufficient.
    - Statements (1) and (2) TOGETHER are not sufficient.

2. Luxo paint contains only alcohol and pigment. What is the ratio of alcohol to pigment in Luxo paint?

(1) Exactly 7 ounces of pigment are contained in a 12-ounce can of Luxo paint.
(2) Exactly 5 ounces of alcohol are contained in a 12-ounce can of Luxo paint.

- Statement (1) ALONE is sufficient, but statement (2) alone is not sufficient.
- Statement (2) ALONE is sufficient, but statement (1) alone is not sufficient.
- BOTH statements TOGETHER are sufficient, but NEITHER statement ALONE is sufficient.
- EACH statement ALONE is sufficient.
- Statements (1) and (2) TOGETHER are not sufficient.

3. A car drives along a straight road from Smithville to Laredo, going through Ferristown along the way. What is the total distance by car from Smithville to Laredo?

(1) The distance from Smithville to Ferristown is $\frac{3}{5}$ of the distance from Smithville to Laredo.
(2) The distance from Ferristown to Laredo is 12 miles.

- Statement (1) ALONE is sufficient, but statement (2) alone is not sufficient.
- Statement (2) ALONE is sufficient, but statement (1) alone is not sufficient.
- BOTH statements TOGETHER are sufficient, but NEITHER statement ALONE is sufficient.
- EACH statement ALONE is sufficient.
- Statements (1) and (2) TOGETHER are not sufficient.

## Challenge Question #13

If Angela is twice as old as the combined ages of Bill and Charlie, then how old is Charlie?

(1) Four years from now, the sum of all three people's ages will be 108.
(2) Five years ago, the average (arithmetic mean) of all three people's ages was 27.

## Data Sufficiency and Geometry

For Problem Solving questions, the figures are generally drawn to scale. Chapter 16 discussed how you can ballpark by using the figure so long as it isn't marked "not drawn to scale."

For Data Sufficiency questions, however, you should be very careful when using the figure. The figures are drawn so that they represent the information in the question stem, but they need not accurately represent the information in the statements. So, you should base your conclusions about whether you have sufficient information on the statements rather than any figures provided with a Data Sufficiency question.

When Data Sufficiency questions are about geometry, however, you can often make very effective use of the Pieces of the Puzzle approach. The Pieces of the Puzzle approach works very well in situations in which you can use formulas and take stock of facts.

Here's an example of a medium question to illustrate:

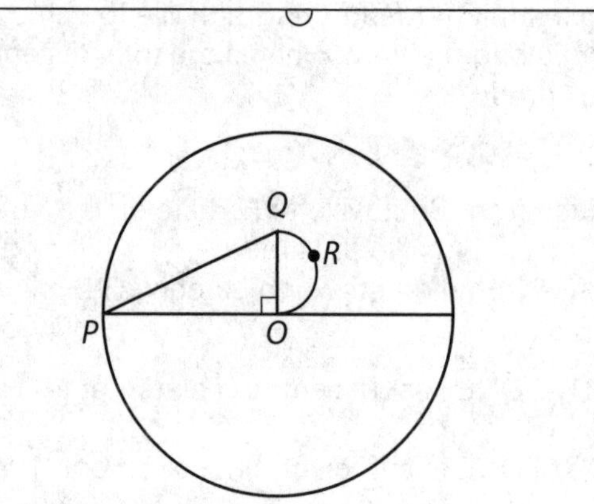


In the figure above, arc *QRO* is a semicircle. What is the area of the circle with center *O* ?

(1) The area of triangle *PQO* is 30.
(2) The length of *QRO* is 2.5π.

### Here's How to Crack It

Apply the Pieces of the Puzzle approach by asking, "What do I know?"

For this problem, you actually know a lot. You know that arc *QRO* is half a circle and that its diameter is one side of a right triangle. Of course, you also know that triangle *PQO* is a right triangle, so the Pythagorean Theorem applies.

Now ask, "What do I need?" The question asks for the area of the circle. Since the formula for the area of a circle is $A = \pi r^2$, you'll need a way to find the radius of the circle. If the statements provide either the length of *PO* or a way to find that length, you'll have sufficient information.

You're ready to look at Statement (1). The formula for the area of a triangle is $A = \frac{base \times height}{2}$. You know the area but neither the base nor the height, so you have insufficient information. Write down BCE.

Next, look only at Statement (2). Now it's time to remember that *QRO* is a semicircle. The statement gives you half of the circumference of a circle. You can use the circumference formula to find the diameter, *QO*. In this case, you actually have half the circumference, so use $2C = \pi d$ or $2(2.5\pi) = \pi d$ and $d = 5$. So, now you know the length of *QO*, but you still don't have the radius of the circle. (You may think that you recognize a 5-12-13 right triangle, but remember that you need two sides of the triangle to use the Pythagorean Theorem.) Cross off (B).

Finally, put the statements together. Now you know both the area of the triangle and its height, so you can plug those values into the formula for the area of a triangle to get $30 = \frac{1}{2}(b)(5)$. Can you use this formula to find *PO*? Yes. So the answer to the problem is (C).

**Pieces of the Puzzle**

*What do you know?*

*QRO* is a semicircle. The triangle is a right triangle. The formulas for the area of a triangle, the circumference of a circle, and the area of a circle.

*What do you need?*

The length of *PO*, the radius of the circle.

---

## Challenge Question #14

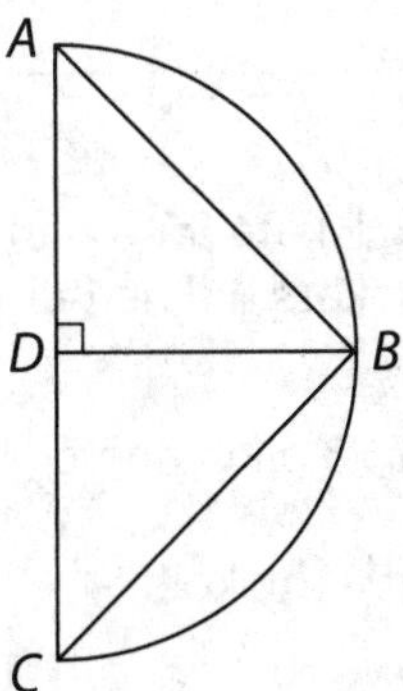


In the figure above, $\overline{AC}$ is the diameter of a circle. Is the area of $\Delta ABD$ equal to the area of $\Delta BCD$ ?

(1) $\overline{AD} = 2$
(2) $\overline{BD} = 5$

## Data Sufficiency and the Strange Powers of Powers

The Data Sufficiency question type is particularly well suited to testing your knowledge of the rules of equations and the strange powers of powers. Let's review this important information:

1. When working with equations, you generally need as many equations as there are variables in those equations.
   - A single equation with two variables cannot be solved,
   - but two distinct equations with the same two variables *can* be solved, using simultaneous equations, as you learned in Chapter 13.

   For example, $x = y + 1$ cannot be solved, but $x = y + 1$ and $2x = -y - 6$ can be added together, eliminating one variable so the other may be solved.

2. Just because there is only one variable doesn't mean that an equation has just one solution.
   - Generally, equations have as many solutions as the greatest exponent in the equation. So, an equation with a squared term will typically have two solutions.
   - Simple equations with a variable raised to an odd power may have only one solution.

   For example, if $x^2 = 4$, then $x$ could equal either 2 or $-2$. If $x^3 = 8$, then $x$ can only equal 2.

3. But sometimes, it's possible to get an answer even if there is only a single equation with two variables—IF the problem asks for an expression that contains both variables.

4. Sometimes you can also get an answer if there is only a single equation with two variables if both of those variables can only take on integer values.

Let's look at some problems that use these rules.

---

Mr. Jones spends $25 on movie tickets for a party of adults and children. How many children's tickets did he buy?

(1) Adult movie tickets cost $3 each and children's tickets cost $2 each.
(2) Mr. Jones buys a total of 11 tickets.

### Here's How to Crack It

Start by asking, "What do I know?" In this case, you know that Mr. Jones spends \$25 and that there are two variables—adult tickets and children's tickets.

Next, ask, "What do I need?" It's time to start thinking "two equations, two unknowns."

Now, evaluate Statement (1). From this statement, you get $3x + 2y = 25$. That's only one equation but two variables, so you do not have sufficient information. So, write down BCE.

Next, evaluate Statement (2), from which you can get the equation $x + y = 11$. Again, there's only one equation and two variables, so cross off (B).

When the statements are combined, you have two distinct equations with two variables, which means that you can solve. So, the answer is (C).

---

Here's a harder example. This example would be an upper-medium problem.

---

What is the value of $\frac{a}{b}$?

(1) $7a - 3b = 0$
(2) $b = 5$

- Statement (1) ALONE is sufficient, but statement (2) alone is not sufficient.
- Statement (2) ALONE is sufficient, but statement (1) alone is not sufficient.
- BOTH statements TOGETHER are sufficient, but NEITHER statement ALONE is sufficient.
- EACH statement ALONE is sufficient.
- Statements (1) and (2) TOGETHER are not sufficient.

### Here's How to Crack It

You're not going to get much mileage out of the Pieces of the Puzzle approach for this question. All you really know is that there are two variables involved.

So, ignore Statement (2). Based on Statement (1) ALONE, can you answer this question? At first glance, you might think not—because there are two variables in one equation. But the question is not asking you to solve for $a$ and for $b$, but for $\frac{a}{b}$. If you add $3b$ to both sides of the equation in Statement (1), you get $7a = 3b$. If you then divide both sides of the equation by $b$, you get $\frac{7a}{b}=\frac{3b}{b}$, which reduces to $\frac{7a}{b}=3$. By dividing both sides by 7, you get $\frac{a}{b}=\frac{3}{7}$, which answers the question. Statement (1) is sufficient, and you are down to AD. Looking at Statement (2) alone, of course, you can't answer the question, so the correct answer to the problem is (A).

---

The problem we just solved made use of the third rule in our review. Notice that (C) was a trap answer for this problem. Sure, you could find the value of *a* and *b* by combining the statements. However, (C) states that you need to put the statements together *because* neither statement provides sufficient information by itself. So, you'll want to remember that it's possible to know the value of an expression without knowing the values of the variables that make up that expression.

Here's one more example. This one doesn't sound that bad, but it's actually a very difficult problem.

---

Mr. Jones spends $76 on movie tickets for a group of adults and children. How many children's tickets did he purchase?

(1) Adult movie tickets cost $11 each and children's movie tickets cost $7 each.
(2) Mr. Jones bought two more adult tickets than children's tickets.

### Here's How to Crack It

As always, start by asking, "What do I know?" In this case, Mr. Jones spends $76 on movie tickets, and there are two variables. But, notice that there is actually one more thing that you know—movie tickets must be bought in integer quantities.

Next, ask, "What do I need?" You'll probably need two equations, but the fact that the variables can only take on integer values may change things.

Now, it's time to look at Statement (1), which gives you the equation $11x + 7y = 76$. Before dismissing this single equation with two variables as insufficient, remember that both $x$ and $y$ must be integers. Also, notice that the coefficients, 11 and 7, are large enough to limit the possibilities. Mr. Jones must buy fewer than 7 adult tickets. It's probably worthwhile to investigate how many of those integer values for $x$ produce an integer value for $y$. As it happens, $y$ is an integer only when $x = 5$. So, Mr. Jones bought 5 adult tickets and 3 children's tickets. So, write down AD.

Statement (2), however, does not provide sufficient information by itself. Remember that you don't even know how much the tickets cost based only on the second statement. So, the answer is (A).

---

So, how was this problem different from the first problem on page 324 in which Mr. Jones bought movie tickets? Why didn't we need to worry about the integer quantities on the first problem? Well, actually, we did. However, for the first problem, the first statement gave us the equation $3x + 2y = 25$. Had we taken some time to investigate this equation, we would have quickly discovered that there are several sets of integer solutions. For example, Mr. Jones could have bought 3 adult tickets and 8 children's tickets, or he could have bought 5 adult tickets and 5 children's tickets.

So, how do you know when to look for a single integer solution? Well, first make sure that the variables can only be integers! Since you can't buy half a movie ticket, that was part of the tip-off. Next, if there is going to be only one integer solution, it is likely that at least one of the coefficients will be a larger prime number like 11 or 17 or 29.

Finally, think about your current scoring level. A problem like that last one would show up only in one of the GMAT's most difficult question bins—because the test-writers think so few people will get it right. You aren't likely to encounter this problem on your computer-adaptive section of the GMAT unless you are scoring in the mid to high 40s on your practice math tests.

## DRILL 15 (Strange Powers of Powers)

The answers can be found in Part VII.

1. What is the value of $x$ ?

   (1) $x^2 = 4$
   (2) $x < 0$

   - Statement (1) ALONE is sufficient, but statement (2) alone is not sufficient.
   - Statement (2) ALONE is sufficient, but statement (1) alone is not sufficient.
   - BOTH statements TOGETHER are sufficient, but NEITHER statement ALONE is sufficient.
   - EACH statement ALONE is sufficient.
   - Statements (1) and (2) TOGETHER are not sufficient.

**Equation Tricks and Traps**

Some equations are not distinct, such as when one equation can be multiplied to equal the other equation.

For example:

$x + y = 4$

$4x + 4y = 16$

These are not distinct equations. There is not enough data yet to solve for $x$ or $y$.

2. What is the value of $xy$ ?

(1) $x^2 = 4$
(2) $y = 0$

- ◯ Statement (1) ALONE is sufficient, but statement (2) alone is not sufficient.
- ◯ Statement (2) ALONE is sufficient, but statement (1) alone is not sufficient.
- ◯ BOTH statements TOGETHER are sufficient, but NEITHER statement ALONE is sufficient.
- ◯ EACH statement ALONE is sufficient.
- ◯ Statements (1) and (2) TOGETHER are not sufficient.

3. What is the value of $xy$ ?

(1) $x^2 = 4$
(2) $y^2 = 9$

- ◯ Statement (1) ALONE is sufficient, but statement (2) alone is not sufficient.
- ◯ Statement (2) ALONE is sufficient, but statement (1) alone is not sufficient.
- ◯ BOTH statements TOGETHER are sufficient, but NEITHER statement ALONE is sufficient.
- ◯ EACH statement ALONE is sufficient.
- ◯ Statements (1) and (2) TOGETHER are not sufficient.

## YES/NO DATA SUFFICIENCY

We covered the basics of Yes/No Data Sufficiency in Chapter 11.

First, let's do a quick review by looking at a problem.

---

Is integer $x$ prime?

(1) $47 < x < 53$
(2) $x > 0$

### Here's How to Crack It

Notice that this question is phrased so that you would need to respond by saying "yes," "no," or "maybe" rather than by giving a numerical answer. That's why this is a yes/no question.

So, start by evaluating only Statement (1). There are 5 integers between 47 and 53—48, 49, 50, 51, and 52. Are any of these integers prime? No. But, notice that means that you can answer the question. Is $x$ prime? No, it isn't. So, you have sufficient information. (Remember that a statement can be sufficient for a yes/no question if it allows you to answer the question in either the affirmative or the negative.) So, write down AD.

Now, look only at Statement (2). Based on Statement (2), you don't know whether $x$ is prime. If $x$ is 3, for example, the answer to the question is yes. However, if $x$ is 4, the answer to the question is no. The best answer you could give to the question "Is $x$ prime?" based on Statement (2) is "maybe." So, the answer to the problem is (A).

---

## Plugging In on Yes/No Questions

Because as many as half of the Data Sufficiency problems you'll see on the GMAT will be Yes/No questions, it's a good idea to have a strategy for these questions. When Yes/No questions involve variables, you can plug into the statement and use those numbers to see if you always get the same answer to the question.

In the problem we just looked at, we plugged into the second statement. Because we were able to find examples of numbers that satisfied the statement but that gave different answers to the question, we knew that Statement (2) wasn't sufficient.

Now, let's look at another example.

---

Is $x$ an integer?

(1) $5x$ is a positive integer.
(2) $5x = 1$

**Statements Must Be True**
You can only plug in numbers that make the statement true. The answer to the QUESTION can be "yes" or "no," but the statements themselves must always be true.
So, for example, if Statement (1) says "$5x$ is a positive integer," then you can't plug $-2$ in for $x$. It would make the statement UNTRUE.

### Here's How to Crack It

As always, ignore Statement (2) and look only at Statement (1). Since this question is phrased as a yes/no question and there are variables involved, let's Plug In.

When you Plug In on a Yes/No Data Sufficiency question, you start by picking a number that satisfies the statement. For example, we can start with a nice, simple number such as $x = 2$. Notice that we can use $x = 2$ because $5 \times 2 = 10$ and 10 is a positive integer.

Now that we've found a number that satisfies the first statement, it's time to use that number to answer the question. Be sure that you use the value that you picked for $x$, not the result of the statement. So, the question becomes "Is 2 a positive integer?" and the answer is, of course, yes. Careful! Don't write down AD yet!

All we've done is find one example of a number that satisfies the first statement and used that number to answer the question. Now that we have an answer of yes, we actually want to see if it's possible to get an answer of no to the question based on a number that satisfies the first statement.

What if we make $x = \frac{1}{5}$? We've satisfied the statement because $5 \times \frac{1}{5} = 1$ and 1 is a positive integer. However, now we need to use our number to get an answer to the question.

Is $\frac{1}{5}$ a positive integer? No.

So, some numbers that satisfy the first statement produce an answer of yes to the question, while other numbers that satisfy the statement produce an answer of no. Therefore, we don't have sufficient information to answer the question, "Is $x$ an integer?" Write down BCE.

Now it's time to look at the second statement. In this case, we have an equation that we can solve to find that $x = \frac{1}{5}$. So we ask, "Is $\frac{1}{5}$ an integer?" and give a definite answer of no.

The answer to the problem is (B).

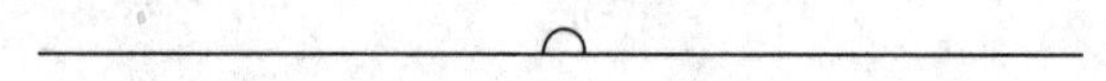

Plugging In is your most important strategy for handling Yes/No Data Sufficiency questions.

To see how effective Plugging In can be, let's try it on a more difficult question.

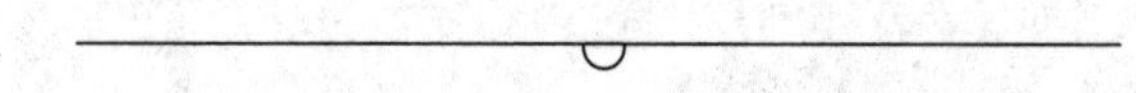

Is $3^n > 2^k$ ?

(1) $k = n + 1$
(2) $n$ is a positive integer.

### Here's How to Crack It

This is a yes/no question involving variables, so Plugging In is a good idea.

Start by evaluating Statement (1) alone. Pick an easy number for $n$. If $n = 2$, then $k = 3$. The numbers satisfy the statement, so it's time to use them to answer the question. Is $3^2 > 2^3$? Yes.

Remember, however, that you can't properly evaluate the statement based on the results from only one set of numbers. Suppose we tried something a little weirder for $n$? If $n = -1$, then $k = 0$. Is $3^{-1} > 2^0$? No. (Remember that negative exponents are just another way of writing a reciprocal and that any nonzero number raised to 0 is 1.)

So, we don't actually know what the answer to the question is based only on Statement (1). It looks as though the answer depends on the numbers we choose. Write down BCE.

For Statement (2), we can also Plug In. Notice that the statement doesn't tell us anything about $k$, however. So we could say that $n = 2$ and $k = 1$ to get an answer of yes to the question. But we could also say that $n = 2$ and $k = 4$ to get an answer of no. Cross off (B).

When we combine the statements, we can still use $n = 2$ and $k = 3$, which, as we saw when we looked at Statement (1), gives us an answer of yes to the question. However, we could also use $n = 1$ and $k = 2$ to satisfy the combined statements. Is $3^1 > 2^2$? No. So, the answer to this problem is (E).

**Don't Do the Work in Your Head**

To remember that you need to Plug In at least twice for each statement, write down the numbers you plugged in and the answers you get to the questions on your scratch pad.

---

### Yes or No Plugging In Checklist

- First, try plugging in a normal number for your variable. The number you pick must satisfy the statement itself. If it doesn't, plug in another number. The number will yield an answer to the question—either yes or no. But you're not done yet.
- Now try plugging in a different number for your variable. This time, you might try one of the "weird" numbers, such as 0, 1, a negative number, or a fraction. If the number still answers the question the same way, then you can begin to suspect that the statement yields a consistent answer and that you're down to AD.
- If you plug in a different number and get a different answer this time (a "yes" after getting a "no," or a "no" after getting a "yes"), then the statement does NOT definitively answer the question, and you're down to BCE.
- Repeat this checklist with Statement (2).

## DRILL 16 (Yes or No)

The answers can be found in Part VII.

1. If $x$ is a positive number, is $x < 1$ ?

   (1) $2x < 1$
   (2) $2x \leq 2$

   - Statement (1) ALONE is sufficient, but statement (2) alone is not sufficient.
   - Statement (2) ALONE is sufficient, but statement (1) alone is not sufficient.
   - BOTH statements TOGETHER are sufficient, but NEITHER statement ALONE is sufficient.
   - EACH statement ALONE is sufficient.
   - Statements (1) and (2) TOGETHER are not sufficient.

2. Is $x$ positive?

   (1) $xy = 6$
   (2) $xy^2 = 12$

   - Statement (1) ALONE is sufficient, but statement (2) alone is not sufficient.
   - Statement (2) ALONE is sufficient, but statement (1) alone is not sufficient.
   - BOTH statements TOGETHER are sufficient, but NEITHER statement ALONE is sufficient.
   - EACH statement ALONE is sufficient.
   - Statements (1) and (2) TOGETHER are not sufficient.

3. Are $x$ and $y$ integers?

   (1) The product $xy$ is an integer.
   (2) $x + y$ is an integer.

   - Statement (1) ALONE is sufficient, but statement (2) alone is not sufficient.
   - Statement (2) ALONE is sufficient, but statement (1) alone is not sufficient.
   - BOTH statements TOGETHER are sufficient, but NEITHER statement ALONE is sufficient.
   - EACH statement ALONE is sufficient.
   - Statements (1) and (2) TOGETHER are not sufficient.

## Challenge Question #15

If $a$ and $b$ are positive integers, is $2\sqrt[3]{a} < \sqrt[3]{a + b}$ ?

1) $7a < b$
2) $7a < a + b$

## More Ways to Plug In

As you have just seen, Plugging In can be a very helpful tool to evaluate whether the statements provide sufficient information to answer the question on Yes/No Data Sufficiency questions. Sometimes, however, Plugging In can also help you discover what the question is asking.

Often, test-writers make a question harder by writing the question stem in a way that hides the concept being tested. After all, if you're having a hard time understanding the question, you'll almost certainly have a hard time answering the question. You should remember, however, that no matter how confusing the question stem appears when you first read it, GMAT questions really test only fairly straightforward math concepts. Plugging In can help you decipher the question stem.

Here's an example of how the test-writers might ask a difficult question:

---

If $l_1$ and $l_2$ are distinct lines in the $xy$ coordinate system such that the equation for $l_1$ is $y = ax + b$ and the equation for $l_2$ is $y = cx + d$, is $ac = a^2$?

(1) $d = b + 2$

(2) For each point $(x, y)$ on $l_1$, there is a corresponding point $(x, y + k)$ on $l_2$ for some constant $k$.

### Here's How to Crack It

One of the hardest things about this question is understanding the question stem. It's going to be impossible to evaluate the information in the statements before we understand what we're being asked.

Let's try applying the Pieces of the Puzzle approach by first asking, "What do we know?" We know there are two lines. And, since the question tells us that the lines are distinct, we know that they are different. We also sort of have the equations for each line, but we recognize that the equations we're given are really just the general equation for any line—$y = mx + b$.

At this point, it might be a good idea to take stock of what we know about lines. In the equation $y = mx + b$, $m$ is the slope and $b$ is the $y$-intercept. For our two lines in question, $a$ and $c$ represent the slopes and $b$ and $d$ represent the $y$-intercepts.

Okay, now we're getting somewhere. The question is asking us something about the slopes of the lines, since $a$ and $c$ represent the slopes. Now ask "What do we need?" We need a way to work with the equations of the two lines. Now, let's Plug In. If we let $a = 2$ and $c = 3$, then $(2)(3) \neq (2)(2)$. How could $ac = a^2$? That could only happen if $a = c$.

Now we've got it. If $a = c$, the slopes of the lines are equal. If the slopes of two lines are equal, the lines are parallel. This question is really just asking, "Is $l_1$ parallel to $l_2$?" If the test-writers had asked the question this way, the difficulty of the question would have dropped.

Let's check out the statements. If we look only at Statement (1), all we know is that the $y$-intercept of $l_2$ is 2 more than the $y$-intercept of $l_1$. In that case, the slopes could be the same—producing an answer of Yes to the question—or the slopes could be different—producing an answer of No. So, Statement (1) is insufficient. Write down BCE.

Now, let's look at Statement (2). Plugging In is a good way to evaluate this statement. Start by picking a value of $k$, which must be a constant. We'll let $k = 2$. Let's say that points (2, 6) and (3, 8) are on line $l_1$, which would mean that (2, 8) and (3, 10) are on $l_2$. Using those points, we can calculate that the slope of each line is 2. Since the slopes are the same, the lines are parallel. We have an answer of Yes to the question.

Of course, when you Plug In on Yes/No Data Sufficiency, you shouldn't stop after plugging in just one set of numbers. This time, let $k = 3$. Let's also say that (2, 8) and (3, 11) are on $l_1$, which would mean that (2, 11) and (3, 14) are on $l_2$. Once again, we can calculate the slope of each line. In this case, both slopes turn out to be 3. Again, since the slopes are the same, the lines are parallel. (Don't be thrown by the fact that the slopes are different for each Plug In. We're only trying to see if the slopes of the lines are the same each time we Plug In.)

If you remain unconvinced, you could try Plugging In again, but you'll again find that the slopes of the lines are equal. In effect, the second statement tells us that for each point on $l_1$ there is a corresponding point on $l_2$ that is a distance of $k$ units away. That can happen only if the lines are parallel. So, the answer is (B).

---

If that question left you shaking your head, you're not alone. It's a very difficult question. Only a handful of test-takers will wind up getting it right. In effect, the test-writers pulled out every trick in their book to make this question difficult. Understanding the various ways that the GMAT test-writers make questions difficult can help you improve your score dramatically.

## POE PRINCIPLES FOR DATA SUFFICIENCY

Data Sufficiency questions that you find difficult and confusing are a distinct possibility when you take the GMAT, so you need to be prepared for them. After all, if the computer is doing its job properly—and you can pretty much count on that—it will keep feeding you progressively harder questions during the computer-adaptive section, in the hopes that it will find one that you don't know how to do.

In other words, almost every GMAT test-taker hits a wall at some point. You've just gotten a string of questions right and suddenly there's a question on your screen that you find confusing. You need to answer it to move on to the next question, but you'd like to do better than a blind guess. In fact, if you narrow your available choices, you may just guess correctly, dodge the bullet, get the next couple of questions right, and wind up with a higher score than if you didn't have a plan for handling those tough, confusing questions. Good test-takers always have a good guessing plan in hand.

Part of the key to using a guessing strategy effectively is to know your current GMAT math score. If your current score indicates that you are answering mostly easy questions (a score up to roughly 25), continue to concentrate on mastering the principles that we've already covered. As you master those principles, you'll start to see more questions on practice tests that will make use of the traps that we'll discuss in a minute. To make further improvements, you'll need to learn how to spot and avoid the test-writers' favorite traps.

If your score is above 25, you're already seeing Data Sufficiency questions on your practice tests that contain the traps we're about to discuss. The first step to avoiding the traps is to learn to spot them. Learning to avoid the traps can be a very effective way to improve your GMAT score.

## Work with What You Know

We've already been using Process of Elimination (POE) throughout this section. On Data Sufficiency questions, a little knowledge can go a long way. Suppose you saw the following Data Sufficiency question:

What is the area of square *ABCD* ?

(1) The length of the side of square *ABCD* is 2.

(2) For square *EFGH*, which has sides that are 6 longer than those of square *ABCD*, the ratio of the perimeter to the area is the reciprocal of the corresponding ratio for square *ABCD*.

When we don't know something about a problem, our first impulse is to just skip the whole thing. Or to assume that there's no way to solve it. However, you can't skip questions on the GMAT, and you may not get your best score possible if you assume that everything that looks hard can't be solved.

Obviously, the second statement of this problem is wordy and confusing. You may not be sure what it says or whether it provides sufficient information to answer the question, but that doesn't mean you need to make a random guess.

Let's focus on what you DO know. To find the area of a square, you need to know the length of the side of the square—exactly what the first statement provides. Since the first statement is sufficient, your possible answers are (A) or (D).

In other words, you have a 50/50 chance of getting the question right. And you get there even if you find the second statement confusing.

As long as you know *something* about a Data Sufficiency question, you can do some shrewd guessing. Take a look at this variation of the problem we've been discussing:

What is the area of square *ABCD* ?

(1) The length of the side of square *ABCD* is greater than 1.

(2) For square *EFGH*, which has sides that are 6 longer than those of square *ABCD*, the ratio of the perimeter to the area is the reciprocal of the corresponding ratio for square *ABCD*.

You still know that you need the length of the side of the square to find its area. However, now the first statement does not provide that length. If the first statement is insufficient, you can narrow your choices down to (B), (C), or (E).

This time, you have a 1 in 3 chance of getting the question right. As before, you didn't need to tackle the second statement to better your odds of getting the question right.

## The Average Test-Taker and Data Sufficiency

Understanding the average test-taker can help you avoid several types of traps on Data Sufficiency questions. The single most important thing to remember about the average test-taker is that he tends to choose his answers very quickly. Any time that you are tempted to answer a Data Sufficiency question in only a few seconds, you may be about to fall for the same sort of trap that sometimes catches the average test-taker. That's not to say that you aren't about to pick the correct answer. However, you should take a few more seconds just to make sure that you aren't missing anything.

There are several common traps that the average test-taker falls for. Let's take a look at them.

Watch out for these common traps!

### Trap #1) Answer Choice E Means "I Don't Know"

Let's revisit that hard question from the More Ways to Plug In section to see how the average test-taker might approach it.

If $l_1$ and $l_2$ are distinct lines in the *xy* coordinate system such that the equation for $l_1$ is $y = ax + b$ and the equation for $l_2$ is $y = cx + d$, is $ac = a^2$ ?

(1) $d = b + 2$

(2) For each point $(x, y)$ on $l_1$, there is a corresponding point $(x, y + k)$ on $l_2$ for some constant $x$.

Many test-takers will find this question confusing. As a result, they have no idea how they are supposed to evaluate the information in the statements. But these test-takers don't want to admit that they don't know what to do. Most people don't like to admit that they don't know how to solve a problem!

Many test-takers will pick (E) on questions that they don't understand. They think that (E) means "I don't know how to do this problem." Of course, that's not what (E) means at all. Choice (E) means "I know exactly how to do this problem and that's why I know that the statements don't provide sufficient information."

If you want to pick (E) on a question that you find confusing, make sure that you can explain why you don't have enough information. You should be able to state exactly the piece of information that you needed but didn't get. If you can't do that, you may be equating (E) with "I don't know how to do this problem."

## Trap #2) The Statements Are Missing Information

Sometimes test-takers pick (E) because the question was designed to make it appear that the statements did not provide sufficient information. This trap is particularly aimed at those test-takers who feel pressed for time. It's always necessary to properly evaluate the information provided by the statements.

Consider this example:

---

What is the value of $r^2 + s$ ?

(1) $t - u = 8$

(2) $r^2t - su + st - r^2u = 24$

### Here's How to Crack It

Many test-takers who try to answer this question too quickly will be tempted by (E). There are two variables in the question stem but four variables in the statements. It is unclear what the variables $t$ and $u$ have to do with finding the values of $r^2$ and $s$. As a result, many test-takers will select (E). Alas, those test-takers have reached their conclusion too quickly.

Just because the statements do not appear to provide the required information, it doesn't mean that there is no way to answer the question.

Here's how this one is solved.

There's no way to determine anything about $r$ and $s$ from information about $t$ and $u$. As a result, Statement (1) is insufficient. So write down BCE.

Now, let's work with Statement (2). The equation provided does contain the two variables in the question stem. Let's try grouping the expressions differently:

$$r^2t - su + st - r^2u = 24$$

$$(r^2t + st) - (r^2u + su) = 24$$

$$t(r^2 + s) - u(r^2 + s) = 24$$

$$(r^2 + s)(t - u) = 24$$

Statement (2) is insufficient. Eliminate (B).

However, if the statements are combined, we can replace the expression $t - u$ with 8 and find that the value of $r^2 + s$ is 3. The correct answer is (C).

---

How can you avoid this mistake? Make sure that you take the time to fairly evaluate the information in each statement. You may need to do a little algebraic manipulation or plug in some numbers to see what's going on, but that is time well spent if you can eliminate some answer choices, or even find the correct one.

## Trap #3) Confusing Statements Are Not Sufficient

Because the GMAT test-writers know that people don't like to pick things that they don't understand, the test-writers will sometimes pair a fairly easy statement with one that is difficult to understand. The test-writers do this because they know that many test-takers will conclude that the difficult to understand statement is insufficient.

---

What is the volume of a certain rectangular solid?

(1) The solid can be cut into 16 cubes, each of which has a volume of 1.

(2) The base of the rectangular solid is a square, which has a diagonal length of $2\sqrt{2}$, and the ratio of the height of the solid to its length is 2:1.

### Here's How to Crack It

It's pretty straightforward to conclude that the volume of the solid is 16 from Statement (1). Most test-takers will quickly, and correctly, determine that Statement (1) is sufficient.

However, most of these test-takers will be confused by the information in Statement (2), So, many will assume that the confusing statement is insufficient and pick (A) as their answer.

However, Statement (2) is also sufficient. Here's how it works:

If the base of the rectangular solid is a square, the diagonal divides the square into two 45-45-90 triangles. For a 45-45-90 triangle, the hypotenuse is $s\sqrt{2}$. In this case, the side of the square turns out to be 2. So, for the rectangular solid, we now know both its length and width. The statement tells us that the ratio of the height of the solid to its length is 2:1, which means that the height of the solid is 4. So, we now know all three dimensions of the solid. Since the second statement was also sufficient, the correct answer is (D).

---

How do you avoid this mistake? This question had a very particular format. An easy to understand statement was matched with a statement that was much harder to understand. Many test-takers didn't want to pick an answer that included a statement that they didn't understand. So, these people picked (A). Typically, however, when the test-writers match an easy statement with a statement that is wordy and confusing, the harder statement is also sufficient. If the hard statement didn't work, the question would be an easy problem.

Obviously, you need to be careful in employing this guessing strategy. The easy statement needs to be so easy that very few people will evaluate it incorrectly. If that's the case, ask yourself why you're tempted to say that the more confusing statement is insufficient. Do you know what information it doesn't supply? Or are you saying, "I really am not sure what this statement says"? If your reason boils down to not fully understanding the statement, your better bet is to say that the confusing statement probably does supply sufficient information.

## Trap #4) Too Many Problems Are Easy

Be wary when you find yourself thinking that many of the questions on the GMAT are easy. GMAT test-writers are very good at disguising hard questions as easy ones. They figure that if a problem looks easy, a test-taker will be less diligent and less careful than when a problem looks hard.

Now, put GMAC's ability to pass off hard questions as easy questions into the context of the adaptive nature of the test. If you start to do well, the computer will feed you a harder question. But if you continue to think that all of the questions are pretty easy, you could wind up getting some hard questions wrong!

---

What was the average (arithmetic mean) attendance for baseball games played at Memorial Stadium during the months of June and July?

(1) The average numbers of people attending baseball games at Memorial Stadium for June and July were 23,100 and 25,200, respectively.

(2) There were 20 baseball games played in June at the stadium and 22 games played in July.

### Here's How to Crack It

This question looks pretty easy. Statement (1) gives us the average attendance for June and the average attendance for July. Many test-takers think this information is sufficient because they think that they can just average the two averages. (You—having completed our chapter on arithmetic—know better.) The same people look at Statement (2) and don't see any attendance figures at all. They quickly pick (A).

Of course, this reasoning is incorrect. The answer to this question is (C). An average is the total sum of values divided by the *total* number of values. We need to know the number of games in each month in order to find out the total number of people attending.

---

How do you avoid this mistake? Slow down! If you are purposeful and diligent when evaluating the information in the statements, you will be less likely to fall for this sort of trap.

## Trap #5) Making Bad Assumptions

Data Sufficiency questions try to get test-takers to make bad assumptions. The test-writers know how most people think about math, and they often write the questions to take advantage of the assumptions that people routinely make.

For example, consider the following question:

---

What is the value of $x$ ?

(1) $x > 8$

(2) $x < 10$

### Here's How to Crack It

Many test-takers assume that the answer is (C) because they assume that numbers are always integers. These test-takers probably also chose (C) very quickly.

Of course, the numbers are not always integers. In this case, the value of $x$ could be 9. But, it also could be 8.5. The correct answer is (E).

---

How can you avoid this mistake? Again, slow down! When a problem seems too easy, go back and reread the information. Are you, for example, assuming anything about the types of numbers that fit the statements? Using the Pieces of the Puzzle approach will also help you to avoid making assumptions about the information provided in the question stem.

## Trap #6) Remembering Statement (1) When Evaluating Statement (2)

Test-takers will often, unknowingly, use the information from Statement (1) as part of their evaluation of Statement (2).

---

At a business dinner, people were offered coffee or tea. If all the diners had either coffee or tea, how many of the diners had tea?

(1) Of the 60 people at the dinner, 10% had tea.

(2) Fifty-four people had coffee.

### Here's How to Crack It

Choice (D) is the most commonly chosen incorrect answer for this question. From Statement (1), it's pretty easy to conclude that 6 people had tea. With that information in mind, it's also pretty easy to look at the second statement and think "54 people had coffee so that means that 6 had tea. Yeah, that works." So, (D) looks like the answer to pick.

There's only one small problem with this line of reasoning—the second statement does not tell us the number of diners. So, based on the second statement, we have no idea how many people had tea. The correct answer is (A).

---

How can you avoid this mistake? *Always evaluate the statements independently.*

You should also be careful when the statements seem to agree. If the second statement had said "two people had coffee," it would have been easy to conclude that the second statement was not sufficient. By choosing a number that agreed with the information from the first statement, the test-writers made it much easier to fall for the trap. So, remember that just because one statement seems to agree with the other, that doesn't mean that they say the same thing.

## Putting It All Together

The biggest reason for falling for any of these traps always boils down to going too fast. We have just run through a list of common ways that test-takers make mistakes when answering Data Sufficiency questions, and all of these ways were different. However, these errors invariably happen from thinking that it's okay to answer Data Sufficiency questions quickly. Just because you don't need to compute an answer to a Data Sufficiency question doesn't mean that you can race through the question.

Recognizing the types of errors that the average test-taker makes on Data Sufficiency questions can sometimes help you guess your way to the right answer. That can be helpful if you find a question confusing or if you are running short on time close to the end of the section.

Let's look at one last example.

---

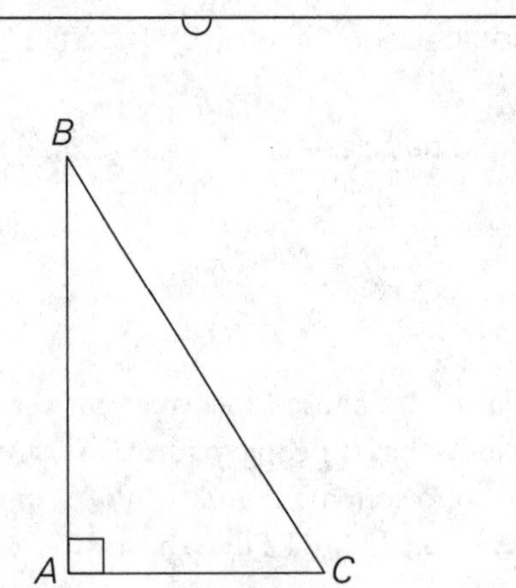


If the perimeter of right triangle *ABC* above is $3+3\sqrt{3}$, what is the area of the triangle?

(1) $AC \neq AB$

(2) Angle $ABC = 30°$

### Here's How to Crack It

The area of a triangle is $\frac{base \times height}{2}$. The average test-taker looks at Statements (1) and (2) and sees neither the base nor the height of the triangle. So, he quickly concludes that the answer is (E) because he doesn't see any way to get the area of the triangle from the information in the statements.

Let's see how close we can get to the answer using Process of Elimination. Ignore Statement (2). The first statement only tells us that the base and height have different lengths. Even with the value for the perimeter, there's no way we're going to get the values of the base or height. So, cross off (A) and (D).

Now, let's look at that second statement. From it, we can conclude that this triangle is a 30-60-90 triangle. If the triangle is 30-60-90, that would also mean that the base and the height of the triangle are different—exactly what the first statement told us. It doesn't sound like combining the statements adds anything that we don't know from just the second statement. So, (C) is unlikely to be the correct answer. This leaves only (B) and (E).

If you were running out of time, what answer choice would you choose? What answer choice would the average test-taker choose? Choice (E) might appeal to someone who did not describe what information is missing from the problem, so they assume that the statements are not sufficient. To a savvy test-taker, this is a signal that the choice might be incorrect, which could lead to the selection of (B).

And the correct answer *is* (B). If you were running out of time or not exactly sure how to solve this question, you can get to the right answer just by knowing how the average test-taker would respond and employing a little deductive reasoning.

---

## Here's How GMAC Wants You to Crack It

Statement (2) tells us that the right triangle is a 30-60-90 triangle. The side lengths of a 30-60-90 triangle are always in the same proportion: $x{:}x\sqrt{3}{:}2x$. (Remember that the $x$ in the proportion is the side opposite the 30-degree angle.) Therefore, the perimeter of a 30-60-90 triangle is $3x + x\sqrt{3}$. Now use the information in the question stem to solve for the short side of the triangle:

$$3x + x\sqrt{3} = 3 + 3\sqrt{3}$$

Remember that you don't need to solve. You just need to know that you can solve, since this is a Data Sufficiency problem. (Just in case you're curious, $x = \sqrt{3}$). Once you've got the length of the base, you can find the height and then find the area of the triangle.

It is possible to solve this problem. So, Statement (2) is sufficient and the answer is (B).

## That Was a Lot of Work

This question was very difficult and very time consuming if you tried to solve it as the test-writers wanted you to. Almost every test-taker battles the clock on the GMAT. Knowing how to use Process of Elimination can help you make informed guesses when you are stuck on a problem and starting to run out of time.

**Need More Practice?**
*Math Workout for the GMAT* contains tons of drills with detailed answer explanations.

# Summary

- The instructions for Data Sufficiency questions are very complicated. Memorize them now. Here is a pared-down checklist:
    - The first statement ALONE answers the question.
    - The second statement ALONE answers the question.
    - You need both statements TOGETHER to answer the question.
    - Both statements SEPARATELY answer the question.
    - Neither statement together or separately answers the question.
- Use POE to narrow down the field. If you know that Statement (1) is sufficient, you are already down to a 50/50 guess: (A) or (D). If you know that Statement (1) is not sufficient, you are already down to a one-in-three guess: (B), (C), or (E).
- If you are stuck on Statement (1), skip it and look at Statement (2). POE will be just as helpful.
- If Statement (2) is sufficient, you will be down to (B) or (D). If Statement (2) is not sufficient, you will be down to (A), (C), or (E).
- The math content of the Data Sufficiency questions is exactly the same as it is on the regular math questions.
- As you would in the regular math problems, look for the clues that tell you how to solve Data Sufficiency problems.
- When a problem asks a yes-or-no question, remember that the answer can be no.
- In yes-or-no questions, a statement is sufficient if it always gives us the *same* answer: always yes or always no. If the answer is sometimes yes and sometimes no, the statement is insufficient.

- In Data Sufficiency questions, look for opportunities to simplify or restate the question. If a question asks, "Did the foreman reject 40% of the 12,000 computers manufactured?" you could simplify that to ask, "Did the foreman reject 4,800 computers?"

- In intermediate and difficult Data Sufficiency problems, you must be on guard against careless assumptions. Take your time and treat every question the way you would the hardest question on the test.

# Chapter 19
# Hard Math

Come test day, chances are that you're going to run into a problem you don't know how to solve. In this chapter, you're going to learn some tools to help you develop a game plan for how to handle questions you're not sure how to solve.

# CRACKING HARD MATH PROBLEMS

## What Is a Hard Math Problem?

Before we discuss how to crack hard math problems, we need to pause for a moment to define the term *hard math problem*. The GMAT test-writers have a very precise definition of a hard math problem. For the test-writers, question difficulty is just a measure of how many people answer the question incorrectly. If a large percentage of test-takers, such as more than 70 percent, answer a question incorrectly, the question is a hard question!

But what are the implications of that definition?

Consider these two questions. Which of these questions do you think is a hard question?

What is the surface area of a rectangular shipping crate that is 12 feet long, 4 feet wide, and for which the greatest possible straight-line distance between any two vertices is 13 feet?

- 96
- 144
- 169
- 192
- 624

The original price of a new tech item is increased by 10 percent. Two months later, the new price is increased by 20 percent. The final price of the item is what percent greater than the original price?

- 10%
- 20%
- 22%
- 30%
- 32%

So, which is the hard question? Both!

We'll review the solutions to these questions in just a moment. First, however, let's talk about why both questions are hard questions and why that matters.

Most test-takers identify the shipping crate question as a hard problem because it tests content that is less familiar. Testing unfamiliar content is certainly one way to make a question hard. However, the difficulty of a question is not exclusively dependent on the content tested by the question. While the tech item question tests more familiar content, it is still a hard question because it has a good trap answer. As discussed in earlier chapters, the inclusion of trap answers can raise the difficulty of the question.

In other words, there's more than one way to create a hard math problem. Sometimes the GMAT creates a hard math problem by testing less familiar content. Other times, they include good trap answers. For that reason, we need to define hard math questions in a way that doesn't depend on the content of the question.

Our definition of a hard math problem is pretty simple: *A hard math question is any math question that you don't know how to solve.*

That means that this chapter is not about content, such as probability, that is sometimes considered hard. Instead, this chapter covers a series of techniques that you can use whenever your first reaction to a problem is "I don't think I know how to solve this problem."

Now, let's review the solutions to those two problems.

---

What is the surface area of a rectangular shipping crate that is 12 feet long, 4 feet wide, and for which the greatest possible straight-line distance between any two vertices is 13 feet?

- ○ 96
- ○ 144
- ○ 169
- ○ 192
- ○ 624

### Here's How to Crack It

Start by drawing a rectangular solid and labeling the length as 12 and the width as 4. Next, the greatest straight-line distance between any two vertices in a rectangular solid is a diagonal that joins a vertex of the top face to the opposite vertex on the bottom face. Add the diagonal to the figure and label its length as 13. Here's what the figure looks like:

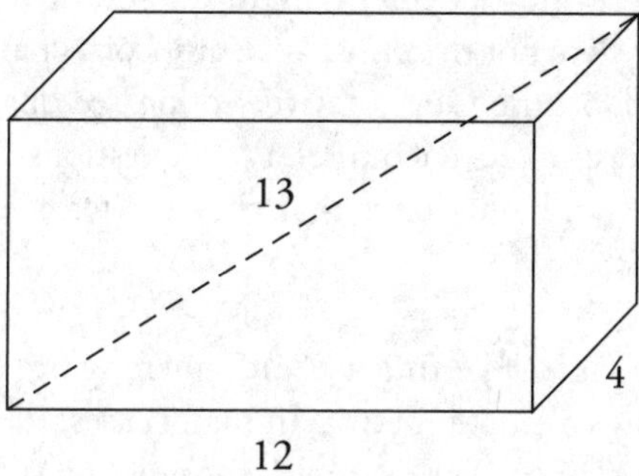


Since all three dimensions of the rectangular solid are needed to find the surface area, you must find its height. To find the height of the rectangular solid from the information provided, use the formula $d^2 = a^2 + b^2 + c^2$, where $a$, $b$, and $c$ are the dimensions of the rectangular solid and $d$ is the length of the diagonal. So, $13^2 = 12^2 + 4^2 + c^2$ and $169 = 160 + c^2$. Solve to find that $c = 3$. To find the surface area of the rectangular solid, start by finding the area of each face. The area of the front (and back) face of the solid is $12 \times 3 = 36$; the area of the right (and left) face is $3 \times 4 = 12$; and the area of the top (and bottom) face is $12 \times 4 = 48$. The surface area of the rectangular solid is $2(36 + 12 + 48) = 192$. The correct answer is (D).

---

The original price of a new tech item is increased by 10 percent. Two months later, the new price is increased by 20 percent. The final price of the item is what percent greater than the original price?

- ⬭ 10%
- ⬭ 20%
- ⬭ 22%
- ⬭ 30%
- ⬭ 32%

### Here's How to Crack It

There are percentages in the answer choices and no starting number so solve by Plugging In. If the original price of the tech item is $100, then the price after the 10 percent increase is $110. After the 20 percent price increase, the final price is $1.2 \times \$110 = \$132$. The original price was $100 and the final price is $132 so the final price is 32% greater. The correct answer is (E).

## Mistakes vs. Hard Questions

Before we start discussing strategies for solving hard questions, we need to take a moment to remember that hard questions are not the only cause of incorrect answers. Even test-takers who get the highest possible score on the Quantitative section see questions mostly about routine topics. While most GMAT test-takers encounter a few questions that they don't know how to answer, those questions aren't the only ones that they get wrong. So we need to distinguish mistakes from hard questions.

Everybody has had the experience of getting a question wrong because they misread something in the question or made a silly calculation error. In many cases, these sorts of errors cause more wrong answers than hard questions. For example, consider a test-taker who gets six questions wrong in the Quantitative section. Four of those errors may have resulted from misreading the question while only two of the errors resulted from not knowing how to do the question.

While it is important to learn how to solve hard questions, it is often easier to improve your score by working to eliminate mistakes on questions that you already know how to solve. Learning good test-taking techniques such as slowing down, reading the question more carefully, and rereading the question before submitting your answer can often add a big boost to your score.

## Common Causes of Mistakes

So what are some of the most common causes of mistakes when solving GMAT math questions? And what are the remedies?

Here are some of the most common causes of mistakes:

- **Going too fast.** The GMAT is, of course, a timed test. And there certainly are problems where it feels like time has accelerated while you are doing that problem! However, you still have, on average, two minutes to solve each question. Because it's likely that you can solve some questions a little faster than two minutes, you'll have an extra minute or so to spend on a few questions. There's no need to race through questions. In fact, if you get an answer to a question very quickly and you've done little or no work, you are almost certainly about to fall for a trap answer. You definitely want to reread the question to see whether you missed anything if you get an answer too quickly.

- **Improper Pacing.** Going too fast is about individual questions. Improper pacing is about the entire section. Some test-takers spend way too much time on some questions and race through others to make up the time spent. Because there's a penalty for leaving questions blank, spending too long on even a handful of questions might damage your score if you don't finish the section. Or, you many need to guess on too many questions at the end which can also damage your score. The remedy is to remember that 3 minutes is the maximum amount of time that you should spend on any one question. If you are at the 3-minute mark and are still trying to figure out how to do the problem, it's time to guess and move on.

- **Doing the Work in Your Head.** It's tempting to try to do the work in your head because it feels like you are saving time. It's also tempting to try to skip a lot of steps even if you are writing down some of your work. However, both of those strategies tend to be false savings of time because they increase the likelihood of making mistakes. Use the noteboards to write down your work and don't skip steps! It's better to take a few extra seconds to answer the question and get it right than to race through it and get it wrong.

- **Misreading the Question.** One of the most common causes of mistakes on GMAT problems actually has nothing to do with math! Many test-takers read problems too quickly and miss key information as a result. Get into the habit of rereading questions before you pick your answer. Spending time practicing GMAT questions can also help you to avoid misreading the question because it gets you familiar with the way that the GMAT constructs questions.

- **Hard Questions.** And, of course, sometimes the cause of a mistake is a hard question that you don't know how to do. In this chapter, we'll be taking a look at some strategies that you can use to solve hard questions.

## What Is a Hard Math Problem (Part II)?

Earlier we defined a hard math question as *any math question that you don't know how to solve.* There are two behaviors that often indicate that you are dealing with a hard math question. If you pay attention to these behaviors, you'll know when to use the strategies described in this chapter.

Some hard problems leave you feeling like you've hit a brick wall. You just don't know what to do. You don't even know how to get the problem started.

Other hard problems leave you feeling like there may be too many ways to get the problem started. You may be afraid to pick an approach because you are afraid that there's a faster approach. Or, a better approach. Alternatively, you may be able to see the first step of the problem but aren't sure what to do next. As a result, you never really get the problem started.

No matter what the situation, it's important to remember that solving a math problem is often an experimental process. Test-takers who get very high scores often don't know all the steps to solve a problem when they get started. They just aren't afraid to try something. If it doesn't work out, they try something else.

## Two Traits of Successful Test-Takers

Good standardized test-takers have two seemingly conflicting characteristics. On the one hand, these successful test-takers tend to be very consistent in how they approach questions. On the other hand, good test-takers tend to be flexible. When their preferred tool for solving a particular type of question doesn't work, they try something else.

Consistency is often key to solving math questions on a standardized test. Good standardized test-takers are good at pattern recognition. They've learned to recognize certain types of problems and to respond with a solution strategy that they know usually works on that type of problem. For example, a test-taker might respond to seeing variables in the answer choices by always Plugging In. This approach allows these test-takers to get to work faster when solving problems. Rather than worrying about whether there's a faster way or a better way to solve the problem, good test-takers just get to work solving the problem. This sort of consistent approach—trying the same tool for every problem that has certain characteristics—saves time in the section overall even if there may be a faster approach for some problems.

However, test-takers who embrace a consistent approach are also flexible in their approach when necessary. Every so often they may discover that their preferred tool doesn't work very well on the type of problem that it usually solves. In those cases, these test-takers look for another way to approach the problem.

Both characteristics—consistency and flexibility—are important to getting a good score on the Quantitative section of the test. Consistency will get you most of the way to a good score and most of this book is about learning consistent approaches, such as Yes-No Plugging In for Data Sufficiency. This chapter is about building some flexibility into your approach.

## Six Strategies for Hard Math Problems

So, what approach can you try when your favorite, consistent approach fails?

We have developed the six strategies listed below for working on hard questions. In most cases, these strategies are designed to help you get problems started. In many cases, if you can get the problem started, you can ultimately find the solution.

Here's a list of the six strategies. In the pages that follow, we'll explain each strategy and how to use it.

1) Use the Word You Know
2) Try a Simpler Example
3) Be Methodical/Look for Patterns
4) Remember What the GMAT Tests
5) Number Savvy
6) Advanced POE for Data Sufficiency

## Strategy 1: Use the Word You Know

When most people encounter a hard math problem, their brain focuses on the part of the problem that seems hard. We may worry about the math term that we aren't sure we understand. Or, we may panic about the complicated looking expression. Or, we may focus on wording that seems confusing.

However, most of these problems also contain math terms or phrases that are far more straightforward. Sometimes the best approach is to simply start with the more understandable part of the problem.

We call that strategy Use the Word You Know. Here's how it works.

---

If the prime factorization of integer $x = 3^a \times 5^b \times 11^c$ and $abc \neq 0$, then which of the following could be a multiple of $x$ ?

- 33
- 45
- 110
- 330
- 385

### Here's How to Crack It

Don't worry about the expression for *x*. We'll get to that. Instead, identify a math term that's easy to work with. In this case, start with the term *multiple*. Once you identify a term that you know, consider the definition or properties of that term. What makes one number a multiple of another? If integer $a$ is a multiple of integer $b$, then $a = nb$, where $n$ is an integer. Based on that definition, if $a$ is a multiple of $b$, then $\frac{a}{b} = n$, where $n$ is an integer. That's our way to work with the answer choices. If the answer choice divided by $x$ results in an integer, then that answer choice is a multiple of $x$. Next, we need to pay attention to the part of the problem that states that $abc \neq 0$. That condition means that none of $a$, $b$, or $c$ can equal zero. Hence, the minimum value of $x$ is $3^1 \times 5^1 \times 11^1 = 165$. Since none of 33, 45, or 110 results in an integer when divided by 165, eliminate choices (A), (B), and (C). Next, try (D). Because $\frac{330}{165} = 2$, an integer, 330 is a multiple of $x$. The correct answer is (D).

The previous problem illustrates how starting with the word you know works. Start by ignoring the part of the problem that seems hard or unfamiliar. Instead, focus on the math terms that you know. Review the definitions or properties of those terms. Use those properties to map out a solution strategy. Or, at the very least, use those properties to find the first step of the solution. Work from that first step to find additional steps to solve the problem.

Here's another:

For $n > 1$, the sequence $x_n$, is defined by $x_n = \sqrt{x_{n-1}}$. If $x_1 > 0$, is the median of the first four even-numbered terms in the sequence greater than the median of the first four odd-numbered terms in the sequence?

(1) $x_4 > \frac{1}{3}$

(2) $x_2 = \frac{1}{9}$

### Here's How to Crack It

The question presents a sequence that contains a square root, which increases the difficulty of this question. The question asks about the median of the first four even-numbered terms in the sequence and the median of the first four odd-numbered terms in the sequence. Focus on the term *median*. The median of an even-numbered list of numbers is the average of the middle two numbers in the ordered list. The first four even-numbered terms in the sequence are $x_2$, $x_4$, $x_6$ and $x_8$, so the median of the first four even-numbered terms in the sequence is found by the expression $\frac{x_4 + x_6}{2}$. The first four odd-numbered terms in the sequence are $x_1$, $x_3$, $x_5$ and $x_7$, so the median of the first four odd-numbered terms in the sequence is found by the expression $\frac{x_3 + x_5}{2}$. Therefore, the question seeks to determine if $\frac{x_4 + x_6}{2} > \frac{x_3 + x_5}{2}$.

The inclusion of the square root in this problem suggests a difficult problem. Before proceeding with the statements, consider the properties of square roots. The square root of a number greater than 1 always results in a lesser number. For instance, $\sqrt{4} = 2$. However, the square root of a number less than 1 always results in a greater number. For instance, $\sqrt{\frac{1}{4}} = \frac{1}{2}$. Because the sequence in the question involves a square root, if the first term in the sequence is greater than one, each subsequent term is less than the previous. If the first term in the sequence is less than one, each subsequent term is greater than the previous. Therefore, if $x_1 > 1$, then $x_1 > x_2 > x_3 > x_4 > x_5 > x_6$. In this case, the answer to the question is "Yes" because $\frac{x_4 + x_6}{2} > \frac{x_3 + x_5}{2}$. If $x_1 < 1$, then $x_1 < x_2 < x_3 < x_4 < x_5 < x_6$ and the answer to the question is "No" because $\frac{x_4 + x_6}{2} < \frac{x_3 + x_5}{2}$.

Evaluate Statement (1). This statement states that $x_4 > \frac{1}{3}$. Plug In a value of $x_4$ that satisfies this statement. If $x_4 = \frac{1}{2}$, then the value of $x_1 = \frac{1}{256}$. According to the information about square roots discussed earlier, this means the answer to the question is "No." Now Plug In again in an attempt to get an answer of "Yes." If $x_4 = 2$, then the value of $x_1 = 256$. According to the information about square roots discussed earlier, this means the answer to the question is "Yes." The statement produces two different answers to the question, so the statement is insufficient. Write down BCE.

Now evaluate Statement (2). Statement (2) provides a definitive value for $x_2$. The value of $x_2$ can be used to calculate that $x_1 = \frac{1}{81}$. Therefore, the answer to the question is "No." This statement cannot produce another answer to the question, so the statement is sufficient. The correct answer is choice (B).

## Strategy 2: Try a Simpler Example

Sometimes the GMAT likes to test familiar concepts in unfamiliar ways. One way that the test-writers accomplish this feat is to ask you to apply standard rules of arithmetic to unusual numbers. For a simple example, consider finding a percentage of a number. It's not very hard to find 10% or 25% of a number. It's a little harder to find 2% of a number but most test-takers can do that. But suppose you were asked to find $\frac{1}{8}\%$ of a number. Now, suppose the number were a fraction and that the answer choices were decimals. That's exactly the sort of situation that the GMAT might use on a harder problem.

For these types of problems, it's important to remember that the standard rules of arithmetic apply no matter how unusual the numbers. However, sometimes you need to remind yourself how the rules work. One good way to do that is to work the problem with easier numbers first. Then, apply those same steps to the harder numbers. We call that strategy Try a Simpler Example.

Here's an example of a problem that we can solve using the Try a Simpler Example strategy.

---

The value of $3^{-19}$ is what percent of the value of $\frac{3^{-16}+3^{-17}+3^{-18}+3^{-19}}{8}$?

- $\frac{1}{5}\%$
- 8%
- 20%
- 40%
- 200%

### Here's How to Crack It

Start with the Use the Word You Know strategy. Rather than focusing on the weird numbers, focus on the recognizable term *percent.* Calculating a percentage involves dividing a part by a whole. While helpful, the weird numbers make it hard to know what should be divided by what. So, it's time to employ the Try a Simpler Example strategy. To use the strategy, replace the weird numbers in the problem with some simpler numbers. Suppose the problem said:

The value of 2 is what percent of the value of 10?

To solve that problem, you would divide 2 by 10 and multiply the result by 100. It's going to work the same way with the weird numbers. Start by dividing the first number by the second number and multiplying the result by 100.

The first step of the solution is:

$$\frac{\left(3^{-19}\right)}{\left(\frac{3^{-16}+3^{-17}+3^{-18}+3^{-19}}{8}\right)}\times 100$$

Now it's time to start working on the calculation. Once again, the intimidating numbers can make it hard to see what needs to be done. However, the numerator of the fraction ($3^{-19}$) is being divided by a fraction. To divide a number by a fraction, multiply the number by the reciprocal of the fraction:

$$3^{-19}\times\frac{8}{3^{-16}+3^{-17}+3^{-18}+3^{-19}}\times 100$$

Or,

$$\frac{3^{-19}\times 8}{3^{-16}+3^{-17}+3^{-18}+3^{-19}}\times 100$$

There's no exponent rule that is immediately applicable, so look for ways to factor. Factoring often provides a way to use one of the three exponent rules when none of those three rules seems to apply. In this case, factor $3^{-19}$ out of the denominator to get:

$$\frac{3^{-19}\times 8}{3^{-19}\left(3^{3}+3^{2}+3+1\right)}\times 100$$

Note that factoring involves using the Multiply-Add exponent rule. For example, $3^{-19}\times 3^{3} = 3^{-16}$. The $3^{-19}$ in the numerator can be used to cancel the $3^{-19}$ in the denominator. By the way, canceling numbers in the numerator and denominator is really just an application of the Divide-Subtract exponent rule.

After cancelling:

$$\frac{8}{3^{3}+3^{2}+3+1}\times 100 =$$

$$\frac{8}{40}\times 100 =$$

$$\frac{1}{5}\times 100 = 20\%$$

The correct answer is (C).

Here's another problem in which the Try a Simpler Example strategy will help us to devise a solution.

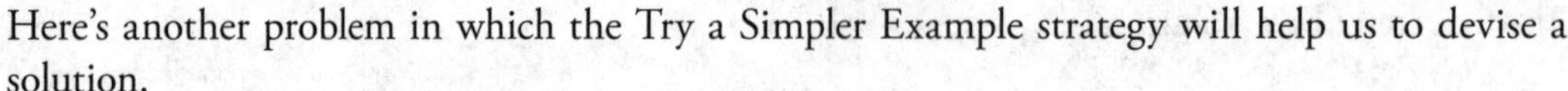

For any positive integer $n$, the sum of the first $n$ positive multiples of 3 equals $\frac{(3n)(n+1)}{2}$. What is the sum of all the multiples of 3 between 299 and 601 ?

- 15,150
- 22,275
- 45,000
- 45,450
- 90,900

### Here's How to Crack It

The test-writers have supplied a formula and they are hoping that you try to solve the problem using the formula. However, the provided formula doesn't exactly match the situation in the problem. The formula can be used to find the sum of the first 200 multiples of 3—600 is the 200th multiple of 3—but the problem asks for the sum of only the multiples of 3 between 299 and 601.

Let's ignore the formula and think about a simpler example. Suppose that you just needed to find the sum of 3, 6, and 9, the first three multiples of 3. That's pretty easy—the sum is 18. However, notice that the sum, 18, is also the product of the average of the three numbers, 6, and the number of numbers, 3. Moreover, because the numbers are evenly spaced, the median and the average are equal. So, to solve the problem, we just need to know how many multiples need to be summed and find the median, which is equal to the average, of those multiples.

There are 301 numbers between 300 and 600, inclusive. One-third of those numbers are multiples of 3. There are 101 numbers between 300 and 600, inclusive, that are multiples of 3.

Now we need the median of those 101 numbers. First, note that 300 is the 100th multiple of 3. We need the value of the 50th multiple of 3 after 300. That value is $300 + (3)(50) = 450$.

To find the sum asked for in the problem: $101 \times 450 = 45{,}450$. The correct answer is (D).

In this problem, the formula didn't really apply to the situation and there were too many numbers to simply add them up. By working with a simpler example first, we were able to determine that the problem was a question about averages. Time-consuming calculations or numbers that are unwieldy can often indicate that using the Try a Simpler Example strategy might be helpful in finding a better way to do the required calculation.

Use the Try a Simple Example strategy when

- Large or otherwise complicated numbers make the problem confusing
- You can only think of a very time-consuming way to work with the numbers in the problem
- You are unsure how to apply standard math rules to the problem

## Strategy 3: Be Methodical/Look for Patterns

The GMAT test-writers view the Quantitative section as a test of quantitative reasoning ability. As a result, they sometimes write problems that try to determine whether you can start from a short list of facts, rules, and operations and reason how to apply those to a new situation. One key facet of mathematical reasoning is looking for patterns. Sometimes the point of a GMAT question is to see whether you can find and apply a pattern for a given situation.

Here's an example:

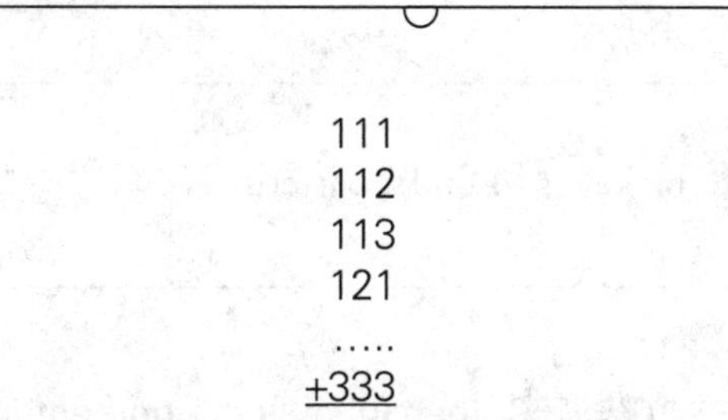

111
112
113
121
.....
+333

The addition problem shown above shows five of the 27 different three-digit integers which can be formed using only the integers 1, 2, and 3. What is the sum of these 27 integers?

- 1,998
- 2,700
- 3,996
- 5,994
- 6,660

### Here's How to Crack It

Obviously, the GMAT test-writers don't expect you to write out the 27 three-digit numbers and add them up. When confronted with a calculation that very few people could complete in two or three minutes, there's going to be a better way to work with the numbers. One way to find that better way is to look for a pattern.

In this problem, take a look at the hundreds digits of the numbers. If you were to write out the next five numbers (122, 123, 131, 132, 133), you'd see that 9 of the 27 numbers have a hundreds digit of 1. That also means that 9 of the numbers have a hundreds digit of 2, and 9 of the numbers have a hundreds digit of 3.

This same logic applies to the tens digits. There are 9 numbers with a tens digit of 1, 9 with a tens digit of 2, and 9 with a tens digit of 3. Of course, the same logic also applies to the units digits of the 27 numbers.

To find the sum of the 27 numbers, find the sums of hundreds, tens, and units digits.

For the hundreds digits: $9(100 + 200 + 300) = 5{,}400$

For the tens digits: $9(10 + 20 + 30) = 540$

For the units digits: $9(1 + 2 + 3) = 54$

The sum of the 27 numbers is $5{,}400 + 540 + 54 = 5{,}994$. The correct answer is (D).

In this problem, the key to the solution was to find the pattern so that 27 numbers could be summed in an efficient way. Without finding the pattern, it would have been difficult to find the sum in the time allotted—especially when you don't have access to a calculator. This problem also illustrates one of the most important tools for finding a pattern—write out enough of the numbers to see the pattern!

---

Here's another question where the key is to find a pattern:

---

If $8^2 + 10^2 + 12^2 + 14^2 + 16^2 = 760$, then what is the percent increase from $8^2 + 10^2 + 12^2 + 14^2 + 16^2$ to $24^2 + 30^2 + 36^2 + 42^2 + 48^2$ ?

- 200%
- 300%
- 600%
- 800%
- 900%

### Here's How to Crack It

Clearly, the test-writers don't expect you to compute the value of $24^2 + 30^2 + 36^2 + 42^2 + 48^2$ by squaring each number and finding the sum of the results. But notice how the brain focuses on the weird numbers in the problem? We can shift the focus away from the numbers by using the Use the Word You Know strategy. In this case, the known math term is percent increase. The formula for calculating a percent increase is $\textit{percent increase} = \frac{\textit{difference}}{\textit{original}} \times 100$. We already know the value of the original number, $8^2 + 10^2 + 12^2 + 14^2 + 16^2$, so we need a way to find the difference between the two numbers.

Now it's time to look for a pattern. Sometimes finding a pattern means matching part of one expression to a corresponding part of another expression. Here we can compare the corresponding parts of each expression by writing the second expression beneath the first:

$$8^2 + 10^2 + 12^2 + 14^2 + 16^2$$

$$24^2 + 30^2 + 36^2 + 42^2 + 48^2$$

It's easy to see that each number in the new expression is 3 times the corresponding number in the original expression. Rewrite the new summation as

$$(3 \times 8)^2 + (3 \times 10)^2 + (3 \times 12)^2 + (3 \times 14)^2 + (3 \times 16)^2$$

$$= (9 \times 8^2) + (9 \times 10^2) + (9 \times 12^2) + (9 \times 14^2) + (9 \times 16^2)$$

$$= 9 \times (8^2 + 10^2 + 12^2 + 14^2 + 16^2)$$

$$= 9 \times 760$$

Resist the urge to do the multiplication in favor of going straight to the percent increase formula:

$$\textit{percent increase} = \frac{(9 \times 760) - 760}{760} \times 100$$

After factoring out 760 in the numerator:

$$\textit{percent increase} = \frac{760(9-1)}{760} \times 100$$

After cancelling:

$$\textit{percent increase} = 8 \times 100 = 800\%$$

The correct answer is (D).

This question illustrates that finding patterns is often about matching corresponding parts of expressions. Matching corresponding parts of expressions makes it easier to see uniform changes from one part of an expression to its corresponding part in another expression. Matching corresponding parts of expressions is also a way of working methodically, which is also often an important part of finding patterns.

Use the Look for Patterns strategy when:

- You start thinking that a complicated formula is necessary to solve a problem
- You can only think of a very time-consuming way to work with the numbers in the problem.

When looking for a pattern, work methodically. You are much more likely to find a pattern when you work in a methodical way.

---

## Strategy 4: Remember What the GMAT Tests

Doctors have a saying: "Think horses, rather than zebras." The saying means that a patient who presents with unusual symptoms is much more likely to have a fairly common disease that just happens to be presenting in an atypical fashion, than to have a rare disease.

The saying also applies to hard math questions on a test such as the GMAT. The GMAT is a standardized test. As such, it needs to routinely test the same, relatively short list of topics. If the GMAT strayed from that list of topics too frequently, it would be impossible to compare scores from test-takers who took the test in different months or years. Therefore, if you see a question and you can't immediately classify the topic, just remember that it is far more likely that the question is testing a standard topic in an unusual way than testing an unusual topic. That's the crux of the Remember What the GMAT Tests strategy.

Here's an example:

---

A terminating decimal is one which has only a finite number of non-zero digits. Which of the following numbers has a reciprocal which is a terminating decimal?

- ◯ $\frac{455}{31}$
- ◯ $\frac{1,045}{43}$
- ◯ $\frac{770}{23}$
- ◯ $\frac{650}{19}$
- ◯ $\frac{800}{13}$

### Here's How to Crack It

Obviously, the GMAT test-writers don't expect you to divide the numbers. The numbers are too messy to work with quickly and the GMAT doesn't test raw calculating ability. However, knowing that the GMAT does not test raw calculating ability does provide a clue about how to proceed.

If the test-writers don't expect you to simply divide the numbers, there's likely some rule at work. So, start reviewing rules that the GMAT does test. The question stem uses the term *terminating decimal*, so start there.

Consider a few different numbers. Division by 3 always produces a non-terminating decimal unless the dividend is divisible by 3. For example, $1 \div 3 = 0.\overline{33}$ and $2 \div 3 = 0.\overline{66}$. Division by 4, on the other hand, always produces a terminating decimal. For example, $1 \div 4 = 0.25$, $2 \div 4 = 0.5$, $3 \div 4 = 0.75$, and $4 \div 4 = 1.0$. Division by 5 always produces terminating decimals. Division by 7 always produces non-terminating decimals unless the dividend is divisible by 7. Other numbers that work like 3 and 7 include 11 and 13.

Now, note that the decimal representation of $\frac{1}{6}$ is $0.1\overline{6}$, a non-terminating decimal. The prime factors of 6 are 2 and 3 so $\frac{1}{6}$ can be written as $\frac{1}{2} \times \frac{1}{3}$, or the product of a terminating decimal and a non-terminating decimal. If you try a few other examples of multiplying a terminating decimal and a non-terminating decimal, you'll see that the product is always a non-terminating decimal. It's also true that the product of two non-terminating decimals is also a non-terminating decimal.

So, now we have the rule that this problem is testing—the product of a terminating and a non-terminating decimal is a non-terminating decimal. This rule is exactly the sort of rule that the GMAT likes to test. The rule can be deduced through some elementary quantitative reasoning. Moreover, the application of the rule depends on looking at prime factors, a favorite GMAT topic.

To apply the rule, first take the reciprocal of an answer choice. Then, look at the prime factorization of the denominator. If the prime factors of the denominator include any numbers that produce non-terminating decimals when used as the divisor, that answer choice is a non-terminating decimal.

For (A), the reciprocal is $\frac{31}{455}$, so look at the prime factorization of 455. The prime factorization of 455 is $455 = 5 \times 7 \times 13$. Because division by either 7 or 13 produces a non-terminating decimal, (A) can be eliminated.

For (B), the reciprocal is $\frac{43}{1{,}045}$. The prime factorization of $1{,}045 = 5 \times 11 \times 19$. Because division by either 11 or 19 results in a non-terminating decimal, (B) can be eliminated.

For (C), the reciprocal is $\frac{23}{770}$. The prime factorization of $770 = 2 \times 5 \times 7 \times 11$. Because division by either 7 or 11 results in a non-terminating decimal, (C) can be eliminated.

For (D), the reciprocal is $\frac{19}{650}$. The prime factorization of $650 = 2 \times 5^2 \times 13$. Because division by 13 results in a non-terminating decimal, (D) can be eliminated.

For (E), the reciprocal is $\frac{13}{800}$. The prime factorization is $800 = 2^4 \times 5^3$. Because division by both 2 and 5 results in terminating decimals, the decimal representation of the reciprocal of this answer choice is a terminating decimal.

The correct answer is (E).

At first glance, this problem might have looked like it was simply testing whether you knew what a reciprocal was and how to divide. However, the numbers didn't divide easily and the GMAT doesn't test raw calculating ability. That led us to consider what the problem was really testing—a rule about multiplication with decimals—a topic that the GMAT does test.

---

Here's another example:

---

Which of the following integers can be written as both the sum of 5 consecutive odd integers and 7 consecutive odd integers?

- ○ 49
- ○ 70
- ○ 140
- ○ 215
- ○ 525

### Here's How to Crack It

If the numbers in the answer choices were smaller, this problem might not seem as intimidating. If the answer turns out to be one of the larger numbers, it's unlikely that you'll be able to quickly find the answer by writing out lists of consecutive odd integers and finding their sums.

Let's try to determine what concept this problem tests. For most GMAT problems, it's clear from the wording which concepts are being tested. For other problems, however, the wording may not make it obvious which concepts are being tested. Remember, however, that it is far more likely that any given GMAT question is testing a regularly tested topic in an unusual way than it is testing an infrequently tested topic.

So, let's see whether we can determine what this problem is testing. Each list of numbers consists of consecutive odd integers, which means that the numbers are evenly spaced. It also means that the numbers are part of an arithmetic sequence. The GMAT does test some basic ideas about sequences, including that the sum of a (finite) arithmetic sequence can be found by multiplying the average of the numbers in the sequence by the number of numbers in the sequence. Moreover, when the numbers in a list of numbers are evenly spaced, the average of the numbers is equal to the median of the numbers.

Now we have a way to solve this problem. In a sense, the problem is just an average question in disguise. The correct answer needs to be both the product of 5 and the average (or median) of a list of 5 consecutive odd integers and the product of 7 and the average (or median) of a list of 7 consecutive odd integers. That means that all we need to do is find an answer that is divisible by both 5 and 7 and ensure that the quotient of each division is an odd integer.

Choice (A) can be eliminated because 49 is not divisible by 5. Choice (B), 70, is divisible by both 5 and 7; however, the quotient in each case is an even number. Eliminate (B). Dividing (C), 140, by 5 or 7 also results in an even quotient. Eliminate (C). Choice (D) can be eliminated because 215 is not divisible by 7. The quotient when (E), 525, is divided by 5 is 105 and the quotient when it is divided by 7 is 75. Because both quotients are odd, 525 is the sum of 5 consecutive odd integers (101 + 103 + 105 + 107 + 109) and 7 consecutive odd integers (69 + 71 + 73 + 75 + 77 + 79 + 81). The correct answer is (E).

Here's what you need to remember about the Remember What the GMAT Tests strategy:

- Just because a problem *looks* like it is testing an unusual topic, doesn't mean that it *is* testing an unusual topic.
- It's more likely that a problem is testing a routine topic in an unusual way than that it is truly testing an unusual topic.
- If you can recast the problem as a familiar topic, you can probably find a way to solve the problem.

---

## Strategy 5: Number Savvy

The time limit is one of the biggest challenges of the GMAT Quant section. Most test-takers wish for an extra 10 or 15 minutes to do the section. Unfortunately, the GMAT test-writers are not likely to accede to the wish any time soon!

However, it is important to remember, as we have mentioned a few times before, that the GMAT does not test raw calculating ability. Every problem on the GMAT is designed so that some percentage of test-takers can do the problem in roughly 2 minutes. The harder the problem, the smaller that percentage of test-takers might be but the GMAT doesn't use problems that no percentage of test-takers can do in the time allotted.

The people who can do the problems that seem to include time-intensive calculations generally find smart, efficient ways to work with the numbers in the problem. We refer to those smart, efficient ways of working with numbers as Number Savvy. Number Savvy is a skill that you can develop. As you practice, be on the lookout for times that you find yourself filling up the page with calculations. You should also be on the lookout for times when you find yourself doing tedious calculations such as division to four decimal places. There are almost always better ways to work with the numbers in those situations. If you look for those ways as you practice, you can develop your Number Savvy.

We'll take a look at some Number Savvy principles, but first, let's look at an example for which Number Savvy is important.

$$\left(\frac{1}{3}\right)^{-2}\left(\frac{1}{9}\right)^{-3}\left(\frac{1}{27}\right)^{-4} =$$

- $\left(\frac{1}{27}\right)^{-9}$
- $\left(\frac{1}{27}\right)^{-24}$
- $\left(\frac{1}{3}\right)^{-144}$
- $\left(\frac{1}{3}\right)^{-20}$
- $\left(\frac{1}{3}\right)^{20}$

### Here's How to Crack It

Sometimes the GMAT likes to write questions that have shock value. In this problem, the numbers were picked to try to shock you into forgetting that basic rules of arithmetic still work even when the numbers get messy! There are only three exponent rules—multiply-add, divide-subtract, power-multiply—and they work no matter how unusual or messy the numbers are. This is another case for using the Remember What the GMAT Tests strategy. The GMAT does not test raw calculating ability. The GMAT does, however, test number savvy. Here, the problem is testing whether you can work with numbers in smart and efficient ways.

First, let's dispose of the fractions. The GMAT knows that many test-takers dislike working with fractions. And, of course, applying a negative exponent to a fraction can make the problem seem all the more confusing. However, we can rewrite the fractions using negative exponents:

$$\left(\frac{1}{3}\right)^{-2}\left(\frac{1}{9}\right)^{-3}\left(\frac{1}{27}\right)^{-4}$$

$$= \left(3^{-1}\right)^{-2}\left(9^{-1}\right)^{-3}\left(27^{-1}\right)^{-4}$$

Now, notice that we are looking for the product of three numbers. The only thing keeping us from using the Multiply-Add exponent rule is that the bases are not the same. However, the

GMAT tends to choose the numbers in a problem for a reason. In this case, notice that the denominators of the fractions are all powers of 3. The fractions can be rewritten so that they all use the same base:

$$\left(3^{-1}\right)^{-2}\left(9^{-1}\right)^{-3}\left(27^{-1}\right)^{-4}$$

$$=\left(3^{-1}\right)^{-2}\left(\left(3^{2}\right)^{-1}\right)^{-3}\left(\left(3^{3}\right)^{-1}\right)^{-4}$$

Now, apply the Power-Multiply rule:

$$\left(3^{-1}\right)^{-2}\left(\left(3^{2}\right)^{-1}\right)^{-3}\left(\left(3^{3}\right)^{-1}\right)^{-4}$$

$$=\left(3^{-1}\right)^{-2}\left(3^{-2}\right)^{-3}\left(3^{-3}\right)^{-4}$$

Apply the Power-Multiply rule again:

$$\left(3^{-1}\right)^{-2}\left(3^{-2}\right)^{-3}\left(3^{-3}\right)^{-4}$$

$$= (3)^{3}\ (3)^{6}\ (3)^{12}$$

It's time to use the Multiply-Add rule:

$$= (3)^{3}\ (3)^{6}\ (3)^{12} = 3^{20}$$

Of course, there's no answer that looks like $3^{20}$, so we'll need to find a way to rewrite $3^{20}$ so that it looks like one of the answer choices. We can use the Power-Multiply rule to do that:

$$3^{20}=\left(3^{-1}\right)^{-20}=\left(\frac{1}{3}\right)^{-20}$$

The correct answer is (D).

There are other ways to work with the numbers in this problem. However, the problem does illustrate two key tenets of Number Savvy. First, basic operations and rules, such as the three exponent rules, work even when the numbers are messy. Second, finding ways to rewrite numbers is often an important part of performing a calculation in an efficient way.

Here are some other Number Savvy principles:

1) Resist the urge to multiply or divide until absolutely necessary.
2) It's often better to work with fractions than decimals because fractions give you the opportunity to cancel.
3) Look for ways to cancel or reduce numbers before multiplying or dividing.
4) Divisibility is about shared prime factors.
5) Multiplying the numerator and denominator of a fraction by the same number doesn't change the value but may give you nicer numbers to work with.
6) Look for ways to factor or distribute.

---

Let's look at a problem that uses some of these principles to simplify a calculation.

---

Jack currently invests $425 per month in a mutual fund. He would like to increase his monthly contribution to the equivalent of $110 per week for a one year period. Rounded to the nearest $0.01, by how much does Jack need to increase his monthly investment?

- ◯ $15.00
- ◯ $33.33
- ◯ $36.67
- ◯ $51.67
- ◯ $76.67

### Here's How to Crack It

Conceptually, the solution to this problem isn't hard. All you need to do is multiply $110 by 52 and divide the result by 12 to find the new monthly investment and subtract $425, the current monthly investment. However, if you go about the calculation in the standard way, you'll be doing more work than is necessary and you'll probably find the calculation time-consuming.

Let's think about using some of those Number Savvy principles. First, we'll resist the urge to multiply or divide until necessary. So, rather than starting by multiplying $110 by 52, we'll just set up a fraction that shows the entire calculation that needs to be completed to find the new monthly investment:

$$\frac{110 \times 52}{12} =$$

Now look for ways to cancel—12 and 52 are both divisible by 4. Cancelling results in:

$$\frac{110 \times 13}{3} =$$

That looks better, but we can rewrite the fraction and use the distributive law to make the calculation a little nicer.

$$\frac{110 \times 13}{3}$$

$$= 110\,\frac{13}{3}$$

$$= 110\left(4 + \frac{1}{3}\right)$$

Then, using the distributive law:

$$= 440 + \frac{110}{3}$$

Finally, divide 110 by 3 to get \$36.67, rounded to the nearest 0.01, and the new monthly investment is 440 + 36.67 = \$476.67. The difference in the monthly investments is \$476.67 – 425 = \$51.67. The correct answer is (D).

---

## Strategy 6: Advanced POE

People who write standardized tests are good at two things: statistics and psychology. Test-writers study the ways that people react to certain kinds of situations that occur in problems. Then they write questions to take advantage of those behaviors.

One of the things that the GMAT test-writers know is that test-takers generally don't pick answers that they don't understand. In the context of a data sufficiency problem, that means that test-takers are likely to select (E) when they don't understand something about the question stem or when they don't understand how the information in the statements applies to the question.

You should pick (E) only when you can identify some piece of information that you needed the statements to provide and that you didn't get. Be careful that you don't fall into the trap of thinking that (E) means "I don't know."

Let's look at an example:

---

Is $k!$ a factor of $n!$ ?

(1) The greatest prime factor of $k!$ is 5.
(2) 7 is a factor of $n!$.

### Here's How to Crack It

Don't be thrown by the factorials. Instead, employ the Use the Word You Know strategy to focus on the word *factor*. How do you know that one number is a factor of another? If necessary, use the Try a Simpler Example strategy. How do you know that 2 is a factor of 10? If you divide 10 by 2, you get 5, an integer.

That means this question stem can be recast as "Is $\frac{n!}{k!}$ an integer?" For this fraction to evaluate to an integer, every number that is part of $k!$ must also be part of $n!$. For that to happen, $n!$ must be greater than $k!$. We'll likely need the statements to provide information about the values of both $k$ and $n$ to answer the question.

Statement (1) provides information about $k!$. If 5 is the greatest prime factor of $k!$, then $k$ either equals 5 or 6 as both 5! and 6! have 5 as their greatest prime factor. However, the statement provides no information about the value of $n$, so the statement is insufficient. Write BCE.

Statement (2) provides information about the value of $n!$. If 7 is a factor of $n!$, then $n \geq 7$. However, Statement (2) provides no information about the value of $k$, so it is insufficient on its own. Eliminate (B).

Combining the two statements shows that $n > k$ and hence that $n! > k!$. The answer to the question is always "Yes" when the statements are combined. The correct answer is (C).

---

The use of the factorials in the previous question stem and statements will confuse some test-takers who might be tempted to pick (E). However, it's a bad idea to pick (E) based on confusion about what the statements or question stem means. In that situation, it's actually better to guess an answer other than (E).

In our chapter on Data Sufficiency, we described the AD/BCE approach. One of the reasons that approach is so effective is that it reminds you to evaluate each statement independently before considering the statements together.

However, many test-takers read the question stem and both statements at the same time. The GMAT test-writers are aware of this behavior and write questions that make it look like the information can be easily combined to yield the answer to the question. It's important to remember that there are really two parts to the description of (C). While (C) does state that the information in the combined statements answers the question, it also stipulates that neither statement alone provides the answer to the question.

Let's take a look at a question for which (C) is the trap answer.

---

If $k$ is the average (arithmetic mean) of prime integers $x$ and $y$, is $k$ prime?

(1) $x = 3$
(2) $y = x + 2$

### Here's How to Crack It

Note that a test-taker who reads both statements at the same time might quickly conclude that the answer is (C). You can answer the question with both statements, but doesn't that just seem a little too easy? Of course, evaluating each statement on its own before evaluating the statements together can help us to avoid this trap!

Plug In to evaluate Statement (1). If $x = 3$ and $y = 7$, then $k = 5$ and the answer to the question is "Yes." However, if $x = 3$ and $y = 13$, then $k = 8$ and the answer to the question is "No." Statement (1) is insufficient. Write down BCE.

Now, Plug In to evaluate Statement (2). When plugging in for this statement, it's also a good idea to be methodical as that might help to identify a pattern. The question stem states that $x$ and $y$ are prime integers, so start by making $x = 3$, the least prime integer that makes $y$ an integer. If $x = 3$, then $y = 5$ and $k = 4$ and the answer to the question is "No." Next, try $x = 5$, the next prime integer greater than 3. If $x = 5$, then $y = 7$ and $k = 6$ and the answer to the question is "No." If $x = 11$, then $x = 13$ and $k = 12$ and the answer to the question is "No." (Note that we had to skip over $x = 7$ because then $y$ is 9, which is not prime.)

We are getting a consistent answer of "No" and we can see the pattern. The statement is producing pairs of consecutive odd numbers that are also prime. Because the values of $x$ and $y$ are consecutive odd numbers, their average is the even number between them. Because all even numbers, except for 2, are not prime, all numbers that satisfy Statement (2) produce an answer of "No" to the question. The correct answer is (B).

---

Finally, let's go back to the idea that people don't like to pick answers that they don't understand. Sometimes the GMAT will give you a data sufficiency problem in which one statement is much easier to understand than the other. In those situations, a good number of test-takers are tempted to pick the answer that states that the easier statement is sufficient but that the harder statement is insufficient. However, in these situations, it's usually a better bet to pick (D); both statements are independently sufficient.

Let's take a look at a problem in which one statement is easier to evaluate than the other.

Five different integers are selected at random from the numbers 1 to 100. Each of the selected numbers is then divided by integer *n*. What is the value of *n* ?

(1) The greatest possible remainder for any selected integer is 4.

(2) For some selected integer, *k*, the quotient when *k* is divided by *n* is 9, the quotient when *k* is divided by *n* + 2 is 6, and the difference of the remainders is 3.

### Here's How to Crack It

Start by evaluating Statement (1). Remainders are always less than the divisor. Use the Look For Patterns strategy by considering the possible remainders when dividing by 3.

When 3 is divided by 3, the remainder is 0.

When 4 is divided by 3, the remainder is 1.

When 5 is divided 3, the remainder is 2.

When 6 is divided by 3, the remainder is 0 again.

The pattern starts to repeat at this point. The possible remainders when dividing by 3 are 0, 1, and 2. So the greatest possible remainder when dividing by 3 is 2. Note that 2 is one less than 3. Now we have the rule—the greatest possible remainder when dividing by integer $n$ is $n - 1$.

Apply that rule to Statement (1). If the greatest possible remainder is 4, then the divisor is $4 + 1 = 5$. The first statement is sufficient. Write down AD.

Evaluate Statement (2). Note that Statement (2) is a lot wordier, and a lot more confusing as a result. If you knew the rule, Statement (1) was easy to evaluate. Even if you didn't know the rule, it wasn't too difficult to determine that Statement (1) meant that $n = 5$. So if you're starting to think that Statement (2) can't be sufficient, it's a good time to remember that when a fairly straightforward statement is paired with a wordier, more confusing statement, the wordier, more confusing statement is also usually sufficient. The better bet for this problem is that the answer is (D). Let's see why.

We can use Statement (2) to write two equations in terms of $k$, the dividend, $n$, the divisor, and $r$, the remainder. The first part of Statement (2) tells us that when $k$ is divided by $n$, the quotient is 9. So, $k$ can be expressed as $k = 9n + r_1$. The second part of Statement (2) tells us that when $k$ is divided by $n + 2$, the quotient is 6. So, $k$ can also be expressed as $k = 6(n + 2) + r_2$. As both expressions equal $k$, the two expressions can be set equal:

$$9n + r_1 = 6(n + 2) + r_2$$

Next, distribute to get:

$$9n + r_1 = 6n + 12 + r_2$$

Rearrange to get:

$$3n = 12 + (r_2 - r_1)$$

Statement (2) also tells us that the difference of the remainders is 3 so $3n = 12 + 3$, and $n = 5$. The correct answer is (D).

# Summary

- The GMAT defines a hard math question as one that most test-takers get wrong.
- The GMAT makes hard math questions by either testing less familiar content or including answer choices that are good trap answers.
- Knowing how to solve hard math questions is important, but most incorrect answers are the result of mistakes due to moving too quickly, not keeping pace, doing math in your head, and misreading the question.
- When you encounter a question you do not know how to solve, try to use one of the six strategies for solving hard math questions:
    - Use the word you know
    - Try a simpler example
    - Be methodical/look for patterns
    - Remember what the GMAT tests
    - Number savvy
    - Advanced POE for Data Sufficiency

# Part IV How to Crack the Verbal GMAT

# Chapter 20
# Grammar Review

Navigating Sentence Correction questions depends on your ability to quickly identify grammatical errors in a sentence. While the GMAT tests only certain errors, it's beneficial to have a strong foundation from which to pull in order to help notice errors.

## Why Grammar Review?

Grammar refers to the way words are used, classified, and structured together to form coherent written or spoken communication. Grammar is the way in which meanings are encoded and structured into words, phrases, clauses, and sentences.

There are approximately 17 sentence correction questions on the GMAT. They vary in terms of complexity of sentence structure and the specific grammar rules being tested. As outlined in the sentence correction chapter of this book, the best way to approach sentence correction questions is to identify errors in the sentence. While the sentence correction chapter looks at the most common types of errors on sentence correction questions, this chapter lays the foundation of the basics for understanding those errors.

Knowing the contents of this chapter can have an impact on your ability to quickly identify errors in sentence correction questions and, by extension, your overall verbal score. For example, can you spot the error in the following sentence?

> *My dog's favorite things to do are to play with a chew toy and barking.*

In this sentence, *to play* is a noun, that is, the infinitive form of the verb *play*, and *barking* is a gerund—that is, a noun made by adding *-ing* to the verb *bark*. The error is that the two activities are not parallel—one is a gerund and one is an infinitive.

How about this one?

> *The crispness of the fall air combined with the warmth of the afternoon sun, and the scent of fresh donuts and cider.*

Here, *crispness of the fall air combined with the warmth of the afternoon sun* and *the scent of fresh donuts and cider* are both phrases and do not form a complete sentence. In this case, *combined*, which can be a verb in some sentences, acts as part of the description rather than a verb that describes what things are doing.

## What's in This Chapter?

This chapter is broken up into three sections. Each section is designed to highlight a grammatical concept. Mastering the contents of each of these sections can only serve to increase your chances of identifying errors on the GMAT's Sentence Correction questions.

The first section covers the 8 basic parts of speech. The second section covers clauses, phrases, and fragments. The last section covers idioms and some common figures of speech—metaphors, similes, and hyperboles. Each of these sections also includes a brief drill to test your comprehension of the topics covered.

## How to Use This Information on the GMAT

Sentence correction questions on the GMAT frequently test the "Big 6"—verb tense, pronouns, idioms, misplaced modifiers, parallel construction, and subject-verb agreement. The content in this chapter is aimed at providing a basic but necessary foundation for keying in on the specific grammar rules tested on each question. Begin by reviewing the parts of speech and the differences between phrases and clauses. Continue to take practice questions on sentence correction. Over time your performance will improve.

## PARTS OF SPEECH

Parts of speech are the fundamental word classes of a language, based on similarities of the words' syntactic, logical, and semantic properties. There are basically 8 different parts of speech: noun, pronoun, adjective, verb, adverb, conjunction, preposition, and interjection. Words can be classified according to the positions they occupy in a sentence, which means that the same word can be classified in more than one way. For example, the word *talk* is a verb in the sentence "Mary will talk this afternoon about galaxies," but is a noun in the sentence "Mary will give a talk about galaxies this afternoon."

Below is a chart that outlines the different parts of speech, the definitions, and a couple examples of each. The remainder of this chapter is devoted to exploring the parts of speech in depth. Instead of providing you with a bunch of text, we've laid out the rest of this chapter in table format. Following the exploration of parts of speech, there is a short drill about identifying the parts of speech of certain words in a sentence.

### The 8 Parts of Speech

| Part of Speech | Definition | Examples |
|---|---|---|
| **Noun** | Name of a person, place, or thing | Robert, town, country, paper, happiness, hope, letters, Washington, sun, stars, Jupiter |
| **Pronoun** | A word used to take the place of a specific noun in a sentence | He, she, it, they, them, our, that, all, who, which |
| **Adjective** | Describes or modifies a noun or pronoun | Large, old, five, blue |
| **Verb** | Shows an action or state of being; describes what someone or something is doing | Speak, run, jump, are, is, was, talk, talking |
| **Adverb** | Describes or modifies a verb, adjective, clause, or another adverb | Gladly, very eagerly |
| **Conjunction** | Joiner for words, phrases, or clauses | And, for, although, but, either…or |
| **Preposition** | Provides information about location in place and time of nouns or pronouns and describes their relationship to other words or parts of sentences | For, under, above, at, between, from |
| **Interjection** | Expresses emotions or sudden feelings such as joy, sorrow, disgust, or excitement | Great!, Whew!, Fantastic!, Whoa! |

## Nouns

There are 10 types of nouns highlighted in the table below. Each type of noun serves a different purpose and provides a name for a person, place, or thing.

| Types of Nouns | Definition | Examples |
|---|---|---|
| **Common** | Used to name a general type of person, place, or thing. | boy, animal, tree, trumpet, house |
| **Proper** | Used to name a specific person, place, or thing. Proper nouns begin with a capital letter. | Fred, Robert, Baltimore, France, Mars, Milky Way |
| **Compound** | Two or more words that create a noun. Compound nouns can be one word (e.g., haircut), words joined by a hyphen (e.g., daughter-in-law), or as separate words (e.g., traffic light). | toothbrush, alarm clock, sailboat, attorney general, commander-in-chief |
| **Countable** | Nouns that can be counted. They can be either singular or plural, and they can be used with a number. | cup, bicycle, gallons, bird, flock |
| **Uncountable** | Nouns that CANNOT be counted. Also referred to as mass nouns. | wood, water, oil, nitrogen, happiness, information |
| **Collective** | Nouns that refer to a set or group of people, animals, or things. | team, group, bunch, staff, assembly |
| **Concrete** | Used to refer to people and things that exist physically and that at least one of the senses can detect (seen, saw, heard, felt, smelled, and/or tasted). | cat, bush, water, smoke, backfire, music |
| **Abstract** | Used to refer to nouns that have no physical existence and are not concrete, such as emotions, concepts, or ideas. | sadness, courage, creativity, excitement |
| **Gerund** | Nouns formed from verbs. All gerunds end in *-ing*, so they are sometimes confused with being a verb. | dancing, writing, thinking, flying |
| **Infinitive** | Nouns made by adding the word *to* in front of a verb. | to run, to play, to walk |

## Pronouns

Pronouns are related to nouns. There are 7 types of pronouns outlined in the table below.

| Types of Pronouns | Definition | Examples |
|---|---|---|
| **Personal** | Refers to a particular person or thing | Harvey trained the dog to shake hands before *it* took the food.<br><br>*Ours* is the car on the end of the row. |
| **Demonstrative** | Words that point to a noun | this, those, these, that<br><br>I'd like to take *that* car for a test drive.<br><br>You should consider taking *these* items for your party |
| **Indefinite** | Pronouns that refer to unspecified things | any, all, each, nobody, everybody, many<br><br>*Many* were invited to the ceremony, but only a *few* attended. |
| **Intensive** | Used to give emphasis to the antecedent | yourself, myself, ourselves, itself<br><br>The vice-president *herself* signed the memo.<br><br>I *myself* knew I had made a mistake. |
| **Interrogative** | Used to ask questions | who, when, whatever, whomever, which<br><br>*Whatever* happened to John Smith?<br><br>To *whom* should the letter be addressed? |
| **Relative** | Words that link a clause or phrase to another | who, whoever, that, which<br><br>*Whoever* wins the drawing will be very lucky.<br><br>The amount is *whichever* of the two is higher. |
| **Reflexive** | Words that refer back to the subject | ourselves, himself, itself, yourself<br><br>Becky taught *herself* how to change a tire.<br><br>We called for roadside assistance but ended up fixing the flat tire *ourselves.* |

## Adjectives

Adjectives are words that give information about nouns or pronouns. Adjectives can be either *determiners* or *descriptors*. *Determiner* adjectives are either articles, quantifiers, or demonstratives. There are no sub-groups of *descriptor* adjectives.

| Types of Adjectives | Definition | Examples |
|---|---|---|
| **Articles** | A determiner adjective. The words *a*, *an*, and *the* are articles. *The* is a definite article because it refers to a particular noun or pronoun. *A* and *an* are called indefinite articles because they refer to a class of noun. | *The* Great Wall of China is a popular tourist destination.<br><br>Clyde is *a* Scotsman.<br><br>Pamela is studying to be *an* engineer. |
| **Quantifiers** | A determiner adjective. Words used to express quantity. It can answer questions like "How many?" or "How much?" | enough, many, any, much, a little, some<br><br>She has *plenty* of money.<br><br>We have *few* alternatives. |
| **Demonstratives** | A determiner adjective. Words that demonstrate and function as an indicator of a speaker's point of view. | this, that, these, those<br><br>*That* car is Jane's.<br><br>*These* pastries taste great. |
| **Descriptive** | Words used to describe size, color, or shape of a noun or pronoun. | He ran down a *long, winding* road.<br><br>*Green, leafy* vegetables are nutritious.<br><br>The *large, black* horse won the race. |

## Verbs

There are three sub-groups of verbs that you should be aware of. There are types of verbs, forms of verbs, and verb tenses.

The different *types of verbs* dictate what is being done in the sentence.

| Types of Verbs | Definition | Examples |
|---|---|---|
| **Action** | Words that give the idea of action | run, fight, study, direct<br><br>Jamie *caught* a fish.<br><br>Corie *plays* tennis. |
| **State** | Words that convey a state of being | is, are, exist, seem<br><br>Amy *seems* studious.<br><br>Navel oranges *are* sweet. |
| **Active Voice** | Sentences in which the subject is performing the action | The detective *followed* the bank robber. |
| **Passive Voice** | Sentences in which the subject is the target or recipient of action | The bank robber *was followed* by the detective. |
| **Transitive** | Requires an object to express a complete thought | Please *bring* the materials.<br><br>Paula *conveyed* the meaning.<br><br>Did you *take* the dog for a walk? |
| **Intransitive** | Does not require an object to act upon | They *sang*.<br><br>Dennis *opined*. |

*Verb forms* are the different structures of verbs. The different structures can dictate certain rules about how the verbs are constructed in a sentence.

| Types of Verb Forms | Definition | Examples |
|---|---|---|
| **Base** | The basic form of a verb | run, play, drive, compete |
| **Infinitive** | The word *to* plus the base form of a verb | to run, to play, to drive, to compete |
| **Participle** | Word formed from a verb and modifies a noun, noun phrase, verb, or verb tense. Participles usually end in *-ed* or *-ing.* | Baked beans, stuffed chicken, crying baby |
| **Present Participle** | Word that can be used as a verb, but it isn't a complete verb when used by itself | guarding, playing, hiking<br><br>The dog has been *sleeping* most of the day.<br><br>Gretchen is *studying* for the test. |
| **Past Participle** | Verb form that usually ends in *-ed* or *-d* and expresses a completed action | played, accelerated, danced<br><br>She *played* for hours.<br><br>Fred *studied* for three months for the certification exam. |
| **Regular Verbs** | Verbs that have set or fixed endings, such as *-ed,* for their Simple Past and Past Participle forms | dress, dressed; close, closed; laugh, laughed; cry, cried<br><br>Jason always *dressed* for success.<br><br>Sherry was *amazed* at how well her Yoga classes went. |
| **Irregular Verbs** | Verbs that have special rules for creating past tense forms. These verbs do not end in *-d, -ed,* or *-ied.* | catch, caught; know, knew; take, took; write, wrote |

*Verb tenses* are a category that express time with reference to the moment of speaking. Tenses are usually manifested using specific forms of verbs, particularly in their conjugation patterns.

| Types of Verb Tenses | Definition | Examples |
|---|---|---|
| **Simple Present** | Subject plus base form of the verb | Jane *plays* chess. |
| **Present Continuous** | Subject plus *is/are* plus Present Participle form of verb | Jane *is playing* chess. |
| **Present Perfect** | Subject plus *has/have* plus Past Participle form of verb. It is used to show something that started in the past and continues into the present or that continued into the recent past. | Jane *has played* chess. |
| **Simple Past** | Subject plus Past Simple form of the verb | Jane *played* chess. |
| **Past Continuous** | Subject plus *was/were* plus Present Participle form of verb | Jane *was playing* chess. |
| **Past Perfect** | Subject plus *had* plus Past Participle form of verb. It is used to show something that started or happened in the past before another past event or activity. | Jane *had played* chess before she learned bridge. |
| **Simple Future** | Subject plus *will* plus base form of verb | Jane *will play* chess. |
| **Future Continuous** | Subject plus *will be* plus Present Participle form of verb | Jane *will be playing* chess. |
| **Future Perfect** | Subject plus *will have* plus Past Participle form of verb | Jane *will have played* chess by the time she gets the message. |

## Adverbs

Adverbs describe a verb, adjective, clause, or another adverb. There are four types of adverbs outlined in the table below.

| Types of Adverbs | Definition | Examples |
|---|---|---|
| **Manner** | Answers the question "How?" | The surveyor measured the area of the parcel *accurately.*<br><br>The man walked *carefully* around the laboratory. |
| **Time** | Answers the questions "When?," "How long?," or "How often?" | I am going to the dentist *tomorrow.*<br><br>He *regularly* lived overseas.<br><br>They received the newspaper *daily.* |
| **Place** | Answers the question "Where?" | The accountant looked *everywhere* for the missing entry.<br><br>The department store was located *nearby.* |
| **Degree** | Answers the question "To what degree?" or "How intensely?" | He didn't run *fast enough.*<br><br>The room temperature was *extremely* low. |

## Conjunctions

Conjunctions are joining words that fall into one of three types.

| Types of Conjunctions | Definition | Examples |
|---|---|---|
| **Coordinating** | Words that join two words, clauses, or phrases that are grammatically equal | for, and, nor, but, or, yet, so<br><br>Caleb is usually not hungry, *but* he can eat cereal anytime.<br><br>We visited cities in Spain, Portugal, *and* Italy. |
| **Subordinating** | Used to link two clauses together | although, whether, as if, how, in case, so that<br><br>*Because* it is so cold outside, Deborah wore her winter coat.<br><br>Bob left extra food out *so that* the dogs would have enough to eat. |
| **Correlative** | Pairs of conjunctions that are used to join equal sentence elements | either…or, neither…nor, so…as<br><br>*Both* my mother *and* I are physicians.<br><br>*Neither* my brother *nor* I won first place. |

## Prepositions

Prepositions provide information about the location in place and time of nouns or pronouns and describe their relationship to other words or parts of a sentence. Prepositional phrases are a group of words that contain a preposition at the beginning and a noun or pronoun at the end. It usually follows this formula: preposition plus modifiers (not required) plus noun or pronoun (object of the preposition). Some common prepositions are *on, in, at, to, for, over, under, except for, because of, instead of,* and *according to.*

Examples of prepositional phrases are: *beyond* the colorful horizon, *from* headquarters, *above* the clouds.

## Interjections

Interjections are used to express emotions and come in three types.

| Types of Interjections | Examples |
|---|---|
| **Adjectives** | *Beautiful!* That is an incredible rainbow.<br><br>*Great!* Now we can go on to the next step. |
| **Nouns** | *Holy smoke!* That was a great catch.<br><br>*Congrats!* You aced the test. |
| **Short Clause** | The food in the refrigerator was moldy. *How gross is that?* |

Interjections can also be followed by a period, comma, or question mark. Examples of this are:

*Ah,* that breeze feels great.
*What?* You got a ticket?
*Hmmm,* is that fresh coffee I smell?

## Parts of Speech Identification Quiz

In the sentences, phrases, or clauses below, identify the part of speech of the word in italics. The answers can be found in Part VII.

| | Sentence, Phrase, or Clause | Part of Speech |
|---|---|---|
| 1. | He always *speaks* the truth. | ____________ |
| 2. | She *frequently* writes articles for the school newspaper. | ____________ |
| 3. | The students dressed *smartly* for the class picture. | ____________ |
| 4. | Clowns, acrobats, *and* elephants | ____________ |
| 5. | *Our* family visited relatives in Florida. | ____________ |
| 6. | *Wow!* This is great! | ____________ |
| 7. | Most of the *yellow* cars are taxis. | ____________ |
| 8. | Helen took the used oil *to* the recycling center. | ____________ |
| 9. | The orders *came* from the colonel. | ____________ |
| 10. | *An* example of a wild animal is a tiger. | ____________ |
| 11. | *Gorillas* can be found at many zoos. | ____________ |
| 12. | It takes a *fast* car to win the Indy 500. | ____________ |
| 13. | His favorite color is *blue.* | ____________ |
| 14. | *Large* trucks on the freeway are frequently called "semis." | ____________ |
| 15. | *She* rarely ate dessert. | ____________ |
| 16. | Camels can *go* for days without water. | ____________ |
| 17. | Dad came back *from* the store. | ____________ |
| 18. | The dog *followed* Paul home. | ____________ |

## SENTENCES, CLAUSES, AND PHRASES

This section explores sentences, clauses, and phrases. These items are combinations of words from all parts of speech that convey a meaning. After introducing sentences, clauses, and phrases, there is a short quiz about identifying them.

### Sentences

A sentence is defined as a group of words that is complete in meaning and expresses a thorough and complete idea by giving a statement, a question, an exclamation, or a command. There are six types of sentence structures and two parts of sentences. Each of the six types of structures must have the two parts of sentences. We'll begin by introducing the two parts of sentences.

The *subject* of a sentence is the doer of the action or to what or whom the sentence is about. The subject can be either a noun or pronoun and is usually located before the predicate. There are three types of subjects: simple, complete, and compound.

| Types of Subjects | Definition | Examples |
|---|---|---|
| **Simple** | Only the main noun or pronoun | *Bobby* went to the market. |
| **Complete** | The subject itself plus any modifying words | *That bright star* is part of the Big Dipper. |
| **Compound** | More than one subject | *Christopher and Winnie-the-Pooh* are lifelong friends. |

The *predicate* says something about the subject and always contains a verb. Each of the types of subjects is associated with a type of predicate.

| Types of Predicates | Definition | Examples |
|---|---|---|
| **Simple** | Uses only the main verb | The robin *ate.* |
| **Complete** | The main verb plus other words that modify the verb | The robin *ate the birdseed.* |
| **Compound** | Multiple verbs plus the words that modify them. | The robin *pecked at* and *ate the birdseed.* |

There are six types of sentence structures. Each sentence structure has a relationship to the subject and the predicate.

| Types of Sentences | Definition | Examples |
|---|---|---|
| **Simple** | A simple sentence has only one subject and one predicate—one independent clause | The lion ran.<br><br>She ate spaghetti.<br><br>The dog played with the ball. |
| **Compound** | A compound sentence has at least two independent clauses. It uses a conjunction to connect the ideas | We had turkey for Thanksgiving, and we had honey-baked ham for New Year's Day. |
| **Complex** | A complex sentence has one independent clause and one or more dependent clauses | While he was on the airplane, the flight attendant brought beverages.<br><br>When you are driving your car, you should never be using your cellphone. |
| **Compound-Complex** | A compound-complex sentence has two or more independent clauses and at least one dependent clause. It uses conjunctions to combine two complete sentences and at least one incomplete sentence. | The man smelled lasagna, which was in the oven, so he immediately washed up for dinner.<br><br>After Wendy and Wanda went to the movie, they stopped for burgers, and then they stopped for gas. |
| **Run-on** | Run-on sentences are too long—they keep going on without the proper use of conjunctions or other connectors. | The raccoon really liked sausages, he went through the garbage every day to find them, he couldn't stop for anything else. |
| **Fragment** | A sentence fragment is merely just a piece of a sentence. It is missing a subject, a predicate, or an independent clause. It's simply incomplete. | If he stays in the water any longer<br><br>When he was stopped by the police officer |

## Clauses

A clause is a set of words that has a subject and a predicate. Every complete sentence has at least one clause. A clause can be as short as only two words, but usually is more than two words. Examples of clauses include:

*Tim sees.*
*Ken runs.*
*Karen ate.*
*They sang.*
*I see you.*
*They sang splendidly.*
*We drank hot chocolate.*

There are two types of clauses. Independent clauses are complete sentences. Essentially, it's a simple sentence. It has a subject and a predicate and makes sense on its own. Examples of independent clauses are:

*The deer ate berries.*
*The bear ate.*
*She ate at the restaurant.*

*Dependent* clauses, also called subordinate clauses, have a subject and a predicate but can't exist as a sentence because they don't express a complete thought. Examples of dependent clauses are:

*After he went bowling*
*Since she turned 25*
*If it rains tomorrow*

There are three different types of dependent clauses: noun clauses, adjective clauses, and adverb clauses.

| Types of Dependent Clauses | Definition | Examples |
|---|---|---|
| **Noun Clause** | A group of words that acts as a noun in a sentence. They begin with relative pronouns like which, who, or what. | She can eat *whatever she wants.* |
| **Adjective Clause** | A group of words that acts as an adjective. It has a pronoun—who, that, which—or an adverb—what, where, why—and a verb. | The book *that the teacher recommended* was not available in the library. |
| **Adverb Clause** | A group of words that acts as an adverb. It answers questions like where, when, how, and why. An adverb clause begins with a subordinate conjunction. | The boy ran *until he got home.* |

## Phrases

A phrase is a group of two or more words that work together but don't form a clause. A phrase is never a complete sentence on its own. There are seven types of phrases.

| Types of Phrases | Definition | Examples |
|---|---|---|
| **Prepositional** | Begins with a preposition and ends with a noun, pronoun, or clause (called the object of the proposition) | Zelda is *at the county fair.* |
| **Participle** | Begins with a past or present participle and is usually combined with an object or modifier | *Running in circles*, the dog tried to catch his tail. |
| **Noun** | Has a noun or pronoun as the main word and acts like a noun in the sentence | Todd bought a *light blue 21-speed bicycle.* |
| **Infinitive** | Infinitive phrases start with an infinitive ("to" plus simple form of verb) | Harry wants *to pet the dog.* |
| **Gerund** | Begins with a gerund (word ending in *-ing*) and includes modifiers or objects | *Bicycling up the hill* made us out of breath. |
| **Appositive** | Noun or noun phrase that gives another name to the noun next to it. It makes a sentence more descriptive. | The duck has an unusual favorite food, *chop suey.*<br><br>I have read my favorite book, *Pride and Prejudice*, many times. |
| **Absolute** | Absolute phrases are optional parts of sentences. The sentence still works normally without them. | *Mouth watering for turkey*, Matt looked forward to Thanksgiving dinner. |

## Clause or Phrase Identification Quiz

The answers can be found in Part VII.

| | Identify whether clause or phrase | Clause or Phrase? |
|---|---|---|
| 1. | He works hard every day. | ______________ |
| 2. | Before the next light. | ______________ |
| 3. | In a dark and dangerous hallway. | ______________ |
| 4. | If I need to call you. | ______________ |
| 5. | After a good day. | ______________ |
| 6. | Because it's the right thing to do. | ______________ |
| 7. | As quickly as possible. | ______________ |
| 8. | This car's not working. | ______________ |
| 9. | Working for himself. | ______________ |
| 10. | Whenever it gets cold. | ______________ |
| 11. | If they want to talk to me. | ______________ |
| 12. | Toward the north. | ______________ |
| 13. | In front of the building. | ______________ |
| 14. | Until the next time. | ______________ |
| 15. | I don't know the answer. | ______________ |

# IDIOMS AND FIGURES OF SPEECH

## Idioms

An idiom is an expression that conveys something different from its literal meaning, and that cannot be guessed from the meanings of its individual words. "Between a rock and a hard place" is an idiom that means "in a difficult or bad position with no good way of getting out of it." What makes an idiom different from a figure of speech is that its nonliteral meaning is already familiar to speakers of the language. Examples of idioms include:

These furniture sales are a *dime a dozen.*
Don't *beat around the bush.*
Don't *jump the gun.*

## Figures of Speech

A figure of speech is a phrase or an expression that expresses an idea by using words in a nonliteral and imaginative way. Unlike an idiom, it is possible to understand a figure of speech even if you have never heard it before. Metaphors, similes, and hyperboles are figures of speech.

| Types of Figures of Speech | Definition | Examples |
|---|---|---|
| Metaphors | A metaphor is a word or phrase typically used to describe one thing but unexpectedly used to describe something different. Metaphors make language interesting and help create imagery. They also make us aware of connections that we may not have thought of before. | *He was drowning in paperwork* is a metaphor that makes a connection between having to deal with a lot of paperwork and drowning in water. |
| Similes | A simile is an expression that uses the words *like* or *as* to describe something by comparing it with something else. A simile is like a metaphor except that a simile uses the words *like* or *as* to signal that a comparison is being made. | *She's as fierce as a tiger* is a simile, but *She's a tiger when she's angry* is a metaphor. |
| Hyperboles | A hyperbole is language that describes something as better or worse than it really is. A hyperbole is just a fancy word for exaggeration. | This suitcase *weighs a ton!*<br><br>I've got *a zillion things to do today.*<br><br>The sand was so hot my feet *were on fire.* |

## Other Figures of Speech

Figures of speech are words or phrases that have meanings other than their literal meanings. They can be metaphors, similes designed to explain a concept, or they can be different ways of pronouncing words or phrases to give them further meaning.

| Other Figures of Speech | Definition | Examples |
|---|---|---|
| **Alliteration** | The repetition of an initial consonant sound | Brenda buys brown basketballs.<br><br>Dennis is a dapper dresser. |
| **Allusion** | An indirect reference to something or someone. The purpose is to stimulate different ideas and associations using only a couple of words. | Gregory is such a scrooge!<br><br>The prisoner was in a Catch-22. |
| **Anaphora** | The repetition of the same word or phrase at the beginning of successive clauses or phrases | "It was the best of times, it was the worst of times, it was the age of foolishness,… ."<br>—Charles Dickens<br><br>"With malice toward none; with charity for all; with firmness in the right… ."—Abraham Lincoln |
| **Antanaclasis** | A rhetorical device in which a word is repeated in order to have different meanings in the same sentence. It is a form of a pun. | "Your argument is sound, nothing but sound."<br>—Benjamin Franklin |
| **Anticlimax** | A figure of speech in which statements gradually descend in order of importance | She won the medal of honor, had a lifelong clean driving record, and baked cookies for the neighborhood. |
| **Antiphrasis** | A figure of speech in which a word or phrase is used to mean the opposite of its normal meaning to create ironic humorous effect | Cyrano is incredibly handsome with his mountain of a nose. |
| **Antithesis** | The juxtaposition of contrasting ideas in balanced phrases | Many make the attempt, but few succeed. |
| **Assonance** | Identity or similarity in sound between internal vowels in neighboring words | "The crumbling thunder of seas"<br>—Robert Louis Stevenson |
| **Cataphora** | A figure of speech in which an earlier expression refers to or describes a forward expression | After she opened her gifts, Kristine made breakfast. |
| **Chiasmus** | A verbal pattern in which the second half of an expression is balanced against the first but with parts reversed | "Live simply so that others may simply live."<br>—Ghandi |

| | | |
|---|---|---|
| **Climax** | A figure of speech in which words, phrases, or clauses are arranged in order of increasing importance | He cooked a great dinner, wrote an antivirus program for the computer, and saved several people in a building fire. |
| **Dysphemism** | The use of a harsh, more offensive word rather than one considered less harsh. Contrasts with euphemism | Cigarettes are cancer sticks. |
| **Ellipsis** | The omission of a word or words whereby the sentence can still be understood | After work I stopped at the gym, which is next to the office, and then came home.<br><br>After work I stopped at the gym … and then came home.<br><br>"I like apples, bananas, cherries…."<br><br>Why would she do that…? |
| **Euphemism** | The substitution of a less harsh word for one considered harsher | Her grandfather passed away peacefully in his sleep. |
| **Irony** | The use of words to convey the opposite of their literal meaning | His commencement speech was clear as mud. |
| **Litotes** | A figure of speech in which an affirmative is expressed by negating its opposite | He is no spring chicken.<br><br>It's not my first rodeo.<br><br>He's not the sharpest knife in the drawer. |
| **Merism** | Conventional phrase that refers to something by naming several of its traits | Flesh and bone<br><br>Nuts and bolts |
| **Metalepsis** | A figure of speech in which reference is made to something by means of another thing that is indirectly related to it | Was this the face that launched a thousand ships?<br><br>I'm being followed by a lead foot. |
| **Metonymy** | A figure of speech whereby one word or phrase is substituted for another that is closely associated | The pen is mightier than the sword.<br><br>The White House has weighed in. |
| **Onomatopoeia** | The use of words that sound much like the actions they refer to | clap of thunder<br><br>murmur, buzz |

| | | |
|---|---|---|
| **Oxymoron** | A figure of speech in which incongruous or contradictory terms appear side by side | dark light<br><br>living dead<br><br>fine mess<br><br>deafening silence |
| **Paradox** | A statement that appears to contradict itself | Nobody goes to the mall anymore—it's too crowded.<br><br>The one rule you need to follow is to ignore all rules.<br><br>"I can resist anything but temptation."—Oscar Wilde |
| **Personification** | A figure of speech in which an inanimate object is endowed with human qualities | Justice is blind.<br><br>Money is the only friend I have.<br><br>The plants all danced as they were being watered. |
| **Pun** | A play on words | A backward poet writes inverse.<br><br>Your nose is the scenter of your face.<br><br>A bad shoemaker's assistant was given the boot.<br><br>A bacteria walked into a bar and was told by the bartender, "We don't serve bacteria here." The bacteria said, "But I work here—I'm staph." |
| **Synecdoche** | A figure of speech in which a part is used to represent a whole | 300 head of cattle<br><br>Twenty sails came into the harbor. |
| **Tautology** | Says the same thing twice in different ways | Forward planning<br><br>It's a free gift. |
| **Understatement** | A saying that downplays the full implications of the described situation | Swimming with those alligators might be a little unpleasant.<br><br>Walking across the state might take a minute or two.<br><br>You have just enough time to fly to Paris for lunch and be back in an hour or so. |

## Figure of Speech Identification Quiz

Identify the type of figure of speech. The answers can be found in Part VII.

| | Sentence, Clause, or Phrase | Figure of Speech |
|---|---|---|
| 1. | He was as brave as a lion. | ____________ |
| 2. | "All the world's a stage." | ____________ |
| 3. | Death lays its icy hands on kings of old. | ____________ |
| 4. | Let's just say that Bozo the Clown is not the brightest bulb in the box. | ____________ |
| 5. | The earth laughed beneath our feet. | ____________ |
| 6. | The ocean looks like a thousand diamonds strewn across a blue blanket. | ____________ |
| 7. | Why do we wait until a pig is dead before we cure it? | ____________ |
| 8. | Necessity is the mother of invention. | ____________ |
| 9. | Humming bee, buzzing saw, and cackling hen are examples of what? | ____________ |
| 10. | My uncle passed away in 1970. | ____________ |
| 11. | "To err is human, to forgive divine." | ____________ |
| 12. | The rancher bought 50 head of cattle last week. | ____________ |
| 13. | The teacher made it clear that cheating was no laughing matter. | ____________ |
| 14. | I'm so hungry I could eat a horse. | ____________ |
| 15. | The old man is long in the tooth. | ____________ |
| 16. | In Crown Hill Cemetery are buried President Benjamin Harrison, three vice-presidents, fifteen senators and governors, and John Dillinger. | ____________ |
| 17. | Phillip fractured five fingers. | ____________ |

# Summary

- Grammar is the way in which meanings are encoded and structured into words, phrases, clauses, and sentences.
- The 8 basic parts of speech are:
  - Noun
  - Pronoun
  - Adjective
  - Verb
  - Adverb
  - Conjunction
  - Preposition
  - Interjection
- A sentence is defined as a group of words that is complete in meaning and expresses a thorough and complete idea by giving a statement, a question, an exclamation, or a command.
- A clause is a set of words that has a subject and a predicate. Every complete sentence has at least one clause.
- A phrase is a group of two or more words that work together but don't form a clause.
- An idiom is an expression that conveys something different from its literal meaning.
- A figure of speech is a phrase or an expression that expresses an idea by using words in a nonliteral and imaginative way.

# Chapter 21
# Sentence Correction

GMAT Sentence Correction involves choosing from among five sentence options the one that is most grammatically correct while maintaining the meaning of the sentence. This chapter will begin with a review of how grammar is tested on the GMAT and then move on to show you the basic approach for handling Sentence Correction questions. Then we'll discuss the different types of grammar errors GMAT loves to test.

Sentence Corrections make up a little more than one-third of the 36 questions on the Verbal portion of the GMAT—approximately 14 questions that will be interspersed throughout the test. A Sentence Correction question consists of one long sentence that is either partially or completely underlined. You have to decide whether the sentence is grammatically correct as it's written, or if it is not, which of the answer choices best replaces the underlined portion.

Before we begin, take a moment to read the following instructions. They are a close approximation of the instructions you'll see on the real GMAT. Be sure you know and understand these instructions before you take the GMAT. If you learn them ahead of time, you won't have to waste valuable seconds reading them on the day of the test.

> Sentence Correction Directions: This question presents a sentence, part of which or all of which is underlined. Beneath the sentence you will find five ways of phrasing the underlined part. The first of these repeats the original; the other four are different. If you think the original is best, choose the first answer; otherwise choose one of the others.
>
> This question tests correctness and effectiveness of expression. In choosing your answer, follow the requirements of standard written English; that is, pay attention to grammar, choice of words, and sentence construction. Choose the answer that produces the most effective sentence; this answer should be clear and exact, without awkwardness, ambiguity, redundancy, or grammatical error.

## The Answers Aren't What You Think

It's important to note the directions specifically mention the "best" answer and that the best answer is based on "grammar, word choice, and sentence construction." What this really means is correct answers for Sentence Correction questions on the GMAT are going to be based on grammar rules of the English language.

If you are a native English speaker, this may sound easy—after all, you grew up speaking, reading, and writing the language. The problem is that few people strictly adhere to the grammatical rules when speaking and even when writing. But, GMAT sentence correction questions do strictly use those rules. So, Sentence Correction questions can be challenging for both native and non-native speakers.

## It's About What's Correct

Confronted with a poorly constructed sentence, most of us could find a way to fix it so that it makes sense. Of course the writers of Sentence Correction questions know this, so they have studied how to make answers sound correct. In other words, they will make answer choices that sound like something you would expect to hear someone say.

Finding a way to fix a poorly constructed sentence, however, is not good enough for the GMAT. You must be able to find the sentence that is correct based on the rules of the English language. As such, unless you are well versed in the grammatical rules of the English language, there will be times that the correct answer sounds incorrect and an incorrect answer sounds correct.

As a result, to do well on Sentence Correction questions, you'll need to stop trusting your ears and rely on a knowledge of English grammar rules to help differentiate correct from incorrect answers.

## The Good News

The people who write the GMAT try to stick to the basics. If they tested a controversial point of grammar, they might be proven wrong. They don't want to have to change their minds after a test is given and mail 20,000 letters explaining why they're changing the answer key (something that has happened from time to time in the past). The easiest way to avoid trouble is to test a handful of the rules of standard written English.

There are huge books devoted exclusively to the correct use of English. You could spend the next six weeks just studying grammar and never even scratch the surface of the subject. The good news is that this won't be necessary. The GMAT concentrates on only a few rules of standard written English. If you are familiar with these rules, then you will be familiar with most of the concepts tested on a given Sentence Correction question.

## An Important Note

That the GMAT typically tests only a handful of rules is not to say that those rules comprise the totality of everything the GMAT does test. The truth is, the GMAT can test any English rules it wants. You may encounter a question that does not have an error that fits into the rules we've covered in this chapter and that you are unfamiliar with. If you do, just do your best, use the POE tools, pick an answer, and move on to another question that tests a rule that is more familiar.

However, the rules we outlined here have proven to be the most likely to show up. If you know them, you'll be able to spot the error in the question much more often than not. So, if you know nothing else about the rules of standard written English, know these rules.

## Before We Get Started

One final note before we get going. This discussion is not designed to be an all-inclusive discussion of English grammar. This chapter is designed to be a discussion of grammar as it appears on the GMAT. Thus, there will be times that we may oversimplify a point, or ignore an arcane exception to a rule. If we do this, its because we feel that particular point did not warrant more, or any, detail.

## Process of Elimination

Most people approach Sentence Correction questions in similar ways. They read the original sentence and then read the entire sentence again with each of the different answer choices. This approach is both laborious and confusing. It's hard to keep five different versions of the same sentence straight, thus increasing the chances that you will make a careless mistake.

The approach we are going to use is based on Process of Elimination. We're going to focus on first identifying any errors in the original sentence, looking to eliminate any obvious repeaters, and then evaluating each remaining answer choice individually.

## Answer Choice (A)

Every Sentence Correction question will have five answer choices. However, (A) will always be a repeat of the underlined portion of the original sentence. So, when you evaluate the original sentence you are really evaluating (A). Therefore, if there is an error in the original sentence, you can eliminate (A) without even looking at it.

## Basic Approach to Sentence Correction

Spotting grammatical errors is important, but you'll need a strategy to get to the credited answer.

The Basic Approach is based on POE.

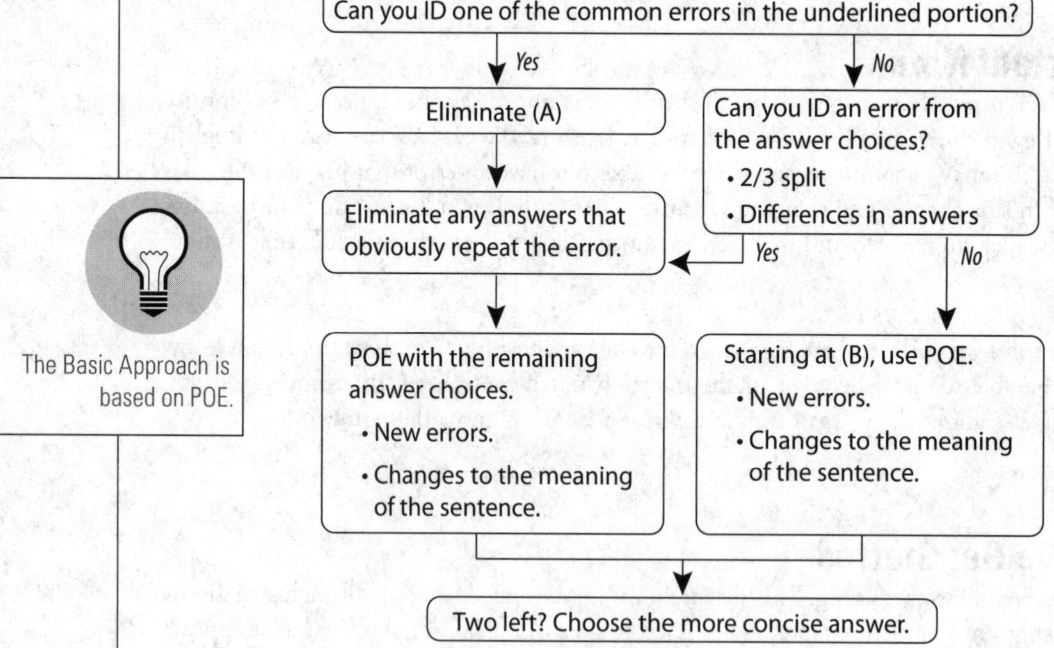


Let's explore each of these steps in a little more detail.

## Identify Any of the Common Errors in the Underlined Portion of the Sentence

When evaluating a Sentence Correction question, start by looking for one of the common errors tested by the GMAT in the underlined portion of the sentence. Those errors are Pronouns, Misplaced Modifiers, Parallel Construction, Comparison, Verb Tense, Subject-Verb Agreement, and Idioms. We'll go over these, and signs to look for to identify them, in more detail later.

**Online Verbal Drills**
Visit your Student Tools and get extra practice using these strategies!

## Obvious Repeaters

If you identified an error in the underlined portion of the sentence, eliminate (A). Then, quickly scan the answer choices looking for any answer choice that obviously repeats the error. An obvious repeater is an answer that you don't even need to read to know that it's wrong. Obvious repeater answer choices include errors that can be identified by the inclusion of only one or two words. If the answer has that word, it's wrong. For example, if the original sentence used the verb *is*, which is singular, but the subject of the sentence is plural, then any answer that includes *is* can be eliminated. The answers that include *is* are obvious repeaters. If you need to read the answer choice to evaluate it, then that answer is not an obvious repeater. At this stage, don't spend time evaluating the answer choices. Just look for the obvious repeaters. When you find an answer choice that obviously repeats the error in the underlined portion of the sentence, eliminate that answer choice.

## Process of Elimination

After you have eliminated any obvious repeaters, move on to working through the remaining answer choices one at a time, looking for reasons to eliminate each.

Begin the Process of Elimination by looking for new errors in the answer choices. Look for the commonly tested errors that you looked for in the underlined portion of the sentence. Start with (B) or the first answer that wasn't eliminated due to the inclusion of obvious repeaters and work your way through the answer choices one at a time. If there were no obvious repeaters, you can first ask whether the answer actually fixes the original error. If it does, then ask whether the answer includes any new errors.

If you do not find a new error in the answer choice, then determine whether the answer choice changes the meaning of the sentence in a substantial way. If the answer choice makes a substantial change to the meaning of the sentence or if the answer choice moves the sentence away from its intended meaning, eliminate it.

If you have two answers left, your final tool is conciseness. In general, the GMAT favors concise language. So, when you have two answers left and neither of them makes a new error or changes the meaning of the sentence, pick the one that's more concise. Recognize that you are essentially making a guess at this point. But, given the GMAT's fondness for concise language, you're making a good guess!

It's important to note here that the first tool you should always use is whether the answer makes a new grammatical error. If you cannot identify a new error, then you should evaluate if the answer choice changes the meaning of the sentence or is not as concise as another.

## The No Side of the Chart

What happens if you can't identify an error in the original sentence? If you can't identify an error in the original sentence, try to find an error by working with the answer choices.

In some cases, the answers will have a characteristic referred to as a 2/3 split. For example, two of the answer choices could start with *is* and the other three could start with *are*. This difference could be an indication that the sentence is testing subject verb agreement. So, look back at the original sentence to see if that's the case. If it is, you can eliminate (A) and any obvious repeaters. From there, just follow the steps described above. Really, the split is just another way to use obvious repeaters.

In other cases, the answers may be more complicated. There may not be a 2/3 split. However, if you scan through the answer choices, you may notice a word or phrase that is constructed differently in some or all of the answer choices. Again, these changes could indicate something that you can look for in the original sentence. If you spot an error in this fashion, you can again follow the steps outlined above.

If you can't find an error by examining the answer choices, then start Process of Elimination with (B). Look for answers that include errors that you can identify or answers that make substantial changes to the meaning of the sentence. If an answer includes an error or changes the meaning of the sentence, you can eliminate it.

If you get down to two answers, choose the one that is more concise. If you eliminate all of the answers for good reasons except (A), it likely means that the sentence was correct as written. You should expect to see some sentences that are correct as written.

Let's take a look at a sample question to illustrate the basic approach.

Registered brokerage firms have been required to record details of all computerized program trades made in the past year so that government agencies <u>will be able to decide whether they should be banned</u>.

- ○ will be able to decide whether they should be banned
- ○ should be able to decide whether they should be banned
- ○ should be able to decide whether they can be banned
- ○ will be able to decide whether program trades should be able to be banned
- ○ will be able to decide whether program trades should be banned

### Here's How to Crack It

Begin by identifying any of the common errors in the underlined portion of the sentence. We'll go over the common errors later in this chapter, so for now just know that one of the common errors is ambiguous pronouns. In this case, the pronoun *they* in the underlined portion of the sentence is ambiguous as it is unclear whether *they* refers to *registered brokerage firms* or *computerized program trades.* There is an error in the underlined portion of the sentence, so eliminate (A) and look for any obvious repeaters. Choices (B) and (C) also used the ambiguous pronoun *they*, so eliminate (B) and (C) as well. Evaluate the remaining answer choices individually, looking for a reason to eliminate each.

Choice (D) fixes the original error by changing the pronoun *they* to *program trades.* Now, determine whether the answer choice makes any other errors. The verb *able to* modifies the phrase *program trade*, meaning that the *program trades* are *able* to do something. This is a misplaced modifier error, so eliminate (D). Choice (E) fixes the original error by changing the pronoun *they* to *program trades* and creates no new errors, so keep (E).

If it was not apparent that (D) contained the misplaced modifier error, then (D) could have been eliminated because it is not as concise as (E). Either way, the correct answer is (E).

**Admissions Insight No. 6: The Interview**

- Always accept an interview opportunity if it is offered.
- Be on time, and dress appropriately.
- Prepare ahead of time—literally practice your responses out loud.
- Put together several points from your essays, and find a way to make these points during the interview.
- If there are any suspicious holes in your résumé, or embarrassing incidents in your past, find a way to bring them up yourself, and have a great explanation.
- When they ask—and they will—about your biggest setback, or your greatest challenge, be prepared to give them a positive spin on a challenging situation that you were able to overcome and learn from.

## COMMON SENTENCE CORRECTION ERRORS

### 1. Pronoun Errors

There are two main types of pronoun errors. The first is called *pronoun ambiguity.* You saw an example of this in the sentence about program trading. Take a look at a simple example:

> *Samantha and Jane went shopping, but she couldn't find anything she liked.*

This sentence contains a pronoun ambiguity error. In the example above, the pronoun *she* could refer to either Samantha or Jane. Because it is unclear who *she* is referring to, the sentence is incorrect.

> *Samantha and Jane went shopping, but Samantha couldn't find anything she liked.*

> *Samantha and Jane went shopping, but Jane couldn't find anything she liked.*

> *Samantha and Jane went shopping, but they couldn't find anything they liked.*

The second type of pronoun error is called *pronoun agreement.* Here is a simple example:

> *The average male moviegoer expects to see at least one scene of violence per film, and they are seldom disappointed.*

In this case, the pronoun *they* clearly refers to the average male moviegoer, so there is no pronoun ambiguity. However, *the average male moviegoer* is a singular noun and the pronoun *they* is a plural pronoun. Therefore, the pronoun and noun are not in agreement.

Pronouns and the nouns they refer to must always be in agreement as either singular or plural.

## How Do You Spot a Pronoun Error?

Whenever you see a pronoun in the sentence, check to make sure the pronoun could refer to only one other noun in the sentence and that the pronoun is in agreement with the noun. If it is unclear which noun the pronoun refers to, the sentence contains a pronoun ambiguity error. If the pronoun and noun are not both singular or both plural, there is a pronoun agreement error.

A pronoun is a word that replaces a noun. Here's a list of common pronouns. (You don't need to memorize these—just be able to recognize them.)

| Singular | Plural | Singular or Plural Depending on Context |
|---|---|---|
| I, me | we, us | some |
| he, him | they, them | none |
| she, her | both | ours |
| it | these | you |
| each | those | who |
| another | | which |
| one | | what |
| other | | that |
| mine | | |
| yours | | |
| his, hers | | |
| this | | |
| either | | |
| neither | | |
| each | | |
| everyone | | |
| nobody | | |
| no one | | |

Let's look at an example.

---

While Brussels has smashed all Western European tourism revenue records this year, they still lag well behind in exports.

- ◯ this year, they still lag well behind in exports
- ◯ in the past year, they still lag well behind in exports
- ◯ in the past year, it lags still well behind in exports
- ◯ this year, they lag still well behind in exports
- ◯ this year, it still lags well behind in exports

### Here's How to Crack It

Identify any of the common errors in the underlined portion of the sentence. The underlined portion of the sentence contains the pronoun *they,* so check to make sure there are no pronoun ambiguity or pronoun agreement errors. The pronoun *they* clearly refers to *Brussels,* so there is no pronoun ambiguity. However, the pronoun *they* is plural and the noun *Brussels* is singular because it is the name of a single city. Therefore, there is a pronoun agreement error. Eliminate (A) and look for any obvious repeaters. Choices (B) and (D) both use the pronoun *they* to refer to *Brussels,* so eliminate (B) and (D). Evaluate the remaining answer choices individually, looking for reasons to eliminate each.

Choice (C) fixes the original error by changing the pronoun *they* to *it.* Choice (C) is an awkwardly constructed sentence, but there may not be an obvious error with the sentence, so do not eliminate it. Instead, evaluate (E). Choice (E) also fixes the original error and doesn't appear to make any further errors. Because no error may be easily identifiable in either answer choices, look for another reason to eliminate an answer. Choice (E) is more concise than (C), so eliminate (C) and select (E), which is the correct answer.

---

**Admissions Insight No. 7: Full Time or Part Time**

Most students find that the experience of attending business school full time is generally more fulfilling than attending part time, because it allows students to build relationships and devote themselves completely to their studies. However, there can be compelling reasons to go part time: for example, if you simply can't afford to take two years off without pay or if your company is willing to pay all or part of your tuition costs.

## 2. Misplaced Modifiers

Misplaced modifiers come in several forms, but the test-writers' favorite looks like this:

*Coming out of the department store, John's wallet was stolen.*

When a sentence begins with a *participial phrase* (just a fancy term for a phrase that starts with a verb), that phrase modifies the noun or pronoun immediately following it.

So, read literally, this sentence means that *John's wallet* was *coming out of the department store.*

This is a misplaced modifier error. The modifying phrase does not modify the correct noun.

Misplaced modifiers come in other forms as well, such as:

A. participial phrases preceded by a preposition:
*On leaving the department store, John's wallet was stolen.*

B. adjectives:
*Frail and weak, the heavy wagon could not be budged by the old horse.*

This sentence indicates that *the heavy wagon* is *frail and weak*. The sentence intended to use the modifying phrase *frail and weak* to describe *the old horse*.

(**Correct**: *Frail and weak, the old horse could not budge the heavy wagon.*)

C. adjectival phrases:
*An organization long devoted to the cause of justice, the mayor awarded a medal to the American Civil Liberties Union.*

This sentence indicates that *the mayor* is *an organization long devoted to the cause of justice*. The sentence intended to use the modifying phrase to describe *the American Civil Liberties Union*.

In each of these examples, the modifying phrase modified the wrong noun or pronoun.

## How Do You Spot a Misplaced Modifier?

Whenever a sentence begins with a modifying phrase that's followed by a comma, the noun or pronoun right after the comma should be what the phrase is referring to. Every single time you see a sentence that begins with a modifying phrase, check to make sure that it modifies the right noun or pronoun. If it doesn't, there is a misplaced modifier error.

Let's look at two examples:

---

Written in 1961, Joseph Heller scored a literary hit with his comedic first novel, *Catch-22*.

- Written in 1961, Joseph Heller scored a literary hit with his comedic first novel, *Catch-22.*
- Written in 1961, Joseph Heller scored a literary hit with *Catch-22*, his comedic first novel.
- Written in 1961, *Catch-22,* the comedic first novel by Joseph Heller, was a literary hit.
- *Catch-22,* which was written in 1961 by Joseph Heller, scored a literary hit with his comedic first novel.
- *Catch-22,* the comedic first novel, scored a literary hit for Joseph Heller by its being written in 1961.

### Here's How to Crack It

Begin by identifying any of the common errors in the underlined portion of the sentence. The entire question is underlined, so look for an error anywhere in the text. There is a modifying phrase, so make sure the phrase properly modifies the noun or pronoun directly following it. In this case, the modifying phrase *written in 1961* modifies *Joseph Heller.* This indicates that Joseph Heller was written in 1961, when the modifying phrase intended to modify *Catch-22.* This is a misplaced modifier error. Eliminate (A) and look for any obvious repeaters. Choice (B) repeats the error, so eliminate (B). Evaluate each remaining answer choice individually, looking for reasons to eliminate each.

Choice (C) fixes the original error by correctly placing the noun *Catch-22* immediately following the modifying phrase, and commits no new errors, so keep (C). Choice (D) also contains a misplaced modifier error that results in pronoun ambiguity. For (D), the construction *Catch-22...scored* creates a modifier error. This sentence suggests that it is *Catch-22* and not *Joseph Heller* that scored a literary hit. Eliminate (D). Choice (E) also contains a misplaced modifier error as the answer choice indicates that *Catch-22...scored*, which is an error because a book cannot score. Eliminate (E). The correct answer is (C).

---

Although not quite as liquid an investment as a money-market account, financial experts recommend a certificate of deposit for its high yield.

- Although not quite as liquid an investment as
- Although it is not quite as liquid an investment as
- While not being quite as liquid an investment as
- While it is not quite as liquid as an investment
- Although not quite liquid an investment as

### Here's How to Crack It

Begin by identifying any common errors in the underlined portion of the sentence. The underlined portion of the sentence is part of a modifying phrase, so make sure the phrase is correctly modifying the noun or pronoun following it. The modifying phrase *Although not quite as liquid an investment* modifies *financial experts.* This is a misplaced modifier error, so eliminate (A) and look for any obvious repeaters. Despite that some of the answer choices begin with *Although,* none of them qualify as obvious repeaters because it is necessary to evaluate them individually to determine if there is an error. There are no obvious repeaters, so evaluate each answer choice individually, looking for reasons to eliminate each.

Choice (B) fixes the original error by inserting the pronoun *it,* which means that the opening phrase is no longer a modifying phrase, and does not appear to create any new errors, so keep (B). Choice (C) does not fix the original error as the modifying phrase still modifies the noun *financial experts.* Eliminate (C). Choice (D) fixes the original error but creates a new error. Choice (D) moves the word *as,* which changes the meaning of the sentence to indicate that the *certificate of deposit* referred to by the pronoun *it* is not *as liquid as an investment,* as opposed to *as liquid an investment as a money-market account.* Eliminate (D). Choice (E) does not fix the original error as the modifying phrase still modifies the noun *financial experts* and creates a new error by eliminating the word *as* from the idiom *as...as.* Eliminate (E). The correct answer is (B).

Remember, while (B) may not sound like a sentence you would speak, the object of Sentence Correction questions is to find the grammatical errors, not to find the sentences that sound correct.

## 3. Parallel Construction

Parallel Construction errors on the GMAT can show up in many different formats, so we're going to focus on the general premise of Parallel Construction and how this type of question most frequently shows up.

Parallel Construction errors on the GMAT exist mostly with verbs. In a Sentence Correction question, the verbs in that sentence must have the same grammatical status. For verbs, that could mean that all the verbs need to be in the same tense. But it could also mean that all the verbs need to have the same form, such as a list of infinitives.

To illustrate this idea for verbs, take a look at the following example:

*The results of the pharmaceutical company's studies reveal that the screening technique may be capable of recognizing the presence of an illness, to identify the appropriate prescription, and monitoring the progress of recovery with subsequent screenings.*

Look at the verbs in that sentence—are all the verbs in the same form? The verbs are in the form *recognizing the presence, to identify,* and *monitoring the progress.* Two of the verbs are in the same form (*recognizing* and *monitoring*), but the other is in the infinitive form *to identify.* As a result the verbs are not parallel, so this is a parallel construction error.

There are a number of ways to fix this error, but all of them require that the verbs be constructed the same way. So, a potential way to fix this sentence is to write:

*The results of the pharmaceutical company's studies reveal that the screening technique may be capable of recognizing the presence of an illness, identifying the appropriate prescription, and monitoring the progress of recovery with subsequent screenings.*

Again, this is not the only way this sentence could be fixed. But the sentence is now correct because all the verbs are constructed in the same way.

Take a look at another example:

*To say that the song patterns of the common robin are less complex than those of the indigo bunting is doing a great disservice to both birds.*

Are the verbs in this sentence constructed in the same way? The first verb, *To say,* is an infinitive but the second verb, *is doing,* is not an infinitive, so this is a parallel construction error.

As before, there are many ways to fix the parallel construction error in the sentence. As long as the verbs are constructed the same way, the parallel construction error is fixed. Here is one way that the sentence could be fixed:

*To say that the song patterns of the common robin are less complex than those of the indigo bunting is to do a great disservice to both birds.*

## How Do You Spot Parallel Construction?

When a sentence has words, usually verbs, that are in a list or related to each other, check to make sure that the words are constructed the same way.

Here's an example:

---

In a recent survey, the Gallup poll discovered that the average American speaks 1.3 languages, buys a new car every 5.2 years, drinks 14 gallons of alcoholic beverages every year, and forgot to pay at least one bill per quarter.

- ○ drinks 14 gallons of alcoholic beverages every year, and forgot to pay at least one bill per quarter
- ○ drinks 14 gallons of alcoholic beverages every year, and forgets to pay at least one bill per quarter
- ○ can drink 14 gallons of alcoholic beverages every quarter and forgot to pay at least one bill per quarter
- ○ drinks 14 gallons of alcoholic beverages every year, and forgets at least to pay one bill per quarter
- ○ drank 14 gallons of alcoholic beverages every year, and forgets to pay at least one bill per quarter

### Here's How to Crack It

Begin by identifying any common errors in the underlined portion of the sentence. The underlined portion of the sentence contains verbs that are in a list, so make sure that they are constructed similarly. The verbs in the list begin with the non-underlined verbs *speaks* and *buys* and then includes the underlined verbs *drinks* and *forgot.* These verbs are not in the same form, so this is a parallel construction error. Because the verbs *speaks* and *buys* are in the non-underlined portion of the sentence, the correct construction of the verbs in the list needs to be in the same form as *speaks* and *buys.* The verb *forgot* is not in the same form, so eliminate (A) and look for any obvious repeaters. Choice (C) also uses the verb *forgot,* so it is an obvious repeater. Eliminate (C). Evaluate each of the remaining answer choices individually, looking for reasons to eliminate each.

Choice (B) fixes the original error by changing the verb *forgot* into *forgets* and makes no new errors, so keep (B). Choice (D) fixes the original error, but changes the meaning of the sentence by putting the adjectival phrase *at least* in front of *to pay,* so eliminate (D). Choice (E) also contains a parallel construction error by changing the word *drinks* to *drank*, so eliminate (E). The correct answer is (B).

---

## Challenge Question #16

There are many skills Karishma wishes to learn, but her parents have reluctantly agreed to buying rock climbing gear, providing sailing lessons, and join a chess club, if she continues to keep up with her schoolwork.

- to buying rock climbing gear, providing sailing lessons, and join a chess club, if she continues to keep up with her schoolwork.
- with buying rock climbing gear, providing lessons for learning to sail, and to join a chess club, if she keeps up with schoolwork.
- having rock climbing gear bought, providing lessons for sailing, and joining a chess club would be allowed if she continues her schoolwork.
- to buy rock climbing gear, provide sailing lessons, and allow her to join a chess club, if she continues to keep up with her schoolwork.
- to having bought rock climbing gear, provided sailing lessons, and allowed her joining of a chess club, if she had continued to keep up with her schoolwork.

## 4. Comparison

Comparison errors are similar to parallel construction errors in that things that are being compared must be the same. Here's an example:

*The people in my office are smarter than other offices.*

Taken literally, this sentence compares *the people in my office* with *other offices.* Therefore, it's an example of faulty comparison—it compares two dissimilar things (in this case, *people* and *offices*). When comparing things within a sentence, the things being compared have to be the same. Because people and offices are not the same, this is a comparison error.

Parallel comparison problems also come up when you compare two actions. Take a look at the following example:

*Synthetic oils burn less efficiently than natural oils.*

While this sentence may not seem to contain an error, and certainly does not sound like it contains an error, there is a comparison error. The first item being compared is how *synthetic oils burn* and the second item being compared is *natural oils.*

There are many ways to fix this comparison error, but the fix will ultimately always be the same—the things being compared have to be similar. The GMAT will often employ pronouns or verbs to indicate back to the thing or action to fix comparison errors. So, for example, the comparison error in the sentence above is fixed by writing the following:

*Synthetic oils burn less efficiently than do natural oils.*

In this case, the verb *do* refers to the action *burn,* thus eliminating the comparison error.

## How Do You Spot Parallel Comparison?

Q: What is an indication of a parallel comparison error?
*Turn to page 418 for the answer.*

Look for sentences that make comparisons. These sentences often include words such as *than*, *as*, *similar to*, and *like*. When you find one of these comparison words, check to see whether the two things compared are really comparable.

Let's look at an example:

---

Doctors sometimes have difficulty diagnosing viral pneumonia because the early symptoms of this potentially deadly illness <u>are often quite similar to the common cold</u>.

- ◯ are often quite similar to the common cold
- ◯ often resemble that of the common cold
- ◯ are often quite similar to those of the common cold
- ◯ are often quite similar to the common cold's symptom
- ◯ quite often are, like the common cold, similar

### Here's How to Crack It

Begin by identifying any of the common errors in the underlined portion of the sentence. The underlined portion of the sentence contains the comparison word *similar,* so look for comparison errors. The first item being compared in the non-underlined portion of the sentence is the *symptoms* of *viral pneumonia.* The second item being compared is *the common cold.* This is a comparison error as the *symptoms* are not being compared to other *symptoms.* Eliminate (A) and look for obvious repeaters. Choice (E) does not compare *symptoms* to other symptoms, so eliminate (E). Evaluate the remaining answer choices, looking for reasons to eliminate each.

**Extra Practice**
Visit your Student Tools to download a free excerpt from *Verbal Workout for the GMAT.*

Choice (B) fixes the original error by introducing the pronoun *that.* However, the noun *symptoms* is plural and the pronoun *that* is singular, so there is a pronoun agreement error. Eliminate (B). Choice (C) fixes the original error and makes no new errors, so keep (C). Choice (D) appears to fix the original error, but actually compares *symptoms* to *symptom,* which is both a parallel construction and comparison error. Eliminate (D). The correct answer is (C).

---

## Challenge Question #17

Unlike Edgar Allan Poe, whose poems have gained recognition over the years as portraying a foreboding tone, Homer's epic volumes of poetry are valued more for the expansive tales they portray.

- ◯ whose poems have gained recognition over the years as portraying a foreboding tone, Homer's epic volumes of poetry are
- ◯ with poems that are recognized portraying a foreboding tone over the years, the epic volumes of poetry written by Homer are
- ◯ the poems of which have been recognized as portraying a foreboding tone, in the example of Homer, his epic volumes of poetry are
- ◯ whose poems have gained recognition over the years for their foreboding tone, Homer produced epic volumes of poetry that are
- ◯ for whom recognition has been gained over the years for poems in a foreboding tone, Homer's epic volumes of poetry are

## 5. Verb Tense

Verb tense problems happen when two verbs in the same sentence are in different tenses, or when a sentence starts in one tense and then shifts to a different tense.

*When he was younger, he walked three miles every day and has lifted weights too.*

The clause *when he was younger* puts the entire sentence firmly in the past. Thus, the two verbs that follow should be in the past tense as well. You may not have known the technical term for *has lifted* (the present perfect tense), but you probably noticed that it was inconsistent with *walked* (the simple past tense). This is a verb tense error.

Here are the tenses that often appear on the GMAT:

| **Tense** | **Example** |
|---|---|
| present | He *walks* three miles a day. |
| simple past | When he was younger, he *walked* three miles a day. |
| present perfect | He *has walked* three miles a day for the last several years. |
| past perfect | He *had walked* three miles a day until he bought his motorcycle. |
| future | He *will walk* three miles a day, starting tomorrow. |

It isn't important that you know the names of these tenses as long as you understand how they're used. For example, a sentence that begins in the present perfect (which describes an action that has happened in the past, but is potentially going on in the present as well) should stay in the present perfect.

*He has walked three miles a day for the last several years and has never complained.*

A: A comparison! Check that the two things being compared are really comparable.

One exception to this rule is a sentence that contains the past perfect (in which one action in the past happened before another action in the past). By definition, any action set in the past perfect must have another action that comes after it, set in the simple past.

*He had ridden his motorcycle for two hours when it ran out of gas.*

The only other exceptions to this rule come up when one action in a sentence clearly precedes another.

*The dinosaurs are extinct now, but they were once present on the Earth in large numbers.*

In this case, the sentence clearly refers to two different time periods: *now*, which requires the present tense, and a period long ago, which requires the past tense.

## How Do You Spot Tense Errors?

When the underlined portion of a sentence contains a verb, check to make sure that the verb is in the same tense as the non-underlined portion of the sentence.

If you read through this book, you might be able to avoid tense errors!

Try the following problem:

A doctor at the Amsterdam Clinic maintains that if children eat a diet high in vitamins and took vitamin supplements, they will be less likely to catch the common cold.

- ○ took vitamin supplements, they will be less likely to catch
- ○ took vitamin supplements, they are less likely to catch
- ○ take vitamin supplements, they were less likely of catching
- ○ take vitamin supplements, they will be less likely of catching
- ○ take vitamin supplements, they are less likely to catch

### Here's How to Crack It

Begin by identifying any common errors in the underlined portion of the sentence. The underlined portion of the sentence contains the verb *took,* so make sure there are no verb tense errors. The verb *took* is in the past tense while the verb *eat* in the non-underlined portion of the sentence is in the present tense. This is a verb tense error, so eliminate (A) and look for any obvious repeaters. Choice (B) also uses the verb *took,* so eliminate (B). Evaluate the remaining answer choices individually, looking for reasons to eliminate each.

Choice (C) fixes the original error by changing the verb *took* to *take* but creates a new error by using the past tense verb *were,* thus creating a new verb tense error. Eliminate (C). Choice (D) fixes the original error by using the future tense verb *will be.* However, this is a verb tense error, so eliminate (D). Choice (E) fixes the original error and commits no new errors, so keep (E). The correct answer is (E).

You may have noticed that the original sentence contained another error in addition to *took.* The verb form *will be* is in the future tense. This is also a verb tense error. GMAT sentence correction questions will sometimes contain more than one error. If you noticed the other error, that is fine—the process for handling the remaining answer choices remains the same.

---

## 6. Subject-Verb Agreement Errors

A singular verb needs to be in agreement with a singular subject (a noun or pronoun). If a singular verb is paired with a plural noun or pronoun, there is a subject-verb agreement error.

Take a look at the following example:

*The number of arrests of drunken drivers are increasing every year.*

The subject of the sentence above is *number,* which is singular. The phrase *of arrests of drunken drivers* modifies the subject. The verb of this sentence is *are,* which is plural. This is a subject-verb agreement error.

If the test-writers had written the sentence *The number are increasing every year,* identifying the subject-verb agreement error would be easy. However, the test-writers will often separate the subject and the verb by using several prepositional phrases to describe or modify the subject. Do not be thrown off by these phrases. Find the subject of the verb and then make sure that they are in agreement.

## How to Spot Subject-Verb Agreement Errors

Find the verb and trace it back to its subject and determine if they are in agreement.

One of the common ways that test-writers will make these questions harder is by using nouns that sound plural but are actually singular.

**Nouns That Sound Plural (But Aren't)**

- The Netherlands (the name of any city, state, or country)
- Tom or John (any two singular nouns connected by *or*)
- the family
- the audience
- politics
- measles
- the number
- the amount

Sometimes pronouns can be the subject of a sentence, in which case the verb has to agree with the pronoun. There are some pronouns that people tend to think are plural when they are in fact singular:

**Pronouns That Sound Plural (But Aren't)**

| | | | |
|---|---|---|---|
| everyone | no one | anyone | none |
| everybody | nobody | anybody | each |
| everything | nothing | anything | |

Let's look at an example of a subject-verb error as it might appear on the GMAT:

Many political insiders now believe that the dissension in Congress over health issues decrease the likelihood for significant action being taken this year to combat the rising costs of healthcare.

- ⬭ decrease the likelihood for significant action being
- ⬭ decrease the likelihood that significant action will be
- ⬭ decrease the likelihood of significant action to be
- ⬭ decreases the likelihood for significant action being
- ⬭ decreases the likelihood that significant action will be

### Here's How to Crack It

Begin by identifying any common errors in the underlined portion of the sentence. The underlined portion of the sentence contains the plural verb *decrease,* so trace that verb back to its subject. The subject of *decrease* is *the dissension*, which is singular, so there is a subject-verb agreement error. Eliminate (A) and look for any obvious repeaters. Choices (B) and (C) repeat the error, so eliminate both choices. Evaluate the remaining answer choices individually, looking for reasons to eliminate each.

Choice (D) fixes the original error with the use of the verb *being* and the unidiomatic expression *likelihood for.* Eliminate (D). Choice (E) fixes the original error and makes no new errors, so keep (E). The correct answer is (E).

---

## 7. Idiom

Idioms, or idiomatic expressions, are expressions, words, or phrases that have commonly understood meanings and constructions. Most idioms tested on the GMAT are pairs of words that must be used together. Often the first word is a verb that needs to be followed by a specific preposition. For example, *I plan to attend business school* is idiomatically correct, while *I plan on attending business school* is not. The biggest problem with idioms is that there are really no rules governing idiomatic errors—you simply must know them—and there are too many to list.

The good news is that in comparison to the other common errors, the GMAT tests idioms less than the other errors. Additionally, if you are familiar with common English constructions, then you know many idioms already.

## How Do You Spot Idiomatic Errors?

Idiomatic errors will appear in sentences that appear to have nothing else wrong with them. Be on the lookout for awkward constructions of sentences or phrases. These could be the sign of an idiom error.

Idioms should also be the last thing that you look for as an error. If the sentence in question has any other error, use that error to work through the Process of Elimination.

Here's an example of what an idiom question on the GMAT may look like:

---

The administration of a small daily dose of aspirin has not only been shown to lower the risk of heart attack, <u>and it has also been shown to help</u> relieve the suffering of arthritis.

- ◯ and it has also been shown to help
- ◯ and it has also been shown helpful to
- ◯ but it has also been shown to help
- ◯ but it has been shown helpful in addition for
- ◯ in addition it has also been shown helping

### Here's How to Crack It

Begin by identifying any common errors in the sentence. The sentence contains the phrase *not only* to introduce one example and then introduces another example. However, when the construction *not only* is used to introduce an example, the next example must be introduced by the phrase *but also.* Therefore, the correct idiomatic construction is *not only...but also.* Choice (A) is an idiom error, so eliminate (A) and look for any obvious repeaters. Because *not only* appears in the non-underlined portion of the sentence, the underlined portion of the sentence must contain *but also.* Choices (B), (D), and (E) do not have the phrase *but also*, so these choices are unidiomatic and can be eliminated. Choice (C) is the only answer choice that uses the proper *not only...but also* construction. The correct answer is (C).

---

## The Idioms Most Commonly Tested on the GMAT

There are, of course, thousands of idiomatic expressions that could be tested on the GMAT. But here are a handful that appear most often.

not only...but also...
not so much...as...
defined as
regard as
neither...nor...
modeled after
based on
a result of
to result in
a debate over
a dispute over
a responsibility to
responsible for
different from
a consequence of
so...as to be...
so (adjective) that
depicted as
define as
as great as
as good as, or better than
credited with

according to
agree with
appear to
because of
choose from
conclude that
contribute to
depend on
due to
in order to
instead of
rather than
subject to
worry about
think of...as
see...as
target...as
prohibit from
distinguish between...and...
distinguish...from...
attributed to

## MINOR GRAMMAR ERRORS ON THE GMAT

The seven errors you've just learned to spot will enable you to answer most of the Sentence Correction problems that come up on the GMAT. However, there is one more error that shows up often enough that you should probably look out for it.

### 8. Quantity Words

GMAC likes to see if you know how to indicate quantity. Here's an example:

> *On the flight to Los Angeles, Nancy had to choose* among *two dinner entrees.*

If there were more than two items being compared, then *among* would be correct. However, if there are only two choices available, the correct quantity word would be *between.*

> *On the flight to Los Angeles, Nancy had to choose* between *two dinner entrees.*

Below are the comparison quantity words that come up on the GMAT most frequently:

| If two items | If more than two items |
|---|---|
| between | among |
| more | most |
| better | best |
| less | least |

Another type of quantity word that shows up on the GMAT from time to time involves things that can be counted as opposed to things that can't. For example, if you were standing in line at a buffet, and you didn't want as big a serving of soup as the person in front of you received, which of the following would be correct?

> *Could I have* fewer *soup, please?*
>
> or
>
> *Could I have* less *soup, please?*

If an item can't be counted, the correct adjective would be "less." However, if we were talking about french fries (which can be counted), the correct adjective would be "fewer."

| Countable items | Uncountable items |
|---|---|
| fewer | less |
| number | amount, quantity |
| many | much |

## How Do You Spot Quantity Word Errors?

Look for quantity words. Whenever you see a "between," check to see if there are only two items discussed in the sentence. (If there are more, you'll need an "among.") Whenever you see an "amount," make sure that whatever is discussed cannot be counted. (If the sentence is talking about the "amount" of people, then you'll need to change it to "number.")

Here's what a "between–among" quantity word error might look like on the GMAT:

Of the many decisions facing the energy commission as it meets to decide on new directions for the next several decades, the question of the future of nuclear energy <u>is for certain the more perplexing</u>.

- ◯ is for certain the more perplexing
- ◯ is certainly the most perplexing
- ◯ it seems certain, is the most perplexed
- ◯ is certainly the more perplexing
- ◯ it seems certain, is perplexing the most

### Here's How to Crack It

Begin by identifying any common errors in the sentence. The sentence uses the word *more*, which is a quantity word, so make sure this use is correct. The sentence says there are *many decisions facing the energy commission*, so the use of the word *more* is incorrect. More can be used to decide between two things, but not three or more. Eliminate (A) and look for any obvious repeaters. Choice (D) also uses the word *more*, so eliminate (D). Evaluate the remaining answer choices individually, looking for reasons to eliminate each.

Choice (B) fixes the original error by using the correct quantity word *most* and makes no new errors, so keep (B). Choice (C) fixes the original error, but changes the tense of the verb *perplexing* to *perplexed*, which changes the meaning of the sentence to indicate that the question is itself *perplexed*. Eliminate (C). Choice (E) fixes the original error but moves the modifying phrase *the most* so that it now modifies *perplexing*, indicating a volume of things that are perplexed. Eliminate (E). The correct answer is (B).

## 9. Redundancy

Redundancy errors on the GMAT are typically well masked, which makes them difficult to identify. A typical redundancy error on the GMAT involves a common phrase paired with a word that shares the phrase's meaning. The meaning of the phrase can be either explicit or implicit and the word and phrase pair can be separated by a long string of text. Here's an example:

> *When asked why the tiger seemed so depressed, the zookeeper stated that the reason is because the tiger did not like captivity.*

In the sentence above, the zookeeper states *the reason is because.* This phrase is redundant as *reason* and *because* share the same meaning. The correct sentence uses either *reason* or *because* but not both.

> *When asked why the tiger seemed so depressed, the zookeeper stated that the reason is the tiger did not like captivity.*

## How to Spot Redundancy Errors

Redundancy errors on the GMAT can show up in many forms, so there is no comprehensive list of redundant phrases. Hence, spotting redundancy errors mostly involves reading carefully and paying close attention to the meaning of phrases and words. If you spot a word or phrase that could be excluded while not changing the meaning of the sentence, then you may have found a redundancy error. Try to remove the word or phrase from the sentence and see whether the sentence remains unchanged.

Here's an example of a redundancy error on the GMAT:

---

Birds of prey have an average wingspan of three feet, but while some have lesser wingspans, <u>some others, such as the Griffon Vulture, have wingspans of at least seven and a half feet or more</u>.

- ○ some others, such as the Griffon Vulture, have wingspans of at least seven and a half feet or more
- ○ the Griffon Vulture, like some others, has wingspans of at least seven and a half feet or more
- ○ some others, such as the Griffon Vulture, have wingspans of at least seven and a half feet
- ○ the Griffon Vulture has a wingspan of at least seven and a half feet or more, greater than some others
- ○ some others, such as the Griffon Vulture, has a wingspan of at least seven and a half feet

### Here's How to Crack It

The underlined portion of the sentence does not contain any of the major errors, so look for minor errors such as redundancy. The underlined portion of the sentence contains the construction *at least...or more.* This phrase is redundant as *at least* implies that the wingspan could also be *or more.* Eliminate (A) and look for obvious repeaters. Choices (B) and (D) both use the construction *at least...or more* so eliminate (B) and (D). Evaluate the remaining answer choices individually.

Choice (C) fixes the original errors and makes no new errors, so keep (C). Choice (E) fixes the original error but creates a subject-verb agreement error as the plural noun *some others* is paired with the singular verb *has.* Eliminate (E). The correct answer is (C).

---

## 10. Subjunctive

Occasionally, the GMAT tests your ability to use the subjunctive mood. On the GMAT, the subjunctive mood is tested in two ways: sentences that convey either a hypothetical idea or an idea that is contrary to fact, and sentences that issue commands, orders, or requests. Sentences that convey hypotheticals typically use a construction such as:

*I **wouldn't** do that if I **were** you.*

*If the game **were** to end in a tie, the home team **would** become the champion.*

When using the subjunctive mood, the verb *were* is used in the *if* clause whether the subject is singular or plural. The verb *would* is used in the *then* (or results) clause. The format of the subjunctive mood in hypothetical situations or an idea that is contrary to fact is:

*If x were, y would*

*Y would if x were*

*Were x, then y would*

Note that the usage of *if* can be optional in a properly phrased subjunctive construction.

When a sentence issues a command, order, or request, the subjunctive pairs the verb expressing the order or demand with the word *that* and then uses the bare infinitive of the following verb:

*The manager **requested that** the staff **stay** late to finish the project.*

*The princess **demanded that** the frog **be brought** to her.*

In the examples above, the verb expressing the order or demand is paired with the word *that* and the second verb is in the bare infinitive, which is just the infinitive form of the verb without the word *to* in front of it. The construction of this type of sentence is:

Subject + Order or demand verb + that + Object + Bare Infinitive + Rest of Sentence

When the GMAT tests subjunctive errors, it often includes the word *should* as part of the second verb. This construction is incorrect. For instance:

**Improper Subjunctive**: The executive stipulated that there should be a broader marketing effort.

**Proper Subjunctive**: The executive stipulated that there be a broader marketing effort.

## How to Spot Subjunctive Errors

To spot subjunctive errors, look for a sentence that issues an order or demand or that states a situation that is either hypothetical or contrary to fact. If a sentence includes any of these concepts, check to make sure the subjunctive mood is constructed correctly.

Here's an example of a subjunctive error on the GMAT:

In ancient Japan, a samurai's honor was so valued that if a samurai were to be dishonored, the samurai's second would help him perform seppuku, a process by which the dishonored samurai requested that his second should decapitate him if the dishonored samurai was incapable of taking his own life.

- ◯ a samurai's honor was so valued that if a samurai were to be dishonored, the samurai's second would help him perform seppuku, a process by which the dishonored samurai requested that his second should decapitate him if the dishonored samurai was incapable of taking his own life
- ◯ a samurai's honor was so valued that if a samurai was to be dishonored, the samurai's second should help him perform seppuku, a process by which the dishonored samurai requested that his second should decapitate him if the dishonored samurai were incapable of taking his own life
- ◯ a samurai's honor was so valued that if a samurai were to be dishonored, the samurai's second would help him perform seppuku, a process by which the dishonored samurai requested that his second decapitate him if the dishonored samurai was incapable of taking his own life
- ◯ a samurai's honor was so valued that if a samurai were to be dishonored, the samurai's second helped him perform seppuku, a process by which the dishonored samurai requested that his second decapitate him if the dishonored samurai was incapable of taking his own life
- ◯ a samurai's honor were so valued that if a samurai were to be dishonored, the samurai's second would help him perform seppuku, a process by which the dishonored samurai requested that his second decapitate him if the dishonored samurai was incapable of taking his own life

### Here's How to Crack It

The underlined portion of the sentence contains no major errors, so look for minor error types. The underlined portion of the sentence contains two subjunctive constructions, so look for errors in either of those. The first subjunctive construction is correct as *if a samurai were...the samurai's second would.* However, the second subjunctive construction contains the word *should,* as it states *the dishonored samurai requested that his second should.* This is an incorrect subjective mood, so eliminate choice (A) and look for obvious repeaters. Choice (B) is an obvious repeater as it also uses the word *should* in an order or demand phrase, so eliminate (B). Evaluate the remaining answer choices individually.

Choice (C) fixes the original error and makes no new errors, so keep (C). Choice (D) fixes the original error but makes a new error by violating the *if x were, then y would* subjunctive construction. The first part of the sentence states *if a samurai were…the samurai's second helped*. Eliminate (D). Choice (E) fixes the original error but creates a subject-verb agreement error by pairing the singular subject *honor* with the plural verb *were*. Eliminate (E). The correct answer is (C).

---

## 11. Passive vs. Active Voice

The usage of passive voice is not, in and of itself, an error. Consider the following two sentences:

> *A goal was met by the team.*
>
> *The team met a goal.*

Both sentences successfully and grammatically express the idea that a goal was met. The first sentence is in the passive voice, as the subject (*team*) is the recipient of the action (*a goal was met*). The second sentence uses the active voice, as the subject (*team*) performs the action (*met a goal*).

Both of these sentences are grammatically correct. However, the GMAT favors sentences that are concise, and the active voice is typically more concise. By itself, the passive voice is not a reason to eliminate an answer choice. If you have two answers left and can't find an error in either of them, the active voice sentence is most likely the correct one. It's likely that the passive voice answer contains an uncommon error, such as a rarely tested idiom. In this case, eliminate the sentence written in the passive voice.

## How to Spot Passive vs. Active Voice Errors

To spot passive voice, look for sentences in which the subject of the sentence is receiving an action instead of performing an action. If you see the passive voice, do not eliminate the choice. Evaluate the remaining answer choices first. If there is another choice written in the active voice that does not contain an error, then eliminate the choice written in passive voice.

Here's a GMAT example:

According to recent genetic analyses comparing the genetic makeup of different types of berries, red berries have more total antioxidants than do non-red berries and less of an enzyme they think causes joint inflammation in humans.

- red berries have more total antioxidants than do non-red berries and less of an enzyme they think causes
- red berries have more total antioxidants than do non-red berries and less of an enzyme thought to cause
- red berries have more total antioxidants than that of non-red berries and have less of an enzyme thought to cause
- more antioxidants are found in red berries than non-red berries and red berries have less of an enzyme thought to cause
- antioxidants are more in red berries than in non-red berries and less of their enzymes are thought to cause

### Here's How to Crack It

The underlined portion of the sentence contains the pronoun *they* so make sure that pronoun is in agreement with its referent and clearly refers to one noun. The pronoun *they* does not clearly refer to any noun, so this pronoun is ambiguous. Eliminate (A) and look for obvious repeaters. There are no obvious repeaters, so evaluate the remaining answer choices individually.

Choice (B) fixes the original error and makes no additional errors, so keep (B). Choice (C) uses the pronoun *that* which is the wrong comparison word for the sentence, so eliminate (C). Choice (D) fixes the original error and does not appear to make any new errors, so keep (D) as well. Choice (E) uses the pronoun *their* which is ambiguous, so eliminate (E). Compare (B) and (D). Choice (D) is written in the passive voice as the subject *red berries* is the recipient of the action *antioxidants are found in.* This is a less concise answer than (B), so eliminate (D). Additionally, (D) contains a comparison error as *antioxidants* is compared to *non-red berries.* The correct answer is (B).

## If You're Really Gung Ho

You can expand your checklist to include as many types of errors as you like. Obviously, the more types of errors you can identify, the better prepared you'll be to take the test. But you should bear in mind that while there are other types of errors that we haven't discussed, these errors don't come up very often on the GMAT. If you're seriously gunning to get every Sentence Correction question correct, you should dig out your old grammar book from high school and study it carefully. You should also do as many of the real GMAT Sentence Correction questions in *The Official Guide for GMAT Review* as you can; pay special attention to the idiomatic expressions that come up in these sections, because these are sometimes repeated.

## DRILL 17 (Sentence Correction)

The answers to the questions in this drill can be found in Part VII.

1. In a company memo, the head of the organization warned that employees should consider contributions to their 401ks or other similar retirement funds as not a luxury item, but as a necessary monthly payment similar to car or bill payments.

   - ⬭ as not a luxury item, but as
   - ⬭ as not a luxury item but
   - ⬭ not a luxury item, rather
   - ⬭ not as a luxury item, but as
   - ⬭ not a luxury item, but

2. Some bird species at first begin migrating from east to west, because daylight hours decrease along a similar westward pattern, but they then turn south to head towards even warmer weather.

   - ⬭ Some bird species at first begin migrating from east to west, because daylight hours decrease along a similar westward pattern, but
   - ⬭ At first, some bird species migrate from east to west, because that is the direction in which daylight hours decrease, but
   - ⬭ While some bird species migrate east to west at first, the direction that daylight hours decrease, and
   - ⬭ Because some bird species migrate east to west, since it is the direction that daylight hours decrease,
   - ⬭ Some bird species, beginning by migrating from east to west, because this is the direction that daylight hours decrease,

3. In a review of hiring practices that date back to the 1950s, modern hiring managers, emphasizing that since most of the hiring practices had struggled to account for rapid changes in technology and employee temperament, none should be considered best practices in the modern workplace.

- ◯ managers, emphasizing that since most hiring practices had struggled to account for rapid changes in technology and employee temperament,
- ◯ managers, emphasizing that most hiring practices struggled in accounting for rapid changes in technology and employee temperament, and
- ◯ managers emphasized that since most hiring practices, having struggled to account for rapid changes in technology and employee temperament,
- ◯ managers emphasized that since most hiring practices struggle to account for rapid changes in technology and employee temperament,
- ◯ managers emphasized that since most hiring practices had struggled to account for rapid changes in technology and employee temperament,

4. A breed of dog now known for its gentle demeanor, the Irish wolfhound's initial purpose included hunting wolves and pulling enemy warriors off moving chariots.

- ◯ A breed of dog now known for its gentle demeanor, the Irish wolfhound's initial purpose included
- ◯ The initial purpose of the Irish wolfhound, a breed of dog now known for its gentle demeanor, included
- ◯ The Irish wolfhound is a breed of dog now known for its gentle demeanor including in its initial purpose
- ◯ Included in the initial purpose of the Irish wolfhound, a breed of dog now known for its gentle demeanor, is
- ◯ A breed of dog now known for its gentle demeanor, initially the Irish wolfhound had the purpose to

5. Especially in the early months, farmers may need to find resourceful ways, such as planting a good diversity of crops or feeding the soil additional nutrients, that ensure their harvests are large and more consistent than they would be otherwise.

- ◯ that ensure their harvests are large
- ◯ to ensure their harvests are larger
- ◯ thus ensuring their harvests are larger
- ◯ so that the harvests are larger
- ◯ of ensuring their harvests are large

6. Tech industry employee benefits, as with other industries, were designed to increase the number of hours employees spend at work and to help attract top talent.

- as with
- as did those of
- as they have in
- like in
- like those of

7. The charitable organization aims to aid local communities and partnering with private industry, supporting access for poor communities for resources such as food and shelter.

- partnering with private industry, supporting access for poor communities for
- partners with private industry to support access for poor communities to
- partner with private industry for supporting of access for poor communities to
- partner with private industry and support accessibility for poor communities for their
- in partnership with private industry to support access for poor communities for

8. Data analysts predict that customers will be equally likely to purchase the new product as the current one.

- equally likely to purchase the new product as
- equally likely to purchase the new product as they are
- equally likely that they will purchase the new product as
- as likely that they will purchase the new product as
- as likely to purchase the new product as they are

9. An increase in the merchandise sales and a decrease in the number of unsold tickets indicate that the show may not be as unpopular as some critics previously speculated.

- tickets indicate that the show may not be as unpopular as some critics previously speculated
- tickets indicates that the show may not be as unpopular as some critics previously speculated
- tickets indicate that the show may not be as unpopular as have been previously speculated by some critics
- tickets, indicating about the show that it may not be so unpopular as previously speculated by some critics
- tickets, indicating the show may not as unpopular as previous speculated to be by some critics

10. In ancient Greece, much of the local worshipper's religious practice was premised on the concept of exchange as gods and goddesses bestowed gifts and humans gave offerings as an expression of thanks and when they constructed sacred precincts for worship.

- ○ much of the local worshipper's religious practice was premised on the concept of exchange as gods and goddesses bestowed gifts and humans gave offerings as an expression of thanks and when they constructed sacred precincts for worship
- ○ much of the local worshipper's religious practice was premised on the concept of exchange as gods and goddesses bestowed gifts while humans gave offerings as an expression of thanks and constructed sacred precincts in which to worship
- ○ much of the local worshipper's religious practice was premised on the concept of exchange as gods and goddesses bestowed gifts and humans gave offerings as an expression of thanks as well as they constructed sacred precincts for worship
- ○ the concept of exchange premised much of the local worshipper's religious practice as the gods and goddesses bestowed gifts while humans to give offerings as an expression of thanks and to construct sacred precincts in which to worship
- ○ the gods and goddesses bestowed gifts as the concept of exchange, which was the premise of much of the local worshipper's religious practice, and humans gave offerings as an expression of thanks and constructed sacred precincts in which to worship

11. The foresight that was evident in the court's selection of an independent trustee to oversee the provisions of the agreement will probably go unremarked by the press.

- ○ that was evident in the court's selection of an independent trustee
- ○ that was evident by the court's selection of an independent trustee
- ○ evidenced with the court's selection of an independent trustee
- ○ evidenced of the court's selection of an independent trustee
- ○ that was evident of the court's selection of an independent trustee

# Summary

- Sentence Correction questions test only a handful of rules. Once you learn them, you will be able to score quite well on this type of question.
- Follow the basic approach and flow chart for Sentence Correction questions.
- Make a checklist of errors to look for when you read a Sentence Correction question. The most common are:
  - **Pronouns:** If a sentence contains a pronoun, check to see whether it clearly refers to the noun it is replacing; also check to see whether the pronoun agrees in number with the noun to which it refers.
  - **Misplaced modifiers:** If the sentence begins with a modifying phrase, check to make sure that the noun it modifies comes directly after the modifying phrase.
  - **Parallel construction:** If a sentence contains a list of things or actions or if the sentence is broken up into two halves, check to make sure the parts of the sentence are parallel.
  - **Comparisons:** When a sentence makes a comparison, check to see whether the two things compared are really comparable.
  - **Verb Tense:** If the answer choices contain different verb tenses, make sure that the tense of the verb or verbs in the original sentence is correct. For the most part, verb tense should be consistent throughout a sentence.
  - **Subject-verb agreement:** GMAT test-writers sometimes put extraneous prepositional phrases between the subject and the verb. Cover up or ignore these phrases so that you can see whether the subject and the verb of each clause in the sentence agree with each other.
  - **Idiom:** If a sentence contains an idiomatic expression that seems wrong to you, try taking the expression out of the sentence and creating a sentence of your own with the suspect expression.
  - **Quantity words:** Whenever you see a quantity word (countable vs. uncountable; two vs. three or more), check to see if it is used correctly.
  - **Redundancy:** If the underlined portion of the sentence contains an idea that is expressed in another part of the sentence, the sentence has a redundancy error.
  - **Subjunctive:** The subjunctive tense shows up in sentences that express something contrary to facts or a hypothetical, and in sentences that express an order or demand.
  - **Passive Voice:** The passive voice occurs when the subject of the sentence is the recipient of the action. The passive voice is not technically incorrect, but typically signals that the sentence is not as concise as it could be.

- If you've spotted the error, go through the answer choices and eliminate any that contain the same error. Then look at the remaining answer choices and find the one that fixes the sentence.
- About one-fifth of the sentences are correct as they are. When a sentence is correct, the answer is (A), which simply repeats the sentence word for word.
- Once you've gained confidence in your ability to spot the major errors, you should expand your checklist to include other types of errors.

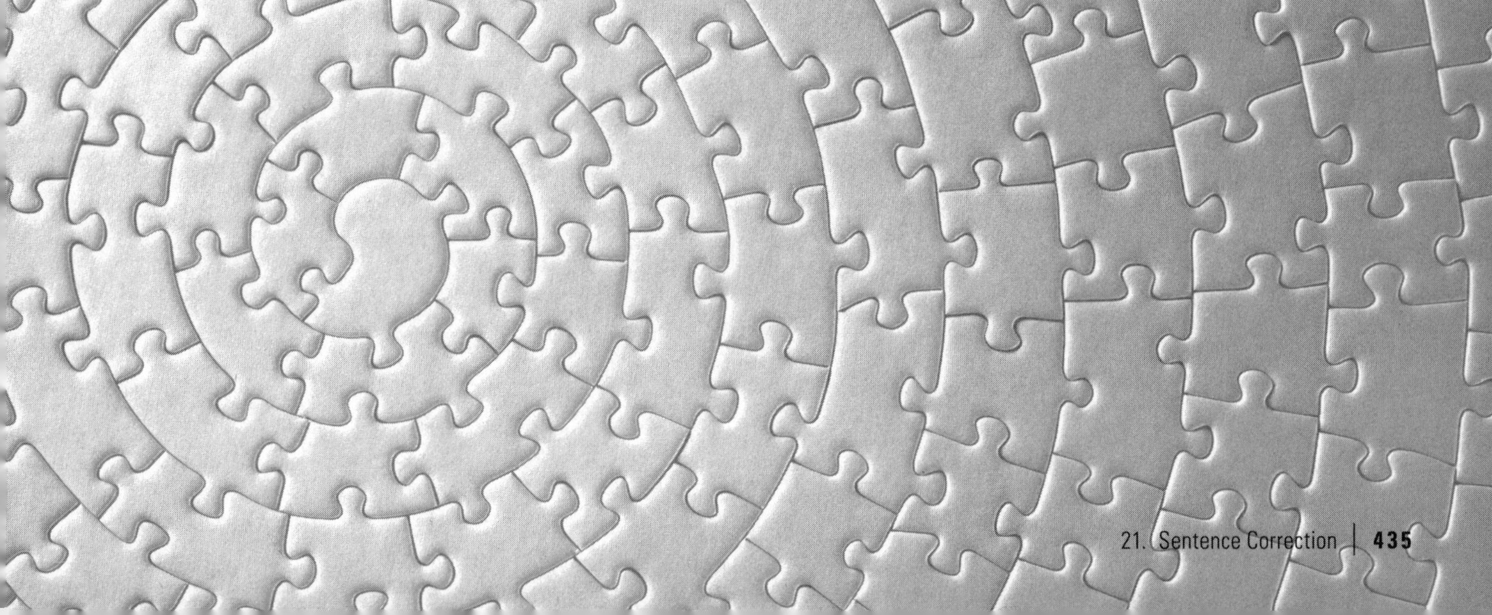

# Chapter 22
# Reading Comprehension

Reading Comprehension questions make up approximately one-third of the questions in the Verbal section. Reading passages occur at any point in the Verbal section, but all questions related to a passage will be presented together.

## READING COMPREHENSION OVERVIEW

In most cases, you'll see four reading passages on the test. There are usually three short passages, which average around 250 words and are typically followed by three questions, and one long passage, which averages around 350 words and is typically followed by four questions. It is possible that you may get two short and two long passages, which means that the total number of questions you will see is most likely around 12 out of 36 total questions.

Reading Comprehension passages can be intimidating to test-takers, as there is a sudden rush of information on the screen and the test-taker prepares for the task of reading and answering questions on a passage that is often dense, wordy, and boring. During Reading Comprehension passages, it is not uncommon for test-takers to feel rushed, which makes it hard to pay attention to a passage that covers a topic area that most find dry. However, contrary to popular belief, everything you need to know to crack Reading Comprehension questions can be found in the text. This chapter is going to teach you how to crack the passages and questions, leading you to the correct answers.

## MORE INFORMATION ON READING COMPREHENSION PASSAGES

GMAT passages cover a variety of topics but typically come from four primary areas.

- *Social Science*: social or historical issues, such as the civil rights movement or World War I.
- *Physical Sciences*: natural science topics, such as photosynthesis or black holes.
- *Biological Sciences:* topics related to living organisms and how they interact with their environment.
- *Business*: business-related topics, such as management strategies or the loosening of international trade restrictions.

The passage appears on the left side of the screen. The passage may be too long to fit in the window, so you may have to use the scroll bar to read it completely. The questions appear on the right side of the screen, one at a time. After you answer the first question, another appears in its place. The passage remains unchanged and in place so you can always refer to it. As with any other type of question on the GMAT, you must answer Reading Comprehension questions in the order that they appear on your screen. So, if a question that asks for the main idea appears first, that's the question you must answer first.

## THE BASIC APPROACH TO CRACKING GMAT READING COMPREHENSION

Before we begin to crack the Reading Comprehension passages and questions, it is important to establish The Basic Approach, which allows you to:

- actively read the passages and seek out the most important information
- understand the different types of questions and what they require you to do
- quickly find the credited response by eliminating incorrect answers

### Don't Be Predictable

The typical test-taker is predictable and approaches questions on the test in a certain way. The people who write the GMAT create questions and passages that are designed with those people in mind. They will make questions that trick and confuse test-takers who follow the typical approach. However, if you approach the test in a better way, you improve your chance of getting a better score. One hard-and-fast rule of test taking is that whenever you do what the test-writers expect, you don't get the best score that you could. When you do things in a different way, you increase your chances of getting a better score. So, our approach to reading needs to be that "different way." The different ways you are going to learn are the Basics of Cracking the Passage, The Basics of Cracking the Questions, and The Basics of Cracking the Answer Choices. These combine to form the foundation that is used for the Basic Approach to Cracking Reading Comprehension.

### The Basics of Cracking the Passage

Let's start with the approach to cracking the passage. The typical test-taker reads the passage without a plan. So to crack the passage, you need to have a plan for reading the passage. The typical test-taker concentrates on the facts in the passage rather than why those facts are there. So to crack the passage, you also need to read for the main idea of the passage.

### The Basics of Cracking the Questions

The typical test-taker reads the question but doesn't identify the question task. To crack the questions, you must learn to locate both the subject and the task of the question. The **subject** of the question is what you need to find in the passage. The **question task** tells you what type of information you need to find about the subject of the question. For example, do you need to locate what the author said about the subject or do you need to find out why the author mentioned the subject?

### The Basics of Cracking the Answer Choices

The typical test-taker is focused on simply finding the correct answer. While that may seem a reasonable goal, it's actually a more effective strategy to utilize Process of Elimination (POE) and eliminate wrong answers. Cracking the answer choices is all about understanding how the

GMAC constructs incorrect answer choices. If you can learn to identify common trap answer choices, you can often eliminate them with confidence.

Additionally, the typical test-taker relies a lot on memory and reads only parts of sentences that are referenced by the question or answer choices. Reading only parts of sentences makes it easy to misconstrue the context of the sentence. Flipping this behavior around by not only reading full sentences but also reading sentences before and after it is crucial to cracking both the question and the answer choices. Remember, the correct answer is always found in the text. Always refer back to the passage and always read full sentences when you do so.

## THE STEPS OF THE BASIC APPROACH TO CRACKING GMAT READING COMPREHENSION

Here are the steps of the Basic Approach:

1. **Work the Passage**

   In this step, apply The Basics of Cracking the Passage. You must have a plan for reading the passage and you must learn to read actively. As you read, always be on the lookout for the main idea of the passage. To find the main idea, ask yourself questions such as what does the author want me to remember or believe about the topic under discussion? What's the author's conclusion? How is that conclusion supported?

2. **Understand the Question Task**

   Apply The Basics of Cracking the Questions**.** Try to break the question down. First, look for the subject of the question. Then, find the words that indicate the task.

3. **Find the Information in the Passage That Addresses the Task of the Question**

   Refer back to the passage. GMAC needs to be able to justify its credited responses by referring to specific information mentioned in the passage. When you understand the task of the question, it becomes easier to find this information. Once you locate the information in the passage that addresses the question task, you're ready to look at the answer choices.

4. **Use POE to Find the Answer**

   Use The Basics of Cracking the Answer Choices. Approach each answer choice with a healthy level of suspicion. Since there are four incorrect answers for every question, you are more likely to be reading a wrong answer than a right answer. Look for signs that are more likely to make an answer wrong, such as the answer sounding too much like the passage. Don't be afraid to just pick the answer that remains if you can find good reasons to eliminate the other four answer choices. An overview of common trap answer choices can be found in the next chapter.

# STEP 1: WORK THE PASSAGE

## Overview

Working the passage is the first step of The Basic Approach to Cracking GMAT Reading Comprehension Passages. By following the recommendations here on how to Work The Passage, you will be able to follow a strategic plan for reading the passage, avoid wasting time by actively reading the passage, learn a little about common passage structures, and map the passage to glean all the relevant information from the passage, which enables you to answer the questions later on. All in all, you will know what it takes to Crack the Passage. From there on, it's time to practice!

## How Do You Plan to Read?

Before we talk about how to Crack the Passage, let's quickly explore how you can plan to read. You saw the idea of planning to read a handful of times in the previous chapter, but what does it mean? Let's first explore how the typical test-taker handles the passage. Typical test-takers approach the Reading Comprehension passage in the same way they would approach any reading assignment. They read as quickly as possible, only barely scratching the surface of the major points of the passage that the author was trying to express. Often about halfway through the passage, they realize they have not retained a single major point of the passage. The test-taker is now either forced to reread the entire passage, or move on to the answer choices without a full comprehension of the material. This strategy is ineffective and wastes a lot of time!

A better way to approach the passage is to plan to read! Central to the plan is the test-taker's ability to comprehend the passage by Active Reading. Active Reading keeps you engaged with the passage, fights off the tendency to let your mind wander away from the task at hand, and leaves you with a better understanding of the author's main point once you are finished. But what is Active Reading and how do you do it?

## The Basics of Cracking the Passage

### Active Reading

The easiest way to define "Active Reading" is to define the opposite, or "Passive Reading." During passive reading, you look at the words but the content just isn't registering. You may remember some of the details from the passage but you probably missed why the author told you about those details. This is common on GMAT passages, as the content is often thick and boring.

Active reading, on the other hand, means that you follow the author's argument. Put another way, you try to separate the author's claims from the facts and other evidence used to back up those claims. This is an essential ingredient for Cracking the Passage.

Effective active reading involves:

- *Asking questions as you read:* Asking questions helps to engage your mind. For example, ask yourself key questions about the passage and its author. What is the author's purpose for writing the passage? What are the big ideas? Where in the passage are the big ideas located? What kind of tone is the author adopting (scholarly, friendly, critical, objective, biased)? At the end of a paragraph, try to predict where the author takes the argument next. These practices help to create a full understanding of the passage.

- *Identifying the Structure of the Passage*: The structure of a passage is an undervalued hint to deciphering the intentions of the author and the main point of the passage. Passages written in a conventional manner usually proceed from the general to the specific and then return to the general. Individual paragraphs are also usually written that way. Authors may open with a topic sentence, elaborate on the topic with explanations and examples, and then conclude the paragraph with a general statement that transitions to the next paragraph. Be on the lookout for trigger words or phrases in the middle of a paragraph (*however, on the contrary, on the other hand*). These words are indicators of the author's perspective of the topic of the passage. Often the author follows up one of these trigger words with the perspective they are trying to convince you to adopt.

- *Look for Topic Sentences*: Topic sentences usually can be found at the start of each paragraph and are not only a great tool to keep you engaged in the passage but also a way to easily find your way back to the appropriate point in the passage when you need to consult the passage to answer a question. A bit further in the paragraph you usually find explanations and examples of that topic. Like before, be on watch for trigger words mid-paragraph. Note how each new paragraph follows the one that precedes it, and look to the end of a paragraph for clues about the next idea. Use the noteboard to record the flow of ideas from one paragraph to the next. Sometimes two or more paragraphs may act as a "chunk" of the passage. Ideas can flow between these chunks in the same way they flow from paragraph to paragraph.

## The Main Idea

One of the central goals of Active Reading is to find the main idea and try to follow it. The main idea of the passage is what the author wants you to believe about the issue being presented in the passage.

Note here that this does not mean that the topic of the passage is the main idea. The topic of the passage—which is usually on one of the four primary areas of GMAT passages outlined in the previous chapter as social science, physical science, biological science, or business—is the overarching theme of the entire passage. The main idea is what the author wants you to believe about the topic. So, if you find yourself agreeing or disagreeing with the author, or noticing the author pushing an opinion or arguing a point, chances are that is the main idea of the passage.

By identifying the main idea of the passage, you can quickly and easily determine the purpose of the passage, which is one of the key components of successfully Cracking the Passage.

## The Purpose of the Passage

The purpose of the passage is what the author wants you to believe after reading the passage. The purpose of most passages is to persuade the reader to accept the author's main point. However, there are other reasons an author may write a passage. Broadly, the purpose behind a passage falls into one of three categories.

- *To Persuade*: The most common purpose for a GMAT passage is to persuade. As stated earlier, the author typically tries to convince you that his or her viewpoint (the main idea) is correct. In that sense, the main idea and the purpose are intimately connected.

- *To Criticize or Evaluate*: The second most common passage purpose is criticism or evaluation. The author may favor a new view over an existing one, or may criticize someone else's ideas. But criticism need not be negative; authors may play up the merits of a particular theory, book, technique, or other idea.

  When the author's purpose is to criticize or evaluate an idea, the passage almost always starts with a review of that idea. The author generally gives a quick overview in a neutral tone. The author's tone changes from neutral to critical (or perhaps complimentary) shortly after the main conclusions of the theory or idea are presented.

- *To Explain or Analyze*: While most passages involve some explanations and some analysis, passages that only explain or analyze are infrequent on the GMAT. Most authors have a point of view about the topic under discussion. However, a passage that deals with some sort of problem or puzzle may be purely explanatory in nature.

## Mapping the Passage

Mapping the Passage is the final tool in learning how to Crack the Passage. By Mapping the Passage you can easily identify the main idea and purpose of the passage, and doing so will keep you engaged and save you time as you move on to the questions. But, to successfully map the passage, you must do something that a typical test-taker never does. You must write things down. Just because you reach a reading comprehension passage does not give you an excuse to stop writing things down. In fact, as a time-saving tactic alone, writing things down while working on a reading comprehension passage is worth the effort. Writing things down also helps you get a better understanding of the topic being presented, which yields a more complete appreciation for the passage and makes answering the questions a lot more manageable!

The best strategy for Mapping the Passage is called Key Sentences. In this approach, read the passage one paragraph at a time. At the end of each paragraph, stop and try to identify the one sentence that seems the most like an opinion, recommendation, conclusion, or reason. Write a short summary of that sentence down on the noteboard. You don't need to write the entire sentence, but you do want to write more than one or two words. It's also a good idea to label the sentence as either a claim (a primary or secondary conclusion of the passage) or a reason that supports a previous claim. The idea of mapping the passage in this fashion is to uncover the author's original outline for the passage. When you are finished mapping the passage, you should be able to string together your key sentences to produce the main idea of the passage.

# STEP 2: UNDERSTAND THE QUESTION TASK

## Overview

Understanding the question task is important to Cracking GMAT Reading Comprehension and it is largely overlooked by the average test-taker. The Basics of Cracking the Questions can be broken down into two parts: identifying the subject and understanding the task.

## The Basics of Cracking the Questions

### Part 1: Identifying the Subject

When cracking GMAT Reading Comprehension questions, you must identify the subject of the question. For example, in the question "The author mentions land management policy in order to," the subject is *land management policy*. The subject helps you locate what you need to read *about* to answer the question.

By identifying the subject, you'll know what the question writer is testing you on. This is important for two reasons. First, by knowing the content that the question writer is testing you on, you are able to locate that information in the passage more easily. This is outlined in Step 3 of the Basic Approach. Secondly, without identifying the subject, you may struggle to eventually answer the question and are susceptible to some of the common trap incorrect answer choices. Identifying the subject is critical to Cracking the Questions, but equally as important is understanding the task of the question.

### Part 2: Understanding the Task

If you have been actively reading, you may have been able to predict that the second part of Cracking the Questions is understanding the task of the question. The task of the question is what you need to find out about the subject. For example, is the question asking for a detail from the passage, or is it asking why that detail is in the passage? Are you required merely to describe something, or does the question expect you to analyze it? Meanwhile, you should also be on the lookout for words such as EXCEPT, LEAST, and NOT.

In the example question given earlier, "The author mentions land management policy in order to," the task words are *in order to*. The tasks that questions can ask about are diverse and can be categorized as *general*, *specific*, or *complex* tasks.

**Specific:** Specific tasks reference a small part of the passage. There are four different ways specific questions can be asked. They are retrieval, inference, purpose, and vocab-in-context.

- **Retrieval** questions ask you to find information in the passage and may make reference to a detail or fact (a person's name, a theory, a time period). The answer is typically just a paraphrase of this information in the passage. These questions are highlighted by phrases such as *According to the passage,* and any reference to things that are mentioned by the author.

- **Inference** questions make test-takers nervous because they appear to suggest that the answer has to be figured out using knowledge about the author. Remember that all answers are found directly in the passage. In fact, inference tasks are a lot like retrieval tasks, particularly since a good portion of inference questions ask about a small detail that is easily overlooked. Keywords that identify a question as an inference include *infer, suggest, conclude,* or *imply,* among others. Because of the nature of these questions, it's easy to go wrong by drawing on outside information or making assumptions. Many wrong answers are based on the ways that people read into or interpret the information in the passage.

- **Purpose** questions ask *why* the author included the subject or some particular piece of information. Typically, the answers to these questions are closely related to the main point of the subject of the question. These questions can be identified by phrases such as *in order to,* and *serves which of the following functions.* To answer these questions, identify what the author said about the subject of the question and find an answer choice that reflects that idea.

- **Vocabulary-in-Context** questions ask you to state what the author means by a certain word or phrase. These questions are very similar to inference questions, because they usually ask what the author is suggesting or implying by the use of a particular term. The correct answer must fit the context of its sentence and the paragraph containing that sentence and match the main point of the passage.

**General:** General tasks ask about the passage as a whole. General questions can be asked in four different ways as well. Those ways are primary purpose, main idea, tone, and structure.

- **Primary Purpose** questions may seem similar to Main Idea questions, but they differ in one critical way. Primary Purpose questions ask *why* the author wrote the passage. Therefore, the answers are typically more general than those for Main Idea questions. The subject of Primary Purpose questions is usually the whole passage. These questions can be identified by the phrase *primary purpose,* and *chiefly concerned.* Not to be confused with Purpose questions, Primary Purpose questions test very broad ideas. This is an instance where, if you have carefully Cracked the Passage, you should be able to answer these questions easily.

- The task of **Main Idea** questions is to figure out what the author wants you to believe. The main idea is the overall claim, supported by the evidence contained in the rest of the text—in other words what does the author want you to accept as true? Main Idea questions differ from Primary Purpose questions in that the former deal with *what* the passage is about rather than *why* the author wrote it. These questions can be identified by any phrase that indicates a need for a general understanding of the passage, such as *overall claims* and *main point.* However, much like Primary Purpose questions, these questions are easily answerable if you have successfully Cracked the Passage.

- **Tone** questions ask you to evaluate how strongly or negatively the author feels about the subject of the question. Find the subject in the passage and look for words that reveal the author's feelings. Examples of such words and phrases include *misrepresenting, unlikely, considerable importance, unfortunately,* and *a poor grasp,* among others. Questions that ask about the author's tone generally use the words *tone* or *attitude.*

- Some **Structure** questions ask about the overall sequence of the passage, while others ask about a smaller piece of it, such as a single paragraph. Either way, these questions test the general flow of the passage. If you can describe the flow of ideas—a task made easier by Mapping the Passage on the noteboard—you'll be able to narrow down the answer choices, crossing off answers that describe things that didn't happen in the passage.

**Complex:** Complex tasks require a good understanding of the main idea, so Cracking the Passage is essential. Complex questions also can be asked in four different ways. Those ways are evaluation, weaken/strengthen, analogy, and application.

- **Evaluation** questions on the GMAT are pretty rare, but they do exist. These questions test your ability to compare or analyze information from the passage. For example, you may be asked to assess the relationship between two pieces of information from the passage. There aren't many common forms of questions like this, so an example of this type of question would be *Which of the following most accurately summarizes the relationship between nineteenth-century American women and eighteenth-century American women in the highlighted text?*

- Slightly more common than evaluation questions, **Weaken/Strengthen** questions ask the test-taker to weaken or strengthen an assertion made in the passage. These questions can be identified by the presence of the word *weaken* or *strengthen* in the question.

- **Analogy** questions typically use the answer choices to draw comparisons to information discussed in the passage. The correct answer is the one that completes a reasonable analogy. Mostly, these questions can be identified by the key phrase *most similar.*

- Sometimes questions ask you to apply information from the passage to a new scenario. These are **Application** questions and can be easily spotted when the question stem refers to the answer choices as either "scenarios," "situations," or "assertions."

## STEP 3: FIND INFORMATION IN THE PASSAGE THAT ADDRESSES THE TASK

### Overview

Step 3 of the Basic Approach to Cracking the GMAT Reading Comprehension is finding the information in the passage that addresses the question task. After you have Cracked the Question by identifying the subject and the task, look for the subject in the passage. Once you locate the subject, find the information about the subject that addresses the task of the question.

This is when Cracking the Passage from Step 1 of The Basic Approach is invaluable. Use your notes to find the appropriate place in the passage that addresses the subject and start reading. Try to read eight to ten lines. Then make sure you understand what you have read. It is important for you to not attempt to answer the question in your own words. Attempting to do so may cause you to interpret the passage, which is not your goal. Your goal is to find the information from the passage that addresses the task of the question. And, as always, the answers to the questions can be found in the passage.

It is important for this step to use the **Active Reading** strategies from Step 1 again. After you have found the appropriate place to begin reading, keep the task of the question in the back of your mind and be on constant lookout for any information that addresses the task of the question. After you have found this information, and have taken measures to ensure you truly understand the information, you are ready to move on to Step 4 of The Basic Approach to Cracking GMAT Reading Comprehension—examining and eliminating the answer choices.

## STEP 4: USE POE TO FIND THE ANSWER

### Overview

The final step of The Basic Approach to Cracking GMAT Reading Comprehension is using POE to find the answer. If you have followed all of the steps up to this point, then you have worked the passage and have a thorough understanding of it through Active Reading, analyzed and achieved understanding of the question subject and task, and located and read the information about the question subject and task in the passage. Now, it's time to look at the answer choices and find the correct answer by using POE (Process of Elimination).

As discussed throughout this entire book thus far, POE is one of the most powerful tools at your disposal on test day. Reading Comprehension is no different as POE is the best tool to help you find the correct answer by eliminating the incorrect ones. Once you understand the task of the question and have been able to locate its information in the passage, eliminating wrong answer choices is the most effective way to answer the question correctly.

Many test-takers do exactly what the writers of the test want them to do—they answer questions based on memory or what sounds correct. However, if you learn how test-takers create incorrect answer choices, you can eliminate answers quickly and stand your best chance at achieving the highest score possible for you.

In light of that, the final step in learning how to crack GMAT Reading Comprehension is learning about the different ways that the test-writers create wrong answer choices. Once you know their methodology, you can learn how to spot wrong answers and then confidently eliminate the offending answer choices.

## The Basics of Cracking the Answer Choices

Knowing the types of answer choices that test-writers use to create wrong answers is the key to being prepared to use POE on test day. Test-writers use certain kinds of answer choices to make an answer choice look attractive. The problem is, even if you have read the passage and followed the steps, a lot of times the incorrect answer choices still look correct! The test-writers have to write hard answer choices like this or else the questions are too easy. Your job is to become familiar with the ways by which they create these wrong answers so that when you read an answer choice constructed in a certain way, it raises suspicion. The more skeptical you are of the answer choices, the more likely you are to be able to eliminate them.

The following are the ways in which test-writers create wrong answers:

Watch out for these tricks and traps!

- Recycled Language and Memory Traps
- Extreme Language
- No Such Comparison
- Reversals
- Emotional Appeals
- Outside Knowledge

Become familiar with these and you are one step closer to cracking GMAT Reading Comprehension.

### Recycled Language and Memory Traps

One of the easiest and most common ways that test-writers create wrong answer choices is by repeating memorable words or phrases from the passage. The correct answers for GMAT Reading Comprehension questions are generally paraphrases of the passage. So the presence of words or phrases that are very reminiscent of the passage is a reason to be skeptical of the answer choice.

Recycled language is one of the most common forms of memory traps. Recycled language in an answer choice is easily identified because recycled language includes words or phrases that are direct quotes from the text. If you see words or phrases that fit the description of recycled language, you should be very skeptical of the answer choice. Did the passage say exactly what the answer choice says regarding the recycled language? If it doesn't, the answer choice is incorrect.

More commonly, memory traps are words or phrases that evoke a strong memory from the passage. These answer choices are designed to make the average test-taker think "Oh, I remember reading that in the passage" and, because of that, they make for very appealing answer choices. Memory traps evoke a stronger memory than actual correct answers do, so if you find yourself attracted to an answer choice because of the mention of something you remember, be wary! Make sure that the answer choice hasn't taken that piece of information out of context or confused it with another part of the passage.

## Extreme Language

Another common way to create wrong answer choices is by using language that is too "powerful" or overt. Common ways to do that are by using words such as *must, always, never, only, best,* and other very strong words, or by answers that use verbs that are really strong, such as *prove* or *fail.*

For instance, a primary purpose question may have answer choices that use a powerful verb such as *defend* or *criticize.* If the passage does not explicitly defend or criticize the main idea, this answer choice is incorrect because it contains the extreme language. Below is a chart of common words that should cause skepticism for extreme language.

| Common Extreme Words | | | |
|---|---|---|---|
| Never | Not | Defend | Contradict |
| Always | No | Attack | Failure |
| Only | Must | Denounce | |
| None | Prove | Counter | |

## No Such Comparison

Comparison words such as *better, more, reconcile, less, decide,* or *more than* are used by test-writers to make answer choices more appealing by drawing a comparison between two items referenced in the passage. If you see them, you should be skeptical. As with every answer choice, make sure to reference them against the information in the passage. Often the ideas being compared in the answer choices were discussed in the passage but not explicitly compared.

## Reversals

Reversal answer choices seek to confuse the test-taker by saying the opposite of the main idea or a detail from the passage. These answer choices are more difficult to spot because there isn't a list of common words. However, if you have successfully Cracked the Passage and found the information in the passage that references the task of the question, then identifying reversals of the answer choices becomes a lot more manageable.

## Emotional Appeals

This answer choice type is fairly rare on the GMAT. However, it is still worth mentioning. Some answer choices may try to appeal to the beliefs of the test-taker. For instance, a political passage may contain an answer choice that values one political stance over another even if the passage made no such claim. If you have successfully followed the steps to Crack the Passage and identified the main idea and the task of the question, these answer choices are easily eliminated.

### Outside Knowledge

Much like emotional appeal answer choices, outside knowledge answer choices are also fairly rare on the GMAT. Correct answer choices on the GMAT contain information that is found only in the passage. However, these answer choices can be very tempting to you because you may know a piece of information that is not mentioned in the passage but is reflected in an answer choice. Remember, you should rely on the information in the passage only to answer questions on the GMAT.

## DRILL 18 (Reading Comprehension)

The answers to the questions in this drill can be found in Part VII.

Questions 1–4 are based on the following passage.

The practice of mindfulness meditation originated as an ancient Buddhist meditation technique in which the meditator focuses on being aware of the present moment and acknowledging feelings and thoughts as they come and go. In recent years, brain imaging techniques have shed light on the effects on the brain and body of those who participate in a couple of hours of mindfulness meditation each week.

MRI scans conducted on the brains of people who engaged in an eight-week meditation practice showed an apparent reduction in the size of the amygdala. Commonly thought of as the primal "fight or flight" center of the brain, the amygdala dictates the response to stress. While the amygdala appears to shrink because of meditation, the prefrontal cortex, the area of the brain associated with concentration and awareness, thickens, and the relationship between the amygdala and the rest of the brain appears to weaken. These findings prompted researchers to hypothesize that increased meditation may be capable of replacing our fearful responses to stress with more rational ones.

While researchers have called for more studies to be done on the mental and physical ramifications of mindfulness meditation, a new debate has emerged over whether meditation itself is a science. Proponents of meditation-as-science argue that science is the study of the natural world through observation and experiment to produce a unified body of knowledge on a given subject. Meditation, says the argument, is the observation of one's own mind, and a body of knowledge has been built over thousands of years as the result of consistent experimentation of techniques to observe and better understand the consciousness of the mind.

1. According to the passage, which of the following is true about the amygdala?

- Extended meditation causes long-term damage to the amygdala.
- The response to stress produced by the amygdala is less valuable than the response produced by the prefrontal cortex.
- There is a direct correlation between the size of the amygdala and the thickness of the prefrontal cortex.
- The size difference of the amygdala between those who practice meditation and those who do not may impact their responses to stress.
- The relationship between the amygdala and the rest of the brain is weakened as a result of the thickening of the prefrontal cortex.

2. The passage is primarily concerned with

- convincing the reader of the benefits of meditation
- outlining the science of the response the brain has to meditation and the debates the practice inspires
- arguing that meditation is the most effective way to depress the "fight or flight" response
- validating the stance of those who believe meditation is a science
- teaching people how to better handle stress

3. Based on the information in the passage, which of the following can be inferred about fearful responses to stress?

- Fearful responses to stress can be replaced with more rational responses if the person engages in a couple of hours of meditation per week.
- Fearful responses to stress occur more regularly in people with a thin prefrontal cortex.
- There is some debate over whether the research behind reducing fearful responses to stress should be considered science.
- Researchers believe that further study regarding fearful responses to stress and the relationship those responses have to mindfulness meditation is warranted.
- Fearful responses to stress can be seen on an MRI scan.

4. Which of the following scenarios would a proponent of meditation-as-science be most likely to argue is not a science?

- A worldwide effort to uncover the secrets of a little-known video game
- A thorough review of popular literature with the goal of analyzing sentence structure and word choice for similarities
- The study of stars and planet movement to notice patterns that correlate to terrestrial events
- The observation of fashion trends over the course of hundreds of years to predict fashion in the future
- Collecting samples of wood used in the construction of log cabins to determine which wood produces the most stable product

Questions 5–7 are based on the following passage.

Artificial neural networks, named so as to distinguish them from real neural networks found inside a brain, are designed to simulate the activity of real neural networks by packing interconnected "brain cells," or units, so a computer can learn and recognize patterns on its own. Artificial neural networks typically consist of three types of units: input units which receive information to learn about, output units which signal how the network has responded to the items it learned about, and hidden units which sit in layers between the input and output units. The connections made between the units are given weight, which dictates the influence of a given connection.

By constructing artificial neural networks in this way, the networks can learn through information flow in a manner similar to how a real brain learns. Information is passed to the input units, which trigger the hidden units. The hidden units are activated and the sum of the inputs it receives triggers the next unit to fire if the sum exceeds a certain threshold. By giving the output units a model to compare the result of the learning process to, the artificial neural network can learn where to place more weight in order to make the result of the output unit more closely resemble that of the model.

5. The primary purpose of the passage is to

- describe artificial neural networks
- contrast artificial neural networks with neural networks found in brains
- illustrate how to build an artificial neural network
- argue for the wider adoption of artificial neural networks
- outline the different units of an artificial neural network and their roles in producing intelligence

6. It can be inferred from the passage that real neural networks

- are to be considered superior to artificial neural networks
- consist of input, hidden, and output units
- inspired the development of artificial neural networks
- are more capable of recognizing patterns than artificial neural networks
- will someday become obsolete

7. According to the passage, which of the following best represents the optimal flow of information through an artificial neural network?

- A model is shown to the input units which pass information to the output units which describe the model.
- Information is fed to the input units which activate the hidden units which then change the input units to more closely resemble the model.
- The input units receive information to give to the hidden units which then forward information to the output units to compare against a model.
- A model is shown to the input units which then attempt to recreate the model using different information.
- The input units are activated by information fed to them via the output units which analyze a model and improve the information before handing it to the input units.

# Summary

- Most likely you will see four Reading Comprehension passages. There are usually three short passages, followed by three questions each, and one long passage, followed by four questions.
- GMAT Reading Comprehension passage topics are usually from four areas: social sciences, biological science, physical science, and business.
- GMAT test-writers create questions in a certain way. For you to be successful, follow the steps of The Basic Approach to Cracking GMAT Reading Comprehension:
    - Step 1: Work the Passage
    - Step 2: Understand the Question Task
    - Step 3: Find Information in the Passage That Addresses the Task
    - Step 4: Use POE to Find the Answer
- The Basics of cracking the passage start with Active Reading. Active Reading enables you to gain a greater understanding of the passage by asking questions, identifying the structure of the passage, and looking for topic sentences.
- Crack the passage by identifying the main point and the purpose of the passage. The main point is what the author wants you to believe about something, and the purpose is why the author wrote the passage (to persuade, to criticize or evaluate, or to explain or analyze).
- Mapping the passage is an effective tool in keeping yourself organized in order to work efficiently while cracking the passage.
- Test-writers deliberately create wrong answers using recycled language and memory traps, extreme language, no such comparison, reversals, emotional appeals, and outside knowledge.

# Chapter 23
# Critical Reasoning

To perform well on Critical Reasoning questions, you need to know how GMAT arguments are constructed and how they are commonly reasoned. It is also helpful to know how incorrect answer choices are typically created so you can recognize them on test day. In this chapter, we will show you how to recognize and master the eight types of argument questions that appear on the GMAT.

# CRITICAL REASONING OVERVIEW

Critical Reasoning questions comprise just over one-quarter of the GMAT's Verbal section—approximately 10 of 36 questions are in this format. Each question consists of a short reading passage, followed by a single question and 5 multiple choice answers. Critical Reasoning passages are based on a short argument, a set of statements, or a plan of action. For each question, select the best answer from among the choices provided.

## The Passage

Critical Reasoning passages tend to be short (usually 20–100 words) and oftentimes take the form of an argument. The subjects they consider don't often fall into neat categories, and the scenarios they present are commonly hypothetical. Read your passages carefully, pay attention to the language employed, and interpret that language literally. It is important to be precise when reading the passage for Critical Reasoning questions. As you'll see in the pages to come, the difference between getting a Critical Reasoning question correct and falling for a trap answer often lies in the particulars of the passage's wording.

## The Question

There are eight types of Critical Reasoning question, each of which involves a different task with respect to the passage. Most questions test your ability to evaluate the reasoning employed in an argument, but some test your ability to reason on the basis of information. This chapter will outline the different types of questions you will see, how to identify them, and what to look for in the passage based on the type of question. So much of your evaluation of the passage depends on what the question is asking you to identify in the passage. Because of this, you should read the question first, and then read the passage.

## The Answer Choices

All things verbal come down to Process of Elimination, and Critical Reasoning is no exception. Each question type for Critical Reasoning questions has its own set of POE tools. These tools are based off the common trap answers constructed by the test-writers. Because the question types all vary, the common trap answers and POE tools to employ also vary based on question type. After mastering the different types of questions, you'll learn how answer choices for those question types are constructed and, with enough practice, you'll be able to spot a bad answer choice with confidence.

## HOW GMAT ARGUMENTS ARE CONSTRUCTED

Most Critical Reasoning passages take the form of *arguments* in which the writer tries to convince the reader of something. Here's an example:

> During the past 10 years, advertising revenues for the magazine *True Investor* have fallen by 30 percent. The magazine has failed to attract new subscribers, and newsstand sales are at an all-time low. Thus, sweeping changes to the editorial board will be necessary for the magazine to survive.

GMAT arguments consist of three connected parts:

- Conclusion—what the author tries to persuade the reader to accept
- Premise—evidence provided in support of a conclusion
- Assumption—unstated ideas upon which an argument's validity rests

### Conclusions

A conclusion is the primary claim made in an argument. The easiest way to identify the conclusion is to ask yourself what its author wants you to believe. In the argument above, the conclusion is found in the last sentence, where the author attempts to persuade the reader that *sweeping changes to the editorial board will be necessary for the magazine to survive.*

In some cases, indicator words can help you to find the conclusion. These include:

| | |
|---|---|
| Therefore | Hence |
| Clearly | Consequently |
| Thus | So |

Indicator words can help you to identify the parts of an argument, but not every argument uses them. However, almost every argument will have a conclusion of some kind. A conclusion can be a plan or course of action, an argument, a statement of supposed truth, or any number of resolutions to the contents of the passage.

Learning to identify the conclusion is the first important step in evaluating the passage. Once you've identified the conclusion, the remaining information in the passage should reveal evidence that is used in support of the conclusion.

### Premises

The premises of an argument include any reasons, statistics, or other evidence provided in support of the conclusion. In the case of GMAT arguments, you must accept the truth of the premises, whether you agree with them or not. The easiest way to identify the premises is to ask what information the author has provided to justify the truth of the conclusion.

In the argument above, the premises can be found in the first two sentences, where the author provides three pieces of evidence in support of the conclusion: *advertising revenues have fallen by 30 percent, the magazine has failed to attract new subscribers*, and *sales are at an all-time low.*

Sometimes you'll see indicator words that can help you to find the premises. These include:

| | |
|---|---|
| Because | In view of |
| Given that | Since |
| As a result of | Supposing that |

## Assumptions

Assumptions are unstated premises on which the author relies to prove his or her conclusion. Even well-reasoned arguments rest on assumptions; because it's impossible to say everything, some things must go unsaid. Therefore, assumptions play a crucial role in the structure of an argument, bridging gaps in reasoning from the premises to the conclusion.

The argument above assumes that the editorial board *caused* the problems now attributed to the magazine. If something other than the editorial board were responsible—had the local population declined by 30 percent, for example—then sweeping changes to the board might do little to improve the magazine's financial situation. In this case, the connection between the premises (the magazine's problems) and the conclusion (changes to the editorial board) falls apart. The reader is no longer persuaded that *changes to the editorial board will be necessary for the magazine to survive.* The argument collapses.

The easiest way to identify an assumption is to distinguish an argument's conclusion from its premises. Then, ask what additional information is required to link the conclusion to the premises.

## Gaps

In many cases, gaps in reasoning are indicated by gaps in language. Look for words or phrases in the conclusion that do not come from the premises. Identify an assumption in the following example:

> Cream cheese contains half as many calories per tablespoon as does butter or margarine. Therefore, a bagel with cream cheese is more healthful than is a bagel with butter.

First, find the conclusion. The word *therefore* gives the conclusion away: *a bagel with cream cheese is more healthful than is a bagel with butter.*

Second, find the premises. What information does the author provide to support the conclusion? The premise states that *cream cheese contains half as many calories per tablespoon.*

Third, look for shifts in language between the premise and conclusion. The premise compares the calorie content of a tablespoon of cream cheese to that of a tablespoon of butter or margarine. The conclusion introduces the word *healthful*, which does not appear in the premise. This shift in the argument's language is indicative of a gap in reasoning—the argument leaps from a thing that *has fewer calories per tablespoon* to a thing that *is more healthful*. Therefore, this argument rests on the assumption that a food with *fewer calories* is a food that is *more healthful*.

Although most Critical Reasoning passages consist of three basic parts—conclusions, premises, and assumptions—some passages also include extraneous ideas, background information, or opposing points of view. The efficiency with which you identify assumptions depends in large part on the accuracy with which you identify conclusions and premises, so don't be distracted by nonessential information.

## COMMON REASONING PATTERNS

Like the other question formats on the GMAT, Critical Reasoning questions tend to be predictable. While you'll never see the same question twice, many Critical Reasoning passages employ similar patterns of reasoning. Learning to recognize these patterns provides you with another means of identifying assumptions.

Not every GMAT argument models one of the common reasoning patterns, so you'll sometimes still need to look for shifts in language. However, when one of the common reasoning patterns is present, it can help you to locate information needed to strengthen or weaken an argument. Each of the five common patterns involves its own standard assumption or assumptions. Learning to recognize these patterns, and the assumptions they incorporate, will help you to identify unstated presuppositions and pinpoint an argument's flaws.

### Causal Patterns

Causal reasoning is the most common type of reasoning you'll encounter in GMAT arguments. Test-writers are fond of causal arguments, and you're likely to see several of them on the GMAT. In a causal argument, the premises usually state that two things happened, from which the author concludes that one thing caused the other. Consider the following simple example:

> A study indicated that adults who listen to classical music regularly are less likely to have anxiety disorders. Clearly, classical music calms the nerves and reduces anxiety.

The author of this argument concludes that *classical music calms the nerves and reduces anxiety*. This conclusion is based on a study indicating that *adults who listen to classical music regularly are less likely to have anxiety disorders*. Thus, the premise posits a correlation between two things—exposure to classical music and reduced likelihood of anxiety disorders—and the conclusion makes a leap from correlation to causation.

Every causal argument involves two standard assumptions:

- There's no other cause.
- It's not a coincidence.

Our argument assumes that it's not a coincidence that adults who listened to classical music were less likely to have anxiety disorders, and that makes sense because it also assumes that nothing other than classical music caused study participants to experience fewer anxiety disorders.

The first standard assumption suggests that classical music, and only classical music, caused participants in the study to experience fewer anxiety disorders. But what if something else was responsible? The passage doesn't rule out the possibility that study participants used anxiety-reducing medication, or that they simply happened to be calm people to begin with. In neither of these cases would it follow that *classical music calms the nerves and reduces anxiety.* Thus, the argument must assume that a causal relationship exists.

The second standard assumption denies that the correlation between classical music and anxiety is a coincidence. But what if a different study indicated that adults who listen to classical music regularly were more likely to have anxiety disorders? In that case, it no longer follows that classical music calms the nerves and reduces anxiety—on the contrary, the counterexample suggests that the first study's results were coincidental. Thus, the argument must assume that the correlation between classical music and lower anxiety is not a coincidence.

When you spot an argument that employs a causal reasoning pattern, remember that the argument relies on two assumptions: first, there's no other cause; and second, it's not a coincidence.

## Planning Patterns

Many GMAT arguments introduce plans that are designed to solve problems: a municipal government's plan to improve water quality, a transit authority's plan to reduce traffic congestion, or a town board's plan to increase voter turnout. The premises of planning arguments describe what the plan is supposed to accomplish and how it is supposed to work. For example:

> During the past 5 years, Meridian Township has seen a dramatic rise in crime. As a result, Meridian's police force plans to install video surveillance cameras at major intersections in neighborhoods that suffer the worst crime rates. Clearly, the crime rate in Meridian Township will drop.

Consider this argument in terms of its parts. Meridian Township has a problem: *a dramatic rise in crime.* To address this problem, the police force plans to *install video surveillance cameras.* These are the premises of the argument because they outline the plan for addressing the problem. The argument concludes that, as a result of instituting the plan, the crime rate will drop. In general, the conclusion of an argument that employs the planning pattern can simply be expressed: *do the plan.*

Every planning argument involves one standard assumption:

- There's no problem with the plan.

Evaluating an argument with a planning reasoning pattern will revolve around the plan itself. For instance, what if there *is* a problem with the plan to reduce crime by installing video cameras at major intersections? After all, crime is not limited to major intersections. Perhaps the cameras will malfunction or produce poor quality images. Perhaps criminals will simply relocate to neighborhoods without cameras. In these cases, our confidence in the conclusion is shaken. On the basis of the premises alone, it no longer seems to follow that *the crime rate will drop*. Thus, in order for the argument to "work," its author must assume that installing the cameras really will reduce crime, or that there's no problem with the plan. A question could ask to identify a potential problem with the plan, or to strengthen the plan with the addition of some other fact.

No matter what the question asks, when you encounter an argument that employs a planning pattern, remember the standard assumption at play: there's no problem with the plan.

## Sampling Patterns

Arguments that exhibit a sampling pattern are less common than causal or planning arguments. In a sampling argument, the author reaches a general conclusion about a population based on evidence about some members of the population. Sampling arguments assume that a smaller group is typical of a larger group and accurately reflects the relevant characteristics or feelings of the larger group. Here is an example:

> Contrary to popular belief, football fans overwhelmingly approve of the decisions made by the administrative staffs of their local teams. We know this to be true because a large group of fans leaving a stadium expressed admiration for their teams' coaches and coordinators in an interview last week.

The author of this argument concludes that *football fans overwhelmingly approve of the decisions made by the administrative staffs of their local teams*. This conclusion is based on the premise that *a large group of fans leaving a stadium expressed admiration for their teams' coaches and coordinators in an interview last week*. Thus, the conclusion makes a leap from the opinion of one group of fans at a particular moment to the opinion of football fans in general.

Every sampling argument involves one standard assumption:

- The sample is representative.

When you encounter a sampling reasoning pattern, look for reasons why the sample itself is either representative or not. What if the opinion of the interviewed group of football fans isn't representative of the opinions of football fans in general? Perhaps the interviewed fans attended a game their team won, and perhaps their local team has long enjoyed a winning record. It does not follow from this that fans of every team approve of the decisions made by their team's administrative staff. To properly link the argument's conclusion to its premise, the author must assume that the opinions of interviewed fans accurately reflect those of football fans in general.

When you run into an argument that employs a sampling pattern, remember that the argument relies on the assumption that a sample is representative of a larger population.

## Interpretation of Evidence Patterns

In some GMAT arguments, the author understands the conclusion to be synonymous with one or more of the premises. In other words, information in the premises is interpreted to mean information in the conclusion. These arguments exhibit the interpretation of evidence pattern.

One particularly common instance of this pattern involves the misinterpretation of statistical data. Not every argument that incorporates statistics is an interpretation of evidence argument, but arguments that exhibit this pattern frequently involve statistics. Most often, the argument confuses percentages with actual values. Consider the following example:

> Local grocer: Ninety percent of customers bought store brand soup last winter, but only eighty percent bought store brand soup this winter. Obviously, more customers bought store brand soup last winter.

The author concludes that *more customers bought store brand soup last winter.* This conclusion is based on the premise that *ninety percent of customers bought soup last winter, but only eighty percent bought soup this winter.* The premise describes a change in the percentage of customers who bought store brand soup, and the conclusion leaps from percentages to actual numbers.

Every interpretation of evidence argument involves one standard assumption:

- There's no other way to interpret the evidence.

What if there's another way to interpret the data? If 100 customers visited the grocer last winter, and ninety percent bought store brand soup, then 90 people bought store brand soup last winter. But if 200 customers visited the grocer this winter, and eighty percent bought store brand soup, then 160 people bought store brand soup this winter. In this case, it no longer follows that more people bought store brand soup last winter—the author misinterprets the statistical data.

When you come across an interpretation of evidence pattern, the argument most likely relies on the standard assumption that there's no other way to interpret the evidence.

## Analogy Patterns

Reasoning by analogy is relatively rare on the GMAT, but that doesn't mean you won't see arguments by analogy. These arguments characteristically assume that what is appropriate in one case is also appropriate in another. They typically rely on the assumption that two things are similar enough to sustain a comparison. Here is a simple example:

> Using this line of products has been shown to cause cancer in laboratory animals. Therefore, you should stop using this line of products.

The author concludes that *you should stop using this line of products.* This conclusion is based on the premise that *this line of products has been shown to cause cancer in laboratory animals.* The premise concerns lab animals, and the conclusion leaps to humans. Thus, the argument relies on the assumption that humans and lab animals are similar: what causes cancer in laboratory animals also causes cancer in humans.

Arguments by analogy involve one standard assumption:

- One thing is similar to another.

What if humans are significantly different from laboratory animals? For example, if a feature of human physiology not shared by lab animals prevented the growth of cancers in humans who used the products, it would no longer follow that you should stop using the products.

When you encounter an argument that employs an analogy pattern, it probably relies on the assumption that one thing is similar to another in some relevant way.

# THE BASIC APPROACH TO CRITICAL REASONING QUESTIONS

Critical Reasoning questions come in eight flavors. The majority of the questions are either *assumption*, *weaken*, *strengthen*, or *inference* questions. However, there are some minor question types, such as *resolve/explain*, *evaluate*, *identify the reasoning*, and *flaw* questions, of which you should be aware. Each of these question types has its own unique task and common trap answers.

Most Critical Reasoning questions will present you with an argument, but not all questions involve arguments. In fact, some Critical Reasoning passages don't look like arguments at all. In order to master the Critical Reasoning format, you need a basic approach that can be applied to any Critical Reasoning question you encounter, no matter what kind of question it is.

Here are the steps of the Basic Approach:

1. **Identify the Question**

   Look for words or phrases in the question stem that can be used to identify the question type. Your knowledge of the question type informs your approach to the passage, so always read the question stem before you read the passage.

2. **Work the Passage**

   For most question types, begin working an argument by distinguishing its conclusion from its premises. Then, look for shifts in language or reasoning patterns that can help you to identify the argument's assumption.

3. **Predict What the Answer Should Do**

   While it's often difficult to predict the answer, it's usually easier to predict what the answer should do. Before turning to the answer choices, use your knowledge of the question and the information in the passage to determine what the correct answer needs to accomplish.

4. **Use POE to Find the Answer**

   It's often easier to identify incorrect answers than it is to identify correct answers, so use POE aggressively. The POE tools change based on the question type, which is why it is critically important for you to become familiar with the different types of questions and how answer choices are constructed for them.

## Step 1: Identify the Question

The surest way to improve performance and boost confidence in your Critical Reasoning ability is to take control of your approach to Critical Reasoning questions. Every question includes a word or phrase that can help you to identify what kind of question it is, and each question type involves a unique task with respect to the passage. Not all tasks are created equally, so it's important to know what's required of you.

Your knowledge of the question type should inform your approach, suggesting what kind of information to look for in the passage and what kind of answers to avoid. For now, we'll introduce the different question types, saving a more detailed discussion for later in the chapter.

### Assumption Questions

Assumptions are necessary but invisible parts of an argument that bridge gaps in reasoning between its premises and conclusion. Here's where all that practice identifying the parts of an argument really begins to pay off. Simply put, assumption questions ask you to identify an unstated premise on which an argument depends.

Assumption questions typically ask:

- The argument above assumes which of the following?
- The author of the argument above presupposes which of the following to be true?
- Which of the following is an assumption on which the truth of the author's conclusion depends?

Different forms of the words *presupposition*, *expectation*, and *assumption* can alert you to the fact that you've encountered an assumption question.

## Weaken Questions

Weaken questions ask to find a reason why the information in the passage could be wrong, or is incomplete. The vast majority of weaken questions require you to undermine the conclusion by attacking one of the argument's assumptions. Most commonly, the real job when answering weaken questions is not to attack the conclusion, but to attack *the way the conclusion follows from the premises.*

Weaken questions typically ask:

- Which of the following, if true, most seriously weakens the argument above?
- Which of the following casts the most doubt on the author's conclusion?
- Which of the following calls into question the reasoning above?

Indicator words such as *weaken*, *undermine*, and *cast doubt* can help you to spot a weaken question.

## Strengthen Questions

Strengthen questions require you to reinforce an argument's conclusion. This is usually accomplished by strengthening one of the argument's assumptions. In order to answer a strengthen question with confidence, therefore, you must first identify an assumption. Once the pivotal assumption has been found, your job is to strengthen it—support the conclusion by strengthening the assumption.

Strengthen questions typically ask:

- Which of the following provides the best support for the claims made above?
- Which of the following statements, if true, most strengthens the argument's conclusion?
- Which of the following, if true, increases the likelihood that the author's claim is also true?

Words such as *strengthen*, *support*, and *justify* can help you to recognize a strengthen question.

## Inference Questions

In one sense, an inference question is like a strengthen question in reverse. In a strengthen question, the correct answer strengthens the passage, but in an inference question, the passage strengthens the correct answer. As a result, many indicator words associated with strengthen questions—words such as *strengthen*, *support*, and *bolster*—are also associated with inference questions. Distinguish an inference question from a strengthen question by determining the direction of support.

In another sense, inference questions are unlike any of the question types we've discussed so far, because they don't require you to break an argument into its parts. In fact, inference passages tend not to resemble arguments at all. Instead, they merely present you with information—usually a collection of facts or opinions that lead to a particular conclusion. Once you're clear on the facts, your job is to select the answer that necessarily follows from them.

Inference questions typically ask:

- Which of the following can be inferred from the information above?
- On the basis of the statements above, which of the following must be true?
- With which of the following statements would the author of the passage most agree?

Words such as *inference*, *support*, and *strengthen* can help you spot an inference question.

## Resolve/Explain Questions

Some Critical Reasoning questions ask you to resolve an apparent discrepancy or explain a paradoxical situation. The passages that accompany these questions almost never resemble arguments. Like inference passages, they merely present you with information. Resolve/Explain questions ask how two seemingly incongruous statements can be true at the same time. Clearly state the two ideas that seem to be opposed, and then select the answer that allows both ideas to be true.

Resolve/Explain questions typically ask:

- Which of the following, if true, resolves the paradox outlined above?
- Which of the following best explains the apparent contradiction?
- Which of the following statements goes farthest in explaining the situation above?

Resolve/Explain questions are easy to recognize because they include the word *resolve* or *explain*. Words such as *paradox* and *discrepancy* can also help you identify resolve/explain questions.

## Evaluate Questions

Evaluate questions target your ability to spot a question (or test) that could be answered (or performed) to *evaluate* or *assess* an argument. Your job is to identify the question that, if answered, would allow you to test the argument's key assumption. Thus, evaluate questions are similar to strengthen and weaken questions in that they first require you to identify an unstated premise.

However, once the key assumption has been found, your task is not to weaken or strengthen it, but to identify the test that could help determine whether the argument is weak or strong.

Evaluate questions typically ask:

- The answer to which of the following questions would most likely yield information that could be used to assess the author's claim?
- Which of the following experiments would be most useful in evaluating the argument above?
- Which of the following tests could be performed to determine the truth of the argument's conclusion?

Indicator words such as *evaluate* and *assess* can help you to recognize an evaluate question.

## Identify the Reasoning Questions

Occasionally, a Critical Reasoning question will ask you to identify the method, technique, or strategy used by the author of an argument, or to describe the roles played by bolded phrases in an argument. Identify the reasoning questions concern the relationships that exist between an argument's parts. Before you can answer a question about that relationship, you must first identify those parts. Distinguish the argument's conclusion from its premises, and then select the answer that accurately describes the structure of the argument.

Identify the reasoning questions typically ask:

- The author provides support for the argument above by...
- Which of the following methods of reasoning does the argument above exhibit?
- The bolded phrases play which of the following roles in the argument above?

Words such as *technique*, *strategy*, *method*, and *by* can help you to spot an identify the reasoning question.

## Flaw Questions

Flaw questions ask you to describe what went wrong in an argument. The question stem already acknowledges that you're dealing with a bad argument. Your job is to identify its vulnerability. Flaw questions tend to resemble a blend of the identify the reasoning and weaken question types. Select the answer that accurately describes a vulnerability in the argument's reasoning.

Flaw questions typically ask:

- Which of the following statements describes a flaw in the argument above?
- The argument above is vulnerable to criticism for which of the following reasons?

To identify a flaw question, look for the words *vulnerable*, *criticism*, and *flaw*.

## Step 2: Work the Argument

After you've read a Critical Reasoning question, read the accompanying passage. Allow your knowledge of the question type to guide you to relevant information.

Most Critical Reasoning questions—assumption, weaken, strengthen, evaluate, flaw, and identify the reasoning questions—provide you with an argument, and then ask you to perform a task related to the reasoning that argument employs.

- **Assumption questions** ask for an assumption required to make the argument valid. The correct answer will bridge a gap in an argument's reasoning from premise to conclusion, so begin by distinguishing the conclusion from the premises that support it. Then, identify the assumption that links the conclusion to the premises, choosing the answer that bridges the gap. Shifts in language and reasoning patterns can help you to spot assumptions.

- **Weaken questions**: Weakening a GMAT argument is almost always accomplished by attacking one of the argument's key assumptions. Therefore, begin a weaken question the same way you begin an assumption question, by using the argument's premises and conclusion to identify unstated information on which the argument depends. Once you've spotted the pivotal assumption, choose the answer that offers good reason to believe it isn't true.

- **Strengthen questions**: Strengthening a GMAT argument is almost always accomplished by reinforcing one of the argument's key assumptions. Begin a strengthen question by identifying the argument's premises and conclusion, as well as any gaps in reasoning between them. Once you've found the pivotal assumption, choose the answer that suggests it's true.

- **Evaluate questions** are similar to weaken and strengthen questions in that they ask you to consider the unstated piece of information that, if you knew it, would tell you whether you're looking at a weak argument or a strong argument. Evaluating a GMAT argument is almost always accomplished by identifying a test you could perform or a question you could answer to determine the truth or falsity of an assumption.

- **Identify the Reasoning questions** ask you to describe the structure of an argument or how it works. Some identify the reasoning questions concern the logical function of bolded phrases in the passage. For any identify the reasoning question, determine which part of the argument functions as its claim and which parts function as evidence. Choose the answer that accurately describes the structure of the argument. There's no need to worry about assumptions.

- **Flaw questions** combine the tasks involved in identify the reasoning and weaken questions. You're looking for the answer that accurately describes the structure of the argument (identify the reasoning), usually by exposing the weakness of an assumption made by the author (weaken). Begin by distinguishing the argument's conclusion from its premises. Use shifts in language or reasoning patterns to identify the faulty assumption.

- **Inference questions**: Passages that accompany inference questions tend to look like collections of facts without any logical progression from premises to conclusion. There's usually no way to differentiate claims from evidence, so don't bother. In fact, you may feel as though the question gives you the evidence and asks you to provide the conclusion. Begin an inference question by familiarizing yourself with the information provided; if it helps, use your noteboard to create a list of facts. Then, choose the answer that must be true on the basis of the facts.

- **Resolve/Explain questions**: Like inference passages, the passages that accompany resolve/explain questions tend not to exhibit the structural elements of an argument. Instead, they present two ideas that seem to be opposed. Rather than looking for premises and conclusions, begin by using your noteboard to clarify the apparent conflict: "On the one hand, *X*, but on the other, *Y*." Indicator words such as *but*, *yet*, and *however* can draw your attention to opposing ideas and help you to articulate the apparent conflict. Choose the answer that explains how *X* and *Y* might both be true at the same time.

## Step 3: Predict What the Answer Should Do

Just as your knowledge of the question type can help you to identify relevant information in a Critical Reasoning passage, your knowledge of the question type can help you to recognize the characteristics of the answer you're looking for.

Predicting the answer to a Critical Reasoning question is often quite difficult. Predicting what the answer should do is usually easier. Before turning to the answers, think about what the correct answer needs to accomplish based on the question type and information in the argument. In this way, you continue to exercise control over a question as you move from information gathering to answer selection.

- **Assumption questions:** Good answers to assumption questions bridge a gap in reasoning between the premises of an argument and its conclusion. For this reason, they often employ words or phrases that appear in the premises, as well as language from the conclusion. A good answer links the author's claim to evidence that supports it, or rules out obstacles to that link.

- **Weaken questions:** Good answers to weaken questions widen a gap in reasoning between the premises of an argument and its conclusion. In order to do so, they often introduce new information that attacks one of the argument's assumptions. A good answer makes the truth of an author's claim seem less likely by disrupting the link between that claim and the evidence that supports it.

- **Strengthen questions:** Good answers to strengthen questions are very similar to those for assumption questions. That's because both question types require you to find an assumption that supports the argument's conclusion. A good answer will confirm the pivotal assumption or introduce new information that rules out obstacles to it.

- **Inference questions:** Like inference questions in the Reading Comprehension format, inference questions in the Critical Reasoning format don't really ask you to make an inference beyond the scope of the information provided. It can be difficult to come up with your own answer to an inference question, so let the test-writers worry about the phrasing. Simply keep in mind that you want the answer best supported by the facts. An answer that paraphrases a fact from the passage is often the credited response.

- **Resolve/Explain questions:** Passages that accompany resolve/explain questions introduce a pair of facts or ideas that seem to oppose one another. Once you've clarified the apparent conflict, look for answer choices that allow both facts to be true simultaneously. Good answers address both sides of the issue, rather than ignoring one side or the other.

- **Evaluate questions:** Evaluate questions require you to select a test you could perform, or a question you could ask, to assess the validity of an argument. If the answer choices are phrased as questions, try answering each question "Yes" and "No" to see whether different answers change your belief in the argument's conclusion. If so, you're probably dealing with the credited response. Good answers make it possible to determine the truth or falsity of an assumption made in the argument.

- **Identify the Reasoning questions:** Once you've identified the premises and conclusion of an identify the reasoning passage, look for answer choices that accurately describe the relationships between an argument's parts. There's no reason to look for gaps or assumptions; the task is purely descriptive. Keep an eye out for answers that focus on the structure of the argument rather than its content. Good answer choices accurately mirror the argument's structure.

- **Flaw questions:** Good answers to flaw questions accurately reflect the structure of the argument. They differ from good answers to identify the reasoning questions only because they invariably describe flaws in reasoning. The correct answer most often articulates a faulty assumption.

## Step 4: Use POE to Find the Answer

This is the last step in the basic approach to Critical Reasoning questions. You've done most of the work required to answer the question. All that remains is to select and confirm your answer. You're already armed with a sense of what the correct answer needs to accomplish. Now, supplement that understanding with an efficient, effective process for weeding out bad answers and avoiding traps—tempting answers that are nevertheless incorrect.

Just as your knowledge of question types can help you find relevant information in a passage and predict what the correct answer should do, it can help you to narrow your search for the correct answer by enabling you to quickly eliminate answers that are flawed. You've read about the characteristics of good answers. It's time to consider the characteristics of poor answers. Each Critical Reasoning question type has its own set of attractor answers that you will learn to anticipate. GMAT arguments are often quite specific, so read them carefully and interpret them literally. Pay close attention to the language used in arguments and answer choices.

**Assumption questions** ask you for the unstated premise in the argument. Correct answers link conclusions to the premises that support them, so ask how each answer affects the author's claim. When you think you've found the correct answer, apply the **Negation Test**. Negate your preferred answer, and if your belief in the argument's conclusion isn't affected, the answer is incorrect. Avoid answers that:

- are out of scope
- use extreme language

**Weaken questions** ask you to select the answer that disrupts the link between the premises and the conclusion. Ask yourself how each choice affects the author's claim. Eliminate answers that:

- are out of scope
- use extreme language
- strengthen the argument

**Strengthen questions** ask you to select the answer that reinforces the link between the premises and the conclusion. Ask yourself how each choice affects the author's claim. Eliminate answers that:

- are out of scope
- use extreme language
- weaken the argument

**Inference questions** ask for the answer choice that follows necessarily from the facts in the passage. The answers to inference questions generally don't stray far from the information provided, so look to eliminate answers that require additional assumptions. Avoid answers that:

- are out of scope
- use extreme language

**Resolve/Explain questions** ask for the answer that resolves an apparent conflict between two ideas, or that explains the conflict away. When you consider the answer choices, adhere closely to the opposing ideas. Avoid answers that:

- are out of scope
- make the conflict worse
- address only one side of the conflict

**Evaluate questions** ask you to select the answer that allows the strength or weakness of an argument to be determined. Incorrect answers offer new information that does not connect the argument's conclusion to its premises in a meaningful way. Eliminate answers that:

- are out of scope

**Identify the Reasoning questions** ask you to find the answer that accurately describes the structure of an argument. Avoid answers that:

- do not match the structure of the argument
- only partially match the structure

**Flaw questions** ask you to choose the answer that accurately describes a flaw in the structure of an argument. Watch out for answers that describe the argument faithfully, but neglect to mention a flaw. Eliminate answers that:

- are out of scope
- cannot be matched to the argument or are only partial matches

## PRACTICE QUESTIONS

Now that you've been introduced to the parts of a GMAT argument, the reasoning patterns typical of GMAT arguments, and the basic approach to Critical Reasoning questions, work through some example questions to bolster your understanding of the Critical Reasoning question format.

Here is an example of an **Assumption question.**

Most people believe that gold and platinum are the most valuable commodities. To the true entrepreneur, however, gold and platinum are less valuable than the knowledge of opportunities is. Thus, in the world of high finance, information is the most valuable commodity.

The author of the passage above makes which of the following assumptions?

- ⬭ Gold and platinum are not the most valuable commodities.
- ⬭ Entrepreneurs are not like most people.
- ⬭ The value of information is incalculably high.
- ⬭ Information about business opportunities is accurate and leads to increased wealth.
- ⬭ Only entrepreneurs feel that information is the most valuable commodity.

### Here's How to Crack It

The question asks for the *assumption* made by the author, so this is an assumption question.

An assumption supports the conclusion of an argument, so when you read the passage, look for the conclusion. The word *thus* in the passage's final sentence gives it away: *in the world of high finance, information is the most valuable commodity.*

Now determine what information in the passage is in support of the conclusion. Two pieces of information are provided in support of the conclusion. One group of people—*most people—believe that gold and platinum are the most valuable commodities.* Another group—*true entrepreneurs* —believe that *gold and platinum are less valuable than is the knowledge of opportunities.*

From the opinions of two groups of people, the author concludes that the opinion of one group is to be preferred, but the passage doesn't say why. Therefore, it's likely that the correct answer will explain why the opinion of *the true entrepreneur* is to be preferred. With that in mind, you're ready to attack the answer choices:

◯ Gold and platinum are not the most valuable commodities.

This answer appears to support the conclusion. If *gold and platinum are not the most valuable commodities,* there's a chance that *information is.* By itself, however, the idea that gold and platinum *are not* the most valuable commodities doesn't mean information *is* the most valuable commodity. This assumption provides no reason why the author should agree with *the true entrepreneur*; it doesn't link the argument's premises to its conclusion. Eliminate (A).

◯ Entrepreneurs are not like most people.

This answer choice doesn't tell you anything you don't already know: if the true entrepreneur doesn't share the opinion of most people, then entrepreneurs aren't like most people (at least not in the way they value commodities). In any case, this answer doesn't provide a reason to favor the opinion of the true entrepreneur. Eliminate (B).

◯ The value of information is incalculably high.

Be wary of the extreme language in this answer choice. The author needn't assume the value of information is incalculable in order to believe that it's the most valuable commodity. On the other hand, the value of many commodities might be incalculable; it doesn't follow from this that information is most valuable. Eliminate (C).

◯ Information about business opportunities is accurate and leads to increased wealth.

This answer links the argument's conclusion to its premises by providing a reason to side with the true entrepreneur. To check whether this assumption is required by the argument, apply the Negation Test. If information *isn't* accurate and *doesn't* lead to increased wealth, it's unclear why the author believes it to be most valuable. Negating this answer disrupts the argument, so keep (D).

◯ Only entrepreneurs feel that information is the most valuable commodity.

This answer is out of scope. It doesn't matter *who* believes information to be most valuable. What matters is *why* the author believes it to be most valuable. Eliminate (E).

The correct answer is (D).

Here is an example of a **Weaken question.**

Given the current economic climate, universal healthcare is an impossibility in the United States. More than half of all U.S. households report feeling overwhelmed by expenses, and many people are struggling to find additional sources of income. Funding such a massive program would require significant tax increases, adding to the financial burden of many individuals. The employer-sponsored healthcare system currently in place keeps taxes low, protecting our nation's economy.

Which of the following, if true, would most weaken the argument above?

- ⬭ Many U.S. citizens enjoy sizeable tax breaks for medical expenses.
- ⬭ Universal healthcare would reduce the financial burden on employers, resulting in significant job growth and wage increases.
- ⬭ A majority of profitable, private health insurers have indicated that they expect to increase their payrolls in the coming quarter.
- ⬭ Pharmaceutical companies have fewer incentives to innovate new drugs in a universal healthcare system.
- ⬭ Most U.S. citizens depend on their employers for health coverage and could not afford comparable coverage under the current system.

### Here's How to Crack It

The question asks you to *weaken* the argument, so this is a weaken question.

Let's break this argument down into its core components. The author concludes that *universal healthcare represents an impossibility in the United States.* Why? Because *funding such a program would require significant tax increases*, and *more than half of all U.S. households already report feeling overwhelmed by expenses....*

Did you spot the gap in the argument's reasoning? The premises refer to the financial burden faced by Americans and to the costs associated with universal healthcare. The conclusion leaps from the cost of such a system to its impossibility. This shift in language exposes a gap in the author's reasoning. Bridging this gap requires an assumption that links the cost of universal healthcare to its impossibility. We know what the correct answer needs to do, and we have a good idea how it might get done. Let's turn to the answer choices.

- ⬭ Many U.S. citizens enjoy sizeable tax breaks for medical expenses.

Under the current healthcare system, many people are compensated for medical expenses via tax breaks. However, there's no information about what will happen to these tax breaks under a universal healthcare system. This answer touches on the financial problem mentioned in the premises, but because it doesn't link this problem to the impossibility of instituting universal healthcare, it can't be used to weaken the argument. This choice is out of scope, so eliminate it.

○ Universal healthcare would reduce the financial burden on employers, resulting in significant job growth and wage increases.

This answer suggests that universal healthcare might lead to positive financial outcomes. If the benefits of universal healthcare outweigh its costs, then those costs don't contribute to the impossibility of universal healthcare. This choice breaks the link between the cost of universal healthcare and its impossibility, so keep (B).

○ A majority of profitable, private health insurers have indicated that they expect to increase their payrolls in the coming quarter.

Are the plans of private health insurers to increase their payrolls relevant to the argument we identified? No, what private insurers do with their payrolls has no bearing on the argument that universal healthcare is impossible because it's expensive. Choice (C) is out of scope. Eliminate it.

○ Pharmaceutical companies have fewer incentives to innovate in a universal healthcare system.

If drug companies have fewer incentives to innovate, then there's evidence to suggest universal healthcare might be a bad idea. This answer addresses the impossibility of universal healthcare by introducing another reason not to pursue it, but that reason doesn't link the impossibility of universal healthcare to its cost. Eliminate (D).

○ Most U.S. citizens depend on their employers for health coverage and could not afford comparable coverage under the current system.

This answer acknowledges the high cost of healthcare under the current system. However, the argument concerns the cost of instituting a universal healthcare system, not the cost of the current system, which is out of scope. Eliminate (E).

The correct answer is (B).

## Challenge Question #18

In an effort to stimulate economic growth, the parliament of Sapland is promoting new legislation which halves the corporate tax rate. Members of parliament claim the move will lead to job creation and investment by the impacted corporations. Critics disagree vocally, pointing to a plethora of studies indicating that such tax savings tend to be kept as profit rather than reinvested, and therefore are unlikely to spur job creation or corporate investment.

Which of the following, if true, most undermines the critics objection to the tax plan promoted by parliament to spur job creation and corporate investment by halving the corporate tax rate?

- ⬭ The legislation halving the corporate tax rate includes a stipulation that funds equal to those owed in the form of taxes must be used by the impacted corporation to promote its primary business purpose.
- ⬭ The tax savings will induce the shareholders of many impacted corporations to increase their personal investment portfolios significantly.
- ⬭ Many corporate shareholders consider their respective corporations' performance to be more than sufficient, and see no reason to expand either their workforces or capital investments.
- ⬭ The majority of the tax revenue lost due to the corporate tax rate reduction can be reclaimed by raising property taxes on large estates.
- ⬭ Sapland currently suffers from high unemployment, brought on by years of government-mandated anti-discrimination policies and environmental regulations.

Here is an example of a **Strengthen question.**

---

It has recently been proposed that Country X adopt an all-volunteer army. This policy was tried on a limited basis several years ago and was a miserable failure. The level of education of the volunteers was unacceptably low, while levels of drug use and crime soared among army personnel. Can Country X trust its national defense to a volunteer army? The answer is clearly "No."

Which of the following statements, if true, provides the most support for the claim that an all-volunteer army should not be implemented?

- The population's level of education has risen since the first time an all-volunteer army was tried.
- The proposal was made by an organization called Citizens for Peace.
- The first attempt to create a volunteer army was carried out according to the same plan now under proposal and under the same conditions as those that exist today.
- A volunteer army would be less expensive than an army that relies on the draft.
- Armies are smaller today than they were when a volunteer army was last proposed.

### Here's How to Crack It

The question asks for the statement that *provides the most support for the claim*, so this is a strengthen question. Begin by distinguishing the argument's conclusion from its premises, and then find the assumption.

The conclusion of the argument is easy to identify because it's stated in the question stem: *an all-volunteer army should not be implemented*. As you read the passage, be on the lookout for premises that support the author's claim.

The author provides only one piece of evidence to suggest that an all-volunteer army shouldn't be implemented: it was *tried on a limited basis several years ago and was a miserable failure*. According to the argument, Country X shouldn't implement an all-volunteer army now because it didn't work out then. This argument exhibits the analogy pattern; it assumes that the current attempt to institute an all-volunteer army will be like the previous attempt.

Because this is a strengthen question, look for answer choices that suggest the two attempts are similar. The more similar they are, the more likely the current attempt will end in failure, and the easier it is to conclude that Country X shouldn't implement an all-volunteer army.

◯ The population's level of education has risen since the first time an all-volunteer army was tried.

This answer choice introduces a difference between the current attempt to implement an all-volunteer army and the past attempt. If the education level of the population increased, there's reason to expect a different result this time around. Rather than strengthen the argument against an all-volunteer army, this answer weakens it. Eliminate (A).

◯ The proposal was made by an organization called Citizens for Peace.

The identity of the group that made the proposal is out of scope. The relevant question asks whether there's good reason to believe that acting on the proposal will end in failure. Eliminate (B).

◯ The first attempt to create a volunteer army was carried out according to the same plan now under proposal and under the same conditions as those that exist today.

Eureka! This answer introduces a relevant similarity between the two attempts to institute an all-volunteer army. If the last attempt ended in disaster, and the current attempt follows the same plan under the same conditions, there's reason to believe the outcome will be similar. Choice (C) strengthens the argument against an all-volunteer army, so keep it.

◯ A volunteer army would be less expensive than an army that relies on the draft.

The cost of a volunteer army is out of scope. The argument concerns the trustworthiness of such an army, not its cost. Eliminate (D).

◯ Armies are smaller today than they were when a volunteer army was last proposed.

Like (A), (E) introduces a dissimilarity between the two attempts to institute a volunteer army. For that reason, it's unlikely to be the correct answer. More importantly, like (B) and (D), it's out of scope. It doesn't matter how big the army is or was, but whether it's staffed by trustworthy people or fools and criminals. Eliminate (E).

The correct answer is (C).

Here is an example of an **Inference question.**

In film and television, it's possible to induce viewers to project their feelings onto characters on the screen. In one study, a camera shot of a woman's face was preceded by images of a baby. The audience thought the woman's face registered contentment. When the same woman's face was preceded by images of a shark attack, the audience thought the woman's face registered fear. Television news teams must be careful to avoid such manipulation of their viewers.

Which of the following is best supported by the information in the passage?

- ○ Television news teams have abused their position of trust in the past.
- ○ The expression on the woman's face was, in actuality, blank.
- ○ Images of a baby engendered feelings of happiness in the audience.
- ○ Audiences should strive to be less gullible.
- ○ The technique for manipulating audiences described in the passage would also work in a radio program that played dramatic music.

### Here's How to Crack It

The question asks for the answer *best supported by the information in the passage.* The direction of support is from the passage to the answer choices, so this is an inference question. Begin by getting clear on the facts.

> Fact 1: *In film and television, it's possible to induce viewers to project their feelings onto characters on the screen, making it possible for news teams to manipulate viewers.*
>
> Fact 2: *When a camera shot of a woman's face was preceded by images of a baby, the audience thought the woman's face registered contentment.*
>
> Fact 3: *When the same woman's face was preceded by images of a shark attack, the audience thought the woman's face registered fear.*

Once you're clear on the facts, look for the answer that must be true on their basis. Be wary of extreme language and eliminate answers that are beyond the scope of the information provided. The correct answer is likely to paraphrase information in the passage.

- ○ Television news teams have abused their position of trust in the past.

This answer goes well beyond the scope of the passage. We have no idea what news teams did in the past based on the information provided. Eliminate (A).

◯ The expression on the woman's face was, in actuality, blank.

Like the previous choice, this answer is out of scope. Based on the information provided, we simply don't know whether the woman's face was expressionless. Eliminate (B).

◯ Images of a baby engendered feelings of happiness in the audience.

Images of a baby led the audience to believe the woman's face registered contentment. If audience members projected their feelings onto the woman, then audience members must have experienced contentment, and it's likely the images of a baby were responsible. Keep (C).

◯ Audiences should strive to be less gullible.

Of course, we should all strive to be less gullible, but we know that simply because we know what "gullible" means, not because of the information provided. Nothing in the passage suggests that audience members were gullible. Eliminate (D).

◯ The technique for manipulating audiences described in the passage would also work in a radio program that played dramatic music.

It's possible that the information in this answer choice is true, but possible isn't good enough. We need an answer that *must be* true, and the passage provides no information about the projection of emotion in the medium of sound. Eliminate (E).

The correct answer is (C).

---

## Challenge Question #19

Glacial ablation is the term for a loss of glacial mass in terms of ice. Ablation rates vary based on a wide number of factors, one of which is submarine melt: ice loss due to contact between the glacier and seawater. While factors such as air temperature, precipitation, and snow accumulation play significant roles, glacial ablation along coastlines tends to proceed at its greatest rate when warm ocean currents come into contact with the base of the glacier and produce a high degree of submarine melt. Warm ocean currents along glacial coastline areas increase in frequency as overall ocean temperatures rise.

Which of the following can be most readily inferred from the information in the passage?

◯ Regions with the greatest rate of glacial ablation have the greatest proximity to the strongest warm ocean currents.
◯ Very few glaciers in regions without warm ocean currents suffer from high rates of glacial ablation.
◯ Glacial ablation due to submarine melt rates was lower on average during periods of lower overall ocean temperatures.
◯ Submarine melt rates have become an important factor to glacial ablation only with the onset of global climatic shifts.
◯ The lower the overall ocean temperature, the more likely that factors such as snow accumulation are to play a significant role in glacial ablation.

Here is an example of a **Resolve/Explain question.**

In 2008, the world's airlines reported an increase in the total number of passengers carried, but a decrease in total revenues, even though prices for airline tickets on all routes remained unchanged from the year before.

Which of the following resolves the paradox described above?

- ⬭ The airline industry was a victim of the recession in 2008.
- ⬭ Total passenger miles were up in 2008.
- ⬭ Fuel costs remained constant from 2007 to 2008.
- ⬭ Passengers traveled shorter distances on less expensive flights in 2008.
- ⬭ No new aircraft were purchased by any carrier in 2008.

### Here's How to Crack It

The question asks for the answer that *resolves the paradox*, so this is a resolve/explain question. Your knowledge of question types suggests that the accompanying passage will present two pieces of information, which seem to be in conflict. State that opposition as clearly as possible.

On the one hand, more passengers traveled by air.

On the other, airline revenues decreased, even though ticket prices remained unchanged.

The correct answer to a resolve/explain question will allow both pieces of information to be true simultaneously. Eliminate answers that are out of scope, address only one side of the conflict, or make the conflict worse.

⬭ The airline industry was a victim of the recession in 2008.

A recession might account for the decrease in revenue, but if ticket prices remained the same, it's unclear how the number of passengers could have increased. Choice (A) addresses only one side of the conflict, so eliminate it.

⬭ Total passenger miles were up in 2008.

If passengers flew farther in 2008 and ticket prices remained the same, it's unclear how revenues could have decreased. Like (A), this answer addresses only one side of the conflict. Eliminate (B).

⬭ Fuel costs remained constant from 2007 to 2008.

Fuel costs are out of scope. An increase in fuel costs might have affected airline profits, but profits are not revenues. This answer has no bearing on either side of the conflict. Eliminate (C).

◯ Passengers traveled shorter distances on less expensive flights in 2008.

This answer looks promising. If the increase in passengers was offset by passengers taking cheaper flights, then revenues could have decreased even as the number of passengers increased. Keep (D).

◯ No new aircraft were purchased by any carrier in 2008.

New aircraft are out of scope. The purchase of new aircraft might have affected airline profits, but if no new aircraft were purchased, then new aircraft affected neither profits nor revenues, and this answer has no relevance at all. Eliminate (E).

The correct answer is (D).

---

Here is an example of an **Evaluate question.**

---

During a period of low growth after a recent and remarkable boom in the solar energy sector, Company X, a major manufacturer of solar-powered generators, attributed its success during the boom to the sale of excess inventory it had discovered in one of its warehouses.

Which of the following tests would most help to evaluate the company's hypothesis as to the cause of its success?

◯ Comparing the length of the low-growth period to the length of the preceding boom
◯ Comparing the boom experienced by Company X to those experienced by similarly-sized manufacturers of solar-powered generators that did not have inventory on hand
◯ Calculating average sales increases within the individual divisions of Company X
◯ Comparing the total number of generators sold by Company X during the boom to the total number sold by Company X during the period of low growth
◯ Using economic theory to predict the next economic boom for Company X

### Here's How to Crack It

The question asks for the test that would most help to *evaluate* the company's hypothesis, so this is an evaluate question. According to the question stem, the hypothesis concerns the cause of Company X's success. As you begin to work the argument, look for claims that provide a reason company X succeeded.

The passage's final sentence states that Company X *attributed its success during the boom to the sale of excess inventory*, but how does Company X come to believe that? The only other piece of information we get from the passage is that there was a *boom in the solar energy sector*, followed by a *period of low growth.*

Without additional information, it's unclear how changes in the solar energy sector relate to the company's claim about its own success. However, if you noticed the word *cause* in the question stem, then you probably recognized that Company X makes a causal argument.

Take advantage of the causal reasoning pattern by recalling its standard assumptions: there's no other cause, and it's not a coincidence. The former assumption seems more relevant here, because Company X assumes the sale of excess inventory alone was responsible for its success.

Evaluate the answer choices one at a time, looking for the test that would allow you to determine whether there isn't another reason for Company X's success.

> ◯ Comparing the length of the low-growth period to the length of the preceding boom

Executing this comparison would tell us how long each of the periods lasted, but connecting that information to the sale of excess inventory would require inferences beyond the scope of the information provided. Eliminate (A).

> ◯ Comparing the boom experienced by Company X to those experienced by similarly-sized manufacturers of solar-powered generators that did not have inventory on hand

This answer choice is tempting. We're looking for a way to determine whether something other than the sale of excess inventory might have caused Company X's success. If competitors without excess inventory to sell experienced booms comparable to that of Company X, then the company's claim might be incorrect. On the other hand, if competitors didn't experience as big a boom, it appears more likely that the sale of excess inventory was responsible for Company X's success. Keep (B).

> ◯ Calculating average sales increases within the individual divisions of Company X

Individual divisions of Company X are out of scope. We already know that the company sold excess inventory; which divisions saw sales increases is irrelevant. Eliminate (C).

> ◯ Comparing the total number of generators sold by Company X during the boom to the total number sold by Company X during the period of low growth

At first glance, this answer choice looks appealing. The comparison described here would allow us to determine how many generators were sold during each period. If more generators were sold during the boom than during the low-growth period, it might seem as though Company X's success during the boom resulted from the sale of excess inventory. However, the passage states that the period of low growth *followed* the boom. If more generators were sold during the boom, then at best, we could infer that a *decline* in sales led to *decreased* success. To determine whether the sale of excess inventory *caused* Company X's success during the boom, we'd need sales numbers from the period *before* the boom, not the period *after* it. Eliminate (D).

◯ Using economic theory to predict when the next economic boom for Company X will occur

Of the five answer choices, this one is most obviously out of scope. An estimate of the time that will elapse before the next boom needn't have any relevance to the cause of the last boom. Eliminate (E).

The correct answer is (B).

---

Here is an example of an **Identify the Reasoning question.**

---

Although measuring the productivity of outside consultants is a complex endeavor, **Company K, which relies heavily on consultants, must find ways to assess the performance of these workers.** The risks to a company that does not review the productivity of its human resources are simply too great. **Last year, Company L was forced into receivership after its productivity declined for three consecutive quarters.**

The bolded clauses play which of the following roles in the argument above?

◯ The first bolded clause states the author's conclusion, and the second introduces unrelated information.
◯ The first bolded clause provides background information, and the second offers evidence to contradict that information.
◯ The first bolded clause states one of the author's premises, while the second states the author's conclusion.
◯ The first bolded clause expresses a position, and the second warns against the adoption of that position.
◯ The first bolded clause represents the author's conclusion, and the second supports the conclusion with an analogy.

### Here's How to Crack It

The bolded clauses in the passage immediately indicate that this is an identify the reasoning question, so begin by distinguishing the argument's conclusion from the premises that support it. Don't worry about finding assumptions.

The phrase *must find ways to assess* is strong language, making the first bolded phrase a good candidate for the argument's conclusion. Why must Company K find ways to assess the performance of its outside consultants? Because companies that don't review the productivity of human resources face risks—just look at Company L! Both of the passage's remaining sentences operate in support of the first bolded phrase. The second bolded clause supports the conclusion by offering the example of a company that was *forced into receivership after its productivity declined.*

Now that you've got a good sense of the argument's structure, look for the answer that correctly mirrors it.

- ◯ The first bolded clause states the author's conclusion, and the second introduces unrelated information.

The first part of this answer looks good, because the first bolded clause *does* state the author's conclusion. However, the second bolded clause supports the conclusion; it does not introduce unrelated information. Choice (A) only partially matches the argument's structure, so eliminate it.

- ◯ The first bolded clause provides background information, and the second offers evidence to contradict that information.

Part of the first bolded clause states that Company K *relies heavily on consultants,* which does resemble background information. However, nothing in the second bolded clause contradicts that information. Choice (B) is a partial match. Eliminate it.

- ◯ The first bolded clause states one of the author's premises, while the second states the author's conclusion.

This answer choice reverses the roles played by the bolded clauses. Since it doesn't match the structure of the argument, eliminate (C).

- ◯ The first bolded clause expresses a position, and the second warns against the adoption of that position.

Like (A) and (B), (D) is a partial match. The first bolded clause expresses a position, but the second doesn't warn against the adoption of that position. Eliminate (D).

- ◯ The first bolded clause represents the author's conclusion, and the second supports the conclusion with an analogy.

This answer accurately reflects the relationship between the bolded clauses: the first is the author's conclusion, and the second supports the conclusion by offering the example of analogous Company L. Keep (E).

The correct answer is (E).

---

Here is an example of a **Flaw question.**

A telephone poll conducted in two states asked respondents whether their homes were cold during the winter months. Ninety-nine percent of respondents said their houses were always warm during the winter. The pollsters published their findings, concluding that ninety-nine percent of all homes in the United States have adequate heating.

Which of the following most accurately describes a questionable technique employed by the pollsters in drawing their conclusion?

- ◯ The poll wrongly ascribes the underlying causes of the problem.
- ◯ The poll assumes conditions in the two states are representative of the entire country.
- ◯ The pollsters conducted the poll by telephone, thereby relying on the veracity of respondents.
- ◯ The pollsters didn't visit respondents' houses in person, so no measure of the temperature in a subject's home was actually made.
- ◯ The pollsters never defined the term "cold" in terms of a specific temperature.

### Here's How to Crack It

The question asks for a *questionable technique* used by the pollsters, so this is a flaw question.

You already know from the question stem that the argument has a serious problem. Your job is to figure out what that problem is. Begin by identifying the argument's premises and conclusion. Then, use a gap in the reasoning to hone in on the assumption. Because this is a flaw question, be on the lookout for common reasoning patterns.

The word *concluding* in the last sentence of the passage gives away the conclusion: *ninety-nine percent of all homes in the United States have adequate heating.* Why did the pollsters conclude this? Their findings were based on the results of *a telephone poll conducted in two states*, in which *ninety-nine percent of respondents said their houses were always warm during the winter.*

Did you recognize the pattern of reasoning in this argument? Information about one group of people (the poll was conducted in two states) is used to make a claim about a much larger group (all households in the United States). This argument employs the sampling pattern. The standard assumption involved in the sampling pattern is that the sample is representative of the larger population. Look for answers that call attention to this assumption.

◯ The poll wrongly ascribes the underlying causes of a problem.

Underlying causes are out of scope. The pollsters ask whether people's homes are cold. The reason they might be cold is irrelevant. Eliminate (A).

◯ The poll assumes conditions in the two states are representative of the entire country.

This answer expresses the standard assumption involved in the sampling pattern. Nothing in the passage suggests that the households surveyed are representative of U.S. householders in general. Keep (B).

◯ The pollsters conducted the poll by telephone, thereby relying on the veracity of respondents.

The information in this answer might betray a weakness in the pollsters' methodology, but it isn't a weakness in the pollsters' reasoning. Eliminate (C).

◯ The pollsters didn't visit respondents' houses in person, so no measurement of the temperature in a subject's home was actually made.

Like (C), this answer describes a problem with the poll, not with the argument. Eliminate (D).

◯ The pollsters never defined the term "cold" in terms of a specific temperature.

It's true that the pollsters never defined the term "cold," but does that represent a flaw in the pollsters' reasoning? The flaw identified here concerns the poll itself, not the argument. Eliminate (E).

The correct answer is (B).

---

Now that you know how to identify and approach each of the eight Critical Reasoning question types, the best way to proceed is to practice. The more you experience through preparation, the less likely you are to be surprised on test day.

As you complete Critical Reasoning drills and exercises, force yourself to follow the basic approach. Your knowledge of the question type informs every step of the basic approach to Critical Reasoning questions, from reading the passage to eliminating incorrect answers, so always read the question first. Memorize the common reasoning patterns and the assumptions that go with them, develop a familiarity with the characteristics of good and bad answers, and you'll be well on your way to mastering the Critical Reasoning format.

## DRILL 19 (Spotting Critical Reasoning Question Types)

The answers to questions in this drill can be found in Part VII.

For each of the questions below, decide which question type it belongs to. For extra credit, list what you should look for in the passage that would normally precede the question.

1. Which of the following, if true, gives the most support to the recommendations above?
2. Which of the following statements can properly be inferred on the basis of the statements above?
3. The answer to which of the following questions would most help the CEO to evaluate the manager's claim?
4. The argument in the passage depends on which of the following assumptions?
5. The argument above is vulnerable to criticism for which of the following reasons?
6. The author's argument would be most seriously weakened if it were true that...
7. The senator responds to the constituent's assertion by...
8. Which of the following statements best explains the apparent discrepancy described above?

### Challenge Question #20

It is widely believed that dogs need to engage in play with other dogs in order to maintain proper socialization as they grow older. In truth, however, merely sharing the same physical space with another dog is sufficient to maintain proper socialization. Supporting evidence to this effect comes from a study demonstrating that the more often a dog shares a physical space with another dog, the better its socialization.

Which of the following, if true, most seriously weakens the influence of the evidence cited?

- ⬭ As dogs age, it is necessary to challenge their physical and mental capacities in order to avoid the deterioration of these capacities.
- ⬭ Many behavioral reasons that negatively impact a dog's proper socialization also increase the likelihood that a dog is not sharing physical space with another dog.
- ⬭ Many dogs are capable of both play and simply sharing space with other dogs.
- ⬭ The study itself did not observe dog socialization, but analyzed observations on the issue from other studies.
- ⬭ The metrics for evaluating socialization that the study measured more resembled play than simply sharing physical space.

# Summary

- Critical Reasoning is made up of short passages. Each of these passages is followed by one question, for a total of roughly 11 questions.
- There are three parts to an argument:
    - Conclusion
    - Premises
    - Assumptions
- Critical Reasoning is **not** like Reading Comprehension.
    - You should never skim; each word is important.
    - Most of the Reading Comprehension techniques we have shown you are inappropriate for Critical Reasoning.
- Follow the basic approach and make sure to read the question first.
- Learn to identify the common reasoning patterns in argument passages:
    - Causal patterns
    - Planning patterns
    - Sampling patterns
    - Interpretation of Evidence patterns
    - Analogy patterns
- There are eight question types. Each type has its own strategy.
    - **Assumption questions**
      Assumptions are unstated premises that support the conclusion.
    - **Strengthen questions**
      Look for an answer choice with information that supports the conclusion.
    - **Weaken questions**
      These questions ask you to find the answer choice that provides information that weakens the conclusion.

- **Inference questions**
  Like Reading Comprehension inference questions, these questions do not actually want you to infer. Unlike most Critical Reasoning questions, these questions typically concern the *premises,* not the conclusion.
- **Resolve/Explain questions**
  This type of question asks you to pick an answer choice that explains an apparent contradiction between two incompatible facts.
- **Evaluate questions**
  This type of question asks you to pick an answer choice that would help to evaluate an unspoken assumption about the argument.
- **Identify the Reasoning questions**
  This type of question asks you to pick an answer choice that identifies the purpose of a word or phrase or the type of reasoning used in an argument.
- **Flaw questions**
  Flaw questions ask you to choose the answer that accurately describes a flaw in the structure of an argument.

# Part V
# How to Crack the Integrated Reasoning GMAT

# Chapter 24 Integrated Reasoning: Basics

This chapter provides an overview of the section. The following chapter provides some specific strategies. We have also included some practice questions to help you prepare.

This chapter reviews the basics of the Integrated Reasoning section, including a rundown on all four question types. Chapter 25 explains some strategies that will help you handle these questions. Finally, Chapter 26 includes two complete Integrated Reasoning sections with explanations so that you can practice.

## MEET THE INTEGRATED REASONING SECTION

The Integrated Reasoning section is 30 minutes long. You'll see it as the second section of your test. Officially, there are only 12 questions, which sounds pretty great. However, most of those questions have multiple parts. For example, a Table Analysis question—one of the question types we'll discuss—usually has three statements that you need to evaluate. So your answer to the question really consists of three separate responses. For the entire section, you'll actually need to select approximately 28 different responses.

### Integrated Reasoning Is Not Adaptive

Unlike the Quantitative and Verbal sections, the Integrated Reasoning section is not adaptive. You won't see harder questions if you keep answering questions correctly. That's good news because it means that you'll more easily be able to focus your attention on the current question rather than worrying whether you got the previous question right!

Test-writers refer to non-adaptive sections as linear. Pacing for a linear section is different from the pacing that we reviewed for the adaptive Quantitative and Verbal sections.

For Integrated Reasoning, pacing is motivated by two general principles.

Following these guidelines can save you time.

Pacing Guidelines

1. Work the easier parts of each question first. As you'll see, many Integrated Reasoning questions call for more than one response per question. Work the easier parts of each question first.

2. Don't get stubborn. With so many questions to answer in only 30 minutes, the Integrated Reasoning section can seem very fast paced. Spending too much time on one question means that you may not get to see all of the questions. Sometimes it's best to guess and move on.

## Integrated Reasoning Scores

The Integrated Reasoning section is scored on a scale from 1 to 8 in one-point increments. While GMAC has not released too many details about the way in which it calculates the score for this section of the test, there are two key facts to keep in mind.

- **Scoring is all or nothing.** Most Integrated Reasoning questions include multiple parts. To get credit for the question, you must select the correct response for each part. For example, Table Analysis questions generally include three statements that you must evaluate. If you select the wrong response for even one of these statements, you get no credit for the entire question.
- **There are experimental questions.** GMAC has stated that the Integrated Reasoning section contains experimental questions that do not count toward your score. GMAC has not, however, stated how many experimental questions there are in the section. It's likely that two or three of the twelve questions in the section are experimental. If you find a question particularly difficult or time-consuming, it is worthwhile to remember that the question could be experimental.

To score the section, GMAC first calculates a raw score. You get one point for each non-experimental question that you get completely correct. Then, your raw score is converted to the 1 to 8 Integrated Reasoning scaled score.

## There's a Calculator

There's an onscreen calculator available for the Integrated Reasoning section. The calculator is not available, however, for the Quantitative section. For the Quantitative section, you still need to perform any necessary calculations by hand.

The calculator for the Integrated Reasoning section is relatively basic. There are buttons to perform the four standard operations: addition, subtraction, multiplication, and division. In addition, buttons to take a square root, find a percent, and take a reciprocal round out the available functions. There are also buttons to store and recall a value in the calculator's memory.

To use the calculator, you'll need to open it by clicking on the "calculator" button in the upper left corner of your screen. The calculator will generally open in the middle of your screen, but you can move it around so that you can see the text of the problem or the numbers on any charts or graphs that are part of the question. The calculator is available for all Integrated Reasoning questions. You can enter a number into the calculator either by clicking on the onscreen number buttons or by typing the number using the keyboard.

Here's what the calculator looks like:

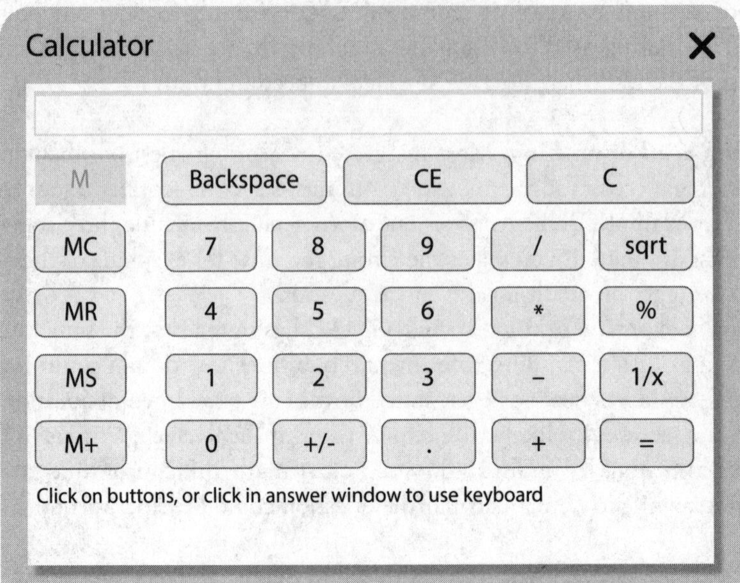


For the most part, the keys on the onscreen calculator work as you might expect. However, a few keys may not work as expected. Oddly enough, that's particularly true if you are accustomed to using a more sophisticated calculator. So, here are few tips about using some of the calculator keys:

MC

MC is the memory clear key. Use this key to wipe out any values that you have stored in the calculator's memory.

MR

MR is the memory recall key. Use this key to return any value that you have stored in the memory to the calculation area. For example, if you want to divide the number currently on your screen by the number in the memory, you would enter the key sequence / MR =.

MS

MS is the memory store key. Use this key to store the number currently on the screen in the calculator's memory.

M+

M+ is the memory addition key. Use this key to add the current onscreen number to the number in the calculator's memory. For example, if 2 is stored in the calculator's memory and 3 is on screen, then clicking M+ will result in 5 being stored in the calculator's memory.

Backspace

Backspace is used to clear the last digit entered. Use this key to correct mistakes when entering numbers without clearing the entire number. For example, if you entered 23 but meant to enter 25, click backspace and then enter 5.

CE — CE is the clear entry button. Use this button to correct a mistake when entering a longer calculation without starting over. For example, suppose you entered 2*3+5 but you meant to enter 2*3+9. If you click on CE right after you enter 5, your screen will show 6, the result of 2*3, and you can now enter +9= to finish your intended calculation.

C — C is the clear key. Use this key when you want to start a calculation over. In our previous example, if you click C after you enter 5, the intermediate result, 6, is not retained.

sqrt — sqrt is the square root key. Click this key after you enter the number for which you want to take the square root. For example, if you enter 4 sqrt, the result 2 will display on your screen.

% — % is the key used to take a percentage without entering a decimal. For example, if you want to take 20% of 400, enter 400*20%. The result 80 will now show on your screen. Note that you do not need to enter = after you click %.

1/x — 1/x is used to take a reciprocal. Click this key after you enter the number for which you want to take the reciprocal. For example, the keystrokes 2 followed by 1/x produces the result 0.5 on your screen. Again, note that you do not need to enter = after you click 1/x.

**Calculator Practice Tip**

When you practice for the Integrated Reasoning section, use a calculator similar to the calculator provided by GMAC. If you are doing online practice, use the onscreen calculator. If you are working problems from this book, use a basic calculator rather than that fancy calculator that you might still have from your high school or college math classes.

Be sure that you thoroughly understand the way the keys for the onscreen calculator work to avoid errors and wasted time when you take your GMAT.

## THE QUESTION TYPES

There are four question types in the Integrated Reasoning section. While some of these questions test Critical Reasoning skills similar to those tested on the Verbal section, these question types are also used to test the same type of content that is tested in the Quantitative section. So, expect to calculate percents and averages. You'll also be asked to make a lot of inferences based on the data presented in the various charts, graphs, and tables that accompany the questions. The format of these questions may take some getting used to but the content will probably seem familiar.

Let's take a more detailed look at each of the question types.

## Table Analysis

Table Analysis questions present data in a table. If you've ever seen a spreadsheet—and really, who hasn't?—you'll feel right at home. Most tables have 5 to 10 columns and anywhere from 6 to 25 rows. You'll be able to sort the data in the table by each column heading. The sort function is fairly basic, however. If you're used to being able to sort first by a column such as state and then a column such as city to produce an alphabetical list of cities by state, you can't do that type of sorting for these questions. You can sort only one column at a time.

Here's what a Table Analysis question looks like:

**Answers for this Question**

We'll discuss how you can solve this Table Analysis question—including which strategies you can apply—in Chapter 25, which is devoted to the Integrated Reasoning section.

Sort By [Select... ▼] ❶

| National Park | | Visitors | | | Area | |
|---|---|---|---|---|---|---|
| Name | State | Number | % Change | Rank | Acres | Rank |
| Grand Canyon | AZ | 4,388,386 | 0.9 | 2 | 1,217,403 | 11 |
| Yosemite | CA | 3,901,408 | 4.4 | 3 | 791,266 | 16 |
| Yellowstone | WY | 3,640,185 | 10.5 | 4 | 2,219,791 | 8 |
| Rocky Mtn. | CO | 2,955,821 | 4.7 | 5 | 265,828 | 26 |
| Zion | UT | 2,665,972 | −2.5 | 8 | 145,598 | 35 |
| Acadia | ME | 2,504,208 | 12.4 | 9 | 47,390 | 47 |
| Bryce | UT | 1,285,492 | 5.7 | 15 | 35,835 | 50 |
| Arches | UT | 1,014,405 | 1.8 | 19 | 76,519 | 42 |
| Badlands | SD | 977,778 | 4.7 | 22 | 242,756 | 28 |
| Mesa Verde | CO | 559,712 | 1.7 | 30 | 52,122 | 46 |
| Canyonlands | UT | 435,908 | −0.1 | 36 | 337,598 | 23 |

The table above gives information for 2010 on total visitors and total acreage for 11 US National Parks. In addition to the numbers of total visitors and total acreage for each National Park, the table also provides the percent increase or decrease over the total visitors for 2009 and the rank of the National Park for total visitors and total acreage in 2010. ❹

Each column of the table can be sorted in ascending order by clicking on the word "Select" above the table and choosing, from the drop-down menu, the heading of the column on which you want the table to be sorted. ❷

Consider each of the following statements about these National Parks. For each statement indicate whether the statement is true or false, based on the information provided in the table. ❸

| True | False ❺ | |
|---|---|---|
| ○ | ○ | The park that experienced the greatest percent increase in visitors from 2009 to 2010 also had the least total acreage. |
| ○ | ○ | The park with the median rank by the number of visitors is larger than only one other park by acreage. |
| ○ | ○ | The total number of visitors at Arches in 2009 was fewer than 1,000,000. |

When you take the Integrated Reasoning section, you will not see the circled numbers shown in the example above. We've added those so we can talk about different parts of a Table Analysis question. Here's what each circled number represents:

❶ This is the Sort By drop-down box. When opened, you'll see all the different ways that you can sort the data in the table. In this table, for example, the possibilities are National Park Name, National Park State, Visitors Number, Visitors % Change, Visitors Rank, Area Acreage, and Area Rank. You can always sort by every column.

2 These are the standard directions for a Table Analysis question. These directions are the same for every Table Analysis question. So, once you've read these directions once, you don't really need to bother reading them again.

3 These lines are additional directions. These additional directions are slightly tailored to the question. However, they'll always tell you to base your answers on the information in the table. They always tell you which type of evaluation you are to make for each statement: true/false, yes/no, agree/disagree, etc. Again, you can probably get by without reading these most of the time.

4 These lines explain the table. Mostly, this information will recap the column headings from the table. Occasionally, you can learn some additional information by reading this explanatory text. For example, the explanatory text for this table states that the Visitors Number column is for 2010 and that % Change column shows the change from 2009 to 2010.

5 These statements are the questions. Typically, there are four statements and you need to evaluate and select an answer for each. The good news is that you can answer these in any order. However, if you try to move to the next question without selecting a response for one or more statements, a pop up window opens to inform you that you have not selected an answer for all statements. You cannot leave any part of the question blank.

If you've read through the statements, you may have noticed that the questions asked you to do things such as calculate a percentage or find a median. That's typical for Table Analysis questions. You've probably also realized just how helpful the sorting function can be in answering some questions.

## Graphics Interpretation

Graphics Interpretation questions give you one chart, graph, or image and ask you to answer two questions based on that information. The questions are statements that include one drop-down box. You select your answer from the drop-down box to complete the statement.

Here's an example of a Graphics Interpretation question:

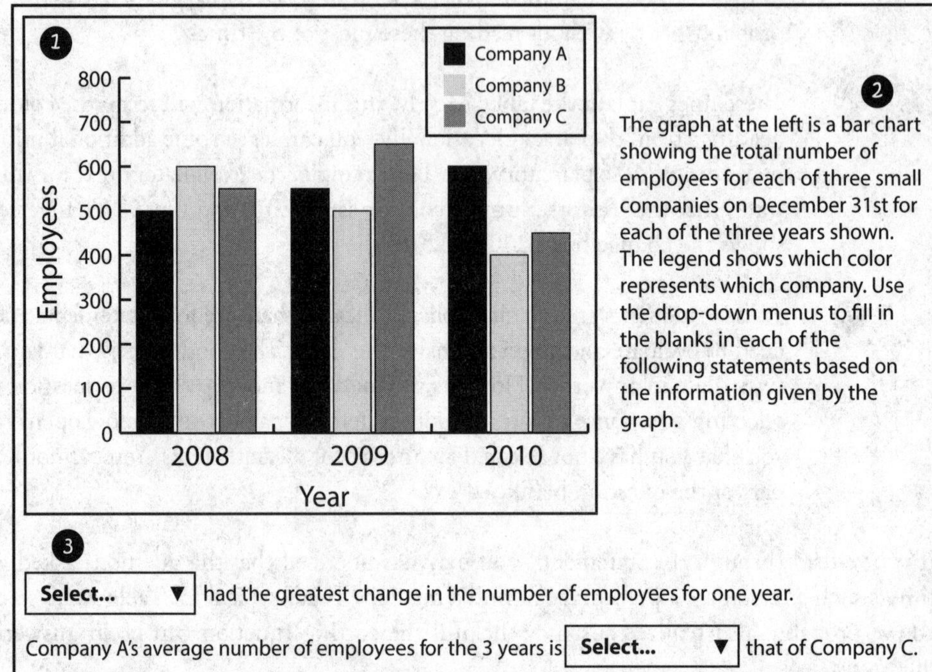


**Want to See What's in the Drop-Downs?**
We'll be discussing how to answer this question in the strategy chapter. We'll expand the drop-down boxes there!

As with the Table Analysis questions, we've added the circled numbers so we can point out the different things that you'll see on your screen for a Graphics Interpretation question. Here's what each circled number represents:

1. The chart, graph, or image is always in the upper left of the screen. As shown here, the chart will take up a good deal of the screen. It will certainly be large enough that you can clearly extract information from it. You can expect to see a variety of different types of charts or graphs including scatterplots, bar charts, line graphs, and circle (or pie) charts. For the most part, you'll see fairly standard types of graphs, however. Be sure to check out any labels on the axes as well as any sort of included legend.

2. These lines provide an explanation of the graph or chart. Mostly, you'll be told what the chart represents as well as what the individual lines, bars, or sectors may represent. Sometimes, you'll be given some additional information such as when measurements were made. For example, here you are told that the bars show the numbers of employees for each firm on December 31 of the year in question. This information is typically extraneous to answering the questions. The explanatory information always ends with the same line about selecting your answers from the drop-down menu.

 These are the questions. Graphics Interpretation questions typically include two statements. You don't have to answer them in order, but you must answer them both to move on to the next question. Each statement is typically a single sentence with one drop-down menu. Each drop-down menu typically includes three to five answer choices. Choose the answer choice that makes the statement true.

Graphics Interpretation questions mostly ask you to find relationships and trends for the data. You can also be asked to calculate percentage increases or decreases, averages, and medians.

## Two-Part Analysis

Next up is the Two-Part Analysis question. In many ways, the Two-Part Analysis question is most similar to a standard math question. You'll typically be presented with a word problem that essentially has two variables in it. You'll need to pick an answer for each variable that makes some condition in the problem true.

Here's an example of a Two-Part Analysis question:

Two families buy new refrigerators using installment plans. Family A makes an initial payment of $750. Family B makes an initial payment of $1200. Both families make five additional payments to pay off the balance. Both families pay the same amount for their refrigerators including all taxes, fees, and finance charges. (1)

In the table below, identify a monthly payment, in dollars, for Family A and a monthly payment, in dollars, for Family B that are consistent with the installment plan described above. Make only one selection in each column. (2)

| Family A | Family B | Monthly payment (in dollars) |
|---|---|---|
| ○ | ○ | 50 |
| ○ | ○ | 80 |
| ○ | ○ | 120 (3) |
| ○ | ○ | 160 |
| ○ | ○ | 250 |
| ○ | ○ | 300 |

**What's the Answer?**
Be sure to read our second chapter on the Integrated Reasoning section to find out!

As you might have surmised, we have once again added the circled numbers so we can described the different parts of the question. Here's what each circled number represents:

 This first block of text is the actual problem. Here, you'll find the description of the two variables in the problem. You'll also find the condition that needs to be made true. As with any word problem, make sure that you read the information carefully. For these problems, you should also make sure that you are clear about which information goes with the first variable and which information goes with the second.

**What's on those Other Tabs?**
We'll show you the other tabs and the answers to these questions in the next chapter on the Integrated Reasoning section.

 This part of the problem tells you how to pick your answers. Mostly this part tells you to pick a value for column A and a value for column B based on the conditions of the problem. This part is mostly boilerplate text that varies slightly from problem to problem.

 These are the answer choices. Two-Part Analysis questions generally have five or six answer choices. You choose only one answer choice for each column. It is possible that the same number is the answer for both columns. So if that's what your calculations indicate, go ahead and choose the same number for both columns.

Most Two-Part Analysis questions can be solved using math that is no more sophisticated than simple arithmetic. There is one exception to that, however. While most Two-Part Analysis questions are math problems, you may see one that looks like a Critical Reasoning question. For these, you'll be given an argument and you'll need to do something like pick one answer that strengthens and one answer that weakens the argument. For these questions, just use the methods from our Critical Reasoning chapter.

## Multi-Source Reasoning

Finally, we come to the Multi-Source Reasoning question. Multi-Source Reasoning questions present information on tabs. The information can be text, charts, graphs, or a combination. In other words, GMAC can put almost anything on the tabs! The layout looks a little bit like Reading Comprehension because the tabbed information is on the left side of your screen while the questions are on the right side.

Here's an example of a Multi-Source Reasoning question:

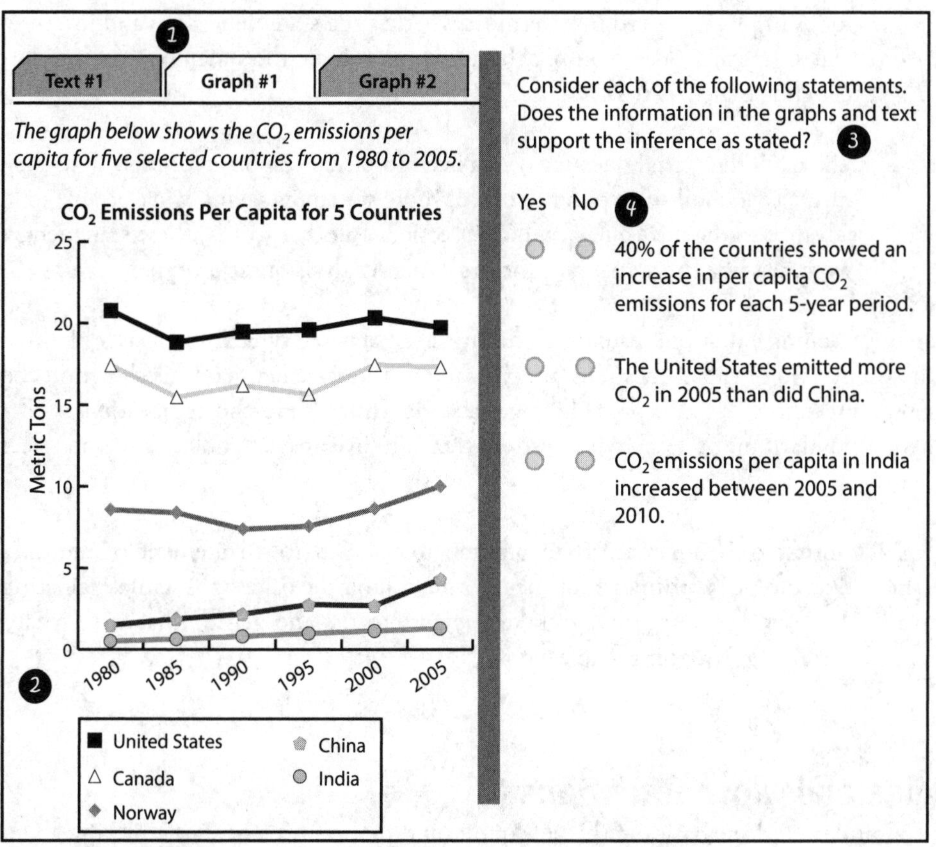


Again, we've added circled numbers to indicate the different parts of the question. Here's what each circled number represents:

1. The tabs appear across the top left of the screen. Some questions have two tabs and some, as in this example, have three. The tabs typically give you some sort of indication about what's on the tab. The currently selected tab is white, while the unselected tabs are grey. GMAC can put almost anything on each tab including graphs, tables, charts, text, or some combination. It's a good idea to take a few seconds to get your bearings before attempting the questions. Make sure you know what is on each tab and how the information on one tab relates to information on the other tab or tabs.

2 The information for each tab appears on the left of the screen. In this case, the information is a graph. When you see a chart or graph, be sure to check out the axes. You should also look for a legend or other information to help explain the information shown by the graph or chart. For tables, check out the column headings so as to better understand the table. Finally, don't neglect to read any supplied headings for the chart, graph, or table. Sometimes that's all you need for the chart to make sense.

3 These are the basic instructions for how to respond to the statements. These instructions help to explain how you need to evaluate each statement. Here, for example, you need to determine whether the statements are valid inferences. In other cases, you may be asked to evaluate the statements for a different choice such as true or false.

4 These are the actual questions. You need to pick a response for each statement. If you fail to respond to one or more statements, you won't be able to advance to the next question in the section. In other words, these statements work just like the statements for the Table Analysis question type.

Multi-Source Reasoning questions usually come in sets. Each set typically consists of three separate questions. Two of those questions are typically in the statement style as shown in the example shown previously. It's also possible to get a standard multiple-choice question as part of the set. For a standard multiple-choice question, there are five answer choices and you select one response.

You may need information from more than one tab to respond to a statement or multiple-choice question. Don't forget to think about the information on the other tabs while evaluating the statements. That's why it's important to take a few moments and get familiar with what's on each tab before starting work on the questions.

## Strategies and More Questions

Now that you understand the basics of the new question types, it's time to start thinking about the best ways to solve these questions. You can find strategies and more practice questions in Chapters 25 and 26, respectively.

# Summary

- The Integrated Reasoning section is 30 minutes long and contains 12 questions, each with multiple parts. This section is not adaptive and you may use an onscreen calculator.
- Work the easier questions first; then tackle the tougher ones. Sometimes your best bet is simply to guess and move along.
- There are four question types. Be sure that you familiarize yourself with these.
    - Table Analysis
    - Graphics Interpretation
    - Two-Part Analysis
    - Multi-Source Reasoning
- Check out these new question types on www.mba.com and practice with the full-length practice GMAT exams available to you once you've registered your book at PrincetonReview.com.

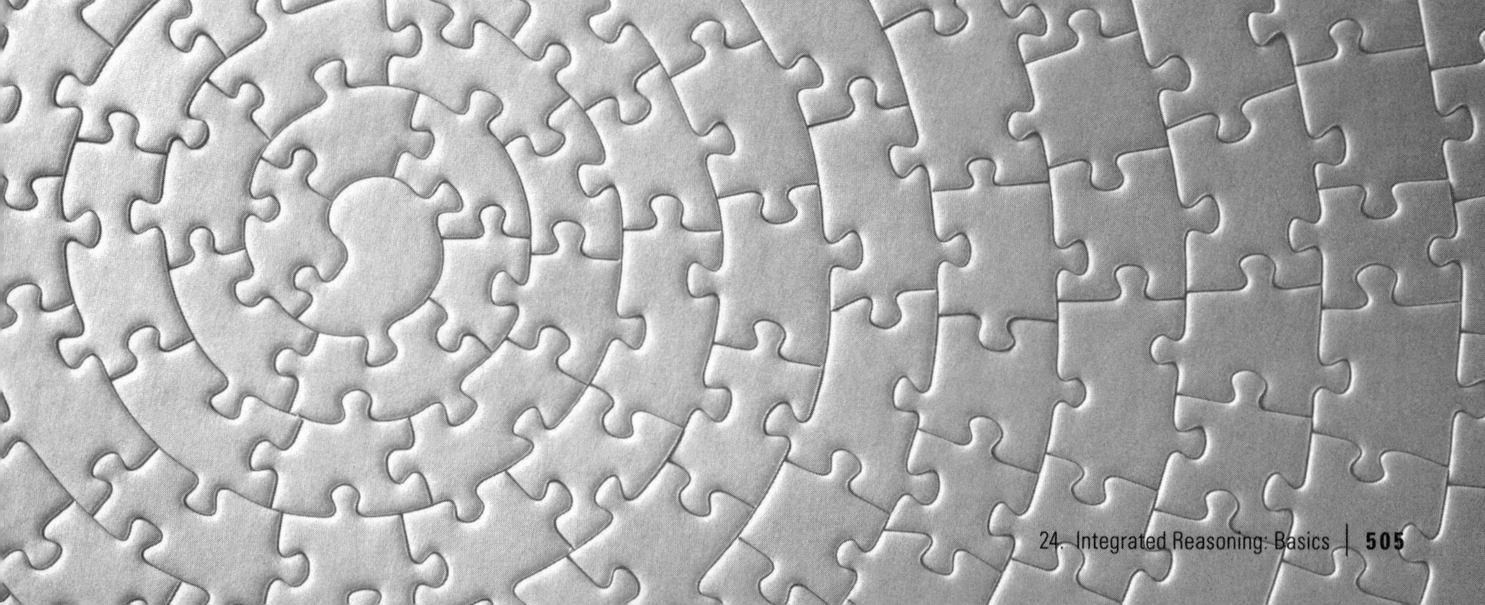

# Chapter 25
# Integrated Reasoning: Strategies

GMAC has devised four question types for the Integrated Reasoning section. As with any section on a standardized test, doing well requires a blend of content knowledge and strategy. Test-takers who approach the Integrated Reasoning section with a firm grasp of strategy will do better than those who haven't thought about strategies for the section.

We'll be looking at two types of strategies in this chapter. Some strategies apply to most or all of the question types that you'll see. Other strategies apply to specific questions types. We'll start by reviewing strategies and pointers for the entire section and then move on to examine some methods for the individual question types.

## GENERAL STRATEGIES

Some strategies apply to the entire section, and you'll use these methods on almost every question. The more consistently you apply these pointers, the better you'll do and the more efficiently you'll use your time.

### Get Your Bearings

Before you can use a chart, graph, or table to answer questions, you need to understand the information on it. So, before you evaluate any statements or answer any questions, take a few moments to review the charts, graphs, and tables.

**What Do the Questions Look Like?**
If you aren't sure what the Integrated Reasoning questions look like, you should reread Chapter 24, Integrated Reasoning: Basics. We introduced the four question types there.

For charts and graphs, make sure you look at the axes. Take note of what each axis measures and the units used to make the measurements. Also, read any headings or titles because those can provide valuable insight into the purpose of the graph. There may be a legend. If there is, take a moment to identify the different items that the chart or graph compares. For tables, make sure that you look at each column heading. This sort of review is essential before you start working on evaluating the statements or answering the questions that go with Table Analysis and Graphics Interpretation questions.

For Multi-Source Reasoning questions, you need to review the information that is on each tab. It's also a good idea to look for connections between the charts on one tab and those on the others. One way that you can do so is to think about what quantities you'd be able to calculate if you used the information from two charts. For example, if one chart shows the number of cars per day that several factories produce and another chart shows the number of days those factories were active in a year, you know that you could calculate the total number of cars each factory produced that year.

## Read What You Need When You Need It

Both Table Analysis and Graphics Interpretation questions include a blurb of text that explains the table or chart. While GMAC includes this information to help you to understand the table or chart, you may not need to take the time to read it.

Most of the charts and tables are understandable without the explanatory text. So if your review of the chart or table doesn't turn up any unusual quantities or units that need further explanation, you're most likely ready to get to work on the actual questions. You can also be guided by the questions. If something about the question or statement isn't making sense, then you can always go back and read the explanatory information.

**Integrated Reasoning Strategies**

Having a solid grasp of the strategies outlined in this chapter will give you an edge. This video highlights one of the most important—pacing. To watch, visit your Student Tools.

## Valid Inferences

Both Table Analysis and Multi-Source Reasoning items include statement style questions. (Reread Chapter 24 to see examples of statement style questions.) In some cases, you'll be asked to decide whether the statement is true or false. In other cases, you'll be asked whether the information supplied supports the inference as stated and then respond yes or no. That's a little different from asking whether the statement is true or false. After all, there's the possibility that there is insufficient information to conclude whether the statement is true or false. If that's the case, you need to pick "no" as your answer.

It's also important to remember that a valid inference is something that you know to be true. You know something is true if you can support it with evidence. GMAC knows, however, that most people start thinking "interpret" or "read into" when they see the word "infer." So, some statements provided on Table Analysis and Multi-Source Reasoning questions attempt to get you to read too much into the information on the chart or table to come up with a conclusion. For example, there may be a clear trend on a chart showing that a company has increased its sales for every year between 2000 and 2008. The statement may try to get you to conclude that the company also increased its sales in 2009 even though 2009 is not shown on the chart. That's not a valid inference! Be careful that you don't mix up "true" and "very likely" when evaluating what can be inferred from the data.

**What's an Inference?**

An inference is a statement that you can prove true using supplied facts or other evidence.

# TABLE ANALYSIS

Table Analysis questions always include one table to display data. You'll be asked to evaluate four statements. You may be asked whether the statements are true or false based on the data in the table. You may also be asked whether the statements represent valid inferences based on the table.

While you won't be called upon to provide numerical answers as part of Table Analysis questions, you may need to perform some calculations to evaluate the statements. For example, you may be asked to verify that a certain percentage of the items in the table have a certain characteristic.

## The Sort Function

The sort function allows you to sort the data in the table by any column. However, the sort function will sort only one column at a time. So forget all those fancy multiple column sorts that you can do with Excel.

To see how the sort function works for Table Analysis questions, let's look at a very simple table. This table is really too simple for a GMAT question, but it will help us to illustrate how the sort function works.

When you first see the table, it is typically sorted by one key statistic from the table. All numerical sorts are always smallest to largest. This table, for example, is sorted by Median Household Income (2014) and represents the original sort for this table.

| City | State | Median Household Income (2014) |
|---|---|---|
| Rochester | NY | $51,086 |
| Philadelphia | PA | $62,171 |
| Salt Lake City | UT | $62,642 |
| New York | NY | $67,066 |

Now, here's what you'll see if you sort by State.

| City | State | Median Household Income (2014) |
|---|---|---|
| Rochester | NY | $51,086 |
| New York | NY | $67,066 |
| Philadelphia | PA | $62,171 |
| Salt Lake City | UT | $62,642 |

If you sort next by City, you might expect that Rochester and New York would exchange positions. That's particularly true if you are used to the way that Excel lets you sort by multiple columns.

**Question Order**
In general, you should just evaluate the statements in order for Table Analysis questions. Of course, if you get stuck on one statement, skip over it, evaluate the other statements, and come back to the one that gave you trouble.

However, what you'll really get is an alphabetical listing by City. Here's what the sort by City looks like.

| City | State | Median Household Income (2014) |
|---|---|---|
| New York | NY | $67,066 |
| Philadelphia | PA | $62,171 |
| Rochester | NY | $51,086 |
| Salt Lake City | UT | $62,642 |

## To Sort or Not to Sort

While the sort feature can be a huge help when answering some questions, you may not need to use it to answer every question. In some cases, you may need to find only one piece of information on the table. In other cases, the table may not have that many rows. Table Analysis questions can have as few as six rows of data. It may be faster to simply scan the table for the information that you need.

On the other hand, remember that sorting the table takes only a few seconds. If you think sorting will help, do it! One thing you shouldn't do, however, is spend time trying to organize the statements so that you do as little sorting as possible. You're actually likely to waste more time trying to come up with the perfect order in which to evaluate the statements than you would if you wind up sorting the same way twice in evaluating the statements.

Let's look at a sample Table Analysis question. Here's the question that we discussed in Chapter 24.

Sort By Select...

| National Park | | Visitors | | | Area | |
|---|---|---|---|---|---|---|
| Name | State | Number | % Change | Rank | Acres | Rank |
| Grand Canyon | AZ | 4,388,386 | 0.9 | 2 | 1,217,403 | 11 |
| Yosemite | CA | 3,901,408 | 4.4 | 3 | 791,266 | 16 |
| Yellowstone | WY | 3,640,185 | 10.5 | 4 | 2,219,791 | 8 |
| Rocky Mtn. | CO | 2,955,821 | 4.7 | 5 | 265,828 | 26 |
| Zion | UT | 2,665,972 | −2.5 | 8 | 145,598 | 35 |
| Acadia | ME | 2,504,208 | 12.4 | 9 | 47,390 | 47 |
| Bryce | UT | 1,285,492 | 5.7 | 15 | 35,835 | 50 |
| Arches | UT | 1,014,405 | 1.8 | 19 | 76,519 | 42 |
| Badlands | SD | 977,778 | 4.7 | 22 | 242,756 | 28 |
| Mesa Verde | CO | 559,712 | 1.7 | 30 | 52,122 | 46 |
| Canyonlands | UT | 435,908 | −0.1 | 36 | 337,598 | 23 |

The table above gives information for 2010 on total visitors and total acreage for 11 U.S. National Parks. In addition to the numbers of total visitors and total acreage for each National Park, the table also provides the percent increase or decrease over the total visitors for 2009 and the rank of the National Park for total visitors and total acreage in 2010.

Each column of the table can be sorted in ascending order by clicking on the word "Select" above the table and choosing, from the drop-down menu, the heading of the column on which you want the table to be sorted.

Consider each of the following statements about these National Parks. For each statement indicate whether the statement is true or false, based on the information provided in the table.

| True | False | |
|---|---|---|
| ○ | ○ | The park that experienced the greatest percent increase in visitors from 2009 to 2010 also had the least total acreage. |
| ○ | ○ | The park with the median rank by the number of visitors is larger than only one other park by acreage. |
| ○ | ○ | The total number of visitors at Arches in 2009 was fewer than 1,000,000. |

**Get Your Bearings**

Step one for any Table Analysis question is to review the information presented by the table.

### Here's How to Crack It

As with any Table Analysis question, the first step is to make sure that you take a moment to understand the information presented by the table. While it might be tempting to jump straight to the statements, you'll be able to evaluate the statements more efficiently when you first take a moment to understand the information on the table. Looking at the column headings can also help you to decide whether you need to read the explanatory information under the table.

The first two columns of this table—National Park Name and National Park State—are self-explanatory. More importantly, however, the first column—National Park Name—tells you that this table provides information about national parks. Next, you get information about visitors to the national parks included in the table. The third column heading—Visitors Number—is pretty clear. However, you don't know the time period for the visitation numbers. The next column—Visitors % Change—shows increases or decreases from some previous time period. Again, you don't know the time period just by looking at the table. Do the time periods matter? Probably not. You'll probably learn the time period from the statements. If the statements seem to indicate that the time periods matter, you can read the explanatory text at that time.

The next column—Visitors Rank—is potentially more confusing, however. Does the rank refer to the number of visitors or the percent change? That's an important distinction for understanding the information in the table. There are two ways to figure out what's being ranked. You could scan the table looking for evidence. Of course, that could be time consuming. Or, you could scan the explanatory text beneath the table. *If you don't understand one of the column headings shown in the table, that's when you want to read the explanatory text.* The explanation indicates that the rank refers to the total number of visitors. As a bonus, you now also know that the visitation numbers are for 2010.

**Step 2**
Decide the best way to sort the table. For some statements, you may be able to sort in more than one way. Sort by the column with the larger numbers or more complex data.

The last two column headings—Area Acres and Area Rank—are also pretty clear. Note that the inclusion of Area Rank means that you won't need to deal with the larger number in the Area Acres column if all you need to do is compare the size of one park to another. The same is also true of the inclusion of the Visitors Rank column. The inclusion of these columns makes it much easier to make some types of comparisons about the parks in the table. That's definitely something to make note of as you finish reviewing the information presented by the chart.

We'll just evaluate the statements in order. First, we'll evaluate:

> The park that experienced the greatest percent increase in visitors from 2009 to 2010 also had the least total acreage.

This statement is typical of the sorts of statements that you are called upon to evaluate for Table Analysis questions. Note that there are two possible sorts that you could perform to evaluate this question. First, you could sort by Visitors % Change. You could also sort by Area Acres. So, what's the best? Sort by only one of those columns? Sort by both? Sort by neither?

With 11 rows of data, you'll probably find it safer to sort by at least one of the columns. But which one? Well, note that the table provides you with ranking information for the areas of the parks. The smaller numbers used to rank the parks by area make it easier to identify the smallest park by area without sorting.

However, you might reasonably be worried about missing which park had the greatest percent increase by visitors. So, sort by Visitors % Change.

Here's what the sorted table looks like:

| National Park | | Visitors | | | Area | |
|---|---|---|---|---|---|---|
| Name | State | Number | % Change | Rank | Acres | Rank |
| Zion | UT | 2,556,972 | −2.5 | 8 | 145,598 | 35 |
| Canyonlands | UT | 435,908 | −0.1 | 36 | 337,598 | 23 |
| Grand Canyon | AZ | 4,388,386 | 0.9 | 2 | 1,217,403 | 11 |
| Mesa Verde | CO | 559,712 | 1.7 | 30 | 52,122 | 46 |
| Arches | UT | 1,014,405 | 1.8 | 19 | 76,519 | 42 |
| Yosemite | CA | 3,901,408 | 4.4 | 3 | 791,266 | 16 |
| Rocky Mtn. | CO | 2,955,821 | 4.7 | 5 | 265,828 | 26 |
| Badlands | SD | 977,778 | 4.7 | 22 | 242,756 | 28 |
| Bryce | UT | 1,285,492 | 5.7 | 15 | 35,835 | 50 |
| Yellowstone | WY | 3,640,185 | 10.5 | 4 | 2,219,791 | 8 |
| Acadia | ME | 2,504,208 | 12.4 | 9 | 47,390 | 47 |

It's clear that Acadia had the greatest percent increase in the number of visitors from 2009 to 2010. Acadia was ranked 47th in terms of overall acreage. You could sort the chart by Area Acres or by Area Rank at this point to finish evaluating the statement. However, since you know Acadia's rank for acreage, it's probably slightly faster to simply scan to see if any park had a higher rank for area. In this case, Bryce was ranked 50th, so this first statement is false.

Now, let's take a look at the second statement:

> The park with the median rank by the number of visitors is larger than only one other park by acreage.

Again, you may be considering several different ways to sort the chart. So, start by asking yourself "What's hardest to see right now?" Remember that your chart will still be sorted as shown above, which is the sort that you did to evaluate the first statement. This sort makes it pretty hard to see which park had the median rank for visitors, so it makes sense to sort by Visitors Rank.

Here's what the sorted chart looks like:

| National Park | | Visitors | | | Area | |
|---|---|---|---|---|---|---|
| Name | State | Number | % Change | Rank | Acres | Rank |
| Grand Canyon | AZ | 4,388,386 | 0.9 | 2 | 1,217,403 | 11 |
| Yosemite | CA | 3,901,408 | 4.4 | 3 | 791,266 | 16 |
| Yellowstone | WY | 3,640,185 | 10.5 | 4 | 2,219,791 | 8 |
| Rocky Mtn. | CO | 2,955,821 | 4.7 | 5 | 265,828 | 26 |
| Zion | UT | 2,665,972 | –2.5 | 8 | 145,598 | 35 |
| Acadia | ME | 2,504,208 | 12.4 | 9 | 47,390 | 47 |
| Bryce | UT | 1,285,492 | 5.7 | 15 | 35,835 | 50 |
| Arches | UT | 1,014,405 | 1.8 | 19 | 76,519 | 42 |
| Badlands | SD | 977,778 | 4.7 | 22 | 242,756 | 28 |
| Mesa Verde | CO | 559,712 | 1.7 | 30 | 52,122 | 46 |
| Canyonlands | UT | 435,908 | –0.1 | 36 | 337,598 | 23 |

With the table sorted by Visitors Rank, it's now fairly easy to find the park with the median rank. To find a median, you start by putting the items on a list into numerical order, which we just did by sorting the list. Then, you can just choose the middle number. In this case, Acadia is the park in the middle position since there are 5 parks ranked before it and 5 parks ranked after it.

**Use Your Noteboards**
For more complicated statements, you may want to make a list of the items that satisfy a condition in the statement.

Note that you could have also sorted the list by Visitors Number. Since data is always sorted from least to greatest, Canyonlands would have been the first row of the table and Grand Canyon would have been the last row. But, Acadia still would have been in the middle. We chose to sort by Visitors Rank because that term was mentioned in the question and it's easier to work with smaller numbers.

Having identified Acadia as the park with the median rank, you now need to decide whether to sort the table again. Since the table provides ranks for the total acreage of the parks on the list, you likely don't need to sort again. Acadia is 47th by acreage. One park, Bryce, with a rank of 50, is smaller. So, Acadia, the median park by visitation, is larger than only one other park on the list. The second statement is true.

Note, however, that if the table had not provided ranks for the parks by total area, then you most likely would have wanted to sort by Area Acres. After all, it's a lot easier to see that only one number is greater than 47 than to see that only one number is less than 47,390. Remember that sorting takes only a few seconds and you should sort whenever you think doing so will help you to accurately find what you need on the table.

Now it's time to finish the question by evaluating the third statement. The third statement claims:

The total number of visitors at Arches in 2009 was fewer than 1,000,000.

Because this statement involves only a single data point, you don't really need to worry about doing any sorting. Even the most involved GMAT tables will have fewer than 30 rows of data. It will never be an issue to quickly scan the table, no matter how it is currently sorted, to find one data point. Just use the current sort which has Arches in the 8th row.

Next, you need some information about Arches to evaluate the statement. The table shows that Arches had 1,014,405 visitors in 2010. The table also shows that the number of visitors in 2010 was 1.8% greater than it was in 2009. To find the number of visitors in 2009, use the percent change formula:

**Calculations Required**
Expect to do some calculations such as computing an average or a percent change to evaluate one or two of the statements in a Table Analysis question.

$$\% \text{ change} = \frac{\text{difference}}{\text{original}} \times 100$$

Next, put the numbers that you know into the formula to get:

$$1.8 = \frac{(1{,}014{,}405 - x)}{x} \times 100$$

We've called the 2009 number that we're trying to find $x$. A little rearranging gives:

$$101.8x = 101{,}440{,}500$$

Finally, just divide through by 101.8 to find that $x$, the 2009 visitation at Arches, was 996,469 rounded to the nearest integer. So, statement three is true.

**Calculator Time!**
Don't forget that you can use the onscreen calculator to perform messy calculations such as dividing through by 101.8!

The following is what your answers should look like just before you click next to move onto the next question in the Integrated Reasoning section.

Sort By Select... ▼

| National Park | | Visitors | | | Area | |
|---|---|---|---|---|---|---|
| Name | State | Number | % Change | Rank | Acres | Rank |
| Grand Canyon | AZ | 4,388,386 | 0.9 | 2 | 1,217,403 | 11 |
| Yosemite | CA | 3,901,408 | 4.4 | 3 | 791,266 | 16 |
| Yellowstone | WY | 3,640,185 | 10.5 | 4 | 2,219,791 | 8 |
| Rocky Mtn. | CO | 2,955,821 | 4.7 | 5 | 265,828 | 26 |
| Zion | UT | 2,665,972 | −2.5 | 8 | 145,598 | 35 |
| Acadia | ME | 2,504,208 | 12.4 | 9 | 47,390 | 47 |
| Bryce | UT | 1,285,492 | 5.7 | 15 | 35,835 | 50 |
| Arches | UT | 1,014,405 | 1.8 | 19 | 76,519 | 42 |
| Badlands | SD | 977,778 | 4.7 | 22 | 242,756 | 28 |
| Mesa Verde | CO | 559,712 | 1.7 | 30 | 52,122 | 46 |
| Canyonlands | UT | 435,908 | −0.1 | 36 | 337,598 | 23 |

The table above gives information for 2010 on total visitors and total acreage for 11 US National Parks. In addition to the numbers of total visitors and total acreage for each National Park, the table also provides the percent increase or decrease over the total visitors for 2009 and the rank of the National Park for total visitors and total acreage in 2010.

Each column of the table can be sorted in ascending order by clicking on the word "Select" above the table and choosing, from the drop-down menu, the heading of the column on which you want the table to be sorted.

Consider each of the following statements about these National Parks. For each statement indicate whether the statement is true or false, based on the information provided in the table.

| True | False | |
|---|---|---|
| ○ | ● | The park that experienced the greatest percent increase in visitors from 2009 to 2010 also had the least total acreage. |
| ● | ○ | The park with the median rank by the number of visitors is larger than only one other park by acreage. |
| ● | ○ | The total number of visitors at Arches in 2009 was fewer than 1,000,000. |

## GRAPHICS INTERPRETATION

Graphics Interpretation questions provide you with one chart, graph, or image. Each chart is followed by two statements. Each statement contains one drop-down list from which you choose one answer. Your job is to pick the answer that makes the statement true. Each drop-down list typically contains between three to five answer choices.

You'll find a few sentences of explanatory text to the right of the chart or graph. As with Table Analysis questions, you may not need to read this explanatory information. Just as with Table Analysis questions, you can be guided by how well you understand the chart or graph. If you understand the chart or graph, then you probably don't need to read the explanatory text.

So, what should you look for when you review the chart or graph? Start by looking at any labels on the axes. Are quantities being measured in common, easily understood units? You should also look to see if the chart or graph has any titles that help to explain the data it shows. Finally, see if there's any sort of legend that helps to differentiate different types of data.

Let's take a look at the sample Graphics Interpretation question that we discussed in Chapter 24.

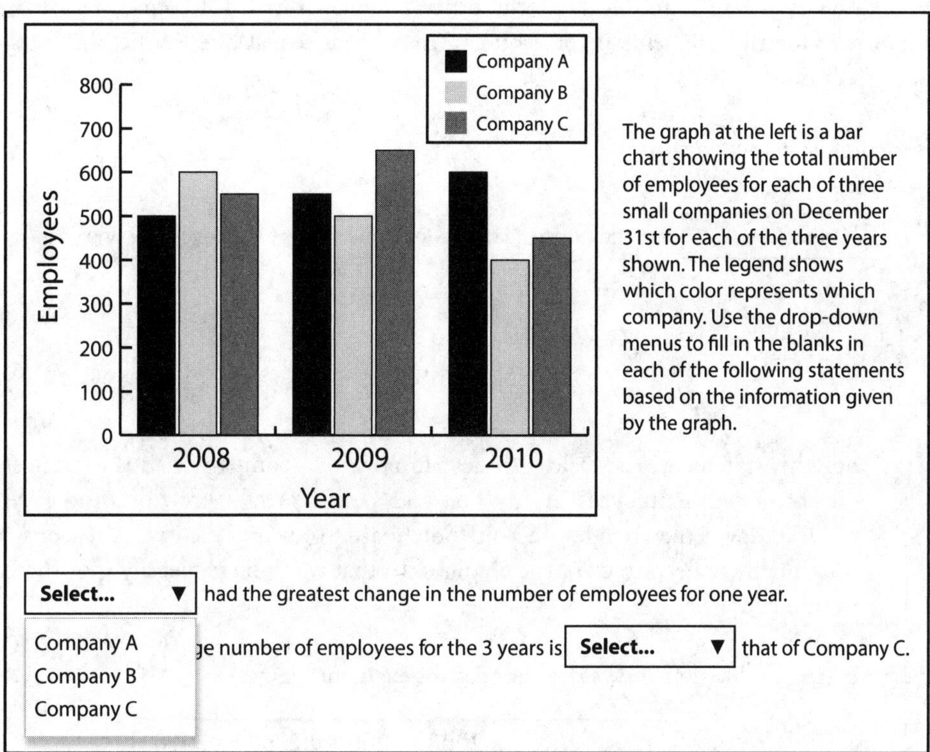


## Here's How to Crack It

Before we get started discussing this question, note that we've expanded the drop down list for the first statement. When the question first appears on the screen, none of the drop-downs are expanded. Here, we just wanted to show what the expanded drop-downs look like in the context of a question.

The first step in answering any Graphics Interpretation question is to review the chart or graph. In this case, there's a bar chart. The vertical axis shows the number of employees, which seems fairly easy to understand. The horizontal axis shows results for three years. The different colored bars are explained by the legend—there are three companies. So, this chart seems fairly straightforward. It shows the number of employees for three companies for three different years.

With everything on the chart so clearly marked, there's little reason to read the explanatory text to the right of the chart. Note that the only piece of information that the explanatory text really adds is that the number of employees for each company was tallied on December 31 of each year. That's the sort of detail that often turns out to be irrelevant in answering the questions. Remember that you can always go back and read the explanatory text if it seems like you need to know something that wasn't clearly reflected on the chart or graph.

Let's take a look at the questions. As with Table Analysis questions, it's best to just evaluate the statements in order. If one of them gives you trouble or seems particularly time consuming, you can always skip over it and evaluate the other statements first. Of course, you'll need to pick an answer for all statements before you can move to the next question in the Integrated Reasoning section.

Here's the first statement again:

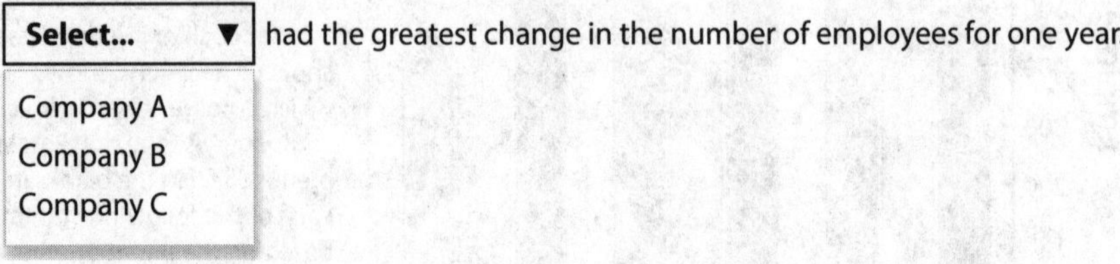


For this statement, the task is to determine which company had the greatest overall changes in employees in any one-year period. You'll probably find it helpful to write down the changes on your noteboard. You may even want to construct a rough table to keep track of the changes. In that way, you can easily spot the largest overall change.

**Avoid Common Errors**

Be careful when you read the chart. Are you looking at the right item? It's also a good idea to write down the data before performing any calculations with the data.

Here's a table that shows the changes for each company:

| | 2008 to 2009 | 2009 to 2010 |
|---|---|---|
| Company A | 50 | 50 |
| Company B | –100 | –100 |
| Company C | 100 | –200 |

For this statement, it's important to note that the question asked for the greatest change. So, you need to include overall decreases in looking for the greatest change. Employment at Company C declined by 200 between 2009 and 2010. The correct answer to statement one is "Company C."

Here's the second statement showing the possible answers:

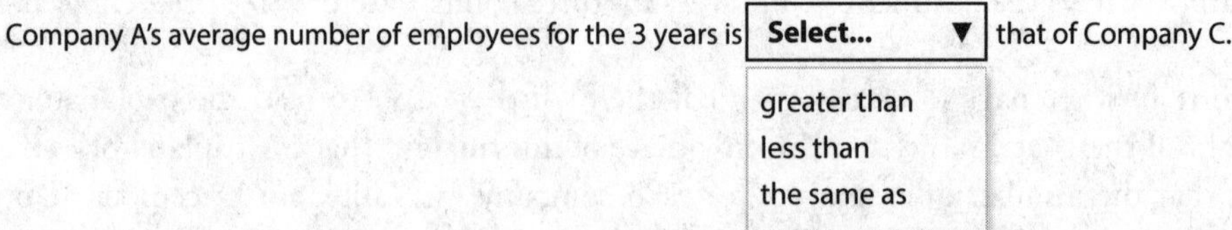


To evaluate this statement, you need to calculate the average number of employees for Companies A and C. Questions that ask you to perform calculations such as finding an average are fairly common for Graphics Interpretation questions. Just be sure to read the information from the chart carefully. Common errors for questions such as this one usually involve reading the information for the wrong company or mixing the information for two companies.

For Company A, the total number of employees for each year was 500, 550, and 600. To find the average, take the sum of the three numbers to get 1,650. Now, just divide by 3 because you want the average over three years. The average number of employees for Company A is 550.

For Company C, the total number of employees for each year was 550, 650, and 450. The average number of employees per year for Company C is also 550. So, the correct answer for the second statement is "the same as."

**Calculator Required?**
While using the calculator is fine, you may be able to do the calculations for some questions faster without the calculator. Make sure you need the calculator before you use it!

Here's what your answers should look like just before you click next to move on to the next question in the Integrated Reasoning section:

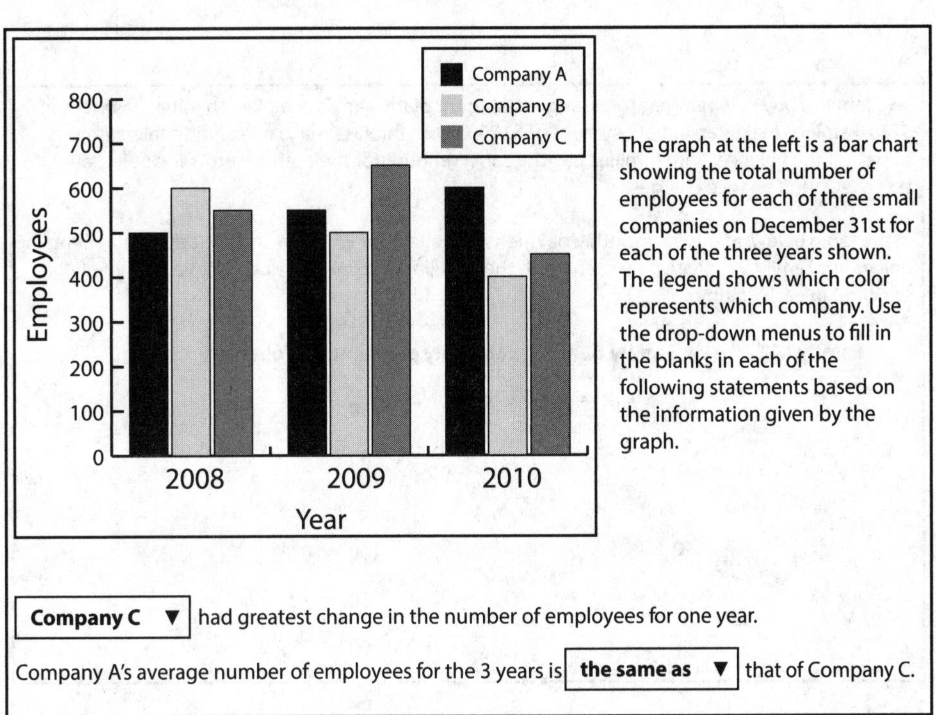


## TWO-PART ANALYSIS

Most Two-Part Analysis questions will remind you of the word problems that are part of the Quantitative section of the GMAT. The only difference is that you'll need to pick two answers rather than one! It's likely that you'll need to do some calculations to solve most Two-Part Analysis questions. For the most part, the math you'll need to do will be fairly straightforward arithmetic. You may find that it's faster to do the calculations without the calculator. However, remember that the calculator is available. Just don't forget to set up your calculations before entering them into the calculator.

For most Two-Part Analysis questions, the two answers that you need to pick are related or linked in some way. When that's the case, you may be able to identify one part as easier to solve than the other. If so, do the easier part first. It's also important to remember that working with the answer choices is often easier for these questions. While some Two-Part Analysis questions can be solved algebraically, it's very often faster to just test out the answer choices. In other words, you'll be able to use a form of PITA (Plugging In the Answers, discussed in Chapter 14) to solve most of these questions. Let's take a look at how to solve the question we saw in Chapter 24.

---

Two families buy new refrigerators using installment plans. Family A makes an initial payment of $750. Family B makes an initial payment of $1200. Both families make five additional payments to pay off the balance. Both families pay the same amount for their refrigerators including all taxes, fees, and finance charges.

In the table below, identify a monthly payment, in dollars, for Family A and a monthly payment, in dollars, for Family B that are consistent with the installment plan described above. Make only one selection in each column.

| Family A | Family B | Monthly payment (in dollars) |
|---|---|---|
| ○ | ○ | 50 |
| ○ | ○ | 80 |
| ○ | ○ | 120 |
| ○ | ○ | 160 |
| ○ | ○ | 250 |
| ○ | ○ | 300 |

### Here's How to Crack It

For this problem, one of the first things to notice is that there is a connection between the payments that each family makes. Since Family B's initial payment is $450 more than that of Family A, Family A's monthly payment is larger than that of Family B. That can help when you start testing the answer choices. Moreover, you can also see that the answer for Family A cannot be either $50 or $80. If Family A's monthly payment were $80, then they would have paid only an additional $400 after 5 months. That's not even enough to make Family A's total payment equal to Family B's initial payment. Of course, Family B makes monthly payments too.

The other thing to notice in this question is that there is a crucial piece of information missing: the cost of the refrigerator. In this case, Plugging In the Answers will enable us to verify that the cost of that fridge is the same for both families. You can set the problem up just like you would a PITA question with one change. So that you can keep track of your Process of

Elimination, write the answer choices down twice, leaving some space between the answers to show any quantities that you needed to calculate. Of course, you'll label your answer choices just as you would with any other PITA question. For this problem, you can label your columns of numbers as "A's payment" and "B's payment." Here's what your initial setup should look like:

| A's payment | | B's payment | |
|---|---|---|---|
| ~~50~~ | | 50 | |
| ~~80~~ | | 80 | |
| 120 | | 120 | |
| 160 | | 160 | |
| 250 | | 250 | |
| 300 | | 300 | |

Note that we've already crossed off 50 and 80 as possible payments for Family A. As discussed, these answers are too small for A's payment. As with any other PITA question, it makes sense to start with a number in the middle. We'll start with $160 for Family A's payment.

If Family A's payment is $160, what can you find? The problem states that Family A makes 5 payments, so the total of those 5 payments is $800. Moreover, the problem also states that Family A made an initial payment of $750. So, if Family A made payments of $160, then the refrigerator cost $750 + $800 = $1,550. That's what goes into the next column for Family A.

What about Family B? If Family A makes payments of $160, then Family B's payments must be less than that amount. So, Family B could make payments of $50, $80, or $120. For each of those numbers, calculate how much Family B would have paid for the refrigerator. Here's what your table should look like at this step:

| A's payment | A's Total | B's payment | B's Total |
|---|---|---|---|
| ~~50~~ | | 50 | $1,450 |
| ~~80~~ | | 80 | $1,600 |
| 120 | | 120 | $1,800 |
| 160 | $1,550 | 160 | |
| 250 | | 250 | |
| 300 | | 300 | |

How do you know if you've found the correct answers? Remember that the problem states that both families pay the same amount for their refrigerators. Since Family B cannot pay $1,550 for their refrigerator, you can eliminate 160 as an answer for Family A.

It's not that clear whether Family A's payment needs to be larger or smaller. So just pick a direction and try it. Let's try $250 for Family A's payment. If Family A's payment is $250, then their refrigerator costs $750 + (5 × $250) = $2,000. For Family B, none of the answers we've already worked out make their refrigerator cost $2,000. However, we can also check what happens if Family B makes monthly payments of $160. In that case, Family B's refrigerator costs $1,200 + (5 × $160) = $2,000. So, the answers are 250 for Family A and 160 for Family B.

Here's what your completed table looks like:

| A's payment | A's Total | B's payment | B's Total |
|---|---|---|---|
| ~~50~~ | | 50 | $1,450 |
| ~~80~~ | | 80 | $1,600 |
| 120 | | 120 | $1,800 |
| ~~160~~ | $1,550 | 160 | $2,000 |
| 250 | $2,000 | 250 | |
| 300 | | 300 | |

Here's what your answers should look like just before you click next to move on to the next question in the Integrated Reasoning section:

**Check Your Answers**
Always double check your answers for a Two-Part Analysis question. Flipping your answers is a very common mistake for these questions. Make sure you have the correct answer for each column.

Two families buy new refrigerators using installment plans. Family A makes an initial payment of $750. Family B makes an initial payment of $1200. Both families make five additional payments to pay off the balance. Both families pay the same amount for their refrigerators including all taxes, fees, and finance charges.

In the table below, identify a monthly payment, in dollars, for Family A and a monthly payment, in dollars, for Family B that are consistent with the installment plan described above. Make only one selection in each column.

| Family A | Family B | Monthly payment (in dollars) |
|---|---|---|
| ○ | ○ | 50 |
| ○ | ○ | 80 |
| ○ | ○ | 120 |
| ○ | ● | 160 |
| ● | ○ | 250 |
| ○ | ○ | 300 |

We used a form of Plugging In the Answers (PITA) to solve the previous question. You can use that approach for most of the Two-Part Analysis questions that you see. Here's a recap of the steps.

## PITA for Two-Part Analysis Questions

1. Write down the answer choices on your noteboard. Make two columns and leave some space between.
2. Decide which variable is easier to work with. For example, you might be able to eliminate some answers for one variable because those answers are too big or too small.
3. Write a label over each column of numbers. Label the first column as the easier variable to work with.
4. Starting with an answer in the middle for the first column, work the steps of the problem. For the second column, remember that you may need to test only the answers that are bigger or smaller than the number you worked with in the first column.
5. Check for a match between the first and second column that makes a condition in the problem true.

For some Two-Part Analysis questions, however, you won't be able to use PITA. For the problem we just discussed, the two monthly payments were linked because both families needed to pay the same amount for a refrigerator. For some Two-Part Analysis questions, however, the variables are either unlinked or, at least, less linked.

Let's look at an example:

Jack divides $30,000 between two investments. He invests 35% of the money in Investment A, which pays 4% simple interest annually for 5 years. He invests the remainder of the money in Investment B, which pays 2% interest compounded semiannually for 4 years.

In the table below, identify the total interest earned, in dollars, for Investment A and the total interest earned, rounded to the nearest dollar, for Investment B that are consistent with the investments described above. Make only one selection in each column.

| Investment A | Investment B | Interest Earned (in dollars) |
|---|---|---|
| ○ | ○ | 392 |
| ○ | ○ | 870 |
| ○ | ○ | 1,560 |
| ○ | ○ | 1,616 |
| ○ | ○ | 2,100 |
| ○ | ○ | 3,347 |

### Here's How to Crack It

For this question, note that there's no common condition that needs to be satisfied. Rather, there are two independent calculations. That's how you know that you can't use PITA to solve this question.

The solution to this question starts with calculating how Jack divides the $30,000 between the two investments. Start by calculating 35% of $30,000. Remember that you can just use the onscreen calculator: 30,000 × 0.35 = 10,500. So, $10,500 is invested in Investment A and the rest, or $19,500, is invested in Investment B.

Next, it's time to calculate the interest earned on each investment. Investment A earns simple interest at a rate of 4% per year for 5 years. To find simple interest, you multiply the principal amount, $10,500, by the interest rate, 0.04, by the time period, 5 years. Here's what the calculation looks like:

$$\$10{,}500 \times 0.04 \times 5 = \$2{,}100$$

The onscreen calculator makes doing the calculation an easy, one-step operation. Just make sure that you use the right numbers from the problem!

For Investment B, the interest is compounded semiannually. That means that every six months the interest is added to the principal so that interest can be earned on the combined amount. There are several ways to calculate compound interest. One of the easiest is to divide the yearly interest rate by the compounding period. For this problem, the investment pays 2% per year, but the interest is compounded twice per year.

So, that's 1% every six months. In four years, there are 8 compounding periods. To find the account balance at the end of 4 years, you'd calculate the interest for the first six months by multiplying by 0.01. Then, you'd add that amount to the principal and repeat the calculation. Keep calculating until you've done all 8 compounding periods. Of course, since you are multiplying each time, there's a shorter way. Here's what the overall calculation looks like.

$$\$19{,}500 \times (1.01)^8 = \$21{,}115.71$$

To find the interest just subtract $19,500 from the account balance. The interest earned is $1,616 rounded to the nearest dollar.

Here's what your answers should look like just before you click next to move on to the next question in the Integrated Reasoning section:

Jack divides $30,000 between two investments. He invests 35% of the money in Investment A, which pays 4% simple interest annually for 5 years. He invests the remainder of the money in Investment B, which pays 2% interest compounded semiannually for 4 years.

In the table below, identify the total interest earned, in dollars, for Investment A and the total interest earned, rounded to the nearest dollar, for Investment B that are consistent with the investments described above. Make only one selection in each column.

| Investment A | Investment B | Interest Earned (in dollars) |
|---|---|---|
| ○ | ○ | 392 |
| ○ | ○ | 870 |
| ○ | ○ | 1,560 |
| ○ | ◉ | 1,616 |
| ◉ | ○ | 2,100 |
| ○ | ○ | 3,347 |

## MULTI-SOURCE REASONING

For Multi-Source Reasoning questions, you'll be given a variety of information that can include text, charts, tables, and graphs. The information is arranged on 2 or 3 tabs. Multi-Source Reasoning questions typically come in sets. So, you'll probably get two sets of statement style questions and perhaps one standard multiple-choice question.

When a new Multi-Source question appears on your screen, you should take a minute to review the information on each tab. As usual, you should check out things like the axes on graphs and any headings for the charts. But, for Multi-Source Reasoning questions, you should also determine how the information on one tab relates to the information on the other tabs.

Let's look at the example that we saw in the previous Integrated Reasoning chapter. This time, we'll take a look at the information on all three tabs. We'll also discuss how to evaluate statements and answer questions.

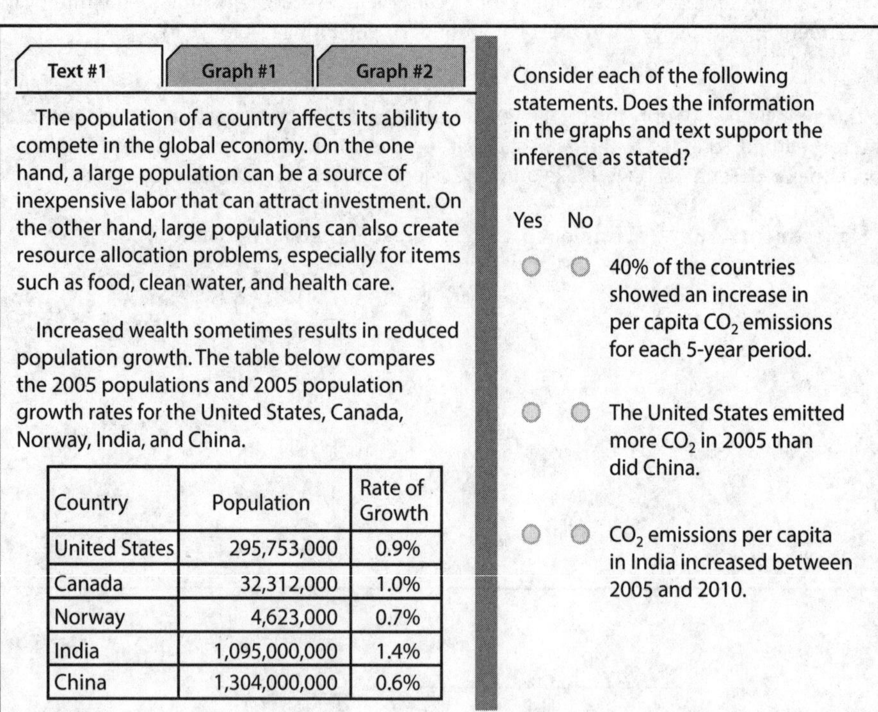

Text #1 | Graph #1 | Graph #2

The population of a country affects its ability to compete in the global economy. On the one hand, a large population can be a source of inexpensive labor that can attract investment. On the other hand, large populations can also create resource allocation problems, especially for items such as food, clean water, and health care.

Increased wealth sometimes results in reduced population growth. The table below compares the 2005 populations and 2005 population growth rates for the United States, Canada, Norway, India, and China.

| Country | Population | Rate of Growth |
|---|---|---|
| United States | 295,753,000 | 0.9% |
| Canada | 32,312,000 | 1.0% |
| Norway | 4,623,000 | 0.7% |
| India | 1,095,000,000 | 1.4% |
| China | 1,304,000,000 | 0.6% |

Consider each of the following statements. Does the information in the graphs and text support the inference as stated?

| Yes | No | |
|---|---|---|
| ○ | ○ | 40% of the countries showed an increase in per capita $CO_2$ emissions for each 5-year period. |
| ○ | ○ | The United States emitted more $CO_2$ in 2005 than did China. |
| ○ | ○ | $CO_2$ emissions per capita in India increased between 2005 and 2010. |

## Here's How to Crack It

We'll review the information one tab at a time before we start evaluating the statements. The first tab, Text #1, provides some background information about the ways in which a country's population can affect its participation in the global economy. This tab also presents a table with population and growth rates for five countries. Notice that you need to read the included information on this tab to determine that the table displays data from 2005. Unlike the other question types that we've discussed, you should always read any text that's included on a tab in a Multi-Source Reasoning question.

Now, here's the information for the second tab:

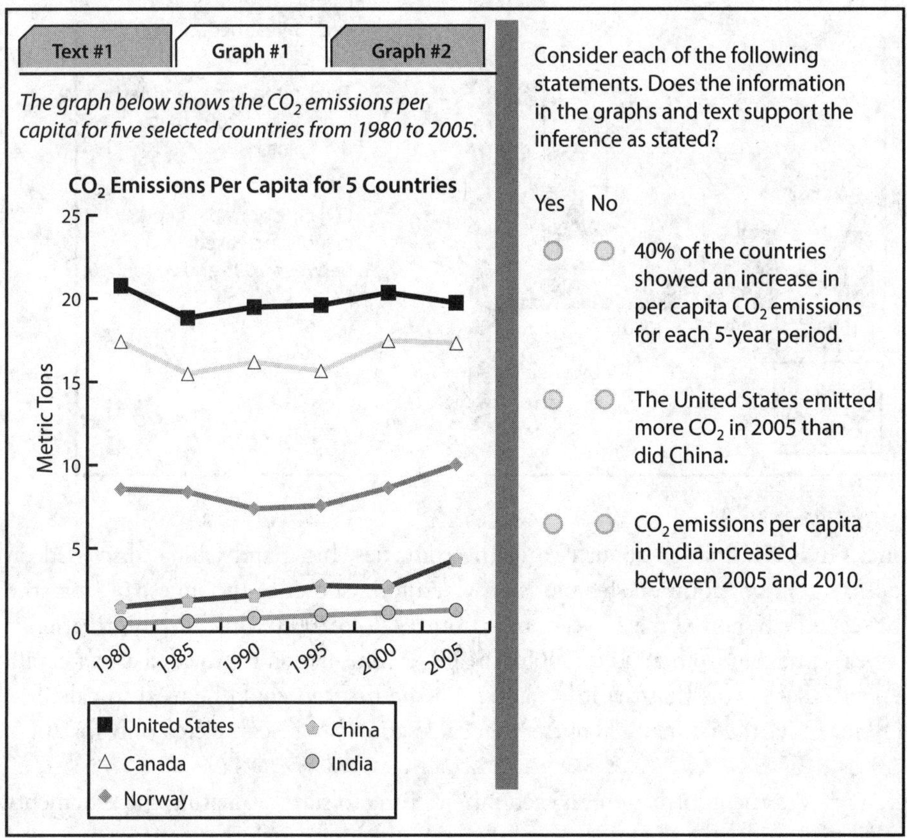


**Make Connections**

As you review the information on each tab, try to find ways that it relates to the information on the other tabs.

This tab shows $CO_2$ emissions for five countries over a 25-year period. Notice that the countries on this tab are the same as the countries on the first tab. It's also important to note that the $CO_2$ emissions on this tab are per capita emissions. Since the first tab provided information about populations for 2005, it would be possible to calculate approximate total $CO_2$ emissions for these five countries for 2005. While you don't necessarily need to consider all the calculations you could perform, thinking about what you could calculate is an excellent way to notice connections between the data provided on the tabs.

Next, let's take a look at the information on the third tab:

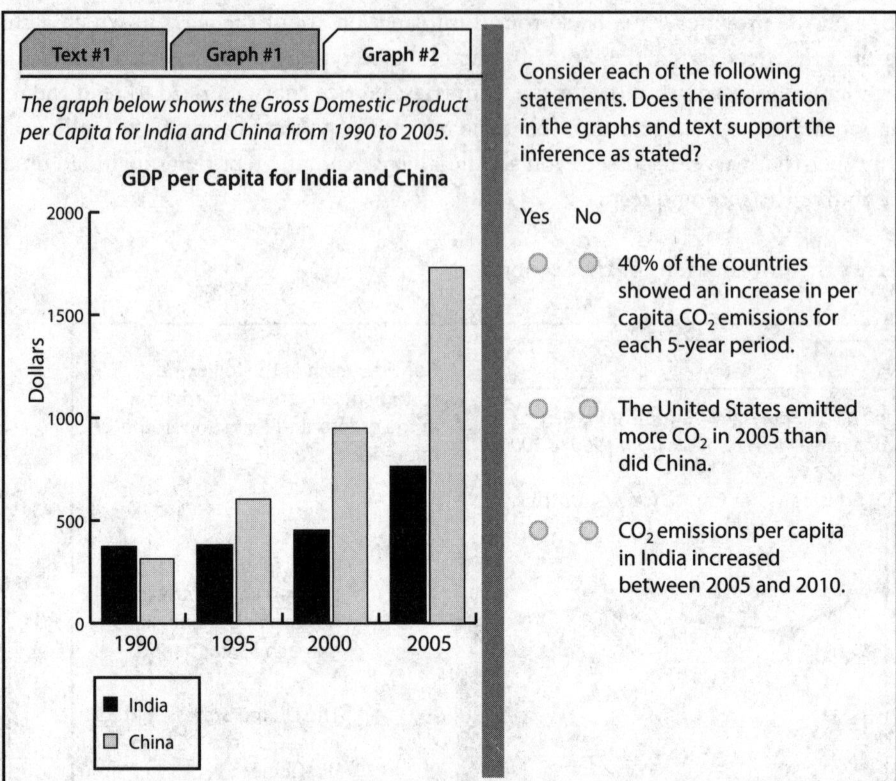


This tab provides GDP information about two of the countries, India and China, discussed on the first two tabs. The information on this tab is provided for a subset of the timespan from the second tab. The second tab showed the 25-year range from 1980 to 2005, while this information is only for the 15-year timespan from 1990 to 2005. The GDP information is provided as per capita information. Again, that means that the information on the first tab could be used to calculate the overall GDP for India and China. Of course, that calculation can be completed only for 2005.

Now that we've reviewed the information on each tab, it's time to start evaluating the statements. But first, we need to consider the directions carefully. The directions state that you are supposed to consider the question "Does the information in the graphs and text support the inference as stated?" Remember our discussion of valid inferences. An inference is a statement that you know to be true because you can back it up with proof.

There are really three cases to consider when evaluating these statements. If the graphs and other information on the tabs are sufficient to show that the statement is true, answer "yes." If the graphs and other information on the tabs are sufficient to show that the statement is false, answer "no." What if there is simply insufficient information to conclusively show that the statement is either true or false? In that case, you answer "no" because the information did not support the inference. In other words, the task here is a little different from simply evaluating whether the statements are true or false. After all, GMAC could have made the answer choices True and False rather than Yes and No.

Remember, however, that most GMAC statements won't try to trick you that way. But, it is important to remember that you need proof to claim that something can be inferred. You will see statements that try to get you to read into or interpret the information. Such activities do not lead to valid inferences!

Let's take a look at the first statement:

> 40% of the countries showed an increase in per capita $CO_2$ emissions for each 5-year period.

The first step in evaluating a statement for a Multi-Source Reasoning question is to determine which tab or tabs contain the information that you need. For this statement, the second tab contains information about per capita $CO_2$ emissions, so select that tab. Next, start checking out the trend lines on the graph. We've reprinted the chart from the second tab below.

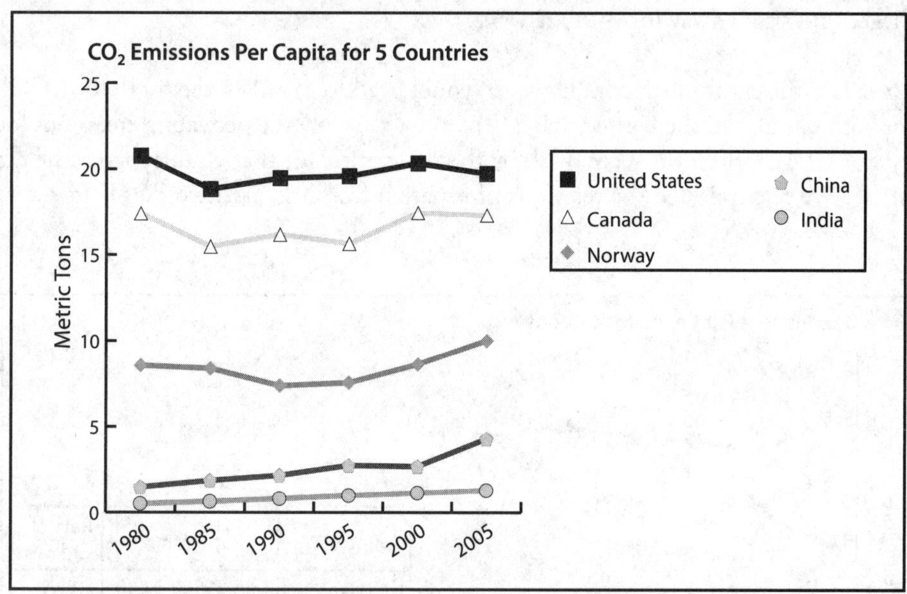


The trend lines for the United States, Canada, and Norway clearly show both increases and decreases between five-year periods, so none of those countries fit the requirements of the statement. The trend line for China needs to be examined carefully. China's $CO_2$ emissions per capita increase for four out of the five five-year periods shown. However, China's emissions decreased slightly between 1995 and 2000. So, China also does not fit the requirements of the statement. Only India's trend line shows an increase for every five-year period depicted on the graph. But that means that only 1 out of 5 or 20% of the countries showed an increase in $CO_2$ emissions for each five-year period. So, the answer to the first statement is "no."

Next, let's take a look at the second statement:

The United States emitted more $CO_2$ in 2005 than did China.

Evaluating this statement is a little trickier than evaluating the first statement. First, be careful of the wording. The statement is about total $CO_2$ emissions rather than the per capita emissions that are shown by the chart on the second tab. So, while the emissions chart does show that per capita emissions for the United States were greater than those for China in 2005, you cannot base your answer only on that piece of information. Remember that the test-writers will try to get you to make hasty conclusions so always check out the wording of the statement carefully.

Since none of the provided charts allows you to simply look up the information for this statement, you need to determine if you have sufficient information to evaluate the statement. To go from per capita $CO_2$ emissions in 2005 to total $CO_2$ emissions in 2005, you need to know the populations for China and the United States in 2005. That information is provided by the table on the first tab. As discussed before, if there had been insufficient information, you could have clicked "no" right away for your answer.

Since there is sufficient information, however, you'll need to calculate the total 2005 $CO_2$ emissions for both China and the United States. To do so, multiply the per capita emissions for each country from the chart on the second tab by the population for that country from the table on the first tab. We've duplicated the relevant information from the first two tabs below.

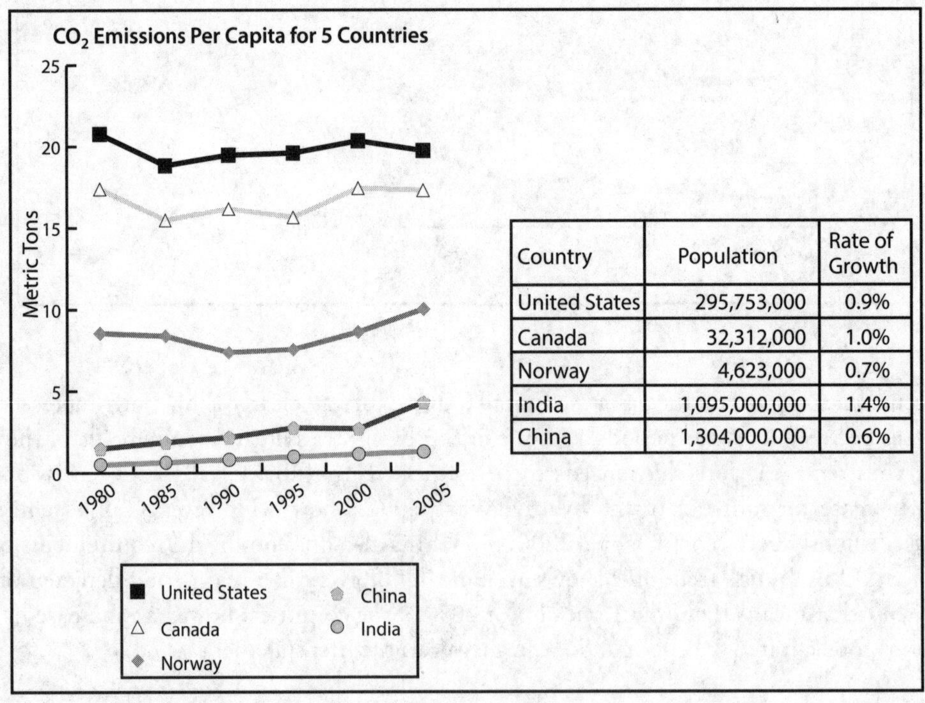


| Country | Population | Rate of Growth |
|---|---|---|
| United States | 295,753,000 | 0.9% |
| Canada | 32,312,000 | 1.0% |
| Norway | 4,623,000 | 0.7% |
| India | 1,095,000,000 | 1.4% |
| China | 1,304,000,000 | 0.6% |

Of course, you won't be able to split the view on your computer screen this way. So, you'll need to write down some of the relevant information on your noteboards. You should use your noteboards to take notes whenever you need information from two different tabs. Simply trying to remember the numbers can cause errors and waste time. For example, to evaluate this statement, you might jot down the 2005 per capita $CO_2$ emissions for the United States and China. Then, go to the first tab to get the population numbers for each country.

For the United States, per capita $CO_2$ emissions in 2005 were approximately 20 metric tons. The U.S. population in 2005 was 295,753,000. So, the total 2005 $CO_2$ emissions for the United States was 20 × 295,753,000 = 5,915,060,000 metric tons. For China, the per capita $CO_2$ emissions are approximately 4.8 and the population was 1,304,000,000. So, China's total $CO_2$ emissions for 2005 were 4.8 × 1,304,000,000 = 6,259,200,000, greater than those of the United States. Therefore, the answer to the second statement is "no."

**Use Your Noteboards**
If the information you need is on two different tabs, use your noteboards to keep track of the information from one of the tabs.

It's time to tackle the third statement:

> $CO_2$ emissions per capita in India increased between 2005 and 2010.

In contrast with the second statement, evaluating this statement is certainly less time-consuming. However, as we'll see, you'll need to remember what is necessary for a valid inference. The necessary information is displayed on the graph on the second tab. Again, we've duplicated the necessary information below.

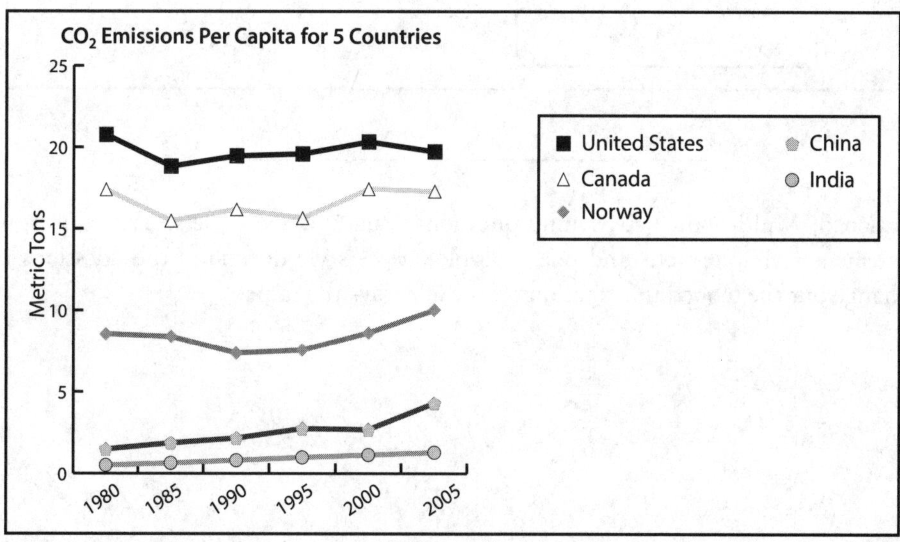


Now it's time to be careful. Notice that the chart displays data only up to 2005. While India's per capita $CO_2$ emissions have shown a steady increase over the 25-year period shown on the chart, that's not sufficient for a valid inference. Since the chart does not display the actual numbers for 2010, the answer to the third statement is "no."

Here's what your answers should look like just before you click next to move on to the next question in the Integrated Reasoning section:

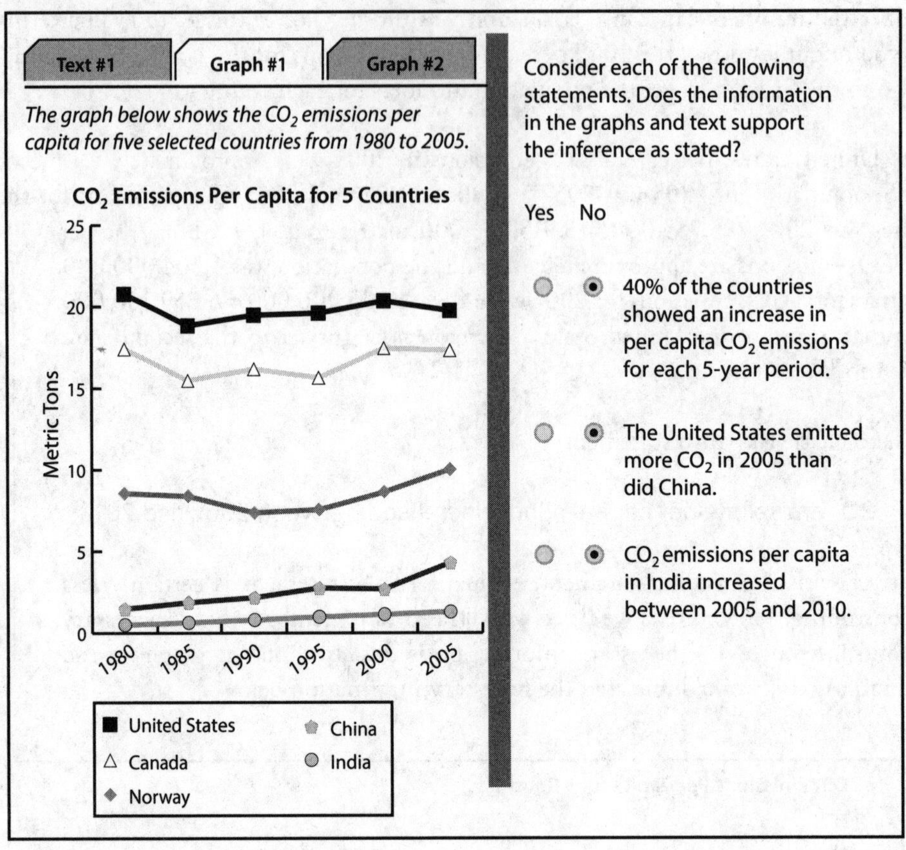


As mentioned, Multi-Source Reasoning questions usually come in sets. Typically, you'll get two statement style questions and one multiple-choice style question. The questions on the right change but the tabbed information on the left stays the same.

Let's take a look at a multiple-choice question for the tabbed information that we just used to evaluate a statement style question.

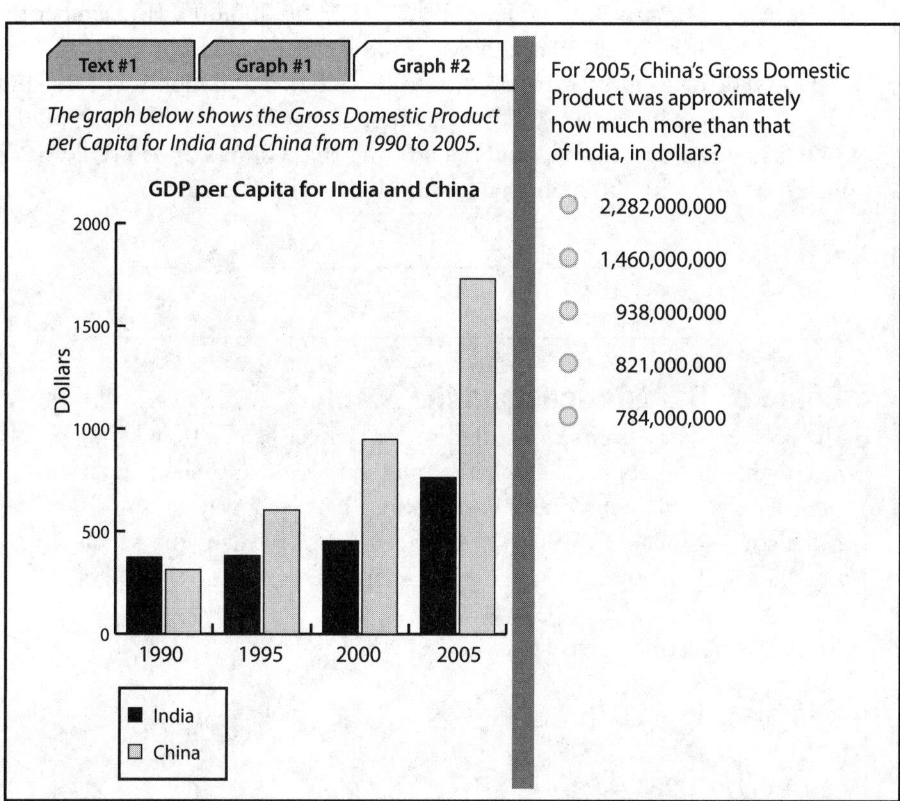


## Here's How to Crack It

As with any other Multi-Source Reasoning question, your first step is to determine which chart or charts contain the relevant data. For this question, you certainly need the bar chart on the third tab because that chart shows information about GDP. The bar chart is shown above. However, the bar chart displays data about GDP per capita and the question asks about overall Gross Domestic Product. So, you'll also need the 2005 population numbers from the table on tab one. We've reproduced the relevant table below.

| Country | Population | Rate of Growth |
|---|---|---|
| United States | 295,753,000 | 0.9% |
| Canada | 32,312,000 | 1.0% |
| Norway | 4,623,000 | 0.7% |
| India | 1,095,000,000 | 1.4% |
| China | 1,304,000,000 | 0.6% |

To answer the question, you need to multiply each country's GDP per capita from 2005 by its population from 2005. Then, subtract India's GDP from that of China.

**Need More Practice?**
Check out *1,138 GMAT Practice Questions, 3rd Edition* for access to 100 more Integrated Reasoning questions!

Based on the bar chart, China's 2005 per capita GDP was approximately \$1,750. Since China's population in 2005 was 1,304,000,000, China's 2005 GDP was approximately \$1,750 × 1,304,000,000 = \$2,282,000,000,000. (Remember that you can use the onscreen calculator to perform the calculation.) For India, the 2005 per capita GDP was approximately \$750, while India's population was 1,095,000,000. That means that India's GDP was approximately \$750 × 1,095,000,000 = \$821,250,000,000. Now, just subtract to find that China's 2005 GDP was approximately \$1,460,750,000 more than that of India. That's closest to (B).

### Complex Calculations and the Memory Keys

The problem just discussed featured several longer calculations. Your calculator at home probably has parentheses, which makes entering such a calculation a one-step operation. Is there a way to do this calculation in one-step using the onscreen GMAT calculator which doesn't have parentheses? Sure, use the memory keys!

Enter the following keystrokes:

1750 * 1304000000 = [MS]

750 * 1095000000 = [+/–] [M+] [MR]

These keystrokes will minimize the number of times you need to enter the large numbers, which helps to avoid errors.

# Summary

- Before you jump into the Integrated Reasoning questions, get your bearings and peruse each tab or piece of information.
- On Table Analysis questions, know that you can sort by only one column at a time. If you think that sorting will help, go for it. But don't waste time devising the perfect order to evaluate statements.
- On Graphics Interpretation questions, start by looking for labels on the axes and finding the legend if there is one.
- On Two-Part Analysis questions, do some algebra or PITA to get to the right answer. Be careful that you select the right button in the right column when answering these questions.
- On Multi-Source Reasoning questions, take a minute to review the information on each tab before you jump in. Think about how the information on one tab relates to the information on other tabs.

# Chapter 26
# Integrated Reasoning: Drills

# PRACTICE INTEGRATED REASONING: SECTION 1

12 Items

Time limit: 30 minutes

This section is a full practice Integrated Reasoning section. Please note that some questions are laid out slightly differently in this book versus what you'll see on the GMAT. Many of the new question formats are interactive. Hence, only approximations can be printed. Specifically,

- Table Analysis questions are shown with a main sort and several alternate sorts. You may not need every sort.
- Graphics Interpretation questions include drop-down boxes. In this book, the box is shown as a fill-in blank and the answers are printed below the blank.
- For Multi-Source Reasoning questions, we've printed what's on each tab consecutively on the page.
- For some questions, you'll see (A), (B), (C), (D), and (E) next to the answer choices. These are included only to make it easier to check your work. These do not appear on the real GMAT.

We've included answers to this section starting on page 618 (Part VII).

## Item 1:

| Subway Station | Riders | % Change | Connecting Subway Lines |
|---|---|---|---|
| Times Square/42nd St. | 58,422,597 | 0.6% | 11 |
| Grand Central/42nd St. | 41,903,210 | –0.2% | 5 |
| 34th St./Herald Square | 37,769,752 | 2.2% | 7 |
| 14th St./Union Square | 34,730,692 | 1.4% | 7 |
| 34th St./Penn Station (Red Lines) | 26,892,243 | –1.1% | 3 |
| 34th St./Penn Station (Blue Lines) | 24,265,016 | 0.3% | 3 |
| 59th St/Columbus Circle | 20,711,058 | 1.4% | 5 |
| Lexington Ave/59th St | 19,553,597 | 3.3% | 6 |
| 86th St. (Green Lines) | 19,147,021 | 1.4% | 3 |

The table above gives information on the ridership in 9 subway stations in New York City for the year 2010. The subway stations were chosen for inclusion in the table because they were the busiest stations in 2010, based on the number of passengers entering the station. In addition to annual ridership (number of passengers) for each station in 2010, the table also gives the percent increase or decrease in ridership from 2009 to 2010 and the number of subway lines that connect to the station.

Each column of the table can be sorted in ascending order by clicking on the word "Select" above the table and choosing, from the drop-down menu, the heading of the column on which you want the table to be sorted.

Alternate Sort 1: *% Change*

| Subway Station | Riders | % Change | Connecting Subway Lines |
|---|---|---|---|
| 34th St./Penn Station (Red Lines) | 26,892,243 | –1.1% | 3 |
| Grand Central/42nd St. | 41,903,210 | –0.2% | 5 |
| 34th St./Penn Station (Blue Lines) | 24,265,016 | 0.3% | 3 |
| Times Square/42nd St | 58,422,597 | 0.6% | 11 |
| 14th St./Union Square | 34,730,692 | 1.4% | 7 |
| 59th St/Columbus Circle | 20,711,058 | 1.4% | 5 |
| 86th St. (Green Lines) | 19,147,021 | 1.4% | 3 |
| 34th St./Herald Square | 37,769,752 | 2.2% | 7 |
| Lexington Ave/59th St | 19,553,597 | 3.3% | 6 |

Alternate Sort 2: *Connecting Subway Lines*

| Subway Station | Riders | % Change | Connecting Subway Lines |
|---|---|---|---|
| 34th St./Penn Station (Red Lines) | 26,892,243 | –1.1% | 3 |
| 34th St./Penn Station (Blue Lines) | 24,265,016 | 0.3% | 3 |
| 86th St. (Green Lines) | 19,147,021 | 1.4% | 3 |
| Grand Central/42nd St. | 41,903,210 | –0.2% | 5 |
| 59th St/Columbus Circle | 20,711,058 | 1.4% | 5 |
| Lexington Ave/59th St | 19,553,597 | 3.3% | 6 |
| 14th St./Union Square | 34,730,692 | 1.4% | 7 |
| 34th St./Herald Square | 37,769,752 | 2.2% | 7 |
| Times Square/42nd St | 58,422,597 | 0.6% | 11 |

Consider each of the following statements about the subway stations. For each statement indicate whether the statement is true or false, based on the information provided in the table.

| | True | False | |
|---|---|---|---|
| Question 1-1 | O | O | The station with the median rank based on annual ridership is also the station with the greatest decrease in annual ridership from 2009 to 2010. |
| Question 1-2 | O | O | The ratio of the average (arithmetic mean) number of riders in 2010 for those subway stations having 5 connecting lines to those having 3 connecting lines is approximately 4:3. |
| Question 1-3 | O | O | The station with the greatest percent increase in riders from 2009 to 2010 had the least annual ridership in 2010. |

## Item 2:

Frank researched the 45 doctors in his local area and found that 8 of them graduated from medical school with honors, but that the services of only 3 of those 8 doctors are covered by his medical plan. He also found that 27 doctors whose services are covered by his medical plan graduated from medical school without honors.

In the table below, for the doctors in Frank's local area, identify the total number of doctors whose services are not covered by Frank's medical plan, and identify the number of doctors who both graduated from medical school without honors and whose services are not covered by Frank's health plan. Make only one selection in each column.

| Services Not Covered by Medical Plan | Graduated Without Honors and Services Not Covered by Medical Plan | Total Number |
|---|---|---|
| (A) ○ | ○ | 10 |
| (B) ○ | ○ | 15 |
| (C) ○ | ○ | 18 |
| (D) ○ | ○ | 30 |
| (E) ○ | ○ | 37 |
| (F) ○ | ○ | 40 |

## Item 3:

A flower market sells orchids for $1.35 and dahlias for $1.80. Faustino spends $18.00 on orchids and dahlias.

In the table below, choose the number of orchids and the number of dahlias that are consistent with the amount spent by Faustino. Make only one selection in each column.

| Orchids | Dahlias | Number Purchased |
|---|---|---|
| (A) ○ | ○ | 0 |
| (B) ○ | ○ | 2 |
| (C) ○ | ○ | 4 |
| (D) ○ | ○ | 5 |
| (E) ○ | ○ | 6 |
| (F) ○ | ○ | 8 |

## Item 4:

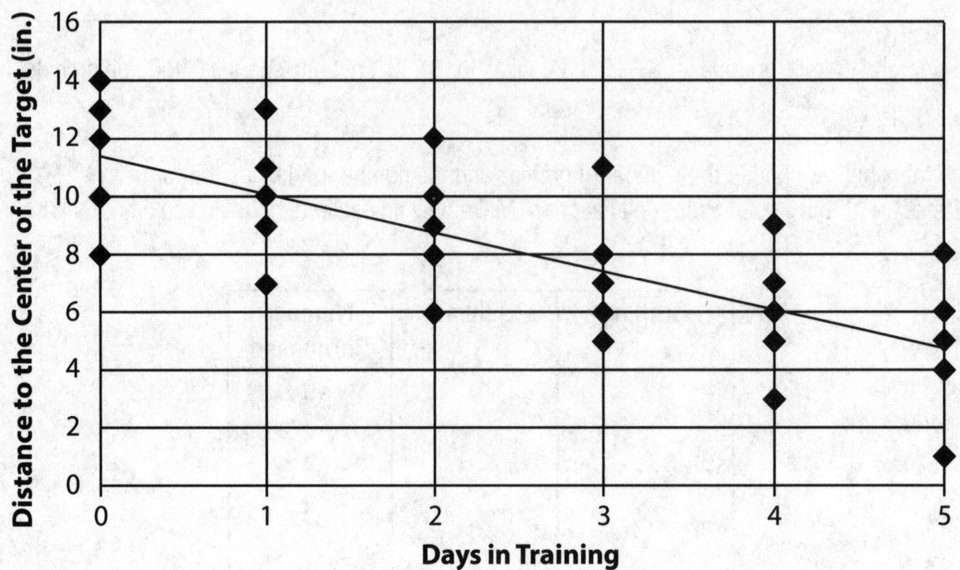


At a certain archery school, each of five students shot a single arrow at the end of each day of training, as well as one arrow before the first day of training. The graph above is a scatterplot, in which each of the 30 points represents the distance from the center of the target to each student's arrow and the number of days the student had been in training at the time the arrow was shot. The solid line is the regression line. Use the drop-down menus to fill in the blanks in each of the following statements based on the information given by the graph.

## Question 4-1:

The slope of the regression line is closest to ________.

(A) –2.6
(B) –1.3
(C) –0.8
(D) 1.2
(E) 2.9

## Question 4-2:

The number of students within 11 inches of the center of the target is ________ after day 2 of training than before any training.

(A) 50% less
(B) 25% less
(C) 50% greater
(D) 100% greater
(E) 200% greater

## Item 5:

The earliest known evidence of seafaring by human ancestors dates to approximately 130,000 years ago. However, in 2010, archaeologists discovered stone tools on the coast of a Mediterranean island that date to the Paleolithic Age (about 2.6 million years ago). Because the Mediterranean Sea, which is more than 40 miles of open water, separates the island from Greece, the archaeologists theorized that some human ancestors developed nautical skills millions of years earlier than previously discovered.

## Question 5-1:

In the table below, identify which statement, if true, most strengthens the argument above, and which statement, if true, most seriously weakens the argument above.

| | Strengthen | Weaken | Statement |
|---|---|---|---|
| (A) | ○ | ○ | In the same area of the island, archaeologists discovered pieces of ancient harpoons and spears used for fishing. |
| (B) | ○ | ○ | The stone tools resemble those made and used by *Homo erectus* and *Homo heidelbergensis*, human ancestors in the Paleolithic Era who lived on the mainland of Greece. |
| (C) | ○ | ○ | The stone tools were probably used primarily for skinning animals. |
| (D) | ○ | ○ | It would be impossible to construct a seaworthy boat solely from the tools discovered by the archaeologists. |
| (E) | ○ | ○ | The Mediterranean Sea dried up approximately 5 million years ago and remained that way for 3 million years. |
| (F) | ○ | ○ | The stone tools were likely used for purposes other than construction of boats or rafts. |

There is no testing material on this page.

# Data for Items 6, 7, and 8:

CD Offerings | **Memo**

This table provides the standard interest rates offered by Central Bank for CDs, listed according to term offering and purchase amount. The interest rates listed are annual rates, compounded annually, to be paid when the CD comes to term. No bonuses or other adjustments are included.

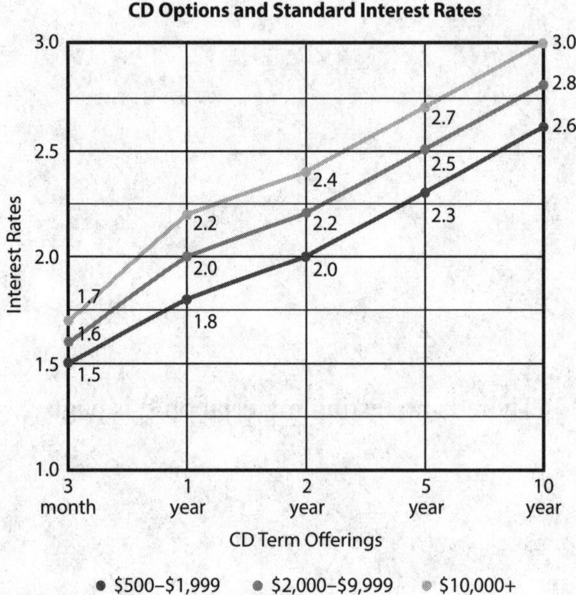


**CD Offerings** | Memo

General memo to employees of Central Bank:

January 15th

In order to improve and stabilize our bank's investment opportunities, we are seeking to shift the balance of our customers' CD accounts towards those with longer maturity terms. We have begun testing two incentive programs. All CDs purchased with terms of at least 5 years now receive, as a bonus, an additional 0.1% interest during the first year to be added to the standard rate. Moreover, preferred customers (those who have previously bought CDs of any term length in amounts of $10,000 or more) will receive a bonus of 0.2% during the first year when they purchase a CD with a term of 5 or 10 years in the amount of at least $10,000. Other CDs continue at the standard rates.

We have also revised the schedule of penalties for early withdrawal and made these applicable to all new CDs. The penalties are as follows: For any CD, early withdrawal less than a year after the CD is purchased results in a loss of all interest. For 2-year CDs, early withdrawal after the first year results in the loss of one year of interest. For 5-year and 10-year CDs, withdrawal after the first year results in the loss of two years of interest and of any accrued bonus interest.

## Item 6:

Determine whether each of the following investments will earn at least $250 of interest in its first year.

| | Yes | No | |
|---|---|---|---|
| Question 6-1 | O | O | $11,000 invested by a new customer in a 1-year CD |
| Question 6-2 | O | O | $9,500 invested by a preferred customer in a 5-year CD |
| Question 6-3 | O | O | $9,500 invested by a new customer in a 10-year CD |

## Item 7:

Determine whether each of these transactions will, according to the new rules and rates described, yield a total interest payment of between $500 and $600.

| | Yes | No | |
|---|---|---|---|
| Question 7-1 | O | O | A new customer's $20,000 1-year CD held for the complete term |
| Question 7-2 | O | O | A new customer's $4,000 5-year CD held for the complete term |
| Question 7-3 | O | O | A preferred customer's $10,000 2-year CD held for the complete term |

## Item 8:

Consider each of the following statements. Does the information in the memo and the table support the inference as stated?

| | Yes | No | |
|---|---|---|---|
| Question 8-1 | O | O | Prior to the policy changes described, there were no penalties for early CD withdrawals. |
| Question 8-2 | O | O | Certain bank policies are designed to reward preferred customers for their loyalty. |
| Question 8-3 | O | O | If the bank accomplishes its stated intentions, it will likely pay a higher average (arithmetic mean) interest rate to customers than if it does not. |

## Item 9:

| Year of Election | President | Political Party | Popular Vote (millions) | % of Popular Vote | Electoral Vote | % of Electoral Vote |
|---|---|---|---|---|---|---|
| 1960 | John Kennedy | Democratic | 34.2 | 49.72% | 303 | 56.40% |
| 1964 | Lyndon Johnson | Democratic | 43.1 | 61.05% | 486 | 90.30% |
| 1968 | Richard Nixon | Republican | 31.8 | 43.42% | 301 | 55.90% |
| 1972 | Richard Nixon | Republican | 47.2 | 60.67% | 520 | 96.70% |
| 1976 | James Carter | Democratic | 40.8 | 50.08% | 297 | 55.20% |
| 1980 | Ronald Reagan | Republican | 43.9 | 50.75% | 489 | 90.90% |
| 1984 | Ronald Reagan | Republican | 54.5 | 58.77% | 525 | 97.60% |
| 1988 | George Bush | Republican | 48.9 | 53.37% | 426 | 79.20% |
| 1992 | William Clinton | Democratic | 44.9 | 43.01% | 370 | 68.80% |
| 1996 | William Clinton | Democratic | 47.4 | 49.23% | 379 | 70.40% |
| 2000 | George W. Bush | Republican | 50.5 | 47.87% | 271 | 50.40% |
| 2004 | George W. Bush | Republican | 62.0 | 50.73% | 286 | 53.20% |
| 2008 | Barack Obama | Democratic | 69.5 | 52.87% | 365 | 67.80% |

The table above gives information about the voting patterns in United States presidential elections from 1960 to 2008. In addition to giving the name and the political party of the president elected in each year, the table provides the total popular vote and electoral vote that the winner received in that election, as well as the percentage of the total vote that each figure represents.
Each column of the table can be sorted in ascending order by clicking on the word "Select" above the table and choosing, from the drop-down menu, the heading of the column on which you want the table to be sorted.

Alternate Sort 1: *Electoral Vote*

| Year of Election | President | Political Party | Popular Vote (millions) | % of Popular Vote | Electoral Vote | % of Electoral Vote |
|---|---|---|---|---|---|---|
| 2000 | George W. Bush | Republican | 50.5 | 47.87% | 271 | 50.40% |
| 2004 | George W. Bush | Republican | 62.0 | 50.73% | 286 | 53.20% |
| 1976 | James Carter | Democratic | 40.8 | 50.08% | 297 | 55.20% |
| 1968 | Richard Nixon | Republican | 31.8 | 43.42% | 301 | 55.90% |
| 1960 | John Kennedy | Democratic | 34.2 | 49.72% | 303 | 56.40% |
| 2008 | Barack Obama | Democratic | 69.5 | 52.87% | 365 | 67.80% |
| 1992 | William Clinton | Democratic | 44.9 | 43.01% | 370 | 68.80% |
| 1996 | William Clinton | Democratic | 47.4 | 49.23% | 379 | 70.40% |
| 1988 | George Bush | Republican | 48.9 | 53.37% | 426 | 79.20% |
| 1964 | Lyndon Johnson | Democratic | 43.1 | 61.05% | 486 | 90.30% |
| 1980 | Ronald Reagan | Republican | 43.9 | 50.75% | 489 | 90.90% |
| 1972 | Richard Nixon | Republican | 47.2 | 60.67% | 520 | 96.70% |
| 1984 | Ronald Reagan | Republican | 54.4 | 58.77% | 525 | 97.60% |

Alternate Sort 2: *Percent of Popular Vote*

| Year of Election | President | Political Party | Popular Vote (millions) | % of Popular Vote | Electoral Vote | % of Electoral Vote |
|---|---|---|---|---|---|---|
| 1992 | William Clinton | Democratic | 44.9 | 43.01% | 370 | 68.80% |
| 1968 | Richard Nixon | Republican | 31.8 | 43.42% | 301 | 55.90% |
| 2000 | George W. Bush | Republican | 50.5 | 47.87% | 271 | 50.40% |
| 1996 | William Clinton | Democratic | 47.4 | 49.23% | 379 | 70.40% |
| 1960 | John Kennedy | Democratic | 34.2 | 49.72% | 303 | 56.40% |
| 1976 | James Carter | Democratic | 40.8 | 50.08% | 297 | 55.20% |
| 2004 | George W. Bush | Republican | 62.0 | 50.73% | 286 | 53.20% |
| 1980 | Ronald Reagan | Republican | 43.9 | 50.75% | 489 | 90.90% |
| 2008 | Barack Obama | Democratic | 69.5 | 52.87% | 365 | 67.80% |
| 1988 | George Bush | Republican | 48.9 | 53.37% | 426 | 79.20% |
| 1984 | Ronald Reagan | Republican | 54.4 | 58.77% | 525 | 97.60% |
| 1972 | Richard Nixon | Republican | 47.2 | 60.67% | 520 | 96.70% |
| 1964 | Lyndon Johnson | Democratic | 43.1 | 61.05% | 486 | 90.30% |

Consider each of the following statements about the Presidential election data. For each statement, indicate whether the statement is true or false, based on the information provided in the table.

| | True | False | |
|---|---|---|---|
| Question 9-1 | ○ | ○ | Of those presidents elected for two terms, William Clinton had the smallest percent increase in popular vote between the two years. |
| Question 9-2 | ○ | ○ | The average (arithmetic mean) number of electoral votes received by Democratic presidents was greater than the average number of electoral votes received by Republican presidents. |
| Question 9-3 | ○ | ○ | The same president was elected in the two election years in which the winner's percentage of the popular vote and percentage of the electoral vote were most nearly equal. |

# Data for Items 10, 11, and 12:

Memo #1 | Memo #2 | Email #1

MEMORANDUM
TO: Regional Office Managers
FROM: Chief Operations Officer
RE: Travel planning

Once again, our annual management retreat will be held in Bloomsbury. In preparation for this year's retreat, all Regional Office Managers (ROMs) will be responsible for arranging the travel reservations for all Level 2 managers within his or her Region. You may delegate that task should you wish.

ROMs will receive a research memorandum from the Logistics Division providing the average (arithmetic mean) airfare from the 6 Regions to Bloomsbury. While ROMs should use that average airfare as a guide, we anticipate that there may be some variation in ticket prices based upon the specifics of travel arrangements. As such, Regional offices will be reimbursed for the full cost of any plane ticket priced within 1 (one) standard deviation of the average airfare from its region to Bloomsbury, inclusive. For any ticket priced more than 1 (one) standard deviation above the mean, regional offices will be reimbursed up to the average airfare from your region to Bloomsbury. For any ticket priced 1 (one) standard deviation or more below average, in addition to full reimbursement of the ticket cost, regional offices will receive a "Budget Bonus" of 50% of the difference between the ticket price and the average airfare from your region to Bloomsbury.

Memo #1 | Memo #2 | Email #1

MEMORANDUM
TO: Regional Office Managers
FROM: Logistics Division
RE: Airfare Research

The attached chart lists the average (arithmetic mean) airfare from the listed Regions to Bloomsbury. The mean airfare was calculated based upon taking a normally distributed sample of airfares. The standard deviation and size of each sample is also listed in the chart.

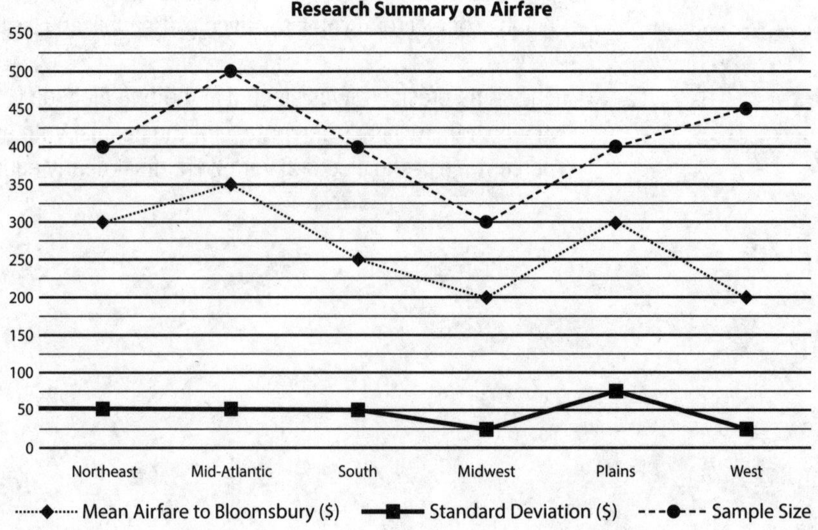


*(See the next page for additional information)*

Memo #1 | Memo #2 | Email #1

*Email from Marco Roland, Human Resources Manager, West Region to Marisa Cortland, Regional Office Manager, West Region*

Dear Marisa,

Tickets have been purchased for all of the Level 2 Managers in the West Region. Below is a summary:

| Airfare | Number of Tickets Purchased |
|---|---|
| $150 | 18 |
| $210 | 4 |
| $230 | 8 |

Best,

Marco

## Item 10:

Consider each of the following statements. Select *Yes* if the information contained in the two memoranda and the email support the inference as stated. Otherwise, select *No*.

| | Yes | No | |
|---|---|---|---|
| Question 10-1 | O | O | No region had a lower average (arithmetic mean) airfare to Bloomsbury than the Midwest. |
| Question 10-2 | O | O | Only Level 2 managers will attend the management retreat. |
| Question 10-3 | O | O | The Regional Office Manager need not make the reservations personally. |

## Item 11:

Consider each of the following statements. Based upon the information contained in the two memoranda and the email, determine whether each statement is true or false as stated.

| | True | False | |
|---|---|---|---|
| Question 11-1 | O | O | The West Region will receive a "Budget Bonus" of $450. |
| Question 11-2 | O | O | The two regions with the least sample size also had the least difference between the most and least expensive airfare found during research. |
| Question 11-3 | O | O | The combined mean airfare of all the researched regions is less than the mean airfare for three of the regions individually. |

## Item 12:

If one of the tickets purchased by the West Region's Level 2 managers were selected at random, what is the probability that it is eligible to be fully reimbursed?

(A) $\frac{4}{15}$

(B) $\frac{9}{15}$

(C) $\frac{11}{15}$

(D) $\frac{12}{15}$

(E) $\frac{14}{15}$

# PRACTICE INTEGRATED REASONING: SECTION 2

12 Items

Time limit: 30 minutes

This section is a full practice Integrated Reasoning section. Please note that some questions are laid out slightly differently in this book versus what you'll see on the GMAT. Many of the new question formats are interactive. Hence, only approximations can be printed. Specifically,

- Table Analysis questions are shown with a main sort and several alternate sorts. You may not need every sort.
- Graphics Interpretation questions include drop-down boxes. In this book, the box is shown as a fill-in blank and the answers printed below the blank.
- For Multi-Source Reasoning questions, we've printed what's on each tab consecutively on the page.
- For some questions, you'll see (A), (B), (C), (D), and (E) next to the answer choices. These are included only to make it easier to check your work. These do not appear on the real GMAT.

We've included answers to this section starting on page 625 (Part VII).

## Item 1:

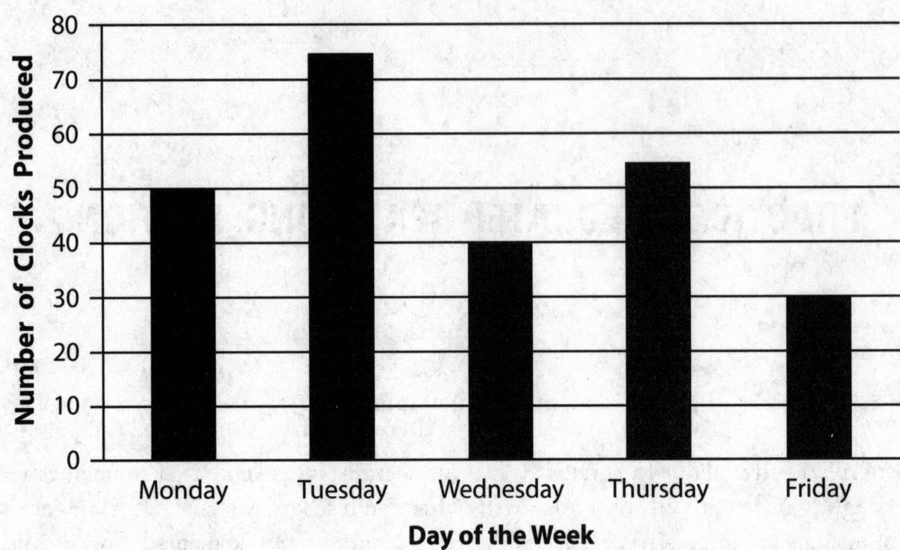


The graph above gives the daily output for five days at a certain clock factory. Use the drop-down menus to fill in the blanks in each of the following statements based on the information given by the graph.

## Question 1-1:

The ratio of the number of clocks produced on Tuesday to those produced on Wednesday is approximately _________.

(A) 15 to 8
(B) 12 to 7
(C) 10 to 9
(D) 8 to 11
(E) 5 to 13

## Question 1-2:

The total number of clocks produced on Monday and Wednesday is approximately _________ of the number of clocks produced for all five days.

(A) 16%
(B) 20%
(C) 28%
(D) 36%
(E) 45%

## Item 2:

Company X: Our company's computer technology is out of date. We will be unable to compete effectively in the modern economy if we are not using current computer technology. We have decided to purchase new computers that run Portals 8, the newest version of the world's best-selling operating system, throughout the entire company.

Technology Consultant: We agree that Company X needs to purchase new computers, but instead of installing Portals 8, Company X should purchase GreenCap, our consulting firm's proprietary operating system. The initial purchase of a GreenCap operating system costs substantially less than does Portals 8, and it provides the same functionality with current computer technology. With the money saved, Company X will be better able to compete effectively in the modern economy.

In the table below, identify which statement, if true, most weakens Company X's argument, and which statement, if true, most weakens the Technology Consultant's argument.

| Weakens Company X | Weakens Technology Consultant | Statement |
|---|---|---|
| (A) ○ | ○ | GreenCap makes more efficient use of computer resources than does Portals 8. |
| (B) ○ | ○ | GreenCap is not the most cutting-edge software available on the market. |
| (C) ○ | ○ | Although Portals 8 was released this year, GreenCap has been available for three years. |
| (D) ○ | ○ | GreenCap requires purchase of an annual maintenance agreement, making it more expensive overall than Portals 8. |
| (E) ○ | ○ | Portals 8 is available in several different versions with different price levels, depending on the proposed use of the operating system. |
| (F) ○ | ○ | Portals 8, which was newly released, contains bugs and design flaws that will impair Company X's ability to compete in the modern economy. |

There is no testing material on this page.

## Item 3:

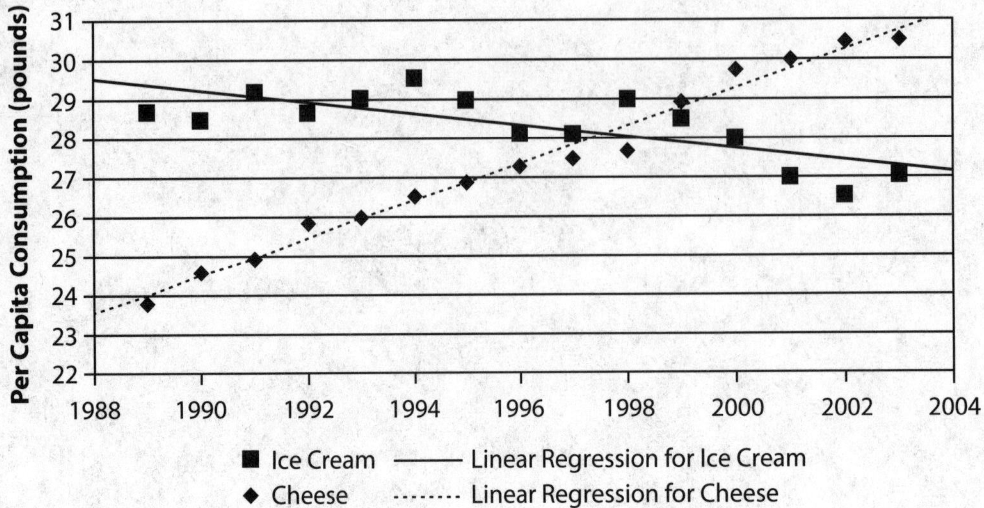


The graph above is a scatterplot with 30 points, each representing the per capita consumption, in pounds, of ice cream and cheese for the years 1989 through 2003 in the United States. The solid line is a regression line for the points representing the per capita consumption of ice cream. The dashed line is a regression line for the points representing the per capita consumption of cheese. Use the drop-down menus to fill in the blanks in each of the following statements based on the information given by the graph.

## Question 3-1:

For the year with the lowest total per capita consumption of both ice cream and cheese combined, the ratio of per capita ice cream consumption to per capita cheese consumption is approximately ________ .

(A) 2 to 3
(B) 3 to 2
(C) 6 to 5
(D) 5 to 6

## Question 3-2:

The slope of the regression line for ice cream is ________ the slope of the regression line for cheese.

(A) greater than
(B) less than
(C) equal to

## Item 4:

XM Representative: Your federal committee thoroughly reviews all of the geo-engineering industry's planned projects and approves only those that meet your guidelines for safety and environmental impact. Since less than two percent of XM projects have ever been rejected, the costly and time-consuming review should be waived so that our latest project can be passed and implemented quickly.

Committee Member: Your request fails to consider that the decisions of our board affect not only the corporation involved, but also the entire field. If we fail to review your project, we also fail to observe innovations in geo-engineering that may need guidelines drafted for the safety of subsequent projects throughout the industry.

In the table below, please identify the additional evidence that most strengthens and the additional evidence that most weakens the committee member's response to the XM representative.

| Strengthens Committee Member's Response | Weakens Committee Member's Response | Additional Evidence |
|---|---|---|
| (A) ○ | ○ | XM's latest project is nearly identical to a previous project by XM that had successfully passed the committee review process. |
| (B) ○ | ○ | The geo-engineering corporation CL, which is XM's biggest competitor, has had less than one percent of its projects rejected by the committee. |
| (C) ○ | ○ | Once a geo-engineering innovation has been passed by the committee, the same innovation is automatically approved in all subsequent projects, without further review. |
| (D) ○ | ○ | Many of XM's geo-engineering projects are peer-reviewed within the industry before they are submitted to the federal committee. |
| (E) ○ | ○ | Geo-engineering is a hazardous field that deserves careful monitoring. |
| (F) ○ | ○ | The federal committee has had to reverse some of its decisions on past projects. |

## Item 5:

A group of entomologists estimates that the population of Insect Species X is decreasing at a constant rate of 10% per year, while the population of Insect Species Y is decreasing at a constant rate of 15% per year. Based on these estimates, in four years, the two species will have equal populations, rounded to the nearest million.

In the table below, identify a number for the current population of Insect Species X, in millions, and a number for the current population of Insect Species Y, in millions, that is consistent with the entomologists' estimates.

| Insect Species X | Insect Species Y | Current Populations (in millions) |
|---|---|---|
| (A) O | O | 450 |
| (B) O | O | 525 |
| (C) O | O | 565 |
| (D) O | O | 600 |
| (E) O | O | 625 |
| (F) O | O | 770 |

# Data for Items 6, 7, and 8:

**Email #1** | **Email #2** | **Memo #1**

*Email from Marketing Director to Marketing Researcher on October 4, 2011.*

As you know, our revenues have declined for each of the past three quarters. To address this issue, I suggest that we initiate a massive advertising buy. On three separate occasions, in 1978, 1987, and 1993, we responded to revenue decreases by increasing our advertising expenditures by 30%. On all three occasions, our revenues began to increase again within one quarter. Therefore, if we increase the number of advertisements targeted at our top consumers by 30%, we will once again increase our revenues.

Since our top consumers are females aged 15–25, determine the top two television programs watched by that group. Also, research the prices for a 30-second commercial for each television program.

**Email #1** | **Email #2** | **Memo #1**

*Email from Marketing Researcher to Marketing Director on October 10, 2011.*

We've hit a slight complication in our research. While we've had no problem determining the top two programs and advertising prices for each, we've realized that there is a fair amount of overlap between the viewers of the two programs. We've found that 80% of the viewers who are females aged 15–25 for *Hart Attack* also watch *Blonde Fury*.

I'll send you the chart summarizing the audience size and advertising prices tomorrow.

**Email #1** | **Email #2** | **Memo #1**

MEMORANDUM
TO: Marketing Director
FROM: Marketing Researcher
DATE: October 11, 2011
RE: Market Research Results

The attached chart presents the results from our research on the top 2 television programs watched by females aged 15–25.

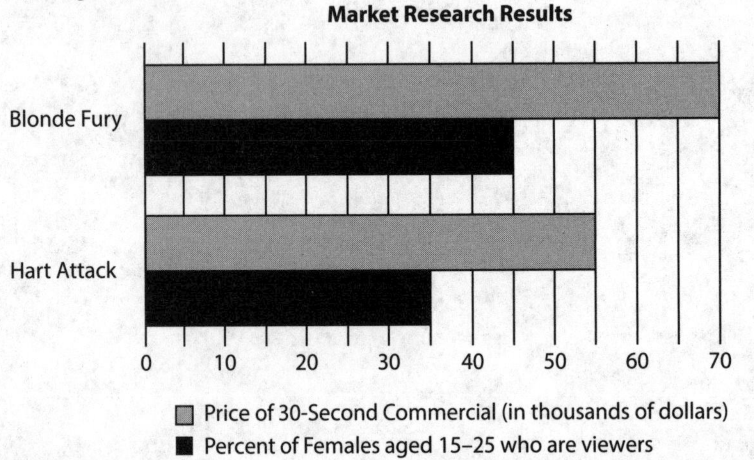

## Item 6:

Consider each of the following statements. Select *Yes* if the information contained in the two emails and the memorandum support the inference as stated. Otherwise, select *No.*

| | Yes | No | |
|---|---|---|---|
| Question 6-1 | O | O | No age and gender group watches *Blonde Fury* more frequently than do females aged 15–25. |
| Question 6-2 | O | O | Thirty second advertisements are more expensive for programs with larger audiences. |
| Question 6-3 | O | O | The ratio of female viewers aged 15 to 25 to dollars spent on advertising for *Hart Attack* is greater than that for *Blonde Fury.* |

## Item 7:

If there are 20,000,000 females aged 15–25, then how many females aged 15–25 (in millions) watch neither *Blonde Fury* nor *Hart Attack*?

(A) 1.4
(B) 4.0
(C) 5.6
(D) 9.6
(E) 11.2

## Item 8:

Consider each of the following statements. Based on the information contained in the two emails and the memorandum, select *Yes* if the statement is an assumption made by the Marketing Director. Otherwise, select *No.*

| | Yes | No | |
|---|---|---|---|
| Question 8-1 | O | O | It is possible for a strategy that succeeded in the past to succeed again. |
| Question 8-2 | O | O | The previous increases in revenues were attributable at least in part to the effect of increased advertising. |
| Question 8-3 | O | O | Increasing the number of advertisements has a similar effect on revenues, to increasing the amount of money spent on advertising expenditures. |

## Item 9:

| Name | Population 2010 | Population 2050 | % of Population Foreign-Born |
|---|---|---|---|
| Andorra | 84,000 | 75,000 | 77.25 |
| Australia | 22,729,000 | 29,013,000 | 19.93 |
| Barbados | 273,000 | 282,000 | 9.31 |
| Brazil | 190,733,000 | 260,692,000 | 0.34 |
| Canada | 34,611,000 | 41,136,000 | 18.76 |
| China | 1,399,725,000 | 1,303,723,000 | 0.29 |
| Egypt | 80,942,000 | 137,873,000 | 0.22 |
| France | 65,822,000 | 69,768,000 | 10.18 |
| India | 1,210,193,000 | 1,656,554,000 | 0.52 |
| Indonesia | 237,556,000 | 313,021,000 | 0.07 |
| Kazakhstan | 16,518,000 | 15,100,000 | 16.88 |
| Laos | 6,230,000 | 10,069,000 | 0.42 |
| Nauru | 10,000 | 12,000 | 38.45 |
| Portugal | 10,637,000 | 9,933,000 | 7.2 |
| Republic of the Congo | 4,043,000 | 9,599,000 | 7.2 |
| Russia | 142,914,000 | 109,187,000 | 8.48 |
| Suriname | 525,000 | 617,000 | 1.11 |
| United Kingdom | 62,436,000 | 71,154,000 | 8.98 |
| United States | 312,399,000 | 439,010,000 | 21.81 |

The table above gives 2010 populations based on UN estimates and 2050 populations based on UN projections for 19 selected countries. The table also gives the UN estimates of the percentage of the population that is foreign-born for each country in 2010.

Each column of the table can be sorted in ascending order by clicking on the word "Select" above the table and choosing, from the drop-down menu, the heading of the column on which you want the table to be sorted.

Alternate Sort 1: *Population 2010*

| Name | Population 2010 | Projected Population 2050 | % of Population Foreign-Born |
|---|---|---|---|
| Nauru | 10,000 | 12,000 | 38.45 |
| Andorra | 84,000 | 75,000 | 77.25 |
| Barbados | 273,000 | 282,000 | 9.31 |
| Suriname | 525,000 | 617,000 | 1.11 |
| Republic of the Congo | 4,043,000 | 9,599,000 | 7.2 |
| Laos | 6,230,000 | 10,069,000 | 0.42 |
| Portugal | 10,637,000 | 9,993,000 | 7.2 |
| Kazakhstan | 16,518,000 | 15,100,000 | 16.88 |
| Australia | 22,729,000 | 29,013,000 | 19.93 |
| Canada | 34,611,000 | 41,136,000 | 18.76 |
| United Kingdom | 62,436,000 | 71,154,000 | 8.98 |
| France | 65,822,000 | 69,768,000 | 10.18 |
| Egypt | 80,942,000 | 137,873,000 | 0.22 |
| Russia | 142,914,000 | 109,187,000 | 8.48 |
| Brazil | 190,733,000 | 260,692,000 | 0.34 |
| Indonesia | 237,556,000 | 313,021,000 | 0.07 |
| United States | 312,399,000 | 439,010,000 | 21.81 |
| India | 1,210,193,000 | 1,656,554,000 | 0.52 |
| China | 1,399,725,000 | 1,303,723,000 | 0.29 |

Consider each of the following statements about these countries. For each statement indicate whether the statement is supported based on the information provided in the table.

| | Supported | Unsupported | |
|---|---|---|---|
| Question 9-1 | O | O | Of the countries with a population greater than 150 million in 2010, the country with the median number of foreign-born inhabitants is China. |
| Question 9-2 | O | O | The total population of Laos is projected to be about 8 million in 2030. |
| Question 9-3 | O | O | Andorra's rank for the percentage of foreign-born inhabitants is greater than that for all other countries listed. |

# Data for Items 10, 11, and 12:

*The following emails come from the Public Relations division of a large nonprofit organization.*

**Email #1** | **Email #2**

Hello Gloria!

We have to choose a caterer for our upcoming gala. Two caterers under consideration are DoxySource and BrightRight. Although DoxySource has delivered satisfactory service in the past, our First Annual Sponsors Gala promises to be the largest event we have ever hosted, and BrightRight is known for large event planning and production. However, I'd like more information before switching from a tried and true contractor. Also, I'd like to consider how to justify any over-budget costs from using BrightRight, if that comes up. I am committed to using only one provider. Please work up a comparison of costs of services and rentals for BrightRight and DoxySource. We require: tables, audio, food, and a punch fountain or fountains (a dessert fountain would be a lovely addition). Our budget is $6,000.00, and we plan for a maximum of 400 people.

Thanks!

Evelyn Schott

Gala Coordinator

**Email #1** | **Email #2**

Hello Evelyn,

I've broken out the data in the following chart:

| | DoxySource | | BrightRight | |
|---|---|---|---|---|
| | Description | Price | Description | Price |
| AUDIO | 200 Watt P.A. System (up to 40 people) | $65.00 | Party Sound System | $650.00 |
| | 500 Watt P.A. System (up to 120 people) | $90.00 | Marquee Sound System | $850.00 |
| CATERING | Choice of appetizers (shrimp or spring roll) | $2.00 per piece | The Classic Western BBQ | $14.00 per person |
| | Choice of entree (chicken or beef w/ rice) | $6.25 per piece | The Greek Feast | $17.50 per person |
| | Choice of dessert (cupcakes or lemon bars) | $3.40 per piece | The Far East Extravaganza | $19.50 per person |
| TABLES | Trestle Table (seats 8) | $15.50 each | Classroom (seats 8) | $20.00 each |
| | Circular Table (seats 7) | $17.00 each | Bistro/Hightop (seats 6) | $22.00 each |
| FOUNTAINS | Chocolate Fountain (supplies not included) | $105.00 | Chocolate Fountain (supplies included) | $500.00 |
| | Punch Fountain (7 gallons, provided, serves approx. 70) | $47.00 | Punch Fountain, waterfall tier (40 gallons, provided) | $350.00 |

BrightRight offers packages that are generally more elegant and comprehensive, and more expensive. For instance, we can choose a single full meal set, such as "The Greek Feast," for the entire gala. Using DoxySource, while more economical and flexible in the catering, does mean more hands-on involvement on our end.

The biggest price difference comes in the audio systems. BrightRight, which consistently hosts events with attendance of several hundred people, offers complex systems that include lights and sound effects, in addition to high-definition audio reproduction. DoxySource offers two standard, large public address systems. I am not sure whether the Gala will need all the flash and sizzle of the high-end sound system; but the projected attendance is above the recommended usage for DoxySource's P.A. systems. Due to electrical concerns, we can have only one P.A. system at the gala.

Gloria Welch

Administrative Assistant, Public Relations

## Item 10:

If the maximum number of guests attend the gala, determine if each of the statements is true or false based on the information in the two emails.

| | True | False | |
|---|---|---|---|
| Question 10-1 | O | O | If the coordinator uses DoxySource and orders one appetizer, one entrée, and one dessert per person, then the least amount that can be spent on tables to seat all guests is approximately 16.6% of the cost of food. |
| Question 10-2 | O | O | If the large punch fountain from BrightRight is sufficient for 400 guests, then using smaller fountains from DoxySource to serve the same number of guests would cost at least 20% less per gallon. |
| Question 10-3 | O | O | If BrightRight is used, the project will go over its present budget by at least 15%. |

## Item 11:

Suppose the Gala Coordinator uses DoxySource for the maximum number of guests. If she wants to use at least one of each type of table, what is the least possible cost for the tables?

(A) \$775.00
(B) \$787.00
(C) \$792.00
(D) \$873.21
(E) \$971.43

## Item 12:

Based on the information in the messages between the Gala Coordinator and the Administrative Assistant, select *Yes* if the statement can be inferred. Otherwise, select *No*.

| | Yes | No | |
|---|---|---|---|
| Question 12-1 | O | O | The Gala Coordinator is willing to ask for a budgetary increase, if necessary. |
| Question 12-2 | O | O | According to the Administrative Assistant, audio costs are not the only determining factor in choosing one event planning service over another. |
| Question 12-3 | O | O | Fountains are an optional element of the gala. |

# Part VI How to Crack the Analytical Writing Assessment

# Chapter 27
# Analytical Writing Assessment

Writing a coherent essay in 30 minutes might seem daunting, but in this chapter, you will learn techniques of pre-construction and pre-structuring that will make the process easy. You will also learn how the essay is scored and the *key factor* the readers are told to look for. (*Hint*: It isn't originality.)

The very first thing you will be asked to do on the GMAT is to write an essay using a word-processing program. You will have 30 minutes for your essay. You will not be given the essay topic in advance, nor will you be given a choice of topics. However, there is a complete list of the most possible writing assessment topics available for you to review on the GMAC website. Simply go to https://www.mba.com/exams/gmat/about-the-gmat-exam/gmat-exam-structure, select the link for the Analytical Writing Assessment section, and follow the directions to download a list of current topics. Oh, and just in case you are wondering, it's free!

Practice writing an essay when you take a full-length GMAT at PrincetonReview.com. You'll have the option of selecting free LiveGrader™ essay scoring.

## Why Have an Essay on the GMAT?

Business schools themselves asked for the essay. Recent studies have indicated that success in business (and in business school) actually depends more on verbal skills than has been traditionally thought.

Business schools have also had to contend with a huge increase in the number of applicants from overseas. Admissions officers at business schools were finding that the application essays they received from outside the United States did not always accurately reflect the abilities of the students who were supposed to have written them. To put it more bluntly, some of these applicants were paying native English speakers to write their essays for them.

The GMAT Analytical Writing Assessment (AWA) is thus at least partly a check on the writing ability of foreign applicants who now make up more than one-third of all applicants to American business schools.

At the business schools' request, all schools to which you apply now receive, in addition to your AWA score, a copy of the actual essay you wrote.

## How Do the Schools Use the Analytical Writing Assessment?

If you are a citizen of a non-English-speaking country, you can expect the schools to look quite closely at both the score you receive on the essay you write and the essay itself. If you are a native English speaker with reasonable Verbal scores and English grades in college, then the AWA is not likely to be a crucial part of your package.

On the other hand, if your verbal skills are *not* adequately reflected by your grades in college or in the other sections of the GMAT, then a strong performance on the AWA could be extremely helpful.

## How Is the Essay Scored?

When you get your GMAT score back from GMAC, you will also receive a separate score for the AWA. Your essay is read by two readers, each of whom will assign your writing a grade from 0 to 6, in half-point increments (6 being the highest score possible). If the two scores are within a point of each other, they will be averaged. If there is more than a one-point spread, the essay will be read by a third reader, and scores will be adjusted to reflect the third scorer's evaluation.

The essay readers use the "holistic" scoring method to grade essays; your writing will be judged not on small details but rather on its overall impact. The readers are supposed to ignore small errors of grammar and spelling. Considering that these readers are going to have to plow through more than 600,000 essays each year, this is probably just as well.

**Admissions Insight No. 8: Financial Aid, Part 1**

The perception is that there is no financial aid available for business school. While this is generally true in the case of grants (money you don't have to pay back), it is not true about government-subsidized student loans

## Who Are These Readers Anyway?

We'll put this in the form of a multiple-choice question:

Your essay will be read by:

(A) captains of industry
(B) leading business school professors
(C) college TAs working part time
(D) a computer

If you guessed (C) and (D), you've got it! Each essay will be read by part-time employees of the testing company, mostly culled from graduate school programs, and a computer that compares your word choice and sentence structure to a database of previously graded essays.

## How Much Time Do They Devote to Each Essay?

The graders get two minutes, tops. They work in eight-hour marathon sessions (nine to five, with an hour off for lunch), and are each required to read 30 essays per hour. Obviously, these poor graders do not have time for an in-depth reading of your essay. They probably aren't going to notice how carefully you thought out your ideas or how clever your analysis was. Under pressure to meet their quota, they are simply going to be giving it a fast skim. By the time your reader gets to your essay, she will probably have already seen more than a hundred essays—and no matter how ingenious you were in coming up with original ideas, she's already seen them.

## So How Do You Score High on the AWA Essays?

On the face of it, you might think it would be pretty difficult to impress these jaded readers, but it turns out that there are some very specific ways to persuade them of your superior writing skills.

## What GMAC Doesn't Want You to Know

In a 1982 internal study, two researchers from one of the big testing companies analyzed a group of essays written by actual test-takers and the grades that those essays received. The most successful essays had one thing in common. Which of the following characteristics do you think it was?

- Good organization
- Proper diction
- Noteworthy ideas
- Good vocabulary
- Sentence variety
- Length
- Number of paragraphs

## What Your Essay Needs in Order to Look Like a Successful Essay

Those researchers discovered that the essays that received the highest grades from the essay graders had one single factor in common: length.

To ace the AWA, you need to take one simple step: *Write as much as you possibly can.* Each essay should include at least four indented paragraphs.

**Admissions Insight No. 9: Financial Aid, Part 2**

The best kind of student loans: low-cost Stafford loans (which don't have to be repaid until the student has graduated or left the program and which generally have much lower rates than regular, unsecured loans). If necessary, borrow the rest through private educational loans.

## How Does the Word-Processing Program Work?

The test-writers have created a simple word-processing program to allow students to compose their essays on the screen.

Here's what your screen will look like during the essay portion of the test:

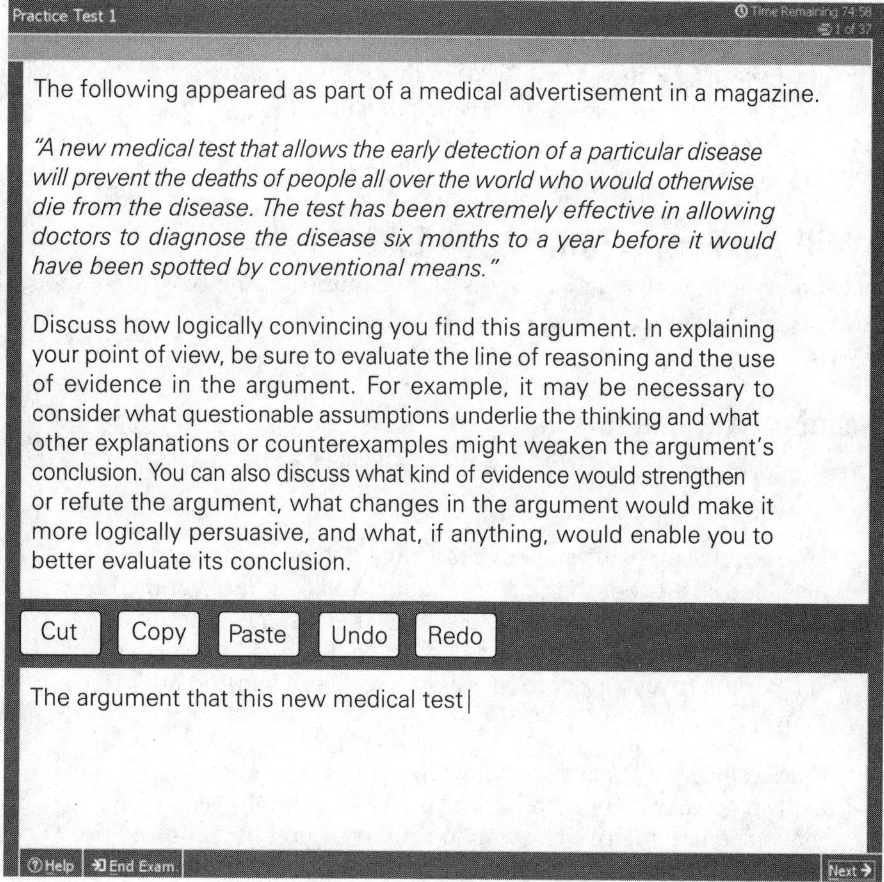


The question always appears at the top of your screen. Below it, in a box, will be your writing area (where you can see a partially completed sentence). When you click inside the box with your mouse, a winking cursor will appear, indicating that you can begin typing. The program supports the use of many of the normal computer keys, plus the following shortcuts:

*Cut:* Ctrl + X and Alt + T
*Copy:* Ctrl + C and Alt + C
*Paste:* Ctrl + V and Alt + A
*Undo:* Ctrl + Z and Alt + U
*Redo:* Ctrl + Y and Alt + R

You can also use the icons above the writing area to copy and paste words, sentences, or paragraphs and to undo and redo actions.

Obviously, this small box is not big enough to display your entire essay. However, you can see your entire essay by using the scroll bar, the up and down arrows, or the Page Up and Page Down keys.

## Does Spelling Count?

Officially, no. Essay readers are supposed to ignore minor errors of spelling and grammar. However, the readers wouldn't be human (so to speak) if they weren't influenced favorably by an essay that had no obvious misspelled words or unwieldy constructions. Unfortunately, there is no spell-check function in the word-processing program.

## What Will the Essay Topic Look Like?

There's only one type of essay topic: Analysis of an Argument. The typical question will look like the text inside the screen on the previous page. Here it is again:

### Analysis of an Argument

The following appeared as part of a medical advertisement in a magazine.

"A new medical test that allows the early detection of a particular disease will prevent the deaths of people all over the world who would otherwise die from the disease. The test has been extremely effective in allowing doctors to diagnose the disease six months to a year before it would have been spotted by conventional means."

Discuss how logically convincing you find this argument. In explaining your point of view, be sure to evaluate the line of reasoning and the use of evidence in the argument. For example, it may be necessary to consider what questionable assumptions underlie the thinking and what other explanations or counter-examples might weaken the argument's conclusion. You can also discuss what kind of evidence would strengthen or refute the argument, what changes in the argument would make it more logically persuasive, and what, if anything, would enable you to better evaluate its conclusion.

## THE AWA: BASIC PRINCIPLES

You might think that there is really no way to prepare for the AWA (other than by practicing writing over a long period of time and by practicing your typing skills). After all, you won't find out the topic of the essay they'll ask you to write until you get there, and there is no way to plan your essay in advance.

However, it turns out there are some very specific ways to prepare for the GMAT essay. Let's take a look.

### Create a Template

When a builder builds a house, the first thing he does is construct a frame. The frame supports the entire house. After the frame is completed, he can nail the walls and windows to the frame. We're going to show you how to build the frame for the perfect GMAT essay. Of course, you won't know the exact topic of the essay until you get there (just as the builder may not know what color his client is going to paint the living room), but you will have an all-purpose frame on which to construct a great essay no matter what the topic is.

We call this frame the *template.*

**Admissions Insight No. 10: Financial Aid, Part 3**
To get student loans, you will probably have to fill out both the FAFSA form (available at www.fafsa.ed.gov) and the PROFILE form (available at https://cssprofile.collegeboard.org). For simple and straightforward advice about making your way through all of that financial aid paperwork, visit PrincetonReview.com.

### Preconstruction

Just as a builder can construct the windows of a house in his workshop weeks before he arrives to install them, so too can you pre-build certain elements of your essay.

We call this *preconstruction.*

In the rest of this chapter, we'll show you how to prepare *ahead of time* to write essays on two topics you won't see until they appear on your screen.

## ANALYSIS OF AN ARGUMENT

The Analysis of an Argument essay must initially be approached just like a logical argument in the Critical Reasoning section.

An Analysis of an Argument topic requires the following steps:

**Step 1**: Read the topic and separate the conclusion from the premises.
**Step 2**: Because they're asking you to critique (i.e., weaken) the argument, concentrate on identifying its assumptions. Brainstorm as many different assumptions as you can think of. It helps to write or type these out.
**Step 3**: Look at the premises. Do they actually help to prove the conclusion?
**Step 4**: Choose a template that allows you to attack the assumptions and premises in an organized way.
**Step 5**: At the end of the essay, take a moment to illustrate how these same assumptions could be used to make the argument more compelling.
**Step 6**: Read over the essay and do some editing.

**Opinions vs. Arguments**
The most common mistake our students make is offering an opinion on the topic presented in the argument. For the Analysis of an Argument essay, you need to analyze the reasoning rather than explain why you agree or disagree.

## What the Readers Look For

An Analysis of an Argument topic presents you with an argument. Your job is to critique the argument's line of reasoning and the evidence supporting it and suggest ways in which the argument could be strengthened. You aren't required to know more about the subject than would any normal person—but you must be able to spot logical weaknesses. This should start to remind you of Critical Reasoning.

The essay readers will look for four things as they skim through your Analysis of an Argument essay at the speed of light. According to GMAC, "an outstanding argument essay...

- clearly identifies and insightfully analyzes important features of the argument;
- develops ideas cogently, organizes them logically, and connects them smoothly with clear transitions;
- effectively supports the main points of the critique; and
- demonstrates superior control of language, including diction, syntactic variety, and the conventions of standard written English. There may be minor flaws."

To put it more simply, the readers look for good organization, good analysis based on a cursory understanding of the rules of logic, and reasonable use of the English language.

## Critical Reasoning in Essay Form

In any GMAT argument, the first thing to do is to separate the conclusion from the premises.

Let's see how this works with an actual essay topic. Check out the Analysis of an Argument topic you saw before.

### Topic:

The following appeared as part of a medical advertisement in a magazine.

"A new medical test that allows the early detection of a particular disease will prevent the deaths of people all over the world who would otherwise die from the disease. The test has been extremely effective in allowing doctors to diagnose the disease six months to a year before it would have been spotted by conventional means."

Discuss how logically convincing you find this argument. In explaining your point of view, be sure to evaluate the line of reasoning and the use of evidence in the argument. For example, it may be necessary to consider what questionable assumptions underlie the thinking and what other explanations or counter-examples might weaken the argument's conclusion. You can also discuss what kind of evidence would strengthen or refute the argument, what changes in the argument would make it more logically persuasive, and what, if anything, would enable you to better evaluate its conclusion.

The conclusion in this argument comes in the first line:

A new medical test that allows the early detection of a particular disease will prevent the deaths of people all over the world who would otherwise die from that disease.

The premises are the evidence in support of this conclusion.

The test has been extremely effective in allowing doctors to diagnose the disease six months to a year before it would have been spotted by conventional means.

The assumptions are the *unspoken* premises of the argument—without which the argument would fall apart. Remember that assumptions are often causal, analogical, or statistical. What are some assumptions of *this* argument? Let's brainstorm.

## Brainstorming for Assumptions

You can often find assumptions by looking for a gap in the reasoning:

**Medical test → early detection**: According to the conclusion, the medical test leads to the early detection of the disease. There doesn't seem to be a gap here.

**Early detection → nonfatal**: In turn, the early detection of the disease allows patients to survive the disease. Well, hold on a minute. Is this necessarily true? Let's brainstorm:

1. First of all, do we know that early detection will necessarily lead to survival? We don't even know if this disease is *curable*. Early detection of an incurable disease is not going to help someone survive it.
2. Second, will the test be widely available and cheap enough for general use? If the test is expensive or available only in certain parts of the world, people will continue to die from the disease.
3. Will doctors and patients interpret the tests correctly? The test may be fine, but if doctors misinterpret the results or if patients ignore the need for treatment, then the test will not save lives.

## The Use of the Evidence

Okay, we've uncovered some assumptions. Now, the essay graders also want to know what we thought of the argument's "use of evidence." In other words, did the premises help to prove the conclusion? Well, in fact, no, they didn't. The premise here (the fact that the test can *spot* the disease six months to a year earlier than conventional tests) does not really help to prove the conclusion that the test will save *lives*.

**B-School Lingo**
*three Cs*: the primary forces considered in marketing—Customer, Competition, Company

Source: *The Best 294 Business Schools*

## Organizing the Analysis of an Argument Essay

We're ready to put this into a ready-made template. In any Analysis of an Argument essay, the template structure will be pretty straightforward: you're simply going to reiterate the argument, attack the argument in three different ways (one to a paragraph), summarize what you've said, and mention how the argument could be strengthened. From an organizational standpoint, this is pretty easy. Try to minimize your use of the word "I." *Your* opinion is not really the point in an Analysis of an Argument essay.

## A Sample Template

Of course, you will want to develop your *own* template for the Analysis of an Argument essay, but to get you started, here's one possible structure:

The argument that (restatement of the conclusion) is not entirely logically convincing, because it ignores certain crucial assumptions.

First, the argument assumes that ______________________________ ______________________________.

Second, the argument never addresses ______________________________ ______________________________.

Finally, the argument omits ______________________________ ______________________________.

Thus, the argument is not completely sound. The evidence in support of the conclusion ______________________________.

Ultimately, the argument might have been strengthened by ______________________________ ______________________________.

## How Would Our Brainstorming Fit Into the Template?

Here's how the assumptions we came up with for this argument would have fit into the template:

**The Analysis of an Argument Essay in Six Steps**

**Step 1**: Read the topic. Isolate the conclusion and premises.

**Step 2**: Identify its assumptions. Brainstorm for five minutes.

**Step 3**: Look at the assumptions. Do they help to prove the conclusion?

**Step 4**: Choose a template that allows you to attack the assumptions in an organized way.

**Step 5**: Illustrate how these same assumptions could be used to make the argument more compelling.

**Step 6**: Do some editing to correct spelling or grammar mistakes.

The argument that the new medical test will prevent deaths that would have occurred in the past is not entirely logically persuasive, because it ignores certain crucial assumptions.

First, the argument assumes that early detection of the disease will lead to a reduced mortality rate. There are a number of reasons this might not be true. For example, the disease might be incurable [etc.].

Second, the argument never addresses the point that the existence of this new test, even if totally effective, is not the same as the widespread use of the test [etc.].

Finally, even supposing the ability of early detection to save lives and the widespread use of the test, the argument still depends on the doctors' correct interpretation of the test and the patients' willingness to undergo treatment. [etc.]

Thus, the argument is not completely sound. The evidence in support of the conclusion (further information about the test itself) does little to prove the conclusion—that the test will save lives—because it does not address the assumptions already raised. Ultimately, the argument might have been strengthened by making it plain that the disease responds to early treatment, that the test will be widely available around the world, and that doctors and patients will make proper use of the test.

## Customizing Your Analysis of an Argument Template

Your organizational structure may vary in some ways, but it will always include the following elements:

- The *first paragraph* should sum up the argument's conclusion.
- In the *second, third, and fourth paragraphs,* you should attack the argument and the supporting evidence.
- In the *last* paragraph, you should summarize what you've said and state how the argument could be strengthened.

Q: What are the most important aspects of writing a good Analysis of an Argument essay?
*Turn to page 586 for the answer.*

Here are some alternate ways of organizing your essay.

## Variation 1:

1st paragraph: Restate the argument.
2nd paragraph: Discuss the link (or lack of one) between the conclusion and the evidence presented in support of it.
3rd paragraph: Show three holes in the reasoning of the argument.
4th paragraph: Show how each of the three holes could be plugged up by explicitly stating the missing assumptions.

## Variation 2:

1st paragraph: Restate the argument and say it has three flaws.
2nd paragraph: Point out a flaw and show how it could be plugged up by explicitly stating the missing assumption.
3rd paragraph: Point out a second flaw and show how it could be plugged up by explicitly stating the missing assumption.
4th paragraph: Point out a third flaw and show how it could be plugged up by explicitly stating the missing assumption.
5th paragraph: Summarize and conclude that because of these three flaws, the argument is weak.

## Analysis of an Argument: Final Thoughts

You've separated the conclusion from the premises. You've brainstormed for the gaps that weaken the argument. You've noted how the premises support (or don't support) the conclusion. Now it's time to write your essay. Start typing, indenting each of the four or five paragraphs. Use all the tools you've learned in this chapter. Remember to keep an eye on the time.

If you have a minute at the end, read over your essay and do any editing that's necessary.

A: Write at least four or five well-organized paragraphs (an introduction, in which you state that you will analyze the reasoning of the topic; a middle, to pick apart the argument by exposing assumptions; and a conclusion in which you state how the argument could be strengthened and sum up your position). Remember, this essay uses the same skills and approach you developed for the Critical Reasoning section of the test.

## PRECONSTRUCTION

The readers will look for evidence of your facility with standard written English. This is where preconstruction comes in. It's amazing how a little elementary preparation can enhance an essay. We'll look at two tricks that almost instantly improve the appearance of a person's writing:

- structure words
- sentence variety

### Structure Words

In our Reading Comprehension chapter, we brought up a problem that most students encounter when they get to the Reading Comprehension section: there isn't enough time to read the passages carefully and answer all the questions. To get around this problem, we showed you some ways to spot the overall organization of a dense reading passage in order to understand the main idea and to find specific points quickly.

When you think about it, the essay readers face almost the identical problem: they have less than two minutes to read your essay and figure out if it's any good. There's no time to appreciate the finer points of your argument. All they want to know is whether it's well organized and reasonably lucid—and to find out, they will look for the *same* structural clues you have learned to look for in the Reading Comprehension passages. Let's mention them again:

- If you have three points to make in a paragraph, it helps to point this out ahead of time:

    There are three reasons why I believe that the Grand Canyon should be preserved for all eternity. First...Second...Third...

- If you want to clue the reader in to the fact that you are about to support the main idea with examples or illustrations, the following words are useful:

    *for example*
    *to illustrate*
    *for instance*
    *because*

- To add yet another example or argument in support of your main idea, you can use one of the following words to indicate your intention:

    *furthermore*
    *in addition*
    *similarly*
    *just as*
    *also*
    *moreover*

- To indicate that the idea you're about to bring up is important, special, or surprising in some way, you can use one of these words:
  *surely*
  *truly*
  *undoubtedly*
  *clearly*
  *certainly*
  *indeed*
  *as a matter of fact*
  *in fact*
  *most important*

**Key to Analysis of an Argument**
Critique the weaknesses in the argument clearly.

- To signal that you're about to reach a conclusion, you might use one of these words:
  *therefore*
  *in summary*
  *consequently*
  *hence*
  *in conclusion*
  *in short*

## The Appearance of Depth

You may have noticed that much of the structure we have discussed thus far has involved contrasting viewpoints. Nothing will give your writing the *appearance* of depth faster than learning to use this technique. The idea is to set up your main idea by first introducing its opposite.

It is a favorite ploy of incoming presidents to blame the federal bureaucracy for the high cost of government, but I believe that bureaucratic waste is only a small part of the problem.

You may have noticed that this sentence contained a "trigger word." In this case, the trigger word *but* tells us that what was expressed in the first half of the sentence is going to be contradicted in the second half. We discussed trigger words in the Reading Comprehension chapter of this book. Here they are again:

| | |
|---|---|
| *but* | *however* |
| *on the contrary* | *although* |
| *yet* | *while* |
| *despite* | *in spite of* |
| *rather* | *nevertheless* |
| *instead* | |

By using these words, you can instantly give your writing the appearance of depth.

### How It Works

Here's a paragraph that consists of a main point and two supporting arguments:

*I believe he is wrong. He doesn't know the facts. He isn't thinking clearly.*

Watch how a few structure words can make this paragraph classier and clearer at the same time:

*I believe he is wrong.* ***For one thing,*** *he doesn't know the facts.* ***For another,*** *he isn't thinking clearly.*

*I believe he is wrong.* ***Obviously,*** *he doesn't know the facts.* ***Moreover,*** *he isn't thinking clearly.*

*I believe he is wrong* ***because, first,*** *he doesn't know the facts, and* ***second,*** *he isn't thinking clearly.*

***Certainly,*** *he doesn't know the facts, and he isn't thinking clearly* ***either.*** ***Consequently,*** *I believe he is wrong.*

**Example:**

Main thought: *I believe that television programs should be censored.*

*While many people believe in the sanctity of free speech, I believe that television programs should be censored.*

*Most people believe in the sanctity of free speech, but I believe that television programs should be censored.*

In addition to trigger words, here are a few other words or phrases you can use to introduce the view you are eventually going to decide *against*:

| | |
|---|---|
| *admittedly* | *true* |
| *certainly* | *granted* |
| *obviously* | *of course* |
| *undoubtedly* | *to be sure* |
| *one cannot deny that* | *it could be argued that* |

Also, don't forget about yin-yang words, which can be used to point directly to two contrasting ideas:

*on the one hand/on the other hand*

*the traditional view/the new view*

## Contrasting Paragraphs

Trigger words can be used to signal the opposing viewpoints of entire paragraphs. Suppose you saw an essay that began:

*Many people believe that youth is wasted on the young. They point out that young people never seem to enjoy, or even think about, the great gifts they have been given but will not always have: physical dexterity, good hearing, good vision. However…*

What do you think is going to happen in the second paragraph? That's right, the author is now going to disagree with the *many people* of the first paragraph.

Setting up one paragraph in opposition to another lets the reader know what's going on right away. The organization of the essay is immediately evident.

## Sentence Variety

Many people think good writing is a mysterious talent that you either have or don't have, like good rhythm. In fact, good writing has a kind of rhythm to it, but there is nothing mysterious about it. Good writing is a matter of mixing up the different kinds of raw materials that you have available to you—phrases, dependent and independent clauses—to build sentences that don't all sound the same.

The graders won't have time to savor your essay, but they will look for variety in your writing. Here's an example of a passage in which all the sentences sound alike:

*Movies cost too much. Everyone agrees about that. Studios need to cut costs. No one is sure exactly how to do it. I have two simple solutions. They can cut costs by paying stars less. They can also cut costs by reducing overhead.*

Why do all the sentences sound alike? Well, for one thing, they are all about the same length. For another thing, the sentences are all made up of independent clauses with the same exact setup: subject, verb, and sometimes object. There are no dependent clauses, almost no phrases, no structure words, and, frankly, no variety at all.

Now let's take a look at the same passage, with some minor modifications.

*Everyone agrees that movies cost too much. Clearly, studios need to cut costs, but no one is sure exactly how to do it. I have two simple solutions: They can cut costs by paying stars less and by reducing overhead.*

In this version of the passage, we've combined some clauses and used conjunctions. This helped to add variety in both sentence structure and sentence length. We also threw in a few structure words as well. As you can see, simple techniques like these can make your writing appear stronger and more polished.

## The AWA

Few people are rejected by a business school based on their writing score, so don't bother feeling intimidated. Think of it this way: the essays present an opportunity if your Verbal score is low, or if English is your second language. For the rest of you, the essay is as good a way as any to warm up (and wake up) before the sections that count.

# Summary

- The GMAT AWA section consists of one essay, written in 30 minutes, using a basic word-processing program and the computer keyboard. The essay will be given scores that range from 0 to 6 in half-point increments.
- Each essay will be evaluated by at least two underpaid, overworked college teaching assistants.
- To score high on the AWA:
    - Write as many words as possible.
    - Use a prebuilt template to organize your thoughts.
    - Use structure words and vary your sentence structure and length to give the appearance of depth to your writing.
    - If possible, refer to a well-known work of literature or nonfiction.
- For the Analysis of an Argument topic:

  **Step 1:** Read the topic and separate the conclusion from the premises.

  **Step 2:** Because they ask you to critique (i.e., weaken) the argument, concentrate on identifying its assumptions. Brainstorm as many different assumptions as you can think of and write them down.

  **Step 3:** Look at the premises. Do they actually help to prove the conclusion?

  **Step 4:** Choose a template that allows you to attack the assumptions and premises in an organized way.

  **Step 5:** At the end of the essay, take a moment to illustrate how these same assumptions could be used to make the argument more compelling.

  **Step 6:** Read over the essay and edit your work.

# Part VII
# Answer Key to Drills

## DRILL 1 (AD/BCE)

1. **BCE** Statement (1) gives a value for $y$ but no information on the value of $x$. Since the problem asks for a value of $x$, Statement (1) is insufficient.

2. **BCE** Statement (1) states that $2y$ is an integer. Consider what values of $y$ are possible. The value of $y$ could be an integer, such as 2, but it could also be a fraction, such as $\frac{1}{2}$. Statement (1) is insufficient.

3. **AD** The question states that there are 12 children in the room. Statement (1) provides the number of girls, so both the number of boys and the difference between the number of boys and the number of girls can be determined. Since the difference can be determined, Statement (1) is sufficient.

4. **AD** Statement (1) can be rewritten as the equation $\left(\frac{10}{100}\right)x = 5$, which can be used to solve for $x$. If the value of $x$ is known, then the question can be answered. Statement (1) is sufficient.

## DRILL 2

1. **77** $74 + (27 - 24) = 74 + 3 = 77$

2. **79** $(8 \times 9) + 7 = 72 + 7 = 79$

3. **10** $2(9 - (8 \div 2)) = 2(9 - 4)$, which simplifies to $2(5) = 10$.

4. **16** $2(7 - 3) + (-4)(5 - 7) = 2(4) + (-4)(-2)$, which simplifies to $8 + 8 = 16$.

5. **B** $4(-3(3 - 5) + 10 - 17) = 4(-3(-2) + 10 - 17)$, which simplifies to $4(6 + 10 - 17) = 4(-1)$, or $-4$. The correct answer is (B).

6. **A** Statement (1) states that $x^3 = 8$. If $x^3 = 8$, then $x$ equals 2. Since there is only one possible value of $x$ that satisfies the equation, Statement (1) is sufficient. Write down AD. Statement (2) states that $x^2 = 4$. In this case, $x$ could be 2 or $-2$. Statement (2) is therefore insufficient. The correct answer is (A).

## DRILL 3

1. $x^2 + x = x(x + 1)$

2. $(55 \times 12) + (55 \times 88) = 55(12 + 88)$, which simplifies to $55(100) = 5{,}500$.

3. $a(b + c - d) = ab + ac - ad$

4. $abc + xyc = c(ab + xy)$

5. **B** If $x = 6$, then $\frac{2xy - xy}{y} = \frac{2(6)y - (6)y}{y}$, which simplifies to $\frac{12y - 6y}{y} = \frac{6y}{y}$, and reduces to 6. The correct answer is (B).

6. **B** Statement (1) provides a value for $x$, but provides no information about $y$ and $z$, so Statement (1) is insufficient. Write down BCE. Statement (2) provides a value for $a$. Factor the equation given to yield $a(x + y + z) = 15$. If $a = 5$, then $x + y + z = 3$, and Statement (2) is sufficient. The correct answer is (B).

## DRILL 4

1. $\mathbf{\frac{49}{8}}$ or $\mathbf{6\frac{1}{8}}$

$5\frac{3}{4}+\frac{3}{8}=\frac{23}{4}+\frac{3}{8}$, which may be rewritten as $\frac{46}{8}+\frac{3}{8}=\frac{49}{8}$.

2. $\mathbf{\frac{1}{5}}$ $\frac{12}{60}=\frac{12\times 1}{12\times 5}$, which reduces to $\frac{1}{5}$.

3. $\mathbf{\frac{29}{3}}$ $9\frac{2}{3}=\frac{9\times 3}{3}+\frac{2}{3}$, which yields $\frac{27}{3}+\frac{2}{3}=\frac{29}{3}$

4. **18** Cross-multiply to get $2x = 36$. Divide both sides of the equation by 2 to get $x = 18$.

5. **C** $\frac{\left(\frac{\frac{4}{5}}{\frac{3}{5}}\right)\left(\frac{\frac{1}{8}}{\frac{2}{3}}\right)}{\frac{3}{4}}=\frac{\left(\frac{4}{5}\times\frac{5}{3}\right)\left(\frac{1}{8}\times\frac{3}{2}\right)}{\frac{3}{4}}$, which yields $\frac{\frac{4}{3}\times\frac{3}{16}}{\frac{3}{4}}=\frac{\frac{4}{16}}{\frac{3}{4}}$, which further yields $\frac{1}{4}\times\frac{4}{3}=\frac{4}{12}$, or $\frac{1}{3}$. The correct answer is (C).

## DRILL 5

1. **33.30** Since the numbers are lined up, just subtract down, remembering to borrow when dealing with the tenths digit.

2. **266.175** Multiply 273 by 975 as normal and then move the decimal point over 3 spots.

3. **6.125** Set up to do long division: $3.2\overline{)19.6}$. Move the decimal point over one to the right to get $32\overline{)196}$. Since 32 goes into 196 a total of 6 times, $32\overline{)196}^{\,6}$. Next, multiply 6 by 32 to get 192 and subtract 192 from 196 to get 4. Then add a decimal point and a 0, bring that 0 down, and see that 32 goes into 40 one time, so multiply 1 by 32 and then subtract 32 from 40 to get 8. Add another 0, bring it down, and see that 32 goes into 80 two times, so multiply 32 by 2 to get 64 and then subtract that from 80. Finally, add one more 0 and see that 32 goes into 160 exactly 5 times:

$$\begin{array}{r} 6.125 \\ 32\overline{)196.000} \\ \underline{192\phantom{.000}} \\ 40\phantom{00} \\ \underline{32\phantom{00}} \\ 80\phantom{0} \\ \underline{64\phantom{0}} \\ 160 \\ \underline{160} \\ 0 \end{array}$$

The correct answer is 6.125.

4. **800** $\dfrac{\frac{4}{0.25}}{\frac{1}{50}} = \dfrac{\frac{4}{\frac{1}{4}}}{\frac{1}{50}}$, which may be rewritten as $\dfrac{4 \times \frac{4}{1}}{\frac{1}{50}} = \dfrac{16}{\frac{1}{50}}$, and yields $16 \times \frac{50}{1} = 800$.

5. **C** $\dfrac{\frac{3}{10} \times 4 \times 0.8}{0.32} = \dfrac{\frac{3}{10} \times \frac{4}{1} \times \frac{8}{10}}{\frac{32}{100}}$, which yields $\dfrac{\frac{96}{100}}{\frac{32}{100}} = \frac{96}{100} \times \frac{100}{32}$, which reduces to $\frac{96}{32} = 3$. The correct answer is (C).

6. **D** The question states that $x$ and $y$ are reciprocals, which means that determining the value of either variable provides the value of the other. Therefore, Statement (1) provides the values of both $x$ and $y$, which allows the question to be answered. Write down AD. Statement (2) also provides the values of both $y$ and $x$, so the correct answer is (D).

## DRILL 6

1. **C** The question involves ratios, so set up a Ratio Box. Since there are 2 ratios given, set up 2 Ratio Boxes—the current situation and the hypothetical if the students drop out.

Current:

| | Men | Women | Total |
|---|---|---|---|
| Ratio | 6 | 5 | 11 |
| Multiplier | | | |
| Actual | | | |

After drop outs:

| | Men | Women | Total |
|---|---|---|---|
| Ratio | 8 | 7 | 15 |
| Multiplier | | | |
| Actual | | | |

Since the algebra seems somewhat complicated, Plug In the Answers. Start with (C). The answers represent the number of men currently in the class. Plugging 18 in gives

Current

| | Men | Women | Total |
|---|---|---|---|
| Ratio | 6 | 5 | 11 |
| Multiplier | 3 | 3 | 3 |
| Actual | 18 | 15 | 33 |

The problem then states that 2 men and 1 woman drop out, so subtract 2 from the total men and 1 from the total women and check if that fits an 8 to 7 ratio in the After drop outs box:

After drop outs:

| | Men | Women | Total |
|---|---|---|---|
| Ratio | 8 | 7 | 15 |
| Multiplier | | | |
| Actual | 16 | 14 | |

16 to 14 is an 8 to 7 ratio. Since the condition is met, the correct answer is (C).

2. **B** If the average of 5 numbers is 7, then the numbers must add up to 35. If three of those numbers average 5, then those 3 numbers must add up to 15. The sum of the two numbers left is therefore 35 – 15 = 20. If the sum of the two numbers is 20, then the average of those two numbers is 10. The correct answer is (B).

3. **D** $\dfrac{\frac{1}{3}^6 - \frac{1}{3}^4}{\frac{1}{3}^5}$ may be factored to yield $\dfrac{\left(\frac{1}{3}\right)^4\left(\left(\frac{1}{3}\right)^2 - 1\right)}{\frac{1}{3}^5} = \dfrac{\left(\frac{1}{3}\right)^4\left(\left(\frac{1}{3}\right)^2 - 1\right)}{\left(\frac{1}{3}\right)^4\left(\frac{1}{3}\right)}$, which reduces to

$\dfrac{\left(\frac{1}{3}\right)^2 - 1}{\frac{1}{3}} = \dfrac{\frac{1}{9} - 1}{\frac{1}{3}}$, which yields $\dfrac{-\frac{8}{9}}{\frac{1}{3}} = -\dfrac{8}{9} \times \dfrac{3}{1}$, which results in $-\dfrac{8 \times 3}{3 \times 3} = -\dfrac{8}{3}$. The correct answer is (D).

4. **D** Factor $\dfrac{\sqrt{147} + \sqrt{75}}{14}$ as $\dfrac{\sqrt{7 \times 7 \times 3} + \sqrt{5 \times 5 \times 3}}{14} = \dfrac{7\sqrt{3} + 5\sqrt{3}}{14}$, which simplifies to

$\dfrac{12\sqrt{3}}{14} = \dfrac{6\sqrt{3}}{7}$. The second expression simplifies to $\dfrac{28}{7\sqrt{3}} = \dfrac{4}{\sqrt{3}}$. In order to evaluate the ratio between the expressions, express them as the fraction $\frac{\frac{6\sqrt{3}}{7}}{\frac{4}{\sqrt{3}}} = \frac{6\sqrt{3}}{7} \times \frac{\sqrt{3}}{4}$, which yields

$\frac{6\sqrt{3 \times 3}}{28} = \frac{6 \times 3}{28}$, and reduces to $\frac{9}{14}$, or a 9 to 14 ratio. The correct answer is (D).

5. **B** Determine the two amounts of interest. \$5,000 earning 8% interest, compounded semiannually, earns 4% interest compounded every 6 months. 4% of 5,000 is $5{,}000 \times \frac{4}{100} = 200$. Then, 4% of the new \$5,200 balance is $5{,}200 \times \frac{4}{100} = 208$, and the account contains \$5,408 at the end of one year. For the other account, 8% of 5,000 is $5{,}000 \times \frac{8}{100} = 400$, so the account contains \$5,400 at the end of one year. The difference is \$5,408 – \$5,400 = \$8. The correct answer is (B).

6. **E** If the average of ten numbers is 10, then the numbers have to add up to 100. However, the numbers could be anything. For example, if all ten numbers are 10, then the standard deviation is 0. However, since standard deviation is defined as the spread of numbers away from the average, the standard deviation could be anything—as the numbers could be negative numbers, really big numbers, and so on—as long as the sum is 100. So, 0, 10, and 20 could all be standard deviations. The correct answer is (E).

7. **D** Start by figuring out the median and mode of List II. The mode is 3 and the median is 5. Their sum is 8. So, the median of List I must also be 8. Since there are 6 elements in List I, the median will be the average of the 3rd and 4th numbers. Therefore, those two numbers must add up to 16. Since 7 is already listed, the only possible way to get a median of 8 is if *y* is 9. The correct answer is (D).

## Algebraic Expressions Quiz

1. $x + 4 = y + 8 - 3$

2. $35 = \left(\frac{x}{100}\right)z$

3. $8 + 3 \times 4 = \left(\frac{x}{100}\right)y$

4. $(x - 8) - 5 = 14$

5. $z = \left(\frac{x}{100}\right)y$

## Substitution Quiz

1. This problem states that $x + 3y = 6$ and $y = \frac{1}{3}x$. Use substitution to solve for $x$: $x + 3\left(\frac{1}{3}x\right) = 6$. This results in $x + x = 6$, so $2x = 6$ and $x = 3$.

2. This problem states that $y = 2x$ and $x + y = 24$ and asks for the value of $3x$. Use substitution to solve: $x + 2x = 24$, so $3x = 24$.

3. This problem states that $4x - 2y = 16$ and $12x + 6y = 48$ and asks for the value of $(x, y)$. Solve for one of the variables first. The first equation can be rewritten as $x = 4 + \frac{1}{2}y$. Solve the second equation for $y$ to produce $y = 8 - 2x$. Use substitution to solve for $x$ in the first equation: $x = 4 + \frac{1}{2}(8 - 2x) = 4 + 4 - x$. Combine like terms to find that $2x = 8$ and $x = 4$. Use this value of $x$ to solve for $y$. In the first equation, $4(4) + 2y = 16$, so $2y = 0$ and $y = 0$. The answer is (4, 0).

4. This problem states that $-6x - 2y = 2$ and $10 = 10x + 10y$ and asks to solve for the value of $x$. Use the second equation and solve for $y$. Isolate $10y$ on one side, which produces $10y = 10 - 10x$. Divide both sides by 10 to produce $y = 1 - x$. Use substitution in the first equation to produce $-6x - 2(1 - x) = 2$. Solve for $x$ by distributing the 2, combining similar terms, and isolating the $x$: $6x - 2 - 2y = 2$ yields $-8x = 4$ and $x = -\frac{1}{2}$.

5. The problem states that the area of a rectangle is 18. The area of a rectangle is found by the expression *length* × *width*. The problem also states that the length is twice the width, which can be written as $l = 2w$. The question asks for the width, so use substitution to solve: $2w \times w = 18$ produces $2w^2 = 18$ and $w^2 = 9$. Therefore, $w = 3$.

6. The problem states that the rate of car $A$ is 3 times that of car $B$, which can be written as $A = 3B$. The problem then states that the combined rate is 88 miles per hour, which can be written as $A + B = 88$. The problem then states that car $A$ travels for 2 hours and car $B$ travels for one hour and asks for the combined distance they each covered. This is a distance problem, so use the distance formula, which is *Distance* = *Rate* × *Time*. The problem provides the time each car traveled and provides formulas that concern the rate. Use substitution to solve for the rate of each car. The first equation defines $A$, so use that information and substitute into the second equation to solve for $B$. This yields $3B + B = 88$ and $4B = 88$, so $B = 22$. Use this information to solve for $A$: $A + 22 = 88$ and $A = 66$. Now use the rate formula to determine the total distance traveled by each car. Car $A$ traveled at a rate of 66 miles per hour for 2 hours, so car $A$ traveled $66 \times 2 = 132$ miles. Car $B$ traveled 22 miles per hour for 1 hour, so car $B$ traveled $22 \times 1 = 22$ miles. The combined distance is $132 + 22 = 154$.

## DRILL 7 (Algebra)

1. **A** There are numbers in the answer choices, so Plug In the Answers. Start with (C) and label the columns as Joe's current age. Draw a new column for Joe's age 5 years ago, which is 27 – 5 = 22. Draw a new column for Jessica's age 5 years ago, which is 22 ÷ 2 = 11. Draw a new column for Jessica's current age, which is 11 + 5 = 16. Draw a new column for Jessica's age in 4 years, which is 16 + 4 = 20. Draw a new column for Joe's age in 4 years, which is 27 + 4 = 31. Finally, evaluate the condition that Joe's age in 4 years *will be one and half times as old* as Jessica's age in 4 years, which is incorrect for (C). Eliminate (C). Because Joe's age in 4 years is greater than *one and a half times* that of Jessica, try (B), which is a smaller number. If Joe's current age is 25, then Joe's age 5 years ago is 25 – 5 = 20, Jessica's age 5 years ago is 20 ÷ 2 = 10, Jessica's current age is 10 + 5 = 15, Jessica's age in 4 years is 15 + 4 = 19, and Joe's age in 4 years is 25 + 4 = 29. Joe's age in 4 years is still greater than *one and half times* that of Jessica, so eliminate (B) and check (A) to confirm that it is the correct answer. If Joe's current age is 23, then Joe's age 5 years ago is 23 – 5 = 18, Jessica's age 5 years ago is 18 ÷ 2 = 9, Jessica's current age is 9 + 5 = 14, Jessica's age in 4 years is 14 + 4 = 18, and Joe's age in 4 years is 27. Since 27 is *one and a half times* 18, (A) meets the condition. The correct answer is (A).

2. **D** $\frac{x^2+2x-9}{3} \leq x+1$ can be rewritten as $x^2+2x-9 \leq 3(x+1)$ or $x^2+2x-9 \leq 3x+3$. Subtract $3x$ and 3 from both sides to yield $x^2+2x-3x-9-3 \leq 0$, or $x^2-x-12 \leq 0$. Factor the quadratic expression to yield $(x-4)(x+3) \leq 0$. Thus, the parabola defined by the quadratic expression has $x$-intercepts of (4, 0) and (–3, 0). Because the term $x^2$ is positive, the $y$-value of the parabola is negative between its $x$-intercepts, and the values of $x$ that satisfy the inequality are those values from –3 to 4, inclusive, which may be represented as $-3 \leq x \leq 4$. The correct answer is (D).

3. **E** There are variables in the answer choices, so Plug In. Let $x = 20$ and $a = 100$. Since 20% of 100 is 20, then $b = 20$. Since 100 is 5 times 20, the target is 5. Now, plug $x = 20$ into the answer choices, looking for the target of 5. Only (E) matches. The correct answer is (E).

4. **E** There are variables in the answer choices, so Plug In. Let $s = 6$. John has 6 pairs of shoes, so Sheila has 18 and James has 3. The *three of them combined* have 27 pairs of shoes, and 27 is the target. Now, plug $s = 6$ into the answer choices, looking for a target of 27. Only (E) matches. The correct answer is (E).

## Which Plugging In Method Should I Use? Quiz

| Question | Should You Plug In? | Plugging In Method |
|---|---|---|
| 1. If Mark's current age is three times greater than Jenny's age was 5 years ago, then, in terms of Jenny's current age, what is Mark's current age? | Yes | Hidden Plug In. Plug In a value for Jenny's current age. |
| 2. What number is 625% of 3,420? | No | None |
| 3. If $x^2 > 17$ and $x^3 > -512$, then which of the following must be true of $x$? | Yes | Plug In more than once using ZONEF numbers. Plug In values of $x$ and use POE. |
| 4. The original price of a shirt was increased by 25% and then decreased by 15% to a final price of $105. What was the original price of the shirt? | Yes | Plug In the Answers. Beginning with (C), Plug in the answer choices for the value of the original price of the shirt. |
| 5. A certain square has an area of 24 and a height that is 1.5 times its width. What is the perimeter of the square? | No | None |

## DRILL 8 (Plugging In)

1. **D** The problem contains a variable and the answer choices provide a specific value for that variable, so Plug In the Answers. Begin with (C). If $x = 2$, then list $L$ is 1, $\sqrt{2}$, 2, 4. This does not meet the requirement that the range of numbers is 4, so eliminate (C). The range needs to be greater, so choose a greater number such as (B), 4. If $x = 4$, then list $L$ is 1, $\sqrt{2}$, 4, 16. This is incorrect as the range is too great, so eliminate (B). Try (D). If $x = \sqrt{5}$, then list $L$ is 1, $\sqrt{2}$, $\sqrt{5}$, 5. The range of this list is 4. The correct answer is (D).

2. **B** There are variables in the question stem and answer choices, so Plug In. This is a "must be" question, so be prepared to Plug In more than once using ZONEF numbers. Begin with easy values for $r$, $s$, and $t$ that abide by the parameters of the problem such as $r = 2$, $s = 3$, and $t = 4$. Plug In these values for the variables into each of the answer choices and eliminate any that are

not true. In this case, (A) is not true because it evalutes to $-4 > 0$, so eliminate (A). Choice (B) is correct, as well as (C) and (D). Choice (E) evaluates to $-4 > -\frac{1}{4}$, which is not true, so eliminate (E). Now Plug In again using ZONEF numbers such as negatives. If $r = -2$, $s = 3$, and $t = 4$, then (B) is still true. Keep (B). Choice (C) is $-8 + 12 > 0$, which is true, so keep (C). Choice (D) is $(4 - 9) \times 4 = -20$, which is less than 0 so eliminate (D). Try Extreme numbers. If $r = -100$, $s = 3$, and $t = 4$, then (B) is still correct but (C) is now $-388 > 0$. This is not true, so eliminate (C). The correct answer is (B).

3. **D** This is a Yes/No Data Sufficiency problem, so be prepared to Plug In more than once. The question asks if $xy > 0$, so be prepared to Plug In for $x$ or $y$ values. Evaluate each statement individually. Statement (1) provides that $|x| + 8|y| = 0$, so Plug In values for $x$ and $y$ that make this statement true. Plugging In various values for $x$ and $y$ reveals that the only way the statement is true is if both $x$ and $y$ are equal to 0. Therefore, the answer to the question is "No" because $xy$ is not greater than 0. Because this statement produces only one correct answer to the question, the statement is sufficient. Write down AD. Now work with Statement (2). Statement (2) states that $8|x| + |y| = 0$. Plug In for values of $x$ and $y$. Plugging In various values for $x$ and $y$ also reveals that the only way the statement is true is if both $x$ and $y$ equal 0. Therefore, the answer to the question is "No" because $xy$ is not greater than 0. Because this statement produces only one correct answer to the question, the statement is sufficient. The correct answer is (D).

4. **B** This is a Hidden Plug In question. Plug In a number for the total number of majors in 2015, such as 100. If there were 100 total majors in 2015 and 18% of them were math majors, then there were 18 math majors in 2015. The problem states that $\frac{2}{6}$ of the math majors focused on statistics, so there are $\frac{2}{6} \times 18 = 6$ majors focused on statistics. Therefore, the correct answer is (B), 6%.

5. **E** This question contains variables in the question stem and answer choices, so Plug In. Begin by establishing what information is provided by the question stem. The stem provides that $x$ and $y$ are integers, $x^2 + y^2 < 46$, and $0 < x \le 5$. So, $x$ is either 1, 2, 3, 4, or 5. Plug In values of $x$ and solve for the possible values of $y$. If $x = 1$, then $y$ can be any of the integers between $-6$ and 6, inclusive, because $1^2 + \pm 6^2 < 46$. So, $-6 \le y \le 6$ is the value of $y$ when $x = 1$. If $x = 2$, then $y$ can be any integer between $-6$ and 6, inclusive, so this is the same information as when $x = 1$. If $x = 3$, then $y$ can be any of the integers between $-6$ and 6, inclusive, which is the same information as when $x = 1$ or 2. However, when $x = 4$, $y$ can only be values between $-5$ and 5, inclusive because $4^2 + \pm 5^2 < 46$, but $4^2 + \pm 6^2 > 46$. So, the possible values of $y$ are represented by $-5 \le y \le 5$. Eliminate (A) and (B). When $x = 5$, $y$ is between the values of $-4$ and 4 because $5^2 + \pm 4^2 < 46$, but $5^2 + \pm 5^2 > 46$. So, the values of $y$ are now restricted to $-4 \le y \le 4$. There are no further values of $x$ possible, so the correct answer is (E).

6. **E** This is a Yes/No Data Sufficiency problem, so be prepared to Plug In more than once. The question asks if the integers $x$, $y$, and $z$ are consecutive. Plug In values for the variables that satisfy the conditions of the statements. Begin with Statement (1), which states that the average (arithmetic mean) of $x$, $y$, and $z$ is $y$. Plug In values that make this statement true. If $x = 2$,

$y = 3$, and $z = 4$, then the average is $\frac{2+3+4}{3} = 3$. This satisfies that statement and the answer to the question is "Yes" because the the integers are consecutive. Now Plug In again and attempt to produce a "No" answer to the question. If $x = 2$, $y = 4$, and $z = 6$, then the average is $\frac{2+4+6}{3} = 4$. This satisfies the statements. However, the answer to the question is now "No" because $x$, $y$, and $z$ are not consecutive. When the statement produces two different answers to the question, the statement is insufficient. Write down BCE. Now evaluate Statement (2). Statement (2) is that $y - x = z - y$. Plug In. If $x = 2$, $y = 3$, and $z = 4$, then the statement is satisfied because $3 - 2 = 4 - 3$. The answer to the question is "Yes" because the integers are consecutive. Plug In again in an attempt to produce a "No" answer. If $x = 2$, $y = 4$, and $z = 6$, then the statement is satisfied because $4 - 2 = 6 - 4$. The answer to the question is now "No" because the integers are not consecutive. Eliminate (B). Now consider the two statements together. The numbers that were Plugged In for both statements individually are the same numbers that can be Plugged In for both statements combined. Therefore, it is possible to produce both a "Yes" and a "No" answer to the question. Eliminate choice (C). The correct answer is (E).

7. **B** The problem contains a variable and the answer choices provide a specific value for that variable, so Plug In the Answers. Begin with (C). If the total number of marbles in the bag is 55, then the probability of pulling 2 red marbles is $\left(\frac{3}{55}\right)\left(\frac{2}{54}\right)$, which does not equal $\frac{3}{55}$. The denominator is too great. Eliminate (C) as well as (D) and (E), as they will make the denominator even greater. Try (B). If the total number of marbles in the bag is 11, then the probability is $\left(\frac{3}{11}\right)\left(\frac{2}{10}\right) = \frac{6}{110} = \frac{3}{55}$. The correct answer is (B).

8. **C** This is a Yes/No Data Sufficiency problem, so be prepared to Plug In more than once. The question states that $y$ is an integer, so Plug In a value for $y$ where possible. Evaluate the statements individually. Statement (1) is that $y > 5$. Plug In for $y$. If $y = 6$, then the answer to the question is "No" because the remainder of $\frac{6}{2}$ is not 1. However, if $y = 7$, then the answer to the question is "Yes" because the remainder of $\frac{7}{2}$ is 1. This statement produces two different answers to the question, so it is insufficient. Write down BCE. Now work with the second statement. Statement (2) is that $y$ is prime. All prime numbers are odd numbers except for the number 2. Plug In. If $y = 2$, then the answer to the question is "No." However, if $y$ is any prime value other than 2, the answer is "Yes." This statement provides two different answers to the question, so it is not sufficient. Eliminate (B). Now combine the statements. All prime numbers greater than 5 are odd numbers, so any value of $y$ that can be Plugged In is going to have a remainder of 1 when divided by 2. The two statements combined are sufficient to answer the question. The correct answer is (C).

9. **A** There are fractions in the answer choices and the question has a missing piece of information (the total number of cars), so this is a Hidden Plug In question. Plug In for the total number of cars that the automobile manufacturer produces. When working with fractions, the best number to Plug In is the product of the denominator of all the fractions in the question stem. The fractions in the question stem are $\frac{1}{4}$, $\frac{1}{5}$, and $\frac{1}{3}$. So, Plug In $4 \times 5 \times 3 = 60$. If the manufacturer produces 60 cars, then $60 \times \frac{1}{4} = 15$ of them are sports cars, which means that $60 - 15 = 45$ are sedans. The problem then states that $60 \times \frac{1}{5} = 12$ of the cars manufactured are red and that $15 \times \frac{1}{3} = 5$ of the sports cars are red. Therefore, $12 - 5 = 7$ of the 45 sedans are red. The fraction of sedans that are red is $\frac{7}{45}$. The correct answer is (A).

10. **A** This is a Yes/No Data Sufficiency problem, so be prepared to Plug In more than once. The question states that line *l* is on the *xy*-plane, so draw the *xy*-plane. The problem asks if line *l* passes through the second quadrant, so label each quadrant. There is no further information about the line, so evaluate each statement independently. Statement (1) states that the slope of line *l* is negative. Plug In for line *l* by either selecting values for the *x*- and *y*-intercept, or by drawing any negative sloped line on the coordinate plane. If the *x*-intercept is 2, then the *y*-intercept must also be a positive number in order to make a negative slope. Plug In 3 for the *y*-intercept. The line that connects these intercepts is a negative line that passes through the second quadrant. Therefore, the answer to the question is "Yes." Plug In again in an attempt to produce a "No" answer to the question. If the *x*-intercept is –2, then the *y*-intercept must be a negative number in order to make a negative slope. Plug In –4 for the *y*-intercept. The line that connects these intercepts is a negative line that passes through the second quadrant. The answer to the question is still "Yes." In fact, no matter what line is drawn on the coordinate plane, if the line has a negative slope it will eventually pass through the second quadrant. This statement produces the same answer, so it is sufficient. Write down AD. Now work with Statement (2). The statement states that the absolute value of the *x*-intercept is greater than 3, so the *x*-intercept is either less than –3 or greater than 3. This statement provides no information about the slope of the line, so Plug In for the *y*-intecept. If the *x*-intercept is –4 and the *y*-intercept is 6, then the line has a positive slope and passes through the second quadrant. In this case, the answer to the question is "Yes." Plug In again in an attempt to get a "No" answer to the question. If the *x*-intercept is 4 and the *y*-intercept is –6, then the slope of the line is positive, but the answer to the question is now "No." The line no longer crosses through the second quadrant. This statement produces two different answers to the question, so it is not sufficient. Eliminate (D). The correct answer is (A).

## DRILL 9 (Applied Arithmetic)

1. **D** When objects move in the same direction, the difference in their rates may be calculated by subtraction. Teena's rate of 55 miles per hour minus Joe's rate of 40 miles per hour yields $55 - 40 = 15$ miles per hour. Thus, Teena travels 15 miles further than Joe every hour. Because Teena is currently 7.5 miles behind Joe, and the question asks in how many minutes she will be

15 miles ahead of Joe, Teena needs to cover a relative distance of 15 + 7.5 = 22.5 miles. Use $D = RT$, and solve for $T$. Therefore, 22.5 = 15 × $T$, which yields that $T = \frac{22.5}{15}$, or $T$ = 1.5 hours. Because there are 60 minutes in each hour, multiply 1.5 by 60 to determine the number of minutes. 1.5 × 60 = 90 minutes. The correct answer is (D).

2. **E** The problem provides the definition of the function $a\Delta b$ and asks for the value of $-1\Delta(1\Delta-1)$, so evaluate the expression in the parenthesis first. $(1\Delta-1)=\frac{(-1-1)^2}{1^2}$, which simplifies to $\frac{(-2)^2}{1}=4$. Now, evaluate $-1\Delta 4$. $-1\Delta 4=\frac{(4-(-1))^2}{(-1)^2}$, which simplifies to $\frac{(5)^2}{1}=25$. The correct answer is (E).

3. **C** The problem does not specify the number of workers or envelopes each worker can stuff, so Plug In. Let the number of full-time workers be 5. There are $\frac{2}{5}$ as many trainees as there are full-time workers, so there are $\frac{2}{5}\times 5=2$ trainees. Let the number of envelopes each full-time worker can stuff per day be 3. Each trainee can stuff $\frac{2}{3}$ as many envelopes as can a full-time worker, so each trainee can stuff $\frac{2}{3}\times 3=2$ envelopes per day. Thus, each day the full-time workers stuff $5\times 3=15$ envelopes, the trainees stuff $2\times 2=4$ envelopes, and together the two groups stuff $15+4=19$ envelopes. The trainees stuff 4 envelopes, so they stuffed $\frac{4}{19}$ of the envelopes. The correct answer is (C).

4. **E** There are variables in the answer choices, so Plug In. Let $x = 3$ and $y = 5$. The larger group consists of $3+2=5$ men and $5+4=9$ women, for a total of $5+9=14$ members. The probability of selecting a man from the larger group is $\frac{5}{14}$, and that is the target. Plug $x = 3$ and $y = 5$ into the answer choices, looking for the target of $\frac{5}{14}$. The correct answer is (E).

## DRILL 10 (Angles and Lengths)

1. $\mathbf{x = 110°}$ There are 180 degrees in a line, so 180 – 70 = 110.

2. $\mathbf{x = 50°; y = 130°; z = 130°}$

   There are 180 degrees in a line, and $y$ and $z$ each form lines with the 50° angle, so they each have a value of 180 – 50 = 130°. $x$ forms a line with either $y$ or $z$, so $x$ has a value of 180 – 130 = 50°.

3. $\mathbf{x = 60°; y = 120°; z = 120°}$

   $x$ forms a line with the 120-degree angle, so it equals 60. Then, with parallel lines, all the small angles are equal and all the big angles are equal. $y$ and $z$ are both big angles, so they both equal 120.

4. $\frac{3}{4}$ There are 360 degrees in a circle. Since the driver has traveled 270 degrees, he has traveled $\frac{270}{360}$ of the track. Reduce to get $\frac{3}{4}$.

5. **D** The question states that $l_1$ and $l_2$ are parallel, so redraw the figure twice, each time with just one of the lines intersecting $l_1$ and $l_2$. When looking at the line that goes down from left to right, notice that both *a* and *d* are "big" angles created as that line crosses $l_1$ and $l_2$ and therefore *a* and *d* must be equal. The correct answer is (D).

6. **C** Statement (1) provides the measure of *y*, but provides no information about angle *x*, so Statement (1) is insufficient. Write down BCE. Statement (2) indicates that $x + y = 180°$, but it provides no information to determine the value of either angle, so Statement (2) is insufficient. Eliminate (B). The statements together provide the relationship between the angles and the value of *y*, so the statements together are sufficient. The correct answer is (C).

## DRILL 11 (Triangles)

1. **8** The legs of a 45-45-90 triangle are the same. Since the other leg is 8, *x* must also be 8.

2. **60** Because all three sides of the triangle are equal, the angles of the triangle must also be equal. There are 180° in a triangle, so $x = 180 \div 3$, or 60°.

3. **5** Notice that this is a 3-4-5 right triangle, so $x = 5$. Alternately, by the Pythagorean Theorem, $3^2 + 4^2 = x^2$ yields $9 + 16 = x^2$, which simplifies to $25 = x^2$, or $x = 5$.

4. **$3 < x < 11$** The third side of a triangle is less than the sum and greater than the difference of the other two sides. Thus, *x* must be less than $7 + 4 = 11$ and greater than $7 - 4 = 3$.

5. **$3\sqrt{2}$** Since the figure is a square and line *AC* is the diagonal of the square, then the two triangles formed must be 45-45-90 triangles. The relationship for the sides of a 45-45-90 triangle is $x{:}x{:}x\sqrt{2}$. Since one of the sides is 3, then the diagonal must be $3\sqrt{2}$.

6. **$2\sqrt{3}$** The triangle is a 30-60-90 triangle, so the relationship of its sides is $x : x\sqrt{3} : 2x$. Since 4 aligns with the 2*x* side, the *x* side equals 2. Line segment *BC* is opposite the 60° angle, so *BC* aligns with the $x\sqrt{3}$ side, so *BC* is $2\sqrt{3}$.

7. **D** The figure is a triangle, and the sum of the interior angles of all triangles is 180. So, it is true that the sum of the values of angles *A, B,* and *C* equals 180, so $A + B + C = 180$. Substitute the values for the angles. Angle *A* is 90, angle *B* is *x*, and angle *C* is $x - 20$, so the equation can be rewritten as $90 + x + x - 20 = 180$. Solve for *x* to find that $x = 55$. The value of angle *C* is $x - 20$, so $C = 55 - 20 = 35$. The question asks for the ratio of the measure of angle *A* to the measure of angle *C*, which is 90 to 35. This can be reduced to a ratio of 9 to 3.5. The correct answer is (D).

8. **C** Recognize that the figure may not be drawn to scale. Statement (1) provides the measure of angle *y*, but it does not provide any way to solve for the value of *x*, so Statement (1) is insufficient. Write down BCE. Statement (2) indicates that $AB = BC$, which provides that *x* and *y* are equal, but it provides no means to determine their values, so Statement (2) is insufficient. Eliminate (B). Together, the statements provide that $x = y = 80$. The correct answer is (C).

## DRILL 12 (Circles)

1. **Area = 25π, Circumference = 10π**
   The formula for area is $\pi r^2$, and the formula for circumference is $2\pi r$. The radius is shown as 5, so area = $25\pi$ and circumference = $10\pi$.

2. **12π** The area of circle is given by $A = \pi r^2$, so the radius is $36\pi = \pi r^2$, which simplifies to $36 = r^2$, or $r = 6$. The circumference of a circle is given by $C = 2\pi r$, so the circumference is $2\pi(6) = 12\pi$.

3. **60** The relationship between arc and circumference is equal to relationship between a central angle which describes the arc and 360°. Thus, since $\frac{\text{arc}}{\text{circumference}} = \frac{1}{6}$, $\frac{x}{360} = \frac{1}{6}$, which yields that $x =$ 60.

4. **B** The area of the unshaded region is determined by subtracting the shaded region from the total region. The radius of the circle with center $N$ is 5, so the area of the circle with center $N$ is $\pi r^2 = \pi(5)^2$, or $25\pi$. The radius of the circle with center $P$ is equal to the diameter of the circle with center $N$, which is $2 \times 5 = 10$, so the area of the circle with center $P$ is $\pi r^2 = \pi(10)^2$, or $100\pi$. Thus, the area of the unshaded region is $100\pi - 25\pi = 75\pi$. The correct answer is (B).

5. **C** Statement (1) provides information about circle $Q$, but it provides no means by which to relate this information to circle $P$, so Statement (1) is insufficient. Write down BCE. Statement (2) provides a relationship between circles $Q$ and $P$, but no values, so Statement (2) is insufficient. Eliminate (B). The statements together provide that the radius of circle $Q$ is $6 \div 2 = 3$, and that the radius of circle $P$ is $3 \div 2 = 1.5$, which allows the question to be answered. The correct answer is (C).

## DRILL 13 (Coordinate Geometry)

1. **A** The problem provides a point on line $l$ and the slope of line $l$. This problem asks for a specific value and that value is represented by the answer choices, so Plug In the Answers. The expression for the slope of a line is $\frac{y_2 - y_1}{x_2 - x_1}$. Use the point (–3, 8) as the $x_2$ and $y_2$ values and the slope, which is –2, and set up the equation for slope. In this case, $\frac{8 - y_1}{-3 - x_1} = -2$. Now Plug In the Answer choices for $x_1$ and $y_1$ and see which produces an answer of –2. Begin with (C). If the point is (1, 4) then the equation is $\frac{8-4}{-3-1} = \frac{4}{-4} = -1$, which is not equal to the slope from the question. Eliminate (C). It is difficult to know which answer choice to try next, so pick one. Try (B). If the point is (–1, 7), then the equation is $\frac{8-7}{-3-(-1)} = \frac{1}{-2} = -\frac{1}{2}$. This is not the same as the slope in the question, so eliminate (B). Try (A). If the point is (–2, 6), then the equation is $\frac{8-6}{-3-(-2)} = \frac{2}{-1} = -2$. This matches the slope in the problem. The correct answer is (A).

2. **B** The vertex of the parabola is at point (–1, 6) and one of the $x$-intercepts is at point (3, 0). The distance between the $x$-intercept and the $x$-coordinate of the vertex is $3 - (-1) = 4$. The distance between the other $x$-intercept and the vertical is also 4, so the $x$-coordinate of the other $x$-intercept is $-1 - 4 = -5$. The correct answer is (B).

3. **C** This is a Yes/No Data Sufficiency question, so Plug In. The question asks if the slope of the line that passes through point $(x, y)$ is negative. Evaluate each of the statements individually, looking for a consistent "Yes" or "No" answer to the question. Statement (1) states that the $x$-intercept of the line is $a$ and $a < x$. Plug In numbers such as $a = 2$ and $x = 3$. This satisfies the statement. However, this statement gives no information about the value of $y$. If $y$ is positive, then the slope of the line is positive. However, if $y$ is negative, then the slope of the line is negative. This statement provides two different answers to the question, so it is insufficient. Write down BCE. Statement (2) states that both $x$ and $y$ are less than 0. This statement is not enough information to determine the slope of the line because it gives information about only one point on the line. To determine if the slope is positive or negative, information about two points is needed. Eliminate (B). Now evaluate both statements together. If $a = -3$ and $x = -2$, then the first statement is satisfied. Plug In $y = -1$ and use the slope formula to find the slope of the line. The slope of the line is $\frac{-1-0}{-2-(-3)} = -\frac{1}{1} = -1$. In this case, the slope of the line is negative and the answer to the question is "Yes." Plug In again in an attempt to get a "No" answer to the question. Plug In extreme numbers such as $a = -100$, $x = -2$, and $y = -5$. In this case, the slope of the line is $\frac{-5-0}{-2-(-100)} = -\frac{5}{102}$. The slope is still negative. In fact, no matter what number is Plugged In for the variables, the slope of the line is always negative. The correct answer is (C).

4. **B** This question asks to solve for the equation of the line that passes through points (18, 5) and (10, 10). The equation for a line is defined as $y = mx + b$, where $m$ is the slope and $b$ is the $y$-intercept. Begin by solving for the slope of the line. The expression for the slope of a line is $\frac{y_2 - y_1}{x_2 - x_1}$, so Plug In the coordinates of the points. The slope of this line is $\frac{10-5}{10-18} = -\frac{5}{8}$. Use this value for the slope and one of the points to solve for a missing point $(x, y)$. The equation is now $\frac{y-5}{x-18} = -\frac{5}{8}$. Cross-multiply to find that $-8y + 40 = 5x - 90$. Write this in the slope intercept form by subtracting 40 to both sides and dividing by $-8$ to reveal that $y = -\frac{5}{8}x - \frac{65}{4}$. The correct answer is (B).

5. **B** This is a Yes/No Data Sufficiency question, so be prepared to Plug In more than once. Before Plugging In, begin by working with the question stem and figure and manipulate them to reveal the information present. The problem asks about the area of the triangles. The area of a triangle is found by the expression $\frac{1}{2}(base)(height)$. The height of both triangles is 4, so rewrite this as $\frac{1}{2}(base)(4)$. The base of triangle $QRS$ is the variable $c$, so the area of triangle $QRS$ is $\frac{1}{2}(c)(4)$. The

base of triangle $STU$ is $d - c$, so the area of triangle $STU$ is $\frac{1}{2}(d-c)(4)$. The question asks if the areas of the triangles are equal, which can be represented by the equation $\frac{1}{2}(c)(4) = \frac{1}{2}(d-c)(4)$. This can be rewritten as $2c = 2(d - c)$ or $c = d - c$, which can be rewritten as $d = 2c$. Therefore, if any of the statements provides information that determines that $d = 2c$, then that statement is sufficient. Evaluate the statements one at a time. Statement (1) states that $b = 2a$. This does not provide any information about the values of $d$ and $c$, so this statement is not sufficient. Write down BCE. Evaluate Statement (2). Statement (2) provides that $d = 2c$, which matches exactly the information determined from the question stem. Therefore, Statement (2) is sufficient. The correct answer is (B).

## DRILL 14 (Data Sufficiency Parts and Wholes)

1. **C** Statement (1) provides the number of people who *paid deposits*, which may seem sufficient, but the question allows for the possibility that a person may pay a deposit and yet not attend, so Statement (1) is insufficient. Write down BCE. Statement (2) provides the percent of people who attended after paying a deposit, but it does not indicate the number of people who paid a deposit, so Statement (2) is insufficient. Eliminate (B). The statements together indicate that 60% of the 70 people who paid deposits attend, which allows the question to be answered. The correct answer is (C).

2. **D** Statement (1) provides an amount of pigment and a total volume, which allows solving for the amount of alcohol and subsequently the ratio of alcohol to pigment, as there are only two ingredients in the paint. Statement (1) is sufficient. Write down AD. Similarly, Statement (2) provides an amount of alcohol and a total volume, which also allows solving for the ratio of alcohol to pigment. Statement (2) is sufficient. The correct answer is (D).

3. **C** Statement (1) provides the proportional distances between the three towns, but no specific values, so Statement (1) is insufficient. Write down BCE. Statement (2) provides the distance from Ferristown to Laredo, but it provides no information about the distance from Smithville to Ferristown, so Statement (2) is insufficient. Eliminate (B). Together, the statements provide that Ferristown to Laredo is 12 miles, which is $\frac{2}{5}$ of the distance from Smithville to Laredo, and allows the question to be answered. The correct answer is (C).

## DRILL 15 (Strange Powers of Powers)

1. **C** Statement (1) provides that $x^2 = 4$, which indicates that $x$ is equal to either 2 or $-2$. Statement (1) is insufficient. Write down BCE. Statement (2) provides only that $x < 0$, so Statement (2) is insufficient. Eliminate (B). Together the statements indicate that $x = -2$. The correct answer is (C).

2. **B** Statement (1) provides that $x^2 = 4$, which indicates that $x$ is equal to either 2 or $-2$, and provides no information about $y$. Statement (1) is insufficient. Write down BCE. Statement (2) provides that $y = 0$. While no information is provided about the value of $x$, any value multiplied by 0 is equal to 0, so Statement (2) is sufficient. The correct answer is (B).

3. **E** Statement (1) provides that $x^2 = 4$, which indicates that $x$ is equal to either 2 or $-2$, and provides no information about $y$. Statement (1) is insufficient. Write down BCE. Statement (2) provides that $y^2 = 9$, which indicates that $y$ is equal to either 3 or $-3$, and provides no information about $x$. Statement (2) is insufficient. Eliminate (B). Together the statements provide possible values for both $x$ and $y$, but allow for both 6 and $-6$ as possible values of $xy$, so the statements together are insufficient. Eliminate (C). The correct answer is (E).

## DRILL 16 (Yes or No)

1. **A** Statement (1) states that $2x < 1$. Divide by 2 to yield that $x < \frac{1}{2}$. The answer to the question is "Yes." Statement (1) is sufficient. Write down AD. Statement (2) states that $2x \leq 2$. Divide by 2 to yield that $x \leq 1$. $x$ can equal 1, and the answer to the question is "No." $x$ can also equal $\frac{1}{2}$, and the answer to the question is "Yes." When two values that satisfy a statement yield different answers to the question, the statement is insufficient. The correct answer is (A).

2. **B** Statement (1) states that $xy = 6$. Let $x = 2$ and $y = 3$. These values satisfy the statement and the answer to the question is "Yes." Try to arrive at an answer of "No." Let $x = -2$ and $y = -3$. These values satisfy the statement and the answer to the question is "No." When two values that satisfy a statement yield different answers to the question, the statement is insufficient. Write down BCE. Statement (2) states that $xy^2 = 12$. Let $x = 3$ and $y = 2$. These values satisfy the statement and the answer to the question is "Yes." Try to arrive at an answer of "No." Because the product is not equal to 0, $y^2$ must be positive. Thus, $x$ must also be positive in order to yield a product of positive 12. Statement (2) is sufficient. The correct answer is (B).

3. **E** Statement (1) states that $xy$ is an integer. Let $x = 2$ and $y = 3$. These values satisfy the statement and the answer to the question is "Yes." Try to arrive at an answer of "No." Let $x = \frac{1}{2}$ and $y = 2$. These values satisfy the statement and the answer to the question is "No." When two values that satisfy a statement yield different answers to the question, the statement is insufficient. Write down BCE. Statement (2) states that $x + y$ is an integer. Let $x = 2$ and $y = 3$. These values satisfy the statement and the answer to the question is "Yes." Try to arrive at an answer of "No." Let $x = \frac{1}{2}$ and $y = \frac{1}{2}$. These values satisfy the statement, and the answer to the question is "No." Statement (2) is insufficient. Eliminate (B). Together, the statements may seem to be sufficient, and the values of $x = 2$ and $y = 3$ will allow a "Yes" answer, but let $x = \sqrt{2}$ and $y = \sqrt{2}$. These values satisfy the statements and the answer to the question is "No." The statements together are insufficient. Eliminate (C). The correct answer is (E).

## Parts of Speech Identification Quiz

| | Sentence, Phrase, or Clause | Part of Speech |
|---|---|---|
| 1. | He always *speaks* the truth. | Verb |
| 2. | She *frequently* writes articles for the school newspaper. | Adverb |
| 3. | The students dressed *smartly* for the class picture. | Adverb |
| 4. | Clowns, acrobats, *and* elephants | Conjunction |
| 5. | *Our* family visited relatives in Florida. | Adjective |
| 6. | *Wow!* This is great! | Interjection |
| 7. | Most of the *yellow* cars are taxis. | Adjective |
| 8. | Helen took the used oil *to* the recycling center. | Preposition |
| 9. | The orders *came* from the colonel. | Verb |
| 10. | *An* example of a wild animal is a tiger. | Article |
| 11. | *Gorillas* can be found at many zoos. | Common noun |
| 12. | It takes a *fast* car to win the Indy 500. | Adjective |
| 13. | His favorite color is *blue.* | Common noun |
| 14. | *Large* trucks on the freeway are frequently called "semis." | Adjective |
| 15. | *She* rarely ate dessert. | Pronoun |
| 16. | Camels can *go* for days without water. | Verb |
| 17. | Dad came back *from* the store. | Preposition |
| 18. | The dog *followed* Paul home. | Verb |

## Clause or Phrase Identification Quiz

| | Identify whether clause or phrase | Clause or Phrase? |
|---|---|---|
| 1. | He works hard every day. | Clause |
| 2. | Before the next light. | Phrase |
| 3. | In a dark and dangerous hallway. | Phrase |
| 4. | If I need to call you. | Clause |
| 5. | After a good day. | Phrase |
| 6. | Because it's the right thing to do. | Clause |
| 7. | As quickly as possible. | Phrase |
| 8. | This car's not working. | Clause |
| 9. | Working for himself. | Phrase |
| 10. | Whenever it gets cold. | Clause |
| 11. | If they want to talk to me. | Clause |
| 12. | Toward the north. | Phrase |
| 13. | In front of the building. | Phrase |
| 14. | Until the next time. | Phrase |
| 15. | I don't know the answer. | Clause |

## Figure of Speech Identification Quiz

| | Sentence, Clause, or Phrase | Figure of Speech |
|---|---|---|
| 1. | He was as brave as a lion. | Simile |
| 2. | "All the world's a stage." | Metaphor |
| 3. | Death lays its icy hands on kings of old. | Personification |
| 4. | Let's just say that Bozo the Clown is not the brightest bulb in the box. | Litotes |
| 5. | The earth laughed beneath our feet. | Personification |
| 6. | The ocean looks like a thousand diamonds strewn across a blue blanket. | Simile |
| 7. | Why do we wait until a pig is dead before we cure it? | Pun |
| 8. | Necessity is the mother of invention. | Personification |
| 9. | Humming bee, buzzing saw, and cackling hen are examples of what? | Onomatopoeia |
| 10. | My uncle passed away in 1970. | Euphemism |
| 11. | "To err is human, to forgive divine." | Antithesis |
| 12. | The rancher bought 50 head of cattle last week. | Synecdoche |
| 13. | The teacher made it clear that cheating was no laughing matter. | Litotes |
| 14. | I'm so hungry I could eat a horse. | Hyperbole |
| 15. | The old man is long in the tooth. | Idiom |
| 16. | In Crown Hill Cemetery are buried President Benjamin Harrison, three vice-presidents, fifteen senators and governors, and John Dillinger. | Anticlimax |
| 17. | Phillip fractured five fingers. | Alliteration |

## DRILL 17 (Sentence Correction)

1. **D** The underlined portion of the sentence contains the construction *as not…but as* which is a parallelism error as the appropriate structure is *not as…but as.* Eliminate (A). There are no obvious repeaters so evaluate each remaining choice individually. Choice (B) drops the *as* after *but* and does not resolve the original error as the sentence is still not parallel in construction. Eliminate (B). Choice (C) eliminates the use of the word *as* entirely, which creates the unidiomatic construction *not…rather.* Eliminate (C). Choice (D) fixes the original error and commits no new errors, so keep (D). Choice (E) eliminates the comparison word *as* which creates an idiom error. Eliminate (E). The correct answer is (D).

2. **B** The underlined portion of the sentence contains the phrase *at first begin* which is redundant, so eliminate (A). There are no obvious repeaters, so evaluate the remaining answer choices individually. Choice (B) fixes the original error and makes no new errors, so keep (B). Choice (C) begins with a dependent clause, which is followed by an independent clause. However, the conjunction *and* is used to link two independent clauses rather than a dependent and independent clause. Eliminate (C). Choice (D) uses the conjunction *Because* which indicates that the migration of the birds from east to west causes them to turn south. This in a conjunction error, so eliminate (D). Choice (E) has a subject verb error as the sentence begins with a main subject, *bird species*, but that subject is not followed by a verb. Eliminate (E). The correct answer is (B).

3. **E** The underlined portion contains the subject of the sentence, *managers.* This subject needs a main verb. However, the sentence uses the present participle form of the verb, *emphasizing*, and the participial form of the verb cannot be the main verb of a sentence. Here, the participle introduces a participial phrase, *emphasizing…temperament*, which modifies *managers.* Eliminate (A) and look for obvious repeaters. Choice (B) obviously repeats the error, so eliminate (B). Evaluate the remaining answers individually. Choice (C) fixes the problem with the main verb. However, *most hiring practices* is the subject of a clause and also needs a verb. Choice (C) uses *having struggled*, a participial form, rather than a main verb form such as *had struggled.* As participles cannot be used as main verbs, eliminate (C). Choice (D) has a parallelism error. The main verb of the sentence, *emphasized*, is in the past tense, so any additional verbs in the sentence need to use some form of the past tense to maintain parallelism. Choice (D) uses *struggle*, the present tense, so eliminate (D). Choice (E) fixes the original error and makes no new errors. The correct answer is (E).

4. **B** The underlined portion of the sentence begins with a modifying phrase. The noun following the modifying phrase is *Irish wolfhound's initial purpose*, which is incorrectly modified by the opening phrase, which describes *a breed of dog.* The noun the modifying phrase needs to modify is *purpose,* as *Irish wolfhound* in this case is in the possessive form and acts as an adjective. Eliminate (A) and look for any obvious repeaters. There are no obvious repeaters, so evaluate the answer choices individually. Choice (B) fixes the original error by rearranging the sentence so that *a breed of dog* modifies *Irish wolfhound* and the main subject of the sentence is *initial purpose.* This choice makes no new errors, so keep (B). Choice (C) makes *Irish wolfhound* the subject of *including,* which is a participle and cannot be used as a main verb. Eliminate (C). Choice (D) has a parallelism error as *included…is* are not in similar verb tenses. Eliminate (D). Choice (E) has a verb form error as *to hunting* is not the correct construction for an infinitive. Eliminate (E). The correct answer is (B).

5. **B** The underlined portion of the sentence contains the word *large* which is part of the phrase *large and more consistent.* The phrase *large and more consistent* is not parallel because *more consistent* is the comparative form of the adjective while *large* is not. To complete the comparison in a way that is also parallel, the comparative form of *large,* which is *larger,* must be used. Eliminate (A) and look for obvious repeaters. Choice (E) obviously repeats the error, so eliminate (E), as well. Evaluate the remaining answer choices individually. Choice (B) fixes the original error and makes no new errors, so keep (B). Choice (C) uses the word *thus* which creates the construction *ways…thus* which does not accurately convey the intended meaning of the sentence. Eliminate (C). Choice (D) pairs *so that* with *ways* creating the incorrect idiom *ways…so that.* Eliminate (D). The correct answer is (B).

6. **E** The underlined portion of the sentence contains the comparison *as with.* As currently constructed, the sentence compares *tech industry employee benefits* to *other industries* which is an incorrect comparison. Eliminate (A) and look for obvious repeaters. There are no obvious repeaters, so evaluate the remaining answer choices individually. Choice (B) fixes the original error by including the pronoun *those* to refer to *employee benefits,* but also uses the verb *did* which is not parallel in tense with the verb *were* used later in the sentence. Eliminate (B). Choice (C) uses the present tense verb phrase *they have,* which does not agree with the past tense verb *were.* This is a verb agreement error. Eliminate (C). Choice (D) does not fix the original error as the sentence still compares *tech industry employee benefits* to *other industries.* Eliminate (D). Choice (E) fixes the original error and makes no additional errors, so keep (E). The correct answer is (E).

7. **B** The sentence contains a conjunction, *and,* so look for a parallelism error. However, it is unclear whether the list consists of two things that the organization does, *aims* and *partnering with,* or two of the organization's aims, *to aid* and *partnering.* In either case, *partnering* is not the same verb form as the first part of the list, so there is a parallelism problem. Eliminate (A). Evaluate the remaining answer choices individually. Choice (B) fixes the original error and makes it clear that the list is comprised of two things the organization does, *aims* and *partners,* and makes no new errors, so keep (B). Choice (C) also fixes the original error as the list could now be *aims to aid…and partner.* However, this choice has an idiom error as the correct idiom is *partner…to (do something)* rather than *partner…for (doing something).* Eliminate (C). Choice (D) also fixes the original error but contains the pronoun *their* which is ambiguous in this sentence. Eliminate (D). Choice (E) uses the phrase *in partnership* which is not parallel with either *aims* or *to aid,* so eliminate (E). The correct answer is (B).

8. **E** The underlined portion of the sentence contains the comparison construction *equally likely to…as.* The correct comparison construction is *as…as.* This is an incorrect comparison, so eliminate (A) and look for obvious repeaters. Choice (B) obviously repeats the error as it contains the construction *equally likely to…as.* Eliminate (B). Evaluate the remaining answer choices individually. Choice (C) contains the comparison construction equally *likely that...as,* which is a comparison idiom error. Eliminate (C). Choice (D) fixes the original error but it does not have a parallel comparison. The construction *they will purchase* is compared to *the current one.* Eliminate (D). Choice (E) fixes the original error and makes no further errors, so keep (E). The correct answer is (E).

9. **A** The sentence is correct as written. The plural verb *indicate* matches with the plural subject *an increase…and a decrease* and the comparison, which uses the proper *as…as* structure, is correct in the sentence. Evaluate the remaining answer choices individually. Choice (B) uses the singular verb *indicates* which creates a subject-verb agreement error. Eliminate (B). Choice (C) uses the verb *have been* which is the incorrect verb tense. Eliminate (C). Choice (D) uses the verb *indicating* which eliminates the main verb of the sentence. Eliminate (D). Choice (E) uses the verb *indicating* which eliminates the main verb of the sentence. Eliminate (E). The correct answer is (A).

10. **B** The underlined portion of the sentence contains a list of items that describes *the concept of exchange* that ancient Greek religious practices were premised on. The list states that *gods and goddesses bestowed...humans gave...and when they.* The final item in this list is not parallel with the other items in the sentence and it contains the ambiguous pronoun *they* which does not clearly refer to either *gods or goddesses* or *humans.* Eliminate (A) and look for obvious repeaters. Choice (C) is an obvious repeater as it also contains the ambiguous pronoun *they,* so eliminate (C), as well. Evaluate the remaining answer choices individually. Choice (B) fixes the original error by eliminating the use of the pronoun *they* and fixes the parallelism error by making the list of items *bestowed...gave...constructed.* Additionally, the use of the conjunction *while* emphasizes the transactional nature of the relationship better than the conjunction *and.* Keep (B). Choice (D) contains the construction *gods and goddesses bestowed...and humans to give...and to construct.* This is a parallelism error, so eliminate (D). Choice (E) eliminates the use of the pronoun *they* and uses the construction *bestowed...gave...constructed,* which is parallel. However, the sentence is rearranged to create a modifier error. As currently constructed, the phrase *bestowed gifts* describes *the concept of exchange.* This is in opposition to the intended meaning in which *the concept of exchange* is described by *gods and goddesses bestowed gifts* and *humans gave... and constructed.* Eliminate (E). The correct answer is (B).

11. **A** The sentence is correct as written. The construction *that was evident* is consistent with the tense of the remainder of the sentence, and the idiom *evident in* is used correctly, so there appear to be no errors in this sentence. Because there appear to be no errors, there are no obvious repeaters. Evaluate the answer choices individually, looking for reasons to eliminate each.

    Choice (B) uses the unidiomatic construction *evident by,* so eliminate (B). Choice (C) changes the tense of the verb to *evidenced* which is not parallel to the rest of the sentence and also uses the unidiomatic construction *evidenced with,* so eliminate (C). Choice (D) commits the same verb tense error as (C) and also uses the unidiomatic construction *evidenced of,* so eliminate (D). Choice (E) uses the unidiomatic construction *evident of,* so eliminate (E). The correct answer is (A).

## DRILL 18 (Reading Comprehension)

1. **D** The subject of the question is the *amygdala* and the task of the question is revealed by the statement *is true,* which indicates this is a purpose question. The question asks which of the answer choices is true. Begin by determining what the passage says about the amygdala. The amygdala is discussed in the second paragraph, which states that *MRI scans* showed a *reduction in the size of the amygdala* for people who engaged in an *eight-week meditation practice.* The passage then goes on to state the purpose of the amygdala as the *"fight or flight" part of the brain* that dictates the *response to stress.* Next, the passage relates the amygdala's response to mindfulness meditation to the prefrontal cortex's response. Evaluate the answer choices one at a time, looking for one that is supported by the information in the passage.

    Choice (A) uses the extreme language *long-term damage,* which is cause for suspicion. The passage mentions that meditation reduces the size of the amygdala but does not state anything about the long-term implications of the reductions in size, nor does the passage suggest any *damage* to the amygdala is caused by meditation. Eliminate (A). Choice (B) uses the extreme language *less valuable,* so be suspicious of this answer choice, as well. While the passage discusses the differences in the responses of the amygdala and the prefrontal cortex, the passage does not make any indication about the value of one over the other. Eliminate (B). Choice (C) also utilizes extreme language with the phrase *direct correlation.* The passage does not state that there is a correlation between the size of the amygdala and the thickness of the prefrontal cortex. The passage mentions both the size of the amygdala and the thickness of the prefrontal cortex but does not state they are correlated, simply that they both occur. Eliminate (C). Choice (D) is supported by the passage, which discusses the size of the amygdala based on a response to meditation and then states that *increased meditation may be capable of replacing our fearful responses to stress.* In other words, the size of the amygdala has some link to the type of response exhibited under stress. Keep (D). Choice (E) utilizes recycled language as the passage does mention the *relationship between the amygdala and the rest of the brain.* However, the passage does not state that this relationship is impacted by the thickness of the prefrontal cortex. Eliminate (E). The correct answer is (D).

2. **B** The subject of the question is the passage as a whole and the task is identified by the phrase *primarily concerned with,* so this is a primary purpose question. Evaluate the statements individually to determine which best describes the primary purpose of the passage.

Choice (A) is an example of extreme language because the passage does not attempt to *convince* the reader of anything. Eliminate (A). Choice (B) is a good description of the primary purpose of the passage, as the passage is *primarily concerned with* spreading information about the science and the debates regarding the brain's response to meditation. Keep (B). Choice (C) is an example of extreme language as the passage does not argue that meditation is the *most effective* way to do anything. The passage is not concerned with the level of effectiveness of meditation. Eliminate (C). Choice (D) is a memory trap because the passage does mention those who believe that meditation should be considered a science in the last paragraph. However, this is not the primary purpose of the passage. Eliminate (D). Choice (E) appeals to outside knowledge and is also a memory trap as the passage is not primarily concerned with ways to better handle stress, but rather that meditation is commonly thought to be a way to handle stress, and the response to stress is discussed in the passage. Eliminate (E). The correct answer is (B).

3. **D** The subject of the passage is the *fearful response to stress,* and the task of the passage is identified by the word *inferred,* so this is an inference question. The correct answer to inference questions must be true based on the information in the passage, so look for an answer choice that is definitely true given the contents of the passage.

While (A) is tempting, it is actually an example of extreme language. The passage states that responses to stress *may be altered* by practicing meditation, from fearful to rational. The passage does not definitively state if fearful responses *can be replaced.* Eliminate (A). Choice (B) is a memory trap from the passage's statement that meditation may cause the thickness of the prefrontal cortex to increase but does not mention the likelihood of having a fearful response to stress based on the thickness of the prefrontal cortex. Eliminate (B). Choice (C) is a memory trap, as the passage discusses whether meditation should be considered a science but does not have that same debate over the research regarding fearful responses. Eliminate (C). Choice (D) is supported by the last sentence of the second paragraph and the first sentence of the third paragraph, which state *These findings prompted researchers to hypothesize that increased meditation may be capable of replacing our fearful responses to stress with more rational ones. While researchers have called for more studies to be done on the mental and physical ramifications of mindfulness meditation....* Keep (D). Choice (E) is a recycled language trap. The word *MRI* is used in the passage, but the passage states that MRIs show the amygdala. The passage does not state that MRI scans show fearful responses. Eliminate (E). The correct answer is (D).

4. **A** The subject of the question is *proponent of meditation-as-science* and the task of the question is found in the phrase *most likely to argue is not a science.* This is an application question, so begin by determining what the passage states about proponents of meditation as a science. The passage states that these individuals define science as *the study of the natural world through observation and experiment to produce a unified body of knowledge on a given subject.* The question asks to identify which one of the answer choices is *not* considered a science based on that definition. Evaluate the answer choices individually.

Choice (A) does not meet the requirement that the study be of the *natural world*, nor does it seek to create a *unified body of knowledge* through *observation and experiment.* Keep (A). Choice (B) pertains to the natural world and produces a unified body of knowledge through observation. This fits the definition of science, so eliminate (B). Choice (C) is a study of the natural world that seeks to explain events based on observation, so eliminate (C). Choice (D) deals with observations of the natural world and experiments to predict future events. This matches the definition of science, so eliminate (D). Choice (E) produces a unified body of knowledge pertaining to the natural world through observation and experimentation with samples of wood. Eliminate (E). The correct answer is (A).

5. **A** The subject of the question is the passage as a whole. The task of the question is found in the phrase *primary purpose,* so this is a primary purpose question. Evaluate the answer choices individually to determine which best describes the primary purpose of the passage.

Choice (A) is a good description of the primary purpose of the passage as the passage does seek to *describe* artificial neural networks, so keep (A). Choice (B) is a no such comparison trap answer. While the passage does discuss artificial neural networks and neural networks found in the brain, the passage does not *contrast* these different networks. Eliminate (B). Choice (C) is a memory trap. The passage does discuss the general construction of artificial neural networks but does not *illustrate how to build* them. Eliminate (C). Choice (D) is an example of extreme language as the passage does not *argue* for anything. The passage only provides information about neural networks. Eliminate (D). Choice (E) is a recycled language trap. The passage does mention the different *units* of an artificial neural network and their roles in producing intelligence, but this is not the primary purpose of the passage. The information about the units of the artificial neural network is only half of the information contained in the passage. Eliminate (E). The correct answer is (A).

6. **C** The subject of the question is *real neural networks.* The task of the question is *inferred,* which indicates this is an inference question. The correct answer for inference questions must be true based on the information in the passage, so determine what the passage states about real neural networks. The passage states that real neural networks are *found inside a brain* and that artificial neural networks *are designed to simulate the activity of real neural networks.* Evaluate the answer choices, looking for one that is true based on this information.

Choice (A) is an example of extreme language as the passage does not suggest that real neural networks *are to be considered superior to artificial neural networks.* Eliminate (A). Choice (B) is a recycled language trap. The passage states that artificial neural networks have *input, hidden, and output units* and are designed to simulate real neural networks. However, the passage does not state that real neural networks contain those units. Eliminate (B). Choice (C) is true based on the information in the passage. If artificial neural networks *are designed to simulate the activity of real neural networks,* then it can be said that real neural networks *inspired the development of artificial neural networks.* Keep (C). Choice (D) is a no such comparison answer as the passage does not compare the capability of real and artificial neural networks. Eliminate (D). Choice (E) is an example of extreme language as the passage does not suggest that real neural networks *will someday become obsolete.* Eliminate (E). The correct answer is (C).

7. **C** The subject of the question is *the optimal flow of information through an artificial neural network.* The task of the question is revealed by the phrase *according to the passage,* so this is a retrieval question. Determine which of the answer choices best represents the subject of the question by first determining what the passage says about the flow of information through an artificial neural network. The second paragraph of the passage gives *the flow of information through* as *Information is passed to the input units, which trigger the hidden units. The hidden units are activated and the sum of the inputs it receives triggers the next unit to fire if the sum exceeds a certain threshold. By giving the output units a model to compare the result of the learning process to, the artificial neural network can learn where to place more weight in order to make the result of the output unit more closely resemble that of the model.* Evaluate the answer choices individually, looking for one that optimizes this path.

   Choice (A) is incorrect, as the input units do not directly pass information to the output units. Eliminate (A). Choice (B) is incorrect as the hidden units do not *change the input units to more closely resemble the model.* Eliminate (B). Choice (C) accurately reflects the optimized path for an artificial neural network as stated in the passage, so keep (C). Choice (D) does not mention the hidden units or the output units, so eliminate (D). Choice (E) states that the output units analyze a model and improve it before handing the model to the input units, which does not match the information in the passage. Eliminate (E). The correct answer is (C).

## DRILL 19 (Spotting Critical Reasoning Question Types)

1. **Strengthen question.**
   Look for the conclusion and premise in the question. The correct answer will strengthen a premise that supports the conclusion.

2. **Inference question.**
   Look for information in the passage that pertains to the subject of the question.

3. **Evaluate question.**
   Look for assumptions in the passage.

4. **Assumption question.**
   To find the correct answer, look for the gap in the argument.

5. **Flaw question.**
   The passage should contain information that can be disputed. Find that information and anything that contradicts it.

6. **Weaken question.**
   Look for the conclusion and premise in the argument. The correct answer will weaken a premise that supports the conclusion.

7. **Identify the reasoning question.**
   The passage will provide a response to an assertion and the correct answer will reveal how the response was made.

8. **Resolve/Explain question.**
   Look for two incongruent facts in the passage and find a way to explain why both facts could be simultaneously true.

### How to Score Your Integrated Reasoning Section

Integrated Reasoning sections are scored on a scale from 1 to 8. Use the chart at the right to approximate your score.

Please note that Integrated Reasoning items are scored all or nothing. For example, Table Analysis items have three parts. You must have picked the correct answer for each part to count the item as correct.

Please also note that Integrated Reasoning sections on the GMAT contain experimental questions that do not count toward your score. The chart has been adjusted to compensate for the fact that these sections do not contain experimental questions.

| Number Correct | Approximate Score |
|---|---|
| 0–1 | 1 |
| 2 | 2 |
| 3–4 | 3 |
| 5–6 | 4 |
| 7–8 | 5 |
| 9–10 | 6 |
| 11 | 7 |
| 12 | 8 |

## INTEGRATED REASONING DRILLS: Section 1

### Item 1: Table Analysis

**1-1. True** Read the text blurb to learn that *% Change* refers to the time period from 2009 to 2010. Sort the table by *Riders* to identify the station with the median annual number of riders: *34th Street/Penn Station (Red Lines).* Note that *Grand Central/42nd Street* is the only other station that experienced a decrease in ridership from 2009 to 2010. Determine the actual decrease in ridership for these two stations.

Approximately 27,000,000 riders visited *34th Street/Penn Station (Red Lines)* in 2010. The number of riders who visited this station decreased by 1.1% from 2009, so 2010 ridership was 98.9% of 2009 ridership. Set up a proportion, $\frac{98.9}{100} = \frac{27,000,000}{x}$, where $x$ represents 2009 ridership. Use the calculator to find that $x \approx 27,300,000$. The actual decrease in ridership for *34th Street/Penn Station (Red Lines)* was approximately 27,300,000 – 27,000,000 = 300,000 riders.

Calculate the actual decrease in ridership at the *Grand Central/42nd Street* station in the same manner. Approximately 85,000 fewer riders visited *Grand Central/42nd Street* in 2010 than had visited the station in 2009. Since the actual decrease was greater at *34th Street/Penn Station (Red Lines),* the statement is true.

**1-2. True** Sort the table by *Connecting Subway Lines* to quickly identify which stations have 3 connecting lines and which have 5. Use the calculator to determine that the average number of riders at stations with 5 connecting lines is 31,307,134, and that the average number of riders at stations with 3 connecting lines is 23,434,760. Use the calculator again to determine that the average at stations with 5 connecting lines is approximately 1.34 times the average at stations with 3 connecting lines. Expressed as a fraction, $1.34 \approx \frac{4}{3}$, so the statement is true.

**1-3. False** Sort the table by *% Change* to quickly identify the station with the greatest percent increase in riders: *Lexington Ave/59th Street.* Now, sort the table by *Riders* to quickly identify the station with the least number of riders: *86th Street (Green Lines).* Since *Lexington Ave/59th Street* does not have the least number of riders, the statement is false.

## Item 2: Two-Part Analysis

### Column 1: Services Not Covered by Medical Plan—Choice (B)

The passage identifies mutually exclusive groups of doctors: doctors who either graduated with honors or who did not, and doctors who are either covered by Frank's medical plan or who are not. Use a group grid to represent the information provided. Since all of the information refers to the same population of doctors, the two columns are linked; a single group grid can be used to find the answer in both columns.

| | Services Covered by Medical Plan | Services Not Covered by Medical Plan | Total |
|---|---|---|---|
| Graduated With Honors | 3 | | 8 |
| Graduated Without Honors | 27 | | |
| Total | | | 45 |

Complete the bottom row of the grid to determine the number of doctors whose services are not covered by Frank's medical plan. If 3 doctors whose services are covered graduated with honors, and 27 doctors whose services are covered graduated without honors, then the services of $3 + 27 = 30$ doctors are covered by Frank's plan. If there are 45 doctors in Frank's area, then the services of $45 - 30 = 15$ doctors are not covered by Frank's plan. The correct answer is (B).

### Column 2: Graduated Without Honors and Services Not Covered by Medical Plan—Choice (A)

Complete the middle row of the grid to determine the number of doctors who didn't graduate with honors and aren't covered by Frank's medical plan. If 8 of the 45 local doctors graduated with honors, then $45 - 8 = 37$ doctors graduated without honors. Of those 37 doctors, 27 of them are covered by Frank's plan. Therefore, $37 - 27 = 10$ doctors without honors aren't covered by Frank's plan. The correct answer is (A).

| | Services Covered by Medical Plan | Services Not Covered by Medical Plan | Total |
|---|---|---|---|
| Graduated With Honors | 3 | | 8 |
| Graduated Without Honors | 27 | | |
| Total | 30 | 15 | 45 |

## Item 3: Two-Part Analysis

**Column 1: Orchids—Choice (F)**

**Column 2: Dahlias—Choice (C)**

The first column asks for the number of orchids purchased, and the second asks for the number of dahlias purchased. Translate the information provided into an algebraic equation, $1.35o + 1.8d = 18$, where $o$ and $d$ represent the number of orchids and dahlias purchased, respectively. Since $o$ and $d$ are related by a single equation, the two columns are linked.

The number of each type of flower must be an integer. Therefore, if Faustino spends $18 on orchids and dahlias, and each orchid costs $1.35, Faustino must buy an even number of orchids (an odd number of orchids would never yield an integer value for the price of the flowers). Eliminate (D) in the first column because it is odd. Plug in the remaining answers to determine the numbers of flowers purchased. Begin with (C), 4 orchids.

If $o = 4$, then $1.35(4) + 1.8d = 18$. Simplify the equation, so that $1.8d = 12.60$. Divide both sides of this equation by 1.8, so that $d = 7$. Since 7 is not an answer choice, eliminate (C) in the first column.

The more orchids Faustino purchases, the fewer dahlias he purchases. Plug in $o = 6$, so that $1.35(6) + 1.8d = 18$. Simplify the equation, so that $1.8d = 9.90$. Dividing both sides of this equation by 1.8 yields a non-integer value of $d$, so eliminate (E) in the first column.

Plug in $o = 8$, so that $1.35(8) + 1.8d = 18$. Simplify the equation, so that $1.8d = 7.2$. Divide both sides of this equation by 1.8, so that $d = 4$. The correct answer in the first column is (F), and the correct answer in the second column is (C).

## Item 4: Graphics Interpretation

4-1. **B** The graph is clearly labeled, so there's no reason to read the text blurb. The first question asks for the slope of the regression line. Open the drop-down box and review the answer choices. The line's slope is negative, so eliminate (D) and (E). The line clearly passes through points (1, 10) and (4, 6), so the slope of the line is approximately equal to $\frac{y - y_1}{x - x_1} = \frac{6-10}{4-1}$, or $-\frac{4}{3}$. Expressed as a decimal, $-\frac{4}{3}$ is approximately equal to −1.3. The correct answer is (B).

4-2. **D** The question asks for the percent by which the number of students within 11 inches of the target's center after day 2 is greater or less than it was before any training. Open the drop-down box and review the answer choices. More students were within 11 inches of the target after 2 days of training, so eliminate (A) and (B). Before any training, 2 students were within 11 inches of the target's center. After 2 days of training, 4 students were within 11 inches of the target's center. Use the percent change formula, $\frac{\textit{difference}}{\textit{original}} \times 100$, to calculate the percent increase, which is equal to $\frac{4-2}{2} \times 100$, or 100%. The correct answer is (D).

## Item 5: Two-Part Analysis

**Column 1: Strengthen—Choice (B)**

**Column 2: Weaken—Choice (E)**

The first column asks for the statement that most strengthens the argument, and the second column asks for the statement that most weakens the argument. Since the questions involve opposite tasks with respect to the same argument, the two columns are linked. Treat this as you would a Critical Reasoning question. Find the argument's premises and conclusion, and then use them to find an assumption.

The archaeologists conclude that *some human ancestors developed nautical skills millions of years earlier than previously discovered.* This conclusion is based on the discovery, on an island *40 miles from Greece*, of *stone tools* dating to *the Paleolithic Age.* The argument assumes the tools were brought to the island by boat from mainland Greece.

Beginning with (A), evaluate the answers one at a time. Whether the tools were *used for fishing* is out of scope. What matters is how the tools got to the island, so eliminate (A). Choice (B) likens the tools to those used by Paleolithic human ancestors who lived on the mainland, reinforcing the assumption that the tools were brought to the island by boat. Keep (B) for the first column. Choices (C) and (D) are out of scope, as how the tools may have been used is irrelevant, so eliminate (C) and (D). Choice (E) suggests the Mediterranean Sea dried up 5 million years ago and remained that way for 3 million years. If this is true, then the answer choice weakens the assumptions that the tools were brought to the island by boat, so eliminate (E). Choice (F) is out of scope. Whether the tools were *used for purposes other than the construction of boats* is irrelevant. The correct answer in the first column is (B), and the correct answer in the second column is (E).

## Item 6: Multi-Source Reasoning

6-1. **No** The *CD Offerings* tab relates the cost and length of an investment to the interest rate it earns. The *Memo* tab explains how the bank uses rewards and penalties to encourage longer-term investment. According to the *CD Offerings* tab, a 1-year, $11,000 investment earns 2.2% interest in the first year. According to the *Memo* tab, a 1-year investment doesn't qualify for bonus interest. Use the calculator to determine that 2.2% of $11,000 is $242. Since $242 < $250, the answer to the first question is "No."

6-2. **No** According to the *CD Offerings* tab, a 5-year, $9,500 investment earns 2.5% interest, compounded annually. According to the *Memo* tab, a 5-year investment earns an additional 0.1% interest in the first year. Use the calculator to determine that 2.6% of $9,500 is $247. Since $247 < $250, the answer to the second question is "No."

6-3. **Yes** According to the *CD Offerings* tab, a 10-year, $9,500 investment earns 2.8% interest, compounded annually. According to the *Memo* tab, CDs with 10-year terms earn an additional 0.1% interest in the first year. Use the calculator to determine that 2.9% of $9,500 is $275.50. Since $275.50 > $250, the answer to the third question is "Yes."

## Item 7: Multi-Source Reasoning

7-1. **No** The *CD Offerings* tab relates the cost and length of an investment to the interest rate it earns. The *Memo* tab explains how the bank uses rewards and penalties to encourage longer-term investment. According to the *CD Offerings* tab, a 1-year, $20,000 investment earns 2.2% interest, compounded annually. According to the *Memo* tab, a 1-year investment doesn't qualify for bonus interest. Use the calculator to determine that 2.2% of $20,000 is $440. Since $440 isn't between $500 and $600, the answer is "No."

7-2. **Yes** According to the *CD Offerings* tab, a 5-year, $4,000 investment earns 2.5% interest, compounded annually. According to the *Memo* tab, a 5-year investment earns an additional 0.1% interest during the first year. Use the calculator to determine that the CD is worth 1.026 × $4,000 = $4,104 at the end of the first year. Similarly, the investment is worth (1.025)4 × $4,104 = $4,530.05 at the end of the fifth year. Thus, the total interest earned is $4,530.05 – $4,000 = $530.05, and the answer is "Yes."

7-3. **No** According to the *CD Offerings* tab, a 2-year, $10,000 investment earns 2.4% interest, compounded annually. According to the *Memo* tab, a 2-year investment doesn't qualify for bonus interest. Use the calculator to determine that the CD is worth (1.024)2 × $10,000 = $10,485.76 at the end of the second year. Thus, the total interest earned is $10,485.76 – $10,000 = $485.76, and the answer is "No."

## Item 8: Multi-Source Reasoning

8-1. **No** The *CD Offerings* tab relates the cost and length of an investment to the interest rate it earns. The *Memo* tab explains how the bank uses rewards and penalties to encourage longer-term investment. According to the *Memo* tab, the schedule of penalties has been *revised*, so penalties for early withdrawals must have existed prior to the policy changes. The statement cannot be inferred from the information provided, so the answer is "No."

8-2. **No** According to the *Memo* tab, the bank policies described are designed to *shift the balance of customers' CD accounts towards those with longer maturity terms*. Although preferred customers receive a bonus that new customers do not receive, there's no indication that the bonus rewards them for their loyalty. The statement cannot be inferred from the information provided, so the answer is "No."

8-3. **Yes** According to the *Memo* tab, the bank intends to steer customers toward CDs with *longer maturity terms*. As an incentive, the bank will reward longer-term investments with bonus interest. If the bank successfully shifts even one customer to a longer-term CD, then it will pay a higher average interest rate to customers. The statement can be inferred from the information provided, so the answer is "Yes."

## Item 9: Table Analysis

9-1. **True** Read the text blurb to learn that *Popular Vote (Millions)* refers to the number of votes earned by the winning candidate. Sort the table by *President* to quickly identify Nixon, Reagan, Clinton, and Bush as the presidents who served two terms. The question asks for the two-term president with the smallest percent increase in *Popular Vote* from one term to the next, so use the percent change formula, $\frac{difference}{original} \times 100$. Compare $\frac{difference}{original}$ for the two-term presidents. William Clinton's $\frac{47.4 - 44.9}{44.9} \times 100 = 5.56$ percent increase in *Popular Vote* was the smallest percent increase for the two-term presidents, so the statement is true.

9-2. **False** Sort the table by *Political Party* to quickly determine that there are 6 Democratic presidents and 7 Republican presidents listed in the table. Use the calculator to determine that the 6 Democratic presidents earned 2,200 electoral votes, averaging $2{,}200 \div 6 \approx 367$ electoral votes per candidate, and the 7 Republican presidents earned a total of 2,818 electoral votes, averaging $2{,}818 \div 7 \approx 403$ per candidate. Since $403 > 367$, the statement is false.

9-3. **True** Sort the table by *% of Popular Vote* to help identify the presidents for whom the difference between *% of Popular Vote* and *% of Electoral Vote* is least. In both 2000 and 2004, the difference between the two percentages is less than 3, much less than the difference for any other president. In both years, George W. Bush was president, so the statement is true.

## Item 10: Multi-Source Reasoning

10-1. **Yes** *Memo #1* explains the company's airfare reimbursement policy, *Memo #2* details the average, standard deviation, and sample size for flights from each region to Bloomsbury, and *Email #1* describes the number of tickets purchased at various prices in the West region. According to the *Memo #2* tab, the West and Midwest regions had the same average ticket price, but no other region had a ticket price lower than that of the Midwest. The statement can be inferred from *Memo #2*, so the answer is "Yes."

10-2. **No** According to *Memo #1*, *Regional Office Managers will be responsible for arranging the travel reservations for all Level 2 managers....* However, no information is provided about who will attend the annual management retreat in addition to Level 2 managers. The statement cannot be inferred from the information in any of the tabs, so the answer is "No."

10-3. **Yes** According to *Memo #1*, Regional Office Managers may *delegate the task* as they wish. Therefore, ROMs *need not make the reservations personally*. The statement can be inferred from *Memo #1*, so the answer is "Yes."

## Item 11: Multi-Source Reasoning

11-1. **True** *Memo #1* explains the company's airfare reimbursement policy, *Memo #2* details the average, standard deviation, and sample size for flights from each region to Bloomsbury, and *Email #1* describes the number of tickets purchased at various prices in the West region. According to *Memo #1, any ticket priced 1 standard deviation or more below average* will be reimbursed a "Budget Bonus" of *50% of the difference between the ticket price and the average airfare* from that region. According to *Memo #2*, airfare from the West region averages \$200 with a standard deviation of \$25. Therefore, the West region will receive a "Budget Bonus" for any flight costing \$175 or less. According to *Email #1*, the West region bought 18 tickets at \$150 per ticket. Thus, the West region will receive \$25 for each one of these 18 tickets. Use the calculator to determine that 18 × \$25 = \$450, which matches the information in the statement. The statement is True.

11-2. **False** Standard deviation is the measure of the spread, or range, of the numbers within a set. Based on *Memo #2,* this may suggest that it is true that the two regions with the least sample size also had the least difference between the most and least expensive airfare found during research; the information provided in the question gives no insight into how many standard deviations were required to encompass all the data points. Therefore, it is impossible to know the distance between the greatest and least values for the information. The statement is False.

11-3. **True** This question asks about the averages of the researched airfare prices, so look at *Memo #2.* Determine the combined mean airfare of the researched regions by finding the sum of total amount for each of the regions individually, and then dividing that number by the total number of the sample size. The combined mean airfare for the researched regions is \$271.42. This is less than the mean airfare for the Northeast, Mid-Atlantic, and Plains regions. The statement is True.

## Item 12: Multi-Source Reasoning

**C** *Memo #1* explains the company's airfare reimbursement policy, *Memo #2* details the average, standard deviation, and sample size for flights from each region to Bloomsbury, and *Email #1* describes the number of tickets purchased at various prices in the West region. According to *Memo #1*, any ticket priced at or below one standard deviation above the mean is eligible for reimbursement. According to *Memo #2*, airfare from the West region averages \$200 per ticket with a standard deviation of \$25. Therefore, any ticket priced at or below \$225 is fully reimbursed. According to *Email #1*, 22 of the 30 tickets purchased in the West region are priced within this range. Thus, the probability a randomly selected ticket is eligible to be fully reimbursed is $\frac{22}{30}$, which reduces to $\frac{11}{15}$. The correct answer is (C).

# INTEGRATED REASONING DRILLS: Section 2

## Item 1: Graphics Interpretation

1-1. **A** Open the drop-down menu and review the answer choices. More clocks are produced on Tuesday than on Wednesday, so eliminate (D) and (E). According to the histogram, 75 clocks are produced on Tuesday and 40 are produced on Wednesday. Express the ratio as a fraction, $\frac{75}{40}$, which can be reduced to $\frac{15}{8}$. The correct answer is (A).

1-2. **D** According to the histogram, 90 clocks are produced on Monday and Wednesday, and 250 clocks are produced during the week, so that $\frac{9}{25}$ of the clocks are produced on Monday and Wednesday. To convert this fraction into a percentage, multiply the numerator and denominator by 4, so that $\frac{36}{100} = 36\%$ of the clocks are produced on Monday and Wednesday. The correct answer is (D).

## Item 2: Two-Part Analysis

**Column 1: Weakens Company X—Choice (F)**

**Column 2: Weakens Technology Consultant—Choice (D)**

The first column asks for the statement that most weakens Company X's argument, and the second column asks for the statement that most weakens the Consultant's argument. Since the tasks involve different arguments, the columns are not linked. Treat these questions as Critical Reasoning questions. Begin with the first column.

Company X concludes that it will *purchase new computers that run Portals 8*, basing its decision on the desire to *compete effectively in the modern economy* and the fact that its *computer technology is out of date.* This argument exhibits the planning pattern, so Company X assumes that there's no problem with its plan to purchase Portals 8. Because this is a weaken question, look for an answer that introduces a problem with the plan.

Choices (A), (B), and (D) are out of scope. Whether GreenCap is *more efficient, the most cutting-edge*, or *more expensive* is irrelevant, since Company X has decided to purchase Portals 8. Choice (C) is also out of scope. Company X bases its decision on its desire to compete in the economy. *When* the operating systems were released is irrelevant. Choice (E) states that Portals 8 is available in *different versions with different price levels*, strengthening Company X's argument by making Portals 8 more appealing. Choice (F) weakens Company X's argument. If Portals 8 *contains bugs and design flaws that will impair its ability to compete in the modern economy*, then there's a problem with Company X's plan to buy Portals 8. The correct answer in the first column is (F).

Now, consider the second column. The Consultant concludes that Company X should *purchase GreenCap* instead of Portals 8, basing the decision on Company X's desire to *complete effectively in the modern economy* and the fact that GreenCap *costs substantially less than does Portals 8*. This argument, too, exhibits the planning pattern. Because this is a weaken question, look for an answer that introduces a problem with the Consultant's plan.

Choices (A), (B), and (C) are out of scope. Whether GreenCap is *more efficient, the most cutting-edge,* or *has been available for three years* is irrelevant. What matters is whether GreenCap will better allow Company X to compete in the economy. Choice (D) weakens the Consultant's argument by challenging the premise that GreenCap *costs substantially less.* If GreenCap *requires an annual maintenance agreement that makes it more expensive overall,* then there's a problem with the Consultant's plan to save Company X money. Choice (E) weakens the Consultant's argument indirectly by making Portals 8 seem more appealing. However, without information describing how *price levels* for Portals 8 will affect Company X, the extent to which this answer weakens the Consultant's argument is unclear. Eliminate (E). Choice (F) strengthens the Consultant's argument by suggesting a reason for Company X to purchase GreenCap instead of Portals 8. The correct answer in the second column is (D).

## Item 3: Graphics Interpretation

3-1. **C** A quick glance at the graph reveals that ice cream consumption is relatively consistent when compared to cheese consumption, which tends to increase over time. Thus, the year with the lowest total consumption will be the year with the lowest cheese consumption, 1989.

Open the drop-down menu to review the answer choices. In 1989, ice cream consumption exceeded cheese consumption, so eliminate (A) and (D). Per capita ice cream consumption was roughly 29 pounds, while per capita cheese consumption was roughly 24 pounds. Express the ratio as a fraction, $\frac{29}{24}$. Since $\frac{29}{24}$ is closer to $\frac{30}{25}$, or $\frac{6}{5}$, than it is to $\frac{36}{24}$, or $\frac{3}{2}$, the correct answer is (C).

3-2. **B** The question asks for the relationship between the slopes of the two regression lines. A quick glance at the graph reveals that the regression line for ice cream slopes downward while the regression line for cheese slopes upward. Open the drop-down menu to review the answer choices. Eliminate (A) and (C), because the slope of the regression line for ice cream is less than the slope of the regression line for cheese. The correct answer is (B).

## Item 4: Two-Part Analysis

**Column 1: Strengthens Committee Member's Response—Choice (C)**

**Column 2: Weakens Committee Member's Response—Choice (A)**

The first column asks for the statement that most strengthens the committee member's response, and the second column asks for the statement that most weakens the committee member's response. Since the questions involve opposite tasks with respect to the same argument, the two columns are linked. Treat this as you would a Critical Reasoning question. Begin with the first column.

The XM representative argues that *the costly and time-consuming review should be waived,* because *less than two percent of XM projects have ever been rejected.* The committee member counters that the review should not be waived, because failing to review the project entails failing *to observe innovations in geo-engineering that may need guidelines drafted for the safety of subsequent projects.* Thus, the committee member is concerned with *safety throughout the industry* and seems to assume that reviews are the only way to observe innovations that can lead to the drafting of guidelines. Because this is a strengthen question, look for answers that reinforce this assumption.

Choice (A) weakens the committee member's response by breaking the link between the review and the observation of innovations. If XM's current project is nearly identical to a project that already passed review, then the committee can expect to see nothing new from a review. Choice (B) is out of scope. The percentage of CL's projects which have been rejected is irrelevant to the argument that XM's project should be reviewed. Choice (C) strengthens the argument that XM's project should be reviewed by suggesting that opportunities for review are limited. If new innovations are reviewed only once, then all new innovations should be reviewed. Choices (D), (E), and (F) are out of scope. Whether *XM's projects are peer-reviewed, Geo-engineering deserves careful monitoring,* or *the committee has had to reverse some of its decisions* is irrelevant to the argument that innovation can be observed, and guidelines drawn up, only when projects are reviewed by the committee. The correct answer in the first column is (C), and the correct answer in the second column is (A).

## Item 5: Two-Part Analysis

**Column 1: Insect Species X—Choice (A)**

**Column 2: Insect Species Y—Choice (C)**

The first column asks for the current population of Insect Species X, and the second column asks for the current population of Insect Species Y. The passage provides the constant rate at which the population of each species changes, and states that in four years, the populations will be equal. Since the information provided can be used to write a single equation relating the current populations of species X and Y, the two columns are linked. Translate the information into an algebraic equation.

The population of species X decreases at a rate of 10% per year, so each year, only 90% of the population survives. The population of species Y decreases at a rate of 15% per year, so each year, only 85% of the population survives. After 4 years, the two populations will be equal, so $x(0.9)^4 = y(0.85)^4$, where $x$ and $y$ represent the current populations of species X and Y, respectively. Note that, because the population of species Y decreases faster than the population of species X, the current population of Y must be greater than that of X.

Manipulate the equation so that the ratio $\frac{x}{y}$ can be determined. Divide both sides of the equation by $y(0.9)^4$, so that $\frac{x}{y} = \frac{0.85^4}{0.9^4}$. Use the calculator to determine that $\frac{x}{y} \approx 0.796$.

In the *Current Population* column, look for two values whose ratio is just under 0.8. Since $\frac{500}{600} = 0.8$, try $\frac{450}{600}$. Expressed as a decimal, $\frac{450}{600} = 0.75$, which is too much less than 0.8. To increase the ratio, either increase the numerator or decrease the denominator. The next least possible numerator is 525. Since $\frac{525}{600} > 0.8$, try decreasing the denominator. Expressed as a decimal, $\frac{450}{565} \approx 0.796$. The correct answer in the first column is (A), and the correct answer in the second column is (C).

## Item 6: Multi-Source Reasoning

6-1. **No** *Email #1* describes the company's plan to increase revenue by ramping up advertising to females aged 15–25. *Email #2* identifies the two most popular programs among females aged 15–25. *Memo #1* presents advertising and viewership data for the two programs. According to *Memo #1*, 45% of females aged 15–25 watch *Blonde Fury*. However, none of the tabs provide information about other age and gender groups. Since the statement cannot be inferred from the information provided, the answer is "No."

6-2. **No** According to *Memo #1*, a greater percentage of females aged 15–25 watches *Blonde Fury* than watches *Hart Attack*. However, none of the tabs provide information sufficient to determine the size of the audience for either program. On the basis of the information provided, it cannot be inferred that 30-second ads are more expensive for programs with larger audiences. The answer is "No."

6-3. **No** According to *Memo #1*, 45% of females aged 15–25 watch *Blonde Fury*, during which a 30-second commercial costs $70,000, and 35% of females aged 15–25 watch *Hart Attack*, during which a 30-second commercial costs $55,000. However, none of the tabs provides information sufficient to determine how much money was actually spent on advertising. The statement cannot be inferred from the information provided, so the answer is "No."

## Item 7: Multi-Source Reasoning

**D** *Email #1* describes the company's plan to increase revenue by ramping up advertising to females aged 15–25. *Email #2* identifies the two most popular programs among females aged 15–25. *Memo #1* presents advertising and viewership data for the two programs.

According to *Memo #1*, 45% of females aged 15–25 watch *Blonde Fury* and 35% of females aged 15–25 watch *Hart Attack*. If there are 20,000,000 females aged 15–25, then $0.45 \times 20{,}000{,}000 = 9{,}000{,}000$ watch *Blonde Fury*, and $0.35 \times 20{,}000{,}000 = 7{,}000{,}000$ watch *Hart Attack*. According to *Email #2*, 80% of female viewers aged 15–25 who watch *Hart Attack* also watch *Blonde Fury*. If 7,000,000 females aged 15–25 watch *Hart Attack*, then $0.80 \times 7{,}000{,}000 = 5{,}600{,}000$ who watch *Hart Attack* also watch *Blonde Fury*.

Use the group formula to answer the question, *group 1* + *group 2* + *neither* – *both* = *total*. Substitute the calculated values into the formula, so that 7,000,000 + 9,000,000 + *neither* – 5,600,000 = 20,000,000. Simplify the equation, so that *neither* = 9,600,000. The correct answer is (D).

## Item 8: Multi-Source Reasoning

8-1. **Yes** *Email #1* describes the company's plan to increase revenue by ramping up advertising to females aged 15–25. *Email #2* identifies the two most popular programs among females aged 15–25. *Memo #1* presents advertising and viewership data for the two programs. In *Email #1*, the Marketing Director writes that *in 1978, 1987, and 1993, we responded to revenue decreases by increasing our advertising expenditures by 30%. On all three occasions, our revenues began to increase again within one quarter.* Since the Director attributes success on all three occasions to increased advertising expenditures, the Director must assume that *it is possible for a strategy that succeeded in the past to succeed again*. The correct answer is "Yes."

8-2. **Yes** In *Email #1*, the Marketing Director writes that *in 1978, 1987, and 1993, we responded to revenue decreases by increasing our advertising expenditures by 30%. On all three occasions, our revenues began to increase again within one quarter.* Since the Director now wants to increase revenue by increasing the number of advertisements by 30%, the Director must assume that *the previous increases in revenues were attributable at least in part to the effect of increased advertising.* The correct answer is "Yes."

8-3. **Yes** In *Email #1*, the Marketing Director states that *in 1978, 1987, and 1993, we responded to revenue decreases by increasing our advertising expenditures by 30%. On all three occasions, our revenues began to increase again within one quarter.* Since the Director now wants to increase revenue by increasing the number of advertisements by 30%, the Director must assume that *increasing the number of advertisements and increasing advertising expenditures have similar effects on revenue.* The correct answer is "Yes."

## Item 9: Table Analysis

9-1. **Supported**

Sort the table by *Population 2010* to quickly identify countries with a population greater than 150 million: Brazil, Indonesia, United States, India, and China. For each of these five countries, use the calculator to determine the number of foreign-born inhabitants.

In Brazil, 0.34% of 190,733,000 inhabitants are foreign-born, so 0.0034 × 190,733,000 = 648,492 inhabitants are foreign born. In Indonesia, 0.07% of 237,556,000 inhabitants are foreign-born, so 0.0007 × 237,556,000 = 166,289 inhabitants are foreign-born. In the United States, 21.81% of 312,399,000 inhabitants are foreign-born, so 0.2181 × 312,399,000 = 68,134,222 inhabitants are foreign-born. In India, 0.52% of 1,210,193,000 inhabitants are foreign-born, so 0.0052 × 1,210,193,000 = 6,293,004 inhabitants are foreign-born. In China, 0.29% of 1,399,725,000 inhabitants are foreign-born, so 0.0029 × 1,399,725,000 = 4,059,203 inhabitants are foreign-born. The country with the median number of foreign-born inhabitants is China, so the statement is supported by the table.

9-2. **Unsupported**

The table doesn't include any information about projected populations for the year 2030, so the statement is not supported by the table.

9-3. **Supported**

Sort the table by *% of Population Foreign-Born* to quickly identify the country with the greatest percentage of foreign-born inhabitants. Of the countries listed, Andorra has the greatest percentage of inhabitants who are foreign-born, so the statement is supported by the table.

## Item 10: Multi-Source Reasoning

10-1. **True** *Email #1* describes what the organization requires for the gala and mentions two catering companies it might hire. *Email #2* compares costs and services for the two companies. According to *Email #1*, the organization expects *a maximum of 400 people.* If 400 people attend a gala catered by DoxySource, then according to *Email #2*, the appetizers cost $2 × 400 = $800, the entrees cost $\$6.25 \times 400 = \$2{,}500$, and the desserts cost $\$3.40 \times 400 = \$1{,}360$. In this case, the total cost of food is $4,660. DoxySource charges $15.50 per 8-person table. Since 50 tables are needed to seat 400 guests, the least amount that can be spent on seating is $\$15.50 \times 50 = \$775$. Finally, seating costs are $\frac{\$775}{\$4{,}660} \times 100 \approx 16.6\%$ of food costs, so the statement is true.

10-2. **True** According to *Email #2,* BrightRight charges $350 for a 40-gallon punch fountain, or $\$350 \div 40 = \$8.75$ per gallon. DoxySource charges $47 for a 7-gallon punch fountain, or $\$47 \div 7 \approx \$6.72$ per gallon. Use the percent change formula, $\frac{\textit{difference}}{\textit{original}} \times 100$, to determine whether DoxySource punch costs at least 20% less per gallon than BrightRight punch. Substitute the costs-per-gallon into the percent change formula, $\frac{8.75 - 6.72}{8.75} \times 100$. Simplify the expression, so that DoxySource punch costs $\frac{2.03}{8.75} \times 100 = 23.2\%$ less per gallon than BrightRight punch. DoxySource fountains cost at least 20% less per gallon, so the statement is true.

10-3. **True** According to *Email #1,* the organization requires *tables, audio, food, and a punch fountain.* The organization's budget is $6,000. To determine whether the organization will go over budget by at least 15%, calculate the cheapest possible cost of using BrightRight.

According to *Email #2,* BrightRight's 8-person tables cost $20 each. Since 50 tables are needed to seat 400 people, the total cost of tables is $\$20 \times 50 = \$1{,}000$. *The Classic Western BBQ* costs $14 per person, so the total cost of food is $\$14 \times 400 = \$5{,}600$. The *Party Sound System* costs $650, and the *Punch Fountain* costs $350. Therefore, the cheapest possible cost of hiring BrightRight to cater the gala is $\$1{,}000 + \$650 + \$5{,}600 + \$350 = \$7{,}600$. In this case, the project will go over budget by $1,600, or by $\frac{\$1{,}600}{\$6{,}000} \times 100 \approx 27\%$. Since the project will go over budget by at least 15%, the statement is true.

## Item 11: Multi-Source Reasoning

**C** *Email #1* describes what the organization requires for the gala and mentions two catering companies it might hire. *Email #2* compares costs and services for the two companies. According to *Email #2,* 8-person DoxySource tables cost $15.50 each, and 7-person tables cost $17 each. The cheapest way to seat 400 people, using at least one of each table type, would be to use only one of the more expensive tables, leaving 393 people to sit at 8-person tables. Seating 393 people requires $393 \div 8 = 49.125$ of the cheaper tables. Since the number of tables should be an integer, and more than 49 cheaper tables are required, the Coordinator should use fifty 8-person tables and one 7-person table, for a total cost of $\$17 + 50(\$15.50) = \$792$. The correct answer is (C).

### Item 12: Multi-Source Reasoning

12-1. **Yes** *Email #1* describes what the organization requires for the gala and mentions two catering companies it might hire. *Email #2* compares costs and services for the two companies. In *Email #1*, the Gala Coordinator states: *I'd like to consider how to justify any over-budget costs from using BrightRight.* If the Coordinator is considering how to justify over-budget costs, then it can be inferred that the Coordinator is willing to ask for a budgetary increase. The answer is "Yes."

12-2. **Yes** In *Email #2*, the Assistant mentions the *price difference* between services offered by the two companies. In addition, the Assistant refers to BrightRight packages as *more elegant and comprehensive*, and to DoxySource packages as *more flexible* and requiring *more hands-on involvement on our end.* Thus, costs are not the only determining factor in choosing one event planning service over the other. The answer is "Yes."

12-3. **No** In *Email #1*, the Coordinator states that *tables, audio, food, and a punch fountain or fountains* are required. Therefore, fountains are not an optional element of the gala. The answer is "No."

## ANSWERS TO CHALLENGE QUESTIONS

### Page 111—Challenge Question #1

**C** Begin by considering the possible values of $x$ and $y$. Prime numbers with squares less than 60 are 2, 3, 5, and 7, for squares of 4, 9, 25, and 49, respectively. Therefore, possible sums of distinct pairs of squares are $4 + 9 = 13$, $4 + 25 = 29$, $4 + 49 = 53$, $9 + 25 = 34$, and $9 + 49 = 58$. Thus, $x$ can be 13, 29, 34, 53, or 58. For $y$, multiples of 17 less than 60 are 17, 34, and 51. Now consider the answer choices. Choice (A) is −19, so look for combinations of answer choices that could result in −19. The only possible values that are close are $13 - 34 = -21$, $29 - 51 = -22$, and $34 - 51 = -17$. None of these values match −19, so eliminate (A). Choice (B) is −7, so consider whether that value might be used. $13 - 17 = -4$ and $29 - 34 = -5$, neither of which matches −7, so eliminate (B). Choice (C) is 0, and $34 - 34 = 0$. The correct answer is (C).

### Page 139—Challenge Question #2

**D** The question asks for the factor by which the value of a gem with a rating of $p$ would have to be multiplied to equal the value of a gem with a rating of $p - r$. According to the rating system described by the question stem, the value of a gem with a rating of $q - 1$ is 5 times greater, and the value of a gem with a rating of $q - 4$ is 625 times greater, than the value of a gem with a rating of $q$. The first example provides the information that subtracting 1 from the rating corresponds to a 5-fold increase in value. The second example provides the value increase by a factor of 625, which can be rewritten as $5^4$. Therefore, the pattern in the question is that for each value subtracted from a rating of $q$, the value is $5^x$, where $x$ is the value subtracted from the rating of $q$. Following the pattern suggested by the question stem, the value of a gem with a $q - 2$ rating is greater than the value of a gem with a $q$ rating by a factor of 25, or $5^2$. Similarly, the value of a gem with a $q - 3$ rating is greater than the value of a gem with a $q$ rating by a factor of 125, or $5^3$. Apply this pattern to gems rated $p - r$ and $p$. The easiest way to do this is to Plug In values for $p$ and $r$. Let $p = 5$ and $r = 2$. In this case, the gems to be compared are rated $5 - 2$ and 5. Based on the pattern above, the value of the gem rated $5 - 2$ is greater than the value of the gem rated 5 by a factor of 25. Substitute $p = 5$ and $r = 2$ into the answer choices, looking for the answer that equals 25. Choice (A) is $5^5 - 2^5$, a number much greater than 25. Eliminate (A). Choice (B) is $2^5 = 32$. Eliminate (B). Choice (C) is $(5 - 2)^5 = 243$. Eliminate (C). Choice (D) is $5^2$, or 25. Keep (D). Choice (E) is $5(2) = 10$. Eliminate (E). The correct answer is (D).

## Page 170—Challenge Question #3

**D** The question asks for the value of $333{,}333.\bar{3}\times\left(10^{-3}-10^{-5}\right)$. Rewrite the expression without the negative exponents, yielding $333{,}333.\bar{3}\times\left(\frac{1}{10^3}-\frac{1}{10^5}\right)$. Use the distributive property of multiplication to rewrite the expression, $\frac{333{,}333.\bar{3}}{10^3}-\frac{333{,}333.\bar{3}}{10^5}$. Eliminate the fractions by shifting the decimal places in the numerators the appropriate number of places to the left, resulting in a subtraction problem, $333.\bar{3}-3.\bar{3}=330$. The correct answer is (D).

## Page 196—Challenge Question #4

**D** The answer choices represent the information directly asked for by the question, so Plug In the Answers. Begin with (C). If the new after-tax price of a car is \$13,500, then the new pretax price is $\frac{\$13{,}500}{1.08}$ = \$12,500, the old pretax price is \$12,500 – \$2,500 = \$10,000, and the old after-tax price is \$10,000 × 1.08 = \$10,800. In this case, the cost of 18 cars at the old after-tax price is 18 × \$10,800 = \$194,400, and the cost of 15 cars at the new after-tax price is 15 × \$13,500 = \$202,500. Since these costs should be equal, eliminate (C).

When the new after-tax price of a car was \$13,500, the cost of 15 cars at the new after-tax price was too great, and the cost of 18 cars at the old after-tax price was less than necessary. Two factors contributed to the unwanted gap between these values. First, fewer cars were purchased at the new price than at the old price. Nothing can be done about this, since the quantities purchased are built into the question. Second, the difference between the new pretax price and the old pretax price is \$2,500. This difference was too great relative to a new after-tax price of \$13,500. To lessen the impact of the \$2,500 pretax price difference, therefore, increase the new after-tax price of per car. Try (D).

If the new after-tax price of a car is \$16,200, then the new pretax price is $\frac{\$16{,}200}{1.08}$ = \$15,000, the old pretax price is \$15,000 – \$2,500 = \$12,500, and the old after-tax price is \$12,500 × 1.08 = \$13,500. In this case, the cost of 18 cars at the old after-tax price is 18 × \$13,500 = \$243,000, and the cost of 15 cars at the new after-tax price is 15 × \$16,200 = \$243,000. Since these costs are equal, the correct answer is (D).

## Page 212—Challenge Question #5

**B** There are variables in the answer choices, so plug in values for $b$, $r$, and $q$. However, there is information in the question stem that should first be considered. The question asks for the value of $p$ in terms of $b$, $r$, and $q$, where $b$ and $r$ represent the point values of blue tokens and red tokens, respectively, and $q$ represents the number of red tokens acquired by Player A expressed as a percentage of all Player A's tokens. Had the question provided the total number of tokens acquired by Player A, then plugging in values of $b$, $r$, and $q$ would have allowed for the calculation of $p$, the percentage of points earned from blue tokens. The question does not provide the number of tokens acquired by Player A, so not only is this a Plug In question, it's also a Hidden Plug In question. Let Player A acquire 10 tokens, and let $b = 5$, $r = 2$, and $q = 80$.

If Player A acquired 10 tokens during the game, and $q = 80\%$ of the tokens that were red, then Player A acquired 8 red tokens and 2 blue tokens. If each blue token is worth 5 points and each red token is worth 2 points, then Player A earned $2 \times 5 = 10$ points from blue tokens and $8 \times 2 = 16$ points from red tokens, for a total of $10 + 16 = 26$ points. In this case, the percentage of points that were earned from blue tokens is $p = \frac{10}{26} \times 100$. Circle the target answer, $\frac{1{,}000}{26}$.

Now, plug $b = 5$, $r = 2$, and $x = 80$ in for each of the answer choices, looking for the choice that equals $\frac{1{,}000}{26}$. Choice (A) is $\frac{100(5)(80)}{(5)(80)+100(2)-(80)(2)} = \frac{40{,}000}{440}$, which reduces to $\frac{4{,}000}{44}$, or $\frac{1{,}000}{11}$. Eliminate (A). Choice (B) is $\frac{10{,}000(5)-100(5)(80)}{100(5)-(5)(80)+(80)(2)} = \frac{10{,}000}{260}$, which reduces to $\frac{1{,}000}{26}$. Keep (B). Choice (C) is $\frac{(5)(80)+100(2)-(80)(2)}{100(5)(80)} = \frac{440}{40{,}000}$. Eliminate (C). Choice (D) is $\frac{100(5)-(5)(80)}{100(2)-100(5)(80)+(80)(2)} = \frac{100}{-39{,}640}$. Eliminate (D). Choice (E) is $\frac{100(5)-(5)(80)+(80)(2)}{10{,}000(5)-100(5)(80)} = \frac{260}{10{,}000}$. Eliminate (E). The correct answer is (B).

## Page 230—Challenge Question #6

**C** If James can complete the job in 6 hours, then James's rate is $\frac{1}{6}$ of a job per hour. If Sarah can complete the job in 4.5 hours, then Sarah's rate is $\frac{1}{4.5}$ or $\frac{2}{9}$ of a job per hour. Together, James and Sarah work at a rate of $\frac{1}{6}+\frac{2}{9}$ or $\frac{3}{18}+\frac{4}{18}=\frac{7}{18}$ of a job per hour.

During the hour that James and Sarah work together, they complete $\frac{7}{18}$ of the job, leaving $\frac{11}{18}$ of the job unfinished. James will complete some of the unfinished work at a rate of $\frac{1}{6}$ per hour, and Sarah will finish the rest at a rate of $\frac{2}{9}$ per hour, such that Sarah works by herself half as long as James does. Translate this information into an algebraic equation. If $t$ represents the number of hours during which James works alone, then $t\times\frac{1}{6}+\frac{t}{2}\times\frac{2}{9}=\frac{11}{18}$. Multiply both sides of the equation by 18 and simplify to find that $3t + 2t = 11$. Simplify the equation further so that $5t = 11$. Divide both sides of the equation by 5, so that $t = 2.2$ hours, or 2 hours and 12 minutes. The correct answer is (C).

## Page 232—Challenge Question #7

**A** First, plug in the values from the question stem. Plug 2 in for $y$ and 144 in for $z$ to get that $\frac{144}{x^2}$ is an integer, while $\frac{144}{x^3}$ is not, which means that $x^2$ divides evenly into 144, but $x^3$ does not. To easily determine if a number divides evenly into another, find the prime factors. In this case, the prime factorization of 144 is $144 = 2^4 * 3^2$. Now Plug In the Answers for the value of $x$ and determine if $\frac{144}{x^2}$ is an integer, while $\frac{144}{x^3}$ is not. Choice (A) is 2 and $2^2$ and $2^3$ are factors of 144. Because the question asks which answer choice is NOT a factor of 144, keep (A). Because the answer choices were used to determine the factors and there can be only one answer choice that works, there is no need to test other answer choices. In fact, if the remaining answer choices are all taken down to their prime factors and plugged in for $x$, they will all abide by the rules in the problem that $\frac{144}{x^2}$ is an integer, while $\frac{144}{x^3}$ is not. The correct answer is (A).

### Page 238—Challenge Question #8

**D** There are variables in the answer choices, so plug values in for $g$ and $b$. Let $g = 2$ and $b = 3$. The question asks for the probability that at least one of two randomly selected players is a girl, which is equivalent to 1 minus the probability that both of the selected players are boys. The probability that the first player selected is a boy is $\frac{3}{5}$, and the probability that the second player selected is a boy is $\frac{2}{4}$. Therefore, the probability that both selected players are boys is $\frac{3}{5} \times \frac{2}{4} = \frac{6}{20}$, and the probability that at least one of the players is a girl is $1 - \frac{6}{20} = \frac{14}{20}$. Plug $g = 2$ and $b = 3$ into each of the answer choices, looking for the answer that equals $\frac{14}{20}$.

Choice (A) is $\frac{2(2-1)}{(3+2)(3+2-1)} = \frac{2}{20}$, so eliminate (A). Choice (B) is $\frac{3(3-1)}{(3+2)(3+2-1)} = \frac{6}{20}$, so eliminate (B). Choice (C) is $\frac{2(3)(2)}{(3+2)(3+2-1)} = \frac{12}{20}$, so eliminate (C). Choice (D) is $\frac{2(2\times3+2-1)}{(3+2)(3+2-1)} = \frac{14}{20}$, so keep (D). Choice (E) is $\frac{3(2\times2+3-1)}{(3+2)(3+2-1)} = \frac{18}{20}$, so eliminate (E). The correct answer is (D).

### Page 244—Challenge Question #9

**B** The answer choices represent the information directly asked for by the question, so Plug In the Answers. However, there is information in the question that should first be considered. Variables $x$ and $y$ represent the number of short and long essays available in Part Two of the test, respectively. The ratio of available long essays to short essays remains a constant in both parts of the test, and the ratio of short to long essays in Part One is 2:1. Therefore, the ratio of short to long essays in Part Two is 2:1, and the value of $x$ must be twice the value of $y$. Eliminate (A) and (D), in which $x$ is an odd number, because they entail non-integer values of $y$. Now, Plug In the Answers, beginning with (C).

If $x = 8$, then there are 8 short essays and 4 long essays available in Part Two, and $8 \times 4 = 32$ ways to select these essays. In this case, because there are $4 \times 2 = 8$ ways to select essays in Part One, there are $8 \times 32 = 256$ different lineups of essays a student can choose. This does not match the criterion in the question stem, which states that there are 144 different lineups. Since the number of essays in Part One is fixed, there must be fewer essays available in Part Two. Try (B).

If $x = 6$, then there are 6 short essays and 3 long essays available in Part Two, and $6 \times 3 = 18$ ways to select these essays. In this case, because there are 8 ways to select essays in Part One, there are $8 \times 18 = 144$ different lineups of essays a student can choose. This matches the criterion in the question stem, so the correct answer is (B).

## Page 260—Challenge Question #10

**A** The problem asks for the value of $z$, so begin manipulating the information in the question to work toward $z$. The sum of the angles in a triangle is 180°, so the equation of the smaller triangle that contains $z$ is $z + 85 + (x + 15) = 180$. Simplify the equation to find that $z + x + 100 = 180$ and $z + x = 80$. Because the larger triangle contains a value of $x$, solve for $x$, so $x = 80 - z$. Now, write the equation for the larger triangle and solve the equation for $x$. The equation for the larger triangle is $z + (2x - 5) + 65 = 180$, which simplifies to $z + 2x + 60 = 180$ and $z + 2x = 120$. Solve for $x$, so $2x = 120 - z$ and $x = \frac{120 - z}{2}$. Next, set the equations equal to each other, so $80 - z = \frac{120 - z}{2}$. Finally, solve for $z$, so $160 - 2z = 120 - z$ and $160 = 120 + z$, so $40 = z$. The correct answer is (A).

## Page 268—Challenge Question #11

**B** Begin by drawing the figure. Drawing the triangle with angles consistent with the information in the problem yields a scalene triangle. When solving for side lengths of unfamiliar triangles, always look for ways to create a more familiar shape. Recognize that the length of $6\sqrt{2}$ for *SR* indicates the possible presence of a 45°-45°-90° triangle. Draw lines vertically down from point *S* and horizontally left from point *R*. Label the new point *Z* for reference.

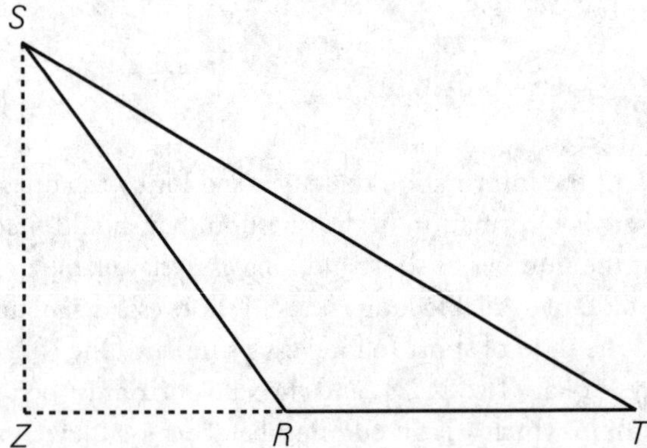


Solving for the measure of angle *SRT* yields $180 - 30 - 15 = 135°$. Because the straight line created by the extension of the figure left from point *R* has to have a degree measure of 180°, the degree measure of angle *ZRS* is $180° - 135° = 45°$. Because $\angle SZT$ is 90°, triangle *ZRS* is a 45°-45°-90° triangle. The problem provides that angle *RST* is 15°, which means that angle *ZST* is $45° + 15° = 60°$. Therefore, triangle *ZST* is a 30°-60°-90° triangle, with sides in a ratio of $x{:}x\sqrt{3}{:}2x$. Because triangle *ZSR* is a 45°-45°-90° triangle, with sides in a ratio of $x{:}x{:}x\sqrt{2}$, and *SR* is $6\sqrt{2}$, *SZ* is 6. *SZ* relates to the $x$ side of the 30°-60°-90° triangle, so *ST*, which relates to the $2x$ side of the 30°-60°-90° triangle, is 12. The correct answer is (B).

## Page 290—Challenge Question #12

**B** There are variables in the answer choices, so plug values in for $h$ and $k$. The value of $k$ must be twice the value of $h$, so let $h = 2$ and $k = 4$. Draw a circle with center (2, 4) that is tangent to the $y$-axis. Create a right triangle by drawing lines from the center of the circle to the $y$-axis and the origin, such that the vertices of the triangle lie at points (0, 0), (0, 4), and (2, 4). Use the Pythagorean Theorem, $a^2 + b^2 = c^2$, to determine the length of the triangle's hypotenuse, $c$. The shorter sides of the triangle are of lengths 2 and 4, so $2^2 + 4^2 = c^2$. Simplify the equation, so that $c^2 = 20$. Take the positive square root of both sides of the equation, so that the distance from the origin to the center of the circle is $2\sqrt{5}$. Now, Plug $k = 4$ in for each of the answer choices, looking for the answer that equals $2\sqrt{5}$.

Choice (A) is $\frac{4\sqrt{3}}{2} = 2\sqrt{3}$, so eliminate (A). Choice (B) is $\frac{4\sqrt{5}}{2} = 2\sqrt{5}$, so keep (B). Choice (C) is 4, so eliminate (C). Choice (D) is $4\sqrt{3}$, so eliminate (D). Choice (E) is $4\sqrt{5}$, so eliminate (E). The correct answer is (B).

## Page 321—Challenge Question #13

**E** This is a Value Data Sufficiency question, so begin by determining what is known and what is needed to answer the question. What is known is that Angela is twice as old as the sum of Bill's and Charlie's ages. This information can be expressed algebraically: let $a$ be Angela's age, $b$ be Bill's age, and $c$ be Charlie's age. Thus, $a = 2(b + c)$. To solve this equation, what is needed are values for both $a$ and $b$ or two more distinct equations with all three variables.

Evaluate Statement (1). In four years, each of the people will have aged, so make sure to include this information in an algebraic equation: $(a + 4) + (b + 4) + (c + 4) = 108$. This equation simplifies into $a + b + c = 96$. This statement gives another equation with all 3 variables. However, there are still 3 variables and only 2 equations. This statement is therefore insufficient. Write down BCE.

Evaluate Statement (2). Remember that an average is calculated by adding the values and dividing by the number of values. Also, "five years ago" will affect each person's age, so make sure this information is included in the algebraic expression: $\frac{(a-5)+(b-5)+(c-5)}{3} = 27$, which simplifies to $a + b + c - 15 = 81$ or $a + b + c = 96$. This statement gives an equation with all 3 variables. But, there are still 3 variables and only 2 equations. This statement is therefore insufficient. Eliminate (B).

Finally, evaluate the two statements combined. The rules for simultaneous equations require that each of the three equations be distinct. Since the equation for Statement (1) is identical to that of Statement (2), the combination of the two statements still gives only 2 equations and 3 variables. The two statements together are therefore insufficient. The correct answer is (E).

## Page 323—Challenge Question #14

**C** This is a Yes/No Data Sufficiency question. However, there is information in the question stem that should be considered, so use the Pieces of the Puzzle approach to assess the question. The question asks whether the area of triangle *ABD* is equal to the area of triangle *BCD*. Since the two triangles share a common height, *BD*, their areas will be equal only if their bases, *AD* and *DC*, are the same length. Therefore, in order to answer the question, the statements must provide information sufficient to determine whether $AD = DC$. The task of a Yes/No Data Sufficiency question is to determine whether the information in the statements produces a consistent "Yes" or "No" answer to the question. Evaluate the statements one at a time.

Evaluate Statement (1). The length of *AD* is 2. However, Statement (1) does not provide the length of *DC*, so it is insufficient to determine whether $AD = DC$. Write down BCE.

Now, evaluate Statement (2). The length of *BD* is 5. However, Statement (2) does not provide the lengths of *AD* and *DC*, so it is insufficient to determine whether $AD = DC$. Eliminate (B).

Now, evaluate both statements together. Recognize that triangles *ABD* and *BCD* together form a larger triangle, triangle *ABC*. The Inscribed Angle Theorem dictates that angle *ABC* must be 90°, so triangle *ABC* is a right triangle, and $(AB)^2 + (BC)^2 = (AC)^2$. From Statement (1), $AD = 2$. Therefore, $AC = DC + 2$. Substitute this value of *AC* into the equation above, so that $(AB)^2 + (BC)^2 = (DC + 2)^2$. If the values of $(AB)^2$ and $(BC)^2$ can be determined, then the length of *DC* can be determined. Determine the value of $(AB)^2$. If $AD = 2$ and $BD = 5$, then $2^2 + 5^2 = (AB)^2$. Simplify the equation, so that $(AB)^2 = 29$. Substitute this value of $(AB)^2$ into the equation above, so that $29 + (BC)^2 = (DC + 2)^2$. Now, determine the value of $(BC)^2$. If $BD = 5$, then $(DC)^2 + 5^2 = (BC)^2$. Simplify the equation, so that $(BC)^2 = (DC)^2 + 25$. Substitute this value of $(BC)^2$ into the equation above, so that $29 + (DC)^2 + 25 = (DC + 2)^2$. Simplify the equation, so that $(DC)^2 + 54 = (DC)^2 + 4(DC) + 4$. Combine like terms, so that $50 = 4(DC)$. Divide both sides of the equation by 4, so that $(DC) = 12.5$. Since $(DC) \neq (AD)$, the areas of triangles *ABD* and *BCD* are not the same, and the answer is "No." Together, both statements are sufficient to answer the question, so eliminate (E). The correct answer is (C).

## Page 332—Challenge Question #15

**A** This is a Yes/No Data Sufficiency question, so be prepared to Plug In more than once. Because both sides of the inequality involve cube roots, take the cube of both sides to remove the cube roots and simplify even further. Therefore, the inequality is $8a < a + b$. Subtract *a* from both sides to find that $7a < b$. Now that the inequality has been simplified as far as possible, evaluate the statements individually. For Statement (1), if it is true that $7a < b$, then the inequality in the question stem is always true, and the answer to the question is "Yes." Write down AD.

For Statement (2), begin by manipulating the statement to produce $6a < b$. Plug in values for *a* and *b* that satisfy that statement. If $a = 1$ and $b = 7$, then the statement is satisfied because $6 < 7$. In this case, the inequality from the question stem, $7a < b$, is not true because $7 = 7$, so the answer is "No." Plug In again to see if there is a way to produce a "Yes" answer to the question. If $a = 1$ and $b = 8$, then the statement is satisfied and the inequality in the question stem is now true because $7 < 8$. Now the answer to the question is "Yes." Because the statement produces two different answers to the question, the statement is insufficient. Eliminate (D). The correct answer is (A).

### Page 415—Challenge Question #16

**D** The sentence as written contains a parallel construction error in the list *buying...providing...join,* so eliminate (A) and any obvious repeaters. Choice (B) adds the word *to* before *join,* but commits the same error as (A), so eliminate (B). Consider the remaining choices. Choice (C) alters the meaning of the original sentence by stating that the parents will [have] *climbing gear bought,* so eliminate (C). Choice (D) fixes the parallel construction error and creates no new errors, so keep (D). Choice (E) contains a parallel construction error in the list *having bought...provided...allowed,* so eliminate (E). The correct answer is (D).

### Page 417—Challenge Question #17

**D** The sentence as written contains an invalid comparison between *Edgar Allan Poe* and *Homer's... poetry.* Eliminate (A) and any obvious repeaters. Choices (B) and (E) repeat the invalid comparison and may be eliminated. Consider the remaining choices. Choice (C) creates the phrase, *Unlike Edgar Allan Poe...in the example of Homer,* which incorrectly compares *Edgar Allan Poe* to *the example of Homer,* so eliminate (C). Choice (D) fixes the invalid comparison by comparing *Edgar Allan Poe* to *Homer* and makes no new errors. The correct answer is (D).

### Page 476—Challenge Question #18

**A** The task of the question is to weaken the objection, which means to provide a reason that the proposed tax plan might work despite the objection. The objection is that *such tax savings tend to be kept as profit rather than reinvested.* This objection is significant, because if the savings are not reinvested, there will be no *job creation or corporate investment* as a result of the savings. Thus, the correct answer needs to change something about what happens to the tax savings. Choice (A) indicates that the savings are required to be reinvested, which addresses the objection. Keep (A). Choice (B) is out of scope, as it discusses *personal* investments, so eliminate (B). Choice (C) is reversal—it strengthens the objection, so eliminate (C). Choice (D) is out of scope. It provides a mechanism by which the lower tax rate may not significantly hurt overall government revenue, which is irrelevant to whether the tax plan will produce *job creation or corporate investment,* so eliminate (D). Choice (E) is out of scope, as it discusses reasons for economic issues that cannot be directly tied to a reason that tax savings would be used to create jobs, so eliminate (E). The correct answer is (A).

### Page 480—Challenge Question #19

**C** Treat the passage as a series of facts and consider whether each answer choice can be proven. Choice (A) is out of scope. Proximity to the strongest warm ocean currents may not mean that any warm ocean currents impact that portion of coastline directly. Eliminate (A). Choice (B) is extreme language, as the other factors of glacial ablation may lead to *high rates* of ablation without warm ocean currents, so eliminate (B). Choice (C) matches the information in the passage. If a rise in ocean temperatures leads to a rise in warm ocean currents along glacial coasts, those currents will cause a rise in submarine melt rates. Thus, submarine melt rates are higher in the presence of warm ocean currents than they are in the absence of warm ocean currents. Keep (C). Choice (D) is extreme. While global climatic shifts may increase the occurrence of submarine melt rates, submarine melt may still have been an important factor in prior periods, so eliminate (D). Choice (E) is extreme language. Lower ocean temperatures may lead to a reduction in submarine melt rates, but that doesn't prove that snow accumulation will be a more significant factor. Eliminate (E). The correct answer is (C).

## Page 488—Challenge Question #20

**B** This is a weaken question, so find the conclusion, premise, and any assumptions in the argument. The conclusion of the argument is that *merely sharing the same physical space with another dog is sufficient to maintain proper socialization* in dogs as they grow older. The premise for the conclusion comes from the last sentence, which cites evidence *from a study demonstrating that the more often a dog shares a physical space with another dog, the better its socialization.* A study shows that the more often a dog shares a physical space, the better its socialization is, so sharing a physical space is sufficient for maintaining proper socialization. This argument exhibits a causal reasoning pattern, in effect stating that shared physical space causes socialization in dogs. The standard assumption for causality is that there is no other cause, and it is not a coincidence. To weaken an argument based on the causality pattern, the correct answer will usually either provide an alternate cause or present a situation in which the supposed cause (shared physical space) is present but the supposed effect (socialization) did not occur. It is also possible that the answer may indicate that the supposed cause and effect have been reversed. Here, that would mean that the answer could indicate that shared physical space is a result of socialization rather than socialization being the result of shared physical space. Evaluate the answer choices one at a time.

Choice (A) is out of scope because challenging a dog's *physical and mental capacities* and avoiding *the deterioration of these capacities.* is not the focus of the argument. Eliminate (A). Choice (B) indicates that the causality may have been reversed. In effect, well-socialized dogs often share physical space with other dogs while poorly socialized dogs (for example, dogs that are aggressive toward other dogs) do not. Keep (B). Choice (C) is out of scope because dogs that are capable of both play and sharing space are not the focus of the passage. Eliminate (C). Choice (D) is out of scope. A study that analyzes other studies is just as valid as a study that collects its own data. Eliminate (D). Choice (E) casts doubt on the validity of the metrics used for measuring socialization, but this is out of scope. Eliminate (E). The correct answer is (B).

# Part VIII
# Diagnostic Test 2

# Chapter 28
# Diagnostic Test 2

## TAKING THE SECOND DIAGNOSTIC

The purpose of the second diagnostic is to gauge how far you've come! Hopefully you took the first diagnostic found at the outset of this book and have a good idea of how you scored. If you took the first diagnostic, you could have used the information gathered from that experience to tailor your study schedule to highlight the areas you struggled with the most.

To maximize the effectiveness of this second diagnostic, don't rush to take it. If there are a couple topics you are still uneasy with, take the time to review them, practice them, and turn them into strengths. Make sure you've overturned every stone this book has to offer before taking this test. Why? Because using this test as a measure of progress is effective only once. If your brain is giving you any sense that you may want to work through another section again before starting this section, listen to that instinct.

Similar to the first diagnostic, there are a couple things you should keep in mind. This test does not include an essay or integrated reasoning section. The diagnostic is separated out into different content sections. Each section has a mix of problem solving and data sufficiency questions ranging in difficulty from easy to hard.

There are two primary ways you can use the diagnostic test to evaluate your progress. The first is by comparing the number of questions you got correct for each content segment in the first diagnostic to the amount you got right in the second diagnostic. The second way to use this tests for timing. On test day, you will need to average about 2 minutes per question to finish each section in the allotted amount of time. While taking the diagnostic, keep track of how long a question has taken you. Getting a correct answer is great! But getting a correct answer in under 2 minutes is fantastic. If you find a problem that is taking you longer than 2 minutes to answer, don't just give up! Continue to solve the problem but make a note for yourself about this content. Once you finish, make sure to give that content area a review to shore up any weaknesses.

## HOW TO SCORE THE SECOND DIAGNOSTIC

At the end of the diagnostic, we provide both an answer key and explanations for each question. Keep track of the number of questions you get correct and the content areas of the questions that you missed. Review the length of time it took you to answer questions, taking note of those content areas for which many questions took you longer than two minutes to answer. The total number of questions you get correct is considered your "score." While this is not an accurate representation of an actual GMAT score, it is a way for you to monitor progress and compare how you perform on this diagnostic with how well you performed on the first diagnostic.

Keeping tabs on the content areas of the questions that you missed provides you the opportunity to seek out those trouble areas in this book and give them the extra attention they need to become areas of strength. This is an incredibly important step to take, so don't skip it.

Once done, compare the content areas that you answer questions incorrectly in the second diagnostic to the content areas of incorrect questions on the first diagnostic. How have you improved? Are there still areas you are still struggling with?

## WHAT TO DO AFTER THE SECOND DIAGNOSTIC?

What happens if the results of this second diagnostic reveal that you are still struggling in some of the same areas you struggled with on the first? If you've read through every page on this topic and answered every practice question in this book about it, then don't fear. You are not out of options. There are many resources from The Princeton Review available to you to continue pushing your studies forward. You can check out one of our other titles that contain even more practice questions. You can contact your local office and inquire about picking up a couple hours of private tutoring. You can email our editorial support team to ask specific questions about what you did wrong on any given question and get another explanation for how to approach a problem.

We are here to help achieve the goal we outlined in the letter at the beginning of this book: to help you achieve the GMAT score of your dreams. Don't be afraid to reach out to us to lament your struggles and celebrate your successes. We will gladly be one of your biggest fans.

Clear your calendar and get ready for the second diagnostic. Best of luck!

## Diagnostic Test 2

**61 Questions**

---

### Arithmetic

1. If $k$ is a positive, two-digit integer, what is the value of $k$ ?

(1) The remainder when $k$ is divided by 9 is 8

(2) The remainder when $k$ is divided by 8 is 7

- Statement (1) ALONE is sufficient, but statement (2) alone is not sufficient.
- Statement (2) ALONE is sufficient, but statement (1) alone is not sufficient.
- BOTH statements TOGETHER are sufficient, but NEITHER statement ALONE is sufficient.
- EACH statement ALONE is sufficient.
- Statements (1) and (2) TOGETHER are not sufficient.

2. If the size of a rug is 25,0000 square millimeters, what is the size of the rug in square centimeters? (1 millimeter = 0.1 centimeter)

- 0.25
- 2.5
- 25
- 250
- 2,500

3. Set $P = \{1, 3, 4, 7, 9\}$

If $d$ is a random two-digit integer formed by any two distinct members chosen from set $P$, what is the probability that $d$ is prime?

- $\frac{7}{20}$
- $\frac{2}{5}$
- $\frac{1}{2}$
- $\frac{3}{5}$
- $\frac{13}{20}$

4. What is the remainder when positive integer $n$ is divided by 17 ?

(1) $n$ divided by 51 has a remainder of 36

(2) $n$ divided by 31 has a remainder of 4

- Statement (1) ALONE is sufficient, but statement (2) alone is not sufficient.
- Statement (2) ALONE is sufficient, but statement (1) alone is not sufficient.
- BOTH statements TOGETHER are sufficient, but NEITHER statement ALONE is sufficient.
- EACH statement ALONE is sufficient.
- Statements (1) and (2) TOGETHER are not sufficient.

GO ON TO THE NEXT PAGE.

5. During a summer Chemistry course, Phyllis earned 1 hour of course credit for every 3 labs she completed and 0.25 hours of course credit for every hour of class she attended. The course lasted 8 weeks, offering 2 three-hour classes per week. If Phyllis went to all classes and completed 9 labs, how much course credit did she earn?

- 3.5
- 5
- 9.5
- 15
- 17

6. If $a + b$ is the average (arithmetic mean) of $c$ and $d$, what is the average of $a$, $b$, $c$, and $d$ ?

(1) $a + b = 2$

(2) $c + d = 4$

- Statement (1) ALONE is sufficient, but statement (2) alone is not sufficient.
- Statement (2) ALONE is sufficient, but statement (1) alone is not sufficient.
- BOTH statements TOGETHER are sufficient, but NEITHER statement ALONE is sufficient.
- EACH statement ALONE is sufficient.
- Statements (1) and (2) TOGETHER are not sufficient.

7. The yield last week from a garden was 15 apples and 20% more pears than apples. How many total pears and apples did the garden yield last week?

- 3
- 6
- 15
- 18
- 33

8. If $x$ is an even integer, then what is the value of $x$ ?

(1) $x + 5$ is prime

(2) $x - 16$ is prime

- Statement (1) ALONE is sufficient, but statement (2) alone is not sufficient.
- Statement (2) ALONE is sufficient, but statement (1) alone is not sufficient.
- BOTH statements TOGETHER are sufficient, but NEITHER statement ALONE is sufficient.
- EACH statement ALONE is sufficient.
- Statements (1) and (2) TOGETHER are not sufficient.

9. In a gumball machine, the probability of not getting a red gumball is 60%. The probability of not getting a lettered gumball is 45%. If none of the red gumballs are lettered, what is the probability of getting a red gumball or a lettered gumball?

- 18%
- 33%
- 51%
- 73%
- 95%

GO ON TO THE NEXT PAGE.

10. The combination of a certain lock is comprised of 5 alpha-numeric characters. The alphabetic characters can be any of the letters A through H of the English alphabet and the numeric characters can be any number 0 through 9. The first character of the combination is a letter, the last two characters are numbers, and the letters and numbers can be used more than once. If a computer can code one possible combination per second, how many hours will it take to code every possible combination?

- 72
- 80
- 104
- 4,320
- 259,200

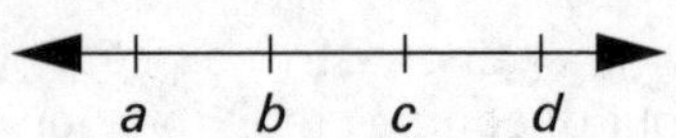


11. $a$, $b$, $c$, and $d$ are numbers on the number line shown. If the distance between each variable is $n$, then what is the value of $a + d$?

(1) $a + 2n = 6$

(2) $b = 2$

- Statement (1) ALONE is sufficient, but statement (2) alone is not sufficient.
- Statement (2) ALONE is sufficient, but statement (1) alone is not sufficient.
- BOTH statements TOGETHER are sufficient, but NEITHER statement ALONE is sufficient.
- EACH statement ALONE is sufficient.
- Statements (1) and (2) TOGETHER are not sufficient.

GO ON TO THE NEXT PAGE.

**Geometry**

1. What is the area of circle $X$?

   (1) The longest chord in circle $X$ has a length of 6.

   (2) The point (2, 3) is on circle $X$.

   - Statement (1) ALONE is sufficient, but statement (2) alone is not sufficient.
   - Statement (2) ALONE is sufficient, but statement (1) alone is not sufficient.
   - BOTH statements TOGETHER are sufficient, but NEITHER statement ALONE is sufficient.
   - EACH statement ALONE is sufficient.
   - Statements (1) and (2) TOGETHER are not sufficient.

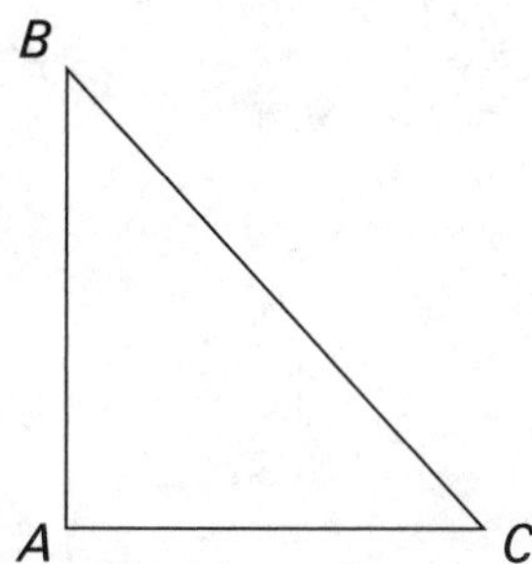


2. What is the area of triangle $ABC$?

   (1) $AB = 12$

   (2) $AC = 5$

   - Statement (1) ALONE is sufficient, but statement (2) alone is not sufficient.
   - Statement (2) ALONE is sufficient, but statement (1) alone is not sufficient.
   - BOTH statements TOGETHER are sufficient, but NEITHER statement ALONE is sufficient.
   - EACH statement ALONE is sufficient.
   - Statements (1) and (2) TOGETHER are not sufficient.

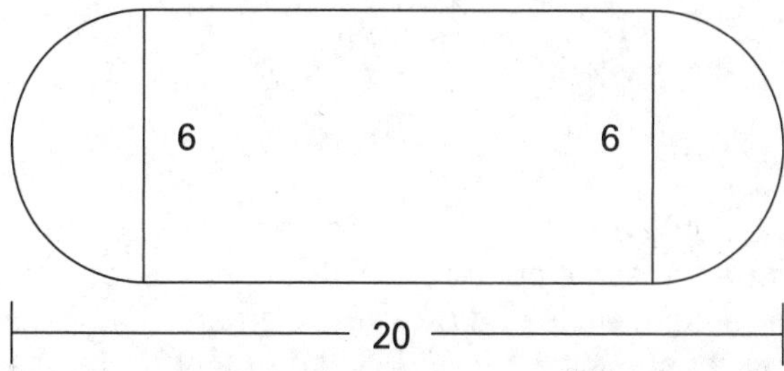


3. A playground consists of a rectangle and two semicircles as shown in the figure above. What is the perimeter of the playground?

   - $28 + 6\pi$
   - $28 + 12\pi$
   - $48 + 6\pi$
   - $48 + 12\pi$
   - $84 + 9\pi$

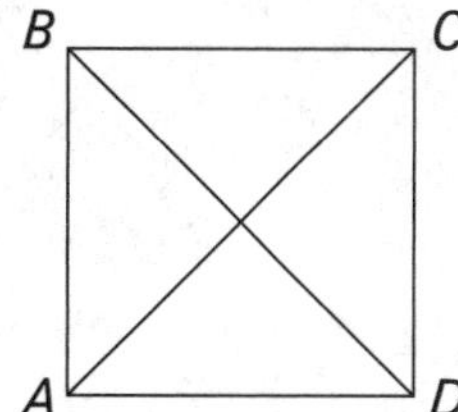


4. In the figure above, the length of the side of square $ABCD$ is 2. What is the ratio of the sum of the lengths of lines $AC$ and $BD$ to the perimeter of $ABCD$?

   - $\sqrt{2} : 1$
   - $1 : \sqrt{2}$
   - $\sqrt{2} : 2$
   - $2 : \sqrt{2}$
   - $1 : 2$

GO ON TO THE NEXT PAGE.

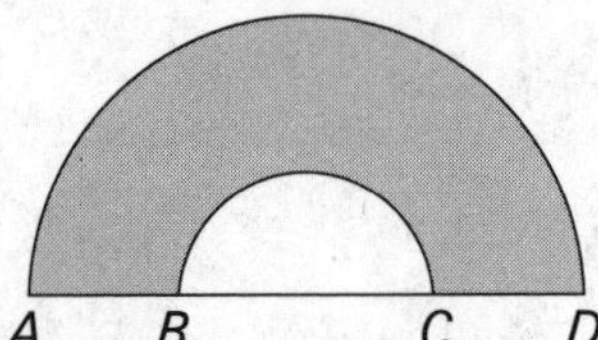


5. The figure above consists of two semicircles that share the same center. *AD* is the diameter of the larger semicircle and *BC* is the diameter of the smaller semicircle. If *AB* = 8 and *AC* = 12. What is the area of the shaded region?

- ◯ $42\pi$
- ◯ $48\pi$
- ◯ $72\pi$
- ◯ $96\pi$
- ◯ $192\pi$

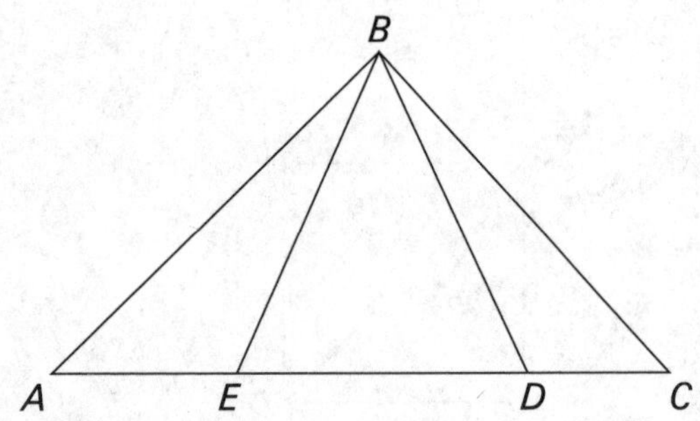


6. In the figure above *EB* = *BD* and *AB* = *BC*. What is the degree measure of angle *ABE* ?

- ◯ 15
- ◯ 17.5
- ◯ 22.5
- ◯ 25
- ◯ 30

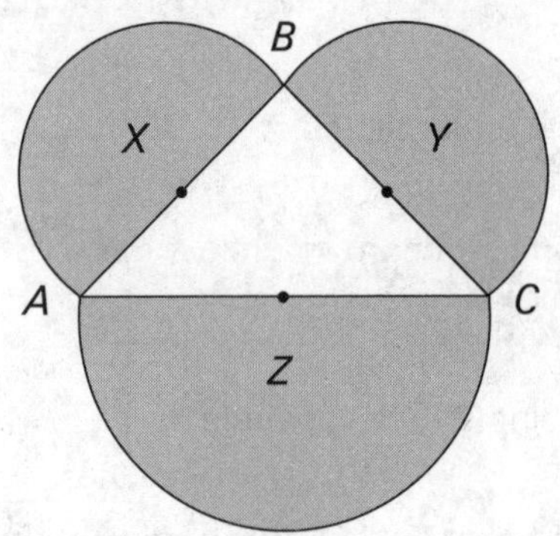


Note: Figure not drawn to scale.

7. In the figure above, triangle *ABC* is surrounded by the semicircles with centers *X*, *Y*, and *Z*. The areas of semicircles *X*, *Y*, and *Z* are $72\pi$, $\frac{25\pi}{2}$, and $\frac{169\pi}{2}$ respectively. What is the area of triangle *ABC* ?

- ◯ 30
- ◯ 72
- ◯ 120
- ◯ 124
- ◯ 169

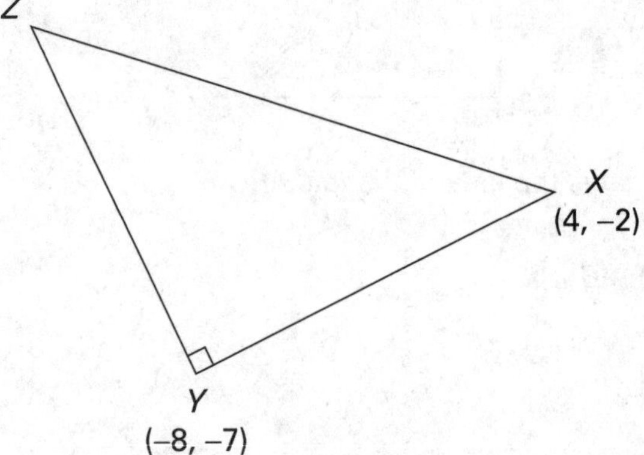


8. What is the perimeter of isosceles right triangle *XYZ*, shown above?

- ◯ $13 + 13\sqrt{2}$
- ◯ 36
- ◯ 39
- ◯ $26 + 13\sqrt{2}$
- ◯ $13 + 26\sqrt{2}$

GO ON TO THE NEXT PAGE.

9. What is the area of a circle with center at (3, –2) ?

(1) The point $\left(\frac{6}{5}, \frac{8}{5}\right)$ is on the circle.

(2) The line $y = \frac{1}{2}x + 1$ is tangent to the circle.

- Statement (1) ALONE is sufficient, but statement (2) alone is not sufficient.
- Statement (2) ALONE is sufficient, but statement (1) alone is not sufficient.
- BOTH statements TOGETHER are sufficient, but NEITHER statement ALONE is sufficient.
- EACH statement ALONE is sufficient.
- Statements (1) and (2) TOGETHER are not sufficient.

10. Is the perimeter of triangle *ABC* greater than 10 ?

(1) The coordinates of point *B* are (1, 2).

(2) The coordinates of point *C* are (–3, –1).

- Statement (1) ALONE is sufficient, but statement (2) alone is not sufficient.
- Statement (2) ALONE is sufficient, but statement (1) alone is not sufficient.
- BOTH statements TOGETHER are sufficient, but NEITHER statement ALONE is sufficient.
- EACH statement ALONE is sufficient.
- Statements (1) and (2) TOGETHER are not sufficient.

GO ON TO THE NEXT PAGE.

## Algebra

1. If $x$ is an integer, is $x^6 = 64$ ?

(1) $x^{-5} = \frac{1}{32}$

(2) $x$ is prime

- Statement (1) ALONE is sufficient, but statement (2) alone is not sufficient.
- Statement (2) ALONE is sufficient, but statement (1) alone is not sufficient.
- BOTH statements TOGETHER are sufficient, but NEITHER statement ALONE is sufficient.
- EACH statement ALONE is sufficient.
- Statements (1) and (2) TOGETHER are not sufficient.

2. If $x$ and $y$ are integers greater than 1, is $x$ prime?

(1) The only factors of integer $y$ are 1 and $y$

(2) The least common multiple of $x$ and $y$ is $xy$

- Statement (1) ALONE is sufficient, but statement (2) alone is not sufficient.
- Statement (2) ALONE is sufficient, but statement (1) alone is not sufficient.
- BOTH statements TOGETHER are sufficient, but NEITHER statement ALONE is sufficient.
- EACH statement ALONE is sufficient.
- Statements (1) and (2) TOGETHER are not sufficient.

3. What is the value of $a + b + c$ ?

(1) $4a - 3b + 5c = 65$

(2) $-2a - 9b - c = 23$

- Statement (1) ALONE is sufficient, but statement (2) alone is not sufficient.
- Statement (2) ALONE is sufficient, but statement (1) alone is not sufficient.
- BOTH statements TOGETHER are sufficient, but NEITHER statement ALONE is sufficient.
- EACH statement ALONE is sufficient.
- Statements (1) and (2) TOGETHER are not sufficient.

4. What is the value of $\frac{g-1}{h+1}$ ?

(1) $7g - 6h = 0$

(2) $h = 42$

- Statement (1) ALONE is sufficient, but statement (2) alone is not sufficient.
- Statement (2) ALONE is sufficient, but statement (1) alone is not sufficient.
- BOTH statements TOGETHER are sufficient, but NEITHER statement ALONE is sufficient.
- EACH statement ALONE is sufficient.
- Statements (1) and (2) TOGETHER are not sufficient.

5. If $x$ and $y$ are integers such that $5 < |y| < 9$ and $4 < |x| < 10$, which of the following represents all possible values of $xy$ ?

- $-90 < xy < 20$
- $-36 < xy < -20$ and $36 < xy < 90$
- $-90 < xy < -20$ and $20 < xy < 90$
- $-50 < xy < 20$ and $-20 < xy < 50$
- $-36 < xy < -20$ and $20 < xy < 36$

GO ON TO THE NEXT PAGE.

6. In 3 years, Calvin will be 3 times as old as Jill. In 6 years, Jill will be half as old as Tom. If Calvin is currently $c$ years old, then, in terms of $c$, how old is Tom?

- $\frac{2c}{3}$
- $\frac{2c}{3}+2$
- $\frac{c+3}{3}+6$
- $\frac{3c+6}{2}$
- $\frac{3c}{2}+2$

7. If $6^{2x+2} = 36^{2x-2}$, then what is the value of $x$ ?

- $\frac{1}{2}$
- 2
- $\frac{3}{2}$
- 3
- 4

8. $r$, $s$, and $t$ are negative consecutive odd digits, and $r < s < t$. All of the following could be the units digit of $s^6$ EXCEPT

- 1
- 3
- 5
- 7
- 9

9. Is $m$ a positive integer?

(1) $-m^3 \leq -1$

(2) $-m^2 \geq -1$

- Statement (1) ALONE is sufficient, but statement (2) alone is not sufficient.
- Statement (2) ALONE is sufficient, but statement (1) alone is not sufficient.
- BOTH statements TOGETHER are sufficient, but NEITHER statement ALONE is sufficient.
- EACH statement ALONE is sufficient.
- Statements (1) and (2) TOGETHER are not sufficient.

10. If $f(x) = 3x + w$ and $g(x) = 4x - w$, then what is the value of $g(f(5)) - f(g(5))$ ?

- $x + 5w$
- $2x - w$
- $5w$
- $-5w$
- $2x + 5w$

GO ON TO THE NEXT PAGE.

**Sentence Correction**

1. Rebuilding and levee development has permitted the seacoast town with increasing its tourist visitation over the past few months, and they are reallocating the budget surplus as a result.

   - has permitted the seacoast town with increasing its tourist visitation over the past few months, and they are reallocating
   - has permitted the seacoast town to increase its tourist visitation over the past few months, and to forecast
   - have permitted the seacoast town to increase its tourist visitation over the past few months, and to reallocate
   - have permitted the seacoast town with increasing its tourist visitation over the past few months, and to reallocate
   - have permitted for the seacoast town to increase its tourist visitation over the past few months, as well as reallocating

2. Using a combination of algebra and ancient Greek to code her clandestine affairs with women, Anne Lister completed a voluminous diary, which also detailed a range of topics from her travels, such as her scaling the mountains of the Pyrenees, and also the improvements made to her properties, notably Shibden Hall in West Yorkshire, England.

   - detailed a range of topics from her travels, such as her scaling the mountains of the Pyrenees, and also the improvements made to her properties, notably
   - covering a range of topics, from her travels such as her scaling the mountains of the Pyrenees and the improvements made to her properties, notably
   - detailing a range of topics, her scaling the mountains of the Pyrenees during her travels, and the improvements made to her properties, notably
   - detailed a range of topics, from her travels, such as scaling the mountains of the Pyrenees, to the improvements made to her properties, notably
   - covered a range of topics, such as her travels such as her scaling the mountains of the Pyrenees plus the improvements made to her properties, notably

GO ON TO THE NEXT PAGE.

3. Alan Turing's reputation as a founder of computer science is now so well-known as to obscure the fact that he was never fully recognized in England, his home country, during his lifetime.

- now so well-known as to obscure the fact that he was never fully recognized in England
- now so well known that it obscures the fact that he was never fully recognized in England
- now so well-known as to obscure the fact that he was never fully recognized in England
- well known enough now that it obscures the fact that he was never fully recognized in England
- well known enough now so as to obscure the fact that he was never fully recognized in England

4. A wild American alligator grows to about 10 feet long, but one kept as a pet can suffer from the cramped housing, which stunts the development of the alligator's jaw, exacerbates the premature loss of teeth, and prevents those teeth from growing back at the proper angles.

- which stunts the development of the alligator's jaw, exacerbates the premature loss of teeth, and prevents those teeth from growing back
- which stunts the development of the alligator's jaw, exacerbates the premature loss of teeth, prevented from growing back
- which stunts the development of the alligator's jaw, exacerbating the premature loss of teeth, only to prevent them from growing back
- stunting the development of the alligator's jaw, exacerbating the premature loss of teeth, only to prevent them from growing back
- stunting the development of the alligator's jaw, exacerbating the premature loss of teeth, and preventing them from growing back

5. With no other work did New Zealand writer Katherine Mansfield inspire such lasting admiration in international literary circles as did her short-story collection *The Garden Party and Other Stories*.

- did her short-story collection *The Garden Party and Other Stories*
- had her short-story collection *The Garden Party and Other Stories*
- with her short-story collection *The Garden Party and Other Stories*
- her short-story collection *The Garden Party and Other Stories did*
- her short-story collection *The Garden Party and Other Stories*

6. During the last month, researchers had narrowed down to two the possible origins that are being discussed in classrooms across the nation to explain the emergence of a new species of caterpillar.

- had narrowed down to two the possible origins that are being discussed in classrooms across the nation to explain the emergence of a new species of caterpillar
- had narrowed down to two the possible origins to explain the emergence of a new species of caterpillar that classrooms are hypothesizing across the nation
- have narrowed down to two the possible origins that classrooms are discussing the emergence of a new species of caterpillar across the nation
- have narrowed down to two the possible origins to explain the emergence of a new species of caterpillar that are being discussed in classrooms across the nation
- have narrowed it down to two possible origins to explain the emergence of a new species of caterpillar that are being discussed in classrooms across the nation

GO ON TO THE NEXT PAGE.

7. To assess the impact of an individual on the community is a conundrum, for there is a limit to the number of consequences of any single course of action that they can be cognizant of.

- ◯ To assess the impact of an individual on the community is a conundrum, for there is a limit to the number of consequences of any single course of action that they can be cognizant of.
- ◯ Assessing the impact of an individual on the community is a conundrum, for one can be cognizant of only a limited number of consequences of any single course of action.
- ◯ It is a conundrum to assess the impact of an individual on the community, for there is only a limited number of consequences of any single course of action, of which one can be cognizant.
- ◯ Just as there are only a limited number of consequences of any single course of action that one can be cognizant of, assessing the impact of an individual on the community is a conundrum.
- ◯ A conundrum is to assess the impact of an individual on the community, for the number of consequences of any single course of action is limited, of which one can be cognizant.

8. The NASA mathematician Mary Jackson, when offered an opportunity to train as an engineer, had to petition the city of Langley to get permission to attend courses at nearby segregated Hampton High School, which only after a special court hearing, they allowed her to attend.

- ◯ which only after a special court hearing, they allowed her to attend
- ◯ allowing her to attend after only a special court hearing
- ◯ which she attended only after a special court hearing they allowed
- ◯ allowing her only to attend after a special court hearing
- ◯ which she was allowed to attend only after a special court hearing

9. The Parks and Recreation office recognizes that by stalling the precise allocation of renovation funds for three months, that it has prevented the commencement of work due to the onset of winter, and thus has use of the department's workforce for other projects until fair weather returns.

- ◯ that it has prevented the commencement of work due to the onset of winter, and thus has
- ◯ the onset of winter has prevented the commencement of work, and thus has
- ◯ it has delayed the commencement of work until the onset of winter, and thus is having
- ◯ the onset of winter has prevented the commencement of work, and thus it is having
- ◯ it has delayed the commencement of work until the onset of winter, and thus has

GO ON TO THE NEXT PAGE.

10. While it causes more damage to wildlife than to urban development to leave more than 10 million acres vulnerable to wildfires, it is the residential and commercial damage that receives the most attention from the media and the most funds for relief and rebuilding.

- ◯ While it causes more damage to wildlife than to urban development to leave more than 10 million acres vulnerable to wildfires, it is the residential and commercial damage that receives the most attention from the media and the most funds for relief and rebuilding.
- ◯ While leaving more than 10 million acres vulnerable to wildfires causes more damage to wildlife than to urban development, the residential and commercial damage from wildfires receives the most attention from the media and the most funds for relief and rebuilding.
- ◯ Even though it causes more damage to wildlife than to urban development to leave more than 10 million acres vulnerable to wildfires, it is the residential and commercial damage that receives the most media attention and funds for relief and rebuilding.
- ◯ The damage caused by leaving more than 10 million acres vulnerable to wildfires is more for wildlife than for urban development, but the residential and commercial damage receives the most media attention and funds for relief and rebuilding.
- ◯ It causes more damage to wildlife than to urban development to leave more than 10 million acres vulnerable to wildfires, but the media attention and funds for relief and rebuilding are the most for residential and commercial damage.

11. Arguably one of the most influential figures in the Silver Age of Comics, Jack Kirby's drawing style, which utilized foreshortening to convey depth and allowed characters to "burst" out of panel frames.

- ◯ Jack Kirby's drawing style, which utilized foreshortening to convey depth and allowed characters to
- ◯ Jack Kirby's drawing style, utilizing foreshortening to convey depth and allowing characters
- ◯ Jack Kirby developed a drawing style which utilized foreshortening to convey depth and allowed characters to
- ◯ Jack Kirby developed a drawing style that utilized foreshortening to convey depth but also allowed characters
- ◯ Jack Kirby developed a drawing style utilizing foreshortening conveying depth and allowing characters to

GO ON TO THE NEXT PAGE.

### Reading Comprehension

Questions 1–3 are based on the following passage:

Creative thinking, adaptability, and collaboration are part of human nature. Unfortunately, however, the hierarchical structures at workplaces unwittingly discourage these traits. Paradoxically, the preeminent organizational strategy designed to maximize efficient productivity may actually be detrimental. The long-term success of a corporation requires flexibility and new ideas to respond to ever-evolving political, social, and economic conditions.

Becoming a "flat organization" will best ensure a company's survival. Such enterprises abolish middle management structures and instead assign most workers to the same level, with only a few superiors. In doing so, corporations must reconsider their view of employees: rather than workers reporting to a manager responsible for making decisions, non-hierarchical committees share in a decentralized decision-making process. Collaboration is encouraged and innovation is rewarded; new ideas can be implemented more quickly without requiring the traditional levels of ascension through middle management. Limiting specialization in job titles fosters flexibility as workers can take on a variety of roles depending on individual project needs, which leads to an increase in employee learning. Simply put, leaders in flat organizations have the responsibility to construct organizations in which members maximize their abilities and directly contribute to the company's success.

1. Which of the following could best serve as an example of how a company might become a flat organization, as such organizations are described in the passage?

   - ○ Outsourcing middle management to a separate company
   - ○ Abolishing job titles and rotating responsibility for leading meetings
   - ○ Denoting specific guidelines for approval of new ideas
   - ○ Hiring a specialist for each stage of a project's completion
   - ○ Assigning each employee another employee to oversee

2. The primary purpose of the passage is to

   - ○ compare various corporate organizational strategies
   - ○ explain and endorse an alternative business structure
   - ○ propose a traditional corporate approach
   - ○ evaluate and then criticize a new method of conducting business
   - ○ acknowledge the similarities between two management theories

3. Which of the following can be inferred from the passage about hierarchical workplaces?

   - ○ They may result in a delayed approval process for new ideas.
   - ○ They often contain more middle managers than upper managers.
   - ○ They maximize efficiency by promoting specialization.
   - ○ They are more beneficial for larger companies than for smaller companies.
   - ○ They do not allow employees to have flexible roles.

GO ON TO THE NEXT PAGE.

Questions 4–6 are based on the following passage:

Eighteenth-century economist Adam Smith introduced the "invisible hand" as a metaphor for the societal results of individuals' self-interested actions. Subsequent theorists expanded Smith's idea to form the "general equilibrium theory," in which invisible market forces guided the interaction of supply and demand toward a natural balance as individuals act in their own interest and firms pursue the goal of maximizing profit.

Despite the ubiquity of this model in both popular and scholarly thinking, there is no evidence for its truth. Although academic economists have demonstrated that an optimal equilibrium of supply and demand exists, the guiding influence of Smith's invisible hand in moving markets toward such a balance has not been shown. The dubious belief that markets actively move toward an equilibrium has been used by proponents of deregulation, who insist that removing government interventions promotes economic strength, and the presumption of its accuracy has prevented some leaders and economists from identifying critical signs of impending crises. The general equilibrium theory presents an optimistic view of self-correction that has not been borne out by actual economic conditions—a defect that calls into question Smith's antecedent hypotheses.

4. The author of the passage implies which of the following regarding the originators of the general equilibrium theory?

- There is ample evidence to support the basis of the theory.
- They developed the theory sometime in the eighteenth century.
- Their theories were immediately popular among the general public.
- They were aware of Smith's beliefs about the relationship between individual actions and the economy.
- Some of them worked closely with Smith during the time in which he formulated his theory.

5. The author of the passage is primarily concerned with

- exploring the argument for economic regulation
- questioning the foundation of the general equilibrium theory
- defending Smith's beliefs with supporting evidence
- asserting that market forces naturally maintain balance
- comparing several economic theories

6. It can be inferred from the passage that defenders of the general equilibrium theory would most likely regard economic regulations as

- imperative
- catastrophic
- salutary
- insufficient
- unnecessary

GO ON TO THE NEXT PAGE.

Questions 7–10 are based on the following passage:

A critical aspect of product advertising is the choice between positive and negative approaches. Positive advertisements tout the benefits of a product to convince consumers that they want or need the item for sale. Negative advertisements, by contrast, involve attacks on competing companies or products to dissuade their audience from considering those options.

An advantage of positive advertising is its ability to evoke emotions such as happiness, nostalgia, and optimism in its audience, creating a psychological association between the brand and feelings of warmth. Despite this, some consumers may view such campaigns as insincere or predatory due to their reliance on manipulating emotions rather than presenting factual information. The resulting distrust can then lead to skepticism regarding appeals that are based more on logic, as consumers assume they are still being manipulated for the goal of producing positive feelings. By contrast, negative advertising can appear more truthful: the company is not painting a rosy sheen over its own products but rather warning consumers of a competitor's flaw. Consumers may thus more readily believe negative information compared to arguments made in favor of a brand or product, and the former often makes a stronger mental impression.

Psychological research explains why such advertising can be more memorable: negativity bias. People tend to give more attention to negative, rather than positive, events, and make more decisions based on negative information. Furthermore, negative advertising has other applications aside from attacking competitors: many firms have found success in advertising by highlighting a problem that the promoted product can solve or by suggesting that it could prevent the consumer from losing something—rather than positive advertising, which might focus on what the audience has to gain.

In spite of these benefits, negativity in advertising is not always more effective than the alternative. For instance, featuring a competitor in an advertisement can inadvertently provide a boost to the competing brand, even if the message is ultimately defamatory. Furthermore, negative advertising poses a risk that the audience will be alienated from both the competitor and the company criticizing it. Consumers who choose a brand simply because the alternative is presented as flawed are not as loyal as those for whom merit guides the decision. A final concern is that consumers may view attacks on competitors as petty and untoward.

7. The primary purpose of the passage is to

- ⬭ argue the inferiority of one advertising approach to another
- ⬭ explore the advantages of different forms of advertising on different audiences
- ⬭ consider the benefits and risks of two marketing strategies
- ⬭ explain what makes a particular advertising strategy effective
- ⬭ illustrate the need for companies to advertise their products

8. All of the following are mentioned as potential risks in advertising EXCEPT

- ⬭ Consumers may lose interest in petty feuds between rival companies.
- ⬭ Consumers may reject both the advertiser and a named competitor.
- ⬭ Consumers may not believe claims made in advertising.
- ⬭ A company could lose its audience's trust.
- ⬭ A company could give attention to a competitor's products.

GO ON TO THE NEXT PAGE.

9. Which of the following could best serve as an example of negative advertising as it is described in the passage?

- ⬭ A packaging company uses a bittersweet story about an animal shelter to provoke an emotional response.
- ⬭ A restaurant advertises that its fruits and vegetables do not contain pesticides.
- ⬭ A beauty company claims its competitor's product has long-term health implications.
- ⬭ An environmental group criticizes the airline industry for its lack of sustainability.
- ⬭ A construction firm provides data and customer reviews to attract new clients.

10. Which of the following best describes the function of the highlighted sentence in the context of the passage as a whole?

- ⬭ It explains why a particular strategy is demonstrably superior to the approach that was previously discussed.
- ⬭ It summarizes the main differences between the two strategies described in the passage and introduces a new perspective.
- ⬭ It refutes the argument made in the first paragraph and provides the foundation for an assertion made in the following paragraph.
- ⬭ It describes an alternative to a potential problem mentioned earlier in the paragraph and previews the topic of the following paragraph.
- ⬭ It suggests that a method mentioned earlier in the paragraph is less effective than most experts believe.

GO ON TO THE NEXT PAGE.

## Critical Reasoning

1. **Physiotherapist:** Although the patient's health would improve with daily outdoor walks, I have advised against it in the health plan. Since she is overweight, an increase in walking exercise would stress the already overstressed knee joints and would therefore put the patient at increased risk of injury.

   The physiotherapist's argument depends on which of the following?

   - The patient would use her knees during daily walks more than she currently does in other activities, such as bicycling.
   - The amount of exercise the patient currently undertakes does not put her at risk of joint injury.
   - Any patient is apt to be healthier with some exercise than with none at all.
   - The patient will not attempt to take daily walks despite the recommendation of the physiotherapist.
   - The physiotherapist should have the patient's best well-being as the foremost concern.

2. Cancer is a disease that involves the uncontrolled division of abnormal cells in the body. It stands to reason that the more cells an organism has, the more likely that organism would get cancer. However, the incidence of cancer in mice is many times that of humans, even though humans have over 1,000 times as many cells as mice do. Furthermore, elephants have even more cells than humans do, but the incidence of cancer in elephants is much lower.

   The statements above, if true, provide the most support for which of the following conclusions?

   - The incidence of cancer in an organism is due in part to factors other than body size.
   - A higher incidence of cancer correlates to an increase in body size.
   - The number of cells in any organism's body is not a predictor of likelihood of cancer.
   - Within a species, the number of abnormal cells in an organism can contribute to the uncontrolled division of those cells.
   - Abnormal cell division is the key to understanding and curing cancer in humans.

GO ON TO THE NEXT PAGE.

3. **Lawyer:** Although there is no eyewitness to the crime, it is evident that it must have been committed by Jones, Alyers, or Singh, all of whom were working in the electronics supply warehouse at the time the theft of the case of new tablets occurred. Electronic timestamps indicate that all three men were checking inventory at the time of the theft. Singh, the more senior employee with the higher pay grade, was supervising Jones and Alyers, who were processing the inventory. Singh has already testified that both Jones and Alyers were out of his sight numerous times throughout the shift. Therefore, Jones or Alyers had the most motive and opportunity to commit the theft.

   The lawyer's argument assumes which of the following?

   ◯ All theft by employees of a company is done during the processing of inventory.
   ◯ Jones was out of Singh's sight more often than Alyers.
   ◯ Any testimony in court should be treated skeptically.
   ◯ The number of trucks with stolen items is growing.
   ◯ Tenure of employment and salary are directly related to the likelihood of committing theft.

4. **Social Media Officer:** Our biggest competitor allows many more advertisements per page view on its website than we currently allow on ours. Because revenue depends on page views, this means that we are not generating as much revenue for our content as we could. I propose that we increase the rotation of banner ads on the header of our homepage as well as include more thumbnail ads on the left margin of each subpage. Although I think this will generate more profits in the long run, be prepared for an initial loss, since ____________________.

   Which of the following is the most logical completion of the passage?

   ◯ our biggest competitor has standing relationships with all the advertisers to whom we are likely to sell the new inventory
   ◯ the percent of ads devoted to our current advertisers will decrease, since the additional ads will be devoted to new advertisers
   ◯ creating the infrastructure to host more advertisements at different locations on our website requires a large up-front investment
   ◯ none of our current customers want to engage with more advertisements
   ◯ the rates we will charge for these new ads will be slightly lower to encourage new advertisers to utilize our site

GO ON TO THE NEXT PAGE.

5. **Store manager:** The majority of the profits in our hardware store during the last quarter depended on the sales of paint and household tools. Regrettably, the reliability of our deliveries has diminished due to nationwide strikes on the part of the truckers' union. Therefore, to keep our store profits at the same level, we will have to raise the prices of products in these categories until the nationwide truckers' strike is over.

   Which of the following is an assumption on which the store manager's argument depends?

   - It is only the actions of the truckers' union that caused the shortages of paint and household tools in the hardware store.
   - Raising prices of paint and household tools until the end of the truckers' strike would not decrease patronage at the grocery store.
   - Raising prices of paint and household tools is more important than diversifying the hardware store's inventory and offering a broader selection of products.
   - Other stores have maintained their profits by raising the prices of their most popular goods to cope with the diminished supply due to the truckers' strike.
   - If the prices of popular goods increase, there will be increased pressure nationwide to end the truckers' strike.

6. **Gardener:** Under normal weather conditions, any major brand of soil provides nutrients to your plants as well as Q-Earth does. However, when conditions are not ideal, Q-Earth's nutrient generation technology provides better support for your plants when natural nutrient formation is inhibited due to lack of sunlight, rain, or heat. So, if you want your garden to thrive under any condition, use Q-Earth.

   Which of the following, if true, most strengthens the gardener's argument?

   - Q-Earth provides about average support for plants that tend to grow quickly.
   - Q-Earth is the preferred soil of interior gardeners—those who build gardens inside homes using plants that typically thrive outside.
   - Q-Earth's share of the soil market has climbed steadily for the past 5 years.
   - Q-Earth, like all branded soil, is more effective under normal weather conditions than conditions that are not ideal.
   - Q-Earth is manufactured at only one location and distributed from there to all markets.

GO ON TO THE NEXT PAGE.

7. **Principal:** The average grade of honors students on the last test was 102 points. Most students in the school are honors students. Furthermore, the amount of extra credit per test earned by any student generally does not fluctuate from test to test. It is clear that most students in the school earn at least some extra credit.

   The principal's conclusion is most vulnerable to which of the following criticisms?

   - It takes for granted that classes with honors students are typical of the classes at the whole school with regard to the average amount of extra credit earned per test.
   - It takes for granted that if a certain average amount of extra credit is earned on a test by each student in the school, then approximately the same amount of extra credit must be earned each test by each honors student.
   - It confuses a claim from which the argument's conclusion about the test scores would necessarily follow with a claim that would follow from the argument's conclusion only with a high degree of probability.
   - It overlooks the possibility that even if, on average, a certain amount of extra credit is earned by some types of students, many students may earn no extra credit at all.
   - It overlooks the possibility that even if most students in the class earn some extra credit each test, any one student may, on some tests, earn no extra credit.

8. The troubling discovery of cheating on the most common college entrance examination should not impact the reputation of the College Admissions Board. **The revelation confirms that the system works**, since the students themselves were the ones who reported their peers for unethical behavior.

   The bolded phrase plays which of the following roles in the argument?

   - It is a claim for which the argument gives evidence, and which is used to support the primary claim.
   - It is the argument's primary position, and another conclusion provides support for it.
   - It is an assumption that has no stated evidence in the argument.
   - It is the main conclusion of the argument.
   - It is a statement that contains both a premise and an assumption that support the conclusion.

GO ON TO THE NEXT PAGE.

9. **Chef:** I have noticed that savory recipes invented by culinary experts with over 20 years of experience in general yield better dishes that enjoy a much broader popularity than savory dishes based on recipes by chefs with less than 20 years of experience. Dishes derived from recipes by less experienced chefs are more prone to error and clashing flavors and, as a result, are not as popular. It seems that more experienced chefs are more precise and careful when designing their savory recipes than their counterparts, who may just be experimenting with trendy cuisines.

   Which of the following, if true, most seriously weakens the chef's argument?

   - The quality of recipes for savory dishes is generally much better than the quality of recipes for sweet dishes, such as cakes and sweetbreads.
   - Savory recipes created by less experienced chefs are generally easier for the domestic cook to follow than savory recipes created by more experienced chefs.
   - Chefs of all experience levels use the same range of spices when creating their savory recipes.
   - The most popular recipes are first discovered by individuals in cooking magazines which often feature recipes by those with industry connections.
   - In general, a culinary expert with over 20 years of experience is older than one with less than 20 years experience.

**END OF DIAGNOSTIC TEST**

# Chapter 29
# Diagnostic Test 2: Answers and Explanations

# DIAGNOSTIC TEST 2 ANSWER KEY

| Arithmetic | Geometry | Algebra |
|---|---|---|
| 1. C | 1. A | 1. A |
| 2. D | 2. E | 2. E |
| 3. D | 3. A | 3. C |
| 4. A | 4. C | 4. C |
| 5. D | 5. B | 5. C |
| 6. D | 6. A | 6. B |
| 7. E | 7. C | 7. D |
| 8. B | 8. D | 8. A |
| 9. E | 9. D | 9. E |
| 10. A | 10. C | 10. C |
| 11. C | | |

| Sentence Correction | Reading Comprehension | Critical Reasoning |
|---|---|---|
| 1. C | 1. B | 1. A |
| 2. D | 2. B | 2. A |
| 3. B | 3. A | 3. E |
| 4. A | 4. D | 4. C |
| 5. C | 5. B | 5. B |
| 6. D | 6. E | 6. B |
| 7. B | 7. C | 7. D |
| 8. E | 8. A | 8. A |
| 9. E | 9. C | 9. D |
| 10. B | 10. D | |
| 11. C | | |

# ARITHMETIC

1. **C** This is a value data sufficiency question, so begin by determining what is known and what is needed to solve the problem. The problem states that $k$ is a two-digit positive integer and asks for the value of $k$. In order to be sufficient, the statements need to provide a way to solve for the value of $k$. Consider Statement (1). For a number to have a remainder of 8 when divided by 9, that number has to be 1 less than a multiple of 9. Therefore, the possible values of $k$ according to this statement are 17, 26, 35, 44, 53, 62, 71, 80, 89, and 98. Because $k$ can be any of those values, the statement is not sufficient. Write down BCE. Consider Statement (2). For a number to have a remainder of 7 when divided by 8, that number has to be 1 less than a multiple of 8. Therefore, the possible values of $k$ according to this statement are 15, 23, 31, 39, 47, 55, 63, 71, 79, 87, and 95. Because $k$ can be any of those values, the statement is not sufficient. Eliminate (B). Consider both statements combined. The only number that is part of both lists is 71. Therefore, $k = 71$. The combined statements provide a single answer to the question, so they are sufficient. The correct answer is (C).

2. **D** Because 1 mm = 0.1 cm, it follows that 1 $mm^2 = 0.1^2\ cm^2 = 0.01\ cm^2$. Therefore, 25,000 $mm^2$ = 25,000(0.01) $cm^2$ = 250 $cm^2$. The correct answer is (D).

3. **D** Begin by determining the number of 2-digit integers that can be formed by distinct members of set $P$. There are 5 options for the first digit and 4 options for the second digit, so there are $5 \times 4 = 20$ possible 2-digit numbers. Next, determine how many possible 2-digit prime numbers can be made from distinct members of set $P$. The prime numbers that can be created are 13, 17, 19, 31, 37, 41, 43, 47, 71, 73, 79, and 97. There are 12 prime numbers and 20 possible numbers, so the probability is $\frac{12}{20} = \frac{3}{5}$. The correct answer is (D).

4. **A** This is a value data sufficiency question, so determine what is known and what is needed to answer the question. The question provides that $n$ is a positive integer. To determine the value of the remainder when $n$ is divided by 17, a value for $n$ needs to be determined or a pattern needs to be revealed by the statements. Consider Statement (1). Statement (1) states that $n$ divided by 51 produces a remainder of 36. In order to determine the value of $n$ that satisfies the statement, add 51 and 36 to produce 87. Dividing 87 by 51 gives a result of 1 with a remainder of 36, so Statement (1) is satisfied. When 87 is divided by 17 the result is 5 with a remainder of 2. When $n = 87$, the remainder is 2. Try another value of $n$. When $n = 138$, then the result of 138 divided by 51 is 2 with a remainder of 36. This value of $n$ satisfies Statement (1). When 138 is divided by 17, the result is 8 with a remainder of 2. This is the same remainder as when $n = 87$. In fact, any value of $n$ that satisfies Statement (1) produces a remainder of 2 for the question. Statement (1) is sufficient. Write down AD. Consider Statement (2). If $n = 35$, then the result of 35 divided by 31 is 1 with a remainder of 4. Statement (2) is satisfied. The result when 35 is divided by 17 is 2 with a remainder of 1. Try another value of $n$. If $n = 66$, then the result of 66 divided by 31 is 2 with a remainder of 4. Statement (2) is satisfied. The result when 66 is divided by 17 is 3 with a remainder of 15. The value of the remainder when $n$ satisfies Statement (2) is at least two different values for the answer to the question. Therefore, Statement (2) is insufficient. Eliminate (D). The correct answer is (A).

5. **D** The problem states there were 2 three-hour classes per week for 8 weeks, which means there was a total of 48 hours of class. If Phyllis attended all classes, she would have earned 48(0.25) = 12 hours of credit for classes. If Phyllis completed 9 labs and received 1 hour of course credit for every 3 labs, she would have earned 9 ÷ 3 = 3 hours of course credit for labs. In total, Phyllis received 12 + 3 = 15 hours of course credit. The correct answer is (D).

6. **D** This is a value data sufficiency question, so determine what is known and what is needed to answer the question. The question states that $a + b$ is the average of $c$ and $d$. Therefore, $a+b=\frac{c+d}{2}$. Simplified, this is $2(a + b) = c + d$. The average of $a$, $b$, $c$, and $d$ can be found by obtaining the sum $a + b + c + d$ and dividing by 4. Thus, since $2(a + b) = c + d$, the statements need to provide values for $(a + b)$ or $(c + d)$. Consider Statement (1). If $a + b = 2$, that means that the average of $c$ and $d$ is 2. In that case, $2 = \frac{c+d}{2}$ and so $c + d = 4$. This means that $a + b + c + d = 6$, and the average can be determined, so Statement (1) is sufficient. Write down AD. Consider Statement (2). If $c + d = 4$, that means that the average of $c$ and $d$ is $\frac{4}{2} = 2$. Since $a + b$ is the average of $c$ and $d$, this means $a + b = 2$, and $a + b + c + d = 6$ and the average can be determined. Statement (2) is sufficient. Eliminate (A). The correct answer is (D).

7. **E** The problem states that the garden yielded 15 apples and 20% more pears than apples. The number of pears is 20% more than apples. The number of pears can be calculated by taking 120% of the number of apples: pears = 1.2 × 15 = 18. The question asks for the number of pears and apples combined, which is 15 + 18 = 33. The correct answer is (E).

8. **B** This is a value data sufficiency question, so begin by determining what is known and what is needed to answer the question. The problem states that $x$ is an even integer and asks for a value of $x$. To answer the question, the statements need to provide a way to determine the value of $x$. Consider Statement (1). Plug In values that satisfy the statement. If $x = 18$, then the statement is satisfied because 18 + 5 = 23. This satisfies the statement. However, if $x = 24$, then the statement is also satisfied because 24 + 5 = 29. Because the statement produces two different values of $x$, the statement is insufficient. Write down BCE. Consider Statement (2). Because $x$ is an even integer and the statement subtracts another even number from it, the result is going to be another even integer because *even – even = even.* The only even prime number is 2. Therefore, $x - 16 = 2$ and $x = 18$. The statement produces one value for the question, so it is sufficient. The correct answer is (B).

9. **E** The probability of getting a red gumball is 100% – 60% = 40%. The probability of getting a lettered gumball is 100% – 45% = 55%. None of the red gumballs are lettered, so the probability of getting one that is both is 0%. Probability is represented by $\frac{want}{total}$, and to find the probability of "A *or* B," *add* the two amounts. The total options that are desired are $\frac{40}{100}$ red gumballs plus $\frac{55}{100}$ lettered gumballs, for a total of $\frac{95}{100}$ gumball options, or 95%. The correct answer is (E).

10. **A** There are 8 possible letters and 10 possible numbers for the combination. The first character in the combination is a letter, so there are 8 possible values for the first slot. The second character can be either a letter or a number. Because the letters and numbers can be used more than once, there are 18 possible letters or numbers for the second character. There are also 18 possible letters or numbers for the third character. The fourth and fifth characters are numbers, so there are 10 possible options for both characters. Therefore, the total number of combinations is 8 × 18 × 18 × 10 × 10. Before multiplying this, work through the rest of the problem and look for ways to simplify. The problem states that one of the combinations can be coded per second and asks for the length of time to code all combinations in hours. There are 60 seconds in a minute and 60 minutes in an hour, so there are 3,600 seconds in an hour. Therefore, the final expression to solve is $\frac{8\times18\times18\times10\times10}{3{,}600}$. Break this down into prime factors to find that $\frac{8\times18\times18\times10\times10}{3{,}600}=\frac{2^3\times(2\times3^2)\times(2\times3^2)\times(2\times5)\times(2\times5)}{2^4\times3^2\times5^2}=\frac{2^7\times3^4\times5^2}{2^4\times3^2\times5^2}=2^3\times3^2=72.$ The correct answer is (A).

11. **C** This is a value data sufficiency question, so determine what is known and what is needed in order to solve the question. The question provides four variables on a number line and states they are all evenly spaced. If the distance between each of the variables is denoted by the variable $n$, then $b = a + n$, $c = a + 2n$, and $d = a + 3n$. The question asks for the value of $a + d$. This can be rewritten as $a + a + 3n = 2a + 3n$. Therefore, the statements need to provide values for the variables. Consider Statement (1). This statement provides an equation containing both $a$ and $n$. This provides enough information to determine that $a = 6 - 2n$. However, this is not enough information to solve for a single value of $n$. This statement is not sufficient. Write down BCE. Consider Statement (2). This statement gives a value of $b$, but does not provide any information about $a$ or $n$. This statement is not sufficient. Eliminate (B). Consider the two statements combined. If $b = 2$ and $b = a + n$, then $2 = 6 - 2n + n$ and $n = 4$. With this value of $n$, it is possible to determine that $a = 2 - 4 = -2$ and $d = 6 + 4 = 10$. Therefore, the value of $a + d$ is $-2 + 10 = 8$. The statements combined produce one possible answer to the question, so the statements are sufficient. The correct answer is (C).

# GEOMETRY

1. **A** This is a value data sufficiency question, so determine what is known and what is needed to solve the problem. The problem does not provide any information about circle *X*. The question asks about the area of circle *X*. The area of a circle is calculated by the formula $area = \pi r^2$, where *r* is the radius of the circle. In order to determine the answer to this question, the statements need to provide a value for the radius, or a way to calculate the value for the radius, of circle *X*. Statement (1) says that the longest chord in circle *X* has a length of 6. The longest chord in a circle is the diameter. Statement (1) provides the diameter which is enough information to determine the radius and the area of circle *X*. Statement (1) is sufficient so write down AD. Statement (2) provides a point on circle *X*. However, this information does not provide any way to solve for the length of the radius and the area of the circle. Statement (2) is not sufficient. Eliminate (D). The answer is (A).

2. **E** This is a value data sufficiency question, so determine what is known and what is needed in order to solve the problem. The problem provides triangle *ABC* and asks for the area of the triangle. The figure provided does provide the measure of any of the angles for triangle *ABC* so it is not known whether the triangle is a right triangle. The area of a triangle is calculated by the formula $area = \frac{1}{2}(base)(height)$. In order to be sufficient, the statements have to provide values for the base and height of the triangle or a way to solve for the base and height and a way to know the measure of the angles. Statement (1) gives the length of one side of the triangle. This is not enough information to determine the area of the triangle, so Statement (1) is not sufficient. Write down BCE. Statement (2) gives the length of one side of the triangle. This is not enough information to determine the area of the triangle, so Statement (2) is not sufficient. Eliminate (B). Evaluate both statements together. The combination of the statements provides the length of two sides of the triangle. However, these statements do not give any information about the measure of the angles of triangle *ABC*. If the triangle is a right triangle then it would be possible to solve for the area because the two sides of the triangle would be perpendicular. If the two sides were perpendicular, then one side would be the base of the triangle and the other the height. However, if the triangle is not a right triangle then this information is not sufficient to solve for the area. The combination of the statements is not sufficient. Eliminate (C). The answer is (E).

3. **A** To determine the perimeter of the playground, find the width of the rectangle and the circumference of each semicircle. Begin with the semicircles. The diameters of the semicircles are 6, so the radii of the semicircles are 3. The combined circumference of the two semicircles is equivalent to the circumference of a single whole circle with the radius of 3. The circumference of a circle is calculated using the formula $C = 2\pi r$, so the circumference is $C = 2\pi(3) = 6\pi$. Now determine the width of the rectangle. Since the width of the entire playground is 20 and the lengths of the two radii are 3, the width of the rectangle is $20 - 3 - 3 = 14$. The perimeter of the playground is made up of two widths of the rectangle and the combined circumference of the semicircles, so the perimeter is $14 + 14 + 6\pi = 28 + 6\pi$. The answer is (A).

4. **C** The perimeter of a square is calculated using the formula $P = 4s$, where $s$ is the side of the square. The perimeter of square $ABCD$ is $4(2) = 8$. Line $AC$ is the diagonal of the square. The diagonal of a square creates a 45-45-90 triangle. The sides of a 45-45-90 triangle are in the ratio $x$: $x$: $x\sqrt{2}$. If the length of a leg of the triangle is 2, then the hypotenuse is $2\sqrt{2}$. Therefore, the sum of the diagonals is $2\sqrt{2} + 2\sqrt{2} = 4\sqrt{2}$. The ratio of the sum of the diagonals to the perimeter of the square is $4\sqrt{2} : 8$ or $\sqrt{2} : 2$. The answer is (C).

5. **B** The area of a shaded region can be found by using the equation *area of shaded region = area of entire figure – area of unshaded* region. Begin by determining the area of the unshaded region. $BC$ is the diameter of the unshaded semicircular region and its length can be found by subtracting $AB$ from $AC$ to yield $12 - 8 = 4$. The area of the unshaded region is half the area of a circle with the same diameter. The diameter is 4 which means the radius is 2 and the area of a full circle with radius 2 is $A = \pi(2^2) = 4\pi$. Therefore, the area of the unshaded region is $2\pi$. Now work to find the area of the entire figure. The area of the entire figure is equal to the area of the larger semicircle. The larger semicircle has a radius of $AD$. Because $AB = CD$, the diameter of the larger semicircle can be found by adding $AB + BC + CD$, which is $8 + 4 + 8 = 20$. The larger semicircle has a diameter of 20 and a radius of 10, which means its area $A = \frac{1}{2}\pi r^2 = \frac{1}{2}\pi(10)^2 = 50\pi$. Solve for the area of the shaded region, which is $50\pi - 2\pi = 48\pi$. The answer is (B).

6. **A** The problem states that $EB = BD$ and $AB = BC$. Because the angle of a side correlates with the length of the side it is opposite from, angle $BDE$ equals angle $BED$ and angle $BCA$ equals angle $BAC$. Therefore, angle $BED$ is 50° and angle $BAC$ is 35°. The question asks for the value of angle $ABE$, which is the top angle of triangle $ABE$. The angles of every triangle add up to 180°. In order to find the value of angle $ABE$, first determine the values of angle $BAE$ and $BEA$. As previously stated, angle $BAE$ is 35°. Angle $BEA$ is formed by line $BE$ intersecting a straight line. Straight lines have an angle of 180° and because angle $BED$ is 50°, angle $BEA$ is 180° – 50° = 130°. Therefore, the measure of angle $ABE$ is 180°– 35°– 130° = 15°. The answer is (A).

7. **C** The formula for the area of a triangle is *area* = $\frac{1}{2}$ (*base*)(*height*). To solve for the area of triangle $ABC$, find the base and height. The legs of triangle $ABC$ are the diameter of semicircles $X$, $Y$, and $Z$. Use the information in the passage about the area of the semicircles to determine the diameters. The area of a semicircle is calculated using the formula $A = \frac{1}{2}\pi r^2$. For semicircle $X$, the area is calculated as $72\pi = 72\pi \frac{1}{2} \pi r^2$, so it has a radius of 12. For semicircle $Y$, the area is calculated as $\frac{25\pi}{2} = \frac{1}{2}\pi r^2$, so it has a radius of 5. For semicircle $Z$, the area is calculated as $\frac{169\pi}{2} = \frac{1}{2}\pi r^2$, so it has a radius of 13. Multiply all the radii by 2 to find that the side lengths of triangle $ABC$ are 10, 24, and 26. These side lengths are multiples of a 5-12-13 special right triangle, so triangle $ABC$ is a right triangle. Use the sides with length 10 and 24 as the base and height of the triangle. The area of the triangle is $\frac{1}{2}(24)(10) = \frac{1}{2}(240) = 120$. The answer is (C).

8. **D** The problem states that triangle *XYZ* is isosceles, which means that the length of *XY* and the length of *YZ* are equal. Because angle *Y* is 90 degrees, this is a 45-45-90 right triangle, with side lengths in the ratio $x$: $x$: $x\sqrt{2}$. Determine the length of side *XY*. The length of side *XY* is the hypotenuse of a triangle that has legs of the vertical distance between *X* and *Y* and the horizontal distance between *X* and *Y*. The vertical distance between *X* and *Y* is $-2 - (-7) = 5$ and the horizontal distance between *X* and *Y* is $-8 - 4 = -12 = 12$. These are the legs of a 5-12-13 right triangle, so *XY* is 13. If *XY* is 13, then *YZ* is 13 and *ZX* is $13\sqrt{2}$. The perimeter of the triangle is $13 + 13 + 13\sqrt{2} = 26 + 13\sqrt{2}$. The answer is (D).

9. **D** This is a value data sufficiency question, so determine what is known and what is needed to answer the question. The question asks about the area of a circle with center (3, –2). The area of a circle is calculated by the formula $area = \pi r^2$. To solve this problem, the statements need to provide the radius of the circle or a way to solve for the radius of the circle. Statement (1) provides a point on the circle. The distance between the center and any point on the circle is the radius. Therefore, Statement (1) can be used to find the radius of the circle and the area of the circle. Statement (1) is sufficient. Write down AD. Now evaluate Statement (2). A line that is tangent to a circle is perpendicular to the radius of the circle that intersects the tangent line at the point where the tangent line touches the circle. The radius that intersects with the tangent line $y = \frac{1}{2}x + 1$ has a slope of –2. This radius line also goes through the center at (3, –2). Plug the slope and point into the equation $y = mx + b$ to reveal that $-2 = -2(3) + b$. The *y*-intercept of this radius line is 4. The equation for this radius line is $y = -2x + 4$. With both the equation of the radius line and the equation of the tangent line, the point of intersection can be found. The point of intersection is a point on the circle. The distance between the center and any point on the circle is the radius. Once the radius is known, it is possible to calculate the area. Statement 2 is sufficient. The answer is (D).

10. **C** This is a Yes/No data sufficiency question, so be prepared to Plug In more than once. The question does not provide a lot of information about triangle *ABC*, so begin working with the statements. Consider Statement (1). This statement provides the coordinates of point *B*, but no information about any other points. This statement is not sufficient to determine the perimeter of triangle *ABC*. Write down BCE. Consider Statement (2). This statement provides the coordinate of point *C*, but no information about any other point. This statement is not sufficient to determine the perimeter of triangle *ABC*. Eliminate (B). Consider the statements combined. The two statements provide the length of a single side of the triangle. Because the third side of a triangle is always less than the sum of the other two sides, $BC < AB + AC$. The length of *BC* is 5, so $5 < AB + AC$. The question asks if $AB + BC + AC > 10$. Because *BC* is 5 *and* $AB + AC > 5$, it is possible to determine that the perimeter of triangle *ABC* is greater than 10. The answer is (C).

# ALGEBRA

1. **A** This is a Yes/No data sufficiency question, so be prepared to Plug In more than once. The question asks if $x^6 = 64$. Break 64 down into its prime factors to reveal that $64 = 2^6$. Therefore, the question is asking if $x^6 = 2^6$. In other words, is $x = 2$. Evaluate the answer choices individually. Consider Statement (1). The term $x^{-5}$ is equal to $\frac{1}{x^5}$, which means that $x^5 =$ 32. Break 32 down into it's prime factors to find that $32 = 2^5$. Statement (1) provides the information that $x = 2$, so the answer to the question is Yes. Because there is no other possible value of $x$ according to this statement, the statement is sufficient. Write down AD. Now consider Statement (2). If $x$ is prime, it could be equal to any of the prime numbers. Therefore, Statement (2) is insufficient. Eliminate (D). The correct answer is (A).

2. **E** This is a Yes/No data sufficiency question, so be prepared to Plug In more than once. The questions asks if $x$ is a prime number and states that both $x$ and $y$ are integers greater than 1. Evaluate the statements individually. Statement (1) provides information about the factors of $y$, but does not give any information about $x$. Without the information about $x$, there is no way to determine if $x$ is prime. Statement (1) is insufficient. Write down BCE. Consider Statement (2). Plug In values of $x$ and $y$. If $x = 5$ and $y = 7$, then Statement (2) is satisfied because 35 is the least common multiple of 5 and 7. In this case, the answer to the question is Yes. Plug In again in an attempt to get an answer of No to the question. If $x = 4$ and $y = 7$, then the statement is satisfied because 28 is the least common multiple of 4 and 7. In this case, the answer to the question is No. The statement produces both a Yes and a No answer to the question, so Statement (2) is insufficient. Eliminate (B). Consider Statements (1) and (2). All of the values used in in Statement (2) satisfy the requirements of Statement (1), which means that Statements (1) and (2) together are insufficient. Eliminate (C). The correct answer is (E).

3. **C** This is a value data sufficiency question, so determine what is known and what is needed to answer the question. The question provides an expression and asks for the value of that expression. There is no further information given about the variables in the expression. To be sufficient, the statements need to provide information about the values of a, $b$, and $c$. Consider Statement (1). There are 3 variables and 1 equation. This means there is no way to solve for the equation, so Statement (1) is insufficient. Write down BCE. Consider Statement (2). Again, there are 3 variables and 1 equation, so Statement (2) is insufficient. Eliminate (B). Now consider Statements (1) and (2) together. There are 3 variables and 2 equations. But if Statement (2) is subtracted from Statement (1), the resulting equation is $6a + 6b + 6c = 42$. Divide by 6 to get $a + b + c = 7$. The correct answer is (C).

4. **C** This is a value data sufficiency question, so determine what is known and what is needed to answer the question. The problem provides an expression and asks for the value of the expression. There are variables in the expression, so the statements need to provide a way to solve for the variables. Consider Statement (1). This statement provides one equation with two variables. There is no way to solve for individual values of the variables in this equation, so this statement is not sufficient. Write down BCE. Consider Statement (2). This statement provides a value for $h$ but does not provide any information about $g$. This statement is insufficient. Eliminate (B). Now consider both statements together. Statement (2) provides a value of $h$ that can be substituted for $h$ in Statement (1). This allows to solve for a value of $g$. The statements

combined provide a way to solve for both variables and a single answer to the question, so the statements together are sufficient. The correct answer is (C).

5. **C** Plug In all possible values for $x$ and $y$. Because the inequalities in the question stem are absolute values, the representation of all possible values of $xy$ has a negative range and a positive range. The least possible negative value of $xy$ is –90 and the greatest possible negative value is –20, so it can be written that $-90 < xy < -20$. The least possible positive value of $xy$ is 20 and the greatest possible positive value is 90, so it can be written that $20 < xy < 90$. Therefore, the possible values of $xy$ are $-90 < xy < -20$ and $20 < xy < 90$. The correct answer is (C).

6. **B** Plug In a value for Calvin's age 3 years from now. If 3 years from now Calvin is 18, then 3 years from now Jill is 6. Therefore, Calvin is currently 15 years old, so $c = 15$, and Jill is currently 3 years old. In 6 years, Jill will be 9, which is half as old as Tom in 6 years. So, in 6 years Tom will be 18, which means that Tom is currently 12. Plug In 15 for $c$ in all the answer choices, looking for one that matches the target answer of 12. Choice (A) results in 10, which is incorrect. Eliminate (A). Choice (B) results in 12, so keep (B). Choice (C) is also 12, so keep (C). Choice (D) is $\frac{51}{2}$, which is not equal to 12 so eliminate (D). Choice (E) is $\frac{45}{2} + 2$, which is not equal to 12, so eliminate (E). Now Plug In again, looking for ways to eliminate either (B) or (C). If Calvin is currently 9, then Jill is currently 1 and Tom is currently 8. In this case, (B) is 8 so keep (B). Choice (C) is 10, so eliminate (C). The correct answer is (B).

7. **D** The question provides an equation with two exponents that have different bases so begin by converting the bases to be equal. Because $6^2 = 36$, the equation can be rewritten as $6^{2x+2} = (6^2)^{2x-2}$. Apply the Power-Multiply rule of exponents to find that $6^{2x+2} = 6^{4x-4}$. Eliminate the bases and write the equation as the exponents equal to one another and solve for $x$. This equation is $2x + 2 = 4x - 4$, so $2x = 6$ and $x = 3$. The correct answer is (D).

8. **A** This question asks about the possible units digit of a number raised to a power. The units digit of a number raised to any power is the same as the units digit of the original number raised to that same power. The question states that $r$, $s$, and $t$ are negative consecutive odd digits and that $r < s < t$. The units digits of any combination of any three negative odd consecutive integers are one of the following sets: {9, 7, 5}; {7, 5, 3}; {5, 3, 1}; {3, 1, 9}; or {1, 9, 7}. Because the question also asks about the value of $s^5$, rewrite all the potential sets of units digits raised to the fifth power. For instance, $9^5$ results in a units digit of 9, $7^5$ results in a units digit of 7, and $5^5$ results in a units digit of 5, and $3^5$ results in a units digit of 3 so the first set can be written as {9, 7, 5, 3}. The only value that is not possible for $s^5$ is 1. In order for the units digit of $s^5$ to be 1, $s$ has to equal 1, which means that $t$ is not a negative odd digit. The correct answer is (A).

9. **E** This is a Yes/No data sufficiency question, so be prepared to Plug In more than once. The question asks if $m$ is a positive integer. The statements need to provide a way to determine if $m$ is a positive or negative integer. Consider Statement (1). Plug In values for $m$ that satisfy the statement. If $m = 2$, then the statement is satisfied because $-2^3 \leq -1$ can be rewritten as $-8 \leq -1$, which is true. In this case, the answer to the question is Yes, because 2 is a positive integer. Plug In again. If $m = \frac{5}{2}$, then the statement is satisfied because $-\frac{5}{2}^3 \leq -1$ can be rewritten as

$-\frac{125}{8} \leq -1$, which is true. In this case the answer to the question is No because $m$ is not an integer. The statement produces two different answer to the question, so it is not sufficient. Write down BCE. Consider Statement (2). Plug In values that satisfy the statement. If $m = 2$, then the statement is $4 \geq 1$, which is true. In this case, the answer to the question is Yes. Plug In again. If $m = \frac{5}{2}$, then the statement is satisfied because $-\frac{5}{2}^2 \leq -1$ can be rewritten as $-\frac{25}{4} \leq -1$, which is true. The answer to the question is now No. Eliminate (B). Consider both statements together. The values that satisfy Statement (1) also satisfy Statement (2). Because of this, it is possible to get an answer of Yes and an answer of No to the question. Eliminate (C). The correct answer is choice (E).

10. **C** This is a function problem, so substitute values into the provided equations. The problem asks for the value of $g(f(5)) - f(g(5))$. Begin with one term at a time. The term $g(f(5))$ results in $g(3(5) + w) = g(15 + w) = 4(15 + w) - w = 60 + 4w - w = 60 + 3w$. The term $f(g(5))$ results in $f(4(5) - w) = f(20 - w) = 3(20 - w) + w = 60 - 3w + w = 60 - 2w$. The expression in the question stem is now $60 + 3w - 60 - 2w = 5w$. The correct answer is (C).

## SENTENCE CORRECTION

1. **C** The underlined portion contains the singular verb *has permitted,* which does not agree with the plural compound noun *Rebuilding and levee development.* Eliminate (A) and look for any obvious repeaters. Choice (B) repeats the error, so eliminate this choice as well. Evaluate the remaining answers individually, looking for reasons to eliminate each. Choice (C) repairs the error in the original sentence and makes no new errors, so keep this choice. Choice (D) has the improper construction *permitted...with.* Since the correct idiom is *permitted...to,* this is an idiom error. Eliminate (D). Choice (E) has the construction *permitted for.* The correct idiom is *permitted...to.* Eliminate this choice. The correct answer is (C).

2. **D** The underlined portion of the sentence contains a list connected by the construction *from...and also* which is not idiomatically correct. The correct idiomatic structure is *from...to.* Therefore, eliminate (A) and look for any obvious repeaters. Choice (B) repeats the error by using the construction *from...and.* Eliminate (B). Evaluate the remaining answer choices individually, looking for reasons to eliminate each. Choice (C) restructures the sentence into a list of three items: *detailing...her scaling...the improvements.* This list is not parallel. Eliminate (C). Choice (D) corrects the list connector by using the construction *from...to* and creates no new errors. Keep (D). Choice (E) uses the construction *such as her travels such as her scaling* which is redundant and not idiomatically correct, as *such as* means "for example." Eliminate (E). The correct answer is (D).

3. **B** The underlined portion of the sentence contains the idiomatic construction *so...as to* which is used to indicate an increasing degree in a condition. However, this sentence offers a contrast between *well known* and *obscure* so the sentence is not framing an increase in degree. Therefore, *so...as to* is idiomatically incorrect. Eliminate (A) and look for any obvious repeaters. Choices (C) and (E) repeat the error so eliminate both of these. Examine the remaining answers, looking for reasons to eliminate each. Choice (B) corrects the idiom by using the more appropriate *so...that* construction and makes no new errors. Keep (B). Choice (D) uses the ambiguous pronoun *it* which may refer to *reputation* or *computer science.* Eliminate this answer. The correct answer is (B).

4. **A** The underlined portion of the sentence contains a list of three items, indicated by the conjunction *and*, detailing the consequences to an alligator from the singular subject *cramped housing*. As written, the list is parallel as each item begins with a singular present tense verb: *stunts, exacerbates*, and *prevents*. Choice (A) has no obvious errors, so keep (A) for now. Evaluate the remaining answer choice individually, looking for reasons to eliminate each. Choice (B) rewords the third list item to begin with *prevented*. This construction begins a modifying phrase for the noun *teeth*. The answer choice also omits the necessary conjunction *and*, so eliminate (B). Choice (C) has the participle *exacerbating* in the second list item, which is not parallel with the verb *stunts* in the first list item, so eliminate (C). Choice (D) rewrites the list so that the first two list items begin with participles: *stunting* and *exacerbating*, but the third list item begins with *only to prevent*, which is not parallel. Eliminate (D). Choice (E) rewrites all the list items so that they begin with participles: *stunting, exacerbating*, and *preventing*. However, this revision constructs the list so that it seems to modify or follow the verb *can suffer*, resulting in a misplaced modifier. Eliminate (E). The correct answer is (A).

5. **C** The underlined portion follows the word *as*, so the underlined portion is the second item in a comparison. The underlined portion starts with the phrase *did her short-story collection*. However, as written this construction is parallel with the phrase *did New Zealand writer Katherine Mansfield* which results in a comparison of *New Zealand writer Katherine Mansfield* to *her short-story collection*. Since it is not proper to compare a work to its author, eliminate (A) and look for any obvious repeaters. Choice (D) repeats the error, so eliminate (D) as well. Evaluate the remaining answer choices individually, looking for reasons to eliminate each. Choice (B) is a parallelism error as the sentence compares *New Zealand writer Katherine Mansfield* to *her short-story collection*. Eliminate (B). Choice (C) corrects the original error by using the phrase *with her short-story collection*. This phrase is parallel to the opening phrase *With no other work*, thus correctly comparing one work of the writer to her other works. Choice (C) also makes no new errors, so keep answer (C). Choice (E) results in a construction that compares the phrase *her short-story collection* to the phrase *lasting admiration*. Since it is not proper to compare a book to an emotion, eliminate (E). The correct answer is (C).

6. **D** The underlined portion of the sentence contains the past perfect verb *had narrowed*, which is the incorrect tense to convey the ongoing action indicated by the opening phrase *During the last month*. Eliminate (A) and look for any obvious repeaters. Choice (B) repeats the error, so eliminate this choice as well. Evaluate the remaining answer choices individually, looking for reasons to eliminate each. Choice (C) places the noun *emergence* adjacent to the phrase *that classrooms are discussing*. This construction indicates that what the *classrooms are discussing* is *the emergence*. This is a misplaced modifier, so eliminate (C). Answer (D) repairs the original error by using the present perfect tense *have narrowed*, and makes no new errors, so keep this choice. Answer (E) includes the pronoun *it* which is ambiguous, as *it* has no proper noun referent in the sentence. Eliminate (E). The correct answer is (D).

7. **B** The underlined portion of the sentence contains the pronoun *they*, so check for agreement or ambiguity errors. The pronoun is preceded by the plural noun *consequences*. This implies that it is the *consequences* that can be *cognizant*. This is a pronoun ambiguity error so eliminate (A) and look for any obvious repeaters. There are no obvious repeaters, so evaluate each answer choice individually, looking for reasons to eliminate each. Choice (B) corrects the original error and makes no other errors, so keep this choice. Choice (C) yields the construction *course of action, of which one can be cognizant*. This indicates one is *cognizant* of a *course of action*, not the *consequences*, which is a misplaced modifier. Eliminate (C). Choice (D) starts with *Just as* which sets up a comparison between *limited number of consequences* and *assessing the impact*. This is a

comparison error, so eliminate this answer. Choice (E) yields the construction *course of action, of which one can be cognizant*, which indicates one is *cognizant* of a *course of action*, not the *consequences*, which is a misplaced modifier. Eliminate (E). The answer is (B).

8. **E** The underlined portion of the sentence contains the plural pronoun *they*, so look for ambiguity or agreement errors. The pronoun refers to *courses*. Since the *courses* could not *allow her to attend*, this pronoun is ambiguous, so eliminate (A) and look for any obvious repeaters. Choice (C) repeats the error, so eliminate it as well. Evaluate the remaining answer choices individually, looking for reasons to eliminate each. Choice (B) has repositioned the word *only* so that it modifies *a special court hearing* instead of *after*. This is a modifier error. Eliminate (B). Choice (D) positions the word *only* so that it modifies *to attend*. This is a modifier error. Eliminate (D). Choice (E) removes the ambiguous pronoun *they* and creates no new errors. The answer is (E).

9. **E** The underlined portion of the sentence contains the phrase *that it has prevented*. This unnecessarily repeats the *that* which is in the prior portion *recognizes that*. This is a redundancy error, so eliminate (A) and look for any obvious repeaters. No other answers repeat this error, so evaluate each answer choice individually, looking for reasons to eliminate each. Choice (B) yields the construction *the onset of winter…has use of the department's workforce*, which suggests that the season is using the workforce. Eliminate this answer. Choice (C) contains the verb *is having* which is not parallel to the prior verb *has delayed*, so eliminate this choice. Choice (D) contains the verb *is having* which is not parallel to the prior verb *has delayed*, so eliminate this choice. Choice (E) does not repeat the redundancy of the original sentence and creates no new errors. The answer is (E).

10. **B** This sentence as written contains the phrase *it causes*, so check for pronoun ambiguity and a greement. The pronoun *it* is ambiguous as it does not refer to any noun but rather to the phrase *to leave more than 10 million acres vulnerable*. Eliminate (A) and look for any obvious repeaters. Choices (C) and (E) repeat the error, so eliminate these choices as well. Examine the remaining answers. Choice (B) avoids the ambiguous pronoun and contains no new errors, so keep (B). Choice (D) contains the construction *the most media attention and funds*, which reads as if the media provides the funds. Eliminate (D). The correct answer is (B).

11. **C** The underlined portion of the sentence contains *Jack Kirby's drawing style*, which follows the modifying phrase *one of the most influential figures*. This is a misplaced modifier error. Eliminate (A) and look for any obvious repeaters. Choice (B) repeats the error, so eliminate this choice. Evaluate the remaining answer choices individually, looking for reasons to eliminate each. Choice (C) repairs the original error by allowing the modifying phrase to refer to *Jack Kirby*, and it makes no other errors. Keep (C). Choice (D) includes the construction *but also* as a connector. This is idiomatically incorrect as it is not preceded by *not only*, so eliminate this answer. Choice (E) uses the phrase *utilizing foreshortening conveying depth* which does not have the idiom *utilize…to*, so eliminate this answer. The correct answer is (C).

## READING COMPREHENSION

1. **B** The subject of the question is *how a company might become a flat organization* and the task is referenced by the phrase *described in the passage,* so this is a retrieval question. Determine what the passage says about the characteristics of flat organizations. The passage notes that flat organizations *abolish middle management structures and instead assign most workers to the same level,* use *non-hierarchical committees* that *share in a decentralized decision-making process,* and limit *specialization in job titles.* Evaluate the answer choices individually, looking for one that reflects these ideas. Choice (A) is a reversal of the information in the passage. *Outsourcing middle management* is not the same as abolishing middle management and would not make an organization flatter. Eliminate (A). Choice (B) is a good description of a step a company could take to become flatter, so keep (B). Choice (C) is a reversal of the information in the passage. Creating *specific guidelines for approval of new ideas* is in opposition to the idea of non-hierarchical committees that share in decision-making. Eliminate (C). Choice (D) is a reversal of the information in the passage. The passage says flat organizations limit job specialization. Eliminate (D). Choice (E) can also be eliminated as it describes a hierarchical structure as opposed to a flat organization. The correct answer is (B).

2. **B** The subject of the question is the entire passage, and the task is referenced by the phrase *primary purpose,* so this is a primary purpose question. The passage begins by stating how *the preeminent organizational strategy designed to maximize efficient productivity may actually be detrimental* and then asserts the *long-term success of a corporation requires flexibility and new ideas to respond to ever-evolving political, social, and economic conditions.* The passage then suggests becoming a "*flat organization*" as the key to unlocking these needs. The remainder of the passage describes the characteristics of flat organizations and their benefits. Evaluate the answer choices individually, looking for one that reflects this content. Choice (A) is a memory trap. The passage does *compare various corporate organizational strategies.* However, the primary purpose of the passage is to advocate for one structure in comparison to another. Eliminate (A). Choice (B) is a good paraphrase of the primary purpose of the passage, so keep it. Choice (C) is a reversal of the information in the passage. The passage states that hierarchical structures are *the preeminent organizational strategy* and the passage is not primarily about hierarchical structures. Eliminate (C). Choice (D) is a reversal of the information in the passage. The passage does not *criticize a new method of conducting business.* Instead, the passage supports a new method. Eliminate (D). Choice (E) is a no-such comparison answer as the passage does not *acknowledge the similarities* between hierarchical and flat structures. Eliminate (E). The correct answer is (B).

3. **A** The subject of the question is *hierarchical workplaces* and the task of the question is referenced by the word *inferred.* This is an inference question. Determine what the passage says about hierarchical workplaces. The passage says these structures *unwittingly discourage* traits such as *creative thinking, adaptability, and collaboration* and that they are *designed to maximize efficient productivity* but *may actually be detrimental.* Evaluate the answer choices individually, looking for one that reflects these descriptions. Choice (A) is a good paraphrase of the information in the passage as delayed approval processes for new ideas is not *adaptable.* Additionally, more streamlined approval processes is listed as one of the benefits of flat structures that is not present in hierarchical structures. Keep (A). Choice (B) is a no-such comparison answer as the passage does not compare the number of middle and upper managers. Eliminate (B). Choice (C) uses the recycled language *maximize efficiency.* This is used to describe the intention of hierarchical structures but is not related to *promoting specialization.* Eliminate (C). Choice (D) is a no-such comparison answer as the passage does not compare large and small companies. Eliminate (D). Choice (E) contains the extreme language *do not allow.* While the passage suggests hierarchical structures make it more difficult to have flexible roles, it does not state that flexible roles are not allowed. Eliminate (E). The correct answer is (A).

4. **D** The subject of the question is the *originators of the general equilibrium theory* and the task of the question is referenced by the word *implies*, so this is an inference question. Determine what the passage says about the originators of the general equilibrium theory. The theory is derived from *Smith's idea* about the "*invisible hand*" and states that *invisible market forces guided the interaction of supply and demand toward a natural balance.* The passage goes on to note the *ubiquity of this model in both popular and scholarly thinking* despite *the guiding influence of Smith's invisible hand in moving markets toward such a balance has not been shown.* The passage concludes that the theory *presents an optimistic view of self-correction that has not been borne out by actual economic conditions.* Evaluate the answer choices individually, looking for one that reflects the information in the passage. Choice (A) is a reversal of the information in the passage which states the theory *has not been borne out by actual economic conditions.* Eliminate (A). Choice (B) is a memory trap. The passage mentions that Adam Smith was around in the eighteenth century, but only states that the originators of the general equilibrium theory were *subsequent theorists.* This does not give a timeframe for when they developed the theory, so eliminate (B). Choice (C) uses the extreme language *immediately.* While the passage does say the theory is ubiquitous *in both popular and scholarly thinking,* it does not state that the theory was immediately popular. Eliminate (C). Choice (D) is a good paraphrase of the information in the passage. Keep (D). Choice (E) is a memory trap. The passage mentions the theory is derived from Adam Smith but does not give any indication if any of the originators worked with Smith. Eliminate (E). The correct answer is (D).

5. **B** The subject of the question is the passage as a whole and the task of the question is referenced by the phrase *primarily concerned with,* so this is a primary purpose question. Determine why the author wrote the passage. The passage introduces Smith's theory of the *"invisible hand"* and then discusses how *subsequent theorists expanded Smith's idea* to create the general equilibrium theory. The passage then states *there is no evidence for [the theory's] truth* and spends the remainder of the passage calling into question the validity of the theory. Evaluate the answer choices individually, looking for one that reflects the primary purpose of the passage. Choice (A) uses the recycled language *economic regulation.* Discussing economic regulation is not the primary purpose of the passage. Eliminate (A). Choice (B) is a good paraphrase of the information in the passage, so keep (B). Choice (C) is a reversal of the information in the passage. The passage seeks to delegitimize Smith's beliefs, not *defend* them. Eliminate (C). Choice (D) is a memory trap. The passage does mention the idea that *market forces naturally maintain balance,* but this is not the primary purpose of the passage. Eliminate (D). Choice (E) is a no-such comparison answer. The passage does not *compare several economic theories.* Eliminate (E). The correct answer is (B).

6. **E** The subject of the question is how *defenders of the general equilibrium theory...regard economic regulations* and the task of the question is referenced by the word *inferred.* This is an inference question. Determine what the passage says about the subject. The passage states that the *belief that markets actively move toward an equilibrium has been used by proponents of deregulation, who insist that removing government interventions promotes economic strength.* So, defenders of the general equilibrium theory most likely regard regulation as ineffective. Evaluate the answer choices individually, looking for one that reflects this idea. Choice (A) is a reversal of the information in the passage and the opposite of "ineffective," so eliminate (A). Choice (B) is an example of extreme language, as the passage does not support the idea that defenders see regulation as *catastrophic.* Eliminate (B). Choice (C) is a reversal of the information in the passage as salutary means producing a good effect. Eliminate (C). Choice (D), *insufficient,* is a reversal of the information in the passage. Eliminate (D). Choice (E) is a good match for "ineffective." The correct answer is (E).

7. **C** The subject of the question is the *passage* as a whole and the task of the question is referenced by the phrase *primary purpose,* so this is a primary purpose question. Determine why the author wrote the passage by using the key sentences approach. The key sentence of the first paragraph is the introduction to the topic of the article, which is *a critical aspect of product advertising is the choice between positive and negative approaches.* The second paragraph discusses the benefits and risks of both positive and negative advertising and concludes *consumers may thus more readily believe negative information compared to arguments made in favor of a brand or product, and the former often makes a stronger mental impression.* The third paragraph *explains why such advertising can be more memorable: negativity bias.* The final paragraph sums up the final conclusion of the passage by stating *In spite of these benefits, negativity in advertising is not always more effective than the alternative.* Evaluate the answer choices individually, looking for one that reflects the primary purpose of the passage. Choice (A) uses the extreme language *argue the inferiority.* The passage does not argue for inferiority of one approach to another, but instead lays out the benefits and risks of each. Eliminate (A). Choice (B) is a memory trap. The passage does *explore the advantages of different forms of advertising,* but it also explores the risks, and the primary purpose is not concerned with *different audiences.* Eliminate (B). Choice (C) is a good paraphrase of the information in the passage, so keep (C). Choice (D) is a memory trap as the passage does spend some time explaining what makes negative advertising *effective,* but this is the subject of only one paragraph and not the primary purpose of the passage. Eliminate (D). Choice (E) is an appeal to outside knowledge. It is true that there is a *need for companies to advertise their products,* but the passage is unconcerned with this need. Eliminate (E). The correct answer is (C).

8. **A** The subject of the question is *potential risks in advertising* and the task of the question is referenced by the phrase *the following are mentioned,* so this is a retrieval question. Determine what the passage says are potential risks in advertising. The passage says that positive advertising can be perceived as *insincere or predatory due to their reliance on manipulating emotions rather than presenting factual information* and that can *lead to skepticism…as consumers assume they are still being manipulated for the goal of producing positive feelings.* Negative advertising that features a competitor *can inadvertently provide a boost to the competing brand* and *poses a risk that the audience will be alienated from both the competitor and the company criticizing it.* The passage also states that consumers who buy based on negative advertising may *not [be] as loyal as those for whom merit guides the decision.* Finally, there is a concern that *consumers may view attacks on competitors as petty and untoward.* This is an except question, so evaluate the answer choices looking for one that is not reflected by the information in the passage. Choice (A) is not mentioned as a potential risk in advertising so keep (A). Choice (B) is listed as a risk when the passage states that negative advertising *poses a risk that the audience will be alienated from both the competitor and the company criticizing it.* Eliminate (B). Choice (C) is listed as a risk of positive advertising. The passage states positive advertising can be perceived as *insincere or predatory.* Eliminate (C). Choice (D) is not explicitly stated in the passage but is implied through statements such as *consumers assume they are still being manipulated for the goal of producing positive feelings.* Eliminate (D). Choice (E) is referenced by the statement that negative advertising *can inadvertently provide a boost to the competing brand.* Eliminate (E). The correct answer is (A).

9. **C** The subject of the passage is *an example of negative advertising* and the task of the question is referenced by the phrase *as it is described in the passage*, so this is a retrieval question. Determine how the passage describes negative advertising. The passage describes negative advertising as *not painting a rosy sheen over its own products but rather warning consumers of a competitor's flaw.* Evaluate the answer choices individually, looking for one that could serve as an example of negative advertising based on this description. Choice (A) is a memory trap as this would be an example of positive advertising. Eliminate (A). Choice (B) is also an example of positive advertising, so eliminate (B). Choice (C) is a good example of negative advertising as described in the passage. Keep (C). Choice (D) is an example of one company criticizing another but is not an example of negative advertising as the environmental group is not trying to sell its product through the negative association with a competitor. Eliminate (D). Choice (E) is not an example of negative advertising as described in the passage, so eliminate (E). The correct answer is (C).

10. **D** The subject of the question is the *highlighted sentence* and the task of the question is referenced by the phrase *describes the function*, so this is a specific purpose question. Determine the role of the highlighted sentence. The highlighted sentence follows a sentence that introduces a *contrast* between positive advertising and negative advertising. The contrast is that *negative advertising can appear more truthful* than positive advertising. This leads to the content of the highlighted sentence, which states that consumers *more readily believe negative information compared to arguments made in favor of a brand or product, and the former often makes a stronger mental impression.* The highlighted sentence closes a paragraph that leads into a conversation regarding *why such advertising can be more memorable.* Evaluate the answer choices individually, looking for one that reflects this idea. Choice (A) contains the extreme language *demonstrably superior.* The sentence does not suggest that negative advertising is demonstrably superior, so eliminate (A). Choice (B) is a memory trap. While the passage does describe *differences between the two strategies,* this sentence does not *summarize* the main differences. Eliminate (B). Choice (C) contains the extreme language *refutes the argument.* The first paragraph does not contain an argument that this sentence could refute. Eliminate (C). Choice (D) is a good description of the function of the sentence, so keep (D). Choice (E) is a memory trap. This sentence states the impact of one strategy in comparison to one from earlier in the paragraph, but evaluating what *most experts believe* is not the function of this sentence. Eliminate (E). The correct answer is (D).

## CRITICAL REASONING

1. **A** The task of this question is referenced by the phrase *argument depends on*, so this is an assumption question. Find the conclusion, premise, and assumption or pattern. The conclusion is *Although the patient's health would improve with daily outdoor walks, I have advised against it in the health plan*. The premise is *an increase in walking exercise would stress the already overstressed knee joints and would therefore put the patient at increased risk of injury*. The argument assumes that *daily* walks mean an *increase* in a byproduct of walking exercise. The correct answer will confirm the assumption in the argument.

   (A) Correct. If *the patient would use her knees more than she currently does* as a result of *daily walks* then the byproduct of the movement would increase.

   (B) No. This choice is out of scope. *The amount of exercise the patient currently undertakes* is not tied to the conclusion or premise of the argument.

   (C) No. The use of the phrase *any patient* is too extreme for this argument, which is just about one patient.

   (D) No. This choice is out of scope. Whether the patient decides to follow the *recommendation of the physiotherapist* is unrelated to the conclusion and premise of the argument.

   (E) No. The use of the phrase *the patient's best well-being as the foremost concern* is out of the scope of the argument.

   The correct answer is (A).

2. **A** The question task is referenced by the phrase *provides the most support for which of the following conclusions*. This is a strengthen question. The conclusion is the answer choices. The premise for the conclusion is *the incidence of cancer in mice is many times that of humans, even though humans have over 1,000 times as many cells as mice do. Furthermore, elephants have even more cells than humans do, but the incidence of cancer in elephants is much lower*. The correct answer will be supported by the premise.

   (A) Correct. The premise in the argument supports the conclusion that cancer *is due in part to factors other than body size*.

   (B) No. This answer is not supported by the premise of the argument.

   (C) No. This answer choice uses the extreme language that *The number of cells in any organism's body is not a predictor*. This is too strong for a passage in which only three species are listed.

   (D) No. The *number of abnormal cells in an organism* is out of scope and is not a conclusion supported by the argument.

   (E) No. *Curing cancer in humans* is out of scope.

   The correct answer is (A).

3. **E** The task of the question is referenced by the phrase *assumes which of the following,* so this is an assumption question. Find the conclusion, premise, and assumption or pattern. The conclusion is *Jones or Alyers had the most motive and opportunity to commit the theft.* The premise is *Singh, the more senior employee with the higher pay grade, was supervising Jones and Alyers, who were processing the inventory* and that *Singh has already testified that both Jones and Alyers were out of his sight numerous times throughout the shift.* The shift of language in this argument is from *senior employee* and *pay grade* in the premise to *motive* in the conclusion, so the argument assumes that these are indicative of *motive.* The correct answer will confirm the missing link between *motive* and *pay grade* or will rule out an alternate cause of the theft.

(A) No. The use of the phrase *all theft* is too extreme for this argument.

(B) No. The relative amount of time Jones and Alyers were out of Singh's sight is out of the scope of the argument.

(C) No. The phrase *Any testimony* is too extreme for this argument.

(D) No. The *number of trucks with stolen items* is out of scope.

(E) Correct. Use the Negation Test. The negated form of the answer indicates that tenure of employment and salary are not directly related to the likelihood of committing theft. This suggests that Singh's status as a senior employee with a higher paygrade does not exclude him from possibly having committed the theft.

The correct answer is (E).

4. **C** The question task is referenced by the phrase *most logical completion of the passage,* so this is an inference question. The passage discusses a proposal to increase ads but warns about an initial loss in profits. The correct answer will provide a reason that an increase in ads would lead to a loss in profits.

(A) No. The relationship between the *biggest competitor* and the advertisers the company *is likely to sell the new inventory* to is out of the scope of the passage.

(B) No. This answer choice is out of scope, as it contrasts ads devoted to new versus current advertisers.

(C) Correct. If *creating the infrastructure to host more advertisements at different locations on our website requires a large up-front investment,* then profits will decrease until the revenue surpasses the cost.

(D) No. The use of the word *none* is an example of extreme language that is not supported by the passage.

(E) No. The revenue from the new ads is in conjunction with the revenue from the old ads. That the rates for the new ads are *slightly lower* is not going to cause a profit loss, only a smaller increase in profits than it would if the new ads were the same price.

The correct answer is (C).

5. **B** The question task is referenced by the phrase *an assumption on which the...argument depends,* so this is an assumption question. Find the conclusion, premise, and assumption or pattern in the argument. The conclusion is *to keep our store profits at the same level, we will have to raise the prices of products in these categories until the nationwide truckers' strike is over.* The premise is *the majority of the profits in our hardware store during the last quarter depended on the sales of paint and household tools.* This argument fits the Planning pattern as the conclusion of the argument is a recommended course of action, so another assumption is that there are no problems with the plan to *raise the prices of products in these categories until the nationwide truckers' strike is over.* The correct answer will contain information that rules out a problem with the plan.

(A) No. The use of the phrase *only the actions of the truckers' union that caused the shortages* is too extreme for this argument.

(B) Correct. Use the Negation Test. The negated form of this answer is *Raising prices of paint and household tools until the end of the truckers' strike would decrease patronage.* Because the negated form of the answer hurts the plan, this answer contains the assumption.

(C) No. The use of the phrase *raising prices of paint and household tools is more important than diversifying the hardware* is too extreme for this argument.

(D) No. What *other stores* do is out of scope.

(E) No. Ending the trucker's strike is out of scope.

The correct answer is (B).

6. **B** The question task is referenced by the phrase *most strengthens,* so this is a strengthen question. Find the conclusion, premise, and pattern or assumption in the argument. The conclusion is *if you want your garden to thrive under any condition, use Q-Earth.* The premise is *Q-Earth's nutrient generation technology provides better support for your plants when natural nutrient formation is inhibited due to lack of sunlight, rain, or heat.* The argument assumes that the best support for plants requires the ability to support plants *under any condition.* Therefore, the correct answer will provide information that supports the assumption.

(A) No. *Plants that tend to grow quickly* is out of the scope of the argument.

(B) Correct. If *Q-Earth is the preferred soil of interior gardeners—those who build gardens inside homes using plants that typically thrive outside,* then people are choosing to use the soil under not ideal conditions.

(C) No. Q-Earth's market share is out of the scope of the argument.

(D) No. This answer uses the extreme language *all branded soil,* which is too strong for the argument.

(E) No. Where Q-Earth is manufactured is out of the scope of the argument.

The correct answer is (B).

7. **D** The task of the question is referenced by the phrase *vulnerable to criticism,* so this is a flaw question. Find the conclusion, premise, and assumption or pattern. The conclusion is *most students in the school earn at least some extra credit,* and the premises are *Most students in the school are honors students* and, *the amount of extra credit per test earned by any student generally does not fluctuate from test to test.* The shift of language in this argument is from *honors students* in the premises to *most students in the school* in the conclusion. The argument is linking the ideas of *honors students* to *most students.* This argument is following a sampling pattern. The standard assumption of a sampling pattern is that the sample is representative. The correct answer will identify a flaw or a bad assumption about the sample of honors representativeness of most students.

(A) No. Specific *classes with honors students* is out of the scope of the passage. The passage discusses only the students as a whole.

(B) No. This answer is out of scope. It targets the premise of the argument that the *certain average score is earned on a test* and *approximately the same amount of extra credit,* instead of identifying the bad assumption or the flaw in the way the argument moves from the premise to the conclusion.

(C) No. This answer cannot be matched to the argument. The conclusion of this argument is not *about test scores,* but rather about the students who earn the scores.

(D) Correct. The argument ignores the fact that extra credit could be earned by *some types of students.* The flaw of the argument is that many students may earn no extra credit at all, so the generalization *most students in the school earn at least some extra credit* is not warranted.

(E) No. The argument does not *overlook* the possibility that any one student may earn no extra credit. The argument acknowledges that the *amount of extra credit per test earned by any student generally does not fluctuate from test to test,* so that amount could be none.

The correct answer is (D).

8. **A** The task of the question is referenced by the phrase *roles in the argument,* so this is an identify the reasoning question. Identify the Conclusion and Premise. The conclusion is *The troubling discovery of cheating on the most common college entrance examination should not impact the reputation of the College Admissions Board.* The bolded phrase is an intermediary claim, *the revelation confirms that the system works,* which is itself supported by the premise *the students themselves were the ones who reported their peers for unethical behavior.* The answer should confirm that the bolded phrase is an intermediary claim that supports the conclusion.

(A) Correct. The argument gives evidence for the bolded claim and the bolded claim supports the primary claim.

(B) No. This answer reverses the roles in the argument. The bolded phrase is not the argument's primary position.

(C) No. This answer does not match the structure of the argument as the argument does have *stated evidence* for the bolded phrase.

(D) No. This answer does not match the structure of the argument as the bolded phrase is not the *main conclusion* of the argument.

(E) No. While the bolded phrase does support the main conclusion of the argument, and the bolded phrase is a part of a sentence that contains a premise, the bolded phrase itself does not contain an assumption. This answer is only a partial match.

The correct answer is (A).

9. **D** The question task is referenced by the phrase *most seriously weakens,* so this is a weaken question. Find the conclusion, premise, and pattern or assumption. The conclusion of the argument is *savory recipes invented by culinary experts with over 20 years of experience in general yield better dishes that enjoy a much broader popularity than savory dishes based on recipes by chefs with less than 20 years of experience.* The premise is *more experienced chefs are more precise and careful when designing their savory recipes than their counterparts, who may just be experimenting with trendy cuisines.* The argument has a causality pattern, assuming the cause of the *better dishes that enjoy a much broader popularity* is that the more experienced chefs are *more precise and careful.* Therefore, the correct answer will provide an alternate cause for the *dishes that enjoy a much broader popularity.*

(A) No. *Recipes for sweet dishes* is out of the scope of the argument.

(B) No. The recipes that are easier *for domestic cooks to follow* are out of the scope of the argument.

(C) No. The *range of spices* used by young and old chefs is out of the scope of the argument.

(D) Correct. This answer choice weakens the argument by giving an alternate cause of a recipe's popularity. If most popular dishes are discovered in cooking magazines and cooking magazines feature recipes by chefs with industry connections, the more experienced chefs are likely to be in magazines as they have been working in the industry for a longer period of time.

(E) No. The age of the culinary expert is out of the scope of the argument.

The correct answer is (D).

# Part IX
# The Princeton Review GMAT Math and Verbal Warm-Up Questions and Explanations

# Chapter 30 GMAT Math and Verbal Warm-Up Questions

The purpose of this 60-minute question set is to get a rough idea of your current scoring range and rough percentiles on the Math and Verbal sections of the GMAT. Using these scores as a guide, you can then select from the bins of practice questions that follow to improve your performance.

According to the test makers, the computer-adaptive sections of the GMAT hone in on your approximate scoring level after only a few questions. You then spend the rest of the test time answering questions from around that level of difficulty, chosen by the computer from bins of potential questions.

To further refine your assessment of where you are right now, we recommend that you take one of The Princeton Review's computer-adaptive tests (available for free online). See the Get More (Free) Content section at the beginning of this book for details. We also highly recommend that you take an actual computer-adaptive GMAT, downloadable for free from the GMAT website at www.mba.com.

**Math Test**
**Time—30 Minutes**
**20 Questions**

**This test is composed of both problem solving questions and data sufficiency questions.**

**Problem Solving Directions**: Solve each problem and choose the best of the answer choices provided.

**Data Sufficiency Directions**: Each data sufficiency problem consists of a question and two statements, labeled (1) and (2), which contain certain data. Using these data and your knowledge of mathematics and everyday facts (such as the number of days in July or the meaning of *counterclockwise*), decide whether the data given are sufficient for answering the question and then indicate one of the following answer choices:

- Statement (1) ALONE is sufficient, but statement (2) alone is not sufficient.
- Statement (2) ALONE is sufficient, but statement (1) alone is not sufficient.
- BOTH statements TOGETHER are sufficient, but NEITHER statement ALONE is sufficient.
- EACH statement ALONE is sufficient.
- Statements (1) and (2) TOGETHER are not sufficient.

---

1. If $(16)(3^2) = x(2^3)$, then $x =$

- 81
- 72
- 18
- 16
- 8

2. By how many dollars is the price of a computer reduced during a sale?

(1) The price of the computer is reduced by 25% during the sale.

(2) The sale price of the computer is \$36.

- Statement (1) ALONE is sufficient, but statement (2) alone is not sufficient.
- Statement (2) ALONE is sufficient, but statement (1) alone is not sufficient.
- BOTH statements TOGETHER are sufficient, but NEITHER statement ALONE is sufficient.
- EACH statement ALONE is sufficient.
- Statements (1) and (2) TOGETHER are not sufficient.

GO ON TO THE NEXT PAGE.

3. Of the 720 players who participated in a softball tournament, 65 percent traveled more than 200 miles to play. What is the difference between the number of participants who traveled more than 200 miles and the number of participants who traveled 200 miles or less?

- 108
- 216
- 252
- 468
- 655

4. If $r - s = 240$, does $r = 320$?

(1) $r = 4s$

(2) $s = 80$

- Statement (1) ALONE is sufficient, but statement (2) alone is not sufficient.
- Statement (2) ALONE is sufficient, but statement (1) alone is not sufficient.
- BOTH statements TOGETHER are sufficient, but NEITHER statement ALONE is sufficient.
- EACH statement ALONE is sufficient.
- Statements (1) and (2) TOGETHER are not sufficient.

5. If a heavy-load trailer travels 7 miles in 1 hour and 10 minutes, what is its speed in miles per hour?

- 6
- 6.5
- 8
- 8.5
- 10

6. If Bob purchases 18 cans of soda, how many of the cans are diet soda?

(1) The number of diet soda cans Bob purchases is equal to the number that are not diet soda.

(2) Bob purchases an odd number of cans of diet soda.

- Statement (1) ALONE is sufficient, but statement (2) alone is not sufficient.
- Statement (2) ALONE is sufficient, but statement (1) alone is not sufficient.
- BOTH statements TOGETHER are sufficient, but NEITHER statement ALONE is sufficient.
- EACH statement ALONE is sufficient.
- Statements (1) and (2) TOGETHER are not sufficient.

GO ON TO THE NEXT PAGE.

7. If $y$ is an odd integer, which of the following must be an even integer?

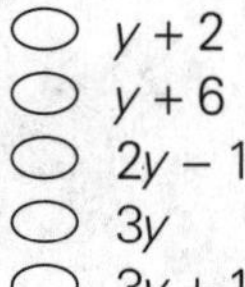

- $y + 2$
- $y + 6$
- $2y - 1$
- $3y$
- $3y + 1$

8. At Perry High School, the ratio of students who participate in either the band program or the choral program to students who participate in neither program is 3 to 8. If 220 students attend Perry High School, how many of them participate in neither program?

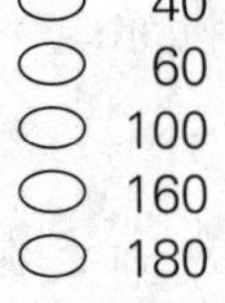

- 40
- 60
- 100
- 160
- 180

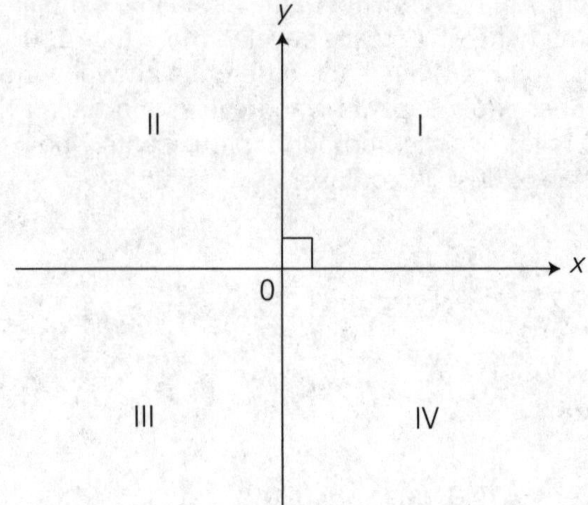


9. The quadrants of the $xy$-plane are shown in the figure above. Does line $d$ (not shown) pass through Quadrant III ?

(1) Line $d$ has a negative $x$-intercept.

(2) Line $f$, which is parallel to line $d$, has a negative $y$-intercept.

- Statement (1) ALONE is sufficient, but statement (2) alone is not sufficient.
- Statement (2) ALONE is sufficient, but statement (1) alone is not sufficient.
- BOTH statements TOGETHER are sufficient, but NEITHER statement ALONE is sufficient.
- EACH statement ALONE is sufficient.
- Statements (1) and (2) TOGETHER are not sufficient.

GO ON TO THE NEXT PAGE.

10. A $240 interest-free loan is to be paid back in equal monthly payments. If a total of $2\frac{1}{2}$ percent of the original amount of the loan is paid back every 6 months, then how many months will it take to pay back $21.00 ?

- 6
- 7
- 18
- 21
- 24

11. If $x$ and $y$ are positive integers, is $x$ a factor of 12 ?

(1) $xy$ is a factor of 12.

(2) $y = 3$

- Statement (1) ALONE is sufficient, but statement (2) alone is not sufficient.
- Statement (2) ALONE is sufficient, but statement (1) alone is not sufficient.
- BOTH statements TOGETHER are sufficient, but NEITHER statement ALONE is sufficient.
- EACH statement ALONE is sufficient.
- Statements (1) and (2) TOGETHER are not sufficient.

12. If a zebra can only get water from either a stream or a pond, which of the two sources of water is closer to the zebra's current position?

(1) Moving at a constant rate from its current position, the zebra reaches the stream in 2 hours.

(2) Moving at a constant rate from the stream, the zebra takes 2 hours to reach the pond.

- Statement (1) ALONE is sufficient, but statement (2) alone is not sufficient.
- Statement (2) ALONE is sufficient, but statement (1) alone is not sufficient.
- BOTH statements TOGETHER are sufficient, but NEITHER statement ALONE is sufficient.
- EACH statement ALONE is sufficient.
- Statements (1) and (2) TOGETHER are not sufficient.

13. What is the value of $x^2 - y^2$ ?

(1) $x - y = 0$

(2) $x + y = 4$

- Statement (1) ALONE is sufficient, but statement (2) alone is not sufficient.
- Statement (2) ALONE is sufficient, but statement (1) alone is not sufficient.
- BOTH statements TOGETHER are sufficient, but NEITHER statement ALONE is sufficient.
- EACH statement ALONE is sufficient.
- Statements (1) and (2) TOGETHER are not sufficient.

GO ON TO THE NEXT PAGE.

14. If the remainder when a certain integer $x$ is divided by 5 is 2, then each of the following could also be an integer, EXCEPT

- $\frac{x}{17}$
- $\frac{x}{11}$
- $\frac{x}{10}$
- $\frac{x}{6}$
- $\frac{x}{3}$

15. A mixture of ground meat consists of 2 pounds of veal that costs $x$ dollars per pound, and 5 pounds of beef that costs $y$ dollars per pound. What is the cost of the mixture in dollars per pound?

- $2x + 5y$
- $\frac{2x+5y}{xy}$
- $5(2x + 5y)$
- $x + y$
- $\frac{2x+5y}{7}$

16. Is $0 < y < 1$ ?

(1) $0 < \sqrt{y} < 1$

(2) $y^2 = \frac{1}{4}$

- Statement (1) ALONE is sufficient, but statement (2) alone is not sufficient.
- Statement (2) ALONE is sufficient, but statement (1) alone is not sufficient.
- BOTH statements TOGETHER are sufficient, but NEITHER statement ALONE is sufficient.
- EACH statement ALONE is sufficient.
- Statements (1) and (2) TOGETHER are not sufficient.

17. If $a$ and $b$ are positive integers, is $ab$ odd?

(1) $b = 3$

(2) $a$ and $b$ are consecutive integers.

- Statement (1) ALONE is sufficient, but statement (2) alone is not sufficient.
- Statement (2) ALONE is sufficient, but statement (1) alone is not sufficient.
- BOTH statements TOGETHER are sufficient, but NEITHER statement ALONE is sufficient.
- EACH statement ALONE is sufficient.
- Statements (1) and (2) TOGETHER are not sufficient.

GO ON TO THE NEXT PAGE.

18. Last year, an appliance store sold an average (arithmetic mean) of 42 microwave ovens per month. In the first 10 months of this year, the store sold an average of only 20 microwaves per month. What is the average number of microwaves sold per month for the entire 22-month period?

- 21
- 30
- 31
- 32
- 44

19. If *AB* is the diameter of the circle with center *X* and *C* is a point on the circle such that $AC = AX = 3$, what is the perimeter of triangle *ABC* ?

- $\frac{9\sqrt{3}}{2}$
- 9
- $6 + 3\sqrt{3}$
- $9 + 3\sqrt{3}$
- $9\sqrt{3}$

| ADVANCE PURCHASE DISCOUNTS FOR AIRLINE TRAVEL | |
|---|---|
| **Days Prior to Departure** | **Percentage Discount** |
| 0–6 days | 0% |
| 7–13 days | 10% |
| 14–29 days | 25% |
| 30 days or more | 40% |

20. The table above shows the discount structure for advance purchase of tickets at a particular airline. A passenger bought a ticket at this airline for $1,050. Had she purchased the ticket one day later, she would have paid $210 more. How many days before her departure did she purchase her ticket?

- 6 days
- 7 days
- 13 days
- 14 days
- 29 days

GO ON TO THE NEXT PAGE.

**Verbal Test**
**Time—30 Minutes**
**20 Questions**

**This test is made up of sentence correction, critical reasoning, and reading comprehension questions.**

**Sentence Correction Directions:** Each of the sentence correction questions presents a sentence, part or all of which is underlined. Beneath the sentence you will find five ways of phrasing the underlined part. The first of these repeats the original; the other four are different. Follow the requirements of standard written English to choose your answer, paying attention to grammar, word choice, and sentence construction. Select the answer that produces the most effective sentence; your answer should make the sentence clear, exact, and free of grammatical errors. It should also minimize awkwardness, ambiguity, and redundancy.

**Reading Comprehension Directions:** Each of the reading comprehension questions is based on the content of a passage. After reading the passage, answer all questions pertaining to it on the basis of what is stated or implied in the passage. For each question, select the best answer of the choices given.

**Critical Reasoning Directions:** Each of the critical reasoning questions is based on a short argument, a set of statements, or a plan of action. For each question, select the best answer of the choices given.

---

21. Unseasonable weather in the months before a wine harvest can cool vineyards in the Bordeaux region enough to affect the overall size of the grapes themselves, create unwanted moisture that can cause mold in some grape varieties and deterioration in others.

- to affect the overall size of the grapes themselves, create
- to affect the overall size of the grapes themselves and create
- that the overall size of the grapes themselves are affected, create
- that it affects the overall size of the grapes themselves, creates
- that the size of the grapes are affected and creates

22. It is posited by some scientists that the near extinction of the sap-eating gray bat of northwestern America was caused by government-sponsored logging operations in the early 1920s that greatly reduced the species' habitat.

Which of the following, if true, most strongly weakens the scientists' claims?

- Logging operations in the 1920s are widely held responsible for the near extinction of other species that lived in the same area.
- A boom in new home construction in the early 1920s led congress to open federal lands to logging operations.
- A 5-year drought in the early 1920s severely reduced the output of sap in trees in northwestern America.
- Numbers of sightings of sap-eating gray bats fell to their lowest numbers in 1926.
- Sightings of sap-eating gray bats in Europe stayed roughly the same during the same period.

GO ON TO THE NEXT PAGE.

23. Upset by the recent downturn in production numbers during the first half of the year, <u>the possibility of adding worker incentives was raised by the board of directors at its quarterly meeting</u>.

- the possibility of adding worker incentives was raised by the board of directors at its quarterly meeting
- the addition of worker incentives was raised as a possibility by the board of directors at its quarterly meeting
- added worker incentives was raised by the board of directors at its quarterly meeting as a possibility
- the board of directors raised at its quarterly meeting the possibility of worker incentives being added
- the board of directors, at its quarterly meeting, raised the possibility of adding worker incentives

24. Whenever a major airplane accident occurs, there is a dramatic increase in the number of airplane mishaps reported in the media, a phenomenon that may last for as long as a few months after the accident. Airline officials assert that the publicity given the gruesomeness of major airplane accidents focuses media attention on the airline industry, and the increase in the number of reported accidents is caused by an increase in the number of news sources covering airline accidents, not by an increase in the number of accidents.

Which of the following, if true, would seriously weaken the assertions of the airline officials?

- The publicity surrounding airline accidents is largely limited to the country in which the crash occurred.
- Airline accidents tend to occur far more often during certain peak travel months.
- Media organizations do not have any guidelines to help them decide how severe an accident must be for it to receive coverage.
- Airplane accidents receive coverage by news sources only when the news sources find it advantageous to do so.
- Studies by government regulators show that the number of airplane flight miles remains relatively constant from month to month.

GO ON TO THE NEXT PAGE.

Questions 25–28 are based on the following passage:

The function of strategic planning is to position a company for long-term growth and expansion in a variety of markets by analyzing its strengths and weaknesses and examining current and potential opportunities. Based on this information, the company develops a strategy for itself. That strategy becomes the basis for supporting strategies for the company's various departments.

This implementation strategy is where all too many strategic plans go astray. Recent business management surveys show that most CEOs who have a strategic plan are concerned with the potential breakdown in the implementation of the plan. Unlike corporations in the 1980s that blindly followed their 5-year plans, even when they were misguided, today's corporations tend to second-guess their long-term plans.

Outsiders can help facilitate the process, but in the final analysis, if the company does not make the plan, the company will not follow the plan. This was one of the problems with strategic planning in the 1980s. In that era, strategic planning was an abstract, top-down process involving only a few top corporate officers and hired guns. Number crunching experts came into a company and generated tome-like volumes filled with a mixture of abstruse facts and grand theories that had little to do with the day-to-day realities of the company. Key middle managers were left out of planning sessions, resulting in lost opportunities and ruffled feelings.

However, more hands-on strategic planning can produce startling results. A recent survey queried more than a thousand small- to medium-sized businesses to compare companies with a strategic plan to companies without one. The survey found that companies with strategic plans had annual revenue growth of 6.2 percent as opposed to 3.8 percent for the other companies.

Perhaps most important, a strategic plan helps companies anticipate—and survive—change. New technology and the mobility of capital means that markets can shift faster than ever before. Some financial analysts wonder why companies should bother planning two years ahead when market dynamics might be transformed by next quarter. However, it is this pace of change that makes planning so crucial. Now, more than ever, companies have to stay alert to the marketplace. In an environment of continual and rapid change, long-range planning expands options and organizational flexibility.

25. The primary purpose of the passage is to

- ◯ refute the idea that change is bad for a corporation's long-term health
- ◯ describe how long-term planning, despite some potential pitfalls, can help a corporation to grow
- ◯ compare and contrast two styles of corporate planning
- ◯ evaluate the strategic planning goals of corporate America today
- ◯ defend a methodology that has come under sharp attack

26. It can be inferred from the passage that strategic planning during the 1980s had all of the following shortcomings EXCEPT

- ◯ a reliance on outside consultants who did not necessarily understand the nuts and bolts of the business
- ◯ a dependence on theoretical models that did not always perfectly describe the workings of the company
- ◯ an inherent weakness in the company's own ability to implement the strategic plan
- ◯ an excess of information and data that made it difficult to get to key concepts
- ◯ the lack of a forum for middle managers to express their ideas

GO ON TO THE NEXT PAGE.

27. The author most likely mentions the results of the survey of 1,000 companies in order to

- put forth an opposing view on strategic plans which is later refuted
- illustrate that when strategic planning is "hands-on," it produces uninspiring results
- give a concrete example of why strategic planning did not work during the 1980s
- support the contention that strategic planning can be very successful when done correctly
- give supporting data to prove that many companies have implemented strategic plans

28. The passage suggests which of the following about the "financial analysts" mentioned in lines 44–47 ?

- They believe that strategic planning is the key to weathering the rapid changes of the marketplace.
- They are working to understand and anticipate market developments that are two years ahead.
- Their study of market dynamics has led them to question the reliability of short-term planning strategies.
- They might not agree with the author that one way to survive rapidly changing conditions comes from long-range planning.
- They consider the mobility of capital to be a necessary condition for the growth of new technology.

29. The Internal Revenue Service has directed that taxpayers who generate no self-employment income can no longer deduct home offices, home office expenses, <u>or nothing that was already</u> depreciated as a business expense the previous year.

- or nothing that was already
- or that was already
- or anything that was already
- and anything
- and nothing that already was

30. Informed people generally assimilate information from several divergent sources before coming to an opinion. However, most popular news organizations view foreign affairs solely through the eyes of our State Department. In reporting the political crisis in a foreign country, news organizations must endeavor to find alternative sources of information.

Which of the following inferences can be drawn from the argument above?

- To the degree that a news source gives an account of another country that mirrors that of our State Department, that reporting is suspect.
- To protect their integrity, news media should avoid the influence of State Department releases in their coverage of foreign affairs.
- Reporting that is not influenced by the State Department is usually more accurate than are other accounts.
- The alternative sources of information mentioned in the passage might not share the same views as the State Department.
- A report cannot be seen as influenced by the State Department if it accurately depicts the events in a foreign country.

GO ON TO THE NEXT PAGE.

31. When automatic teller machines were first installed in the 1980s, bank officials promised they would be faster, more reliable, and less prone to make errors than their human counterparts.

- they would be faster, more reliable, and less prone to make errors
- they would be faster, more reliable, and that they would be less prone for making errors
- the machines would be faster, more reliable, and less prone to errors
- the machines were faster, more reliable, and errors would occur much less
- faster, more reliable machines, and that errors would be less prone

32. With its plan to create a wildlife sanctuary out of previously unused landfill, Sweden is but one of a number of industrialized nations that is accepting its responsibility to protect endangered species and promote conservation.

- is accepting its responsibility to protect endangered species and promote
- is accepting its responsibility for protecting endangered species and promoting
- are accepting its responsibility to protect endangered species and promoting
- are accepting of their responsibility to protect endangered species and to promote
- are accepting their responsibility to protect endangered species and promote

33. A decade after a logging operation in India began cutting down trees in a territory that serves as a sanctuary for Bengal tigers, the incidence of tigers attacking humans in nearby villages has increased by 300 percent. Because the logging operation has reduced the number of acres of woodland per tiger on average from 15 acres to approximately 12 acres, scientists have theorized that tigers must need a minimum number of acres of woodland in order to remain content.

Which of the following statements, if true, would most strengthen the scientists' hypothesis?

- In other wildlife areas in India where the number of acres of woodland per tiger remains at least 15 acres, there has been no increase in the number of tiger attacks on humans.
- Before the logging operation began, there were many fewer humans living in the area.
- The largest number of acres per tiger before the logging operation began was 32 acres per tiger in one area of the sanctuary, whereas the smallest number of acres per tiger after the logging operation was 9 acres.
- Other species of wild animals have begun competing with the Bengal tigers for the dwindling food supply.
- The Bengal tiger has become completely extinct in other areas of Asia.

GO ON TO THE NEXT PAGE.

34. The machine press union and company management were not able to communicate effectively, and it was a major cause of the 1999 strike in Seattle.

- ⬭ The machine press union and company management were not able to communicate effectively, and it
- ⬭ Communications between the machine press union and company management were not effective, and it
- ⬭ For the machine press union and company management, to be unable to communicate effectively
- ⬭ The inability of the machine press union and company management to communicate effectively
- ⬭ The machine press union, being unable to communicate effectively with company management,

35. A greater number of fresh vegetables are sold in City *X* than in City *Y*. Therefore, the people in City *X* have better nutritional habits than those in City *Y*.

Each of the following, if true, weakens the conclusion above EXCEPT:

- ⬭ City *X* has more people living in it than City *Y*.
- ⬭ Most of the people in City *Y* work in City *X* and buy their vegetables there.
- ⬭ The people in City *X* buy many of their vegetables as decorations, not to eat.
- ⬭ The per capita consumption of junk food in City *X* is three times that of City *Y*.
- ⬭ The average price per pound of vegetables in City *Y* is lower than the average price per pound of vegetables in City *X*.

36. Heavy metals, toxic waste by-products that can cause tumors in fish, are generally found in the waters off industrial shorelines, but have been discovered in trace amounts even in the relatively pristine waters of the South Pacific.

- ⬭ are generally found in the waters off industrial shorelines, but have been discovered in trace amounts even
- ⬭ are generally to be found in the waters off industrial shorelines, and have even been discovered in trace amounts
- ⬭ can, in general, be found in the waters off industrial shorelines, and have been discovered in trace amounts even
- ⬭ had generally been found in the waters off industrial shorelines, but have even been discovered in trace amounts
- ⬭ are found generally in the waters off industrial shorelines, but have been discovered in a trace amount even

GO ON TO THE NEXT PAGE.

Questions 37–40 are based on the following passage:

In Roman times, defeated enemies were generally put to death as criminals for having offended the emperor of Rome. In the Middle Ages, however, the practice of ransoming, or returning prisoners in exchange for money, became common. Though some saw this custom as a step toward a more humane society, the primary reasons behind it were economic rather than humanitarian.

In those times, rulers had only a limited ability to raise taxes. They could neither force their subjects to fight nor pay them to do so. The promise of material compensation in the form of goods and ransom was therefore the only way of inducing combatants to participate in a war. In the Middle Ages, the predominant incentive for the individual soldier was the expectation of spoils. Although collecting ransom clearly brought financial gain, keeping a prisoner and arranging for his exchange had its costs. Consequently, procedures were devised to reduce transaction costs.

One such device was a rule asserting that the prisoner had to assess his own value. This compelled the prisoner to establish a value without too much distortion; indicating too low a value would increase the captive's chances of being killed, while indicating too high a value would either ruin him financially or create a prohibitively expensive ransom that would also result in death.

37. The primary purpose of the passage is to

- ◯ discuss the economic basis of the medieval practice of exchanging prisoners for ransom
- ◯ examine the history of the treatment of prisoners of war
- ◯ emphasize the importance of a warrior's code of honor during the Middle Ages
- ◯ explore a way of reducing the costs of ransom
- ◯ demonstrate why warriors of the Middle Ages looked forward to battles

38. It can be inferred from the passage that a medieval soldier

- ◯ was less likely to kill captured members of opposing armies than was a soldier of the Roman Empire
- ◯ operated on a basically independent level and was motivated solely by economic incentives
- ◯ had few economic options and chose to fight because it was the only way to earn an adequate living
- ◯ was motivated to spare prisoners' lives by humanitarian rather than economic ideals
- ◯ had no respect for his captured enemies since captives were typically regarded as weak

GO ON TO THE NEXT PAGE.

39. Which of the following best describes the change in policy from executing prisoners in Roman times to ransoming prisoners in the Middle Ages?

- The emperors of Rome demanded more respect than did medieval rulers, and thus Roman subjects went to greater lengths to defend their nation.
- It was a reflection of the lesser degree of direct control medieval rulers had over their subjects.
- It became a show of strength and honor for warriors of the Middle Ages to be able to capture and return their enemies.
- Medieval soldiers were not as humanitarian as their ransoming practices might have indicated.
- Medieval soldiers demonstrated more concern about economic policy than did their Roman counterparts.

40. The author uses the phrase "without too much distortion" (lines 24–25) in order to

- indicate that prisoners would fairly assess their worth
- emphasize the important role medieval prisoners played in determining whether they should be ransomed
- explain how prisoners often paid more than an appropriate ransom in order to increase their chances for survival
- suggest that captors and captives often had understanding relationships
- show that when in prison a soldier's view could become distorted

**END OF WARM-UP TEST**

# Chapter 31
# GMAT Math and Verbal Warm-Up Questions: Answers and Explanations

## GMAT WARM-UP QUESTIONS SCORING GUIDE

Detailed explanations to these answers can be found on page 710.

### ANSWER KEY

| MATH | | VERBAL | |
|---|---|---|---|
| 1. | C | 21. | B |
| 2. | C | 22. | C |
| 3. | B | 23. | E |
| 4. | D | 24. | B |
| 5. | A | 25. | B |
| 6. | A | 26. | C |
| 7. | E | 27. | D |
| 8. | D | 28. | D |
| 9. | A | 29. | C |
| 10. | D | 30. | D |
| 11. | A | 31. | C |
| 12. | E | 32. | E |
| 13. | A | 33. | A |
| 14. | C | 34. | D |
| 15. | E | 35. | E |
| 16. | A | 36. | A |
| 17. | B | 37. | A |
| 18. | D | 38. | A |
| 19. | D | 39. | B |
| 20. | D | 40. | A |

## The Math Score

**If you got 6 or fewer math questions correct:** Your percentile rank is in the lower one-third of the testing group and you should begin by practicing the problems in Math Bin 1. Once you've mastered the material in Math Bin 1, you should move on to the questions in Math Bin 2.

**If you got between 6 and 13 math questions correct:** Your percentile rank is in the middle one-third of the testing group and you should begin by practicing the problems in Math Bin 2. Once you've mastered the material in Math Bin 2, you should move on to the questions in Math Bin 3.

**If you got 14 or more math questions correct:** Your percentile rank is in the top one-third of the testing group and you should begin by practicing the problems in Math Bins 3 and 4.

## The Verbal Score

**If you got 6 or fewer verbal questions correct:** Your percentile rank is in the lower one-third of the testing group and you should begin by practicing the problems in Verbal Bin 1. Once you've mastered the material in Verbal Bin 1, you should move on to the questions in Verbal Bin 2.

**If you got between 6 and 13 verbal questions correct:** Your percentile rank is in the middle one-third of the testing group and you should begin by practicing the problems in Verbal Bin 2. Once you've mastered the material in Verbal Bin 2, you should move on to the questions in Verbal Bin 3.

**If you got 14 or more verbal questions correct:** Your percentile rank is in the top one-third of the testing group and you should begin by practicing the problems in Verbal Bin 3.

(If you want additional practice for either the Math or the Verbal section, you may find it helpful to do the problems in a bin with a lower number than the one suggested. So if your math diagnostic score indicates that you should do the questions in Math Bin 2, you might want to do the questions in Math Bin 1 as well.)

## The Combined Score

**If you got 12 or fewer of the 40 total questions correct:** Your combined score at the moment is less than 450.

**If you got between 12 and 31 of the 40 total questions correct:** Your combined score at the moment is between 450 and 550.

**If you got 32 or more of the 40 total questions correct:** Your combined score at the moment is more than 550.

## QUESTIONS

1. If $(16)(3^2) = x(2^3)$, then $x =$

- 81
- 72
- 18
- 16
- 8

2. By how many dollars is the price of a computer reduced during a sale?

(1) The price of the computer is reduced by 25% during the sale.

(2) The sale price of the computer is $36.

- Statement (1) ALONE is sufficient, but statement (2) alone is not sufficient.
- Statement (2) ALONE is sufficient, but statement (1) alone is not sufficient.
- BOTH statements TOGETHER are sufficient, but NEITHER statement ALONE is sufficient.
- EACH statement ALONE is sufficient.
- Statements (1) and (2) TOGETHER are not sufficient.

3. Of the 720 players who participated in a softball tournament, 65 percent traveled more than 200 miles to play. What is the difference between the number of participants who traveled more than 200 miles and the number of participants who traveled 200 miles or less?

- 108
- 216
- 252
- 468
- 655

## MATH EXPLANATIONS

1. **C** Before doing the algebra to uncover the value of $x$, recognize that the algebra is made easier by breaking 16 down into its prime factors. The prime factorization of 16 is $2^4$, so this equation can be rewritten as $(2^4)(3^2) = x(2^3)$. Now solve for $x$ by dividing $2^3$ from each side of the equation to find that $x = 2(3^2)$. Solve to find that $x = 18$ and the correct answer is (C).

2. **C** This is a Value Data Sufficiency question, so start by determining what is known from the question and what is needed from the statements to answer the question. What is known is that a computer's price is reduced during a sale. The statements need to provide a way to determine the original price and the sale price. Evaluate each statement individually. Statement (1) gives the percent reduction in price, but the actual price or sale price is not given. Statement (1) is insufficient, so write down BCE. Statement (2) gives the sale price of the computer, but no information about the original price, so statement (2) is insufficient. Eliminate (B). The statements combined give the percent reduction and the sale price, which is enough information to determine the original price. Because the original price is lowered by 25%, the sale price is 75% of the original. Therefore, the sale price can be determined with the equation $36 = \frac{75}{100}x$ and $x = 48$. The statements combined are sufficient. The correct answer is (C).

3. **B** This is a percent problem, so start by finding the number of players who traveled more than 200 miles: 65% of 720 is 468. The number of players who traveled 200 miles or less, then, is $720 - 468 = 252$ (or, alternatively, 35% of 720 is 252). Although both 468 and 252 are answer choices, the question asks for the difference between the two types of participants: $468 - 252 = 216$. The correct answer is (B).

## QUESTIONS

4. If $r - s = 240$, does $r = 320$ ?

(1) $r = 4s$

(2) $s = 80$

- Statement (1) ALONE is sufficient, but statement (2) alone is not sufficient.
- Statement (2) ALONE is sufficient, but statement (1) alone is not sufficient.
- BOTH statements TOGETHER are sufficient, but NEITHER statement ALONE is sufficient.
- EACH statement ALONE is sufficient.
- Statements (1) and (2) TOGETHER are not sufficient.

5. If a heavy-load trailer travels 7 miles in 1 hour and 10 minutes, what is its speed in miles per hour?

- 6
- 6.5
- 8
- 8.5
- 10

6. If Bob purchases 18 cans of soda, how many of the cans are not diet soda?

(1) The number of diet soda cans Bob purchases is equal to the number that are not diet soda.

(2) Bob purchases an odd number of cans of diet soda.

- Statement (1) ALONE is sufficient, but statement (2) alone is not sufficient.
- Statement (2) ALONE is sufficient, but statement (1) alone is not sufficient.
- BOTH statements TOGETHER are sufficient, but NEITHER statement ALONE is sufficient.
- EACH statement ALONE is sufficient.
- Statements (1) and (2) TOGETHER are not sufficient.

## MATH EXPLANATIONS

4. **D** This is a Yes/No Data Sufficiency question, so look to Plug In. The question provides variables and asks to solve for one of the variables, so look for a way to consistently answer the question "Yes" or "No." Evaluate Statement (1). If $r = 4s$, then substitute $4s$ into $r$ in the original equation to find that $4s - s = 240$. Therefore, $3s = 240$ and $s = 80$. So, $r = 320$. Write down AD. Statement (2) provides a value for $s$ that can be used in the original equation to solve and find that $r = 320$. The correct answer is (D).

5. **A** The question mentions distances and rates, so make a Rate Pie. The distance is 7 miles. The time is 1 hour and 10 minutes. Convert 1 hour and 10 minutes to hours. 10 minutes is $\frac{1}{6}$ of an hour. So, the time is $1\frac{1}{6}$. Divide to find time: $\frac{7}{1\frac{1}{6}} = \frac{7}{\frac{7}{6}} = 7 \times \frac{6}{7} = 6$. The correct answer is (A).

6. **A** This is a Value Data Sufficiency question, so begin by determining what is known and what is needed to answer the question. What is known is that Bob purchased 18 cans of soda. The question asks how many cans are not diet soda. The statements need to provide a way to determine the number of cans that contain diet and non-diet soda. Statement (1) states there is an equal number of diet and non-diet cans, which means that there are 9 cans of each. Statement (1) is sufficient. Write AD.
Statement (2) states that Bob purchased an odd number of cans of diet soda. However, there is no way to tell if that means he purchased 5 cans of diet soda or 11 cans of diet soda. Statement (2) is insufficient. The correct answer is (A).

## QUESTIONS

7. If $y$ is an odd integer, which of the following must be an even integer?

- ○ $y + 2$
- ○ $y + 6$
- ○ $2y - 1$
- ○ $3y$
- ○ $3y + 1$

8. At Perry High School, the ratio of students who participate in either the band program or the choral program to students who participate in neither program is 3 to 8. If 220 students attend Perry High School, how many of them participate in neither program?

- ○ 40
- ○ 60
- ○ 100
- ○ 160
- ○ 180

## MATH EXPLANATIONS

7. **E** This question is a must be question with variables, so be prepared to Plug In more than once. Since $y$ is odd, try $y = 3$. If $y = 3$, then (A) is 5, which is not even, so eliminate (A). Choice (B) is 9, which is not even, so eliminate (B). Choice (C) is 5, which is not even. Eliminate (C). Choice (D) is 9, which is not even. Eliminate (D). Choice (E) is 10, which is even. The correct answer is (E).

8. **D** The question involves ratios, so set up a Ratio Box. The ratio of the students who participate to those who don't is 3 to 8 and the total number of students is 220. Filling those into the box gives a total ratio of 11, which results in a multiplier of 20, because $11 \times 20 = 220$. Then, multiply 8 by 20 to get 160 students who don't participate in either program. The Ratio Box looks like this:

| | Participate | Don't Participate | Total |
|---|---|---|---|
| Ratio | 3 | 8 | 11 |
| Multiplier | 20 | 20 | 20 |
| Actual | 60 | 160 | 220 |

The correct answer is (D).

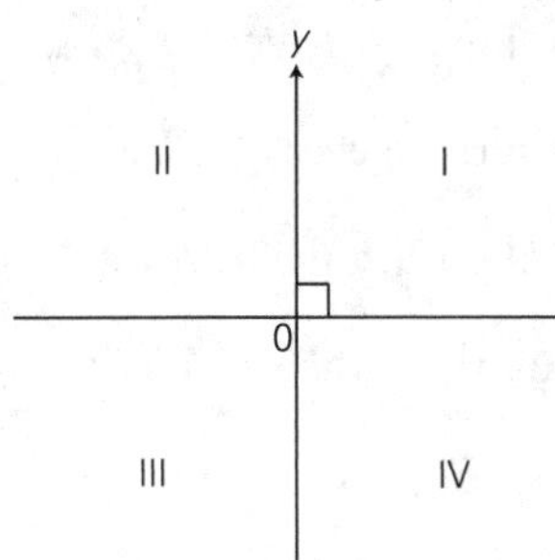


9. The quadrants of the $xy$-plane are shown in the figure above. Does line $d$ (not shown) pass through Quadrant III ?

(1) Line $d$ has a negative $x$-intercept.

(2) Line $f$, which is parallel to line $d$, has a negative $y$-intercept.

- Statement (1) ALONE is sufficient, but statement (2) alone is not sufficient.
- Statement (2) ALONE is sufficient, but statement (1) alone is not sufficient.
- BOTH statements TOGETHER are sufficient, but NEITHER statement ALONE is sufficient.
- EACH statement ALONE is sufficient.
- Statements (1) and (2) TOGETHER are not sufficient.

9. **A** This is a Yes/No Data Sufficiency question, so be prepared to Plug In more than once. The question asks about line $d$, which is not shown, so the statements need to provide information about line $d$. Statement (1) states that line $d$ has a negative $x$-intercept. The $x$-intercept is where the line passes through the $x$-axis. Pick a negative $x$-axis, such as $x = -2$, and draw the line. If $x = -2$, then if line $d$ has a positive slope, it passes through Quadrant III. If line $d$ has a negative slope, then it passes through Quadrant III. In fact, no matter what the $x$-intercept is, if it is negative then line $d$ is going to pass through Quadrant III. Statement (1) is sufficient. Write AD. Statement (2) states that line $f$ has a negative $y$-intercept and that line $f$ is parallel to line $d$. The $y$-intercept is where the line passes through the $y$-axis. Because the lines are parallel, they have the same slope. Draw line $f$. If line $f$ has a positive slope with $y$-intercept of $-2$, then line $d$ also has a positive slope and eventually passes through Quadrant III. If line $f$ has a negative slope with $y$-intercept of $-2$, then line $d$ also has a negative slope. In this case, if line $d$ also has a negative $y$-intercept then line $d$ passes through Quadrant III and the answer to the question is "Yes." If line $d$ has a positive $y$-intercept, then it does not pass through Quadrant III and the answer to the question is "No." Because Statement (2) provides two different answers to the question, the statement is insufficient. The correct answer is (A).

## QUESTIONS

10. A $240 interest-free loan is to be paid back in equal monthly payments. If a total of $2\frac{1}{2}$ percent of the original amount of the loan is paid every 6 months, then how many months will it take to pay back $21.00 ?

- 6
- 7
- 18
- 21
- 24

11. If $x$ and $y$ are positive integers, then is $x$ a factor of 12 ?

(1) $xy$ is a factor of 12.

(2) $y = 3$

- Statement (1) ALONE is sufficient, but statement (2) alone is not sufficient.
- Statement (2) ALONE is sufficient, but statement (1) alone is not sufficient.
- BOTH statements TOGETHER are sufficient, but NEITHER statement ALONE is sufficient.
- EACH statement ALONE is sufficient.
- Statements (1) and (2) TOGETHER are not sufficient.

## MATH EXPLANATIONS

**10. D** Start by finding $2\frac{1}{2}$ percent of $240, which is $\frac{2.5}{100} \times 240 = 6$. So every 6 months a total of $6 is repaid. If these amounts are paid back in equal monthly payments, then each month $1 is paid toward the loan. So, to pay back $21.00 would take 21 months, and the correct answer is (D).

**11. A** This is a Yes/No Data Sufficiency question, so Plug In for the variables. Evaluate Statement (1). If the product of $xy$ is a factor of 12, then $xy$ is equal to 1, 2, 3, 4, 6, or 12. Plug In. If $x = 2$ and $y = 3$, then the answer to the question is "Yes." Plug In again to try and get an answer of "No." In fact, as long as the product of $xy$ is a factor of 12, and $x$ and $y$ are integers, $x$ is a factor of 12. Write down AD. Evaluate Statement (2). This statement provides no information about the value of $x$. Therefore, it is impossible to know if $x$ is a factor of 12. The correct answer is (A).

## QUESTIONS

12. If a zebra can only get water from either a stream or a pond, which of the two sources of water is closer to the zebra's current position?

    (1) Moving at a constant rate from its current position, the zebra reaches the stream in 2 hours.

    (2) Moving at a constant rate from the stream, the zebra takes 2 hours to reach the pond.

    ◯ Statement (1) ALONE is sufficient, but statement (2) alone is not sufficient.
    ◯ Statement (2) ALONE is sufficient, but statement (1) alone is not sufficient.
    ◯ BOTH statements TOGETHER are sufficient, but NEITHER statement ALONE is sufficient.
    ◯ EACH statement ALONE is sufficient.
    ◯ Statements (1) and (2) TOGETHER are not sufficient.

## MATH EXPLANATIONS

12. **E** This is a Value Data Sufficiency question, so begin by determining what is known and what is needed to answer the question. The question provides that there are two locations to reach and asks which is closer. The statements must provide a way to determine the distance between the two points and the current position. Statement (1) gives the time it takes the zebra to reach the stream from its current position; however, it gives no information about the time required to reach the pond. Statement (1) is insufficient. Write down BCE.

Similarly, Statement (2) only gives the time it takes the zebra to get from the pond to the stream—and doesn't mention the zebra's current position. Statement (2) is insufficient. Eliminate (B).

Statements (1) and (2) together give how long it takes for the zebra to reach the stream and then how long it takes the zebra to reach the pond from the stream. However, no information is given about the direction. For example, the zebra, pond, and stream might be in a straight line, they could form many different triangles, or the zebra could even double back from the stream to the pond. The two statements together are insufficient. The correct answer to this question is (E).

13. What is the value of $x^2 - y^2$?

(1) $x - y = 0$

(2) $x + y = 4$

- Statement (1) ALONE is sufficient, but statement (2) alone is not sufficient.
- Statement (2) ALONE is sufficient, but statement (1) alone is not sufficient.
- BOTH statements TOGETHER are sufficient, but NEITHER statement ALONE is sufficient.
- EACH statement ALONE is sufficient.
- Statements (1) and (2) TOGETHER are not sufficient.

**13. A** This is a Value Data Sufficiency question, so determine what is known and what is needed. Start by noticing that $x^2 - y^2$ is the common quadratic $(x + y)(x - y)$. The question asks for the value of the expression, so the statements need to provide a way to determine the value of the variables or the expression as a whole. Statement (1) gives that $x - y = 0$. If $x - y = 0$, the value of $(x + y)(x - y)$ is also 0. Statement (1) is sufficient. Write AD.

Statement (2) says that $x + y = 4$. No information is given about $x - y$. For example, $x$ and $y$ could both be 2 or $x$ could be 3 and $y$ could be 1, both of which yield a different value for $x^2 - y^2$. Statement (2) is insufficient. The correct answer is (A).

14. If the remainder when a certain integer $x$ is divided by 5 is 2, then each of the following could also be an integer, EXCEPT

- $\frac{x}{17}$
- $\frac{x}{11}$
- $\frac{x}{10}$
- $\frac{x}{6}$
- $\frac{x}{3}$

**14. C** There are variables in the answer choices, so Plug In. To get a remainder of 2 when $x$ is divided by 5, $x$ must be a multiple of 5 plus 2 more. In other words, $x$ could be 7 or 12 or 17 or 22, etc. Now, go through the answer choices, plugging in numbers for $x$ that allow them to be integers as well. For example, if $x = 17$, then (A) is $\frac{17}{17}$, which is an integer. Eliminate (A).

If $x = 22$, then the result is $\frac{22}{11}$, which is an integer. Eliminate (B). Choice (C) is not an integer, so keep (C). Choices (D) and (E) are also not integers, so keep (D) and (E). Plug In again. If $x = 12$, then (C) is not an integer but (D) and (E) are. Eliminate (D) and (E). The correct answer is (C).

## QUESTIONS

15. A mixture of ground meat consists of 2 pounds of veal that costs $x$ dollars per pound, and 5 pounds of beef that costs $y$ dollars per pound. What is the cost of the mixture in dollars per pound?

- $2x + 5y$
- $\frac{2x+5y}{xy}$
- $5(2x + 5y)$
- $x + y$
- $\frac{2x+5y}{7}$

16. Is $0 < y < 1$ ?

(1) $0 < \sqrt{y} < 1$

(2) $y^2 = \frac{1}{4}$

- Statement (1) ALONE is sufficient, but statement (2) alone is not sufficient.
- Statement (2) ALONE is sufficient, but statement (1) alone is not sufficient.
- BOTH statements TOGETHER are sufficient, but NEITHER statement ALONE is sufficient.
- EACH statement ALONE is sufficient.
- Statements (1) and (2) TOGETHER are not sufficient.

## MATH EXPLANATIONS

15. **E** There are variables in the answer choices, so Plug In. The question asks for the cost of the mixture in dollars per pound. Because there are 7 total pounds of meat, plug in numbers that are divisible by 7, such as $x = 14$ and $y = 7$. In that case, the total cost of the mixture is (2)(14) + (5)(7) = 63. Divide by 7 to get the cost per pound, which is \$9. Plug $x = 14$ and $y = 7$ into the answers, looking for one that equals 9. Only (E) equals 9, so the correct answer is (E).

16. **A** This is a Yes/No Data Sufficiency question, so be prepared to Plug In more than once. Statement (1) states that $0 < \sqrt{y} < 1$, so test out possible values of $y$. The only values of $y$ that will satisfy $0 < \sqrt{y} < 1$ are fractions (such as $\frac{1}{4}, \frac{1}{2}, \frac{4}{9}$, etc.). Therefore, the value of $y$ is always between 0 and 1 and the answer to the question is "Yes." Statement (1) is sufficient. Write AD. Statement (2) states that $y^2 = \frac{1}{4}$, so $y$ could be either $\frac{1}{2}$ or $-\frac{1}{2}$. In one case, the answer to the question is a "Yes" and in the other it is a "No." Statement (2) is insufficient. The correct answer is (A).

## QUESTIONS

17. If $a$ and $b$ are positive integers, is $ab$ odd?

(1) $b = 3$

(2) $a$ and $b$ are consecutive integers.

- Statement (1) ALONE is sufficient, but statement (2) alone is not sufficient.
- Statement (2) ALONE is sufficient, but statement (1) alone is not sufficient.
- BOTH statements TOGETHER are sufficient, but NEITHER statement ALONE is sufficient.
- EACH statement ALONE is sufficient.
- Statements (1) and (2) TOGETHER are not sufficient.

## MATH EXPLANATIONS

17. **B** This is a Yes/No Data Sufficiency question, so be prepared to Plug In more than once. The question asks if $ab$ is odd if $a$ and $b$ are positive integers. Evaluate the statements individually. Statement (1) states that $b = 3$. Plug in different values for $a$. If $a = 2$, then $ab = 6$ and the answer to the question is "No." If $a = 3$, then $ab = 9$ and the answer to the question is a "Yes." Statement (1) is insufficient. Write BCE.

Statement (2) states that $a$ and $b$ are consecutive integers. Plug in some values for $a$ and $b$. If $a = 2$ and $b = 3$, then $ab = 6$ and the answer to the question is "No." If $a = 3$ and $b = 4$, then $ab = 12$ and the answer is still "No." The product of any two consecutive integers is even and the answer to the question is always "No." Statement (2) is sufficient. The correct answer is (B).

18. Last year, an appliance store sold an average (arithmetic mean) of 42 microwave ovens per month. In the first 10 months of this year, the store sold an average of only 20 microwaves per month. What is the average number of microwaves sold per month for the entire 22-month period?

- 21
- 30
- 31
- 32
- 44

18. **D** If the appliance store sold an average of 42 microwaves per month last year, then the total microwaves sold for the year was $42 \times 12 = 504$. For the first 10 months of this year, the total sold was $20 \times 10 = 200$. So, the total sold for the 22-month period is 704. Divide 704 by 22 to get the average. $704 \div 22 = 32$. The correct answer is (D).

## QUESTIONS

19. If $AB$ is the diameter of the circle with center $X$ and $C$ is a point on the circle such that $AC = AX = 3$, what is the perimeter of triangle $ABC$ ?

- $\frac{9\sqrt{3}}{2}$
- 9
- $6 + 3\sqrt{3}$
- $9 + 3\sqrt{3}$
- $9\sqrt{3}$

| ADVANCE PURCHASE DISCOUNTS FOR AIRLINE TRAVEL | |
|---|---|
| **Days Prior to Departure** | **Percentage Discount** |
| 0–6 days | 0% |
| 7–13 days | 10% |
| 14–29 days | 25% |
| 30 days or more | 40% |

20. The table above shows the discount structure for advanced purchase of tickets at a particular airline. A passenger bought a ticket at this airline for \$1,050. Had she purchased the ticket one day later, she would have paid \$210 more. How many days before her departure did she purchase her ticket?

- 6 days
- 7 days
- 13 days
- 14 days
- 29 days

## MATH EXPLANATIONS

19. **D** First, draw the picture. It looks something like this:

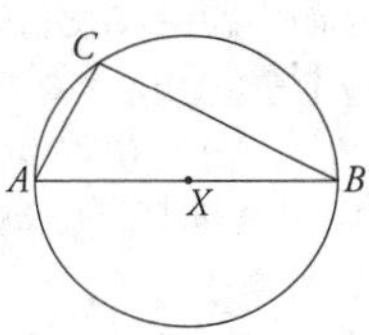


The problem states that $AB$ is the diameter of the circle and that $X$ is the center of the circle. $ABC$ is the triangle that connects the 3 points. $AC$ and $AX$ can be labeled as 3—as can $BX$, since, like $AX$, it's a radius.

To find the 3rd side, recognize that triangle $ABC$, because it's inscribed in a semicircle, is a right triangle, with the right angle at point $C$.

Now use the Pythagorean Theorem—recognize $ABC$ as a 30-60-90 triangle—to determine that $BC$ is $3\sqrt{3}$. The perimeter is $6+3+3\sqrt{3}$, or $9+3\sqrt{3}$. The correct answer is (D).

20. **D** The problem asks for a specific value, and that value is represented by the answer choices, so Plug In the Answers. Start with (C). If the passenger bought a ticket 13 days in advance versus 12 days in advance (one day later), then there would be no savings (discount is the same for 13 days and 12 days), so eliminate (C). Try (D). If the passenger bought a ticket 14 days in advance, then the discount is 25%. So, the cost of the ticket is 75% of the undiscounted cost. Set up an equation to find the undiscounted cost, which is $\frac{75}{100}x = 1{,}050$. Solving for $x$ gives an undiscounted cost of \$1,400. The discount if the ticket had been bought one day later is 10%. 10% of \$1,400 is \$140, so the cost of the ticket is \$1,260. The difference in cost is \$1,260 – \$1,050 = \$210, which meets the condition of a \$210 savings. The correct answer is (D).

## QUESTIONS

21. Unseasonable weather in the months before a wine harvest can cool vineyards in the Bordeaux region enough to affect the overall size of the grapes themselves, create unwanted moisture that can cause mold in some grape varieties and deterioration in others.

- to affect the overall size of the grapes themselves, create
- to affect the overall size of the grapes themselves and create
- that the overall size of the grapes themselves are affected, create
- that it affects the overall size of the grapes themselves, creates
- that the size of the grapes are affected and creates

## VERBAL EXPLANATIONS

21. **B** The underlined portion of the sentence contains part of a list of the effects of *unseasonable weather.* The list is *to affect…create.* This list is not parallel, as there is no connector word joining the two ideas, which creates an unparallel fragment. Eliminate (A) and look for any obvious repeaters. Neither (C) nor (D) contains a connector word, so the sentence remains not parallel. Eliminate (C) and (D). Evaluate the remaining answer choices individually.
Choice (B) fixes the original error by placing the connector word *and* before the verb *create,* which is the second part of the list that begins with *to affect.* This choice makes no new errors, so keep (B). Choice (E) fixes the original error but creates new errors by changing the form of the verbs in the list to *affected* and *creates.* These verbs are not parallel and not in the same form, so eliminate (E). The correct answer is (B).

## QUESTIONS

22. It is posited by some scientists that the near extinction of the sap-eating gray bat of northwestern America was caused by government-sponsored logging operations in the early 1920s that greatly reduced the species' habitat.

Which of the following, if true, most strongly weakens the scientists' claims?

- ◯ Logging operations in the 1920s are widely held responsible for the near extinction of other species that lived in the same area.
- ◯ A boom in new home construction in the early 1920s led congress to open federal lands to logging operations.
- ◯ A 5-year drought in the early 1920s severely reduced the output of sap in trees in northwestern America.
- ◯ Numbers of sightings of sap-eating gray bats fell to their lowest numbers in 1926.
- ◯ Sightings of sap-eating gray bats in Europe stayed roughly the same during the same period.

## VERBAL EXPLANATIONS

22. **C** The question asks which of the answer choices *most strongly weakens the scientists' claims,* so this is a weaken question. This is a causal argument, as the scientists' claim is that the bat's near extinction was caused by logging. The standard assumptions of a causal argument are that there are no other causes and it's not a coincidence. The argument is weakened by presenting an alternate cause or providing evidence that the argument presented is a coincidence. Evaluate each answer choice individually. Choice (A) strengthens the argument by presenting evidence that logging was responsible for the extinction of other species. Eliminate (A). Choice (B) is out of scope because the reasons for the logging are not the concern of the scientists. The scientists are concerned only about the link between the logging and the extinction of the bats. Eliminate (B). Choice (C) provides an alternate cause for the extinction of the bats. If there was no food source for the bats, then that could be the reason for their extinction. Keep (C). Choice (D) is out of scope because the *sightings* of the bats is not the concern of the scientists. Eliminate (D). Choice (E) is out of scope because it concerns the population of the bats on another continent. Eliminate (E). The correct answer is (C).

## QUESTIONS

23. Upset by the recent downturn in production numbers during the first half of the year, the possibility of adding worker incentives was raised by the board of directors at its quarterly meeting.

- the possibility of adding worker incentives was raised by the board of directors at its quarterly meeting
- the addition of worker incentives was raised as a possibility by the board of directors at its quarterly meeting
- added worker incentives was raised by the board of directors at its quarterly meeting as a possibility
- the board of directors raised at its quarterly meeting the possibility of worker incentives being added
- the board of directors, at its quarterly meeting, raised the possibility of adding worker incentives

## VERBAL EXPLANATIONS

23. **E** The underlined portion of the sentence follows a leading descriptive opening phrase, so look for a misplaced modifier error. The sentence currently reads that *the possibility* is *upset by the recent downturn*. This is a misplaced modifier error, so eliminate (A) and look for obvious repeaters. There are no obvious repeaters, so evaluate each answer choice individually.

Choice (B) does not fix the original error because *the addition* is not *upset by the recent downturn*, so eliminate (B). Choice (C) does not fix the original error because *added worker incentives* is not *upset by the recent downturn*, so eliminate (C). Choice (D) fixes the original error by placing the *board members* as the noun that is described as *upset by the recent downturn*. However, this choice utilizes the passive voice with the phrasing *raised at its quarterly meeting the possibility of worker incentives being added*. Eliminate (D). Choice (E) fixes the original error by placing the *board members* as the noun that is described as *upset by the recent downturn*. This choice makes no additional errors, so keep (E).

## QUESTIONS

24. Whenever a major airplane accident occurs, there is a dramatic increase in the number of airplane mishaps reported in the media, a phenomenon that may last for as long as a few months after the accident. Airline officials assert that the publicity given the gruesomeness of major airplane accidents focuses media attention on the airline industry, and the increase in the number of reported accidents is caused by an increase in the number of news sources covering airline accidents, not by an increase in the number of accidents.

    Which of the following, if true, would seriously weaken the assertions of the airline officials?

    - ◯ The publicity surrounding airline accidents is largely limited to the country in which the crash occurred.
    - ◯ Airline accidents tend to occur far more often during certain peak travel months.
    - ◯ News organizations do not have any guidelines to help them decide how severe an accident must be for it to receive coverage.
    - ◯ Airplane accidents receive coverage by news sources only when the news sources find it advantageous to do so.
    - ◯ Studies by government regulators show that the number of airplane flight miles remains relatively constant from month to month.

## VERBAL EXPLANATIONS

24. **B** The question asks which of the answer choices *would seriously weaken the assertion of the airline officials,* so this is a weaken question. This argument uses a sampling reasoning pattern as the official asserts that there is no increase in mishaps during the months after an accident, but an increase in the number of news sources reporting mishaps. Therefore, the claim that *there is a dramatic increase in the number of airline mishaps* is contested by the airline officials. The standard assumption of a sampling reasoning pattern is that the sample is representative. Because the airline officials are challenging the assumption to weaken the assertion of the airline officials, the correct answer will show that the sample is representative. Choice (A) discusses the *country in which the crash occurred,* which is out of scope, so eliminate (A). Choice (B) weakens the claim of the airline officials by implying that certain months are more likely to have frequent accidents due to the high volume of flights. Keep (B). Choice (C) strengthens the argument because if there is no standard definition for what an accident is, then news organizations can use a broad definition of accident to inflate the number of accidents. Eliminate (C). Choice (D) strengthens the argument by providing evidence to suggest the sample is not representative because accidents are covered only *when the news sources find it advantageous to do so.* Eliminate (D). Choice (E) also strengthens the argument because if the *number of airplane flight miles remains relatively constant,* then the officials' commentary is correct, as the number of accidents would then be expected to be relatively constant, as well. Eliminate (E). The correct answer is (B).

## QUESTIONS

## VERBAL EXPLANATIONS

Questions 25–28 are based on the following passage:

The function of strategic planning is to position a company for long-term growth and expansion in a variety of markets by analyzing its strengths and weaknesses and examining current and potential opportunities. Based on this information, the company develops a strategy for itself. That strategy becomes the basis for supporting strategies for the company's various departments.

This implementation stage is where all too many strategic plans go astray. Recent business management surveys show that most CEOs who have a strategic plan are concerned with the potential breakdown in the implementation of the plan. Unlike corporations in the 1980s that blindly followed their 5-year plans, even when they were misguided, today's corporations tend to second-guess their long-term plans.

Outsiders can help facilitate the process, but in the final analysis, if the company does not make the plan, the company will not follow the plan. This was one of the problems with strategic planning in the 1980s. In that era, strategic planning was an abstract, top-down process involving only a few top corporate officers and hired guns. Number crunching experts came into a company and generated tome-like volumes filled with a mixture of abstruse facts and grand theories that had little to do with the day-to-day realities of the company. Key middle managers were left out of planning sessions, resulting in lost opportunities and ruffled feelings.

However, more hands-on strategic planning can produce startling results. A recent survey queried more than a thousand small- to medium-sized businesses to compare companies with a strategic plan to companies without one. The survey found that companies with strategic plans had annual revenue growth of 6.2 percent as opposed to 3.8 percent for the other companies.

Perhaps most important, a strategic plan helps companies anticipate—and survive—change. New technology and the mobility of capital means that markets can shift faster than ever before. Some financial analysts wonder why companies should bother planning two years ahead when market dynamics might be transformed by next quarter. However, it is this pace of change that makes planning so crucial. Now, more than ever, companies have to stay alert to the marketplace. In an environment of continual and rapid change, long-range planning expands options and organizational flexibility.

## QUESTIONS

25. The primary purpose of the passage is to

- ◯ refute the idea that change is bad for a corporation's long-term health
- ◯ describe how long-term planning, despite some potential pitfalls, can help a corporation to grow
- ◯ compare and contrast two styles of corporate planning
- ◯ evaluate the strategic planning goals of corporate America today
- ◯ defend a methodology that has come under sharp attack

## VERBAL EXPLANATIONS

25. **B** This is a primary purpose question. The subject of the question is the passage itself and the task is to determine the primary purpose of the passage. The first paragraph of the passage states the *function of strategic planning* and that the strategy *becomes the basis for supporting strategies for the company's various departments.* The rest of the passage expands on the virtues and drawbacks of strategic planning. This is the primary purpose of the passage, so look for an answer choice that reflects this idea. Choice (A) is an example of extreme language, as the passage does not indicate that *change is bad*. Eliminate (A). Choice (B) effectively summarizes the main idea of the passage that despite some potential problems, strategic planning can allow a company to expand and grow. Keep (B). Choice (C) is a no such comparison answer, as the passage does not seek to *compare and contrast two styles of corporate planning.* Eliminate (C). Choice (D) is a memory trap as the passage does discuss the evaluation of goals, but the primary purpose is not to evaluate the *goals of corporate America.* Eliminate (D). Choice (E) is extreme language, as the passage does not seek to *defend* anything. Eliminate (E). The correct answer is (B).

## QUESTIONS

26. It can be inferred from the passage that strategic planning during the 1980s had all of the following shortcomings EXCEPT

- ⬭ a reliance on outside consultants who did not necessarily understand the nuts and bolts of the business
- ⬭ a dependence on theoretical models that did not always perfectly describe the workings of the company
- ⬭ an inherent weakness in the company's own ability to implement the strategic plan
- ⬭ an excess of information and data that made it difficult to get to key concepts
- ⬭ the lack of a forum for middle managers to express their ideas

## VERBAL EXPLANATIONS

26. **C** The subject of the question is the *shortcomings* of *strategic planning during the 1980s.* This is an inference question, so the task is to determine what is true from the passage. This is an Except question, so the correct answer is the choice that is not true based on the information in the passage. Choice (A) is true because the third paragraph of the passage states that the use of outsiders was *one of the problems with strategic planning in the 1980s.* Eliminate (A). Choice (B) is also verified in the third paragraph which states that one of the problems was *abstruse facts and grand theories that had little to do with the day-to-day realities of the company.* Eliminate (B). Choice (C) is a memory trap from the second paragraph, which states that *today's corporations tend to second-guess their long-term plans* is a modern phenomenon, not one related to companies in the 1980s. Keep (C). Choice (D) is supported by the third paragraph, which states that *number crunching experts came into a company and generated tome-like volumes filled with a mixture of abstruse facts and grand theories.* Eliminate (D). Choice (E) is also supported by the third paragraph, which states *key middle managers were left out of planning sessions.* Eliminate (E). The correct answer is (C).

## QUESTIONS

27. The author most likely mentions the results of the survey of 1,000 companies in order to

- put forth an opposing view on strategic plans which is later refuted
- illustrate that when strategic planning is "hands-on," it produces uninspiring results
- give a concrete example of why strategic planning did not work during the 1980s
- support the contention that strategic planning can be very successful when done correctly
- give supporting data to prove that many companies have implemented strategic plans

## VERBAL EXPLANATIONS

27. **D** The subject of the question is the *survey of 1,000 companies* and the task of the question is *most likely mentions,* so this is a purpose question. The passage states that the survey was to *compare companies with a strategic plan to companies without one* and that the survey *found that companies with strategic plans had annual revenue growth of 6.2 percent as opposed to 3.8 percent for the other companies.* This information bolsters the stance that strategic planning is valuable. Choice (A) is a reversal of the point of including the survey, so eliminate (A). Choice (B) contains recycled language as the passage does discuss *"hands-on"* but not in the context of the survey. Eliminate (B). Choice (C) is a memory trap as the passage does discuss companies during the 1980s, but not in the context of the survey. Eliminate (C). Choice (D) is a good summary of the value of including the information about the survey, so keep (D). Choice (E) uses the extreme language *prove.* The survey does not prove that *many companies have implemented strategic plans,* only that companies that have experience higher annual growth. Eliminate (E). The correct answer is (D).

## QUESTIONS

28. The passage suggests which of the following about the "financial analysts" mentioned in lines 44–47 ?

- They believe that strategic planning is the key to weathering the rapid changes of the marketplace.
- They are working to understand and anticipate market developments that are two years ahead.
- Their study of market dynamics has led them to question the reliability of short-term planning strategies.
- They might not agree with the author that one way to survive rapidly changing conditions comes from long-range planning.
- They consider the mobility of capital to be a necessary condition for the growth of new technology.

## VERBAL EXPLANATIONS

28. **D** The subject of the question is the financial analysts in lines 44–47 and the task of the question is the word *suggests*, which means this is an inference question. Determine which of the answer choices is true based on the information in the passage. The passage states that *financial analysts wonder why companies should bother planning two years ahead* and then goes on to state that *it is this pace of change that makes planning so crucial. Now, more than ever, companies have to stay alert to the marketplace.* The financial analysts' argument is presented and the author provides a reason why that argument is incorrect. Choice (A) is a reversal of the stance of the financial analysts, so eliminate (A). Choice (B) is a reversal of the stance of the financial analysts, so eliminate (B). Choice (C) is a reversal, as *short-term planning* is not the focus of the passage. Eliminate (C). Choice (D) is a good summary of the financial analysts mentioned in the passage, so keep (D). Choice (E) uses the recycled language *mobility of capital,* but this is not used in the context of the financial analysts. Eliminate (E). The correct answer is (D).

## QUESTIONS

29. The Internal Revenue Service has directed that taxpayers who generate no self-employment income can no longer deduct home offices, home office expenses, <u>or nothing that was already</u> depreciated as a business expense the previous year.

- ⬭ or nothing that was already
- ⬭ or that was already
- ⬭ or anything that was already
- ⬭ and anything
- ⬭ and nothing that already was

## VERBAL EXPLANATIONS

29. **C** The underlined portion of the sentence contains the idiom *or nothing* so check for idiom errors. The idiom *no...nothing* is an incorrect idiom. Eliminate (A) and look for obvious repeaters. Choice (E) also contains the incorrect idiom *no... nothing,* so eliminate (E) as well. Evaluate the remaining answer choices individually looking for reasons to eliminate each.

Choice (B) eliminates the noun *nothing* which creates a parallel construction error as the list *home offices, home office expenses,* or *that* is not parallel. Eliminate (B) for a parallel construction error. Choice (C) fixes the original error by using the proper idiom *no...anything,* and commits no new errors, so keep (C). Choice (D) fixes the original error by using the proper idiom *no...anything,* but commits another error with the use of the word *and* which is a clauses and connectors error. Eliminate (D).

## QUESTIONS

30. Informed people generally assimilate information from several divergent sources before coming to an opinion. However, most popular news organizations view foreign affairs solely through the eyes of our State Department. In reporting the political crisis in a foreign country, news organizations must endeavor to find alternative sources of information.

Which of the following inferences can be drawn from the argument above?

- To the degree that a news source gives an account of another country that mirrors that of our State Department, that reporting is suspect.
- To protect their integrity, news media should avoid the influence of State Department releases in their coverage of foreign affairs.
- Reporting that is not influenced by the State Department is usually more accurate than are other accounts.
- The alternative sources of information mentioned in the passage might not share the same views as the State Department.
- A report cannot be seen as influenced by the State Department if it accurately depicts the events in a foreign country.

## VERBAL EXPLANATIONS

30. **D** The question stem asks which of the answer choices is true based on the information in the passage. The question uses the word *inference* to describe the answer choices, so the correct answer has to be provable based on the passage. Choice (A) implies that the State Department's views are always likely to diverge from other news sources, which is extreme language. Eliminate (A). Choice (B) implies that the State Department should never be used as a news source, which is also extreme language that is not supported by the passage. Eliminate (B). Choice (C) is out of scope because the passage gives no information about *reporting that is not influenced by the State Department.* Eliminate (C). Choice (D) is supported by the passage because the *alternative sources* are akin to the *divergent sources* mentioned in the passage as necessary for coming to an opinion. Keep (D). Choice (E) uses the extreme language *cannot* and the conversation about accuracy is out of scope. Eliminate (E). The correct answer is (D).

## QUESTIONS

31. When automatic teller machines were first installed in the 1980s, bank officials promised they would be faster, more reliable, and less prone to make errors than their human counterparts.

- they would be faster, more reliable, and less prone to make errors
- they would be faster, more reliable, and that they would be less prone for making errors
- the machines would be faster, more reliable, and less prone to errors
- the machines were faster, more reliable, and errors would occur much less
- faster, more reliable machines, and that errors would be less prone

## VERBAL EXPLANATIONS

31. **C** The underlined portion of the sentence contains the pronoun *they* so check to make sure that the pronoun has a clear referent and is in agreement. The pronoun *they* could refer to either *automatic teller machines* or *bank officials.* This is an ambiguous pronoun, so eliminate (A) and look for obvious repeaters. Choice (B) is an obvious repeater as it also uses the pronoun *they,* so eliminate (B). Evaluate the remaining answer choices individually. Choice (C) fixes the original error by replacing *they* with *the machines* and commits no further errors, so keep (C). Choice (D) also fixes the original error but contains the construction *faster, more reliable...errors would occur much less* which is not parallel, so eliminate choice (D). Choice (E) contains the construction *faster, more reliable...that errors would be less prone,* which is not parallel, so eliminate (E). The correct answer is (C).

32. With its plan to create a wildlife sanctuary out of previously unused landfill, Sweden is but one of a number of industrialized nations that is accepting its responsibility to protect endangered species and promote conservation.

- is accepting its responsibility to protect endangered species and promote
- is accepting its responsibility for protecting endangered species and promoting
- are accepting its responsibility to protect endangered species and promoting
- are accepting of their responsibility to protect endangered species and to promote
- are accepting their responsibility to protect endangered species and promote

32. **E** The underlined portion of the sentence contains the verb *is* so check to make sure the verb agrees with its intended subject. The verb *is* in the underlined portion seems to agree with the subject of the sentence, *Sweden,* but in fact, the noun *is* must agree with *nations,* which is plural. Eliminate (A) and look for obvious repeaters. Choice (B) uses the verb *is* so eliminate (B). Evaluate the remaining answer choices individually. Choice (C) keeps the singular pronoun *its,* which is a pronoun agreement error with the noun nations. Eliminate (C). Choice (D) contains the clunky phrase *accepting of.* The *of* is an unnecessary preposition that is an incorrect idiom. Eliminate (D). Choice (E) fixes the original error and commits no new errors. The correct answer is (E).

## QUESTIONS

33. A decade after a logging operation in India began cutting down trees in a territory that serves as a sanctuary for Bengal tigers, the incidence of tigers attacking humans in nearby villages has increased by 300 percent. Because the logging operation has reduced the number of acres of woodland per tiger on average from 15 acres to approximately 12 acres, scientists have theorized that tigers must need a minimum number of acres of woodland in order to remain content.

Which of the following statements, if true, would most strengthen the scientists' hypothesis?

- In other wildlife areas in India where the number of acres of woodland per tiger remains at least 15 acres, there has been no increase in the number of tiger attacks on humans.
- Before the logging operation began, there were many fewer humans living in the area.
- The largest number of acres per tiger before the logging operation began was 32 acres per tiger in one area of the sanctuary, whereas the smallest number of acres per tiger after the logging operation was 9 acres.
- Other species of wild animals have begun competing with the Bengal tigers for the dwindling food supply.
- The Bengal tiger has become completely extinct in other areas of Asia.

## VERBAL EXPLANATIONS

33. **A** The question asks which of the answer choices *would most strengthen the scientists hypothesis*, so this is a strengthen question. The argument uses a causal reasoning pattern, so identify the conclusion, premise, and any assumptions. The conclusion is that *tigers must need a minimum number of acres of woodland...to remain content.* The premise is that the *logging operation* which has *reduced the number of acres of woodland per tiger* has caused the increase in the *incidence of tigers attacking humans in nearby villages.* That standard assumption of a causal argument is that there is no other cause and it is not a coincidence. To strengthen the argument, the answer choices need to provide evidence that there is no other cause for the tiger attacks or it is not a coincidence that the logging and the tiger attacks are not related. Choice (A) provides evidence that it is not a coincidence, so keep (A). Choice (B) gives an alternate cause for the increase in tiger attacks—in other words, it weakens the argument instead of strengthening it. Eliminate (B). Choice (C) adds details without really strengthening the argument, so (C) is out of scope. Eliminate (C). Choice (D) weakens the scientists' hypothesis by presenting a possible alternate cause for the tigers' attacks on humans. Eliminate (D). Choice (E) emphasizes the seriousness of the problem without shedding light on its cause, so (E) is out of scope. Eliminate (E). The correct answer is (A).

## QUESTIONS

34. The machine press union and company management were not able to communicate effectively, and it was a major cause of the 1999 strike in Seattle.

- The machine press union and company management were not able to communicate effectively, and it
- Communications between the machine press union and company management were not effective, and it
- For the machine press union and company management, to be unable to communicate effectively
- The inability of the machine press union and company management to communicate effectively
- The machine press union, being unable to communicate effectively with company management,

## VERBAL EXPLANATIONS

34. **D** The underlined portion of the sentence contains the pronoun *it,* so check for agreement and ambiguity. The word *it* could refer to either *union* or *management,* but neither of those options makes sense. Instead, what *it* intends to refer to is that the two sides were *not able to communicate effectively.* This is not clear from the current construction, so eliminate (A) for a pronoun ambiguity error and look for obvious repeaters. Choice (B) obviously repeats the error, so eliminate (B) as well. Evaluate each remaining choice individually. Choice (C) contains a verb tense error with the verb *to be* which does not match tense with the past tense verb *was.* Eliminate (C). Choice (D) fixes the original error by removing the pronoun *it* and referring directly to the *inability…to communicate.* This choice does not commit any new errors, so keep (D). Choice (E) fixes the original error but is overly wordy and awkward in comparison to (D). Eliminate (E). The correct answer is (D).

## QUESTIONS

35. A greater number of fresh vegetables are sold in City *X* than in City *Y*. Therefore, the people in City *X* have better nutritional habits than those in City *Y*.

Each of the following, if true, weakens the conclusion above EXCEPT:

- City *X* has more people living in it than City *Y*.
- Most of the people in City *Y* work in City *X* and buy their vegetables there.
- The people in City *X* buy many of their vegetables as decorations, not to eat.
- The per capita consumption of junk food in City *X* is three times that of City *Y*.
- The average price per pound of vegetables in City *Y* is lower than the average price per pound of vegetables in City *X*.

## VERBAL EXPLANATIONS

35. **E** The question stem states *weakens the conclusion* so this is a weaken question. The question stem also uses the word *EXCEPT* so the task of the question is to determine which of the answer choices does not weaken the conclusion. The conclusion of the argument is that *the people in City X have better nutritional habits than those in City Y.* The premise of the argument is that the *greater number of fresh vegetables are sold in City X than in City Y.* Evaluate the answer choices individually, looking for one that does not weaken the conclusion. Choice (A) weakens the conclusion because if there are more people in City *X* than in City *Y*, then that explains why there are more fresh vegetables sold. Eliminate (A). Choice (B) weakens the argument because it provides another reason why more vegetables are sold in City *X* than in City *Y*. Eliminate (B). Choice (C) weakens the argument because it provides an alternate reason why more vegetables are sold in City *X* than are sold in City *Y* that is independent of *better nutritional habits.* Eliminate (C). Choice (D) also weakens the conclusion because it challenges the statement that *people in City X have better nutritional habits.* Eliminate (D). Choice (E) suggests that vegetables are cheaper in City *Y*, which does not weaken the argument. The correct answer is (E).

## QUESTIONS

36. Heavy metals, toxic waste by-products that can cause tumors in fish, are generally found in the waters off industrial shorelines, but have been discovered in trace amounts even in the relatively pristine waters of the South Pacific.

- ⬭ are generally found in the waters off industrial shorelines, but have been discovered in trace amounts even
- ⬭ are generally to be found in the waters off industrial shorelines, and have even been discovered in trace amounts
- ⬭ can, in general, be found in the waters off industrial shorelines, and have been discovered in trace amounts even
- ⬭ had generally been found in the waters off industrial shorelines, but have even been discovered in trace amounts
- ⬭ are found generally in the waters off industrial shorelines, but have been discovered in a trace amount even

## VERBAL EXPLANATIONS

36. **A** The sentence is correct as written. The underlined portion of the sentence contains the plural verb *are* which is the correct tense and the conjunction *but* which properly connects the two ideas in the sentence. Evaluate the remaining answer choices individually. Choice (B) replaces the conjunction *but* with the conjunction *and* which gives the impression that the second half of the sentence is an added thought instead of a new development. This changes the meaning of the sentence. Eliminate (B). Choice (C) makes the same error as (B), so eliminate (C). Choice (D) changes the verb tense from the present *are* to the past tense *had,* which is not parallel with the remainder of the sentence. Eliminate (D). Choice (E) uses the phrase *in a trace amount,* which does not agree with the plural *heavy metals.* Eliminate (E). The correct answer is (A).

Questions 37–40 are based on the following passage:

In Roman times, defeated enemies were generally put to death as criminals for having offended the emperor of Rome. In the Middle Ages, however, the practice of ransoming, or returning prisoners in exchange for money, became common. Though some saw this custom as a step toward a more humane society, the primary reasons behind it were economic rather than humanitarian.

In those times, rulers had only a limited ability to raise taxes. They could neither force their subjects to fight nor pay them to do so. The promise of material compensation in the form of goods and ransom was therefore the only way of inducing combatants to participate in a war. In the Middle Ages, the predominant incentive for the individual soldier was the expectation of spoils. Although collecting ransom clearly brought financial gain, keeping a prisoner and arranging for his exchange had its costs. Consequently, procedures were devised to reduce transaction costs.

One such device was a rule asserting that the prisoner had to assess his own value. This compelled the prisoner to establish a value without too much distortion; indicating too low a value would increase the captive's chances of being killed, while indicating too high a value would either ruin him financially or create a prohibitively expensive ransom that would also result in death.

## QUESTIONS

37. The primary purpose of the passage is to

- ⬭ discuss the economic basis of the medieval practice of exchanging prisoners for ransom
- ⬭ examine the history of the treatment of prisoners of war
- ⬭ emphasize the importance of a warrior's code of honor during the Middle Ages
- ⬭ explore a way of reducing the costs of ransom
- ⬭ demonstrate why warriors of the Middle Ages looked forward to battles

## VERBAL EXPLANATIONS

37. **A** The subject of the question is the passage as a whole and the task of the question is to determine the *primary purpose* of the passage. The passage is focused on discussing the *primary reasons* behind *ransoming* prisoners. Evaluate the answer choices individually. Choice (A) correctly summarizes the primary purpose of the passage, which is stated in the first paragraph sentence that states *the primary reasons behind* [ransoming] *were economic rather than humanitarian.* Choice (B) is a memory trap as the passage begins by discussing the historical treatment of prisoners of war, but this is not the primary purpose. Eliminate (B). Choice (C) discusses the *warrior's code of honor,* which is out of scope of the passage. Eliminate (C). Choice (D) is a memory trap as reducing the costs of ransom is part of the passage but not the primary purpose. Eliminate (D). Choice (E) is out of scope of the passage. Eliminate (E). The correct answer is (A).

## QUESTIONS

38. It can be inferred from the passage that a medieval soldier

- ◯ was less likely to kill captured members of opposing armies than was a soldier of the Roman Empire
- ◯ operated on a basically independent level and was motivated solely by economic incentives
- ◯ had few economic options and chose to fight because it was the only way to earn an adequate living
- ◯ was motivated to spare prisoners' lives by humanitarian rather than economic ideals
- ◯ had no respect for his captured enemies since captives were typically regarded as weak

## VERBAL EXPLANATIONS

38. **A** The subject of the question is the *medieval soldier* and the task of the question is found in the word *inference.* Determine what is true about the medieval soldier based on the information in the passage. Choice (A) is supported by the information in the first paragraph of the passage, so keep (A). Choice (B) is an example of extreme language because the soldiers are not *basically independent.* Eliminate (B). Choice (C) is a memory trap from the passage, but it is also an example of extreme language because the passage does not state that combat was the *only way to earn an adequate living.* Eliminate (C). Choice (D) is a reversal of the information in the passage from the first paragraph. Eliminate (D). Choice (E) is extreme language, as the passage does not support the idea that medieval soldiers had *no respect* for captured enemies. Eliminate (E). The correct answer is (A).

## QUESTIONS

39. Which of the following best describes the change in policy from executing prisoners in Roman times to ransoming prisoners in the Middle Ages?

- ⬭ The emperors of Rome demanded more respect than did medieval rulers, and thus Roman subjects went to greater lengths to defend their nation.
- ⬭ It was a reflection of the lesser degree of direct control medieval rulers had over their subjects.
- ⬭ It became a show of strength and honor for warriors of the Middle Ages to be able to capture and return their enemies.
- ⬭ Medieval soldiers were not as humanitarian as their ransoming practices might have indicated.
- ⬭ Medieval soldiers demonstrated more concern about economic policy than did their Roman counterparts.

## VERBAL EXPLANATIONS

39. **B** The subject of the question is the *change in policy from executing prisoners in Roman times to ransoming prisoners in the Middle Ages* and the task of the question is to determine which of the answer choices *best describes* the change. The passage states that *rulers...could neither force their subjects to fight nor pay them to do so* and that *the promise of material compensation in the form of goods and random was...the only way of inducing combatants to participate in a war.* Evaluate the answer choices individually. Choice (A) is out of scope, as the passage is not concerned with how much *respect* the rulers of the different time periods demanded. Eliminate (A). Choice (B) is a good summary of the information in the passage. Keep (B). Choice (C) is out of scope as *strength and honor of the Middle Ages* is not reflective of the reason for the change in policy. Eliminate (C). Choice (D) is a memory trap as the passage does discuss the word *humanitarian,* but this is not a description of the change in policy. Eliminate (D). Choice (E) is also out of scope, so eliminate (E). The correct answer is (B).

## QUESTIONS

40. The author uses the phrase "without too much distortion" (lines 24–25) in order to

- ◯ indicate that prisoners would fairly assess their worth
- ◯ emphasize the important role medieval prisoners played in determining whether they should be ransomed
- ◯ explain how prisoners often paid more than an appropriate ransom in order to increase their chances for survival
- ◯ suggest that captors and captives often had understanding relationships
- ◯ show that when in prison a soldier's view could become distorted

## VERBAL EXPLANATIONS

40. **A** The subject of the question is the quoted phrase and the task is to determine why the author uses the phrase. The phrase from the passage is mentioned in relationship with the concept that a prisoner had to *assess his own value.* The phrase is part of a description of a ransom value that was neither too low nor too high. Evaluate the answer choices individually. Choice (A) is a good summary of the reason for using the phrase, so keep (A). Choice (B) is a reversal of the information in the passage because the prisoners were not able to determine *whether they should be ransomed,* only how much they were ransomed for. Eliminate (B). Choice (C) is a reversal of the information in the passage because the prisoners did not pay more; they only set the value. Eliminate (C). Choice (D) is an example of extreme language, as captors and captives did not have an *understanding* relationship. Eliminate (D). Choice (E) is a reversal, as the information in the passage shows that prisoners do not become distorted. Eliminate (E). The correct answer is (A).

# Part X The Princeton Review GMAT Math and Verbal Practice Bins and Explanations

# Chapter 32 GMAT Math and Verbal Practice Bins

Once you know your current scoring level from taking the Warm-Up Questions, use the "bins" in the following pages to improve your performance.

If you got six or fewer math questions correct on the Warm-Up Questions, start by practicing with the problems in Math Bin 1. If you got 6–13 math questions correct on the Warm-Up Questions, start by practicing with the problems in Math Bin 2. If you got 14 or more math questions correct, practice with the problems in Math Bins 3 and 4.

If you got six or fewer verbal questions correct on the Warm-up Questions, start by practicing with the problems in Verbal Bin 1. If you got 6–13 verbal questions correct on the Warm-Up Questions, start by practicing with the problems in Verbal Bin 2. If you got 14 or more verbal questions correct, practice with the problems in Verbal Bin 3.

## Math Test
## Bin 1—Easier Questions
## 26 Questions

**This test is composed of both problem solving questions and data sufficiency questions.**

**Problem Solving Directions:** Solve each problem and choose the best of the answer choices provided.

**Data Sufficiency Directions:** Each data sufficiency problem consists of a question and two statements, labeled (1) and (2), which contain certain data. Using these data and your knowledge of mathematics and everyday facts (such as the number of days in July or the meaning of *counterclockwise*), decide whether the data given are sufficient for answering the question and then indicate one of the following answer choices:

- Statement (1) ALONE is sufficient, but statement (2) alone is not sufficient.
- Statement (2) ALONE is sufficient, but statement (1) alone is not sufficient.
- BOTH statements TOGETHER are sufficient, but NEITHER statement ALONE is sufficient.
- EACH statement ALONE is sufficient.
- Statements (1) and (2) TOGETHER are not sufficient.

---

1. What percent of 112 is 14 ?

- 0.125%
- 8%
- 12.5%
- 125%
- 800%

2. The number of flights leaving a certain airport doubles during every one-hour period between 9 A.M. and noon; after noon, the number of flights leaving from the airport doubles during every two-hour period. If 4 flights left from the airport between 9 and 10 A.M., how many flights left the airport between 2 and 4 P.M. ?

- 32
- 48
- 64
- 128
- 256

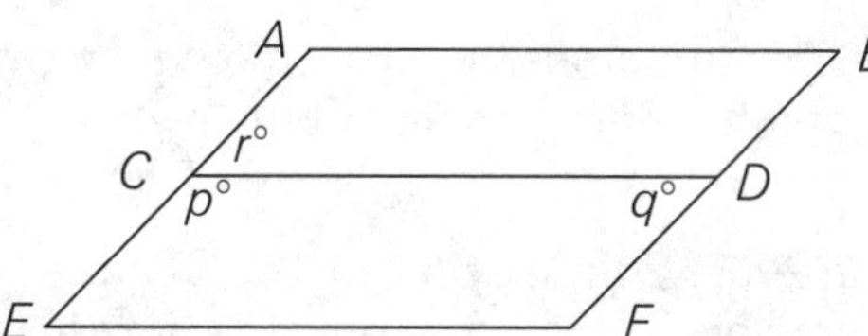


3. If both *ABDC* and *CDFE* are parallelograms, what is $q + r$ ?

(1) $r = 70$

(2) $p = 110$

- Statement (1) ALONE is sufficient, but statement (2) alone is not sufficient.
- Statement (2) ALONE is sufficient, but statement (1) alone is not sufficient.
- BOTH statements TOGETHER are sufficient, but NEITHER statement ALONE is sufficient.
- EACH statement ALONE is sufficient.
- Statements (1) and (2) TOGETHER are not sufficient.

GO ON TO THE NEXT PAGE.

4. Chris's convertible gets gas mileage that is 40 percent greater than that of Stan's SUV. If Harry's hatchback gets gas mileage that is 15 percent greater than that of Chris's convertible, then Harry's hatchback gets gas mileage that is what percent greater than that of Stan's SUV?

- ○ 25%
- ○ 46%
- ○ 55%
- ○ 61%
- ○ 66%

5. If $x$ is equal to 1 more than the product of 3 and $z$, and $y$ is equal to 1 less than the product of 2 and $z$, then $2x$ is how much greater than $3y$ when $z$ is 4 ?

- ○ 1
- ○ 2
- ○ 3
- ○ 5
- ○ 6

6. In 2005, did Company *A* have more than twice the number of employees that Company *B* did?

(1) In 2005, Company *A* had 11,500 more employees than did Company *B*.

(2) In 2005, the 3,000 employees with advanced degrees at Company *A* made up 12.5 percent of that company's total number employees, and the 2,500 employees with advanced degrees at Company *B* made up 20 percent of that company's total number of employees.

- ○ Statement (1) ALONE is sufficient, but statement (2) alone is not sufficient.
- ○ Statement (2) ALONE is sufficient, but statement (1) alone is not sufficient.
- ○ BOTH statements TOGETHER are sufficient, but NEITHER statement ALONE is sufficient.
- ○ EACH statement ALONE is sufficient.
- ○ Statements (1) and (2) TOGETHER are not sufficient.

7. Is $x^3$ equal to 125 ?

(1) $x > 4$

(2) $x < 6$

- ○ Statement (1) ALONE is sufficient, but statement (2) alone is not sufficient.
- ○ Statement (2) ALONE is sufficient, but statement (1) alone is not sufficient.
- ○ BOTH statements TOGETHER are sufficient, but NEITHER statement ALONE is sufficient.
- ○ EACH statement ALONE is sufficient.
- ○ Statements (1) and (2) TOGETHER are not sufficient.

8. Bob leaves point *A* and drives due west to point *B*. From point *B*, he drives due south to point *C*. How far is Bob from his original location?

(1) Point *A* is 24 miles from point *B*.

(2) Point *B* is 18 miles from point *C*.

- ○ Statement (1) ALONE is sufficient, but statement (2) alone is not sufficient.
- ○ Statement (2) ALONE is sufficient, but statement (1) alone is not sufficient.
- ○ BOTH statements TOGETHER are sufficient, but NEITHER statement ALONE is sufficient.
- ○ EACH statement ALONE is sufficient.
- ○ Statements (1) and (2) TOGETHER are not sufficient.

GO ON TO THE NEXT PAGE.

9. The formula $M = \sqrt{l^2 + w^2 + d^2}$ describes the relationship between the length of $M$, which is the longest line that can be drawn in a rectangular solid, and the length, $l$, width, $w$, and depth, $d$, of that rectangular solid. The longest line that can be drawn in a rectangular solid with a length of 12, a width of 4, and a depth of 3 is how much longer than the longest line that can drawn in a rectangular solid with a length of 6, a width of 3, and a depth of 2 ?

- 5
- 6
- 7
- 9
- 13

10. Is the average (arithmetic mean) of $a$, $b$, and $c$ equal to 8 ?

(1) Three times the sum of $a$, $b$, and $c$ is equal to 72.

(2) The sum of $2a$, $2b$, and $2c$ is equal to 48.

- Statement (1) ALONE is sufficient, but statement (2) alone is not sufficient.
- Statement (2) ALONE is sufficient, but statement (1) alone is not sufficient.
- BOTH statements TOGETHER are sufficient, but NEITHER statement ALONE is sufficient.
- EACH statement ALONE is sufficient.
- Statements (1) and (2) TOGETHER are not sufficient.

11. $\sqrt{\sqrt{\left(1 + \frac{17}{64}\right)}} =$

- $\frac{\sqrt{34}}{8}$
- $\frac{3\sqrt{2}}{4}$
- $\frac{9}{8}$
- $\frac{\sqrt{68}}{4}$
- $\frac{3\sqrt{2}}{2}$

12. A certain stadium is currently full to $\frac{13}{16}$ of its maximum seating capacity. What is the maximum seating capacity of the stadium?

(1) If 1,250 people were to enter the stadium, the stadium would be full to $\frac{15}{16}$ of its maximum seating capacity.

(2) If 2,500 people were to leave the stadium, the stadium would be full to $\frac{9}{16}$ of its maximum seating capacity.

- Statement (1) ALONE is sufficient, but statement (2) alone is not sufficient.
- Statement (2) ALONE is sufficient, but statement (1) alone is not sufficient.
- BOTH statements TOGETHER are sufficient, but NEITHER statement ALONE is sufficient.
- EACH statement ALONE is sufficient.
- Statements (1) and (2) TOGETHER are not sufficient.

GO ON TO THE NEXT PAGE.

13. Andre has already saved $\frac{3}{7}$ of the cost of a new car, and he has calculated that he will be able to save $\frac{2}{5}$ of the remaining amount before the end of the summer. What fraction of the cost of the new car will he still need to save after the end of the summer?

- $\frac{6}{35}$
- $\frac{8}{35}$
- $\frac{12}{35}$
- $\frac{23}{35}$
- $\frac{29}{35}$

{1, 4, 6, *y*}

14. If the average (arithmetic mean) of the set of numbers above is 6, then what is the median?

- 5
- 6
- 7
- 13
- 24

15. A store sells a six-pack of soda for $2.70. If this represents a savings of 10 percent of the individual price of cans of soda, then what is the price of a single can of soda?

- $ 0.35
- $ 0.40
- $ 0.45
- $ 0.50
- $ 0.55

16. If Beth spent $400 of her earnings last month on rent, how much did Beth earn last month?

(1) Beth saved $\frac{1}{3}$ of her earnings last month and spent half of the remainder on rent.

(2) Beth earned twice as much this month as last month.

- Statement (1) ALONE is sufficient, but statement (2) alone is not sufficient.
- Statement (2) ALONE is sufficient, but statement (1) alone is not sufficient.
- BOTH statements TOGETHER are sufficient, but NEITHER statement ALONE is sufficient.
- EACH statement ALONE is sufficient.
- Statements (1) and (2) TOGETHER are not sufficient.

17. If *n* is an integer, is *n* even?

(1) 2*n* is an even integer.

(2) $n - 1$ is an odd integer.

- Statement (1) ALONE is sufficient, but statement (2) alone is not sufficient.
- Statement (2) ALONE is sufficient, but statement (1) alone is not sufficient.
- BOTH statements TOGETHER are sufficient, but NEITHER statement ALONE is sufficient.
- EACH statement ALONE is sufficient.
- Statements (1) and (2) TOGETHER are not sufficient.

GO ON TO THE NEXT PAGE.

18. At apartment complex $Z$, 30 percent of the residents are men over the age of 18, and 40 percent are women over the age of 18. If there are 24 children living in the complex, how many total residents live in apartment complex $Z$?

- ◯ 32
- ◯ 80
- ◯ 94
- ◯ 112
- ◯ 124

19. Over the course of a soccer season, 30 percent of the players on a team scored goals. What is the ratio of players on the team who scored goals to those who did not?

- ◯ 3 to 10
- ◯ 1 to 3
- ◯ 3 to 7
- ◯ 1 to 1
- ◯ 3 to 1

20. At a restaurant, Luis left a tip for his waiter equal to 20 percent of his entire dinner check, including tax. What was the amount of the dinner check?

(1) The sum of the dinner check and the tip was $16.80.

(2) Luis's tip consisted of two bills and four coins.

- ◯ Statement (1) ALONE is sufficient, but statement (2) alone is not sufficient.
- ◯ Statement (2) ALONE is sufficient, but statement (1) alone is not sufficient.
- ◯ BOTH statements TOGETHER are sufficient, but NEITHER statement ALONE is sufficient.
- ◯ EACH statement ALONE is sufficient.
- ◯ Statements (1) and (2) TOGETHER are not sufficient.

21. Which sport utility vehicle has a higher list price, the Touristo or the Leisure?

(1) The list price of the Leisure is $\frac{5}{6}$ the list price of the Touristo.

(2) The list price of the Touristo is 1.2 times the list price of the Leisure.

- ◯ Statement (1) ALONE is sufficient, but statement (2) alone is not sufficient.
- ◯ Statement (2) ALONE is sufficient, but statement (1) alone is not sufficient.
- ◯ BOTH statements TOGETHER are sufficient, but NEITHER statement ALONE is sufficient.
- ◯ EACH statement ALONE is sufficient.
- ◯ Statements (1) and (2) TOGETHER are not sufficient.

GO ON TO THE NEXT PAGE.

22. In the circle above, center $O$ is intersected by 2 straight lines, and $3a = b$. What is the value of $b - a$ ?

- 2
- 30
- 45
- 90
- 135

23. What is the value of integer $w$ ?

(1) $w$ is a multiple of 3.

(2) $420 < w < 425$

- Statement (1) ALONE is sufficient, but statement (2) alone is not sufficient.
- Statement (2) ALONE is sufficient, but statement (1) alone is not sufficient.
- BOTH statements TOGETHER are sufficient, but NEITHER statement ALONE is sufficient.
- EACH statement ALONE is sufficient.
- Statements (1) and (2) TOGETHER are not sufficient.

24. What is the quotient when 0.25% of 600 is divided by 0.25 of 600 ?

- 10
- 1
- 0.1
- 0.01
- 0.001

25. A certain town's economic development council has 21 members. If the number of females on the council is 3 less than 3 times the number of males on the council, then the town's economic development council has how many male members?

- 5
- 6
- 7
- 9
- 15

26. Roger can chop down 4 trees in an hour. How long does it take Vincent to chop down 4 trees?

(1) Vincent spends 6 hours per day chopping down trees.

(2) Vincent takes twice as long as Roger to chop down trees.

- Statement (1) ALONE is sufficient, but statement (2) alone is not sufficient.
- Statement (2) ALONE is sufficient, but statement (1) alone is not sufficient.
- BOTH statements TOGETHER are sufficient, but NEITHER statement ALONE is sufficient.
- EACH statement ALONE is sufficient.
- Statements (1) and (2) TOGETHER are not sufficient.

END OF BIN.

## Math Test
## Bin 2—Medium Questions
## 27 Questions

**This test is composed of both problem solving questions and data sufficiency questions.**

**Problem Solving Directions:** Solve each problem and choose the best of the answer choices provided.

**Data Sufficiency Directions:** Each data sufficiency problem consists of a question and two statements, labeled (1) and (2), which contain certain data. Using these data and your knowledge of mathematics and everyday facts (such as the number of days in July or the meaning of *counterclockwise*), decide whether the data given are sufficient for answering the question and then indicate one of the following answer choices:

- ◯ Statement (1) ALONE is sufficient, but statement (2) alone is not sufficient.
- ◯ Statement (2) ALONE is sufficient, but statement (1) alone is not sufficient.
- ◯ BOTH statements TOGETHER are sufficient, but NEITHER statement ALONE is sufficient.
- ◯ EACH statement ALONE is sufficient.
- ◯ Statements (1) and (2) TOGETHER are not sufficient.

---

1. If $x = \dfrac{\frac{5}{9}+\frac{15}{27}+\frac{45}{81}}{3}$, then $\sqrt{1-x} =$

- ◯ $\dfrac{\sqrt{5}}{9}$
- ◯ $\dfrac{5}{9}$
- ◯ $\dfrac{2}{3}$
- ◯ $\dfrac{\sqrt{5}}{3}$
- ◯ $\dfrac{15}{9}$

2. Steven has run a certain number of laps around a track at an average (arithmetic mean) time per lap of 51 seconds. If he runs one additional lap in 39 seconds and reduces his average time per lap to 49 seconds, how many laps did he run at an average time per lap of 51 seconds?

- ◯ 2
- ◯ 5
- ◯ 6
- ◯ 10
- ◯ 12

3. $200^2 - 2(200)(199) + 199^2 =$

- ◯ –79,201
- ◯ –200
- ◯ 1
- ◯ 200
- ◯ 79,999

GO ON TO THE NEXT PAGE.

4. If $x \neq \frac{1}{2}$, then $\frac{6x^2 + 11x - 7}{2x - 1} =$

- $3x + 7$
- $3x - 7$
- $3x + 1$
- $x + 7$
- $x - 7$

5. If Amy drove the distance from her home to the beach in less than 2 hours, was her average speed greater than 60 miles per hour?

(1) The distance that Amy drove from her home to the beach was less than 125 miles.

(2) The distance that Amy drove from her home to the beach was greater than 122 miles.

- Statement (1) ALONE is sufficient, but statement (2) alone is not sufficient.
- Statement (2) ALONE is sufficient, but statement (1) alone is not sufficient.
- BOTH statements TOGETHER are sufficient, but NEITHER statement ALONE is sufficient.
- EACH statement ALONE is sufficient.
- Statements (1) and (2) TOGETHER are not sufficient.

6. If $x = m - 1$, which of the following is true when $m = \frac{1}{2}$?

- $x^0 > x^2 > x^3 > x^1$
- $x^0 > x^2 > x^1 > x^3$
- $x^0 > x^1 > x^2 > x^3$
- $x^2 > x^0 > x^3 > x^1$
- $x^3 > x^2 > x^1 > x^0$

7. If a comedian plays two shows and twice as many tickets are available for the evening show as for the afternoon show, what percentage of the total number of tickets available for both shows has been sold?

(1) A total of 450 tickets are available for both shows.

(2) Exactly $\frac{3}{5}$ of the tickets available for the afternoon show have been sold, and exactly $\frac{1}{5}$ of the tickets available for the evening show have been sold.

- Statement (1) ALONE is sufficient, but statement (2) alone is not sufficient.
- Statement (2) ALONE is sufficient, but statement (1) alone is not sufficient.
- BOTH statements TOGETHER are sufficient, but NEITHER statement ALONE is sufficient.
- EACH statement ALONE is sufficient.
- Statements (1) and (2) TOGETHER are not sufficient.

8. If $\frac{1}{y} = 2\frac{2}{3}$, then $\left(\frac{1}{y+1}\right)^2 =$

- $\frac{9}{64}$
- $\frac{3}{8}$
- $\frac{64}{121}$
- $\frac{121}{64}$
- $\frac{64}{9}$

GO ON TO THE NEXT PAGE.

9. An operation $\sim$ is defined by $a \sim b = \frac{a+b}{(ab)^2}$ for all numbers $a$ and $b$ such that $ab \neq 0$. If $c \neq 0$ and $a \sim c = 0$, then $c =$

- $-a$
- 0
- $\sqrt{a}$
- $a$
- $a^2$

10. If $x$ is a positive integer, is the greatest common factor of 150 and $x$ a prime number?

(1) $x$ is a prime number.

(2) $x < 4$

- Statement (1) ALONE is sufficient, but statement (2) alone is not sufficient.
- Statement (2) ALONE is sufficient, but statement (1) alone is not sufficient.
- BOTH statements TOGETHER are sufficient, but NEITHER statement ALONE is sufficient.
- EACH statement ALONE is sufficient.
- Statements (1) and (2) TOGETHER are not sufficient.

$X = \{9, 10, 11, 12\}$

$Y = \{2, 3, 4, 5\}$

11. If one number is chosen at random from each of the sets above and the number from Set $X$ is divided by the number from Set $Y$, what is the probability that the result is an integer?

- $\frac{1}{16}$
- $\frac{3}{8}$
- $\frac{1}{2}$
- $\frac{3}{4}$
- $\frac{15}{16}$

12. If $p$ and $q$ are integers, is $\frac{p+q}{2}$ an integer?

(1) $p < 17$

(2) $p = q$

- Statement (1) ALONE is sufficient, but statement (2) alone is not sufficient.
- Statement (2) ALONE is sufficient, but statement (1) alone is not sufficient.
- BOTH statements TOGETHER are sufficient, but NEITHER statement ALONE is sufficient.
- EACH statement ALONE is sufficient.
- Statements (1) and (2) TOGETHER are not sufficient.

GO ON TO THE NEXT PAGE.

13. A perfectly spherical satellite with a radius of 4 feet is being packed for shipment to its launch site. If the inside dimensions of the rectangular crates available for shipment, when measured in feet, are consecutive even integers, then what is the volume of the smallest available crate that can be used? (Note: the volume of a sphere is given by the equation $V = \frac{4}{3}\pi r^3$.)

- 48
- 192
- 480
- 960
- 1,680

14. Richard is 6 years older than David, and David is 8 years older than Scott. In 8 years, if Richard will be twice as old as Scott, then how old was David 4 years ago?

- 8
- 10
- 12
- 14
- 16

15. What is the value of $x$ ?

(1) $x^2 - 5x + 4 = 0$

(2) $x$ is not prime.

- Statement (1) ALONE is sufficient, but statement (2) alone is not sufficient.
- Statement (2) ALONE is sufficient, but statement (1) alone is not sufficient.
- BOTH statements TOGETHER are sufficient, but NEITHER statement ALONE is sufficient.
- EACH statement ALONE is sufficient.
- Statements (1) and (2) TOGETHER are not sufficient.

16. Sam and Jessica are invited to a dance. If there are 7 men and 7 women in total at the dance, and one woman and one man are chosen to lead the dance, what is the probability that Sam and Jessica will NOT be the pair chosen to lead the dance?

- $\frac{1}{49}$
- $\frac{1}{7}$
- $\frac{6}{7}$
- $\frac{47}{49}$
- $\frac{48}{49}$

17. What is the surface area of rectangular solid $Y$ ?

(1) The dimensions of one face of rectangular solid $Y$ are 2 by 3.

(2) The volume of rectangular solid $Y$ is 12.

- Statement (1) ALONE is sufficient, but statement (2) alone is not sufficient.
- Statement (2) ALONE is sufficient, but statement (1) alone is not sufficient.
- BOTH statements TOGETHER are sufficient, but NEITHER statement ALONE is sufficient.
- EACH statement ALONE is sufficient.
- Statements (1) and (2) TOGETHER are not sufficient.

GO ON TO THE NEXT PAGE.

18. A six-sided die with faces numbered one through six is rolled three times. What is the probability that the face with the number 6 on it will NOT be facing upward on all three rolls?

- ⬭ $\frac{1}{216}$
- ⬭ $\frac{1}{6}$
- ⬭ $\frac{2}{3}$
- ⬭ $\frac{17}{18}$
- ⬭ $\frac{215}{216}$

19. What is the sum of $x$, $y$, and $z$ ?

(1) $2x + y + 3z = 45$

(2) $x + 2y = 30$

- ⬭ Statement (1) ALONE is sufficient, but statement (2) alone is not sufficient.
- ⬭ Statement (2) ALONE is sufficient, but statement (1) alone is not sufficient.
- ⬭ BOTH statements TOGETHER are sufficient, but NEITHER statement ALONE is sufficient.
- ⬭ EACH statement ALONE is sufficient.
- ⬭ Statements (1) and (2) TOGETHER are not sufficient.

20. A department store receives a shipment of 1,000 shirts, for which it pays $9,000. The store sells the shirts at a price 80 percent above cost for one month, after which it reduces the price of the shirts to 20 percent above cost. The store sells 75 percent of the shirts during the first month and 50 percent of the remaining shirts afterward. How much gross income did sales of the shirts generate?

- ⬭ $10,000
- ⬭ $10,800
- ⬭ $12,150
- ⬭ $13,500
- ⬭ $16,200

21. David has three credit cards: a Passport card, an EverywhereCard, and an American Local card. He owes balances on all three cards. Does he owe the greatest balance on the EverywhereCard?

(1) The sum of the balances on his EverywhereCard and American Local card is $1,350, which is three times the balance on his Passport card.

(2) The balance on his EverywhereCard is $\frac{4}{3}$ of the balance on his Passport card and $\frac{4}{5}$ of the balance on his American Local card.

- ⬭ Statement (1) ALONE is sufficient, but statement (2) alone is not sufficient.
- ⬭ Statement (2) ALONE is sufficient, but statement (1) alone is not sufficient.
- ⬭ BOTH statements TOGETHER are sufficient, but NEITHER statement ALONE is sufficient.
- ⬭ EACH statement ALONE is sufficient.
- ⬭ Statements (1) and (2) TOGETHER are not sufficient.

GO ON TO THE NEXT PAGE.

22. Automobile $A$ is traveling at two-thirds the speed that Automobile $B$ is traveling. At what speed is Automobile $A$ traveling?

(1) If both automobiles increased their speed by 10 miles per hour, Automobile $A$ would be traveling at three-quarters the speed that Automobile $B$ would be traveling.

(2) If both automobiles decreased their speed by 10 miles per hour, Automobile $A$ would be traveling at half the speed that Automobile $B$ would be traveling.

- ◯ Statement (1) ALONE is sufficient, but statement (2) alone is not sufficient.
- ◯ Statement (2) ALONE is sufficient, but statement (1) alone is not sufficient.
- ◯ BOTH statements TOGETHER are sufficient, but NEITHER statement ALONE is sufficient.
- ◯ EACH statement ALONE is sufficient.
- ◯ Statements (1) and (2) TOGETHER are not sufficient.

23. $a$ and $b$ are nonzero integers such that $0.35a = 0.2b$. What is the value of $b$ in terms of $a$ ?

- ◯ $0.07a$
- ◯ $0.57a$
- ◯ $0.7a$
- ◯ $1.75a$
- ◯ $17.5a$

24. The Binary Ice Cream Shoppe sells two flavors of cones, vanilla and chocolate. On Friday, the ratio of vanilla cones sold to chocolate cones sold was 2 to 3. If the store sold 4 more vanilla cones, the ratio of vanilla cones sold to chocolate cones sold would have been 3 to 4. How many vanilla cones did the store sell on Friday?

- ◯ 32
- ◯ 35
- ◯ 42
- ◯ 48
- ◯ 54

25. Is integer $a$ a prime number?

(1) $2a$ has exactly three factors.

(2) $a$ is an even number.

- ◯ Statement (1) ALONE is sufficient, but statement (2) alone is not sufficient.
- ◯ Statement (2) ALONE is sufficient, but statement (1) alone is not sufficient.
- ◯ BOTH statements TOGETHER are sufficient, but NEITHER statement ALONE is sufficient.
- ◯ EACH statement ALONE is sufficient.
- ◯ Statements (1) and (2) TOGETHER are not sufficient.

26. Renee rides her bicycle 20 miles in $m$ minutes. If she rides $x$ miles in 10 minutes at the same rate, which of the following is an expression for $x$, in terms of $m$ ?

- ◯ $\frac{m}{200}$
- ◯ $\frac{m}{20}$
- ◯ $\frac{m}{2}$
- ◯ $2m$
- ◯ $\frac{200}{m}$

27. If $s$ and $w$ are integers, is $\frac{w}{5}$ an integer?

(1) $4s + 2$ is divisible by 5.

(2) $w + 3 = 4s$

- ◯ Statement (1) ALONE is sufficient, but statement (2) alone is not sufficient.
- ◯ Statement (2) ALONE is sufficient, but statement (1) alone is not sufficient.
- ◯ BOTH statements TOGETHER are sufficient, but NEITHER statement ALONE is sufficient.
- ◯ EACH statement ALONE is sufficient.
- ◯ Statements (1) and (2) TOGETHER are not sufficient.

END OF BIN.

## Math Test
## Bin 3—Medium-Hard Questions
## 26 Questions

**This test is composed of both problem solving questions and data sufficiency questions.**

**Problem Solving Directions:** Solve each problem and choose the best of the answer choices provided.

**Data Sufficiency Directions:** Each data sufficiency problem consists of a question and two statements, labeled (1) and (2), which contain certain data. Using these data and your knowledge of mathematics and everyday facts (such as the number of days in July or the meaning of *counterclockwise*), decide whether the data given are sufficient for answering the question and then indicate one of the following answer choices:

- Statement (1) ALONE is sufficient, but statement (2) alone is not sufficient.
- Statement (2) ALONE is sufficient, but statement (1) alone is not sufficient.
- BOTH statements TOGETHER are sufficient, but NEITHER statement ALONE is sufficient.
- EACH statement ALONE is sufficient.
- Statements (1) and (2) TOGETHER are not sufficient.

---

1. An electronics store normally sells all its merchandise at a 10 percent to 30 percent discount from the suggested retail price. During a sale, if the store were to deduct an additional 20 percent from the discounted price, what is the lowest price possible for an item with a suggested retail price of $260 ?

- $130.00
- $145.60
- $163.80
- $182.00
- $210.00

2. A certain gas station discounts the price per gallon of all gasoline purchased after the first 10 gallons by 10 percent. The total per gallon discount for 25 gallons of gas purchased at this station is what percent of the total per gallon discount for 20 gallons of gas?

- 80%
- 100%
- 116.7%
- 120%
- 140%

GO ON TO THE NEXT PAGE.

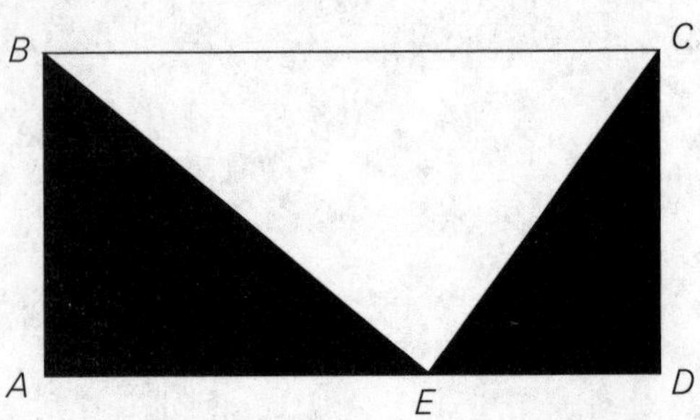


3. What is the area of the shaded region in the figure shown above?

(1) The area of rectangle $ABCD$ is 54.

(2) $AE = 2ED$

- Statement (1) ALONE is sufficient, but statement (2) alone is not sufficient.
- Statement (2) ALONE is sufficient, but statement (1) alone is not sufficient.
- BOTH statements TOGETHER are sufficient, but NEITHER statement ALONE is sufficient.
- EACH statement ALONE is sufficient.
- Statements (1) and (2) TOGETHER are not sufficient.

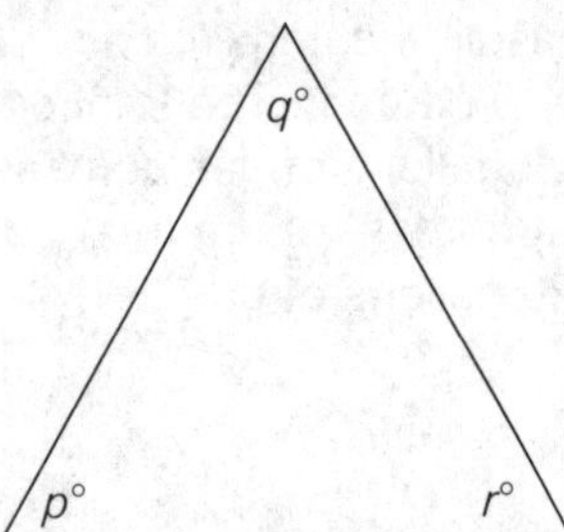


4. For the triangle shown above, does $p = q = 60$ ?

(1) $r = 180 - (p + r)$

(2) $p = 60$

- Statement (1) ALONE is sufficient, but statement (2) alone is not sufficient.
- Statement (2) ALONE is sufficient, but statement (1) alone is not sufficient.
- BOTH statements TOGETHER are sufficient, but NEITHER statement ALONE is sufficient.
- EACH statement ALONE is sufficient.
- Statements (1) and (2) TOGETHER are not sufficient.

5. During a certain two-week period, a video rental store rented only comedies, dramas, and action movies. If 70 percent of the movies rented were comedies, and of the remaining movies rented, 5 times as many dramas as action movies were rented and $A$ action movies were rented, then, in terms of $A$, how many of the movies rented were comedies?

- $\frac{A}{14}$
- $\frac{5A}{7}$
- $\frac{7A}{5}$
- $14A$
- $35A$

6. $x$, $y$, and $z$ are consecutive positive integers such that $x < y < z$. If the units digit of $x^2$ is 6 and the units digit of $y^2$ is 9, what is the units digit of $z^2$ ?

- 0
- 1
- 2
- 4
- 5

GO ON TO THE NEXT PAGE.

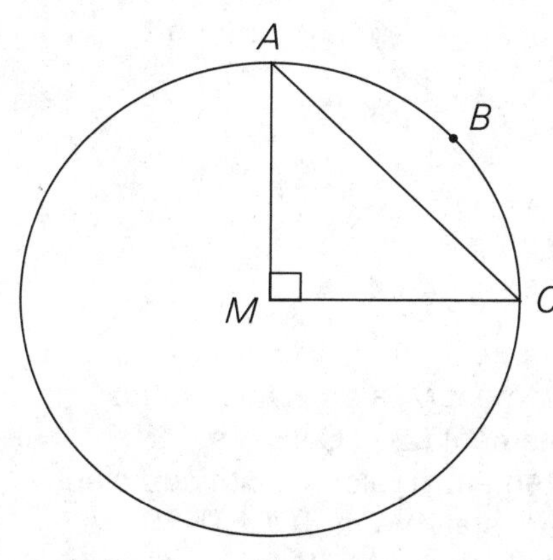


7. What is the area of the circle with center $M$ shown above?

(1) The length of $AC$ is $8\sqrt{2}$.

(2) The length of arc $ABC$ is $4\pi$.

- Statement (1) ALONE is sufficient, but statement (2) alone is not sufficient.
- Statement (2) ALONE is sufficient, but statement (1) alone is not sufficient.
- BOTH statements TOGETHER are sufficient, but NEITHER statement ALONE is sufficient.
- EACH statement ALONE is sufficient.
- Statements (1) and (2) TOGETHER are not sufficient.

8. If 70 percent of the female and 90 percent of the male students in the senior class at a certain school are going on the senior trip and the senior class is 60 percent female, what percent of the senior class is going on the senior trip?

- 82%
- 80%
- 78%
- 76%
- 72%

9. If $P$ is a set of integers and 3 is in $P$, is every positive multiple of 3 in $P$?

(1) For any integer in $P$, the sum of 3 and that integer is also in $P$.

(2) For any integer in $P$, that integer minus 3 is also in $P$.

- Statement (1) ALONE is sufficient, but statement (2) alone is not sufficient.
- Statement (2) ALONE is sufficient, but statement (1) alone is not sufficient.
- BOTH statements TOGETHER are sufficient, but NEITHER statement ALONE is sufficient.
- EACH statement ALONE is sufficient.
- Statements (1) and (2) TOGETHER are not sufficient.

10. A certain seafood restaurant gets a delivery of fresh seafood every day of the week. If the delivery company charges $d$ dollars per delivery and $c$ cents per delivered item and the restaurant has an average (arithmetic mean) of $x$ items delivered per day, then which of the following is an expression for the total cost, in dollars, of one week's deliveries?

- $\frac{7cdx}{100}$
- $d+\frac{7cx}{100}$
- $7d+\frac{xc}{100}$
- $7d+\frac{7xc}{100}$
- $7cdx$

GO ON TO THE NEXT PAGE.

11. Which of the following contains the interval two standard deviations from the mean of a set of data with an arithmetic mean of 46 and a standard deviation of 4 ?

- 38 to 46
- 38 to 54
- 42 to 50
- 44 to 48
- 46 to 50

12. If $a$ and $b$ are positive integers, is $a$ a multiple of $b$ ?

(1) Every distinct prime factor of $b$ is also a distinct prime factor of $a$.

(2) Every factor of $b$ is also a factor of $a$.

- Statement (1) ALONE is sufficient, but statement (2) alone is not sufficient.
- Statement (2) ALONE is sufficient, but statement (1) alone is not sufficient.
- BOTH statements TOGETHER are sufficient, but NEITHER statement alone is sufficient.
- EACH statement ALONE is sufficient.
- Statements (1) and (2) TOGETHER are NOT sufficient.

13. If Set $X$ contains 10 consecutive integers and the sum of the 5 least members of the set is 265, then what is the sum of the 5 greatest members of the set?

- 290
- 285
- 280
- 275
- 270

14. If $a - b = c$, what is the value of $b$ ?

(1) $c + 6 = a$

(2) $a = 6$

- Statement (1) ALONE is sufficient, but statement (2) alone is not sufficient.
- Statement (2) ALONE is sufficient, but statement (1) alone is not sufficient.
- BOTH statements TOGETHER are sufficient, but NEITHER statement ALONE is sufficient.
- EACH statement ALONE is sufficient.
- Statements (1) and (2) TOGETHER are not sufficient.

$\{3, 5, 9, 13, y\}$

15. If the average (arithmetic mean) and the median of the set of numbers shown above are equal, then what is the value of $y$ ?

- 7
- 8
- 10
- 15
- 17

16. For a certain foot race, how many different arrangements of medal winners are possible?

(1) Medals will be given for 1st, 2nd, and 3rd place.

(2) There are 10 runners in the race.

- Statement (1) ALONE is sufficient, but statement (2) alone is not sufficient.
- Statement (2) ALONE is sufficient, but statement (1) alone is not sufficient.
- BOTH statements TOGETHER are sufficient, but NEITHER statement ALONE is sufficient.
- EACH statement ALONE is sufficient.
- Statements (1) and (2) TOGETHER are not sufficient.

GO ON TO THE NEXT PAGE.

17. For the set of measurements 3, $x_2$, $x_3$, what is the value of $x_3$ ?

(1) The range of the set of measurements is 0.

(2) The standard deviation of the set of measurements is 0.

- Statement (1) ALONE is sufficient, but statement (2) alone is not sufficient.
- Statement (2) ALONE is sufficient, but statement (1) alone is not sufficient.
- BOTH statements TOGETHER are sufficient, but NEITHER statement ALONE is sufficient.
- EACH statement ALONE is sufficient.
- Statements (1) and (2) TOGETHER are not sufficient.

18. An employer has 6 applicants for a programming position and 4 applicants for a manager position. If the employer must hire 3 programmers and 2 managers, what is the total number of ways the employer can make the selection?

- 1,490
- 132
- 120
- 60
- 23

19. On Monday, an animal shelter housed 55 cats and dogs, and by Friday exactly $\frac{1}{5}$ of the cats and $\frac{1}{4}$ of the dogs had been adopted. If no new cats or dogs were brought to the shelter during this period, what is the greatest possible number of pets that could have been adopted from the animal shelter between Monday and Friday?

- 11
- 12
- 13
- 14
- 20

20. If $x$ is an integer, then which of the following statements about $x^2 - x - 1$ is true?

- It is always odd.
- It is always even.
- It is always positive.
- It is even when $x$ is even and odd when $x$ is odd.
- It is even when $x$ is odd and odd when $x$ is even.

21. During a five-day period, Monday through Friday, the average (arithmetic mean) high temperature was 86 degrees Fahrenheit. What was the high temperature on Friday?

(1) The average high temperature for Monday through Thursday was 87 degrees Fahrenheit.

(2) The high temperature on Friday reduced the average high temperature for the five-day period by 1 degree Fahrenheit.

- Statement (1) ALONE is sufficient, but statement (2) alone is not sufficient.
- Statement (2) ALONE is sufficient, but statement (1) alone is not sufficient.
- BOTH statements TOGETHER are sufficient, but NEITHER statement ALONE is sufficient.
- EACH statement ALONE is sufficient.
- Statements (1) and (2) TOGETHER are not sufficient.

GO ON TO THE NEXT PAGE.

22. What is the value of $x^2 - y^2$?

(1) $x + y = 0$

(2) $x - y = 2$

- Statement (1) ALONE is sufficient, but statement (2) alone is not sufficient.
- Statement (2) ALONE is sufficient, but statement (1) alone is not sufficient.
- BOTH statements TOGETHER are sufficient, but NEITHER statement ALONE is sufficient.
- EACH statement ALONE is sufficient.
- Statements (1) and (2) TOGETHER are not sufficient.

23. If $P$ is the perimeter of an equilateral triangle, which of the following represents the height of the triangle?

- $\frac{P}{3}$
- $\frac{P\sqrt{3}}{3}$
- $\frac{P}{4}$
- $\frac{P\sqrt{3}}{6}$
- $\frac{P}{6}$

24. If 75 percent of all Americans own an automobile, 15 percent of all Americans own a bicycle, and 20 percent of all Americans own neither an automobile nor a bicycle, then what percent of Americans own *both* an automobile and a bicycle?

- 0%
- 1.33%
- 3.75%
- 5%
- 10%

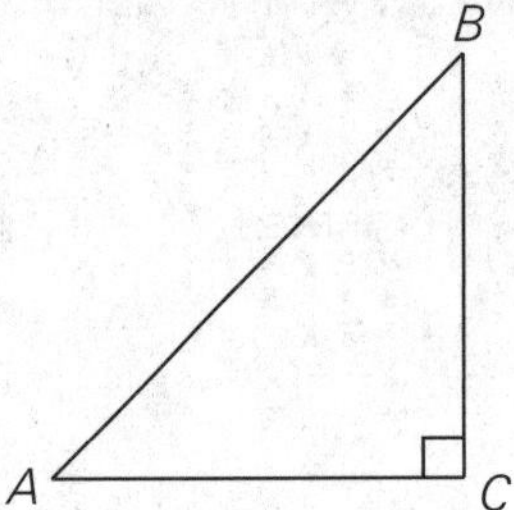


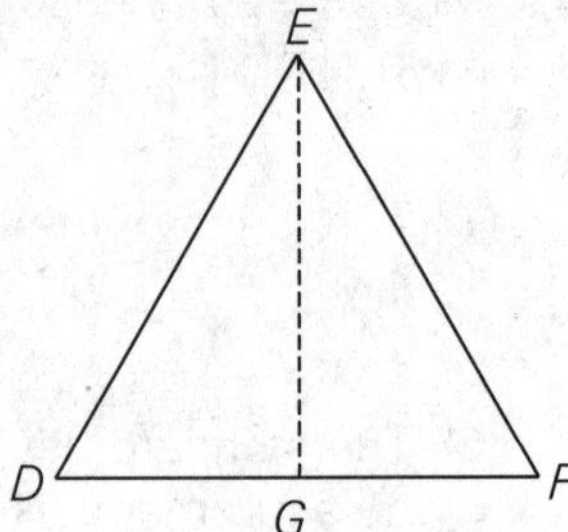


25. Triangle *ABC* above is an isosceles right triangle and triangle *DEF* above is an equilateral triangle with height *EG*. What is the ratio of the area of *ABC* to the area of *DEF* ?

(1) The ratio of *BC* to *EG* is 1:1.

(2) The ratio of *AC* to *DF* is $\sqrt{3}:2$.

- Statement (1) ALONE is sufficient, but statement (2) alone is not sufficient.
- Statement (2) ALONE is sufficient, but statement (1) alone is not sufficient.
- BOTH statements TOGETHER are sufficient, but NEITHER statement ALONE is sufficient.
- EACH statement ALONE is sufficient.
- Statements (1) and (2) TOGETHER are not sufficient.

26. What is the value of integer $x$ ?

(1) $\sqrt[x]{64} = 4$

(2) $x^2 = x + 6$

- Statement (1) ALONE is sufficient, but statement (2) alone is not sufficient.
- Statement (2) ALONE is sufficient, but statement (1) alone is not sufficient.
- BOTH statements TOGETHER are sufficient, but NEITHER statement ALONE is sufficient.
- EACH statement ALONE is sufficient.
- Statements (1) and (2) TOGETHER are not sufficient.

END OF BIN.

## Math Test
## Bin 4—Hard Questions
## 25 Questions

**This test is composed of both problem solving questions and data sufficiency questions.**

**Problem Solving Directions:** Solve each problem and choose the best of the answer choices provided.

**Data Sufficiency Directions:** Each data sufficiency problem consists of a question and two statements, labeled (1) and (2), which contain certain data. Using these data and your knowledge of mathematics and everyday facts (such as the number of days in July or the meaning of *counterclockwise*), decide whether the data given are sufficient for answering the question and then indicate one of the following answer choices:

- ○ Statement (1) ALONE is sufficient, but statement (2) alone is not sufficient.
- ○ Statement (2) ALONE is sufficient, but statement (1) alone is not sufficient.
- ○ BOTH statements TOGETHER are sufficient, but NEITHER statement ALONE is sufficient.
- ○ EACH statement ALONE is sufficient.
- ○ Statements (1) and (2) TOGETHER are not sufficient.

---

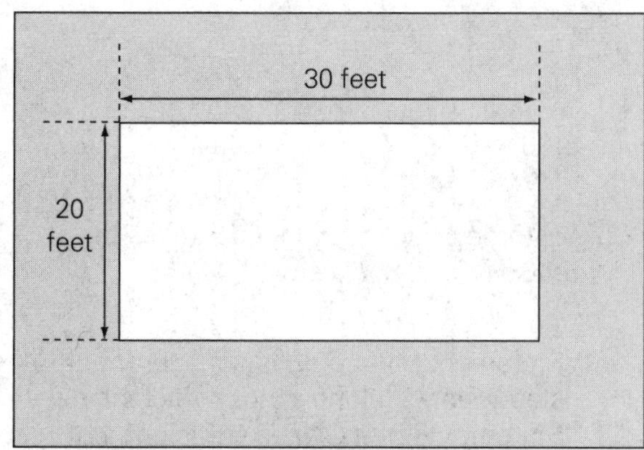


1. A rectangular garden with dimensions 20 feet by 30 feet is surrounded by a rectangular brick walkway of uniform width, as shown by the figure above. If the area of the walkway equals the area of the garden, what is the width of the walkway?

- ○ 1 foot
- ○ 3 feet
- ○ 5 feet
- ○ 8 feet
- ○ 10 feet

2. If a fair two-sided coin is flipped 6 times, what is the probability that tails is the result at least twice but at most 5 times?

- ○ $\frac{5}{8}$
- ○ $\frac{3}{4}$
- ○ $\frac{7}{8}$
- ○ $\frac{57}{64}$
- ○ $\frac{15}{16}$

GO ON TO THE NEXT PAGE.

3. The new recruits of a military organization who score in the bottom 16 percent on their physical conditioning tests are required to retest. If the test scores are normally distributed and have an arithmetic mean of 72, what is the score at or below which the recruits are required to retest?

(1) There are 500 new recruits.

(2) 10 new recruits scored at least 82 on the physical conditioning test.

- Statement (1) ALONE is sufficient, but statement (2) alone is not sufficient.
- Statement (2) ALONE is sufficient, but statement (1) alone is not sufficient.
- BOTH statements TOGETHER are sufficient, but NEITHER statement ALONE is sufficient.
- EACH statement ALONE is sufficient.
- Statements (1) and (2) TOGETHER are not sufficient.

4. Each of the integers from 1 to 20 is written on a separate index card and placed in a box. If the cards are drawn from the box at random without replacement, how many cards must be drawn to ensure that the product of all the integers drawn is even?

- 19
- 12
- 11
- 10
- 3

5. The average (arithmetic mean) of integers $r$, $s$, $t$, $u$, and $v$ is 100. Are exactly two of the integers greater than 100 ?

(1) Three of the integers are less than 50.

(2) None of the integers is equal to 100.

- Statement (1) ALONE is sufficient, but statement (2) alone is not sufficient.
- Statement (2) ALONE is sufficient, but statement (1) alone is not sufficient.
- BOTH statements TOGETHER are sufficient, but NEITHER statement ALONE is sufficient.
- EACH statement ALONE is sufficient.
- Statements (1) and (2) TOGETHER are not sufficient.

6. Paul jogs along the same route every day at a constant rate for 80 minutes. What distance does he jog?

(1) Yesterday, Paul began jogging at 5:00 P.M.

(2) Yesterday, Paul had jogged 5 miles by 5:40 P.M. and 8 miles by 6:04 P.M.

- Statement (1) ALONE is sufficient, but statement (2) alone is not sufficient.
- Statement (2) ALONE is sufficient, but statement (1) alone is not sufficient.
- BOTH statements TOGETHER are sufficient, but NEITHER statement ALONE is sufficient.
- EACH statement ALONE is sufficient.
- Statements (1) and (2) TOGETHER are not sufficient.

GO ON TO THE NEXT PAGE.

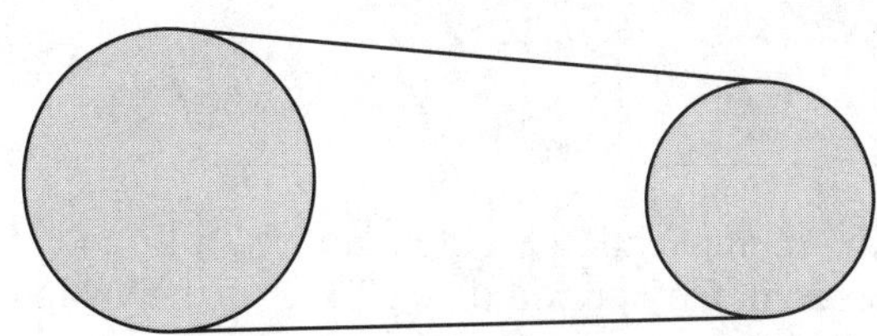

7. The diagram above shows two wheels that drive a conveyor belt. The larger wheel has a diameter of 40 centimeters, and the smaller wheel has a diameter of 32 centimeters. If each wheel must rotate the exact same number of centimeters per minute, and the larger wheel makes *r* revolutions per minute, then, in terms of *r*, how many revolutions does the smaller wheel make per hour?

- ◯ $\frac{1{,}280\pi}{3}$
- ◯ $75r$
- ◯ $48r$
- ◯ $24r$
- ◯ $\frac{64\pi}{3}$

8. An automobile dealership sells only sedans and coupes. It sells each in only two colors: red and blue. Last year, the dealership sold 9,000 vehicles, half of which were red. How many coupes did the dealership sell last year?

(1) The dealership sold three times as many blue coupes as red sedans last year.

(2) The dealership sold half as many blue sedans as blue coupes last year.

- ◯ Statement (1) ALONE is sufficient, but statement (2) alone is not sufficient.
- ◯ Statement (2) ALONE is sufficient, but statement (1) alone is not sufficient.
- ◯ BOTH statements TOGETHER are sufficient, but NEITHER statement ALONE is sufficient.
- ◯ EACH statement ALONE is sufficient.
- ◯ Statements (1) and (2) TOGETHER are not sufficient.

9. At a college football game, $\frac{4}{5}$ of the seats in the lower deck of the stadium were sold. If $\frac{1}{4}$ of all the seats in the stadium are located in the lower deck, and if $\frac{2}{3}$ of all the seats in the stadium were sold, what fraction of the unsold seats in the stadium are in the lower deck?

- ◯ $\frac{3}{20}$
- ◯ $\frac{1}{6}$
- ◯ $\frac{1}{5}$
- ◯ $\frac{1}{3}$
- ◯ $\frac{7}{15}$

10. At Company *R*, the average (arithmetic mean) age of executive employees is 54 years old and the average age of non-executive employees is 34 years old. What is the average age of all the employees at Company *R* ?

(1) There are 10 executive employees at Company *R*.

(2) The number of non-executive employees at Company *R* is four times the number of executive employees at Company *R*.

- ◯ Statement (1) ALONE is sufficient, but statement (2) alone is not sufficient.
- ◯ Statement (2) ALONE is sufficient, but statement (1) alone is not sufficient.
- ◯ BOTH statements TOGETHER are sufficient, but NEITHER statement ALONE is sufficient.
- ◯ EACH statement ALONE is sufficient.
- ◯ Statements (1) and (2) TOGETHER are not sufficient.

GO ON TO THE NEXT PAGE.

11. If $a, b, c, d$, and $x$ are all nonzero integers, is the product $ax \cdot (bx)^2 \cdot (cx)^3 \cdot (dx)^4$ negative?

(1) $a < c < x < 0$

(2) $b < d < x < 0$

- Statement (1) ALONE is sufficient, but statement (2) alone is not sufficient.
- Statement (2) ALONE is sufficient, but statement (1) alone is not sufficient.
- BOTH statements TOGETHER are sufficient, but NEITHER statement ALONE is sufficient.
- EACH statement ALONE is sufficient.
- Statements (1) and (2) TOGETHER are not sufficient.

12. A four-character password consists of one letter from the English alphabet and three different digits from 0 to 9. If the letter is the second or third character of the password, how many different passwords are possible?

- 5,040
- 18,720
- 26,000
- 37,440
- 52,000

13. If $x$ is a positive integer, is $x$ divisible by 48 ?

(1) $x$ is divisible by 8.

(2) $x$ is divisible by 6.

- Statement (1) ALONE is sufficient, but statement (2) alone is not sufficient.
- Statement (2) ALONE is sufficient, but statement (1) alone is not sufficient.
- BOTH statements TOGETHER are sufficient, but NEITHER statement ALONE is sufficient.
- EACH statement ALONE is sufficient.
- Statements (1) and (2) TOGETHER are not sufficient.

$$\begin{array}{r} FGF \\ \times\, G \\ \hline HGG \end{array}$$

14. In the multiplication problem above, $F$, $G$, and $H$ represent distinct odd digits. What is the value of the three-digit number $FGF$ ?

- 151
- 161
- 171
- 313
- 353

15. A group of 20 friends formed an investment club, with each member contributing an equal amount to the general fund. The club then invested the entire fund, which amounted to $d$ dollars, in Stock $X$. The value of the stock subsequently increased 40 percent, at which point the stock was sold and the proceeds divided evenly among the members. In terms of $d$, how much money did each member of the club receive from the sale? (Assume that transaction fees and other associated costs were negligible.)

- $800d$
- $\frac{7d}{5}$
- $\frac{d}{20} + 40$
- $\frac{d}{2}$
- $\frac{7d}{100}$

GO ON TO THE NEXT PAGE.

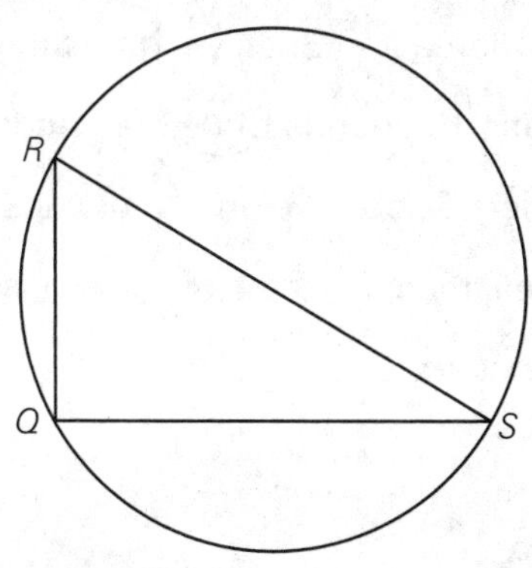


16. Triangle $QRS$ is inscribed in a circle as shown above. Is $QRS$ a right triangle?

    (1) $RS$ is a diameter of the circle.

    (2) $QR = 3$ and $RS = 5$

    - Statement (1) ALONE is sufficient, but statement (2) alone is not sufficient.
    - Statement (2) ALONE is sufficient, but statement (1) alone is not sufficient.
    - BOTH statements TOGETHER are sufficient, but NEITHER statement ALONE is sufficient.
    - EACH statement ALONE is sufficient.
    - Statements (1) and (2) TOGETHER are not sufficient.

17. Square $G$ has sides of length 4 inches. Is the area of Square $H$ exactly one half the area of Square $G$ ?

    (1) The length of the diagonal of Square $H$ equals the length of one side of Square $G$.

    (2) The perimeter of Square $H$ is twice the length of the diagonal of Square $G$.

    - Statement (1) ALONE is sufficient, but statement (2) alone is not sufficient.
    - Statement (2) ALONE is sufficient, but statement (1) alone is not sufficient.
    - BOTH statements TOGETHER are sufficient, but NEITHER statement ALONE is sufficient.
    - EACH statement ALONE is sufficient.
    - Statements (1) and (2) TOGETHER are not sufficient.

18. In a certain state, 70 percent of the counties received some rain on Monday, and 65 percent of the counties received some rain on Tuesday. No rain fell either day in 25 percent of the counties in the state. What percent of the counties received some rain on Monday and Tuesday?

    - 12.5%
    - 40%
    - 50%
    - 60%
    - 67.5%

GO ON TO THE NEXT PAGE.

B C x z A y D

19. *ABCD* is a rectangle with sides of length $x$ centimeters and width $y$ centimeters and a diagonal of length $z$ centimeters. What is the perimeter, in centimeters, of *ABCD* ?

(1) $x - y = 7$

(2) $z = 13$

- Statement (1) ALONE is sufficient, but statement (2) alone is not sufficient.
- Statement (2) ALONE is sufficient, but statement (1) alone is not sufficient.
- BOTH statements TOGETHER are sufficient, but NEITHER statement ALONE is sufficient.
- EACH statement ALONE is sufficient.
- Statements (1) and (2) TOGETHER are not sufficient.

20. Together, Andrea and Brian weigh $p$ pounds and Brian weighs 10 pounds more than Andrea. If Andrea's dog, Cubby, weighs $\frac{p}{4}$ pounds more than Andrea, then, in terms of $p$, what is Cubby's weight in pounds?

- $\frac{p}{2} - 10$
- $\frac{3p}{4} - 5$
- $\frac{3p}{2} - 5$
- $\frac{5p}{4} - 10$
- $5p - 5$

21. A first-grade teacher uses ten flash cards, numbered 1 through 10, to teach her students to order numbers correctly. She has students choose four flash cards at random and arrange the cards in ascending order. If she removes the cards numbered 2 and 4, how many different correctly ordered arrangements of the four selected cards are possible?

- 70
- 210
- 336
- 840
- 1,680

GO ON TO THE NEXT PAGE.

22. If $A$ and $B$ are two-digit integers that share the same digits, except in reverse order, then what is the sum of $A$ and $B$ ?

(1) $A - B = 45$

(2) The difference between the two digits in each number is 5.

- Statement (1) ALONE is sufficient, but statement (2) alone is not sufficient.
- Statement (2) ALONE is sufficient, but statement (1) alone is not sufficient.
- BOTH statements TOGETHER are sufficient, but NEITHER statement ALONE is sufficient.
- EACH statement ALONE is sufficient.
- Statements (1) and (2) TOGETHER are not sufficient.

23. A university awarded grants in the amount of either \$7,000 or \$10,000 to selected incoming freshmen. If the total amount of all such awards is \$2,300,000, did the university award more \$7,000 grants than \$10,000 grants to the selected incoming freshmen?

(1) A total of 275 freshmen received grants in one of the two amounts.

(2) The amount of money awarded in \$10,000 grants was \$200,000 more than the amount of money awarded in \$7,000 grants.

- Statement (1) ALONE is sufficient, but statement (2) alone is not sufficient.
- Statement (2) ALONE is sufficient, but statement (1) alone is not sufficient.
- BOTH statements TOGETHER are sufficient, but NEITHER statement ALONE is sufficient.
- EACH statement ALONE is sufficient.
- Statements (1) and (2) TOGETHER are not sufficient.

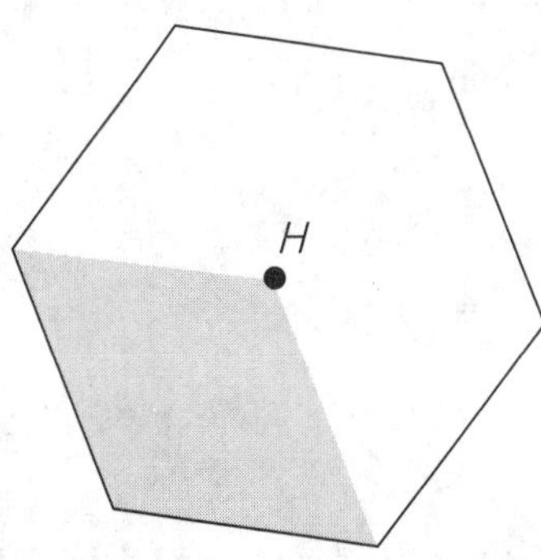


24. The figure shown above is a regular hexagon with center $H$. The shaded area is a parallelogram that shares three vertices with the hexagon and its fourth vertex is the center of the hexagon. If the length of one side of the hexagon is 8 centimeters, what is the area of the unshaded region?

- $16\sqrt{3}$ cm$^2$
- 96 cm$^2$
- $64\sqrt{3}$ cm$^2$
- $96\sqrt{3}$ cm$^2$
- 256 cm$^2$

25. A fish tank contains a number of fish, including 5 Fantails. If two fish are selected from the tank at random, what is the probability that both will be Fantails?

(1) The probability that the first fish chosen is a Fantail is $\frac{1}{2}$.

(2) The probability that the second fish chosen is a Fantail is $\frac{4}{9}$.

- Statement (1) ALONE is sufficient, but statement (2) alone is not sufficient.
- Statement (2) ALONE is sufficient, but statement (1) alone is not sufficient.
- BOTH statements TOGETHER are sufficient, but NEITHER statement ALONE is sufficient.
- EACH statement ALONE is sufficient.
- Statements (1) and (2) TOGETHER are not sufficient.

END OF BIN.

## Verbal Test
## Bin 1—Easy Questions
## 25 Questions

**This test is made up of sentence correction, critical reasoning, and reading comprehension questions.**

**Sentence Correction Directions:** Each of the sentence correction questions presents a sentence, part or all of which is underlined. Beneath the sentence you will find five ways of phrasing the underlined part. The first of these repeats the original; the other four are different. Follow the requirements of standard written English to choose your answer, paying attention to grammar, word choice, and sentence construction. Select the answer that produces the most effective sentence; your answer should make the sentence clear, exact, and free of grammatical errors. It should also minimize awkwardness, ambiguity, and redundancy.

**Reading Comprehension Directions:** Each of the reading comprehension questions is based on the content of a passage. After reading the passage, answer all questions pertaining to it on the basis of what is stated or implied in the passage. For each question, select the best answer of the choices given.

**Critical Reasoning Directions:** Each of the critical reasoning questions is based on a short argument, a set of statements, or a plan of action. For each question, select the best answer of the choices given.

---

1. As its reputation for making acquisitions of important masterpieces has grown, the museum has increasingly turned down gifts of lesser-known paintings they would in the past have accepted gratefully.

- they would in the past have accepted gratefully
- they would have accepted gratefully in the past
- it would in the past have accepted gratefully
- it previously would have accepted gratefully in the past
- that previously would have been accepted in the past

2. Over the past few decades, despite periodic attempts to reign in spending, currencies in South America are devalued by rampant inflation.

- are devalued
- are becoming more devalued
- which have lost value
- have become devalued
- have since become devalued

3. A fashion designer's fall line for women utilizing new soft fabrics broke all sales records last year. To capitalize on her success, the designer plans to launch a line of clothing for men this year that makes use of the same new soft fabrics.

The designer's plan assumes that

- other designers are not planning to introduce new lines for men utilizing the same soft fabrics
- men will be as interested in the new soft fabrics as women were the year before
- the designer will have time to develop new lines for both men and women
- the line for men will be considered innovative and daring because of its use of fabrics
- women who bought the new line last year will continue to buy it this year

GO ON TO THE NEXT PAGE.

4. The standard lamp is becoming outmoded, and so too is the incandescent light bulb, it is Edison's miraculous invention to use so much more energy than the new low-wattage halogen bulbs.

- so too is the incandescent light bulb, it is Edison's miraculous invention to use
- so too is the incandescent light bulb, Edison's miraculous invention that uses
- so too the incandescent light bulb, Edison's miraculous invention using
- also the incandescent light bulb, it is Edison's miraculous invention that uses
- also the incandescent light bulb, which is Edison's miraculous invention to use

5. Over the last 20 years, the growth of information technology has been more rapid than any other business field, but has recently begun to lag behind as newly emerging fields seem more enticing to new graduates.

- the growth of information technology has been more rapid than any other business field
- the growth of information technology has been more rapid than any other fields of business
- information technology's growth has been more rapid than any other fields of business
- the growing of information technology has been more rapid than that of any other business field
- the growth of information technology has been more rapid than that of any other business field

6. According to mutual fund sales experts, a successful year for a stock fund should result not only in increased investor dollars flowing into the fund, but also in increased investor dollars flowing into other mutual stock funds offered by the same company. However, while last year the Grafton Mutual Company's "Growth Stock Fund" beat average market returns by a factor of two and recorded substantial new investment, the other stock funds offered by Grafton did not report any increase whatsoever.

Which of the following conclusions can properly be drawn from the statements above?

- When one of the mutual funds offered by a company beats average market returns, the other mutual funds offered by that company will beat average market returns.
- The mutual fund sales experts neglected to consider bond funds in formulating their theory.
- The performance of the Grafton "Growth Stock Fund" was a result of a wave of mergers and acquisitions that year.
- Investors currently dislike all stock mutual funds because of market volatility.
- The success of one mutual fund is not the only factor affecting whether investors will invest in other mutual funds run by the same company.

7. With less than thirty thousand dollars in advance ticket sales and fewer acceptances by guest speakers than expected, the one-day symposium on art and religion was canceled for lack of interest.

- less than thirty thousand dollars in advance ticket sales and fewer
- fewer than thirty thousand dollars in advance ticket sales and less
- fewer than thirty thousand dollars in advance ticket sales and fewer
- lesser than thirty thousand dollars in advance ticket sales and fewer
- less than thirty thousand dollars in advance ticket sales and as few

GO ON TO THE NEXT PAGE.

8. New technology now makes it feasible for computer call-in help desk services to route calls they receive to almost anywhere, theoretically allowing employees to work from home, without the need for a daily commute.

   The adoption of this policy would be most likely to increase productivity if employees did not ____________.

   - ⬭ commute from a distance of fewer than 10 miles
   - ⬭ commute by car as opposed to by rail
   - ⬭ live in areas with dependable phone service
   - ⬭ need to consult frequently with each other to solve callers' problems
   - ⬭ have more than one telephone line

9. The port cities of England in the 19th century saw a renaissance of ship construction, with some innovative designs breaking new ground, stretching the limits of ship-building theory, and <u>received</u> acclaim from around the world.

   - ⬭ received
   - ⬭ it received
   - ⬭ receiving
   - ⬭ would receive
   - ⬭ it had received

10. According to a consumer research group survey, the majority of kitchen appliances purchased in the United States are purchased by men. This appears to belie the myth that women spend more time in the kitchen than men.

    The argument is flawed primarily because the author ____________.

    - ⬭ fails to differentiate between buying and using
    - ⬭ does not provide information about the types of kitchen appliances surveyed
    - ⬭ depends on the results of one survey
    - ⬭ does not give exact statistics to back up his case
    - ⬭ does not provide information on other appliances such as washers and dryers

11. <u>A contribution to a favorite charity being sent instead</u> of flowers when a colleague dies is becoming more the rule than the exception when it comes to funeral etiquette.

    - ⬭ A contribution to a favorite charity being sent instead
    - ⬭ A contribution being sent to a favorite charity as opposed
    - ⬭ To send a contribution for a favorite charity instead
    - ⬭ Sending a contribution to a favorite charity instead
    - ⬭ Sending a contribution to a favorite charity as opposed

GO ON TO THE NEXT PAGE.

Questions 12–15 are based on the following passage:

As a business model, the world of publishing has always been a somewhat sleepy enclave, but now all that seems poised to change. Several companies have moved aggressively into a new business endeavor whose genesis comes from the question: Who owns the great works of literature?

Text-on-demand is not a completely new idea, of course. In the 1990s, the Gutenberg project sought volunteers to type literary classics that had expired copyrights into word processing files so that scholars would have searchable databases for their research. Most of the works of Shakespeare, Cervantes, Proust, and Molière were to be found free online by as early as 1995.

However, now large-scale companies have moved into the market, with scanners and business plans, and are looking for bargain basement content. These companies are striking deals with libraries, and some publishers, to be able to provide their content, for a price, to individual buyers over the Internet.

At stake are the rights to an estimated store of 30 million books, most of which are now out of print. Many of these books are now also in the public domain, giving any company the right to sell them online. Still, a good portion of the books a general audience might actually want to buy is still under copyright. The urgent question: Who owns those copyrights? In the case of all too many books put out more than 20 years ago by now-defunct publishing companies, the answer is unclear—a situation the new text-on-demand companies are eager to exploit. An association of publishers has sued, claiming massive copyright infringement. The case is several years away from trial.

12. The primary purpose of the passage is to

- ◯ present the results of a statistical analysis and propose further study
- ◯ explain a recent development and explore its consequences
- ◯ identify the reasons for a trend and recommend measures to address it
- ◯ outline several theories about a phenomenon and advocate one of them
- ◯ describe the potential consequences of implementing a new policy and argue in favor of that policy

13. It can be inferred from the passage that the works of Shakespeare, Cervantes, and Molière

- ◯ are some of the most popular works of literature
- ◯ are no longer copyrighted
- ◯ are among the works for which the association of publishers is suing text-on-demand companies
- ◯ do not currently exist as searchable databases
- ◯ were owned by now-defunct publishing companies

14. Which of the following is an example of a book that a text-on-demand company would not have to acquire the rights to?

- ◯ A book still under copyright
- ◯ A book more than 20 years old
- ◯ A book in the public domain
- ◯ A book a general audience might want to buy
- ◯ A book not already owned by publishers the company has a deal with

15. It can be inferred from the passage that a common practice of text-on-demand companies is to

- ◯ use scanners to find books they want to acquire
- ◯ create business plans well before they have any actual business
- ◯ buy content at premium prices
- ◯ acquire the rights to books for as little as possible
- ◯ attempt to supplant the role of traditional publishers

GO ON TO THE NEXT PAGE.

16. Exit polls, conducted by an independent organization among voters at five polling locations during a recent election, suggested that the incumbent mayor—a Democrat—was going to lose the election by a wide margin. But, in fact, by the time the final results were tabulated, the incumbent had won the election by a narrow margin.

    Which of the following, if true, would explain the apparent contradiction in the results of the exit polls?

    - ⬭ The people chosen at random to be polled by the independent organization happened to be Democrats.
    - ⬭ The exit poll locations chosen by the independent organization were in predominantly Republican districts.
    - ⬭ The exit polls were conducted during the afternoon, when most of the districts' younger voters, who did not support the incumbent mayor, were at work.
    - ⬭ The incumbent mayor ran on a platform that promised to lower taxes if elected.
    - ⬭ An earlier poll, conducted the week before the election, had predicted that the incumbent mayor would win.

17. The spread of Avian flu from animals to humans has been well-documented, but less understood is the mechanism by which it is spread from one bird species to another. **In order to avoid a worldwide epidemic of Avian flu, scientists must make that study a first priority.** To solely tackle the human dimension of this possible pandemic is to miss half of the problem: its spread from one hemisphere to another.

    The bolded phrase plays which of the following roles in the argument above?

    - ⬭ The bolded phrase states a premise of the argument.
    - ⬭ The bolded phrase contradicts the author's main point.
    - ⬭ The bolded phrase makes a statement that the author is about to contradict.
    - ⬭ The bolded phrase states the author's conclusion.
    - ⬭ The bolded phrase states an assumption the author is making.

18. Successful business leaders not only anticipate potential problems and have contingency plans <u>ready, instead proceeding as if they are likely to occur at any time</u>.

    - ⬭ ready, instead proceeding as if they are likely to occur at any time
    - ⬭ ready, but also proceed as if such problems are likely to occur at any time
    - ⬭ ready, but also proceeding as if the occurrence of them is at any time likely
    - ⬭ ready; they instead proceed as if their occurrence is likely at any time
    - ⬭ ready; such problems are likely to occur at any time, is how they proceed

19. An artist who sells her paintings for a fixed price decides that she must increase her income. Because she does not believe that customers will pay more for her paintings, she decides to cut costs by using cheaper paints and canvases. She expects that, by cutting costs, she will increase her profit margin per painting and thus increase her annual net income.

    Which of the following, if true, most weakens the argument above?

    - ⬭ Other area artists charge more for their paintings than the artist charges for hers.
    - ⬭ The artist has failed to consider other options, such as renting cheaper studio space.
    - ⬭ The artist's plan will result in the production of inferior paintings which, in turn, will cause a reduction in sales.
    - ⬭ If the economy were to enter a period of inflation, the artist's projected increase in income could be wiped out by increases in the price of art supplies.
    - ⬭ The artist considered trying to complete paintings more quickly and thus increase production, but concluded that it would be impossible.

GO ON TO THE NEXT PAGE.

20. Although tapirs reared in captivity are generally docile and have even been kept as pets by South American villagers, <u>it is nonetheless a volatile creature</u> prone to unpredictable and dangerous temper tantrums.

- ◯ it is nonetheless a volatile creature
- ◯ it is nonetheless volatile creatures
- ◯ being nonetheless volatile creatures
- ◯ they are nonetheless a volatile creature
- ◯ they are nonetheless volatile creatures

21. According to a recent report, the original tires supplied with the Impressivo, a new sedan-class automobile, wore much more quickly than tires conventionally wear. The report suggested two possible causes: (1) defects in the tires and (2) improper wheel alignment of the automobile.

Which of the following would best help the authors of the report determine which of the two causes identified was responsible for the extra wear?

- ◯ A study in which the rate of tire wear in the Impressivo is compared to the rate of tire wear in all automobiles in the same class
- ◯ A study in which a second set of tires, manufactured by a different company from the one that made the first set, is installed on all Impressivos and the rate of wear is measured
- ◯ A study in which the level of satisfaction of workers in the Impressivo manufacturing plant is measured and compared to that of workers at other automobile manufacturing plants
- ◯ A study that determines how often improper wheel alignment results in major problems for manufacturers of other automobiles in the Impressivo's class
- ◯ A study that determines the degree to which faulty driving techniques employed by Impressivo drivers contributed to tire wear

<u>Questions 22–25</u> are based on the following passage:

Founded at the dawn of the modern industrial era, the nearly forgotten Women's Trade Union League (WTUL) played an instrumental role in advancing the cause of working women throughout the early part of the twentieth century. In the face of considerable adversity, the WTUL made a contribution far greater than did most historical footnotes.

The organization's successes did not come easily; conflict beset the WTUL in many forms. During those early days of American unions, organized labor was aggressively opposed by both industry and government. The WTUL, which represented a largely unskilled labor force, had little leverage against these powerful opponents. Also, because of the skill level of its workers as well as inherent societal gender bias, the WTUL had great difficulty finding allies among other unions. Even the large and powerful American Federation of Labor (AFL), which nominally took the WTUL under its wing, kept it at a distance. Because the AFL's power stemmed from its highly skilled labor force, the organization saw little economic benefit in working with the WTUL. The affiliation provided the AFL with political cover, allowing it to claim support for women workers; in return, the WTUL gained a potent but largely absent ally.

The WTUL also had to overcome internal discord. While the majority of the group's members were working women, a sizeable and powerful minority consisted of middle- and upper-class social reformers whose goals extended beyond labor reform. While workers argued that the WTUL should focus its efforts on collective bargaining and working conditions, the reformers looked beyond the workplace, seeking state and national legislation aimed at education reform and urban poverty relief as well as workplace issues.

Despite these obstacles, the WTUL accomplished a great deal. The organization was instrumental in the passage of state laws mandating an eight-hour workday, a minimum wage for women, and a ban on child labor. It provided seed money to women who organized workers in specific plants and industries, and it also established strike funds and soup kitchens to support striking unionists. After the tragic Triangle Shirtwaist Company fire of 1911, the WTUL launched a four-year investigation whose

GO ON TO THE NEXT PAGE.

conclusions formed the basis of much subsequent workplace safety legislation. The organization also offered a political base for all reform-minded women, and thus helped develop the next generation of American leaders. Eleanor Roosevelt was one of many prominent figures to emerge from the WTUL.

The organization began a slow death in the late 1920s, when the Great Depression choked off its funding. The organization limped through the 1940s; the death knell eventually rang in 1950, at the onset of the McCarthy era. A turn-of-the-century labor organization dedicated to social reform, one that during its heyday was regarded by many as "radical," stood little chance of weathering that storm. This humble ending, however, does nothing to diminish the accomplishments of an organization that is yet to receive its historical due.

22. The primary purpose of this passage is to

- describe the barriers confronting women in the contemporary workplace
- compare and contrast the methods of two labor unions of the early industrial era
- critique the methods employed by an important labor union
- rebuke historians for failing to cover the women's labor movement adequately
- call readers' attention to an overlooked contributor to American history

23. Which of the following best characterizes the American Federation of Labor's view of the Women's Trade Union League, as it is presented in the passage?

- The WTUL was an important component of the AFL's multifront assault on industry and its treatment of workers.
- Because of Eleanor Roosevelt's affiliation with the organization, the WTUL was a vehicle through which the AFL could gain access to the White House.
- The WTUL was to be avoided because the radical element within it attracted unwanted government scrutiny.
- The WTUL offered the AFL some political capital but little that would assist it in labor negotiations.
- The WTUL was weakened by its hesitance in pursuing widespread social reform beyond the workplace.

24. Each of the following is cited in the passage as an accomplishment of the Women's Trade Union League EXCEPT

- it organized a highly skilled workforce to increase its bargaining power
- it contributed to the development of a group of leaders in America
- it provided essential support to striking women
- it helped fund start-up unions for women
- it contributed to the passage of important social and labor reform legislation

GO ON TO THE NEXT PAGE.

25. The passage suggests which of the following about the "middle- and upper-class social reformers" mentioned in lines 32–33 ?

- ⬭ They did not understand, nor were they sympathetic to, the plight of poor women workers.
- ⬭ Their naive interest in Communism was ultimately detrimental to the Women's Trade Union League.
- ⬭ It was because of their social and political power that the Women's Trade Union League was able to form an alliance with the American Federation of Labor.
- ⬭ They represented only an insignificant fraction of the leadership of Women's Trade Union League.
- ⬭ They sought to advance a broad political agenda of societal improvement.

END OF BIN.

# Verbal Test
## Bin 2—Medium Questions
## 27 Questions

**This test is made up of sentence correction, critical reasoning, and reading comprehension questions.**

**Sentence Correction Directions:** Each of the sentence correction questions presents a sentence, part or all of which is underlined. Beneath the sentence you will find five ways of phrasing the underlined part. The first of these repeats the original; the other four are different. Follow the requirements of standard written English to choose your answer, paying attention to grammar, word choice, and sentence construction. Select the answer that produces the most effective sentence; your answer should make the sentence clear, exact, and free of grammatical errors. It should also minimize awkwardness, ambiguity, and redundancy.

**Reading Comprehension Directions:** Each of the reading comprehension questions is based on the content of a passage. After reading the passage, answer all questions pertaining to it on the basis of what is stated or implied in the passage. For each question, select the best answer of the choices given.

**Critical Reasoning Directions:** Each of the critical reasoning questions is based on a short argument, a set of statements, or a plan of action. For each question, select the best answer of the choices given.

---

1. As its performance has risen on all the stock indexes, the bio-tech start-up has branched out into new markets to look for opportunities they would previously have had to ignore.

   - they would previously have had to ignore
   - they would have had to ignore previously
   - that previously they would have had to ignore
   - it previously would have had to ignore in past years
   - it would previously have had to ignore

2. Scientists wishing to understand the kinetic movements of ancient dinosaurs are today studying the movements of modern-day birds, which many scientists believe are descended from dinosaurs. A flaw in this strategy is that birds, although once genetically linked to dinosaurs, have evolved so far that any comparison is effectively meaningless.

   Which of the following, if true, would most weaken the criticism made above of the scientists' strategy?

   - Birds and dinosaurs have a number of important features in common that exist in no other living species.
   - Birds are separated from dinosaurs by 65 million years of evolution.
   - Our theories of dinosaur movements have recently undergone a radical reappraisal.
   - The study of kinetic movement is a relatively new discipline.
   - Many bird experts do not study dinosaurs to draw inferences about birds.

GO ON TO THE NEXT PAGE.

3. A factory in China has two options to improve efficiency: adding robotic assembly lines and subcontracting out certain small production goals that could be done more efficiently elsewhere. Adding robotic assembly lines will improve efficiency more than subcontracting some small production goals. Therefore, by adding robotic assembly lines, the factory will be doing the most that can be done to improve efficiency.

   Which of the following is an assumption on which the argument depends?

   - Adding robotic assembly lines will be more expensive than subcontracting some small production goals.
   - The factory has a choice of robotic assembly lines, some of which might be better suited to this factory than others.
   - The factory may or may not decide to choose either alternative.
   - Efficiency cannot be improved more by using both methods together than by adding robotic assembly lines alone.
   - This particular factory is already the third most efficient factory in China.

4. <u>Just as the early NASA space explorers attempted on each flight to push the frontiers of our knowledge, so too</u> are the new private-consortium space explorers seeking to add to man's general understanding of the cosmos.

   - Just as the early NASA space explorers attempted on each flight to push the frontiers of our knowledge, so too
   - The early NASA space explorers attempted on each flight to push the frontiers of our knowledge, and in the same way
   - Like the case of the early NASA space explorers who attempted on each flight to push the frontiers of our knowledge, so too
   - As in the early NASA space explorers' attempts on each flight to push the frontiers of our knowledge, so too
   - Similar to the early NASA space explorers attempted on each flight to push the frontiers of our knowledge, so too

5. A proposal for a new building fire safety code requires that fire-retardant insulation no longer be sprayed on steel girders in the factory, but be sprayed on once the girders have arrived at the building site. This will eliminate the dislodging of the insulation in transit and reduce fatalities in catastrophic fires by an estimated 20%.

   Which of the following, if true, represents the strongest challenge to the new proposal?

   - The fire-retardant insulation will also be required to be one inch thicker than in the past.
   - Studies have shown that most dislodgement of insulation occurs after the girders arrive on site.
   - Catastrophic fires represent only 4% of the fires reported nationally.
   - The proposed safety code will add considerably to the cost of new construction.
   - In most of Europe, spraying fire-retardant insulation onto steel girders at the building site has been required for the past ten years.

6. An effort <u>to control the crippling effects of poverty in Brazil's interior cities, begun almost thirty years ago,</u> has been partially successful, despite the setback of a major drought and the interruption of aid during an extended economic crisis.

   - to control the crippling effects of poverty in Brazil's interior cities, begun almost thirty years ago,
   - begun almost thirty years ago for controlling the crippling effects of poverty in Brazil's interior cities,
   - begun for controlling the crippling effects of poverty in Brazil's interior cities almost thirty years ago,
   - at controlling the crippling effects of poverty in Brazil's interior cities begun almost thirty years ago,
   - that has begun almost thirty years ago to control the crippling effects of poverty in Brazil's interior cities,

GO ON TO THE NEXT PAGE.

7. A newly discovered disease is thought to be caused by a certain bacterium. However, recently released data note that the bacterium thrives in the presence of a certain virus, implying that it is actually the virus that causes the new disease.

   Which of the following pieces of evidence would most support the data's implication?

   - ◯ In the absence of the virus, the disease has been observed to follow infection by the bacterium.
   - ◯ The virus has been shown to aid the growth of bacteria, a process which often leads to the onset of the disease.
   - ◯ The virus alone has been observed in many cases of the disease.
   - ◯ In cases where the disease does not develop, infection by the bacterium is usually preceded by infection by the virus.
   - ◯ Onset of the disease usually follows infection by both the virus and the bacterium.

8. The company was not even publicly traded until 1968, when the owner and founder sold it to David P. Markham, a private investor, <u>who took the company public and established a long and generous policy of stock options for</u> valued employees.

   - ◯ who took the company public and established a long and generous policy of stock options for
   - ◯ who, taking the company public, established a long and generous policy of stock options to
   - ◯ who, when he took the company public, established a long and generous policy of stock options to
   - ◯ who had taken the company public, establishing a long and generous policy of stock options as
   - ◯ taking the company public and establishing a long and generous policy of stock options for

9. Because of a quality control problem, a supplier of flu vaccines will not be able to ship any supplies of the vaccine for the upcoming flu season. This will create a shortage of flu vaccines and result in a loss of productivity as workers call in sick.

   Which of the following, if true, most seriously weakens the argument above?

   - ◯ The quality control problem of the supplier is not as severe as some experts had initially predicted.
   - ◯ Other suppliers of flu vaccine have not been affected by the quality control problem.
   - ◯ Last year there was also a shortage of flu vaccine available.
   - ◯ The price of flu vaccines is expected to fall in the next ten years.
   - ◯ The flu season is expected to last longer than usual this year.

10. Never before had the navy defeated <u>so many foes at once as it had in</u> the battle of Trafalgar in 1805.

    - ◯ so many foes at once as it had in
    - ◯ at once as many foes as
    - ◯ at once as many foes that there were in
    - ◯ as many foes at once as it did in
    - ◯ so many foes at once as that it defeated in

11. The changes that may be part of a general global warming trend include an increase in the frequency and severity of hurricanes, a gradual rise in sea level, <u>depleting the ozone layer, and raising the temperature of the Earth</u>.

    - ◯ depleting the ozone layer, and raising the temperature of the Earth
    - ◯ depleting the ozone layer, and a rise in the Earth's temperature
    - ◯ a depletion of the ozone layer, and raising the Earth's temperature
    - ◯ a depletion of the ozone layer, and a raise of the temperature of the Earth
    - ◯ a depletion of the ozone layer, and a rise in the temperature of the Earth

GO ON TO THE NEXT PAGE.

Questions 12–16 are based on the following passage:

It has long been a tenet of business theory that the best decisions are made after careful review and consideration. Only after weighing all the options and studying projections, say most professors of business, can a practical decision be made.

Now, that model is being questioned by some business thinkers in the light of the theories of Malcolm Gladwell, who states that human beings often make better decisions in the blink of an eye.

It is, at first glance, a theory so counter-intuitive as to seem almost ludicrous. Behind any decision, Gladwell posits, there is a behind-the-scenes subconscious process in which the brain analyzes; ranks in order of importance; compares and contrasts vast amounts of information; and dismisses extraneous factors, seemingly almost instantaneously, often arriving at a conclusion in less than two seconds. Citing a multitude of studies and examples from life, Gladwell shows how that split-second decision is often better informed than a drawn-out examination.

Evanston and Cramer were the first to apply this theory to the business world. Evanston videotaped the job interviews of 400 applicants at different firms. He then played only 10 seconds of each videotape to independent human resources specialists. The specialists were able to pick out the applicants who were hired with an accuracy of over 90%.

Cramer took the experiment even further, using only five seconds of videotape, without sound. To his astonishment, the rate of accuracy with which the HR specialists were able to predict the successful applicants fell only to 82%.

Critics argue that these results illustrate a problem with stereotyping that impedes human resources specialists from hiring the best candidates even when they have the time to get below the surface: going for the candidate who "looks the part." Gladwell argues that, on the contrary, the human mind is able to make complicated decisions quickly and that intuition often trumps an extended decision-making process.

12. The primary purpose of the passage is to

- ◯ discuss reasons an accepted business theory is being reexamined
- ◯ present evidence that resolves a contradiction in business theory
- ◯ describe a tenet of business practices and how that tenet can be tested in today's economic environment
- ◯ argue that a counter-intuitive new business idea is, in the final analysis, incorrect
- ◯ present evidence that invalidates a new business model

13. According to the passage, all of the following are examples of the subconscious processes by which the brain makes a decision EXCEPT

- ◯ analysis of information
- ◯ ranking of information
- ◯ comparison and contrast of information
- ◯ rejecting information that is not pertinent
- ◯ consulting a multitude of studies and examples

14. The author's attitude toward the long-held view that decisions should be made carefully over time expressed in lines 1–5 can best be described as

- ◯ dismissive and scornful
- ◯ respectful but questioning
- ◯ admiring and deferential
- ◯ uncertain but optimistic
- ◯ condescending and impatient

GO ON TO THE NEXT PAGE.

15. The author most likely mentions the results of Cramer's extension of Evanston's experiment in order to

- ⬭ show that Cramer's hypothesis was correct, while Evanston's hypothesis turned out to be incorrect
- ⬭ show that Evanston's hypothesis was correct, while Cramer's hypothesis turned out to be incorrect
- ⬭ demonstrate that while both experiments were scientifically rigorous, neither ended up being scientifically valid
- ⬭ illustrate that the principle of subconscious decisions continues to work even when less information is available
- ⬭ demonstrate that Cramer's experiment was 8% more accurate than Evanston's, even though his subjects had less information to work with

16. It can be inferred that the critics referred to in line 36 believed the results of the two experiments had less to do with the innate decision-making of the subjects than with

- ⬭ the excellent decision-making of Evanston and Cramer
- ⬭ the expertise of Malcolm Gladwell, who originated the theory
- ⬭ not choosing candidates who "looked the part"
- ⬭ the use of videotape as a method of choosing candidates
- ⬭ their unconscious use of visual stereotypes in making their selections

17. The women's volleyball team at a local college finished fifth in its division, prompting the college to fire the team's general manager. The manager responded by suing the college, saying that the team's performance put it among the top teams in the country.

Which of the following statements, if true, would support the claim of the team's manager, and resolve the apparent contradiction?

- ⬭ The team won all of its "away" games during the season in question.
- ⬭ Attendance at the volleyball team's games was up 35% from the year before.
- ⬭ Of the starting team, three team members were unable to play for at least half the season because of injuries.
- ⬭ There are 80 teams in this particular volleyball team's division.
- ⬭ The team lost more games this year than it did the year before.

18. Country A recently broke off diplomatic relations with Country B when it was reported that Country B had been running a covert intelligence operation within the borders of Country A. While a spokesperson for Country B admitted the charge, the spokesperson said that it was common knowledge that all countries do this, and that Country A was no exception.

Which of the following inferences can be drawn from the argument above?

- ⬭ Country B should apologize and dismantle its intelligence operation in Country A.
- ⬭ The spokesperson for Country B claims that Country A engages in intelligence gathering too.
- ⬭ Because all countries engage in this practice, Country A's outrage was disingenuous.
- ⬭ Relations between Country A and Country B will be strained for some time.
- ⬭ Country B would be just as outraged if it was reported that Country A was running a covert intelligence operation with Country B's borders.

GO ON TO THE NEXT PAGE.

19. Because cellular telephones emit signals that can interfere with cockpit-to-control-tower transmissions, airplane passengers' use of these instruments at all times that the airplane is in motion, even while on the ground, are prohibited.

- ◯ at all times that the airplane is in motion, even while on the ground, are
- ◯ at all times during which the airplane, even while on the ground, is in motion, are
- ◯ during airplane motion, even when it is on the ground, are
- ◯ during times of the airplane being in motion, even on the ground, is
- ◯ when the airplane is in motion, even while on the ground, is

20. In contrast to classical guitars, whose owners prefer the dulcet, rounded tones produced by nylon strings, folk guitar owners prefer the bright and brassy sound that only bronze or steel can create.

- ◯ folk guitar owners prefer the bright and brassy sound
- ◯ folk guitar owners prefer to get a sound that is bright and brassy
- ◯ with a folk guitar, the owner gets the preferably bright and brassy sound
- ◯ folk guitars produce a bright and brassy sound, which their owners prefer,
- ◯ folk guitars produce a preferred bright and brassy sound for their owners

Questions 21–22 are based on the following passage:

A system-wide county school anti-smoking education program was instituted last year. The program was clearly a success. Last year, the incidence of students smoking on school premises decreased by over 70 percent.

21. Which of the following assumptions underlies the argument in the passage?

- ◯ Cigarettes are detrimental to one's health; once people understand this, they will quit smoking.
- ◯ The doubling of the price of a pack of cigarettes last year was not the only cause of the students' altered smoking habits.
- ◯ The teachers chosen to lead the anti-smoking education program were the most effective teachers in the school system.
- ◯ The number of cigarettes smoked each day by those students who continued to smoke last year did not greatly increase.
- ◯ School policy enforcers were less vigilant in seeking out smokers last year than they were in previous years.

22. Which of the following, if true, would most seriously weaken the argument in the passage?

- ◯ The author of this statement is a school system official hoping to generate good publicity for the anti-smoking program.
- ◯ Most students who smoke stopped smoking on school premises last year continued to smoke when away from school.
- ◯ Last year, another policy change made it much easier for students to leave and return to school grounds during the school day.
- ◯ The school system spent more on anti-smoking education programs last year than it did in all previous years.
- ◯ The amount of time students spent in anti-smoking education programs last year resulted in a reduction of in-class hours devoted to academic subjects.

GO ON TO THE NEXT PAGE.

23. Mild exercise throughout pregnancy <u>may reduce the discomfort associated with pregnancy and result in</u> a speedier, easier birth, according to a recent study.

- may reduce the discomfort associated with pregnancy and result in
- may reduce the discomfort associated with pregnancy, with the result
- may cause a reduction in the discomfort associated with pregnancy and as a result
- might lead to a reduction in the discomfort associated with pregnancy and as a result
- might reduce the discomfort associated with pregnancy and resulting in

<u>Questions 24–27</u> are based on the following passage:

What is it that keeps the developing world in an apparent state of perpetual poverty? Poor education, lack of basic medical care, and the absence of democratic structures all certainly contribute to these nations' plight. However, according to Peruvian economist Hernando de Soto, the overriding cause is the overwhelming prevalence of black market activity, well outside the formal economy, in these countries. The losses incurred from this condition are twofold. First, they deny the government tax revenues which could be used to improve education, medical treatment, and government efficiency. More important, however, they deny earners the chance to accumulate assets recognized by law and thus prevent them from leveraging those assets to borrow. Reforming these nations' legal systems in order to confer ownership through titling, De Soto argues, would help the poor there access the assets their work should be generating. These assets could then be used to buy homes and construct businesses, thus building a more stable and prosperous economy. De Soto estimates the value of these assets, which he terms "dead capital," at nearly $10 trillion worldwide.

De Soto is not the first to locate the developing world's problems in the domain of property rights. Others have tried property rights reform and failed. According to de Soto, this is because his predecessors attempted to model their plans on existing, successful property rights systems. In other words, they tried to transplant American and British property law to an inhospitable host. De Soto argues that within many of the extralegal markets of the developing world, mutually agreed-upon rules for distributing assets and recognizing property rights already exist. Rather than force these markets to adjust to a new, foreign system of property titling, reformers should focus on codifying the existing systems wherever it is practical to do so. This would facilitate a quicker, more natural transition to an economy that builds wealth rather than squanders it.

GO ON TO THE NEXT PAGE.

24. The author's primary goal in the passage is to

- ⬭ compare several failed attempts to address a problem
- ⬭ respond to criticism of a new theory
- ⬭ identify the problems inherent in a new economic theory
- ⬭ describe a novel approach to an old problem
- ⬭ compare different property rights systems in the industrial world

25. According to the passage, de Soto believes that the quickest way to address poverty in the developing world is to

- ⬭ increase funding for education
- ⬭ build the infrastructure to support lending
- ⬭ ensure medical care for all citizens
- ⬭ aggressively root out corruption in government
- ⬭ increase tax rates on all citizens in developing countries

26. The author's assertion that "reformers should focus on codifying the existing systems wherever it is practical to do so" (lines 39–41) suggests that

- ⬭ in some instances, current systems are inadequate to meet the needs of a market economy
- ⬭ these systems are already written down and need only be enacted as law
- ⬭ where it is impractical to codify existing systems, countries should adopt American property law
- ⬭ the existing systems are superior to those currently in use in modern industrialized countries
- ⬭ improving education and medical care in these countries should take priority over reforming property laws

27. The term "dead capital" (line 24) refers to

- ⬭ loans that are never repaid
- ⬭ failed investments in new businesses
- ⬭ cities ruined by over-industrialization
- ⬭ the proceeds of extralegal commerce
- ⬭ property passed from generation to generation

END OF BIN.

## Verbal Test
## Bin 3—Hard Questions
## 26 Questions

**This test is made up of sentence correction, critical reasoning, and reading comprehension questions.**

**Sentence Correction Directions**: Each of the sentence correction questions presents a sentence, part or all of which is underlined. Beneath the sentence you will find five ways of phrasing the underlined part. The first of these repeats the original; the other four are different. Follow the requirements of standard written English to choose your answer, paying attention to grammar, word choice, and sentence construction. Select the answer that produces the most effective sentence; your answer should make the sentence clear, exact, and free of grammatical errors. It should also minimize awkwardness, ambiguity, and redundancy.

**Reading Comprehension Directions**: Each of the reading comprehension questions is based on the content of a passage. After reading the passage, answer all questions pertaining to it on the basis of what is stated or implied in the passage. For each question, select the best answer of the choices given.

**Critical Reasoning Directions**: Each of the critical reasoning questions is based on a short argument, a set of statements, or a plan of action. For each question, select the best answer of the choices given.

---

1. Unlike Franklin D. Roosevelt's bootstrap program that helped to restart economic growth in the 1930s through public works, Ronald Reagan proposed a program of trickle-down economics to restart the economy.

   - ⬭ Franklin D. Roosevelt's bootstrap program that helped
   - ⬭ Franklin D. Roosevelt and his bootstrap program which helped
   - ⬭ Franklin D. Roosevelt, whose bootstrap program helped
   - ⬭ the bootstrap program of Franklin D. Roosevelt that has helped
   - ⬭ Franklin D. Roosevelt and his bootstrap program helping

2. In the 1970s, it became evident that writing about someone else's research was much easier for social scientists who wanted to make a quick name for themselves than it was to do their own research.

   - ⬭ that writing about someone else's research was much easier for social scientists who wanted to make a quick name for themselves
   - ⬭ that for social scientists who wanted to make a quick name for themselves, it was much easier to write about someone else's research
   - ⬭ that for social scientists wanting to make a quick name for themselves, writing about someone else's research was much easier
   - ⬭ for social scientists who wanted to make a quick name for themselves that writing about someone else's research was much easier
   - ⬭ for social scientists who wanted to make a quick name for themselves, writing about someone else's research was much easier

GO ON TO THE NEXT PAGE.

Questions 3–4 are based on the following passage:

To improve the town's overcrowded school system, the town council has proposed an ambitious education plan to reduce classroom size and make capital improvements—a plan they intend to pay for with an increase in property taxes for homes valued over $500,000. Although the school system desperately needs improving, the town council's plan should be defeated because the majority of the people who would end up paying for the improvements receive no benefit from them.

3. Which of the following, if true, most strengthens the argument above?

- ◯ The town's school system is currently ranked among the worst in the state.
- ◯ Other towns nearby that have made similar capital improvements did not find that the improvements translated to a better quality of education.
- ◯ The town will need to spend additional money on an architect's plans for the capital improvements.
- ◯ An examination of the tax rolls shows that most homeowners in this category no longer have school-age children.
- ◯ Some homeowners will delay home improvement projects in order to keep the value of their homes below $500,000.

4. Which of the following, if true, provides the town council with the strongest counter to the objection that its plan is unfair?

- ◯ Even with the proposed increase, property taxes in the town are well below the national average.
- ◯ Paying for the school system improvements using existing town funds will result in shortfalls that will force the town into arrears.
- ◯ The teachers in the town's school system receive some of the lowest salary packages in the immediate area, which is a major cause of attrition.
- ◯ Smaller class sizes and capital improvements in a school system tend to increase property values in the surrounding community.
- ◯ A feasibility study has shown that the cost of the improvements will likely be 20% higher than projected.

5. The rules of engagement under which a border patrol station can decide to use deadly force <u>includes responding to an invasionary incursion and the return of</u> hostile fire.

- ◯ includes responding to an invasionary incursion and the return of
- ◯ includes responding to an invasionary incursion and returning
- ◯ include responding to an invasionary incursion and the return of
- ◯ include a response to an invasionary incursion and the return of
- ◯ include a response to an invasionary incursion and returning

6. Although the word "phonetician" is popularly associated with Henry Higgins's task of improving the diction of Eliza Doolittle in *My Fair Lady*, in linguistics, <u>it is someone who studies</u> the formation of language.

- ◯ it is someone who studies
- ◯ it is a person studying
- ◯ it refers to someone who studies
- ◯ they are people who study
- ◯ it is in reference to people who study

GO ON TO THE NEXT PAGE.

7. Experts studying patterns of shark attacks on humans have noted that attacks tend to diminish when the water temperature drops below 65 degrees Fahrenheit. Until recently, researchers believed this was because sharks prefer warmer water, and thus are present in fewer numbers in colder water. However, new research shows that sharks are present in equal numbers in cold and warm water.

Which of the following, if true, best explains the apparent paradox?

- ⬭ In general, humans prefer warm water.
- ⬭ Sharks' keen sense of smell is enhanced in cold water.
- ⬭ In the Pacific, shark attacks tend to occur more frequently in the daytime.
- ⬭ Of the more than 200 types of sharks present in the ocean, only three attack humans.
- ⬭ The average temperature of the Earth's oceans is 55 degrees.

8. As a result of surging economic indicators, most analysts upgraded the company's stock to a strong "buy," ignoring the advice of the head of a watchdog organization <u>who warned that the company's product would prove not only dangerous but</u> ineffective in the long run.

- ⬭ who warned that the company's product would prove not only dangerous but
- ⬭ warning that the company's product would prove not only dangerous and also
- ⬭ warning that the company's product would prove itself to be both dangerous and
- ⬭ who warned that the company's product would prove to be both dangerous and
- ⬭ who was warning that the company's product would prove not only dangerous but

9. MoviesNow! streaming service is projected to buy more licenses to stream more movies in the next 5 years than in any previous 5-year window. This is because MoviesNow!'s board of directors has encouraged the pursuit of subscribers who are parents of children under the age of 12 and the current selection of movies to stream in the MoviesNow! database is targeted at subscribers ages 18–35.

Which of the following, if true, would most strengthen the argument from MoviesNow!'s board of directors that they should pursue subscribers who are parents of children under the age of 12?

- ⬭ The board monitors the demographic targets of large advertising companies and chooses target audiences for their streaming service based on those trends.
- ⬭ A population study conducted by an independent research group has uncovered a large uptick in the number of parents who are raising children under the age of 12.
- ⬭ People aged 18–35 generally have less disposable income than other age demographics.
- ⬭ The licensing agreement MoviesNow! has with the largest movie production company is set to expire within the next 5 years.
- ⬭ The board of MoviesNow! is comprised of parents of children under the age of 12.

GO ON TO THE NEXT PAGE.

10. A new influx of unprecedented private investment should create a bright new future for manned space exploration, <u>making the possibility of commercial space tourism much more viable than 10 years ago</u>.

- ⬭ making the possibility of commercial space tourism much more viable than 10 years ago
- ⬭ and make the possibility of commercial space tourism much more viable than 10 years ago
- ⬭ making the possibility of commercial space tourism much more viable than it was 10 years ago
- ⬭ and make the possibility of commercial space tourism much more viable than it was 10 years in the past
- ⬭ making the possibility of commercial space tourism much more viable than 10 years in the past

<u>Questions 11–15</u> are based on the following passage:

As the American workforce gets grayer, age discrimination will likely become a more prominent issue in the courts. It is, of course, illegal to discriminate against an employee because of his or her age, and yet it is not illegal to dismiss a worker because he has a high salary and expensive health care.

This apparent contradiction is at the heart of a raft of cases now making their way through the courts. The outcome of these cases will have broad implications for the workplace in the coming years. By 2020, the Bureau of Labor Statistics has projected that more than half of all workers will be over 40—many of whom, by dint of seniority and promotions, will be earning higher than median salaries, eligible for more stock options, and carrying higher health care costs as a result of a larger number of dependents and the increased cost of health care for older workers.

Is it any wonder that a bottom-line oriented business might want to shed these workers, whose productivity is likely to plummet in the next few years, even as they become more expensive employees?

Still, the legal challenges of implementing this policy are daunting. Businesses have the right to rate workers on their productivity and to rank them against their peers. But they are not allowed to prejudge individuals based on their sex, race, or age. Each worker must be treated on his or her own merits, rather than by how they fit into a larger profile of the group they belong to.

For companies looking to lay off these workers, the cost of making a mistake is high; while only one in three age discrimination suits is won by the plaintiff, the awards tend to be steep and the political fall-out harsh.

GO ON TO THE NEXT PAGE.

11. The primary purpose of the passage is to

- ⬭ advocate on behalf of the older American worker who could soon face dismissal
- ⬭ describe the origin of two theories of labor law and their effects on the workplace
- ⬭ present an overview of the legal ramifications of a practice some call discriminatory
- ⬭ describe the process by which America's workforce is getting older
- ⬭ describe the methods by which a company could reduce its bottom line

12. Which of the following best describes the organization of the second paragraph of the passage?

- ⬭ An assertion is made and then briefly contradicted.
- ⬭ A contradiction is stated and then quickly resolved.
- ⬭ A new theory is described and then qualified.
- ⬭ An apparent inconsistency is stated and its consequences outlined.
- ⬭ A conventional model is described and an alternative is introduced.

13. Which of the following, if true, would most effectively weaken the author's assertion that a "bottom-line oriented business" might want to lay off older workers?

- ⬭ A new study shows that, on average, younger workers earn less and have lower associated medical costs than older workers.
- ⬭ Older workers have a higher rate of absenteeism than younger workers.
- ⬭ A new study shows that older workers are in fact more productive and have fewer medical expenses compared to younger workers.
- ⬭ A forecasted downturn in the economy will erode profits in many American businesses.
- ⬭ A new bill scheduled to become law will make it easier for employers to employ undocumented immigrants.

14. It can be inferred from the passage regarding the relationship between American companies and older Americans that

- ⬭ what is good for American companies is not necessarily good for older Americans
- ⬭ American companies are prohibited by law from practices that discriminate based on age
- ⬭ large monetary judgments from age discrimination suits might prove more expensive than paying older employees' salaries
- ⬭ by the year 2030, the percentage of older employees will be even higher than in the year 2020
- ⬭ some older employees may well be more productive than some younger employees

15. The author mentions all of the following as driving up the cost to employers for employing workers over the age of 40 EXCEPT

- ⬭ the cost of out-placement services
- ⬭ a larger number of dependents
- ⬭ increased cost of health care
- ⬭ higher median salaries
- ⬭ the cost of employee stock options

GO ON TO THE NEXT PAGE.

16. A pharmaceutical company claims that its new drug promotes learning in children. To back up its claims, the company points to a study of 300 children who were given the drug, along with a control group of 300 children who were given a placebo. The 300 children who were given the drug reported that they were able to retain new information much more easily.

Which of the following statements, if true, would most tend to weaken the claims of the pharmaceutical company?

- ⬭ The 300 children in the control group also reported that they were able to retain new information much more easily.
- ⬭ The drug has also been shown to prevent common skin rashes.
- ⬭ The drug has been proven to have severe side-effects.
- ⬭ The children in the study were not given any other medications during the study.
- ⬭ The children who were given the drug did better on cognitive measurement tests after the drug therapy than before.

17. In order to understand the dangers of the current real-estate bubble in Country Y, one has only to look to the real-estate bubble of the last decade in Country Z. In that country, incautious investors used the inflated value of their real estate as collateral in risky margin loans. When the real-estate market collapsed, many investors went bankrupt, creating a major recession. Country Y is in real danger of a similar recession if more-stringent laws restricting margin loans are not enacted promptly.

The answer to which of the following questions would be most useful in evaluating the significance of the author's claims?

- ⬭ Was the real estate in Country Z located principally in rural areas or was it located in more urban communities?
- ⬭ Could the bankruptcies in Country Z have been prevented by a private bailout plan by the nation's banks?
- ⬭ Does Country Y currently have any laws on its books regarding margin loans?
- ⬭ Are there business ties and connections between Country Y and Country Z?
- ⬭ Were there other factors in the case of Country Y that would make the comparison with Country Z less meaningful?

18. Rules governing participation in a new extreme sports fantasy camp require <u>that applicants should be physically fit enough to endure the demanding</u> activities in which they will be engaging.

- ⬭ that applicants should be physically fit enough to endure the demanding
- ⬭ that applicants be physically fit enough to endure the demanding
- ⬭ applicants should have enough physical fitness to allow enduring the demands of
- ⬭ applicants are physically fit enough as to endure the demands of
- ⬭ physical fitness in applicants, enough for endurance of demanding

GO ON TO THE NEXT PAGE.

19. During the summer of 2002, the Outer Banks suffered a massive toad infestation, discouraging many vacationers from visiting the area.

- suffered a massive toad infestation, discouraging
- suffered from a massive toad infestation and discouraged
- suffered a massive infestation of toads, which discouraged
- was suffering a massive infestation of toads and discouraging
- had suffered from a massive toad infestation and this discouraged

20. A prolonged period of low mortgage rates resulted in a period of the most robust home sales ever. At the same time, the average sale price of resale homes actually dropped, when adjusted for inflation.

Which of the following, if true, would explain the apparent contradiction between the robust home sales and the drop in the average sale price of resale homes?

- The inflation rate during this period exceeded the increase in the average salary, thus preventing many buyers from securing mortgages.
- Resale homes represent the best value on the real estate market.
- Without the adjustment for inflation, the price of resale homes actually increased by a very slight amount.
- The decrease in mortgage rates was accompanied by a widening of the types of mortgages from which borrowers could choose.
- The increase in home sales was due entirely to an increase in the sale of new homes.

21. Luis is taller than Rei. Kiko is taller than Marcus. Therefore, Kiko is taller than Rei.

The conclusion drawn above is not supported by the argument; however, the addition of one additional piece of information would make the conclusion logically sound. All of the following could be that additional piece of information EXCEPT

- Kiko is taller than Luis.
- Luis is taller than Marcus.
- Luis and Marcus are the same height.
- Marcus and Rei are the same height.
- Marcus is taller than Rei.

22. It has been estimated that an increase in average regional temperature of even 0.5 degrees Fahrenheit could cost the southern United States more than $10 billion in lost agricultural income annually.

- an increase in average regional temperature of even 0.5 degrees Fahrenheit could cost the southern United States more than $10 billion in lost agricultural income annually
- every year, $10 billion in agricultural income could be the cost to the southern United States as a result of an increase in the average temperature of the region of even 0.5 degrees Fahrenheit
- the cost to the southern United States could be more than $10 billion in income from agriculture that results from a regional increase in average temperature of even 0.5 degrees Fahrenheit annually
- annual income losses in agriculture of more than $10 billion could be the cost from increasing average temperatures in the southern United States of even 0.5 degrees Fahrenheit
- annual income losses to the southern United States from the increase in average regional temperature of even 0.5 degrees Fahrenheit costing more than $10 billion in agricultural income each year

GO ON TO THE NEXT PAGE.

23. Within the Green Party, an internal debate is raging among those who believe in compromising with mainstream politicians in order to achieve some goals with those who believe the party must not abandon any of its principles.

- among those who believe in compromising with mainstream politicians in order to achieve some goals with those who believe the party must not abandon any of its principles
- among those who believe that achieving some goals requires compromise with mainstream politicians and those believing that none of the party's principles must be abandoned
- between those believing in compromising with mainstream politicians in order to achieve some goals with those who believe the party must not abandon any of its principles
- between those who believe in compromising with mainstream politicians in order to achieve some goals and those who believe the party must not abandon any of its principles
- between those believing that achieving some goals means compromising with mainstream politicians and those who believe that the principles of the party must not be abandoned

24. In comparison to the drivers who live in Mountainview, a greater proportion of the drivers who live in Oak Valley exceed the speed limit regularly. This explains why there are more accidents each year in Oak Valley than in Mountainview.

All of the following statements, if true, weaken the conclusion drawn above EXCEPT

- Oak Valley has a greater proportion of blind intersections and sharp turns than has Mountainview.
- There is a greater number of drivers in Oak Valley than in Mountainview.
- Drivers in Mountainview must travel to Oak Valley to shop and work.
- Per capita, there are fewer police officers monitoring traffic in Oak Valley than there are in Mountainview.
- The roads are icier for a greater portion of the year in Oak Valley than in Mountainview.

GO ON TO THE NEXT PAGE.

25. A study showed that only ten percent of American dog owners enroll their dogs in formal obedience training classes. More than twenty percent of these dog owners, the study also showed, participate in dog shows. Thus, it is obvious that people who train their dogs are more likely to participate in dog shows than are people who do not train their dogs.

    The conclusion above is correct provided which of the following statements is also true?

    ◯ It is impossible for a dog to compete in a dog show if the dog has not completed at least one formal obedience training class.
    ◯ The proportion of dog owners who enroll their dogs in formal obedience training classes is representative of the proportion who train their dogs outside such classes.
    ◯ Dog owners who participate in dog shows only train their dogs by enrolling them in formal obedience training lessons.
    ◯ Participation in dog shows is a reliable indicator of how much attention a dog owner pays to his dog.
    ◯ Only purebred dogs can participate in dog shows, so many owners who enroll their dogs in formal obedience training classes are excluded from this activity.

26. A bullet train travels in excess of 150 miles per hour. Therefore, if a train travels slower than 150 miles per hour, it is not a bullet train.

    Which of the following most closely parallels the reasoning used in the argument above?

    ◯ An orange ripens only on the vine. If it ripens on the vine, then it is not an orange.
    ◯ Newspapers are often read by more than one person. Therefore, magazines are also likely to be read by more than one person.
    ◯ An earthquake of 5.0 or above on the Richter scale causes massive damage. If there is not massive damage, then the earthquake did not attain a 5.0 or above.
    ◯ A supersonic plane travels at speeds in excess of Mach 1. If it is not supersonic, then it will travel at speeds below Mach 1.
    ◯ Fluoride generally prevents cavities. If there are no cavities, then there was no fluoride used.

## END OF EXAMINATION

# Chapter 33
# GMAT Math and Verbal Practice Bins: Answers and Explanations

If you really want to improve your score, then you should read *all* the explanations for *all* the questions on the pages that follow, not just the ones you got wrong. It's important to make sure you're getting questions correct for the right reasons and even more important that you are recognizing opportunities to use The Princeton Review techniques, which can save you time and eliminate the possibility of careless errors.

# ANSWER KEY

| MATH | | | | VERBAL | | |
|---|---|---|---|---|---|---|
| **Bin 1** | **Bin 2** | **Bin 3** | **Bin 4** | **Bin 1** | **Bin 2** | **Bin 3** |
| 1. C | 1. C | 1. B | 1. C | 1. C | 1. E | 1. C |
| 2. C | 2. B | 2. D | 2. C | 2. D | 2. A | 2. B |
| 3. D | 3. C | 3. A | 3. C | 3. B | 3. D | 3. D |
| 4. D | 4. A | 4. C | 4. C | 4. B | 4. A | 4. D |
| 5. D | 5. B | 5. D | 5. E | 5. E | 5. B | 5. D |
| 6. B | 6. A | 6. D | 6. B | 6. E | 6. A | 6. C |
| 7. E | 7. B | 7. D | 7. B | 7. A | 7. C | 7. A |
| 8. C | 8. C | 8. C | 8. C | 8. D | 8. A | 8. D |
| 9. B | 9. A | 9. A | 9. A | 9. C | 9. B | 9. B |
| 10. D | 10. C | 10. D | 10. B | 10. A | 10. D | 10. C |
| 11. B | 11. B | 11. B | 11. A | 11. D | 11. E | 11. C |
| 12. D | 12. B | 12. B | 12. D | 12. B | 12. A | 12. D |
| 13. C | 13. D | 13. A | 13. E | 13. B | 13. E | 13. C |
| 14. A | 14. B | 14. A | 14. A | 14. C | 14. B | 14. B |
| 15. D | 15. E | 15. D | 15. E | 15. D | 15. D | 15. A |
| 16. A | 16. E | 16. C | 16. A | 16. B | 16. E | 16. A |
| 17. B | 17. C | 17. D | 17. D | 17. D | 17. D | 17. E |
| 18. B | 18. E | 18. C | 18. D | 18. B | 18. B | 18. B |
| 19. C | 19. C | 19. C | 19. C | 19. C | 19. E | 19. C |
| 20. A | 20. D | 20. A | 20. B | 20. E | 20. D | 20. E |
| 21. D | 21. B | 21. D | 21. A | 21. B | 21. B | 21. B |
| 22. D | 22. D | 22. A | 22. E | 22. E | 22. C | 22. A |
| 23. C | 23. D | 23. D | 23. D | 23. D | 23. A | 23. D |
| 24. D | 24. A | 24. E | 24. C | 24. A | 24. D | 24. D |
| 25. B | 25. A | 25. D | 25. D | 25. E | 25. B | 25. B |
| 26. B | 26. E | 26. A | | | 26. A | 26. C |
| | 27. C | | | | 27. D | |

# MATH BIN 1

## QUESTIONS

1. What percent of 112 is 14 ?

- 0.125%
- 8%
- 12.5%
- 125%
- 800%

2. The number of flights leaving a certain airport doubles during every one-hour period between 9 A.M. and noon; after noon, the number of flights leaving from the airport doubles during every two-hour period. If 4 flights left from the airport between 9 and 10 A.M., how many flights left the airport between 2 and 4 P.M. ?

- 32
- 48
- 64
- 128
- 256

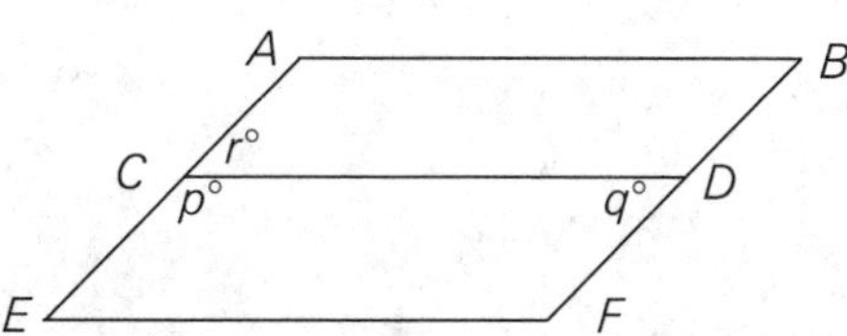


3. If both *ABDC* and *CDFE* are parallelograms, what is $q + r$ ?

(1) $r = 70$

(2) $p = 110$

- Statement (1) ALONE is sufficient, but statement (2) alone is not sufficient.
- Statement (2) ALONE is sufficient, but statement (1) alone is not sufficient.
- BOTH statements TOGETHER are sufficient, but NEITHER statement ALONE is sufficient.
- EACH statement ALONE is sufficient.
- Statements (1) and (2) TOGETHER are not sufficient.

## EXPLANATIONS

1. **C** Since this is a percent problem, you can solve it by thinking in terms of $\frac{part}{whole}$. In this case, $\frac{part}{whole} = \frac{14}{112} = \frac{x}{100}$; cross-multiply to get $112x = 1{,}400$, so $x = \frac{1{,}400}{112}$, and $x = 12.5$.

Like most percent questions on the GMAT, you can also find the answer using POE. Since 14 is a little bigger than $\frac{1}{10}$, or 10%, of 112—11.2 is exactly 10%—so the answer can only be (C).

2. **C** Rather than try to rely on high school-style exponential growth formulas, let's just count this one out. If 4 flights left the airport between 9 and 10 A.M., then 8 left between 10 and 11 A.M., and 16 left between 11 A.M. and noon. Starting at noon, the flights begin to double every *two* hours, so 32 left between noon and 2 P.M. and 64 left between 2 P.M. and 4 P.M. The correct answer is (C). If you chose (E), you may have forgotten to account for the afternoon change in the rate of increase, and the test-writers, of course, made sure that the answer you came up with was there waiting for you.

3. **D** Since you have parallelograms, you really have only two angles, big ones and small ones, and a big angle plus a small one equals 180. Statement (1) gives the value of *r; q,* like *r,* is a small angle, so $q + r = 70 + 70$, or 140. You're down to AD.

Statement (2) gives the value of a big angle, which you can subtract from 180 to get the value of a small angle. You now have the same information you had in Statement (1), and the answer is (D).

## QUESTIONS

4. Chris's convertible gets gas mileage that is 40% greater than that of Stan's SUV. If Harry's hatchback gets gas mileage that is 15% greater than that of Chris's convertible, then Harry's hatchback gets gas mileage that is what percent greater than that of Stan's SUV?

- 25%
- 46%
- 55%
- 61%
- 66%

5. If $x$ is equal to 1 more than the product of 3 and $z$, and $y$ is equal to 1 less than the product of 2 and $z$, then $2x$ is how much greater than $3y$ when $z$ is 4 ?

- 1
- 2
- 3
- 5
- 6

## EXPLANATIONS

4. **D** This is a Plugging In problem. Since it's a percent problem, too, and the question asks you to find a percentage greater than the mileage of Stan's SUV, make Stan's mileage 100. Chris's mileage is therefore 140; 15% of 140 is 21, so Harry's mileage is 161. Since 161 is 61% greater than 100, the correct answer is (D).

   Choices (A) and (C) are both traps, since they're simple addition and subtraction, respectively, of the numbers in the problem. If you got (B), you probably increased Chris's mileage by 15% of 40, rather than 15% of 140.

5. **D** Start by translating the two original equations: $x = 3z + 1$ and $y = 2z - 1$. If $z$ is 4, then $x = 13$ and $y = 7$. Thus, $2x$ is 26 and $3y$ is 21. The difference between the two values is 5, so the correct answer is (D).

   If you chose (A), you may have mistakenly added when the problem asked for a product. If you got (E), you may have solved for $x - y$ when the problem asked for $2x - 3y$. And if you got (C), you may have done both.

## MATH BIN 1

### QUESTIONS

6. In 2005, did Company *A* have more than twice the number of employees that Company *B* did?

(1) In 2005, Company *A* had 11,500 more employees than did Company *B*.

(2) In 2005, the 3,000 employees with advanced degrees at Company *A* made up 12.5% of that company's total number employees, and the 2,500 employees with advanced degrees at Company *B* made up 20% of that company's total number of employees.

- Statement (1) ALONE is sufficient, but statement (2) alone is not sufficient.
- Statement (2) ALONE is sufficient, but statement (1) alone is not sufficient.
- BOTH statements TOGETHER are sufficient, but NEITHER statement ALONE is sufficient.
- EACH statement ALONE is sufficient.
- Statements (1) and (2) TOGETHER are not sufficient.

### EXPLANATIONS

6. **B** Statement (1) gives the difference between the numbers of employees at the two companies. Without the actual number of employees at either company, though, this information isn't sufficient to answer this yes-or-no question, so you're down to BCE.

Statement (2), on the other hand, gives you the part-to-whole relationship you need to solve for the actual number of employees at each of the companies. You therefore know you can answer the question with a definitive "yes" or "no"—it doesn't matter which one is actually correct—so the answer is (B).

(If you really want to crunch the numbers, that 12.5% at Company *A* is the same as $\frac{1}{8}$, and Company *A* had 24,000 employees; that 20% at Company *B* is the same as $\frac{1}{5}$, and Company *B* had 12,500 employees. The answer to the original question is "no"; Company *A* did not have more than twice the number of employees as did Company *B*.)

### QUESTIONS

7. Is $x^3$ equal to 125 ?

(1) $x > 4$

(2) $x < 6$

- Statement (1) ALONE is sufficient, but statement (2) alone is not sufficient.
- Statement (2) ALONE is sufficient, but statement (1) alone is not sufficient.
- BOTH statements TOGETHER are sufficient, but NEITHER statement ALONE is sufficient.
- EACH statement ALONE is sufficient.
- Statements (1) and (2) TOGETHER are not sufficient.

### EXPLANATIONS

7. **E** The question "Is $x^3$ equal to 125?" can be rewritten as "Is $x = 5$?" This is a yes-or-no question, and the best way to tackle it is to Plug In twice. In Statement (1), you can plug in 5, in which case the answer to the question "Is $x^3$ equal to 125?" is "yes." Or, you can plug in 6, in which case the answer is "no." Thus, because you get two different answers depending on the numbers you plug in, Statement (1) is not sufficient. You're down to BCE.

In Statement (2), you can plug in 5, in which case the answer is "yes," or 4, in which case the answer is "no." Eliminate (B).

## QUESTIONS

## EXPLANATIONS

To see if the answer is (C), choose a number that satisfies the conditions of both Statements (1) and (2) at the same time. You can plug in 5, in which case the answer is "yes." You might have been tempted to choose (C) at this point because no other integer will satisfy the two equations at the same time, but does this problem limit you to picking integers? Nope. What about 4.5? Or 5.2? In either of these cases, the answer is "no." Because you get two different answers depending on what numbers you plug in, the combination of Statements (1) and (2) is not sufficient either, and the correct answer is (E).

8. Bob leaves point $A$ and drives due west to point $B$. From point $B$, he drives due south to point $C$. How far is Bob from his original location?

(1) Point $A$ is 24 miles from point $B$.

(2) Point $B$ is 18 miles from point $C$.

- Statement (1) ALONE is sufficient, but statement (2) alone is not sufficient.
- Statement (2) ALONE is sufficient, but statement (1) alone is not sufficient.
- BOTH statements TOGETHER are sufficient, but NEITHER statement ALONE is sufficient.
- EACH statement ALONE is sufficient.
- Statements (1) and (2) TOGETHER are not sufficient.

8. **C** When a geometry problem comes without a diagram, always start by drawing one of your own. In this case, your diagram should look like this:

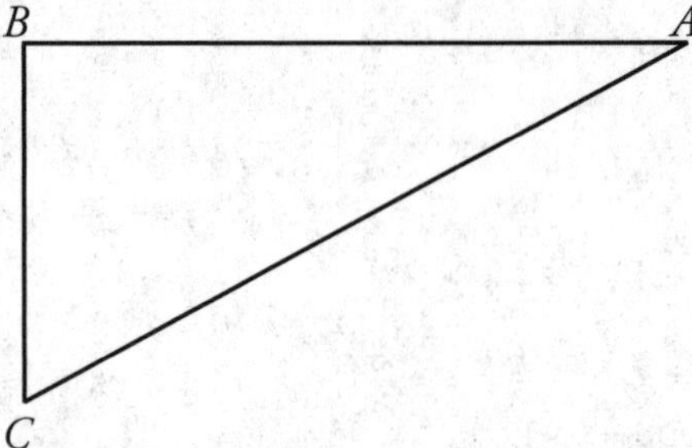


Statement (1) tells you the length of one side of the triangle, the distance from $A$ to $B$. Since you know you have a right triangle (because Bob drove due west and due south), any two sides would be enough to find the remaining side. And *if* you knew that you had a "special" right triangle, one side might be enough. Neither of these cases applies, though, so you're down to BCE. Statement (2) gives you, again, a single side. Remember, though, that you can no longer consider the information from Statement (1), so this statement alone is also insufficient. You're down to (C) or (E).

## QUESTIONS

## EXPLANATIONS

When you put the 2 statements together, you know you *could* solve for the remaining side using the Pythagorean Theorem—although, since this is a Data Sufficiency question, there's no reason you would. The correct answer is (C). Incidentally, if you did want to solve for the third side, you could save a lot of unnecessary calculation by recognizing this as a multiple of the old GMAT favorite, the 3-4-5 triangle. The two shorter sides of the triangle are multiplied by 6, so the remaining side must be 30.

9. The formula $M = \sqrt{l^2 + w^2 + d^2}$ describes the relationship between the length of $M$, which is the longest line that can be drawn in a rectangular solid, and the length, $l$, width, $w$, and depth, $d$, of that rectangular solid. The longest line that can be drawn in a rectangular solid with a length of 12, a width of 4, and a depth of 3 is how much longer than the longest line that can drawn in a rectangular solid with a length of 6, a width of 3, and a depth of 2 ?

- 5
- 6
- 7
- 9
- 13

9. **B** Although the relationship provided in the problem is based on geometry, this isn't really a geometry problem: you can simply plug the given numbers into the formula. Starting with the larger rectangular solid, $\sqrt{12^2 + 4^2 + 3^2} = \sqrt{144 + 16 + 9} = \sqrt{169} = 13$. For the smaller rectangular solid, $\sqrt{6^2 + 3^2 + 2^2} = \sqrt{36 + 9 + 4} = \sqrt{49} = 7$. Both 13 and 7 are, of course, answer choices, but the problem asked you for the *difference* between the two values, so the correct answer is 6, (B).

## QUESTIONS

10. Is the average (arithmetic mean) of *a, b,* and *c* equal to 8 ?

(1) Three times the sum of *a, b,* and *c* is equal to 72.

(2) The sum of 2*a,* 2*b,* and 2*c* is equal to 48.

- Statement (1) ALONE is sufficient, but statement (2) alone is not sufficient.
- Statement (2) ALONE is sufficient, but statement (1) alone is not sufficient.
- BOTH statements TOGETHER are sufficient, but NEITHER statement ALONE is sufficient.
- EACH statement ALONE is sufficient.
- Statements (1) and (2) TOGETHER are not sufficient.

## EXPLANATIONS

10. **D** This is a yes-or-no question, and you need to recognize that it's not asking about the individual values of *a, b,* and *c*—it's asking only about the average of those values. Of course, you could easily find the average if you knew the individual values. But, you can also find the average if you know the sum of the values, since the average of any group of values is their sum divided by the number of values in the group. Therefore, the question is asking whether $\frac{a+b+c}{3} = 8$. To simplify this equation, multiply both sides by 3 to get $a + b + c = 24$. If the sum is 24, then the average is 8.

Statement (1) says that $3(a + b + c) = 72$. You can divide both sides by 3 to find out that the sum is, indeed, 24; the average is 8; and the answer to the question is "yes." Since this is a Data Sufficiency problem, though, you can stop as soon as you know that you can find the sum of *a, b,* and *c,* and you're down to AD.

Statement (2) says that $2a + 2b + 2c = 48$. If you factor a 2 out of the left side of the equation, you get $2(a + b + c) = 48$ and once again see that you can find the sum. The correct answer is (D).

## QUESTIONS

11. $\sqrt{\sqrt{\left(1+\frac{17}{64}\right)}}=$

- $\frac{\sqrt{34}}{8}$
- $\frac{3\sqrt{2}}{4}$
- $\frac{9}{8}$
- $\frac{\sqrt{68}}{4}$
- $\frac{3\sqrt{2}}{2}$

## EXPLANATIONS

11. **B** Since you should always calculate things inside the parentheses first—don't forget PEMDAS!—start by adding 1 and $\frac{17}{64}$ to get $\frac{81}{64}$. Those are both perfect squares, so the inner root sign will be easy to handle: $\sqrt{\frac{81}{64}}=\frac{\sqrt{81}}{\sqrt{64}}=\frac{9}{8}$. Don't grab (C), though—you still need to work the outer sign: $\sqrt{\frac{9}{8}}=\frac{\sqrt{9}}{\sqrt{8}}=\frac{3}{2\sqrt{2}}$. Like in high school, you can't leave a radical on the bottom of a fraction, so you'll need to multiply your answer by $\frac{\sqrt{2}}{\sqrt{2}}$ to get the final answer of (B), $\frac{3\sqrt{2}}{4}$.

If you're comfortable estimating fractions and roots, you can apply POE to this question. $1+\frac{17}{64}$ is a little greater than 1; the square root of something a little greater than 1 is also something a little greater than 1; and the square root of that number is, again, something a little greater than 1. Only (B) and (C) are a little greater than 1.

## QUESTIONS

12. A certain stadium is currently full to $\frac{13}{16}$ of its maximum seating capacity. What is the maximum seating capacity of the stadium?

(1) If 1,250 people were to enter the stadium, the stadium would be full to $\frac{15}{16}$ of its maximum seating capacity.

(2) If 2,500 people were to leave the stadium, the stadium would be full to $\frac{9}{16}$ of its maximum seating capacity.

- Statement (1) ALONE is sufficient, but statement (2) alone is not sufficient.
- Statement (2) ALONE is sufficient, but statement (1) alone is not sufficient.
- BOTH statements TOGETHER are sufficient, but NEITHER statement ALONE is sufficient.
- EACH statement ALONE is sufficient.
- Statements (1) and (2) TOGETHER are not sufficient.

## EXPLANATIONS

12. **D** This is a fraction problem, so the key is to convert fractions to actual numbers. Statement (1) says that 1,250 people will take the stadium from $\frac{13}{16}$ full to $\frac{15}{16}$ full; that's a difference of $\frac{2}{16}$, or $\frac{1}{8}$, so 1,250 represents $\frac{1}{8}$ of the total seating capacity of the stadium. The stadium must, therefore, hold $8 \times 1,250$, or 10,000 people, and you're down to AD.

Statement (2) allows you to find a similar equivalence: a change of 2,500 represents the difference between $\frac{9}{16}$ and $\frac{13}{16}$, that is, $\frac{4}{16}$, or $\frac{1}{4}$ of the stadium's total seating capacity. So you know you can find the total seating capacity ($4 \times 2,500$, or 10,000 people) with Statement (2) as well, making (D) the correct answer.

## QUESTIONS

13. Andre has already saved $\frac{3}{7}$ of the cost of a new car, and he has calculated that he will be able to save $\frac{2}{5}$ of the remaining amount before the end of the summer. What fraction of the cost of the new car will he still need to save after the end of the summer?

- $\frac{6}{35}$
- $\frac{8}{35}$
- $\frac{12}{35}$
- $\frac{23}{35}$
- $\frac{29}{35}$

{1, 4, 6, $y$}

14. If the average (arithmetic mean) of the set of numbers above is 6, then what is the median?

- 5
- 6
- 7
- 13
- 24

## EXPLANATIONS

13. **C** Because there are fractions in the answer choices, and they're fractions of an unspecified amount, the quickest way to solve this problem is to Plug In. Make the price of Andre's dream car $35—the denominators of the fractions in the problem are 7 and 5 (both factors of 35) and, moreover, 35 is in the denominator of *all* of the answer choices.

If the car costs $35, and Andre has already saved $\frac{3}{7}$ of that, or $15, he currently has $20 left to save. Before the end of the summer, he'll be able to save $\frac{2}{5}$ of that remaining $20, or $8. That will give him a total of $23 saved toward his car, leaving him $12 to go. Expressed as a fraction of the cost of the car, that's $\frac{12}{35}$, and the correct answer is (C).

As always, watch those trap answers. Choice (D) is the fraction of the cost that Andre will have saved by the end of the summer. Choice (A) is what you'd get if you calculated Andre's summer earnings as two-fifths of the total cost of the car instead of two-fifths of what Andre has left to save. Choice (E) is what you'd get if you made both mistakes.

14. **A** The average of all four numbers is 6, so the numbers must add up to 6 times 4, or 24. That means $y$ must equal 13. And if $y$ equals 13, the median must be 5—that is, the average of the two middle numbers in the set. Even if $y$ is very large, the middle numbers will still be 4 and 6, so (D) and (E) are much too large. The correct answer is (A).

## QUESTIONS

15. A store sells a six-pack of soda for \$2.70. If this represents a savings of 10 percent of the individual price of cans of soda, then what is the price of a single can of soda?

- \$ 0.35
- \$ 0.40
- \$ 0.45
- \$ 0.50
- \$ 0.55

16. If Beth spent \$400 of her earnings last month on rent, how much did Beth earn last month?

(1) Beth saved $\frac{1}{3}$ of her earnings last month and spent half of the remainder on rent.

(2) Beth earned twice as much this month as last month.

- Statement (1) ALONE is sufficient, but statement (2) alone is not sufficient.
- Statement (2) ALONE is sufficient, but statement (1) alone is not sufficient.
- BOTH statements TOGETHER are sufficient, but NEITHER statement ALONE is sufficient.
- EACH statement ALONE is sufficient.
- Statements (1) and (2) TOGETHER are not sufficient.

## EXPLANATIONS

**15. D** If a six-pack sells for \$2.70, then each can costs 45 cents when purchased together. When purchased individually, the price is higher than 45 cents, so cross off (A), (B), and (C). Let's plug in (D). Choice (D) says the price of an individual can is 50 cents. 10% of 50 cents is 5 cents, so the price per can of a six-pack would be 50 – 5 = 45 cents. Therefore, (D) is correct.

**16. A** Covering up Statement (2) and looking only at Statement (1), you can see that Beth saved one-third of her earnings and spent half of the two-thirds that remained on rent. Half of two-thirds is one-third. So set up the equation:

$$\frac{1}{3} = \frac{400}{x}$$

And $x$ equals \$1,200. Note that you didn't actually need to find out how much Beth earned. You just needed to know that you *could* find out. You're down to AD. Now, looking at Statement (2), you can see that it tells you how Beth did THIS month. But do you care? Nope. The question asks about LAST month. The correct answer is (A).

# MATH BIN 1

## QUESTIONS

17. If $n$ is an integer, is $n$ even?

(1) $2n$ is an even integer.

(2) $n - 1$ is an odd integer.

- Statement (1) ALONE is sufficient, but statement (2) alone is not sufficient.
- Statement (2) ALONE is sufficient, but statement (1) alone is not sufficient.
- BOTH statements TOGETHER are sufficient, but NEITHER statement ALONE is sufficient.
- EACH statement ALONE is sufficient.
- Statements (1) and (2) TOGETHER are not sufficient.

## EXPLANATIONS

17. **B** To answer this yes-or-no question, you must plug in values that make the statements true. Starting with Statement (1), let's plug in 4 for $n$, which makes the statement "$2n$ is an even integer" true, and gives a "yes" to the overall question. Now, plug in 3 for $n$, which still makes the statement true, but gives a "no" to our overall question. Because the answer is sometimes "yes" and sometimes "no," you're down to BCE.

Looking at Statement (2) only, let's plug in values that make the statement true. If $n = 2$, the statement is true, and the answer to our overall question is a tentative "yes." Now, if you can find even one case where you can plug a number into this statement that makes the statement true but answers the question "no," then you'll be down to CE. But as you try different numbers, you'll realize that in order to make Statement (2) true, $n$ has to be even. So the answer to this question is (B).

18. At apartment complex $Z$, 30 percent of the residents are men over the age of 18, and 40 percent are women over the age of 18. If there are 24 children living in the complex, how many total residents live in apartment complex $Z$?

- 32
- 80
- 94
- 112
- 124

18. **B** Altogether, the percentages of men and women add up to 70%, so that means 30% of the residents at this complex are children. Just set up an equation:

$$\frac{30}{100} = \frac{24}{Z}$$

Solving for $Z$, the total number of residents is 80. The answer is (B).

You could also Plug In the Answers. Choice (C) seems difficult, so why not start with (B), which has an easy number to work with? 30% of 80 = 24, and 40% of 80 = 32. So there are a total of 24 + 32 = 56 adults. If (B) is correct, there should be 24 kids. And guess what? That's just what the problem says.

## QUESTIONS

19. Over the course of a soccer season, 30 percent of the players on a team scored goals. What is the ratio of players on the team who scored goals to those who did not?

- 3 to 10
- 1 to 3
- 3 to 7
- 1 to 1
- 3 to 1

20. At a restaurant, Luis left a tip for his waiter equal to 20 percent of his entire dinner check, including tax. What was the amount of the dinner check?

(1) The sum of the dinner check and the tip was $16.80.

(2) Luis's tip consisted of two bills and four coins.

- Statement (1) ALONE is sufficient, but statement (2) alone is not sufficient.
- Statement (2) ALONE is sufficient, but statement (1) alone is not sufficient.
- BOTH statements TOGETHER are sufficient, but NEITHER statement ALONE is sufficient.
- EACH statement ALONE is sufficient.
- Statements (1) and (2) TOGETHER are not sufficient.

## EXPLANATIONS

19. **C** If 30% of the players on the soccer team scored goals during the season, then 70% did not score goals. The ratio of those who scored to those who did not is 30 to 70, which reduces to 3 to 7. Some will find that Plugging In is the easiest way to solve this problem. Plug in 10 for the number of players on the team (choose this number because it is easy to work with in a percentage problem). 30% of the 10 players—that is to say, 3 players—scored goals. The other 7, it then follows, did not score goals. The ratio of those who scored to those who did not is 3 to 7. The correct answer is (C).

20. **A** Because Luis tipped the waiter 20%, the sum of the check and tip equals 1.2 times the amount of the check. Thus, you can write the equation

$$1.2x = 16.80$$

and solve for $x$ to determine both the amount of the check and the amount of Luis's tip. The answer must be (A) or (D). Statement (2) is insufficient because it does not identify either the bills or the coins. The correct answer is (A).

## QUESTIONS

21. Which sport utility vehicle has a higher list price, the Touristo or the Leisure?

(1) The list price of the Leisure is $\frac{5}{6}$ the list price of the Touristo.

(2) The list price of the Touristo is 1.2 times the list price of the Leisure.

- Statement (1) ALONE is sufficient, but statement (2) alone is not sufficient.
- Statement (2) ALONE is sufficient, but statement (1) alone is not sufficient.
- BOTH statements TOGETHER are sufficient, but NEITHER statement ALONE is sufficient.
- EACH statement ALONE is sufficient.
- Statements (1) and (2) TOGETHER are not sufficient.

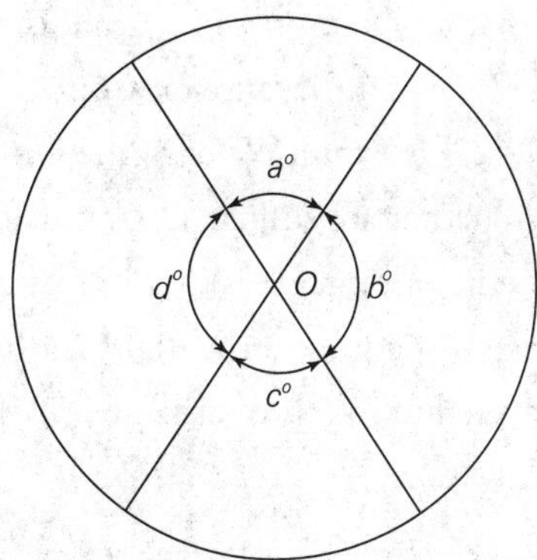


22. In the circle above, center $O$ is intersected by 2 straight lines, and $3a = b$. What is the value of $b - a$?

- 2
- 30
- 45
- 90
- 135

## EXPLANATIONS

21. **D** According to Statement (1), the list price of the Leisure is $\frac{5}{6}$ the list price of the Touristo. The list price of the Touristo is therefore greater than the list price of the Leisure. Statement (1) is sufficient; the answer must be (A) or (D). Statement (2) tells you that the list price of the Touristo is 1.2 times the list price of the Leisure. So Statement (2) also tells you that the list price of the Touristo is greater than the list price of the Leisure. The correct answer is (D).

22. **D** If you look carefully at the drawing, you should notice that $a$ and $b$ are supplementary angles; that is, together they make up a line. The sum of these angles, therefore, is 180°. Or, to put this in math-speak:

$$a + b = 180$$

Now, return to the equation in the question stem, $3a = b$. You can use this information to rewrite the equation $a + b = 180$ as

$$a + 3a = 180$$

$$4a = 180$$

$$a = 45$$

## QUESTIONS

## EXPLANATIONS

Because $a + b = 180$, and $a = 45$, $b$ must equal 135, which is (E). Wait, though, you're not done yet: the question asks for the solution $b - a$. Because $b - a = 135 - 45$, the answer to this question is 90. The correct answer is (D).

23. What is the value of integer $w$ ?

(1) $w$ is a multiple of 3.

(2) $420 < w < 425$

- Statement (1) ALONE is sufficient, but statement (2) alone is not sufficient.
- Statement (2) ALONE is sufficient, but statement (1) alone is not sufficient.
- BOTH statements TOGETHER are sufficient, but NEITHER statement ALONE is sufficient.
- EACH statement ALONE is sufficient.
- Statements (1) and (2) TOGETHER are not sufficient.

23. **C** Because there are an infinite number of multiples of 3, it is clear that Statement (1) is not sufficient to answer the question. The answer must be (B), (C), or (E). Statement (2) narrows the range of possible answers to 421, 422, 423, or 424. However, because it does not narrow the answer to a single solution, it is not sufficient. Eliminate (B). When you put the two statements together, you know that $w$ is a multiple of 3 that is either 421, 422, 423, or 424. Because only one of these values, 423, is a multiple of 3, the two statements together are sufficient. (A quick way to test whether an integer is divisible by 3 is to add its digits; if the sum of the digits is divisible by 3, then the number is divisible by 3.) The correct answer is (C).

24. What is the quotient when 0.25% of 600 is divided by 0.25 of 600 ?

- 10
- 1
- 0.1
- 0.01
- 0.001

24. **D** Before you worry about the division, solve for the two values. The second one is easier, so start there: "of" means multiply, so $0.25 \times 600 = 150$. With the first value, you have to be sure to take into account both the decimal *and* the percent sign: 0.25% can be represented as $\frac{0.25}{100}$, or 0.0025. Either way, when you multiply by 600, the result is 1.5. The quotient is thus 1.5 divided by 150, or 0.01. The answer is (D).

## QUESTIONS

## EXPLANATIONS

If you're really comfortable with manipulating fractions, you can save yourself a lot of math. The whole question translates into $\frac{\frac{0.25}{100}\times 600}{0.25\times 600}$, which easily cancels down to $\frac{1}{100}$, or 0.01.

25. A certain town's economic development council has 21 members. If the number of females on the council is 3 less than 3 times the number of males on the council, then the town's economic development council has how many male members?

- 5
- 6
- 7
- 9
- 15

25. **B** Although you could solve this by writing a pair of algebraic equations ($f + m = 21$ and $f = m - 3$), it's simpler to Plug In the Answers. Start with (C), 7 men. The number of women would be 3 less than 3 times that number, or 21 – 3 = 18 women. That's a total of 25 council members altogether, and you're looking for 21. Now that you know that (C) is too big, eliminate (C), (D), and (E). If you try (B), 6 men, then you have 18 – 3 = 15 women. This gives the desired total of 21 council members, so the correct answer is (B). If you got (E), by the way, you solved for the number of *female* members on the board.

26. Roger can chop down 4 trees in an hour. How long does it take Vincent to chop down 4 trees?

(1) Vincent spends 6 hours per day chopping down trees.

(2) Vincent takes twice as long as Roger to chop down trees.

- Statement (1) ALONE is sufficient, but statement (2) alone is not sufficient.
- Statement (2) ALONE is sufficient, but statement (1) alone is not sufficient.
- BOTH statements TOGETHER are sufficient, but NEITHER statement ALONE is sufficient.
- EACH statement ALONE is sufficient.
- Statements (1) and (2) TOGETHER are not sufficient.

26. **B** Statement (1) tells you how many hours Vincent spends chopping down trees in a day, but it provides no data to help you determine how long it takes him to chop down 4 trees. This statement is clearly insufficient to answer the question. The answer must be (B), (C), or (E).
Statement (2) tells you that Vincent takes twice as long as Roger to chop down trees. Because the question stem tells you that Roger chops down 4 trees per hour, you can deduce that Vincent chops down 4 trees every 2 hours. Thus, Statement (2) is sufficient to answer the question. The correct answer is (B).

# MATH BIN 2

## QUESTIONS

1. If $x = \dfrac{\frac{5}{9}+\frac{15}{27}+\frac{45}{81}}{3}$, then $\sqrt{1-x}=$

- $\frac{\sqrt{5}}{9}$
- $\frac{5}{9}$
- $\frac{2}{3}$
- $\frac{\sqrt{5}}{3}$
- $\frac{15}{9}$

2. Steven has run a certain number of laps around a track at an average (arithmetic mean) time per lap of 51 seconds. If he runs one additional lap in 39 seconds and reduces his average time per lap to 49 seconds, how many laps did he run at an average time per lap of 51 seconds?

- 2
- 5
- 6
- 10
- 12

## EXPLANATIONS

1. **C** You could start by converting all the fractions to their least common denominator of 81—an understandable temptation. However, in this case, it's quicker and simpler to reduce the fractions instead. They all reduce to $\frac{5}{9}$, so $x = \dfrac{\frac{5}{9}+\frac{5}{9}+\frac{5}{9}}{3}$, or $\dfrac{3\left(\frac{5}{9}\right)}{3}$…or $\frac{5}{9}$. Now that you know the value of $x$, you can solve for $\sqrt{(1-x)}$ : $\sqrt{\left(1-\frac{5}{9}\right)} = \sqrt{\frac{4}{9}} = \frac{\sqrt{4}}{\sqrt{9}} = \frac{2}{3}$. The correct answer is (C). Choice (B), of course, is $x$ itself, and (D) is $\sqrt{x}$.

2. **B** This is a multistep average problem involving an unknown quantity—in short, a perfect place to Plug In the Answers! Start with (C). If Steven has already run 6 laps, then he has run for a total of $6 \times 51$, or 306, seconds. One more lap in 39 seconds gives him a total of 7 laps in 345 seconds, and the average works out to be a little greater than 49 seconds ($49\frac{2}{7}$, to be exact). Close, but not quite. Fewer laps will reduce Steven's average speed, so (B) is the next logical choice to try. Five laps in 51 seconds means Steven has run $5 \times 51$, or 255, seconds so far, and the additional 39-second lap gives a total of 6 laps run in 294 seconds. The average is now $\frac{294}{6} = 49$ seconds, and (B) is the correct answer.

# MATH BIN 2

## QUESTIONS

3. $200^2 - 2(200)(199) + 199^2 =$

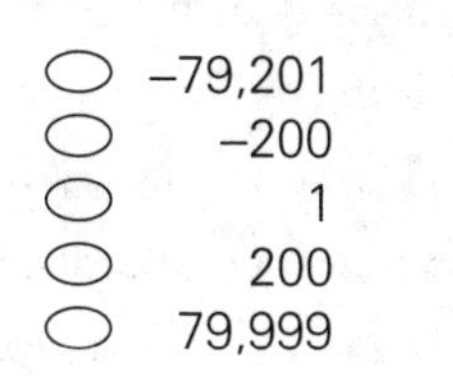

- −79,201
- −200
- 1
- 200
- 79,999

4. If $x \neq \frac{1}{2}$, then $\frac{6x^2 + 11x - 7}{2x - 1} =$

- $3x + 7$
- $3x - 7$
- $3x + 1$
- $x + 7$
- $x - 7$

## EXPLANATIONS

3. **C** Although you could solve this problem with lots of tedious multiplication, it's much faster to recognize the common quadratic hidden in the numbers: $x^2 - 2xy + y^2 = (x - y)(x - y)$. That means this calculation can be rewritten as $(200 - 199)(200 - 199)$, or $(1)(1)$. The correct answer is (C).

Since the answer choices vary so widely, you could have applied some POE to the most extreme answer choices, (A) and (E). The product of 200 and 199, which you have to double, is not too different from either $200^2$ or $199^2$. Thus, the negative value in the equation is roughly equal to the sum of the two positive values in the equation. If you did the math, by the way, and *got* one of those answers, you must have reversed an addition or subtraction sign.

4. **A** Since this problem has variables in the answer choices, the simplest way to solve it is to Plug In. If $x = 2$, the equation becomes $\frac{6(2)^2 + 11(2) - 7}{2(2) - 1} = \frac{24 + 22 - 7}{4 - 1} = \frac{39}{3} = 13$. Now plug in 2 for $x$ in the answer choices—only (A) yields 13, so it must be the correct answer.

You could also try Plugging In the Answers. Try multiplying the answer choices by the expression in the denominator of the fraction and see which one yields the expression in the numerator. Only (A) does, so it is the correct answer.

## QUESTIONS

5. If Amy drove the distance from her home to the beach in less than 2 hours, was her average speed greater than 60 miles per hour?

(1) The distance that Amy drove from her home to the beach was less than 125 miles.

(2) The distance that Amy drove from her home to the beach was greater than 122 miles.

- Statement (1) ALONE is sufficient, but statement (2) alone is not sufficient.
- Statement (2) ALONE is sufficient, but statement (1) alone is not sufficient.
- BOTH statements TOGETHER are sufficient, but NEITHER statement ALONE is sufficient.
- EACH statement ALONE is sufficient.
- Statements (1) and (2) TOGETHER are not sufficient.

## EXPLANATIONS

5. **B** Take a moment to translate what this question is really asking: is the distance Amy drove greater than 120 miles? This rate problem is also a yes-or-no question, so you don't need to know Amy's exact speed, just whether her average speed was greater than 60 miles per hour. The simplest way to find out whether Statement (1) is sufficient is to try different possible times and distances. If her total driving time was, for instance, 1 hour, a distance of 61 miles yields an answer of "yes." Meanwhile, a distance of 59 miles yields an answer of "no." That means the possible answers are BCE.

Regardless of what times and distances you plug in for Statement (2), you will always get an answer of "yes." Even if Amy were to have driven the *full* 2 hours and gone *only* 122 miles, she would be driving at a rate of 61 miles per hour; since she actually drove a greater distance in less time, her rate must be greater than 61. Since Statement (2) always gives the same answer, it is sufficient, and the answer is (B).

## QUESTIONS

6. If $x = m - 1$, which of the following is true when $m = \frac{1}{2}$?

- $x^0 > x^2 > x^3 > x^1$
- $x^0 > x^2 > x^1 > x^3$
- $x^0 > x^1 > x^2 > x^3$
- $x^2 > x^0 > x^3 > x^1$
- $x^3 > x^2 > x^1 > x^0$

## EXPLANATIONS

6. **A** Once you've solved for *x*, which equals $-\frac{1}{2}$, this question is just a matter of putting the four values in order. Even better, you already know two of them: $x = -\frac{1}{2}$ and $x^0 = 1$. With the other two values, be especially careful about the negative sign: $x^2 = \frac{1}{4}$ and $x^3 = -\frac{1}{8}$. The correct order is $x^0 > x^2 > x^3 > x^1$, and the answer is (A).

# MATH BIN 2

## QUESTIONS

7. If a comedian plays two shows and twice as many tickets are available for the evening show as for the afternoon show, what percentage of the total number of tickets available for both shows has been sold?

   (1) A total of 450 tickets are available for both shows.

   (2) Exactly $\frac{3}{5}$ of the tickets available for the afternoon show have been sold, and exactly $\frac{1}{5}$ of the tickets available for the evening show have been sold.

   - Statement (1) ALONE is sufficient, but statement (2) alone is not sufficient.
   - Statement (2) ALONE is sufficient, but statement (1) alone is not sufficient.
   - BOTH statements TOGETHER are sufficient, but NEITHER statement ALONE is sufficient.
   - EACH statement ALONE is sufficient.
   - Statements (1) and (2) TOGETHER are not sufficient.

8. If $\frac{1}{y}=2\frac{2}{3}$, then $\left(\frac{1}{y+1}\right)^2=$

   - $\frac{9}{64}$
   - $\frac{3}{8}$
   - $\frac{64}{121}$
   - $\frac{121}{64}$
   - $\frac{64}{9}$

## EXPLANATIONS

7. **B** The information in Statement (1), along with that in the question itself, is enough for you to find the number of tickets issued for each show. Without any information about the number of tickets that were sold, though, you can't answer the question, and you're down to BCE.

   Statement (2), along with the information in the question, is sufficient—even without the information in Statement (1). If you have the fraction of each type of ticket that was sold, and the ratio of one type of ticket to the other, you can figure out the overall percentage of tickets sold. The correct answer is (B).

   Want to prove it? Try Plugging In. In Statement (2), the denominator of both fractions is 5, so let's say that 25 tickets have been issued for the afternoon show and 50 have been issued for the evening show. That means 15 tickets have been sold for the afternoon show and 10 have been sold for the evening show, for a total of 25 tickets sold out of a total of 75 tickets issued. The answer is $\frac{1}{3}$, as it will always be if you meet the requirements of Statement (2) and the question itself.

8. **C** First, solve for *y*. Since $2\frac{2}{3}=\frac{8}{3}$, $\frac{1}{y}=\frac{8}{3}$ and thus $y=\frac{3}{8}$. Now plug the value for *y* into the expression:

$$\left(\frac{1}{\frac{3}{8}+1}\right)^2=\left(\frac{1}{\left(\frac{11}{8}\right)}\right)^2=\frac{1^2}{\left(\frac{11}{8}\right)^2}=\frac{1}{\frac{121}{64}}=\frac{64}{121}.$$

   The correct answer is (C).

   Choice (B), of course, is the value of *y*. Choice (D) is the reciprocal of the correct answer, which

## QUESTIONS

## EXPLANATIONS

could indicate that you didn't do the last step of the calculation. If you chose (A), you forgot to add 1 when you put the value for $y$ into the expression. And if you chose (E), you did both.

9. An operation ~ is defined by $a \sim b = \frac{a+b}{(ab)^2}$ for all numbers $a$ and $b$ such that $ab \neq 0$. If $c \neq 0$ and $a \sim c = 0$, then $c =$

- ◯ $-a$
- ◯ 0
- ◯ $\sqrt{a}$
- ◯ $a$
- ◯ $a^2$

9. **A** Answering a function problem on the GMAT is simply a matter of following the directions provided by the definition of the function. In this case, the operation signified by two numbers with the ~ between them is defined as the sum of the numbers on either side of the ~ sign divided by the square of the product of the two numbers. If $a \sim c = 0$, then $\frac{a+c}{(ac)^2} = 0$; since the numerator must be zero in order for the fraction itself to equal zero, you know that $a + c = 0$. Subtract $a$ from both sides and $c = -a$. The answer is (A).

10. If $x$ is a positive integer, is the greatest common factor of 150 and $x$ a prime number?

(1) $x$ is a prime number.

(2) $x < 4$

- ◯ Statement (1) ALONE is sufficient, but statement (2) alone is not sufficient.
- ◯ Statement (2) ALONE is sufficient, but statement (1) alone is not sufficient.
- ◯ BOTH statements TOGETHER are sufficient, but NEITHER statement ALONE is sufficient.
- ◯ EACH statement ALONE is sufficient.
- ◯ Statements (1) and (2) TOGETHER are not sufficient.

10. **C** The easiest way to determine whether Statement (1) by itself is sufficient is to plug in different values for $x$. If $x = 2$, the greatest common factor is 2, and the answer to this yes-or-no question is "yes." If $x = 7$, on the other hand, the greatest common factor is 1, and since 1 is not prime, the answer is "no." The possible answers are BCE.
Statement (2) by itself is also not sufficient. If $x$ is equal to 1, 2, or 3, then the greatest common factor of $x$ and 150 is $x$ itself. But since 2 and 3 are prime, and 1 is not, the possible answers are (C) and (E).

## QUESTIONS

## EXPLANATIONS

If the statements are put together, the only possible values for $x$ are 2 and 3. With either one, the greatest common factor is equal to $x$ itself and is, therefore, prime. The correct answer is (C).

$X = \{9, 10, 11, 12\}$

$Y = \{2, 3, 4, 5\}$

11. If one number is chosen at random from each of the sets above and the number from Set $X$ is divided by the number from Set $Y$, what is the probability that the result is an integer?

○ $\frac{1}{16}$

○ $\frac{3}{8}$

○ $\frac{1}{2}$

○ $\frac{3}{4}$

○ $\frac{15}{16}$

11. **B** As with all probability problems, find a fraction that has the total number of possibilities in the denominator and the number of those possibilities that meet a certain requirement in the numerator. The denominator is the easy part: because there are 4 members of each set, there are $4 \times 4 = 16$ total possibilities for the quotient when one member of $X$ is divided by one member of $Y$. Now just figure out how many of those possibilities meet the requirement.

The requirement, in this case, is that the quotient is an integer—in other words, that the member chosen from $X$ is divisible by the member chosen from $Y$—and you can count out all of the combinations that meet that requirement quickly and easily. The first member of Set $X$, 9, is divisible by only one member of Set $Y$, 3, so that's one. Then, working through Set $X$: 10 is divisible by both 2 and 5, so there are two other possibilities; 11 is prime, so it's not divisible by any members of Set $Y$; and 12 gives three other possibilities, because it's divisible by 2, 3, and 4. Thus, 6 of the total of 16 possibilities meet our requirement, and our probability is $\frac{6}{16}$, or $\frac{3}{8}$. The answer is (B).

# MATH BIN 2

## QUESTIONS

12. If $p$ and $q$ are integers, is $\frac{p+q}{2}$ an integer?

(1) $p < 17$

(2) $p = q$

- Statement (1) ALONE is sufficient, but statement (2) alone is not sufficient.
- Statement (2) ALONE is sufficient, but statement (1) alone is not sufficient.
- BOTH statements TOGETHER are sufficient, but NEITHER statement ALONE is sufficient.
- EACH statement ALONE is sufficient.
- Statements (1) and (2) TOGETHER are not sufficient.

## EXPLANATIONS

**12. B** Since Statement (1) doesn't say anything about the value of $q$, and very little about the value of $p$, it is, by itself, insufficient to answer this yes-or-no question. Statement (2), though, while it gives no new specifics about the values of $p$ or $q$, gives enough information to know the answer to the question. If $p = q$, then $\frac{p+q}{2} = \frac{p+p}{2} = \frac{2p}{2} = p$ since you know from the question that $p$ is an integer, the answer to the question is "yes," and the answer is (B). Of course, you can easily show the sufficiency of Statement (2) by plugging in values for $p$ and $q$: as long as the values are equal integers, the answer is always "yes."

13. A perfectly spherical satellite with a radius of 4 feet is being packed for shipment to its launch site. If the inside dimensions of the rectangular crates available for shipment, when measured in feet, are consecutive even integers, then what is the volume of the smallest available crate that can be used? (The volume of a sphere is $V = \frac{4}{3}\pi r^3$.)

- 48
- 192
- 480
- 960
- 1,680

**13. D** Although this may seem like a volume question, it's really about being able to fit the diameter of the satellite inside the crate—you can entirely disregard the formula for the volume of a sphere. Start with what you know: since the radius of the sphere is 4, the diameter is 8. Therefore, every dimension in the crate must be at least 8 and the smallest available crate will measure $8 \times 10 \times 12$. The volume of that crate is 960, and the correct answer is (D).

In fact, if you try to use the volume formula, you can easily go astray. Using a rough value of 3 for $\pi$, you can approximate the value of the sphere to be a little greater than 250 (replacing $\pi$ with 3 in the formula gives a value of 256, and the exact value is a little greater than 268). You might be tempted, therefore, to select (C), but don't: the only set of three consecutive integers that yields a volume of 480 is $6 \times 8 \times 10$, and you can't put a spherical object with a diameter of 8 feet into a crate that's only 6 feet across in one direction.

## QUESTIONS

14. Richard is 6 years older than David, and David is 8 years older than Scott. In 8 years, if Richard will be twice as old as Scott, then how old was David 4 years ago?

- 8
- 10
- 12
- 14
- 16

15. What is the value of $x$ ?

(1) $x^2 - 5x + 4 = 0$

(2) $x$ is not prime.

- Statement (1) ALONE is sufficient, but statement (2) alone is not sufficient.
- Statement (2) ALONE is sufficient, but statement (1) alone is not sufficient.
- BOTH statements TOGETHER are sufficient, but NEITHER statement ALONE is sufficient.
- EACH statement ALONE is sufficient.
- Statements (1) and (2) TOGETHER are not sufficient.

## EXPLANATIONS

14. **B** This problem could be an algebraic nightmare, so Plug In the Answers, starting with (C), 12. If David was 12 years old 4 years ago, he's 16 now, and that means Richard is 22 and Scott is 8. In 8 years, then, Richard will be 30 and Scott will be 16; since Richard won't be twice as old as Scott at that point, this can't be the answer.

Now try (B), 10, using the same process. If David was 10 years old 4 years ago, he's 14 now, so Richard is 20 and Scott is 6. In 8 years, then, Richard will be 28 and Scott will be 14; since Richard will then be twice as old as Scott, the answer is (B).

15. **E** Statement (1) is a quadratic equation, so factor it and see what the options are for $x$:

$x^2 - 5x + 4 = 0$ factors into $(x - 4)(x - 1) = 0$, so $x$ could be 4 or 1. Since there's more than one value for $x$, Statement (1) alone is insufficient, and you're down to BCE.

Statement (2) alone leaves you with the vast majority of all numbers—this statement is *definitely* not sufficient, so you're down to (C) or (E).

When you combine the statements, they're still not sufficient. Be careful not to fall for one of the classic GMAT traps: 1 is *not* prime. Because 4 is also not prime, you're left with both values, and the correct answer is (E).

## QUESTIONS

16. Sam and Jessica are invited to a dance. If there are 7 men and 7 women in total at the dance, and one woman and one man are chosen to lead the dance, what is the probability that Sam and Jessica will NOT be the pair chosen to lead the dance?

- ◯ $\frac{1}{49}$
- ◯ $\frac{1}{7}$
- ◯ $\frac{6}{7}$
- ◯ $\frac{47}{49}$
- ◯ $\frac{48}{49}$

## EXPLANATIONS

16. **E** The probability that Sam will be chosen is $\frac{1}{7}$. The probability that Jessica will be chosen is also $\frac{1}{7}$. The probability that they will both be chosen is $\frac{1}{7} \times \frac{1}{7} = \frac{1}{49}$ This is (A), but you aren't done yet. The question asks for the probability that they will NOT both be chosen. The probability that an event does NOT happen can be expressed as 1 minus the probability that the event DOES happen. So $1 - \frac{1}{49} = \frac{48}{49}$, or (E).

## QUESTIONS

17. What is the surface area of rectangular solid *Y*?

(1) The dimensions of one face of rectangular solid *Y* are 2 by 3.

(2) The volume of rectangular solid *Y* is 12.

- ◯ Statement (1) ALONE is sufficient, but statement (2) alone is not sufficient.
- ◯ Statement (2) ALONE is sufficient, but statement (1) alone is not sufficient.
- ◯ BOTH statements TOGETHER are sufficient, but NEITHER statement ALONE is sufficient.
- ◯ EACH statement ALONE is sufficient.
- ◯ Statements (1) and (2) TOGETHER are not sufficient.

## EXPLANATIONS

17. **C** Whenever you see a geometry problem without a diagram, it's a good idea to make one. Statement (1) gives only two of the three dimensions you need to find the surface area. You're down to BCE.

Statement (2) gives the volume of the rectangular solid. By itself, the volume does not give any of the three dimensions that you need to find the surface area, so you're down to (C) and (E).

Putting the two statements together, you have all three dimensions. Statement (1) says that two of the dimensions are 2 and 3. Since the formula for the volume of a rectangular solid is $V = lwh$, the third dimension of the solid is 2. With all three dimensions, the surface area can be calculated. The answer is (C).

## QUESTIONS

18. A six-sided die with faces numbered 1 through 6 is rolled three times. What is the probability that the face with the number 6 on it will NOT face upward on all three rolls?

- $\frac{1}{216}$
- $\frac{1}{6}$
- $\frac{2}{3}$
- $\frac{17}{18}$
- $\frac{215}{216}$

## EXPLANATIONS

18. **E** Before you start calculating, it is always helpful to think about what is reasonable. The probability that the number 6 is going to come up three times in a row is pretty low, which is another way of saying that the probability that 6 is NOT going to come up three times in a row is pretty high. So eliminate (A), (B), and (C). Now, figure out the problem. The probability that the first roll yields the number 6 is $\frac{1}{6}$. The probability that the second roll yields the number 6 is also $\frac{1}{6}$. The probability that the third roll yields the number 6? You guessed it: $\frac{1}{6}$. To find the probability of the series of these three events happening, you multiply the probabilities of each of the individual events: $\frac{1}{6} \times \frac{1}{6} \times \frac{1}{6} = \frac{1}{216}$. That's (A), but you aren't done yet. $\frac{1}{216}$ is the probability that the number 6 WILL land face up on all three rolls. The probability that an event does NOT happen can be expressed as 1 minus the probability that the event DOES happen: $1 - \frac{1}{216} = \frac{215}{216}$. The correct answer is (E).

## QUESTIONS

19. What is the sum of $x$, $y$, and $z$ ?

(1) $2x + y + 3z = 45$

(2) $x + 2y = 30$

- Statement (1) ALONE is sufficient, but statement (2) alone is not sufficient.
- Statement (2) ALONE is sufficient, but statement (1) alone is not sufficient.
- BOTH statements TOGETHER are sufficient, but NEITHER statement ALONE is sufficient.
- EACH statement ALONE is sufficient.
- Statements (1) and (2) TOGETHER are not sufficient.

20. A department store receives a shipment of 1,000 shirts, for which it pays $9,000. The store sells the shirts at a price 80 percent above cost for one month, after which it reduces the price of the shirts to 20 percent above cost. The store sells 75 percent of the shirts during the first month and 50 percent of the remaining shirts afterward. How much gross income did sales of the shirts generate?

- $10,000
- $10,800
- $12,150
- $13,500
- $16,200

## EXPLANATIONS

19. **C** Gut instinct may lead to you select (E) on this one; after all, Statement (1) provides a three-variable equation, which does not have a unique solution. Statement (2) refers to only two of the three variables mentioned in the question stem, so clearly it cannot be sufficient. At first glance, it may be hard to imagine how the two statements together could be any more helpful than each is on its own.

Statement (1) is, in fact, insufficient on its own, for the reason stated above. The possible answers are BCE. Statement (2) is also insufficient, again for the reason stated above. Eliminate (B). The answer is (C) or (E).

Now, add the two equations provided by Statements (1) and (2) to get $3x + 3y + 3z = 75$. Factor a 3 out of both sides of the equation and you end up with $x + y + z = 25$. Thus, the two statements together *are* sufficient to answer the question. The correct answer is (C).

20. **D** To answer this question, break the problem down into small, manageable steps. The first job at hand is to determine the selling price of the shirt, both during the first month they were on sale and then during subsequent months. Because the store bought 1,000 shirts for $9,000, the cost of each shirt was $9.00. The store sold the shirts at an 80% markup during the first month. 1.8 × $9.00 = $16.20, so during the first month, the shirts sold for $16.20 each. After the first month, the selling price was 20% above cost. 1.20 × $9.00 = $10.80, so that was the selling price after the first month.

The store sold 75% of the shirts during the first month. 75% of 1,000 is 750; the store sold 750 shirts at $16.20 each. 750 × $16.20 = $12,150. Note that this partial answer is (C). Test-takers who only half-finish their work will choose this incorrect answer. The store then sold 50% of its remaining stock at $10.80 per shirt. The remaining

## QUESTIONS

## EXPLANATIONS

stock is 250 shirts (1,000 – 750), half of which is 125. The store, then, sold 125 shirts at \$10.80 each. 125 × \$10.80 = \$1,350. The store's gross income from the sale of these shirts, then, is \$12,150 + \$1,350 = \$13,500. The correct answer is (D).

21. David has three credit cards: a Passport card, an EverywhereCard, and an American Local card. He owes balances on all three cards. Does he owe the greatest balance on the EverywhereCard?

(1) The sum of the balances on his EverywhereCard and American Local card is \$1,350, which is three times the balance on his Passport card.

(2) The balance on his EverywhereCard is $\frac{4}{3}$ of the balance on his Passport card and $\frac{4}{5}$ of the balance on his American Local card.

- Statement (1) ALONE is sufficient, but statement (2) alone is not sufficient.
- Statement (2) ALONE is sufficient, but statement (1) alone is not sufficient.
- BOTH statements TOGETHER are sufficient, but NEITHER statement ALONE is sufficient.
- EACH statement ALONE is sufficient.
- Statements (1) and (2) TOGETHER are not sufficient.

21. **B** Statement (1) provides information only about the sum of the balances on David's EverywhereCard and his American Local card. Therefore, the statement is insufficient to determine whether the balance on David's EverywhereCard is his highest balance, because it does not provide any information that allows you to compare the balance on the EverywhereCard to the balances on the other two cards. The possible answers are BCE.

Statement (2) tells you that the balance on David's EverywhereCard is greater than the balance on his Passport card and less than the balance on his American Local card. Thus, it provides enough information to answer the question. The correct answer is (B).

There are a couple of places where you can go wrong on this question. The first involves the fact that Statement (2) answers the question this way: "No, he does not owe the greatest balance on the EverywhereCard." Some test-takers get confused and use a "no" answer to decide that a statement is insufficient. Remember, it doesn't matter how you answer a yes-or-no question, just so long as you can answer it conclusively.

Some test-takers might realize that Statements (1) and (2) together provide enough information to calculate the exact balance on each credit card, and thus may choose (C). But because Statement (2) is sufficient on its own, (C) cannot be the correct answer to this question.

## QUESTIONS

22. Automobile $A$ is traveling at two-thirds the speed that Automobile $B$ is traveling. At what speed is Automobile $A$ traveling?

(1) If both automobiles increased their speed by 10 miles per hour, Automobile $A$ would be traveling at three-quarters the speed that Automobile $B$ would be traveling.

(2) If both automobiles decreased their speed by 10 miles per hour, Automobile $A$ would be traveling at half the speed that Automobile $B$ would be traveling.

- Statement (1) ALONE is sufficient, but statement (2) alone is not sufficient.
- Statement (2) ALONE is sufficient, but statement (1) alone is not sufficient.
- BOTH statements TOGETHER are sufficient, but NEITHER statement ALONE is sufficient.
- EACH statement ALONE is sufficient.
- Statements (1) and (2) TOGETHER are not sufficient.

## EXPLANATIONS

22. **D** To solve this problem, you need to write some equations. Let's call Automobile *A*'s current speed *A* and Automobile *B*'s current speed *B*. The question stem tells you that $A = \frac{2}{3}B$. Statement (1) tells you that $A + 10 = \frac{3}{4}(B + 10)$. Thus, between the question stem and Statement (1), you have two distinct equations, which means you can solve for the two variables. The possible answers are (A) or (D). Statement (2) tells you that $A - 10 = \frac{1}{2}(B - 10)$. Once again, you have two distinct equations and two variables. Statement (2) is sufficient, and the correct answer is (D).

23. $a$ and $b$ are nonzero integers such that $0.35a = 0.2b$. What is the value of $b$ in terms of $a$ ?

- $0.07a$
- $0.57a$
- $0.7a$
- $1.75a$
- $17.5a$

23. **D** What makes this problem tricky is the presence of decimals, so the best thing to do is to convert the decimals to integers. Multiply both sides of the equation by 100 to produce the equation $35a = 20b$. (If you don't multiply both sides carefully, you could end up with (E).) Now, simply solve for $b$ by dividing both sides by 20 to get $b = \frac{35}{20}a$. Convert the fraction to a decimal by dividing 35 by 20 to yield $b = 1.75a$. The correct answer is (D).

# MATH BIN 2

## QUESTIONS

24. The Binary Ice Cream Shoppe sells two flavors of cones, vanilla and chocolate. On Friday, the ratio of vanilla cones sold to chocolate cones sold was 2 to 3. If the store sold 4 more vanilla cones, the ratio of vanilla cones sold to chocolate cones sold would have been 3 to 4. How many vanilla cones did the store sell on Friday?

- 32
- 35
- 42
- 48
- 54

25. Is integer *a* a prime number?

(1) 2*a* has exactly three factors.

(2) *a* is an even number.

- Statement (1) ALONE is sufficient, but statement (2) alone is not sufficient.
- Statement (2) ALONE is sufficient, but statement (1) alone is not sufficient.
- BOTH statements TOGETHER are sufficient, but NEITHER statement ALONE is sufficient.
- EACH statement ALONE is sufficient.
- Statements (1) and (2) TOGETHER are not sufficient.

## EXPLANATIONS

24. **A** Plug In the Answers! Start with (C). If this is the correct answer, then the Binary Ice Cream Shoppe sold 42 vanilla cones on Friday. Because vanilla cones sold at a 2-to-3 ratio to chocolate cones, this means that the shop sold 63 chocolate cones $\left(\frac{2}{3}=\frac{42}{63}\right)$. If this is the correct answer, then the ratio of 46, the result of adding 4 to the number of vanilla cones sold, to 63 is 3 to 4. It is not, so this answer is incorrect.

You must decide next whether the correct answer is more or less than 42. Since the situation is complicated, you may not be sure in which direction to go so just pick a direction; you'll find the correct answer soon enough. Note that the answer cannot be (B) because 35 is not divisible by 2; thus it cannot be the number of vanilla cones sold. Choice (A) is the correct answer. 32 to 48 is a 2-to-3 ratio; add 4 more vanilla cones to get a ratio of 36 to 48, which reduces to 3 to 4.

25. **A** In order to answer this yes-or-no question correctly, you must remember that 2 is a prime number. Statement (1) tells you that 2*a* has exactly 3 distinct factors. Plug in some numbers. If you choose 3 for *a*, then $2a = 6$. What are the factors of 6? 1, 6, 2, and 3. In other words, there are 4 factors. Is there any number you can plug in for *a* that gives only 3 factors for the number 2*a*? As a matter of fact, there is only one: 2. Only 2 times 2, or 4, has exactly three factors: 1, 2, and 4. This tells you that *a* is 2; any other multiple of 2 has at least 4 factors (itself, 1, 2, and the product of itself and 2.) So if *a* can only be 2, can you definitely answer this yes-or-no question? Yes, 2 is a prime number. Write down AD.

## QUESTIONS

## EXPLANATIONS

Statement (2) is tempting for several reasons. If you forgot that 2 is prime, you would incorrectly conclude that this statement alone is sufficient to answer the question "No." If you figured out that $a = 2$ from Statement (1), you may be tempted to choose this because it confirms the information given in Statement (1). However, because it is not sufficient to answer the question on its own, you must resist temptation. The correct answer is (A).

26. Renee rides her bicycle 20 miles in $m$ minutes. If she rides $x$ miles in 10 minutes at the same rate, which of the following is an expression for $x$, in terms of $m$ ?

- $\frac{m}{200}$
- $\frac{m}{20}$
- $\frac{m}{2}$
- $2m$
- $\frac{200}{m}$

**26. E** Solve this problem by Plugging In. Set $m$ equal to a value that turns the question into an easy arithmetic problem. For example, $m = 40$ is a good, easy value. It tells you that Renee can ride 1 mile every 2 minutes. How many miles, then, can she ride in 10 minutes? She can ride 5 miles in 10 minutes.

Now, plug in 40 for $m$ in each of the answer choices. The correct answer will calculate to 5, the value of $x$ when $m = 40$. Because (E) is the only answer that equals 5, (E) is the correct answer.

27. If $s$ and $w$ are integers, is $\frac{w}{5}$ an integer?

(1) $4s + 2$ is divisible by 5.

(2) $w + 3 = 4s$

- Statement (1) ALONE is sufficient, but statement (2) alone is not sufficient.
- Statement (2) ALONE is sufficient, but statement (1) alone is not sufficient.
- BOTH statements TOGETHER are sufficient, but NEITHER statement ALONE is sufficient.
- EACH statement ALONE is sufficient.
- Statements (1) and (2) TOGETHER are not sufficient.

**27. C** Since this question is a yes-no question, use Plugging In to evaluate the statements. Note that Statement (1) does not provide any information about $w$. So, while you can say that $s = 2$ is a value that satisfies Statement (1), you can pick any value for $w$. If $s = 2$ and $w = 5$, the answer to the question is "yes." However, if $s = 2$ and $w = 7$, the answer to the question is "no." Thus, Statement (1) is insufficient. The possible answers are BCE.

For Statement (2), $s = 2$ and $w = 5$ satisfy the statement and produce an answer of "yes" to the question. However, $s = 4$ and $w = 13$ also satisfy the statement and produce an answer of "no"

## QUESTIONS

## EXPLANATIONS

to the question. The possible answers are (C) or (E). Now, pick numbers that satisfy both statements. Start by using a pair that you've already used: $s = 2$ and $w = 5$. These numbers satisfy both statements and produce an answer of "yes" to the question. Now, try $s = 7$ and $w = 25$. These numbers also satisfy both statements and produce an answer of "yes" to the question. If you keep trying to pick numbers that satisfy both statements, you'll discover that you must pick values for $w$ that are divisible by 5. The correct answer is (C).

You might also note the algebraic reason the combined statements ensure that $w$ is divisible by 5. Statement (2) provides an expression for $4s$ that can be substituted into the expression in Statement (1): $w + 3 + 2 = w + 5$ is divisible by 5. Both parts of this expression must be divisible by 5 for $w + 5$ to be divisible by 5. So, $w$ is divisible by 5.

# MATH BIN 3

## QUESTIONS

1. An electronics store normally sells all its merchandise at a 10 percent to 30 percent discount from the suggested retail price. During a sale, if the store were to deduct an additional 20 percent from the discounted price, what is the lowest price possible for an item with a suggested retail price of $260 ?

- $130.00
- $145.60
- $163.80
- $182.00
- $210.00

2. A certain gas station discounts the price per gallon of all gasoline purchased after the first 10 gallons by 10 percent. The total per gallon discount for 25 gallons of gas purchased at this station is what percent of the total per gallon discount for 20 gallons of gas?

- 80%
- 100%
- 116.7%
- 120%
- 140%

## EXPLANATIONS

1. **B** You don't need to worry about that range for the initial discount: since you want the *lowest* possible price, you want the *greatest* possible discount. Thirty percent of 260 is 78, so the price after the initial discount is $260 – $78, or $182. The additional 20% discount amounts to $36.40—remember, the 20% discount is 20% of the already-discounted price. $182 – $36.40 = $145.60, and the correct answer is (B).

2. **D** This problem never specifies the cost of a gallon of gas, so plug in $1. If the price per gallon is $1 for the first 10 gallons, then the price for every subsequent gallon is $0.90. Now calculate the per gallon discount for 20 gallons. First, calculate the total cost for 20 gallons. The cost is $10 for the first 10 gallons and 10 × $0.90 = $9 for the next 10 gallons, for a total of $19 and an average price per gallon of $0.95. So the per gallon discount is 5 cents. Repeat this process to calculate the per gallon discount for 25 gallons. The total price for 25 gallons is $23.50, for an average per gallon price of $0.94 and a discount of 6 cents. The question asks you to relate the per gallon discounts as a percentage, so 6 is 120% of 5 and the correct answer is (D).

# MATH BIN 3

## QUESTIONS

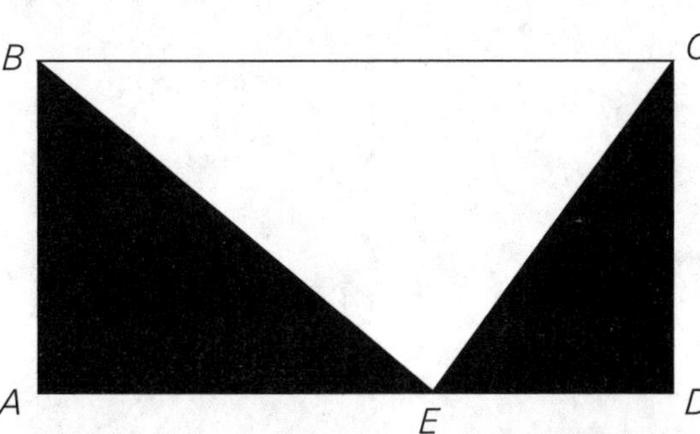


3. What is the area of the shaded region in the figure shown above?

(1) The area of rectangle *ABCD* is 54.

(2) $AE = 2ED$

- Statement (1) ALONE is sufficient, but statement (2) alone is not sufficient.
- Statement (2) ALONE is sufficient, but statement (1) alone is not sufficient.
- BOTH statements TOGETHER are sufficient, but NEITHER statement ALONE is sufficient.
- EACH statement ALONE is sufficient.
- Statements (1) and (2) TOGETHER are not sufficient.

## EXPLANATIONS

3. **A** Statement (1) is sufficient, by itself, to answer the question. Although you can't determine, from Statement (1), the individual areas of the two triangular shaded regions, when combined they equal 27 (half of the total area of rectangle *ABCD*). The easiest way to see this is to draw a vertical line through point *E*, cutting the rectangle into two smaller ones. Now you have two rectangles that are divided by diagonals, and diagonals, by definition, cut rectangles in half. If half of the two smaller rectangles are shaded, then so is half of the larger rectangle. You're down to AD.
Statement (2) gives the relationship between the two smaller shaded regions, but it doesn't allow you to determine anything about their individual areas. Statement (2) is insufficient, and the correct answer is (A).

## QUESTIONS

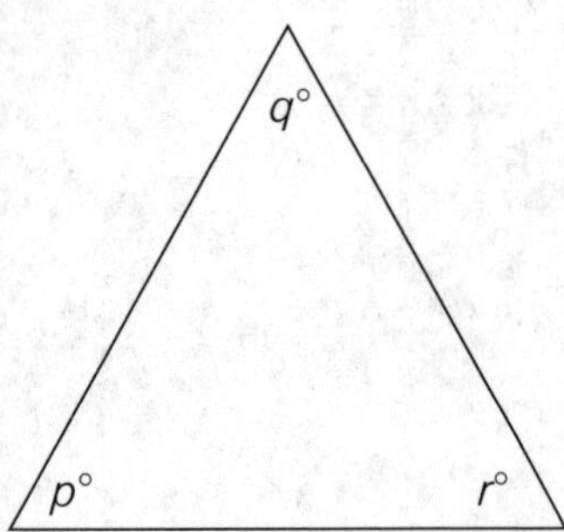


4. For the triangle shown above, does $p = q = 60$ ?

(1) $r = 180 - (p + r)$

(2) $p = 60$

- Statement (1) ALONE is sufficient, but statement (2) alone is not sufficient.
- Statement (2) ALONE is sufficient, but statement (1) alone is not sufficient.
- BOTH statements TOGETHER are sufficient, but NEITHER statement ALONE is sufficient.
- EACH statement ALONE is sufficient.
- Statements (1) and (2) TOGETHER are not sufficient.

## EXPLANATIONS

4. **C** First, take a moment to rephrase the question. If $p = q = 60$, the triangle is equilateral. So, the question is equivalent to asking "Is the triangle equilateral?" Statement (1) is, by itself, insufficient to answer the question, although it does provide the very useful information that $r = q$. If you're comfortable working with triangles, you may have immediately read "180 minus the sum of $p$ and $r$" as being equal to $q$. If not, you can prove this by doing some algebraic manipulation. Add $(p + r)$ to both sides to yield $r + p + r = 180$, but since 180 also equals $p + q + r$, you can combine the equations to get $r + p + r = p + q + r$. Subtract a $p$ and a $q$ from each side, and you're left with $r = q$. Nonetheless, this is still insufficient to answer the question. If $r$ and $q$ are both 60, the answer is "yes"; if they're both 45—remember, you can't trust the diagrams in Data Sufficiency—the answer is "no." You're down to BCE.

Statement (2), by itself, is also insufficient to answer the question; the only thing it says about $q$ and $r$ is their sum, which equals 120. Eliminate (B).

When you combine the statements, though, you can determine whether the triangle is equilateral. If $r$ and $q$ are equal and their sum is 120, then they, like $p$, equal 60. If all three angles equal 60, the triangle is equilateral, and the correct answer is (C).

## QUESTIONS

5. During a certain two-week period, a video rental store rented only comedies, dramas, and action movies. If 70 percent of the movies rented were comedies, and of the remaining movies rented, 5 times as many dramas as action movies were rented and *A* action movies were rented, then, in terms of *A*, how many of the movies rented were comedies?

- $\frac{A}{14}$
- $\frac{5A}{7}$
- $\frac{7A}{5}$
- $14A$
- $35A$

6. $x$, $y$, and $z$ are consecutive positive integers such that $x < y < z$. If the units digit of $x^2$ is 6 and the units digit of $y^2$ is 9, what is the units digit of $z^2$ ?

- 0
- 1
- 2
- 4
- 5

## EXPLANATIONS

5. **D** Since the problem never specifies how many videos were rented during the two-week period, this is a good opportunity to plug in. Rather than plugging in a value for *A* and trying to determine the total number of videos rented—possible but problematic—plug in an easy number, such as 100, for the total, and calculate the rest of the numbers from there.

If a total of 100 videos were rented in the two-week period, then 70 were comedies. Of the remaining 30, there were 5 times as many dramas as action movies, so that means 25 dramas and 5 action movies. You now know both the value for *A*, 5, and the target answer, 70. Only (D) yields 70 when 5 is plugged in for (A), so (D) is the correct answer.

6. **D** Because the units digit of $x^2$ is 6, the units digit of $x$ must be either 4 or 6. Because $x$, $y$, and $z$ are consecutive positive integers, the units digit of $y$ is 5 if the units digit of $x$ is 4. However, the units digit of $y$ *can't* be 5 because the problem says that the units digit of $y^2$ is 9; if the units digit of $y$ were 5, then the units digit of $y^2$ would also be 5. Therefore, the units digit of $x$ is 6, the units digit of $y$ is 7, and the units digit of $z$ is 8. The units digit of $z^2$, then, is 4. The correct answer is (D).

## QUESTIONS

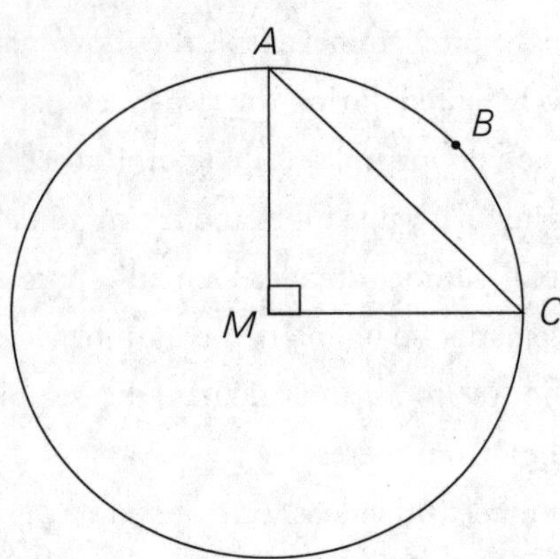


7. What is the area of the circle with center $M$ shown above ?

(1) The length of $AC$ is $8\sqrt{2}$.

(2) The length of arc $ABC$ is $4\pi$.

- Statement (1) ALONE is sufficient, but statement (2) alone is not sufficient.
- Statement (2) ALONE is sufficient, but statement (1) alone is not sufficient.
- BOTH statements TOGETHER are sufficient, but NEITHER statement ALONE is sufficient.
- EACH statement ALONE is sufficient.
- Statements (1) and (2) TOGETHER are not sufficient.

## EXPLANATIONS

7. **D** Statement (1) alone is sufficient to answer the question. Ordinarily, having one side of a right triangle isn't enough to solve for all three sides. However, since two of the sides of this triangle are also radii of the circle, this is no ordinary right triangle: it's an isosceles right triangle, also known as a 45-45-90 triangle. As such, knowing that the long side of the triangle is $8\sqrt{2}$ is enough to tell you that the short sides are both 8. Once you know the radius, you can solve for the area—$64\pi$, if you were wondering—and you're down to AD.

Statement (2) alone is also sufficient to answer the question. Arc *ABC*, since it's subtended (or "cut out") by a 90° angle, must represent $\frac{90}{360}$, or $\frac{1}{4}$, of the entire circumference. That gives an entire circumference of $16\pi$; from the circumference, you can find the radius, 8, and from there the area. The correct answer is (D).

# MATH BIN 3

## QUESTIONS

8. If 70 percent of the female and 90 percent of the male students in the senior class at a certain school are going on the senior trip and the senior class is 60 percent female, what percent of the senior class is going on the senior trip?

- ◯ 82%
- ◯ 80%
- ◯ 78%
- ◯ 76%
- ◯ 72%

## EXPLANATIONS

8. **C** This is a question about an unspecified amount, so it is a great opportunity to Plug In! Since the answers are percentages, let's plug in 100 for the total number of seniors. That means there are 60 females, of whom 70%, or 42, are going on the senior trip; they'll be joined by 90% of the 40 males, which gives 36 males on the trip. That's a total of $42 + 36 = 78$ students who are going on the trip. Seventy-eight out of our senior class of 100 is, of course, 78%, so the correct answer is (C).

9. If *P* is a set of integers and 3 is in *P*, is every positive multiple of 3 in *P* ?

(1) For any integer in *P*, the sum of 3 and that integer is also in *P*.

(2) For any integer in *P*, that integer minus 3 is also in *P*.

- ◯ Statement (1) ALONE is sufficient, but statement (2) alone is not sufficient.
- ◯ Statement (2) ALONE is sufficient, but statement (1) alone is not sufficient.
- ◯ BOTH statements TOGETHER are sufficient, but NEITHER statement ALONE is sufficient.
- ◯ EACH statement ALONE is sufficient.
- ◯ Statements (1) and (2) TOGETHER are not sufficient.

9. **A** To find the answer to this yes-or-no question, plug in for the two statements, starting with the one number that you know is in the set: 3. For Statement (1), if 3 is in the set, then 6 is in the set. If 6 is in the set, then 9 is also in the set. Using similar reasoning, it can be shown that every positive multiple of 3 is in the set. So, the answer to the question is "yes" and Statement (1) is sufficient. The possible answers are AD. For Statement (2), it can be shown that 3, 0, −3, −6 are in the set. But the positive multiples of 3 can be in the set, in which case the answer to the question is "yes," or not in the set in which case the answer to the question is "no." So, Statement (2) is not sufficient. The answer is (A).

## QUESTIONS

10. A certain seafood restaurant gets a delivery of fresh seafood every day of the week. If the delivery company charges *d* dollars per delivery and *c* cents per delivered item and the restaurant has an average (arithmetic mean) of *x* items delivered per day, then which of the following is an expression for the total cost, in dollars, of one week's deliveries?

- $\frac{7cdx}{100}$
- $d+\frac{7cx}{100}$
- $7d+\frac{xc}{100}$
- $7d+\frac{7xc}{100}$
- $7cdx$

## EXPLANATIONS

10. **D** Since the answer choices contain variables, this is a good place to Plug In. Make $d = 10$, $c = 200$ (a particularly helpful number, because it allows you to work the problem in whole dollar amounts), and $x = 5$. If the restaurant has an average of 5 items per day delivered, then it had a total of 35 items delivered for the week. Multiplied by the 200 cents (or $2) charge per item, that's a total of $70 in per-item charges. When you add that amount to the $70 total for the per-delivery charges—7 deliveries at $10 per delivery—you get a total of $140 for the week. The target answer, then, is 140; only (D) gives 140 when you plug the values into the answer choices, and, therefore, (D) is the correct answer.

If you got (C), by the way, check your calculations for your target answer. You likely calculated the per-item charges as though *x* were the total, rather than the daily average, of the items delivered.

## QUESTIONS

11. Which of the following contains the interval two standard deviations from the mean of a set of data with an arithmetic mean of 46 and a standard deviation of 4 ?

- ◯ 38 to 46
- ◯ 38 to 54
- ◯ 42 to 50
- ◯ 44 to 48
- ◯ 46 to 50

## EXPLANATIONS

11. **B** Standard deviation is the measure of how greatly the individual elements in a data set vary from the arithmetic mean of the set. As a general rule, the more widely dispersed the data in a set, the greater the standard deviation.

For the GMAT, you mostly need to know that standard deviation is measured from the arithmetic mean of a data set. If a data set has an arithmetic mean of 10 and a standard deviation of 2, then 8 and 12 are the values that are exactly one standard deviation from the arithmetic mean of the set.

In this problem, the standard deviation is 4, and the question asks for an interval that covers two standard deviations from the arithmetic mean of 46. It's key here to remember that "two standard deviations" means two *in each direction*—that is, both above *and* below the mean. Thus, you need an interval that covers $2 \times 4$, or 8, from the mean in each direction: $46 - 8 = 38$, so the bottom end of the interval is 38, and $46 + 8 = 54$, so the top end of the interval is 54. The correct answer is (B).

If you chose (A), by the way, you accounted for only the two standard deviations below the mean. If you chose (E), you accounted only for the two standard deviations above the mean. And if you chose (C), you forgot to take two standard deviations in each direction.

## QUESTIONS

12. If $a$ and $b$ are positive integers, is $a$ a multiple of $b$ ?

(1) Every distinct prime factor of $b$ is also a distinct prime factor of $a$.

(2) Every factor of $b$ is also a factor of $a$.

- ◯ Statement (1) ALONE is sufficient, but statement (2) alone is not sufficient.
- ◯ Statement (2) ALONE is sufficient, but statement (1) alone is not sufficient.
- ◯ BOTH statements TOGETHER are sufficient, but NEITHER statement ALONE is sufficient.
- ◯ EACH statement ALONE is sufficient.
- ◯ Statements (1) and (2) TOGETHER are not sufficient.

## EXPLANATIONS

12. **B** To solve this yes-or-no problem, your best bet is to plug in values that meet the requirements given in the statements to determine whether Plugging In always yields the same answer to the question.

For Statement (1), for example, you could plug in 4 for both $a$ and $b$—that's one easy way to make sure that every prime factor of $b$ is also a prime factor of $a$—and since every number is a multiple of itself, the answer to the question is "yes." However, if you leave $b = 4$ but make $a = 2$, you can still satisfy the requirement of Statement (1)—4 has only one prime factor, 2, which is also a prime factor of 2—but now the answer is "no." Since Statement (1) yields different answers, it's insufficient, and the possible answers are BCE.

Similar attempts in Statement (2), however, will always yield the answer "yes." You could, of course, again plug 4 in for both variables, and get the first "yes." If you leave $b = 4$, though, you can't make $a = 2$, since 4 isn't a factor of 2; $a$ is a number such as 4 (which we've already used), 12, 16, or some other number that has 1, 2, and 4 as factors. Whichever one you pick, though, the answer is "yes"; Statement (2) is therefore sufficient, and the answer to the problem is (B).

## MATH BIN 3

### QUESTIONS

13. If Set $X$ contains 10 consecutive integers and the sum of the 5 least members of the set is 265, then what is the sum of the 5 greatest members of the set?

- 290
- 285
- 280
- 275
- 270

14. If $a - b = c$, what is the value of $b$ ?

(1) $c + 6 = a$

(2) $a = 6$

- Statement (1) ALONE is sufficient, but statement (2) alone is not sufficient.
- Statement (2) ALONE is sufficient, but statement (1) alone is not sufficient.
- BOTH statements TOGETHER are sufficient, but NEITHER statement ALONE is sufficient.
- EACH statement ALONE is sufficient.
- Statements (1) and (2) TOGETHER are not sufficient.

### EXPLANATIONS

13. **A** You *could* solve this problem algebraically, although it's a bit of a chore. If you assign $x$ to represent the smallest integer in the set, then $x + (x + 1) + (x + 2) + (x + 3) + (x + 4) = 265$, so $5x + 10 = 265$, $5x = 255$, and $x = 51$. The five least consecutive integers are thus 51 through 55; you can now add the five greatest consecutive integers, which are 56 through 60. The total is 290, and the correct answer is (A).
A much simpler way to solve the problem, though, is to recognize that the difference between the sums of *any* two adjacent sets of five consecutive integers is the same; you can, therefore, find this difference using much smaller, easier-to-work-with numbers, and then add this difference to the total given in the problem. The sum of the integers from 1 to 5 is 15, and the sum of the integers from 6 to 10 is 40; our difference, thus, is 25, and $265 + 25 = 290$.

14. **A** It can be a good idea to simplify before heading into the statements. If you have the equation $a - b = c$ and want $b$, then you could simply write it as $b = a - c$. Now, consider Statement (1) on its own. Statement (1) can be rewritten as $a - c = 6$. Since $a - c = b$ from the question stem, you know that $b = 6$. Statement (1) is sufficient, and you're down to AD. Statement (2) provides information about only one of the three variables in the original equation, so it cannot be sufficient on its own. The correct answer is (A).

## QUESTIONS

{3, 5, 9, 13, *y*}

15. If the average (arithmetic mean) and the median of the set of numbers shown above are equal, then what is the value of *y* ?

- 7
- 8
- 10
- 15
- 17

16. For a certain foot race, how many different arrangements of medal winners are possible?

(1) Medals will be given for 1st, 2nd, and 3rd place.

(2) There are 10 runners in the race.

- Statement (1) ALONE is sufficient, but statement (2) alone is not sufficient.
- Statement (2) ALONE is sufficient, but statement (1) alone is not sufficient.
- BOTH statements TOGETHER are sufficient, but NEITHER statement ALONE is sufficient.
- EACH statement ALONE is sufficient.
- Statements (1) and (2) TOGETHER are not sufficient.

## EXPLANATIONS

15. **D** This problem is a great opportunity to Plug In the Answers. Start with (C) and substitute 10 for *y* in the problem. The average of the numbers {3, 5, 9, 13, 10} is 8, but the median of those numbers is 9. Eliminate (C). The value of *y* needs to be greater, so try (D), 15. The average of the numbers {3, 5, 9, 13, 15} is 9, and the median of those numbers is also 9. You're done. The correct answer is (D).

16. **C** This is a permutation problem. Looking at Statement (1), it might seem enough to know that medals will be awarded for 1st, 2nd, and 3rd place. While some test-takers might be quick to assume that there are $3 \times 2 \times 1$ possible arrangements of medal winners, until you know the number of runners, you don't know enough. The possible answers are BCE.
Statement (2) gives the number of runners. Since you cannot use the information from Statement (1) while evaluating Statement (2), you now do not know how many medals are to be given. You're down to (C) or (E).
Putting the two statements together, you can now find out how many different arrangements of medal winners there are: $10 \times 9 \times 8 = 720$. The correct answer is (C).

## QUESTIONS

17. For the set of measurements 3, $x_2$, $x_3$, what is the value of $x_3$ ?

(1) The range of the set of measurements is 0.

(2) The standard deviation of the set of measurements is 0.

- Statement (1) ALONE is sufficient, but statement (2) alone is not sufficient.
- Statement (2) ALONE is sufficient, but statement (1) alone is not sufficient.
- BOTH statements TOGETHER are sufficient, but NEITHER statement ALONE is sufficient.
- EACH statement ALONE is sufficient.
- Statements (1) and (2) TOGETHER are not sufficient.

## EXPLANATIONS

17. **D** The range of any set of measurements is equal to the greatest item in the set minus the least. Statement (1) gives a value for the range. If that value were anything other than 0, you would not be able to solve the problem based only on this statement. Because Statement (1) says that the range is 0, you actually know more than you might think about these three numbers. Because the problem says that the first measurement is 3, plug in values for $x_2$ and $x_3$, just to see what happens. For example, if $x_2$ and $x_3$ both equal 5, the range does not equal 0. When you start plugging in numbers, you realize that the only way for the range of these three numbers to be 0 is if each of the numbers is exactly the same. And because you know the first value is 3, that means both $x_2$ and $x_3$ equal 3 as well. The possible answers are AD.
Statement (2) says that all the measurements correspond exactly to the arithmetic mean—which says that all three measurements are equal to 3. Statement (2) is also sufficient, so the correct answer is (D).

## QUESTIONS

18. An employer has 6 applicants for a programming position and 4 applicants for a manager position. If the employer must hire 3 programmers and 2 managers, what is the total number of ways the employer can make the selection?

- 1,490
- 132
- 120
- 60
- 23

## EXPLANATIONS

18. **C** In this combination problem, the employer's choice of a programmer can be written as

$$\frac{6\times5\times4}{3\times2\times1} \text{ or } 20$$

The employer's choice of a manager can be written as

$$\frac{4\times3}{2\times1} \text{ or } 6$$

To find the total number of ways she could make her selection, multiply the respective number of possibilities: $6 \times 20 = 120$. The correct answer is (C).

## QUESTIONS

19. On Monday, an animal shelter housed 55 cats and dogs, and by Friday exactly $\frac{1}{5}$ of the cats and $\frac{1}{4}$ of the dogs had been adopted. If no new cats or dogs were brought to the shelter during this period, what is the greatest possible number of pets that could have been adopted from the animal shelter between Monday and Friday?

- 11
- 12
- 13
- 14
- 20

## EXPLANATIONS

19. **C** The question asks you for the greatest number of animals that could have been adopted from the shelter within the parameters of the problem. Because a greater proportion of dogs than cats was adopted, you should seek a scenario that maximizes the number of dogs adopted. You must also satisfy the other conditions of the problem, however; the number of cats, for example, must be a multiple of 5, because that is the only way that $\frac{1}{5}$ of the cats can be adopted.

Because you want to maximize the number of dogs in the shelter, start by assuming the minimum possible number of cats, 5. This would leave 50 dogs in the shelter. This solution, unfortunately, is impossible; because 50 is not evenly divisible by 4, there cannot be 50 dogs in the shelter. Could there be 10 cats at the shelter? No, because this would leave 45 dogs, again making it impossible for exactly $\frac{1}{4}$ of the dogs to be adopted. 15 cats is the magic number, as it means there are 40 dogs. $\left(\frac{1}{5}\times 15\right)+\left(\frac{1}{4}\times 40\right)=$ $3 + 10 = 13$ animals. The correct answer is (C).

# MATH BIN 3

## QUESTIONS

20. If $x$ is an integer, then which of the following statements about $x^2 - x - 1$ is true?

- It is always odd.
- It is always even.
- It is always positive.
- It is even when $x$ is even and odd when $x$ is odd.
- It is even when $x$ is odd and odd when $x$ is even.

21. During a five-day period, Monday through Friday, the average (arithmetic mean) high temperature was 86 degrees Fahrenheit. What was the high temperature on Friday?

(1) The average high temperature for Monday through Thursday was 87 degrees Fahrenheit.

(2) The high temperature on Friday reduced the average high temperature for the five-day period by 1 degree Fahrenheit.

- Statement (1) ALONE is sufficient, but statement (2) alone is not sufficient.
- Statement (2) ALONE is sufficient, but statement (1) alone is not sufficient.
- BOTH statements TOGETHER are sufficient, but NEITHER statement ALONE is sufficient.
- EACH statement ALONE is sufficient.
- Statements (1) and (2) TOGETHER are not sufficient.

## EXPLANATIONS

20. **A** Because $x$ is an integer, $x$ must be either even or odd. If $x$ is even, then $x^2 - x$ must also be even, and therefore $x^2 - x - 1$ is always odd. If $x$ is odd, then $x^2 - x$ must be even, and again, $x^2 - x - 1$ is always odd.

You can also solve this problem by Plugging In. After plugging in several values for $x$ and calculating $x^2 - x - 1$, you will discover that the result is always odd. The correct answer is (A).

21. **D** The question stem states that the average high temperature for the five-day period was 86°; therefore, the sum of the high temperatures for those days was $5 \times 86 = 430°$. Statement (1) says that the average high temperature for the first four days was 87°; therefore, the sum of the high temperatures for those days was $4 \times 87 = 348°$. $430 - 348 = 82°$, the high temperature on Friday. Statement (1) is sufficient; the answer is AD. Statement (2) says that Friday's temperature reduced the average high for the five-day period by 1 degree. This means that the average high for the first four days was 87°; thus, Statement (2) is sufficient for the same reason that Statement (1) is sufficient. The correct answer is (D).

## QUESTIONS

22. What is the value of $x^2 - y^2$?

(1) $x + y = 0$

(2) $x - y = 2$

- Statement (1) ALONE is sufficient, but statement (2) alone is not sufficient.
- Statement (2) ALONE is sufficient, but statement (1) alone is not sufficient.
- BOTH statements TOGETHER are sufficient, but NEITHER statement ALONE is sufficient.
- EACH statement ALONE is sufficient.
- Statements (1) and (2) TOGETHER are not sufficient.

23. If $P$ is the perimeter of an equilateral triangle, which of the following represents the height of the triangle?

- $\frac{P}{3}$
- $\frac{P\sqrt{3}}{3}$
- $\frac{P}{4}$
- $\frac{P\sqrt{3}}{6}$
- $\frac{P}{6}$

## EXPLANATIONS

22. **A** Don't get caught making a careless assumption on this question. You may have immediately recognized that $x^2 - y^2$ factors to $(x + y)(x - y)$. Seeing that Statement (1) provides a value for $(x + y)$ and Statement (2) provides a value for $(x - y)$, you might have automatically assumed that the correct answer to this question is (C). Look more closely, however; Statement (1) tells you that $(x + y) = 0$. Zero times any number equals zero. Therefore, Statement (1) is sufficient to tell you that $(x + y)(x - y) = 0$. Statement (2), however, is not sufficient. Since Statement (2) says that $x - y = 2$, plug this number back into the factored expression from the question stem. Without the value for the other factor (or the values of $x$ and $y$), Statement (2) cannot be used on its own to answer the question. The correct answer is (A).

23. **D** This is an excellent Plugging In problem. Plug in a value that is easily divisible by 3 for $P$: use 18. That would make the length of each side of the equilateral triangle 6.

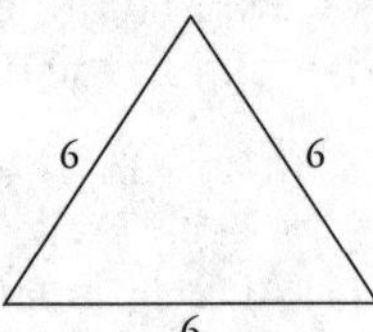


Draw a height for the triangle. Note that the height of an equilateral triangle divides the triangle into two 30-60-90 triangles, each with a base of 3.

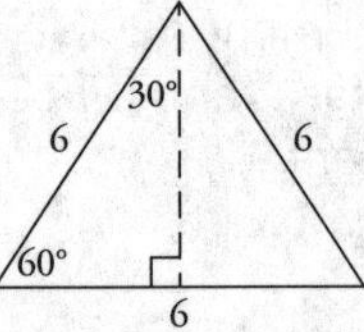


Now you can use the formula for the sides of a 30-60-90 triangle to determine that the height of the triangle is $3\sqrt{3}$ when $P = 18$. Finally, simply plug in 18 for $P$ in every answer choice and eliminate those that do not yield a result of $3\sqrt{3}$. The correct answer is (D).

## QUESTIONS

24. If 75 percent of all Americans own an automobile, 15 percent of all Americans own a bicycle, and 20 percent of all Americans own neither an automobile nor a bicycle, then what percent of Americans own *both* an automobile and a bicycle?

- 0%
- 1.33%
- 3.75%
- 5%
- 10%

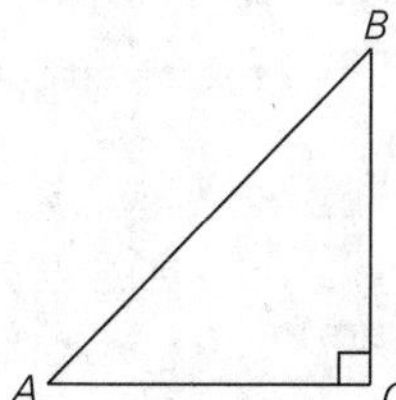


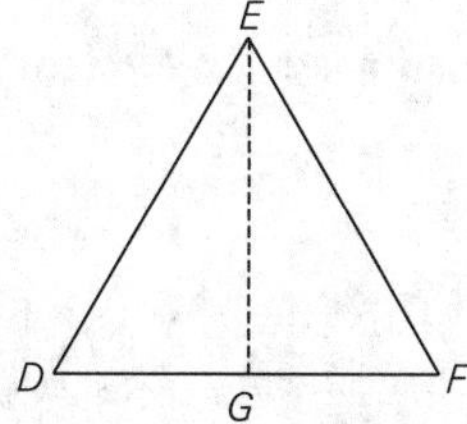


25. Triangle *ABC* is an isosceles right triangle and triangle *DEF* is an equilateral triangle with height *EG*. What is the ratio of the area of *ABC* to the area of *DEF* ?

(1) The ratio of *BC* to *EG* is 1:1.

(2) The ratio of *AC* to *DF* is $\sqrt{3}:2$.

- Statement (1) ALONE is sufficient, but statement (2) alone is not sufficient.
- Statement (2) ALONE is sufficient, but statement (1) alone is not sufficient.
- BOTH statements TOGETHER are sufficient, but NEITHER statement ALONE is sufficient.
- EACH statement ALONE is sufficient.
- Statements (1) and (2) TOGETHER are not sufficient.

## EXPLANATIONS

24. **E** This is a group formula problem. The group formula is Total = Group 1 + Group 2 – Both + Neither. Assume the total is 100. If there are 100 total Americans, then 75 own an automobile (which is Group 1), 15 own a bicycle (Group 2), and 20 own neither. So the equation now reads 100 = 75 + 15 – Both + 20. Solve for Both and discover that it equals 10. Since 10 is 10% of 100, the correct answer is (E).

25. **D** The formula for the area of a triangle is $A = \frac{base \times height}{2}$. Therefore, if you know the ratio of the bases and the heights of these triangles, it would be safe to assume that you know enough to calculate the ratios of their areas. This makes (C) a very tempting answer, because Statement (1) provides the ratio of the heights of the two triangles and Statement (2) provides the ratio of the bases of the two triangles.

The reason that the answer to this question is (D) lies in the special nature of isosceles right triangles and equilateral triangles. Their sides are in a fixed proportion to one another, so when you have information about one side, you have information about all the sides and, consequently, the area of the triangles. For this reason, each statement is sufficient on its own.

To prove that to yourself, you can plug in values for the sides of the triangles. For example, in Statement (1), the ratio of *BC* to *EG* is 1 to 1. So, let's say *BC* and *EG* are both one meter long. Since

## QUESTIONS

## EXPLANATIONS

*ABC* is isosceles, that means $AC = 1$, too, and the area of *ABC* is $\frac{1}{2}$. Since *DEF* is equilateral, that means *DG* and *GF* are each $\sqrt{3}$ and *DF* is $2\sqrt{3}$. Therefore, you can find the area of *DEF* ($\sqrt{3}$).

26. What is the value of integer $x$ ?

(1) $\sqrt[x]{64} = 4$

(2) $x^2 = x + 6$

- Statement (1) ALONE is sufficient, but statement (2) alone is not sufficient.
- Statement (2) ALONE is sufficient, but statement (1) alone is not sufficient.
- BOTH statements TOGETHER are sufficient, but NEITHER statement ALONE is sufficient.
- EACH statement ALONE is sufficient.
- Statements (1) and (2) TOGETHER are not sufficient.

26. **A** The only solution to the equation in Statement (1) is $x = 3$. That narrows it down to AD.
To determine whether Statement (2) is sufficient, subtract $2x + 8$ from both sides of the equation to get

$$x^2 - x - 6 = 0$$

This equation can be factored to

$$(x - 3)(x + 2) = 0$$

Thus, the equation has two solutions: $x$ can equal 3 or –2. Statement (2) is not sufficient. The correct answer is (A).

# MATH BIN 4

## QUESTIONS

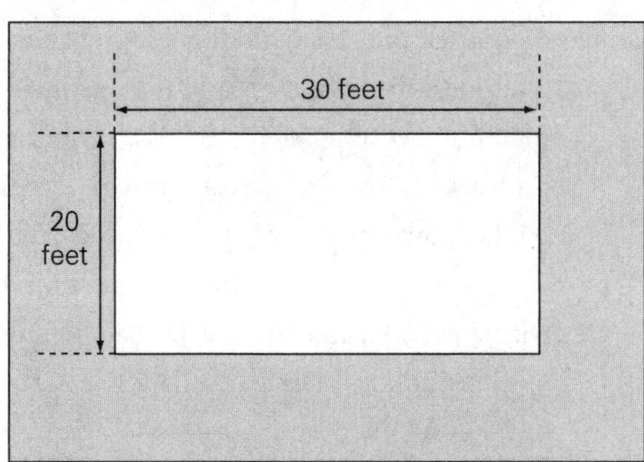


1. A rectangular garden with dimensions 20 feet by 30 feet is surrounded by a rectangular brick walkway of uniform width, as shown in the figure above. If the area of the walkway equals the area of the garden, what is the width of the walkway?

- 1 foot
- 3 feet
- 5 feet
- 8 feet
- 10 feet

## EXPLANATIONS

1. **C** To answer this question, first recognize that the area of the walkway can be calculated by subtracting the area of the smaller (white) rectangle from the larger rectangle in the figure. The difference between the areas of the two rectangles equals the area of the shaded region. This problem is ideal for Plugging In the Answers. Start with (C); if it is incorrect, you may be able to tell whether it is too large or too small, and you will be able to eliminate not only (C) but also two other answers.

   If (C) is correct, then the walkway is 5 feet wide. With a walkway of that width, the dimensions of the large rectangle in the figure are 30 feet (the width of the garden—20 feet—plus 5 feet on each side to account for the width of the walkway) by 40 feet (the length of the garden—30 feet—plus 5 feet on each side to account for the width of the walkway). The area of the large rectangle, then, is $40 \times 30 = 1{,}200$ square feet, and the area of the shaded region is $1{,}200 - (20 \times 30) = 1{,}200 - 600 = 600$ square feet.

   When the width of the walkway is 5 feet, the area of the walkway equals the area of the garden. That's the result you're looking for, so the correct answer is (C).

## QUESTIONS

2. If a fair two-sided coin is flipped 6 times, what is the probability that tails is the result at least twice but at most 5 times?

- $\frac{5}{8}$
- $\frac{3}{4}$
- $\frac{7}{8}$
- $\frac{57}{64}$
- $\frac{15}{16}$

## EXPLANATIONS

2. **C** As is often the case with difficult probability questions, the bottom part of the fraction—the total number of possibilities—is a permutation problem in itself. In this case, you need to figure out how many different outcomes you can get if you flip a coin 6 times. Since you have 6 events with 2 possible outcomes each, the total number of different outcomes is $2 \times 2 \times 2 \times 2 \times 2 \times 2$, or $2^6$, or 64. Now you just need to figure out how many of those possibilities meet the requirement.

For this problem, however, since there are so many different ways to meet the requirement, you'll be better off figuring out how many outcomes *don't* meet the requirement; you can then subtract this number from the total of 64. There are only three ways to *not* meet the requirement of 2 to 5 tails on 6 flips—you could get 0, 1, or 6 tails—and these can be quickly and easily counted out. There is only one way to get 6 tails, and, likewise, there is only one way to get 0 tails, which is another way of saying 6 heads. That's two possibilities. And there are only six different ways to get tails once: the single tails can come up in the first spot, the second spot, and so on. That's 8 out of the total of 64 possible outcomes that don't meet our requirement, so 56 do. The probability, therefore, is $\frac{56}{64}$, which reduces to $\frac{7}{8}$. The correct answer is (C).

# MATH BIN 4

## QUESTIONS

3. The new recruits of a military organization who score in the bottom 16 percent on their physical conditioning tests are required to retest. If the scores are normally distributed and have an arithmetic mean of 72, what is the score at or below which the recruits are required to retest?

(1) There are 500 new recruits.

(2) 10 new recruits scored at least 82 on the physical conditioning test.

- ◯ Statement (1) ALONE is sufficient, but statement (2) alone is not sufficient.
- ◯ Statement (2) ALONE is sufficient, but statement (1) alone is not sufficient.
- ◯ BOTH statements TOGETHER are sufficient, but NEITHER statement ALONE is sufficient.
- ◯ EACH statement ALONE is sufficient.
- ◯ Statements (1) and (2) TOGETHER are not sufficient.

## EXPLANATIONS

3. **C** Statement (1) is not sufficient to answer the question by itself. It does let you determine *how many* recruits will have to retake the test, but you don't know anything about their scores. The possible answers are BCE. Statement (2) is also insufficient by itself—while those 10 recruits are certainly impressive, you don't know what part of the overall recruiting class they represent. You're down to (C) or (E).

When you combine the statements, though, you have enough information to answer the question. From Statements (1) and (2), it is possible to calculate that the 10 new recruits who scored at least 82 on the physical conditioning test make up the top 2% of the whole. Since the scores are normally distributed, the top 2% represents the third standard deviation above the mean. Because the top 2% represents the third standard deviation above the mean, there are two full standard deviations that occur before the top 2%. On a normally distributed curve, the first standard deviation is marked by 34% of the population, the second is marked by 14%, and the third is 2%. So, there are two full standard deviations in between the mean (72) and the beginning of the third standard deviation (82). Because standard deviations in a normal curve are consistent values, each standard deviation begins 5 away from the last. So, the first standard deviation is represented by the values 72–77, the second is represented by 77–82, and the third is represented by 82–87. Now look at the question. The question is asking for the score that represents the bottom 16%, which is represented by the bottom two standard deviations. Since each standard deviation is worth 5, those who score at or below 67 represent the bottom 16%. The correct answer is (C).

## QUESTIONS

4. Each of the integers from 1 to 20 is written on a separate index card and placed in a box. If the cards are drawn from the box at random without replacement, how many cards must be drawn to ensure that the product of all the integers drawn is even?

- 19
- 12
- 11
- 10
- 3

## EXPLANATIONS

4. **C** To determine how many cards must be drawn to ensure that the product is even, determine the worst-case scenario. Start by figuring out the maximum number of cards that can be drawn so that the product of the numbers on the cards is odd. The first card, obviously, is an odd-numbered card. If the second card is an odd-numbered card, then the product of the numbers on the cards is odd. If the third card is odd, then the product remains odd. As long as the numbers on the cards drawn are odd, the product of those numbers is odd. Thus, in the worst-case scenario, all ten odd numbered cards are drawn in succession. At this point, the eleventh card must be even, which would make the product of the 11 cards even. Therefore, 11 cards must be drawn to ensure an even product. The correct answer is (C).

## QUESTIONS

5. The average (arithmetic mean) of integers *r*, *s*, *t*, *u*, and *v* is 100. Are exactly two of the integers greater than 100 ?

(1) Three of the integers are less than 50.

(2) None of the integers is equal to 100.

- Statement (1) ALONE is sufficient, but statement (2) alone is not sufficient.
- Statement (2) ALONE is sufficient, but statement (1) alone is not sufficient.
- BOTH statements TOGETHER are sufficient, but NEITHER statement ALONE is sufficient.
- EACH statement ALONE is sufficient.
- Statements (1) and (2) TOGETHER are not sufficient.

## EXPLANATIONS

5. **E** This is a yes-or-no question. Statement (1) says that three of the five integers are less than 50. This information by itself does not ensure that the other two integers *are* greater than 100. Both remaining values *could* be greater than 100; the solution set {10, 20, 30, 140, 300}, for example, satisfies this condition. However, the set {1, 2, 3, 4, 490} *also* satisfies the conditions of the problem, and it contains only one value greater than 100. Statement (1) is insufficient on its own; the correct answer must be BCE. Statement (2) says only that none of the integers is equal to 100. By itself, this is clearly not sufficient to tell you that exactly two of the integers are greater than 100; eliminate (B). In fact, the statement provides no more useful information than that provided in Statement (1); both of the solutions provided above satisfy this statement as well. The correct answer is (E).

## QUESTIONS

6. Paul jogs along the same route every day at a constant rate for 80 minutes. What distance does he jog?

(1) Yesterday, Paul began jogging at 5:00 P.M.

(2) Yesterday, Paul had jogged 5 miles by 5:40 P.M. and 8 miles by 6:04 P.M.

- ⬭ Statement (1) ALONE is sufficient, but statement (2) alone is not sufficient.
- ⬭ Statement (2) ALONE is sufficient, but statement (1) alone is not sufficient.
- ⬭ BOTH statements TOGETHER are sufficient, but NEITHER statement ALONE is sufficient.
- ⬭ EACH statement ALONE is sufficient.
- ⬭ Statements (1) and (2) TOGETHER are not sufficient.

## EXPLANATIONS

6. **B** Statement (1) clearly is not sufficient to answer the question because the only information it provides is Paul's starting time. The correct answer to this question must be BCE. Statement (2) says that Paul had jogged 5 miles by 5:40 P.M. and 8 miles by 6:04 P.M. You might be tempted to choose (C) at this point; after all, you now know when Paul began jogging and how far he had jogged at various intervals, so you could easily figure out how far he had run by 6:20 P.M., the end of the 80-minute period beginning at 5:00 P.M. Resist the temptation! Look more closely at Statement (2). It says that Paul covered 3 miles between 5:40 P.M. and 6:04 P.M. Thus, you know that Paul ran eight-minute miles during that 24-minute period. The question stem says that Paul jogs at a constant rate, and that he jogs for 80 minutes. Therefore, Statement (2), in combination with the question stem, provides all the information you need; Paul jogs eight-minute miles for 80 minutes, so the route along which he jogs is 10 miles long. The correct answer is (B).

## QUESTIONS

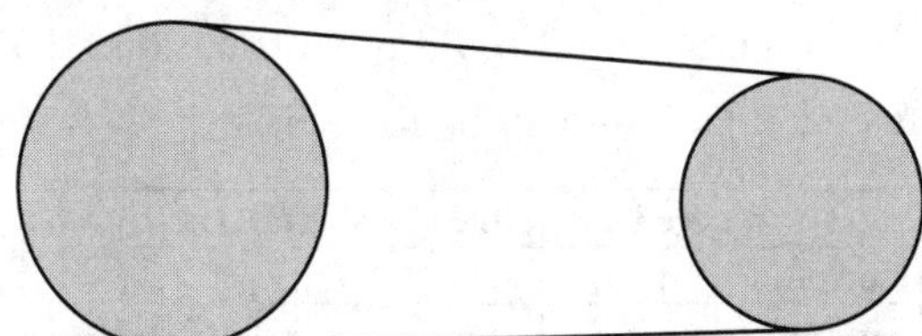

7. The diagram above shows two wheels that drive a conveyor belt. The larger wheel has a diameter of 40 centimeters, and the smaller wheel has a diameter of 32 centimeters. If each wheel must rotate the exact same number of centimeters per minute, and the larger wheel makes $r$ revolutions per minute, then, in terms of $r$, how many revolutions does the smaller wheel make per hour?

- $\frac{1,280\pi}{3}$
- $75r$
- $48r$
- $24r$
- $\frac{64\pi}{3}$

## EXPLANATIONS

7. **B** Because the problem has variables in the answer choices, Plugging In is a great way to solve. Plug in an easy number, one that will make your calculations and answer checking simple. For the purposes of this explanation, let's set $r$ equal to 2. With each rotation, each wheel rotates the length of its circumference. Thus, the wheel with diameter 40 centimeters rotates $40\pi$ centimeters with each rotation; the wheel with diameter 32 centimeters rotates $32\pi$ centimeters with each rotation. The larger wheel makes $r$ revolutions per minute; because we've set $r$ equal to 2, it makes 2 revolutions per minute and thus rotates $80\pi$ centimeters per minute. According to the problem, the smaller wheel must rotate the same distance. Therefore, the smaller wheel also rotates $80\pi$ centimeters per minute, meaning it rotates $60 \times 80\pi = 4,800\pi$ centimeters per hour. The smaller wheel covers $32\pi$ centimeters per rotation, so it must rotate $4,800\pi \div 32\pi = 150$ times per hour. Plug 2 in for $r$ in each of the answer choices to see which one gives you 150. The correct answer is (B), $75r$.

## QUESTIONS

8. An automobile dealership sells only sedans and coupes. It sells each in only two colors: red and blue. Last year, the dealership sold 9,000 vehicles, half of which were red. How many coupes did the dealership sell last year?

(1) The dealership sold three times as many blue coupes as red sedans last year.

(2) The dealership sold half as many blue sedans as blue coupes last year.

- Statement (1) ALONE is sufficient, but statement (2) alone is not sufficient.
- Statement (2) ALONE is sufficient, but statement (1) alone is not sufficient.
- BOTH statements TOGETHER are sufficient, but NEITHER statement ALONE is sufficient.
- EACH statement ALONE is sufficient.
- Statements (1) and (2) TOGETHER are not sufficient.

## EXPLANATIONS

8. **C** Create a table to solve this proportions question. It should look something like this:

| | **Red** | **Blue** | **TOTAL** |
|---|---|---|---|
| **Coupes** | | | |
| **Sedans** | | | |
| **TOTAL** | 4,500 | 4,500 | 9,000 |

The question stem says how many cars were sold last year. Because it says that half the cars sold were red, it also says the number of blue cars sold last year.

Statement (1) says, "The dealership sold three times as many blue coupes as red sedans last year." Enter this information into the table in algebraic terms:

| | **Red** | **Blue** | **TOTAL** |
|---|---|---|---|
| **Coupes** | | $3x$ | |
| **Sedans** | $x$ | | |
| **TOTAL** | 4,500 | 4,500 | 9,000 |

Because two unknowns—red coupes and blue sedans—remain, Statement (1) does not provide enough information to solve the problem. The correct answer is BCE.

Use the same procedure to test Statement (2): "The dealership sold half as many blue sedans as blue coupes last year":

| | **Red** | **Blue** | **TOTAL** |
|---|---|---|---|
| **Coupes** | | $2x$ | |
| **Sedans** | | $x$ | |
| **TOTAL** | 4,500 | 4,500 | 9,000 |

Again, two unknowns remain. *This* time, though, you have all the information you need to write a solvable equation. You know that $2x + x =$ 4,500. Therefore, $x$ equals 1,500. You now know the following:

| | **Red** | **Blue** | **TOTAL** |
|---|---|---|---|
| Coupes | | 3,000 | |
| Sedans | | 1,500 | |
| **TOTAL** | 4,500 | 4,500 | 9,500 |

## QUESTIONS

## EXPLANATIONS

Unfortunately, this still isn't enough information to answer the question. The answer is (C) or (E). Combine the information from the two statements. Statement (2) says that the dealership sold 3,000 blue coupes; combined with Statement (1), this says that the dealership sold 1,000 red sedans. Now subtract 1,000 from 4,500 to determine that the dealership sold 3,500 red coupes. Therefore, it sold 6,500 coupes last year. The correct answer is (C).

9. At a college football game, $\frac{4}{5}$ of the seats in the lower deck of the stadium were sold. If $\frac{1}{4}$ of all the seats in the stadium are located in the lower deck, and if $\frac{2}{3}$ of all the seats in the stadium were sold, what fraction of the unsold seats in the stadium are in the lower deck?

- ○ $\frac{3}{20}$
- ○ $\frac{1}{6}$
- ○ $\frac{1}{5}$
- ○ $\frac{1}{3}$
- ○ $\frac{7}{15}$

9. **A** Solve this one using Plugging In. First, plug in a number of seats for the entire stadium. Choose a number that divides easily by 3, 4, and 5. For the purposes of this explanation, let's say the stadium seats 60,000 people. The problem states that $\frac{2}{3}$ of all the seating in the stadium was sold, meaning that 40,000 of the 60,000 seats were sold. It also states that $\frac{1}{4}$ of the seating is located in the lower deck. Because $\frac{1}{4}$ of 60,000 is 15,000, that means the stadium has 15,000 seats in the lower deck. Of those 15,000 seats, according to the problem, $\frac{4}{5}$, or 12,000, were sold. The question asks what fraction of the unsold seats in the stadium were in the lower deck. Because 40,000 seats were sold in the entire stadium, a total of 20,000 were unsold; of the 20,000 unsold seats, $15,000 - 12,000 = 3,000$ were in the lower deck. The fraction $\frac{3,000}{20,000}$ reduces to $\frac{3}{20}$, so the correct answer is (A).

## QUESTIONS

10. At Company $R$, the average (arithmetic mean) age of executive employees is 54 years old and the average age of non-executive employees is 34 years old. What is the average age of all the employees at Company $R$?

(1) There are 10 executive employees at Company $R$.

(2) The number of non-executive employees at Company $R$ is four times the number of executive employees at Company $R$.

- Statement (1) ALONE is sufficient, but statement (2) alone is not sufficient.
- Statement (2) ALONE is sufficient, but statement (1) alone is not sufficient.
- BOTH statements TOGETHER are sufficient, but NEITHER statement ALONE is sufficient.
- EACH statement ALONE is sufficient.
- Statements (1) and (2) TOGETHER are not sufficient.

## EXPLANATIONS

10. **B** Statement (1) provides no information about the non-executive employees at Company *R*. It is not sufficient by itself, so you're down to BCE. Statement (2) provides a ratio of executive employees to non-executive employees at Company *R*. This information is sufficient on its own to determine the average age of all employees at Company *R*. Regardless of whether Company *R* has 2 executives and 8 non-executives or 200 executives and 800 non-executives, the resulting average for all employees is the same, because the proportional contribution of each group to the average remains fixed. The best way to prove this is simply to plug in some numbers and see for yourself. The average age of 1 executive and 4 non-executives is $\frac{54+4(34)}{5}=38$. The average age of 30 executives and 120 non-executives is $\frac{30(54)+120(34)}{150}=38$. Thus, the correct answer is (B).

# MATH BIN 4

## QUESTIONS

11. If $a$, $b$, $c$, $d$, and $x$ are all nonzero integers, is the product $ax \cdot (bx)^2 \cdot (cx)^3 \cdot (dx)^4$ negative?

(1) $a < c < x < 0$

(2) $b < d < x < 0$

- Statement (1) ALONE is sufficient, but statement (2) alone is not sufficient.
- Statement (2) ALONE is sufficient, but statement (1) alone is not sufficient.
- BOTH statements TOGETHER are sufficient, but NEITHER statement ALONE is sufficient.
- EACH statement ALONE is sufficient.
- Statements (1) and (2) TOGETHER are not sufficient.

12. A four-character password consists of one letter from the English alphabet and three different digits from 0 to 9. If the letter is the second or third character of the password, how many different passwords are possible?

- 5,040
- 18,720
- 26,000
- 37,440
- 52,000

## EXPLANATIONS

11. **A** Statement (1) says that $a$, $c$, and $x$ are negative. Instinctively, you might conclude that this isn't enough information, because it says nothing about $b$ or $d$. Look at the expression in the question stem again, though; $b$ and $d$ appear only in the expressions $(bx)^2$ and $(dx)^4$. Both of these expressions contain even exponents; you know, therefore, that these expressions are positive regardless of the values $b$ and $d$ represent, because nonzero integers raised to an even power are always positive. From Statement (1), you know that $ax$ is positive (a negative times a negative equals a positive) and, similarly, that $(cx)^3$ is positive. Statement (1) is sufficient even though the answer to the question is "no." The possible answers are AD. Statement (2) provides no valuable information. The values of $b$ and $d$ do not matter, as they are only used in expressions that result in positive numbers. The values of $a$ and $c$, however, do matter because they are raised to an odd exponent. Any number raised to an odd exponent retains the positive or negative nature of the original number. There is no way to ensure, then, that $ax$ or $cx$, when raised to an odd exponent, is positive or negative. The correct answer is (A).

12. **D** According to the problem, an acceptable password consists of either *DLDD* or *DDLD*, where *D* represents a digit and *L* represents a letter of the alphabet. Remember also that the digits must be different. First, consider *DLDD*. The first character can be any of the ten digits, 0 through 9. The second character can be any of the 26 letters of the English alphabet. There are only 9 possible digits for the third character, because the third character cannot repeat the digit used for the first character. By the same reasoning, there are only 8 possible digits for the fourth character. Thus, there are $10 \times 26 \times 9 \times 8 = 18{,}720$ possible

## QUESTIONS

## EXPLANATIONS

passwords that follow the *DLDD* pattern. Now consider *DDLD*. There are an equal number of possible passwords that follow this pattern. The first character can be any of 10 digits; the second character can be any of the 9 remaining digits; the third character can be any of the 26 letters of the alphabet; and the fourth character can be any of the remaining 8 digits: $10 \times 9 \times 26 \times 8 =$ 18,720. There are 18,720 + 18,720 = 37,440 different passwords possible, and the correct answer is (D).

13. If $x$ is a positive integer, is $x$ divisible by 48 ?

(1) $x$ is divisible by 8.

(2) $x$ is divisible by 6.

- Statement (1) ALONE is sufficient, but statement (2) alone is not sufficient.
- Statement (2) ALONE is sufficient, but statement (1) alone is not sufficient.
- BOTH statements TOGETHER are sufficient, but NEITHER statement ALONE is sufficient.
- EACH statement ALONE is sufficient.
- Statements (1) and (2) TOGETHER are not sufficient.

**13. E** This is a yes-or-no question. If you plug in numbers for $x$ in Statement (1), you can get both a "yes" answer (by Plugging In 48) and a "no" answer (by Plugging In 16), so the possible answers are BCE. The same is true with Statement (2). If $x = 48$, which is divisible by 6, the answer to the question is "yes." But, if $x = 6$, the answer to the question is "no." The possible answers are (C) or (E). Now, combine the statements. If $x = 48$, which is divisible by both 6 and 8, the answer to the question is "yes." However, if $x =$ 24, which is also divisible by both 6 and 8, the answer to the question is "no." So, the statements are not sufficient when combined. Therefore, the correct answer is (E).

# MATH BIN 4

## QUESTIONS

$$\begin{array}{r} FGF \\ \times G \\ \hline HGG \end{array}$$

14. In the multiplication problem above, *F, G,* and *H* represent distinct odd digits. What is the value of the three-digit number *FGF* ?

- 151
- 161
- 171
- 313
- 353

## EXPLANATIONS

14. **A** At first it looks as though you'll have to substitute every odd digit for the three variables until you stumble onto the correct answer, but there's a trick to this problem that eliminates such guesswork. Look at the units column of the problem and you'll see that $F \times G$ yields a product with a units digit of *G*; therefore, it is quite possible that *F* is 1. Actually, you can go even further: *F must* equal 1, because *G* cannot equal 1 (otherwise, the product of this multiplication problem would be *FGF*, not *HGG*). Plus, if both *F* and *G* were odd digits greater than 1, the product of this multiplication problem would be a four-digit number. Because the product is the three-digit number *HGG*, *F* equals 1. You can now eliminate (D) and (E), and you also know that *G* must equal 5 or 7 (*G* cannot equal 6 because the problem says *G* must be an odd digit). When *G* equals 7, the product is a four-digit number; therefore, *G* is 5, and the correct answer is (A).

But you could have just plugged the answer choices into the problem, one at a time, to see which one works.

## QUESTIONS

15. A group of 20 friends formed an investment club, with each member contributing an equal amount to the general fund. The club then invested the entire fund, which amounted to *d* dollars, in Stock *X*. The value of the stock subsequently increased 40 percent, at which point the stock was sold and the proceeds divided evenly among the members. In terms of *d*, how much money did each member of the club receive from the sale? (Assume that transaction fees and other associated costs were negligible.)

- $800d$
- $\frac{7d}{5}$
- $\frac{d}{20}+40$
- $\frac{d}{2}$
- $\frac{7d}{100}$

## EXPLANATIONS

15. **E** The variables in the answer choices should tell you that this is a great problem for Plugging In. Choose a value easily divisible by 20 (the number of friends in the group) and one for which percentages are easy to calculate (because the value of the stock increases by a percentage). Set *d* equal to 100. The general fund of \$100, then, was invested in Stock *X*, which subsequently increased in value by 40 percent; thus, its value increased to \$140. At this point, the club sold the stock and divvied up the proceeds. Each member received \$140 ÷ 20 = \$7 in the process. Therefore, when *d* equals 100, the correct answer choice yields a result of 7. Check each answer choice, plugging in 100 for *d*. The correct answer is (E).

## QUESTIONS

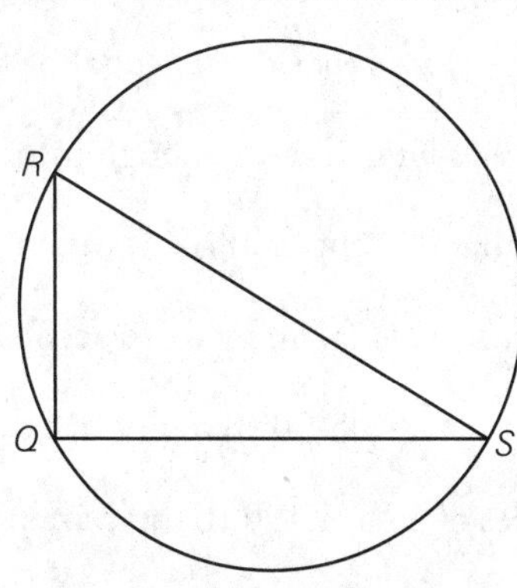


16. Triangle *QRS* is inscribed in a circle as shown above. Is *QRS* a right triangle?

(1) *RS* is a diameter of the circle.

(2) $QR = 3$ and $RS = 5$

- Statement (1) ALONE is sufficient, but statement (2) alone is not sufficient.
- Statement (2) ALONE is sufficient, but statement (1) alone is not sufficient.
- BOTH statements TOGETHER are sufficient, but NEITHER statement ALONE is sufficient.
- EACH statement ALONE is sufficient.
- Statements (1) and (2) TOGETHER are not sufficient.

## EXPLANATIONS

**16. A** This problem requires you to clear two hurdles. First, you must remember a rule about inscribed angles in semicircles. Then, you must avoid succumbing to the power of suggestion. First, the rule about inscribed angles. Statement (1) says that *RS* is a diameter of the circle. That means you are dealing with two semicircles. The question stem says that triangle *QRS* is inscribed in a circle; thus, $\angle RQS$ is inscribed. A triangle inscribed in a semicircle is always a right triangle. Therefore, $\angle RQS$ measures 90°. Statement (1) is sufficient, and you're down to AD. Statement (2) can trick you if you don't forget all about Statement (1) first. It suggests that *QSR* is a right triangle, because the ratio of *QR* to *RS* recalls the familiar 3-4-5 triangle that satisfies the Pythagorean Theorem. However, Statement (2) does not preclude the possibility that *RS* is *not* a diameter and that therefore side *QS* does *not* measure 4. There is no way to determine whether *QRS* is a right triangle from Statement (2). The correct answer is (A).

## QUESTIONS

17. Square $G$ has sides of length 4 inches. Is the area of Square $H$ exactly one half the area of Square $G$ ?

(1) The length of the diagonal of Square $H$ equals the length of one side of Square $G$.

(2) The perimeter of Square $H$ is twice the length of the diagonal of Square $G$.

- Statement (1) ALONE is sufficient, but statement (2) alone is not sufficient.
- Statement (2) ALONE is sufficient, but statement (1) alone is not sufficient.
- BOTH statements TOGETHER are sufficient, but NEITHER statement ALONE is sufficient.
- EACH statement ALONE is sufficient.
- Statements (1) and (2) TOGETHER are not sufficient.

## EXPLANATIONS

17. **D** Statement (1) says that the diagonal of Square $H$ is 4 inches long. That is enough information to determine the length of a side of Square $H$, because the diagonal and two adjacent sides of a square form a 45-45-90 triangle, and the lengths of the sides of a 45-45-90 triangle are in the proportion $1:1:\sqrt{2}$. One side of Square $H$ has a length of $\frac{4}{\sqrt{2}} = \frac{4\sqrt{2}}{2} = 2\sqrt{2}$ inches. The area of Square $H$ is 8 square inches, which is indeed half the area of Square $G$. You're down to AD. Statement (2) mentions the diagonal of Square $G$, which is $4\sqrt{2}$ inches because the question stem says that the length of one side of Square $G$ is 4 inches. Thus, the perimeter of Square $H$ is $8\sqrt{2}$ inches, and the length of one side of Square $H$ is $2\sqrt{2}$ inches. As in Statement (1), this information is sufficient to answer the question. The correct answer is (D).

# MATH BIN 4

## QUESTIONS

18. In a certain state, 70 percent of the counties received some rain on Monday, and 65 percent of the counties received some rain on Tuesday. No rain fell either day in 25 percent of the counties in the state. What percent of the counties received some rain on Monday and Tuesday?

- 12.5%
- 40%
- 50%
- 60%
- 67.5%

## EXPLANATIONS

18. **D** Use the group formula to solve this problem. The group formula is Total = Group 1 + Group 2 – Both + Neither. The problem specifies that the answer is the percent of counties that got rain on both days, so the answer depends on finding the "Both" category of the formula. Now, fill in the values for the formula. Plug in 100 for the total number of counties. Therefore, 70 counties received rain on Monday (which is Group 1), 65 counties received rain on Tuesday (Group 2), and 25 counties received no rain. Put these into the formula, so 100 = 70 + 65 – Both + 25. Solve the equation to find that Both = 60. Since 60 is 60% of 100, the correct answer is (D).

## QUESTIONS

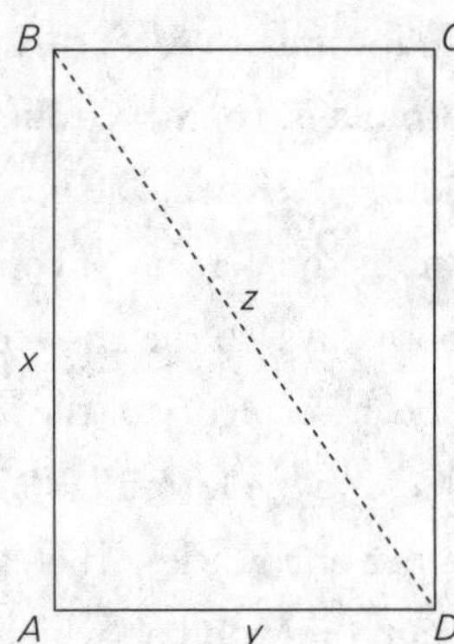


19. *ABCD* is a rectangle with sides of length $x$ centimeters and width $y$ centimeters and a diagonal of length $z$ centimeters. What is the perimeter, in centimeters, of *ABCD* ?

(1) $x - y = 7$

(2) $z = 13$

- Statement (1) ALONE is sufficient, but statement (2) alone is not sufficient.
- Statement (2) ALONE is sufficient, but statement (1) alone is not sufficient.
- BOTH statements TOGETHER are sufficient, but NEITHER statement ALONE is sufficient.
- EACH statement ALONE is sufficient.
- Statements (1) and (2) TOGETHER are not sufficient.

## EXPLANATIONS

19. **C** Statement (1) says that $x - y = 7$. An infinite number of combinations satisfy this equation, yielding an infinite number of perimeters for *ABCD*. Statement (1) is not sufficient, and you're down to BCE. Similarly, there are many different ways to draw a rectangle with diagonal 13. Not all of these rectangles have the same perimeter. Statement (2) is not sufficient by itself, and the correct answer is (C) or (E). At first glance, the two statements together don't appear to offer much more help. However, by applying a bit of algebraic trickery and the Pythagorean Theorem, you can wring more information from these two statements than is immediately apparent. Start by squaring Statement (1); this yields the equation $x^2 - 2xy + y^2 = 49$. The Pythagorean Theorem says that $x^2 + y^2 = z^2$, so use Statement (2) to substitute $13^2$, or 169, for $x^2 + y^2$. This yields the equation $169 - 2xy = 49$, which can be simplified to $xy = 60$. There's just one more step.
You know that $x^2 + y^2 = 169$, and you know that $xy = 60$. Thus, you know that $x^2 + 2xy + y^2 = 289$. The square root of $x^2 + 2xy + y^2$ is $(x + y)$, so you also know that $x + y = 17$ (it cannot equal $-17$ because $x$ and $y$ are centimeter lengths). This equation can be used in conjunction with Statement (1) to solve simultaneously for $x$ and $y$, thus allowing you a way to calculate the perimeter of the rectangle. The correct answer is (C).

## MATH BIN 4

### QUESTIONS

20. Together, Andrea and Brian weigh $p$ pounds and Brian weighs 10 pounds more than Andrea. If Andrea's dog, Cubby, weighs $\frac{p}{4}$ pounds more than Andrea, then, in terms of $p$, what is Cubby's weight in pounds?

- $\frac{p}{2}-10$
- $\frac{3p}{4}-5$
- $\frac{3p}{2}-5$
- $\frac{5p}{4}-10$
- $5p-5$

### EXPLANATIONS

20. **B** Variables in the answer choices mean it's time to Plug In. For the purposes of this problem, it's probably easiest to plug in weights for Andrea and Brian, add them, and use the sum for the value of $p$. Remember to plug in values that conform to the rules of the problem; Brian must weigh exactly 10 pounds more than Andrea. Try to make $p$ a value that is divisible by 4; that will make it easier to calculate Cubby's weight. Let's say Andrea weighs 45 pounds and Brian weighs 55 pounds. That makes $p$ equal to 100, a nice, round number that is easily divisible by 4. Cubby weighs $\frac{p}{4}$ pounds more than Andrea, so he weighs 25 pounds more than Andrea, or 70 pounds. Plug 100 in for $p$ in each of the answer choices and eliminate those that do not yield an answer of 70. The correct answer is (B).

## QUESTIONS

21. A first-grade teacher uses ten flash cards, numbered 1 through 10, to teach her students to order numbers correctly. She has students choose four flash cards at random and arrange the cards in ascending order. If she removes the cards numbered 2 and 4, how many different correctly ordered arrangements of the four selected cards are possible?

- 70
- 210
- 336
- 840
- 1,680

## EXPLANATIONS

21. **A** This question is easier than it first appears. At first glance, the restrictive rules—the cards must be arranged in order, some cards have been removed from the deck—seem to complicate the problem. In fact, they do not; because there is only one correct solution for each set of cards chosen, you must determine only the number of possible combinations of the cards in order to determine the number of possible correct arrangements. The one-to-one correlation between combinations and correct solutions actually simplifies the problem. Because the teacher has removed two cards from the deck, only 8 cards remain. The values on the selected cards are immaterial and are presented merely as a distractor; the answer to this question is the same regardless of the values written on the two cards she removes. Make four spots for the cards chosen; then fill in the number of options for each spot: $8 \times 7 \times 6 \times 5$. Then, divide by the number of ways to arrange these four cards: $4 \times 3 \times 2 \times 1$. Reduce and solve to find 70. The correct answer is (A).

## MATH BIN 4

### QUESTIONS

22. If $A$ and $B$ are two-digit integers that share the same digits, except in reverse order, then what is the sum of $A$ and $B$ ?

(1) $A - B = 45$

(2) The difference between the two digits in each number is 5.

- Statement (1) ALONE is sufficient, but statement (2) alone is not sufficient.
- Statement (2) ALONE is sufficient, but statement (1) alone is not sufficient.
- BOTH statements TOGETHER are sufficient, but NEITHER statement ALONE is sufficient.
- EACH statement ALONE is sufficient.
- Statements (1) and (2) TOGETHER are not sufficient.

### EXPLANATIONS

22. **E** As you consider each statement, you might be tempted to think, "How many numbers can possibly satisfy all the constraints of the question stem *and* this statement?" Or, you may figure that both statements together, in addition to the information in the question stem, *must* be sufficient to answer the question. That, of course, is just what the test-writers *expect* you to think. It turns out that several values satisfy each of the statements: 61 and 16; 72 and 27; 83 and 38; and 94 and 49 all satisfy Statements (1) and (2). Thus, neither statement is sufficient on its own, nor are they sufficient together. The correct answer is (E).

23. A university awarded grants in the amount of either \$7,000 or \$10,000 to selected incoming freshmen. If the total amount of all such awards is \$2,300,000, did the university award more \$7,000 grants than \$10,000 grants to its incoming freshmen?

(1) A total of 275 freshmen received grants in one of the two amounts.

(2) The amount of money awarded in \$10,000 grants was \$200,000 more than the amount of money awarded in \$7,000 grants.

- Statement (1) ALONE is sufficient, but statement (2) alone is not sufficient.
- Statement (2) ALONE is sufficient, but statement (1) alone is not sufficient.
- BOTH statements TOGETHER are sufficient, but NEITHER statement ALONE is sufficient.
- EACH statement ALONE is sufficient.
- Statements (1) and (2) TOGETHER are not sufficient.

23. **D** This is a simultaneous equation problem dressed up as a word problem. The question stem says that two types of grants were awarded; it also provides the sum of the grants. Let's call the group of freshmen who received \$7,000 grants $x$ and the group of freshmen who received \$10,000 grants $y$. The question stem says that $7{,}000x + 10{,}000y = 2{,}300{,}000$. That's one equation; to solve simultaneous equations, you need two equations. Statement (1) provides a second equation. That equation is $x + y = 275$. You can solve simultaneously—although, of course, you don't have to because this is Data Sufficiency, not Problem Solving—to determine that $x = 150$ and $y = 125$. Statement (1) is sufficient; the answer is (A) or (D). Statement (2) also provides a second equation. That equation is $10{,}000y = 7{,}000x + 200{,}000$. Again, you can solve to determine that $x = 150$ and $y = 125$. Choice (D) is the correct answer.

## QUESTIONS

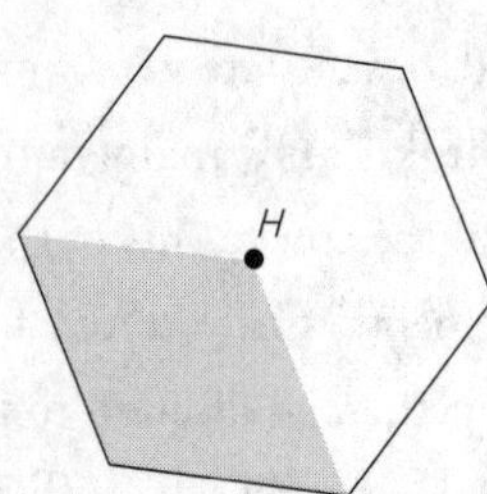


24. The figure shown above is a regular hexagon with center $H$. The shaded area is a parallelogram that shares three vertices with the hexagon and its fourth vertex is the center of the hexagon. If the length of one side of the hexagon is 8 centimeters, what is the area of the unshaded region?

- ○ $16\sqrt{3}$ cm$^2$
- ○ 96 cm$^2$
- ○ $64\sqrt{3}$ cm$^2$
- ○ $96\sqrt{3}$ cm$^2$
- ○ 256 cm$^2$

## EXPLANATIONS

24. **C** When a problem includes a regular hexagon, you know a lot more than you might think. That's because you can divide a regular hexagon into 6 congruent equilateral triangles, all meeting at the center of the hexagon. Furthermore, if you know the length of one side of an equilateral triangle, you can determine its area by dividing the equilateral triangle into two 30-60-90 triangles and applying the 30-60-90 ratios to determine the height of the equilateral triangle (the ratio of the sides of a 30-60-90 triangle is $1:\sqrt{3}:2$). The problem tells you that the length of one side of the hexagon is 8 centimeters. That means that the equilateral triangles that make up the hexagon have sides of 8 centimeters. Divide one into a 30-60-90 triangle and you'll get a triangle with sides $4 : 4\sqrt{3} : 8$; this tells you that the height of the equilateral triangle is $4\sqrt{3}$ and that its area is $\frac{8\left(4\sqrt{3}\right)}{2} = 16\sqrt{3}\text{ cm}^2$. The area of the unshaded region consists of four of the six equilateral triangles (the shaded region consists of the other two), so the area of the unshaded region is $4 \times 16\sqrt{3} = 64\sqrt{3}\text{ cm}^2$. The correct answer is (C).

## QUESTIONS

25. A fish tank contains a number of fish, including 5 Fantails. If two fish are selected from the tank at random, what is the probability that both will be Fantails?

(1) The probability that the first fish chosen is a Fantail is $\frac{1}{2}$.

(2) The probability that the second fish chosen is a Fantail is $\frac{4}{9}$.

- Statement (1) ALONE is sufficient, but statement (2) alone is not sufficient.
- Statement (2) ALONE is sufficient, but statement (1) alone is not sufficient.
- BOTH statements TOGETHER are sufficient, but NEITHER statement ALONE is sufficient.
- EACH statement ALONE is sufficient.
- Statements (1) and (2) TOGETHER are not sufficient.

## EXPLANATIONS

25. **D** To figure out this problem, you need to know the total number of fish. Looking at Statement (1) in combination with the question itself, you can see that if there are 5 Fantails, and the probability that the first selection is a Fantail is $\frac{1}{2}$; that means you actually know the total number of fish: $\frac{1}{2} = \frac{5}{x}$ or 10. You might think that the probability of the second fish being a Fantail is also $\frac{1}{2}$, but in fact that's not the case. There are only 9 fish left in total when the second selection is made, and there are only 4 possible Fantails from which to chose. So the probability of them both being chosen is $\frac{1}{2} \times \frac{4}{9}$, or $\frac{2}{9}$. You are down to AD. Now, looking at Statement (2), if the probability that the second fish will be a Fantail is $\frac{4}{9}$, that means that the probability of the first fish being a Fantail is $\frac{5}{10}$, which means you can answer the question based on Statement (2) alone as well. The correct answer is (D).

# VERBAL BIN 1

## QUESTIONS

1. As its reputation for making acquisitions of important masterpieces has grown, the museum has increasingly turned down gifts of lesser-known paintings they would in the past have accepted gratefully.

- they would in the past have accepted gratefully
- they would have accepted gratefully in the past
- it would in the past have accepted gratefully
- it previously would have accepted gratefully in the past
- that previously would have been accepted in the past

2. Over the past few decades, despite periodic attempts to reign in spending, currencies in South America are devalued by rampant inflation.

- are devalued
- are becoming more devalued
- which have lost value
- have become devalued
- have since become devalued

3. A fashion designer's fall line for women utilizing new soft fabrics broke all sales records last year. To capitalize on her success, the designer plans to launch a line of clothing for men this year that makes use of the same new soft fabrics.

The designer's plan assumes that

- other designers are not planning to introduce new lines for men utilizing the same soft fabrics
- men will be as interested in the new soft fabrics as women were the year before
- the designer will have time to develop new lines for both men and women
- the line for men will be considered innovative and daring because of its use of fabrics
- women who bought the new line last year will continue to buy it this year

## EXPLANATIONS

1. **C** The pronoun *they* in this stem sentence doesn't agree with the noun it refers to: the museum. In everyday speech, of course, you often say "they" when you are referring to a large institution—but on the GMAT, the test-writers won't let you get away with such imprecision. Choices (A) and (B) can both be eliminated because they use the plural pronoun. Choices (D) and (E) both fix the problem in different ways, but both add a redundancy: there is no need to have "previously" and "in the past" in the same sentence. The correct answer is (C).

2. **D** This is a tense question. *Over the past few decades* implies a continued action over time—which needs the perfect tense. This eliminates choices (A) and (B). Choice (C) creates a sentence fragment. Choice (E) isn't bad, but the word *since* is a bit redundant because the sentence began with *over the past few decades.* The correct answer is (D).

3. **B** This is an analogy argument. The men's line is being introduced in the hope that men will like the new soft fabrics as much as women did the year before. The key word in the passage that might have alerted you to the analogy was the word *same.* The assumption on which this argument depends is that men and women will like the same new fabric. Choices (A), (C), (D), and (E) are all outside the scope of the argument. The correct answer is (B).

## VERBAL BIN 1

### QUESTIONS

4. The standard lamp is becoming outmoded, and so too is the incandescent light bulb, it is Edison's miraculous invention to use so much more energy than the new low-wattage halogen bulbs.

 - so too is the incandescent light bulb, it is Edison's miraculous invention to use
 - so too is the incandescent light bulb, Edison's miraculous invention that uses
 - so too the incandescent light bulb, Edison's miraculous invention using
 - also the incandescent light bulb, it is Edison's miraculous invention that uses
 - also the incandescent light bulb, which is Edison's miraculous invention to use

5. Over the last 20 years, the growth of information technology has been more rapid than any other business field, but has recently begun to lag behind as newly emerging fields seem more enticing to new graduates.

 - the growth of information technology has been more rapid than any other business field
 - the growth of information technology has been more rapid than any other fields of business
 - information technology's growth has been more rapid than any other fields of business
 - the growing of information technology has been more rapid than that of any other business field
 - the growth of information technology has been more rapid than that of any other business field

### EXPLANATIONS

4. **B** This is basically an idiom question, but your checklist may first uncover a pronoun issue. The pronoun *it* clearly refers back to *light bulb*, but in this case the pronoun isn't actually necessary: *Edison's miraculous invention* refers directly back to *light bulb* without the need of a pronoun. This eliminates (A) and (D), both of which are actually run-on sentences. Next, you should turn your attention to the end of the underlined phrase. Do you have an invention *to use* energy ((A) and (E)), an invention *that uses* energy ((B) and (D)), or an invention *using* energy ((C))? If you said *that uses*, then you are doing just fine. Since we've already eliminated (D), the correct answer is (B).

5. **E** The clue that tells you this is a potential parallel construction problem is the word *than*. This sentence is supposed to compare the *growth* of information technology to the *growth* in other fields. However, as written, the sentence is comparing the *growth* of information technology directly to other fields. Once you spot this, you should immediately start looking for the replacement phrase, *that of*. Only two answer choices contain it, (D) and (E). However, (D) uses the awkward and unidiomatic phrase *the growing of information technology*. The correct answer is (E).

## QUESTIONS

6. According to mutual fund sales experts, a successful year for a stock fund should result not only in increased investor dollars flowing into the fund, but also in increased investor dollars flowing into other mutual stock funds offered by the same company. However, while last year the Grafton Mutual Company's "Growth Stock Fund" beat average market returns by a factor of two and recorded substantial new investment, the other stock funds offered by Grafton did not report any increase whatsoever.

   Which of the following conclusions can properly be drawn from the statements above?

   - When one of the mutual funds offered by a company beats average market returns, the other mutual funds offered by that company will beat average market returns.
   - The mutual fund sales experts neglected to consider bond funds in formulating their theory.
   - The performance of the Grafton "Growth Stock Fund" was a result of a wave of mergers and acquisitions that year.
   - Investors currently dislike all stock mutual funds because of market volatility.
   - The success of one mutual fund is not the only factor affecting whether investors will invest in other mutual funds run by the same company.

7. With <u>less than thirty thousand dollars in advance ticket sales and fewer</u> acceptances by guest speakers than expected, the one-day symposium on art and religion was canceled for lack of interest.

   - less than thirty thousand dollars in advance ticket sales and fewer
   - fewer than thirty thousand dollars in advance ticket sales and less
   - fewer than thirty thousand dollars in advance ticket sales and fewer
   - lesser than thirty thousand dollars in advance ticket sales and fewer
   - less than thirty thousand dollars in advance ticket sales and as few

## EXPLANATIONS

6. **E** This is a causal argument. According to experts, the high returns of one mutual fund *cause* investors to invest in other mutual funds run by the same company. However, in the case of the Grafton "family" of mutual funds, that was not the case. What conclusion can you draw from this? Keep (E), which asks you to consider that there might be alternate causes. Choices (A), (B), and (C) are outside the scope of the argument, while (D) is too extreme and illogical because the argument makes it clear that investors liked at least *one* stock mutual fund: Grafton's "Growth Stock Fund." The correct answer is (E).

7. **A** This question is about quantity words, as you probably suspected just from looking at the answer choices. When it comes to money, you use *fewer* if you are referring to the number of actual bills you have, but *less* if you are referring to the total amount and don't know the actual number of bills. This would get you down to (A) and (E). Acceptances, however, can be counted, so in the second half of the underlined portion of the underlined sentence, you would use *fewer.* If you were tempted by (E), you didn't notice that it created a new idiomatic error: would you say as few *than* or as few *as*? That is, with (E) you would be

## QUESTIONS

## EXPLANATIONS

saying "and as few acceptances by guest speakers than expected" when the idiom is "as few as" not "as few than." The correct answer is (A).

8. New technology now makes it feasible for computer call-in help desk services to route calls they receive to almost anywhere, theoretically allowing employees to work from home, without the need for a daily commute.

   The adoption of this policy would be most likely to increase productivity if employees did not ___________.

   - ○ commute from a distance of fewer than 10 miles
   - ○ commute by car as opposed to by rail
   - ○ live in areas with dependable phone service
   - ○ need to consult frequently with each other to solve callers' problems
   - ○ have more than one telephone line

8. **D** The tricky part of this inference question is dealing with the "did not." Choice (A) is outside the scope of the argument because eliminating such a short commute would presumably not have much effect on productivity. Choice (B) is also outside the scope since the *method* of the commute employees would no longer have to make is probably irrelevant. If employees did not live in areas of dependable phone service, that would likely *decrease* productivity, so that eliminates (C). For similar reasons, eliminate (E); if employees did not have more than one phone line, it might decrease productivity since they would presumably get some personal calls at their place of residence. For (D), if employees needed to consult each other to answer callers' questions, they would be at a distinct disadvantage if they were all in separate locations. The correct answer is (D).

9. The port cities of England in the 19th century saw a renaissance of ship construction, with some innovative designs breaking new ground, stretching the limits of ship-building theory, and <u>received</u> acclaim from around the world.

   - ○ received
   - ○ it received
   - ○ receiving
   - ○ would receive
   - ○ it had received

9. **C** This is a parallel construction question, in which the second half of the sentence contains a list of three actions, all of which must be expressed in the same way. The three actions are *breaking, stretching,* and *received. Received* is underlined and does not match the other actions, so it must be changed to *receiving.* Eliminate (A), (B), (D), and (E), as they are not parallel to the other two verbs. The correct answer is (C).

## QUESTIONS

10. According to a consumer research group survey, the majority of kitchen appliances purchased in the United States are purchased by men. This appears to belie the myth that women spend more time in the kitchen than men.

The argument is flawed primarily because the author ________.

- ◯ fails to differentiate between buying and using
- ◯ does not provide information about the types of kitchen appliances surveyed
- ◯ depends on the results of one survey
- ◯ does not give exact statistics to back up his case
- ◯ does not provide information on other appliances such as washers and dryers

11. <u>A contribution to a favorite charity being sent instead</u> of flowers when a colleague dies is becoming more the rule than the exception when it comes to funeral etiquette.

- ◯ A contribution to a favorite charity being sent instead
- ◯ A contribution being sent to a favorite charity as opposed
- ◯ To send a contribution for a favorite charity instead
- ◯ Sending a contribution to a favorite charity instead
- ◯ Sending a contribution to a favorite charity as opposed

## EXPLANATIONS

**10. A** The faulty assumption of this argument is that the buyers of the kitchen appliances are also the users of the kitchen appliances. You do not know that this is true. While more men may buy kitchen appliances, they are not necessarily the ones who use them. Choice (B) is wrong because knowing the individual types of kitchen appliances would not enhance the argument. Although (C) and (D) might seem tempting, the problem with this argument is not so much that the survey might not be representative, but rather that the author is using information about buying patterns to extrapolate how these appliances are later going to be used and by whom. Choice (E) is outside the scope of the argument. The correct answer is (A).

**11. D** The GMAT test-writers have an aversion to the word *being*, which usually creates a passive voice. This eliminates (A) and (B). Generally, when a sentence begins with the infinitive verb form (*To send…*), you would need a parallel infinitive verb form in the second half of the sentence, which is not the case in (C) (which also uses the incorrect idiomatic expression *contribution for*). Choice (E) might seem tempting, except that the last two words—*as opposed*—don't go idiomatically with *of*. The correct answer is (D).

## QUESTIONS

## EXPLANATIONS

Questions 12–15 are based on the following passage:

As a business model, the world of publishing has always been a somewhat sleepy enclave, but now all that seems poised to change. Several companies have moved aggressively into a new business endeavor whose genesis comes from the question: Who owns the great works of literature?

Text-on-demand is not a completely new idea, of course. In the 1990s, the Gutenberg project sought volunteers to type literary classics that had expired copyrights into word processing files so that scholars would have searchable databases for their research. Most of the works of Shakespeare, Cervantes, Proust, and Molière were to be found free online by as early as 1995.

However, now large-scale companies have moved into the market, with scanners and business plans, and are looking for bargain basement content. These companies are striking deals with libraries, and some publishers, to be able to provide their content, for a price, to individual buyers over the Internet.

At stake are the rights to an estimated store of 30 million books, most of which are now out of print. Many of these books are now also in the public domain, giving any company the right to sell them online. Still, a good portion of the books a general audience might actually want to buy is still under copyright. The urgent question: Who owns those copyrights? In the case of all too many books put out more than 20 years ago by now-defunct publishing companies, the answer is unclear—a situation the new text-on-demand companies are eager to exploit. An association of publishers has sued, claiming massive copyright infringement. The case is several years away from trial.

12. The primary purpose of the passage is to

- present the results of a statistical analysis and propose further study
- explain a recent development and explore its consequences
- identify the reasons for a trend and recommend measures to address it
- outline several theories about a phenomenon and advocate one of them
- describe the potential consequences of implementing a new policy and argue in favor of that policy

12. **B** Process of Elimination is useful here. Does the author present a statistical analysis? No, so eliminate (A). While the author might be said to identify the reasons for a trend, does she recommend measures to address it? No, so eliminate (C). Does the author advocate anything whatsoever? No, so eliminate (D). Does the author argue in favor of any policy? No, so eliminate (E). The correct answer is (B).

## QUESTIONS

13. It can be inferred from the passage that the works of Shakespeare, Cervantes, and Molière

- ⬭ are some of the most popular works of literature
- ⬭ are no longer copyrighted
- ⬭ are among the works for which the association of publishers is suing text-on-demand companies
- ⬭ do not currently exist as searchable databases
- ⬭ were owned by now-defunct publishing companies

14. Which of the following is an example of a book that a text-on-demand company would not have to acquire the rights to?

- ⬭ A book still under copyright
- ⬭ A book more than 20 years old
- ⬭ A book in the public domain
- ⬭ A book a general audience might want to buy
- ⬭ A book not already owned by publishers the company has a deal with

## EXPLANATIONS

13. **B** Look for information about the authors mentioned in the question: it's in the end of the second paragraph. Make sure to read the context and not just those lines. Based on the previous sentence, these books are examples of ones with expired copyrights that were typed and put online. This supports (B). Choices (A) and (E) might be true but cannot be inferred. Choice (C) is out of scope, as lawsuits apply to other works than the subject of this question. Choice (D) directly contradicts the passage. The correct answer is (B).

14. **C** The passage states in the last paragraph that these companies want to exploit the unclear situation of who owns the copyrights to certain books. They would want to print something that is not under copyright, so it would be in the public domain, as the passage indicates in lines 24–26. For (B), the passage does not say that all books over 20 years old may be freely printed. The correct answer is (C).

## QUESTIONS

15. It can be inferred from the passage that a common practice of text-on-demand companies is to

- ⬭ use scanners to find books they want to acquire
- ⬭ create business plans well before they have any actual business
- ⬭ buy content at premium prices
- ⬭ acquire the rights to books for as little as possible
- ⬭ attempt to supplant the role of traditional publishers

## EXPLANATIONS

15. **D** Use Process of Elimination. Choices (A) and (B) are recycled language—the passage mentions scanners and business plans but not in the same way as these two choices. Choice (C) is a reversal—the passage states that these companies are *looking for bargain basement content.* Choice (D) fits with this statement. Choice (E) is not supported because the passage doesn't explain what these practices have to do with *the role of traditional publishers.* The correct answer is (D).

16. Exit polls, conducted by an independent organization among voters at five polling locations during a recent election, suggested that the incumbent mayor—a Democrat—was going to lose the election by a wide margin. But, in fact, by the time the final results were tabulated, the incumbent had won the election by a narrow margin.

Which of the following, if true, would explain the apparent contradiction in the results of the exit polls?

- ⬭ The people chosen at random to be polled by the independent organization happened to be Democrats.
- ⬭ The exit poll locations chosen by the independent organization were in predominantly Republican districts.
- ⬭ The exit polls were conducted during the afternoon, when most of the districts' younger voters, who did not support the incumbent mayor, were at work.
- ⬭ The incumbent mayor ran on a platform that promised to lower taxes if elected.
- ⬭ An earlier poll, conducted the week before the election, had predicted that the incumbent mayor would win.

16. **B** The key to this statistical argument is to understand that the sampling of the voters might not be representative of ALL the voters. Choice (A) says the voters chosen by the pollsters happened to be Democrats. But in that case, you would expect that the incumbent mayor, a Democrat, would have been predicted the winner of the election. Choice (C) says the exit poll was conducted at a time of day in which many people who disliked the mayor could not vote, implying that the actual election results for the incumbent would be worse, or at least no better. Choices (D) and (E) are outside the scope of the argument. Choice (B) gives a statistical reason for the skewed results: the exit polls were conducted in locations where the incumbent had little support—leaving open the possibility that his results would be stronger elsewhere. The correct answer is (B).

## QUESTIONS

17. The spread of Avian flu from animals to humans has been well-documented, but less understood is the mechanism by which it is spread from one bird species to another. **In order to avoid a world-wide epidemic of Avian flu, scientists must make that study a first priority.** To solely tackle the human dimension of this possible pandemic is to miss half of the problem: its spread from one hemisphere to another.

 The bolded phrase plays which of the following roles in the argument above?

 - The bolded phrase states a premise of the argument.
 - The bolded phrase contradicts the author's main point.
 - The bolded phrase makes a statement that the author is about to contradict.
 - The bolded phrase states the author's conclusion.
 - The bolded phrase states an assumption the author is making.

18. Successful business leaders not only anticipate potential problems and have contingency plans ready, instead proceeding as if they are likely to occur at any time.

 - ready, instead proceeding as if they are likely to occur at any time
 - ready, but also proceed as if such problems are likely to occur at any time
 - ready, but also proceeding as if the occurrence of them is at any time likely
 - ready; they instead proceed as if their occurrence is likely at any time
 - ready; such problems are likely to occur at any time, is how they proceed

## EXPLANATIONS

17. **D** Although there is no "therefore" or "hence" in front of it, the bolded phrase is the conclusion of the argument. The other phrases are premises of the argument. If you suspect a phrase may be the conclusion, it sometimes helps to imagine a "therefore" in front of it, to see if the sentence would make sense. If it does, chances are that's your conclusion. The correct answer is (D).

18. **B** The phrase *not only* must be followed by the phrase *but also* in order to complete the sentence properly. The answer must therefore be either (B) or (C). Choice (C) lacks parallel structure in the words *anticipate* and *proceeding.* Correctly formulated, this sentence should read *business leaders not only anticipate...but also proceed....* The correct answer is (B).

## QUESTIONS

19. An artist who sells her paintings for a fixed price decides that she must increase her income. Because she does not believe that customers will pay more for her paintings, she decides to cut costs by using cheaper paints and canvases. She expects that, by cutting costs, she will increase her profit margin per painting and thus increase her annual net income.

Which of the following, if true, most weakens the argument above?

- ⬭ Other area artists charge more for their paintings than the artist charges for hers.
- ⬭ The artist has failed to consider other options, such as renting cheaper studio space.
- ⬭ The artist's plan will result in the production of inferior paintings which, in turn, will cause a reduction in sales.
- ⬭ If the economy were to enter a period of inflation, the artist's projected increase in income could be wiped out by increases in the price of art supplies.
- ⬭ The artist considered trying to complete paintings more quickly and thus increase production, but concluded that it would be impossible.

20. Although tapirs reared in captivity are generally docile and have even been kept as pets by South American villagers, it is nonetheless a volatile creature prone to unpredictable and dangerous temper tantrums.

- ⬭ it is nonetheless a volatile creature
- ⬭ it is nonetheless volatile creatures
- ⬭ being nonetheless volatile creatures
- ⬭ they are nonetheless a volatile creature
- ⬭ they are nonetheless volatile creatures

## EXPLANATIONS

19. **C** To weaken an argument, look first at its conclusion. This argument concludes that the artist will *increase her profit margin...and thus increase her annual income* by using cheaper art supplies. Which answer choice undercuts this conclusion? Choice (C) does; if the artist's sales decrease, then her increased profit margin may not lead to an increase in annual income, because the decrease in sales may offset the increase in per-painting profit. The correct answer is (C).

20. **E** This is a pronoun agreement question. The subject of the sentence is *tapirs*; therefore, the pronoun that refers to the subject must be plural. The answer, therefore, must be (D) or (E). Choice (D) contains a new pronoun agreement error, because *they* is plural and *a volatile creature* is singular. Choice (C) has no pronoun at all. The correct answer is (E).

## QUESTIONS

21. According to a recent report, the original tires supplied with the Impressivo, a new sedan-class automobile, wore much more quickly than tires conventionally wear. The report suggested two possible causes: (1) defects in the tires and (2) improper wheel alignment of the automobile.

Which of the following would best help the authors of the report determine which of the two causes identified was responsible for the extra wear?

- A study in which the rate of tire wear in the Impressivo is compared to the rate of tire wear in all automobiles in the same class
- A study in which a second set of tires, manufactured by a different company than the one that made the first set, is installed on all Impressivos and the rate of wear is measured
- A study in which the level of satisfaction of workers in the Impressivo manufacturing plant is measured and compared to that of workers at other automobile manufacturing plants
- A study that determines how often improper wheel alignment results in major problems for manufacturers of other automobiles in the Impressivo's class
- A study that determines the degree to which faulty driving techniques employed by Impressivo drivers contributed to tire wear

## EXPLANATIONS

21. **B** Because the report identifies two possible causes of the tire wear, the best answer must identify a study that focuses on one of these possible causes. Studies focusing on car models other than the Impressivo, (A) and (D), worker satisfaction, (C), or driver error, (E), are all irrelevant to this study. The study described in (B) removes one of the two possible causes. If the newly installed tires made by another manufacturer also turn out to wear abnormally, then the authors will have good reason to suspect that faulty alignment caused the initial problem. If the new tires wear normally, then they will know that the original tires were faulty. The correct answer is (B).

## QUESTIONS

## EXPLANATIONS

Questions 22–25 are based on the following passage:

Founded at the dawn of the modern industrial era, the nearly forgotten Women's Trade Union League (WTUL) played an instrumental role in advancing the cause of working women throughout the early part of the twentieth century. In the face of considerable adversity, the WTUL made a contribution far greater than did most historical footnotes.

The organization's successes did not come easily; conflict beset the WTUL in many forms. During those early days of American unions, organized labor was aggressively opposed by both industry and government. The WTUL, which represented a largely unskilled labor force, had little leverage against these powerful opponents. Also, because of the skill level of its workers as well as inherent societal gender bias, the WTUL had great difficulty finding allies among other unions. Even the large and powerful American Federation of Labor (AFL), which nominally took the WTUL under its wing, kept it at a distance. Because the AFL's power stemmed from its highly skilled labor force, the organization saw little economic benefit in working with the WTUL. The affiliation provided the AFL with political cover, allowing it to claim support for women workers; in return, the WTUL gained a potent but largely absent ally.

The WTUL also had to overcome internal discord. While the majority of the group's members were working women, a sizeable and powerful minority consisted of middle- and upper-class social reformers whose goals extended beyond labor reform. While workers argued that the WTUL should focus its efforts on collective bargaining and working conditions, the reformers looked beyond the workplace, seeking state and national legislation aimed at education reform and urban poverty relief as well as workplace issues.

Despite these obstacles, the WTUL accomplished a great deal. The organization was instrumental in the passage of state laws mandating an eight-hour workday, a minimum wage for women, and a ban on child labor. It provided seed money to women who organized workers in specific plants and industries, and it also established strike funds and soup kitchens to support striking unionists. After the tragic Triangle Shirtwaist Company fire of 1911, the WTUL launched a four-year investigation whose conclusions formed the basis of much subsequent workplace safety legislation. The organization also offered a political base for all reform-minded women, and thus helped develop the next generation of American leaders. Eleanor Roosevelt was one of many prominent figures to emerge from the WTUL.

The organization began a slow death in the late 1920s, when the Great Depression choked off its funding. The organization limped through the 1940s; the death knell eventually rang in 1950, at the onset of the McCarthy era. A turn-of-the-century labor organization dedicated to social reform, one that during its heyday was regarded by many as "radical," stood little chance of weathering that storm. This humble ending, however, does nothing to diminish the accomplishments of an organization that is yet to receive its historical due.

## QUESTIONS

22. The primary purpose of this passage is to

- ⬭ describe the barriers confronting women in the contemporary workplace
- ⬭ compare and contrast the methods of two labor unions of the early industrial era
- ⬭ critique the methods employed by an important labor union
- ⬭ rebuke historians for failing to cover the women's labor movement adequately
- ⬭ call readers' attention to an overlooked contributor to American history

## EXPLANATIONS

22. **E** Use Process of Elimination. Choice (A) is incorrect because the passage is focused on a historical group, not contemporary conditions. Choice (B) is incorrect because the passage is about only one union. Choice (C) is incorrect because the author doesn't critique the union's methods. Choice (D) is close but highlights why (E) is correct. The author notes that the WTUL is *nearly forgotten* but doesn't criticize historians for not drawing attention to it. The passage serves to remind readers of the WTUL. The correct answer is (E).

## QUESTIONS

23. Which of the following best characterizes the American Federation of Labor's view of the Women's Trade Union League, as it is presented in the passage?

- ⬭ The WTUL was an important component of the AFL's multifront assault on industry and its treatment of workers.
- ⬭ Because of Eleanor Roosevelt's affiliation with the organization, the WTUL was a vehicle through which the AFL could gain access to the White House.
- ⬭ The WTUL was to be avoided because the radical element within it attracted unwanted government scrutiny.
- ⬭ The WTUL offered the AFL some political capital but little that would assist it in labor negotiations.
- ⬭ The WTUL was weakened by its hesitance in pursuing widespread social reform beyond the workplace.

## EXPLANATIONS

23. **D** The passage states that the AFL was a *potent but largely absent ally,* and that the AFL *saw little economic benefit in working with the WTUL,* which served as *political cover* for the AFL. This does not support (A), (B), (C), or (E). The correct answer is (D).

## QUESTIONS

24. Each of the following is cited in the passage as an accomplishment of the Women's Trade Union League EXCEPT

- it organized a highly skilled workforce to increase its bargaining power
- it contributed to the development of a group of leaders in America
- it provided essential support to striking women
- it helped fund start-up unions for women
- it contributed to the passage of important social and labor reform legislation

25. The passage suggests which of the following about the "middle- and upper-class social reformers" mentioned in lines 32–33 ?

- They did not understand, nor were they sympathetic to, the plight of poor women workers.
- Their naive interest in Communism was ultimately detrimental to the Women's Trade Union League.
- It was because of their social and political power that the Women's Trade Union League was able to form an alliance with the American Federation of Labor.
- They represented only an insignificant fraction of the leadership of Women's Trade Union League.
- They sought to advance a broad political agenda of societal improvement.

## EXPLANATIONS

24. **A** Search the passage for each answer choice. Choice (B) is in lines 54–55. Choice (C) is in lines 47–48. Choice (D) is in lines 45–46. Choice (E) is in lines 42–44. Choice (A) is not supported by the passage because in line 14 it states that the WTUL *represented a largely unskilled labor force.* The correct answer is (A).

25. **E** The passage states that these women were a *powerful minority* within the WTUL and that they were *looking beyond the workplace* to influence legislation. Choices (A), (B), (C), and (D) are not supported by the text in this part of the passage, whereas (E) matches the meaning of the passage. The correct answer is (E).

# VERBAL BIN 2

## QUESTIONS

1. As its performance has risen on all the stock indexes, the bio-tech start-up has branched out into new markets to look for opportunities <u>they would previously have had to ignore</u>.

   - they would previously have had to ignore
   - they would have had to ignore previously
   - that previously they would have had to ignore
   - it previously would have had to ignore in past years
   - it would previously have had to ignore

2. Scientists wishing to understand the kinetic movements of ancient dinosaurs are today studying the movements of modern-day birds, which many scientists believe are descended from dinosaurs. A flaw in this strategy is that birds, although once genetically linked to dinosaurs, have evolved so far that any comparison is effectively meaningless.

   Which of the following, if true, would most weaken the criticism made above of the scientists' strategy?

   - Birds and dinosaurs have a number of important features in common that exist in no other living species.
   - Birds are separated from dinosaurs by 65 million years of evolution.
   - Our theories of dinosaur movements have recently undergone a radical reappraisal.
   - The study of kinetic movement is a relatively new discipline.
   - Many bird experts do not study dinosaurs to draw inferences about birds.

## EXPLANATIONS

1. **E** If you go through your mental checklist, you will probably spot the pronoun *they*. To whom does that pronoun refer? Even though there are a lot of plural nouns in the front half of the sentence, *they* must refer to the start-up company, which is singular. Never mind that many people in spoken English refer to a large company as *they*. On the GMAT, a singular noun needs a singular pronoun. That eliminates (A), (B), and (C). To choose between (D) and (E), look for a new error. That's what you'll find in (D), which uses both the word *previously* and the phrase *in the past*, creating a redundancy error. The correct answer is (E).

2. **A** In this passage, the author is questioning an analogical argument. To understand the kinetic movement of dinosaurs, says the argument, you should study the kinetic movement of birds, which are a lot like dinosaurs. The author is trying to weaken this analogy by saying that dinosaurs and birds are actually not very similar. Your job is to weaken the author's attempt to demonstrate that the argument is flawed. How do you do that? By showing that dinosaurs and birds *are* in fact alike. Choice (B), if anything, actually strengthens the author's criticism of the analogy. Choices (C) and (D) are outside the scope of the argument. Choice (E) seems to strengthen the author's criticism of the analogy. It is also out of scope since the fact that some bird experts don't study dinosaurs doesn't mean that dinosaur experts shouldn't study birds. Choice (A) shows how birds and dinosaurs are alike. The correct answer is (A).

# VERBAL BIN 2

## QUESTIONS

3. A factory in China has two options to improve efficiency: adding robotic assembly lines and subcontracting out certain small production goals that could be done more efficiently elsewhere. Adding robotic assembly lines will improve efficiency more than subcontracting some small production goals. Therefore, by adding robotic assembly lines, the factory will be doing the most that can be done to improve efficiency.

   Which of the following is an assumption on which the argument depends?

   - Adding robotic assembly lines will be more expensive than subcontracting some small production goals.
   - The factory has a choice of robotic assembly lines, some of which might be better suited to this factory than others.
   - The factory may or may not decide to choose either alternative.
   - Efficiency cannot be improved more by using both methods together than by adding robotic assembly lines alone.
   - This particular factory is already the third most efficient factory in China.

4. <u>Just as the early NASA space explorers attempted on each flight to push the frontiers of our knowledge, so too</u> are the new private-consortium space explorers seeking to add to man's general understanding of the cosmos.

   - Just as the early NASA space explorers attempted on each flight to push the frontiers of our knowledge, so too
   - The early NASA space explorers attempted on each flight to push the frontiers of our knowledge, and in the same way
   - Like the case of the early NASA space explorers who attempted on each flight to push the frontiers of our knowledge, so too
   - As in the early NASA space explorers' attempts on each flight to push the frontiers of our knowledge, so too
   - Similar to the early NASA space explorers attempted on each flight to push the frontiers of our knowledge, so too

## EXPLANATIONS

3. **D** As always, if you don't immediately grasp the reasoning behind an argument, scope is key to eliminating wrong answers. For example, the expense of implementing these goals, (A), was never mentioned and thus is outside the scope of the argument. The same goes for (B): choosing between different types of robotic assembly lines is not part of this argument. As for (C), the argument does not depend on whether the two actions being considered are ever actually implemented—again it is outside the scope. And, come to think of it, so is (E), which tells us that the factory is already quite efficient; the argument is about making it *more* efficient. By using POE, you have your answer. However, here's the logic: the conclusion of the argument is that choosing *one* of these two methods will result in the factory becoming the most efficient that it can be. What the argument is ignoring is the possibility that the factory could be even more efficient if it implemented *both* changes. The correct answer is (D).

4. **A** The idiom *just as...so too* is correct as written. Each of the other choices uses variations on an unidiomatic expression instead. The correct answer is (A).

# VERBAL BIN 2

## QUESTIONS

5. A proposal for a new building fire safety code requires that fire-retardant insulation no longer be sprayed on steel girders in the factory, but be sprayed on once the girders have arrived at the building site. This will eliminate the dislodging of the insulation in transit and reduce fatalities in catastrophic fires by an estimated 20%.

Which of the following, if true, represents the strongest challenge to the new proposal?

- The fire-retardant insulation will also be required to be one inch thicker than in the past.
- Studies have shown that most dislodgement of insulation occurs after the girders arrive on site.
- Catastrophic fires represent only 4% of the fires reported nationally.
- The proposed safety code will add considerably to the cost of new construction.
- In most of Europe, spraying fire-retardant insulation onto steel girders at the building site has been required for the past ten years.

6. An effort <u>to control the crippling effects of poverty in Brazil's interior cities, begun almost thirty years ago,</u> has been partially successful, despite the setback of a major drought and the interruption of aid during an extended economic crisis.

- to control the crippling effects of poverty in Brazil's interior cities, begun almost thirty years ago,
- begun almost thirty years ago for controlling the crippling effects of poverty in Brazil's interior cities,
- begun for controlling the crippling effects of poverty in Brazil's interior cities almost thirty years ago,
- at controlling the crippling effects of poverty in Brazil's interior cities begun almost thirty years ago,
- that has begun almost thirty years ago to control the crippling effects of poverty in Brazil's interior cities,

## EXPLANATIONS

5. **B** The words *strongest challenge* in the question mean that you are trying to weaken the argument. Choice (A), if anything, appears to support the argument rather than weaken it, so you can eliminate it. Choices (C) and (D) do seem negative toward the argument, but both are outside the scope, as is (E). For (B), if the insulation comes loose *after* the girders arrive on site, then making an effort to prevent its dislodgement in transit to the building site will not have any effect and will not necessarily reduce fatalities. The correct answer is (B).

6. **A** This is an idiom question. Do you attempt *to* do something, do you attempt *at* something, or do you attempt *for* something? Choice (E) uses the idiom correctly but creates a new tense error. The correct answer is (A).

## QUESTIONS

7. A newly discovered disease is thought to be caused by a certain bacterium. However, recently released data note that the bacterium thrives in the presence of a certain virus, implying that it is actually the virus that causes the new disease.

Which of the following pieces of evidence would most support the data's implication?

- In the absence of the virus, the disease has been observed to follow infection by the bacterium.
- The virus has been shown to aid the growth of bacteria, a process which often leads to the onset of the disease.
- The virus alone has been observed in many cases of the disease.
- In cases where the disease does not develop, infection by the bacterium is usually preceded by infection by the virus.
- Onset of the disease usually follows infection by both the virus and the bacterium.

8. The company was not even publicly traded until 1968, when the owner and founder sold it to David P. Markham, a private investor, who took the company public and established a long and generous policy of stock options for valued employees.

- who took the company public and established a long and generous policy of stock options for
- who, taking the company public, established a long and generous policy of stock options to
- who, when he took the company public, established a long and generous policy of stock options to
- who had taken the company public, establishing a long and generous policy of stock options as
- taking the company public and establishing a long and generous policy of stock options for

## EXPLANATIONS

7. **C** The last line of this argument gives away its type: *...the virus that causes....* The cause of a certain disease was thought to be one thing, but now is believed to be something else. Recent evidence suggests that the cause is a virus (which also nourishes the bacterium once thought to be the cause of the disease). To support a causal argument, you take away possible alternate causes. Choice (C) does this by showing that while both virus and bacterium are often present at the same time, the virus has been found *without* the bacterium in many cases of the disease. Choice (A) directly contradicts this, suggesting that the bacterium is the sole cause. Choices (B) and (E) suggest that the virus plays a supporting role to the bacterium. Choice (D) is outside the scope of the argument. The correct answer is (C).

8. **A** The second half of this sentence contains a correctly constructed parallel list. The private investor *took* and *established*, both verbs in the simple past. In (B) and (D), the construction is less than parallel. In addition, several choices also use the unidiomatic *established...for* as opposed to *established... to.* In (E), the construction is parallel, but it now seems to modify *the owner and founder* rather than *Markham*. The correct answer is (A).

## QUESTIONS

9. Because of a quality control problem, a supplier of flu vaccines will not be able to ship any supplies of the vaccine for the upcoming flu season. This will create a shortage of flu vaccines and result in a loss of productivity as workers call in sick.

Which of the following, if true, most seriously weakens the argument above?

- ◯ The quality control problem of the supplier is not as severe as some experts had initially predicted.
- ◯ Other suppliers of flu vaccine have not been affected by the quality control problem.
- ◯ Last year there was also a shortage of flu vaccine available.
- ◯ The price of flu vaccines is expected to fall in the next ten years.
- ◯ The flu season is expected to last longer than usual this year.

## EXPLANATIONS

9. **B** You might have been tempted by (A), which seems to weaken the argument by saying the quality control problem of the supplier is not as severe as experts had predicted. However, the initial predictions of experts are outside the scope of the argument, because they don't change the fact that this supplier will not be supplying any vaccines, regardless of how minor the problems might be. Similarly, what happened last year, (C), or what will happen in the next 10 years, (D), is also outside the scope of the argument; you want to know what will happen *this* year. Choice (E) seems to strengthen the argument since a longer flu season will presumably result in more people getting sick. For (B), if other suppliers have not been affected by quality control problems, then the overall shortage may be less severe. The correct answer is (B).

## VERBAL BIN 2

### QUESTIONS

10. Never before had the navy defeated so many foes at once as it had in the battle of Trafalgar in 1805.

- so many foes at once as it had in
- at once as many foes as
- at once as many foes that there were in
- as many foes at once as it did in
- so many foes at once as that it defeated in

### EXPLANATIONS

10. **D** This question is a swirling mixture of idiom and parallel comparison. The correct idiom in question: *as many…as*. When you say it out loud, does *so many…as* seem right? Of course, it's much easier to notice that it doesn't when the expression has already been pulled out of the problem for you. During the GMAT, you have to do your own pulling, but remember, you always have five sensational clues: the answer choices. Even if you initially have no idea what might or might not be wrong with this sentence, you can figure it out by scanning the answers; you'll see that you have a collection of *so many as*'s and *as many as*'s to choose from.

The other thing going on in this sentence, of course, is parallel comparison. Words such as *as* or *than* often mean a comparison is being made. The correct comparison would read "Never before had a navy defeated as many foes at once as it *defeated…*," but as you know from reading our chapter on Sentence Correction, the test-writers like to see if you know that you can replace the second verb with a replacement verb: *did*. The correct answer is (D).

11. The changes that may be part of a general global warming trend include an increase in the frequency and severity of hurricanes, a gradual rise in sea level, depleting the ozone layer, and raising the temperature of the Earth.

- depleting the ozone layer, and raising the temperature of the Earth
- depleting the ozone layer, and a rise in the Earth's temperature
- a depletion of the ozone layer, and raising the Earth's temperature
- a depletion of the ozone layer, and a raise of the temperature of the Earth
- a depletion of the ozone layer, and a rise in the temperature of the Earth

11. **E** This sentence has what should be a parallel list of nouns, beginning with *an increase* and *a rise*, but then the last two items on the list are suddenly verb-like things: *depleting* and *raising*. Since it is the last two items that are underlined, these are the items that must change. Choices (A), (B), and (C) all have verb-like things in them. Choice (D), with two noun-like things, seems tempting at first, but do you say *a raise of the temperature*? Nope, it's unidiomatic. The correct answer is (E).

## QUESTIONS

## EXPLANATIONS

Questions 12–16 are based on the following passage:

It has long been a tenet of business theory that the best decisions are made after careful review and consideration. Only after weighing all the options and studying projections, say most professors of business, can a practical decision be made.

Now, that model is being questioned by some business thinkers in the light of the theories of Malcolm Gladwell, who states that human beings often make better decisions in the blink of an eye.

It is, at first glance, a theory so counter-intuitive as to seem almost ludicrous. Behind any decision, Gladwell posits, there is a behind-the-scenes subconscious process in which the brain analyzes; ranks in order of importance; compares and contrasts vast amounts of information; and dismisses extraneous factors, seemingly almost instantaneously, often arriving at a conclusion in less than two seconds. Citing a multitude of studies and examples from life, Gladwell shows how that split-second decision is often better informed than a drawn-out examination.

Evanston and Cramer were the first to apply this theory to the business world. Evanston videotaped the job interviews of 400 applicants at different firms. He then played only 10 seconds of each videotape to independent human resources specialists. The specialists were able to pick out the applicants who were hired with an accuracy of over 90%.

Cramer took the experiment even further, using only five seconds of videotape, without sound. To his astonishment, the rate of accuracy with which the HR specialists were able to predict the successful applicants fell only to 82%.

Critics argue that these results illustrate a problem with stereotyping that impedes human resources specialists from hiring the best candidates even when they have the time to get below the surface: going for the candidate who "looks the part." Gladwell argues that, on the contrary, the human mind is able to make complicated decisions quickly and that intuition often trumps an extended decision-making process.

## QUESTIONS / EXPLANATIONS

12. The primary purpose of the passage is to

- ⬭ discuss reasons an accepted business theory is being reexamined
- ⬭ present evidence that resolves a contradiction in business theory
- ⬭ describe a tenet of business practices and how that tenet can be tested in today's economic environment
- ⬭ argue that a counter-intuitive new business idea is, in the final analysis, incorrect
- ⬭ present evidence that invalidates a new business model

12. **A** In this passage, the accepted practice of making thoughtful business decisions based on careful review is being questioned in light of a new theory. Both (D) and (E) imply that the author has rejected this new model. Choice (C) uses a catchy word from the passage (*tenet*) and fails to indicate that there is a new idea that goes against that tenet. Choice (B) implies that the contradiction between the theory of making decisions based on careful review and the theory of making split-second decisions has in fact been resolved. The correct answer is (A).

13. According to the passage, all of the following are examples of the subconscious processes by which the brain makes a decision EXCEPT

- ⬭ analysis of information
- ⬭ ranking of information
- ⬭ comparison and contrast of information
- ⬭ rejecting information that is not pertinent
- ⬭ consulting a multitude of studies and examples

13. **E** Where do you find the key words *subconscious process*? In the third paragraph. Choices (A), (B), (C), and (D) are all paraphrases of examples of the processes cited in that paragraph. Only (E) is not. In fact, the multitude of studies and examples are cited in support of Gladwell's hypothesis. The correct answer is (E).

14. The author's attitude toward the long-held view that decisions should be made carefully over time expressed in lines 1–5 can best be described as

- ⬭ dismissive and scornful
- ⬭ respectful but questioning
- ⬭ admiring and deferential
- ⬭ uncertain but optimistic
- ⬭ condescending and impatient

14. **B** Both (A) and (E) are too extreme to be the correct answer on the GMAT. But clearly, the new theory being described is an attempt to go beyond the conventional wisdom. The correct answer is (B).

## QUESTIONS

15. The author most likely mentions the results of Cramer's extension of Evanston's experiment in order to

- ⬭ show that Cramer's hypothesis was correct, while Evanston's hypothesis turned out to be incorrect
- ⬭ show that Evanston's hypothesis was correct, while Cramer's hypothesis turned out to be incorrect
- ⬭ demonstrate that while both experiments were scientifically rigorous, neither ended up being scientifically valid
- ⬭ illustrate that the principle of subconscious decisions continues to work even when less information is available
- ⬭ demonstrate that Cramer's experiment was 8% more accurate than Evanston's, even though his subjects had less information to work with

## EXPLANATIONS

15. **D** The information about Cramer's *extension* is in lines 31–35. Choices (A) and (B) are incorrect because the passage doesn't mention what the researchers' hypotheses were. Choice (C) is incorrect because the author doesn't say their work was invalid. Choice (D) is supported by the passage because Cramer found that with even less information the specialists were still highly successful at predicting. Choice (E) is incorrect; in Cramer's study the participants did somewhat worse with less information, not better. The correct answer is (D).

16. It can be inferred that the critics referred to in line 36 believed the results of the two experiments had less to do with the innate decision-making of the subjects than with

- ⬭ the excellent decision-making of Evanston and Cramer
- ⬭ the expertise of Malcolm Gladwell, who originated the theory
- ⬭ not choosing candidates who "looked the part"
- ⬭ the use of videotape as a method of choosing candidates
- ⬭ their unconscious use of visual stereotypes in making their selections

16. **E** The passage states that the critics believe that human resources specialists prefer someone *who looks the part* and that is the reason successful candidates can be predicted from brief observations. This supports (E) because [looking] *the part* is the same as *visual stereotypes.* Watch out for trap answer (C), which is a reversal. The correct answer is (E).

## QUESTIONS

17. The women's volleyball team at a local college finished fifth in its division, prompting the college to fire the team's general manager. The manager responded by suing the college, saying that the team's performance put it among the top teams in the country.

Which of the following statements, if true, would support the claim of the team's manager, and resolve the apparent contradiction?

- The team won all of its "away" games during the season in question.
- Attendance at the volleyball team's games was up 35% from the year before.
- Of the starting team, three team members were unable to play for at least half the season because of injuries.
- There are 80 teams in this particular volleyball team's division.
- The team lost more games this year than it did the year before.

18. Country A recently broke off diplomatic relations with Country B when it was reported that Country B had been running a covert intelligence operation within the borders of Country A. While a spokesperson for Country B admitted the charge, the spokesperson said that it was common knowledge that all countries do this, and that Country A was no exception.

Which of the following inferences can be drawn from the argument above?

- Country B should apologize and dismantle its intelligence operation in Country A.
- The spokesperson for Country B claims that Country A engages in intelligence gathering too.
- Because all countries engage in this practice, Country A's outrage was disingenuous.
- Relations between Country A and Country B will be strained for some time.
- Country B would be just as outraged if it was reported that Country A was running a covert intelligence operation with Country B's borders.

## EXPLANATIONS

17. **D** The manager was apparently fired because of his team's end-of-season statistics. If this made you wonder if the statistics were actually representative, your thinking was right on the money. To support the manager's claim, you have to show that the team's fifth-place finish was actually better than it looked. Choices (A), (B), and (C), while generally positive about the team (and by extension, perhaps, its manager), are outside the scope of the argument. Choice (E) actually puts the team's performance in a more negative light. On the other hand, (D) puts the team's fifth-place finish in a very positive perspective: if the division was made up of 80 teams, finishing in fifth place is actually extremely good. The correct answer is (D).

18. **B** All of the answers to this inference question infer way too much to be the correct answer to a GMAT question—except for (B), which simply restates a sentence from the argument itself. Choice (A) says an apology is needed, which is way beyond the scope of this argument. Choice (C) goes further than the argument to make a value judgment. Choice (D) looks into the future, and (E) takes a "what if" position and builds on it. The correct answer is (B).

## QUESTIONS

19. Because cellular telephones emit signals that can interfere with cockpit-to-control-tower transmissions, airplane passengers' use of these instruments at all times that the airplane is in motion, even while on the ground, are prohibited.

   - at all times that the airplane is in motion, even while on the ground, are
   - at all times during which the airplane, even while on the ground, is in motion, are
   - during airplane motion, even when it is on the ground, are
   - during times of the airplane being in motion, even on the ground, is
   - when the airplane is in motion, even while on the ground, is

## EXPLANATIONS

19. **E** The subject of this sentence, *use*, is singular. Therefore, (A), (B), and (C) are incorrect; each states that *the passengers' use of these instruments… are prohibited.* Choice (D) is unidiomatic, and the phrase *even on the ground* is unnecessarily vague. Choice (E) is concise, clear, and employs the correct verb. The correct answer is (E).

20. In contrast to classical guitars, whose owners prefer the dulcet, rounded tones produced by nylon strings, folk guitar owners prefer the bright and brassy sound that only bronze or steel can create.

   - folk guitar owners prefer the bright and brassy sound
   - folk guitar owners prefer to get a sound that is bright and brassy
   - with a folk guitar, the owner gets the preferably bright and brassy sound
   - folk guitars produce a bright and brassy sound, which their owners prefer,
   - folk guitars produce a preferred bright and brassy sound for their owners

20. **D** Choices (A), (B), and (C) include a parallel comparison error; (A) and (B) compare *classical guitars* and *folk guitar owners*, while (C) compares a plural (*classical guitars*) and a singular (*a folk guitar*) noun. Choice (E) incorrectly suggests that the *bright and brassy* sound is universally preferred rather than preferred specifically by folk guitar owners. Furthermore, the placement of *for their owners* is unnecessarily confusing, as it separates two elements of the sentence that should be closely connected (*bright and brassy sound…that only bronze and steel can create*). Choice (D) corrects this error by setting the interceding phrase off with commas. The correct answer is (D).

# VERBAL BIN 2

## QUESTIONS

Questions 21–22 are based on the following passage:

A system-wide county school anti-smoking education program was instituted last year. The program was clearly a success. Last year, the incidence of students smoking on school premises decreased by over 70 percent.

21. Which of the following assumptions underlies the argument in the passage?

- Cigarettes are detrimental to one's health; once people understand this, they will quit smoking.
- The doubling of the price of a pack of cigarettes last year was not the only cause of the students' altered smoking habits.
- The teachers chosen to lead the anti-smoking education program were the most effective teachers in the school system.
- The number of cigarettes smoked each day by those students who continued to smoke last year did not greatly increase.
- School policy enforcers were less vigilant in seeking out smokers last year than they were in previous years.

## EXPLANATIONS

21. **B** The argument presented is a causal argument. The significant underlying assumption of the argument, therefore, relates to the causal link between the anti-smoking education program and the reduction in smoking on school premises. The argument assumes that the program, and not some other set of circumstances, caused the reduction. It thus assumes that other possible causes—such as an increase in the price of cigarettes—were not substantial contributors to this result.

Process of Elimination is effective on this question, as it is on all Critical Reasoning questions. Because the argument hinges on one crucial piece of evidence—a decrease in the incidence of smoking on school premises—you can eliminate all answers that do not speak directly to that reduction. Thus, you can eliminate (A), (C), and (D). Choice (E), if true, would weaken the argument and therefore cannot be correct. The correct answer is (B).

## QUESTIONS

22. Which of the following, if true, would most seriously weaken the argument in the passage?

- The author of this statement is a school system official hoping to generate good publicity for the anti-smoking program.
- Most students who smoke stopped smoking on school premises last year continued to smoke when away from school.
- Last year, another policy change made it much easier for students to leave and return to school grounds during the school day.
- The school system spent more on anti-smoking education programs last year than it did in all previous years.
- The amount of time students spent in anti-smoking education programs last year resulted in a reduction of in-class hours devoted to academic subjects.

## EXPLANATIONS

22. **C** Once again, your focus should be on the evidence supporting the causal link between the anti-smoking education program and the reduction in smoking on school premises. What, other than the effectiveness of the program, would explain the reduced incidence of smoking on school premises? Choice (C) provides a possible alternate explanation: school policy made it easier for students to leave and return to campus. It is therefore possible, then, that the reduction in smoking on school premises was simply the result of students leaving school premises to smoke and then returning afterward.

Choice (B), while tempting, does not provide an alternate cause for the observed result. None of the other answers address the evidence supporting the conclusion of the passage; therefore, none of them truly weaken the argument. The correct answer is (C).

## QUESTIONS

23. Mild exercise throughout pregnancy <u>may reduce the discomfort associated with pregnancy and result in</u> a speedier, easier birth, according to a recent study.

- may reduce the discomfort associated with pregnancy and result in
- may reduce the discomfort associated with pregnancy, with the result
- may cause a reduction in the discomfort associated with pregnancy and as a result
- might lead to a reduction in the discomfort associated with pregnancy and as a result
- might reduce the discomfort associated with pregnancy and resulting in

## EXPLANATIONS

23. **A** The sentence, as written, maintains correct parallel construction between *reduce the discomfort*...and *result in a speedier*.... Each of the incorrect answers violates the rule of parallel construction. The correct answer is (A).

## QUESTIONS

## EXPLANATIONS

Questions 24–27 are based on the following passage:

What is it that keeps the developing world in an apparent state of perpetual poverty? Poor education, lack of basic medical care, and the absence of democratic structures all certainly contribute to these nations' plight. However, according to Peruvian economist Hernando de Soto, the overriding cause is the overwhelming prevalence of black market activity, well outside the formal economy, in these countries. The losses incurred from this condition are twofold. First, they deny the government tax revenues which could be used to improve education, medical treatment, and government efficiency. More important, however, they deny earners the chance to accumulate assets recognized by law and thus prevent them from leveraging those assets to borrow. Reforming these nations' legal systems in order to confer ownership through titling, de Soto argues, would help the poor there access the assets their work should be generating. These assets could then be used to buy homes and construct businesses, thus building a more stable and prosperous economy. De Soto estimates the value of these assets, which he terms "dead capital," at nearly $10 trillion worldwide.

De Soto is not the first to locate the developing world's problems in the domain of property rights. Others have tried property rights reform and failed. According to de Soto, this is because his predecessors attempted to model their plans on existing, successful property rights systems. In other words, they tried to transplant American and British property law to an inhospitable host. De Soto argues that, within many of the extralegal markets of the developing world, mutually agreed-upon rules for distributing assets and recognizing property rights already exist. Rather than force these markets to adjust to a new, foreign system of property titling, reformers should focus on codifying the existing systems wherever it is practical to do so. This would facilitate a quicker, more natural transition to an economy that builds wealth rather than squanders it.

## QUESTIONS

24. The author's primary goal in the passage is to

- ⬭ compare several failed attempts to address a problem
- ⬭ respond to criticism of a new theory
- ⬭ identify the problems inherent in a new economic theory
- ⬭ describe a novel approach to an old problem
- ⬭ compare different property rights systems in the industrial world

## EXPLANATIONS

24. **D** Use POE. The author briefly mentions failed attempts, but it's not the main point of the passage, so (A) is incorrect. Choices (B) and (C) are incorrect because the author doesn't mention any criticisms or problems with the new theory. Choice (D) is supported by the passage because the author says that poverty is a *perpetual* problem and that de Soto's approach is different, or *novel*. Choice (E) is incorrect because while it is briefly mentioned, it's not the main point of the passage. The correct answer is (D).

25. According to the passage, de Soto believes that the quickest way to address poverty in the developing world is to

- ⬭ increase funding for education
- ⬭ build the infrastructure to support lending
- ⬭ ensure medical care for all citizens
- ⬭ aggressively root out corruption in government
- ⬭ increase tax rates on all citizens in developing countries

25. **B** The passage states that de Soto feels it's a problem that the poor are prevented from borrowing (lines 15–16) and that by *reforming…legal systems… to confer ownership through titling* (16–20), the poverty would decrease. This supports (B). Some of the other answer choices are mentioned as problems in the developing world, but they aren't attributed to de Soto. The correct answer is (B).

## VERBAL BIN 2

### QUESTIONS

26. The author's assertion that "reformers should focus on codifying the existing systems wherever it is practical to do so" (lines 39–41) suggests that

- in some instances, current systems are inadequate to meet the needs of a market economy
- these systems are already written down and need only be enacted as law
- where it is impractical to codify existing systems, countries should adopt American property law
- the existing systems are superior to those currently in use in modern industrialized countries
- improving education and medical care in these countries should take priority over reforming property laws

### EXPLANATIONS

26. **A** The passage indicates that many of the black markets are already systems but aren't written into law. Choice (A) is supported by the quotation because it states *wherever possible*, so there may be some places that do not have sufficient systems to make into law. Choice (B) is a reversal—the passage states that the systems are not written. Choice (C) is incorrect because the author states that adopting such a strategy *failed*. Eliminate (D) because the author makes no such comparison to those in industrialized countries. Choice (E) is the opposite of what is stated in the passage. The correct answer is (A).

27. The term "dead capital" (line 24) refers to

- loans that are never repaid
- failed investments in new businesses
- cities ruined by over-industrialization
- the proceeds of extralegal commerce
- property passed from generation to generation

27. **D** The passage refers *dead capital* back to these assets which ultimately are *the assets* [the poor's] *work should be generating*. The poor use black markets and thus do not receive the assets they would if their work were legal. This supports (D) because *extralegal* means outside of the law. The correct answer is (D).

# VERBAL BIN 3

## QUESTIONS

1. Unlike Franklin D. Roosevelt's bootstrap program that helped to restart economic growth in the 1930s through public works, Ronald Reagan proposed a program of trickle-down economics to restart the economy.

- Franklin D. Roosevelt's bootstrap program that helped
- Franklin D. Roosevelt and his bootstrap program which helped
- Franklin D. Roosevelt, whose bootstrap program helped
- the bootstrap program of Franklin D. Roosevelt that has helped
- Franklin D. Roosevelt and his bootstrap program helping

2. In the 1970s, it became evident that writing about someone else's research was much easier for social scientists who wanted to make a quick name for themselves than it was to do their own research.

- that writing about someone else's research was much easier for social scientists who wanted to make a quick name for themselves
- that for social scientists who wanted to make a quick name for themselves, it was much easier to write about someone else's research
- that for social scientists wanting to make a quick name for themselves, writing about someone else's research was much easier
- for social scientists who wanted to make a quick name for themselves that writing about someone else's research was much easier
- for social scientists who wanted to make a quick name for themselves, writing about someone else's research was much easier

## EXPLANATIONS

1. **C** Part of what normally makes misplaced modifiers easy to spot is that the test-writers generally ask you to fix the second phrase; this time, you have to fix the first phrase. The modifying phrase *Unlike FDR's bootstrap program* is supposed to modify the noun *Ronald Reagan*, which, of course, is not possible. You can't directly compare a program to a person. You could fix the second half of the sentence (*unlike FDR's program… Reagan's program…*), but since the second half of the sentence isn't underlined, we'll have to fix the first half. Choices (B) and (E) still directly compare FDR's program to Ronald Reagan. So does (D). Only (C) avoids the modifier error by directly comparing FDR to Reagan. The correct answer is (C).

2. **B** The problem in the stem sentence is that there are two actions that ought to be parallel but are not. *Writing* (about someone else's research) was easier than *to do* the research themselves. You could fix this two ways in the real world: *writing* was easier than *doing*, or it was easier *to write* than *to do.* Each of the other answer choices mixes and matches these two ways incorrectly, except for (B). Putting the phrase *for social scientists* first, as (D) and (E) do, would not necessarily be wrong if the verbs were parallel. Choices (D) and (E) also do not have the idiom *evident that.* The correct answer is (B).

# VERBAL BIN 3

## QUESTIONS

Questions 3–4 are based on the following passage:

To improve the town's overcrowded school system, the town council has proposed an ambitious education plan to reduce classroom size and make capital improvements—a plan they intend to pay for with an increase in property taxes for homes valued over $500,000. Although the school system desperately needs improving, the town council's plan should be defeated because the majority of the people who would end up paying for the improvements receive no benefit from them.

3. Which of the following, if true, most strengthens the argument above?

- ⬭ The town's school system is currently ranked among the worst in the state.
- ⬭ Other towns nearby that have made similar capital improvements did not find that the improvements translated to a better quality of education.
- ⬭ The town will need to spend additional money on an architect's plans for the capital improvements.
- ⬭ An examination of the tax rolls shows that most homeowners in this category no longer have school-age children.
- ⬭ Some homeowners will delay home improvement projects in order to keep the value of their homes below $500,000.

## EXPLANATIONS

3. **D** The author is arguing to nix the plan to improve the schools. You want to strengthen his argument, but before you do, there is usually at least one answer choice that actually weakens the argument. It is helpful to get rid of these first, since they are usually easier to spot. In this case, (A) gives a compelling reason to *improve* the school system; eliminate it. Now, the reason the author gives for defeating the plan is that the people who pay for it will not benefit. To strengthen this argument, you need to show why this would be true. Choice (B) is against the school improvements, but for a different reason: in other towns, similar improvements didn't increase the quality of education. While important in the real world, this is slightly outside the scope of this argument. Choice (C) provides another possible negative of the plan, but again it doesn't show why the people who pay for it will not benefit. Choice (E) implies that taxpayers will delay their own capital improvements to avoid paying for the schools' capital improvements, but again this doesn't strengthen the author's particular argument—that the plan should be defeated because the people who must pay for it do not benefit. Choice (D) explains how this could be true: most of the people slotted to pay for the school improvements don't even have school-age children. The correct answer is (D).

## QUESTIONS

4. Which of the following, if true, provides the town council with the strongest counter to the objection that its plan is unfair?

- ⬭ Even with the proposed increase, property taxes in the town are well below the national average.
- ⬭ Paying for the school system improvements using existing town funds will result in shortfalls that will force the town into arrears.
- ⬭ The teachers in the town's school system receive some of the lowest salary packages in the immediate area, which is a major cause of attrition.
- ⬭ Smaller class sizes and capital improvements in a school system tend to increase property values in the surrounding community.
- ⬭ A feasibility study has shown that the cost of the improvements will likely be 20% higher than projected.

5. The rules of engagement under which a border patrol station can decide to use deadly force <u>includes responding to an invasionary incursion and the return of</u> hostile fire.

- ⬭ includes responding to an invasionary incursion and the return of
- ⬭ includes responding to an invasionary incursion and returning
- ⬭ include responding to an invasionary incursion and the return of
- ⬭ include a response to an invasionary incursion and the return of
- ⬭ include a response to an invasionary incursion and returning

## EXPLANATIONS

4. **D** The author says the plan is unfair to the people who must pay for it. How do you counter that? By showing that they actually do receive a benefit. Before you weaken the author's argument, eliminate any answers that strengthen it. In this case, that means only (E). Now, (A) points out that property taxes would still be quite low even after the increase, but that doesn't mean the increase is fair. Choice (B) states why an alternate way to finance the improvements won't work, but it doesn't address the fairness of the way being discussed. Choice (C) states why the funds are urgently needed, but again doesn't show that the people who have to supply the funds actually would receive a benefit. Choice (D) finally gives a reason the property tax increase might actually benefit those who pay for it: good schools translates to higher property values. The correct answer is (D).

5. **D** As you know, GMAT test-writers like to put as many words between the subject and the verb of a sentence as they can, in hopes that you will forget to check for agreement. The subject of this sentence was the plural *rules*. The verb was the singular *includes*. This eliminates (A) and (B). Choices (C) and (E) are not parallel because they mix verb-like forms with noun-like forms. The correct answer is (D).

# VERBAL BIN 3

## QUESTIONS

6. Although the word "phonetician" is popularly associated with Henry Higgins's task of improving the diction of Eliza Doolittle in *My Fair Lady*, in linguistics, it is someone who studies the formation of language.

- it is someone who studies
- it is a person studying
- it refers to someone who studies
- they are people who study
- it is in reference to people who study

7. Experts studying patterns of shark attacks on humans have noted that attacks tend to diminish when the water temperature drops below 65 degrees Fahrenheit. Until recently, researchers believed this was because sharks prefer warmer water, and thus are present in fewer numbers in colder water. However, new research shows that sharks are present in equal numbers in cold and warm water.

Which of the following, if true, best explains the apparent paradox?

- In general, humans prefer warm water.
- Sharks' keen sense of smell is enhanced in cold water.
- In the Pacific, shark attacks tend to occur more frequently in the daytime.
- Of the more than 200 types of sharks present in the ocean, only three attack humans.
- The average temperature of the Earth's oceans is 55 degrees.

## EXPLANATIONS

6. **C** The question here is: to what does the pronoun *it* refer? You might think it refers to *phonetician* (in which case you might have thought the sentence was fine the way it was), but in fact it refers to *the word*. Choices (A), (B), and (D) could give the impression that *the word* is a person or persons. Choice (E) is awkward, and, like (D), needlessly uses the plural *people*. The correct answer is (C).

7. **A** People tend to try to explain shark attacks by thinking about the *shark's* behavior. But (A) points out that it takes two to tango. A shark attack requires one shark and one human to be attacked. One reason there might be fewer shark attacks on humans in cold water is that there are fewer humans swimming in cold water in the first place. If you were looking at (B) and saying, "Hmm, if a shark's olfactory powers were enhanced by cold water, then presumably he'd be better at attacking," or if you were thinking that if his olfactory powers were enhanced, he would know enough *not* to attack a human, then either way, you were having to think way too hard for this to be inside the scope. Choice (C) is outside the scope, too, since it is dealing with only one ocean and does not address temperature at all. Choice (D) provides extraneous information, and (E) does not help to explain the apparent paradox. The correct answer is (A).

## QUESTIONS

8. As a result of surging economic indicators, most analysts upgraded the company's stock to a strong "buy," ignoring the advice of the head of a watchdog organization who warned that the company's product would prove not only dangerous but ineffective in the long run.

- who warned that the company's product would prove not only dangerous but
- warning that the company's product would prove not only dangerous and also
- warning that the company's product would prove itself to be both dangerous and
- who warned that the company's product would prove to be both dangerous and
- who was warning that the company's product would prove not only dangerous but

## EXPLANATIONS

8. **D** The sentence, as written, needs a *but also* to complement its *not only*. Choices (A) and (E) bite the dust. In (B), the same idiom comes into play, but this choice has bigger problems: without the *who warned*, it is no longer clear who is doing the warning. Choice (C) can be eliminated for the same reason. Choice (D) uses the correct combination of *both . . . and*. The correct answer is (D).

# VERBAL BIN 3

## QUESTIONS

9. MoviesNow! streaming service is projected to buy more licenses to stream more movies in the next 5 years than in any previous 5-year window. This is because MoviesNow!'s board of directors has encouraged the pursuit of subscribers who are parents of children under the age of 12 and the current selection of movies to stream in the MoviesNow! database is targeted at subscribers ages 18–35.

   Which of the following, if true, would most strengthen the argument from MoviesNow!'s board of directors that they should pursue subscribers who are parents of children under the age of 12 ?

   - The board monitors the demographic targets of large advertising companies and chooses target audiences for their streaming service based on those trends.
   - A population study conducted by an independent research group has uncovered a large uptick in the number of parents who are raising children under the age of 12.
   - People aged 18–35 generally have less disposable income than other age demographics.
   - The licensing agreement MoviesNow! has with the largest movie production company is set to expire within the next 5 years.
   - The board of MoviesNow! is comprised of parents of children under the age of 12.

## EXPLANATIONS

9. **B** This is a strengthen problem, as evidenced by the question asking which answer choice *would most strengthen the argument.* This argument uses a planning pattern, as evidenced by the presence of the plan of *MovieNow!'s board of directors.* The assumption of a planning reasoning pattern is that there are no problems with the plan. In this case, the assumption is that there are no problems with the plan to pursue *subscribers who are parents of children under the age of 12.* Because this is a strengthen question, the correct answer will provide information that makes the plan stronger, or removes a potential objection to the plan. Evaluate the answer choices individually. Choice (A) introduces *large advertising companies* and states that *the board monitors the demographic targets* of those companies to help *choose target audiences for their streaming service.* This choice is out of scope because it is not possible to know that the demographic targets of large advertising companies are the same demographics that the board of MoviesNow! is interested in pursuing. Eliminate (A). Choice (B) mentions a *population study conducted by an independent research group* that *uncovered a large uptick* in the demographic that the board of directors wants to pursue. If this information is true, then this is a good justification for the plan. Keep (B). Choice (C) mentions *people aged 18–35,* which is out of the scope of the question. Eliminate (C). Choice (D) mentions the *licensing agreement MoviesNow! has with the largest movie production company,* which is out of scope, so eliminate (D). Choice (E) could potentially weaken the argument, as if the board of directors is making choices based on their own demographic information and biases, then that is an alternate cause for the recommendation. Eliminate (E). The correct answer is (B).

## QUESTIONS

10. A new influx of unprecedented private investment should create a bright new future for manned space exploration, making the possibility of commercial space tourism much more viable than 10 years ago.

- making the possibility of commercial space tourism much more viable than 10 years ago
- and make the possibility of commercial space tourism much more viable than 10 years ago
- making the possibility of commercial space tourism much more viable than it was 10 years ago
- and make the possibility of commercial space tourism much more viable than it was 10 years in the past
- making the possibility of commercial space tourism much more viable than 10 years in the past

## EXPLANATIONS

10. **C** The key word here is *than*—and if you spotted it, you knew to look for a parallel comparison problem. Two actions are being compared in this sentence, so you need the words "it was" after *than* to make that clear. If you spotted this error, you could eliminate (A), (B), and (E). Choice (D) might seem possible (and parallel in a different kind of way) until you get to the last words: *10 years in the past.* This is just not the same as *ago.* The correct answer is (C).

## QUESTIONS

Questions 11–15 are based on the following passage:

As the American workforce gets grayer, age discrimination will likely become a more prominent issue in the courts. It is, of course, illegal to discriminate against an employee because of his or her age, and yet it is not illegal to dismiss a worker because he has a high salary and expensive health care.

This apparent contradiction is at the heart of a raft of cases now making their way through the courts. The outcome of these cases will have broad implications for the workplace in the coming years. By 2020, the Bureau of Labor Statistics has projected that more than half of all workers will be over 40—many of whom, by dint of seniority and promotions, will be earning higher than median salaries, eligible for more stock options, and carrying higher health care costs as a result of a larger number of dependents and the increased cost of health care for older workers.

Is it any wonder that a bottom-line oriented business might want to shed these workers, whose productivity is likely to plummet in the next few years, even as they become more expensive employees?

Still, the legal challenges of implementing this policy are daunting. Businesses have the right to rate workers on their productivity and to rank them against their peers. But they are not allowed to prejudge individuals based on their sex, race, or age. Each worker must be treated on his or her own merits, rather than by how they fit into a larger profile of the group they belong to.

For companies looking to lay off these workers, the cost of making a mistake is high; while only one in three age discrimination suits is won by the plaintiff, the awards tend to be steep and the political fall-out harsh.

11. The primary purpose of the passage is to

- advocate on behalf of the older American worker who could soon face dismissal
- describe the origin of two theories of labor law and their effects on the workplace
- present an overview of the legal ramifications of a practice some call discriminatory
- describe the process by which America's workforce is getting older
- describe the methods by which a company could reduce its bottom line

## EXPLANATIONS

11. **C** Use POE. Choice (A) is incorrect because the passage describes a problem but doesn't *advocate*. Choice (B) is incorrect because the passage doesn't describe the origins of the ideas. Choice (C) is supported because the author maintains focus on the legal issues and states that some feel the practice is discriminatory. Choice (D) is incorrect because the passage isn't just about how people get older. Choice (E) is incorrect because it isn't the main focus of the passage. The correct answer is (C).

## QUESTIONS

12. Which of the following best describes the organization of the second paragraph of the passage?

- An assertion is made and then briefly contradicted.
- A contradiction is stated and then quickly resolved.
- A new theory is described and then qualified.
- An apparent inconsistency is stated and its consequences outlined.
- A conventional model is described and an alternative is introduced.

## EXPLANATIONS

12. **D** The contradiction highlighted at the beginning of the second paragraph is not resolved or qualified; it is stated, and then its ramifications are outlined. The correct answer is (D).

13. Which of the following, if true, would most effectively weaken the author's assertion that a "bottom-line oriented business" might want to lay off older workers?

- A new study shows that, on average, younger workers earn less and have lower associated medical costs than older workers.
- Older workers have a higher rate of absenteeism than younger workers.
- A new study shows that older workers are in fact more productive and have fewer medical expenses compared to younger workers.
- A forecasted downturn in the economy will erode profits in many American businesses.
- A new bill scheduled to become law will make it easier for employers to employ undocumented immigrants.

13. **C** To weaken the assertion that it might be in the interest of employers to lay off older people, it is necessary to show why employing older people would be good for companies. Choice (C) is the only answer that does so, suggesting that older employees are actually more productive and have fewer health care costs. The correct answer is (C).

# VERBAL BIN 3

## QUESTIONS

14. It can be inferred from the passage regarding the relationship between American companies and older Americans that

- what is good for American companies is not necessarily good for older Americans
- American companies are prohibited by law from practices that discriminate based on age
- large monetary judgments from age discrimination suits might prove more expensive than paying older employees' salaries
- by the year 2030, the percentage of older employees will be even higher than in the year 2020
- some older employees may well be more productive than some younger employees

15. The author mentions all of the following as driving up the cost to employers for employing workers over the age of 40 EXCEPT

- the cost of out-placement services
- a larger number of dependents
- increased cost of health care
- higher median salaries
- the cost of employee stock options

## EXPLANATIONS

14. **B** Choice (A) is unsupported by the passage, so eliminate (A). Choice (B) is directly supported by the first paragraph of the passage, so keep (B). Choice (C) is a bit of an appeal to outside knowledge, and as true as it may be, it is not supported by the passage, so eliminate (C). Choices (D) and (E) are both out of the scope of the passage, so eliminate them both. The correct answer is (B).

15. **A** Use Process of Elimination. Choice (B) is mentioned in line 18. Choice (C) is in line 17. Choice (D) is in lines 15–16. Choice (E) is in line 16. The correct answer is (A).

## QUESTIONS

16. A pharmaceutical company claims that its new drug promotes learning in children. To back up its claims, the company points to a study of 300 children who were given the drug, along with a control group of 300 children who were given a placebo. The 300 children who were given the drug reported that they were able to retain new information much more easily.

Which of the following statements, if true, would most tend to weaken the claims of the pharmaceutical company?

- ⬭ The 300 children in the control group also reported that they were able to retain new information much more easily.
- ⬭ The drug has also been shown to prevent common skin rashes.
- ⬭ The drug has been proven to have severe side-effects.
- ⬭ The children in the study were not given any other medications during the study.
- ⬭ The children who were given the drug did better on cognitive measurement tests after the drug therapy than before.

## EXPLANATIONS

16. **A** The drug company says its drug caused enhanced learning ability. To weaken this causal argument, look for an alternate cause. Choices (B), (D), and (E) appear to strengthen the argument, so you can eliminate them. Choice (C), while clearly a negative aspect of the drug, does not weaken the argument itself, which states simply that the drug enhances learning capability in children. Side effects are outside the scope of the argument. Choice (A) may not seem at first like an alternate cause, but if the control group (which did not receive the medicine) reported the exact same results as the children who did receive the drug, then clearly there is some other, as yet unnamed, alternate cause. The correct answer is (A).

## QUESTIONS

17. In order to understand the dangers of the current real-estate bubble in Country Y, one has only to look to the real-estate bubble of the last decade in Country Z. In that country, incautious investors used the inflated value of their real estate as collateral in risky margin loans. When the real-estate market collapsed, many investors went bankrupt, creating a major recession. Country Y is in real danger of a similar recession if more-stringent laws restricting margin loans are not enacted promptly.

    The answer to which of the following questions would be most useful in evaluating the significance of the author's claims?

    - Was the real estate in Country Z located principally in rural areas or was it located in more urban communities?
    - Could the bankruptcies in Country Z have been prevented by a private bailout plan by the nation's banks?
    - Does Country Y currently have any laws on its books regarding margin loans?
    - Are there business ties and connections between Country Y and Country Z?
    - Were there other factors in the case of Country Y that would make the comparison with Country Z less meaningful?

18. Rules governing participation in a new extreme sports fantasy camp require that applicants should be physically fit enough to endure the demanding activities in which they will be engaging.

    - that applicants should be physically fit enough to endure the demanding
    - that applicants be physically fit enough to endure the demanding
    - applicants should have enough physical fitness to allow enduring the demands of
    - applicants are physically fit enough as to endure the demands of
    - physical fitness in applicants, enough for endurance of demanding

## EXPLANATIONS

17. **E** To evaluate the significance of the author's claims, you need to recognize what kind of argument it is: an analogy. The author is saying that the situation in Country Y is analogous to that of Country Z. To weaken an analogy, you merely have to question whether the two situations were really analogous. Choices (A) and (B) are outside the scope of the argument. Choice (C) is incorrect because the author's argument stated that more-stringent laws were needed, making it irrelevant whether Country Y had any laws about this in the first place. Choice (D) goes off on an interesting tangent by asking if there were business ties between the two countries, but it does not weaken the argument's analogy. Only (E) questions whether the two situations are in fact analogous. The correct answer is (E).

18. **B** This question tests two concepts. The first is idiomatic and concerns the word *require*. Because the word *require* indicates something that is compulsory (as opposed to optional), it cannot be followed by the word *should*; in other words, you can't require that something should happen, because then it's not really a requirement. This eliminates (A) and (C).

    The second concept is a little more arcane. Requirements, like hypothetical situations posited in the future, take the subjunctive mood. In the subjunctive, the proper way to phrase the idea expressed in this sentence is *the rules require that applicants be physically fit*. The correct answer is (B).

## QUESTIONS

19. During the summer of 2002, the Outer Banks suffered a massive toad infestation, discouraging many vacationers from visiting the area.

- suffered a massive toad infestation, discouraging
- suffered from a massive toad infestation and discouraged
- suffered a massive infestation of toads, which discouraged
- was suffering a massive infestation of toads and discouraging
- had suffered from a massive toad infestation and this discouraged

## EXPLANATIONS

19. **C** This question presents two ways to discuss the unfortunate toad incident on the Outer Banks. Was there a *massive toad infestation* or a *massive infestation of toads*? The second option is better, because the first leaves it unclear whether *massive* refers to the infestation or the toads themselves. Under the first option, it is theoretically possible that the Outer Banks was infested by a single 50-foot-tall toad. Thus, (A), (B), and (E) are all incorrect. Choice (D) incorrectly suggests that the Outer Banks, not the infestation of toads, discouraged vacationers. The correct answer is (C).

20. A prolonged period of low mortgage rates resulted in a period of the most robust home sales ever. At the same time, the average sale price of resale homes actually dropped, when adjusted for inflation.

Which of the following, if true, would explain the apparent contradiction between the robust home sales and the drop in the average sale price of resale homes?

- The inflation rate during this period exceeded the increase in the average salary, thus preventing many buyers from securing mortgages.
- Resale homes represent the best value on the real estate market.
- Without the adjustment for inflation, the price of resale homes actually increased by a very slight amount.
- The decrease in mortgage rates was accompanied by a widening of the types of mortgages from which borrowers could choose.
- The increase in home sales was due entirely to an increase in the sale of new homes.

20. **E** During a period of robust home sales, one would expect the prices of all homes to increase; that would be the natural effect of the law of supply and demand. The question states, however, that the real price of resale homes during this period actually decreased. Thus, it is reasonable to assume that the demand for resale homes decreased. How can you resolve this apparent contradiction? If all the increased demand for homes was in the new home market, then it would be possible that the overall increase in home sales would not result in an increase in resale home prices and may, in fact, even accompany a drop in those prices. The correct answer is (E).

## QUESTIONS

21. Luis is taller than Rei. Kiko is taller than Marcus. Therefore, Kiko is taller than Rei.

The conclusion drawn above is not supported by the argument; however, the addition of one additional piece of information would make the conclusion logically sound. All of the following could be that additional piece of information EXCEPT

- Kiko is taller than Luis.
- Luis is taller than Marcus.
- Luis and Marcus are the same height.
- Marcus and Rei are the same height.
- Marcus is taller than Rei.

## EXPLANATIONS

21. **B** This question is best solved by drawing a diagram to represent the information in the question stem.

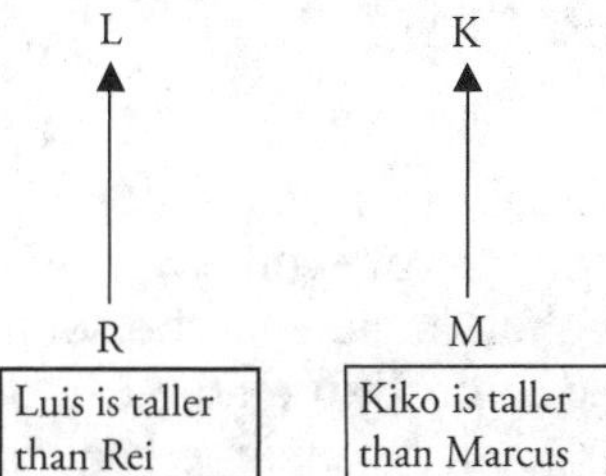


Look for information that will allow you to draw the diagram

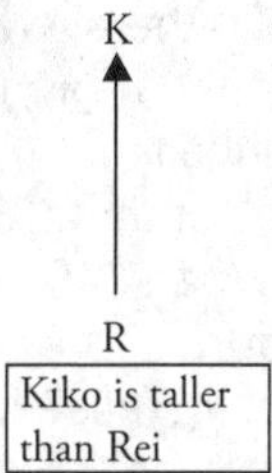


According to the question stem, four of the answer choices are sufficient to accomplish this. Your job is to find the one that is NOT sufficient.

Choice (A) is sufficient; if Kiko is taller than Luis and Luis is taller than Rei, Kiko must be taller than Rei.

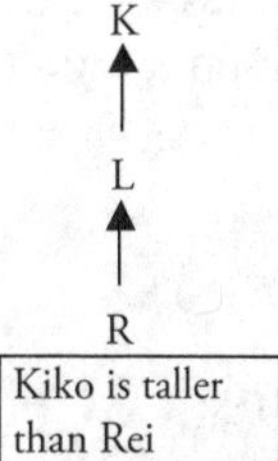


Choice (B) is NOT sufficient; if Luis is taller than Marcus, then it is conceivable that Luis is taller than Kiko. Consequently, it is also possible that Rei, who is shorter than Luis, is also taller than Kiko; however, Rei may also be shorter. Use the diagrams you have already created to demonstrate, on your own, that (C), (D), and (E) are sufficient to make the conclusion logically sound. The correct answer is (B).

## QUESTIONS

22. It has been estimated that an increase in average regional temperature of even 0.5 degrees Fahrenheit could cost the southern United States more than $10 billion in lost agricultural income annually.

- an increase in average regional temperature of even 0.5 degrees Fahrenheit could cost the southern United States more than $10 billion in lost agricultural income annually
- every year, $10 billion in agricultural income could be the cost to the southern United States as a result of an increase in the average temperature of the region of even 0.5 degrees Fahrenheit
- the cost to the southern United States could be more than $10 billion in income from agriculture that results from a regional increase in average temperature of even 0.5 degrees Fahrenheit annually
- annual income losses in agriculture of more than $10 billion could be the cost from increasing average temperatures in the southern United States of even 0.5 degrees Fahrenheit
- annual income losses to the southern United States from the increase in average regional temperature of even 0.5 degrees Fahrenheit costing more than $10 billion in agricultural income each year

## EXPLANATIONS

22. **A** Well, you've got five choices here and none is particularly good. Only four, however, contain grammatical errors, so the best way to proceed on a question like this one is to eliminate as many answer choices as you can, take your best guess from among the remaining answers, and move on. Choice (B) is an endless string of prepositions; furthermore, the placement of the phrase *of the region* between *increase in the average temperature* and *of even 0.5 degrees Fahrenheit* is needlessly confusing. Choice (C) incorrectly suggests that it is agriculture, and not lost income, that results from the temperature increase. In (D), *cost from* is unidiomatic; the correct phrasing is *cost of.* Choice (E) is redundant, as it refers to *annual losses* that occur *each year.* The correct answer is (A).

## QUESTIONS

23. Within the Green Party, an internal debate is raging among those who believe in compromising with mainstream politicians in order to achieve some goals with those who believe the party must not abandon any of its principles.

- among those who believe in compromising with mainstream politicians in order to achieve some goals with those who believe the party must not abandon any of its principles
- among those who believe that achieving some goals requires compromise with mainstream politicians and those believing that none of the party's principles must be abandoned
- between those believing in compromising with mainstream politicians in order to achieve some goals with those who believe the party must not abandon any of its principles
- between those who believe in compromising with mainstream politicians in order to achieve some goals and those who believe the party must not abandon any of its principles
- between those believing that achieving some goals means compromising with mainstream politicians and those who believe that the principles of the party must not be abandoned

## EXPLANATIONS

23. **D** This is a tricky *between/among* question. The rule is that *between* is used to compare two items, *among* to compare three or more. Here you are talking about thousands of people, so you might think that *among* is the correct choice. However, because the sentence compares two groups of people, the correct answer is *between.* The argument is between the two groups, not among the thousands of people who make up those groups. Eliminate (A) and (B).

Eliminate (C) because it is unidiomatic: it draws a comparison between one group *with* another when it should draw a comparison between one group *and* another. Choice (E) can be eliminated because it lacks parallel structure: it compares *those* ***believing*** *that achieving some goals*...and *those who* ***believe*** *that the principles of the party must not be abandoned.* The correct answer is (D).

## QUESTIONS

24. In comparison to the drivers who live in Mountainview, a greater proportion of the drivers who live in Oak Valley exceed the speed limit regularly. This explains why there are more accidents each year in Oak Valley than in Mountainview.

All of the following statements, if true, weaken the conclusion drawn above EXCEPT

- Oak Valley has a greater proportion of blind intersections and sharp turns than has Mountainview.
- There is a greater number of drivers in Oak Valley than in Mountainview.
- Drivers in Mountainview must travel to Oak Valley to shop and work.
- Per capita, there are fewer police officers monitoring traffic in Oak Valley than there are in Mountainview.
- The roads are icier for a greater proportion of the year in Oak Valley than in Mountainview.

25. A study showed that only ten percent of American dog owners enroll their dogs in formal obedience training classes. More than 20 percent of these dog owners, the study also showed, participate in dog shows. Thus, it is obvious that people who train their dogs are more likely to participate in dog shows than are people who do not train their dogs.

The conclusion above is correct provided which of the following statements is also true?

- It is impossible for a dog to compete in a dog show if the dog has not completed at least one formal obedience training class.
- The proportion of dog owners who enroll their dogs in formal obedience training classes is representative of the proportion who train their dogs outside such classes.
- Dog owners who participate in dog shows only train their dogs by enrolling them in formal obedience training lessons.
- Participation in dog shows is a reliable indicator of how much attention a dog owner pays to his dog.
- Only purebred dogs can participate in dog shows, so many owners who enroll their dogs in formal obedience training classes are excluded from this activity.

## EXPLANATIONS

24. **D** Choice (D) may explain why people are more likely to exceed the speed limit in Oak Valley than in Mountainview, but it has no necessary correlation to the number of accidents in the two towns; therefore, it does nothing to weaken the conclusion that the greater proportion of speeders in Oak Valley results in a greater number of accidents there.
Choices (A) and (E) provide an alternate explanation: driving conditions are poor, which certainly could contribute to accidents. Choice (B) indicates that there is much more traffic in Oak Valley, which could well explain why there are more traffic accidents there. Choice (C) states that many Mountainview residents travel to Oak Valley regularly; it is possible, then, that they, not the drivers who live in Oak Valley, cause the accidents. The correct answer is (D).

25. **B** The statement draws a conclusion about *people who train their dogs* based on statistics relating only to people who take their dogs to formal obedience training classes. In order for the statement to be correct, then, these statistics must be valid for all people who train their dogs, not only those who train them in formal classes. Choice (B) plugs this hole in the argument, thus making the conclusion necessarily true. The correct answer is (B).

# VERBAL BIN 3

## QUESTIONS

26. A bullet train travels in excess of 150 miles per hour. Therefore, if a train travels slower than 150 miles per hour, it is not a bullet train.

Which of the following most closely parallels the reasoning used in the argument above?

- An orange ripens only on the vine. If it ripens on the vine, then it is not an orange.
- Newspapers are often read by more than one person. Therefore, magazines are also likely to be read by more than one person.
- An Earthquake of 5.0 or above on the Richter scale causes massive damage. If there is not massive damage, then the Earthquake did not attain a 5.0 or above.
- A supersonic plane travels at speeds in excess of Mach 1. If it is not supersonic, then it will travel at speeds below Mach 1.
- Fluoride generally prevents cavities. If there are no cavities, then there was no fluoride used.

## EXPLANATIONS

26. **C** To answer this parallel-the-reasoning question, you have to break down the original argument, and then find an answer choice that mimics it exactly. In this case, the argument says a bullet train travels in excess of 150 miles per hour (if A, then B). Therefore, if a train travels less than 150 miles per hour, then it is not a bullet train (if not B, then not A). Now all you have to do is find an answer choice that mimics that reasoning exactly. Choice (A), broken down, reads, "if A, then B…so if B, then not A." This isn't it. Eliminate it. Choice (B) breaks down to "if A, then B… therefore C will also cause B." That's not it either. Choice (C) breaks down to "if A, then B…therefore if not B, then not A." Keep (C).
Choice (D) might seem tempting because it also has to do with a fast means of transportation, but what counts here is the reasoning: "if A, then B…if not A, then not B." This is close, but no cigar. Choice (E) is also appealing; you may even think it mimics the argument exactly. But there's a trick. The first half of the sentence reads, *Fluoride generally prevents cavities* (if A, then B). Note that the B part is about the prevention—not the presence—of cavities. So the second half, *If there are no cavities, there was no fluoride*, actually breaks down to "if B, then not A." The correct answer is (C).